2000 EDITION

Panorama of European Business

Data 1989-1999

4

EUROPEAN
COMMISSION

eurostat

THEME 4
Industry, trade
and services

·········· Immediate access to **harmonized statistical data**

Eurostat Data Shops:

A personalised data retrieval service

In order to provide the greatest possible number of people with access to high-quality statistical information, Eurostat has developed an extensive network of Data Shops ([1]).

Data Shops provide a wide range of **tailor-made services**:

- ★ immediate information searches undertaken by a team of experts in European statistics;
- ★ rapid and personalised response that takes account of the specified search requirements and intended use;
- ★ a choice of data carrier depending on the type of information required.

Information can be requested by phone, mail, fax or e-mail.

([1]) See list of Eurostat Data Shops at the end of the publication.

Internet:

Essentials on Community statistical news

- ★ Euro indicators: more than 100 indicators on the euro-zone; harmonized, comparable, and free of charge;
- ★ About Eurostat: what it does and how it works;
- ★ Products and databases: a detailed description of what Eurostat has to offer;
- ★ Indicators on the European Union: convergence criteria; euro yield curve and further main indicators on the European Union at your disposal;
- ★ Press releases: direct access to all Eurostat press releases.

For further information, visit us on the Internet at: **www.europa.eu.int/comm/eurostat**

A great deal of additional information on the European Union is available on the Internet.
It can be accessed through the Europa server (http://europa.eu.int).

Cataloguing data can be found at the end of this publication.

Luxembourg: Office for Official Publications of the European Communities, 2000

ISBN 92-894-0180-X

EUROSTAT

L-2920 Luxembourg — Tel. (352) 43 01-1 — Telex COMEUR LU 3423
Rue de la Loi 200, B-1049 Bruxelles — Tel. (32-2) 299 11 11

Eurostat is the Statistical Office of the European Communities. Its task is to provide the European Union with statistics at a European level, that allow comparisons to be made between countries and regions. Eurostat consolidates and harmonizes the data collected by the Member States.

To ensure that the vast quantity of accessible data is made widely available, and to help each user make proper use of the information, Eurostat has set up a publications and services programme.

This programme makes a clear distinction between general and specialist users and particular collections have been developed for these different groups. The collections *Press releases*, *Statistics in focus*, *Panorama of the European Union*, *Key indicators* and *Catalogues* are aimed at general users. They give immediate key information through analyses, tables, graphs and maps.

The collections *Methods and nomenclatures, Detailed tables* and *Studies and research* suit the needs of the specialist who is prepared to spend more time analysing and using very detailed information and tables.

All Eurostat products are disseminated through the Data Shop network or the sales agents of the Office for Official Publications of the European Communities. Data Shops are available in 12 of the 15 Member States as well as in Switzerland, Norway and the United States. They provide a wide range of services from simple database extracts to tailor-made investigations. The information is provided on paper and/or in electronic form via e-mail, on diskette or CD-ROM.

As part of the new programme Eurostat has developed its website. It includes a broad range of on-line information on Eurostat products and services, newsletters, catalogues, on-line publications as well as indicators on the euro-zone.

Yves Franchet
Director-General

Panorama of European Business, 2000
This publication was funded by the Enterprise DG. It has been managed and is under the responsibility of unit D2 of Eurostat, responsible for structural business statistics (Head of Unit, Mr. Bernard Langevin). The opinions expressed are those of the individual authors alone and do not necessarily reflect the position of the European Commission.

Co-ordinators:
August Götzfried
Jean Lienhardt
Emmanuel Raulin
Eurostat D2
Statistical Office of the European Communities
Bâtiment Joseph Bech
Rue Alphonse Weicker, 5
L-2721 Luxembourg
august.goetzfried@cec.eu.int
jean.lienhardt@cec.eu.int
emmanuel.raulin@cec.eu.int

Production:
data processing, statistical analysis, economic analysis, design and desktop publishing
Informa sàrl
Giovanni Albertone, Simon Allen, Laurence Bastin, Iain Christopher, Stephen Evans, Sabine Joham, Andrew Redpath, Martin Schaaper, Markus Voget, Daniel Waterschoot
informa@informa.lu

Translation:
translation service of the European Commission, Luxembourg

Published by:
Office for Official Publications of the European Communities, Luxembourg 2001

Enquiries regarding the purchase of data should be addressed to:
Eurostat Datashop
Rue Alphonse Weicker, 4
L-2721 Luxembourg
tel: (352) 43 35 22 51
fax: (352) 43 35 22 221
dslux@eurostat.datashop.lu
http://europa.eu.int/comm/eurostat/

A great deal of additional information on the European Union is available on the Internet. It can be accessed through the Europa server at http://europa.eu.int

Guide to the publication

CONTENTS OF THE PUBLICATION

"Panorama of European Business, 2000" aims to provide a standard set of information for industrial and market service activities within the European Union. The data provided in Panorama traces the major developments in production, employment and external trade for the EU, as well as providing more in-depth descriptions of the performance and competitiveness of European business. The information presented concentrates largely on the 3-digit level of the NACE Rev. 1 classification of economic activities[1].

Publication format

The publication is available in three different formats. Firstly, there is a "professional" CD-ROM that contains all three language (German, English and French) versions of the accompanying text, all the tables and figures found in the paper publication, as well as a comprehensive set of additional data (longer time-series, breakdown by Member State, EU estimates for the most recent periods, additional variables). Furthermore, the CD-Rom provides a large amount of background information on the underlying legislation, sources, classifications, as well as a glossary of terms; all components can be accessed through a single harmonised interface designed to help the user navigate around the product. The professional CD-ROM is aimed at specialist users who want a large data set and a fully comprehensive set of background information (for example, banks, research institutes and universities).

Secondly, there is a "standard" CD-ROM. This product mirrors the "professional" CD-ROM, other than the exhaustive data sets. The main data series that accompany the text are nevertheless provided in electronic format and can be easily accessed (using Eurostat's dedicated database browser, EVA). As with the professional version, data can be extracted and exported for further use in database or spreadsheet applications. The standard CD-ROM is aimed at generalists who want a broad overview of the structure of European business (for example, SMEs, individuals and schools).

Thirdly, there is a paper publication (available in separate German, English and French versions). This product contains all of the text provided on the CD-ROMs. However, due to space constraints, a limited set of data (focusing on a set of key variables) is presented. The paper product provides only a subset of the underlying background information that is available on the CD-ROMs. Eurostat plan to release the paper publication in a number of different volumes for users that wish to have a limited amount of information on a particular area of the business economy.

---

(1) Published by Eurostat, ISBN 92-826-8767-8, available from the usual outlets for Commission publications.

Structure of the publication
Panorama is divided into three main sections.

1. The first provides a general overview of the evolution of the European business economy (industry and services), looking at the changes in production, value added and employment both between and within the different sectors of the economy, as well as the geographical distribution/concentration of European business.

2. The second section provides a sectoral description of industrial activities, broken down into 15 separate chapters. Each chapter contains a number of sub-chapters, which are usually based on he 3-digit level of the NACE Rev. 1 classification. In addition, each chapter concludes with a statistical annex which provides the key figures for each activity.

3. The final section provides a description of services, broken down into 6 separate chapters (again with sub-chapters and a statistical annex).

Structure of an individual chapter within the publication
The chapters in Panorama are structured largely on the basis of their NACE Rev. 1 coding, starting with energy and the extractive industries and finishing with business services and the "new economy". Each chapter begins with a preliminary section explaining the sectoral coverage of the data provided. NACE Rev. 1 is a hierarchical classification made up of Sections (1-letter codes), Sub-sections (2-letter codes), Divisions (2-digit codes), Groups (3-digit codes) and Classes (4-digit codes). NACE Rev. 1 establishes a direct link between the European classification and the internationally recognised ISIC Rev. 3 developed under the auspices of the United Nations. These two classifications are directly compatible at the 2-digit level and the lower levels of ISIC Rev. 3 can be calculated by aggregating the more detailed levels from NACE Rev. 1. Users should be aware that if an observation unit has its production split between three industries X, Y and Z, all the data provided are assigned to the so-called "principal activity". The principal activity is chosen by the enterprise when replying to the enquiry. In other words, secondary activities are taken into account within the principal activity. This is, however, not the case for foreign trade data. As such, structural business statistics and foreign trade indicators should not be combined. For this reason, it was decided to drop the notion of apparent consumption from Panorama 2000.

The compilation of industry and services data has followed a different historical development, and furthermore it is generally easier to compile product statistics about goods than knowledge or information-based services. Hence, there is a great deal more information currently available for industrial activities and goods than for service activities and products. For this reason, a different form of presentation is employed for these two broad activity groupings. It should be noted that the improvement in data availability for services during the last few years has been enormous and most EU Member States now compile annual statistics for most of the service activities covered in this publication. Clearly it will take a number of years to build up robust time-series and considerable work still needs to be done in the area of product statistics for services.

Within the specific chapters for industry and services, every effort has been made to present a coherent set of information that should allow comparisons across industries or services. The information in services' chapters, is more often supplemented by figures originating from professional trade associations (FEBIs/FEBS).

Industrial chapters
Within industrial chapters the most relevant economic and labour-related variables and international comparisons are provided alongside the text. The vast majority of this data is derived from the SBS database, Eurostat's reference database on structural business statistics. For more detailed coverage, each chapter contains a statistical annex (at the 3-digit level of the NACE Rev. 1 classification). This annex presents a set of five standardised tables per activity (subject to data availability). The tables take two forms, either a time-series presentation for the EU aggregate or a snapshot of the latest year available for each individual Member State. Three types of information are provided. The first concerns production-related indicators, which are of use for analysing the structure of an industry: production value, domestic producer prices, value added at factor cost, gross operating surplus and the number of persons employed. The second set of information relates to external trade: exports, imports, the trade balance and the cover ratio (exports/imports). The third set of information concerns labour-related indicators, which are of use for example for analysing competitiveness: unit personnel costs (personnel costs per employee), social charges as a share of personnel costs, apparent labour productivity (value added/persons employed), wage adjusted labour productivity (value added/personnel costs, adjusted to take account of the share of unpaid persons employed) and personnel costs as a share of total operating costs.

Services chapters
Within services chapters the (non-) availability of data often renders it difficult to provide a standard set of information. Where this is the case, functional databases from within Eurostat have been used to complement structural business statistics. Non-official sources have been used in chapters where very little official data exists. Services chapters are also supplemented by a statistical annex (at the 3-digit level of the NACE Rev. 1 classification)[2]. These tables are given for the most recent reference period available (normally 1997), as insufficient information exists to publish time-series. The tables provided are snapshots, giving information by Member State. Three types of information are provided: the first concerns employment-related indicators, the number of persons employed, the share of the number of employees in the number of persons employed and the average number of persons employed per enterprise. The second set of information relates to turnover (sales): total turnover, average turnover per enterprise and average turnover per person employed. The third set of information concerns performance-related indicators: value added at factor cost, value added as a share of turnover, apparent labour productivity (value added/persons employed), unit personnel costs (personnel costs per employee), wage adjusted labour productivity and the gross operating surplus (value added - personnel costs).

---

(2) The annexes for energy (chapter 1), transport services (chapter 18) and information and audio-visual services (chapter 21) are supplemented with information derived from Eurostat's functional databases.

GUIDE TO THE STATISTICS

Two main data sources should be distinguished when using this publication: those originating from official sources (collected by the national statistical authorities in each Member State and harmonised by Eurostat) and those provided by professional trade associations (industry representatives) and other non-official bodies. Wherever possible official data sources have been used. Non-official sources are easily recognised as tables and figures that are derived from these sources always appear in a shaded box.

SBS database

The bulk of the information contained within Panorama is derived from the SBS (structural business statistics) database. This data has been collected within the legal framework provided by the SBS Regulation[3]. There are two main collections of SBS data that have been used in this publication. The first covers long time-series[4] for enterprises with 20 or more persons employed (often available from 1985 onwards). These series are only published for industrial activities and they are used predominantly in the second section of this publication[5]. However, not all Member States have transmitted data relating to the enterprise as the statistical unit and the specified size threshold. Table 1 presents the main discrepancies with respect to these standards.

The second collection covers all enterprises[6] and these series have been used for service sectors[7]. The data generally starts in 1995 although for some services a small number of Member States have provided longer time-series. However, not all Member States have transmitted data relating to this population. In particular, some Member States can only provide data for units with employment above a certain size threshold. Table 2 presents the main deviations from the standard population as laid down in the SBS Regulation (enterprise with 1 person employed or more).

---

(3) Council Regulation (EC, EURATOM) No. 58/97 of 20 December 1996 concerning structural business statistics.
(4) Public access is available via the Eurostat Datashop network: NewCronos, domain SBS, collection Enterpr, table Enter_L.
(5) Except for energy (chapter 1) where there is poor data availability.
(6) Public access is available via the Eurostat Datashop network: NewCronos, domain SBS, collection Enterpr, table Enter.
(7) As well as construction (chapter 15) where due to the high number of small and medium-sized enterprises it is more important to have complete coverage of enterprises of all size classes.

―――――――――――――――――――――――――――――――――――――Table 1

Country	Year	Population covered
Belgium	1995-1998	Enterprises with 1 person employed or more.
Greece	1985-1996	Local kind-of-activity units employing 20 persons or more.
Spain	1985-1998	Enterprises with 1 employee or more.
France	1985-1995	Enterprises with 20 employees or more.
Ireland	1985-1998	Enterprises with 3 persons employed or more for NACE Rev. 1 Divisions 10 to 41.
Luxembourg	1985-1994 1995-1998	Kind-of-activity units with 20 persons employed or more Kind-of-activity units with 1 person employed or more.
Netherlands	1997	Number of enterprises: data for this variable are rounded to multiples of 5. A "0" therefore means 2 or less enterprises.
Austria	1985-1994	Establishments with 20 persons employed or more for NACE Rev. 1 Divisions 10 to 37.
Portugal	1985-1998	Enterprises with 1 person employed or more.
Finland	1986-1994 1995-1998	Establishments with 5 persons employed or more. Enterprises with 1 person employed or more.
Japan	1985-1997	Local kind-of-activity units with 4 persons employed or more (30 for investment).
United States	1985-1997	Local kind-of-activity units with 1 person employed or more.

―――――――――――――――――――――――――――――――――――――Table 2

Country	Statistical unit and size coverage used from 1995 onwards			
	Industry (NACE Rev. 1 Sections C, D and E)	Construction (NACE Rev. 1 Section F)	Trade (NACE Rev. 1 Section G)	Services (NACE Rev. 1 Sections H to K)
Greece	No major deviations	No major deviations	Enterprises with a turnover of 15 million GDR or more	Enterprises with a turnover of 15 million GDR or more
Spain	Enterprises with 1 employee or more	Enterprises with 1 employee or more	No data	No major deviations
France	No major deviations	No major deviations	No major deviations	In transport activities NACE Rev. 1 61.2Z and 61.2B, enterprises with 6 employees or more
Ireland	Enterprises with 3 persons employed or more	No major deviations	No major deviations	No major deviations
Italy	1996: turnover from the principal activity at the NACE Rev. 1 4-digit level: this code is supplied only for enterprises with 200 employees and over	No major deviations	No major deviations	No major deviations
Luxembourg	1995 onwards: kind-of-activity units with 1 person employed or more	1995 onwards: kind-of-activity units with 1 person employed or more	No major deviations	No major deviations
Netherlands	Number of enterprises: data for this variable are rounded to multiples of 5. A "0" therefore means 2 or less enterprises			
	Enterprises with 20 employees or more for NACE Rev. 1 Section E			Survey on holdings (NACE Rev. 1 74.11): enterprises with 5 employees or more

The series come from a combination of regular or ad hoc surveys conducted by the Member States and administrative sources. Data in the publication are generally available at the 3-digit NACE Rev. 1 level. More detailed information is available within the SBS Enter table covering 4-digit activity codes.

The definitions are standardised, and so the figures are largely comparable across industries and countries. Variable definitions do however vary somewhat between the countries. Until the reference year 1994 inclusive, EU Member States transmitted the data to Eurostat according to either the previous legal basis for industry or on a voluntary basis for services. As far as possible Eurostat and Member States have converted these data in line with the variable definitions as implemented in the SBS Regulation. However, the results of the conversion are not of the same quality as the data collected from the 1995 reference year onwards. For France, this conversion is applied until the reference year 1995 inclusive. For Greece, this conversion is applied until the reference year 1996 inclusive. Table 3 presents the main discrepancies with the standard variable definitions.

Estimates
EU-15 data for 1998 and 1999 are estimated. Estimates are made using individual country information and short-term indicators such as indices of production, producer prices and employment. The individual country estimates are not published and as a result the information by Member State is only available up until 1997 and is normally the final data provided by Member States rather than estimates. Estimates are only made for the series concerning 20 or more persons employed and hence only for industrial activities. As such, the time-series presented for industrial activities normally under-report the true values for absolute values. This can be particularly important in industries where small and medium-sized enterprises (SMEs) play an important role (textiles, for example, where small enterprises employing less than 20 persons are estimated to have accounted for 18.5% of production in 1997). In addition, these estimates are revised twice a year. Moreover, the 1999 estimates are to be revised at the beginning of 2001 as soon as the definitive (actual) data for reference year 1998 is available.

Eurostat estimates have also been made in order to provide economic ratios (not absolute values) for more recent years when country coverage or confidentiality has prevented fresh EU totals from being created. This was done by extracting a common set of core variables from which the ratios were derived. A consistent set of countries and variables were used for each activity-ratio paring in order to allow the broadest possible estimates to be made. Ratios were only calculated if at least two of the four largest EU Member States (France, Germany, Italy and the United Kingdom) were present, as well as a majority of the 15 Member States (in other words at least 8 individual countries). These ratios are only used within the text, where they are specifically referred to as Eurostat estimates.

Table 3

Long time-series: enterprises employing 20 or more persons			
Country	Year	Variable	Discrepancy
Spain	1995-1997	Gross investment in tangible goods	Gross investment in land and gross investment in machinery and equipment
Finland	1995	Value added at facctor cost	Value added at market price
		Gross operating surplus	Value added at market price - personnel costs
Sweden	1995-1996	Number of persons employed: since self-employed are not included and since the variable collected for enterprises with less than 10 employees is the number of employees "full time equivalent", then the number of persons employed and number of employees are very close.	

Enterprises employing 1 or more persons			
Country	Year	Variable	Discrepancy
Denmark	1990-1997	Value added at factor cost	Value added at basic prices
		Gross operating surplus	Value added at basic prices - personnel costs
Spain	1985-1997	Gross investment in tangible goods	Gross investment in land and gross investment I machinery and equipment
Ireland	1991-1994	Value added at factor cost	Gross value added excluding VAT
		Gross operating surplus	Gross value added excluding VAT - personnel costs
Italy	1992-1995	Number of persons employed	Number of employees
Finland	1986-1995	Value added at factor cost	Value added at market price
		Gross operating surplus	Value added at market price - personnel costs
United Kingdom	all years	Value added for Sections G to K	Value added at factor cost, but before deduction of indirect taxes linked to production

Other Eurostat data sources
employed within this publication

Whilst this publication relies to a large degree upon the use of SBS data there are a number of additional data sources that have been used, in order to present the reader with as broad a picture as possible of the European business economy. Details follow concerning the main additional Eurostat data sources that have been employed within this publication.

Comext

European foreign trade data is available in the Comext database, broken down according to the combined nomenclature (CN) of several thousand products. Trade data is available until 1999. No estimates are made, although it is possible that subsequent revisions will occur. The data are processed by summing together product statistics (using a conversion table from the CN product classification to NACE Rev. 1). The data for EU-15 are reported in terms of trade flows with the rest of the world, in other words extra-EU trade. However, for the individual Member States total trade flows are used (in other words intra and extra-EU trade). All trade figures are given in current ECU/euro terms.

European Business Trends (EBT)

Tracking the business cycle is indispensable for many economic actors. The European Business Trends (EBT) database provides politicians, government agencies, bankers, business owners, consumers and trade unionists with information that is crucial when making decisions on whether industries grow, stagnate or decline. The legal base of the European system of quantitative Short Term Statistics is the Council Regulation No.1165/98 concerning short-term statistics, which was adopted on 19th May 1998.

One variable from the EBT database is directly presented in this publication, namely the domestic producer price index. Producer price indices report the short-term changes in the prices of commodities produced and sold in a given Member State. Converted to an annual series this index has also been used to deflate SBS turnover, production value and value added data, using appropriate activity indices to create series in constant price (or volume) terms. Production and employment indices from the EBT database also provide valuable information that used to "nowcast" structural business statistics for 1998 and 1999.

Capacity utilisation data was also extracted from the EBT database. However, the original source of this information is the Directorate General of Economic and Financial Affairs (DG ECFIN). The information is collected as part of the Directorate General of Economic and Financial Affairs monthly survey of business opinions.

Labour Force Survey (LFS)

The methodological basis and the contents of this survey are described in the publication "Labour Force Survey - Methods and Definitions", 1998 edition. The main statistical objective of the Labour Force Survey is to divide the population of working age (generally 15 years and above[8]) into three mutually exclusive and exhaustive groups (persons in employment, unemployed persons and inactive persons) and to provide descriptive and explanatory data on each of these categories. Respondents are assigned to one of these groups on the basis of the most objective information possible, obtained through a survey questionnaire, which relates principally to their actual activity within a defined reference week.

It is important to note that the information is not collected from enterprises (as with the SBS database) but through a survey addressed to individual households. The National Statistical Institutes are responsible for selecting the sample, preparing the questionnaires, conducting the interviews and forwarding the results to Eurostat in accordance with a common coding scheme. Eurostat devises the programme for analysing the results and is responsible for processing and disseminating the information forwarded by the National Statistical Institutes.

The Community Labour Force Survey[9], is based upon a sample of the population. The results are therefore subject to the usual types of errors associated with sampling techniques. Eurostat implement basic guidelines intended to avoid the publication of figures which are statistically unreliable. Figures below these thresholds (column A, table 4) are not published. A second threshold is applied to data that may only be published with a warning concerning its reliability (column B). These data are presented in bold in the tables that use LFS data within this publication. In the case that non-response (unknown) to the breakdown characteristics of the labour force (educational attainment, sex and full-time / part-time) exceeded 5% of the total, data have not been published.

---

(8) For the classification of the labour force by educational attainment, use was made of the age group 25-59.
(9) Council Regulation (EC) No. 577/98 of 9 March 1998 on the organisation of a labour force sample survey in the Community.

_____Table 4

Sample thresholds for publication of LFS data
(minimum sample size)

	A	B
EU-15	54,000	-
Belgium	2,500	4,500
Denmark	2,500	4,500
Germany	8,000	-
Greece	2,500	4,500
Spain	2,500	5,000
France	3,500	8,500
Ireland	2,500	4,500
Italy	3,500	7,500
Luxembourg	500	1,500
Netherlands	4,500	10,000
Austria	2,000	-
Portugal	2,500	4,500
Finland	2,500	4,500
Sweden	9,000	-
United Kingdom	10,000	-

A: thresholds for publishing data;
B: thresholds for reliable data.

There was a methodological change between 1998 and 1999 in the collection of Belgian Labour Force Survey data. As such there may well be a rupture in the series in 1999.

National Accounts

The National Accounts data published are in accordance with the ESA-79 (European System of Integrated Economic Accounts), which is the European Union version of the United Nations' system of National Accounts (SNA). It gives common definitions for the complete set of National Accounts, input-output tables and financial (flow or funds) accounts. The basic classification NACE-CLIO, which is used to build the input-output tables that are employed to detail the aggregates by branch. This data may be found in Eurostat's SEC2 database.

The occupied population covers all the persons engaged in some activity which is considered as productive (in the national accounts sense) whether these persons are civilian or military personnel. It comprises both the residents and the non-residents (wage and salary earners, self-employed persons, unpaid family workers, armed forces) who work for resident producer units.

The final consumption of households represents the value of goods and services used for the direct satisfaction of individual human wants. For each branch, the gross value added is the difference between the value of actual output and the value of intermediate consumption. The flow contains the final consumption of resident households and non-residents households on the economic territory.

The ESA-79 has recently been replaced by ESA-95 which, for the purposes of industrial activity, uses a classification based on NACE Rev. 1. At the present time only a limited amount of sectoral data is available from this source, but in future years this should allow National Accounts data to be more comparable with SBS data.

Small and medium-sized enterprises (SME)

The SME tabular data are structural enterprise data, broken down by employment size class and economic activity at national and regional levels. For most (but not all) of the countries, data have been produced by the national statistical authority. In many cases they integrate different official data sources such as business censuses, the VAT register, the statistical business register, results of various surveys and data from social security authorities, notably for employment data.

The main characteristic of the SME data is its breakdown by employment size class. The size class boundaries are expressed in terms of the number of employees (paid employment) hence creating a size class "0" separate from the rest of the enterprise population.

Time frame

The data within this publication was extracted from various Eurostat databases during May 2000. Fresher data may well be available on the CD-ROM products or by consulting the Eurostat Datashop network (see back page or CD-ROM booklet for details), as the SBS database is frequently updated. The text was written during the second and third quarters of 2000.

The time-series for industrial activities are ideally presented for the EU between 1989 and 1999. Gaps in the data were filled (wherever possible) by estimates made by Eurostat. The estimation procedures do not currently extend to cover services (data available generally up until 1997). Individual Member State data was also available up until 1997.

Exchange rates

All data are reported in ECU/euro terms, with national currencies converted using average exchange rates prevailing for the year in question. As of January 1st 1999, eleven of the Member States entered into an economic and monetary union (EMU). These countries form what has become known as the euro-zone (indicated in tables and figures as EUR-11). Technically data available prior to that date should continue to be denominated in ECU terms, whilst data available afterwards should be denominated in euro (EUR). However, as the conversion rate was equal to 1 ECU = 1 EUR, for practical purposes the two terms are used interchangeably (when referring to a series that covers both periods).

Whilst the conversion of data expressed in national currencies to a common currency facilitates comparison, large fluctuations in currency markets are partially responsible for movements identified when looking at the evolution of a series in ECU/EUR terms (especially at the level of an individual country). A table with currency conversion rates may be found on page 38.

Geographical coverage

EU totals given in this publication cover all 15 Member States (they are not aggregates of the available data, unless this is specified in a footnote).

Figures for Germany are on a post-unification basis, unless otherwise stated.

The source of the American data is the Federal Administration, whilst the source of Japanese data is the Ministry of International Trade and Industry (MITI). To compare the EU data with that of the other two Triad members, Eurostat use correspondence tables between NACE Rev. 1 and the US SIC or NAICS activity classifications and the Japanese JSIC activity classification.

Non-availability

Data given as "0" in tables are real zeros. Data presented as ":" are not available, either because the data has not been provided to Eurostat or because it is confidential. In figures, data that are not available are left blank (i.e. no shading), these data are also footnoted. If there is no footnote associated with a value in a figure that looks close to zero, this denotes a real value that is close (or equal) to zero.

GLOSSARY OF TERMS

There follows a brief list of the main terms employed within this publication.

Annual average growth rate: calculated using constant price series (unless otherwise stated). In other words, these growth rates have the effect of price fluctuations over time removed and may be used as a proxy for volume increases/decreases. Annual average growth rates are provided in percentage per annum terms.

Apparent labour productivity: value added at factor cost/number of persons employed (usually expressed in thousand ECU per person employed); care should be taken in the interpretation of this ratio between different activities and countries because of the use of a simple head count for the labour input measure, as a proxy for the volume of work done. Values may exceptionally be negative.

Constant prices: refers to data that have had the effect of price fluctuations over time removed from them (deflated). This is generally done by applying specific producer price indices to current price series. By removing the price effect constant price series may be used as a proxy for volume increases/decreases. The text in this publication only refers to whether a series is in current or constant prices when it is in constant price terms, otherwise the reader should infer that the series presented is in current prices.

Cover ratio: exports / imports (expressed as a percentage).

Current prices: data which are presented including the effects of price changes. In this publication the majority of series are reported in current price terms. The text in this publication only refers to whether a series is in current or constant prices when it is in constant price terms, otherwise the reader should infer that the series presented is in current prices.

Domestic producer price index: covers the prices of all commodities produced in a given country which are sold within the country. Producer price indices are often used to deflate production data (in value) in order to obtain production in constant price terms. The index of producer prices aims to show the changes in ex-works selling prices of all products sold on domestic markets of the various countries, excluding VAT and similar deductible taxes.

Employees: are defined as those persons who work for an employer and who have a contract of employment and receive compensation in the form of wages, salaries, fees, gratuities, piecework pay or remuneration in kind. The relationship of employer to employee exists when there is an agreement, which may be formal or informal, between an enterprise and a person, normally entered into voluntarily by both parties, whereby the person works for the enterprise in return for remuneration in cash or in kind. Employees include part-time workers, seasonal workers, persons on strike or on short-term leave, but excludes those persons on long-term leave. Employees does not include voluntary workers.

Enterprise: an enterprise is the smallest combination of legal units that is an organisational unit producing goods or services, which benefits from a certain degree of autonomy in decision-making, especially for the allocation of its current resources. An enterprise carries out one or more activities at one or more locations. An enterprise may be a sole legal unit.

Export specialisation: relative index that compares the export share of an industrial activity in total manufacturing exports for a given country with the same ratio for the EU (expressed as a percentage). If a country displays a ratio above 100 then it is relatively more specialised than the EU as a whole within the industry being studied. The EU export specialisation figures are calculated as the share of extra-EU exports in total extra-EU manufacturing exports compared to the same ratio for the sum of all Member States (in other words using total trade rather than just extra-EU trade). Hence, if the EU figure is greater than 100% for any given activity, the EU is more orientated towards non-member country markets. If the ratio is less than 100% then the EU is generally more orientated towards the Internal Market.

Extra-EU exports: goods which leave the statistical territory of a Member State bound for a non-member country, having gone through; the customs export procedure (final export, export following inward processing, etc.); or the customs outward-processing procedure (usually goods destined to be processed, transformed or repaired for subsequent re-import).

Extra-EU imports: goods which enter the statistical territory of a Member State from a non-member country and are placed under the customs procedure for release into free circulation (goods intended to be consumed in the importing Member State or dispatched to another Member State), either immediately or after a period in a customs warehouse; or goods which are placed under the customs procedure for inward processing (including inward processing in a customs warehouse) or processing under customs control (usually goods destined to be processed, transformed or repaired for subsequent re-export) either immediately or after a period in a customs warehouse.

Gross investment in tangible goods: investment made during the reference period in all tangible goods. Included are new and existing tangible capital goods, whether bought from third parties or produced for own use (in other words capitalised production of tangible capital goods), having a useful life of more than one year including non-produced tangible goods such as land.

Gross margin: gross operating surplus/value added at factor cost (performance measure, expressed as a percentage). Values may be negative.

Gross operating surplus: is the surplus generated by operating activities after the labour factor input has been recompensed. It can be calculated from the value added at factor cost less the personnel costs. It is the balance available to the unit which allows it to recompense the providers of own funds and debt, to pay taxes and eventually to finance all or a part of its investment. Values may be negative.

Gross operating rate: gross operating surplus/turnover (profitability measure, expressed as a percentage). May be negative.

Investment rate: investment/value added at factor cost (expressed as a percentage). Values may exceptionally be negative.

Nominal terms: refers to a non-deflated series.

Number of persons employed (employment): is defined as the total number of persons who work in the observation unit (inclusive of working proprietors, partners working regularly in the unit and unpaid family workers), as well as persons who work outside the unit who belong to it and are paid by it (e.g. sales representatives, delivery personnel, repair and maintenance teams). It includes persons absent for a short period (e.g. sick leave, paid leave or special leave), and also those on strike, but not those absent for an indefinite period. It also includes part-time workers who are regarded as such under the laws of the country concerned and who are on the pay-roll, as well as seasonal workers, apprentices and home workers on the pay-roll.

Total operating costs: sum of total purchases of goods and services and personnel costs.

Personnel costs: the total remuneration, in cash or in kind, payable by an employer to an employee (regular and temporary employees as well as home workers) in return for work done by the latter during the reference period. Personnel costs also include taxes and employees' social security contributions retained by the unit as well as the employer's compulsory and voluntary social contributions. Personnel costs are made up of: wages and salaries and employers' social security costs.

Production specialisation: relative index that compares the production share of an industrial activity in total manufacturing production for a given country with the same ratio for the EU (expressed as a percentage - if a country displays a ratio above 100 then it is relatively more specialised than the EU as a whole within the industry being studied).

Production value: measures the amount actually produced by the unit, based on sales adjusted for changes in stocks and the resale of goods and services. The production value is defined as turnover, plus or minus the changes in stocks of finished products, work in progress and goods and services purchased for resale, minus the purchases of goods and services for resale, plus capitalised production, plus other operating income (excluding subsidies). Values may very exceptionally be negative.

Real terms: used as a synonym for a deflated series (i.e. with the effect of price fluctuations removed).

Simple wage adjusted labour productivity: value added at factor cost/personnel costs * 100 (expressed as a ratio). Values may exceptionally be negative.

Social security costs: correspond to an amount equal to the value of the social contributions incurred by employers in order to secure for their employees the entitlement to social benefits. Social security costs include the employer's social security contributions to schemes for retirement pensions, sickness, maternity, disability, unemployment, occupational accidents and diseases, family allowances as well as other schemes.

Total purchases of goods and services: include the value of all goods and services purchased during the accounting period for resale or consumption in the production process, excluding capital goods the consumption of which is registered as consumption of fixed capital. The goods and services concerned may be either resold with or without further transformation, completely used up in the production process or, finally, be stocked.

Trade balance: exports - imports (values may be negative).

Turnover: comprises the totals invoiced by the observation unit during the reference period, and this corresponds to market sales of goods or services supplied to third parties. Turnover includes all duties and taxes on the goods or services invoiced by the unit with the exception of the VAT invoiced by the unit vis-à-vis its customer and other similar deductible taxes directly linked to turnover. It also includes all other charges (transport, packaging, etc.) passed on to the customer, even if these charges are listed separately in the invoice. Reduction in prices, rebates and discounts as well as the value of returned packing must be deducted.

Unit personnel costs: personnel costs/number of employees in nominal terms (usually expressed in thousand ECU per employee).

Value added at factor cost: is the gross income from operating activities after adjusting for operating subsidies and indirect taxes. It can be calculated from turnover, plus capitalised production, plus other operating income, plus or minus the changes in stocks, minus the purchases of goods and services, minus other taxes on products which are linked to turnover but not deductible, minus the duties and taxes linked to production. Alternatively it can be calculated from gross operating surplus by adding personnel costs. Income and expenditure classified as financial or extraordinary in company accounts is excluded from value added. Values may exceptionally be negative.

Wage adjusted labour productivity: (value added at factor cost/personnel costs) * (number of employees/number of persons employed) * 100 (expressed as a ratio). Values may exceptionally be negative.

ABBREVIATIONS

A	Austria
B	Belgium
B/L	Belgo-Luxembourg Economic Union
BLEU	Belgo-Luxembourg Economic Union
CN	Combined Nomenclature (product classification for foreign trade)
COMEXT	Eurostat reference database containing external trade statistics (commerce extérieur)
D	Germany
DK	Denmark
EBT	European Business Trends (Eurostat database of short-term indicators)
ECU	European currency unit
E	Spain
EL	Greece
EU	European Union
EU-15	fifteen Member States of the European Union
EUR	euro
EUR-11	eleven Member States participating in the euro
Eurostat	Eurostat is one of the Directorates-General of the European Commission; also known as ESTAT
Euro-zone	geographical entity covered by the eleven Member States participating in the euro
F	France
FDI	Foreign Direct Investment
FIN	Finland
GDP	Gross Domestic Product
IRL	Ireland
I	Italy
JAP	Japan
L	Luxembourg
LFS	Labour Force Survey
NACE/CLIO	General Industrial Classification of Economic Activities in the European Communities - version used for the input-output tables (European System of Accounts 1979). Used in National Accounts to divide the economy into different sectors
NACE Rev. 1	Statistical Classification of Economic Activities in the European Community, Revision 1.
NL	Netherlands
P	Portugal
S	Sweden
SBS	Structural Business Statistics
SME	Small and Medium-sized Enterprises
Triad	EU-15, Japan and the USA
UK	United Kingdom
USA	United States of America
:	not available

Overview: evolution of the European business economy

The aim of this publication is to delineate the structure of industrial and service activities within the European Union. Before going into the detail of individual industries and services, this introductory chapter provides a brief overview of the structure of the EU economy in comparison to that of the other members of the Triad, Japan and the USA, before looking at developments in EU manufacturing, illustrating in particular the relative performance of the different activities and Member States.

1. GENERAL ECONOMIC DEVELOPMENTS WITHIN THE TRIAD

For the purpose of this study the data concentrates upon six branches of the economy (agriculture[1], fuel and power, manufacturing, construction, market services and non-market services) and two variables (value added in constant prices using a purchasing power standard and the number of persons employed). The data given in this section come from National Accounts (stored within Eurostat's SEC2 database). The NACE-CLIO nomenclature used in National Accounts means that no comparison can be made between data presented in this section and that which follows for industrial and service sectors (based on the NACE Rev. 1 classification of economic activities).

(1) This term is used as an abbreviation for the complete title of agriculture, forestry and fishery products.

EU accounted for more than 40% of the Triad's GDP, GDP totalled 16,649 billion PPS within the Triad in 1996. The breakdown of GDP between the three Triad members showed that the EU accounted for 40.6% of total GDP, just behind the USA (43.0%), but well ahead of Japan (16.4%). Whilst the EU had higher absolute GDP than Japan, the ratio of value added per capita (which may be used as an indicator to measure the standard of living) showed that the EU lagged behind both the USA and Japan. Value added per capita stood at 18.1 thousand PPS in the EU in 1996, compared to 21.8 thousand PPS in Japan and 26.9 thousand PPS in the USA. Lower activity rates may be cited as one of the underlying causes of the lower EU per capita figure, as only 55.3% of the total population aged 15 or over were active in the EU in 1996 . Activity rates across the EU varied considerably, from above 60% in Denmark, Sweden and the United Kingdom to below 50% in Italy, Greece and Spain.

(2) Within the labour force (in other words persons employed or actively seeking work).

Box 1

Currency fluctuations play an important role in the competitiveness of international economies. The majority of the growth rates given in this publication for Triad comparisons are based upon the period 1987 to 1997. Between these years there was a fairly small change in the ECU-dollar exchange rate from 1.15445 to 1.13404[3], an appreciation of 4.1% for the dollar. The change in the ECU-Yen exchange rate was more substantial, with the Yen appreciating by 9.5%.

Figure 1

Changes in the exchange rates of the ECU/euro (% change on the previous year) (1)

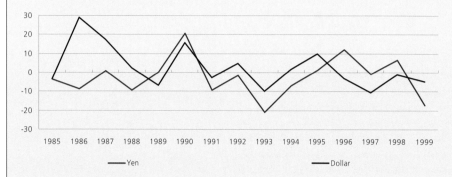

(1) A positive figure implies an appreciation of the ECU/euro.

Source: Eurostat (MNY)

As of January 1st 1999[4], the euro entered into force, creating a common currency with irrevocably fixed conversion rates between 11 Member States[5]. As such, currency differentials between the 11 participating countries have been eliminated. This change is of particular importance as more than 63% of the EU's trade was conducted on an intra-EU basis in 1999 (in other words, trade between EU Member States).

The ECU/euro[6] is used as the common currency unit throughout this publication. The interpretation of ECU/euro based series should be treated with caution, especially when making inter-temporal comparisons, as volatility in currency markets has resulted in annual changes in excess of +/-10% being common place[7].

(3) Expressed in terms of 1 ECU=X national currency.
(4) Council Regulation (EC) No 2866/98 of 31 December 1998 on the conversion rates between the euro and the currencies of the Member States adopting the euro.
(5) At the time of writing (summer 2000) DK, EL, S and UK were not members of the euro-zone.
(6) From January 1st 1999, ECU values were converted to euro on the basis of a 1:1 exchange rate. Data post-1999 use the euro as their unit of currency, whilst pre-1999 series continue to employ the ECU as their unit of currency.
(7) The standard deviation of the annual change in relation to the ECU/euro between 1985 and 1999 was equal to 10.6% for the yen and 11.1% for the dollar.

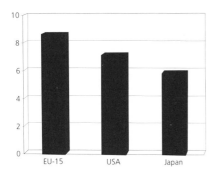

_____ Figure 2

**Annual average growth rates of labour
productivity in the Triad, 1985-1996 (%) (1)**

(1) Value added in constant prices for agriculture, energy,
manufacturing, construction, market and non-market
services.

Source: Eurostat (SEC2)

*Market services are the largest and fastest
growing branch of the Triad economy*

The largest share of value added in the Triad was generated by the market services' branch of the economy.
In 1996 this branch was responsible for an absolute
majority of total value added in all three Triad
economies: ranging from 52.7% in the USA to 51.0%
in the EU-6 (founder Member States, no other data
was available in constant price terms). Market services
were the only branch of the EU economy where the
relative share of value added rose between 1985 and
1996. A similar picture was seen in Japan, if the minor
increase of 0.1% for manufactured products is dis-
counted.

EU-6 data recorded the fastest shift towards market
services from other branches of the economy between
1985 and 1996, with the share of market services in
total value added increasing by 4.6 percentage points.
The speed of transformation towards a service-based
economy in the EU may in part be explained by the
fact that the USA (and to a lesser degree Japan) had
already seen a large amount of economic activity
switch to services prior to 1985.

*The share of EU manufacturing in the total value
added recorded the largest decline*

Nowhere was the decline in the relative share of EU
value added more noticeable than in the manufacturing sector ((-2.2 percentage points, again in constant
price terms for EU-6). Between 1985 and 1996, the
manufacturing sector of the EU fared worse than in
the other two Triad economies, where relative increases of 2.3 percentage points and 0.1 percentage points
were recorded in the USA and Japan respectively.
Manufacturing did however remain the second largest
branch in the EU-6 economy, accounting for 22.4% of
total value added in 1996, a share between those of
the USA (20.6%) and Japan (25.7%).

Data for all 15 Member States in current price terms
support the changes observed in constant prices for 6
Member States - with a more rapid switch from manufacturing to market services.

_____Table 1

Structure and evolution of value added in the Triad (% share of value added in constant prices)

	EU-6		Japan		USA	
	1996	1985/1996 (points change)	1996	1985/1996 (points change)	1996	1985/1996 (points change)
Market services	51.0	4.6	51.3	2.5	52.7	-0.5
Manufactured products	22.4	-2.2	25.7	0.1	20.6	2.3
Non-market services	14.8	-0.6	8.7	-2.1	16.7	-1.4
Building and construction	4.7	-1.1	9.0	0.7	3.9	-0.6
Fuel and power products	4.3	-0.7	3.3	-0.3	3.9	0.0
Agricultural, forestry and fishery products	2.7	-0.3	1.9	-1.0	2.1	0.1

Source: Eurostat (SEC2)

Table 2 ───

Structure and evolution of employment in the Triad (% share of total employment) (1)

	EU-15		Japan		USA	
	1997	1985/1997 (points change)	1997	1985/1997 (points change)	1997	1985/1997 (points change)
Market services	46.2	7.4	52.4	4.2	53.7	4.7
Manufactured products	19.6	-4.7	22.5	-1.9	14.7	-3.8
Non-market services	21.3	0.4	6.1	-0.4	22.3	0.0
Building and construction	6.6	:	10.9	1.7	5.7	0.0
Agricultural, forestry and fishery products	5.2	-3.1	7.3	-3.7	2.8	-0.3
Fuel and power products	1.2	:	0.7	0.1	0.9	-0.6

(1) The change in employment for manufactured products includes building and construction and fuel and power for the EU.

Source: Eurostat (SEC2)

Evolution of employment in the Triad,
strong growth for market services

There were approximately 340 million persons employed within the Triad in 1997. This represented a 13.2% increase compared to 1985. The number of additional persons employed rose at a fast rate in the USA (an increase of 23.4%), whilst the EU and Japan reported much lower overall growth (7.5% and 10.5% respectively).

The highest share of employment was unsurprisingly accounted for by market services (50.2% of total Triad employment). At the same time the corresponding share of market services in total value added was higher in all three Triad economies, and hence, apparent labour productivity for this branch was superior to that of the total economy as a whole. As well as providing the most jobs and recording the highest net increase in the number of occupied persons, market services were therefore the most productive by this measure.

The net gain of 24.2 million persons occupied in the USA was almost two and a half times the improvement recorded in the EU (10.2 million persons) and nearly four times the net increase recorded in Japan (6.3 million persons)[8]. These absolute figures translated into annual average growth rates of 1.8% in the USA, 0.8% in Japan and 0.6% in the EU between 1985 and 1997. Hence, whilst value added in the EU appeared to be catching up on the levels recorded in Japan and the USA, employment was growing at a slower pace.

Market services account for a net
gain of almost 15 million jobs

Market services recorded a 7.4 percentage point increase in their share of total EU employment between 1985 and 1997, equivalent to a gain of 14.8 million persons. Despite this rapid rate of increase (faster than in either Japan or the USA), this branch accounted for only 46.2% of total employment in the EU in 1997, a lower share than either the USA or Japan (53.7% and 52.4%).

Of the remaining branches, only non-market services reported a slight increase in their share of total EU employment (up by 0.4 percentage points). On the downside there was a decline of 3.6 million persons employed within energy, manufacturing and construction between 1985 and 1997. Manufacturing continued to account for around one-fifth of the total number of persons occupied in the EU in 1997 (19.6%), which was a considerably higher share than in the USA (14.7%).

Summary

This brief introductory section has shown that the majority of growth over the last decade and a half in the EU economy (be it in terms of value added or employment) has been generated within the service sector (or more specifically the market services economy). This was not a common trend observed throughout the Triad, as manufactured products made relative gains within the USA economy.

It would appear that both higher national income (standards of living), as well as the creation of more jobs depend strongly upon the performance of the market services' sector of the economy. Whilst it is true that many new service activities have witnessed rapid growth in recent years, it is also true that some changes are of a structural nature. Two or three decades ago industrial enterprises may have had their own catering, security, industrial cleaning and personnel services, as well as an accounting and legal departments. Nowadays, many of these services are outsourced or sub-contracted to enterprises that specialise in their provision. Whilst the tasks carried out may have remained quite similar, there has been a shift in the economic activity under which they are classified.

───────────────────────────────

(8) Note that these figures do not take account of the differences in the size of population.

2. EU MANUFACTURING PERFORMANCE

Production value of the EU's manufacturing sector reached nearly 4,000 billion EUR in 1999. The late 1980s and the mid- to late 1990s were the two periods with the most rapid growth. Nevertheless, compared to long-term historical developments, the last decade and a half has seen fairly modest annual average growth rates in real terms for both production and value added. Production in constant prices accelerated towards the end of the 1990s, recording an expansion of 4.9% per annum in the five-year period to 1998 (value added grew by 3.1% per annum in real terms over the same period). The EU generated considerably less value added than either the USA or Japan, and the differential between real production and value added growth rates provided further evidence that the European industrial economy has further potential to specialise in high added value industries.

The relative weight of the EU's manufacturing sector increased during the last 15 years

The EU's share of Triad manufacturing output grew by 2.8 percentage points between 1985 and 1997, whilst the relative shares of both the USA and Japan decreased[9]. In 1997, the EU accounted for 40.0% of manufacturing output in the Triad (compared to 36.9% in the USA and 23.0% in Japan). Nevertheless, the same breakdown of value added provided evidence that American manufacturing concentrated on high value added products or processes, as the USA accounted for 45.6% of Triad value added in 1985. Japan and the EU had caught-up to some degree, as the American share fell by 4.1 percentage points between 1985 and 1996 (Japan gaining 3.5 percentage points).

The EU was by far the leading manufacturing employer in the Triad

There were around 23.3 million persons employed in the manufacturing sector in the EU in 1999. This was a significant decline compared to the number of persons employed in 1985, down by almost 2.5 million persons. However, there has been little evolution in the level of European employment since 1994 as all the losses were experienced before this date. The EU's relative share of Triad employment declined at a moderate pace between 1985 and 1996. The EU accounted for almost half of the Triad manufacturing workforce in 1985 (47.8%), a relative share that fell to 45.9% by 1996. Japan's share remained constant over the whole period, whilst the USA recorded a 2 percentage point gain.

(9) The loss of approximately 1.4 percentage points for both JAP and the USA hides the fact that the Japanese share of Triad output fell by 7.1 percentage points between 1993 and 1997.

2.1. SHARES OF MANUFACTURING ACTIVITY BY MEMBER STATE

As would be expected, the largest EU Member States (in terms of population and GDP) were the main contributors to EU manufacturing output in 1997. The four largest economies[10] together produced 72.2% of the EU manufacturing total in 1997 (down from 74.0% in 1987).

Modest shift in production away from the largest Member States towards the periphery of the EU…

Germany was by far the leading producer within the EU, accounting for 26.6% of the EU total, although the German share of EU manufacturing fell by 2.6 percentage points over this period. The remaining larger countries showed less of a change in their production shares. The fastest growth rates for production were recorded in Spain, Ireland and Portugal, as EU production shifted somewhat away from its centre towards the periphery of the European Union.

(10) D (26.6%), F (16.3%), UK (15.1%) and I (14.2%, 1996).

Figure 3

Manufacturing production as a share of the EU total, 1987 and 1997 (%)

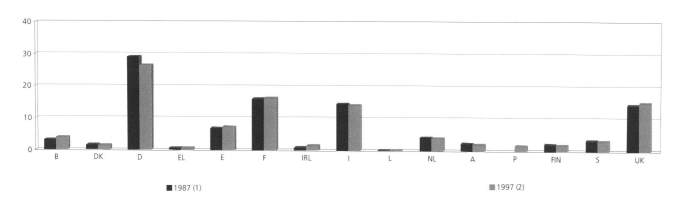

■ 1987 (1)　　　　■ 1997 (2)

(1) FIN, 1988; P, not available.
(2) EL and I, 1996.

Source: Eurostat (SBS)

Figure 4

Manufacturing employment as a share of the EU total, 1987 and 1997 (%)

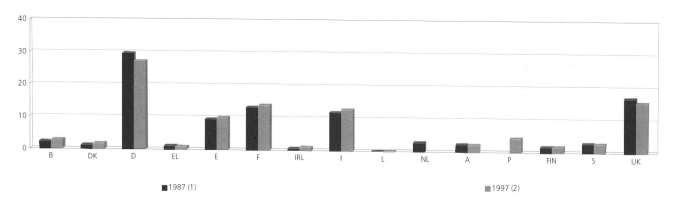

■ 1987 (1)   ■ 1997 (2)

(1) FIN, 1988; P, not available.
(2) EL and I, 1996; NL, not available.

Source: Eurostat (SBS)

2.2 SHARES OF MANUFACTURING ACTIVITY BY INDUSTRY

... likewise for value added

The shares registered by each of the Member States in the EU's total manufacturing value added largely followed the trend seen for EU production. Ireland was the country with the largest relative gain, recording an increase of 0.8 percentage points in its share of total value added between 1987 and 1997. Germany and France were the two countries that recorded the largest declines in their respective shares. As such, value added was also seen to be shifting at a moderate pace away from the four largest EU economies towards the smaller Member States.

... as well as employment

Total EU manufacturing employment stood at 23.3 million persons in 1997 (down 8.9% on the figure for 1987). Looking at the shares of each Member State in the EU total between 1987 and 1997 a similar phenomena was seen as for production and value added. Germany (-2.4 percentage points) and the United Kingdom (-1.4 points) recorded the largest declines in their relative shares, whilst some of the southern Member States (Spain, Italy and Portugal) benefited.

The growth rates of production and value added across different industries varied considerably from one Member State to another. This would seem to be evidence that there is scope for restructuring and allocation of resources within the European Union. These differences may be attributed to different business cultures within national economies, as well as to the processes of specialisation and concentration across the Union. With the increasing trend of globalisation, it is common for enterprises (particularly large enterprises) to re-structure their productive capacity and to locate in a reduced number of locations (where competitive and comparative advantages exist). This trend may explain to some degree the shift in production from the larger EU economies.

Food, beverages and tobacco was the largest industry in terms of production value...

The largest industry when ranking the Panorama 2000 manufacturing chapters by production value was food, beverages and tobacco (chapter 3), which accounted for 16.0% of the EU total in 1997. Chemicals, rubber and plastics (chapter 6) had a 14.7% of EU manufacturing output, whilst transport equipment (chapter 13) followed in third place with a 13.2% share. None of the remaining chapter headings accounted for more than 10% of EU production value.

At the other end of the ranking, furniture manufacture and other manufacturing (chapter 14), made-up besides furniture of jewellery, musical instruments, sports goods and games and toys, accounted for just 2.5% of total EU manufacturing output, whilst instrument engineering (chapter 12) had a 1.9% share.

Figure 5

Share of total manufacturing production in the EU, 1997 (%) (1)

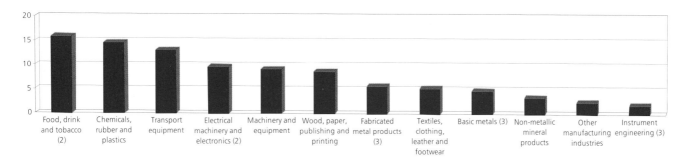

(1) The shares in total manufacturing production do not sum to 100% as mixed reference years had to be used to provide information for all activities; excluding NACE Rev. 1 23.
(2) Estimates.
(3) 1996.

Source: Eurostat (SBS)

... but was a distant third in terms of value added
A similar ranking by chapter heading for value added at factor costs showed notable differences. Activities with the fastest growth rates for value added tended to have a much higher relative share of total EU value added compared to their respective shares of production value. In other words, there was a tendency for the EU to increasingly concentrate production in activities that generated higher added value. It is nevertheless important to note that the EU's share of total Triad value added remained considerably below its corresponding shares of either production value or employment.

Chemicals, rubber and plastics generated the highest share of manufacturing value added in the EU in 1997, accounting for 16.3% of the total, some 2.1 percentage points more than its corresponding production share. This figure was well above the second-placed industry, transport equipment, which registered an 11.8% share. Food, beverages and tobacco followed close behind in third place (11.4%), whilst machinery and equipment (chapter 10), wood, paper, publishing and printing (chapter 5) and electrical machinery and electronics (chapter 11) also accounted for more than 10% of EU manufacturing added value in 1997.

The industries that recorded a loss in their respective shares of total EU value added could generally be grouped together as mature, labour-intensive industries. The largest decline was recorded by textiles, clothing, leather and footwear (chapter 4), where a loss of 1.7 percentage points was recorded between 1987 and 1997, followed by the basic treatment of metals (chapter 8), where there was a 1.1 percentage point reduction.

Figure 6

Share of total manufacturing value added in the EU, 1997 (%) (1)

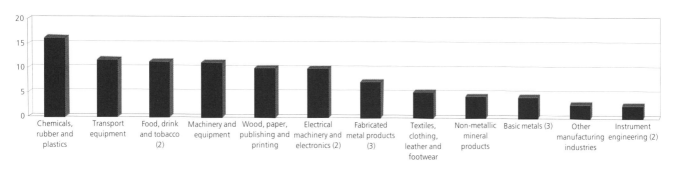

(1) The shares in total manufacturing value added do not sum to 100% as mixed reference years had to be used to provide information for all activities; excluding NACE Rev. 1 23.
(2) Estimates.
(3) 1996.

Source: Eurostat (SBS)

2.3 SPECIALISATION AND CONCENTRATION
TRENDS IN EU MANUFACTURING

The degree of specialisation has grown within the EU during the last decade[11]. Taking the specialisation of the five most important activities at the level of NACE Rev. 1 Divisions, there was an increase in the specialisation ratios for 10 out of the 11 Member States for which data was available during the latest ten-year period (1987-1997). Greece was the only exception, with the output share of its top five industries in the domestic manufacturing total falling by 5.7 percentage points. In general the larger Member States reported the lowest absolute differences between the shares of the top five industries in 1987 and 1997.

Structural change slowest in the large Member States
One measure for studying the rate of structural change within EU manufacturing is to look at the individual shares of each NACE Rev. 1 Division in the manufacturing total for each Member State and to see how these shares evolve over time. Taking the sum of the absolute changes between 1987 and 1997 it is possible to show which Member States adapted their manufacturing sector at the fastest pace[12].

(11) The term specialisation is defined in this context as the share of the top five industries within the domestic manufacturing total of a particular country. The indicator uses value added at factor cost as its measure for output. There were incomplete time-series for B, L, A and P. Data for EL and I in 1997 were replaced with 1996 data. Data for FIN in 1987 was replaced with 1988 data.
(12) Again this indicator is based upon changes in value added at factor cost between 1987 and 1997, subject to data availability - details of which are given in footnote 11.

Ireland was the country to report the most rapid changes in the composition of its manufacturing sector, closely followed by Greece. Sweden and Finland were the next countries in the ranking. At the bottom of the ranking were a group of countries with very similar results: including (in descending order) Spain, the Netherlands, the United Kingdom, France and Germany. The results for this indicator were consistent with those measuring the evolution of specialisation within the Member States. It is revealing that the countries with the highest growth rates for manufacturing value added over the period 1987 to 1997 were generally the same as those that reported increasing levels of specialisation and an ability to adapt their manufacturing structure quickly (with the exception of Finland and Sweden).

These aggregate figures should not necessarily mean that the larger Member States were not specialising production in a number of key industries where they benefited from competitive advantages. In Germany the share of the motor vehicles industry rose from 12.4% of domestic manufacturing in 1987 to 13.7% by 1997, whilst the share of food, drink and tobacco increased from 12.4% to 13.8% in the United Kingdom and the chemicals industry registered a net gain of 1.6 percentage points in France, attaining a 13.2% share in 1997. In the smaller EU countries, specialisation has led to the development of niche markets. There is probably a higher degree of risk attached to this policy in smaller economies, as external shocks may have more serious repercussions when production is concentrated in a limited number of industries.

Figure 7

Value added of the top five manufacturing activities, 1987 and 1997 (%) (1)

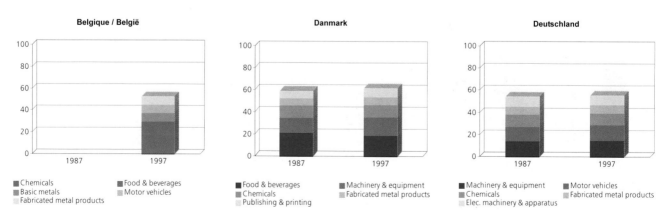

(1) B, L, A and P, incomplete time-series; FIN, 1988 instead of 1987; EL and I, 1996 instead of 1997.

Source: Eurostat (SBS)

———Figure 7 (continued)

Value added of the top five manufacturing activities, 1987 and 1997 (%) (1)

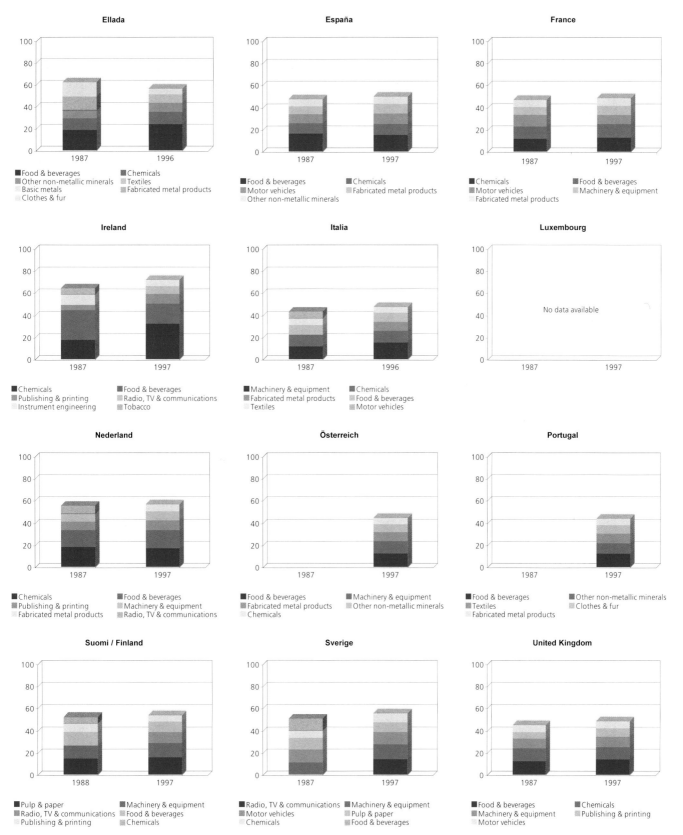

(1) B, L, A and P, incomplete time-series; FIN, 1988 instead of 1987; EL and I, 1996 instead of 1997.

Source: Eurostat (SBS)

Figure 8

Geographical concentration of value added, 1987 and 1997 (%) (1)

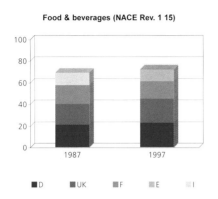

Food & beverages (NACE Rev. 1 15)

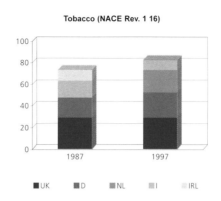

Tobacco (NACE Rev. 1 16)

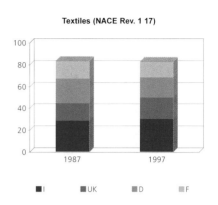

Textiles (NACE Rev. 1 17)

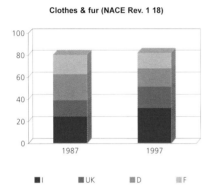

Clothes & fur (NACE Rev. 1 18)

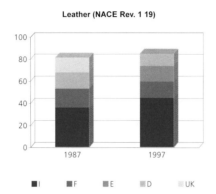

Leather (NACE Rev. 1 19)

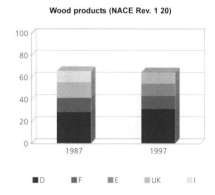

Wood products (NACE Rev. 1 20)

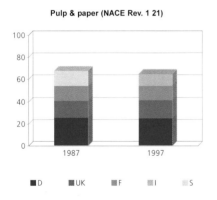

Pulp & paper (NACE Rev. 1 21)

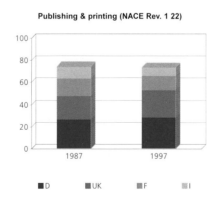

Publishing & printing (NACE Rev. 1 22)

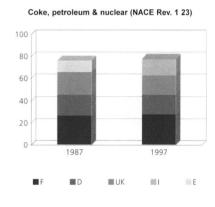

Coke, petroleum & nuclear (NACE Rev. 1 23)

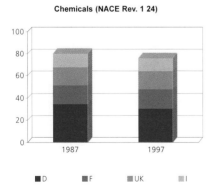

Chemicals (NACE Rev. 1 24)

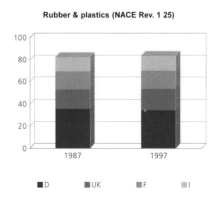

Rubber & plastics (NACE Rev. 1 25)

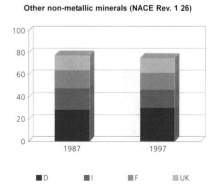

Other non-metallic minerals (NACE Rev. 1 26)

(1) B, L, A and P, incomplete time-series; EL and I, 1997 instead of 1996.

Source: Eurostat (SBS)

Figure 8 (continued)

Geographical concentration of value added, 1987 and 1997 (%) (1)

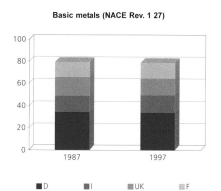

Basic metals (NACE Rev. 1 27)

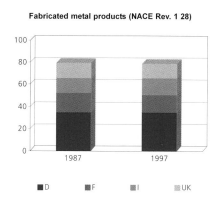

Fabricated metal products (NACE Rev. 1 28)

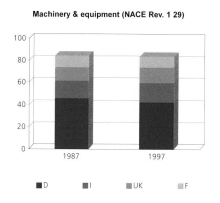

Machinery & equipment (NACE Rev. 1 29)

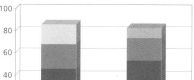

Office machinery & computers (NACE Rev. 1 30)

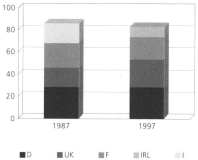

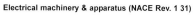

Electrical machinery & apparatus (NACE Rev. 1 31)

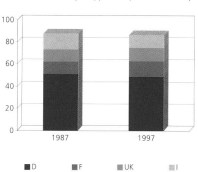

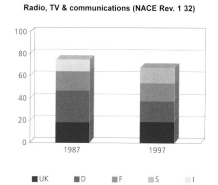

Radio, TV & communications (NACE Rev. 1 32)

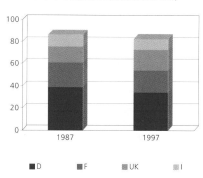

Instrument engineering (NACE Rev. 1 33)

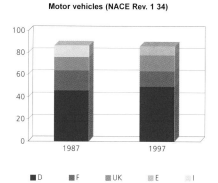

Motor vehicles (NACE Rev. 1 34)

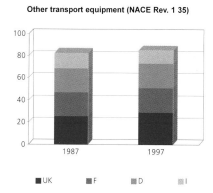

Other transport equipment (NACE Rev. 1 35)

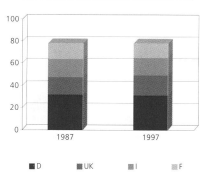

Furniture & other manufacturing (NACE Rev. 1 36)

(1) B, L, A and P, incomplete time-series; FIN, 1988 instead of 1987; EL and I, 1996 instead of 1997.

Source: Eurostat (SBS)

Geographical concentration lessens in the 1990s

The change in the geographical distribution of industrial activities over time may be studied by looking at the sum of the differences of country shares in total EU output between two given periods (1987 and 1997)[13]. Looking at the evolution of shares of total value added by country, there was some diversity in the composition over time. There was a high degree of change in the distribution of output in the tobacco industry (NACE Rev. 1 16), radio, television and communication equipment (NACE Rev. 1 32), office machinery and computers (NACE Rev. 1 30) and wearing apparel and fur (NACE Rev. 1 18), whilst on the other hand there was a low degree of re-allocation of productive capacity in machinery and equipment (NACE Rev. 1 29), other transport equipment (NACE Rev. 1 35) and rubber and plastics (NACE Rev. 1 25).

Taking the share of the largest four producing countries for each NACE Rev. 1 Division, it is possible to create a concentration ratio (referred to here as CR4). The CR4 was over 85% in 1987 in the manufacture of electrical machinery and apparatus n.e.c. (NACE Rev. 1 31), instrument engineering (NACE Rev. 1 33), the manufacture of motor vehicles (NACE Rev. 1 34) and the manufacture of office machinery and computers (NACE Rev. 1 30).

---

(13) Again value added at factor cost is used as an indicator for output. There were incomplete time-series for B, L, A and P. FIN, 1988 instead of 1987. Data for EL and I in 1997 were replaced with 1996 data.

The CR4 fell between 1987 and 1997 in the majority of industries. The highest CR4s in 1997 were recorded by other transport equipment (NACE Rev. 1 35), where the top four producing Member States had an 82.3% share of EU output. The least concentrated industries were wood (NACE Rev. 1 20) and pulp and paper (NACE Rev. 1 21), where less than 65% of output was generated by the four largest producers.

The largest geographical shift in production was in the tobacco communication equipment industries

The largest absolute change in the CR4 between 1987 and 1997 was recorded in the tobacco (NACE Rev. 1 16) and radio, television and communication equipment industry (NACE Rev. 1 32).

In conclusion, the distribution of value added across the EU does not appear to have created asymmetries between countries, rather the smaller countries and the periphery of the Union have benefited as there has been a diversification of output. The main driving forces behind this change would appear to be higher growth rates and quicker adaptability, resulting in the smaller Member States becoming specialised producers, whilst the larger Member States see their relative share of output decline, as productive capacity switches to more economically favourable regions of the Union. Whilst globalisation widens the horizon for production-related decision making, it also increases the speed with which information, technology and ultimately competition are diffused.

2.4 EXPORT TRENDS IN EU MANUFACTURING

Whilst this section has, so far, focused upon the productive capacity within the EU and the shift in output between industries and countries, exports offer an alternative means of gaining market shares. This penultimate section of the introductory overview provides a general description of the main trends that have been witnessed within the EU as regards the export of manufactured goods.

Whilst production specialisation has increased within the Member States, it would appear that the same cannot be said for exports. This may appear an anomaly as the share of production destined for domestic consumption has generally declined at the expense of production for export as a result of the globalisation process and the opening up of the Internal Market. However, these changes in the structure of the global economy may only explain partially the trends observed, as it is often difficult to measure the trade of goods and services between units contained within the same enterprise group, whilst it is easier to measure their output.

Machinery and equipment is Europe's leading export sector, with 15.2% of extra-EU exports

Extra-EU exports totalled 708.9 billion EUR in 1999. The leading export sector was machinery and equipment (NACE Rev. 1 29), which accounted for a 15.2% of the EU's manufacturing exports to non-Community countries, just ahead of the chemicals industry (NACE Rev. 1 24) with 14.3%. There was only one other industry that had a double-digit share of manufacturing exports in 1999, motor vehicles (NACE Rev. 1 34) with exactly 10.0%.

The five leading EU export sectors accounted for more than half of manufacturing exports...

The top five exporting sectors[14] accounted for over half (54.0%) of total EU manufacturing exports in 1999. This figure was down by 0.2 percentage points when compared to the corresponding share of the top five export industries in 1989. By Member State, the share of the top five exporting industries in total manufacturing exports showed a share of at least 50% in every Member State (although Italy, Portugal and Austria had shares just above 50%).

... a share that rose as high as 86.0% in Ireland

Germany was the only one of the five largest EU economies to report that more than 60% of its exports were accounted for by its top five exporting sectors (60.7%). The main exporting industries within Germany were motor vehicles (19.8% of manufacturing exports), machinery and equipment (16.2%) and chemicals (12.1%) - these three activities were also the three leading export activities for the EU as a whole. Amongst the remaining countries, Belgium/Luxembourg, Sweden, Finland and Greece also reported between 60% and 70% of their manufacturing exports accounted for by their top five export earners in 1999, whilst the share in Ireland reached as high as 86.0%.

_____

(14) This description is based upon the evolution of exports in value terms between 1989 and 1999. Extra-EU exports are used as the measure for the EU, whilst total exports (intra and extra-EU) are used for the individual Member States. The study is based upon the 22 NACE Rev. 1 Divisions that form manufacturing. Data presented for B and L is aggregated due to the economic and monetary union between these countries.

Figure 9

Share of EU manufacturing exports to non-Community countries, 1999 (%)

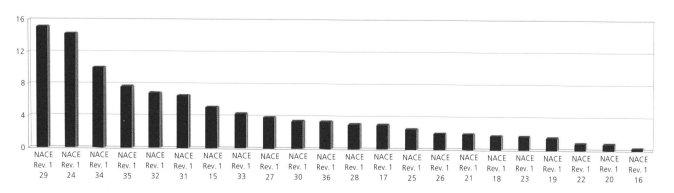

Source: Eurostat (COMEXT)

Figure 10

Top five manufacturing export sectors, 1989 and 1999 (%)

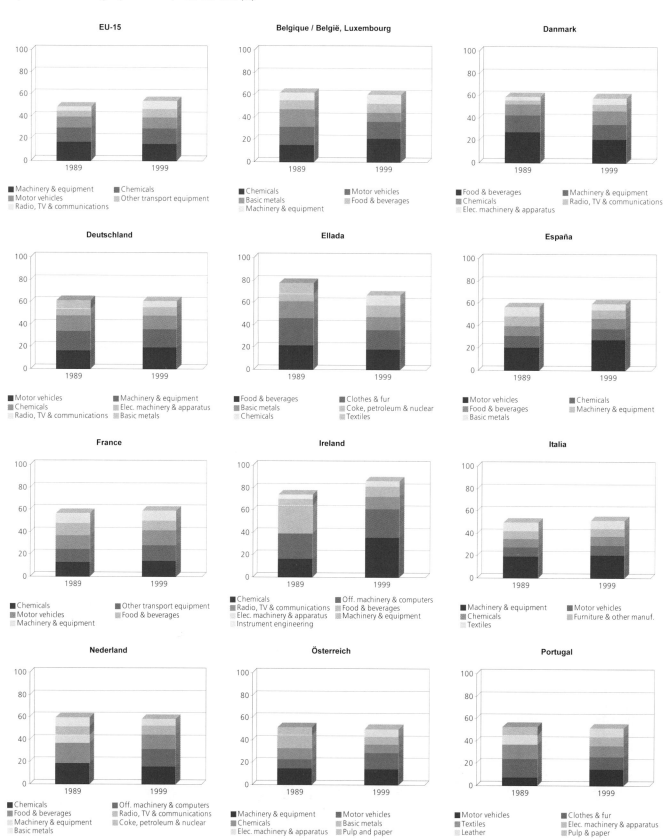

Source: Eurostat (COMEXT)

—————————————————————————————————Figure 10 (continued)

Top five manufacturing export sectors, 1989 and 1999 (%)

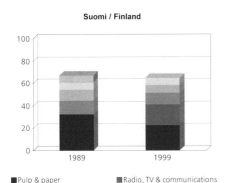

Suomi / Finland

■ Pulp & paper
■ Machinery & equipment
▨ Wood products
■ Radio, TV & communications
▨ Basic metals
▨ Chemicals

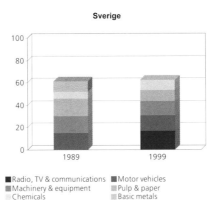

Sverige

■ Radio, TV & communications
▨ Machinery & equipment
▨ Chemicals
■ Motor vehicles
▨ Pulp & paper
▨ Basic metals

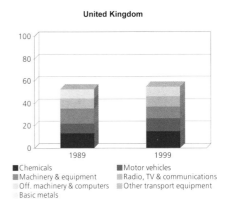

United Kingdom

■ Chemicals
■ Machinery & equipment
▨ Off. machinery & computers
▨ Basic metals
■ Motor vehicles
■ Radio, TV & communications
▨ Other transport equipment

Source: Eurostat (COMEXT)

*However, mixed results concerning the evolution
of export specialisation over time*

The share of the top five export industries increased in 6 of the 15 Member States between 1989 and 1999. The largest increase was recorded in Ireland with a gain of 12.0 percentage points (mainly due to the performance of the chemicals and radio, television and communication equipment industries). With the exception of Germany (-0.8 percentage points), the remaining four largest EU economies also reported increasing export specialisation, with gains above 1.5 percentage points. Sweden and Ireland were the only smaller Member States to follow this trend. On the other hand, the top five exporting industries lost 10.8 percentage points in Greece (mainly due to a reduction in the importance of wearing apparel, textiles, basic metals and food and beverages), resulting in 66.4% of exports being generated by the top five activities in 1999.

*Tobacco and other transport equipment register
the highest geographical concentration of exports*

The tobacco industry had 87.7% of its exports concentrated within four Member States in 1999. Only one other industry had more than 80% of its exports accounted for by the top four exporters, other transport equipment (86.5%). Exports were least concentrated in the wood, food and beverages and radio, television and communication equipment industries, where less than 61.0% of EU exports were accounted for by the leading four exporters. All of these industries were characterised by the fact that smaller Member States had a considerable share of production (reducing the weight of the larger EU economies, which normally formed the group of top exporters).

*Exports become less concentrated
within the European Union*

In 1989, 10 out of the 22 NACE Rev. 1 manufacturing Divisions had more than 70% of their exports concentrated within the four largest exporting countries. By 1999, this figure had dropped to just 6 out of 22. The share of the top four (CR4) exporting countries within total EU exports declined in all but two industries studied, office machinery and computers (NACE Rev. 1 30) and other transport equipment (NACE Rev. 1 35). These are the same two industries that had recorded the highest CR4 for production in1997. Within the office machinery and computers industry the majority of the gains were due to the Netherlands and Ireland, whilst in other transport equipment, France and Germany had the largest increases.

Nevertheless, it was more common to find exports being more widely distributed across the EU. This was especially the case in leather (NACE Rev. 1 19), chemicals (NACE Rev. 1 24) and electrical machinery and apparatus (NACE Rev. 1 31), where there was a reduction of more than 6 percentage points in the weight of the top four exporters.

Figure 11

Geographical concentration of exports, 1989 and 1999 (%)

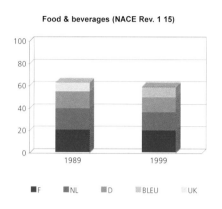

Food & beverages (NACE Rev. 1 15)

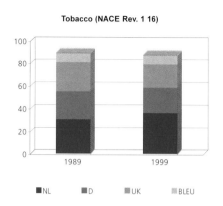

Tobacco (NACE Rev. 1 16)

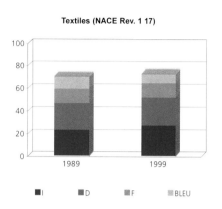

Textiles (NACE Rev. 1 17)

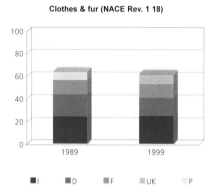

Clothes & fur (NACE Rev. 1 18)

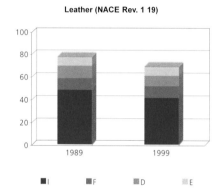

Leather (NACE Rev. 1 19)

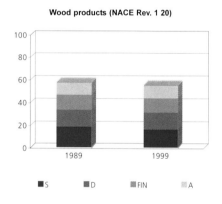

Wood products (NACE Rev. 1 20)

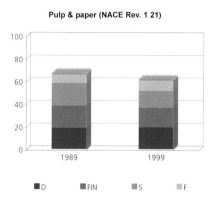

Pulp & paper (NACE Rev. 1 21)

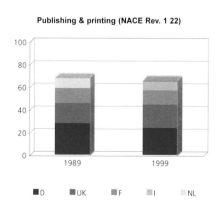

Publishing & printing (NACE Rev. 1 22)

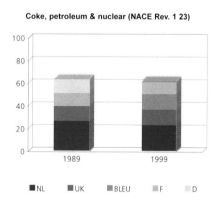

Coke, petroleum & nuclear (NACE Rev. 1 23)

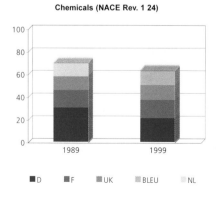

Chemicals (NACE Rev. 1 24)

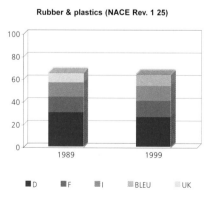

Rubber & plastics (NACE Rev. 1 25)

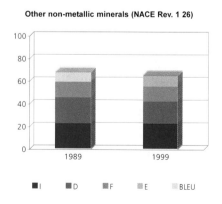

Other non-metallic minerals (NACE Rev. 1 26)

Source: Eurostat (SBS)

Figure 11 (continued)

Geographical concentration of exports, 1989 and 1999 (%)

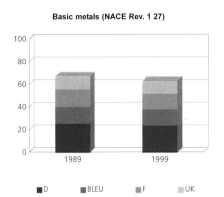

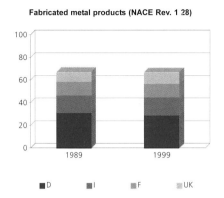

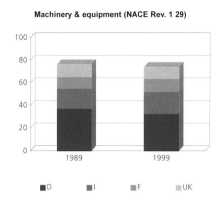

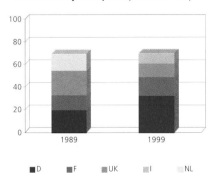

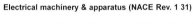

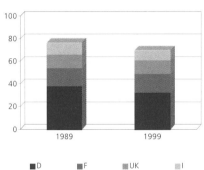

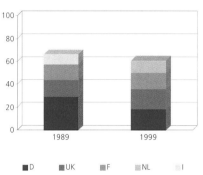

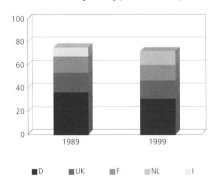

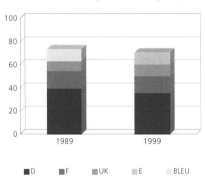

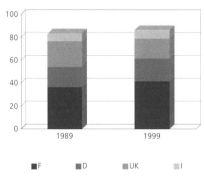

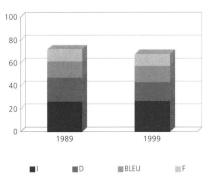

Source: Eurostat (SBS)

2.5 DESTINATION OF MANUFACTURING EXPORTS AND ORIGIN OF IMPORTS

This final section will look at the trade flows of the EU with the rest of the world. The EU is taken as a single trading entity and therefore the study looks only at the flow of extra-EU imports and extra-EU exports.

USA accounts for more than one fifth of extra-EU trade in manufacturing

The largest trading partner of the EU was the USA, accounting for 24.7% of extra-EU exports and 23.3% of extra-EU imports. These shares were far ahead of the second placed country in each of the rankings. However, whilst the share of European manufacturing exports to the USA increased by 2.4 percentage points between 1989 and 1999, the American share of EU imports declined by 0.8 percentage points.

Switzerland (8.3%), Japan (4.8%) and Poland (3.9%) were the next most important countries in terms of export markets for EU manufactured products. Further down the ranking were mostly neighbouring European countries (Norway, Turkey, the Czech Republic and Hungary) as well as China and Canada. In 1999 the USA and Switzerland featured amongst the top five destinations for EU exports in all of the 22 manufacturing NACE Rev. 1 Divisions except the tobacco industry (neither USA nor Switzerland) and the radio, television and communication equipment industry (not Switzerland).

China is an emerging player in terms of imports into the EU

Whilst the largest share of the EU's imports originated from the USA, Japan (11.1%) accounted for a considerable but declining share (5.4 percentage points down on 1989). China (7.7%) was the third largest origin of imports into the EU, just ahead of Switzerland (7.5%). A combination of south-east Asian economies and Eastern European economies (Taiwan, South Korea, Hungary, the Czech Republic and Poland) continued this ranking. The Chinese share of EU imports rose by 4.9 percentage points between 1989 and 1999 (within 7 manufacturing Divisions in 1999, China accounted for more than 10% of all EU imports). South Korea, Hungary, the Czech Republic and Poland also made relative gains.

Concentration of both exports and imports reduced during the nineties

The concentration of trade related indicators may be expected to reduce over time as a result of increasingly globalised markets resulting in more trading partners. Looking at the importance of the top five countries (CR5) of origin for imports and the top five destinations for EU exports, just 3 out of the 22 NACE Rev. 1 manufacturing Divisions reported an increase in their concentration of exports between 1989 and 1999 (food and beverages; chemicals; other transport equipment). The EU industries that showed the biggest reductions in the relative importance of their largest export partners were largely traditional industries (tobacco, wearing apparel and coke, refined petroleum and nuclear fuel; furniture manufacture and other manufacturing; wood).

On the import side there were just 4 of the 22 NACE Rev. 1 Divisions that reported increasing concentration (tobacco; leather; coke, refined petroleum and nuclear fuel; furniture manufacture and other manufacturing).

Figure 12

Destination of EU manufacturing exports, 1989 (%)

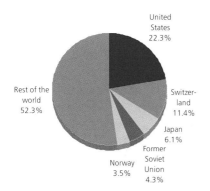

Source: Eurostat (COMEXT)

Figure 13

Destination of EU manufacturing exports, 1999 (%)

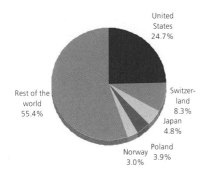

Source: Eurostat (COMEXT)

Figure 14

Origin of EU manufacturing imports, 1989 (%)

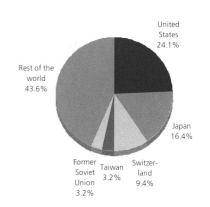

Source: Eurostat (COMEXT)

Figure 15

Origin of EU manufacturing imports, 1999 (%)

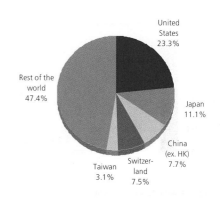

Source: Eurostat (COMEXT)

Statistical annex

There follows a short set of tables and graphs giving some general information which may be of use in interpreting the data that follows in the remaining chapters. This data is of a horizontal nature and may prove relevant for a number of chapters.

Table 1

Gross domestic product in constant prices, annual changes (%)

	1988	1989	1990	1991	1992	1993	1994	1995	1996	1997	1998	1999 (1)	2000 (2)
EU-15	:	:	:	:	1.3	-0.5	2.8	2.3	1.6	2.4	2.7	2.4	3.3
EUR-11	:	:	:	:	1.6	-0.8	2.4	2.2	1.4	2.3	2.7	2.4	3.4
B	4.6	3.6	2.7	2.0	1.6	-1.5	3.0	2.5	1.0	3.5	2.7	2.5	3.5
DK	1.2	0.2	1.0	1.1	0.6	0.0	5.5	2.8	2.5	3.1	2.5	1.7	2.0
D	:	:	:	:	2.2	-1.1	2.4	1.7	0.8	1.4	2.1	1.6	2.9
EL	:	:	:	:	:	:	:	:	2.4	3.4	3.7	3.5	3.9
E	:	:	:	:	:	:	:	:	2.3	3.8	4.0	3.8	3.8
F	4.6	4.2	2.6	1.0	1.5	-0.9	2.1	1.7	1.1	1.9	3.1	2.9	3.7
IRL	:	:	:	1.9	3.3	2.7	5.8	9.7	7.7	10.7	8.6	9.8	7.5
I	4.0	2.9	2.0	1.4	0.8	-0.9	2.2	2.9	1.1	1.8	1.5	1.4	2.7
L	:	:	:	:	:	:	:	:	2.9	7.3	5.0	7.5	5.6
NL	2.6	4.7	4.1	2.3	2.0	0.8	3.2	2.3	3.0	3.8	3.7	3.6	4.1
A	:	:	:	:	:	:	:	:	2.0	1.2	2.9	2.1	3.2
P	:	5.4	4.8	2.4	1.9	-1.4	2.5	3.7	3.6	3.7	3.5	2.9	3.6
FIN	4.7	5.1	0.0	-6.3	-3.3	-1.2	4.0	3.8	4.0	6.3	5.5	4.0	4.9
S	:	:	:	:	:	:	4.1	3.7	1.1	2.0	3.0	3.8	3.9
UK	5.2	2.1	0.7	-1.5	0.1	2.3	4.4	2.8	2.6	3.5	2.6	2.1	3.3
JAP	6.2	4.8	5.1	3.8	1.0	0.3	0.6	1.5	5.1	1.4	-2.8	0.3	1.1
USA	4.2	3.5	1.8	-0.5	3.1	2.7	4.0	2.7	3.6	4.4	4.4	4.2	3.6

(1) EU-15, EUR-11, EL, P, FIN and JAP, estimates.
(2) Forecasts.

Source: Eurostat (NA SEC1)

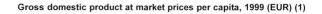

Figure 1

Gross domestic product at market prices per capita, 1999 (EUR) (1)

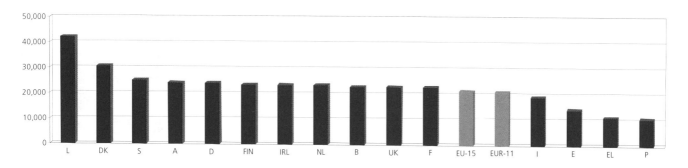

(1) EU-15, EUR-11, EL and P, estimates.

Source: Eurostat (NA SEC1)

Table 2

Final consumption expenditure of households in constant prices, annual change (%)

	1988	1989	1990	1991	1992	1993	1994	1995	1996	1997	1998 (1)	1999 (2)	2000 (3)
EU-15	:	:	:	:	1.7	-0.4	1.7	1.8	1.9	1.9	3.0	2.9	2.8
EUR-11	:	:	:	:	2.0	-0.8	1.3	1.9	1.6	1.5	2.9	2.7	2.7
B	3.7	3.9	3.2	3.0	2.2	-1.0	2.0	0.7	0.7	2.2	3.8	2.0	2.2
DK	0.0	-0.1	0.1	1.6	1.9	0.5	6.5	1.2	2.5	3.8	3.5	0.7	1.4
D	:	:	:	:	2.7	0.1	1.1	2.1	1.0	0.7	2.0	2.6	2.2
EL	:	:	:	:	:	:	:	:	2.1	3.1	2.2	2.6	3.0
E	:	:	:	:	:	:	:	:	2.1	2.9	4.1	4.4	3.8
F	2.7	3.0	2.7	0.7	1.0	-0.4	1.2	1.2	1.3	0.2	3.3	2.1	3.1
IRL	:	:	:	1.8	2.9	2.9	4.4	4.1	6.4	7.5	7.8	7.8	7.2
I	4.0	3.8	2.1	2.9	1.9	-3.7	1.6	1.7	1.3	3.0	2.3	1.7	1.9
L	:	:	:	:	:	:	:	:	4.4	3.8	2.3	4.2	3.2
NL	0.8	3.3	4.6	3.0	1.8	0.5	2.3	2.1	4.0	2.7	4.2	4.2	3.9
A	:	:	:	:	:	:	:	:	3.2	0.2	1.5	2.7	2.7
P	:	3.1	6.0	3.6	3.6	0.9	2.2	5.3	3.9	3.1	5.7	4.4	3.5
FIN	5.3	4.6	-0.7	-3.8	-4.4	-3.1	2.6	4.4	4.2	3.5	4.9	3.6	3.0
S	:	:	:	:	:	:	1.8	0.6	1.4	1.7	2.4	4.1	3.7
UK	7.6	3.2	0.8	-1.7	0.5	2.9	2.9	1.7	3.6	3.9	4.0	4.3	3.1
JAP	5.3	4.8	4.4	2.5	2.1	1.2	1.9	2.1	2.9	1.0	-0.5	1.2	0.6
USA	4.0	2.7	1.8	-0.2	2.9	3.4	3.8	3.0	3.2	3.6	4.7	5.3	4.4

(1) JAP, estimate.
(2) EU-15, EUR-11, EL, P, FIN and JAP, estimates.
(3) Forecasts.

Source: Eurostat (SEC2)

Figure 2

Breakdown of final consumption expenditure of households in the EU (%)

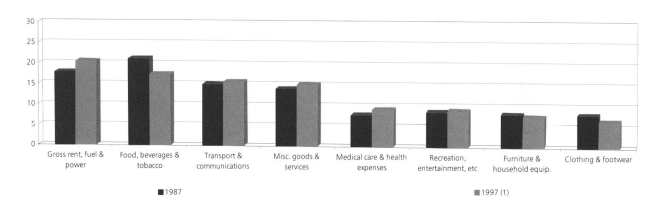

(1) Estimates.

Source: Eurostat (SEC2)

——Table 3

Final consumption expenditure of government in constant prices, annual change (%)

	1988	1989	1990	1991	1992	1993	1994	1995	1996	1997	1998	1999 (1)	2000 (2)
EU-15	:	:	:	:	2.8	1.3	1.2	0.8	1.6	0.6	1.1	1.6	1.4
EUR-11	:	:	:	:	3.5	1.6	1.2	0.6	1.6	1.0	0.9	1.4	1.2
B	-0.7	0.8	-0.4	3.9	1.4	-0.2	1.5	1.2	2.3	0.0	1.4	2.8	1.3
DK	-0.2	-0.8	-0.2	0.6	0.8	4.1	3.0	2.1	3.4	1.3	3.0	1.4	1.4
D	:	:	:	:	5.0	0.1	2.4	1.5	1.8	-0.9	0.5	-0.1	0.7
EL	:	:	:	:	:	:	:	:	0.9	1.7	2.1	0.5	0.7
E	:	:	:	:	:	:	:	:	1.3	2.7	2.0	1.8	1.7
F	3.2	1.6	2.6	2.7	3.8	4.6	0.7	-0.1	2.3	2.1	0.1	2.6	1.7
IRL	:	:	:	2.7	3.0	0.1	4.1	3.8	3.2	5.6	5.3	5.2	4.7
I	4.0	0.2	2.5	1.7	0.6	-0.2	-0.9	-2.2	1.0	0.8	0.7	0.6	0.5
L	:	:	:	:	:	:	:	:	4.4	2.1	2.8	12.9	3.2
NL	1.2	2.8	2.0	2.4	3.6	2.2	1.1	0.7	-0.4	3.3	3.3	2.6	2.0
A	:	:	:	:	:	:	:	:	1.3	-0.4	2.0	1.0	0.7
P	:	6.6	5.5	10.3	1.1	0.9	2.1	2.7	-0.3	2.6	3.4	4.0	2.0
FIN	1.9	2.2	4.0	2.1	-2.4	-4.2	0.3	2.0	2.5	4.1	1.7	2.0	0.3
S	:	:	:	:	:	:	-0.9	-0.6	0.9	-1.0	2.2	1.8	1.4
UK	0.0	0.8	2.5	2.9	0.5	-0.9	1.4	1.6	1.7	-1.4	1.1	3.0	3.1
JAP	2.3	2.0	1.5	2.0	2.0	2.4	2.4	3.3	1.9	1.5	0.7	1.3	1.2
USA	1.5	2.6	2.6	1.3	0.4	-0.4	0.2	0.0	0.5	1.8	1.5	2.1	1.8

(1) EU-15, EUR-11, EL, P, FIN and JAP, estimates.
(2) Forecasts.

Source: Eurostat (NA AGGR)

——Figure 3

Mean equivalised total net income per person, 1996 (ECU)

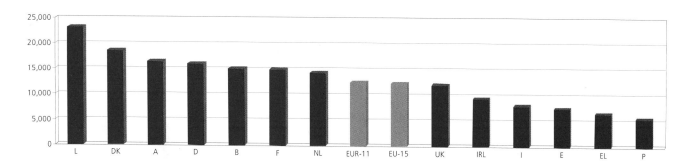

Source: Eurostat (ILC)

Table 4

Harmonised indices of consumer prices, 12-month average rate (%)

	1990 (1)	1991 (1)	1992 (1)	1993 (1)	1994 (1)	1995 (1)	1996 (2)	1997 (3)	1998	1999
EU-15	5.1	5.2	4.0	3.4	2.8	:	2.4	1.7	1.3	1.2
EUR-11	:	4.1	3.6	3.2	2.7	:	2.2	1.6	1.1	1.1
B	:	:	2.3	2.5	2.4	1.3	1.8	1.5	0.9	1.1
DK	2.5	2.2	1.9	0.9	1.8	2.0	2.1	1.9	1.3	2.1
D	:	:	:	:	:	:	1.2	1.5	0.6	0.6
EL	:	:	:	:	:	:	7.9	5.4	4.5	2.1
E	:	:	:	4.9	4.6	:	3.6	1.9	1.8	2.2
F	:	3.4	2.4	2.2	1.7	:	2.1	1.3	0.7	0.6
IRL	:	:	:	:	:	:	2.2	1.2	2.1	2.5
I	6.2	6.2	5.0	4.5	4.2	:	4.0	1.9	2.0	1.7
L	:	:	:	:	:	:	1.2	1.4	1.0	1.0
NL	2.4	3.1	2.8	1.7	2.2	1.6	1.4	1.9	1.8	2.0
A	2.8	3.1	3.5	3.2	2.7	:	1.8	1.2	0.8	0.5
P	13.3	11.4	8.9	5.9	5.0	:	2.9	1.9	2.2	2.2
FIN	5.8	4.5	3.3	3.3	1.6	:	1.1	1.2	1.4	1.3
S	:	:	:	:	:	:	0.8	1.8	1.0	0.6
UK	7.0	7.5	4.2	2.5	2.0	:	2.5	1.8	1.6	1.3

(1) Estimates.
(2) EU-15, EUR-11, IRL and UK, estimates.
(3) EU-15, EUR-11 and IRL, estimates.

Source: Eurostat (PRICE)

Table 5

Exchange rates, annual average rates (1 ECU/EUR=... national currency)

	1986	1987	1988	1989	1990	1991	1992	1993	1994	1995	1996	1997	1998	1999
BEF	43.7979	43.0410	43.4285	43.3806	42.4257	42.2233	41.5932	40.4713	39.6565	38.5519	39.2986	40.5332	40.6207	40.3399
DKK	7.93565	7.88472	7.95153	8.04929	7.85652	7.90859	7.80925	7.59359	7.54328	7.32804	7.35934	7.48361	7.49930	7.43556
DEM	2.12819	2.07153	2.07440	2.07015	2.05209	2.05076	2.02031	1.93639	1.92453	1.87375	1.90954	1.96438	1.96913	1.95583
GRD	137.425	156.269	167.576	178.841	201.412	225.216	247.026	268.568	288.026	302.989	305.546	309.355	330.731	325.763
ESP	137.456	142.165	137.601	130.406	129.411	128.469	132.526	149.124	158.918	163.000	160.748	165.887	167.184	166.386
FRF	6.79976	6.92910	7.03644	7.02387	6.91412	6.97332	6.84839	6.63368	6.58262	6.52506	6.49300	6.61260	6.60141	6.55957
IEP	0.733526	0.775448	0.775673	0.776818	0.767768	0.767809	0.760718	0.799952	0.793618	0.815525	0.793448	0.747516	0.786245	0.787564
ITL	1,461.88	1,494.91	1,537.33	1,510.47	1,521.98	1,533.24	1,595.52	1,841.23	1,915.06	2,130.14	1,958.96	1,929.30	1,943.65	1,936.27
NLG	2.40090	2.33418	2.33479	2.33526	2.31212	2.31098	2.27482	2.17521	2.15827	2.09891	2.13973	2.21081	2.21967	2.20371
ATS	14.9643	14.5710	14.5861	14.5695	14.4399	14.4309	14.2169	13.6238	13.5396	13.1824	13.4345	13.8240	13.8545	13.7603
PTE	147.089	162.616	170.059	173.413	181.109	178.614	174.714	188.370	196.896	196.105	195.761	198.589	201.695	200.482
FIM	4.97974	5.06518	4.94362	4.72301	4.85496	5.00211	5.80703	6.69628	6.19077	5.70855	5.82817	5.88064	5.98251	5.94573
SEK	6.99567	7.31001	7.24192	7.09939	7.52051	7.47927	7.53295	9.12151	9.16308	9.33192	8.51472	8.65117	8.91593	8.80752
GBP	0.671543	0.704571	0.664434	0.673302	0.713851	0.701012	0.737650	0.779988	0.775903	0.828789	0.813798	0.692304	0.676434	0.658735
JPY	164.997	166.598	151.459	151.938	183.660	166.493	164.223	130.148	121.322	123.012	138.084	137.077	146.415	121.317
USD	0.98417	1.15445	1.18248	1.10175	1.27343	1.23916	1.29810	1.17100	1.18952	1.30801	1.26975	1.13404	1.12109	1.06578

Source: Eurostat (MNY)

Figure 4

Stock market indices (1991=100)

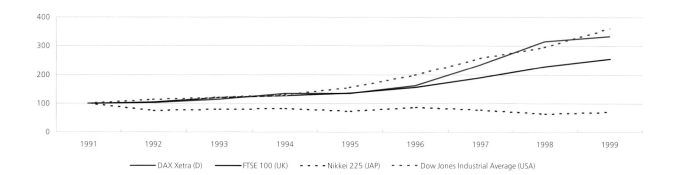

DAX Xetra (D) —— FTSE 100 (UK) - - - - Nikkei 225 (JAP) - - - - Dow Jones Industrial Average (USA)

Source: Eurostat (MNY)

Figure 5

Long-term interest rate for central government bond yields, average annual data (%)

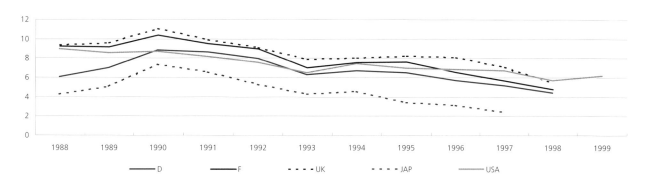

—— D —— F - - - - UK - - - - JAP —— USA

Source: Eurostat (MNY)

Figure 6

Taxes and social contributions as a percentage of GDP (%)

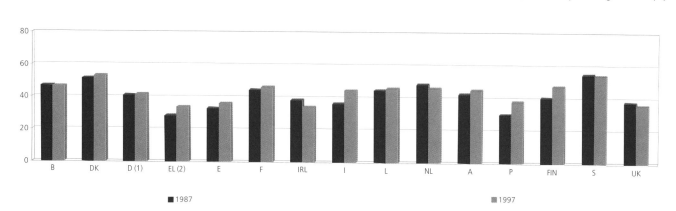

■ 1987   ■ 1997

(1) Excluding former East Germany in 1987.
(2) 1989 instead of 1987; 1996 instead of 1997.

Source: Eurostat (GOV)

Table 6

EU foreign direct investment positions with the continents, as of 31/12/1997 (million ECU)

	Europe (1)	Asia	America	Africa	Australia and Pacific
Assets	107,237	74,413	403,744	23,621	35,884
Liabilities	119,336	50,097	310,384	4,245	14,881

(1) Excluding with other EU countries.

Source: Eurostat (BOP)

Table 7

EU foreign direct investment positions in major sectors, as of 31/12/1997 (million ECU)

	Assets			Liabilities		
	Extra-EU	JAP	USA	Extra-EU	JAP	USA
Agriculture and fishing	826	1	401	409	11	160
Mining and quarrying	53,591	325	18,926	33,283	51	28,517
Manufacturing	280,448	6,615	132,991	169,480	7,596	100,901
Food products	46,541	1,063	18,590	22,982	212	12,167
Textiles and wood	20,149	156	11,772	18,295	787	5,970
Petroleum, chemicals, rubber and plastics	88,103	3,058	42,370	53,422	831	35,872
Metal and mechanical products	27,667	749	13,394	21,917	989	12,927
Machinery, electrical and electronic products	29,234	986	11,941	22,670	2,957	13,370
Transport equipment	18,370	279	5,986	12,183	1,350	8,807
Electricity, gas and water	8,755	27	2,811	14,805	-258	13,502
Construction	7,590	39	3,312	4,159	-290	1,413
Services	303,061	4,974	139,490	277,761	27,909	125,072
Trade and repair	44,736	2,241	15,208	55,921	14,138	20,777
Hotels and restaurants	6,149	20	3,552	6,441	-340	2,425
Transport and communication services	45,699	20	5,124	7,723	100	4,025
Financial intermediation	127,336	2,022	50,345	110,428	11,650	43,129
Real estate and business activities	98,398	518	57,445	88,390	2,030	48,652
Other services	10,742	153	7,817	8,858	26	6,063
TOTAL	658,570	12,005	298,167	500,955	35,334	270,100

Source: Eurostat (BOP)

Figure 7

Trade balance of goods and services at constant prices (million EUR)

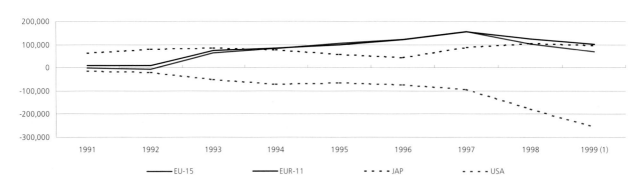

(1) EU-15, EUR-11 and JAP, estimates.

Source: Eurostat (BOP)

Table 8

Gross domestic expenditure on R&D as a percentage of GDP (%)

	1988	1989	1990	1991	1992	1993	1994	1995	1996	1997	1998	1999
EU-15 (1)	1.9	2.0	2.0	1.9	1.9	1.9	1.8	1.8	1.8	1.8	1.8	:
B	1.6	1.6	:	1.6	:	1.6	1.6	1.6	:	:	:	:
DK	1.5	1.5	1.6	1.6	1.7	1.7	:	1.8	1.9	1.9	1.9	2.0
D (1)	2.9	2.9	2.8	2.5	2.4	2.4	2.3	2.3	2.3	2.3	2.3	:
EL	0.3	0.4	:	0.4	:	0.5	:	0.5	:	0.5	:	:
E	0.7	0.8	0.9	0.9	0.9	0.9	0.9	0.8	0.8	0.8	0.9	0.9
F	2.2	2.3	2.4	2.4	2.4	2.4	2.3	2.3	2.3	2.2	2.2	:
IRL	0.8	0.8	0.8	0.9	1.0	1.2	1.3	1.4	1.4	1.4	:	:
I	1.2	1.2	1.3	1.2	1.2	1.1	1.1	1.0	1.0	1.0	1.0	1.1
L	:	:	:	:	:	:	:	:	:	:	:	:
NL	2.2	2.1	2.2	2.1	2.0	2.0	2.0	2.0	2.0	2.0	:	:
A	1.4	1.4	1.4	1.5	1.5	1.5	1.6	1.6	1.6	1.6	1.6	1.6
P	0.4	:	0.5	:	0.6	:	:	0.6	:	0.6	:	:
FIN	1.8	1.8	1.9	2.0	2.1	2.2	2.3	2.3	2.5	2.7	2.9	3.1
S	:	2.9	:	2.9	:	3.3	:	3.5	:	3.7	:	:
UK	2.2	2.2	2.2	2.1	2.1	2.1	2.1	2.0	1.9	1.8	1.8	:
JAP	2.8	3.0	3.0	3.0	3.0	2.9	2.8	3.0	2.8	2.9	3.1	:
USA	2.8	2.7	2.8	2.8	2.7	2.6	2.5	2.6	2.7	2.7	2.7	2.8

(1) Excluding former East Germany, 1988 to 1990.

Source: Eurostat (MSTI)

Table 9

Gross fixed capital formation, as a percentage of GDP (%)

	1987	1988	1989	1990	1991 (1)	1992 (1)	1993 (1)	1994 (2)	1995 (3)	1996 (4)	1997 (5)
EU-15	19.6	20.5	21.2	21.2	20.5	19.5	18.0	17.6	:	:	:
EUR-11	20.0	20.7	21.3	21.6	21.2	20.4	18.7	18.3	:	:	:
B	16.1	17.8	19.1	20.3	18.8	18.6	17.8	17.4	17.7	17.5	17.8
DK	19.7	18.3	18.2	17.5	16.5	15.6	15.0	14.6	15.8	16.5	17.4
D	19.8	20.0	20.6	21.4	21.7	21.1	19.3	18.7	:	:	:
EL	17.6	17.7	19.1	19.4	22.5	21.2	20.2	18.6	18.5	19.3	20.0
E	20.2	22.0	23.4	23.8	23.1	21.2	19.3	19.3	20.1	19.6	19.8
F	19.8	20.7	21.4	21.4	21.2	20.1	18.6	18.1	18.0	17.5	17.2
IRL	16.5	16.4	17.5	18.9	17.2	16.7	15.3	16.1	16.6	17.8	18.7
I	19.7	20.1	20.2	20.3	19.8	19.2	16.9	16.6	17.3	17.0	16.7
L	22.1	23.2	22.9	22.5	23.7	22.5	23.2	20.1	20.8	19.5	21.2
NL	21.3	21.3	21.5	21.0	20.4	20.1	19.3	18.9	19.2	19.6	20.1
A	22.0	22.8	22.1	22.3	22.4	22.6	22.0	21.8	21.8	21.9	22.1
P	26.8	28.7	27.7	27.6	26.2	25.0	23.4	23.5	23.6	23.8	25.1
FIN	23.9	25.2	28.0	27.0	22.4	18.4	14.8	14.5	15.5	16.0	16.9
S	19.4	20.3	22.1	21.6	19.2	16.8	14.1	13.6	14.5	14.7	13.6
UK	17.8	20.0	20.9	19.7	17.1	15.7	15.0	15.1	15.5	15.5	15.4
JAP	28.4	29.7	30.7	31.8	31.3	30.2	29.2	28.3	28.2	29.3	28.0
USA	18.3	18.2	17.5	16.7	15.4	15.3	16.0	16.7	17.2	17.9	:

(1) EU-15, EUR-11 and D, estimates.
(2) EU-15, EUR-11, D, JAP and USA, estimates.
(3) JAP and USA, estimates.
(4) L, P, JAP and USA, estimates.
(5) DK, E, I, L, P, S, UK and JAP, estimates.

Source: Eurostat (NA SEC1)

Figure 8

Capacity utilisation rates in the EU (%)

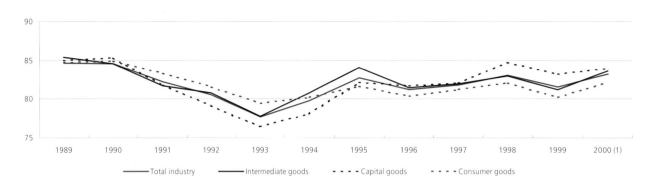

(1) Average based on the first three quarters of 2000.

Source: DG ECFIN

Table 10

Business and consumer confidence in the EU (balance)

	1995	1996	1997	1998	1999	2000 1st quarter	2nd quarter
Industrial confidence indicator	-1	-14	-4	-3	-8	2	4
Construction confidence indicator	-27	-35	-30	-17	-8	-2	1
Consumer confidence indicator	-13	-17	-11	-4	-2	0	0

Source: DG ECFIN

Figure 9

Electricity prices for large industrial consumers (using more than 24 GWh per year), as of 01/07/1999 (EUR per 100 kWh) (1)

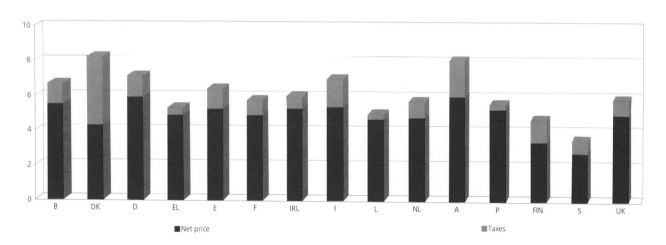

(1) EL, E, F, IRL, P and UK, price in the capital city; D, Westliches Gebiet; L, using more than 12 GWh per year; NL, Rotterdam; A, Oberösterreich/Tyrol/Vienna, as of 01/01/1999.

Source: Eurostat (SIRENE)

Table 11

Estimates of emissions of main air pollutants, 2000

	Sulphur oxides (thousand tonnes)	1990/2000 (%)	Nitrogen oxides (thousand tonnes)	1990/2000 (%)	Carbon monoxide (thousand tonnes)	1990/2000 (%)	Carbon dioxide (thousand tonnes)	1990/2000 (%)	Methane (thousand tonnes)	1990/2000 (%)
B	216	-3.9	310	-1.0	981	-3.8	116,000	1.0	578	0.1
DK	109	-6.7	248	-1.3	557	-2.3	63,207	1.9	423	0.0
D	1,468	-12.1	1,803	-4.0	6,374	-5.5	894,000	-1.3	3,564	-4.4
EL	507	0.0	369	0.7	1,375	0.3	82,970	-0.3	458	0.4
E	1,927	-1.6	1,243	0.5	4,372	-0.8	242,800	0.2	2,377	0.8
F	947	-2.8	1,698	-1.0	8,253	-2.3	358,650	0.5	2,566	-1.4
IRL	165	-0.8	124	0.7	333	-2.5	36,150	2.0	755	-0.6
I	1,322	-2.2	1,768	-0.9	7,755	-0.1	402,350	0.3	2,555	0.9
L	6	-8.8	20	-1.4	82	-7.3	8,450	-2.6	23	-0.4
NL	125	-4.7	445	-2.6	826	-3.6	178,289	0.9	1,112	-1.5
A	57	-4.6	172	-1.2	1,012	-2.4	:	:	440	-2.8
P	359	0.4	373	1.9	1,320	2.4	47,910	-2.1	834	12.6
FIN	100	-9.1	260	-1.4	430	-2.5	60,500	1.3	246	-0.1
S	91	-3.9	337	-1.4	968	-2.3	51,550	-0.7	260	-2.2
UK	1,660	-7.9	1,835	-4.0	5,090	-2.7	529,600	-1.0	2,727	-4.8

Source: Eurostat (MILIEU)

Figure 10

Population, as of 01/01/1999 (thousands)

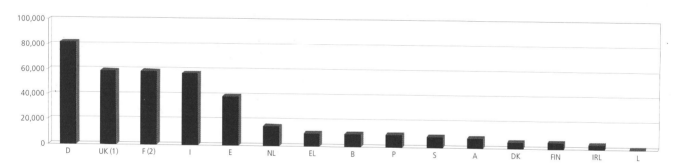

(1) Estimate.
(2) Provisional.

Source: Eurostat (DEMO)

Figure 11

Breakdown of population by age and gender in the EU (%)

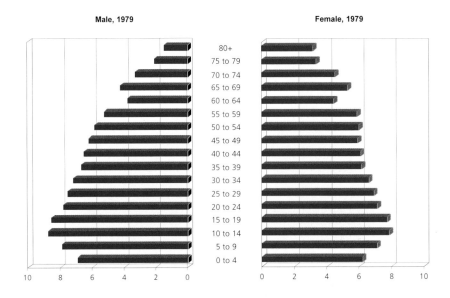

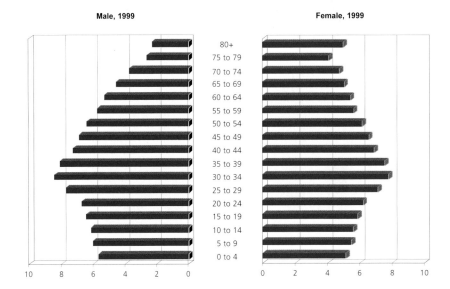

Source: Eurostat (DEMO)

eurostat

Table 12

Labour force indicators for the EU

	1995	1996	1997	1998	1999
Labour force (thousands)	166,172	167,397	168,213	169,752	171,687
Men (thousands)	95,915	96,233	96,488	97,169	97,697
Women (thousands)	70,257	71,163	71,724	72,582	73,990
Activity rate (%) (1)	55.3	55.3	55.4	55.6	55.9
Men (%)	66.3	66.0	65.9	65.9	66.0
Women (%)	45.1	45.3	45.6	45.9	46.6
Share of part-time employment in total employment (%)	16.0	16.3	16.9	17.4	17.6
Men (%)	5.2	5.5	5.8	6.1	6.1
Women (%)	31.2	31.5	32.3	33.0	33.3
Unemployment rate (%) (2)	10.7	10.8	10.6	9.9	9.2
Men (%)	9.4	9.6	9.3	8.6	7.9
Women (%)	12.5	12.4	12.3	11.7	10.9

(1) Share of the labour force in the total population.
(2) Expressed as a percentage of the labour force.

Source: Eurostat (LFS and UNEMPLOY)

Table 13

Share of women working in the labour force (%) (1)

	1987	1988	1989	1990	1991	1992	1993	1994	1995	1996	1997	1998	1999
EU-15	:	:	:	:	:	:	:	:	42.3	42.5	42.6	42.8	43.1
EUR-11	:	:	:	:	:	:	:	:	41.8	42.1	42.2	42.3	42.7
B	38.5	38.7	38.8	39.2	40.0	40.6	41.2	41.2	41.4	41.5	41.9	42.3	42.9
DK	46.1	45.9	45.8	46.2	46.6	46.8	46.9	46.2	45.5	45.7	45.9	46.6	46.4
D (2)	39.5	39.7	39.8	40.9	42.5	42.6	42.5	42.7	42.9	43.1	43.2	43.4	43.7
EL	35.8	36.8	37.0	37.1	35.8	36.8	37.0	37.3	37.8	38.7	39.0	39.4	40.2
E	32.9	34.2	34.6	35.2	35.3	36.1	36.6	37.5	38.2	38.5	38.8	39.2	39.7
F	43.3	43.6	43.8	43.8	44.3	44.6	45.0	45.2	45.5	45.5	45.4	45.7	45.7
IRL	32.8	32.6	33.0	33.6	34.1	35.4	36.5	37.2	37.6	38.4	39.0	39.7	40.4
I	35.6	36.0	36.6	36.6	37.1	36.8	36.7	37.1	37.3	37.8	37.9	37.8	38.4
L	35.4	34.8	34.6	35.0	35.8	37.5	36.1	37.1	35.9	36.8	38.2	38.3	39.4
NL	37.6	38.1	38.4	39.1	39.5	40.4	40.6	41.1	41.3	41.8	42.1	42.3	43.0
A	:	:	:	:	:	:	:	:	43.5	43.4	43.6	43.9	43.9
P	41.8	42.4	42.6	42.8	43.8	44.4	44.7	45.0	45.0	45.2	45.4	45.1	45.4
FIN	:	:	:	:	:	:	:	:	47.9	47.8	47.5	47.6	48.0
S	:	:	:	:	:	:	:	:	47.7	47.7	47.4	46.6	47.2
UK	42.2	42.4	42.9	43.1	43.2	43.3	43.7	43.7	43.8	44.0	44.2	44.3	44.4

(1) Aged 15 and over.
(2) Including former East Germany from 1991 onwards.

Source: Eurostat (LFS)

Table 14

Unemployment rate, expressed as a percentage of the labour force, annual average (%)

	1988	1989	1990	1991	1992	1993	1994	1995	1996	1997	1998	1999
EU-15 (1)	9.5	8.7	8.1	8.5	9.4	10.8	11.2	10.7	10.8	10.6	9.9	9.2
EUR-11	:	:	:	8.2	9.2	10.8	11.6	11.3	11.5	11.5	10.9	10.0
B (2)	9.0	7.5	6.7	6.6	7.2	8.8	10.0	9.9	9.7	9.4	9.5	9.1
DK	6.1	7.3	7.7	8.4	9.2	10.2	8.2	7.2	6.8	5.6	5.2	5.2
D (3)	:	:	:	5.6	6.6	7.8	8.4	8.2	8.9	9.9	9.4	8.8
EL (2)	6.8	6.7	6.4	7.0	7.9	8.6	8.9	9.2	9.6	9.8	10.9	11.7
E	19.5	17.2	16.2	16.4	18.4	22.7	24.1	22.9	22.2	20.8	18.8	15.9
F	9.9	9.4	9.0	9.5	10.4	11.7	12.3	11.7	12.4	12.3	11.8	11.3
IRL (2)	16.2	14.7	13.4	14.7	15.4	15.6	14.3	12.3	11.7	9.9	7.6	5.7
I (4)	9.8	9.8	9.0	8.6	8.8	10.2	11.1	11.6	11.7	11.7	11.8	11.3
L	2.0	1.8	1.7	1.7	2.1	2.6	3.2	2.9	3.0	2.7	2.7	2.3
NL (4)	7.6	6.9	6.2	5.8	5.6	6.5	7.1	6.9	6.3	5.2	4.0	3.3
A	:	:	:	:	:	4.0	3.8	3.9	4.3	4.4	4.5	3.8
P	5.9	5.2	4.8	4.2	4.3	5.7	6.9	7.3	7.3	6.8	5.2	4.5
FIN	4.2	3.1	3.2	6.6	11.7	16.3	16.6	15.4	14.6	12.7	11.4	10.2
S	1.8	1.6	1.7	3.1	5.6	9.1	9.4	8.8	9.6	9.9	8.3	7.2
UK	8.7	7.3	7.0	8.8	10.0	10.5	9.6	8.7	8.2	7.0	6.3	6.1
JAP	2.3	2.3	2.1	2.1	2.2	2.5	2.9	3.1	3.4	3.4	4.1	4.7
USA	5.5	5.3	5.5	6.7	7.4	6.8	6.1	5.6	5.4	4.9	4.5	4.2

(1) 1988-1995, excluding A, FIN and S.
(2) 1988-1991, estimates.
(3) 1991-1992, estimates.
(4) 1988-1992, estimates.

Source: Eurostat (UNEMPLOY)

Table 15

Average hourly labour costs in total industry (ECU)

	B (1)	DK	D (2)	EL (1)	E (1)	F (1)	IRL	I	L (1)	NL	A	P (1)	FIN	S	UK
1988	17.0	15.5	18.3	5.4	9.1	15.3	10.6	14.2	13.6	16.4	:	3.0	:	:	11.0
1992	21.3	19.3	21.7	7.0	15.1	19.1	12.8	18.7	17.2	19.3	:	5.6	:	:	13.1
1996	25.8	23.0	26.5	9.6	14.9	22.5	13.9	:	19.9	22.6	24.6	6.1	19.7	23.1	:
1999	26.2	:	27.5	11.8	15.4	24.1	:	:	20.0	:	25.9	6.3	:	25.5	:

(1) 1998, instead of 1999.
(2) Excluding former East Germany, 1988.

Source: Eurostat (LACOSTS)

Figure 12

Statutory monthly minimum wages, 1999 (EUR) (1)

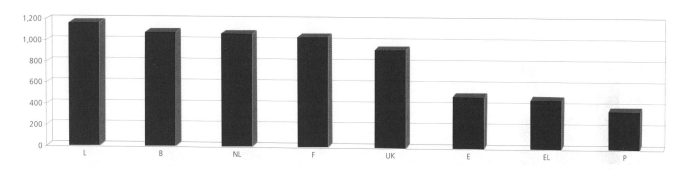

(1) DK, D, IRL, I, A, FIN, S, no data available.

Source: Eurostat (MINWAGES)

—Figure 13

Usual hours worked per week by employees aged 15 years and over, 1999 (hours)

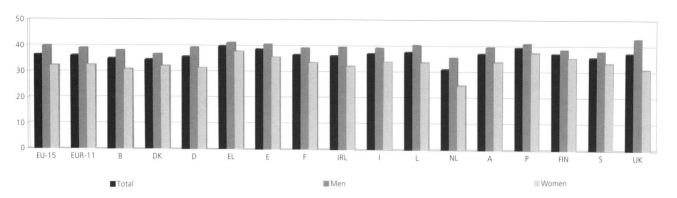

■ Total　　　　　　　　　■ Men　　　　　　　　　■ Women

Source: Eurostat (LFS)

—Table 16

Working days lost due to labour disputes (days per thousand workers)

	1993	1994	1995	1996	1997	1998	1999
B	17.8	23.2	32.3	47.1	12.6	27.5	8.0
DK	50.2	33.0	84.3	32.0	42.3	1,321.0	37.5
D	:	:	7.8	3.1	1.7	0.5	:
EL	116.3	47.4	31.4	52.4	26.5	18.1	:
E	247.2	731.8	163.6	171.7	186.3	86.5	84.5
F	49.1	40.1	309.4	59.0	20.4	17.6	:
IRL	69.8	27.5	133.4	111.5	68.9	31.5	169.0
I	236.1	237.3	64.5	136.2	83.2	40.2	61.8
L	0.0	0.0	83.2	2.1	0.0	0.0	0.0
NL	7.7	8.1	117.1	1.2	2.3	5.1	11.3
A	:	:	0.0	0.0	0.0	0.0	0.0
P	24.5	30.4	19.9	16.9	25.1	28.3	:
FIN	:	:	513.5	11.7	58.0	71.7	9.4
S	:	:	204.0	17.6	7.0	0.5	22.0
UK	29.8	12.8	18.8	58.1	10.3	12.2	10.2

Source: Eurostat (STRIKES)

—Figure 14

Standardised incidence rate of accidents at work, 1996 (accidents per 100,000 persons in employment)

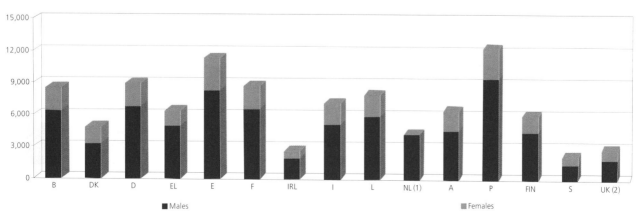

■ Males　　　　　　　　　■ Females

(1) No breakdown by gender available.
(2) Excluding Northern Ireland.

Source: Eurostat (HEALTH)

Energy (NACE Rev. 1 10, 11, 12, 23, 40 and 41)

The activities covered in this chapter are classified under Sub-section CA of NACE Rev. 1 (mining and quarrying of energy producing materials), Sub-section DF (the manufacture of coke, refined petroleum products and nuclear fuel) and Section E (electricity, gas and water supply). The first three sub-chapters cover the mining and processing of three main fuel types, namely solid fuels, crude oil (and natural gas) and nuclear fuels. The fourth looks at the generation and distribution of electricity from these fuel types and other sources, such as hydroelectric and renewable sources. The final sub-chapter looks at water supply and distribution.

The energy sector plays a significant role in the European economy. According to National Accounts the 1.7 million persons employed in the energy branch of the EU economy generated value added of 305 billion ECU in 1997, which represented some 4.5% of GDP. In addition to its economic weight, the energy sector is of strategic importance as most economic activities and households use energy. Indeed, energy production, distribution and use have a great impact on the physical and social environment, as well as the economy. The availability and cost of energy affect the competitiveness of businesses and standards of living of households, but the sector is also implicated in environmental and sustainable development issues (which are not addressed within this publication).

The energy sector is facing major changes, notably through technology, environmental regulation and political regulation of the sector. At a world level technological developments are reducing barriers to entry and changing the way that electricity is generated. Most notably combined-cycle gas turbines (CCGT) can come on stream faster than traditional coal powered turbines, they are more efficient and can operate at a lower scale.

It is expected that distribution of energy to consumers will also undergo significant changes in the near future with developments in fuel cells and micro-cogeneration. The main driving force for more rigorous environmental regulation has been the commitment made at the Kyoto conference in 1997 by many countries, including all EU Member States, to limit or reduce emissions of greenhouse gases.

Gas and electricity Directives expected
to open-up energy markets

The main changes to the regulatory regime of the sector are the EU-wide liberalisation of electricity and gas markets that started in the late 1990s. The Gas and Electricity Directives[1] require Member States to progressively open-up national markets by allowing consumer's with an annual consumption above a specific threshold to choose their supplier. It is believed that the implementation of these Directives will lead to the development of an internal energy market stimulating both competition and cross-border trade.

(1) Gas Market Directive (98/30/EC) and Electricity Market Directive (96/92/EC).

The activities covered in this chapter (in terms of NACE Rev. 1) include:

- 10: mining of coal and lignite; extraction of peat;
- 10.1: mining and agglomeration of hard coal;
- 10.2: mining and agglomeration of lignite;
- 10.3: extraction and agglomeration of peat;
- 11: extraction of crude petroleum and natural gas; service activities incidental to oil and gas extraction, excluding surveying;
- 11.1: extraction of crude petroleum and natural gas;
- 11.2: service activities incidental to oil and gas extraction, excluding surveying;
- 12: mining of uranium and thorium ores;
- 23: manufacture of coke, refined petroleum products and nuclear fuel;
- 23.1: manufacture of coke oven products;
- 23.2: manufacture of refined petroleum products;
- 23.3: processing of nuclear fuel;
- 40: electricity, gas, steam and hot water supply;
- 40.1: production and distribution of electricity;
- 40.2: manufacture of gas; distribution of gaseous fuels through mains;
- 40.3: steam and hot water supply;
- 41: collection, purification and distribution of water.

Table 1.1

Structural indicators of the energy market, 1998

		EU-15	B	DK	D	EL	E	F	IRL	I	L	NL	A	P	FIN	S	UK
Coal	Underground employment	74,800	0	0	45,700	0	17,800	5,100	0	0	0	0	0	0	0	0	6,200
Oil	Refinery capacity (thousand tonnes)	641,670	32,000	11,900	109,900	19,870	64,100	93,200	3,100	100,800	:	59,400	10,500	15,200	10,000	21,400	90,300
Natural gas	Length of distribution network (km)	:	48,220	17,748	347,700	2,174	30,131	178,517	6,752	197,100	1,080	:	:	2,189	2,000	3,500	421,000
Electricity	Installed net capacity (MW)	561,376	15,395	12,544	113,624	10,017	50,010	112,347	4,457	72,352	1,210	20,158	17,456	9,789	16,143	33,029	72,845

Source: Eurostat (SIRENE)

Table 1.2

Electricity, gas and water supply (NACE Rev. 1 40 and 41)

Breakdown of turnover and employment by employment size class, 1996 (%)

	Micro (0-9)		Small (10-49)		Medium (50-249)		Large (250+)	
	Turnover (1)	Employment (2)	Turnover (1)	Employment (2)	Turnover (3)	Employment (4)	Turnover (3)	Employment (4)
EU-15	5.9	3.0	4.2	4.4	28.3	8.3	61.7	84.4
B	:	:	:	:	0.0	0.0	:	:
DK	:	:	:	:	:	:	54.2	48.0
D	1.6	4.2	6.5	8.2	67.0	12.2	24.9	75.3
EL	:	:	:	:	:	:	:	:
E	2.7	7.6	3.9	6.9	6.8	14.0	86.7	71.6
F	3.1	1.0	1.4	1.6	3.1	3.2	92.4	94.3
IRL	:	:	:	:	:	:	:	:
I	1.3	1.8	3.3	3.7	5.2	7.8	90.2	86.7
L	:	:	:	:	:	:	:	:
NL	:	:	:	0.0	:	20.8	:	78.5
A	1.5	3.9	3.4	5.0	11.7	10.2	:	:
P	5.3	3.4	:	3.2	:	:	:	:
FIN	17.4	6.1	11.5	12.2	28.8	28.1	42.4	53.6
S	9.4	:	:	:	:	:	:	:
UK	:	0.3	0.4	0.5	4.5	2.0	:	97.2

(1) D, A and FIN, 1997.
(2) D, E, A and FIN, 1997.
(3) D and FIN, 1997.
(4) D, E and FIN, 1997.

Source: Eurostat (SME)

Box 1.1

Many of the statistical indicators used to assess the energy sector are different from the traditional business statistics measures. A distinction is sometimes made between different types of energy consumption. A commonly used measure of consumption is "gross inland energy consumption", which is the key aggregate in the energy balance sheet. This term refers to the quantity of energy necessary to satisfy inland consumption of the geographical entity under consideration, and corresponds to the sum of distribution and transformation losses and consumption. As regards "energy available for final consumption", this term refers to the sum of all energy placed at the disposal of the final consumers, including electricity produced from other fuels, and excludes transformation and distribution losses.

STRUCTURE AND PERFORMANCE

Gross inland energy consumption of the EU was equal to about 1.4 billion TOE[2] in 1998, a level 6.6% higher than in 1991. This corresponded to an average growth rate of just over 0.9% per annum. Growth occurred initially between 1994 and 1996 and more recently growth of 1.9% was recorded between 1997 and 1998.

Energy intensity, defined as gross inland energy consumption per unit of GDP, has witnessed a strong decline[3] in the EU. In 1998 this ratio was nearly 6 percentage points lower than in 1991. The improvements in energy intensity can be explained by the maturity of EU energy markets, where growth has been primarily in sectors with low energy intensity (such as service activities), as well as investment in more energy-efficient capital.

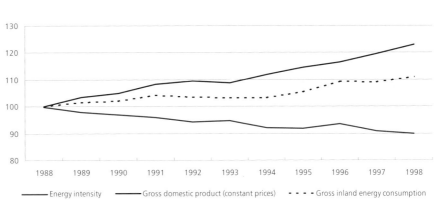

Figure 1.1

Energy intensity of the EU (1988=100) (1)

—— Energy intensity　　—— Gross domestic product (constant prices)　　- - - - Gross inland energy consumption

(1) Data for EU-15 includes former East Germany for 1991 and subsequent years.

Source: Eurostat (SIRENE)

Oil accounts for the largest share of the energy mix
Crude oil and petroleum products accounted for 41.9% of total gross inland consumption of the EU in 1998, a share that has hardly changed over the past seven years (41.8% in 1991). Levels of crude oil and petroleum products consumption showed an average annual increase of more than 0.9% between 1991 and 1998, to reach 601 million TOE in 1998. Natural gas experienced much stronger growth, averaging 4.0% growth over the same period, to attain 315 million TOE in 1998. Gross inland gas consumption was equivalent to 22.0% of total gross inland consumption in 1998, up from 17.8% in 1991. Solid fuels, in

contrast, demonstrated a continuous decrease in absolute levels of consumption from 1991 and saw their share in total gross inland consumption fall to 15.5% in 1998 from 21.3% in 1991. New electric power plants have increasingly tended to be fuelled by natural gas in the 1990s. The other sources of energy, including nuclear and renewable ones, increased their share of the energy mix from 19.0% in 1991 to 20.5% in 1998 (of which 5.9% could be attributed to renewable sources). Some of the renewable sources have recorded the fastest growth rates of gross inland consumption over the seven-year period to 1998. Consumption of energy from wind power has increased at an annual average rate of 40.8% and biogas by 11.2% per annum, but in levels both remain very small, with a combined share of gross inland consumption around 0.2%.

(2) The tonne of oil equivalent (TOE) is a standardised conventional unit defined on the basis of one tonne of oil having a calorific value of 41,868 kilojoules per kilogram.
(3) From a qualitative point of view, a lowering of energy intensity is considered as an improvement, meaning that less energy was required to produce the same amount of domestic product.

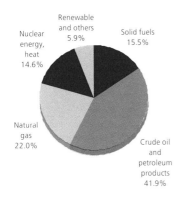

Figure 1.2

Gross inland energy consumption by fuel in the EU, 1998 (%)

Nuclear energy, heat 14.6%
Renewable and others 5.9%
Solid fuels 15.5%
Natural gas 22.0%
Crude oil and petroleum products 41.9%

Source: Eurostat (SIRENE)

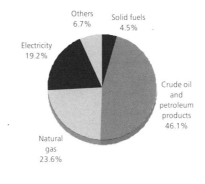

Figure 1.3

Final energy consumption by fuel in the EU, 1998 (%)

Others 6.7%
Solid fuels 4.5%
Electricity 19.2%
Crude oil and petroleum products 46.1%
Natural gas 23.6%

Source: Eurostat (SIRENE)

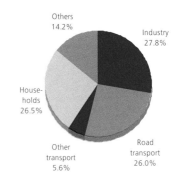

Figure 1.4

Final energy consumption by user in the EU, 1998 (%)

Others 14.2%
Industry 27.8%
Households 26.5%
Road transport 26.0%
Other transport 5.6%

Source: Eurostat (SIRENE)

Natural gas and electricity increase their
share of final energy consumption

As regards final consumption of energy, the mix has also evolved over the last seven years. Natural gas and electricity substantially increased their share at the expense of solid fuels and, to some extent, crude oil and petroleum products. The latest figures for 1998 show that crude oil and petroleum products represented 46.1% of final energy consumption ahead of natural gas with 23.6% (up from 21.9% in 1991) and electricity with 19.2% (up from 18.0%). Coal and other solid fuels accounted for only 4.5% of final energy consumption, a share that has fallen by more than 40% since 1991. Again biogas showed significant growth over the seven-year period from 1991 to 1998 as did solar heat, both recording an annual average growth rate in excess of 10%.

The principal sectors of final energy demand are industry, transport, households and others. All of these end-users reported growth in their final energy consumption between 1991 and 1998. The relative share of the household and other sectors fell from 41.8% in 1991 to 40.7% in 1998, and that of industry declined to 27.8%, or 262.5 million TOE, down from 29.0%. In contrast, the transport sector increased its share and, since 1991, has consumed more energy than industry. By 1998 it accounted for 31.6% of final energy consumption (298.6 million TOE).

LABOUR AND PRODUCTIVITY

Approximating the energy industry as NACE Rev. 1 Divisions 10, 11, 12, 23 and 40 and the water industry (collection, purification and distribution) to NACE Rev. 1 Division 41, the Labour Force Survey estimates that total employment in the EU for the energy and water industries was around 1.74 million persons in 1998. Of these, 253 thousand were in the water industry and 1.49 million in the energy industry. Between 1995 and 1998 employment in the EU energy industry fell by a total of 9.7%, mainly due to a net reduction in employment of 93 thousand in electricity, gas and hot water supply and 36 thousand persons in the mining of coal and lignite. Employment in the water industry fell over the same period by 4.2%, equivalent to 11 thousand persons.

Figure 1.5

Final energy consumption by user in the EU (million TOE) (1)

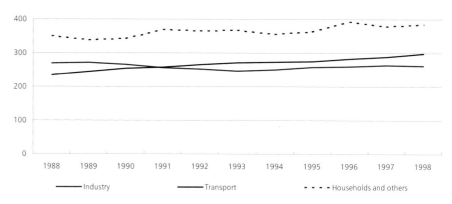

(1) Data for EU-15 includes former East Germany for 1991 and subsequent years.

Source: Eurostat (SIRENE)

Figure 1.6

Gross inland consumption by fuel in the EU (million TOE) (1)

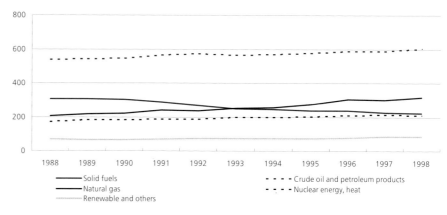

(1) Data for EU-15 includes former East Germany for 1991 and subsequent years.

Source: Eurostat (SIRENE)

——————————————————————————————————Figure 1.7

Electricity, gas and water supply (NACE Rev. 1 40 and 41)

Apparent labour productivity and unit personnel costs, 1997 (thousand ECU)

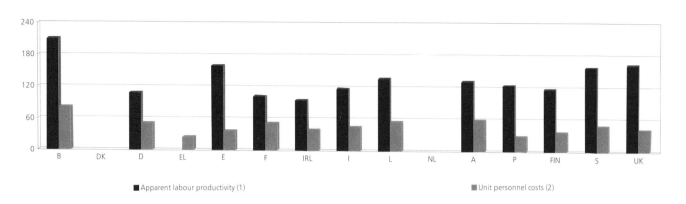

■ Apparent labour productivity (1)   ■ Unit personnel costs (2)

(1) IRL and I, 1996; DK, EL and NL, not available.
(2) EL, IRL and I, 1996; DK and NL, not available.

Source: Eurostat (SBS)

—————————————————Table 1.3

Energy (NACE Rev. 1 10, 11, 12, 23, 40 and 41)
Composition of the labour force, 1999 (%)

	Men (1)	Full-time (2)	Highly-educated (3)
EU-15	82.8	95.6	25.3
B	86.2	94.7	29.5
DK	82.6	95.4	37.1
D	83.7	95.7	28.0
EL	85.3	99.6	18.6
E	88.5	98.2	37.9
F	77.6	93.7	24.7
IRL	85.4	95.2	22.9
I	87.4	97.1	7.9
L	87.0	93.9	:
NL	80.8	83.0	23.2
A	84.0	94.2	8.3
P	89.2	97.7	10.5
FIN	80.3	97.0	37.2
S	79.3	96.8	:
UK	76.3	94.4	36.2

(1) EU-15 and EL, 1998.
(2) EU-15, B and EL, 1998.
(3) EL, 1998; EU-15, IRL and UK, 1997.

Source: Eurostat (LFS)

INTERNATIONAL TRENDS AND FOREIGN TRADE

The EU has significant trade in energy, but imports outstrip exports considerably. In 1991 net imports were equal to 668 million TOE and had risen to 723 million TOE seven years later. As a share of gross inland consumption, net imports represented between 47% and 51% of the total during the period from 1991 to 1998.

EU relies heavily on oil imports

Imports of solid fuels, crude oil and petroleum products, gas and electricity have all risen as rising demand has outstripped production growth. The share of crude oil and petroleum products in energy imports has fallen from 74.4% in 1991 to 72.8% in 1998, whilst the share of gas has increased from 13.2% to 15.6%, reflecting the change in the energy mix over this period. Exports of solid fuels fell in absolute terms and accounted for 2.6% of total EU energy exports in 1998, one-quarter less than their share from 1991 (3.7%). EU exports of other products rose in absolute terms.

The trade deficit of the EU increased over the seven-year period to 1998 for each of the main energy products, except electricity, where the balance was volatile. The electricity balance ranged from a surplus of 136 thousand TOE in 1996 to a deficit of 1.9 million TOE in 1993. Crude oil and petroleum products were the largest contributors to the deficit, although their share of the total fell from 71.3% in 1991 to 67.7% in 1998.

The Middle East and Norway remain the principal sources of crude oil imports, whilst Algeria, Norway and the former Soviet Union were the most important natural gas suppliers from outside the EU. Imports of solid fuels were dominated by supplies from the USA, Australia and South Africa.

—————————————————Figure 1.8

Gross inland energy consumption by world region, 1997 (% of TOE)

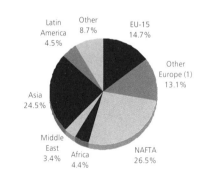

(1) Including EFTA, Central and Eastern European Countries, the CIS and Baltic States.

Source: Eurostat, DG TREN

SUB-CHAPTER 1.1
SOLID FUELS (NACE Rev. 1 10 AND 23.1)

This sub-chapter covers the extraction, washing, grading and ranking of solid fuels, which include hard coal (NACE Rev. 1 Group 10.1), lignite (Group 10.2) and peat (10.3). Furthermore, it covers the processing of these products, namely the manufacture of coke oven products (Group 23.1).

Gross inland consumption of solid fuels, of which hard coal represents more than three-quarters, has fallen every year since 1991 in the EU. The production of solid fuels has fallen faster than both consumption and exports and this has lead to an increase in imports despite falling demand. The main market for solid fuels is still conventional thermal power stations, where its share of transformation input fell from 67.2% in 1991 to 54.9% in 1998, largely displaced by gas (whose share increased by 13.0 percentage points over the same period).

STRUCTURE AND PERFORMANCE

Without exception, the EU's primary production of solid fuels fell every year from 1991 to a level of 113.6 million TOE in 1998, a total reduction of just under 40%, equivalent to 7.0% per annum on average. In 1998, primary production fell by just over 9% compared to the previous year, less than the reductions experienced in 1993 and 1994 (both 11.6%).

Coal represented 58.4% of the primary production of solid fuels in the EU in 1998. Between 1991 and 1998 the EU's primary production of coal fell by 42.7% to reach 66.4 million TOE. Germany accounted for almost half (46.2%) of the EU's primary coal production in 1998, the United Kingdom for 37.9%, Spain for 11.5% and France for the remaining 4.4%[4].

Primary coal production fell in all of these Member States in 1998, with France (15.9%) and the United Kingdom (15.0%) recording the largest contractions. Over the seven years to 1998 primary production more than halved in France (-53.7%) and in the United Kingdom (-53.0%) and fell significantly in Germany (-35.2%). By contrast, in Spain, primary coal production recorded a sequence of increases and falls, ending the period with primary production some 5.7% lower in 1998 than in 1991.

---

(4) IRL and P stopped production in 1994; I and S stopped production in 1993; B stopped production in 1992.

Figure 1.9

Main indicators for solid fuels in the EU (million TOE) (1)

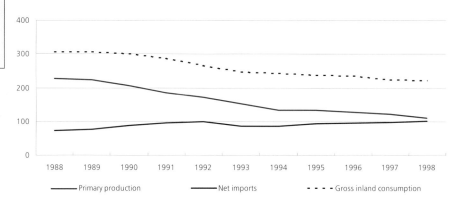

(1) Data for EU-15 includes former East Germany for 1991 and subsequent years.

Source: Eurostat (SIRENE)

Figure 1.10

Breakdown of final energy consumption of solid fuels in the EU (%) (1)

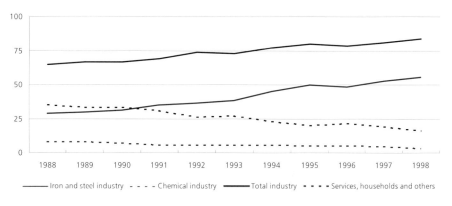

(1) Data for EU-15 includes former East Germany for 1991 and subsequent years.

Source: Eurostat (SIRENE)

Increased dependency on conventional thermal power stations; a market where solid fuels are losing ground to gas

Just less than 70% of the EU's gross inland consumption of solid fuels in 1998 was input for transformation in conventional thermal power stations, 16.7% was input for coke-oven plants, 5.3% for blast furnace plants and just 1.6% for patent fuel and briquetting plants. Compared to seven years earlier, there had been a shift in these transformation markets away from patent fuel and briquetting plants (-3.6 percentage points from 5.2%) towards a greater concentration in conventional thermal power stations (+5.4 percentage points from 64.4%).

In 1998, 45.2 million TOE of solid fuels was available for consumption in the EU, just 20.3% of gross inland consumption. Although final energy consumption by industry fell to 35.5 million TOE in 1998 from 47.7 million TOE seven years earlier, its share of final energy consumption rose from 69.2% to 84.0%. The principal industrial users were the iron and steel industry (56.1% of final energy consumption) and the manufacture of non-metallic mineral products (12.2%). The other main user of solid fuels in 1998 were households, but their final energy consumption fell from 18.8 million TOE in 1991 to just 5.8 million TOE seven years later and their share of final energy consumption nearly halved to 13.7%. The use of solid fuels in transport was already very small in 1991, just 24.0 thousand TOE, and by 1998 it had fallen to an insignificant 1.9 thousand TOE.

LABOUR AND PRODUCTIVITY

Underground employment in coal mining in the EU in 1998 was equal to 74.8 thousand persons, 6.1 thousand (-7.5%) less than in 1997 and 94.5 thousand less than seven years earlier, a fall in employment of more than one-half. Most of this reduction was registered in Germany (37.9 thousand net job losses) and the United Kingdom (35.8 thousand). In relative terms the most significant losses were in the United Kingdom, where the 6.2 thousand underground employees remaining in this industry in 1998 represented less than 15% of the total seven years earlier. The fall in underground employment levels has been the least severe in Spain, with the Spanish underground coal workforce equal to 17.8 thousand persons in 1998.

Increases in productivity

The reduction in employment levels have generally been faster than the falls in production, and as a result productivity measured as kilograms of output per man hour has increased across the EU from 664.8 in 1991 to 704.0 Kg per man hour in 1998. This seven-year period however hides an increase to a temporary peak of 777.6 Kg per man hour in 1994 and a higher peak of 803.9 Kg per man hour in 1997.

In 1998, productivity (using this measure) was highest in the United Kingdom at 1,198 Kg per man hour, although this had fallen steadily from a high of 1,857 Kg per man hour in 1994. The Spanish workforce consistently recorded the lowest levels of productivity by this measure during the period from 1993 to 1998.

The share of men in employment in Division 10 of NACE Rev. 1 (mining of coal and lignite; extraction of peat) was 93.1% in 1998 according to the Labour Force Survey, the highest proportion of any Division, and a share which rose 2.3 percentage points since 1995.

INTERNATIONAL TRENDS AND FOREIGN TRADE

The falling consumption of solid fuels in the EU goes against world trends where coal consumption has continued to grow. Global growth is almost exclusively due to its use in electricity generation, not because of an increase in its share of the energy mix, but rather due to a general increase in electricity generation as a whole.

Increase of 24.5% in total imports of solid fuels

As noted, gross inland consumption (-22.2%) and primary production (-39.6%) of solid fuels fell substantially in the EU between 1991 and 1998 (in volume terms). Although exports also fell (-12.0%), their rate of decline was slower than for production and hence a smaller proportion of domestic primary production has been available for gross inland consumption. As a result, the negative trade balance, or net imports, has risen from 96.1 million TOE in 1991 to 101.0 million TOE (+ 5.2%) in 1998, as total imports have climbed to 110.4 million TOE.

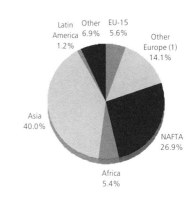

Figure 1.11

Production of solid fuels by world region, 1997 (% of TOE)

(1) Including EFTA, Central and Eastern European Countries, the CIS and Baltic States.

Source: Eurostat, DG TREN

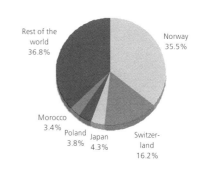

Figure 1.12

Solid fuels (NACE Rev. 1 10 and 23.1) Destination of EU exports, 1999 (%)

Source: Eurostat (COMEXT)

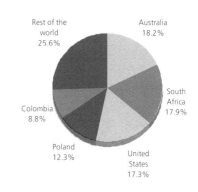

Figure 1.13

Solid fuels (NACE Rev. 1 10 and 23.1) Origin of EU imports, 1999 (%)

Source: Eurostat (COMEXT)

Table 1.4

Solid fuels (NACE Rev. 1 10) Composition of the labour force, 1999 (%)

	Men (1)	Full-time (2)	Highly-educated
EU-15	93.1	97.8	:
B	:	:	:
DK	:	:	:
D	96.4	99.7	16.6
EL	92.5	98.1	:
E	98.7	100.0	20.7
F	96.0	96.0	:
IRL	:	:	:
I	:	100.0	:
L	:	:	:
NL	:	:	:
A	:	:	:
P	:	:	:
FIN	100.0	100.0	:
S	:	100.0	:
UK	94.3	100.0	:

(1) EU-15, EL and FIN, 1998.
(2) EU-15, EL, E, FIN and UK, 1998; I and S, 1997.

Source: Eurostat (LFS)

SUB-CHAPTER 1.2
CRUDE OIL AND NATURAL GAS
(NACE Rev. 1 11 AND 23.2)

This sub-chapter covers the exploration for and production of crude oil and natural gas and the production of condensates and other liquids resulting from gas processing operations, as well as related supporting service activities (excluding surveying) (NACE Rev. 1 Division 11). Furthermore, it includes information on the manufacture of refined petroleum products (Group 23.2), but excludes retail sale of petroleum products (see Chapter 16).

Two recent mergers within the petroleum industry have resulted in the creation of a new tier of companies. On 31st December 1998, BP Amoco was created by the merger of Amoco Corporation (USA) and the British Petroleum Company p.l.c. (UK). On 30th November 1999, Exxon Corporation and Mobil Corporation (both USA) merged to form Exxon Mobil Corporation. Exxon and Mobil together had (in 1998) 123 thousand employees worldwide.

Box 1.2

The petroleum industry has faced a high degree of volatility in crude oil prices in recent times. 1998 saw prices fall as demand fell for the first time in 10 years and there was excess supply. The spot price for Brent crude started the year at 15.89 USD (per barrel) rose quickly to a year high of 16.03 USD (29th January 1998) and finished the year at 10.44 USD, just above the year's low of 9.17 (10th December 1998). The main causes of this fall over the year were mild climatic conditions, a more severe than expected recession in Japan and elsewhere in south-east Asia and an increase in exports by Iraq. In 1999, prices rose rapidly, pausing only in May and October, before finishing the year at 25.1 USD. The rise experienced in 1999 continued into 2000 and had reached a year high of 34.27 USD at the time of writing (30th August 2000). This rise has been attributed to a resurgence in demand and agreements by OPEC and a number of other producing countries on production levels. The result of this was that throughout 1999 world demand for oil exceeded production by more than 800 thousand barrels per day.

STRUCTURE AND PERFORMANCE

Production of crude oil and natural gas in the EU increased steadily up until the middle of the 1980s, stimulated by rising oil prices, following the oil price shocks of the 1970s. However, the collapse of oil prices in 1986 reduced the attractiveness of upstream investment and set output on a downward trend. By 1989, primary production of crude oil, petroleum products and gas had fallen to pre-1983 levels at under 250 million TOE in the EU. Since then, output increased to 343.1 million TOE in 1998, with both crude oil and natural gas production on a rising trend from 1991 until 1996, since when gas production has fallen slightly.

Production trends

The output of the EU crude oil and petroleum industry experienced strong growth in the first half of the 1990s and has remained between 159 million TOE and 162 million TOE since 1995. In 1998, production was 36.9% higher than 1991. The United Kingdom accounted for 83.3% of the EU's production in 1998. Indeed, the increase in EU output between 1991 and 1998 was largely due to the United Kingdom's crude oil production, which rose by 45.2% over the period.

Figure 1.14

Main indicators for crude oil and petroleum products in the EU (million TOE) (1)

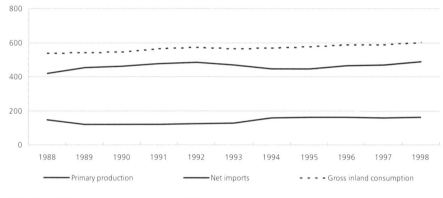

(1) Data for EU-15 includes former East Germany for 1991 and subsequent years.

Source: Eurostat (SIRENE)

Figure 1.15

Main indicators for natural gas in the EU (million TOE) (1)

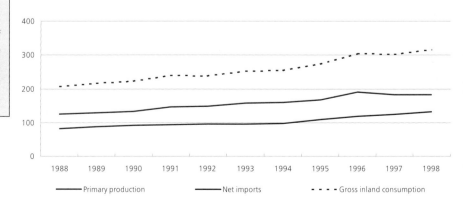

(1) Data for EU-15 includes former East Germany for 1991 and subsequent years.

Source: Eurostat (SIRENE)

Box 1.3

The major change in the European gas market has been the adoption in June 1998 by the European Parliament and the Council of a directive on common rules for the internal market in natural gas, which Member States must implement by August 2000. The directive establishes common rules for the transmission, distribution, supply and storage of natural gas. Member States will be able to specify which customers will have the legal capacity to contract for natural gas. With some exceptions this will initially cover all gas-fired power generators, as well as other final customers consuming more than 25 million m³ of gas annually, leading to an opening of the market equal to at least 20% of national gas consumption. In two further stages after 5 and 10 years, the annual consumption threshold will fall to 5 million m³. The directive regulates for access to the system based on objective, transparent and non-discriminatory criteria. A further aim of the directive is to unbundle the industry and hence it requires accounts of integrated undertakings to be as transparent as possible to detect any abuse of a dominant position (tariffs or discriminatory practices); separate accounts are required for natural gas transmission, distribution and storage activities.

Recent falls in natural gas production against long term growth

As regards natural gas, EU production grew by an average of 3.2% per annum between 1991 and 1998, to 181.5 million TOE, despite a 3.5% decline in 1997 and a further 0.4% decrease in 1998. The two principal EU gas producers in 1998 were the United Kingdom (44.7% of EU primary production) and the Netherlands (31.7%), followed by Germany and Italy (8.6% each).

Consumption trends

Turning to demand, EU gross inland consumption of crude oil, petroleum products and gas reached 917.0 million TOE in 1998, an increase of 3.0% compared to 1997. Crude oil accounted for nearly two-thirds of consumption, and natural gas just over one-third. Gross inland consumption of crude oil and petroleum products progressed by 0.9% per annum on average between 1991 and 1998, whilst gas consumption grew much more quickly (4.0% per annum).

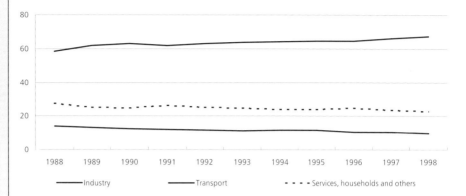

Figure 1.16

Breakdown of final energy consumption of crude oil and petroleum products in the EU (%) (1)

Industry ——— Transport ——— Services, households and others

(1) Data for EU-15 includes former East Germany for 1991 and subsequent years.

Source: Eurostat (SIRENE)

Figure 1.17

Breakdown of final energy consumption of natural gas in the EU (%) (1)

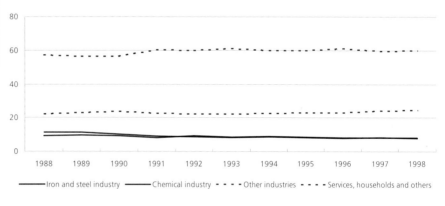

Iron and steel industry ——— Chemical industry - - - Other industries - - - Services, households and others

(1) Data for EU-15 includes former East Germany for 1991 and subsequent years.

Source: Eurostat (SIRENE)

Crude oil refined mainly into gas/diesel oil and motor spirit

Practically all crude oil (and feedstocks) is used as an input for transformation in refineries. The breakdown of output of petroleum products from refineries in 1998 was: gas/diesel oil 34.6%, motor spirit 22.5%, residual fuel oils 16.7%, kerosene and jet fuels 6.8%, naphtha 6.4%, refinery gas 3.5%, liquefied petroleum gases (LPG) 2.9% and various other petroleum products 6.7%. The energy branch itself consumes most refinery gas and residual fuel oil is often used as an input for conventional thermal power stations. The majority of the remaining output from oil refineries is available for final consumption.

Large increases in the use of natural gas as an input for conventional thermal power stations

Less than a quarter (22.4%) of gross inland consumption of natural gas was used in transformation in 1998, but this share has grown steadily since 1991 when it had been 14.9%. Its main use in transformation is in conventional thermal power stations (97.0% of the transformation input total). In 1998, 74.8 million TOE of natural gas was used as an input for conventional power stations, compared to just 36.7 million TOE seven years earlier. The amount of natural gas used for transformation in gasworks and district heating was less in absolute terms in 1998 than it had been seven years earlier.

Transport was the main final energy user of petroleum products and households the main user of natural gas

After transformation (and losses and own consumption by the energy branch), 760.6 million TOE of crude oil, petrochemical products and gas were available for final consumption in the EU in 1998, of which 30.6% was natural gas and 29.5% was gas/diesel oil. Non-energy final consumption (in other words use as raw materials rather than fuel) accounted for 12.3%, whilst final energy consumption accounted for the rest. The transport sector was the main market for petroleum products, accounting for 74.4% of final energy consumption of gas/diesel oil, motor spirit and kerosene combined. Households took a 13.9% share of final consumption of petroleum products, and as much as 44.7% of final energy consumption of natural gas (both shares above those of industry, 9.8% and 37.7% respectively).

LABOUR AND PRODUCTIVITY

Restricting the activity coverage to NACE Rev. 1 Division 11 (the extraction of crude petroleum and natural gas and related service activities), the Labour Force Survey estimates that total employment in the EU was 109.4 thousand persons in 1998, 12.7% less than in 1995. Just under half of the persons employed in this industry were recorded in the United Kingdom and just under one-fifth in Italy. The share of men in employment was equal to 83.0% in 1998, approximately 6 percentage points less than the average for mining and quarrying.

Figure 1.18

Proportion of gross inland consumption used for transformation by conventional thermal power stations, in the EU (%) (1)

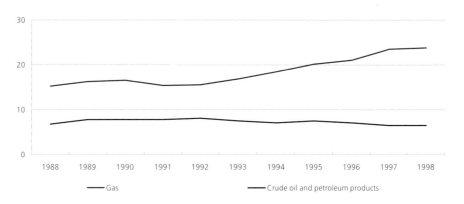

(1) Data for EU-15 includes former East Germany for 1991 and subsequent years.

Source: Eurostat (SIRENE)

INTERNATIONAL TRENDS AND FOREIGN TRADE

Despite rising crude oil production, the EU is still heavily dependent on imports, with net imports covering as much as 75.4% of gross inland consumption in 1998. This marked a slight increase compared to 1997, but was below shares recorded between 1989 and 1993, after which North Sea output increased. Imports of crude oil stood at 564.0 million TOE in 1998, 5.1% higher than a year before, and the highest level over the seven-year period studied. The Middle East is by far the most important supplier of crude oil to the EU, together with a number of African countries (mainly Nigeria, Libya and Algeria), as well as Norway.

As regards natural gas, the share of EU gross inland consumption met by EU production (primary production minus exports) has risen from 47.4% in 1991 and 1992 to 48.9% in 1994, only to fall back further to 45.8% in 1998. Net imports of natural gas by the EU rose by 5.9% to 131.5 million TOE in 1998, a level nearly 40% higher than seven years earlier. The main suppliers of natural gas to the EU are the CIS, Algeria and Norway.

Table 1.5

Crude oil and natural gas (NACE Rev. 1 11)
Composition of the labour force, 1999 (%)

	Men (1)	Full-time (2)	Highly-educated (3)
EU-15	83.0	95.9	:
B	90.6	90.1	:
DK	:	100.0	:
D	88.2	95.2	:
EL	:	:	:
E	60.7	97.7	:
F	83.4	96.1	:
IRL	:	:	:
I	82.5	100.0	18.6
L	:	:	:
NL	74.9	85.4	:
A	:	:	:
P	:	100.0	:
FIN	:	:	:
S	:	:	:
UK	83.7	96.5	41.2

(1) EU-15, 1998; D, 1997.
(2) EU-15 and B, 1998; D and P, 1997.
(3) UK, 1997.

Source: Eurostat (LFS)

Table 1.6

Proven reserves of crude oil relative to production (years)

	1996	1999
Algeria	20.9	21.3
Angola	21.0	19.7
Argentina	7.5	8.0
Australia	7.9	14.5
Brazil	14.2	19.4
Brunei	22.7	23.9
Canada	7.3	6.7
China	20.7	20.5
Colombia	14.7	9.0
Ecuador	14.4	14.7
Egypt	11.7	11.1
Gabon	10.1	19.2
India	22.7	14.9
Indonesia	9.1	9.4
Iran	65.5	65.2
Iraq	:	145.8
Kuwait	122.8	122.4
Libya	58.2	58.2
Malaysia	17.2	15.4
Mexico	41.5	36.3
Nigeria	26.8	28.9
Norway	7.3	9.9
Oman	15.8	16.1
Qatar	23.2	13.7
Russia	22.1	22.6
Saudi Arabia	83.1	80.5
United Arab Emirates	114.1	109.9
United Kingdom	4.5	5.3
USA	8.0	8.2
Venezuela	54.2	57.7
World	41.2	40.4

Source: CPDP

————————————————Figure 1.19

Oil production by world region, 1997
(% of TOE)

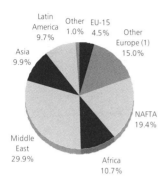

(1) Including EFTA, Central and Eastern European Countries,
the CIS and Baltic States.

Source: Eurostat, DG TREN

————————————————Figure 1.20

Natural gas production by world region, 1997
(% of TOE)

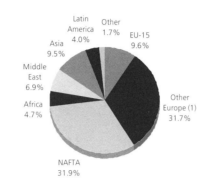

(1) Including EFTA, Central and Eastern European Countries,
the CIS and Baltic States.

Source: Eurostat, DG TREN

————————————————Figure 1.21

Crude oil and natural gas
(NACE Rev. 1 11 and 23.2)
Destination of EU exports, 1999 (%)

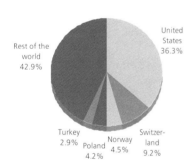

Source: Eurostat (COMEXT)

————————————————Figure 1.22

Crude oil and natural gas
(NACE Rev. 1 11 and 23.2)
Origin of EU imports, 1999 (%)

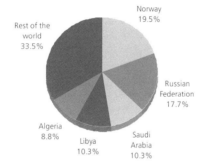

Source: Eurostat (COMEXT)

SUB-CHAPTER 1.3
NUCLEAR FUELS
(NACE Rev. 1 12 AND 23.3)

This sub-chapter covers the mining and processing of nuclear fuels. Mining of uranium and thorium ores is covered by NACE Rev. 1 Division 12. Processing, which involves the production of enriched uranium, fuel elements for nuclear reactors and radioactive elements for industrial and medical use is covered by NACE Rev. 1 Group 23.3, as is the treatment of nuclear waste. The generation of electricity from nuclear fuels is treated in sub-chapter 1.4.

The mining and processing of nuclear fuels is directly related to demand for electricity from nuclear power stations and the supply of material from secondary sources. The factors affecting the nuclear fuels industries are therefore dependent on the main issues facing electricity generation: deregulation of the electricity market, competition and sustainable development. The contribution of nuclear energy remains however controversial and the political impact of this can be witnessed by the premature shut down of one nuclear reactor power station in Sweden at the end of November 1999.

STRUCTURE AND PERFORMANCE

Mining of uranium and thorium ores does not exist in most EU Member States with only France, Spain and Portugal having any natural production. In quantity terms, uranium production within the EU has been on a downward trend since the early 1990s. According to the Uranium Institute, production in France, Spain and Portugal together decreased from 1,921 tonnes in 1993 to 782 tonnes five years later, with a 23.3% fall between 1997 and 1998. France was still the largest producer in 1998, but its output had fallen by 70% compared to 1993.

The Euratom Supply Agency estimates average reactor needs of the EU for natural uranium until 2009 at about 21.4 thousand tonnes/year. Net requirements, after accounting for recycling and stock changes, are estimated at about 19.1 thousand tonnes/year and hence the EU is heavily dependent on non-Community countries for natural uranium supplies.

EU processing of nuclear fuels in 1999 regains the loses of 1998
The processing of nuclear fuels was also an activity which only existed in a limited number of countries, with seven[5] of the Member States reporting no activity in 1996 or 1997. Estimated EU output for 1999 for the remaining Member States was 8.4 billion ECU, an increase of 15.4% compared to 1998 (but comparable with the 1997 figure). France's share of the EU total in 1997 was 59.1%.

(5) DK, EL, IRL, L, A, P and FIN.

LABOUR AND PRODUCTIVITY

The most recent estimates of employment in the EU nuclear fuels processing industry was 28.1 thousand persons in 1995. The two Member States with the largest workforce in this industry are the United Kingdom (around 12 thousand in 1997) and France (11.4 thousand, 1997).

INTERNATIONAL TRENDS AND FOREIGN TRADE

World production of natural uranium has been below consumption since at least 1990 and the shortfall has been met by reductions in stocks and recycling. World production of natural uranium in 1999 was estimated (provisional figures) to be 31 thousand tonnes, below the 1998 figure (source: Euratom Supply Agency). According to the Uranium Institute the largest world producers in 1998 were Canada and Australia with 32.2% and 14.4% of world production respectively. Between 1994 and 1995 Australian output increased significantly, whilst production in Kazakhstan, Niger and Russia fell, such that Australia went from the fifth largest producer to the second largest, a position which it has maintained since then. Australia, Kazakhstan, Canada and South Africa all had reasonably assured reserves[6] (as of 1st January 1997) in excess of 200 thousand tonnes.

Like production, conversion has also seen reduced worldwide activity because of the use of secondary sources, although there has been less impact on the final processing stages of enrichment and fabrication. Increased competition in the electricity market has lead to increased competition in the nuclear fuels industry, with prices and stocks falling and restructuring through a number of international mergers and acquisitions.

(6) The uranium that occurs in known mineral deposits of such size, grade, and configuration that it could be recovered within a given production cost ranges (<80$/kg), with currently proven mining and processing technology.

Table 1.7

Forecasts of uranium and separative work requirements in the EU

	2000	2001	2002	2003	2004	2005	2006	2007	2008	2009	Average 2000-2009
Uranium (tU)											
Reactor needs	21,200	21,900	21,600	21,300	22,000	21,400	21,300	21,600	21,000	21,000	21,400
Net requirements	17,400	17,500	18,600	19,900	19,600	19,200	19,400	19,700	19,600	19,900	19,100
Separative work (tSW)											
Reactor needs	11,900	12,100	12,200	12,000	12,500	12,300	12,200	12,400	12,100	12,100	12,200
Net requirements	11,000	10,700	10,900	10,900	11,500	11,200	11,300	11,500	11,300	11,500	11,200

Source: Euratom Supply Agency

South Africa and Australia are the largest exporters of nuclear ores to the EU

The EU is largely dependent upon imports to satisfy its demand for uranium, whether natural or processed. Australia's exports to the EU fell from 39.0 million ECU in 1998 to 24.9 million EUR in 1999, but it remained the largest (in value terms) supplier of uranium and thorium ores to the EU. South Africa was the second largest exporter to the EU (but its exports also fell, from 27.0 million ECU to 19.8 million EUR). In 1999, Uzbekistan was the third most important origin of EU imports, valued at over 15.3 million EUR compared to 0.8 million ECU the previous year. Large increases were also recorded by Russia, Kazakhstan and the United States whilst imports from Ukraine fell below 5 million EUR and imports from Canada and Niger fell below 10 million EUR.

The United States and Russia are the largest exporters of processed nuclear fuels to the EU

Just under 72% of the EU's processed nuclear fuel imports in 1999 were from the United States and Russia, a slightly lower proportion than in 1998. Notably EU imports from the United States fell from 265.2 million ECU to 190.3 million EUR in 1999. A significant increase between 1998 and 1999 was recorded for EU imports from Kazakhstan (8.1 million ECU to 53.7 million EUR) and from the Czech Republic (0.3 million ECU to 4.1 million EUR).

Table 1.8

Production of uranium in the world (tonnes)

	1993	1994	1995	1996	1997	1998
Total	32,512	32,188	32,916	34,996	35,692	33,932
Canada	9,178	9,694	10,515	11,788	12,029	10,924
Australia	2,268	2,183	3,712	4,974	5,520	4,885
Niger	2,914	2,975	2,970	3,160	3,497	3,731
Namibia	1,665	1,901	2,007	2,452	2,905	2,762
Russia (1)	2,399	2,968	2,250	2,000	2,000	2,000
USA	1,192	1,400	2,324	2,420	2,170	1,872
Kazakhstan	2,700	2,240	1,630	1,320	1,000	1,250
South Africa	1,700	1,690	1,424	1,436	1,100	962
Gabon	556	650	630	560	472	731
Czech Republic	950	541	600	598	590	610
France	1,710	1,028	980	940	748	508
China (1)	780	780	500	500	500	500
Ukraine (1)	500	500	500	500	500	500
España	183	255	255	255	255	255
India (1)	290	200	200	200	200	200
Romania (1)	120	120	100	100	100	100
Deutschland (2)	116	395	40	40	40	40
Argentina	125	64	65	28	35	35
Pakistan (1)	23	23	23	23	23	23
Portugal	28	24	18	15	17	19
Belgique/België	34	40	23	28	27	15
Hungary	381	402	205	200	200	10
Brazil	50	50	125	0	0	0
Bulgaria	50	50	20	0	0	0

(1) UI estimate.
(2) From decommissioning.

Source: UI, IAEA

Figure 1.23

Mining of uranium and thorium ores (NACE Rev. 1 12)

Origin of EU imports, 1999 (%)

Source: Eurostat (COMEXT)

Figure 1.24

Processing of nuclear fuel (NACE Rev. 1 23.3)

Destination of EU exports, 1999 (%)

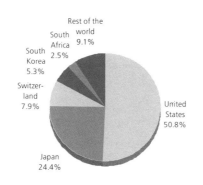

Source: Eurostat (COMEXT)

Figure 1.25

Processing of nuclear fuel (NACE Rev. 1 23.3)

Origin of EU imports, 1999 (%)

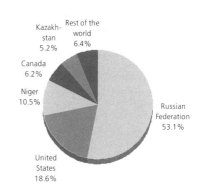

Source: Eurostat (COMEXT)

SUB-CHAPTER 1.4
ELECTRICITY GENERATION AND
DISTRIBUTION (NACE Rev. 1 40.1)

This sub-chapter covers production, transmission and
distribution of electricity generated from all sources,
notably thermal, nuclear, hydro-electric, gas turbine,
diesel and renewable energies. These activities are
classified in Group 40.1 of NACE Rev. 1.

STRUCTURE AND PERFORMANCE

Total net installed capacity in the EU in 1998 was
561.4 thousand MW[7], an increase of 0.5% compared
to 1997. Indeed, capacity increased every year in the
EU between 1991 and 1998, with the exception of a
very slight fall in 1992 (0.2%), such that in 1998
capacity was 7.8% higher than in 1991. Thermal supply power stations accounted for 56.3% of this capacity, nuclear power stations for 21.9% and hydro-electric 20.7%. Geothermal and wind energy accounted
for the remaining 1.2%. Compared to 1991 this represented a small increase in the share of thermal supply power stations (+0.3 percentage points) and a
more significant increase, albeit from a very small
base, for geothermal and wind energy (+1.0 percentage points).

*Introduction of combined cycle, internal
combustion engine and gas turbine power plants*
Although total capacity for thermal power plants has
not changed greatly, the type of plant providing this
capacity has changed greatly. In 1991 only eight
Member States reported capacity for combined cycle
power plants, but by 1998 all except France,
Luxembourg and Finland had some capacity from this
type of plant and total EU capacity had increased more
than seven-fold. Internal combustion engine power
plants and gas turbine power plants have also seen
large increases in capacity, particularly in Spain.

*Increased capacity for generation
from renewable sources*
In 1991 only Denmark, Germany, the Netherlands, the
United Kingdom and Sweden reported a significant
capacity for wind energy, but by 1998 all countries
had capacity for this type of electricity generation
totalling 6.2 thousand MW. Geothermal energy
remained limited to Greece, Italy and Portugal in
1998, as it had in 1991.

France and the United Kingdom recorded the largest
increase in capacity for nuclear power plants between
1991 and 1998, together adding 6.1 thousand MW of
capacity, though both recorded slight falls between
1997 and 1998.

(7) Megawatts.

Figure 1.26 —————
**Breakdown of net electricity capacity in the EU,
1998 (%)**

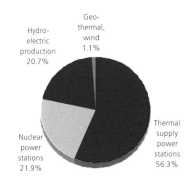

Source: Eurostat (SIRENE)

Figure 1.27 —————
Net production mix of electricity in the EU, 1998 (%)

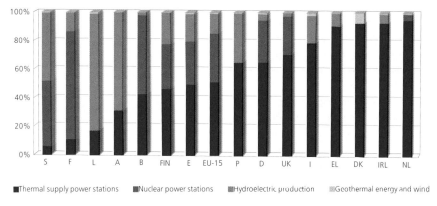

Source: Eurostat (SIRENE)

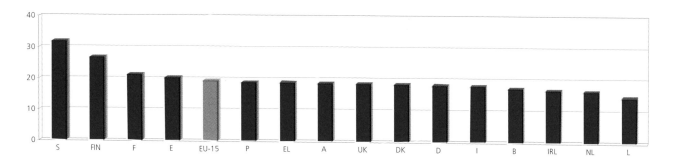

—————Figure 1.28

Share of electricity in final energy consumption, 1998 (%)

Source: Eurostat (SIRENE)

It has been the intention of the European Commission since the beginning of the 1990s to stimulate greater competition in electricity markets. Directive 96/92/EC concerning common rules of the internal market in electricity was adopted in December 1996. The directive legislates for access to networks to be based on objective, transparent and non-discriminatory criteria. From the consumers' perspective, the core part of the directive concerns market opening in three steps between February 1999[8] and February 2003. These steps are based on access for large final consumers exceeding a certain threshold of annual consumption. For the first step the threshold was 40 GWh[9], for the second 20 GWh and for the third 9 GWh, implying that initially about 26% of each national market should have been opened for competition, reaching about 33% after the third step. Some Member States had already liberalised their electricity markets (notably Finland, Sweden and the United Kingdom) and some others have chosen to move faster and further than the common EU requirements (notably Spain and Portugal).

The greater network access and opening-up of markets for distributors and consumers should allow the choice of suppliers to be made on an economic basis, irrespective of national boundaries and may lead to an important increase in electricity trade amongst EU Member States.

(8) B and IRL have a one-year extension; EL has a two-year extension.
(9) Gigawatthours.

—————Figure 1.29

Breakdown of final energy consumption of electricity in the EU (%) (1)

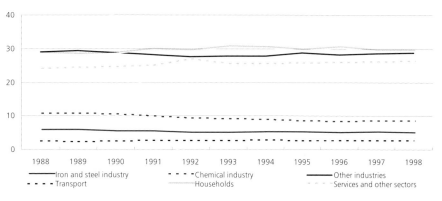

(1) Data for EU-15 includes the former East Germany for 1991 and subsequent years.

Source: Eurostat (SIRENE)

Widespread increases in electricity generation

In 1998 net electricity production in the EU was 2.36 TWh[10], an increase of 2.7% compared to 1997 and of 12.6% compared to 1991. Net production increased in every Member State between 1997 and 1998, except in Denmark where a fall of 6.4% was reported. Over a seven-year period (1991 to 1998) only Luxembourg recorded a fall (around 7%) and most Member States recorded increases in net production of between 12% and 30%. Germany had a 21.9% share of EU net production in 1998, followed by France (20.6%) and the United Kingdom (14.4%).

(10) Terawatthours (thousand gigawatthours).

Differences in the mix of sources for electricity generation across the EU are significant, reflecting access to the various primary energy sources, as well as differing policies concerning, for example, the provision of supply. Conventional thermal power stations accounted for more than half (51.5%) of net electricity production in the EU in 1998. However, this type of power plant supplied less than 10% of electricity production in Sweden, but more than 90% in the Netherlands, Ireland, Denmark and Greece. Similarly, nuclear power accounted for 75.6% of net electricity production in France (second in the world only to Lithuania), but less than 30% in the Netherlands, the United Kingdom and Germany. Seven Member States reported no electricity produced from nuclear power. Hydro-electric sources accounted for a large share of net production in Luxembourg (81.9%) and Austria (68.5%), as well as Sweden (47.8%). Some other renewable sources exceeded 1% of net electricity production, for example, in Italy (geothermal 1.6%), Denmark (wind 7.1%) and Spain (wind 1.1%).

Substitution of coal and petroleum by natural gas
Coal fired power plants have recorded a 12.3 percentage point fall in their share of EU net production from conventional thermal power stations between 1991 and 1998, whilst lignite and petroleum fired power stations have seen their shares fall by 2.6 and 2.8 percentage points respectively. Most of these reductions have been taken up by the 16.5 percentage point rise in the share of natural gas fired power stations, whilst there was also a 1.1 percentage point increase in the share of biomass[11]-fired power plants. The reduction in the share of EU electricity derived from coal fired power stations has taken place despite an increase in production in Portugal, Ireland, the Netherlands and Germany.

The production of electricity derived from petroleum fired power stations fell significantly in Germany (56.7%) and the United Kingdom (81.6%)[12] between 1991 and 1998, bringing down the EU total, although output increased in most other Member States. The United Kingdom's increased reliance on natural gas fired power stations (from 3.9 TWh in 1991 to 114.0 TWh in 1998) accounts for more than half of the EU's increase in production from this type of power station.

(11) Biomass/waste is organic, non-fossil material of biological origin. It comprises purpose-grown energy crops and waste.
(12) L reported no electricity production from petroleum fired power stations since 1998.

2.4% annual average growth rate in demand over 5 years
Due to the economic slowdown of 1992-93, slower growth in demand for electricity was recorded at the start of the 1990s, but in the 5 years since 1993 consumption within the internal market has grown on average by 2.4% per year.

Electricity steadily increased its share of final energy consumption over the 1980s, rising from less than 15.0% in the early 1980s to reach 19.2% by 1998. The share of electricity in final energy consumption varies substantially between countries, between 14.3% in Luxembourg and 31.6% in Sweden. In 1998, the largest share of electricity consumption was concentrated within industry (41.9%) and households (29.4%), with only 2.6% used in transport.

LABOUR AND PRODUCTIVITY

Employment in the electricity generation and distribution industry exceeded 700 thousand persons in 1997, of which practically all (99.9%, Eurostat estimate) were paid employees. Eurostat estimates that turnover per person employed was equal to 342.0 thousand ECU in 1997 and that apparent labour productivity was 132.8 thousand ECU. Another measure, simple wage adjusted labour productivity (262.7% in 1997) confirmed the relatively high productivity of this industry.

Table 1.9 ──────────────────────

Electricity, gas, steam and hot water supply (NACE Rev. 1 40)
Composition of the labour force, 1999 (%)

	Men (1)	Full-time (2)	Highly-educated (3)
EU-15	81.1	95.1	25.6
B	83.3	96.5	33.4
DK	87.5	98.0	24.0
D	79.3	94.1	31.4
EL	82.4	99.6	19.4
E	85.9	97.1	45.4
F	78.1	94.0	24.5
IRL	83.6	94.6	:
I	88.4	98.1	6.0
L	86.7	93.8	:
NL	82.0	80.4	16.0
A	87.0	95.9	7.2
P	92.7	100.0	:
FIN	80.6	100.0	36.3
S	79.4	96.3	:
UK	72.1	92.1	35.4

(1) EU-15 and EL, 1998.
(2) EU-15, B, and EL 1998; D and P, 1997.
(3) DK and EL, 1998; EU-15 and UK, 1997.

Source: Eurostat (LFS)

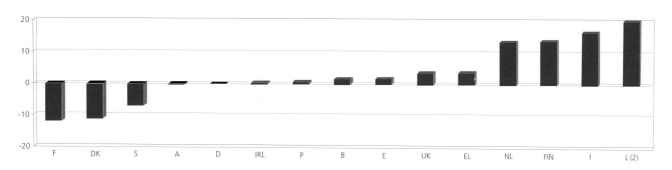

———Figure 1.30

Net electricity imports as a share of national net production, 1998 (%) (1)

(1) A negative sign indicates net exports.
(2) Luxembourg = 433.1.

Source: Eurostat (SIRENE)

INTERNATIONAL TRENDS AND FOREIGN TRADE

Trade with countries outside the EU is still very limited owing to the lack of interconnections between countries. Only Switzerland and Norway currently exchange significant amounts of electricity with the EU. Opportunities for electricity trade with Central and Eastern European countries have improved through the link between the Centrel grid[13] and the continental European UCPTE grid[14] .

Foreign trade limited geographically

Total imports in 1998 were equal to 168.4 TWh, a fall of 2.1% compared to 1997, but 20.9% higher than in 1991. The EU's net imports were equal to 13.1 TWh in 1998 which represented only 0.6% of net production. The EU has run a small trade deficit every year since 1991, except in 1996. As a proportion of net production, France (11.8%) and Denmark (11.0%) were the largest net exporters within the EU, whilst Luxembourg (433.1%) and Italy (16.5%) were the largest net importers. The main origins for EU imports in 1999 were Switzerland (52.6%) and the Russian Federation (18.1%), with the vast majority (88.4%) of the EU's exports going to Switzerland.

(13) Poland, the Czech Republic, Slovakia and Hungary.
(14) B, D, EL, E, F, I, L, NL, A, P and former Yugoslavia.

—————————————————————————————————Figure 1.31

Electricity generation and distribution
(NACE Rev. 1 40.1)
Destination of EU exports, 1999 (%)

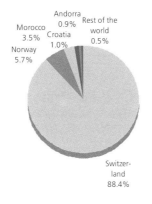

Source: Eurostat (COMEXT)

—————————————————————————————————Figure 1.32

Electricity generation and distribution
(NACE Rev. 1 40.1)
Origin of EU imports, 1999 (%)

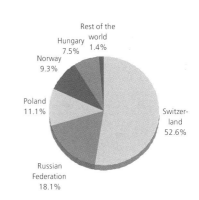

Source: Eurostat (COMEXT)

SUB-CHAPTER 1.5
WATER SUPPLY AND DISTRIBUTION
(NACE Rev. 1 41)

Water supply and distribution (NACE Rev. 1 Division 41) encompasses collection, purification, desalinisation and distribution. The operation of irrigation systems for agricultural purposes and the treatment of waste water purely for pollution prevention are not covered.

The organisation of the supply of drinking water in the EU is varied and evolving, essentially covering: direct public administration management (local administrative bodies or groups thereof); publicly owned enterprises with varying degrees of autonomy; public administration ownership with fixed period operating contracts for private enterprises; and private enterprises operating under independent regulatory authorities.

There has been a tendency for enterprises/public service bodies operating in the water industry (Division 41) to expand into waste water treatment activities (part of Division 90) or to merge with enterprises/public service bodies from that industry. Générale des Eaux and Suez Lyonnaise des Eaux (both F) are examples of two groups that are active in both of these industries and are the largest European enterprises operating in the supply of drinking water and waste water treatment.

Box 1.5
The European Commission presented proposals for a Water Framework Directive in 1997/98 and, at the time of writing, this is under a joint decision process by the European Parliament and the Council. Some of the aims of this draft Directive are expanding the scope of water protection to all waters, a combined approach of emission limit values and quality standards and "getting the prices right". Concerning the last issue, the need to conserve adequate supplies of a resource for which demand is continuously increasing is one of the drivers behind the introduction of pricing reflecting costs. Member States will be required (with some exceptions) to ensure that the price charged to water consumers - such as for the abstraction and distribution of fresh water and the collection and treatment of waste water - reflects true costs.

Table 1.10

Total fresh water resources, long term annual average: potential renewable sources (km³)

B	16.5
DK	6.1
D	178.0
EL	72.0
E	111.0
F	170.0
IRL	52.2
I	175.0
L	1.6
NL	91.0
A	84.0
P	72.9
FIN	110.0
S	179.0
UK	147.0

Source: Eurostat (MILIEU); Eurostat (not specified) for NL and UK

Table 1.11

Fresh water abstraction (million m³)

	Year	Total surface and ground water	For public water supply
B	1996	7,449	740
DK	1996	961	514
D	1995	43,374	5,810
EL (1)	1997	8,461	861
E	1997	40,855	5,393
F	1994	40,670	5,931
IRL	1994	1,176	470
I	1989	56,200	7,925
L	1995	57	33
NL	1996	4,425	1,267
A	1997	3,529	604
P	1989	7,288	578
FIN	1994	2,437	419
S	1995	2,709	37
UK (2)	1997	13,530	6,140

(1) Estimate.
(2) Excluding Scotland and Northern Ireland.

Source: Eurostat (MILIEU)

STRUCTURE AND PERFORMANCE
The 1997 EU production value in the water industry was 24.9 billion ECU[15]. Of this aggregate, France accounted for 32.7%, Germany 24.9% and the United Kingdom 24.3%.

In quantity terms, total abstraction of fresh water in the EU is in the order of 200 billion m³ to 250 billion m³ of water per year. Italy accounts for nearly one-quarter of this total and Germany, Spain and France just less than one-fifth each. The volume abstracted for public water supply is around 30 billion m³ to 40 billion m³ in the EU. Italy accounts for over 20% of this amount, while England and Wales (together), France, Germany and Spain each account for between 14% and 17%. The International Water Association's (IWA) figures indicate that public water supply in EU Member States in 1997 had fallen compared to 1980 levels in Denmark, Germany and Sweden and increased elsewhere[16].

(15) DK, EL, NL, not available; I, 1996.
(16) 1980 data not available for FIN.

LABOUR AND PRODUCTIVITY

Employment in Division 41 of NACE Rev. 1 was 144.3[17] thousand persons in 1997, of which practically all were paid employees. Eurostat estimates turnover per head was equal to 167.7 thousand ECU in 1997 and apparent labour productivity was 81.6 thousand ECU. Simple wage adjusted labour productivity was estimated at 220.1%, in other words value added was 2.2 times higher than personnel costs.

The share of men in employment in the water industry was 81.3% in 1998, marginally higher than the average for electricity, gas and water supply (81.2%), according to the Labour Force Survey. Nearly one-quarter (24.5%) of the persons in employment in the water industry in 1997 had completed a higher education degree, typical of the averages reported for the whole of electricity, gas and water supply, but considerably higher than the proportion recorded for the whole of manufacturing (16.3%). Close to 94.8% of persons worked full-time in 1998 in the water industry, a slight fall compared to 1995 and slightly below the average for the whole of electricity, gas and water supply (95.0% in 1998).

(17) DK, EL, NL, not available; I, 1996.

Table 1.12

Collection, purification and distribution of water (NACE Rev. 1 41)

Composition of the labour force, 1999 (%)

	Men (1)	Full-time (2)	Highly-educated (3)
EU-15	81.3	94.8	24.5
B	89.2	96.1	:
DK	:	:	:
D	77.3	95.9	:
EL	85.8	100.0	:
E	92.1	98.5	32.7
F	68.2	91.5	25.2
IRL	:	:	:
I	84.3	91.9	:
L	:	:	:
NL	82.0	91.5	:
A	81.7	89.4	:
P	88.3	90.0	:
FIN	88.2	95.8	:
S	:	:	:
UK	72.8	93.8	39.7

(1) EU-15, EL and A, 1998.
(2) EU-15, B, EL and A, 1998.
(3) EU-15 and UK, 1997.

Source: Eurostat (LFS)

Table 1.13

Interior flows of solid fuels, 1998 (thousand TOE)

	EU-15	B	DK	D	EL	E	F	IRL	I	L	NL	A (1)	P	FIN	S	UK
Primary production	113,571	0	0	65,690	8,353	9,301	3,222	813	6	0	0	267	0	430	333	25,156
Recovery	1,202	132	0	0	0	6	197	0	0	0	0	0	0	0	0	867
Total imports	110,367	9,587	4,844	17,832	895	9,101	12,961	1,834	11,611	106	14,497	2,983	3,257	3,169	2,318	15,369
Variation of stocks	6,903	-235	902	2,391	-46	-327	678	213	152	0	581	-102	-33	1,858	100	770
Total exports	9,323	1,045	103	486	46	307	371	11	63	0	5,842	0	54	17	56	921
Net imports	101,043	8,542	4,741	17,346	849	8,794	12,590	1,823	11,548	106	8,656	2,983	3,203	3,152	2,262	14,448
Cover ratio (%)	8.4	10.9	2.1	2.7	5.2	3.4	2.9	0.6	0.5	0.0	40.3	0.0	1.6	0.5	2.4	6.0
Gross inland consumption	222,719	8,439	5,643	85,426	9,156	17,775	16,687	2,849	11,706	106	9,237	3,148	3,171	5,441	2,695	41,241
Transformation input	209,056	6,756	5,263	82,901	8,207	17,884	14,353	2,165	11,061	0	9,013	2,773	3,015	4,807	2,382	38,475
-conventional thermal power stations	*155,533*	*3,040*	*5,260*	*66,558*	*8,189*	*14,655*	*7,914*	*2,038*	*4,944*	*0*	*5,425*	*862*	*2,646*	*3,359*	*647*	*29,998*
Transformation output	32,168	2,218	0	10,410	37	1,971	3,997	147	3,719	0	2,009	1,088	244	621	781	4,927
Consumption of the energy branch	600	7	0	331	0	3	189	0	36	0	0	0	0	0	0	35
Available for final consumption	45,231	3,893	380	12,605	985	1,858	6,142	831	4,329	106	2,232	1,463	399	1,254	1,094	7,659
Final non-energy consumption	1,627	167	0	337	0	180	117	0	359	0	173	12	0	0	16	266
Chemical industry	1,063	167	0	72	0	180	117	0	185	0	77	0	0	0	0	266
Others	563	0	0	265	0	0	0	0	175	0	96	12	0	0	16	0
Final energy consumption	42,335	3,313	340	11,281	964	1,814	6,706	857	3,939	106	1,472	1,512	413	1,162	1,070	7,387
Industry	35,546	3,085	314	9,580	917	1,609	5,839	77	3,872	106	1,448	1,179	413	1,134	1,068	4,905
-iron and steel industry	*23,768*	*2,666*	*0*	*6,125*	*0*	*1,265*	*4,489*	*0*	*2,998*	*29*	*1,339*	*914*	*109*	*427*	*629*	*2,777*
-non ferrous metals industry	*724*	*20*	*0*	*132*	*146*	*56*	*0*	*0*	*64*	*0*	*0*	*5*	*0*	*0*	*40*	*261*
-chemical industry	*1,629*	*21*	*11*	*486*	*1*	*74*	*314*	*0*	*0*	*0*	*40*	*46*	*13*	*23*	*103*	*497*
-non-metallic mineral products	*5,162*	*264*	*202*	*1,962*	*/67*	*195*	*240*	*51*	*32*	*77*	*40*	*118*	*291*	*161*	*180*	*580*
-ore extraction industry	*167*	*0*	*35*	*72*	*0*	*4*	*0*	*0*	*0*	*0*	*0*	*0*	*0*	*0*	*56*	*0*
-food, drink and tobacco industry	*866*	*42*	*65*	*268*	*0*	*14*	*47*	*26*	*180*	*0*	*26*	*3*	*0*	*0*	*16*	*178*
-textile, leather and clothing industry	*114*	*6*	*0*	*46*	*0*	*0*	*3*	*0*	*13*	*0*	*0*	*0*	*0*	*0*	*0*	*46*
-paper and printing industry	*1,322*	*34*	*0*	*413*	*0*	*6*	*196*	*0*	*0*	*0*	*0*	*80*	*0*	*478*	*19*	*98*
-engineering and others metal industry	*196*	*10*	*0*	*6*	*2*	*37*	*0*	*0*	*52*	*0*	*0*	*0*	*0*	*0*	*11*	*78*
-others industries	*1,272*	*23*	*0*	*69*	*0*	*0*	*369*	*0*	*373*	*0*	*0*	*13*	*0*	*46*	*0*	*379*
-adjustment	*326*	*0*	*1*	*0*	*0*	*-42*	*180*	*0*	*158*	*0*	*3*	*0*	*0*	*0*	*15*	*10*
Transport	2	0	0	1	0	0	0	0	0	0	0	1	0	0	0	0
-railways	*2*	*0*	*0*	*1*	*0*	*0*	*0*	*0*	*0*	*0*	*0*	*1*	*0*	*0*	*0*	*0*
Households, etc.	6,787	228	26	1,700	48	205	867	780	67	0	24	332	0	27	3	2,482
-households	*5,801*	*228*	*5*	*1,385*	*39*	*194*	*874*	*773*	*67*	*0*	*6*	*20*	*0*	*16*	*0*	*2,194*
-agriculture	*31*	*0*	*22*	*0*	*8*	*0*	*0*	*0*	*0*	*0*	*0*	*0*	*0*	*0*	*1*	*0*
-others	*955*	*0*	*0*	*315*	*0*	*11*	*-7*	*7*	*0*	*0*	*17*	*313*	*0*	*11*	*1*	*287*
Statistical divergence	1,269	414	40	987	21	-136	-681	-26	30	0	588	-61	-14	93	8	6

(1) Most data are provisional.

Source: Eurostat (SIRENE)

Table 1.14

Evolution of interior flows of solid fuels, EU-15 (thousand TOE) (1)

	1988	1989	1990	1991	1992	1993	1994	1995	1996	1997	1998
Primary production	228,834	225,728	208,219	188,121	175,011	154,746	136,769	136,607	130,165	125,122	113,571
Recovery	1,801	1,580	1,656	1,965	1,047	1,040	728	1,416	1,255	1,147	1,202
Total imports	88,631	93,192	102,316	106,673	106,404	93,590	94,932	101,344	101,291	105,334	110,367
Variation of stocks	1,586	1,274	3,028	107	-8,086	4,667	18,822	5,342	8,276	-1,244	6,903
Total exports	15,489	15,721	14,068	10,596	7,766	6,984	8,591	6,936	6,100	6,872	9,323
Net imports	73,142	77,471	88,248	96,077	98,639	86,606	86,341	94,408	95,190	98,462	101,043
Cover ratio (%)	17.5	16.9	13.7	9.9	7.3	7.5	9.0	6.8	6.0	6.5	8.4
Gross inland consumption	305,363	306,052	301,152	286,270	266,611	247,059	242,660	237,773	234,887	223,487	222,719
Transformation input	286,088	289,220	282,744	266,424	248,340	227,759	223,493	220,589	216,296	204,787	209,056
-conventional thermal power stations	*173,749*	*178,264*	*182,318*	*184,349*	*176,327*	*163,185*	*162,824*	*161,820*	*160,862*	*149,973*	*155,533*
Transformation output	75,127	73,091	66,028	52,734	45,077	40,017	37,495	34,714	34,275	33,624	32,168
Consumption of the energy branch	1,121	1,054	952	1,222	863	753	768	493	521	506	600
Available for final consumption	93,281	88,869	83,483	71,358	62,485	58,564	55,895	51,406	52,344	51,818	45,231
Final non-energy consumption	3,625	3,783	3,401	2,890	2,913	2,474	2,756	1,737	1,599	1,589	1,627
Chemical industry	1,947	1,992	1,971	1,915	1,932	1,719	1,729	1,166	1,093	1,087	1,063
Others	1,679	1,791	1,430	975	981	755	1,027	571	506	503	563
Final energy consumption	89,213	85,265	80,124	68,890	61,282	54,966	51,894	48,981	46,305	46,435	42,335
Industry	57,642	56,872	53,486	47,672	45,185	40,126	40,133	39,138	36,332	37,684	35,546
-iron and steel industry	*26,226*	*26,110*	*25,661*	*24,447*	*22,712*	*21,374*	*23,720*	*24,619*	*22,772*	*24,872*	*23,768*
-non ferrous metals industry	*1,246*	*1,389*	*1,167*	*865*	*1,011*	*944*	*868*	*730*	*694*	*656*	*724*
-chemical industry	*7,690*	*7,335*	*6,277*	*4,387*	*3,899*	*3,341*	*3,253*	*2,724*	*2,555*	*2,518*	*1,629*
-non-metallic mineral products	*10,900*	*10,564*	*10,312*	*9,993*	*9,622*	*8,083*	*7,657*	*6,907*	*6,432*	*5,892*	*5,162*
-ore extraction industry	*659*	*645*	*506*	*219*	*225*	*144*	*91*	*158*	*92*	*122*	*167*
-food, drink and tobacco industry	*2,659*	*2,628*	*2,238*	*1,701*	*1,561*	*1,412*	*1,294*	*987*	*835*	*716*	*866*
-textile, leather and clothing industry	*1,035*	*1,012*	*857*	*615*	*536*	*388*	*341*	*260*	*181*	*132*	*114*
-paper and printing industry	*1,970*	*1,797*	*1,820*	*1,568*	*2,240*	*2,057*	*1,608*	*1,591*	*1,302*	*1,268*	*1,322*
-engineering and others metal industry	*3,341*	*3,207*	*2,584*	*1,774*	*1,443*	*1,041*	*796*	*501*	*380*	*260*	*196*
-others industries	*1,842*	*1,604*	*1,747*	*1,211*	*1,485*	*1,135*	*400*	*339*	*845*	*948*	*1,272*
-adjustment	*73*	*582*	*317*	*892*	*449*	*205*	*107*	*322*	*244*	*300*	*326*
Transport	43	36	32	24	21	14	12	14	15	7	2
-railways	*43*	*36*	*32*	*24*	*21*	*14*	*12*	*14*	*15*	*7*	*2*
Households, etc.	31,528	28,357	26,606	21,193	16,076	14,826	11,749	9,828	9,958	8,744	6,787
-households	*23,499*	*20,427*	*19,751*	*18,789*	*12,667*	*12,089*	*10,148*	*8,086*	*8,294*	*7,646*	*5,801*
-agriculture	*129*	*112*	*100*	*108*	*128*	*119*	*117*	*114*	*103*	*39*	*31*
-others	*7,900*	*7,817*	*6,755*	*2,296*	*3,281*	*2,618*	*1,484*	*1,628*	*1,562*	*1,059*	*955*
Statistical divergence	443	-179	-42	-422	-1,710	1,123	1,245	687	4,440	3,794	1,269

(1) Data for EU-15 includes former East Germany for 1991 and subsequent years.

Source: Eurostat (SIRENE)

Table 1.15

Mining and agglomeration of hard coal (NACE Rev. 1 10.1)

Trade related indicators in the EU (1)

	1989	1990	1991	1992	1993	1994	1995	1996	1997	1998	1999
Exports (million EUR)	72	69	39	21	30	28	27	30	46	41	32
Imports (million EUR)	5,313	5,610	6,290	5,991	4,683	5,126	5,246	5,408	5,682	5,713	5,062
Trade balance (million EUR)	-5,242	-5,541	-6,251	-5,971	-4,652	-5,097	-5,219	-5,379	-5,636	-5,672	-5,031
Cover ratio (%)	1.4	1.2	0.6	0.3	0.7	0.6	0.5	0.5	0.8	0.7	0.6

(1) Technically, data before 01/01/1999 are in ECU and after this date in euro. However, as the conversion rate was 1 ECU =1 EUR, for practical purposes the two terms can be used interchangeably.

Table 1.16

Mining and agglomeration of hard coal (NACE Rev. 1 10.1)

Production related indicators, 1997

	B	DK	D	EL (1)	E	F	IRL	I	L	NL	A	P	FIN	S	UK (1)
Number of persons employed (thousands)	:	0.0	82.7	0.0	23.7	:	:	:	0.0	:	0.0	0.0	0.0	0.0	17.9
Production (million ECU)	:	0	3,124	0	1,244	:	:	:	0	0	0	0	0	0	2,630
Value added (million ECU)	:	0	3,452	0	757	:	:	:	0	0	0	0	0	0	1,079
Gross operating surplus (million ECU)	:	0.0	-494.2	0.0	-26.0	:	:	:	0.0	0.0	0.0	0.0	0.0	0.0	473.1

(1) 1996.

Table 1.17

Mining and agglomeration of hard coal (NACE Rev. 1 10.1)

Trade related indicators, 1999

	B	DK	D	EL	E	F	IRL	I	L	NL	A	P	FIN	S	UK
Exports (million EUR)	109	6	30	0	1	7	5	2	0	169	0	0	0	0	66
Imports (million EUR)	455	14	722	30	643	679	113	678	5	606	150	179	131	130	878
Trade balance (million EUR)	-347	-7	-692	-30	-641	-672	-108	-676	-5	-438	-150	-179	-131	-129	-813
Cover ratio (%)	23.9	47.6	4.1	0.2	0.2	1.1	4.4	0.3	0.0	27.8	0.1	0.0	0.0	0.3	7.5

Table 1.18

Mining and agglomeration of lignite (NACE Rev. 1 10.2)

Trade related indicators in the EU (1)

	1989	1990	1991	1992	1993	1994	1995	1996	1997	1998	1999
Exports (million EUR)	2	2	18	6	3	4	2	2	4	3	3
Imports (million EUR)	61	46	88	92	83	77	73	73	64	51	45
Trade balance (million EUR)	-59	-44	-70	-85	-80	-73	-71	-71	-61	-48	-42
Cover ratio (%)	3.1	3.4	20.3	7.1	3.3	5.3	3.4	3.4	5.6	5.7	7.2

(1) Technically, data before 01/01/1999 are in ECU and after this date in euro. However, as the conversion rate was 1 ECU =1 EUR, for practical purposes the two terms can be used interchangeably.

Table 1.19

Mining and agglomeration of lignite (NACE Rev. 1 10.2)

Production related indicators, 1997

	B	DK	D	EL (1)	E	F	IRL	I (1)	L	NL	A	P	FIN	S	UK
Number of persons employed (thousands)	0.0	0.0	28.6	7.1	:	0.0	0.0	0.0	0.0	:	:	0.0	0.0	0.0	:
Production (million ECU)	0	0	3,259	:	:	0	0	0	0	0	:	0	0	0	:
Value added (million ECU)	0	0	1,872	:	:	0	0	0	0	0	:	0	0	0	:
Gross operating surplus (million ECU)	0.0	0.0	468.6	:	:	0.0	0.0	0.0	0.0	0.0	:	0.0	0.0	0.0	:

(1) 1996.

Table 1.20

Mining and agglomeration of lignite (NACE Rev. 1 10.2)

Trade related indicators, 1999

	B	DK	D	EL	E	F	IRL	I	L	NL	A	P	FIN	S	UK
Exports (million EUR)	0	0	27	1	0	0	1	0	0	1	0	:	:	0	1
Imports (million EUR)	8	0	44	0	0	3	2	2	1	2	14	:	0	1	:
Trade balance (million EUR)	-8	0	-16	1	0	-3	-1	-2	-1	-1	-14	:	:	-1	:
Cover ratio (%)	0.8	27.2	62.8	44,704.0	100.0	1.9	61.4	0.2	0.1	34.6	0.4	:	:	26.2	:

Source: Eurostat (SBS, COMEXT)

eurostat

Table 1.21

Extraction and agglomeration of peat (NACE Rev. 1 10.3)

Trade related indicators in the EU (1)

	1989	1990	1991	1992	1993	1994	1995	1996	1997	1998	1999
Exports (million EUR)	24	26	29	29	33	35	40	42	40	44	47
Imports (million EUR)	15	16	18	21	23	45	46	48	55	76	76
Trade balance (million EUR)	9	10	11	9	10	-10	-6	-6	-16	-32	-29
Cover ratio (%)	159.4	163.9	162.6	142.6	142.4	78.2	86.2	87.6	71.9	57.7	61.9

(1) Technically, data before 01/01/1999 are in ECU and after this date in euro. However, as the conversion rate was 1 ECU =1 EUR, for practical purposes the two terms can be used interchangeably.

Table 1.22

Extraction and agglomeration of peat (NACE Rev. 1 10.3)

Production related indicators, 1997

	B	DK	D	EL (1)	E	F	IRL	I (1)	L	NL	A	P	FIN	S	UK
Number of persons employed (thousands)	:	:	1.9	0.0	:	0.2	:	0.0	0.0	:	:	0.0	1.7	0.3	:
Production (million ECU)	:	:	219	0	:	33	:	0	0	:	:	0	287	60	:
Value added (million ECU)	:	:	79	0	:	7	:	0	0	:	:	0	109	21	:
Gross operating surplus (million ECU)	:	:	20.7	0.0	:	1.3	:	0.0	0.0	:	:	0.0	75.9	8.7	:

(1) 1996.

Table 1.23

Extraction and agglomeration of peat (NACE Rev. 1 10.3)

Trade related indicators, 1999

	B	DK	D	EL	E	F	IRL	I	L	NL	A	P	FIN	S	UK
Exports (million EUR)	9	6	149	0	0	2	54	0	0	54	3	0	13	8	6
Imports (million EUR)	20	8	23	6	20	50	1	53	1	65	14	2	0	7	32
Trade balance (million EUR)	-11	-2	126	-6	-19	-48	53	-53	-1	-10	-12	-2	13	1	-26
Cover ratio (%)	45.1	75.9	638.5	0.6	1.7	4.0	3,756.1	0.8	0.5	84.0	19.7	0.1	6,977.2	120.7	17.3

Table 1.24

Manufacture of coke oven products (NACE Rev. 1 23.1)

Trade related indicators in the EU (1)

	1989	1990	1991	1992	1993	1994	1995	1996	1997	1998	1999
Exports (million EUR)	212	67	52	50	48	48	42	35	50	52	37
Imports (million EUR)	263	248	298	278	344	466	644	544	585	656	535
Trade balance (million EUR)	-51	-181	-247	-229	-296	-418	-602	-509	-535	-604	-498
Cover ratio (%)	80.6	27.0	17.3	17.8	13.9	10.2	6.5	6.5	8.5	7.9	7.0

(1) Technically, data before 01/01/1999 are in ECU and after this date in euro. However, as the conversion rate was 1 ECU =1 EUR, for practical purposes the two terms can be used interchangeably.

Table 1.25

Manufacture of coke oven products (NACE Rev. 1 23.1)

Production related indicators, 1997

	B	DK	D	EL (1)	E	F	IRL	I	L	NL	A	P	FIN	S	UK
Number of persons employed (thousands)	0.5	0.0	:	0.0	:	0.5	0.0	:	0.0	:	0.0	0.0	0.0	0.0	0.6
Production (million ECU)	107	0	:	0	:	71	0	:	0	:	0	0	0	0	81
Value added (million ECU)	27	0	:	0	:	13	0	:	0	:	0	0	0	0	25
Gross operating surplus (million ECU)	-8.5	0.0	:	0.0	:	-1.9	0.0	:	0.0	:	0.0	0.0	0.0	0.0	7.7

(1) 1996.

Table 1.26

Manufacture of coke oven products (NACE Rev. 1 23.1)

Trade related indicators, 1999

	B	DK	D	EL	E	F	IRL	I	L	NL	A	P	FIN	S	UK
Exports (million EUR)	63	:	18	0	38	60	0	22	:	146	5	9	3	6	29
Imports (million EUR)	86	3	319	3	29	102	1	35	0	85	35	3	46	32	34
Trade balance (million EUR)	-23	:	-302	-3	9	-42	-1	-13	:	62	-30	6	-43	-26	-5
Cover ratio (%)	73.4	:	5.5	0.1	130.2	58.4	4.4	63.3	:	172.8	13.5	285.5	6.2	17.5	85.6

Source: Eurostat (SBS, COMEXT)

Table 1.27

Interior flows of crude oil and petroleum products, 1998 (thousand TOE)

	EU-15	B	DK	D	EL	E	F	IRL	I	L	NL	A (1)	P	FIN	S	UK
Primary production	161,683	0	11,661	2,964	316	522	2,135	0	5,671	0	2,680	989	0	68	0	134,679
Recovery	281	0	0	212	0	0	69	0	0	0	0	0	0	0	0	0
Total imports	783,947	49,826	11,601	155,852	22,641	74,728	114,423	8,643	113,404	2,065	97,548	13,108	17,425	15,848	26,799	60,035
Variation of stocks	-8,245	-517	-369	-2,919	-753	-1,059	-1,046	-119	-559	-36	123	-137	217	245	-650	-668
Total exports	294,678	20,937	11,639	16,415	3,214	8,661	21,117	1,243	22,975	17	61,067	1,532	1,928	4,812	8,842	110,280
Net imports	489,269	28,889	-38	139,437	19,428	66,067	93,306	7,400	90,429	2,048	36,482	11,576	15,497	11,036	17,957	-50,245
Cover ratio (%)	37.6	42.0	100.3	10.5	14.2	11.6	18.5	14.4	20.3	0.8	62.6	11.7	11.1	30.4	33.0	183.7
Marine bunkers	41,513	5,403	1,378	2,034	3,465	5,953	2,836	157	2,626	0	12,194	0	380	514	1,553	3,019
Gross inland consumption	601,476	22,969	9,875	137,660	15,525	59,577	91,628	7,125	92,914	2,013	27,091	12,428	15,334	10,835	15,754	80,747
Transformation input	725,571	37,731	9,510	122,546	23,139	64,855	97,520	4,272	123,576	0	82,243	10,824	16,223	14,155	22,457	96,520
-conventional thermal power stations	39,270	550	1,476	1,263	1,905	3,280	2,054	1,088	21,925	0	709	784	2,110	236	632	1,258
-refineries	684,271	37,173	7,985	120,299	21,220	61,482	95,387	3,184	101,646	0	81,534	9,960	14,105	13,728	21,357	95,211
Transformation output	679,561	36,896	7,956	118,475	21,129	62,109	94,677	3,170	100,740	0	80,863	9,817	14,093	13,623	21,029	94,983
Exchanges, transfers, returns	1,617	1,097	0	208	72	79	90	-1	-117	0	-182	0	22	15	-49	385
Consumption of the energy branch	38,458	1,673	347	7,011	920	4,085	5,598	101	5,496	0	3,749	794	693	589	470	6,933
Available for final consumption	518,626	21,558	7,974	126,786	12,667	52,825	83,277	5,921	64,465	2,013	21,780	10,628	12,533	9,729	13,807	72,662
Final non-energy consumption	81,932	3,692	392	22,397	379	8,495	13,165	265	9,434	17	5,720	1,254	2,444	1,291	2,263	10,724
Chemical industry	54,041	3,157	0	17,406	16	4,147	9,157	0	5,766	0	3,779	640	1,386	547	1,161	6,880
Others	27,892	535	392	4,991	363	4,348	4,008	265	3,668	17	1,941	614	1,059	744	1,102	3,844
Final energy consumption	436,058	17,942	7,329	104,758	12,669	42,644	72,232	5,750	54,499	1,985	16,017	9,242	9,639	7,444	12,292	61,616
Industry	42,645	2,107	719	6,959	2,060	5,794	5,993	738	5,185	79	1,137	660	2,415	888	1,818	6,094
-iron and steel industry	3,201	57	4	1,398	47	321	158	7	87	18	5	242	43	137	325	352
-non ferrous metals industry	1,424	25	0	149	233	129	383	242	121	0	0	13	41	25	28	36
-chemical industry	5,269	380	53	414	246	982	477	109	545	8	864	32	375	116	135	535
-non-metallic mineral products	8,076	240	135	1,285	358	2,343	986	32	1,489	0	50	122	572	89	150	224
-ore extraction industry	1,004	0	28	98	102	113	18	29	103	0	30	8	50	44	72	309
-food, drink and tobacco industry	4,739	175	201	1,011	302	669	863	155	327	4	25	47	277	121	184	377
-textile, leather and clothing industry	1,478	24	8	165	103	205	120	31	348	0	0	25	286	36	36	93
-paper and printing industry	2,198	38	10	365	92	293	250	10	73	0	2	69	332	62	491	111
-engineering and others metal industry	3,205	51	73	923	32	258	309	67	642	0	23	34	41	90	203	460
-others industries	10,400	643	204	1,152	546	349	1,429	55	1,450	37	136	69	395	143	192	3,599
-adjustment	1,652	472	3	0	0	133	1,000	1	1	12	1	0	3	26	0	0
Transport	293,529	9,447	4,715	63,313	7,277	30,130	47,663	3,293	39,960	1,545	13,468	5,967	5,673	4,252	7,539	49,286
-railways	2,623	63	79	624	42	455	455	102	192	5	0	0	47	54	16	489
-road transport	245,646	7,504	3,679	55,687	5,164	24,029	40,944	2,706	36,382	1,258	9,545	5,415	4,929	3,635	6,510	38,260
-air transport	38,908	1,591	829	6,633	1,201	3,974	5,493	449	3,173	282	3,266	553	650	483	883	9,449
-inland navigation	6,352	290	129	369	870	1,673	772	36	213	0	657	0	46	81	129	1,089
Households, etc.	99,884	6,388	1,895	34,486	3,332	6,721	18,576	1,720	9,354	361	1,412	2,615	1,551	2,303	2,936	6,236
-households	60,690	4,087	1,024	23,343	2,249	3,827	10,606	776	6,393	333	92	1,320	686	1,406	1,249	3,301
-fisheries	0	0	0	0	0	0	0	0	0	0	0	0	0	0	0	0
-agriculture	14,387	932	708	1,755	835	1,532	2,651	239	2,660	7	275	459	543	527	474	790
-others	24,807	1,369	163	9,387	248	1,363	5,318	704	301	21	1,046	836	323	371	1,213	2,145
Statistical divergence	636	-75	253	-369	-380	1,685	-2,119	-94	532	10	44	132	450	994	-748	322

(1) Most data are provisional.

Source: Eurostat (SIRENE)

Table 1.28

Evolution of interior flows of crude oil and petroleum products, EU-15 (thousand TOE) (1)

	1988	1989	1990	1991	1992	1993	1994	1995	1996	1997	1998
Primary production	143,478	119,850	116,798	118,074	121,315	126,993	156,242	159,341	158,870	158,016	161,683
Recovery	67	155	166	200	182	176	175	313	310	266	281
Total imports	661,492	677,145	698,867	712,094	730,345	727,716	726,677	719,088	745,833	756,308	783,947
Variation of stocks	4,001	-1,574	1,397	2,363	519	4,716	-1,311	4,390	-83	313	-8,245
Total exports	240,841	223,715	238,011	235,759	246,519	260,152	280,338	272,375	280,432	287,043	294,678
Net imports	420,652	453,430	460,856	476,335	483,826	467,564	446,339	446,713	465,401	469,265	489,269
Cover ratio (%)	36.4	33.0	34.1	33.1	33.8	35.7	38.6	37.9	37.6	38.0	37.6
Marine bunkers	31,852	31,840	34,166	33,893	34,177	35,082	33,746	34,714	36,834	40,108	41,513
Gross inland consumption	**536,345**	**540,020**	**545,051**	**563,079**	**571,665**	**564,368**	**567,700**	**576,043**	**587,662**	**587,753**	**601,476**
Transformation input	620,106	630,077	639,232	651,778	671,449	674,132	681,600	680,860	698,813	707,510	725,571
-conventional thermal power stations	*36,686*	*42,201*	*42,559*	*44,275*	*46,114*	*42,247*	*40,390*	*43,650*	*41,630*	*38,430*	*39,270*
-refineries	*580,065*	*584,922*	*593,671*	*603,850*	*622,006*	*628,729*	*638,267*	*635,179*	*655,063*	*666,697*	*684,271*
Transformation output	575,636	581,189	589,768	600,820	618,642	625,898	634,492	631,283	649,482	661,868	679,561
Exchanges, transfers, returns	1,201	1,408	1,568	1,953	2,392	6,006	6,681	6,159	5,713	5,166	1,617
Consumption of the energy branch	31,782	32,232	32,320	32,394	34,172	35,348	36,599	36,823	38,317	37,060	38,458
Available for final consumption	**461,293**	**460,308**	**464,835**	**481,679**	**487,078**	**486,792**	**490,674**	**495,802**	**505,728**	**510,217**	**518,626**
Final non-energy consumption	**68,609**	**68,223**	**69,315**	**73,328**	**77,007**	**72,525**	**79,025**	**82,022**	**80,827**	**85,816**	**81,932**
Chemical industry	42,801	42,215	44,089	46,403	50,504	47,516	51,380	56,075	55,542	57,693	54,041
Others	25,808	26,008	25,226	26,925	26,504	25,009	27,645	25,947	25,285	28,122	27,892
Final energy consumption	**394,749**	**390,494**	**396,805**	**408,321**	**412,824**	**416,826**	**415,430**	**418,422**	**430,115**	**429,538**	**436,058**
Industry	55,528	51,953	48,885	48,287	47,732	46,602	48,243	47,815	45,308	44,724	42,645
-iron and steel industry	*4,247*	*4,398*	*3,730*	*3,597*	*3,479*	*3,634*	*3,834*	*3,793*	*3,341*	*3,399*	*3,201*
-non ferrous metals industry	*1,703*	*1,413*	*1,965*	*1,397*	*1,347*	*1,316*	*1,333*	*1,283*	*1,328*	*1,465*	*1,424*
-chemical industry	*11,943*	*11,302*	*10,338*	*9,527*	*9,628*	*9,057*	*9,335*	*8,498*	*6,702*	*6,827*	*5,269*
-non-metallic mineral products	*9,408*	*9,625*	*9,605*	*9,355*	*9,027*	*8,540*	*8,654*	*8,410*	*8,262*	*8,546*	*8,076*
-ore extraction industry	*823*	*769*	*759*	*750*	*803*	*761*	*769*	*938*	*902*	*891*	*1,004*
-food, drink and tobacco industry	*6,562*	*6,047*	*5,968*	*6,165*	*6,082*	*5,782*	*5,870*	*5,659*	*5,301*	*4,852*	*4,739*
-textile, leather and clothing industry	*2,549*	*2,412*	*2,291*	*2,102*	*1,889*	*1,832*	*2,005*	*1,645*	*1,593*	*1,514*	*1,478*
-paper and printing industry	*3,252*	*3,112*	*2,938*	*2,916*	*2,701*	*2,549*	*2,852*	*2,827*	*2,745*	*2,613*	*2,198*
-engineering and others metal industry	*5,621*	*4,727*	*4,474*	*4,643*	*4,328*	*3,880*	*3,767*	*3,514*	*3,714*	*3,437*	*3,205*
-others industries	*8,974*	*7,715*	*7,273*	*7,853*	*8,216*	*8,307*	*8,830*	*10,200*	*10,342*	*10,096*	*10,400*
-adjustment	*446*	*432*	*-457*	*-17*	*233*	*943*	*995*	*1,049*	*1,077*	*1,085*	*1,652*
Transport	*230,846*	*241,072*	*249,603*	*252,649*	*260,789*	*266,487*	*267,283*	*270,716*	*278,247*	*283,575*	*293,529*
-railways	*3,144*	*3,006*	*2,852*	*2,821*	*2,829*	*2,847*	*2,674*	*2,732*	*2,726*	*2,724*	*2,623*
-road transport	*197,261*	*205,176*	*212,260*	*215,108*	*222,024*	*226,690*	*226,337*	*228,753*	*234,291*	*238,276*	*245,646*
-air transport	*25,435*	*26,815*	*27,808*	*27,877*	*28,796*	*30,049*	*31,303*	*32,545*	*34,367*	*36,060*	*38,908*
-inland navigation	*5,005*	*6,076*	*6,683*	*6,843*	*7,140*	*6,901*	*6,969*	*6,686*	*6,862*	*6,515*	*6,352*
Households, etc.	108,375	97,469	98,318	107,384	104,303	103,736	99,904	99,891	106,561	101,239	99,884
-households	*64,348*	*62,846*	*59,841*	*65,411*	*61,999*	*62,309*	*58,790*	*59,216*	*64,034*	*60,073*	*60,690*
-fisheries	*1,278*	*496*	*372*	*135*	*0*	*0*	*0*	*0*	*0*	*0*	*0*
Source: Eurostat (SIRENE)	*13,064*	*12,138*	*12,155*	*13,257*	*13,341*	*13,188*	*13,470*	*13,716*	*14,196*	*13,928*	*14,387*
-others	*29,685*	*21,989*	*25,950*	*28,582*	*28,963*	*28,240*	*27,644*	*26,960*	*28,331*	*27,239*	*24,807*
Statistical divergence	-2,065	1,591	-1,285	31	-2,753	-2,559	-3,781	-4,643	-5,215	-5,137	636

(1) Data for EU-15 includes former East Germany for 1991 and subsequent years.

Source: Eurostat (SIRENE)

Table 1.29

Interior flows of gas, 1998 (thousand TOE)

	EU-15	B	DK	D (1)	EL (1)	E	F	IRL	I	L	NL	A (1)	P	FIN	S	UK
Primary production	181,464	0	6,763	15,670	40	102	1,837	1,407	15,568	0	57,613	1,335	0	0	0	81,128
Total imports	168,328	12,432	0	59,333	690	12,058	30,834	1,396	34,927	633	5,164	5,297	697	3,336	712	819
Variation of stocks	2,541	43	-34	1,014	-5	-551	1,448	0	669	0	22	99	0	0	0	-162
Total exports	36,837	0	2,506	3,289	0	0	706	0	38	0	27,853	0	0	0	0	2,446
Net imports	131,491	12,432	-2,506	56,045	690	12,058	30,128	1,396	34,889	633	-22,688	5,297	697	3,336	712	-1,627
Cover ratio (%)	21.9	0.0	:	5.5	0.0	0.0	2.3	0.0	0.1	0.0	539.3	0.0	0.0	0.0	0.0	298.7
Gross inland consumption	315,497	12,474	4,224	72,729	725	11,609	33,413	2,803	51,126	633	34,946	6,730	697	3,336	712	79,339
Transformation input	76,921	3,727	1,851	14,089	352	2,446	1,601	1,353	14,578	41	11,132	2,497	504	1,953	526	20,271
-conventional thermal power stations	74,766	3,661	1,762	12,576	352	2,438	1,601	1,353	14,578	41	11,132	2,298	426	1,808	467	20,271
Transformation output	18,867	1,424	0	5,764	0	1,012	2,548	0	1,959	0	1,401	689	180	564	629	2,698
Exchanges, transfers, returns	31	0	-2	0	0	0	32	0	0	0	0	0	0	0	0	0
Consumption of the energy branch	13,418	303	515	1,894	29	279	796	0	851	0	1,741	329	30	195	98	6,360
Distribution losses	2,049	0	4	631	1	262	79	28	119	2	0	216	10	0	71	625
Available for final consumption	242,007	9,868	1,853	61,879	344	9,634	33,517	1,421	37,537	590	23,474	4,378	333	1,752	647	54,781
Final non-energy consumption	11,319	731	0	2,150	201	499	2,347	459	944	0	2,555	250	0	31	0	1,152
Chemical industry	11,319	731	0	2,150	201	499	2,347	459	944	0	2,555	250	0	31	0	1,152
Final energy consumption	222,769	9,175	1,861	53,878	142	9,135	30,233	962	36,595	590	21,480	4,029	327	1,722	616	52,025
Industry	89,191	4,281	879	20,924	129	7,131	12,910	398	15,714	374	6,239	2,495	247	1,662	449	15,359
-iron and steel industry	16,953	1,250	43	4,927	29	1,002	2,001	18	2,077	131	758	734	42	418	212	3,310
-non ferrous metals industry	2,467	96	4	805	6	165	514	0	346	0	91	43	0	0	7	391
-chemical industry	18,270	1,184	74	4,/17	3	1,246	1,843	131	2,777	0	2,265	245	15	42	49	3,678
-non-metallic mineral products	12,580	408	141	2,949	26	1,811	1,533	47	3,327	0	593	284	171	148	19	1,122
-ore extraction industry	464	0	9	116	0	87	135	12	25	0	15	54	0	0	10	0
-food, drink and tobacco industry	10,901	167	341	1,830	39	658	2,213	151	1,706	0	1,257	218	8	44	83	2,185
-textile, leather and clothing industry	3,467	66	26	442	16	529	431	0	1,218	0	162	49	0	0	3	524
-paper and printing industry	8,420	87	71	1,716	9	866	1,361	0	1,485	0	365	276	0	980	31	1,172
-engineering and others metal industry	9,262	142	107	2,599	2	685	1,538	0	2,008	0	535	87	9	0	20	1,531
-others industries	6,407	880	62	823	0	82	1,340	37	746	242	199	503	2	29	13	1,447
-adjustment	1	0	0	0	0	0	1	0	0	0	0	0	0	0	0	0
Transport	312	0	0	0	0	6	0	0	286	0	0	21	0	0	0	0
-road transport	312	0	0	0	0	6	0	0	286	0	0	21	0	0	0	0
Households, etc.	133,265	4,894	982	32,954	13	1,998	17,323	564	20,595	216	15,241	1,514	79	60	167	36,666
-households	95,789	3,377	698	23,667	13	1,466	8,772	338	20,478	216	8,052	1,019	27	19	105	27,541
-agriculture	4,327	0	112	258	0	38	252	0	117	0	3,418	12	1	15	0	104
-others	33,149	1,517	172	9,028	0	494	8,299	226	0	0	3,771	483	51	25	62	9,020
Statistical divergence	7,919	-38	-7	5,852	0	0	937	0	-2	0	-562	99	6	-1	31	1,604

(1) Most data are provisional.

Source: Eurostat (SIRENE)

Table 1.30

Evolution of interior flows of gas, EU-15 (thousand TOE) (1)

	1988	1989	1990	1991	1992	1993	1994	1995	1996	1997	1998
Primary production	124,723	129,085	132,871	145,680	146,838	157,894	159,737	166,597	188,632	182,123	181,464
Total imports	105,540	116,100	120,293	126,321	129,721	130,511	132,974	143,163	159,808	163,241	168,328
Variation of stocks	-566	-2,301	-3,112	-322	-4,946	-609	-3,448	-1,872	-1,953	-3,750	2,541
Total exports	23,175	27,233	28,000	31,986	34,500	35,566	35,628	34,536	41,350	39,074	36,837
Net imports	82,364	88,867	92,293	94,335	95,221	94,945	97,345	108,626	118,458	124,167	131,491
Cover ratio (%)	22.0	23.5	23.3	25.3	26.6	27.3	26.8	24.1	25.9	23.9	21.9
Gross inland consumption	206,521	215,651	222,052	239,693	237,113	252,230	253,635	273,351	305,137	302,540	315,497
Transformation input	37,163	40,447	41,865	42,076	41,735	47,172	51,746	61,223	68,879	72,643	76,921
-conventional thermal power stations	31,344	34,908	36,530	36,708	36,839	42,462	46,843	55,170	64,156	70,825	74,766
Transformation output	27,648	28,198	26,283	23,698	21,680	20,598	20,036	20,033	19,653	19,573	18,867
Exchanges, transfers, returns	40	46	39	17	73	26	31	40	40	31	31
Consumption of the energy branch	12,105	12,074	11,628	11,536	10,930	11,252	11,574	12,478	13,294	12,982	13,418
Distribution losses	2,061	2,517	2,877	3,126	2,665	1,497	1,583	1,635	3,090	2,524	2,049
Available for final consumption	182,881	188,856	192,005	206,670	203,536	212,933	208,797	218,088	239,568	233,995	242,007
Final non-energy consumption	13,191	13,354	12,487	11,925	9,821	10,307	11,254	11,417	10,419	11,081	11,319
Chemical industry	13,191	13,354	12,487	11,925	9,821	10,307	11,254	11,417	10,419	11,081	11,319
Final energy consumption	169,644	175,559	178,233	193,559	193,108	198,393	195,423	205,745	227,713	216,667	222,769
Industry	72,234	76,580	77,160	76,435	77,248	77,302	78,106	82,008	88,238	87,053	89,191
-iron and steel industry	19,021	19,704	18,014	17,176	16,344	16,088	16,964	17,083	17,470	17,580	16,953
-non ferrous metals industry	1,743	1,867	1,839	1,836	1,816	1,784	1,791	1,931	2,035	2,120	2,467
-chemical industry	15,739	17,016	16,795	15,749	18,000	17,132	17,016	17,620	18,674	17,798	18,270
-non-metallic mineral products	10,021	10,722	10,771	10,495	10,500	10,711	10,754	11,574	12,329	12,145	12,580
-ore extraction industry	480	520	535	653	546	554	530	621	675	488	464
-food, drink and tobacco industry	7,007	7,575	7,614	8,235	8,538	8,740	8,929	9,598	10,536	10,561	10,901
-textile, leather and clothing industry	2,129	2,305	2,526	2,849	2,807	3,042	2,919	3,304	3,489	3,414	3,467
-paper and printing industry	4,169	4,669	5,267	5,596	5,803	6,316	6,765	6,960	7,547	8,160	8,420
-engineering and others metal industry	7,638	7,923	7,978	9,196	8,847	8,669	8,060	9,073	8,727	8,372	9,262
-others industries	4,335	4,296	5,636	4,661	4,043	4,239	4,320	4,231	6,762	6,413	6,407
-adjustment	-49	-17	184	-11	4	28	57	13	-7	3	1
Transport	223	212	208	213	236	239	250	267	289	298	312
-road transport	223	212	208	213	236	239	250	267	289	298	312
Households, etc.	97,187	98,767	100,865	116,911	115,624	120,852	117,067	123,470	139,187	129,316	133,265
-households	67,690	74,148	76,039	84,126	83,305	87,232	84,319	88,664	100,897	92,723·	95,789
-agriculture	2,858	3,034	3,508	4,023	4,048	4,295	3,945	4,385	4,205	4,249	4,327
-others	26,640	21,584	21,318	28,762	28,271	29,326	28,803	30,420	34,084	32,345	33,149
Statistical divergence	47	-57	1,285	1,185	607	4,233	2,121	926	1,436	6,247	7,919

(1) Data for EU-15 includes former East Germany for 1991 and subsequent years.

Source: Eurostat (SIRENE)

Table 1.31

Extraction of crude petroleum and natural gas (NACE Rev. 1 11.1)

Trade related indicators in the EU (1)

	1989	1990	1991	1992	1993	1994	1995	1996	1997	1998	1999
Exports (million EUR)	2,303	2,814	2,120	2,351	3,189	3,758	3,338	2,786	2,530	1,863	3,545
Imports (million EUR)	47,229	53,814	53,947	50,288	51,443	52,339	47,377	58,159	66,241	46,017	59,416
Trade balance (million EUR)	-44,925	-51,001	-51,827	-47,938	-48,254	-48,581	-44,039	-55,372	-63,711	-44,154	-55,871
Cover ratio (%)	4.9	5.2	3.9	4.7	6.2	7.2	7.0	4.8	3.8	4.0	6.0

(1) Technically, data before 01/01/1999 are in ECU and after this date in euro. However, as the conversion rate was 1 ECU =1 EUR, for practical purposes the two terms can be used interchangeably.

Table 1.32

Extraction of crude petroleum and natural gas (NACE Rev. 1 11.1)

Production related indicators, 1997

	B (1)	DK	D	EL	E	F (1)	IRL	I	L	NL	A	P	FIN	S	UK
Number of persons employed (thousands)	0.0	:	3.4	:	:	8.2	:	:	0.0	:	:	0.0	0.0	0.0	16.3
Production (million ECU)	0	:	1,493	:	:	2,101	:	:	0	:	:	0	0	0	25,321
Value added (million ECU)	0	:	597	:	:	1,235	:	:	0	:	:	0	0	0	20,600
Gross operating surplus (million ECU)	0.0	:	319.0	:	:	592.5	:	:	0.0	:	:	0.0	0.0	0.0	19,155.4

(1) 1996.

Table 1.33

Extraction of crude petroleum and natural gas (NACE Rev. 1 11.1)

Trade related indicators, 1999

	B	DK	D	EL	E	F	IRL	I	L	NL	A	P	FIN	S	UK
Exports (million EUR)	89	1,137	772	127	3	119	1	23	0	4,508	7	0	0	0	9,553
Imports (million EUR)	5,019	565	17,940	969	6,547	12,516	391	9,370	0	8,830	1,384	1,707	1,622	2,384	3,509
Trade balance (million EUR)	-4,930	572	-17,168	-842	-6,544	-12,397	-391	-9,347	0	-4,322	-1,377	-1,707	-1,622	-2,384	6,044
Cover ratio (%)	1.8	201.2	4.3	13.1	0.0	1.0	0.1	0.2	441.6	51.1	0.5	0.0	0.0	0.0	272.3

Source: Eurostat (SBS, COMEXT)

Table 1.34

Manufacture of refined petroleum products (NACE Rev. 1 23.2)

Production related indicators in the EU (1)

	1989	1990	1991	1992	1993	1994	1995	1996	1997	1998	1999
Number of persons employed (thousands)	:	:	:	:	:	:	105.8	:	:	:	:
Production (million EUR)	:	:	:	:	:	:	162,055	198,072	201,901	188,462	205,315
Domestic producer price index (1995=100)	:	:	:	:	:	:	:	:	:	95.7	109.9
Value added (million EUR)	:	:	:	:	:	:	11,878	13,967	14,953	13,608	15,301

(1) Technically, data before 01/01/1999 are in ECU and after this date in euro. However, as the conversion rate was 1 ECU =1 EUR, for practical purposes the two terms can be used interchangeably.

Table 1.35

Manufacture of refined petroleum products (NACE Rev. 1 23.2)

Trade related indicators in the EU (1)

	1989	1990	1991	1992	1993	1994	1995	1996	1997	1998	1999
Exports (million EUR)	5,490	6,198	6,365	6,102	9,722	10,218	8,374	10,403	12,432	9,929	10,732
Imports (million EUR)	12,463	14,580	14,656	11,358	10,690	10,037	10,640	10,940	11,754	8,278	10,900
Trade balance (million EUR)	-6,973	-8,382	-8,292	-5,257	-968	181	-2,267	-537	678	1,651	-169
Cover ratio (%)	44.1	42.5	43.4	53.7	90.9	101.8	78.7	95.1	105.8	119.9	98.5

(1) Technically, data before 01/01/1999 are in ECU and after this date in euro. However, as the conversion rate was 1 ECU =1 EUR, for practical purposes the two terms can be used interchangeably.

Table 1.36

Manufacture of refined petroleum products (NACE Rev. 1 23.2)

Production related indicators, 1997

	B	DK	D	EL (1)	E	F	IRL	I (1)	L	NL	A	P	FIN	S	UK (1)
Number of persons employed (thousands)	4.2	0.3	:	3.6	8.5	19.2	:	22.4	0.0	:	:	3.1	4.6	:	12.7
Production (million ECU)	10,250	54	:	2,712	10,572	37,714	:	30,484	0	:	:	4,093	1,922	:	43,253
Value added (million ECU)	942	19	:	275	1,492	2,378	:	2,465	0	:	:	433	288	:	1,890
Gross operating surplus (million ECU)	613.3	8.3	:	148.1	1,036.4	980.4	:	1,516.0	0.0	:	:	319.9	84.2	:	1,407.0

(1) 1996.

Table 1.37

Manufacture of refined petroleum products (NACE Rev. 1 23.2)

Trade related indicators, 1999

	B	DK	D	EL	E	F	IRL	I	L	NL	A	P	FIN	S	UK
Exports (million EUR)	4,055	471	3,201	802	2,132	2,883	122	2,526	3	7,380	285	306	927	1,643	4,219
Imports (million EUR)	3,047	634	4,987	416	1,601	4,036	669	3,062	359	2,701	1,035	615	522	1,164	2,821
Trade balance (million EUR)	1,008	-163	-1,786	386	532	-1,153	-547	-535	-356	4,679	-750	-309	404	479	1,398
Cover ratio (%)	133.1	74.3	64.2	192.6	133.2	71.4	18.2	82.5	0.8	273.3	27.5	49.8	177.4	141.1	149.6

Table 1.38

Manufacture of refined petroleum products (NACE Rev. 1 23.2)

Labour related indicators, 1997

	B	DK (1)	D	EL (2)	E	F	IRL	I (2)	L	NL	A	P	FIN	S	UK (2)
Unit personnel costs (thousand ECU per employee)	78.1	52.2	:	34.8	44.0	72.8	:	42.7	:	:	:	36.1	42.2	:	38.1
Social charges as a share of personnel costs (%)	39.5	9.0	:	28.3	22.8	63.5	:	51.3	:	:	:	43.1	23.4	:	16.5
Apparent labour productivity (thousand ECU/pers. empl.)	223.3	75.9	:	75.4	175.2	123.9	:	110.2	:	:	:	137.8	62.6	:	149.0
Wage adjusted labour productivity (%)	286.0	179.6	:	216.8	398.0	170.2	:	258.3	:	:	:	381.9	148.3	:	391.2
Personnel costs as a share of total operating costs (%)	3.5	19.9	:	4.6	2.9	5.3	:	2.8	:	:	:	5.1	4.5	:	3.5

(1) Unit personnel costs and wage adjusted labour productivity, 1996; (2) 1996.

Source: Eurostat (SBS, EBT, COMEXT)

Table 1.39

Manufacture of gas; distribution of gaseous fuels through mains (NACE Rev. 1 40.2)

Production related indicators, 1997

	B	DK	D	EL (1)	E	F	IRL	I	L	NL	A	P	FIN	S	UK
Number of persons employed (thousands)	1.4	:	31.4	0.0	4.1	27.0	:	:	:	:	3.1	1.0	0.0	0.2	30.1
Production (million ECU)	2,575	:	25,776	0	2,484	9,188	:	:	:	:	1,196	142	6	278	15,619
Value added (million ECU)	510	:	4,120	0	929	3,184	:	:	:	:	347	75	3	61	4,883
Gross operating surplus (million ECU)	406.8	:	2,533.6	0.0	759.5	1,770.1	:	:	:	:	204.1	43.2	1.2	48.5	3,440.8

(1) 1996.

Table 1.40

Manufacture of gas; distribution of gaseous fuels through mains (NACE Rev. 1 40.2)

Labour related indicators, 1997

	B	DK	D	EL	E	F	IRL	I	L	NL	A	P	FIN	S	UK
Unit personnel costs (thousand ECU per employee)	74.1	:	50.6	:	38.5	52.4	:	:	:	:	46.6	31.3	37.4	53.2	47.9
Social charges as a share of personnel costs (%)	44.4	:	34.3	:	25.5	70.9	:	:	:	:	45.2	42.9	30.8	44.7	18.2
Apparent labour productivity (thousand ECU/pers. empl.)	362.5	:	131.3	:	226.8	118.1	:	:	:	:	113.0	74.3	65.2	263.0	162.3
Wage adjusted labour productivity (%)	489.5	:	259.7	:	588.5	225.2	:	:	:	:	242.4	237.1	174.4	494.1	338.6
Personnel costs as a share of total operating costs (%)	4.7	:	6.9	:	7.0	19.1	:	:	:	:	16.3	25.8	26.2	5.4	12.2

Source: Eurostat (SBS)

Table 1.41

Interior flows of other energy sources, 1998 (thousand TOE)

	EU-15	B	DK	D	EL	E	F	IRL	I	L	NL	A	P	FIN	S	UK
Nuclear energy																
Primary production	**209,664**	**11,394**	**0**	**38,912**	**0**	**14,418**	**96,636**	**0**	**0**	**0**	**937**	**0**	**0**	**5,370**	**16,166**	**25,831**
Transformation input	209,666	11,394	0	38,915	0	14,418	96,636	0	0	0	937	0	0	5,370	16,166	25,831
-nuclear power stations	209,666	11,394	0	38,915	0	14,418	96,636	0	0	0	937	0	0	5,370	16,166	25,831
Available for final consumption	-2	0	0	-2	0	0	0	0	0	0	0	0	0	0	0	0
Statistical divergence	-2	0	0	-2	0	0	0	0	0	0	0	0	0	0	0	0
Derived heat (1)																
Transformation output	23,575	290	3,007	9,950	0	69	0	0	0	24	2,333	1,141	80	2,814	3,867	0
-conventional thermal power stations	17,216	290	2,409	7,101	0	69	0	0	0	24	2,333	768	80	2,185	1,956	0
Consumption of the energy branch	471	0	143	232	0	0	0	0	0	0	0	1	0	0	96	0
Distribution losses	2,576	28	575	982	0	0	0	0	0	0	350	133	0	227	282	0
Available for final consumption	**20,528**	**262**	**2,289**	**8,737**	**0**	**69**	**0**	**0**	**0**	**24**	**1,983**	**1,007**	**80**	**2,587**	**3,489**	**0**
Final energy consumption	**20,748**	**323**	**2,292**	**8,737**	**0**	**69**	**0**	**0**	**0**	**24**	**1,983**	**1,007**	**80**	**2,517**	**3,714**	**0**
Industry	3,888	281	143	1,672	0	69	0	0	0	19	812	114	80	341	356	0
-iron and steel industry	18	11	2	5	0	0	0	0	0	0	0	0	0	0	0	0
-chemical industry	678	90	22	475	0	20	0	0	0	0	0	22	47	0	0	0
-non-metallic mineral products	54	0	1	53	0	0	0	0	0	0	0	0	0	0	0	0
-food, drink and tobacco industry	193	0	29	134	0	0	0	0	0	0	0	17	13	0	0	0
-textile, leather and clothing industry	66	0	3	49	0	0	0	0	0	0	0	0	14	0	0	0
-paper and printing industry	174	0	40	92	0	0	0	0	0	0	0	42	0	0	0	0
-engineering and others metal industry	565	0	34	518	0	0	0	0	0	0	0	14	0	0	0	0
-others industries	1,173	179	11	282	0	0	0	0	0	0	0	4	0	341	356	0
-adjustment	967	0	1	64	0	49	0	0	0	19	812	16	6	0	0	0
Households, etc.	16,860	42	2,150	7,065	0	0	0	0	0	5	1,171	893	0	2,176	3,358	0
-households	9,675	11	1,496	4,081	0	0	0	0	0	5	197	351	0	1,340	2,195	0
-agriculture	45	0	45	0	0	0	0	0	0	0	0	0	0	0	0	0
-others	7,140	32	609	2,984	0	0	0	0	0	0	974	542	0	836	1,163	0
Statistical divergence	-220	-61	-3	0	0	0	0	0	0	0	0	0	0	70	-225	0
Renewable energies																
Primary production	**84,816**	**660**	**1,768**	**8,501**	**1,355**	**7,001**	**16,890**	**259**	**13,278**	**50**	**1,454**	**6,765**	**3,591**	**7,247**	**13,734**	**2,263**
Transformation input	15,340	367	992	1,758	0	595	1,899	30	3,129	24	1,097	772	198	1,444	2,015	1,020
-conventional thermal power stations	13,256	367	520	1,138	0	595	1,882	30	3,118	24	1,097	639	198	1,282	1,344	1,020
Exchanges, transfers, returns	-27,300	-34	-241	-1,906	-326	-3,109	-5,392	-93	-3,564	-11	-64	-3,196	-1,124	-1,296	-6,418	-526
Consumption of the energy branch	0	0	0	0	0	0	0	0	0	0	0	0	0	0	0	0
Distribution losses	0	0	0	0	0	0	0	0	0	0	0	0	0	0	0	0
Available for final consumption	**42,176**	**258**	**535**	**4,837**	**1,029**	**3,298**	**9,599**	**136**	**6,585**	**15**	**293**	**2,797**	**2,269**	**4,507**	**5,301**	**717**
Final energy consumption	**42,175**	**258**	**522**	**4,837**	**1,029**	**3,295**	**9,599**	**136**	**6,585**	**15**	**293**	**2,797**	**2,269**	**4,522**	**5,301**	**718**
Industry	15,205	88	115	388	205	1,270	1,844	92	946	0	79	867	1,102	3,382	4,321	506
Households, etc.	26,971	170	407	4,450	824	2,024	7,754	44	5,639	15	214	1,930	1,166	1,140	980	212
-households	25,028	170	306	3,868	824	2,024	7,754	44	5,467	15	212	971	1,160	1,041	962	209
-agriculture	1,014	0	57	0	0	0	0	0	0	0	0	953	0	0	4	0
-others	929	0	45	582	0	0	0	0	173	0	2	7	6	98	13	3
Statistical divergence	1	0	13	0	0	3	0	0	0	0	0	0	0	-15	0	-1

(1) EU-15 and D, provisional data.

Source: Eurostat (SIRENE)

Table 1.42

Evolution of interior flows of other energy sources, EU-15 (thousand TOE) (1)

	1988	1989	1990	1991	1992	1993	1994	1995	1996	1997	1998
Nuclear energy											
Primary production	**173,332**	**182,429**	**181,439**	**187,021**	**188,267**	**197,558**	**197,271**	**201,239**	**208,864**	**212,615**	**209,664**
Transformation input	173,227	182,328	181,351	187,021	188,267	197,558	197,271	201,239	208,864	212,615	209,666
-nuclear power stations	173,227	182,328	181,351	187,021	188,267	197,558	197,271	201,239	208,864	212,615	209,666
Available for final consumption	105	101	88	0	0	0	0	0	0	0	-2
Statistical divergence	105	101	88	0	0	0	0	0	0	0	-2
Derived heat											
Transformation output	18,713	17,839	18,840	18,914	17,985	19,968	20,421	21,885	23,791	23,334	23,575
-conventional thermal power stations	4,776	4,005	4,884	5,736	5,524	6,071	6,949	15,184	17,082	16,945	17,216
Consumption of the energy branch	493	438	376	225	237	256	313	317	345	473	471
Distribution losses	1,654	1,527	2,074	1,993	1,914	2,177	2,102	2,441	2,542	2,533	2,576
Available for final consumption	**16,566**	**15,873**	**16,391**	**16,696**	**15,834**	**17,535**	**18,006**	**19,127**	**20,904**	**20,328**	**20,528**
Final energy consumption	**16,517**	**15,877**	**16,394**	**16,657**	**15,798**	**17,524**	**18,004**	**19,089**	**20,692**	**20,510**	**20,748**
Industry	3,749	3,691	3,824	3,179	2,371	2,521	2,583	3,091	4,078	4,162	3,888
-iron and steel industry	116	135	101	70	70	60	60	14	15	18	18
-chemical industry	844	860	837	663	640	654	636	631	722	667	678
-non-metallic mineral products	229	195	89	64	44	43	51	53	54	54	54
-food, drink and tobacco industry	251	247	332	267	147	155	166	163	162	181	193
-textile, leather and clothing industry	125	132	75	55	36	41	46	55	59	64	66
-paper and printing industry	44	56	95	87	78	119	149	162	163	168	174
-engineering and others metal industry	722	711	934	911	717	691	686	572	577	574	565
-others industries	496	454	432	423	427	532	557	760	841	848	1,173
-adjustment	923	900	927	639	213	226	232	681	1,485	1,589	967
Households, etc.	12,768	12,186	12,570	13,477	13,426	15,003	15,422	15,998	16,614	16,348	16,860
-households	6,729	6,470	6,926	7,816	7,745	9,821	10,095	9,787	10,028	9,520	9,675
-agriculture	45	0	0	45	45	45	45	45	40	45	45
-others	5,994	5,716	5,644	5,617	5,637	5,138	5,282	6,167	6,546	6,783	7,140
Statistical divergence	50	-4	-3	39	37	10	1	38	212	-182	-220
Renewable energies											
Primary production	**69,145**	**65,040**	**65,804**	**68,916**	**70,834**	**72,430**	**72,636**	**73,348**	**76,052**	**81,771**	**84,816**
Transformation input	8,191	8,798	8,839	9,241	10,644	11,553	11,851	12,622	14,148	15,003	15,340
-conventional thermal power stations	7,785	8,341	8,387	8,747	10,030	10,798	10,924	11,635	12,019	12,961	13,256
Exchanges, transfers, returns	-26,798	-21,664	-22,341	-23,177	-24,720	-25,085	-25,835	-25,297	-25,232	-26,084	-27,300
Consumption of the energy branch	0	0	0	0	0	0	0	0	0	0	0
Distribution losses	0	1	0	0	0	0	0	1	0	0	0
Available for final consumption	**34,156**	**34,577**	**34,624**	**36,497**	**35,470**	**35,791**	**34,950**	**35,429**	**36,672**	**40,684**	**42,176**
Final energy consumption	**34,179**	**34,641**	**34,692**	**36,575**	**35,543**	**35,838**	**35,019**	**35,897**	**36,517**	**40,817**	**42,175**
Industry	12,377	12,885	12,585	12,692	12,188	13,017	13,783	14,052	13,889	14,754	15,205
Households, etc.	21,802	21,756	22,108	23,882	23,355	22,821	21,237	21,845	22,628	26,063	26,971
-households	20,787	20,557	20,891	22,622	22,057	21,706	20,192	20,683	21,378	24,749	25,028
-agriculture	1,003	1,016	1,032	1,080	1,098	920	849	954	987	1,012	1,014
-others	12	184	184	180	200	195	195	209	263	302	929
Statistical divergence	-23	-64	-69	-78	-73	-47	-69	-469	155	-134	1

(1) Data for EU-15 includes former East Germany for 1991 and subsequent years.

Source: Eurostat (SIRENE)

———Table 1.43

Processing of nuclear fuels (NACE Rev. 1 23.3)

Trade related indicators in the EU (1)

	1989	1990	1991	1992	1993	1994	1995	1996	1997	1998	1999
Exports (million EUR)	733	855	754	772	921	832	869	777	834	684	1,013
Imports (million EUR)	1,164	920	952	898	837	1,059	1,017	1,004	1,209	1,100	1,025
Trade balance (million EUR)	-431	-65	-198	-126	84	-227	-148	-227	-375	-416	-13
Cover ratio (%)	63.0	92.9	79.2	86.0	110.1	78.6	85.4	77.4	69.0	62.2	98.8

(1) Technically, data before 01/01/1999 are in ECU and after this date in euro. However, as the conversion rate was 1 ECU =1 EUR, for practical purposes the two terms can be used interchangeably.

———Table 1.44

Processing of nuclear fuels (NACE Rev. 1 23.3)

Production related indicators, 1997

	B	DK	D	EL (1)	E	F	IRL	I	L	NL	A	P	FIN	S	UK
Number of persons employed (thousands)	1.1	0.0	:	0.0	:	11.4	0.0	:	0.0	:	0.0	0.0	0.0	:	:
Production (million ECU)	465	0	:	0	:	4,919	0	:	0	:	0	0	0	:	:
Value added (million ECU)	209	0	:	0	:	2,046	0	:	0	:	0	0	0	:	:
Gross operating surplus (million ECU)	143.7	0.0	:	0.0	:	1,423.8	0.0	:	0.0	:	0.0	0.0	0.0	:	:

(1) 1996.

———Table 1.45

Processing of nuclear fuels (NACE Rev. 1 23.3)

Trade related indicators, 1999

	B	DK	D	EL	E	F	IRL	I	L	NL	A	P	FIN	S	UK
Exports (million EUR)	582	0	266	0	31	1,011	0	16	0	202	1	:	3	74	471
Imports (million EUR)	600	8	499	5	130	894	2	33	0	70	11	2	67	140	443
Trade balance (million EUR)	-18	-7	-233	-5	-99	117	-1	-18	0	132	-10	:	-64	-66	28
Cover ratio (%)	97.0	1.2	53.3	3.3	24.1	113.0	23.1	46.8	0.0	287.7	10.2	:	4.3	52.8	106.4

Source: Eurostat (SBS, COMEXT)

Table 1.46

Interior flows of electricity, 1998 (thousand TOE)

	EU-15	B	DK	D	EL	E	F	IRL	I	L	NL	A	P	FIN	S	UK
Total imports	**14,482**	**673**	**282**	**3,294**	**215**	**771**	**395**	**13**	**3,580**	**545**	**1,052**	**886**	**342**	**824**	**525**	**1,086**
Total exports	13,355	553	653	3,349	77	478	5,344	6	77	79	36	900	318	24	1,444	14
Net imports	1,127	120	-371	-55	138	293	-4,949	7	3,502	466	1,016	-14	24	800	-920	1,072
Cover ratio (%)	7.8	17.8	-131.7	-1.7	64.4	38.0	-1,254.3	51.5	97.8	85.4	96.6	-1.6	6.9	97.1	-175.3	98.7
Gross inland consumption	**1,127**	**120**	**-371**	**-55**	**138**	**293**	**-4,949**	**7**	**3,502**	**466**	**1,016**	**-14**	**24**	**800**	**-920**	**1,072**
Transformation output	184,945	7,028	3,291	45,620	3,645	13,579	38,148	1,702	18,245	21	7,770	1,610	2,222	4,737	7,187	30,139
-conventional thermal power stations	111,498	3,058	3,291	31,722	3,645	8,506	4,787	1,702	18,245	21	7,442	1,610	2,222	2,858	860	21,528
-nuclear power stations	73,446	3,969	0	13,899	0	5,072	33,361	0	0	0	328	0	0	1,879	6,327	8,610
Exchanges, transfers, returns	27,300	34	741	1,906	326	3,109	5,392	93	3,564	11	64	3,196	1,124	1,296	6,418	526
Consumption of the energy branch	18,701	488	211	5,286	456	1,133	4,392	118	1,816	30	543	311	181	319	1,155	2,263
Distribution losses	13,249	335	200	2,075	273	1,576	2,625	165	1,591	9	333	287	279	255	912	2,333
Available for final consumption	**181,422**	**6,359**	**2,750**	**40,110**	**3,380**	**14,271**	**31,574**	**1,519**	**21,904**	**458**	**7,975**	**4,193**	**2,910**	**6,260**	**10,618**	**27,140**
Final energy consumption	**181,422**	**6,359**	**2,750**	**40,110**	**3,380**	**14,271**	**31,574**	**1,519**	**21,904**	**455**	**7,975**	**4,193**	**2,910**	**6,260**	**10,621**	**27,140**
Industry	76,023	3,215	856	17,910	1,110	6,141	11,349	609	10,924	283	3,386	1,676	1,253	3,506	4,675	9,129
-iron and steel industry	8,853	554	53	1,995	75	1,046	1,359	26	1,618	149	197	183	63	210	430	896
-non ferrous metals industry	5,423	161	0	1,543	296	757	774	28	468	0	470	30	9	166	232	488
-chemical industry	14,904	1,097	99	4,565	107	877	2,221	81	1,754	23	1,054	218	178	371	515	1,742
-non-metallic mineral products	5,540	210	73	1,279	173	662	765	50	1,083	27	130	125	179	68	96	621
-ore extraction industry	883	31	0	172	24	125	74	24	95	1	15	30	36	43	214	0
-food, drink and tobacco industry	7,008	313	197	1,193	90	610	1,439	148	921	7	554	94	123	131	209	979
-textile, leather and clothing industry	2,988	166	17	377	84	318	336	32	961	27	55	46	200	23	31	314
-paper and printing industry	9,858	204	63	1,693	38	456	1,015	14	797	0	308	365	168	2,099	1,813	827
-engineering and others metal industry	10,822	260	175	2,377	61	714	2,119	80	1,994	50	367	218	115	206	367	1,718
-others industries	9,727	220	164	2,716	161	576	1,246	126	1,235	0	235	367	182	188	768	1,543
-adjustment	16	0	16	0	0	0	0	0	0	0	0	0	0	0	0	0
Transport	4,795	117	26	1,383	15	322	955	2	676	7	140	188	31	44	241	645
-railways	4,795	117	26	1,383	15	322	955	2	676	7	140	188	31	44	241	645
Households, etc.	100,604	3,026	1,867	20,817	2,255	7,807	19,270	908	10,304	165	4,448	2,329	1,626	2,710	5,705	17,366
-households	53,337	2,011	880	11,250	1,099	3,586	10,589	475	5,097	65	1,788	1,118	755	1,560	3,640	9,425
-agriculture	4,060	995	165	672	223	361	233	0	386	7	284	132	54	71	145	333
-others	43,207	21	822	8,895	932	3,860	8,448	433	4,822	93	2,376	1,079	816	1,080	1,920	7,609
Statistical divergence	0	0	0	0	0	0	0	0	0	3	0	0	0	0	-3	0

Source: Eurostat (SIRENE)

_____Table 1.47

Evolution of interior flows of electricity, EU-15 (thousand TOE) (1)

	1988	1989	1990	1991	1992	1993	1994	1995	1996	1997	1998
Total imports	**11,083**	**12,342**	**13,265**	**11,979**	**12,784**	**13,315**	**13,083**	**13,988**	**14,666**	**14,790**	**14,482**
Total exports	8,997	10,046	10,932	10,760	11,169	11,434	11,532	12,492	14,802	14,121	13,355
Net imports	2,086	2,297	2,333	1,218	1,616	1,881	1,552	1,496	-136	669	1,127
Cover ratio (%)	18.8	18.6	17.6	10.2	12.6	14.1	11.9	10.7	-0.9	4.5	7.8
Gross inland consumption	**2,086**	**2,297**	**2,333**	**1,218**	**1,616**	**1,881**	**1,552**	**1,496**	**-136**	**669**	**1,127**
Transformation output	150,336	159,580	161,617	165,963	165,109	165,114	167,283	173,214	180,213	180,830	184,945
-conventional thermal power stations	_91,693_	_97,380_	_99,692_	_101,702_	_99,767_	_96,817_	_99,187_	_103,544_	_107,023_	_106,893_	_111,498_
-nuclear power stations	_58,643_	_62,200_	_61,925_	_64,261_	_65,342_	_68,296_	_68,096_	_69,670_	_73,190_	_73,937_	_73,446_
Exchanges, transfers, returns	26,790	21,664	22,342	23,176	24,708	25,066	25,835	25,297	25,227	26,085	27,300
Consumption of the energy branch	17,764	17,595	17,982	18,341	18,226	17,714	17,373	18,016	18,305	18,338	18,701
Distribution losses	11,535	11,365	11,583	12,012	11,624	11,866	12,380	12,623	13,147	12,217	13,249
Available for final consumption	**149,913**	**154,582**	**156,727**	**160,004**	**161,583**	**162,481**	**164,917**	**169,369**	**173,852**	**177,030**	**181,422**
Final energy consumption	**148,986**	**153,761**	**155,972**	**158,810**	**163,740**	**161,053**	**163,632**	**169,369**	**173,851**	**177,046**	**181,422**
Industry	67,287	69,584	69,287	68,142	67,815	66,935	67,983	71,356	71,734	74,264	76,023
-iron and steel industry	_8,459_	_8,596_	_8,209_	_8,160_	_7,914_	_7,802_	_8,352_	_8,586_	_8,458_	_8,881_	_8,853_
-non ferrous metals industry	_5,814_	_5,839_	_5,819_	_5,634_	_5,450_	_5,108_	_4,792_	_4,979_	_5,093_	_5,168_	_5,423_
-chemical industry	_15,584_	_15,908_	_16,059_	_15,283_	_14,799_	_14,436_	_14,080_	_14,165_	_14,178_	_14,596_	_14,904_
-non-metallic mineral products	_4,936_	_5,208_	_5,002_	_4,947_	_4,998_	_4,862_	_5,100_	_5,316_	_5,421_	_5,471_	_5,540_
-ore extraction industry	_1,076_	_907_	_1,136_	_1,110_	_1,053_	_964_	_779_	_933_	_925_	_912_	_883_
-food, drink and tobacco industry	_5,241_	_5,507_	_5,793_	_5,965_	_6,120_	_6,231_	_6,217_	_6,570_	_6,737_	_6,926_	_7,008_
-textile, leather and clothing industry	_2,899_	_3,078_	_3,003_	_2,964_	_2,929_	_2,808_	_2,936_	_2,871_	_2,857_	_2,961_	_2,988_
-paper and printing industry	_7,411_	_7,678_	_7,867_	_7,869_	_7,948_	_8,191_	_8,495_	_9,253_	_9,173_	_9,698_	_9,858_
-engineering and others metal industry	_10,663_	_11,229_	_11,434_	_11,148_	_11,123_	_10,652_	_10,949_	_9,902_	_10,137_	_10,358_	_10,822_
-others industries	_5,202_	_5,633_	_4,921_	_5,060_	_5,473_	_5,880_	_6,269_	_8,767_	_8,742_	_9,288_	_9,727_
-adjustment	_0_	_0_	_45_	_3_	_7_	_2_	_14_	_14_	_15_	_3_	_16_
Transport	3,626	3,697	4,004	4,237	4,283	4,469	4,609	4,691	4,831	4,886	4,795
-railways	_3,626_	_3,697_	_4,004_	_4,237_	_4,283_	_4,469_	_4,609_	_4,691_	_4,831_	_4,886_	_4,795_
Households, etc.	78,073	80,480	82,680	86,431	91,642	89,649	91,040	93,321	97,285	97,896	100,604
-households	_42,614_	_43,274_	_44,618_	_47,291_	_47,952_	_49,032_	_49,554_	_50,046_	_52,662_	_52,146_	_53,337_
-agriculture	_2,544_	_2,593_	_2,696_	_2,822_	_2,804_	_2,822_	_2,860_	_2,960_	_3,006_	_3,973_	_4,060_
-others	_32,916_	_34,614_	_35,366_	_36,318_	_40,886_	_37,795_	_38,626_	_40,315_	_41,618_	_41,778_	_43,207_
Statistical divergence	927	821	755	1,194	-2,156	1,428	1,285	0	1	-16	0

(1) Data for EU-15 includes former East Germany for 1991 and subsequent years.

Source: Eurostat (SIRENE)

Table 1.48

Production and distribution of electricity (NACE Rev. 1 40.1)

Trade related indicators in the EU (1)

	1989	1990	1991	1992	1993	1994	1995	1996	1997	1998	1999
Exports (million EUR)	450	552	659	699	824	903	1,115	1,427	1,185	1,225	1,191
Imports (million EUR)	499	545	605	510	515	562	526	546	567	651	727
Trade balance (million EUR)	-49	8	54	189	308	341	588	882	618	574	464
Cover ratio (%)	90.2	101.4	108.9	137.1	159.9	160.7	211.9	261.6	209.1	188.1	163.9

(1) Technically, data before 01/01/1999 are in ECU and after this date in euro. However, as the conversion rate was 1 ECU =1 EUR, for practical purposes the two terms can be used interchangeably.

Table 1.49

Production and distribution of electricity (NACE Rev. 1 40.1)

Production related indicators, 1997

	B	DK	D	EL	E	F	IRL	I (1)	L	NL	A	P	FIN	S	UK
Number of persons employed (thousands)	19.0	:	249.4	:	43.3	122.2	:	116.3	0.9	:	29.8	16.7	16.8	23.4	72.5
Production (million ECU)	17,560	:	82,082	:	14,034	31,003	:	25,245	189	:	8,262	6,206	3,873	11,524	41,181
Value added (million ECU)	4,733	:	26,953	:	8,616	14,236	:	13,909	144	:	3,948	2,237	1,956	3,786	13,230
Gross operating surplus (million ECU)	2,930.3	:	13,855.3	:	6,632.2	7,601.2	:	8,396.6	89.6	:	2,128.0	1,775.9	1,432.4	2,646.4	10,161.2

(1) 1996.

Table 1.50

Production and distribution of electricity (NACE Rev. 1 40.1)

Trade related indicators, 1999

	B	DK	D	EL	E	F	IRL	I	L	NL	A	P	FIN	S	UK
Exports (million EUR)	237	122	484	:	45	2,754	0	0	0	15	345	35	2	142	13
Imports (million EUR)	242	59	600	10	103	279	12	0	:	217	238	15	190	112	599
Trade balance (million EUR)	-4	62	-116	:	-57	2,475	-12	0	:	-201	107	20	-188	29	-586
Cover ratio (%)	98.2	204.6	80.7	:	44.0	985.8	0.3	4.0	:	7.1	145.2	233.0	1.3	126.1	2.1

Table 1.51

Production and distribution of electricity (NACE Rev. 1 40.1)

Labour related indicators, 1997

	B	DK	D	EL	E	F	IRL	I (1)	L	NL	A	P	FIN	S	UK
Unit personnel costs (thousand ECU per employee)	94.9	:	52.5	:	40.2	54.3	:	47.4	59.4	:	61.2	27.9	36.1	48.7	42.4
Social charges as a share of personnel costs (%)	86.1	:	39.0	:	25.0	66.6	:	54.3	:	:	47.3	51.8	29.2	64.0	14.4
Apparent labour productivity (thousand ECU/pers. empl.)	248.8	:	108.1	:	198.8	116.5	:	119.6	156.5	:	132.7	134.2	116.5	161.9	182.6
Wage adjusted labour productivity (%)	262.2	:	205.8	:	495.1	214.6	:	252.2	263.3	:	216.8	482.0	322.4	332.2	430.8
Personnel costs as a share of total operating costs (%)	12.4	:	20.4	:	16.5	32.2	:	33.1	15.3	:	30.1	10.9	11.6	12.8	10.0

(1) 1996.

Source: Eurostat (SBS, EBT, COMEXT)

————————————————Table 1.52

Steam and hot water supply (NACE Rev. 1 40.3)

Production related indicators, 1997

	B	DK	D	EL (1)	E	F	IRL	I	L	NL	A	P	FIN	S	UK
Number of persons employed (thousands)	0.0	:	8.7	0.0	0.7	15.5	0.0	:	:	:	1.5	0.1	0.6	3.2	0.0
Production (million ECU)	2	:	2,341	0	31	2,650	0	:	:	:	436	4	107	1,349	0
Value added (million ECU)	1	:	755	0	16	648	0	:	:	:	201	1	62	397	0
Gross operating surplus (million ECU)	0.1	:	423.8	0.0	5.3	16.9	0.0	:	:	:	136.2	0.5	41.3	292.1	0.0

(1) 1996.

————————————————Table 1.53

Steam and hot water supply (NACE Rev. 1 40.3)

Labour related indicators, 1997

	B	DK	D	EL	E	F	IRL	I	L	NL	A	P	FIN	S	UK
Unit personnel costs (thousand ECU per employee)	30.5	:	37.8	:	16.7	40.8	:	:	:	:	44.0	12.4	34.3	33.0	:
Social charges as a share of personnel costs (%)	33.3	:	25.0	:	29.1	43.6	:	:	:	:	30.8	20.0	37.3	51.2	:
Apparent labour productivity (thousand ECU/pers. empl.)	33.1	:	86.3	:	22.2	41.9	:	:	:	:	136.2	18.5	97.1	124.5	:
Wage adjusted labour productivity (%)	108.7	:	228.1	:	133.2	102.7	:	:	:	:	309.7	149.1	283.0	377.7	:
Personnel costs as a share of total operating costs (%)	44.4	:	17.7	:	35.2	23.0	:	:	:	:	22.0	20.0	14.6	10.0	:

Source: Eurostat (SBS)

Table 1.54

Collection, purification and distribution of water (NACE Rev. 1 41)

Production related indicators in the EU (1)

	1989	1990	1991	1992	1993	1994	1995	1996	1997	1998	1999
Number of persons employed (thousands)	152.3	154.5	152.9	163.1	154.6	160.3	:	:	:	:	:
Production (million EUR)	17,996	20,414	21,965	23,960	24,827	27,394	:	:	:	:	:
Domestic producer price index (1995=100)	:	:	:	:	:	:	100.0	105.4	109.7	113.3	115.7
Value added (million EUR)	7,767	8,629	9,438	10,122	10,477	11,556	:	:	:	:	:

(1) Technically, data before 01/01/1999 are in ECU and after this date in euro. However, as the conversion rate was 1 ECU =1 EUR, for practical purposes the two terms can be used interchangeably.

Table 1.55

Collection, purification and distribution of water (NACE Rev. 1 41)

Production related indicators, 1997

	B	DK	D	EL	E	F	IRL	I (1)	L	NL	A	P	FIN	S	UK
Number of persons employed (thousands)	7.0	:	31.4	:	17.9	33.1	0.0	15.6	0.4	:	1.2	1.6	2.0	0.8	33.2
Production (million ECU)	1,030	:	4,968	:	1,954	8,139	0	1,846	38	:	224	130	335	167	6,032
Value added (million ECU)	517	:	2,869	:	945	2,100	0	833	30	:	155	82	253	101	3,901
Gross operating surplus (million ECU)	198.7	:	1,698.4	:	399.5	602.9	0.0	213.3	13.5	:	100.6	51.7	191.0	61.8	2,851.8

(1) 1996.

Table 1.56

Collection, purification and distribution of water (NACE Rev. 1 41)

Labour related indicators, 1997

	B	DK	D	EL	E	F	IRL	I (1)	L	NL	A	P	FIN	S	UK
Unit personnel costs (thousand ECU per employee)	45.7	:	37.3	:	27.4	45.2	:	40.0	44.0	:	44.2	19.4	30.8	47.9	31.6
Social charges as a share of personnel costs (%)	38.9	:	28.1	:	28.2	51.5	:	48.5	:	:	49.7	34.4	32.1	58.0	15.2
Apparent labour productivity (thousand ECU/pers. empl.)	74.1	:	91.4	:	52.7	63.4	:	53.3	80.1	:	126.5	50.7	123.9	123.0	117.7
Wage adjusted labour productivity (%)	162.3	:	245.0	:	192.0	140.3	:	133.3	182.0	:	286.6	261.8	402.7	256.7	371.9
Personnel costs as a share of total operating costs (%)	38.8	:	37.4	:	31.6	21.7	:	38.3	32.6	:	42.6	39.0	42.6	37.3	36.5

(1) 1996.

Source: Eurostat (SBS, EBT)

Non-energy mining and quarrying (NACE Rev. 1 13 and 14)

This chapter on non-energy mining and quarrying covers both underground and open-cast mining. The first sub-chapter deals with the mining of iron ores (NACE Rev. 1 13.1), it is followed by the mining of non-ferrous metal ores (NACE Rev. 1 13.2), which excludes the mining of uranium and thorium. Finally, there is a sub-chapter that covers other mining and quarrying (NACE Rev. 1 14), which includes the extraction of a variety of basic materials including stone, sand, salt and other minerals.

These industries (for example, the quarrying of sand and clay) are characterised by a large number of family-run SME's, some of which only extract minerals part of the year. As such, the collection of reliable production statistics is a difficult task.

Non-energy mining and quarrying industries are actively present across the European Union. The extraction of industrial and construction minerals is relatively evenly spread within the EU with, for example, the extraction of aggregates (crushed stone) and sand and gravel for construction purposes being carried out in all Member States. On the other hand, production is more concentrated within the area of metallic minerals, where Finland, Greece, Ireland, Portugal, Spain and Sweden together account for some 75% of total EU production in volume terms.

Worldwide demand for ores, minerals and building materials is likely to increase as the global economy expands. Most metals and minerals are traded globally, and their markets are characterised by high price volatility. These characteristics should be borne in mind when assessing trends on the basis of production value data.

The vast majority of iron ore is used in steel making. Iron ore is often the only source of primary iron, with scrap being an alternative for some processing techniques. The fortunes of the iron ore industry are strongly linked to demand from downstream metal processing industries (see chapter 8). Demand for non-ferrous metals follows a similar pattern, as illustrated by the use of bauxite (the basic form of aluminium) in packaging, vehicle manufacture and construction, copper (used principally within electronic goods) and lead (a main component in the manufacture of batteries).

Sand, gravel, chalk and lime are used in the fabrication of road aggregates and cement, whereby demand is often linked to construction activity. The abundance of construction aggregates and cement deposits throughout the EU leads in part to the existence of many small enterprises which service local markets with materials specific to the region they are located in.

Products such as salt and minerals have different demand patterns, as the use of potash, phosphates and sulphur depends to a large degree on agricultural demand for fertilisers, whilst one of the principal uses of salt (around a fifth of the EU's sales to end-users) is as a de-icing agent (demand being therefore dependent upon climatic conditions). The other main end uses of salt are the chemicals industry (almost half the sales in the EU) and food grade salt (around a sixth of total EU sales).

The activities covered in this chapter (in terms of NACE Rev. 1) include:

13:    mining of metal ores;
13.1: mining of iron ores;
13.2: mining of non-ferrous metal ores, except uranium and thorium ores;
14:    other mining and quarrying;
14.1: quarrying of stone;
14.2: quarrying of sand and clay;
14.3: mining of chemical and fertilizer minerals;
14.4: production of salt;
14.5: other mining and quarrying n.e.c.

Table 2.1

Non-energy mining and quarrying (NACE Rev. 1 13 and 14)

Breakdown of turnover and employment by employment size class, 1996 (%)

	Micro (0-9)		Small (10-49)		Medium (50-249)		Large (250+)	
	Turnover (1)	Employment (1)	Turnover (2)	Employment (3)	Turnover (4)	Employment (1)	Turnover (1)	Employment (1)
EU-15	21.1	18.7	29.6	38.1	22.4	19.5	26.9	23.7
B	:	:	:	:	21.6	:	:	:
DK	30.2	34.6	26.2	36.2	:	:	:	:
D	38.0	11.2	14.1	31.5	12.3	19.9	35.6	37.4
EL	:	:	:	:	:	:	:	:
E	21.2	27.4	:	43.0	:	:	:	:
F	15.4	17.4	35.6	38.4	22.1	18.1	27.0	26.1
IRL	:	:	:	:	:	:	:	:
I	:	:	:	:	:	:	:	:
L	:	:	:	:	:	:	:	:
NL	:	:	:	79.5	:	0.0	:	0.0
A	:	:	:	:	:	:	:	:
P	:	:	:	:	:	:	:	:
FIN	15.0	17.1	13.9	15.9	:	:	:	:
S	13.9	5.5	:	:	:	:	:	79.8
UK	8.4	14.7	:	37.3	:	:	26.2	:

(1) D, 1997.
(2) D and FIN, 1997.
(3) D and E, 1997.
(4) B and D, 1997.

Source: Eurostat (SME)

Total output of non-energy mining and quarrying products amounted to approximately 19.3 billion ECU[1] in 1997, approximately a quarter of mining and quarrying output (which was equal to some 70 billion ECU[2] in 1997). Production value of the non-energy mining and quarrying industry represented approximately 0.5% of total manufacturing output[3].

Relatively high labour intensity

There were around 152 thousand persons employed in 1997[4], some 40% of the mining and quarrying total[5]. When compared to total manufacturing employment, non-energy mining and quarrying represented 0.7% of the total number of persons employed (a share somewhat higher than the corresponding share of production).

(1) EL, I and P, 1996; IRL, no data available.
(2) EL, I and P, 1996; NL, 1995; IRL, no data available.
(3) It is important to note that non-energy mining and quarrying is not part of the manufacturing Division with the NACE Rev. 1 classification.
(4) EL, I and P, 1996; IRL and NL, no data available.
(5) EL and I, 1996; NL, no data available.

Other mining and quarrying by far the largest activity in terms of production

Of the three industries studied in this chapter, the residual grouping of other mining and quarrying (NACE Rev. 1 14), which includes activities such as the quarrying of stone, sand, clay, minerals and salt, was the largest. It reported output equal to 16.3 billion ECU[6] in 1996, some 85% of the production value generated by the activities covered in this chapter[7].

Judging the relative size of the other two sub-chapters is a difficult task, as many Member States have not reported data, including one of the larger EU economies, the United Kingdom. Only Spain and France reported production data for the mining of iron ores (NACE Rev. 1 13.1) in 1996[8], with total output equal to 40.0 million ECU. More Member States[9] reported figures within the activity of non-ferrous metal ores (NACE Rev. 1 13.2), where output reached 562 million ECU[10] in 1996.

(6) B, IRL, L and A, no data available.
(7) EL, I and P, 1996; IRL, no data available.
(8) Six Member States reported that they had no domestic production.
(9) EL, E, F, I and FIN.
(10) P, 1995; IRL, S and UK, no data available.

Almost three-quarters of the enterprises employed fewer than 10 persons

Of all the EU enterprises covered by this chapter, nearly three-quarters (13.1 thousand) had fewer than ten employees in 1996, of which 4.0 thousand had no employees at all. Small firms (10 to 49 employees) accounted for the bulk of the remainder of enterprises (21.9%), whilst there were only 80 enterprises with more than 250 employees (0.5% of the total).

However, large enterprises together employed 49.4 thousand persons, or almost a quarter (23.7%) of the total number of persons employed. Small firms were the largest employers (79.4 thousand persons), representing 38.1% of the total, whilst medium-sized enterprises employed almost a fifth of those employed (19.5% or 40.7 thousand persons).

STRUCTURE AND PERFORMANCE

United Kingdom data is only available for 1997, and hence estimates for EU totals prior to this date are not possible. EU production volumes rose during the 1990s - although it is important to note that production values are largely a function of world prices. As such, value data shows EU output declining over the same period.

In France output declined in real terms on average by 1.0% per annum between 1990 and 1997. This was not a substantial decrease when compared to Italy, where annual average rates of change were equal to -5.1% during the ten-year period to 1996. German output also fell at a rapid pace, down by 10.8% in 1996 and 23.8% in 1997 (again in real terms). These losses meant that the United Kingdom was the largest producer in the EU in 1997, with production equal to 4.1 billion ECU. Spain (2.0 billion ECU) and Sweden (1.6 billion ECU) had the fourth and fifth highest production levels in 1997. Both these countries reported rising output during the course of the 1990s.

LABOUR AND PRODUCTIVITY

Due to a lack of data, the analysis in this chapter concentrates upon the individual Member States.

Employment fell in nearly all Member States
The United Kingdom was the largest employer in 1997, with 27.2 thousand persons employed, an increase on the 24.9 thousand persons employed in 1995. This rising trend was not common across the rest of the EU, as over the same period the number of persons employed in Germany fell from 38.7 thousand to 26.5 thousand.

France was the third largest employer in 1997 (24.7 thousand persons). Nevertheless, French employment fell from 28.8 thousand persons in 1990. The decline was larger in Italy, with the workforce almost halved between 1986 and 1996, falling from 21.2 thousand persons to 11.2 thousand. Spanish employment fell at a more gradual pace from 20.9 thousand persons in 1993 to 19.9 thousand in 1997.

Apparent labour productivity was highest in the United Kingdom, where each person employed generated 69.1 thousand ECU of value added in 1997. Germany also reported quite high levels of apparent labour productivity (63.0 thousand ECU per person employed).

High proportion of males in the workforce
In 1998, the proportion of men in the workforce of the non-energy mining and quarrying industries (88.9%) was one of the highest in the EU economy. It ranked alongside the mining of coal and lignite and the extraction of peat (NACE Rev. 1 10) at 93.1%, construction (NACE Rev. 1 45) at 91.5% and the manufacture of basic metals (NACE Rev. 1 27) at 87.9%.

Figure 2.1

Non-energy mining and quarrying (NACE Rev. 1 13 and 14)

Apparent labour productivity and unit personnel costs, 1997 (thousand ECU)

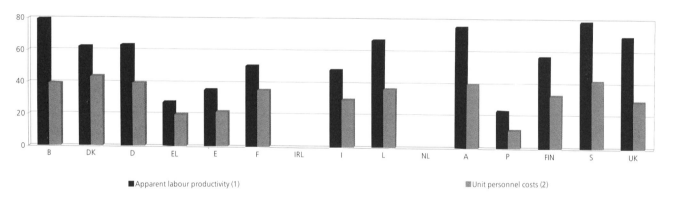

■ Apparent labour productivity (1)   ■ Unit personnel costs (2)

(1) EL, I and P, 1996; IRL and NL, not available.
(2) DK, EL, I and P, 1996; IRL and NL, not available.

Source: Eurostat (SBS)

INTERNATIONAL TRENDS AND FOREIGN TRADE

The EU's ran a trade deficit that increased during the 1990s, from the 5.6 billion ECU in 1989 to 8.4 billion EUR in 1999. The value of exports rose steadily from 4.7 billion ECU in 1991 to 9.1 billion EUR in 1999. There was a similar trend to the development of imports, which more than doubled between 1992 (8.6 billion ECU) and 1999 (17.5 billion EUR).

The Japanese trade deficit fell from 8.0 billion ECU in 1989 to 6.1 billion ECU in 1993. It remained close to that figure for the rest of the 1990s (with the exception of 1997 when it rose back to 7.5 billion ECU). In the USA, a trade deficit of 1.2 billion ECU was reported in both 1989 and 1998, with somewhat lower values in between these two dates.

Swiss imports to the EU increased rapidly in the 1990s

Switzerland was the main origin of EU imports in 1999, with a value of 3.5 billion EUR, over a fifth of the total (20.1%). This marked a substantial increase compared to 1989, when Switzerland accounted for only 0.6% of total EU imports. It is important to note that Switzerland is not a major producer of minerals. Rather, these high figures are likely to be a result of many traders being located in Switzerland.

The relative share of Brazilian imports also rose, with the value of imports originating from Brazil multiplied by five between 1989 and 1999 from 300 million ECU to 1.5 billion EUR (8.8% of the total). The value of imports from South Africa fell slightly to 1.4 billion EUR in 1999 (7.9% of the total), whilst the share of Australian imports remained fairly constant in 1999 (7.2%).

India was the main destination for EU exports in both 1989 and 1999, accounting for more than a third of the EU's exports in both of these reference years (37.9% and 38.6% respectively). Israel became an increasingly important destination, with its share of EU exports rising from 22.5% in 1989 to 29.1% in 1999, whilst the share of the USA fell from 10.2% to 7.9%.

Figure 2.2

Non-energy mining and quarrying (NACE Rev. 1 13 and 14)
Destination of EU exports, 1999 (%)

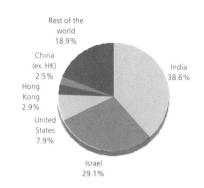

Source: Eurostat (COMEXT)

Figure 2.3

Non-energy mining and quarrying (NACE Rev. 1 13 and 14)
Origin of EU imports, 1999 (%)

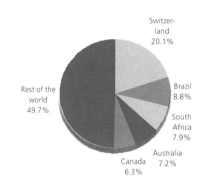

Source: Eurostat (COMEXT)

SUB-CHAPTER 2.1
IRON ORE (NACE Rev. 1 13.1)

The mining of iron ores (NACE Rev. 1 13.1) comprises mining, beneficiation and agglomeration activities. It does not include the preparation or mining of pyrites, which are covered under NACE Rev. 1 14.3 (see sub-chapter 2.3).

Many of the Member States reported that they had no production in this activity during the mid-1990s, including Denmark, Germany, Greece, Ireland, Italy, Luxembourg, the Netherlands and Finland[11].

STRUCTURE AND PERFORMANCE

The production data available for France and Spain points to a declining iron ore industry in those Member States that maintain an industry. In France, output declined from 63.0 million ECU in 1992 to 18.5 million ECU in 1996. Spanish output declined at a rapid pace between 1993 and 1997, falling from 38.0 million ECU to 10.8 million ECU. Taking producer price variations into account, the severity of the decline was illustrated even more, as real output fell by 17.9% in 1994, 31.2% in 1996 and 49.0% in 1997.

LABOUR AND PRODUCTIVITY

Given the size of the iron ore industry, there were very few people employed in this industry across the EU. Where employment data does exist, there have been large declines in the respective workforces during the 1990s. Spain employed just 259 persons in 1997, well down on the 771 persons employed in 1993. There was a similar decline in France, where the number of persons employed fell from 938 in 1992 to just 244 by 1996.

(11) It is important to note that data was not available for a number of other countries.

_____ Box 2.1

Sweden was the largest EU producer (in volume terms) with 21 million tons of iron ore produced in 1999. Globally, the production of iron ore is concentrated in about a dozen countries. It is estimated that global output in volume terms reached 992 million tons of usable ore in 1999, of which 205 million tons originated from China, 190 million tons from Brazil and 150 million tons from Australia.

Reserves of iron ore appear to be plentiful as it is estimated that there are at least 800 billion tons of crude ore, containing 230 billion tons of iron yet to be exploited.

INTERNATIONAL TRENDS AND FOREIGN TRADE

The EU's trade deficit was relatively unchanged between 1989 and 1999, moving from 2.8 billion ECU to 2.6 billion EUR (with the principal exception being a reduction to 2.0 billion ECU in 1993). There were relatively few EU exports (as production was so low), although the value of these did rise from 78.5 million ECU in 1989 to 187 million ECU in 1997 (falling away to 117 million EUR two years later). During the same ten-year period, the value of imports varied between 3.0 billion ECU in 1998 and 2.1 billion ECU in 1993, with the most recent value 2.7 billion EUR in 1999. The large difference in the level of imports and exports leads to a cover ratio which was equal to just 4.3% in 1999.

Japan runs a trade deficit almost equivalent to that of the EU's

The trade deficit in Japan was similar to that in the EU, 2.7 billion ECU in 1998. This figure was broadly in line with the values recorded during the rest of the 1990s. There were practically no exports of iron ore from Japan. The USA ran a much smaller trade deficit throughout the 1990s, which never exceeded 410 million ECU (1990). By 1998, the deficit had fallen to 322 million ECU.

Brazil supplied nearly half of the EU's imports of iron ore

In 1999, 46.6% of all imports to the EU came from Brazil, with a value of 1.2 billion EUR. This marked a moderate increase when compared to the 1.0 billion ECU of imports that originated from Brazil in 1989 (34.9%). The absolute value of Canadian and Australian imports fell between 1989 and 1999 to 404 million EUR and 363 million EUR respectively. Nevertheless, their relative shares of total EU imports increased to 15.7% and 14.1%. In 1999, the next most important origins of EU imports were Mauritania (231 million EUR, 9.0% of the total) and South Africa (115 million EUR, 4.5%).

The level of EU exports to non-Community countries was very limited. The majority of exports in 1999 went to Saudi Arabia (31.6 million EUR, 27% of the total), Libya (20.6 million EUR, 17.6%) and Egypt (19.6 million EUR, 16.7%).

_____ Figure 2.4

Iron ore (NACE Rev. 1 13.1)

Destination of EU exports, 1999 (%)

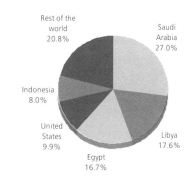

Source: Eurostat (COMEXT)

_____ Figure 2.5

Iron ore (NACE Rev. 1 13.1)

Origin of EU imports, 1999 (%)

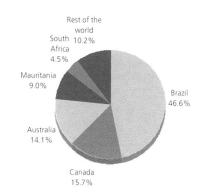

Source: Eurostat (COMEXT)

SUB-CHAPTER 2.2
NON-FERROUS METAL ORES
(NACE Rev. 1 13.2)

This sub-chapter covers the activities of mining and preparation of non-ferrous ores, including metals such as aluminium (bauxite), copper, lead, zinc, tin, manganese, nickel and cobalt. The extraction of precious metals such as gold, silver and platinum are also included.

In 1996, total output of non-ferrous metal ore mining was equal to 562 million ECU[12], equivalent to about 3% of the non-energy mining and quarrying total. Production is largely determined by the abundance of natural metal reserves. As a result many mines across the EU have closed within the last 20 or 30 years as natural stocks have been depleted and the EU has turned increasingly towards imports to satisfy demand. Twelve Member States supplied data covering these industries for 1996 or 1997. However, 6 of these reported that they had zero production[13].

STRUCTURE AND PERFORMANCE

Portugal was the largest producer of non-ferrous metal ores in the EU with production valued at 218 million ECU in 1995. Greece followed, with output of 89 million ECU in 1996, a figure that was down from the 129 million ECU in 1991, with the largest decline being recorded in 1995, down some 24.8% in real terms. There was a moderate recovery in 1996, when real output rose by 3.9%. Spain was the second largest producer of non-ferrous metal ores in the EU with output equal to 88 million ECU in 1997. Spanish output fell during the course of the 1990s, with one of the largest losses being recorded in 1997 (-37.9% in real terms). There were similar trends in Finland, where production values fell from 137 million ECU in 1991 to 74 million ECU in 1995 (with a one-off reduction of 28.6% in the latter of these years). As with the Greek figures, there was a recovery to almost 86 million ECU by 1997. The only country to buck the negative trend over a period of more than two years was France, where output rose from 26.3 million ECU in 1992 to 66.5 million ECU in 1996. Italy was one of the smallest producing countries in the EU, with output dwindling to 6.4 million ECU in 1996.

(12) P, 1995; IRL, S and UK, no data available.
(13) B, DK, D, L, NL and A had no production.

LABOUR AND PRODUCTIVITY

Most Member States reported employment levels falling significantly during the 1990s, often with their respective workforces being halved (largely as a result of rising productivity, rationalisation and automation). Greece had the largest workforce in 1996 with 2.2 thousand persons employed (compared to 5.3 thousand persons in 1986). In Spain, the 1.8 thousand persons employed in 1993 fell to 1.2 thousand by 1995, staying at that level over the next two years. Portugal saw employment fall sharply, from 2.8 thousand in 1990 to 1.3 thousand in 1995 (the most recent figure available), whilst in Finland the workforce was reduced from 1.4 thousand persons in 1989 to 545 persons by 1997.

INTERNATIONAL TRENDS AND FOREIGN TRADE

The EU trade deficit of 3.2 billion EUR in 1999 showed little evolution when compared to that of ten years earlier (3.3 billion ECU). There had been a reduction in the deficit to 1.9 billion ECU in 1993, although following the general economic recession imports increased once more at a rapid pace and the deficit returned to near the 3 billion ECU mark in 1996.

The value of exports was relatively small, and declined further as the EU produced less non-ferrous metal ores during the course of the 1990s, extra-EU exports fell from 346 million ECU in 1989 to only 193 million EUR by 1999.

The Japanese trade deficit was of a similar magnitude to that of the EU, with the latest figure available for 1998 (2.6 billion ECU) synonymous of Japan's trade position during the 1990s. In the USA there was less reliance on imports. During the 1990s, the American trade balance generally fluctuated between extremes of -279 million ECU in 1993 and +144 million ECU in 1995. However, in 1998 the deficit widened to 415 million ECU.

EU imports originate largely from the southern hemisphere

The value of EU imports originating from Australia rose from 384 million ECU to 496 million EUR between 1989 and 1999. This made Australia the main origin of imports at the end of the 1990s, accounting for 14.7% of the EU total. Indonesia (12.4%) followed close behind, with imports originating in this country rising from 11.6 million ECU in 1989 to 416 million EUR ten years later. South Africa followed, accounting for 10.5% of the EU's imports of non-ferrous metal ores, just ahead of Canada (which

had been the main origin of imports in 1989). The main export destinations for EU non-ferrous metal ores were Norway (40.0 million EUR, 21.4%), Canada (24.3 million EUR, 13.0%) and Japan (16.0 million EUR, 8.5%) in 1999.

Figure 2.6

Non-ferrous metal ores (NACE Rev. 1 13.2)
Destination of EU exports, 1999 (%)

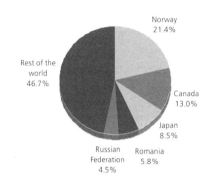

Source: Eurostat (COMEXT)

Figure 2.7

Non-ferrous metal ores (NACE Rev. 1 13.2)
Origin of EU imports, 1999 (%)

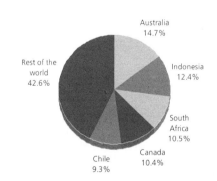

Source: Eurostat (COMEXT)

SUB-CHAPTER 2.3
MINING OF MINERALS (NACE Rev. 1 14)

Other mining and quarrying encompasses a variety of extractive industries, from the quarrying of stone (NACE Rev. 1 14.1), sand and clay (NACE Rev. 1 14.2) to the mining of minerals (NACE Rev. 1 14.3) and salt (NACE Rev. 1 14.4). Other mining and quarrying not elsewhere classified (NACE Rev. 1 14.5) completes the activities in this sub-chapter, including minerals as diverse as quartz, asphalt, asbestos, talc and graphite.

The mining of minerals in the EU had a production value of 16.3 billion ECU[14] in 1996, around 85% of the activities covered in this chapter[15]. The workforce totalled 140 thousand persons[16] in 1996, equivalent to 92% of the total number of persons employed in the activities covered by this chapter[17].

German production declined rapidly in 1997
Germany had the highest production value in the EU within the mining of minerals industry in 1996 (4.9 billion ECU), accounting for well over a quarter of the EU's output (29.9%)[18]. The level of German production was dramatically reduced in 1997 to 3.6 billion ECU. The United Kingdom and France each accounted for almost one-fifth of the EU's production (19.8%) with production valued at 3.2 billion ECU in 1996 for both countries. France maintained the value of its output in 1997. Spain reported a share of 10% of the EU total in 1996, as output reached 1.9 billion ECU in 1997.

INTERNATIONAL TRENDS AND FOREIGN TRADE
Up until 1993, the EU ran a trade surplus within the mining of minerals industry (equal to 921 million ECU in 1992). The trade deficit of 1993 (1.3 billion ECU) remained broadly stable through until 1997. However, in 1998 imports grew at a rapid pace resulting in a trade deficit of 2.3 billion ECU, a trend which continued in 1999 (-2.6 billion EUR). EU imports totalled 11.4 billion EUR in 1999, rising from 6.8 billion ECU in 1993. Exports followed a similar trend, doubling between 1990 (4.4 billion ECU) and 1999 (8.8 billion EUR).

In Japan there was a trade deficit of 1.2 billion ECU reported in 1998. This figure was consistent with the trade position of Japan throughout the 1990s, as the largest deficit was recorded in 1997 (1.4 billion ECU). There was little change in the USA either, as trade deficits between 1989 and 1998 varied between 684 million ECU (1989) and 338 million ECU (1991), with the latest figure available for 1998 showing a trade deficit of 446 million ECU.

_____
(14) B, IRL, L and A, no data available.
(15) The comparison is generally made with 1997 as a reference year; EL, I and P, 1996; IRL, no data available.
(16) B, IRL, L, NL and A, no data available.
(17) The comparison is generally made with 1997 as a reference year; EL, I and P, 1996; IRL and NL, no data available.
(18) B, IRL, L and A, no data available.

Table 2.2

Consumption of bitumen by the road industry (thousand tonnes)

	1997	1998	Growth rate, 97/98 (%)
EU-15	13,440	13,700	1.9
B	220	210	-4.5
DK	180	180	0.0
D	2,680	2,570	-4.1
EL	370	380	2.7
E	1,320	1,410	6.8
F	2,900	2,900	0.0
IRL	210	220	4.8
I	1,950	2,000	2.6
NL	330	320	-3.0
A	320	340	6.3
P	580	740	27.6
FIN	250	250	0.0
S	320	370	15.6
UK	1,810	1,810	0.0

Source: EAPA

With imports valued at 3.5 billion EUR in 1999, Switzerland accounted for almost one-third (30.5%) of the EU's imports, which was a higher share than the combined value of imports from the four next most important countries. Again it is important to note that Switzerland is not a major producer of minerals. Rather, the high share of Switzerland is likely to be a result of many traders being located in this country. South Africa was displaced as the principal origin of the EU's imports (a position held in 1989) despite a moderate increase in the value of its imports, which rose to 898 million EUR in 1999 (7.9%). Other countries that accounted for a significant share of EU imports in 1999 included Russia (778 million EUR, 6.8%), the Democratic Republic of Congo[19] (712 million EUR, 6.3%) and Israel (663 million EUR, 5.8%).

India was the main destination for EU exports, accounting for around two-fifths of the minerals that left the EU to non-Community countries in both 1989 (41.0%) and 1999 (39.9%). The relative importance of the second and third most important export destinations between these two dates moved in opposite directions, with Israel becoming more important (24.4% in 1989 and 30.1% in 1999) and the USA relatively less important (10.7% and 8.0%).

(19) Formerly Zaire.

Figure 2.8

Mining of minerals (NACE Rev. 1 14)
Destination of EU exports, 1999 (%)

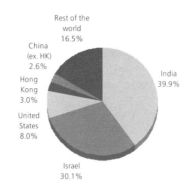

Source: Eurostat (COMEXT)

Figure 2.9

Mining of minerals (NACE Rev. 1 14)
Origin of EU imports, 1999 (%)

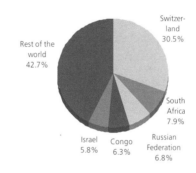

Source: Eurostat (COMEXT)

Table 2.3

Mining of iron ores (NACE Rev. 1 13.1)

Trade related indicators in the EU (1)

	1989	1990	1991	1992	1993	1994	1995	1996	1997	1998	1999
Exports (million EUR)	79	90	71	81	86	85	120	138	187	144	117
Imports (million EUR)	2,904	2,773	2,988	2,661	2,045	2,640	2,774	2,288	2,997	3,027	2,711
Trade balance (million EUR)	-2,825	-2,682	-2,917	-2,580	-1,958	-2,555	-2,655	-2,150	-2,810	-2,884	-2,594
Cover ratio (%)	2.7	3.3	2.4	3.0	4.2	3.2	4.3	6.0	6.3	4.7	4.3

(1) Technically, data before 01/01/1999 are in ECU and after this date in euro. However, as the conversion rate was 1 ECU =1 EUR, for practical purposes the two terms can be used interchangeably.

Table 2.4

Mining of iron ores (NACE Rev. 1 13.1)

Trade related indicators, 1999

	B	DK	D	EL	E	F	IRL	I	L	NL	A	P	FIN	S	UK
Exports (million EUR)	3	0	1	0	1	2	0	0	0	531	0	:	:	333	0
Imports (million EUR)	264	1	1,047	0	156	418	0	389	0	543	136	12	98	6	424
Trade balance (million EUR)	-262	-1	-1,046	0	-155	-417	0	-389	0	-11	-136	:	:	327	-423
Cover ratio (%)	1.0	1.3	0.1	243.4	0.5	0.4	5.7	0.0	0.1	97.9	0.0	:	:	5,239.1	0.1

Source: Eurostat (COMEXT)

Table 2.5

Mining of non-ferrous metal ores, except uranium and thorium ores (NACE Rev. 1 13.2)

Trade related indicators in the EU (1)

	1989	1990	1991	1992	1993	1994	1995	1996	1997	1998	1999
Exports (million EUR)	346	289	207	215	217	195	241	194	234	180	193
Imports (million EUR)	3,648	2,956	2,522	2,438	2,087	2,591	3,059	3,262	3,770	3,432	3,391
Trade balance (million EUR)	-3,301	-2,667	-2,315	-2,222	-1,870	-2,396	-2,818	-3,068	-3,536	-3,252	-3,198
Cover ratio (%)	9.5	9.8	8.2	8.8	10.4	7.5	7.9	6.0	6.2	5.2	5.7

(1) Technically, data before 01/01/1999 are in ECU and after this date in euro. However, as the conversion rate was 1 ECU =1 EUR, for practical purposes the two terms can be used interchangeably.

Table 2.6

Mining of non-ferrous metal ores, except uranium and thorium ores (NACE Rev. 1 13.2)

Production related indicators, 1997

	B	DK	D	EL (1)	E	F (1)	IRL	I (1)	L	NL	A	P	FIN	S	UK
Number of persons employed (thousands)	0.0	0.0	0.0	2.1	1.2	0.7	:	0.3	0.0	:	0.0	:	0.5	:	:
Production (million ECU)	0	0	0	89	88	67	:	6	0	0	0	:	86	:	:
Value added (million ECU)	0	0	0	47	30	24	:	3	0	0	0	:	24	:	:
Gross operating surplus (million ECU)	0.0	0.0	0.0	1.4	0.9	4.8	:	-5.2	0.0	0.0	0.0	:	1.6	:	:

(1) 1996.

Table 2.7

Mining of non-ferrous metal ores, except uranium and thorium ores (NACE Rev. 1 13.2)

Trade related indicators, 1999

	B	DK	D	EL	E	F	IRL	I	L	NL	A	P	FIN	S	UK
Exports (million EUR)	292	0	39	15	66	22	101	21	0	94	1	110	14	145	10
Imports (million EUR)	434	2	826	2	785	392	96	247	0	251	35	3	552	60	285
Trade balance (million EUR)	-142	-1	-787	12	-720	-370	5	-226	0	-157	-34	107	-539	84	-275
Cover ratio (%)	67.3	24.6	4.7	660.8	8.4	5.6	105.7	8.5	8.5	37.4	2.6	3,425.9	2.4	239.8	3.5

Table 2.8

Mining of non-ferrous metal ores, except uranium and thorium ores (NACE Rev. 1 13.2)

Labour related indicators, 1997

	B	DK	D	EL (1)	E	F (1)	IRL	I (1)	L	NL	A	P	FIN	S	UK
Unit personnel costs (thousand ECU per employee)	:	:	:	21.1	24.4	28.9	:	25.6	:	:	:	.	43.4	:	:
Social charges as a share of personnel costs (%)	:	:	:	30.2	28.2	44.1	:	42.9	:	:	:	:	34.1	:	:
Apparent labour productivity (thousand ECU/pers. empl.)	:	:	:	21.8	25.0	36.0	:	9.0	:	:	:	:	44.7	:	:
Wage adjusted labour productivity (%)	:	:	:	103.1	102.4	124.4	:	35.2	:	:	:	:	102.9	:	:
Personnel costs as a share of total operating costs (%)	:	:	:	49.7	30.9	32.1	:	58.3	:	:	:	:	27.7	:	:

(1) 1996.

Source: Eurostat (SBS, EBT, COMEXT)

_____Table 2.9

Quarrying of stone (NACE Rev. 1 14.1)

Production related indicators in the EU (1)

	1989	1990	1991	1992	1993	1994	1995	1996	1997	1998	1999
Number of persons employed (thousands)	:	:	:	:	40.7	37.3	:	:	:	:	:
Production (million ECU)	:	:	:	:	3,065	2,972	:	:	:	:	:
Domestic producer price index (1995=100)	:	:	:	:	:	:	100.0	103.0	104.1	105.3	107.0
Value added (million ECU)	:	:	:	:	1,373	1,374	:	:	:	:	:

(1) Technically, data before 01/01/1999 are in ECU and after this date in euro. However, as the conversion rate was 1 ECU =1 EUR, for practical purposes the two terms can be used interchangeably.

_____Table 2.10

Quarrying of stone (NACE Rev. 1 14.1)

Trade related indicators in the EU (1)

	1989	1990	1991	1992	1993	1994	1995	1996	1997	1998	1999
Exports (million EUR)	216	185	212	208	238	263	252	312	417	383	393
Imports (million EUR)	343	358	386	374	416	448	496	513	592	622	643
Trade balance (million EUR)	-127	-173	-174	-166	-178	-185	-244	-202	-175	-239	-250
Cover ratio (%)	62.9	51.7	54.9	55.6	57.1	58.7	50.8	60.7	70.4	61.6	61.1

(1) Technically, data before 01/01/1999 are in ECU and after this date in euro. However, as the conversion rate was 1 ECU =1 EUR, for practical purposes the two terms can be used interchangeably.

_____Table 2.11

Quarrying of stone (NACE Rev. 1 14.1)

Production related indicators, 1997

	B	DK	D	EL (1)	E	F	IRL	I (1)	L	NL	A	P	FIN	S	UK
Number of persons employed (thousands)	1.8	:	1.3	0.8	7.6	3.8	:	4.1	:	:	:	9.5	1.1	:	3.3
Production (million ECU)	263	:	195	34	592	491	:	339	:	0	:	522	163	:	440
Value added (million ECU)	122	:	105	20	248	181	:	155	:	0	:	191	70	:	171
Gross operating surplus (million ECU)	61.0	:	56.5	7.2	112.5	52.3	:	40.0	:	0.0	:	95.5	38.0	:	92.4

(1) 1996.

_____Table 2.12

Quarrying of stone (NACE Rev. 1 14.1)

Trade related indicators, 1999

	B	DK	D	EL	E	F	IRL	I	L	NL	A	P	FIN	S	UK
Exports (million EUR)	128	14	29	21	223	82	5	194	1	16	8	40	33	40	29
Imports (million EUR)	88	24	132	13	117	107	10	406	10	98	15	13	34	27	92
Trade balance (million EUR)	40	-11	-103	8	107	-25	-5	-212	-9	-82	-6	27	-1	13	-62
Cover ratio (%)	146.2	55.5	22.0	162.4	191.7	77.1	46.0	47.7	12.8	16.3	57.5	306.6	97.1	148.5	32.0

_____Table 2.13

Quarrying of stone (NACE Rev. 1 14.1)

Labour related indicators, 1997

	B	DK	D	EL (1)	E	F	IRL	I (1)	L	NL	A	P	FIN	S	UK
Unit personnel costs (thousand ECU per employee)	36.9	:	37.2	16.8	19.0	33.9	:	28.9	:	:	:	10.7	30.6	:	24.3
Social charges as a share of personnel costs (%)	42.2	:	24.7	29.2	31.1	44.7	:	63.9	:	:	:	31.9	29.0	:	15.4
Apparent labour productivity (thousand ECU/pers. empl.)	69.6	:	79.7	23.1	32.7	47.7	:	37.3	:	:	:	20.2	63.0	:	51.8
Wage adjusted labour productivity (%)	188.4	:	213.9	138.1	172.0	140.7	:	129.4	:	:	:	188.5	205.9	:	213.3
Personnel costs as a share of total operating costs (%)	31.2	:	26.2	45.1	27.4	29.2	:	38.3	:	:	:	22.2	25.0	:	20.0

(1) 1996.

Source: Eurostat (SBS, EBT, COMEXT)

Table 2.14

Quarrying of sand and clay (NACE Rev. 1 14.2)

Production related indicators in the EU (1)

	1989	1990	1991	1992	1993	1994	1995	1996	1997	1998	1999
Number of persons employed (thousands)	:	:	:	:	80.6	83.1	:	:	:	:	:
Production (million ECU)	:	:	:	:	9,998	11,349	:	:	:	:	:
Domestic producer price index (1995=100)	:	:	:	:	:	:	100.0	101.8	103.0	104.1	105.3
Value added (million ECU)	:	:	:	:	4,050	4,478	:	:	:	:	:

(1) Technically, data before 01/01/1999 are in ECU and after this date in euro. However, as the conversion rate was 1 ECU =1 EUR, for practical purposes the two terms can be used interchangeably.

Table 2.15

Quarrying of sand and clay (NACE Rev. 1 14.2)

Trade related indicators in the EU (1)

	1989	1990	1991	1992	1993	1994	1995	1996	1997	1998	1999
Exports (million EUR)	97	102	104	113	127	146	134	138	162	173	171
Imports (million EUR)	279	274	286	313	332	382	347	363	444	500	527
Trade balance (million EUR)	-182	-172	-182	-200	-205	-236	-213	-225	-282	-327	-355
Cover ratio (%)	34.7	37.2	36.2	36.1	38.3	38.2	38.5	38.0	36.4	34.6	32.6

(1) Technically, data before 01/01/1999 are in ECU and after this date in euro. However, as the conversion rate was 1 ECU =1 EUR, for practical purposes the two terms can be used interchangeably.

Table 2.16

Quarrying of sand and clay (NACE Rev. 1 14.2)

Production related indicators, 1997

	B	DK	D	EL (1)	E	F	IRL	I (1)	L	NL	A	P	FIN	S	UK
Number of persons employed (thousands)	2.0	0.3	22.4	1.3	7.4	15.3	:	4.2	:	:	2.1	4.2	1.2	1.4	20.8
Production (million ECU)	429	48	2,998	98	704	2,312	:	598	:	177	276	303	145	252	3,291
Value added (million ECU)	176	20	1,385	47	259	855	:	245	:	68	140	106	56	85	1,515
Gross operating surplus (million ECU)	95.5	8.8	530.5	20.9	120.3	358.2	:	128.8	:	39.0	62.6	63.7	28.6	36.3	919.7

(1) 1996.

Table 2.17

Quarrying of sand and clay (NACE Rev. 1 14.2)

Trade related indicators, 1999

	B	DK	D	EL	E	F	IRL	I	L	NL	A	P	FIN	S	UK
Exports (million EUR)	45	2	158	2	22	79	0	24	0	76	2	2	3	4	375
Imports (million EUR)	88	11	158	7	72	91	4	243	3	100	41	17	165	94	69
Trade balance (million EUR)	-42	-9	1	-5	-51	-12	-4	-219	-3	-24	-40	-16	-162	-90	306
Cover ratio (%)	51.6	15.0	100.4	22.0	30.0	86.7	1.0	10.0	11.6	75.8	3.7	10.8	1.9	4.6	544.5

Table 2.18

Quarrying of sand and clay (NACE Rev. 1 14.2)

Labour related indicators, 1997

	B	DK (1)	D	EL (2)	E	F	IRL	I (2)	L	NL	A	P	FIN	S	UK
Unit personnel costs (thousand ECU per employee)	40.7	32.7	38.6	20.1	19.9	32.5	:	29.0	:	:	37.0	10.7	26.9	34.1	28.8
Social charges as a share of personnel costs (%)	40.0	3.6	25.2	27.4	28.9	46.0	:	58.0	:	20.7	31.2	32.3	30.7	37.3	14.1
Apparent labour productivity (thousand ECU/pers. empl.)	88.7	63.9	61.8	36.3	35.2	55.9	:	57.7	:	:	66.3	25.3	47.0	59.4	73.0
Wage adjusted labour productivity (%)	218.3	169.3	160.2	180.6	176.6	172.1	:	198.9	:	:	179.2	235.9	174.5	174.1	253.1
Personnel costs as a share of total operating costs (%)	24.8	29.3	32.3	33.0	23.1	24.9	:	24.8	:	19.2	33.7	17.5	23.1	22.2	24.4

(1) Unit personnel costs and wage adjusted labour productivity, 1996; (2) 1996.

Source: Eurostat (SBS, EBT, COMEXT)

eurostat

_____Table 2.19

Mining of chemical and fertilizer minerals (NACE Rev. 1 14.3)

Production related indicators in the EU

	1989	1990	1991	1992	1993	1994	1995	1996	1997	1998	1999
Number of persons employed (thousands)	:	:	:	:	15.6	16.4	:	:	:	:	:
Production (million ECU)	:	:	:	:	1,231	1,541	:	:	:	:	:
Domestic producer price index (1995=100)	:	:	:	:	:	:	100.0	103.7	105.1	:	:
Value added (million ECU)	:	:	:	:	528	671	:	:	:	:	:

_____Table 2.20

Mining of chemical and fertilizer minerals (NACE Rev. 1 14.3)

Trade related indicators in the EU (1)

	1989	1990	1991	1992	1993	1994	1995	1996	1997	1998	1999
Exports (million EUR)	128	123	106	103	102	115	138	136	172	158	165
Imports (million EUR)	1,116	891	793	581	451	500	535	536	662	687	681
Trade balance (million EUR)	-988	-768	-687	-478	-349	-384	-397	-400	-490	-529	-515
Cover ratio (%)	11.4	13.8	13.4	17.7	22.7	23.1	25.8	25.4	26.0	23.0	24.3

(1) Technically, data before 01/01/1999 are in ECU and after this date in euro. However, as the conversion rate was 1 ECU =1 EUR, for practical purposes the two terms can be used interchangeably.

_____Table 2.21

Mining of chemical and fertilizer minerals (NACE Rev. 1 14.3)

Production related indicators, 1997

	B	DK	D	EL (1)	E	F	IRL	I	L	NL	A	P (1)	FIN	S (1)	UK
Number of persons employed (thousands)	:	0.0	0.4	0.0	1.5	2.5	0.0	:	0.0	:	:	0.0	0.0	0.0	1.3
Production (million ECU)	:	0	41	0	162	141	0	:	0	0	:	1	0	0	215
Value added (million ECU)	:	0	16	0	59	69	0	:	0	0	:	0	0	0	89
Gross operating surplus (million ECU)	:	0.0	-1.0	0.0	5.2	-79.3	0.0	:	0.0	0.0	:	0.2	0.0	0.0	33.6

(1) 1996.

_____Table 2.22

Mining of chemical and fertilizer minerals (NACE Rev. 1 14.3)

Trade related indicators, 1999

	B	DK	D	EL	E	F	IRL	I	L	NL	A	P	FIN	S	UK
Exports (million EUR)	55	1	184	2	82	23	0	31	0	108	8	1	11	4	26
Imports (million EUR)	158	10	121	31	143	150	4	90	5	121	35	15	10	38	39
Trade balance (million EUR)	-103	-9	63	-29	-61	-127	-4	-60	-5	-12	-27	-14	1	-35	-13
Cover ratio (%)	34.6	7.1	152.0	6.3	57.1	15.4	1.4	33.9	4.6	90.0	23.6	6.4	114.2	9.7	66.1

_____Table 2.23

Mining of chemical and fertilizer minerals (NACE Rev. 1 14.3)

Labour related indicators, 1997

	B	DK	D	EL	E	F	IRL	I	L	NL	A	P (1)	FIN	S	UK
Unit personnel costs (thousand ECU per employee)	:	:	43.3	:	33.7	58.6	:	:	:	:	:	3.9	:	:	41.5
Social charges as a share of personnel costs (%)	:	:	38.0	:	27.0	50.8	:	:	:	:	:	0.0	:	:	12.3
Apparent labour productivity (thousand ECU/pers. empl.)	:	:	40.7	:	38.5	27.3	:	:	:	:	:	10.5	:	:	66.6
Wage adjusted labour productivity (%)	:	:	93.9	:	114.3	46.5	:	:	:	:	:	270.4	:	:	160.5
Personnel costs as a share of total operating costs (%)	:	:	34.5	:	31.7	58.5	:	:	:	:	:	20.0	:	:	27.1

(1) 1996.

Source: Eurostat (SBS, EBT, COMEXT)

Table 2.24

Production of salt (NACE Rev. 1 14.4)

Production related indicators in the EU (1)

	1989	1990	1991	1992	1993	1994	1995	1996	1997	1998	1999
Number of persons employed (thousands)	:	:	:	:	8.5	7.6	:	:	:	:	:
Production (million ECU)	:	:	:	:	935	913	:	:	:	:	:
Domestic producer price index (1995=100)	:	:	:	:	:	:	:	:	:	101.3	100.5
Value added (million ECU)	:	:	:	:	413	389	:	:	:	:	:

(1) Technically, data before 01/01/1999 are in ECU and after this date in euro. However, as the conversion rate was 1 ECU =1 EUR, for practical purposes the two terms can be used interchangeably.

Table 2.25

Production of salt (NACE Rev. 1 14.4)

Trade related indicators in the EU (1)

	1989	1990	1991	1992	1993	1994	1995	1996	1997	1998	1999
Exports (million EUR)	36	34	46	78	78	78	60	62	66	73	80
Imports (million EUR)	20	19	14	14	19	21	23	20	25	24	26
Trade balance (million EUR)	16	15	32	64	59	56	37	42	41	48	53
Cover ratio (%)	177.5	181.5	323.0	554.6	412.3	362.9	257.6	306.1	264.8	296.8	302.1

(1) Technically, data before 01/01/1999 are in ECU and after this date in euro. However, as the conversion rate was 1 ECU =1 EUR, for practical purposes the two terms can be used interchangeably.

Table 2.26

Production of salt (NACE Rev. 1 14.4)

Production related indicators, 1997

	B	DK	D	EL (1)	E	F	IRL	I	L	NL	A	P	FIN	S	UK
Number of persons employed (thousands)	0.0	:	1.9	0.4	0.7	1.5	0.0	:	0.0	:	:	0.5	0.0	0.0	:
Production (million ECU)	0	:	272	22	93	110	0	:	0	:	:	18	0	0	:
Value added (million ECU)	0	:	127	8	41	67	0	:	0	:	:	6	0	0	:
Gross operating surplus (million ECU)	0.0	:	34.7	1.3	21.4	30.1	0.0	:	0.0	:	:	1.3	0.0	0.0	:

(1) 1996.

Table 2.27

Production of salt (NACE Rev. 1 14.4)

Trade related indicators, 1999

	B	DK	D	EL	E	F	IRL	I	L	NL	A	P	FIN	S	UK
Exports (million EUR)	5	16	85	2	19	43	0	10	0	113	13	1	1	1	35
Imports (million EUR)	53	16	61	5	4	36	10	29	3	19	10	5	14	43	18
Trade balance (million EUR)	-48	0	24	-3	14	7	-10	-18	-3	95	3	-4	-13	-42	18
Cover ratio (%)	9.6	102.9	139.6	45.9	446.8	119.3	0.3	36.0	1.0	605.2	131.3	12.2	3.8	3.0	200.2

Table 2.28

Production of salt (NACE Rev. 1 14.4)

Labour related indicators, 1997

	B	DK	D	EL (1)	E	F	IRL	I	L	NL	A	P	FIN	S	UK
Unit personnel costs (thousand ECU per employee)	:	:	49.2	16.8	25.5	23.7	:	:	:	:	:	11.0	:	:	:
Social charges as a share of personnel costs (%)	:	:	31.9	26.4	30.6	49.8	:	:	:	:	:	28.2	:	:	:
Apparent labour productivity (thousand ECU/pers. empl.)	:	:	67.7	19.6	54.4	43.2	:	:	:	:	:	13.0	:	:	:
Wage adjusted labour productivity (%)	:	:	137.7	117.1	213.6	182.1	:	:	:	:	:	118.1	:	:	:
Personnel costs as a share of total operating costs (%)	:	:	28.8	27.6	22.6	40.3	:	:	:	:	:	11.1	:	:	:

(1) 1996.

Source: Eurostat (SBS, EBT, COMEXT)

_____Table 2.29

Other mining and quarrying (NACE Rev. 1 14.5)

Production related indicators in the EU

	1989	1990	1991	1992	1993	1994	1995	1996	1997	1998	1999
Number of persons employed (thousands)	:	:	:	:	6.4	6.5	:	:	:	:	:
Production (million ECU)	:	:	:	:	690	844	:	:	:	:	:
Domestic producer price index (1995=100)	:	:	:	:	:	:	:	:	:	:	:
Value added (million ECU)	:	:	:	:	325	364	:	:	:	:	:

_____Table 2.30

Other mining and quarrying (NACE Rev. 1 14.5)

Trade related indicators in the EU (1)

	1989	1990	1991	1992	1993	1994	1995	1996	1997	1998	1999
Exports (million EUR)	4,654	3,922	3,896	3,882	4,991	5,428	5,621	6,222	7,014	5,760	7,954
Imports (million EUR)	2,713	2,381	2,199	2,180	5,591	5,926	6,264	6,801	7,836	7,043	9,533
Trade balance (million EUR)	1,940	1,541	1,696	1,702	-600	-498	-643	-579	-822	-1,283	-1,579
Cover ratio (%)	171.5	164.7	177.1	178.1	89.3	91.6	89.7	91.5	89.5	81.8	83.4

(1) Technically, data before 01/01/1999 are in ECU and after this date in euro. However, as the conversion rate was 1 ECU =1 EUR, for practical purposes the two terms can be used interchangeably.

_____Table 2.31

Other mining and quarrying (NACE Rev. 1 14.5)

Production related indicators, 1997

	B	DK	D	EL (1)	E	F	IRL	I (1)	L	NL	A	P (1)	FIN	S	UK
Number of persons employed (thousands)	:	:	0.5	1.2	1.2	0.8	:	2.0	0.0	:	0.3	0.3	0.2	:	0.7
Production (million ECU)	:	:	80	79	300	113	:	251	0	:	41	10	68	:	25
Value added (million ECU)	:	:	37	39	61	48	:	112	0	:	20	4	21	:	6
Gross operating surplus (million ECU)	:	:	15.4	16.1	30.7	15.3	:	50.9	0.0	:	6.7	0.8	14.1	:	-0.4

(1) 1996.

_____Table 2.32

Other mining and quarrying (NACE Rev. 1 14.5)

Trade related indicators, 1999

	B	DK	D	EL	E	F	IRL	I	L	NL	A	P	FIN	S	UK
Exports (million EUR)	6,446	18	84	58	53	87	39	54	1	90	51	4	36	13	4,304
Imports (million EUR)	6,633	51	243	5	83	96	16	201	3	118	73	48	8	30	5,553
Trade balance (million EUR)	-187	-34	-158	53	-30	-9	23	-147	-1	-28	-22	-45	28	-17	-1,249
Cover ratio (%)	97.2	34.6	34.8	1,270.1	64.1	90.7	248.1	27.1	48.3	76.5	70.0	7.5	472.2	43.6	77.5

_____Table 2.33

Other mining and quarrying (NACE Rev. 1 14.5)

Labour related indicators, 1997

	B	DK	D	EL (1)	E	F	IRL	I (1)	L	NL	A	P (1)	FIN	S	UK
Unit personnel costs (thousand ECU per employee)	:	:	39.7	19.1	24.4	41.7	:	32.5	:	:	44.8	8.9	39.9	:	13.2
Social charges as a share of personnel costs (%)	:	:	26.0	26.8	28.2	47.7	:	60.3	:	:	35.6	31.8	28.1	:	46.8
Apparent labour productivity (thousand ECU/pers. empl.)	:	:	67.9	32.7	50.4	61.4	:	56.9	:	:	66.8	11.4	116.8	:	8.8
Wage adjusted labour productivity (%)	:	:	171.1	171.4	207.0	147.3	:	174.8	:	:	149.2	127.7	292.6	:	66.9
Personnel costs as a share of total operating costs (%)	:	:	25.4	34.5	10.7	34.2	:	27.5	:	:	37.7	30.2	14.1	:	22.5

(1) 1996.

Source: Eurostat (SBS, EBT, COMEXT)

Food, drink and tobacco (NACE Rev. 1 15 and 16)

This chapter includes information on the manufacture of food products, beverages and tobacco, which is broken down into two Divisions within the NACE Rev. 1 activity classification: the manufacture of food products and beverages (NACE Rev. 1 Division 15) and the manufacture of tobacco products (NACE Rev. 1 Division 16). Food and beverages can be further subdivided into nine Groups covering meat, fish, fruit and vegetables, oils and fats, dairy products and beverages (all of which are classified as individual NACE Rev. 1 Groups). For the purpose of this chapter grain mill products, starches and starch products, prepared animal feeds and other food products (NACE Rev. 1 Groups 15.6 to 15.8) are analysed together in sub-chapter 3.8.

Food, beverages and tobacco the largest manufacturing activity in the EU

In 1996, food, beverages and tobacco accounted for a 16.2% share of manufacturing activity in the EU in terms of production value, totalling 570.9 billion ECU. Using Sub-sections within the NACE classification (of which there are 14 in manufacturing), food, beverages and tobacco had the largest share of manufacturing output in the EU, preceding transport equipment by 3.6 percentage points. In terms of value added (122.7 billion ECU in 1996), this industry accounted for a considerably lower share of the EU manufacturing total, 11.4%.

Food and beverages (NACE Rev. 1 15) dominate the data presented in this chapter, no matter which measure of size is used (production or value added). Based on estimated data the tobacco industry (NACE Rev. 1 16) accounted for between 7% and 8% of the production total for activities presented in this chapter, whilst beverages (NACE Rev. 1 15.9) accounted for almost 15% of the total. However, it was within the food industry that the largest activities were found.

---Figure 3.1

**Food, beverages and tobacco
(NACE Rev. 1 15 and 16)
Share of total manufacturing value added
in the EU, 1995 (%)**

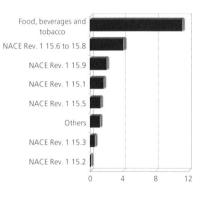

Source: Eurostat (SBS)

The most important sub-chapter was grain mill products, starches and starch products, the manufacture of prepared animal feeds and the manufacture of other food products (NACE Rev. 1 15.6 to 15.8), which together accounted for 31.6%[1] of output within food, beverages and tobacco (other food products alone accounted for 22.0%[2]). Production, processing and preserving of meat and meat products had a 17.6[3] share of production amongst the industries covered in this chapter, and was closely followed by the manufacture of dairy products (15.0%[4]).

---

(1) IRL, L, A and S, no data available.
(2) IRL, no data available.
(3) L, no data available.
(4) L, no data available.

The activities covered in this chapter (in terms of NACE Rev. 1) include:

15:    manufacture of food products and beverages;
15.1: production, processing and preserving of meat and meat products;
15.2: processing and preserving of fish and fish products;
15.3: processing and preserving of fruit and vegetables;
15.4: manufacture of vegetable and animal oils and fats;
15.5: manufacture of dairy products;
15.6: manufacture of grain mill products, starches and starch products;
15.7: manufacture of prepared animal feeds;
15.8: manufacture of other food products;
15.9: manufacture of beverages;
16:    manufacture of tobacco products.

Box 3.1

There are a few large multi-nationals which play a significant role in the performance of this industry. The largest company in the food, beverages and tobacco industry in early 2000 in terms of market capitalisation was Coca-Cola (USA), followed by Nestle (CH), Philip Morris (USA) and Unilever (UK/NL).

The largest EU company, Unilever, produces a vast array of products, which may be divided into two main categories, food and home and personal care, both accounting for around 50% of sales. In 1999, Unilever estimated sales reached 37.2 billion EUR, whilst 267 thousand persons were employed in 1998.

Another large European company was the Danone Group (FR). It is the largest producer of fresh dairy products in the world and also produces grocery products, pasta, biscuits, sweets, savoury snacks, sauces and condiments, beer and mineral water. Estimated worldwide sales in 1999 reached 12.0 billion EUR, whilst almost 79 thousand persons were employed in 1998.

The largest tobacco manufacturer with headquarters in the EU (UK) was British American Tobacco, an international cigarette manufacturer with processing operations in over 50 countries. Worldwide sales in 1999 were estimated at 12.5 billion EUR, with an employment figure of over 100 thousand in 1998.

Figure 3.2

Share of food, beverages and tobacco in total household consumption in the EU (%)

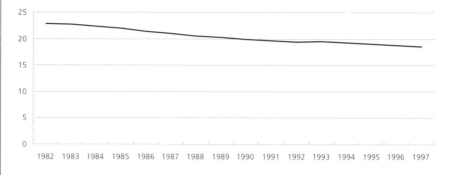

Source: Eurostat (SEC2)

Table 3.1

Food, beverages and tobacco (NACE Rev. 1 15 and 16)

Breakdown of turnover and employment by employment size class, 1996 (%)

	Micro (0-9)		Small (10-49)		Medium (50-249)		Large (250+)	
	Turnover (1)	Employment (2)	Turnover (1)	Employment (2)	Turnover (1)	Employment (2)	Turnover (1)	Employment (2)
EU-15	7.8	21.6	14.0	19.8	23.5	18.3	54.6	40.3
B	11.0	29.3	19.4	20.1	25.3	17.7	44.2	32.9
DK	:	:	:	:	14.6	16.4	:	:
D	4.3	18.8	10.1	23.9	18.3	17.0	67.4	40.3
EL	:	:	:	:	:	:	:	:
E	12.9	22.7	:	26.5	26.3	22.4	:	28.4
F	:	30.7	:	18.9	:	18.4	:	32.1
IRL	:	:	:	:	:	:	:	:
I	:	38.6	26.2	22.6	24.6	17.4	34.7	21.4
L	:	:	:	:	:	:	:	:
NL	:	12.6	:	11.7	:	:	:	:
A	:	:	:	:	:	:	:	:
P	:	:	:	:	:	:	:	:
FIN	:	:	:	:	:	:	:	:
S	:	:	:	:	:	:	:	:
UK	4.2	5.3	7.1	8.5	14.0	:	74.7	:

(1) B and D, 1997.
(2) B, D and E, 1997.

Source: Eurostat (SME)

STRUCTURE AND PERFORMANCE

In absolute terms, during the ten-year period 1986 to 1996, EU production value increased from 374.3 billion ECU to 570.9 billion ECU, a nominal gain of 52.5%, somewhat below the manufacturing average of 60.5%. The annual average growth rate of production in constant prices between 1991 and 1996 was equal to just 0.8% per annum for food, beverages and tobacco, which was 0.7 percentage points lower than the equivalent figure for total manufacturing. As the standard of living in Europe increases, it is normal to find relative expenditure on basic commodities such as food, beverages and tobacco remaining stable or falling.

Large expansion in 1991, followed
by more moderate growth

The annual average growth rates given above hide the most significant period of growth in recent years, which was registered in 1991, when EU production value rose by 7.2% in real terms, whilst value added rose by 8.9% (also in real terms). After the rapid growth of 1991, this industry was subsequently characterised by more moderate growth rates of between -3.3% and 4.7%.

Denmark and Greece record more than a quarter of
their national manufacturing output in this sector

The production share of the four largest Member States in the Union accounted for 65.9% of the food, beverages and tobacco industry in 1996, which was well below their corresponding share in total manufacturing output (72.2%). This may in part be explained by the fact that the food industry often processes fresh products with a relatively low value, which often remain within national markets. Furthermore, regional preferences for national dishes and products reinforce local production (although there is a trend towards exporting high value speciality products to other countries, aided by the opening up of the Single Market).

In Denmark (1997), no less than 28.6% of total manufacturing output was generated by the food, beverages and tobacco industry. In Greece (1996) this industry accounted for 27.0% of domestic manufacturing output. The lowest share was reported in Luxembourg (1997), where food, beverages and tobacco contributed just 8.6% to the national manufacturing total. Sweden (1997) was next lowest with a 10.2% share of national manufacturing production.

Box 3.2

In 1997, food, beverages and tobacco (National Accounts data) accounted for 18.6% of EU household consumption (measured in constant PPS). This was 1.2 percentage points less than the equivalent share in Japan, but 7.1 percentage points more than in the USA.

The share of food, beverages and tobacco in total household consumption has been gradually declining since 1970 (when individual Member State series begin). In 1985, food, beverages and tobacco accounted for the highest share of household consumption in the EU, at 22.0%, followed by gross rent, fuel and power (18.5%) and transport and communications (14.4%). By 1997, the share of food, beverages and tobacco had fallen by 3.4 percentage points to 18.6%, and was now very closely followed by gross rent, fuel and power (18.3%).

The Member States where food, beverages and tobacco accounted for the highest share of total household consumption were Greece (35.3%), Portugal (29.7%), and Ireland (29.2%). The lowest shares were found in Germany (15.6%) and the Netherlands (14.7%).

Figure 3.3

Food, beverages and tobacco (NACE Rev. 1 15 and 16)

EU production and value-added in constant prices and employment compared to total manufacturing (1990=100)

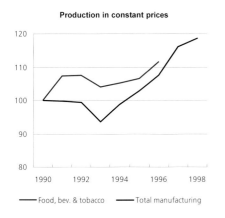

Production in constant prices

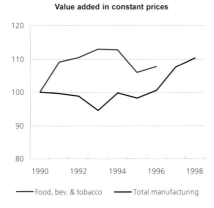

Value added in constant prices

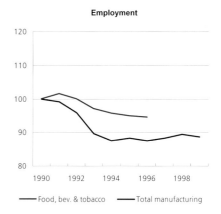

Employment

Source: Eurostat (SBS)

LABOUR AND PRODUCTIVITY

The number of persons employed in the EU in the food, beverages and tobacco industry went down from 2.7 million to 2.6 million between 1986 and 1996, an overall reduction of 2.7%. This industry accounted for 11.5% of the European manufacturing workforce in 1996.

Job losses were at a slower pace than in manufacturing as a whole

The decline in European employment within the food, beverages and tobacco industry was at a relatively slow pace when compared to the performance of total manufacturing (where a nominal decline of 10.0% was registered between 1986 and 1996). Employment fell in each year between 1991 and 1996 in the EU. Between 1991 and 1996, the annual average decline in the number of persons employed in the EU was equal to 1.4% per annum for food, beverages and tobacco, against 2.4% in total manufacturing.

Labour force lowly-skilled

The food, beverages and tobacco industry is generally considered a mature, low-tech industry. This is reflected in the average skill level of the labour force. In 1997, just 11.0% of those employed in the food, beverages and tobacco industry had completed a higher education degree, whilst as many as 44.7% had a primary or lower secondary education.

The food, beverages and tobacco industry was also characterised by the fact that in 1998 most Member States reported a higher reliance on temporary work contracts. In the EU some 12.0% of those employed did not possess a permanent contract. This may be due to the seasonal nature of some food processing industries, whereby production may be correlated with harvest periods. Female participation in this industry was generally higher than national manufacturing averages. In the EU as a whole, women accounted for 37.7% of the total number of persons employed in food, beverages and tobacco in 1998.

Low skills matched by low unit personnel costs

With a generally low skill level, it was not surprising to find that unit personnel costs were also below the manufacturing average within the food, beverages and tobacco industry. Eurostat estimate that unit personnel costs were equal to 26.9 thousand ECU per employee within the food, beverages and tobacco industry in 1997, whilst the corresponding figure for total manufacturing was 33.7 thousand ECU per employee.

Nevertheless, total personnel costs rose by 49.6% in nominal terms during the period 1986-1996, whilst in total manufacturing the equivalent nominal growth rate was 44.0%. Food, beverages and tobacco processing is in many cases reliant on a fairly high degree of automation. This may be seen when looking at the share of personnel costs in production value, which stood at just 12.6% in 1996 in the EU (well below the equivalent figure for total manufacturing of 21.0%).

Table 3.2

Food, beverages and tobacco
(NACE Rev. 1 15 and 16)
Composition of the labour force, 1999 (%)

	Women (1)	Part-time (2)	Highly-educated (3)
EU-15	37.7	12.0	11.0
B	25.5	8.0	17.3
DK	37.6	20.1	9.6
D	49.1	19.7	14.6
EL	33.7	2.9	10.7
E	31.6	3.3	14.0
F	39.7	11.0	10.5
IRL	27.5	7.2	19.6
I	31.8	4.9	2.9
L	36.8	:	:
NL	35.5	25.5	14.6
A	31.0	11.4	3.5
P	46.0	5.8	4.5
FIN	58.2	9.1	16.2
S	29.6	13.3	:
UK	33.0	12.2	12.1

(1) EU-15 and EL, 1998.
(2) EU-15, B and EL, 1998.
(3) EL, 1998; EU-15, IRL, P and UK, 1997.

Source: Eurostat (LFS)

Apparent labour productivity for food, beverages and tobacco was almost identical to the EU manufacturing average in 1996 (46.5 thousand ECU per head compared to 46.3 thousand ECU). Whilst apparent labour productivity figures were roughly comparable, the same was not true once the relatively low unit personnel costs were taken into account. Eurostat estimate that wage adjusted labour productivity for the food, beverages and tobacco industry reached 170.7% in 1996.

Figure 3.4

Food, beverages and tobacco (NACE Rev. 1 15 and 16)
Apparent labour productivity and unit personnel costs, 1997 (thousand ECU)

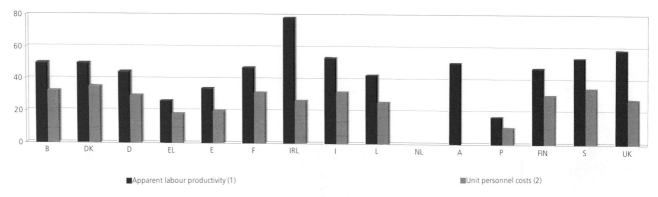

■ Apparent labour productivity (1)   ■ Unit personnel costs (2)

(1) EL, I and A, 1996; NL, not available.
(2) DK, EL and I, 1996; NL and A, not available.

Source: Eurostat (SBS)

INTERNATIONAL TRENDS AND FOREIGN TRADE

The EU was the largest producer in the Triad, with production value more than 100 billion ECU higher than in the USA (457.6 billion ECU in 1997) and more than 300 billion ECU higher than in Japan (258.6 billion ECU in 1997). The USA however, generated more value added than the EU (195.0 billion ECU in 1997 versus 122.7 billion ECU in the EU in 1996), whilst Japan followed with 89.2 billion ECU (1996).

The distribution of the number of persons employed across the Triad closely followed that of production. In 1996, 48.7% of the total number of persons employed in the Triad were working in the EU. The USA accounted for 28.4% of persons employed, whilst generating 32.2% of Triad output and 43.2% of Triad value added.

EU runs a positive trade balance

In 1999, the trade balance for the EU food, beverages and tobacco industry was positive. Extra-EU exports reached 38.4 billion EUR, which was 6.6 billion EUR more than imports originating from non-Community countries. The EU was the largest exporter within the Triad, accounting for 56.9% of total Triad exports in 1998. The EU was also the largest importer, with a 36.2% share of total Triad imports. Japan ran a large trade deficit, 26.6 billion ECU in 1998.

The share of extra-EU exports in the manufacturing total went down from 7.2% in 1989 to 5.4% in 1999 and the share of imports from 7.2% to 5.0%. Intra-EU trade accounted for 73.5% of total imports in the EU in 1999.

Box 3.3

In 1997, the EU held 46.8 billion ECU of stocks of foreign direct investment (FDI) in the food industry in third countries outside the EU, of which 39.7% was in the USA. EU enterprises had a fairly outward orientation to non-Community markets, as intra-EU stocks of EU enterprises were equal to 42.0 billion ECU in 1997.

Non-EU countries had FDI stocks equal to 23.3 billion ECU in 1997 within the EU, of which more than half (52.2%) was held by American enterprises. As such European enterprises were more active in the food industry in terms of investment abroad than foreign competitors were within the EU.

_____Figure 3.5

Food, beverages and tobacco (NACE Rev. 1 15 and 16)

International comparison of production, value added and employment

Production (million ECU) (1)	Value added (million ECU) (2)	Employment (units) (2)

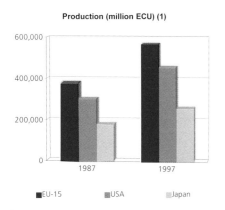

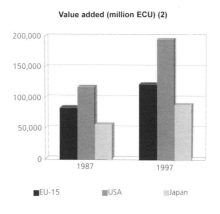

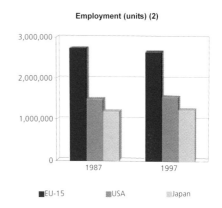

(1) EU-15, 1996.
(2) EU-15 and JAP, 1996.

Source: Eurostat (SBS)

_____Figure 3.6

Food, beverages and tobacco (NACE Rev. 1 15 and 16)

Destination of EU exports, 1999 (%)

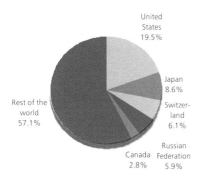

Source: Eurostat (COMEXT)

_____Figure 3.7

Food, beverages and tobacco (NACE Rev. 1 15 and 16)

Origin of EU imports, 1999 (%)

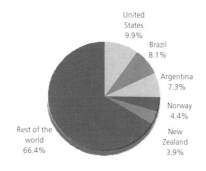

Source: Eurostat (COMEXT)

SUB-CHAPTER 3.1
MEAT (NACE Rev. 1 15.1)

This Group of the NACE classification consists of three Classes. The data presented cover the production of fresh, chilled or frozen meat, in carcasses and in cuts, the production of hides and skins, rendering of edible fats of animal origin, the processing of animal offal, the production of feathers and down, the production of dried, salted or smoked meat, as well as the production of prepared meat dishes. The data does not cover the wholesale trade activities of packaging meat and poultry meat (see chapter 16).

Eurostat estimate that the meat industry accounted for 104.3 billion EUR of production value in 1999, whilst generating 18.7 billion EUR of value added and employing 571 thousand persons. The meat industry produced 2.6% of total manufacturing output in the EU in 1999, with an employment share of 2.4% and a value added share of 1.6% in 1997. In terms of its importance to the food and beverages (NACE Rev. 1 15) sector as a whole, the meat industry was, in 1999, responsible for 19.9%[5] of production.

Denmark specialised in meat production

In absolute terms, France had the highest share of output in 1997, 22.7% of total EU production, followed by Germany with 17.4% and the United Kingdom with 14.0%. In relative terms however, the meat industry was of much more importance to Denmark, where it accounted for 9.7% of total manufacturing activity (and hence a production specialisation ratio of 342.6%, in other words almost three and half times the average of all Member States). Ireland (201.3%) and the Netherlands (167.4%) were also relatively specialised in the production and processing of meat in 1997.

In these three countries the share of meat production in total manufacturing output decreased during the ten-year period 1987 to 1997. In Denmark the share was down by 2.0 percentage points, in Ireland by 4.3 points and in the Netherlands by just 0.1 points.

(5) L, no data available.

Figure 3.8

Meat (NACE Rev. 1 15.1)

Production and export specialisation (%)

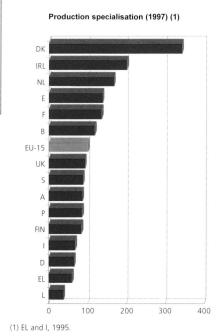

Production specialisation (1997) (1)

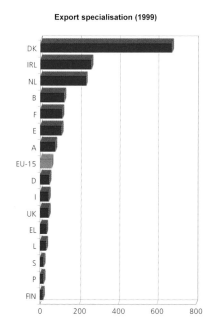

Export specialisation (1999)

(1) EL and I, 1995.

Source: Eurostat (SBS, COMEXT)

Box 3.4

Total meat production in the EU in 1999 reached 36,046 billion tonnes. This was an increase of 9.3% compared with 1990. Almost half of the total meat production (49.6%) in 1999 consisted of pork. Poultry accounted for 23.5% and beef and veal for 21.1%. During the nineties a shift away from red meat could be observed. Compared with 1990, beef and veal lost 6.0 percentage points. In the same period, pork gained 2.7 points and poultry 3.8 points.

Table 3.3

Breakdown of meat production in the EU (%)

	1990	1991	1992	1993	1994	1995	1996	1997	1998	1999
Beef and veal	27.1	28.2	26.6	24.4	23.3	23.4	22.8	22.7	21.5	21.1
Pig meat	46.9	45.3	45.8	47.7	47.9	47.1	47.3	47.2	48.9	49.6
Poultry meat	19.7	20.2	21.3	21.6	22.7	23.2	23.7	24.1	23.8	23.5
Sheep and goat meat	3.7	3.7	3.6	3.6	3.5	3.5	3.4	3.2	3.1	3.2
Others	2.5	2.5	2.6	2.6	2.6	2.8	2.8	2.8	2.7	2.7

Source: FAO

STRUCTURE AND PERFORMANCE

Between 1989 and 1999 the meat industry reported a nominal production increase of 30.2%, which was 13.1 percentage points less than the equivalent figure for total manufacturing. After a large expansion of production in 1991 (9.6% in real terms), the recession led to a slowdown in output growth in 1992 and 1993. Between 1993 and 1998 the industry followed a path of moderate expansion, with an average annual growth rate of 1.9%, some 3.0 percentage points lower than the equivalent rate for total manufacturing. This evolution could be attributed to several factors: consumption of food generally increases at a slower pace in developed economies than GDP; there has in recent years been a shift in nutritional patterns away from meat; health and safety issues have affected demand within the meat industry (see box 3.5).

Low profits

The gross operating rate (defined as value added minus personnel costs divided by turnover) may be used as a proxy for the profitability of an activity. For the meat industry this indicator gives low values when compared to manufacturing averages. The 1999 gross operating rate was 4.2%, whilst the figure for manufacturing was 9.4%. These ratios have been quite stable over the past decade. Looking in more detail by Member State, the meat industry in the United Kingdom had the highest "profitability rate" (subject to data availability) at 9.4% in 1997 (national manufacturing average of 12.4%). The lowest gross operating rates were reported in France (2.6%, compared to 6.3% for total manufacturing) and Sweden (2.5%, compared to 11.9% for total manufacturing).

Box 3.5

After the BSE-crisis of 1996, in May 1999 the Belgian government announced that excessive levels of the cancer-causing chemical dioxin had been discovered in eggs, meat and dairy products. More than 1,200 farms were closed and the government promised to destroy all suspect pork, beef and poultry. By October 1999, almost 6,200 tonnes of meat had been destroyed.

Figure 3.9

Meat (NACE Rev. 1 15.1)

International comparison of production and employment (1990=100)

Production in constant prices

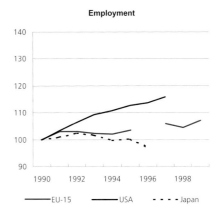

Employment

Source: Eurostat (SBS)

LABOUR AND PRODUCTIVITY

Contrary to the developments seen for the whole of food, beverages and tobacco, employment levels rose in the meat industry during the last 10 years. Between 1989 and 1999, a net gain of 42,600 persons was recorded, equal to an increase of 8.1%. This figure represented growth of 0.8% per annum in terms of an annual average, compared to the -1.1% per annum figure recorded for the whole of manufacturing.

*Low personnel costs and low
apparent labour productivity*

Personnel costs form a smaller share of production value in the meat industry than in manufacturing as a whole, 13.4% in 1999 compared to 20.0% in manufacturing. Whilst total personnel costs were comparatively low as a share of production value, they were also low in terms of unit costs per employee. In 1997, unit personnel costs in the EU equalled 23.2 thousand ECU per employee[6], whilst Eurostat estimate that the corresponding figure for the whole of food, beverages and tobacco in the EU was 26.9 thousand ECU per employee. These relatively low unit personnel costs may well be a result of the type of work being performed in this activity, often highly automated work that is carried out by a fairly low-skilled workforce.

---

(6) DK, EL, I and NL, no data available.

In the meat industry apparent labour productivity was considerably below the food, beverages and tobacco average. In 1997 each person employed generated 32.8 thousand ECU of value added, which was 13.5 thousand ECU below the food, beverages and tobacco average.

Whilst the food, beverages and tobacco industry reported wage adjusted labour productivity figures above the manufacturing average, this was not the case in the meat industry, where in 1997 this ratio was equal to 140.7%[7], just below the manufacturing average.

---

(7) DK, EL, I and NL, no data available.

INTERNATIONAL TRENDS AND FOREIGN TRADE

The EU was responsible for 47.8% of meat production in the Triad in 1997, whilst the USA produced 44.0% and Japan was a distant third with only 8.2%. As such, the meat industry represented equivalent shares of total manufacturing output in both the EU and USA (2.8%). However, in terms of value added, the EU generated just 76.1% of the value added recorded in the USA. There was almost no evolution in the respective shares of production or value added during the ten-year period 1987 to 1997, with the EU and the USA maintaining constant shares of Triad output. During the ten-year period 1987-1997, net employment gains were higher in the USA than in the EU, with an annual average growth rate of 2.6% (EU, 1.2%). In Japan employment fell by 0.3% per annum during the period 1986-1996.

Low levels of trade

Meat products accounted for only 0.7% of EU manufacturing exports in 1999 and 12.8% of exports from the food, beverages and tobacco industry. This share was lower than ten years earlier, when 14.5% of food, beverages and tobacco exports were accounted for by the meat industry. Imports from non-Community countries were of a similar relative magnitude, accounting for 14.4% of all food, beverages and tobacco imports in 1999. The decrease in this share was more pronounced, coming down from 19.6% in 1989.

The three Member States with the highest production specialisation ratios in the meat industry also recorded the three highest export specialisation ratios: Denmark (675.4%), Ireland (260.2%) and the Netherlands (232.7%).

Figure 3.10 ───────────────

Meat (NACE Rev. 1 15.1)
Destination of EU exports, 1999 (%)

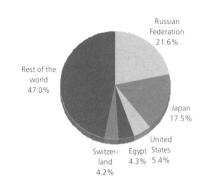

Source: Eurostat (COMEXT)

Figure 13.11 ───────────────

Meat (NACE Rev. 1 15.1)
Origin of EU imports, 1999 (%)

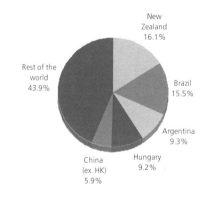

Source: Eurostat (COMEXT)

SUB-CHAPTER 3.2
FISH (NACE Rev. 1 15.2)

This Group of the NACE Rev. 1 classification consists of the preparation and preservation of fish, crustaceans and molluscs (freezing, deep-freezing, drying, smoking, salting, immersing in brine, canning, etc.), the production of fish, crustacean and mollusc products (cooked fish, fish fillets, roes, caviar, caviar substitutes, etc.), the production of prepared fish dishes, and the activities of shipping vessels only engaged in the processing and preserving of fish. The activities of shipping vessels engaged both in fishing and in processing and preserving of fish (included in fishing, NACE Rev. 1 Section B), as well as the production of oils and fats from marine material (see sub-chapter 3.4) and the manufacture of fish soups (see sub-chapter 3.8) are excluded from the data presented in this chapter.

Denmark not only specialised in meat, but also in fish
Based on the data of 14 Member States[8] the estimated production value amounts to 11.0 billion ECU for the fish processing and preserving industry in 1996. This was equivalent to a 2.0% share in the production value of the food, beverages and tobacco industry or a 0.3% share of total EU manufacturing (both excluding Austria).

The largest producers in 1996 were France (producing 16.3% of total output), Spain (16.2%) and the United Kingdom (15.2%). However, as a share of production value in its national manufacturing total, Danish output was the highest, at 2.0%, followed by Spain (0.8%) and Ireland (0.6%). These shares led to relative production specialisation ratios of more than 600% in Denmark and more than 200% in both Spain and Ireland.

Employment in the fish industry accounted for a 3.3% share of the food, beverages and tobacco industry and for a 0.4% share of total manufacturing[9], substantially higher than the equivalent shares of either production or value added.

(8) Excluding A, which had an estimated share of only 0.1% of total EU production.
(9) NL and A, no data available.

Figure 3.12
Fish (NACE Rev. 1 15.2)
Production and export specialisation (%)

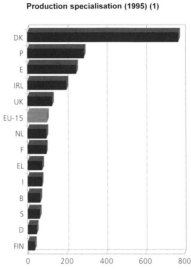
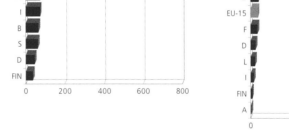

(1) L and A, not available.

Source: Eurostat (SBS, COMEXT)

STRUCTURE AND PERFORMANCE

Unfortunately, there are no recent statistics for the EU-15 aggregate available. However, using data from the individual Member States it is possible to make estimates for a number of economic ratios for 1997.

Declining gross operating rate
During the decade between 1987 and 1997, the gross operating rate has been declining in the fish industry, from 8.4% to 6.0%, contrary to relatively stable figures in the whole of food, beverages and tobacco during the same period. Taking personnel costs out of this measure leaves the share of value added in turnover, which showed similar figures for fish and for the whole of food, beverages and tobacco (19.9% and 19.8%). The fall in the gross operating rate of the fish industry could therefore be attributed to rising personnel costs. Nevertheless, the share of personnel costs in total operating costs was at 14.8% (1997) some 6.5 percentage points below the manufacturing average.

Figure 3.13

Fish (NACE Rev. 1 15.2)

International comparison of production in constant prices and employment (1990=100)

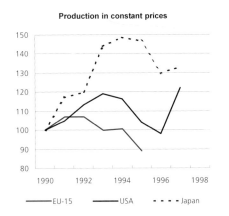

Production in constant prices

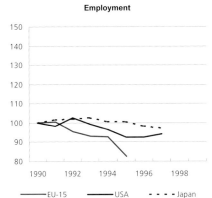

Employment

Source: Eurostat (SBS)

LABOUR AND PRODUCTIVITY

Personnel costs accounted for 69.9% of turnover in 1997 within the fish industry, compared to 58.1% for food, beverages and tobacco. Again, the importance of personnel costs was seen to be rising, as in 1987 this share was equal to only 62.1%.

Personnel costs rising, but still
below manufacturing average

Despite the growing importance of personnel costs, unit personnel costs per employee in the fish industry (21.0 thousand ECU per employee) were still well below the average levels recorded for food, beverages and tobacco (26.9 thousand ECU per employee). Apparent labour productivity in the fish industry was estimated at 30.0 thousand ECU per person employed in 1997, also well below the average for food, beverages and tobacco (46.9 thousand ECU per person employed).

The gross operating surplus per person employed (9.0 thousand ECU per person employed in 1997) further supported the evidence of weaker performance than food, beverages and tobacco (19.3 thousand ECU per person employed). In the period 1987-1997, this ratio recorded a nominal increase of just 12.7% in the fish industry compared to 53.7% in the whole of food, beverages and tobacco.

INTERNATIONAL TRENDS AND FOREIGN TRADE

The EU was responsible for 25.1% of Triad output in the fish industry in 1996, ahead of Japan (13.7%), but far behind the USA (61.2%). Compared with ten years earlier, the USA gained 3.3 percentage points and the EU added 1.8 points at the expense of Japan, who lost 5.1 points. In terms of value added the gap was even wider, with the USA responsible for 65.6% of the value added generated in the Triad in 1996, the EU 18.5% and Japan 15.9%.

EU has a large trade deficit...

The EU ran a deficit of 7.3 billion EUR in 1999. Exports to non-Community countries stood at 1.5 billion EUR, whilst imports from non-Community countries reached 8.8 billion EUR. The deficit was higher than a decade earlier, when exports were valued at 1.1 billion ECU and imports 5.5 billion ECU. During this ten-year period the EU cover ratio (exports divided by imports) declined by 2.5 percentage points, moving from 20.0% in 1989 to 17.2% in 1999.

... but remains the largest exporter in the Triad

Despite the trade deficit and despite being a much smaller producer than the USA, the EU was responsible for 42.8% of Triad exports in 1998, 1.2 percentage points more than the USA. Japan exported only 15.6% of Triad exports. Japan was the largest importer, accounting for 37.4% of Triad imports, closely followed by the EU (37.1%).

Amongst the EU Member States, Denmark had the highest export specialisation rate (1,159.2%). Spain (332.7%) and Portugal (226.5%), like Denmark both relatively specialised in fish production, were the next two Member States in the ranking. The same three countries were also relatively specialised in fish imports compared to the other Member States: Denmark (327.6%), Portugal (312.7%) and Spain (244.0%).

Figure 3.14

Fish (NACE Rev. 1 15.2)

Destination of EU exports, 1999 (%)

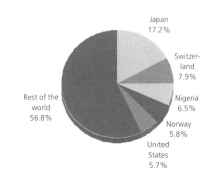

Source: Eurostat (COMEXT)

Figure 3.15

Fish (NACE Rev. 1 15.2)

Origin of EU imports, 1999 (%)

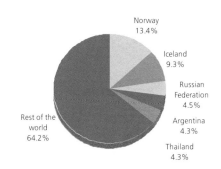

Source: Eurostat (COMEXT)

SUB-CHAPTER 3.3
FRUIT AND VEGETABLES
(NACE Rev. 1 15.3)

The main categories in this NACE Rev. 1 Group are the processing and preserving of potatoes (including the production of potato snacks and crisps), the manufacture of fruit and vegetable juice (including production of concentrates and nectars), and other processing and preserving of fruit and vegetables (including the preserving of fruit, nuts or vegetables, the manufacture of fruit or vegetable food products and the manufacture of jams, marmalades and table jellies). The manufacture of flour or meal and the preservation of fruit and nuts in sugar are excluded.

The production value of the fruit and vegetables industry reached 31.5 billion EUR in 1999, whilst the industry employed 175.6 thousand persons. As such, fruit and vegetable processing and preserving accounted for 5.9% of output in the food and beverages industry[10] and its share in total manufacturing was 0.8%. The equivalent employment shares were 6.6% and 0.8%.

Modest specialisation ratios, except Greece
Germany had the largest output share of the EU Member States in 1997 accounting for 18.4% of the Union's production, followed by the United Kingdom (17.1%) and France (14.1%)[11]. In relative terms, the industry was important in southern Member States and the Netherlands (relative production specialisation ratios of 166.5% in Spain and 162.1% in the Netherlands). These were however modest specialisation rates when compared to the rates found in other industries, except for Greece (where the latest figure for 1995 was 439.1%).

(10) Excluding tobacco.
(11) No 1997 data are available for I, which on the basis of 1996 data would be in the top three EU producers.

Figure 3.16

Fruit and vegetables (NACE Rev. 1 15.3)
Production and export specialisation (%)

Production specialisation (1997) (1)

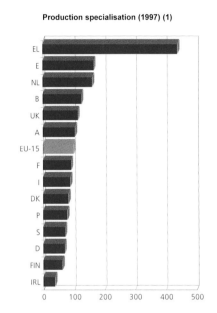

(1) EL and I, 1995; L, not available.

Export specialisation (1999)

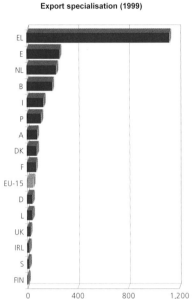

Source: Eurostat (SBS, COMEXT)

STRUCTURE AND PERFORMANCE

The output of the fruit and vegetables industry showed a large increase in 1991, growing 9.5% in real terms, outperforming total food and beverages by 2.4 percentage points. However, after this date output growth slowed. Between 1992 and 1997 the annual average growth rate was equal to just 0.8%, 0.5 percentage points below the average figure for food and beverages activities.

Large expansion of output in Finland
The largest fruit and vegetable processing industries were located in Germany and the United Kingdom (with output of 5.6 and 5.2 billion ECU respectively in 1997). For those Member States for which data were available, the highest growth rates of production in constant price terms between 1992 and 1997 were recorded in Finland and neighbouring Sweden, with average increases of 16.0% and 7.2% per annum[12].

(12) It is important to note the small size of this industry in these two countries (especially in FIN, which probably accounts for less than 1.0% of the EU's output).

Turnover per person employed was equal to 186.2 thousand EUR in 1999, which was substantially below the average figure for food and beverages (220.1 thousand EUR). However, the gross operating rate in the fruit and vegetables industry was somewhat higher than the average rate for the whole of food and beverages, 8.9% compared to 8.1%. This figure was only marginally below the 1989 figure, which stood at 9.1%. The share of value added in production showed similar results, with fruit and vegetables having a higher ratio than the average for food and beverages, 23.5% compared to 22.4% in 1999.

Table 3.4

Consumption of raw potatoes used for processing, 1998 (thousand tonnes)

	Pre-fried, frozen/chilled products	Dehydrated products	Snacks	Other products	Total
B	446	:	198	:	645
D	301	137	85	177	699
F	321	65	47	70	503
I	43	0	26	:	69
NL	1,315	81	38	18	1,452
S	:	:	12	:	47
UK	619	14	183	:	816

Source: UEITP

Figure 3.17

Fruit and vegetables (NACE Rev. 1 15.3)

International comparison of production in constant prices and employment (1990=100)

Production in constant prices

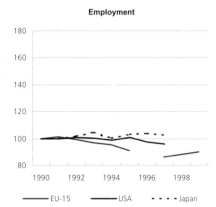

Employment

Source: Eurostat (SBS)

LABOUR AND PRODUCTIVITY

Between 1989 and 1999 employment in the EU went down by 7.6 thousand persons, from 183.2 thousand persons to 175.6 thousand persons. This was equivalent to an annual average decline of 0.4%. In the same period, employment in the food and beverages industry as a whole remained stable.

Lower personnel costs and lower apparent labour productivity than in food and beverages
Unit personnel costs stood at an estimated 24.3 thousand ECU per employee (1997) in the fruit and vegetables industry, which was 2.6 thousand ECU less

than in food and beverages. Apparent labour productivity grew from 28.9 thousand ECU per person employed to 42.1 thousand EUR per person employed between 1989 and 1999, somewhat below the figures for food and beverages, where productivity increased from 34.0 thousand ECU per person employed to 45.3 thousand EUR per person employed. When combining these two measures to produce the simple wage adjusted labour productivity ratio (value added divided by personnel costs), fruit and vegetables were found to be more productive than the whole of food and beverages (165.2% in 1999 compared to 150.9%).

INTERNATIONAL TRENDS AND FOREIGN TRADE

In 1989 the USA was responsible for almost half of the Triad's output of fruit and vegetables processing and preserving. By 1997 this share had dropped to 36.5%, and the USA was overtaken by the EU (38.1%) as the leading producer within the Triad. The relative share of the EU increased by 7.3 percentage points during this period.

Large trade deficit in the EU

The EU ran a large deficit in 1999, when extra-EU exports (2.1 billion EUR) attained only 43.2% of the value of extra-EU imports (4.8 billion EUR). Ten years earlier, the cover ratio was even lower at 42.5%. The USA was the largest exporter within the Triad, accounting for 54.4% of total Triad exports in 1998. The EU followed with 44.7%.

Fruit and vegetables account more than half of Greek food, beverages and tobacco exports

Greek fruit and vegetable exports accounted for more than half (54.1%) of all Greek food, beverages and tobacco exports to non-Community countries in 1999. Spain (26.6%) and Portugal (21.5%) also reported that fruit and vegetables accounted for a high share of total food, beverages and tobacco exports. Indeed, if the Benelux countries are excluded from the analysis of export specialisation ratios, then just four of the Member States were relatively specialised in this industry, the three noted above, as well as Italy.

Figure 3.18

Fruit and vegetables (NACE Rev. 1 15.3)
Destination of EU exports, 1999 (%)

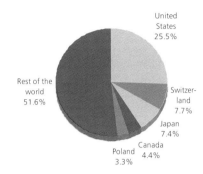

Source: Eurostat (COMEXT)

Figure 3.19

Fruit and vegetables (NACE Rev. 1 15.3)
Destination of EU exports, 1999 (%)

Source: Eurostat (COMEXT)

SUB-CHAPTER 3.4
OILS AND FATS (NACE Rev. 1 15.4)

This Group of the NACE classification consists of three Classes, covering the manufacture of crude oils and fats, the manufacture of refined oils and fats and the manufacture of margarine and similar edible fats. Excluded from this activity are the rendering and refining of lard and other edible animal fats (see sub-chapter 3.1), wet corn milling (see sub-chapter 3.8), the production of essential oils (see sub-chapter 6.1) and the production of olive oil from self-produced olives (NACE Rev. 1 Section A).

In 1996, Eurostat estimate that the production value of the EU oils and fats industry was equal to 22.4 billion ECU, generating 2.5 billion ECU of value added, whilst offering employment to 43.7 thousand persons. As such this industry accounted for 3.9% of output in the food, beverages and tobacco industry, but only for 2.0% of value added and 1.6% of employment.

Spain, an important producer of oils and fats
Spain was the largest producer of oils and fats in 1996, contributing almost a quarter (23.3%) of the EU total, followed by Germany with a 19.2% share. This industry is of importance in Spain not only in absolute terms, but also in relative terms, as Spain recorded the highest production specialisation ratio of the EU Member States (317.6%). Greece (290.2%) and the Netherlands (275.3%) followed in the ranking.

Box 3.7
Between 1990 and 1998, the consumption of margarine in the EU went down by 400g from 6.1kg per capita in 1990 to 5.7kg per capita in 1998. The decrease in consumption could not be attributed to a substitution effect towards butter (the manufacture of which is covered in the next sub-chapter), as the consumption of butter also declined from 4.6kg per capita in 1994 to 4.4kg per capita in 1999. The largest consumers of margarine in the EU in 1998 were the three Nordic countries (Denmark, Finland and Sweden) and the Low Countries (Belgium and the Netherlands).

Figure 3.20

Oils and fats (NACE Rev. 1 15.4)

Production and export specialisation (%)

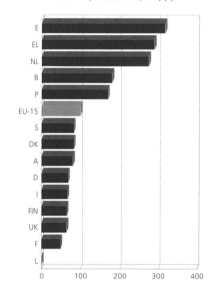

Production specialisation (1996) (1)

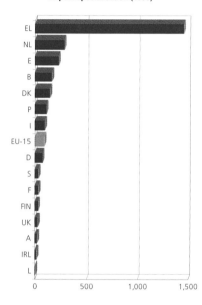

Export specialisation (1999)

(1) DK, F and A, 1994; IRL, not available.

Source: Eurostat (SBS, COMEXT)

STRUCTURE AND PERFORMANCE

Production value of the EU oils and fats industry increased by 5.8 billion ECU between 1986 and 1996, nominal growth of 35.0%. However, over the same period value added decreased, down by 107 million ECU (a decline of 4.0%). The equivalent growth rates for the whole of food, beverages and tobacco were 52.5% for production and 17.2% for value added.

*Significant contractions of production
and value added in the 1990s*
In real terms, between 1991 and 1996, the production value of the oils and fats industry contracted on average by 2.5% per annum. In the same period value added decreased by 8.4% on average each year. The decline in production was 3.3 percentage points below the equivalent rate for total food, beverages and tobacco, whilst for value added the difference was even more pronounced, at 8.6 percentage points.

Table 3.5

**Production of oil products, 1998
(thousand tonnes)**

	Oilseeds processed	Crude oil and fats produced (1)	Cakes and meals produced
EU-15	30,980	8,874	21,639
B	2,160	599	1,523
DK	461	157	281
D	8,663	2,700	5,921
EL (2)	875	152	661
E	4,433	1,098	3,195
F	2,909	1,129	1,831
I	2,221	542	1,670
NL	4,993	1,146	3,745
A	184	74	100
P (3)	935	217	693
FIN	298	78	208
S (2)	217	85	124
UK	2,631	897	1,687

(1) Excluding olives, maize germs, grape and tomato pips.
(2) Estimates for oilseeds processed and cakes and meats produced.
(3) Estimates for oilseeds processed.

Source: Fediol

Table 3.6

Main indicators of vegetable oils in the EU, 1998 (thousand tonnes)

	Production	Imports	Exports	Apparent consumption	Self-sufficiency ratio (%)
Liquid oils	8,583	372	2,301	6,654	129
Lauric oils	64	1,162	36	1,190	5
Linseed oil	220	4	57	167	132
Castor oil	7	96	1	102	7
Palm oil	:	2,027	69	1,958	:

Source: Fediol

Low and decreasing profits

The share of value added in production went down by 4.6 percentage points between 1986 and 1996, from 15.8% to 11.2%. The equivalent shares in food, beverages and tobacco were higher and more stable (21.5% in 1996), although still considerably below manufacturing averages (30.4% in 1996). The profitability of this industry, as estimated by the gross operating rate, was relatively low in 1986 at 6.2%. However, by 1996 the gross operating rate had declined still further and was 4.0 percentage points below the average for food, beverages and tobacco at 4.2%.

Table 3.7

Main indicators of margarine and blends, 1998 (thousand tonnes)

	Production	Imports	Exports	Apparent consumption	Self-sufficiency ratio (%)	Per capita margarine consumption (kg)
B	252.5	69.8	210.3	112.1	225.3	11.0
DK	92.0	1.4	37.8	77.0	119.5	14.5
D	785.1	19.8	239.8	565.1	138.9	6.9
EL	39.1	14.0	2.0	51.0	76.6	4.9
E	87.0	16.0	12.1	90.9	95.7	2.3
F	154.9	108.8	33.4	211.0	73.4	3.6
IRL (1)	14.3	1.4	3.7	12.1	118.4	3.3
I	96.6	21.4	14.3	103.6	93.2	1.8
NL	289.7	29.7	155.6	160.7	180.3	10.2
A	43.2	5.7	9.0	39.8	108.5	4.9
P (1)	44.7	0.2	2.6	42.3	105.7	4.2
FIN	78.8	23.4	47.8	57.6	136.8	11.2
S	157.5	:	47.6	109.9	143.3	12.4
UK	456.7	2.6	9.2	450.1	101.5	7.6

(1) Estimates for production, imports and exports.

Source: IMACE, IFMA

Figure 3.21

Production of animal fats and meals, 1998 (thousand tonnes)

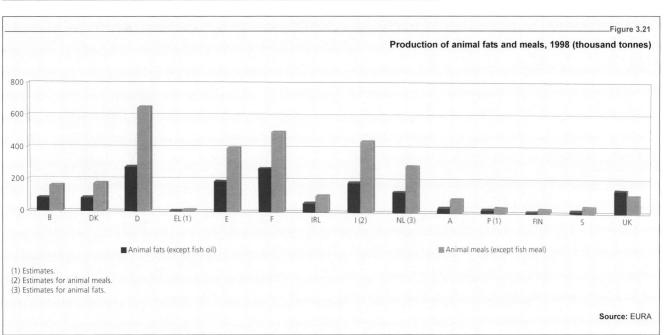

- ■ Animal fats (except fish oil)
- ■ Animal meals (except fish meal)

(1) Estimates.
(2) Estimates for animal meals.
(3) Estimates for animal fats.

Source: EURA

Figure 3.22

Oils and fats (NACE Rev. 1 15.4)

International comparison of production in constant prices and employment (1990=100)

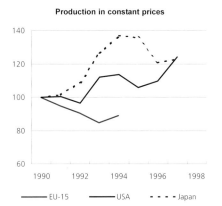

Production in constant prices

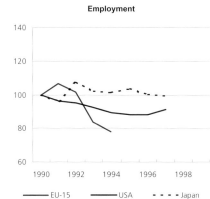

Employment

Source: Eurostat (SBS)

Compared to the breakdown of total manufacturing trade between intra and extra-EU, oils and fats were exported more to fellow Member States, whilst there was a higher influx of imports from non-Community countries. Within the Member States, Greece stood out with a relative export specialisation ratio of 1,454% in 1999. The most popular export destinations for EU exports in 1999 were Russia (12.6%), followed by the USA (12.3%) and Poland (8.4%). The main origins of imports were South America and south-east Asia, with Argentina (28.3%) at the top of the ranking, followed by Brazil (19.5%), Indonesia (12.5%) and Malaysia (9.7%).

Figure 3.23

Oils and fats (NACE Rev. 1 15.4)

Destination of EU exports, 1999 (%)

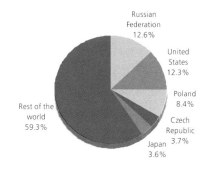

Source: Eurostat (COMEXT)

LABOUR AND PRODUCTIVITY

A large number of jobs were lost between 1986 and 1996 in the oils and fats industry. After the number of persons employed rose from 64.6 thousand in 1986 to 72.0 thousand in 1991, employment fell at a rapid pace in the early 1990s to 43.7 thousand persons by 1996. This was equivalent to an annual average reduction of 9.5% between 1991 and 1996 (whilst the food, beverages and tobacco average fell by 6.8% per annum). The largest reduction was recorded in 1993, when the number of persons employed in the oils and fats industry fell by 17.5%.

High apparent labour productivity

With extensive job losses, apparent labour productivity did not suffer from the contraction in value added, rising from 40.5 thousand ECU per person employed in 1986 to 57.4 thousand ECU per person employed in 1996. Labour productivity differentials compared to the average for food, beverages and tobacco remained constant over time, some 11.1 thousand ECU per person employed higher for oils and fats in both 1986 and 1996.

Personnel costs, measured as a share of production value, stood at 6.5% in 1996, which was just over half of the equivalent figure for food, beverages and tobacco (12.6%) and less than one third of the figure for total manufacturing (21.0%).

INTERNATIONAL TRENDS AND FOREIGN TRADE

The EU produced 48.5% of the Triad's output in 1996, ahead of the USA (39.9%) and Japan (11.6%), whilst employing a higher share (56.0% of the total), compared to 33.1% in the USA and 10.9% in Japan. However, the USA generated the highest share of Triad value added (44.8%), well above the EU (33.3%) or Japan (21.9%). This phenomenon, of high Triad production and employment shares but lower value added shares for the EU was observed across the majority of the food, beverages and tobacco industry.

Oils and fats account for just under 7% of food, beverages and tobacco exports

In 1999, 6.8% of exports within the food, beverages and tobacco industry were accounted for by oils and fats, well above the corresponding production share of 3.9% (in 1996). The equivalent share of imports was higher, at 15.3% of the food, beverages and tobacco total. Extra-EU exports were equal to 2.6 billion EUR in 1999, whilst imports reached 4.9 billion EUR. As such, the EU ran a deficit of 2.3 billion EUR (or a corresponding cover ratio of 53.6%). During the 1990s, exports expanded at a more rapid pace than imports (which remained relatively stable in nominal terms), resulting in an increase of the cover ratio equal to 24.6 percentage points between 1989 and 1999.

Figure 3.24

Oils and fats (NACE Rev. 1 15.4)

Origin of EU imports, 1999 (%)

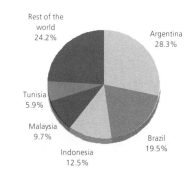

Source: Eurostat (COMEXT)

SUB-CHAPTER 3.5
DAIRY PRODUCTS (NACE Rev. 1 15.5)

This industry covers the operation of dairies and cheese making and the manufacture of ice cream. Included are activities such as the production of fresh milk, the production of cream, the manufacture of dried or concentrated milk and the production of butter, yoghurt, cheese and curd, as well as ice cream.

Summing up over the 14 Member States for which data are available[13], production value in the EU in the dairy industry reached 85.7 billion ECU in 1996, whilst generating 13.8 billion ECU of value added. Dairy products therefore accounted for 15.0% of the production value of the EU's food, beverages and tobacco industry (11.2% of value added). Employment reached 283.2 thousand persons employed in 1999, equivalent to a 10.6% share in food and beverages (excluding tobacco).

Ireland is the most specialised dairy products manufacturer, followed by Denmark
France was the largest producer of dairy products in 1997, with a production value of 18.6 billion ECU in 1997, followed by Germany (17.5 billion ECU) and Italy with 10.7 billion ECU (in 1996). However, relative to the share of total manufacturing, Ireland reported the highest production specialisation ratio in 1997[14], at 264.5%, followed by Denmark (257.7%) and Greece (182.5% in 1996). It is interesting to note that ten years earlier in 1987, Ireland also had the highest specialisation ratio (447.5%), whilst the ratio for Greece was below 100% (92.2%).

---

(13) L, no data available.
(14) L, no data available; EL and I, 1996.

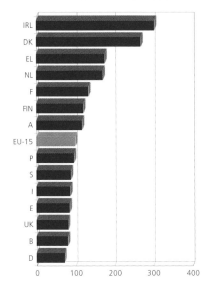

Production specialisation (1995) (1)

Export specialisation (1999)

(1) L, not available.

Source: Eurostat (SBS, COMEXT)

STRUCTURE AND PERFORMANCE

Between 1986 and 1996, production value in the dairy industry increased by 21.1 billion ECU in nominal terms[15], or by 32.7%. In the same period, the nominal growth rate for the whole of food, beverages and tobacco was 52.5%.

Low profits continue to be recorded
The gross operating rate, a proxy for the profitability of an activity, was estimated to be 5.4% within the dairy industry in 1997, which was considerably lower than the corresponding figure for the whole of food, beverages and tobacco (8.2%) or total manufacturing (9.2%). Almost no change was observed in this rate during the preceding decade.

Leaving out personnel costs from the previous equation gives the share of value added in turnover, where similar results were reported. The 1997 ratio of value added to turnover was 14.9% for dairy products, again well below the figures for food, beverages and tobacco (19.8%) and total manufacturing (27.9%). Turnover per person employed in the dairy industry reached 326.8 thousand ECU.

---

(15) L, no data available for 1996.

Table 3.8

Consumption of dairy products, 1998 (kg/capita)

	Cheese	Butter	Liquid milk
B/L	:	6.1	:
DK	16.4	2.1	138.5
D	20.5	6.8	88.5
EL	23.8	1.0	:
E	:	1.0	:
F	23.6	8.3	95.1
IRL	:	3.5	175.0
I	19.0	2.2	85.3
NL	16.6	3.3	126.4
A	16.0	4.7	100.0
P	:	1.6	:
FIN	17.0	5.9	185.0
S	16.8	1.6	149.2
UK	9.7	3.0	117.9

Source: ZMP

Figure 3.26

Dairy products (NACE Rev. 1 15.5)

International comparison of production in constant prices and employment (1990=100)

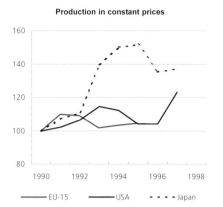

Production in constant prices

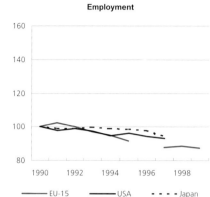

Employment

Source: Eurostat (SBS)

LABOUR AND PRODUCTIVITY

Between 1989 and 1999 employment levels fell by 33.8 thousand persons, a decline of 10.7%, equivalent to an annual average reduction of 1.1%. In the same ten-year period, employment in the food and drink industry (excluding tobacco) remained almost unchanged. Apparent labour productivity was estimated to be 48.6 thousand ECU per person employed in 1997, slightly higher than the average for food, beverages and tobacco (46.3 thousand ECU per person employed).

Unit personnel costs higher than for food, beverages and tobacco

Personnel costs in the dairy industry were estimated to be equal to 30.8 thousand ECU per employee in 1997, higher than the food, beverages and tobacco average (26.9 thousand ECU per employee). The ratio of the gross operating surplus per person employed was equal to 17.7 thousand ECU per person employed in 1997 in the dairy products industry, some 1.6 thousand ECU per person employed below the average figure for food, beverages and tobacco.

INTERNATIONAL TRENDS AND FOREIGN TRADE

In 1996, the EU was the largest producer of dairy products in the Triad, with output 39.9 billion ECU higher than in the USA and 68.7 billion ECU higher than in Japan. The EU also recorded the highest level of value added, just above that of the USA (13.8 billion ECU compared to 12.4 billion ECU).

During the ten-year period between 1986 and 1996, the EU's share of Triad output (in terms of production value and value added) increased at a rapid pace. The production share went up by 8.7 percentage points, from 49.0% in 1986 to 57.7% in 1996 (at the same time, the Japanese share went up from 9.1% to 11.4%). The EU recorded a 6.3 percentage point gain in terms of value added over the same period (from 37.4% to 43.7%, becoming the largest contributor within the Triad). There was little evolution in the relative shares of Triad employment.

EU runs a large trade surplus of 3.4 billion EUR in 1999

EU exports to non-Community countries stood at 4.4 billion EUR in 1999, whilst imports reached only 1.0 billion EUR. The EU cover ratio declined somewhat over the ten-year period 1989-1999, from 543.2% to 443.3%, remaining strongly positive. Despite the large surplus with respect to non-Community countries, the majority of the EU's trade remained within the Internal Market, with the intra-EU exports accounting for 76.8% of total trade, above the food, beverages and tobacco average of 71.6%. The EU accounted for the overwhelming share of Triad trade in this industry, 89.1% of Triad exports in 1998, the USA had just 10.8%, whilst the share of Japan was negligible. In terms of export destinations, the USA was the largest

partner for EU exporters accounting for 13.0% of the extra-EU total in 1999, followed by Saudi Arabia (8.2%) and Algeria (6.2%).

The USA was the largest importer of dairy products within the Triad, with a 39.1% share of Triad imports in 1998, followed by the EU (33.3%) and Japan (27.6%). Two partner countries accounted for more than half of the EU's imports, New Zealand (32.1%) and Switzerland (28.8%).

Figure 3.27

Dairy products (NACE Rev. 1 15.5)

Destination of EU exports, 1999 (%)

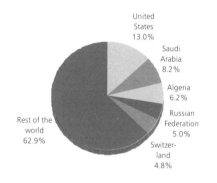

Source: Eurostat (COMEXT)

Figure 3.28

Dairy products (NACE Rev. 1 15.5)

Origin of EU imports, 1999 (%)

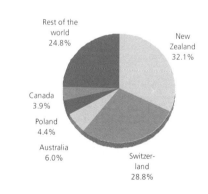

Source: Eurostat (COMEXT)

SUB-CHAPTER 3.6
BEVERAGES (NACE Rev. 1 15.9)

This industry covers the manufacture of distilled alcoholic beverages (whisky, brandy, gin, liqueurs, etc.), the manufacture of wines, cider and other fruit wines (including vermouth and the like), the manufacture of beer, the manufacture of malt and the production of mineral waters and soft drinks. Neither bottling, packaging nor the production of fruit and vegetable juice (see sub-chapter 3.3) are covered.

High value added rate for beverages

This industry is characterised by the fact that it generates a high level of value added, contrary to the general trends observed for the whole of food, drink and tobacco. The beverages industry accounted for nearly a fifth of the value added generated in the whole of food, beverages and tobacco, well above its corresponding share of production value, 14.9%.

Production value reached 84.8 billion ECU in 1996 for the 14 Member States for which data are available[16], whilst value added stood at 22.8 billion ECU. The employment share of beverages was lower than the corresponding production and value added shares, accounting for 12.2% of the food, beverages and tobacco total[17].

Germany was the largest producer in the EU, with a contribution to total output of 23.5%, followed by the United Kingdom (20.1%) and France (15.4%). Relative production specialisation rates were not particular high in this industry, with Greece reporting the highest (234.6%), followed by Ireland (196.6%) and the United Kingdom (152.0%).

Non-alcoholic beverages generally account for around a quarter of beverages production value in the EU

In the majority of countries the production share of non-alcoholic drinks was between 20% and 35% of the beverages total in 1997. The share in the United Kingdom was somewhat lower at 17.2%, although the main exception was Finland (where non-alcoholic drinks accounted for just 1.8% of beverage output). Value added shares of non-alcoholic beverages were generally lower than their corresponding production shares.

(16) L, no data available (contribution to EU production in 1995 was less than 0.3% of the EU total).
(17) L and NL, no data available.

Figure 3.29

Beverages (NACE Rev. 1 15.9)

Production and export specialisation (%)

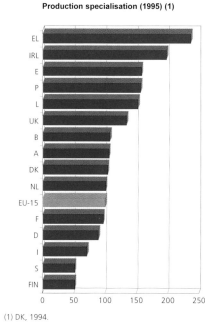

Production specialisation (1995) (1)

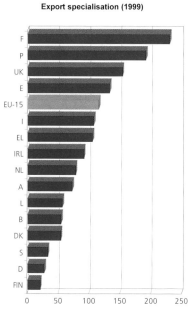

Export specialisation (1999)

(1) DK, 1994.

Source: Eurostat (SBS, COMEXT)

Box 3.8

In 1997, tap water was the most consumed beverage in Europe, accounting for almost half of total consumption. However, in the USA soft drinks were the most consumed beverage, accounting for 29.5% of American consumption in 1997 (compared to just 6.2% in Europe). Mineral waters, soft drinks and beer had similar shares of total EU beverage consumption in 1998, between 70 and 77 litres per capita. The highest consumption of mineral water was in Italy (136 litres per capita) and Belgium (117 litres per capita). Low consumption of mineral water was found in Ireland (17 litres per capita), the Netherlands (15 litres per capita) and the United Kingdom (11 litres per capita). The differences in soft drinks were less pronounced, ranging from a high of 93 litres per capita in Belgium to a low of 37 litres per capita in France.

Germans were the largest consumers of beer, drinking 127 litres per capita in 1998, closely followed by the Irish (124 litres per capita). In Italy, beer consumption was very low, at 27 litres per capita. The highest wine consumption was recorded in France (60 litres per capita), Italy (58 litres per capita) and Portugal (53 litres per capita)[18].

(18) The highest figure was recorded in L (63 litres per capita), although this could be attributed in part to a low tax regime resulting in a large number of purchases being made by tourists and day-trippers.

Table 3.9

Consumption of beer (litres/capita)

	1990	1998
D	142.7	127.4
IRL	123.9	124.2
L	116.8	111.0
A	121.3	108.1
DK	127.2	107.7
UK	113.2	99.4
B	121.6	98.0
NL	90.0	84.3
FIN	84.2	79.1
EU-15	80.7	77.8
E	71.9	66.4
P	69.3	65.3
CH	70.7	59.9
S	60.1	57.3
NO	52.3	49.7
EL	41.0	42.0
F	41.5	38.6
I	23.0	26.9

Source: CBMC

Table 3.10

Consumption of soft drinks (litres/capita)

	1990	1998 (1)
IRL (2)	67.9	99.9
B	80.2	93.3
E	73.1	89.6
UK	73.0	85.6
DK	56.9	83.1
D	82.6	82.9
NL	76.1	82.4
A	77.5	82.3
S	55.2	66.5
EL	55.1	65.9
FIN	41.7	49.7
I	46.9	49.6
P	33.8	45.6
F	30.4	37.0

(1) Estimates.
(2) 1997 instead of 1998.

Source: UNESDA/CISDA

Table 3.11

Production of mineral waters, 1998 (million litres)

	Flat mineral water	Sparkling mineral water
B (1)	727.3	311.7
D	:	7,480.3
E	2,629.0	153.0
F (2)	4,237.0	1,413.0
IRL (1)	42.3	18.5
I	4,300.0	3,500.0
NL (1)	74.5	51.6
A	:	601.0
P	344.6	92.6
UK	340.0	139.0

(1) Including water direct from a source.
(2) Estimates.

Source: UNESEM

STRUCTURE AND PERFORMANCE

Production value in the beverages industry increased by 30.4 billion ECU in nominal terms between 1986 and 1996[19], equivalent to a 55.8% increase (consistent with the average growth rate for the whole of food, beverages and tobacco, 52.5%). Value added increased by just 34.0% during the same ten-year period (against a 53.3% increase for food, beverages and tobacco).

High profit rate in beverages

Profit rates (the gross operating rate) were higher in beverages than the average for food, beverages and tobacco. In 1996, the profit rate for beverages was equal to 12.4%[20], whilst in food, beverages and tobacco it was just 8.2%. Ten years earlier the gap had been even wider, 14.0% compared to 7.9%. The gross operating surplus per person employed in beverages was equal to 34.5 thousand ECU per person employed in 1996[21], high when compared with the food, beverages and tobacco average of just 19.2 thousand ECU per person employed.

The slower growth of value added compared with production value resulted in the share of value added in production falling from 31.3% in 1986 to 26.9% in 1996. This reduction was in keeping with the general trends reported within the whole of manufacturing, although contrary to the trend for food, beverages and tobacco where a constant, but considerably lower share was maintained.

(19) L, no data available for 1996.
(20) L, no data available.
(21) L and NL, no data available.

Figure 3.30

Beverages (NACE Rev. 1 15.9)

International comparison of production in constant prices and employment (1990=100)

Production in constant prices

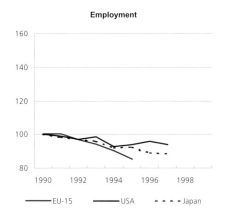

Employment

Source: Eurostat (SBS)

LABOUR AND PRODUCTIVITY

Excluding Luxembourg and the Netherlands, the remaining 13 Member States saw their employment levels reduced by 19.8% between 1986 and 1996 in the beverages industry, to 309.8 thousand persons employed. In keeping with the general trends in food, beverages and tobacco, personnel costs accounted for a relatively low share of production value in the beverages industry in 1996, 13.6%[22].

With this industry generating relatively high levels of value added, it is perhaps not surprising to find that apparent labour productivity reached 70.3 thousand ECU per person employed[23] in 1996. The differential to average apparent labour productivity for the whole of food, beverages and tobacco was maintained between 1986 and 1996 (and stood at 24.0 thousand ECU per person employed in 1996).

_____
(22) L, no data available.
(23) L and the NL, no data available.

INTERNATIONAL TRENDS AND FOREIGN TRADE

The EU was the largest producer of beverages in the Triad in 1996, accounting for 48.4% of total production value[24]. The USA accounted for 27.1% and Japan for 24.5%. In terms of value added however, the EU (37.7%) and the USA (37.6%) had almost identical shares.

EU has a large, but decreasing trade
surplus, 8.3 billion EUR in 1999

EU exports to non-Community countries reached 10.9 billion EUR in 1999, whilst the level of imports from non-Community countries stood at 2.7 billion EUR. Imports increased at a more rapid pace during the latest ten-year period, resulting in the cover ratio being halved, from 913.4% to 412.3% by 1999. The rapid growth in EU imports was seen when analysing the share of EU imports in total Triad imports, a ratio that increased by 9.2 percentage points between 1989 and 1998, to reach 20.6%.

Contrary to almost all other industries within this chapter, a relatively high share of beverages was exported to non-Community countries. This share was however declining, as trade within the Internal Market became increasingly important (56.8% of exports in 1999 stayed within the EU). The main destination of EU exports in 1999 was the USA (39.4%), whilst Japan accounted for 11.0% and Switzerland for 7.4%. The USA was also the most important origin of imports, accounting for 23.1% of the EU total, followed by Australia (18.5%) and Chile (9.3%).

_____
(24) L, no data available.

_____Figure 3.31

Beverages (NACE Rev. 1 15.9)
Destination of EU exports, 1999 (%)

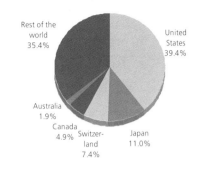

Source: Eurostat (COMEXT)

_____Figure 3.32

Beverages (NACE Rev. 1 15.9)
Origin of EU imports, 1999 (%)

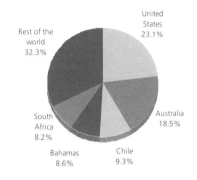

Source: Eurostat (COMEXT)

SUB-CHAPTER 3.7
TOBACCO (NACE Rev. 1 16)

This Division of the NACE Rev. 1 classification covers the manufacture of tobacco products (cigarettes, cigarette tobacco, cigars, pipe tobacco, chewing tobacco and snuff). Growing and the preliminary processing of tobacco are not included under this heading, but within agriculture (Section A of NACE Rev. 1).

There are no recent estimates of structural business statistics for the EU aggregate for this industry. The latest total is for 1994, when tobacco production value accounted for 8.0% of the food, beverages and tobacco output, 10.0% of EU value added, but just 2.7% of employment.

The United Kingdom is the largest producer, but not the largest employer
The largest manufacturer of tobacco products in 1997 in the EU was the United Kingdom, with output equal to 22.3 billion ECU. Germany was the second largest producer with some 13.1 billion ECU, followed by Italy (6.8 billion ECU in 1996).

In terms of employment the United Kingdom was only the fourth largest employer in the EU, with 8.4 thousand persons employed in 1997, proceeded by Spain (9.3 thousand persons employed), Germany (13.3 thousand persons employed) and Italy (13.7 thousand persons employed in 1996).

Figure 3.33

Tobacco (NACE Rev. 1 16)
Production and export specialisation (%)

Production specialisation (1994) (1)

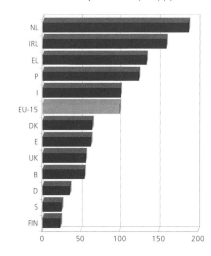

Export specialisation (1999)

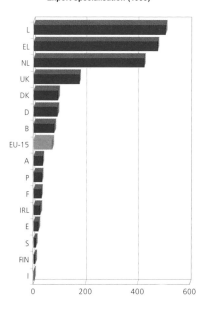

(1) F, L and A, not available.

Source: Eurostat (SBS, COMEXT)

In 1998, there were 92.6 million cigarette smokers in the EU, some 2.7 million less than in 1995. The share of the population that smoke cigarettes fell in the EU from 25.6% in 1995 to 24.7% in 1998. Respective shares within the Member States varied from as high as 36.1% in Greece to as low as 13.6% in Sweden. The decrease in the share of smokers in total EU population was not universal across the Member States. Indeed, six countries (EL, E, IRL, I, NL and A) reported that the share of smokers rose between 1995 and 1998. The largest reductions were recorded in Sweden (-7.9 percentage points) and Portugal (-6.2 points). However, the highest daily consumption per smoker was found in Portugal, with an average of 32.0 cigarettes per smoker per day in 1998, well ahead of Austria and Spain (both at 22.5 cigarettes per smoker per day). The lowest average number of cigarettes smoked per day was recorded in the Netherlands, the only Member State with a figure below 10 cigarettes (9.9).

STRUCTURE AND PERFORMANCE
In the Netherlands, the annual average growth rate of production value in constant prices between 1987 and 1997 was equal to 4.4%. In the United Kingdom growth was not as pronounced, reaching 2.8%[25]. In Spain, the manufacture of tobacco products declined by 0.4% on average per annum in real terms over the same period, whilst in Germany the decline was equal to 0.5% per annum. Italian production also decreased in real terms (during the ten-year period 1986-1996), by as much as 4.1% on average per year.

High turnover, but low profit rates
Using data from the individual Member States, estimates for a number of economic ratios for 1997 can be analysed. The share of value added in turnover was only 9.5% in the tobacco industry, less than half of its corresponding share in food, beverages and tobacco (19.8%). As a result of such high turnover relative to value added, the gross operating rate in the tobacco industry was equal to just 5.3% in 1997, well below the average for food, beverages and tobacco (8.2%).

Many governments spend a large share of their health and education budgets on trying to dissuade people from smoking, pointing out the health hazards involved. At the end of June 2000, European Union health ministers voted in favour of new laws to tighten controls on the tar and carbon monoxide content of cigarettes, as well as on the labelling (prohibiting the use of terms such as "light" and "mild" and forcing manufacturers to print "smoking kills" on each pack).

(25) The large jump in the level of output in the UK between 1995 and 1996 may well be a result of a classification problem (with a large company declaring tobacco as its principal activity in 1996). This change severely hampers the analysis of time-series data.

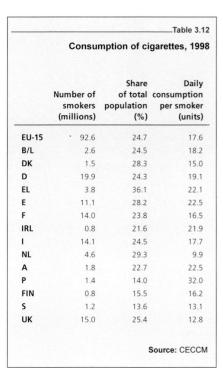

Table 3.12

Consumption of cigarettes, 1998

	Number of smokers (millions)	Share of total population (%)	Daily consumption per smoker (units)
EU-15	92.6	24.7	17.6
B/L	2.6	24.5	18.2
DK	1.5	28.3	15.0
D	19.9	24.3	19.1
EL	3.8	36.1	22.1
E	11.1	28.2	22.5
F	14.0	23.8	16.5
IRL	0.8	21.6	21.9
I	14.1	24.5	17.7
NL	4.6	29.3	9.9
A	1.8	22.7	22.5
P	1.4	14.0	32.0
FIN	0.8	15.5	16.2
S	1.2	13.6	13.1
UK	15.0	25.4	12.8

Source: CECCM

Figure 3.34

Tobacco (NACE Rev. 1 16)

International comparison of production in constant prices and employment (1990=100)

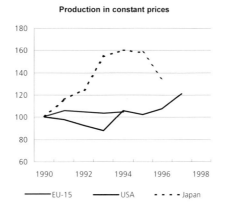

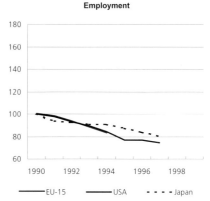

Source: Eurostat (SBS)

LABOUR AND PRODUCTIVITY

Although there are no recent employment figures for the EU as a whole, from the available data it is clear that employment followed a significantly downward trend between 1987 and 1997. Between 1987 and 1994, employment fell by 29.1 thousand persons, to 72.3 thousand, equivalent to a reduction of 28.7%. Furthermore, between 1994 and 1997, in the Member States for which data is available[26], employment went down by a further 8.6%.

Low employment levels...

Tobacco is a fairly capital-intensive industry, especially when compared to the majority of the other industries covered by this chapter. As a result of the relatively low level of employees and despite considerably higher unit personnel costs per employee than for food, beverages and tobacco (41.2 thousand ECU against 26.9 thousand ECU in 1997), the share of personnel costs in total operating costs (10.5%) in 1997 was well below the manufacturing average of 21.3%.

... high apparent labour productivity

Apparent labour productivity stood at 94.3 thousand ECU per person employed in 1997, whilst in food, beverages and tobacco it was less than half of this level at 46.3 thousand ECU per person employed. Labour productivity has increased at a rapid pace in the tobacco industry, more than doubling in nominal terms between 1987 (42.9 thousand ECU per person employed) and 1997.

(26) B, D, E, IRL, P, FIN and UK.

INTERNATIONAL TRENDS AND FOREIGN TRADE

Although there are no complete data for the EU in 1997, it is still possible to state that the EU was the largest producer in the Triad. USA production reached 32.0 billion ECU and Japanese output was equal to 17.7 billion ECU (both of these figures were below the sum of production value for the 7 Member States for which data are available). In 1994 the EU accounted for 47.4% of total Triad production, the USA for 28.9% and Japan for 23.7%. As in many manufacturing industries, the USA had a far higher share of value added in 1994 (54.4%), ahead of the EU (36.6%) and Japan (8.9%). In 1997, value added had gone up by 29.9% nominally in the USA and by 12.2% in Japan. Based on the limited data available, it seems unlikely that the increases in the EU were as large.

*USA largest exporter, Japan largest
importer within the Triad*
EU exports to non-Community countries stood at 2.0 billion EUR in 1999. In 1998, the EU's share in total Triad exports was 30.0%, well behind the USA, where exports equal to 4.3 billion ECU accounted for 67.4% of the Triad's exports. Whilst Japan's share of Triad exports was negligible (2.6%), it accounted for almost three-quarters of Triad imports in 1998 (71.1%), ahead of the USA (19.6%) and the EU (9.3%). There was little evolution in the level of extra-EU imports the following year (still 0.2 billion EUR in 1999).

*Exports to south-east Asia,
imports from the Americas*
In 1999, south-east Asia was one of the main destinations for extra-EU tobacco exports: Taiwan (9.0%), Singapore (6.5%) and Hong Kong (5.4%) were the three most important destinations. In terms of the origin of imports, the largest share was located in the Americas, with the USA the leading non-Community country from which tobacco was imported in 1999 (29.0%), followed by Cuba (27.1%), the Dominican Republic (9.5%), Zimbabwe (8.4%) and Brazil (5.3%).

Figure 3.35 ——————————————

Tobacco (NACE Rev. 1 16)

Destination of EU exports, 1999 (%)

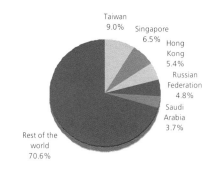

Source: Eurostat (COMEXT)

Figure 3.36 ——————————————

Tobacco (NACE Rev. 1 16)

Origin of EU imports, 1999 (%)

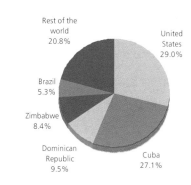

Source: Eurostat (COMEXT)

SUB-CHAPTER 3.8
MISCELLANEOUS FOOD PRODUCTS
(NACE Rev. 1 15.6, 15.7 AND 15.8)

In this sub-chapter, three Groups of the NACE Rev. 1 classification are analysed. The first covers milling, flours, cereal breakfast foods, starches and corn oil (NACE Rev. 1 15.6). The second Group includes prepared animal feed for both farm animals and pets, excluding fishmeal and oilseed cake (NACE Rev. 1 15.7). The final Group covers a variety of other food products such as bread, cakes, biscuits, snacks, sugar, chocolate, pasta, condiments, dietetic food, soups, yeast and the processing of coffee and tea, excluding salt, herbal medical products and the harvesting of tea, coffee and spices (NACE Rev. 1 15.8). It should be noted that because the NACE classification is only revised periodically, it is possible that over time a large number of new food products are classified within this final Group.

Data are available for 11 of the Member States[27] for 1996, together their production value for miscellaneous food products contributed 31.6% to total food, beverages and tobacco output, with considerably higher shares of value added (39.4%) and employment (42.8%)[28]. More recent data is available for 1997 in certain countries, with Germany the largest producer (40.2 billion ECU), followed by the United Kingdom (33.3 billion ECU) and France (32.9 billion ECU)[29].

Other food products by far the largest
NACE Group in this sub-chapter
Using data for the same 11 Member States in 1996, the breakdown of production between the three activities covered was heavily weighted in favour of the heterogeneous other food products (NACE Rev. 1 15.8), with 69.6% of output. In terms of employment and value added other food products was even more important, accounting for 80.5% of the value added generated and 86.9% of the total number of persons employed in 1996. Prepared animal feeds (19.1%) had a production value almost twice that of grain mill products and starches (11.3%).

(27) IRL, L, A and S, no data available.
(28) IRL, L, NL, A and S, no data available.
(29) Output in I reached 20.2 billion ECU in 1996.

_____Figure 3.37

Miscellaneous food products (NACE Rev. 1 15.6, 15.7 and 15.8)

Production and export specialisation (%)

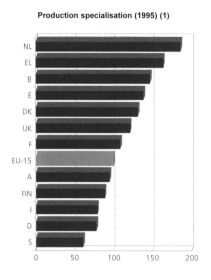

Production specialisation (1995) (1)

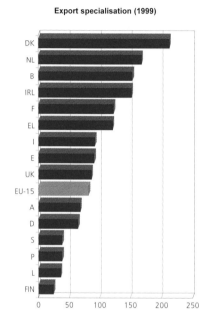

Export specialisation (1999)

(1) DK, A and S, 1994; IRL, L and P, not available.

Source: Eurostat (SBS, COMEXT)

_____Table 3.13

Consumption of grain mill products, 1998 (%)

	Bakeries	Biscuits and rusk manufacturers	Households	Other users
B	85.5	9.0	1.5	4.0
DK (1)	90.0	:	10.0	:
D	71.0	15.0	6.0	7.0
E	79.8	15.7	1.6	2.9
F	67.6	18.8	4.8	8.8
I (2)	74.0	26.0	:	:
NL	63.3	22.9	0.7	13.1
A	67.0	16.0	15.0	2.0
P	:	:	6.0	:
FIN	60.0	5.0	26.0	9.0
S	56.0	15.0	18.0	11.0
UK	61.4	14.9	4.1	19.6

(1) Biscuits and rusks manufacturers are included in bakeries.
(2) Households and other users are included in biscuits and rusk manufacturers.

Source: GAM

STRUCTURE AND PERFORMANCE

Between 1990 and 1995, production value of miscellaneous food products grew on average by 1.9% in real terms, which was 0.6 percentage points higher than in total food, beverages and tobacco. Growth rates of production in 1996 and 1997 (subject to data availability) showed that output was rising at a similar pace to that of the whole of food, beverages and tobacco (around 6.3% in real terms in 1997[30]). The fastest growing activity of those covered in this sub-chapter was other food products, which had an annual average growth rate of 4.1% in real terms between 1990 and 1997[31].

High value added rate in comparison to other food, beverage and tobacco activities

The share of value added in production was higher in miscellaneous food products than in food, beverages and tobacco. There was little evolution in this ratio over time as it fell by just 0.1 percentage points between 1987 and 1997 to 27.2%[32], well above the food, beverages and tobacco average of 21.7%[33]. Other food products again recorded the highest ratio, with value added accounting for 31.4% of production value[34]. Eurostat estimate that the gross operating rate for miscellaneous food products was equal to 9.8% in 1997, 1.6 percentage points above the food, beverages and tobacco average.

(30) DK, EL, IRL, I, L, A and S, no data available.
(31) EL, IRL, I, A and P, no data available.
(32) DK, EL, I, IRL, L and S, no data available.
(33) EL, I and A, no data available.
(34) EL, IRL and I, no data available.

Table 3.14

Market breakdown for compound animal feed in the EU, 1998 (%) (1)

Pigs	35.6
Poultry	29.3
Cattle	26.8
Other compound feed	6.9
Milk replacers	1.4

(1) Excluding EL and L.

Source: FEFAC

Table 3.15

Production of biscuits, cocoa and confectionery in the EU, 1998 (%)

Biscuits	35.4
Other baked goods	22.0
Chocolate confectionery	22.0
Other chocolate products	4.4
Sugar confectionery	16.2

Source: CAOBISCO

Table 3.16

Consumption of pasta, 1998 (kg/capita)

I	26.7
EL	8.8
F	7.3
P	6.8
S	6.0
Benelux	5.4
D	5.3
S	4.6
UK	2.5

Source: UNAFPA

Table 3.17

Consumption of fermented vinegar, 1998 (litres/capita)

A (1)	2.4
D	2.1
B	2.0
F	1.8
E	1.4
DK (1)	1.1
P	0.8
FIN	0.5

(1) 1997.

Source: CPIV

Figure 3.38

Miscellaneous food products (NACE Rev. 1 15.6, 15.7 and 15.8)

International comparison of production in constant prices and employment (1990=100)

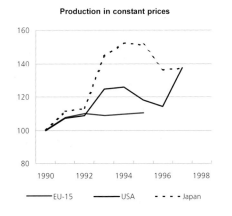

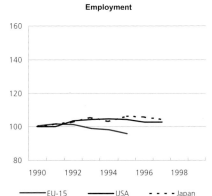

Source: Eurostat (SBS)

	1988	1989	1990	1991	1992	1993	1994	1995	1996	1997	1998
B	100.0	121.7	134.8	115.2	110.9	60.9	34.8	34.8	50.2	41.5	39.1
D	100.0	102.8	116.3	135.4	141.4	146.7	146.2	144.8	145.1	157.4	151.9
E	100.0	108.3	91.7	100.0	108.3	108.3	108.3	116.7	114.7	167.6	122.3
F	100.0	103.6	103.8	105.1	97.9	100.3	105.3	114.5	102.8	123.4	114.3
I	100.0	100.0	100.0	100.0	122.2	144.4	133.3	133.3	138.3	136.9	140.4
UK	100.0	100.0	25.8	28.9	27.0	28.3	27.7	29.6	29.6	29.6	29.6

Table 3.18

Production of mustard (1988=100)

Source: CIMCEE

LABOUR AND PRODUCTIVITY

Between 1985 and 1995, employment was stable in these miscellaneous food industries, with an annual average reduction of less than 0.1%. Between 1995 and 1997 the number of persons employed increased within those countries for which data is available[35]. As such miscellaneous food products consistently reported employment growth rates above the food, beverages and tobacco average.

Miscellaneous food products
a labour-intensive industry

It has already been noted that the industries covered in this sub-chapter accounted for 42.8% of all persons employed in food, beverages and tobacco. The importance of labour was confirmed by the relatively high share of personnel costs in total operating costs (Eurostat estimate, 16.6%).

Nevertheless, the average cost of labour was relatively low in 1997, at 25.0 thousand ECU per employee (Eurostat estimate). Apparent labour productivity stood at 41.6 thousand ECU per person employed in 1997 (Eurostat estimate). As such this industry was characterised by a high reliance on relatively cheap labour, with fairly low productivity levels. When combined these two measures gave a wage adjusted labour productivity figure of 158.9% (Eurostat estimate).

(35) Increases of 1.1% in 1996 (excluding DK, IRL, L, NL, A, P and S) and 5.2% in 1997 (excluding DK, EL, IRL, I, L, NL, A and S).

INTERNATIONAL TRENDS AND FOREIGN TRADE

Although complete EU statistics for 1997 are missing, it is certain that the EU was the largest producer of miscellaneous food products in the Triad. Production value for the USA was 161.1 billion ECU in 1997, whilst in Japan it stood at 106.2 billion ECU. In the EU, only 9 of the 15 Member States[36] reported output almost equal to that of the USA (157.1 billion ECU). However, in terms of value added, the USA accounted for the largest share in 1995 (43.9%), ahead of Japan (28.9%) and the EU (27.2%).

EU largest trading bloc in the Triad,
but intra-EU trade more important

EU exports to non-Community countries reached 9.9 billion EUR in 1999, whilst imports were equal to just 4.8 billion EUR. Extra-EU exports accounted for 57.4% of the Triad total in 1998, far ahead of the USA (38.9%) and Japan (3.7%). The top five non-Community destinations were the USA (13.2%), Switzerland (7.2%), Norway (4.8%), Japan (4.4%) and Poland (3.6%). Whilst being the largest exporter within the Triad, the majority of the EU's trade was within the Internal Market, 69.3% of total EU exports in 1999.

The USA was the largest importer within the Triad in 1998, accounting for a 44.5% share, followed by the EU (31.3%) and Japan (24.2%). However, it is important to note that more than 80% of EU imports originated from inside the European Union in 1999. The top five countries of origin for extra-EU imports of miscellaneous food products in 1999 were the USA (23.7%), Switzerland (13.3%), Mauritius (6.0%), the Ivory Coast (4.4%) and India (3.6%).

(36) DK, EL, IRL, I, L and S, no data available.

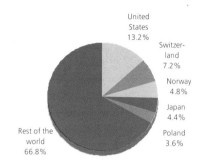

Figure 3.39

Miscellaneous food products
(NACE Rev. 1 15.6, 15.7 and 15.8)
Destination of EU exports, 1999 (%)

United States 13.2%
Switzerland 7.2%
Norway 4.8%
Japan 4.4%
Poland 3.6%
Rest of the world 66.8%

Source: Eurostat (COMEXT)

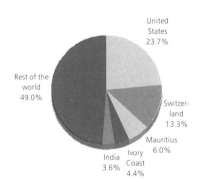

Figure 3.40

Miscellaneous food products
(NACE Rev. 1 15.6, 15.7 and 15.8)
Origin of EU imports, 1999 (%)

United States 23.7%
Switzerland 13.3%
Mauritius 6.0%
Ivory Coast 4.4%
India 3.6%
Rest of the world 49.0%

Source: Eurostat (COMEXT)

Table 3.19

Production, processing and preserving of meat and meat products (NACE Rev. 1 15.1)

Production related indicators in the EU (1)

	1989	1990	1991	1992	1993	1994	1995	1996	1997	1998	1999
Number of persons employed (thousands)	528.2	534.1	548.9	549.0	545.4	544.4	551.4	:	565.1	556.4	570.8
Production (million EUR)	80,106	84,617	91,657	96,029	93,830	94,607	98,567	:	108,120	103,143	104,321
Domestic producer price index (1995=100)	:	99.9	98.3	101.6	100.8	100.0	100.0	102.7	105.5	100.7	97.3
Value added (million EUR)	13,823	15,029	16,354	16,761	17,348	17,079	17,492	:	19,555	18,748	18,721

(1) Technically, data before 01/01/1999 are in ECU and after this date in euro. However, as the conversion rate was 1 ECU =1 EUR, for practical purposes the two terms can be used interchangeably.

Table 3.20

Production, processing and preserving of meat and meat products (NACE Rev. 1 15.1)

Trade related indicators in the EU (1)

	1989	1990	1991	1992	1993	1994	1995	1996	1997	1998	1999
Exports (million EUR)	3,629	3,404	3,792	3,765	4,317	4,871	4,834	5,115	5,623	4,912	4,927
Imports (million EUR)	4,454	4,127	3,866	4,191	4,019	4,579	4,493	4,631	5,022	4,653	4,563
Trade balance (million EUR)	-825	-723	-74	-426	298	292	342	484	601	260	365
Cover ratio (%)	81.5	82.5	98.1	89.8	107.4	106.4	107.6	110.5	112.0	105.6	108.0

(1) Technically, data before 01/01/1999 are in ECU and after this date in euro. However, as the conversion rate was 1 ECU =1 EUR, for practical purposes the two terms can be used interchangeably.

Table 3.21

Production, processing and preserving of meat and meat products (NACE Rev. 1 15.1)

Production related indicators, 1997

	B	DK	D	EL (1)	E	F	IRL	I (1)	L	NL	A	P	FIN	S	UK
Number of persons employed (thousands)	16.7	25.2	107.5	3.6	60.5	118.3	13.5	36.6	0.5	:	11.2	15.7	11.2	13.9	109.3
Production (million ECU)	5,086	5,146	18,831	358	10,880	24,053	3,179	9,793	69	7,164	1,791	1,472	1,704	2,939	15,136
Value added (million ECU)	813	1,087	3,663	73	1,614	3,667	465	1,722	14	926	424	214	441	536	3,794
Gross operating surplus (million ECU)	323.2	323.9	1,024.0	18.0	567.3	681.2	203.7	668.3	3.2	301.3	119.6	80.1	118.1	82.5	1,449.0

(1) 1996.

Table 3.22

Production, processing and preserving of meat and meat products (NACE Rev. 1 15.1)

Trade related indicators, 1999

	B	DK	D	EL	E	F	IRL	I	L	NL	A	P	FIN	S	UK
Exports (million EUR)	2,219	3,307	2,669	30	1,190	3,905	1,867	1,141	28	4,541	543	48	75	161	1,198
Imports (million EUR)	1,109	527	4,114	661	930	3,110	249	3,836	108	1,495	583	499	116	398	3,559
Trade balance (million EUR)	1,110	2,780	-1,446	-630	260	795	1,618	-2,695	-80	3,045	-39	-452	-41	-237	-2,360
Cover ratio (%)	200.0	627.6	64.9	4.6	127.9	125.6	748.8	29.7	26.1	303.7	93.3	9.6	64.3	40.4	33.7

Table 3.23

Production, processing and preserving of meat and meat products (NACE Rev. 1 15.1)

Labour related indicators, 1997

	B	DK (1)	D	EL (2)	E	F	IRL	I (2)	L	NL	A	P	FIN	S	UK
Unit personnel costs (thousand ECU per employee)	30.9	34.4	24.7	15.0	18.0	25.2	19.4	29.5	23.4	:	27.5	8.6	28.8	32.7	21.5
Social charges as a share of personnel costs (%)	39.9	5.6	21.5	32.0	29.0	40.1	14.8	48.5	:	17.8	30.7	31.2	29.8	40.6	10.1
Apparent labour productivity (thousand ECU/pers. empl.)	48.6	43.1	34.1	19.9	26.7	31.0	34.4	47.1	30.0	:	37.9	13.6	39.2	38.6	34.7
Wage adjusted labour productivity (%)	157.2	143.7	137.7	132.4	147.9	122.8	177.1	159.5	127.9	:	137.8	157.9	135.9	118.2	161.2
Personnel costs as a share of total operating costs (%)	10.3	15.7	13.8	15.5	9.4	11.9	8.1	10.2	16.5	8.6	16.8	8.8	19.9	13.8	16.6

(1) Unit personnel costs and wage adjusted labour productivity, 1996; (2) 1996.

Source: Eurostat (SBS, EBT, COMEXT)

Table 3.24

Processing and preserving of fish and fish products (NACE Rev. 1 15.2)

Production related indicators in the EU (1)

	1989	1990	1991	1992	1993	1994	1995	1996	1997	1998	1999
Number of persons employed (thousands)	111.0	107.2	107.4	102.1	99.6	99.2	88.2	:	:	:	:
Production (million ECU)	10,422	11,054	12,098	12,410	11,736	12,009	10,903	:	:	:	:
Domestic producer price index (1995=100)	:	:	:	:	:	:	100.0	101.9	104.3	110.7	115.5
Value added (million ECU)	2,621	2,643	2,871	2,900	2,866	2,692	2,420	:	:	:	:

(1) Technically, data before 01/01/1999 are in ECU and after this date in euro. However, as the conversion rate was 1 ECU =1 EUR, for practical purposes the two terms can be used interchangeably.

Table 3.25

Processing and preserving of fish and fish products (NACE Rev. 1 15.2)

Trade related indicators in the EU (1)

	1989	1990	1991	1992	1993	1994	1995	1996	1997	1998	1999
Exports (million EUR)	1,110	1,016	1,111	1,074	1,147	1,305	1,409	1,475	1,610	1,581	1,520
Imports (million EUR)	5,541	5,797	6,599	6,504	5,945	6,753	6,754	7,067	7,928	9,383	8,819
Trade balance (million EUR)	-4,431	-4,781	-5,489	-5,429	-4,798	-5,448	-5,346	-5,591	-6,318	-7,802	-7,299
Cover ratio (%)	20.0	17.5	16.8	16.5	19.3	19.3	20.9	20.9	20.3	16.8	17.2

(1) Technically, data before 01/01/1999 are in ECU and after this date in euro. However, as the conversion rate was 1 ECU =1 EUR, for practical purposes the two terms can be used interchangeably.

Table 3.26

Processing and preserving of fish and fish products (NACE Rev. 1 15.2)

Production related indicators, 1997

	B	DK	D	EL (1)	E	F (1)	IRL	I (1)	L	NL	A	P	FIN	S	UK
Number of persons employed (thousands)	1.3	6.5	15.4	0.8	17.7	11.7	2.8	4.9	0.0	:	0.2	5.6	0.6	1.7	16.0
Production (million ECU)	341	1,055	1,659	44	2,193	1,785	333	1,093	0	443	11	328	86	289	2,081
Value added (million ECU)	59	224	523	9	416	382	88	202	0	92	3	62	21	74	467
Gross operating surplus (million ECU)	20.5	53.3	108.9	1.4	160.1	80.5	43.5	72.9	0.0	30.2	-0.1	18.5	7.5	23.7	155.3

(1) 1996.

Table 3.27

Processing and preserving of fish and fish products (NACE Rev. 1 15.2)

Trade related indicators, 1999

	B	DK	D	EL	E	F	IRL	I	L	NL	A	P	FIN	S	UK
Exports (million EUR)	360	1,816	682	45	1,159	604	169	186	10	1,193	6	195	18	218	674
Imports (million EUR)	708	1,042	1,689	215	2,242	2,104	73	1,922	40	876	160	828	84	433	1,860
Trade balance (million EUR)	-348	774	-1,007	-171	-1,083	-1,501	96	-1,735	-31	318	-154	-633	-66	-215	-1,187
Cover ratio (%)	50.8	174.2	40.4	20.7	51.7	28.7	232.0	9.7	23.7	136.3	3.9	23.5	21.5	50.4	36.2

Table 3.28

Processing and preserving of fish and fish products (NACE Rev. 1 15.2)

Labour related indicators, 1997

	B	DK (1)	D	EL (2)	E	F (2)	IRL	I (2)	L	NL	A	P	FIN	S	UK
Unit personnel costs (thousand ECU per employee)	29.7	27.6	27.0	9.7	14.4	25.8	16.4	26.8	:	:	14.8	7.9	24.1	29.4	19.6
Social charges as a share of personnel costs (%)	34.4	4.0	26.0	29.3	28.9	38.5	13.3	44.6	:	10.8	26.1	29.7	27.4	42.3	9.5
Apparent labour productivity (thousand ECU/pers. empl.)	44.7	34.6	34.1	11.6	23.5	32.7	31.8	41.1	:	:	14.4	11.2	33.6	43.1	29.2
Wage adjusted labour productivity (%)	150.6	148.6	126.1	119.3	162.9	126.7	194.2	153.3	:	:	97.1	141.3	139.5	146.8	149.4
Personnel costs as a share of total operating costs (%)	11.9	14.5	21.0	17.1	10.5	14.7	15.0	10.6	:	14.0	24.3	11.9	13.7	17.8	15.0

(1) Unit personnel costs and wage adjusted labour productivity, 1996; (2) 1996.

Source: Eurostat (SBS, EBT, COMEXT)

Table 3.29

Processing and preserving of fruit and vegetables (NACE Rev. 1 15.3)

Production related indicators in the EU (1)

	1989	1990	1991	1992	1993	1994	1995	1996	1997	1998	1999
Number of persons employed (thousands)	183.2	194.5	196.9	193.2	188.5	185.2	177.3	:	167.9	171.9	175.6
Production (million EUR)	21,595	24,003	26,992	27,721	26,351	27,199	27,476	:	30,562	31,105	31,490
Domestic producer price index (1995=100)	:	:	:	:	:	:	100.0	101.3	100.6	102.3	104.9
Value added (million EUR)	5,291	5,657	6,464	6,779	6,625	7,040	6,795	:	7,287	7,420	7,388

(1) Technically, data before 01/01/1999 are in ECU and after this date in euro. However, as the conversion rate was 1 ECU =1 EUR, for practical purposes the two terms can be used interchangeably.

Table 3.30

Processing and preserving of fruit and vegetables (NACE Rev. 1 15.3)

Trade related indicators in the EU (1)

	1989	1990	1991	1992	1993	1994	1995	1996	1997	1998	1999
Exports (million EUR)	1,438	1,270	1,338	1,356	1,508	1,781	1,828	1,910	2,022	2,153	2,072
Imports (million EUR)	3,384	3,555	3,998	3,893	3,593	3,992	4,023	4,340	4,333	4,556	4,791
Trade balance (million EUR)	-1,946	-2,285	-2,660	-2,537	-2,086	-2,212	-2,194	-2,429	-2,312	-2,403	-2,719
Cover ratio (%)	42.5	35.7	33.5	34.8	42.0	44.6	45.5	44.0	46.7	47.3	43.2

(1) Technically, data before 01/01/1999 are in ECU and after this date in euro. However, as the conversion rate was 1 ECU =1 EUR, for practical purposes the two terms can be used interchangeably.

Table 3.31

Processing and preserving of fruit and vegetables (NACE Rev. 1 15.3)

Production related indicators, 1997

	B	DK	D	EL (1)	E	F	IRL	I (1)	L	NL	A	P	FIN	S	UK
Number of persons employed (thousands)	5.7	2.0	27.4	7.6	32.1	22.6	1.7	21.7	:	:	2.2	4.4	2.1	3.4	33.6
Production (million ECU)	1,527	350	5,628	715	3,701	4,584	169	4,800	:	1,960	612	384	357	673	5,230
Value added (million ECU)	304	95	1,259	123	861	839	61	972	:	486	142	102	107	200	1,773
Gross operating surplus (million ECU)	132.6	36.2	463.9	26.8	354.2	216.0	22.5	387.4	:	216.8	58.8	45.4	50.3	75.6	912.1

(1) 1996.

Table 3.32

Processing and preserving of fruit and vegetables (NACE Rev. 1 15.3)

Trade related indicators, 1999

	B	DK	D	EL	E	F	IRL	I	L	NL	A	P	FIN	S	UK
Exports (million EUR)	1,842	191	1,211	508	1,415	1,211	66	1,675	19	2,280	281	151	19	79	363
Imports (million EUR)	1,155	309	3,355	142	558	2,202	264	972	46	1,604	398	202	167	416	2,238
Trade balance (million EUR)	687	-118	-2,144	366	857	-992	-197	702	-27	676	-117	-51	-148	-337	-1,874
Cover ratio (%)	159.5	61.7	36.1	357.7	253.5	55.0	25.1	172.2	41.0	142.2	70.6	74.6	11.6	18.9	16.2

Table 3.33

Processing and preserving of fruit and vegetables (NACE Rev. 1 15.3)

Labour related indicators, 1997

	B	DK (1)	D	EL (2)	E	F	IRL	I (2)	L	NL	A	P	FIN	S	UK
Unit personnel costs (thousand ECU per employee)	30.2	30.4	29.1	12.7	15.8	27.6	22.7	27.4	:	:	37.2	12.9	27.9	36.1	25.8
Social charges as a share of personnel costs (%)	35.2	5.0	22.6	29.0	28.8	38.8	19.8	41.9	:	17.3	30.0	29.4	25.4	42.4	11.0
Apparent labour productivity (thousand ECU/pers. empl.)	52.9	47.0	45.9	16.2	26.8	37.1	35.4	44.9	:	:	63.5	23.0	50.2	58.2	52.7
Wage adjusted labour productivity (%)	175.4	153.4	157.7	127.5	170.3	134.7	156.1	163.7	:	:	170.9	177.4	179.7	161.0	204.3
Personnel costs as a share of total operating costs (%)	12.2	16.2	14.6	14.1	12.9	13.4	20.9	12.5	:	14.3	14.0	14.5	14.5	19.2	19.6

(1) Unit personnel costs and wage adjusted labour productivity, 1996; (2) 1996.

Source: Eurostat (SBS, EBT, COMEXT)

Table 3.34

Manufacture of vegetable and animal oils and fats (NACE Rev. 1 15.4)

Production related indicators in the EU (1)

	1989	1990	1991	1992	1993	1994	1995	1996	1997	1998	1999
Number of persons employed (thousands)	63.9	67.4	72.0	68.5	56.5	52.7	:	43.7	:	:	:
Production (million ECU)	20,187	22,240	21,626	21,195	20,057	21,484	:	22,384	:	:	:
Domestic producer price index (1995=100)	:	:	:	:	:	:	99.9	108.4	109.1	105.2	101.8
Value added (million ECU)	2,954	3,762	3,323	3,785	3,056	2,830	:	2,509	:	:	:

(1) Technically, data before 01/01/1999 are in ECU and after this date in euro. However, as the conversion rate was 1 ECU =1 EUR, for practical purposes the two terms can be used interchangeably.

Table 3.35

Manufacture of vegetable and animal oils and fats (NACE Rev. 1 15.4)

Trade related indicators in the EU (1)

	1989	1990	1991	1992	1993	1994	1995	1996	1997	1998	1999
Exports (million EUR)	1,397	1,415	1,348	1,554	1,503	1,923	2,486	2,262	3,048	3,251	2,612
Imports (million EUR)	4,811	4,113	4,165	4,132	4,397	5,212	4,810	5,172	5,364	5,341	4,873
Trade balance (million EUR)	-3,414	-2,698	-2,816	-2,579	-2,893	-3,289	-2,324	-2,910	-2,316	-2,090	-2,261
Cover ratio (%)	29.0	34.4	32.4	37.6	34.2	36.9	51.7	43.7	56.8	60.9	53.6

(1) Technically, data before 01/01/1999 are in ECU and after this date in euro. However, as the conversion rate was 1 ECU =1 EUR, for practical purposes the two terms can be used interchangeably.

Table 3.36

Manufacture of vegetable and animal oils and fats (NACE Rev. 1 15.4)

Production related indicators, 1997

	B	DK	D	EL (1)	E	F	IRL	I (1)	L	NL	A	P	FIN	S	UK
Number of persons employed (thousands)	1.4	1.0	8.0	1.6	13.2	4.6	:	3.3	0.0	:	0.8	4.2	0.8	1.7	2.2
Production (million ECU)	1,887	267	4,856	378	6,006	2,350	:	2,126	0	2,714	330	856	286	593	1,766
Value added (million ECU)	123	56	577	60	527	341	:	201	0	306	103	92	66	142	265
Gross operating surplus (million ECU)	54.2	21.4	208.0	19.2	276.7	139.4	:	105.9	0.0	180.1	45.1	46.6	36.9	75.2	168.3

(1) 1996.

Table 3.37

Manufacture of vegetable and animal oils and fats (NACE Rev. 1 15.4)

Trade related indicators, 1999

	B	DK	D	EL	E	F	IRL	I	L	NL	A	P	FIN	S	UK
Exports (million EUR)	1,026	244	1,392	445	843	412	41	822	2	1,864	58	101	51	108	284
Imports (million EUR)	866	463	1,287	86	828	1,612	241	1,657	16	1,142	187	257	81	207	1,176
Trade balance (million EUR)	159	-220	105	359	15	-1,199	-200	-835	-15	722	-129	-156	-30	-99	-892
Cover ratio (%)	118.4	52.6	108.2	519.2	101.8	25.6	16.9	49.6	9.7	163.2	31.0	39.4	62.8	52.1	24.2

Table 3.38

Manufacture of vegetable and animal oils and fats (NACE Rev. 1 15.4)

Labour related indicators, 1997

	B	DK	D	EL (1)	E	F	IRL	I (1)	L	NL	A	P	FIN	S	UK
Unit personnel costs (thousand ECU per employee)	48.3	:	46.0	25.6	18.9	43.4	:	29.8	:	:	68.2	13.4	35.7	38.5	45.0
Social charges as a share of personnel costs (%)	38.2	9.9	31.0	28.8	25.3	44.6	:	47.6	:	12.6	22.2	36.8	29.7	43.1	9.4
Apparent labour productivity (thousand ECU/pers. empl.)	85.5	57.3	71.9	37.3	40.0	73.4	:	60.9	:	:	121.3	22.0	82.6	81.9	123.1
Wage adjusted labour productivity (%)	177.2	:	156.3	145.9	211.6	169.1	:	204.1	:	:	178.0	163.7	231.3	212.8	273.2
Personnel costs as a share of total operating costs (%)	3.7	13.1	7.5	10.2	3.7	8.2	:	4.7	:	3.0	13.4	4.9	10.9	12.1	5.4

(1) 1996.

Source: Eurostat (SBS, EBT, COMEXT)

Table 3.39

Manufacture of dairy products (NACE Rev. 1 15.5)

Production related indicators in the EU (1)

	1989	1990	1991	1992	1993	1994	1995	1996	1997	1998	1999
Number of persons employed (thousands)	317.0	323.8	331.7	323.5	313.7	308.1	297.1	:	284.0	286.9	283.2
Production (million ECU)	74,896	77,732	83,286	84,775	80,384	82,828	85,607	:	:	:	:
Domestic producer price index (1995=100)	:	97.0	93.2	95.2	96.5	97.6	100.0	100.8	100.9	101.8	100.8
Value added (million ECU)	11,969	12,476	14,106	14,246	13,875	13,965	13,912	:	:	:	:

(1) Technically, data before 01/01/1999 are in ECU and after this date in euro. However, as the conversion rate was 1 ECU =1 EUR, for practical purposes the two terms can be used interchangeably.

Table 3.40

Manufacture of dairy products (NACE Rev. 1 15.5)

Trade related indicators in the EU (1)

	1989	1990	1991	1992	1993	1994	1995	1996	1997	1998	1999
Exports (million EUR)	4,434	3,761	3,795	4,043	4,202	3,994	4,665	4,641	4,962	4,580	4,361
Imports (million EUR)	816	759	714	709	790	818	872	836	920	961	984
Trade balance (million EUR)	3,618	3,002	3,081	3,335	3,411	3,176	3,794	3,805	4,041	3,619	3,377
Cover ratio (%)	543.2	495.4	531.4	570.7	531.6	488.4	535.3	555.1	539.1	476.6	443.3

(1) Technically, data before 01/01/1999 are in ECU and after this date in euro. However, as the conversion rate was 1 ECU =1 EUR, for practical purposes the two terms can be used interchangeably.

Table 3.41

Manufacture of dairy products (NACE Rev. 1 15.5)

Production related indicators, 1997

	B	DK	D	EL (1)	E	F	IRL	I (1)	L	NL	A	P	FIN	S	UK
Number of persons employed (thousands)	7.3	12.4	44.6	6.8	25.5	60.1	10.0	38.3	:	:	5.1	9.9	5.9	9.8	37.5
Production (million ECU)	2,680	3,110	17,530	911	5,600	18,580	3,356	10,666	:	5,809	1,665	1,442	1,758	2,310	9,565
Value added (million ECU)	347	595	2,390	186	1,179	2,612	566	2,030	:	842	295	216	296	412	1,984
Gross operating surplus (million ECU)	99.6	229.9	769.5	60.1	549.8	683.8	268.4	728.9	:	324.8	86.9	97.4	109.1	100.1	927.2

(1) 1996.

Table 3.42

Manufacture of dairy products (NACE Rev. 1 15.5)

Trade related indicators, 1999

	B	DK	D	EL	E	F	IRL	I	L	NL	A	P	FIN	S	UK
Exports (million EUR)	1,853	1,301	3,993	103	435	3,866	1,139	962	86	3,152	410	131	199	167	1,011
Imports (million EUR)	1,903	270	2,716	434	836	1,997	279	2,487	75	1,836	350	190	112	194	1,782
Trade balance (million EUR)	-50	1,031	1,277	-331	-401	1,869	860	-1,526	11	1,316	60	-59	87	-27	-771
Cover ratio (%)	97.4	482.2	147.0	23.7	52.0	193.6	407.8	38.7	114.2	171.7	117.2	68.8	178.1	86.1	56.7

Table 3.43

Manufacture of dairy products (NACE Rev. 1 15.5)

Labour related indicators, 1997

	B	DK (1)	D	EL (2)	E	F	IRL	I (2)	L	NL	A	P	FIN	S	UK
Unit personnel costs (thousand ECU per employee)	35.1	33.7	36.4	18.6	24.2	32.1	30.0	34.4	:	:	40.8	12.2	31.8	31.8	28.5
Social charges as a share of personnel costs (%)	38.9	3.8	24.7	29.3	28.5	41.0	17.5	47.0	:	30.3	30.8	30.9	31.6	49.5	10.8
Apparent labour productivity (thousand ECU/pers. empl.)	47.3	47.9	53.6	27.4	46.3	43.4	56.8	53.0	:	:	57.9	21.8	49.9	42.1	52.9
Wage adjusted labour productivity (%)	134.8	164.4	147.2	147.4	191.1	135.5	189.6	154.0	:	:	141.7	178.1	156.9	132.0	185.2
Personnel costs as a share of total operating costs (%)	9.2	9.7	8.5	14.5	11.0	9.4	8.2	11.8	:	8.1	11.4	8.4	10.7	12.5	11.2

(1) Unit personnel costs and wage adjusted labour productivity, 1996; (2) 1996.

Source: Eurostat (SBS, EBT, COMEXT)

_____Table 3.44

Manufacture of grain mill products, starches and starch products (NACE Rev. 1 15.6)

Production related indicators in the EU (1)

	1989	1990	1991	1992	1993	1994	1995	1996	1997	1998	1999
Number of persons employed (thousands)	69.5	67.0	68.5	64.2	62.9	61.2	55.4	:	:	:	:
Production (million ECU)	16,729	16,536	18,034	18,147	18,031	17,441	18,264	:	:	:	:
Domestic producer price index (1995=100)	:	102.1	94.6	96.9	100.3	100.1	100.0	102.1	99.6	97.3	94.2
Value added (million ECU)	3,401	3,490	3,715	3,704	3,758	3,721	3,997	:	:	:	:

(1) Technically, data before 01/01/1999 are in ECU and after this date in euro. However, as the conversion rate was 1 ECU =1 EUR, for practical purposes the two terms can be used interchangeably.

_____Table 3.45

Manufacture of grain mill products, starches and starch products (NACE Rev. 1 15.6)

Trade related indicators in the EU (1)

	1989	1990	1991	1992	1993	1994	1995	1996	1997	1998	1999
Exports (million EUR)	1,024	970	1,064	1,224	1,215	1,202	1,190	1,063	1,462	1,182	1,042
Imports (million EUR)	380	338	360	379	380	548	415	521	602	610	569
Trade balance (million EUR)	645	632	705	845	835	654	775	542	860	572	473
Cover ratio (%)	269.8	286.7	295.8	323.2	319.7	219.3	286.9	204.1	242.9	193.7	183.1

(1) Technically, data before 01/01/1999 are in ECU and after this date in euro. However, as the conversion rate was 1 ECU =1 EUR, for practical purposes the two terms can be used interchangeably.

_____Table 3.46

Manufacture of grain mill products, starches and starch products (NACE Rev. 1 15.6)

Production related indicators, 1997

	B	DK (1)	D	EL (1)	E	F	IRL	I (1)	L	NL	A	P	FIN	S	UK
Number of persons employed (thousands)	2.7	0.8	10.5	1.7	7.9	11.7	0.5	4.7	:	:	1.0	3.4	0.9	1.2	12.9
Production (million ECU)	1,315	290	2,981	376	2,229	3,849	144	2,286	:	1,493	206	514	278	401	4,364
Value added (million ECU)	239	65	642	51	399	825	21	358	:	340	40	70	53	101	1,294
Gross operating surplus (million ECU)	115.7	28.1	240.3	16.5	231.9	369.2	7.0	206.8	:	180.2	1.8	34.6	21.1	51.8	825.6

(1) 1996.

_____Table 3.47

Manufacture of grain mill products, starches and starch products (NACE Rev. 1 15.6)

Trade related indicators, 1999

	B	DK	D	EL	E	F	IRL	I	L	NL	A	P	FIN	S	UK
Exports (million EUR)	457	103	480	33	238	619	41	542	16	321	38	13	8	28	623
Imports (million EUR)	292	130	434	35	116	544	148	137	15	271	73	88	55	114	456
Trade balance (million EUR)	166	-26	46	-3	122	75	-107	406	0	50	-35	-76	-47	-86	167
Cover ratio (%)	156.8	79.8	110.6	92.3	204.7	113.8	27.6	396.4	101.9	118.6	51.8	14.2	14.1	24.6	136.7

_____Table 3.48

Manufacture of grain mill products, starches and starch products (NACE Rev. 1 15.6)

Labour related indicators, 1997

	B	DK (1)	D	EL (1)	E	F	IRL	I (1)	L	NL	A	P	FIN	S	UK
Unit personnel costs (thousand ECU per employee)	49.2	43.5	38.2	20.1	21.3	39.1	30.7	33.3	:	:	38.0	12.2	34.0	39.7	36.6
Social charges as a share of personnel costs (%)	39.6	7.3	25.3	30.8	27.4	44.4	21.2	48.8	:	16.4	33.7	32.3	29.7	43.4	14.6
Apparent labour productivity (thousand ECU/pers. empl.)	89.5	76.7	60.8	29.5	50.3	70.7	45.8	75.6	:	:	39.2	20.3	56.1	82.0	100.5
Wage adjusted labour productivity (%)	182.0	176.2	159.4	147.1	236.0	181.0	149.3	227.2	:	:	103.2	166.2	164.9	206.5	275.0
Personnel costs as a share of total operating costs (%)	10.3	13.5	13.5	11.2	7.0	12.2	8.6	6.8	:	11.1	17.7	7.1	11.6	12.5	12.5

(1) 1996.

Source: Eurostat (SBS, EBT, COMEXT)

Table 3.49

Manufacture of prepared animal feeds (NACE Rev. 1 15.7)

Production related indicators in the EU (1)

	1989	1990	1991	1992	1993	1994	1995	1996	1997	1998	1999
Number of persons employed (thousands)	96.2	97.3	97.3	95.9	93.0	91.4	91.2	88.5	:	:	:
Production (million ECU)	30,398	29,639	30,502	30,522	30,952	31,127	32,111	33,397	:	:	:
Domestic producer price index (1995=100)	:	:	:	:	:	:	100.0	104.3	104.1	98.8	94.8
Value added (million ECU)	4,692	4,755	4,819	4,959	4,862	5,025	4,763	4,949	:	:	:

(1) Technically, data before 01/01/1999 are in ECU and after this date in euro. However, as the conversion rate was 1 ECU =1 EUR, for practical purposes the two terms can be used interchangeably.

Table 3.50

Manufacture of prepared animal feeds (NACE Rev. 1 15.7)

Trade related indicators in the EU (1)

	1989	1990	1991	1992	1993	1994	1995	1996	1997	1998	1999
Exports (million EUR)	506	505	569	702	813	851	953	977	1,109	1,176	1,073
Imports (million EUR)	146	185	226	268	284	328	339	787	961	925	843
Trade balance (million EUR)	360	320	343	434	529	523	614	190	147	251	230
Cover ratio (%)	345.7	272.5	251.6	261.7	286.3	259.3	281.4	124.1	115.3	127.1	127.3

(1) Technically, data before 01/01/1999 are in ECU and after this date in euro. However, as the conversion rate was 1 ECU =1 EUR, for practical purposes the two terms can be used interchangeably.

Table 3.51

Manufacture of prepared animal feeds (NACE Rev. 1 15.7)

Production related indicators, 1997

	B	DK	D	EL (1)	E	F	IRL	I (1)	L	NL	A	P	FIN	S	UK
Number of persons employed (thousands)	4.2	1.5	11.3	1.0	12.8	17.3	1.7	6.9	0.0	:	1.2	4.6	1.4	:	17.3
Production (million ECU)	2,494	325	4,219	180	5,134	6,884	554	4,056	0	4,142	294	1,053	501	:	5,766
Value added (million ECU)	262	59	765	19	572	819	75	456	0	598	61	134	85	:	1,234
Gross operating surplus (million ECU)	103.4	13.4	258.4	1.4	292.1	165.0	30.4	213.0	0.0	291.0	18.0	71.6	35.3	:	636.8

(1) 1996.

Table 3.52

Manufacture of prepared animal feeds (NACE Rev. 1 15.7)

Trade related indicators, 1999

	B	DK	D	EL	E	F	IRL	I	L	NL	A	P	FIN	S	UK
Exports (million EUR)	560	308	614	5	133	1,047	88	109	1	957	85	9	16	12	420
Imports (million EUR)	439	124	664	105	241	358	137	454	24	375	98	160	47	100	413
Trade balance (million EUR)	121	184	-50	-100	-108	689	-50	-345	-23	582	-13	-151	-31	-88	8
Cover ratio (%)	127.5	248.7	92.5	4.9	55.3	292.3	63.8	24.0	4.1	255.0	86.4	5.7	33.3	11.8	101.9

Table 3.53

Manufacture of prepared animal feeds (NACE Rev. 1 15.7)

Labour related indicators, 1997

	B	DK (1)	D	EL (2)	E	F	IRL	I (2)	L	NL	A	P	FIN	S	UK
Unit personnel costs (thousand ECU per employee)	40.4	38.7	45.0	16.7	22.1	37.9	26.9	36.0	:	:	35.0	13.4	38.0	:	34.7
Social charges as a share of personnel costs (%)	36.9	3.9	26.7	29.3	27.8	43.8	19.0	47.3	:	21.4	29.3	31.8	29.1	:	14.0
Apparent labour productivity (thousand ECU/pers. empl.)	63.0	39.6	67.5	18.1	44.8	47.4	44.9	66.1	:	:	49.5	28.9	61.7	:	71.4
Wage adjusted labour productivity (%)	155.9	164.3	150.1	107.8	202.3	125.2	167.0	183.6	:	:	141.2	215.0	162.4	:	205.5
Personnel costs as a share of total operating costs (%)	6.6	14.0	11.1	8.2	4.9	8.3	8.1	6.1	:	6.4	14.2	6.1	10.8	:	8.4

(1) Unit personnel costs and wage adjusted labour productivity, 1996; (2) 1996.

Source: Eurostat (SBS, EBT, COMEXT)

Table 3.54

Manufacture of other food products (NACE Rev. 1 15.8)
Production related indicators in the EU (1)

	1989	1990	1991	1992	1993	1994	1995	1996	1997	1998	1999
Number of persons employed (thousands)	907.8	929.4	940.2	943.4	920.8	917.8	896.2	:	:	:	:
Production (million ECU)	86,202	91,863	98,497	104,568	106,035	110,734	113,462	:	:	:	:
Domestic producer price index (1995=100)	:	88.2	89.4	92.0	94.0	96.8	100.0	101.0	102.9	104.2	103.8
Value added (million ECU)	25,937	28,740	31,438	33,357	34,471	35,652	35,166	:	:	:	:

(1) Technically, data before 01/01/1999 are in ECU and after this date in euro. However, as the conversion rate was 1 ECU =1 EUR, for practical purposes the two terms can be used interchangeably.

Table 3.55

Manufacture of other food products (NACE Rev. 1 15.8)
Trade related indicators in the EU (1)

	1989	1990	1991	1992	1993	1994	1995	1996	1997	1998	1999
Exports (million EUR)	4,351	4,909	4,779	5,268	6,229	7,477	7,981	8,289	9,021	8,798	7,770
Imports (million EUR)	2,175	2,252	2,392	2,510	2,600	2,839	2,868	3,139	3,085	3,197	3,351
Trade balance (million EUR)	2,176	2,657	2,387	2,758	3,629	4,638	5,113	5,150	5,937	5,601	4,419
Cover ratio (%)	200.0	218.0	199.8	209.9	239.6	263.4	278.3	264.1	292.5	275.2	231.9

(1) Technically, data before 01/01/1999 are in ECU and after this date in euro. However, as the conversion rate was 1 ECU =1 EUR, for practical purposes the two terms can be used interchangeably.

Table 3.56

Manufacture of other food products (NACE Rev. 1 15.8)
Production related indicators, 1997

	B	DK	D	EL (1)	E	F	IRL	I (1)	L	NL	A	P	FIN	S	UK
Number of persons employed (thousands)	47.7	20.1	281.9	13.4	146.1	108.6	:	67.0	2.2	:	23.5	57.7	17.2	19.8	172.2
Production (million ECU)	6,826	2,969	33,041	1,068	10,185	22,166	:	13,888	115	7,528	2,421	1,991	2,090	2,956	23,160
Value added (million ECU)	1,838	957	9,910	302	3,616	5,170	:	3,773	59	2,259	937	620	731	1,044	9,054
Gross operating surplus (million ECU)	796.2	338.5	3,043.3	74.7	1,317.9	1,715.3	:	1,610.9	17.5	1,020.6	229.8	227.0	280.2	362.8	4,501.9

(1) 1996.

Table 3.57

Manufacture of other food products (NACE Rev. 1 15.8)
Trade related indicators, 1999

	B	DK	D	EL	E	F	IRL	I	L	NL	A	P	FIN	S	UK
Exports (million EUR)	2,914	1,048	3,922	117	1,024	4,328	1,396	2,636	28	3,313	558	123	136	445	2,299
Imports (million EUR)	1,981	588	3,831	285	1,377	3,305	583	1,263	108	1,452	761	506	325	628	3,633
Trade balance (million EUR)	933	460	91	-168	-353	1,023	813	1,373	-80	1,861	-203	-383	-189	-183	-1,334
Cover ratio (%)	147.1	178.2	102.4	41.0	74.3	131.0	239.3	208.7	25.9	228.2	73.3	24.4	41.8	70.8	63.3

Table 3.58

Manufacture of other food products (NACE Rev. 1 15.8)
Labour related indicators, 1997

	B	DK (1)	D	EL (2)	E	F	IRL	I (2)	L	NL	A	P	FIN	S	UK
Unit personnel costs (thousand ECU per employee)	26.4	38.6	24.5	17.0	17.5	31.8	:	32.9	21.5	:	30.4	7.5	27.6	34.5	26.8
Social charges as a share of personnel costs (%)	38.1	5.9	23.6	29.6	28.3	40.3	:	51.1	:	20.3	31.4	31.6	26.5	43.6	12.5
Apparent labour productivity (thousand ECU/pers. empl.)	38.5	47.7	35.2	22.5	24.8	47.6	:	56.3	27.2	:	39.9	10.7	42.4	52.8	52.6
Wage adjusted labour productivity (%)	146.0	153.0	143.4	132.1	141.7	149.6	:	171.0	126.3	:	131.2	143.4	154.0	153.2	196.4
Personnel costs as a share of total operating costs (%)	17.4	22.6	21.4	21.9	22.3	15.8	:	16.7	40.9	16.2	26.9	20.5	22.8	24.1	22.4

(1) Unit personnel costs and wage adjusted labour productivity, 1996; (2) 1996.

Source: Eurostat (SBS, EBT, COMEXT)

Table 3.59

Manufacture of beverages (NACE Rev. 1 15.9)

Production related indicators in the EU (1)

	1989	1990	1991	1992	1993	1994	1995	1996	1997	1998	1999
Number of persons employed (thousands)	377.2	384.3	384.6	371.0	361.2	346.1	326.8	:	:	:	:
Production (million ECU)	63,892	70,370	75,019	76,447	74,702	76,767	79,816	:	:	:	:
Domestic producer price index (1995=100)	:	85.0	87.0	91.2	94.2	96.6	100.0	103.0	104.9	106.5	107.4
Value added (million ECU)	19,526	21,226	22,260	22,943	22,889	22,747	22,550	:	:	:	:

(1) Technically, data before 01/01/1999 are in ECU and after this date in euro. However, as the conversion rate was 1 ECU =1 EUR, for practical purposes the two terms can be used interchangeably.

Table 3.60

Manufacture of beverages (NACE Rev. 1 15.9)

Trade related indicators in the EU (1)

	1989	1990	1991	1992	1993	1994	1995	1996	1997	1998	1999
Exports (million EUR)	6,334	6,692	6,883	7,261	7,963	8,873	8,838	9,499	10,697	10,091	10,941
Imports (million EUR)	693	870	1,007	1,143	1,216	1,323	1,307	1,603	2,015	2,286	2,654
Trade balance (million EUR)	5,640	5,822	5,877	6,118	6,746	7,549	7,531	7,896	8,682	7,805	8,288
Cover ratio (%)	913.4	769.5	683.8	635.1	654.6	670.6	676.3	592.5	531.0	441.4	412.3

(1) Technically, data before 01/01/1999 are in ECU and after this date in euro. However, as the conversion rate was 1 ECU =1 EUR, for practical purposes the two terms can be used interchangeably.

Table 3.61

Manufacture of beverages (NACE Rev. 1 15.9)

Production related indicators, 1997

	B	DK	D	EL (1)	E	F	IRL	I (1)	L	NL	A (1)	P	FIN	S	UK
Number of persons employed (thousands)	10.7	6.9	80.1	7.8	45.6	39.9	4.7	28.1	0.7	:	10.2	15.5	3.6	6.3	51.7
Production (million ECU)	3,011	1,236	19,420	1,160	9,563	13,464	2,417	8,655	130	3,366	1,911	1,819	790	1,332	21,510
Value added (million ECU)	833	531	5,376	323	2,935	3,605	958	1,688	52	1,094	706	501	261	474	5,146
Gross operating surplus (million ECU)	345.6	299.5	2,040.2	137.0	1,566.1	1,879.7	762.3	726.9	29.2	608.5	252.9	269.1	154.9	234.3	3,364.7

(1) 1996.

Table 3.62

Manufacture of beverages (NACE Rev. 1 15.9)

Trade related indicators, 1999

	B	DK	D	EL	E	F	IRL	I	L	NL	A	P	FIN	S	UK
Exports (million EUR)	1,100	292	1,669	106	1,596	8,847	727	3,011	56	1,694	570	570	107	323	4,684
Imports (million EUR)	1,466	514	3,222	267	988	1,656	460	871	169	1,089	269	376	172	478	4,395
Trade balance (million EUR)	-366	-222	-1,553	-161	608	7,192	268	2,140	-113	604	301	194	-65	-155	289
Cover ratio (%)	75.0	56.9	51.8	39.8	161.5	534.4	158.2	345.6	32.9	155.5	212.1	151.6	62.4	67.6	106.6

Table 3.63

Manufacture of beverages (NACE Rev. 1 15.9)

Labour related indicators, 1997

	B	DK (1)	D	EL (2)	E	F	IRL	I (2)	L	NL	A (2)	P	FIN	S	UK
Unit personnel costs (thousand ECU per employee)	46.2	40.2	41.9	24.0	28.5	43.3	41.3	34.9	31.6	:	:	15.1	37.4	38.0	34.5
Social charges as a share of personnel costs (%)	45.2	7.6	24.6	33.5	24.7	42.5	22.8	50.4	:	27.9	30.1	36.2	33.2	45.2	15.5
Apparent labour productivity (thousand ECU/pers. empl.)	78.1	77.1	67.1	41.6	64.3	90.4	201.9	60.1	70.3	:	69.2	32.2	72.2	75.3	99.5
Wage adjusted labour productivity (%)	169.0	175.7	160.2	173.5	226.1	209.0	489.2	172.3	222.4	:	:	213.8	193.0	197.9	288.0
Personnel costs as a share of total toperating costs (%)	19.8	22.9	18.7	18.4	14.4	15.1	15.0	11.2	18.1	19.1	27.7	13.2	20.1	20.3	14.8

(1) Unit personnel costs and wage adjusted labour productivity, 1996; (2) 1996.

Source: Eurostat (SBS, EBT, COMEXT)

Table 3.64

Manufacture of tobacco products (NACE Rev. 1 16)

Production related indicators in the EU (1)

	1989	1990	1991	1992	1993	1994	1995	1996	1997	1998	1999
Number of persons employed (thousands)	91.5	87.4	85.2	81.4	77.0	72.3	:	:	:	:	:
Production (million ECU)	35,061	37,067	40,407	40,187	40,288	41,455	:	:	:	:	:
Domestic producer price index (1995=100)	:	:	:	:	:	:	100.4	102.4	107.7	111.8	114.7
Value added (million ECU)	5,045	5,191	6,778	7,311	11,599	12,483	:	:	:	:	:

(1) Technically, data before 01/01/1999 are in ECU and after this date in euro. However, as the conversion rate was 1 ECU =1 EUR, for practical purposes the two terms can be used interchangeably.

Table 3.65

Manufacture of tobacco products (NACE Rev. 1 16)

Trade related indicators in the EU (1)

	1989	1990	1991	1992	1993	1994	1995	1996	1997	1998	1999
Exports (million EUR)	739	886	1,218	1,445	1,422	958	857	1,299	1,999	1,902	1,952
Imports (million EUR)	362	402	571	592	949	924	404	386	204	219	207
Trade balance (million EUR)	376	484	647	854	473	35	453	913	1,794	1,683	1,745
Cover ratio (%)	203.8	220.4	213.3	244.3	149.8	103.7	212.2	336.3	978.2	869.0	944.2

(1) Technically, data before 01/01/1999 are in ECU and after this date in euro. However, as the conversion rate was 1 ECU =1 EUR, for practical purposes the two terms can be used interchangeably.

Table 3.66

Manufacture of tobacco products (NACE Rev. 1 16)

Production related indicators, 1997

	B	DK	D	EL (1)	E	F	IRL	I (1)	L	NL	A	P	FIN	S	UK
Number of persons employed (thousands)	2.8	:	13.3	2.8	9.3	:	1.0	13.7	:	:	:	1.2	0.7	:	8.4
Production (million ECU)	1,625	:	13,118	350	1,952	:	937	6,760	:	3,929	:	1,025	109	:	22,258
Value added (million ECU)	209	:	1,527	96	501	:	162	609	:	1,329	:	34	34	:	1,858
Gross operating surplus (million ECU)	96.9	:	793.5	33.2	193.5	:	121.8	237.9	:	1,082.7	:	5.3	4.9	:	1,341.1

(1) 1996.

Table 3.67

Manufacture of tobacco products (NACE Rev. 1 16)

Trade related indicators, 1999

	B	DK	D	EL	E	F	IRL	I	L	NL	A	P	FIN	S	UK
Exports (million EUR)	462	147	1,605	137	66	329	59	15	143	2,622	78	28	11	24	1,534
Imports (million EUR)	393	17	644	139	481	1,557	53	1,185	193	385	49	34	46	77	200
Trade balance (million EUR)	68	130	961	-2	-415	-1,229	6	-1,171	-50	2,237	29	-7	-35	-52	1,334
Cover ratio (%)	117.4	844.1	249.2	98.6	13.8	21.1	111.5	1.2	74.3	680.3	158.1	80.7	23.5	32.0	767.5

Table 3.68

Manufacture of tobacco products (NACE Rev. 1 16)

Labour related indicators, 1997

	B	DK	D	EL (1)	E	F	IRL	I (1)	L	NL	A	P	FIN	S	UK
Unit personnel costs (thousand ECU per employee)	39.7	:	55.3	22.7	30.2	:	42.2	27.2	:	:	:	24.1	35.9	:	61.8
Social charges as a share of personnel costs (%)	44.0	:	32.4	33.0	28.6	:	31.8	35.9	:	23.6	:	88.9	29.5	:	20.9
Apparent labour productivity (thousand ECU/pers. empl.)	73.5	:	115.2	34.7	53.9	:	168.9	44.5	:	:	:	28.5	46.8	:	221.9
Wage adjusted labour productivity (%)	185.1	:	208.1	152.7	178.7	:	400.2	163.9	:	:	:	118.4	130.5	:	359.2
Personnel costs as a share of total operating costs (%)	7.3	:	14.6	14.7	10.0	:	17.7	5.1	:	12.8	:	17.2	25.2	:	16.1

(1) 1996.

Source: Eurostat (SBS, EBT, COMEXT)

Textiles, clothing, leather and footwear (NACE Rev. 1 17, 18, and 19)

This chapter covers the manufacture of textiles through to the production of finished items such as clothing and footwear. The manufacture of textiles (NACE Rev. 1 17) encompasses activities such as the processing of fibres, weaving and finishing. Clothing production is covered by NACE Rev. 1 18 and comprises of clothes which are made from leather, textiles and fur. The tanning and dressing of leather (NACE Rev. 1 19) is classified separately, and includes the manufacture of footwear, luggage and other leather products.

It is important to note that the vast majority of data reported upon in this chapter concerns information that relates to enterprises with 20 or more persons employed (see the guide to statistics at the start of this publication for specific country details). This decision was taken as it allows time-series to be shown. Nevertheless, in industries where small enterprises have a relatively important economic weight the under-reporting of the true level of the economic activity in question should be borne in mind.

For example, within the manufacture of textiles, clothing, leather and footwear small enterprises (employing less than 20 persons) are estimated to have accounted for 18.5% of total production in 1997[1].

---

(1) D and EL, no data available; I, 1996.

Low-wage production centres in developing economies have taken an increasing share of production in these activities. As a result, EU manufacturers of textiles, clothing, leather and footwear have responded by switching their production to high value goods, using modern technologies to innovate new materials and fibres.

Figure 4.1

**Textiles, clothing, leather and footwear
(NACE Rev. 1 17, 18 and 19)
Share of total manufacturing value added
in the EU, 1999 (%)**

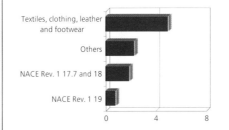

Source: Eurostat (SBS)

EU enterprises have adapted to new realities...
Nevertheless, substantial rationalisation has taken place. Many EU producers have followed these global trends and re-located their production facilities to regions such as Asia, North Africa and Eastern Europe. These changes have boosted world production levels, increased economic activity in less industrialised countries and often resulted in lower prices.

... whilst remaining relatively labour-intensive
EU production of textiles, clothing, leather and footwear reached 193.3 billion EUR in 1999, which was equivalent to 4.8% of total manufacturing output. This share was well below the corresponding share of persons employed, 8.7% (or just over 2 million persons).

The activities covered in this chapter (in terms of NACE Rev. 1) include:

17: manufacture of textiles;
17.1: preparation and spinning of textile fibres;
17.2: textile weaving;
17.3: finishing of textiles;
17.4: manufacture of made-up textile articles, except apparel;
17.5: manufacture of other textiles;
17.6: manufacture of knitted and crocheted fabrics;
17.7: manufacture of knitted and crocheted articles;
18: manufacture of wearing apparel; dressing and dyeing of fur;
18.1: manufacture of leather clothes;
18.2: manufacture of other wearing apparel and accessories;
18.3: dressing and dyeing of fur; manufacture of articles of fur;
19: tanning and dressing of leather; manufacture of luggage, handbags, saddlery, harness and footwear;
19.1: tanning and dressing of leather;
19.2: manufacture of luggage, handbags and the like, saddlery and harness;
19.3: manufacture of footwear.

Figure 4.2

Share of clothing and footwear in total household consumption in the EU (%)

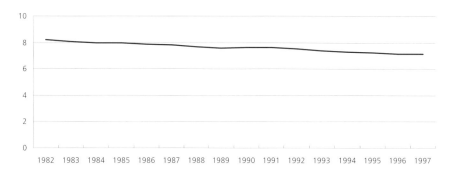

Source: Eurostat (SEC2)

In 1996, clothing (sub-chapter 4.3) was the largest of the industries covered in this chapter, with approximately 67.8 billion ECU of output[2], equivalent to just over a third of the total (37%). It was followed by the manufacture of textiles (sub-chapter 4.1) with approximately 52.2 billion ECU of output[3] (or 28% of the total). There were smaller, but still significant levels of output within the leather and footwear industries (sub-chapter 4.4), where production was valued at 35.0 billion ECU (19% of the total) and the made-up

textiles and other textiles industries (sub-chapter 4.2), with output equal to 29.0 billion ECU (16% of the total)[4].

Italy was by far the largest producer, but Portugal and Greece were relatively more specialised
Textiles, clothing, leather and footwear accounted of 11.9% of Italy's total manufacturing output in 1996, equivalent to 59.7 billion ECU. Italy reported a relative production specialisation ratio of 226.6% in 1995.

Germany was much less specialised, despite 28.4 billion ECU of output in 1997, which made it the second largest producer in the EU. Nearly a fifth of Portugal's manufacturing output (19.0%) was generated in these industries in 1997. Production of 11.5 billion ECU made Portugal the sixth largest manufacturer of textiles, clothing, leather and footwear in the EU, with a relative production specialisation ratio of 360.6% in 1997. Greek output totalled 2.3 billion ECU in 1996, which was equivalent to more than a tenth of the domestic manufacturing total (11.2%).

Almost 14% of EU enterprises were found to be manufacturing textiles, clothing, leather or footwear
The industries covered by this chapter accounted for 13.9% of all manufacturing enterprises in the EU in 1996, a proportionately large number considering that they contributed just over 5% of total manufacturing output. More than four-fifths of the 279 thousand textiles, clothing, leather and footwear enterprises covered by in this chapter were very small in size (with between 0 and 9 employees), whilst 16.3% were small (with between 10 and 49 employees). Their respective shares of total employment were considerably different, as the workforce was distributed quite evenly between enterprises of different size classes. Just under a fifth of the persons employed (19.0%) worked in a very small enterprise, slightly less than a third (31.3%) in a small enterprise, whilst 26.6% were working for medium-sized enterprises and 23.0% in large enterprises.

(2) L, no data available for NACE Rev. 1 18; IRL, no data available for NACE Rev. 1 17.7.
(3) S, no data available for NACE Rev. 1 17.1; IRL, no data available for NACE Rev. 1 17.3 and 17.6.

(4) IRL, L and S, no data available for NACE Rev. 1 17.4; L, no data available for NACE Rev. 1 17.5.

Table 4.1

Textiles, clothing, leather and footwear (NACE Rev. 1 17, 18 and 19)

Breakdown of turnover and employment by employment size class, 1997 (%)

	Micro (0-9)		Small (10-49)		Medium (50-249)		Large (250+)	
	Turnover (1)	Employment (2)	Turnover (1)	Employment (1)	Turnover (3)	Employment (4)	Turnover (5)	Employment (5)
EU-15	11.8	19.0	27.8	31.3	30.3	26.6	30.1	23.0
B	11.0	18.0	:	26.4	24.1	27.1	:	:
DK	:	:	:	:	:	:	:	:
D	4.3	16.3	11.8	18.3	31.3	27.7	52.7	37.7
EL	:	:	:	:	:	:	:	:
E	:	:	:	:	:	:	:	:
F	10.6	13.8	27.8	27.1	33.6	35.3	28.1	23.8
IRL	:	:	:	:	:	:	:	:
I	14.7	25.4	37.9	43.5	28.6	20.1	18.8	11.0
L	:	:	:	:	:	:	:	:
NL	:	:	:	:	:	:	:	:
A	4.7	11.2	14.2	18.3	29.7	27.6	52.0	44.6
P	6.8	10.8	24.5	28.6	41.5	36.4	27.2	24.2
FIN	15.9	18.4	21.9	25.4	32.5	32.4	:	:
S	15.4	:	35.6	27.9	:	:	:	:
UK	14.7	15.7	16.8	17.5	:	:	:	:

(1) EU-15, F, I, P and S, 1996.
(2) EU-15, F, I and P, 1996.
(3) EU-15, F, I, A, P and FIN, 1996.
(4) EU-15, B, F, I, A, P and FIN, 1996.
(5) EU-15, F, I, A and P, 1996.

Source: Eurostat (SME)

Figure 4.3

Textiles, clothing, leather and footwear (NACE Rev. 1 17, 18 and 19)
EU production and value-added in constant prices and employment compared to total manufacturing (1990=100)

Production in constant prices

Value added in constant prices

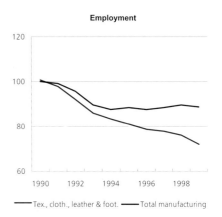

Employment

Source: Eurostat (SBS)

STRUCTURE AND PERFORMANCE

Between 1989 and 1999, EU production in current prices increased by 19.9 billion ECU to 193.3 billion EUR, whilst value added at factor cost rose by 2.6 billion ECU to 60.3 billion EUR. Growth rates were below manufacturing averages for both production and value added during the whole of the 1990s. Production in constant prices rose by 1.2% per annum during the five years to 1998 (3.7 percentage points below the EU manufacturing average).

Profitability was usually below
the manufacturing average

In 1999, the gross operating rate for textiles, clothing, leather and footwear industries was equal to 8.7%, some 0.7 percentage points lower than the manufacturing average. There was little volatility in the figures reported over the period 1989 to 1999, as the operating rate for the industries covered by this chapter varied between a high of 8.9% in 1994 and a low of 8.1% in 1991.

LABOUR AND PRODUCTIVITY

Almost a third of the net reduction in total manufacturing employment in the EU between 1989 and 1999 could be attributed to losses within this industry. Between these dates, the textiles, clothing, leather and footwear workforce fell from 2.8 to 2.0 million persons. This was equivalent to a 29.9% reduction, which resulted in this industry's share of total manufacturing employment falling from 10.8% to 8.7%.

The size of the workforce declined steadily over the decade. Employment fell at an average annual rate of 3.2% during the ten-year period 1989 to 1999. The largest losses were recorded in 1992 and 1993 with reductions of 6.1% and 6.6% respectively (whilst there was also a 5.3% decline in 1999).

Productivity consistently lower than
the manufacturing average

The employment losses contributed towards the increase in apparent labour productivity, which rose from 20.5 thousand ECU in 1989 to 29.9 thousand EUR in 1999. As such, labour productivity grew at a slower rate than the manufacturing average, with the difference rising from 14.8 thousand ECU in 1989 to 21.9 thousand EUR by 1999. Wage adjusted labour productivity ratios remained relatively constant, rising somewhat from 134.1% in 1991 to 141.4% in 1995, whilst finishing the decade at 140.9% in 1999.

Table 4.2

Textiles, clothing, leather and footwear
(NACE Rev. 1 17, 18 and 19)
Composition of the labour force, 1999 (%)

	Women (1)	Part-time (2)	Highly-educated (3)
EU-15	60.4	10.0	6.0
B	51.0	6.0	12.3
DK	67.0	13.2	17.9
D	60.9	18.5	12.6
EL	57.2	4.4	5.5
E	57.9	7.7	8.4
F	60.4	6.1	8.5
IRL	56.2	13.7	:
I	59.4	6.2	2.4
L	:	:	:
NL	45.0	27.8	:
A	62.1	15.0	:
P	72.3	5.4	1.2
FIN	67.0	12.5	16.7
S	:	:	:
UK	57.0	15.3	7.3

(1) EU-15 and EL, 1998.
(2) EU-15, B, EL and FIN, 1998.
(3) DK and EL, 1998; EU-15, 1997.

Source: Eurostat (LFS)

Figure 4.4

Textiles, clothing, leather and footwear (NACE Rev. 1 17, 18 and 19)

Apparent labour productivity and unit personnel costs, 1997 (thousand ECU)

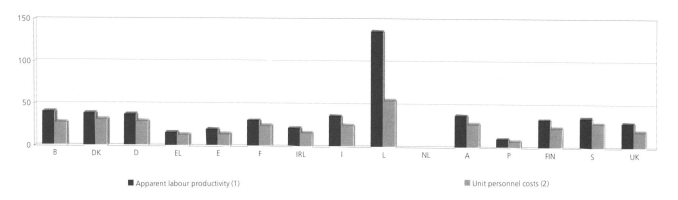

■ Apparent labour productivity (1)　　　　■ Unit personnel costs (2)

(1) EL and I, 1996; NL, not available.
(2) DK, EL and I, 1996; NL, not available.

Source: Eurostat (SBS)

A predominantly female workforce

In 1999, women made up 60.8% of the EU workforce in these industries[5], the highest proportion of any of the industries covered in this publication (at the level of chapter headings employed in this publication). The average participation rate of women in the manufacturing workforce was 28.3%. Indeed, the high proportion of women employed in these activities exceeded the shares of other female-dominated sectors of the economy, such as retail trade (NACE Rev. 1 52), where women made up the 57.0% of the workforce.

(5) EL, no data available.

INTERNATIONAL TRENDS AND FOREIGN TRADE

In 1997, nearly half of the 412.8 billion ECU of Triad production came from the EU (48.5%), over a third from the USA (34.2%) and under a fifth (17.4%) from Japan. The EU increased its share of output when compared to ten years earlier from 44.1% in 1987, largely to the detriment of Japan (whose share declined from 22.6%). All three Triad members reported that textiles, clothing, leather and footwear had a declining share of their domestic manufacturing output between 1989 and 1999, with the global figure for the Triad falling from 5.8% in 1987 to 4.3% by 1997.

Employment fell at a similar rate throughout the Triad

Employment levels fell at a rapid pace throughout the Triad, with ten-year average annual rates equal to -2.8% in the EU (to 1997), -2.4% in the USA (to 1997) and -3.5% in Japan (to 1996). The total Triad workforce fell from 6.1 million persons in 1985 to 4.9 million persons in 1995, with the following respective shares for each Triad member in 1995: 46.8% in the EU, 33.4% in the USA and 19.8% in Japan.

Figure 4.5

Textiles, clothing, leather and footwear (NACE Rev. 1 17, 18 and 19)

International comparison of production, value added and employment

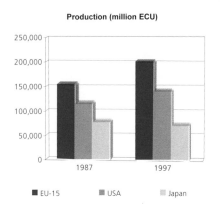
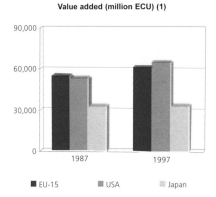
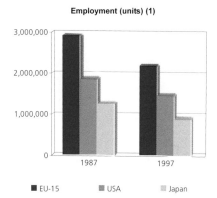

(1) JAP, 1996.

Source: Eurostat (SBS)

EU trade deficit widened

The EU trade deficit reached 27.2 billion EUR in 1999, a figure almost twice that reported in 1997, and over three times the 1989 figure. Although exports increased from 26.1 billion ECU in 1989 to 44.2 billion EUR in 1999, imports grew at a quicker pace, more than doubling between 1989 and 1999 from 35.1 billion ECU to 71.4 billion EUR. Similar trends prevailed in the USA, where the trade deficit grew from 33.8 billion ECU in 1989 to 60.3 billion ECU in 1998. The Japanese trade deficit more than doubled between 1989 and 1996 to reach 20.6 billion ECU, although it had subsequently fallen to 16.4 billion ECU by 1998.

China, the principal origin of imports

China was the most important origin for EU imports in 1999, with goods valued at 12.4 billion EUR. Turkey was the second most important origin in 1999, accounting for almost a tenth of the total (9.2%). India was relegated to third place, with its imports to the value of 8.8 billion EUR (or 6.2% of the total).

The principal markets for EU textiles, clothes, leather and footwear exports remained the USA (7.2 billion EUR), Switzerland (4.0 billion EUR) and Japan (3.1 billion EUR). Each of their relative shares declined in comparison to 1989, as EU enterprises developed new markets in Central and Eastern Europe, in particular in Poland (2.7 billion EUR) and Romania (2.1 billion EUR).

Figure 4.6

**Textiles, clothing, leather and footwear
(NACE Rev. 1 17, 18 and 19)
Destination of EU exports, 1999 (%)**

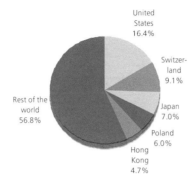

Source: Eurostat (COMEXT)

Figure 4.7

**Textiles, clothing, leather and footwear
(NACE Rev. 1 17, 18 and 19)
Origin of EU imports, 1999 (%)**

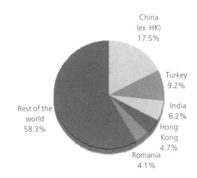

Source: Eurostat (COMEXT)

SUB-CHAPTER 4.1
MANUFACTURE OF TEXTILES
(NACE Rev. 1 17.1, 17.2, 17.3 AND 17.6)

The manufacture of textiles consists of the preparation and spinning of fibres (NACE Rev. 1 17.1), the weaving and knitting of fabrics (NACE Rev. 1 17.2 and 17.6) and the finishing of textiles (NACE Rev. 1 17.3). All types of fibre are included, in other words both natural and synthetic fibres. The finishing of textiles includes processes such as bleaching and printing of textiles.

The success of one or other textile is often based on price and fashion. Innovations such as polyester/cotton or acrylic/wool blends and wrinkle resistant cotton have served to offer consumers more choice. Clothing manufactures (the main downstream industry) are continually seeking the ideal material that combines ease of wear with ease of care.

In 1996, the European textiles industry reported output equal to 52.2 billion ECU[6]. This figure represented around 28% of textiles, clothing, leather and footwear production[7]. Textile weaving (NACE Rev. 1 17.2) was the largest single activity amongst those covered by this sub-chapter, with a 41% share, followed by the preparation and spinning of textile fibres (NACE Rev. 1 17.1) with around 31%[8], the finishing of textiles (NACE Rev. 1 17.3) with approximately 19%[9] and the manufacture of knitted and crocheted articles (NACE Rev. 1 17.6) with 9%.

There were just over half a million persons employed in the EU textiles industry (506.5 thousand)[10], which was equivalent to just under a quarter (23%) of the textiles, clothing, leather and footwear total[11] - somewhat lower than the corresponding share of output.

(6) S, no data available for NACE Rev. 1 17.1; IRL, no data available for NACE Rev. 1 17.3 and 17.6.
(7) IRL and S, no data available for NACE Rev. 1 17.1 to 17.3 and 17.6; IRL, L and S, no data available for NACE Rev. 1 17.4 and 17.5; IRL and L, no data available for NACE Rev. 1 17.7 and 18.
(8) S, no data available..
(9) IRL, no data available.
(10) IRL, no data available for NACE Rev. 1 17.3 and 17.6; NL, no data available.
(11) IRL, NL and S, no data available for NACE Rev. 1 17.1 to 17.3 and 17.6; IRL, L, NL and S, no data available for NACE Rev. 1 17.4 and 17.5; IRL, L and NL, no data available for NACE Rev. 1 17.7 and 18.

Figure 4.8

Manufacture of textiles (NACE Rev. 1 17.1, 17.2, 17.3 and 17.6)

Production and export specialisation (%)

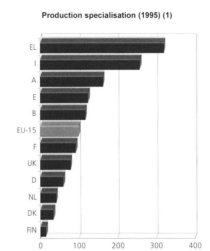

Production specialisation (1995) (1)

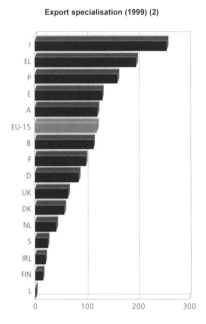

Export specialisation (1999) (2)

(1) DK, 1994; IRL, L, P and S, not available.
(2) Excluding NACE Rev. 1 17.3.

Source: Eurostat (SBS, COMEXT)

STRUCTURE AND PERFORMANCE

There were similar levels of production for the manufacture of textiles in Germany (7.8 billion ECU) and France (7.6 billion ECU) in 1997, where textiles accounted for 0.8% and 1.2% respectively of domestic manufacturing output. The United Kingdom (5.6 billion ECU) and Spain (5.2 billion ECU) followed in the ranking of output.

A key industry in southern Member States
However, the by far the largest textile industry in the EU was in Italy, with production valued at 18.5 billion ECU in 1996, equivalent to 3.7% of domestic manufacturing. Portugal was also relatively specialised in the manufacture of textiles, with production of 2.8 billion ECU in 1997 (or 4.6% of domestic manufacturing), somewhat higher than the relative share of textiles in Greece (4.2% in 1996).

The gross operating rate of the EU textiles industry was 9.6% in 1995, 0.4 percentage points above the manufacturing average. More recent data was available for textile weaving (NACE Rev. 1 17.2), where the gross operating rate followed a steady path between 1995 and 1999, fluctuating between 9.1% and 10.0%.

LABOUR AND PRODUCTIVITY

Employment fell by 118 thousand persons between 1993 and 1995, resulting in 449 thousand persons being employed. As a result of the reduction in employment, apparent labour productivity increased from 28.2 thousand ECU to 35.0 thousand ECU per person employed, whilst wage adjusted labour productivity rose from 134.0% to 144.2%.

Again more recent data is available for textile weaving, where the average annual decline in employment between 1994 and 1999 was equal to 2.3%. Apparent labour productivity did not evolve from its 1995 level of 37.4 thousand ECU, and finished just 0.5 thousand ECU higher in 1999.

INTERNATIONAL TRENDS AND FOREIGN TRADE

The EU was the largest producer of textiles in the Triad. In 1995, the relative shares of Triad textiles' production were 43.0% in the EU, 29.5% in Japan and 27.5% in the USA. There was a diverging trend in the data reported by the other two members of the Triad, as output declined in Japan during the 1990s (to 27.0 billion ECU in 1997), whilst there was growth in the USA (35.8 billion ECU in 1997).

─────────────────────────**Box 4.1**

World output of synthetic fibres totalled 29.9 million tons in 1998. Production in volume terms more than doubled between 1978 (14.3 million tons) and 1998. Production was concentrated within the manufacture of polyester (16.0 million tons), olefin (4.9 million tons), nylon (3.9 million tons) and acrylics (2.7 million tons). Asia was the main centre for world synthetic fibre production in 1998, producing 15.8 million tons, compared to 5.4 million tons in North America.

Rising EU exports lead to an increasing trade surplus
Textiles was the only industry covered in this chapter that reported a trade surplus in 1999[12]. The EU surplus grew from 857 million ECU in 1989 to 4.8 billion EUR in 1999. Imports rose by about 1.5 billion ECU to 8.3 billion EUR over this period, whilst exports almost doubled to 13.1 billion EUR.

Japan also reported a trade surplus in the textiles industry, 1.2 billion ECU in 1998 (its second highest surplus of the 1990s). There was little change in the USA, where a 1.8 billion ECU trade deficit in 1998 was synonymous with trade performance during the 1990s.

Eastern Europe and North Africa become important export markets for the EU
In 1999, Poland (1.3 billion EUR), Tunisia (1.2 billion EUR), the USA (1.1 billion EUR), Morocco (also 1.1 billion EUR) and Romania (1.0 billion EUR) were the top five destinations for EU exports, suggesting that EU firms were exporting textiles to be made-up into garments and articles, before re-importing finished goods.

Turkey was the main origin of EU imports in 1999, accounting for more than a tenth of the total (11.7%). India increased its share of the EU market between 1989 and 1999 (9.4% of the total). The level of imports originating from China was similar in 1989 and 1999 (the latter figure being 719 million EUR or 8.7%).

(12) All external trade data in this section exclude NACE Rev. 1 17.3.

─────────────────────────**Figure 4.9**

Manufacture of textiles
(NACE Rev. 1 17.1, 17.2 and 17.6)
Destination of EU exports, 1999 (%)

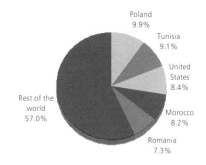

Source: Eurostat (COMEXT)

─────────────────────────**Figure 4.10**

Manufacture of textiles
(NACE Rev. 1 17.1, 17.2 and 17.6)
Origin of EU imports, 1999 (%)

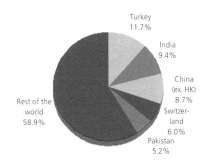

Source: Eurostat (COMEXT)

SUB-CHAPTER 4.2
MADE-UP TEXTILES AND OTHER TEXTILES
(NACE Rev. 1 17.4 AND 17.5)

The manufacture of made-up textiles and other textiles covers all final textile processing activities, except for the manufacture of clothes. The production of made-up textile articles (NACE Rev. 1 17.4) encompasses a wide variety of articles, including household products (blankets, table linen, bed clothes, curtains and so on) as well as outdoor products (camping goods, sails and tarpaulins). Other textile production (NACE Rev. 1 17.5) includes the manufacture of carpets and rugs, various types of rope, netting and non-woven apparel.

In 1996, EU output was close to 29 billion ECU[13], approximately 16% of the activities covered in this chapter[14], with a workforce of 292 thousand persons[15], approximately 13% of the total number of persons employed in the whole of textiles, clothing, leather and footwear[16].

The breakdown of this industry was divided into approximately 70% for made-up textile production (NACE Rev. 1 17.4) and 30% for other textile production (NACE Rev. 1 17.5).

Germany and the United Kingdom
the largest producers
In 1997, both Germany and the United Kingdom accounted for one fifth of the EU's output of made-up and other textile production (valued at 5.8 billion ECU in each country). France was the third ranking producer (4.5 billion ECU), followed by Italy (3.9 billion ECU, 1996).

With the exception of Luxembourg (378 million ECU of output, which is equivalent to 6.0% of the domestic manufacturing total) there were two other countries that were relatively specialised in the manufacture of made-up and other textiles: Belgium (4.3 billion ECU, or 2.8% of domestic manufacturing output) and Portugal (1.1 billion ECU, equivalent to 1.8%).

(13) IRL, L and S, no data available for NACE Rev. 1 17.4; L, no data available for NACE Rev. 1 17.5.
(14) IRL and S, no data available for NACE Rev. 1 17.1 to 17.3 and 17.6; IRL, L and S, no data available for NACE Rev. 1 17.4 and 17.5; IRL and L, no data available for NACE Rev. 1 17.7 and 18.
(15) IRL, L, NL and S, no data available for NACE Rev. 1 17.4; L and NL, no data available for NACE Rev. 1 17.5.
(16) IRL, NL and S, no data available for NACE Rev. 1 17.1 to 17.3 and 17.6; IRL, L, NL and S, no data available for NACE Rev. 1 17.4 and 17.5; IRL, L and NL, no data available for NACE Rev. 1 17.7 and 18.

Figure 4.11

Made-up textiles and other textiles (NACE Rev. 1 17.4 and 17.5)
Production and export specialisation (%)

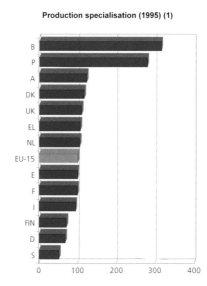

Production specialisation (1995) (1)

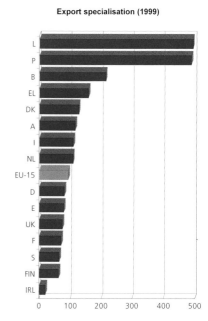

Export specialisation (1999)

(1) S, 1994; IRL and L, not available.

Source: Eurostat (SBS, COMEXT)

STRUCTURE AND PERFORMANCE

Production increased by 11.5 billion ECU in current prices between 1985 and 1996, with output equal to around 29.0 billion ECU[17]. The average annual growth rate of production in constant prices during the five years to 1995 was 0.6%, 0.1 percentage points higher than the manufacturing average.

More recent data was reported for the manufacture of made-up textile articles (NACE Rev. 1 17.4), where production fell on average by 0.3% per annum between 1990 and 1996. The manufacture of other textiles (NACE Rev. 1 17.5) recorded real production growth of 2.9% per annum between 1990 and 1998.

(17) IRL, L and S, no data available for NACE Rev. 1 17.4; L, no data available for NACE Rev. 1 17.5.

LABOUR AND PRODUCTIVITY

Employment fell at a relatively slow pace when compared to other industries within this chapter. Between 1985 and 1995, 10.6 thousand jobs were lost, leaving 294.5 thousand persons employed. The average annual rate of change over this period was -0.4%, which was 0.7 percentage points above the manufacturing average.

Productivity lagged behind manufacturing averages
Apparent labour productivity of the made-up textiles and other textiles industries was below the EU manufacturing average between 1985 and 1995. Indeed, the difference in the two levels increased from 7.9 thousand ECU per person employed in 1985 to 14.5 thousand ECU by 1995. Apparent labour productivity of the made-up textiles and other textiles industries increased from 19.4 thousand ECU to 30.8 thousand ECU.

—————————————————————————— Figure 4.12

Made-up textiles and other textiles (NACE Rev. 1 17.4 and 17.5)

International comparison of production in constant prices and employment (1990=100)

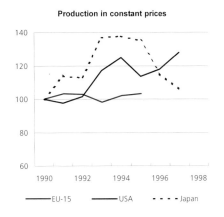

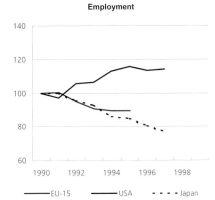

Source: Eurostat (SBS)

INTERNATIONAL TRENDS AND FOREIGN TRADE

The USA was the largest producer of made-up and other textiles in the Triad in 1995, despite its share of Triad output falling from 48.8% in 1985 to 42.1%. Subsequently, American output grew to 39.6 billion ECU in 1997. The EU increased its share of Triad production, up from 29.6% in 1985 to 34.1% in 1995, whilst the Japanese share rose by 2.2 percentage points to 23.8% (or 19.6 billion ECU) in 1995, before falling to 15.9 billion ECU by 1997.

EU trade deficit worsens towards the end of the 1990s

Imports and exports were almost balanced in the EU in 1996 (with a small trade deficit of 46.6 million ECU). This deficit widened to 864 million EUR by 1999, as imports rose at a rapid pace. The other two Triad members also recorded trade deficits, equal to 2.4 billion ECU in the USA and 884 million ECU in Japan (both 1998).

The USA was the main export destination for EU made-up and other textile products in both 1989 and 1999 (when EU exports were valued at 1.1 billion EUR). Switzerland maintained its position as the second most important export destination, with a value of 573 million EUR in 1999. Poland and the Czech Republic followed, with exports valued at 506 million EUR and 330 million EUR respectively.

China (1.0 billion EUR) and India (847 million EUR) were the two main origins of EU imports of made-up and other textiles in 1999. However, looking at the growth of imports between 1989 and 1999, imports from Turkey expanded at a rapid pace, rising from 244 million ECU to 750 million EUR.

—————————————————————————— Figure 4.13

Made-up textiles and other textiles

(NACE Rev. 1 17.4 and 17.5)

Destination of EU exports, 1999 (%)

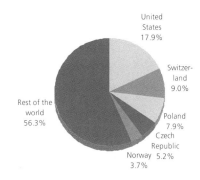

Source: Eurostat (COMEXT)

—————————————————————————— Figure 4.14

Made-up textiles and other textiles

(NACE Rev. 1 17.4 and 17.5)

Origin of EU imports, 1999 (%)

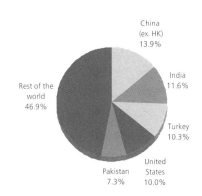

Source: Eurostat (COMEXT)

SUB-CHAPTER 4.3
CLOTHING INCLUDING KNITTED ARTICLES
(NACE Rev. 1 17.7 AND 18)

This sub-chapter deals with the manufacture of clothing and furs (NACE Rev. 1 18), as well as the manufacture of knitted and crocheted articles (such as pullovers and cardigans), which are classified under the heading of NACE Rev. 1 17.7. The clothing activities classified within NACE Rev. 1 18 are broken down into three different Groups covering leather clothes; workwear, outerwear, underwear and accessories; and fur.

The clothing industry is the largest of those covered within this chapter, with production valued at 71.7 billion ECU in 1999 (around 37% of the textiles, clothing, leather and footwear total). In 1999, almost 904 thousand persons were employed in the EU, which was equivalent to around 45% of those employed within the activities covered by this chapter.

The speed with which enterprises identify fashion trends and translate these observations into high quality, affordable garments is an increasingly important factor of competitiveness. In the past, this process could take over a year, but enterprises now seek response times equal to a matter of weeks, thanks to the development of new manufacturing technologies.

STRUCTURE AND PERFORMANCE
The average annual growth rate of production in constant prices during the five years to 1998 was equal to 0.7%, which was 4.2 percentage points lower than the manufacturing average.

Portugal, Greece and Italy specialised
in clothing manufacture
For most Member States, this industry accounted for less than 2% of manufacturing output (the EU average was 1.8% in 1999). The principal exceptions to this rule were Portugal, where clothing industries accounted for 8.1% of manufacturing output in 1997, Greece (5.1% in 1996) and Italy (4.2% in 1996). Italy had by far the highest value of production in the EU (21.2 billion ECU, 1996), with output almost double the value recorded in Germany (11.4 billion ECU) in 1997.

Figure 4.15

Clothing including knitted articles (NACE Rev. 1 17.7 and 18)
Production and export specialisation (%)

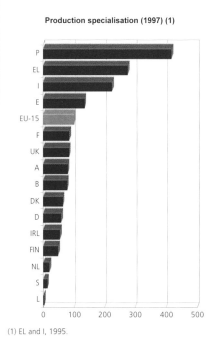

Production specialisation (1997) (1)

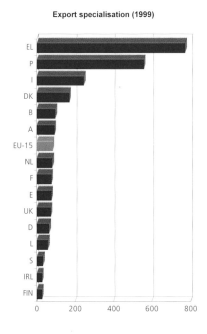

Export specialisation (1999)

(1) EL and I, 1995.

Source: Eurostat (SBS, COMEXT)

LABOUR AND PRODUCTIVITY
Between 1993 and 1999 there were 226.6 thousand fewer persons employed in the clothing industry. The annual average rate of decline during the five years to 1999 was equal to 3.4%, which was 3.6 percentage points below the EU manufacturing average. The largest decline recorded during this period was in 1999, when employment fell by 6.8% (to reach 904 thousand persons).

Slow growth in productivity
Apparent labour productivity edged upwards from 20.1 thousand ECU in 1993 to 25.1 thousand EUR in 1999. Over the same period, there was a significant increase in the apparent labour productivity of the EU manufacturing sector as a whole, which led to a widening of the difference between the two levels from 20.1 thousand ECU in 1993 to 26.7 thousand EUR by 1999.

Taking personnel costs into account there was a similar trend, as wage adjusted labour productivity rose gradually in the clothing industry to 133.2% in 1999, whilst the difference with manufacturing grew from 4.2 percentage points in 1993 to 17.8 points by 1999.

INTERNATIONAL TRENDS AND FOREIGN TRADE

In 1997, the EU accounted for almost half (48.7%) of total Triad output, followed by the USA (57.6 billion ECU, 38.1%) and Japan (20.0 billion ECU, 13.2%). Employment fell at a slower rate in the EU than in the other Triad countries. The EU textiles industry saw its employment levels reduced by 3.0% per annum on average during the five years to 1997, compared to annual average reductions of 7.6% in Japan and 4.3% in the USA. The EU accounted for almost half of the workforce in the Triad, with its share rising from 44.8% in 1993 to 47.9% in 1997, whilst Japan lost 2.6 percentage points over the same period, down to 16.7%.

EU trade deficit widened

The EU's trade deficit almost tripled between 1989 and 1999, moving from 9.9 billion ECU to 28.7 billion EUR. EU exports increased by almost 6 billion ECU between 1989 and 1999, to reach 14.1 billion EUR, whilst imports rose by 24.4 billion ECU to 42.7 billion EUR in 1999. The other two Triad members also recorded widening trade deficits in the clothing industry. In the USA, the deficit grew from 21.3 billion ECU in 1989 to 40.2 billion ECU in 1998, whilst in Japan the deficit almost doubled during the 1990s to reach 12.6 billion ECU in 1998.

Imports from Asia, Turkey and northern Africa, exports to the Triad and neighbouring European countries

China (16.6%), Turkey (11.3%) and Hong Kong (6.7%) were the main origins for EU imports in 1999 (as had been the case in 1989). In fourth and fifth place were Tunisia and Morocco whose respective shares of EU imports had increased between 1989 and 1999 (to reach 5.6% and 5.0%).

In 1999, the most important export destinations for the EU clothing industry were the USA (2.3 billion EUR), Switzerland (2.1 billion EUR), Japan (1.4 billion EUR) and Norway (672 million EUR). The same four countries had also been the top four export destinations in 1989, although Switzerland had been the leading country in that year (1.9 billion ECU).

Figure 4.16

**Clothing including knitted articles
(NACE Rev. 1 17.7 and 18)
Destination of EU exports, 1999 (%)**

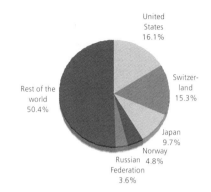

Source: Eurostat (COMEXT)

Figure 4.17

**Clothing including knitted articles
(NACE Rev. 1 17.7 and 18)
Origin of EU imports, 1999 (%)**

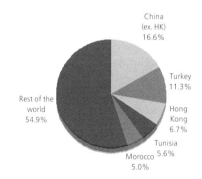

Source: Eurostat (COMEXT)

SUB-CHAPTER 4.4
LEATHER AND FOOTWEAR
(NACE Rev. 1 19)

This sub-chapter deals with leather processing and footwear industries, covering the initial processing, tanning and dressing of leather (NACE Rev. 1 19.1), the manufacture of luggage, bags and accessories (NACE Rev. 1 19.2) and the footwear industry (NACE Rev. 1 19.3). Substitute materials that are used in the manufacture of luggage, bags and footwear are also included in these NACE Rev. 1 Groups.

In 1999, the production value of the leather and footwear industries reached 35.7 billion EUR in the EU. There were 359 thousand persons employed in the EU. As such, leather and footwear industries are labour-intensive, demonstrated by the fact that they employed 1.5% of EU's manufacturing workforce, whilst they accounted for just 0.9% of its output.

EU production dominated by Italy, whilst
Portugal was more specialised
Italian leather and footwear production reached 16.0 billion ECU in 1996. This figure was higher than the combined total of the next three largest European producers, Spain (6.0 billion ECU), France (3.4 billion ECU) and Germany (3.3 billion ECU) in 1997. There was also a significant level of activity in Portugal (2.7 billion ECU) in 1997. Leather and footwear industries generally accounted for less than 1% of manufacturing output in the Member States in 1997, a share which rose as high as 4.5% in Portugal, 3.2% in Italy (1996) and 2.2% in Spain.

STRUCTURE AND PERFORMANCE
There was a fluctuating trend to production growth in the EU during the 1990s. Production fell by between 5.0% and 6.0% in real terms in 1992, 1993, 1995 and 1998, whilst positive rates of growth were recorded in 1994 (7.8%), 1996 and 1997 (up by more than 4.0%). The average growth rate of production between 1993 and 1998 was equal to 0.9% per annum, which was 4.0 percentage points below the manufacturing average.

Profitability declined to 1997, but has
since recovered some of the lost ground
The gross operating rate of the leather and footwear industries remained between 7% and 9% during the 1990s, falling from a high of 8.8% in 1995 to 7.2% in 1997, whilst recovering to 8.2% by 1999. The gross operating rate remained below the EU manufacturing average throughout the 1990s, finishing 1.2 percentage points lower in 1999.

Figure 4.18 ───────────────────────

Leather and footwear (NACE Rev. 1 19)

Production and export specialisation (%)

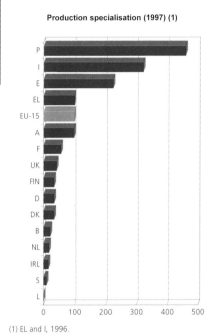
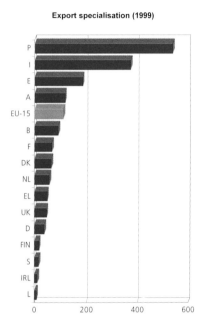

(1) EL and I, 1996.

Source: Eurostat (SBS, COMEXT)

Figure 4.19 ───────────────────────

Leather and footwear (NACE Rev. 1 19)

International comparison of production in constant prices and employment (1990=100)

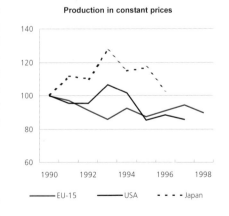
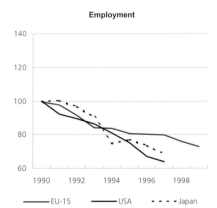

Source: Eurostat (SBS)

LABOUR AND PRODUCTIVITY

Leather and footwear industries experienced a substantial reduction in their employment levels, with almost 125 thousand net jobs lost between 1989 and 1999, resulting in almost 359 thousand persons employed. The average annual rate of decline between these two dates was equal to 2.7%, which was nearly 2 percentage points below the manufacturing average. The largest reductions were recorded at the beginning and end of the 1990s, for example 1992 (-6.3%) and 1993 (-8.0%), as well as 1998 (-4.6%) and 1999 (-4.1%).

Productivity rose slowly

The 1990s saw apparent labour productivity increase from 20.0 thousand ECU in 1990 to 26.9 thousand EUR in 1999. This fairly modest evolution meant that the leather and footwear industries showed a result that was nearly half the level of total manufacturing (51.8 thousand EUR) in 1999. However, when taking personnel costs into account, wage adjusted labour productivity progressed at a more rapid pace than the manufacturing average, rising from 137.5% in 1989 to 146.8% in 1999. This increase meant that the difference between leather and footwear wage adjusted labour productivity and the EU manufacturing average was reduced from 11.5 percentage points in 1989 to 4.2 points by 1999.

INTERNATIONAL TRENDS AND FOREIGN TRADE

In 1997, the EU accounted for 68.7% of the Triad's output of leather goods and footwear, which was up from 61.9% in 1987. The corresponding shares of the other two Triad members were the USA (15.0%) and Japan (16.3%).

EU production in constant prices rose by an average of 0.9% per annum over the five years to 1998. Japanese production fell by 1.6% per annum in real terms between 1991 and 1996, whilst in the USA output fell by 2.1% per annum in real terms between 1992 and 1997.

EU employs more than 7 out of 10 persons in the Triad

The average annual rates of employment reduction between 1987 and 1997 showed that the EU workforce was contracting at a slower speed than in either Japan or the USA. Employment fell by 2.5% per annum in the EU, whilst the corresponding rates were 3.9% in Japan and 5.2% in the USA. Consequently, the EU's share of total Triad employment rose from 66.4% to 71.1%.

Deficits were common in the EU during the 1990s

The EU leather and footwear industries recorded a trade deficit of 2.5 billion EUR in 1999, which marked a deterioration in its trade position compared to the majority of the 1990s. Japan recorded a trade deficit that grew from 1.8 billion ECU in 1989 to 4.2 billion ECU in 1998. The USA recorded by far the largest deficit within the Triad, equal to 15.8 billion ECU in 1998 (compared to 9.8 billion ECU in 1989).

China once again the principal importer into the EU

China jumped from being the third largest origin of EU imports in 1989 to become the most important partner country in 1999 (3.6 billion EUR), accounting for more than a quarter of the EU total (27.9%). Vietnam was the second most important origin of imports, with a rapidly increasing share of the EU market (up from 0.01% to 10.7% between 1989 and 1999).

The USA remained the largest export market for the EU with exports valued at 2.7 billion EUR in 1999, followed by Japan (1.1 billion EUR) and Hong Kong (883 million EUR).

Figure 4.20

Leather and footwear (NACE Rev. 1 19)
Destination of EU exports, 1999 (%)

Source: Eurostat (COMEXT)

Figure 4.21

Leather and footwear (NACE Rev. 1 19)
Origin of EU imports, 1999 (%)

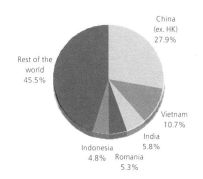

Source: Eurostat (COMEXT)

Table 4.3

Preparation and spinning of textile fibres (NACE Rev. 1 17.1)

Production related indicators in the EU

	1989	1990	1991	1992	1993	1994	1995	1996	1997	1998	1999
Number of persons employed (thousands)	:	:	:	:	187.9	186.4	144.3	:	:	:	:
Production (million ECU)	:	:	:	:	15,447	17,456	15,908	:	:	:	:
Domestic producer price index (1995=100)	:	:	:	:	:	:	:	:	:	:	:
Value added (million ECU)	:	:	:	:	4,903	5,508	4,787	:	:	:	:

Table 4.4

Preparation and spinning of textile fibres (NACE Rev. 1 17.1)

Trade related indicators in the EU (1)

	1989	1990	1991	1992	1993	1994	1995	1996	1997	1998	1999
Exports (million EUR)	1,670	1,495	1,454	1,448	1,589	1,862	1,858	1,861	1,986	1,863	1,880
Imports (million EUR)	2,638	2,570	2,393	2,240	2,005	2,758	2,605	2,533	3,142	3,103	2,805
Trade balance (million EUR)	-969	-1,075	-939	-792	-416	-896	-748	-671	-1,157	-1,240	-924
Cover ratio (%)	63.3	58.2	60.8	64.7	79.3	67.5	71.3	73.5	63.2	60.1	67.0

(1) Technically, data before 01/01/1999 are in ECU and after this date in euro. However, as the conversion rate was 1 ECU =1 EUR, for practical purposes the two terms can be used interchangeably.

Table 4.5

Preparation and spinning of textile fibres (NACE Rev. 1 17.1)

Production related indicators, 1997

	B	DK	D	EL (1)	E	F	IRL	I (1)	L	NL	A	P	FIN	S	UK
Number of persons employed (thousands)	4.7	0.3	16.0	7.6	17.8	17.5	1.0	41.2	0.0	:	2.9	19.0	0.4	:	21.5
Production (million ECU)	570	27	2,041	515	1,602	2,208	100	5,944	0	55	385	881	30	:	1,964
Value added (million ECU)	169	10	616	151	490	554	36	1,620	0	18	135	269	10	:	654
Gross operating surplus (million ECU)	53.4	3.2	102.1	30.5	177.1	102.7	13.7	612.5	0.0	3.2	45.5	102.6	1.5	:	199.6

(1) 1996.

Table 4.6

Preparation and spinning of textile fibres (NACE Rev. 1 17.1)

Trade related indicators, 1999

	B	DK	D	EL	E	F	IRL	I	L	NL	A	P	FIN	S	UK
Exports (million EUR)	571	40	1,065	134	447	909	78	1,647	0	80	267	117	10	16	580
Imports (million EUR)	716	141	1,102	149	425	773	102	1,585	2	189	234	445	40	56	778
Trade balance (million EUR)	-145	-100	-37	-15	21	137	-23	62	-2	-109	33	-328	-29	-39	-198
Cover ratio (%)	79.7	28.7	96.6	89.6	105.0	117.7	77.1	103.9	2.2	42.4	114.1	26.3	26.3	28.9	74.5

Table 4.7

Preparation and spinning of textile fibres (NACE Rev. 1 17.1)

Labour related indicators, 1997

	B	DK (1)	D	EL (2)	E	F	IRL	I (2)	L	NL	A	P	FIN	S	UK
Unit personnel costs (thousand ECU per employee)	25.8	33.9	32.2	15.8	17.4	25.8	21.4	25.0	:	:	30.2	8.8	22.3	:	21.4
Social charges as a share of personnel costs (%)	42.9	4.4	23.3	31.8	28.9	34.3	20.4	52.4	:	14.4	31.3	30.9	27.5	:	12.0
Apparent labour productivity (thousand ECU/pers. empl.)	35.7	37.7	38.5	19.9	27.5	31.6	34.8	39.4	:	:	45.6	14.2	25.3	:	30.5
Wage adjusted labour productivity (%)	138.4	161.3	119.6	125.3	158.0	122.8	163.0	157.6	:	:	151.1	161.3	113.5	:	142.1
Personnel costs as a share of total operating costs (%)	22.5	30.5	23.5	27.5	18.1	20.7	25.1	18.6	:	29.0	25.6	20.4	31.0	:	24.5

(1) Unit personnel costs and wage adjusted labour productivity, 1996; (2) 1996.

Source: Eurostat (SBS, EBT, COMEXT)

Table 4.8

Textile weaving (NACE Rev. 1 17.2)

Production related indicators in the EU (1)

	1989	1990	1991	1992	1993	1994	1995	1996	1997	1998	1999
Number of persons employed (thousands)	:	:	:	:	205.0	195.3	163.9	191.2	179.6	182.9	173.8
Production (million EUR)	:	:	:	:	18,935	20,171	19,773	21,498	22,972	21,997	21,548
Domestic producer price index (1995=100)	:	:	:	:	:	:	100.0	99.8	100.0	:	:
Value added (million EUR)	:	:	:	:	6,013	6,272	6,137	6,491	6,746	6,609	6,580

(1) Technically, data before 01/01/1999 are in ECU and after this date in euro. However, as the conversion rate was 1 ECU =1 EUR, for practical purposes the two terms can be used interchangeably.

Table 4.9

Textile weaving (NACE Rev. 1 17.2)

Trade related indicators in the EU (1)

	1989	1990	1991	1992	1993	1994	1995	1996	1997	1998	1999
Exports (million EUR)	5,421	5,779	5,983	6,409	7,028	7,838	8,486	8,905	9,922	10,163	9,627
Imports (million EUR)	3,876	4,126	3,995	3,762	3,731	4,238	4,324	4,354	4,994	5,116	4,711
Trade balance (million EUR)	1,545	1,653	1,988	2,647	3,298	3,599	4,162	4,550	4,928	5,047	4,917
Cover ratio (%)	139.9	140.1	149.8	170.4	188.4	184.9	196.2	204.5	198.7	198.7	204.4

(1) Technically, data before 01/01/1999 are in ECU and after this date in euro. However, as the conversion rate was 1 ECU =1 EUR, for practical purposes the two terms can be used interchangeably.

Table 4.10

Textile weaving (NACE Rev. 1 17.2)

Production related indicators, 1997

	B	DK	D	EL (1)	E	F	IRL	I (1)	L	NL	A	P	FIN	S	UK
Number of persons employed (thousands)	9.6	0.8	26.0	1.8	17.3	20.0	1.1	55.3	0.0	:	3.9	21.3	0.4	1.5	18.7
Production (million ECU)	1,318	77	3,489	144	2,110	3,024	114	8,140	0	306	462	937	47	163	1,780
Value added (million ECU)	424	29	1,106	29	480	762	36	2,422	0	95	152	283	14	61	622
Gross operating surplus (million ECU)	137.3	6.1	266.7	-3.5	183.6	209.3	4.8	968.9	0.0	31.6	32.6	107.0	5.0	16.5	176.4

(1) 1996.

Table 4.11

Textile weaving (NACE Rev. 1 17.2)

Trade related indicators, 1999

	B	DK	D	EL	E	F	IRL	I	L	NL	A	P	FIN	S	UK
Exports (million EUR)	1,937	199	3,990	58	1,105	2,868	97	5,737	2	815	582	404	62	213	1,443
Imports (million EUR)	941	311	2,794	295	957	1,900	118	1,730	7	619	442	663	135	221	2,391
Trade balance (million EUR)	997	-112	1,196	-237	148	968	-20	4,007	-5	196	140	-259	-73	-9	-949
Cover ratio (%)	206.0	63.9	142.8	19.7	115.4	151.0	82.7	331.6	23.7	131.7	131.6	60.9	46.1	96.1	60.3

Table 4.12

Textile weaving (NACE Rev. 1 17.2)

Labour related indicators, 1997

	B	DK (1)	D	EL (2)	E	F	IRL	I (2)	L	NL	A	P	FIN	S	UK
Unit personnel costs (thousand ECU per employee)	30.3	32.2	32.4	18.2	17.5	27.7	29.6	26.8	:	:	30.4	8.3	24.5	30.2	24.0
Social charges as a share of personnel costs (%)	42.1	4.6	23.0	32.6	29.3	35.7	51.7	50.8	:	22.0	28.8	28.9	25.0	42.0	13.1
Apparent labour productivity (thousand ECU/pers. empl.)	44.3	37.9	42.5	16.2	27.7	38.2	33.9	43.8	:	:	38.6	13.3	36.6	41.5	33.3
Wage adjusted labour productivity (%)	146.2	128.9	131.4	89.0	158.4	137.9	114.7	163.8	:	:	127.1	159.9	149.2	137.3	138.5
Personnel costs as a share of total operating costs (%)	24.5	31.9	24.3	22.2	15.1	19.1	28.7	20.5	:	22.7	26.5	21.2	20.0	30.0	26.9

(1) Unit personnel costs and wage adjusted labour productivity, 1996; (2) 1996.

Source: Eurostat (SBS, EBT, COMEXT)

Table 4.13

Finishing of textiles (NACE Rev. 1 17.3)

Production related indicators in the EU (1)

	1989	1990	1991	1992	1993	1994	1995	1996	1997	1998	1999
Number of persons employed (thousands)	151.4	150.5	147.2	136.2	126.3	125.2	111.3	:	120.8	117.3	114.7
Production (million EUR)	10,637	10,654	10,742	9,865	9,171	9,760	9,438	:	11,201	10,630	10,597
Domestic producer price index (1995=100)	:	:	:	:	:	:	:	:	:	:	:
Value added (million EUR)	4,107	4,112	3,590	4,160	3,763	3,937	3,746	:	4,241	4,017	3,991

(1) Technically, data before 01/01/1999 are in ECU and after this date in euro. However, as the conversion rate was 1 ECU =1 EUR, for practical purposes the two terms can be used interchangeably.

Table 4.14

Finishing of textiles (NACE Rev. 1 17.3)

Production related indicators, 1997

	B	DK	D	EL (1)	E	F	IRL	I (1)	L	NL	A	P	FIN	S (1)	UK
Number of persons employed (thousands)	4.3	0.6	16.4	2.2	14.0	15.6	:	36.6	0.0	:	2.0	10.1	0.4	0.4	14.8
Production (million ECU)	459	39	1,625	126	870	1,812	:	3,564	0	331	223	362	28	32	1,094
Value added (million ECU)	145	20	578	53	382	547	:	1,398	0	140	84	142	12	13	511
Gross operating surplus (million ECU)	37.4	3.6	45.5	15.3	115.1	105.8	:	385.4	0.0	49.3	12.2	53.2	4.3	2.1	163.9

(1) 1996.

Table 4.15

Finishing of textiles (NACE Rev. 1 17.3)

Labour related indicators, 1997

	B	DK (1)	D	EL (2)	E	F	IRL	I (2)	L	NL	A	P	FIN	S (2)	UK
Unit personnel costs (thousand ECU per employee)	25.3	32.8	32.7	17.5	19.5	28.3	:	28.4	:	:	35.2	8.9	23.9	29.2	23.8
Social charges as a share of personnel costs (%)	38.3	3.2	23.4	30.7	28.9	37.2	:	54.3	:	17.9	30.7	31.4	25.9	:	12.9
Apparent labour productivity (thousand ECU/pers. empl.)	33.6	33.6	35.3	24.5	27.2	35.1	:	38.1	:	:	41.1	14.1	32.2	35.1	34.5
Wage adjusted labour productivity (%)	133.2	125.6	108.0	139.9	139.8	124.0	:	134.5	:	:	116.7	158.0	134.7	120.3	144.9
Personnel costs as a share of total operating costs (%)	25.5	46.3	32.5	36.8	34.2	26.2	:	31.9	:	30.7	33.1	27.6	30.9	35.0	36.7

(1) Unit personnel costs and wage adjusted labour productivity, 1996; (2) 1996.

Source: Eurostat (SBS, EBT)

Table 4.16

Manufacture of made-up textile articles, except apparel (NACE Rev. 1 17.4)
Production related indicators in the EU (1)

	1989	1990	1991	1992	1993	1994	1995	1996	1997	1998	1999
Number of persons employed (thousands)	132.2	132.8	134.2	125.6	122.3	122.6	103.2	114.1	:	:	:
Production (million ECU)	7,708	8,282	8,807	9,146	8,719	9,217	8,397	9,104	:	:	:
Domestic producer price index (1995=100)	:	90.7	92.5	94.3	95.3	97.1	100.0	101.5	102.2	103.6	104.3
Value added (million ECU)	2,707	2,756	3,131	3,215	3,109	3,253	2,853	3,032	:	:	:

(1) Technically, data before 01/01/1999 are in ECU and after this date in euro. However, as the conversion rate was 1 ECU =1 EUR, for practical purposes the two terms can be used interchangeably.

Table 4.17

Manufacture of made-up textile articles, except apparel (NACE Rev. 1 17.4)
Trade related indicators in the EU (1)

	1989	1990	1991	1992	1993	1994	1995	1996	1997	1998	1999
Exports (million EUR)	756	740	799	787	892	985	1,089	1,196	1,305	1,399	1,471
Imports (million EUR)	1,326	1,491	1,899	1,981	2,207	2,444	2,568	2,878	3,187	3,650	4,051
Trade balance (million EUR)	-570	-750	-1,100	-1,194	-1,315	-1,459	-1,479	-1,682	-1,882	-2,252	-2,580
Cover ratio (%)	57.0	49.7	42.1	39.7	40.4	40.3	42.4	41.6	41.0	38.3	36.3

(1) Technically, data before 01/01/1999 are in ECU and after this date in euro. However, as the conversion rate was 1 ECU =1 EUR, for practical purposes the two terms can be used interchangeably.

Table 4.18

Manufacture of made-up textile articles, except apparel (NACE Rev. 1 17.4)
Production related indicators, 1997

	B	DK	D	EL (1)	E	F	IRL	I (1)	L	NL	A	P	FIN	S	UK
Number of persons employed (thousands)	6.4	2.2	19.4	1.8	16.8	13.4	:	9.7	0.1	:	2.1	8.8	1.1	1.1	29.5
Production (million ECU)	1,076	190	1,850	104	1,157	1,292	:	1,191	11	245	215	350	100	118	2,051
Value added (million ECU)	310	69	645	29	336	397	:	381	7	83	107	94	34	43	799
Gross operating surplus (million ECU)	80.1	11.9	142.4	6.5	116.4	80.0	:	132.9	4.7	21.6	47.6	33.9	13.3	14.4	271.8

(1) 1996.

Table 4.19

Manufacture of made-up textile articles, except apparel (NACE Rev. 1 17.4)
Trade related indicators, 1999

	B	DK	D	EL	E	F	IRL	I	L	NL	A	P	FIN	S	UK
Exports (million EUR)	494	216	741	66	262	451	39	464	14	350	173	762	29	160	420
Imports (million EUR)	460	220	1,777	96	281	1,081	115	422	26	568	316	63	98	295	974
Trade balance (million EUR)	34	-5	-1,036	-29	-19	-630	-76	43	-12	-218	-144	699	-69	-135	-555
Cover ratio (%)	107.4	97.9	41.7	69.5	93.1	41.7	34.2	110.1	53.1	61.7	54.6	1,201.9	29.6	54.1	43.1

Table 4.20

Manufacture of made-up textile articles, except apparel (NACE Rev. 1 17.4)
Labour related indicators, 1997

	B	DK (1)	D	EL (2)	E	F	IRL	I (2)	L	NL	A	P	FIN	S	UK
Unit personnel costs (thousand ECU per employee)	38.0	30.2	25.9	12.3	14.2	23.6	:	26.6	17.5	:	28.2	7.4	20.8	27.2	18.3
Social charges as a share of personnel costs (%)	19.3	4.2	22.0	29.7	27.5	33.9	:	48.5	:	16.0	28.8	27.3	23.7	41.7	12.3
Apparent labour productivity (thousand ECU/pers. empl.)	48.1	31.7	33.2	15.8	20.0	29.6	:	39.1	48.1	:	50.5	10.8	30.7	40.7	27.1
Wage adjusted labour productivity (%)	126.5	135.6	128.3	128.9	140.3	125.2	:	147.1	275.4	:	179.2	146.2	147.4	149.7	148.0
Personnel costs as a share of total operating costs (%)	23.0	30.9	26.8	23.7	19.5	24.5	:	22.4	28.4	24.4	31.4	18.6	24.1	24.3	28.1

(1) Unit personnel costs and wage adjusted labour productivity, 1996; (2) 1996.

Source: Eurostat (SBS, EBT, COMEXT)

Table 4.21

Manufacture of other textiles (NACE Rev. 1 17.5)

Production related indicators in the EU (1)

	1989	1990	1991	1992	1993	1994	1995	1996	1997	1998	1999
Number of persons employed (thousands)	189.7	197.1	196.5	187.4	176.1	171.9	191.3	:	189.1	191.3	183.2
Production (million EUR)	15,120	16,104	16,699	16,919	16,385	17,371	19,561	:	22,643	22,679	22,786
Domestic producer price index (1995=100)	:	:	:	:	:	:	100.0	101.2	100.8	100.7	101.1
Value added (million EUR)	5,201	5,642	5,842	5,831	5,701	5,842	6,220	:	7,634	7,527	7,751

(1) Technically, data before 01/01/1999 are in ECU and after this date in euro. However, as the conversion rate was 1 ECU =1 EUR, for practical purposes the two terms can be used interchangeably.

Table 4.22

Manufacture of other textiles (NACE Rev. 1 17.5)

Trade related indicators in the EU (1)

	1989	1990	1991	1992	1993	1994	1995	1996	1997	1998	1999
Exports (million EUR)	2,839	2,837	2,957	3,074	3,406	3,808	4,135	4,467	4,917	4,910	4,970
Imports (million EUR)	2,297	2,332	2,584	2,585	2,721	2,875	2,779	2,831	3,139	3,206	3,254
Trade balance (million EUR)	541	505	373	490	686	932	1,355	1,635	1,778	1,704	1,716
Cover ratio (%)	123.6	121.7	114.4	118.9	125.2	132.4	148.8	157.8	156.7	153.2	152.7

(1) Technically, data before 01/01/1999 are in ECU and after this date in euro. However, as the conversion rate was 1 ECU =1 EUR, for practical purposes the two terms can be used interchangeably.

Table 4.23

Manufacture of other textiles (NACE Rev. 1 17.5)

Production related indicators, 1997

	B	DK	D	EL (1)	E	F	IRL	I (1)	L	NL	A	P	FIN	S	UK
Number of persons employed (thousands)	15.0	2.0	32.5	1.6	14.4	26.1	1.8	20.1	1.0	:	3.4	23.5	2.8	2.9	37.4
Production (million ECU)	3,181	285	3,987	84	1,160	3,193	144	2,714	367	1,103	375	735	328	333	3,770
Value added (million ECU)	825	93	1,430	27	363	988	61	938	155	299	151	251	152	148	1,407
Gross operating surplus (million ECU)	367.7	27.6	347.9	7.0	120.1	268.8	19.6	347.8	94.4	117.7	44.8	85.7	77.1	46.2	462.4

(1) 1996.

Table 4.24

Manufacture of other textiles (NACE Rev. 1 17.5)

Trade related indicators, 1999

	B	DK	D	EL	E	F	IRL	I	L	NL	A	P	FIN	S	UK
Exports (million EUR)	2,686	286	2,862	51	436	1,531	76	1,784	345	1,364	494	305	210	305	1,253
Imports (million EUR)	748	256	2,556	158	637	1,439	155	1,027	55	755	448	343	194	307	1,811
Trade balance (million EUR)	1,938	29	306	-108	-201	91	-79	757	290	608	45	-38	15	-2	-558
Cover ratio (%)	359.2	111.5	112.0	32.0	68.5	106.4	48.9	173.7	628.4	180.6	110.1	88.8	108.0	99.4	69.2

Table 4.25

Manufacture of other textiles (NACE Rev. 1 17.5)

Labour related indicators, 1997

	B	DK (1)	D	EL (2)	E	F	IRL	I (2)	L	NL	A	P	FIN	S	UK
Unit personnel costs (thousand ECU per employee)	31.1	35.9	33.3	13.0	17.2	27.5	23.0	30.4	60.2	:	31.1	7.4	29.5	34.8	25.6
Social charges as a share of personnel costs (%)	36.9	6.8	23.4	31.2	28.2	37.1	15.5	49.7	:	19.5	29.8	28.8	26.4	44.4	12.3
Apparent labour productivity (thousand ECU/pers. empl.)	55.0	46.0	44.1	17.4	25.2	37.8	33.9	46.7	153.4	:	43.9	10.7	53.4	50.6	37.6
Wage adjusted labour productivity (%)	176.7	153.1	132.5	134.0	146.3	137.4	147.0	153.8	255.1	:	141.4	145.2	180.9	145.6	146.9
Personnel costs as a share of total operating costs (%)	16.4	23.4	26.8	24.5	22.2	23.4	28.9	24.9	22.1	17.1	28.3	24.5	30.0	32.6	26.7

(1) Unit personnel costs and wage adjusted labour productivity, 1996; (2) 1996.

Source: Eurostat (SBS, EBT, COMEXT)

Table 4.26

Manufacture of knitted and crocheted fabrics (NACE Rev. 1 17.6)

Production related indicators in the EU (1)

	1989	1990	1991	1992	1993	1994	1995	1996	1997	1998	1999
Number of persons employed (thousands)	:	:	:	:	48.0	45.5	29.5	:	38.5	36.2	34.8
Production (million EUR)	:	:	:	:	4,331	4,198	3,505	:	4,879	4,723	4,968
Domestic producer price index (1995=100)	:	:	:	:	:	:	100.0	100.7	100.8	100.8	99.0
Value added (million EUR)	:	:	:	:	1,332	1,306	1,030	:	1,410	1,396	1,445

(1) Technically, data before 01/01/1999 are in ECU and after this date in euro. However, as the conversion rate was 1 ECU =1 EUR, for practical purposes the two terms can be used interchangeably.

Table 4.27

Manufacture of knitted and crocheted fabrics (NACE Rev. 1 17.6)

Trade related indicators in the EU (1)

	1989	1990	1991	1992	1993	1994	1995	1996	1997	1998	1999
Exports (million EUR)	478	543	592	642	728	888	997	1,134	1,329	1,553	1,619
Imports (million EUR)	197	256	341	331	365	471	434	457	702	814	774
Trade balance (million EUR)	281	288	251	311	363	417	563	677	627	740	846
Cover ratio (%)	242.5	212.6	173.4	194.0	199.5	188.5	229.5	248.2	189.4	190.9	209.3

(1) Technically, data before 01/01/1999 are in ECU and after this date in euro. However, as the conversion rate was 1 ECU =1 EUR, for practical purposes the two terms can be used interchangeably.

Table 4.28

Manufacture of knitted and crocheted fabrics (NACE Rev. 1 17.6)

Production related indicators, 1997

	B	DK	D	EL (1)	E	F	IRL	I (1)	L	NL	A	P	FIN	S	UK
Number of persons employed (thousands)	0.6	0.7	5.0	0.7	6.9	3.4	0.0	5.3	0.0	:	1.1	8.2	0.3	0.4	6.0
Production (million ECU)	81	94	647	85	620	545	0	869	0	38	246	638	33	67	768
Value added (million ECU)	25	34	210	17	173	140	0	231	0	14	65	118	10	18	268
Gross operating surplus (million ECU)	10.1	11.8	61.4	7.6	60.1	41.9	0.0	102.3	0.0	4.2	30.2	53.6	3.1	6.5	117.8

(1) 1996.

Table 4.29

Manufacture of knitted and crocheted fabrics (NACE Rev. 1 17.6)

Trade related indicators, 1999

	B	DK	D	EL	E	F	IRL	I	L	NL	A	P	FIN	S	UK
Exports (million EUR)	141	116	926	36	258	595	6	909	0	128	247	28	17	54	237
Imports (million EUR)	174	81	416	258	149	491	35	295	1	143	101	151	19	31	343
Trade balance (million EUR)	-33	35	510	-221	109	105	-29	614	-1	-15	146	-124	-3	22	-106
Cover ratio (%)	80.9	143.9	222.7	14.1	173.5	121.3	17.6	307.9	10.2	89.7	245.6	18.2	86.6	170.5	69.1

Table 4.30

Manufacture of knitted and crocheted fabrics (NACE Rev. 1 17.6)

Labour related indicators, 1997

	B	DK (1)	D	EL (2)	E	F	IRL	I (2)	L	NL	A	P	FIN	S	UK
Unit personnel costs (thousand ECU per employee)	26.1	33.2	30.2	14.5	17.3	28.8	:	25.4	:	:	32.5	8.0	22.6	32.2	25.4
Social charges as a share of personnel costs (%)	44.8	4.3	21.9	32.0	27.9	37.9	:	46.8	:	23.8	30.7	26.8	23.6	41.5	11.8
Apparent labour productivity (thousand ECU/pers. empl.)	43.1	50.1	42.3	25.4	25.2	41.2	:	43.8	:	:	60.8	14.5	32.4	50.1	44.8
Wage adjusted labour productivity (%)	165.3	151.9	140.3	175.5	146.0	142.9	:	172.2	:	:	187.3	180.0	143.6	155.7	176.6
Personnel costs as a share of total operating costs (%)	21.3	26.7	23.7	13.3	19.6	19.6	:	16.6	:	28.7	15.2	10.6	23.0	19.2	22.8

(1) Unit personnel costs and wage adjusted labour productivity, 1996; (2) 1996.

Source: Eurostat (SBS, EBT, COMEXT)

Table 4.31

Manufacture of knitted and crocheted articles (NACE Rev. 1 17.7)

Production related indicators in the EU (1)

	1989	1990	1991	1992	1993	1994	1995	1996	1997	1998	1999
Number of persons employed (thousands)	:	:	:	:	199.4	189.1	170.1	:	161.3	155.1	145.4
Production (million EUR)	:	:	:	:	13,964	12,357	11,827	:	12,887	11,856	11,899
Domestic producer price index (1995=100)	:	:	:	:	:	:	100.0	101.3	101.7	103.4	:
Value added (million EUR)	:	:	:	:	4,742	4,269	4,220	:	4,275	4,061	4,197

(1) Technically, data before 01/01/1999 are in ECU and after this date in euro. However, as the conversion rate was 1 ECU =1 EUR, for practical purposes the two terms can be used interchangeably.

Table 4.32

Manufacture of knitted and crocheted articles (NACE Rev. 1 17.7)

Trade related indicators in the EU (1)

	1989	1990	1991	1992	1993	1994	1995	1996	1997	1998	1999
Exports (million EUR)	1,334	1,300	1,137	1,202	1,254	1,419	1,503	1,719	1,886	1,847	1,822
Imports (million EUR)	2,168	2,275	3,114	3,625	3,873	3,906	3,656	4,193	5,285	5,429	6,318
Trade balance (million EUR)	-833	-975	-1,977	-2,423	-2,620	-2,487	-2,153	-2,475	-3,399	-3,582	-4,496
Cover ratio (%)	61.6	57.1	36.5	33.2	32.4	36.3	41.1	41.0	35.7	34.0	28.8

(1) Technically, data before 01/01/1999 are in ECU and after this date in euro. However, as the conversion rate was 1 ECU =1 EUR, for practical purposes the two terms can be used interchangeably.

Table 4.33

Manufacture of knitted and crocheted articles (NACE Rev. 1 17.7)

Production related indicators, 1997

	B	DK	D	EL (1)	E	F	IRL	I (1)	L	NL	A	P	FIN	S	UK
Number of persons employed (thousands)	2.6	1.2	14.6	3.6	12.5	21.3	3.4	36.4	0.0	:	3.4	24.1	1.8	0.6	37.0
Production (million ECU)	128	130	1,169	186	690	1,584	102	4,264	0	151	239	733	107	42	1,956
Value added (million ECU)	51	39	476	57	243	555	43	1,126	0	43	128	233	57	19	944
Gross operating surplus (million ECU)	7.3	7.6	105.8	14.2	69.4	61.9	11.0	346.7	0.0	11.9	25.3	71.6	16.8	5.0	279.4

(1) 1996.

Table 4.34

Manufacture of knitted and crocheted articles (NACE Rev. 1 17.7)

Trade related indicators, 1999

	B	DK	D	EL	E	F	IRL	I	L	NL	A	P	FIN	S	UK
Exports (million EUR)	449	279	896	77	206	642	78	3,322	10	426	202	661	19	97	611
Imports (million EUR)	637	354	3,364	97	409	1,883	225	813	45	833	488	183	130	335	1,812
Trade balance (million EUR)	-188	-74	-2,468	-19	-203	-1,241	-147	2,508	-35	-407	-286	478	-111	-238	-1,201
Cover ratio (%)	70.5	79.0	26.6	79.9	50.4	34.1	34.6	408.4	23.3	51.2	41.4	362.1	14.4	29.0	33.7

Table 4.35

Manufacture of knitted and crocheted articles (NACE Rev. 1 17.7)

Labour related indicators, 1997

	B	DK (1)	D	EL (2)	E	F	IRL	I (2)	L	NL	A	P	FIN	S	UK
Unit personnel costs (thousand ECU per employee)	17.6	29.3	25.4	11.9	14.5	23.1	9.6	22.2	:	:	30.4	6.9	23.3	24.4	18.1
Social charges as a share of personnel costs (%)	39.7	5.1	22.5	28.5	28.5	32.0	13.1	47.9	:	17.3	30.3	26.7	27.3	40.6	10.3
Apparent labour productivity (thousand ECU/pers. empl.)	19.3	32.8	32.6	15.7	19.5	26.0	12.8	30.9	:	:	37.7	9.7	31.5	33.0	25.6
Wage adjusted labour productivity (%)	109.9	129.8	128.2	131.5	134.6	112.5	133.5	139.5	:	:	124.1	139.6	135.1	135.4	141.3
Personnel costs as a share of total operating costs (%)	36.0	24.8	31.0	26.6	26.4	33.0	30.2	19.8	:	20.7	43.0	23.9	43.1	37.8	34.9

(1) Unit personnel costs and wage adjusted labour productivity, 1996; (2) 1996.

Source: Eurostat (SBS, EBT, COMEXT)

Table 4.36

Manufacture of leather clothes (NACE Rev. 1 18.1)

Production related indicators in the EU (1)

	1989	1990	1991	1992	1993	1994	1995	1996	1997	1998	1999
Number of persons employed (thousands)	:	:	:	:	12.1	10.8	6.5	:	:	:	:
Production (million EUR)	:	:	:	:	780	764	582	:	577	579	625
Domestic producer price index (1995=100)	:	:	:	:	:	:	:	:	:	:	:
Value added (million EUR)	:	:	:	:	225	207	137	:	148	149	160

(1) Technically, data before 01/01/1999 are in ECU and after this date in euro. However, as the conversion rate was 1 ECU =1 EUR, for practical purposes the two terms can be used interchangeably.

Table 4.37

Manufacture of leather clothes (NACE Rev. 1 18.1)

Trade related indicators in the EU (1)

	1989	1990	1991	1992	1993	1994	1995	1996	1997	1998	1999
Exports (million EUR)	260	238	186	157	149	168	163	186	200	198	181
Imports (million EUR)	1,095	1,261	1,312	1,144	1,299	1,376	1,212	1,204	1,366	1,198	1,092
Trade balance (million EUR)	-835	-1,023	-1,126	-987	-1,150	-1,208	-1,049	-1,017	-1,166	-1,000	-912
Cover ratio (%)	23.8	18.9	14.2	13.7	11.4	12.2	13.4	15.5	14.7	16.5	16.6

(1) Technically, data before 01/01/1999 are in ECU and after this date in euro. However, as the conversion rate was 1 ECU =1 EUR, for practical purposes the two terms can be used interchangeably.

Table 4.38

Manufacture of leather clothes (NACE Rev. 1 18.1)

Production related indicators, 1997

	B	DK	D	EL	E	F	IRL	I (1)	L	NL	A	P	FIN	S	UK
Number of persons employed (thousands)	0.1	0.0	0.6	:	1.5	0.6	:	2.0	0.0	:	0.0	0.7	0.3	:	:
Production (million ECU)	10	0	74	:	109	71	:	251	0	:	0	16	19	:	:
Value added (million ECU)	2	0	17	:	27	19	:	61	0	:	0	5	6	:	:
Gross operating surplus (million ECU)	0.8	0.0	3.0	:	6.9	4.8	:	4.6	0.0	:	0.0	0.9	1.9	:	:

(1) 1996.

Table 4.39

Manufacture of leather clothes (NACE Rev. 1 18.1)

Trade related indicators, 1999

	B	DK	D	EL	E	F	IRL	I	L	NL	A	P	FIN	S	UK
Exports (million EUR)	27	17	141	4	33	68	0	200	1	35	15	1	5	11	28
Imports (million EUR)	56	26	527	24	97	174	8	115	4	84	73	18	9	29	155
Trade balance (million EUR)	-29	-9	-386	-19	-64	-106	-8	85	-3	-48	-58	-17	-3	-18	-127
Cover ratio (%)	47.9	66.2	26.8	17.7	33.7	39.2	5.7	173.4	33.9	42.1	20.0	5.8	59.4	38.6	18.0

Table 4.40

Manufacture of leather clothes (NACE Rev. 1 18.1)

Labour related indicators, 1997

	B	DK	D	EL	E	F	IRL	I (1)	L	NL	A	P	FIN	S	UK
Unit personnel costs (thousand ECU per employee)	14.9	:	23.4	:	14.9	24.9	:	29.6	:	:	:	6.0	19.4	:	:
Social charges as a share of personnel costs (%)	30.0	:	24.1	:	25.2	34.3	:	48.7	:	:	:	25.8	27.3	:	:
Apparent labour productivity (thousand ECU/pers. empl.)	21.8	:	27.5	:	17.7	33.2	:	30.3	:	:	:	6.6	23.7	:	:
Wage adjusted labour productivity (%)	146.1	:	117.9	:	118.9	133.6	:	102.5	:	:	:	110.0	122.1	:	:
Personnel costs as a share of total operating costs (%)	13.5	:	16.2	:	16.0	20.9	:	23.0	:	:	:	27.0	25.2	:	:

(1) 1996.

Source: Eurostat (SBS, EBT, COMEXT)

Table 4.41

Manufacture of other wearing apparel and accessories (NACE Rev. 1 18.2)

Production related indicators in the EU (1)

	1989	1990	1991	1992	1993	1994	1995	1996	1997	1998	1999
Number of persons employed (thousands)	:	:	:	:	910.2	865.9	707.2	:	:	:	:
Production (million EUR)	:	:	:	:	50,677	52,822	52,175	55,002	59,434	59,365	58,483
Domestic producer price index (1995=100)	:	:	:	:	:	:	100.0	100.8	101.3	102.0	101.9
Value added (million EUR)	:	:	:	:	17,600	17,694	16,594	17,941	18,226	18,880	18,168

(1) Technically, data before 01/01/1999 are in ECU and after this date in euro. However, as the conversion rate was 1 ECU =1 EUR, for practical purposes the two terms can be used interchangeably.

Table 4.42

Manufacture of other wearing apparel and accessories (NACE Rev. 1 18.2)

Trade related indicators in the EU (1)

	1989	1990	1991	1992	1993	1994	1995	1996	1997	1998	1999
Exports (million EUR)	6,357	6,855	6,882	7,248	7,747	9,028	9,732	10,956	11,688	12,062	11,627
Imports (million EUR)	14,816	17,323	21,501	22,159	24,137	25,411	25,569	27,352	31,207	33,386	35,046
Trade balance (million EUR)	-8,459	-10,468	-14,619	-14,911	-16,390	-16,383	-15,836	-16,396	-19,519	-21,324	-23,419
Cover ratio (%)	42.9	39.6	32.0	32.7	32.1	35.5	38.1	40.1	37.5	36.1	33.2

(1) Technically, data before 01/01/1999 are in ECU and after this date in euro. However, as the conversion rate was 1 ECU =1 EUR, for practical purposes the two terms can be used interchangeably.

Table 4.43

Manufacture of other wearing apparel and accessories (NACE Rev. 1 18.2)

Production related indicators, 1997

	B	DK	D	EL (1)	E	F	IRL	I (1)	L	NL	A	P	FIN	S	UK
Number of persons employed (thousands)	15.7	:	80.9	21.4	125.9	91.9	:	163.6	:	:	:	155.9	7.1	:	133.1
Production (million ECU)	2,066	:	10,158	818	6,086	8,414	:	16,615	:	:	:	4,126	502	:	7,318
Value added (million ECU)	432	:	2,723	263	1,929	2,400	:	5,139	:	:	:	1,279	181	:	3,212
Gross operating surplus (million ECU)	125.9	:	555.9	22.9	428.2	308.4	:	1,231.2	:	:	:	310.0	41.0	:	1,185.7

(1) 1996.

Table 4.44

Manufacture of other wearing apparel and accessories (NACE Rev. 1 18.2)

Trade related indicators, 1999

	B	DK	D	EL	E	F	IRL	I	L	NL	A	P	FIN	S	UK
Exports (million EUR)	3,040	1,349	5,951	1,126	1,303	4,513	300	8,859	92	2,623	1,072	2,342	183	450	3,327
Imports (million EUR)	3,651	1,763	15,232	739	2,439	8,530	834	4,439	234	4,535	2,254	716	692	1,616	9,123
Trade balance (million EUR)	-612	-414	-9,281	387	-1,136	-4,018	-534	4,420	-142	-1,912	-1,182	1,626	-509	-1,166	-5,797
Cover ratio (%)	83.3	76.5	39.1	152.3	53.4	52.9	36.0	199.6	39.2	57.8	47.6	327.0	26.4	27.9	36.5

Table 4.45

Manufacture of other wearing apparel and accessories (NACE Rev. 1 18.2)

Labour related indicators, 1997

	B	DK	D	EL (1)	E	F	IRL	I (1)	L	NL	A	P	FIN	S	UK
Unit personnel costs (thousand ECU per employee)	21.3	:	26.8	11.4	12.9	22.8	:	24.7	:	:	:	6.6	21.1	:	15.6
Social charges as a share of personnel costs (%)	31.2	:	21.9	28.9	27.7	31.5	:	47.9	:	:	:	28.1	25.7	:	10.2
Apparent labour productivity (thousand ECU/pers. empl.)	27.5	:	33.7	12.3	15.3	26.1	:	31.4	:	:	:	8.2	25.4	:	24.1
Wage adjusted labour productivity (%)	128.9	:	125.6	108.2	118.9	114.7	:	127.2	:	:	:	125.2	120.9	:	154.5
Personnel costs as a share of total operating costs (%)	15.7	:	20.6	31.2	25.5	25.0	:	24.7	:	:	:	24.8	26.8	:	30.9

(1) 1996.

Source: Eurostat (SBS, EBT, COMEXT)

_____Table 4.46

Dressing and dyeing of fur, manufacture of articles of fur (NACE Rev. 1 18.3)

Production related indicators in the EU (1)

	1989	1990	1991	1992	1993	1994	1995	1996	1997	1998	1999
Number of persons employed (thousands)	15.3	11.7	10.5	9.6	9.0	8.6	7.5	:	:	7.4	6.5
Production (million EUR)	934	802	848	707	585	609	698	709	739	740	689
Domestic producer price index (1995=100)	:	:	:	:	:	:	100.0	103.3	106.5	105.0	102.5
Value added (million EUR)	301	271	273	240	201	197	166	173	163	160	149

(1) Technically, data before 01/01/1999 are in ECU and after this date in euro. However, as the conversion rate was 1 ECU =1 EUR, for practical purposes the two terms can be used interchangeably.

_____Table 4.47

Dressing and dyeing of fur, manufacture of articles of fur (NACE Rev. 1 18.3)

Trade related indicators in the EU (1)

	1989	1990	1991	1992	1993	1994	1995	1996	1997	1998	1999
Exports (million EUR)	497	373	345	328	389	418	472	683	787	522	418
Imports (million EUR)	264	199	241	266	251	257	247	322	358	347	281
Trade balance (million EUR)	233	174	104	61	138	160	225	361	429	174	137
Cover ratio (%)	188.2	187.1	143.0	122.9	155.2	162.3	190.9	212.1	220.1	150.1	148.7

(1) Technically, data before 01/01/1999 are in ECU and after this date in euro. However, as the conversion rate was 1 ECU =1 EUR, for practical purposes the two terms can be used interchangeably.

_____Table 4.48

Dressing and dyeing of fur, manufacture of articles of fur (NACE Rev. 1 18.3)

Production related indicators, 1997

	B	DK	D	EL	E	F	IRL	I (1)	L	NL	A	P	FIN	S	UK
Number of persons employed (thousands)	0.3	:	0.5	:	3.3	0.6	0.1	1.0	:	:	:	0.6	0.4	0.0	:
Production (million ECU)	54	:	36	:	318	70	3	144	:	0	:	31	29	0	:
Value added (million ECU)	12	:	16	:	60	15	2	26	:	0	:	8	11	0	:
Gross operating surplus (million ECU)	5.8	:	4.3	:	8.6	-0.8	0.6	7.8	:	0.0	:	2.6	3.0	0.0	:

(1) 1996.

_____Table 4.49

Dressing and dyeing of fur, manufacture of articles of fur (NACE Rev. 1 18.3)

Trade related indicators, 1999

	B	DK	D	EL	E	F	IRL	I	L	NL	A	P	FIN	S	UK
Exports (million EUR)	22	17	134	201	105	52	0	145	0	14	7	8	40	8	47
Imports (million EUR)	10	19	154	103	43	44	0	113	1	15	21	4	12	12	31
Trade balance (million EUR)	11	-2	-21	98	62	8	0	32	-1	-1	-14	4	29	-4	17
Cover ratio (%)	210.0	89.3	86.5	195.1	246.0	117.1	309.7	128.5	12.7	94.2	34.9	193.5	347.9	68.0	154.0

_____Table 4.50

Dressing and dyeing of fur, manufacture of articles of fur (NACE Rev. 1 18.3)

Labour related indicators, 1997

	B	DK	D	EL	E	F	IRL	I (1)	L	NL	A	P	FIN	S	UK
Unit personnel costs (thousand ECU per employee)	22.2	:	23.5	:	17.0	26.9	19.1	21.1	:	:	:	9.2	25.8	:	:
Social charges as a share of personnel costs (%)	33.3	:	20.4	:	27.8	33.9	12.5	52.5	:	:	:	28.9	25.8	:	:
Apparent labour productivity (thousand ECU/pers. empl.)	42.6	:	31.8	:	18.0	25.5	28.2	26.1	:	:	:	13.1	28.3	:	:
Wage adjusted labour productivity (%)	191.7	:	134.9	:	106.1	94.7	148.3	123.7	:	:	:	142.7	109.9	:	:
Personnel costs as a share of total operating costs (%)	12.8	:	25.8	:	16.3	22.2	37.0	13.8	:	:	:	16.0	29.9	:	:

(1) 1996.

Source: Eurostat (SBS, EBT, COMEXT)

Table 4.51

Tanning and dressing of leather (NACE Rev. 1 19.1)

Production related indicators in the EU (1)

	1989	1990	1991	1992	1993	1994	1995	1996	1997	1998	1999
Number of persons employed (thousands)	56.4	52.8	50.0	47.4	43.1	42.3	41.0	40.3	40.7	39.4	39.3
Production (million EUR)	7,986	7,349	6,642	6,341	6,042	7,002	6,628	6,994	7,507	7,235	7,401
Domestic producer price index (1995=100)	:	:	:	:	:	:	:	:	:	102.6	102.1
Value added (million EUR)	1,623	1,550	1,655	1,527	1,444	1,419	1,331	1,443	1,393	1,362	1,437

(1) Technically, data before 01/01/1999 are in ECU and after this date in euro. However, as the conversion rate was 1 ECU =1 EUR, for practical purposes the two terms can be used interchangeably.

Table 4.52

Tanning and dressing of leather (NACE Rev. 1 19.1)

Trade related indicators in the EU (1)

	1989	1990	1991	1992	1993	1994	1995	1996	1997	1998	1999
Exports (million EUR)	1,642	1,554	1,471	1,473	1,816	2,229	2,388	2,785	2,935	2,771	2,885
Imports (million EUR)	1,638	1,788	1,414	1,307	1,334	2,046	2,018	2,027	2,278	2,105	1,727
Trade balance (million EUR)	4	-234	56	166	483	183	370	758	657	666	1,158
Cover ratio (%)	100.3	86.9	104.0	112.7	136.2	108.9	118.3	137.4	128.8	131.6	167.1

(1) Technically, data before 01/01/1999 are in ECU and after this date in euro. However, as the conversion rate was 1 ECU =1 EUR, for practical purposes the two terms can be used interchangeably.

Table 4.53

Tanning and dressing of leather (NACE Rev. 1 19.1)

Production related indicators, 1997

	B	DK	D	EL (1)	E	F	IRL	I (1)	L	NL	A	P	FIN	S	UK
Number of persons employed (thousands)	0.2	:	2.5	0.4	7.3	2.4	:	16.6	0.0	:	1.3	3.6	0.3	0.4	3.6
Production (million ECU)	41	:	408	51	1,007	299	:	4,010	0	109	194	313	31	68	539
Value added (million ECU)	7	:	101	10	202	58	:	759	0	22	24	62	8	20	117
Gross operating surplus (million ECU)	0.8	:	21.3	2.1	57.6	-6.4	:	317.2	0.0	8.9	-2.7	23.4	2.9	6.3	30.7

(1) 1996.

Table 4.54

Tanning and dressing of leather (NACE Rev. 1 19.1)

Trade related indicators, 1999

	B	DK	D	EL	E	F	IRL	I	L	NL	A	P	FIN	S	UK
Exports (million EUR)	61	35	655	18	302	279	46	2,684	0	117	240	48	17	58	339
Imports (million EUR)	94	39	558	27	423	395	5	1,240	0	99	154	325	26	25	185
Trade balance (million EUR)	-33	-3	98	-10	-121	-116	40	1,444	0	18	86	-276	-10	34	154
Cover ratio (%)	64.4	91.2	117.5	64.2	71.5	70.6	855.5	216.4	16.8	118.2	155.6	14.9	63.9	236.7	183.3

Table 4.55

Tanning and dressing of leather (NACE Rev. 1 19.1)

Labour related indicators, 1997

	B	DK	D	EL (1)	E	F	IRL	I (1)	L	NL	A	P	FIN	S	UK
Unit personnel costs (thousand ECU per employee)	24.3	:	31.6	19.2	20.1	27.3	:	27.6	:	:	20.8	10.8	18.8	32.4	23.9
Social charges as a share of personnel costs (%)	31.8	:	23.3	31.7	29.1	37.3	:	48.9	:	17.4	31.7	25.4	27.3	38.9	13.2
Apparent labour productivity (thousand ECU/pers. empl.)	27.6	:	39.8	24.3	27.5	24.6	:	45.6	:	:	18.7	17.1	28.0	47.7	32.3
Wage adjusted labour productivity (%)	113.4	:	125.9	126.6	137.1	90.0	:	165.4	:	:	89.7	158.3	148.7	147.3	135.1
Personnel costs as a share of total operating costs (%)	15.4	:	20.1	18.7	14.7	21.5	:	11.9	:	13.3	13.5	13.4	19.7	21.5	17.1

(1) 1996.

Source: Eurostat (SBS, EBT, COMEXT)

_____Table 4.56

Manufacture of luggage, handbags and the like, saddlery and harness (NACE Rev. 1 19.2)

Production related indicators in the EU (1)

	1989	1990	1991	1992	1993	1994	1995	1996	1997	1998	1999
Number of persons employed (thousands)	82.0	83.0	82.1	75.0	66.4	65.8	:	58.5	:	:	:
Production (million ECU)	5,240	5,256	5,559	5,550	5,015	5,454	:	5,036	:	:	:
Domestic producer price index (1995=100)	:	:	:	:	:	:	:	:	:	108.2	109.3
Value added (million ECU)	1,883	1,986	2,059	1,996	1,770	1,907	:	1,742	:	:	:

(1) Technically, data before 01/01/1999 are in ECU and after this date in euro. However, as the conversion rate was 1 ECU =1 EUR, for practical purposes the two terms can be used interchangeably.

_____Table 4.57

Manufacture of luggage, handbags and the like, saddlery and harness (NACE Rev. 1 19.2)

Trade related indicators in the EU (1)

	1989	1990	1991	1992	1993	1994	1995	1996	1997	1998	1999
Exports (million EUR)	1,370	1,386	1,292	1,350	1,443	1,848	2,092	2,318	2,270	2,034	2,262
Imports (million EUR)	1,625	1,717	2,085	2,099	2,214	2,313	2,461	2,704	3,071	3,280	3,588
Trade balance (million EUR)	-255	-331	-793	-749	-771	-465	-369	-387	-801	-1,246	-1,326
Cover ratio (%)	84.3	80.7	62.0	64.3	65.2	79.9	85.0	85.7	73.9	62.0	63.0

(1) Technically, data before 01/01/1999 are in ECU and after this date in euro. However, as the conversion rate was 1 ECU =1 EUR, for practical purposes the two terms can be used interchangeably.

_____Table 4.58

Manufacture of luggage, handbags and the like, saddlery and harness (NACE Rev. 1 19.2)

Production related indicators, 1997

	B	DK	D	EL (1)	E	F	IRL	I (1)	L	NL	A	P	FIN	S	UK
Number of persons employed (thousands)	:	:	7.2	0.1	9.6	11.9	:	12.5	0.0	:	0.7	4.0	0.5	0.3	5.8
Production (million ECU)	:	:	595	4	533	969	:	2,111	0	32	45	85	44	17	279
Value added (million ECU)	:	:	231	1	169	444	:	600	0	10	21	29	15	8	138
Gross operating surplus (million ECU)	:	:	47.9	0.5	45.7	139.6	:	266.9	0.0	1.1	2.5	4.8	6.9	1.4	38.3

(1) 1996.

_____Table 4.59

Manufacture of luggage, handbags and the like, saddlery and harness (NACE Rev. 1 19.2)

Trade related indicators, 1999

	B	DK	D	EL	E	F	IRL	I	L	NL	A	P	FIN	S	UK
Exports (million EUR)	433	39	352	6	157	1,323	23	1,252	3	210	146	11	12	33	282
Imports (million EUR)	360	117	1,108	67	314	909	57	577	14	360	161	75	51	133	937
Trade balance (million EUR)	73	-78	-755	-61	-157	414	-33	675	-11	-150	-15	-64	-39	-100	-655
Cover ratio (%)	120.4	33.1	31.8	8.9	50.1	145.5	41.4	217.0	18.8	58.2	90.5	14.5	23.6	25.0	30.1

_____Table 4.60

Manufacture of luggage, handbags and the like, saddlery and harness (NACE Rev. 1 19.2)

Labour related indicators, 1997

	B	DK	D	EL (1)	E	F	IRL	I (1)	L	NL	A	P	FIN	S	UK
Unit personnel costs (thousand ECU per employee)	:	:	25.2	10.0	14.3	25.4	:	27.7	:	:	25.3	6.5	20.6	25.3	17.5
Social charges as a share of personnel costs (%)	:	:	22.3	33.3	27.9	35.4	:	44.2	:	20.8	29.1	27.6	26.6	43.2	10.0
Apparent labour productivity (thousand ECU/pers. empl.)	:	:	32.1	15.7	17.6	37.1	:	48.0	:	:	28.8	7.1	30.0	30.6	23.8
Wage adjusted labour productivity (%)	:	:	127.3	156.6	123.3	145.9	:	173.2	:	:	113.5	107.7	145.7	121.2	136.0
Personnel costs as a share of total operating costs (%)	:	:	28.4	21.6	22.2	29.8	:	17.4	:	27.4	39.0	29.3	21.2	37.0	34.3

(1) 1996.

Source: Eurostat (SBS, EBT, COMEXT)

Table 4.61

Manufacture of footwear (NACE Rev. 1 19.3)

Production related indicators in the EU (1)

	1989	1990	1991	1992	1993	1994	1995	1996	1997	1998	1999
Number of persons employed (thousands)	344.9	354.0	346.9	326.5	303.4	302.9	293.4	296.6	:	:	:
Production (million ECU)	18,833	20,570	21,152	20,166	19,688	21,278	21,233	22,914	:	:	:
Domestic producer price index (1995=100)	:	87.8	90.7	93.3	95.4	97.1	100.0	102.0	103.6	105.0	105.5
Value added (million ECU)	6,072	6,248	6,631	6,334	6,143	6,305	6,030	6,528	:	:	:

(1) Technically, data before 01/01/1999 are in ECU and after this date in euro. However, as the conversion rate was 1 ECU =1 EUR, for practical purposes the two terms can be used interchangeably.

Table 4.62

Manufacture of footwear (NACE Rev. 1 19.3)

Trade related indicators in the EU (1)

	1989	1990	1991	1992	1993	1994	1995	1996	1997	1998	1999
Exports (million EUR)	3,471	3,654	3,503	3,769	3,992	4,797	5,027	5,639	6,033	5,778	5,457
Imports (million EUR)	3,116	3,455	4,582	4,646	5,030	5,455	5,250	5,910	7,035	6,989	7,761
Trade balance (million EUR)	355	199	-1,078	-877	-1,038	-658	-222	-272	-1,002	-1,211	-2,304
Cover ratio (%)	111.4	105.8	76.5	81.1	79.4	87.9	95.8	95.4	85.8	82.7	70.3

(1) Technically, data before 01/01/1999 are in ECU and after this date in euro. However, as the conversion rate was 1 ECU =1 EUR, for practical purposes the two terms can be used interchangeably.

Table 4.63

Manufacture of footwear (NACE Rev. 1 19.3)

Production related indicators, 1997

	B (1)	DK	D	EL (1)	E	F	IRL	I (1)	L	NL	A	P	FIN	S	UK
Number of persons employed (thousands)	1.1	1.0	16.9	3.3	52.6	29.7	0.5	83.2	0.0	:	4.6	72.4	2.1	0.3	21.2
Production (million ECU)	66	143	2,295	148	4,493	2,137	21	9,842	0	111	458	2,310	159	26	1,532
Value added (million ECU)	26	51	651	43	883	767	10	2,496	0	45	168	690	66	10	713
Gross operating surplus (million ECU)	3.1	21.6	140.5	2.4	277.3	131.1	2.4	719.5	0.0	13.4	49.3	200.8	19.2	1.1	313.8

(1) 1996.

Table 4.64

Manufacture of footwear (NACE Rev. 1 19.3)

Trade related indicators, 1999

	B	DK	D	EL	E	F	IRL	I	L	NL	A	P	FIN	S	UK
Exports (million EUR)	1,369	276	1,293	26	1,774	989	25	6,506	5	907	539	1,540	62	66	800
Imports (million EUR)	1,049	426	4,045	228	522	2,543	234	2,133	44	1,533	773	306	168	368	3,114
Trade balance (million EUR)	321	-150	-2,752	-202	1,253	-1,554	-209	4,373	-39	-626	-233	1,234	-105	-302	-2,314
Cover ratio (%)	130.6	64.8	32.0	11.5	340.1	38.9	10.8	305.0	12.0	59.2	69.8	503.8	37.2	18.0	25.7

Table 4.65

Manufacture of footwear (NACE Rev. 1 19.3)

Labour related indicators, 1997

	B (1)	DK (2)	D	EL (1)	E	F	IRL	I (1)	L	NL	A	P	FIN	S	UK
Unit personnel costs (thousand ECU per employee)	23.6	31.3	30.0	12.7	12.1	21.4	14.6	22.1	:	:	25.9	6.9	22.2	28.3	19.2
Social charges as a share of personnel costs (%)	37.8	3.6	27.0	31.2	27.9	31.4	13.2	45.7	:	14.3	30.2	27.4	26.6	39.7	11.6
Apparent labour productivity (thousand ECU/pers. empl.)	24.4	49.6	38.4	13.2	16.8	25.8	19.1	30.0	:	:	36.6	9.5	30.8	31.8	33.6
Wage adjusted labour productivity (%)	103.3	164.0	128.1	103.7	138.7	120.6	130.7	135.6	:	:	141.4	138.4	138.8	112.3	175.3
Personnel costs as a share of total operating costs (%)	34.9	11.4	21.1	27.1	13.7	28.9	35.2	18.1	:	29.5	25.9	22.2	33.1	35.8	25.3

(1) 1996; (2) Unit personnel costs and wage adjusted labour productivity, 1996.

Source: Eurostat (SBS, EBT, COMEXT)

Wood, paper, publishing and printing (NACE Rev. 1 20, 21 and 22)

This chapter concerns the production and processing of wood and paper, through to the creation of finished products, such as books and magazines. Sawing and first processing of wood (NACE Rev. 1 20.1) and the manufacture of pulp and paper (NACE Rev. 1 21) are the initial processing stages in this chain of vertically-integrated activities, followed by intermediate activities such as the manufacture of veneer sheets or builders carpentry (NACE Rev. 1 20.2 and 20.3), with activities such as publishing and printing (NACE Rev. 1 22.1 and 22.2) at the end of the chain. The reproduction of recorded media (NACE Rev. 1 22.3) is excluded, it may be found within the final chapter on information and audio-visual services.

—Figure 5.1

Wood, paper, publishing and printing (NACE Rev. 1 20, 21 and 22) Share of total manufacturing value added in the EU, 1996 (%)

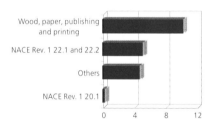

Source: Eurostat (SBS)

The activities covered in this chapter (in terms of NACE Rev. 1) include:

20: manufacture of wood and of products of wood and cork, except furniture; manufacture of articles of straw and plaiting materials;
20.1: sawmilling and planing of wood; impregnation of wood;
20.2: manufacture of veneer sheets; manufacture of plywood, laminboard, particle board, fibre board and other panels and boards;
20.3: manufacture of builders' carpentry and joinery;
20.4: manufacture of wooden containers;
20.5: manufacture of other products of wood; manufacture of articles of cork, straw and plaiting materials;
21: manufacture of pulp, paper and paper products;
21.1: manufacture of pulp, paper and paperboard;
21.2: manufacture of articles of paper and paperboard;
22: publishing, printing and reproduction of recorded media;
22.1: publishing;
22.2: printing and service activities related to printing;
22.3: reproduction of recorded media.

EU production of wood, paper, publishing and printing[1] was equal to 355 billion EUR in 1999, or 8.9% of total manufacturing output, whilst its share of manufacturing value added was significantly higher at 10.3% (125 billion EUR). There were 2.4 million persons employed in 1999 (10.1% of the manufacturing total).

Publishing and printing had a significantly higher share of value added, with 55.8 billion ECU of value added generated in 1996, which represented more than half (50.5%) of the total for the activities covered in this chapter.

Publishing and printing the largest activity

The publishing and printing industry (NACE Rev. 1 22.1 and 22.2) was the largest covered in this chapter (138.2 billion ECU of production in 1996, or 44.3% of the total), followed by pulp, paper and paperboard (111.9 billion ECU[2] in 1996 or 35.9% of the total). Semi-finished and finished wood products (NACE Rev. 1 20.2 to 20.5) accounted for 12.8% of the total (39.9 billion ECU[3] in 1996), whilst the sawing and first processing of wood made-up 4.4% of total wood, paper, publishing and printing activity (13.9 billion ECU).

Finland, Sweden and Austria the most specialised countries

In 1997, Germany reported production equal to 78.2 billion ECU, making it the largest producer in the EU. Wood, paper, publishing and printing accounted for 7.7% of German manufacturing output in 1997. The United Kingdom was the second largest producer in the EU, with 50.8 billion ECU of output (equivalent to 8.9% of the national manufacturing total).

---

(1) The totals used in this overview include the reproduction of recorded media (NACE Rev. 1 22.3). A detailed analysis of this industry is provided in chapter 21.
(2) L, no data available.
(3) L and A, no data available.

Table 5.1

Wood, paper, publishing and printing (NACE Rev. 1 20, 21 and 22)

Breakdown of turnover and employment by employment size class, 1997 (%)

	Micro (0-9)		Small (10-49)		Medium (50-249)		Large (250+)	
	Turnover (1)	Employment (2)	Turnover (1)	Employment (2)	Turnover (3)	Employment (4)	Turnover (3)	Employment (4)
EU-15	12.5	23.5	20.4	24.7	23.5	20.6	43.5	31.1
B	16.8	26.4	24.0	25.4	24.2	20.6	34.9	27.5
DK	:	:	:	:	:	:	:	:
D	8.1	17.0	15.0	20.9	19.3	20.7	57.6	41.4
EL	:	:	:	:	:	:	:	:
E	:	36.3	:	31.4	:	19.5	:	12.9
F	12.2	21.9	25.1	28.5	27.0	23.9	35.8	25.7
IRL	:	:	:	:	:	:	:	:
I	19.0	39.0	30.3	31.8	25.3	15.9	25.4	13.3
L	:	:	:	:	:	:	:	:
NL	:	:	:	:	:	:	:	:
A	8.9	15.3	16.9	26.0	29.0	28.6	45.4	30.0
P	17.0	28.8	27.2	35.2	27.2	22.6	28.7	13.4
FIN	4.1	9.4	6.9	12.3	12.1	16.8	76.9	61.6
S	7.2	:	14.4	:	21.0	23.9	57.4	44.2
UK	16.3	23.7	18.6	20.8	:	21.2	:	33.8

(1) EU-15, F, I, P and S, 1996.
(2) EU-15, F, I and P, 1996.
(3) EU-15, F, I, A, P and S, 1996.
(4) EU-15, F, I, A, P, S and UK, 1996.

Source: Eurostat (SME)

However, the three most recent Member States to join the Union reported that the wood and paper industries were particularly important for their respective manufacturing sectors. The production value of Finland was equal to 20.6 billion ECU in 1997, which was equivalent to more than a quarter (28.9%) of national manufacturing output. Sweden was also relatively specialised, with 21.0 billion ECU of production equating to almost a fifth (17.9%) of the national manufacturing total. Austria (9.5 billion ECU and 13.1% of manufacturing) and in addition Portugal (7.2 billion ECU and 11.9% of manufacturing) were the other Member States that were relatively specialised.

Almost one in five jobs were accounted for by enterprises with less than 10 employees
In 1996, there were 306.7 thousand very small enterprises (0 to 9 employees) and 41.5 thousand small enterprises (10 to 49 employees) in the wood, paper, publishing and printing industries of the EU, equal to 18.8% and 13.9% of the total number of manufacturing enterprises within these two size classes. Wood, paper, publishing and printing enterprises accounted for lower shares of the total manufacturing enterprise population within medium and large-sized enterprises, accounting for 11.9% and 10.7% of each respective total.

The proportion of persons employed in manufacturing totals were similar, with wood, paper, publishing and printing accounting for much higher shares of manufacturing employment in very small enterprises (17.6% of the manufacturing total or 793.2 thousand persons) and small enterprises (13.8% of the total or 834.3 thousand persons).

Box 5.1

Manufacturers of wood, paper, publishing and printing industries have become increasingly concerned with the protection of timber resources. They are seeking to develop a common certification scheme that will be clear and informative for both downstream industries and consumers.

CEPI (the Confederation of European Paper Industries) estimates that there has been a substantial increase in the consumption of recovered paper, with usage up by 3.8% in 1999 (to 38.5 million tonnes). The breakdown of consumption by the paper and board industry in 1999 was made-up as follows: virgin fibres (44%), recycled fibres (40%), non-fibrous materials (15%) and other pulp (1%).

Figure 5.2

Wood, paper, publishing and printing (NACE Rev. 1 20, 21 and 22)

EU production and value-added in constant prices and employment compared to total manufacturing (1990=100)

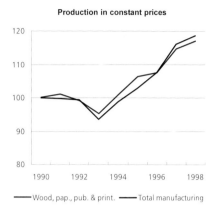

Production in constant prices

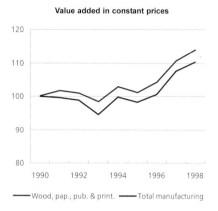

Value added in constant prices

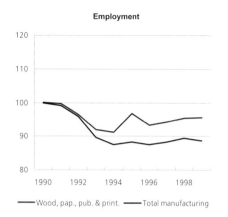

Employment

Source: Eurostat (SBS)

STRUCTURE AND PERFORMANCE

Output of wood, paper, publishing and printing increased by 43.5% in nominal terms between 1989 to 1999, from 247 billion ECU to 355 billion EUR. In real terms, recent growth was similar to the EU's manufacturing average, with annual increases in excess of 5.0% in three of the five years between 1993 and 1998. The average annual growth rate of production in constant prices was equal to 4.2% between 1993 and 1998, just below the manufacturing average of 4.9% per annum. This represented a significant increase of the figures from the early 1990s, when output within wood, paper, publishing and printing fell in real terms by 2.0% (1992) and 3.8% (1993). These were however the only negative rates of change reported during the 1990s.

The average annual growth rates over the ten years to 1997 showed that Spain (4.2%), Germany (3.8%) and the United Kingdom (2.8%) all reported production in constant prices rising at a faster pace within the wood, paper, publishing and printing industries than their respective manufacturing averages (differences between +0.7 percentage points and +1.2 percentage points).

Figure 5.3

Wood, paper, publishing and printing (NACE Rev. 1 20, 21 and 22)

Capacity utilisation rates in the EU (%)

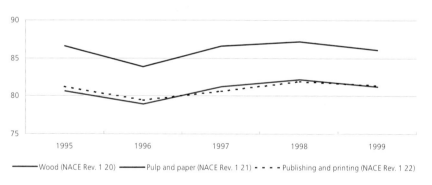

Source: DG ECFIN

Figure 5.4

Wood (NACE Rev.1 20)

Capacity utilisation rates, 1999 (%)

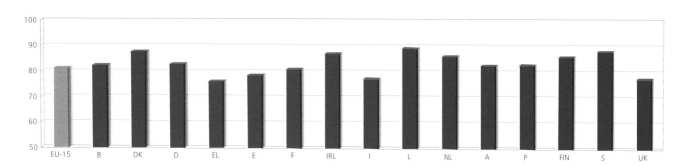

Source: DG ECFIN

Figure 5.5

Pulp and paper (NACE Rev.1 21)

Capacity utilisation rates, 1999 (%) (1)

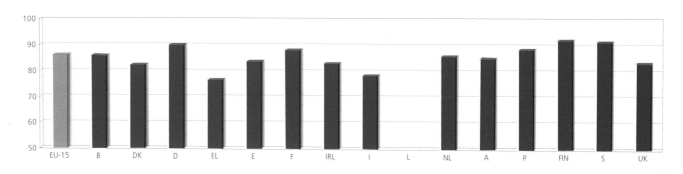

(1) L, not available.

Source: DG ECFIN

Figure 5.6

Publishing and printing (NACE Rev.1 22)

Capacity utilisation rates, 1999 (%)

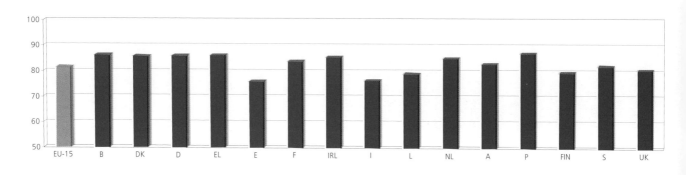

Source: DG ECFIN

LABOUR AND PRODUCTIVITY

The size of the EU workforce declined from 2.47 million persons employed in 1989 to 2.37 million persons by 1999. This reduction of 93.9 thousand persons was at a slower pace than the manufacturing average. As a result, the proportion of persons employed in wood, paper, publishing and printing increased from 9.5% of the manufacturing total to 10.2% over the ten-year period considered.

The largest losses in employment were recorded in 1992 (-3.2%) and 1993 (-4.7%), with the total number of persons employed falling to 2.28 million persons. There was a moderate recovery during the mid- to late-1990s, with a 6.3% increase in the number of persons employed in 1995, as well as growth in excess of 1.0% in both 1997 and 1998.

Productivity levels just above manufacturing averages
Apparent labour productivity in the wood, paper, printing and publishing industries was consistently just above the manufacturing average during the 1990s. There was a steady increase in apparent labour productivity from the 36.6 thousand ECU per person employed in 1989 to 52.9 thousand ECU by 1999. Wage adjusted labour productivity remained almost unchanged during the ten-year period considered, with ratios of 156.0% in 1989 and 157.4% in 1999. However, between these dates the ratio fell to 142.3% in 1992.

More than one in ten persons self-employed
The proportion of men employed in EU wood, paper, publishing and printing industries was equal to 71.3% in 1998, an almost identical figure to that for manufacturing as a whole. Since 1995 there was a slight increase in this proportion, which rose by almost 1 percentage point.

The breakdown of the educational attainment of the workforce also posted similar results to manufacturing averages. In 1997, 16.3% of the workforce had completed a higher education degree, whilst 36.5% finished education at a primary or lower secondary level (manufacturing averages were 16.3% and 38.8% respectively).

The proportion of self-employed was higher in wood, paper, printing and publishing activities in 1998, with more than one in ten persons (11.4%) working for themselves in the 25 to 59 age group (as opposed to 7.8% for manufacturing as a whole). There were similar figures for the incidence of part-time work, with 11.5% of the wood, paper, printing and publishing workforce employed on a part-time basis in 1998 (as opposed to 7.3% for manufacturing as a whole).

Table 5.2

**Wood, paper, publishing and printing
(NACE Rev. 1 20, 21 and 22)
Composition of the labour force, 1999 (%)**

	Women (1)	Part-time (2)	Highly-educated (3)
EU-15	28.7	11.5	16.3
B	27.0	6.7	28.7
DK	29.8	14.3	15.1
D	32.7	16.7	17.4
EL	23.3	3.8	12.9
E	18.6	4.0	22.3
F	30.9	8.0	19.2
IRL	28.6	:	23.3
I	23.1	4.9	4.8
L	22.6	:	:
NL	28.5	32.0	17.2
A	24.6	9.2	5.6
P	26.4	3.2	6.7
FIN	30.1	6.9	28.5
S	29.0	11.1	18.7
UK	31.6	13.4	19.9

(1) EU-15 and EL, 1998.
(2) EU-15, B and EL, 1998.
(3) EL, 1998; EU-15, IRL and UK, 1997.

Source: Eurostat (LFS)

Figure 5.7

**Wood, paper, publishing and printing (NACE Rev. 1 20, 21 and 22)
Apparent labour productivity and unit personnel costs, 1997 (thousand ECU)**

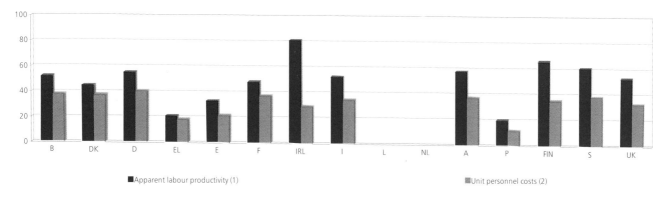

■ Apparent labour productivity (1)   ■ Unit personnel costs (2)

(1) EL and I, 1996; L and NL, not available.
(2) DK, EL and I, 1996; L and NL, not available.

Source: Eurostat (SBS)

Figure 5.8

Wood, paper, publishing and printing (NACE Rev. 1 20, 21 and 22)

International comparison of production, value added and employment

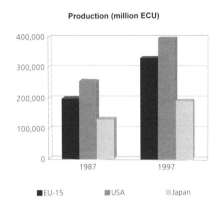

Production (million ECU)

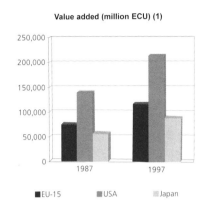

Value added (million ECU) (1)

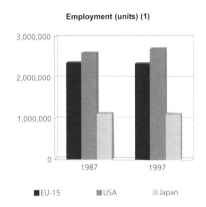

Employment (units) (1)

(1) JAP, 1996.

Source: Eurostat (SBS)

INTERNATIONAL TRENDS AND FOREIGN TRADE

The USA was responsible for 394.7 billion ECU of production in 1997 or 43.0% of the Triad total, higher than the 36.1% of output accounted for by the EU, with the remaining 20.9% produced in Japan. Annual average growth of production in constant prices was equal to 4.7% in the USA between 1992 and 1997 (which was higher than in the other Triad countries), as a result the USA's share of total Triad production rose from 39.1% in 1992 to 43.0% in 1997.

*EU ran a trade surplus throughout
the second half of the 1990s*

Exports from the EU almost doubled in nominal terms between 1989 and 1999, whilst imports grew at a much slower pace, hence transforming a 2.1 billion ECU trade deficit into a 1.6 billion EUR surplus. Exports totalled 25.1 billion EUR in 1999 (3.5% of the manufacturing total). As a proportion of the manufacturing total this was a reduction compared to 1989, when wood, paper, publishing and printing accounted for 4.0% of manufacturing exports. Imports rose by around 7.5 billion ECU in nominal terms between 1989 and 1999, to reach 23.5 billion EUR.

In Japan, the trade deficit (8.1 billion ECU) showed little evolution between 1989 and 1998. However, this masks the fact that up until 1997 the Japanese deficit had widened considerably to reach 12.5 billion ECU, only to fall back again in 1998. A small surplus in the early 1990s in the USA turned into an increasing deficit as the economic recovery took hold and imports were sucked into the American economy. By 1998 the trade deficit was equal to 7.6 billion ECU.

*North America and near neighbours
were the EU's main trading partners*

The USA was the largest origin of EU imports in 1999, with 4.7 billion EUR of imports amounting to almost a fifth (19.9%) of the total. This proportion was down on the figures from 1989, when US imports accounted for 23.9% of the EU total. The second most important origin of EU imports in 1999 was Canada, although the relative proportion of Canadian imports declined from 18.5% in 1989 to 10.0% by 1999. Switzerland (1.9 billion EUR, 8.3%) and Norway (1.6 billion EUR, 6.8%) followed in terms of being the next largest origin of EU imports.

The USA was the most important destination for EU exports in 1999 (3.7 billion EUR, 14.8%), with its share of total EU exports remaining fairly constant (15.1% in 1989). Switzerland had been the most important destination in 1989 (18.0% of the total). Despite EU exports to Switzerland rising in nominal terms between 1989 and 1999 to 3.3 billion EUR, the Swiss share of the total fell by 5.0 percentage points to 13.1%.

Figure 5.9

**Wood, paper, publishing and printing
(NACE Rev. 1 20, 21 and 22)**

Destination of EU exports, 1999 (%)

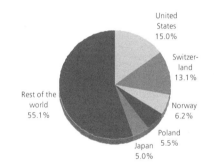

Source: Eurostat (COMEXT)

Figure 5.10

**Wood, paper, publishing and printing
(NACE Rev. 1 20, 21 and 22)**

Origin of EU imports, 1999 (%)

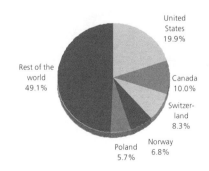

Source: Eurostat (COMEXT)

SUB-CHAPTER 5.1
SAWING AND FIRST PROCESSING OF WOOD (NACE Rev. 1 20.1)

Sawing, planing and machining of wood is the principal manufacturing process covered in this sub-chapter, but the production of basic wooden products such as railway sleepers, unassembled wooden flooring, wooden particles and wooden chips are also included, as are the activities of drying, impregnating and chemically treating wood.

This sub-chapter has the smallest share of total wood, paper, printing and publishing output. Sawing and first processing of wood accounted for almost a quarter (24.8%) of the EU's wood industry in terms of production value in 1996, when production was equal to 13.9 billion ECU. The relative share of employment was lower, at just under a fifth (19.8%) of the wood industry total, with some 107.7 thousand persons employed in 1996.

An important industry for Sweden and Finland
The sawing and first processing of wood was an important industry for Sweden and Finland, accounting for well over half (69.4% and 57.1%) of domestic wood production in 1997, with output equal to 3.9 billion ECU and 2.5 billion ECU respectively. As such Swedish output was the highest in the EU, followed by Germany (3.0 billion ECU), where the share in total wood output was equal to 20.5% (more than 4 percentage points below the EU average). Austria was the only other country that was highly specialised in the sawing and first processing of wood, with 1.1 billion ECU of production in 1997, equivalent to just over a third (35.9%) of domestic production in the wood industry.

STRUCTURE AND PERFORMANCE

There was nominal production growth of 59.0% (or 5.1 billion ECU) between 1986 and 1996 in the EU sawing and first processing of wood industry. Average annual growth of production in constant prices was equal to 3.6% between 1991 and 1996. This overall positive picture was due largely to two years of strong growth in the mid-1990s, when production rose by 21.3% and 10.5% respectively in 1994 and 1996. There was however a fluctuating trend to output, as production fell by 10.0% (1991), 5.5% (1993) and 4.4% (1995) in alternating years. The trend of value added was even more erratic, with a large gain in 1994 (22.6%), as well as losses of 14.6% in 1991 and 16.0% in 1995 (all in real terms).

_____Figure 5.11

Sawing and first processing of wood (NACE Rev. 1 20.1)
Production and export specialisation (%)

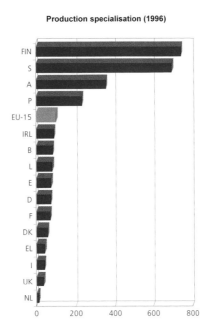

Production specialisation (1996)

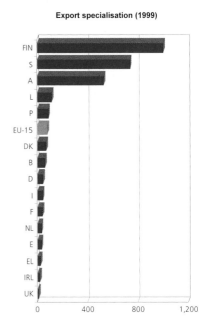

Export specialisation (1999)

Source: Eurostat (SBS, COMEXT)

Profitability high in Nordic countries
The gross operating rate (the gross operating surplus divided by turnover) was in double-digits for just three of the Member States in 1997 in the sawing and first processing of wood industry. The gross operating rate was as high as 14.8% in Finland, 12.3% in the Netherlands and 12.1% in Sweden. These figures were considerably above the EU average of 6.7% in 1996[4].

_____

(4) However the EU figure rose to 9.6% in 1997, excluding EL, IRL and I.

LABOUR AND PRODUCTIVITY

The number of persons employed in the sawing and first processing of wood industries fell by 15.4 thousand in the EU during the ten-year period 1986 to 1996. There were 107.7 thousand persons employed in 1996, which was equivalent to a net decline of 12.5%. This rate of decline was larger than that for the whole of the wood industry, where the overall loss in employment was equal to 2.0% between 1986 and 1996.

Apparent labour productivity well below the EU manufacturing average

From 1986 to 1995, apparent labour productivity in the sawing and first processing of wood industry consistently lagged behind the EU manufacturing average by between 7.2 (1994) and 11.3 (1991) thousand ECU per person employed. In 1996 the difference widened still further to 14.7 thousand ECU per person employed. Apparent labour productivity in the sawing and first processing of wood industry was equal to 21.0 thousand ECU per person employed in 1986 in the EU and increased steadily (with the exception of 1991) to reach 37.4 thousand ECU per person employed by 1995 (only to fall to 31.8 thousand ECU the following year).

Conversely, simple wage adjusted productivity (value added divided by personnel costs) was frequently above the manufacturing average, as a result of comparatively low unit personnel costs. Simple wage adjusted labour productivity rose as high as 171.6% in 1994 (more than 25 percentage points above the EU manufacturing average), but fell at a rapid pace to below the manufacturing average by 1996 (139.8%).

INTERNATIONAL TRENDS AND FOREIGN TRADE

EU exports of sawing and first processing of wood products totalled 2.1 billion EUR in 1999 (up from 863 million ECU in 1989). This was a relatively low level of exports, as it was equal to just 0.3% of total manufacturing exports from the EU in 1999. Imports did not grow at such a rapid pace over the ten-year period considered. The EU imported goods to the value of 4.8 billion EUR in 1999. As a result, the trade deficit fell from 3.3 billion ECU in 1989 to 2.7 billion EUR in 1999.

The USA was the largest source of imports, Japan the principal destination for exports

The USA was the main origin of EU imports in 1999 (734 million EUR in 1999), accounting for 15.3% of total imports of sawing and first processing of wood products. There was a nominal increase of 149 million ECU in the value of imports from the USA between 1989 and 1999, which resulted in the USA moving up from being the third most important to being the most important partner country. Canada had been the main origin of imports in 1989, however the Canadian share of total EU imports fell from 16.9% to 8.3% between 1989 and 1999. The Soviet Union accounted for 16.9% of EU imports in 1989, whilst in 1999 Latvia and Russia were still important trading partners (both with respective shares of 8.1%).

Japan was the main destination for EU exports in 1999, accounting for almost a quarter (22.4%) of the total, some 456 billion EUR in value terms. Norway (10.7%) and Switzerland (8.5%) followed, with Egypt and the USA also accounting for more than 7.0% of the EU's exports in 1999.

Figure 5.12

Sawing and first processing of wood (NACE Rev. 1 20.1)

International comparison of production in constant prices and employment (1990=100)

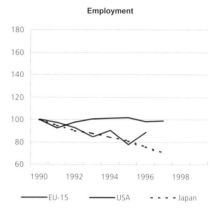

Source: Eurostat (SBS)

Figure 5.13

Sawing and first processing of wood (NACE Rev. 1 20.1)

Destination of EU exports, 1999 (%)

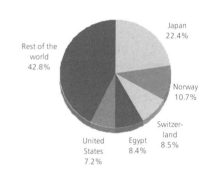

Source: Eurostat (COMEXT)

Figure 5.14

Sawing and first processing of wood (NACE Rev. 1 20.1)

Origin of EU imports, 1999 (%)

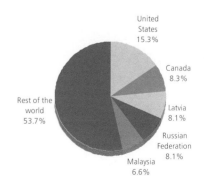

Source: Eurostat (COMEXT)

SUB-CHAPTER 5.2
SEMI-FINISHED AND FINISHED WOOD PRODUCTS
(NACE Rev. 1 20.2, 20.3, 20.4 AND 20.5)

This sub-chapter covers basic materials used in the building trade and the manufacture of furniture, such as veneer sheets, plywood, laminboard and particleboard (NACE Rev. 1 20.2). It also includes information on carpentry and joinery products such as doors, windows and stairs (NACE Rev. 1 20.3), as well as wooden cases and boxes, pallets and drums (NACE Rev. 1 20.4). The final NACE Rev. 1 Group, 20.5, covers a diverse selection of other wood products, such as cork, straw, wooden brooms, ornaments and wickerwork.

Production value of these diverse wood industries was equal to 39.9 billion ECU[5] in 1996, whilst there were 406 thousand persons employed[6]. In 1999, the manufacture of builders' carpentry and joinery (NACE Rev. 1 20.3) accounted for more than a third (34.1%) of total output in the EU wood industry, whilst just over a tenth (11.3%) of the total was generated by the manufacture of other wood products (NACE Rev. 1 20.5). Wooden containers (NACE Rev. 1 20.4) is a relatively small industry (7.5% share of wood processing output in 1996), whilst just over a fifth (21.7%) of the production of wood in 1994 was derived within the manufacture of veneer sheets and boards (NACE Rev. 1 20.2).

Portugal the most specialised Member State
Semi-finished and finished wood products accounted for 4.1% of total Portuguese manufacturing output in 1997 and just over a third of all wood, paper, publishing and printing activities in Portugal in the same year. Portuguese output was equal to 2.5 billion ECU in 1997. Denmark (1.2 billion ECU of production value), Finland (1.9 billion ECU) and Austria (2.0 billion ECU) also reported relatively high specialisation in these industries. However, Germany was by far the largest producer amongst the Member States in 1997, with 11.7 billion ECU of output, followed by France (5.3 billion ECU).

(5) L and A, no data available.
(6) L, NL and A, no data available.

———————————————————Figure 5.15
Semi-finished and finished wood products (NACE Rev. 1 20.2, 20.3, 20.4 and 20.5)
Production and export specialisation (%)

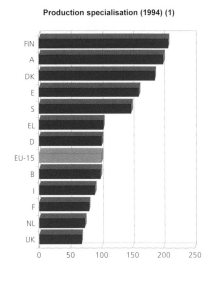

Production specialisation (1994) (1)

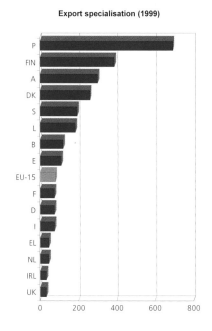

Export specialisation (1999)

(1) IRL, L and P, not available.

Source: Eurostat (SBS, COMEXT)

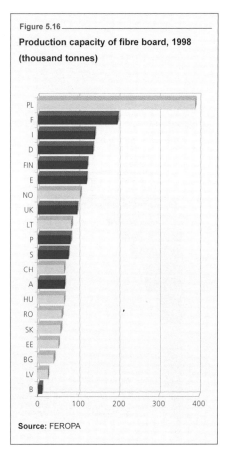

Figure 5.16

Production capacity of fibre board, 1998 (thousand tonnes)

Source: FEROPA

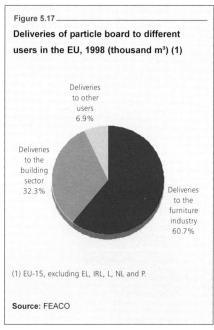

Figure 5.17

Deliveries of particle board to different users in the EU, 1998 (thousand m³) (1)

Deliveries to other users 6.9%

Deliveries to the building sector 32.3%

Deliveries to the furniture industry 60.7%

(1) EU-15, excluding EL, IRL, L, NL and P.

Source: FEACO

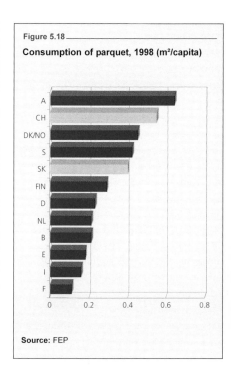

Figure 5.18

Consumption of parquet, 1998 (m²/capita)

Source: FEP

Figure 5.19

Semi-finished and finished wood products (NACE Rev. 1 20.2, 20.3, 20.4 and 20.5)
International comparison of production in constant prices and employment (1990=100)

Production in constant prices

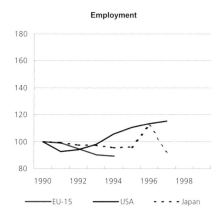

Employment

Source: Eurostat (SBS)

STRUCTURE AND PERFORMANCE

Nominal production rose from 25.0 billion ECU in 1986 to around 39.9 billion ECU[7] in 1996, a rate of increase (59.6%) that was somewhat lower than that for the whole of wood, paper, printing and publishing (70.2%).

Structure of output varies considerably between Member States

The breakdown of production between the different activities that make-up the semi-finished and finished wood products industry varied considerably across the Union. The principal activity in Portugal was the manufacture of other wood products, which accounted for more than half (51.0%) of the domestic output of semi-finished and finished wood products in 1997. The second highest share was recorded in Spain (13.4% of total semi-finished and finished wood products' output within the manufacture of other wood products). No other country generated more than a tenth of its output of semi-finished and finished wood products within this activity.

(7) L and A, no data available.

In 1997, the highest relative shares for the veneer sheets and boards industry (NACE Rev. 1 20.2) were recorded in the largest Member States. Other than Belgium (36.0%), the most specialised Member States were the United Kingdom (25.6%), Germany and Spain (both 23.6%) and France (20.0%). The manufacture of builders' carpentry and joinery (NACE Rev. 1 20.3) was a domain in which Denmark and the Netherlands specialised, this industry accounting for 69.2% and 66.7% of total semi-finished and finished wood products output in 1997. The Netherlands and France specialised in the manufacture of wooden containers (NACE Rev. 1 20.4), accounting for 17.2% and 15.4% of their respective domestic totals for semi-finished and finished wood products in 1997.

LABOUR AND PRODUCTIVITY

The share of total wood, paper, printing and publishing employment accounted for by semi-finished and finished wood products industries fell from 19.0% in 1985 to 17.4% in 1994, as the number of persons employed was reduced by 53.2 thousand to 394.6 thousands. Most of these jobs were lost in 1992 and 1993 when employment fell by 4.6% and 4.7%.

INTERNATIONAL TRENDS AND FOREIGN TRADE

Exports from and imports to the EU more than doubled in current prices over the ten years to 1999, when the value of exports reached 3.5 billion EUR and the value of imports was equal to 5.5 billion EUR. As such, the trade deficit widened from 1.1 billion in 1989.

All three Triad members recorded trade deficits in the 1990s. In Japan, the deficit more than doubled between 1989 and 1997 to reach 4.0 billion ECU. The deterioration of the Japanese deficit stopped abruptly in 1998 when it was reduced to 2.3 billion ECU. In the USA, strong domestic demand in the mid-to-late 1990s led to a rapid increase in imports. The American deficit rose from 1.6 billion ECU in 1993 to over 4 billion ECU by 1998.

Polish imports increase at a rapid pace
Only 2.6% of the EU's imports of semi-finished and finished wood products originated from Poland in 1989. However, ten years later Poland accounted for 13.5% of total EU imports (equivalent to 789 million EUR in value terms). Indonesia and China were the second and third most important origins of imports in 1999 (as they had been in 1989), with little change reported in their respective shares (10.5% and 10.1% in 1999). The USA fell from first to fourth place, as the American share of imports fell from 15.4% to 9.0% between 1989 and 1999.

Switzerland was the principal destination for EU exports in 1989 (31.9% of the total). However, the Swiss share fell to just 15.8% by 1999. The most important destination for EU exports of semi-finished and finished wood products became the USA, with exports valued at 593 million EUR in 1999 (17.3% of the total).

Figure 5.20

Semi-finished and finished wood products
(NACE Rev. 1 20.2, 20.3, 20.4 and 20.5)
Destination of EU exports, 1999 (%)

Source: Eurostat (COMEXT)

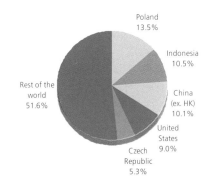

Figure 5.21

Semi-finished and finished wood products
(NACE Rev. 1 20.2, 20.3, 20.4 and 20.5)
Origin of EU imports, 1999 (%)

Source: Eurostat (COMEXT)

SUB-CHAPTER 5.3
PULP, PAPER AND PAPERBOARD
(NACE Rev. 1 21)

The production of both pulp (NACE Rev. 1 21.11) and paper for further industrial processing (NACE Rev. 1 21.12) is covered by this sub-chapter, as is the manufacture of articles of paper and paperboard (NACE Rev. 1 21.2). The latter Group includes the whole spectrum of paper products from paperboard containers, bags and sacks to household paper products, such as stationary and wallpaper.

The production value of the EU pulp, paper and paperboard industry was equal to approximately 112 billion ECU[8] in 1996, representing well over a third (35.9%) of the total output of wood, paper, printing and publishing. The share of value added was almost 4 percentage points lower at 32.0%[9] (or 35.3 billion ECU of value added). In terms of employment pulp, paper and paperboard industries accounted for just over a quarter (26.5%[10]) of all those employed in wood, paper, printing and publishing (equivalent to 615 thousand persons) in 1996.

Nearly 18% of Finnish manufacturing output
In 1997, Finland produced pulp, paper and paperboard to the value of 12.6 billion ECU. This was equivalent to 17.8% of total manufacturing output in Finland. Sweden was also relatively specialised, with output equal to 10.3 billion ECU in 1997, almost a tenth (8.8%) of the Swedish manufacturing total.

(8) L, no data available.
(9) L, no data available.
(10) L and NL, no data available.

Box 5.2
CEPI[11] (the Confederation of European Paper Industries) estimates that during 1999 its members produced over 85.2 million tonnes of paper and board, 3% more in volume terms than in 1998. More than a third (35%) of the paper and board produced in 1999 was used for packaging. The remaining uses were broken down as follows: more than a fifth (22%) for coated graphics, just under a fifth (19%) for uncoated graphics, 13% for newsprint, 6% for sanitary and household use and 5% for other uses.

(11) EU-15 (excluding EL and L), Norway and Switzerland.

Figure 5.22

Pulp, paper and paperboard (NACE Rev. 1 21)
Production and export specialisation (%)

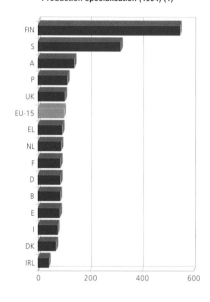

Production specialisation (1994) (1)

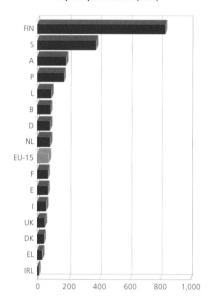

Export specialisation (1999)

(1) L, not available.

Source: Eurostat (SBS, COMEXT)

Germany (25.6 billion ECU), France (16.1 billion ECU) and the United Kingdom (15.5 billion ECU) were the largest EU producers in 1997, with the pulp, paper and paperboard industries accounting for around 2.5% of total manufacturing activity in all three countries in 1997. Most of the other Member States reported similar shares in total manufacturing output, although Austrian was also relatively specialised, with the production of pulp, paper and paperboard valued at 3.7 billion ECU in 1997 (equivalent to 5.1% of total manufacturing output).

STRUCTURE AND PERFORMANCE
EU production in current prices increased from 73.0 billion ECU in 1986 to approximately 112 billion ECU[12] in 1996, an increase of around 53% (below the average rate for the wood, paper, printing and publishing industry in the EU, 70.2%).

Operating surplus as a share of value added,
consistently above the manufacturing average
The share of gross operating surplus in value added for the pulp, paper and paperboard industries was at least 4.3 percentage points higher than the manufacturing average between 1985 and 1994. The highest difference between the two rates was recorded in 1986 (10.1 percentage points), whilst this ratio peaked at 41.3% in 1988 (the lowest share being recorded in 1992, 31.0%). From 1994 (37.4%) onwards the ratio rose again, reaching 40.4% by 1997[13].

(12) L, no data available.
(13) EL, I and L, no data available.

LABOUR AND PRODUCTIVITY

The number of persons employed in this industry fell from 712.7 thousand in 1985 to 658.8 thousand by 1994, a net loss of 53.9 thousand posts. The decline was even more considerable if one considers that the workforce grew to as many as 743.1 thousand persons by 1990. However, there were successive reductions of the workforce between 1991 and 1994, of which the largest was 6.9% in 1993.

High apparent labour productivity

Apparent labour productivity within the pulp, paper and paperboard industries reached 50.0 thousand ECU per person employed in 1994. Throughout the period 1985 to 1994, the EU's pulp, paper and paperboard industry recorded apparent labour productivity figures which were higher than the manufacturing average (by between 3.6 and 6.3 thousand ECU per person employed). In 1994, the simple wage adjusted labour productivity ratio was equal to 159.8% (again considerably higher than EU manufacturing average of 146.0%).

INTERNATIONAL TRENDS AND FOREIGN TRADE

Exports of pulp, paper and paperboard from the EU grew by more than 5 billion EUR between 1989 and 1999, ending the period with a value of 13.8 billion EUR. As a result of expanding exports, the EU's trade position strengthened, with the trade surplus of 631 million ECU in 1989 expanding to 4.0 billion EUR by 1999. Despite this growth, the proportion of total manufacturing exports accounted for by the pulp, paper, printing and publishing industries fell from 2.4% in 1989 to 1.9% of the total by 1999.

The EU's largest trading partners
were NAFTA and EFTA

The USA was the largest origin of EU imports (22.2%) and the principal destination for EU exports (13.7%) in 1999. As with other industries within this chapter, Canada had been the largest importer into the EU in 1989, but the Canadian share fell by nearly 10 percentage points to 18.1% in 1999. Switzerland (12.6%) and Norway (12.4%) were the next most important origins of pulp, paper and paperboard products in 1999.

Switzerland was the second most important destination for EU exports, despite a reduction in its share of total exports from 12.7% to 10.3% between 1989 and 1999. The most significant change occurred with respect to Poland, which accounted for 7.1% of the EU's exports of pulp, paper and paperboard in 1999 (965 million EUR). This was a large increase when compared to 1989, when the EU exported goods valued at 82.9 million ECU to Poland (just 1.0% of the total).

Figure 5.23

Pulp, paper and paperboard (NACE Rev. 1 21)
International comparison of production in constant prices and employment (1990=100)

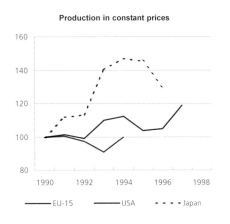
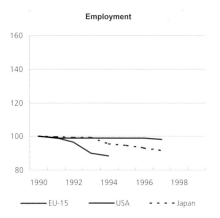

Source: Eurostat (SBS)

Figure 5.24

Pulp, paper and paperboard (NACE Rev. 1 21)
Destination of EU exports, 1999 (%)

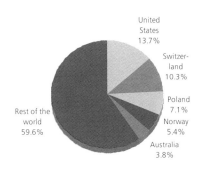

Source: Eurostat (COMEXT)

Figure 5.25

Pulp, paper and paperboard (NACE Rev. 1 21)
Origin of EU imports, 1999 (%)

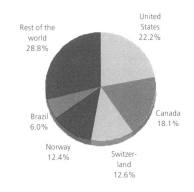

Source: Eurostat (COMEXT)

SUB-CHAPTER 5.4
PUBLISHING AND PRINTING
(NACE Rev. 1 22.1 AND 22.2)

The principal activities covered by this sub-chapter are the printing and publishing of books, newspapers and brochures. Printing activities also encompass the activities of bookbinding, composition and plate making, as well as the manufacture of overhead projection foils and the preparation of digital data. Publishing activities cover sound recordings, as well as printed matter. The manufacture of diverse recording media (NACE Rev. 1 22.3), such as tapes, CDs and computer storage systems are not covered (see chapter 21).

Publishing and printing was the largest activity within the wood, paper, publishing and printing activities in terms of production, value added or employment. EU production was valued at 138.2 billion ECU in 1996, which was equivalent to 44.3% of the wood, paper, printing and publishing total, whilst value added (55.8 billion ECU) and employment (1.1 million persons) represented shares of 50.5% and 48.3% respectively.

Box 5.3

Publishers and printers are anxious to see how the so-called "information revolution" will affect their industry. So far, the Internet and CD-ROMs largely exist as compliments to paper copies of newspapers, magazines and books. There is little sign that new media are replacing old ones, rather new media forms are driving demand for more information. At present, many on-line newspapers and magazines are used as a marketing tool to encourage people to take out subscriptions for paper versions of publications (whilst at the same time allowing subscribers access to back issues).

Figure 5.26

Publishing and printing (NACE Rev. 1 22.1 and 22.2)

Production and export specialisation (%)

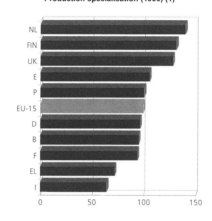

Production specialisation (1996) (1)

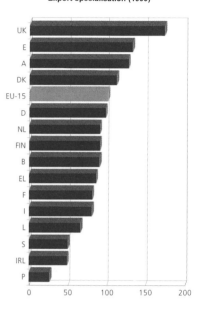

Export specialisation (1999)

(1) DK, IRL, L, A and S, not available.

Source: Eurostat (SBS, COMEXT)

Denmark, the Netherlands and the United Kingdom specialise in publishing and printing

Germany was the largest producer within the publishing and printing industries in the EU, with output to the value of 37.2 billion ECU in 1997, a figure that represented 3.7% of the German manufacturing total or almost half (47.6%) of German production within the activities covered by this chapter. There were several countries where publishing and printing accounted for more than 5.0% of the domestic manufacturing output in 1997, including the United Kingdom (which was the second largest producer with 29.3 billion ECU, equivalent to 5.1% of the manufacturing total). Denmark was the most specialised country within the EU, with 5.8% of Danish manufacturing output derived from printing and publishing activities (3.1 billion ECU in value terms), followed by the Netherlands as the second most specialised country, with production valued at 3.5 billion ECU (or 5.2% of manufacturing).

STRUCTURE AND PERFORMANCE

Based on the EU data for 1995 (135.7 billion ECU) and 1996 (138.2 billion ECU), the cost structure of the publishing and printing industries is in many ways similar to that for total manufacturing. Personnel costs accounted for 69.6% of value added in 1996 (which was just 0.3 percentage points higher than in total manufacturing), whilst the gross operating surplus was 30.4% of value added. However, in relation to turnover the EU's publishing and printing industries generated a much higher gross operating surplus than manufacturing in general. The gross operating rate for publishing and printing was equal to 12.0% in 1996 (3.4 percentage points above the manufacturing average). The value added rate (40.4%), which measures the share of value added in production, was also considerably above the manufacturing average (10.0 percentage points higher), reflecting a somewhat vertically integrated industry.

LABOUR AND PRODUCTIVITY

In 1995 and 1996 the number of persons employed in the EU publishing and printing industry fell by 5.4% to 1.1 million persons. Almost a quarter (23.8%) of the EU's workforce was employed in Germany (267 thousand persons) in 1996, just over a fifth (20.7%) in the United Kingdom, whilst France (12.9%) and Spain (11.0%) were the only other Member States to record double-digit shares in the total.

Printing provides more jobs in southern Europe
In 1996, just over half a million (504 thousand persons) were employed in the EU's publishing industry (45.1% of the total for publishing and printing), whilst some 615 thousand persons were employed in the printing industry. Printing was relatively more important in the southern Member States[14], with much higher shares in domestic publishing and printing totals being recorded in Spain (66.9%), Italy (59.9%) and Portugal (73.4%), as well as in Belgium (71.5%).

EU apparent labour productivity for the publishing and printing industry was equal to 49.9 thousand ECU per person employed in 1996, which was 4.6 thousand ECU above the manufacturing average. This marked a reversal compared to 1995, when apparent labour productivity was 1.6 thousand ECU per person employed higher in total manufacturing.

(14) Other than EL, where printing accounted for only 27.1% of total employment.

INTERNATIONAL TRENDS AND FOREIGN TRADE

Exports of publishing and printing goods grew at a faster pace than imports between 1989 and 1997. As a result the EU's trade surplus reached 3.0 billion ECU in 1997, up from 1.6 billion ECU in 1989. This figure fell somewhat in the subsequent two years, resulting in a 2.5 billion EUR surplus by 1999. Publishing and printing accounted for 0.8% of the EU's total manufacturing exports in 1999, down from 1.0% of the total in 1989.

USA and Switzerland the main trading partners
The principal origins of EU imports and destinations for EU exports were the USA and Switzerland. Whilst in nominal terms imports from these two countries increased between 1989 and 1999, their relative shares of total EU imports declined. Imports from the USA were valued at 1.3 billion EUR in 1999, whilst those from Switzerland were worth 404 million EUR. In relative terms, the proportion of imports from the USA fell from 44.2% to 38.0% between 1989 and 1999, whilst the share of Switzerland fell from 20.2% to 12.0%.

Switzerland was the largest EU export destination, accounting for almost a fifth (19.6%) of the EU's exports in 1999. This figure was down 4.5 percentage points on the corresponding share of 1989. There was little change in the share of exports to the USA over the ten-year period considered, with a reduction of 0.5 percentage points to 19.2%.

Figure 5.27

**Publishing and printing
(NACE Rev. 1 22.1 and 22.2)
Destination of EU exports, 1999 (%)**

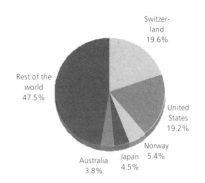

Source: Eurostat (COMEXT)

Figure 5.28

**Publishing and printing
(NACE Rev. 1 22.1 and 22.2)
Origin of EU imports, 1999 (%)**

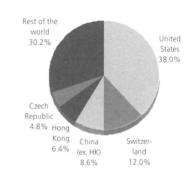

Source: Eurostat (COMEXT)

Table 5.3

Sawmilling and planing of wood, impregnation of wood (NACE Rev. 1 20.1)

Production related indicators in the EU (1)

	1989	1990	1991	1992	1993	1994	1995	1996	1997	1998	1999
Number of persons employed (thousands)	122.0	121.8	118.4	112.7	103.0	109.5	94.5	107.7	:	:	:
Production (million ECU)	11,540	12,267	11,394	11,331	10,838	13,378	13,303	13,851	:	:	:
Domestic producer price index (1995=100)	:	:	:	:	:	:	100.0	94.2	98.2	97.2	96.7
Value added (million ECU)	3,329	3,512	3,095	3,171	3,243	4,045	3,533	3,424	:	:	:

(1) Technically, data before 01/01/1999 are in ECU and after this date in euro. However, as the conversion rate was 1 ECU =1 EUR, for practical purposes the two terms can be used interchangeably.

Table 5.4

Sawmilling and planing of wood, impregnation of wood (NACE Rev. 1 20.1)

Trade related indicators in the EU (1)

	1989	1990	1991	1992	1993	1994	1995	1996	1997	1998	1999
Exports (million EUR)	863	937	824	772	981	1,224	1,408	1,407	1,766	1,680	2,063
Imports (million EUR)	4,139	4,222	3,633	3,500	3,371	3,969	3,868	3,544	4,443	4,411	4,801
Trade balance (million EUR)	-3,276	-3,285	-2,809	-2,729	-2,390	-2,745	-2,460	-2,136	-2,676	-2,730	-2,738
Cover ratio (%)	20.9	22.2	22.7	22.0	29.1	30.8	36.4	39.7	39.8	38.1	43.0

(1) Technically, data before 01/01/1999 are in ECU and after this date in euro. However, as the conversion rate was 1 ECU =1 EUR, for practical purposes the two terms can be used interchangeably.

Table 5.5

Sawmilling and planing of wood, impregnation of wood (NACE Rev. 1 20.1)

Production related indicators, 1997

	B	DK	D	EL (1)	E	F	IRL (1)	I (1)	L	NL	A	P	FIN	S	UK
Number of persons employed (thousands)	2.8	1.4	20.2	0.6	12.4	14.7	1.3	4.9	0.2	:	5.6	13.4	9.6	14.4	8.7
Production (million ECU)	474	144	3,029	33	885	1,643	158	768	19	34	1,143	561	2,519	3,917	768
Value added (million ECU)	99	49	872	8	234	448	37	191	5	11	263	145	638	976	255
Gross operating surplus (million ECU)	38.7	12.9	227.4	0.4	79.9	70.2	14.2	81.1	1.1	4.2	113.6	54.1	371.7	473.9	82.6

(1) 1996.

Table 5.6

Sawmilling and planing of wood, impregnation of wood (NACE Rev. 1 20.1)

Trade related indicators, 1999

	B	DK	D	EL	E	F	IRL	I	L	NL	A	P	FIN	S	UK
Exports (million EUR)	327	104	741	7	105	432	45	324	32	193	1,176	72	1,483	2,081	79
Imports (million EUR)	610	541	1,371	145	706	815	206	1,803	24	845	339	149	101	162	1,679
Trade balance (million EUR)	-283	-437	-630	-138	-601	-384	-161	-1,479	7	-652	837	-78	1,382	1,919	-1,600
Cover ratio (%)	53.6	19.2	54.0	4.7	14.9	52.9	21.7	18.0	129.7	22.8	346.6	48.0	1,472.9	1,286.8	4.7

Table 5.7

Sawmilling and planing of wood, impregnation of wood (NACE Rev. 1 20.1)

Labour related indicators, 1997

	B	DK (1)	D	EL (2)	E	F	IRL (2)	I (2)	L	NL	A	P	FIN	S	UK
Unit personnel costs (thousand ECU per employee)	25.2	31.7	32.2	14.2	14.2	25.8	18.7	23.5	23.4	:	26.8	7.1	29.0	34.9	20.7
Social charges as a share of personnel costs (%)	36.9	4.7	23.4	31.7	30.7	40.3	19.2	53.5	:	15.0	30.7	32.6	28.7	43.3	14.0
Apparent labour productivity (thousand ECU/pers. empl.)	34.8	35.3	43.1	14.5	18.9	30.6	29.8	39.0	28.0	:	46.9	10.9	66.4	67.8	29.3
Wage adjusted labour productivity (%)	138.4	123.2	133.7	102.1	133.2	118.5	158.9	165.7	119.8	:	174.9	153.0	228.8	194.4	141.7
Personnel costs as a share of total operating costs (%)	13.9	25.8	20.7	23.8	18.3	23.0	14.7	14.4	20.3	22.0	13.8	15.7	12.1	14.1	18.2

(1) Unit personnel costs and wage adjusted labour productivity, 1996; (2) 1996.

Source: Eurostat (SBS, EBT, COMEXT)

_____Table 5.8

Manufacture of veneer sheets; manufacture of plywood, laminboard, particle board, fibre board and other panels and boards (NACE Rev. 1 20.2)

Production related indicators in the EU (1)

	1989	1990	1991	1992	1993	1994	1995	1996	1997	1998	1999
Number of persons employed (thousands)	93.3	84.6	82.4	80.1	76.8	77.2	:	:	:	:	:
Production (million ECU)	10,397	9,660	9,738	9,741	9,756	10,621	:	:	:	:	:
Domestic producer price index (1995=100)	:	:	:	:	:	:	100.0	96.4	95.8	97.0	94.4
Value added (million ECU)	3,412	3,006	3,035	3,028	3,046	3,186	:	:	:	:	:

(1) Technically, data before 01/01/1999 are in ECU and after this date in euro. However, as the conversion rate was 1 ECU =1 EUR, for practical purposes the two terms can be used interchangeably.

_____Table 5.9

Manufacture of veneer sheets; manufacture of plywood, laminboard, particle board, fibre board and other panels and boards (NACE Rev. 1 20.2)

Trade related indicators in the EU (1)

	1989	1990	1991	1992	1993	1994	1995	1996	1997	1998	1999
Exports (million EUR)	475	485	444	445	625	780	883	977	1,224	1,388	1,423
Imports (million EUR)	1,538	1,612	1,545	1,616	1,596	1,810	1,937	1,791	2,124	2,220	2,205
Trade balance (million EUR)	-1,064	-1,126	-1,101	-1,171	-971	-1,030	-1,054	-814	-901	-831	-782
Cover ratio (%)	30.9	30.1	28.7	27.5	39.2	43.1	45.6	54.6	57.6	62.5	64.5

(1) Technically, data before 01/01/1999 are in ECU and after this date in euro. However, as the conversion rate was 1 ECU =1 EUR, for practical purposes the two terms can be used interchangeably.

_____Table 5.10

Manufacture of veneer sheets; manufacture of plywood, laminboard, particle board, fibre board and other panels and boards (NACE Rev. 1 20.2)

Production related indicators, 1997

	B	DK	D	EL (1)	E	F	IRL (1)	I (1)	L	NL	A	P	FIN	S	UK
Number of persons employed (thousands)	2.8	1.2	20.7	2.3	10.3	8.2	0.6	10.7	:	:	3.5	2.7	7.1	2.0	7.2
Production (million ECU)	792	143	3,485	209	1,440	1,392	110	1,980	:	59	587	341	836	271	1,200
Value added (million ECU)	181	49	1,091	56	380	335	33	518	:	16	169	87	332	80	435
Gross operating surplus (million ECU)	84.4	15.5	300.4	10.6	191.5	94.1	17.4	246.7	:	3.6	42.5	51.7	137.3	14.8	245.8

(1) 1996.

_____Table 5.11

Manufacture of veneer sheets; manufacture of plywood, laminboard, particle board, fibre board and other panels and boards (NACE Rev. 1 20.2)

Trade related indicators, 1999

	B	DK	D	EL	E	F	IRL	I	L	NL	A	P	FIN	S	UK
Exports (million EUR)	633	69	1,398	15	231	689	109	409	78	95	566	147	589	230	119
Imports (million EUR)	417	241	1,231	98	351	549	82	573	21	512	270	79	56	234	958
Trade balance (million EUR)	216	-171	166	-83	-120	140	27	-164	58	-417	296	68	533	-4	-839
Cover ratio (%)	151.8	28.8	113.5	15.2	65.8	125.5	132.6	71.4	379.1	18.5	209.4	186.2	1,056.8	98.3	12.4

_____Table 5.12

Manufacture of veneer sheets; manufacture of plywood, laminboard, particle board, fibre board and other panels and boards (NACE Rev. 1 20.2)

Labour related indicators, 1997

	B	DK (1)	D	EL (2)	E	F	IRL (2)	I (2)	L	NL	A	P	FIN	S	UK
Unit personnel costs (thousand ECU per employee)	35.0	31.8	38.2	19.7	18.6	29.3	27.9	25.9	:	:	36.7	13.2	28.6	33.3	26.5
Social charges as a share of personnel costs (%)	51.3	5.4	22.9	30.1	30.2	40.6	14.9	52.6	:	15.5	31.3	31.6	27.3	40.7	14.7
Apparent labour productivity (thousand ECU/pers. empl.)	64.2	39.4	52.6	24.3	37.0	40.8	59.5	48.3	:	:	49.0	32.7	46.5	40.8	60.8
Wage adjusted labour productivity (%)	183.3	155.3	137.6	123.3	198.5	139.0	212.9	186.1	:	:	133.5	246.9	162.7	122.6	229.0
Personnel costs as a share of total operating costs (%)	13.6	25.6	23.7	22.7	13.2	18.2	16.1	15.7	:	21.4	22.1	11.7	28.2	23.7	18.8

(1) Unit personnel costs and wage adjusted labour productivity, 1996. (2) 1996.

Source: Eurostat (SBS, EBT, COMEXT)

Table 5.13

Manufacture of builders' carpentry and joinery (NACE Rev. 1 20.3)

Production related indicators in the EU (1)

	1989	1990	1991	1992	1993	1994	1995	1996	1997	1998	1999
Number of persons employed (thousands)	227.5	228.7	222.8	211.5	206.1	198.1	:	:	237.1	242.3	237.3
Production (million EUR)	15,804	16,727	16,614	16,378	16,357	16,243	:	:	20,767	22,180	22,942
Domestic producer price index (1995=100)	:	:	:	:	:	:	100.0	100.8	101.8	103.3	104.6
Value added (million EUR)	5,637	5,773	5,762	5,841	5,969	5,800	:	:	7,281	7,671	7,900

(1) Technically, data before 01/01/1999 are in ECU and after this date in euro. However, as the conversion rate was 1 ECU =1 EUR, for practical purposes the two terms can be used interchangeably.

Table 5.14

Manufacture of builders' carpentry and joinery (NACE Rev. 1 20.3)

Trade related indicators in the EU (1)

	1989	1990	1991	1992	1993	1994	1995	1996	1997	1998	1999
Exports (million EUR)	449	443	410	397	395	538	678	808	933	932	969
Imports (million EUR)	315	374	471	598	766	969	995	1,013	1,141	1,173	1,341
Trade balance (million EUR)	134	69	-61	-201	-372	-431	-317	-206	-209	-242	-372
Cover ratio (%)	142.6	118.4	87.1	66.4	51.5	55.5	68.1	79.7	81.7	79.4	72.2

(1) Technically, data before 01/01/1999 are in ECU and after this date in euro. However, as the conversion rate was 1 ECU =1 EUR, for practical purposes the two terms can be used interchangeably.

Table 5.15

Manufacture of builders' carpentry and joinery (NACE Rev. 1 20.3)

Production related indicators, 1997

	B	DK	D	EL (1)	E	F	IRL	I (1)	L	NL	A	P	FIN	S	UK
Number of persons employed (thousands)	6.0	9.8	58.2	0.5	46.5	17.7	2.5	13.4	0.0	:	14.4	20.9	9.0	10.4	22.2
Production (million ECU)	587	955	6,496	30	2,317	2,316	198	1,437	2	885	1,327	541	904	1,257	1,686
Value added (million ECU)	182	375	2,330	6	798	648	78	493	1	292	564	172	287	416	624
Gross operating surplus (million ECU)	38.1	95.6	402.2	-0.8	218.6	176.5	37.1	162.5	0.5	70.6	163.4	54.8	74.5	85.4	183.4

(1) 1996.

Table 5.16

Manufacture of builders' carpentry and joinery (NACE Rev. 1 20.3)

Trade related indicators, 1999

	B	DK	D	EL	E	F	IRL	I	L	NL	A	P	FIN	S	UK
Exports (million EUR)	273	490	370	3	118	193	6	174	1	200	432	35	343	542	113
Imports (million EUR)	149	171	1,131	14	94	222	62	181	35	199	281	50	28	53	390
Trade balance (million EUR)	124	319	-761	-11	24	-29	-56	-7	-34	0	151	-15	315	489	-277
Cover ratio (%)	183.0	286.7	32.7	19.2	125.7	86.8	10.3	96.2	3.9	100.2	153.6	69.5	1,236.4	1,023.2	28.9

Table 5.17

Manufacture of builders' carpentry and joinery (NACE Rev. 1 20.3)

Labour related indicators, 1997

	B	DK (1)	D	EL (2)	E	F	IRL	I (2)	L	NL	A	P	FIN	S	UK
Unit personnel costs (thousand ECU per employee)	27.1	31.4	33.4	13.2	15.1	26.6	17.2	25.9	25.5	:	28.1	7.1	25.2	31.7	20.8
Social charges as a share of personnel costs (%)	54.0	4.8	22.7	30.9	29.1	41.8	14.2	50.7	:	16.7	30.5	34.8	27.8	40.5	11.3
Apparent labour productivity (thousand ECU/pers. empl.)	30.6	38.3	40.0	11.5	17.2	36.6	31.8	36.7	47.5	:	39.2	8.2	32.1	39.9	28.1
Wage adjusted labour productivity (%)	112.9	131.8	119.9	86.8	113.7	137.4	185.0	141.4	186.0	:	139.5	116.0	127.6	125.8	135.1
Personnel costs as a share of total operating costs (%)	26.4	31.8	30.4	24.3	26.1	21.5	21.9	25.6	31.3	26.6	31.3	23.4	24.4	27.5	26.6

(1) Unit personnel costs and wage adjusted labour productivity, 1996; (2) 1996.

Source: Eurostat (SBS, EBT, COMEXT)

_____Table 5.18

Manufacture of wooden containers (NACE Rev. 1 20.4)

Production related indicators in the EU (1)

	1989	1990	1991	1992	1993	1994	1995	1996	1997	1998	1999
Number of persons employed (thousands)	46.6	47.7	48.7	46.2	43.2	42.9	:	44.6	42.8	42.9	45.4
Production (million ECU)	3,312	3,764	3,890	3,667	3,369	3,559	:	4,160	:	:	:
Domestic producer price index (1995=100)	:	97.4	99.1	97.8	96.2	96.4	100.0	98.6	98.6	99.1	99.3
Value added (million EUR)	1,091	1,233	1,264	1,245	1,135	1,124	:	1,265	1,328	1,373	1,455

(1) Technically, data before 01/01/1999 are in ECU and after this date in euro. However, as the conversion rate was 1 ECU =1 EUR, for practical purposes the two terms can be used interchangeably.

_____Table 5.19

Manufacture of wooden containers (NACE Rev. 1 20.4)

Trade related indicators in the EU (1)

	1989	1990	1991	1992	1993	1994	1995	1996	1997	1998	1999
Exports (million EUR)	72	82	89	83	94	118	139	164	203	251	277
Imports (million EUR)	68	134	177	177	148	184	225	226	265	319	352
Trade balance (million EUR)	4	-52	-88	-93	-54	-65	-86	-62	-62	-68	-75
Cover ratio (%)	105.7	61.5	50.5	47.3	63.5	64.4	61.6	72.5	76.6	78.6	78.7

(1) Technically, data before 01/01/1999 are in ECU and after this date in euro. However, as the conversion rate was 1 ECU =1 EUR, for practical purposes the two terms can be used interchangeably.

_____Table 5.20

Manufacture of wooden containers (NACE Rev. 1 20.4)

Production related indicators, 1997

	B	DK	D	EL (1)	E	F	IRL	I (1)	L	NL	A	P	FIN	S	UK
Number of persons employed (thousands)	1.2	0.5	5.3	0.2	9.0	10.7	0.3	4.9	:	:	0.4	1.0	0.9	1.0	6.5
Production (million ECU)	214	53	577	10	650	1,067	29	504	:	228	32	42	103	119	580
Value added (million ECU)	52	17	228	3	167	335	7	146	:	61	15	10	36	41	203
Gross operating surplus (million ECU)	15.0	2.4	68.7	0.9	48.6	64.1	2.4	38.5	:	16.5	4.8	3.5	12.5	8.9	64.3

(1) 1996.

_____Table 5.21

Manufacture of wooden containers (NACE Rev. 1 20.4)

Trade related indicators, 1999

	B	DK	D	EL	E	F	IRL	I	L	NL	A	P	FIN	S	UK
Exports (million EUR)	85	13	103	2	65	287	1	66	4	65	24	22	5	44	121
Imports (million EUR)	83	23	191	9	57	143	10	103	4	61	48	8	15	18	151
Trade balance (million EUR)	2	-10	-87	-7	8	144	-9	-37	0	4	-23	15	-10	27	-31
Cover ratio (%)	102.6	57.4	54.3	20.5	114.2	200.7	10.4	63.9	106.1	106.0	51.1	297.7	35.2	253.0	79.8

_____Table 5.22

Manufacture of wooden containers (NACE Rev. 1 20.4)

Labour related indicators, 1997

	B	DK (1)	D	EL (2)	E	F	IRL	I (2)	L	NL	A	P	FIN	S	UK
Unit personnel costs (thousand ECU per employee)	31.8	30.0	30.5	8.7	14.6	25.4	16.4	23.2	:	:	24.9	7.0	28.5	31.0	22.3
Social charges as a share of personnel costs (%)	40.9	5.8	21.1	30.8	28.4	41.0	14.0	50.6	:	12.3	25.6	33.3	27.9	40.0	11.6
Apparent labour productivity (thousand ECU/pers. empl.)	42.6	31.7	43.1	13.1	18.5	31.4	23.9	29.6	:	:	36.6	9.4	39.4	39.6	31.5
Wage adjusted labour productivity (%)	133.9	116.7	141.5	150.6	127.0	123.7	145.4	127.3	:	:	147.2	134.5	138.2	127.6	141.5
Personnel costs as a share of total operating costs (%)	18.7	28.1	26.9	16.2	18.6	25.7	18.4	22.4	:	19.8	32.6	15.7	25.9	28.8	26.0

(1) Unit personnel costs and wage adjusted labour productivity, 1996. (2) 1996.

Source: Eurostat (SBS, EBT, COMEXT)

Table 5.23

Manufacture of other products of wood; manufacture of articles of cork, straw and plaiting materials (NACE Rev. 1 20.5)

Production related indicators in the EU (1)

	1989	1990	1991	1992	1993	1994	1995	1996	1997	1998	1999
Number of persons employed (thousands)	83.0	82.3	85.0	80.7	72.6	76.4	72.0	:	77.0	76.4	77.3
Production (million EUR)	4,458	4,655	4,988	5,201	4,998	5,230	5,323	:	6,019	6,515	7,549
Domestic producer price index (1995=100)	:	:	:	:	:	:	100.0	104.1	106.6	109.3	112.3
Value added (million EUR)	1,670	1,766	1,878	1,944	1,858	1,933	1,796	:	2,004	2,283	2,394

(1) Technically, data before 01/01/1999 are in ECU and after this date in euro. However, as the conversion rate was 1 ECU =1 EUR, for practical purposes the two terms can be used interchangeably.

Table 5.24

Manufacture of other products of wood; manufacture of articles of cork, straw and plaiting materials (NACE Rev. 1 20.5)

Trade related indicators in the EU (1)

	1989	1990	1991	1992	1993	1994	1995	1996	1997	1998	1999
Exports (million EUR)	449	431	431	447	439	494	545	632	718	770	787
Imports (million EUR)	614	663	811	862	961	1,054	1,144	1,202	1,382	1,434	1,636
Trade balance (million EUR)	-165	-232	-381	-416	-522	-560	-598	-570	-664	-663	-850
Cover ratio (%)	73.1	65.1	53.1	51.8	45.7	46.9	47.7	52.6	52.0	53.7	48.1

(1) Technically, data before 01/01/1999 are in ECU and after this date in euro. However, as the conversion rate was 1 ECU =1 EUR, for practical purposes the two terms can be used interchangeably.

Table 5.25

Manufacture of other products of wood; manufacture of articles of cork, straw and plaiting materials (NACE Rev. 1 20.5)

Production related indicators, 1997

	B	DK	D	EL (1)	E	F	IRL	I (1)	L	NL	A	P	FIN	S	UK
Number of persons employed (thousands)	1.6	0.9	12.3	0.1	13.8	5.8	0.6	10.4	:	:	1.1	22.7	0.8	1.0	5.5
Production (million ECU)	134	86	1,153	4	822	529	42	1,030	:	120	93	1,548	49	83	400
Value added (million ECU)	50	32	456	1	277	186	16	339	:	43	43	313	23	39	173
Gross operating surplus (million ECU)	12.5	7.5	69.2	0.2	88.1	38.1	8.1	104.7	:	15.1	12.3	125.1	8.3	9.5	65.3

(1) 1996.

Table 5.26

Manufacture of other products of wood; manufacture of articles of cork, straw and plaiting materials (NACE Rev. 1 20.5)

Trade related indicators, 1999

	B	DK	D	EL	E	F	IRL	I	L	NL	A	P	FIN	S	UK
Exports (million EUR)	129	85	236	2	195	167	1	310	1	89	75	753	6	80	86
Imports (million EUR)	176	64	797	26	163	588	23	248	8	185	121	70	20	85	340
Trade balance (million EUR)	-47	21	-560	-24	33	-421	-22	62	-7	-96	-46	683	-14	-5	-254
Cover ratio (%)	73.5	132.3	29.7	7.4	120.0	28.3	6.0	124.8	10.4	48.0	62.3	1,073.4	30.6	94.2	25.3

Table 5.27

Manufacture of other products of wood; manufacture of articles of cork, straw and plaiting materials (NACE Rev. 1 20.5)

Labour related indicators, 1997

	B	DK (1)	D	EL (2)	E	F	IRL	I (2)	L	NL	A	P	FIN	S	UK
Unit personnel costs (thousand ECU per employee)	27.3	31.4	31.8	10.2	15.1	25.6	15.1	23.6	:	:	27.7	9.0	25.4	28.7	21.6
Social charges as a share of personnel costs (%)	43.1	4.2	21.9	33.3	27.9	38.7	15.9	52.5	:	13.3	32.6	30.3	27.0	40.4	11.6
Apparent labour productivity (thousand ECU/pers. empl.)	31.0	34.1	37.2	10.8	20.0	32.2	29.0	32.5	:	:	38.5	13.8	30.2	38.0	31.5
Wage adjusted labour productivity (%)	113.7	151.6	117.0	105.9	132.6	125.8	192.9	137.6	:	:	139.4	153.3	119.0	132.5	145.7
Personnel costs as a share of total operating costs (%)	30.8	31.2	32.6	30.0	23.7	27.8	22.3	25.2	:	21.0	34.7	12.6	32.3	39.0	29.2

(1) Unit personnel costs and wage adjusted labour productivity, 1996; (2) 1996.

Source: Eurostat (SBS, EBT, COMEXT)

Table 5.28

Manufacture of pulp, paper and paperboard (NACE Rev. 1 21.1)

Production related indicators in the EU (1)

	1989	1990	1991	1992	1993	1994	1995	1996	1997	1998	1999
Number of persons employed (thousands)	296.1	296.1	286.9	273.1	248.7	240.4	:	:	232.2	233.3	226.7
Production (million EUR)	52,643	50,615	48,069	45,434	41,165	48,122	:	:	56,923	57,380	58,993
Domestic producer price index (1995=100)	:	:	:	:	:	:	100.0	87.6	83.6	84.5	82.6
Value added (million EUR)	16,373	15,184	14,358	13,056	12,051	14,975	:	:	17,194	17,410	17,924

(1) Technically, data before 01/01/1999 are in ECU and after this date in euro. However, as the conversion rate was 1 ECU =1 EUR, for practical purposes the two terms can be used interchangeably.

Table 5.29

Manufacture of pulp, paper and paperboard (NACE Rev. 1 21.1)

Trade related indicators in the EU (1)

	1989	1990	1991	1992	1993	1994	1995	1996	1997	1998	1999
Exports (million EUR)	6,665	5,934	5,618	5,643	6,293	7,342	9,540	9,061	10,161	9,972	10,729
Imports (million EUR)	7,104	6,553	6,253	6,097	5,379	6,801	9,280	7,481	7,962	8,359	8,341
Trade balance (million EUR)	-439	-619	-636	-454	914	540	260	1,580	2,199	1,614	2,388
Cover ratio (%)	93.8	90.6	89.8	92.6	117.0	107.9	102.8	121.1	127.6	119.3	128.6

(1) Technically, data before 01/01/1999 are in ECU and after this date in euro. However, as the conversion rate was 1 ECU =1 EUR, for practical purposes the two terms can be used interchangeably.

Table 5.30

Manufacture of pulp, paper and paperboard (NACE Rev. 1 21.1)

Production related indicators, 1997

	B	DK	D	EL (1)	E	F	IRL	I (1)	L	NL	A	P	FIN	S	UK
Number of persons employed (thousands)	5.5	1.4	45.7	2.6	14.7	28.6	0.1	18.3	0.0	:	8.1	6.1	37.7	31.8	23.9
Production (million ECU)	1,663	221	10,849	192	2,697	6,871	31	4,067	0	1,634	2,089	1,208	12,009	8,324	4,856
Value added (million ECU)	432	70	3,284	13	832	1,723	10	1,296	0	541	697	407	3,506	2,697	1,612
Gross operating surplus (million ECU)	160.5	21.9	1,330.4	-39.3	384.7	563.0	4.3	643.6	0.0	273.8	326.1	269.9	2,514.3	1,356.6	787.4

(1) 1996.

Table 5.31

Manufacture of pulp, paper and paperboard (NACE Rev. 1 21.1)

Trade related indicators, 1999

	B	DK	D	EL	E	F	IRL	I	L	NL	A	P	FIN	S	UK
Exports (million EUR)	2,084	205	6,995	33	1,204	3,831	66	1,883	172	2,412	2,215	889	8,162	6,747	1,782
Imports (million EUR)	2,586	869	7,436	468	2,372	5,290	400	4,137	113	3,023	1,270	485	313	673	5,854
Trade balance (million EUR)	-502	-664	-441	-435	-1,168	-1,459	-334	-2,253	59	-610	945	404	7,849	6,074	-4,073
Cover ratio (%)	80.6	23.6	94.1	7.1	50.7	72.4	16.4	45.5	151.6	79.8	174.4	183.5	2,607.2	1,002.6	30.4

Table 5.32

Manufacture of pulp, paper and paperboard (NACE Rev. 1 21.1)

Labour related indicators, 1997

	B	DK (1)	D	EL (2)	E	F	IRL	I (2)	L	NL	A	P	FIN	S	UK
Unit personnel costs (thousand ECU per employee)	49.6	40.3	42.8	20.3	29.4	40.6	37.8	36.0	:	:	45.9	22.7	41.9	42.2	34.7
Social charges as a share of personnel costs (%)	40.4	5.5	25.1	35.5	27.7	43.4	25.6	52.6	:	14.7	31.9	43.6	30.3	44.9	14.4
Apparent labour productivity (thousand ECU/pers. empl.)	78.8	50.9	71.9	4.9	56.7	60.3	66.2	70.8	:	:	86.2	67.3	93.1	84.8	67.5
Wage adjusted labour productivity (%)	159.0	151.5	167.9	24.3	193.3	148.6	175.0	196.7	:	:	187.9	296.3	222.1	201.2	194.6
Personnel costs as a share of total operating costs (%)	18.2	24.1	19.4	26.9	17.3	18.4	18.8	18.4	:	19.5	18.8	14.5	14.5	18.7	20.1

(1) Unit personnel costs and wage adjusted labour productivity, 1996. (2) 1996.

Source: Eurostat (SBS, EBT, COMEXT)

Table 5.33

Manufacture of articles of paper and paperboard (NACE Rev. 1 21.2)

Production related indicators in the EU (1)

	1989	1990	1991	1992	1993	1994	1995	1996	1997	1998	1999
Number of persons employed (thousands)	438.6	447.0	452.0	446.3	421.0	418.2	393.3	:	:	:	:
Production (million ECU)	43,780	47,937	50,841	51,298	48,795	52,471	56,050	:	:	:	:
Domestic producer price index (1995=100)	:	88.8	88.2	88.5	87.8	88.7	100.0	97.3	94.4	95.0	94.6
Value added (million ECU)	14,210	15,716	16,824	17,795	17,254	17,938	17,570	:	:	:	:

(1) Technically, data before 01/01/1999 are in ECU and after this date in euro. However, as the conversion rate was 1 ECU =1 EUR, for practical purposes the two terms can be used interchangeably.

Table 5.34

Manufacture of articles of paper and paperboard (NACE Rev. 1 21.2)

Trade related indicators in the EU (1)

	1989	1990	1991	1992	1993	1994	1995	1996	1997	1998	1999
Exports (million EUR)	1,555	1,550	1,608	1,755	1,930	2,249	2,529	2,890	3,169	3,116	2,951
Imports (million EUR)	485	564	717	681	693	784	904	996	1,158	1,257	1,456
Trade balance (million EUR)	1,069	986	891	1,074	1,237	1,465	1,625	1,893	2,011	1,859	1,494
Cover ratio (%)	320.3	274.7	224.2	257.6	278.6	286.7	279.7	290.0	273.6	247.8	202.6

(1) Technically, data before 01/01/1999 are in ECU and after this date in euro. However, as the conversion rate was 1 ECU =1 EUR, for practical purposes the two terms can be used interchangeably.

Table 5.35

Manufacture of articles of paper and paperboard (NACE Rev. 1 21.2)

Production related indicators, 1997

	B	DK	D	EL (1)	E	F	IRL	I (1)	L	NL	A	P	FIN	S	UK
Number of persons employed (thousands)	9.0	7.3	105.1	5.1	36.9	60.3	4.6	43.7	:	:	9.1	9.4	4.6	13.1	83.7
Production (million ECU)	1,615	856	14,748	460	4,729	9,200	655	8,253	:	2,746	1,625	667	633	1,968	10,598
Value added (million ECU)	490	334	4,979	123	1,501	2,667	269	2,503	:	946	598	192	237	720	3,849
Gross operating surplus (million ECU)	163.6	94.7	1,079.1	38.1	673.3	636.9	132.5	1,176.2	:	359.9	232.0	81.3	94.6	220.9	1,419.6

(1) 1996.

Table 5.36

Manufacture of articles of paper and paperboard (NACE Rev. 1 21.2)

Trade related indicators, 1999

	B	DK	D	EL	E	F	IRL	I	L	NL	A	P	FIN	S	UK
Exports (million EUR)	1,114	255	2,955	30	415	1,364	87	1,309	4	1,074	676	118	531	752	1,117
Imports (million EUR)	996	401	1,731	185	417	1,898	354	442	59	949	447	219	133	302	1,360
Trade balance (million EUR)	119	-147	1,224	-155	-3	-534	-268	867	-55	125	229	-101	399	450	-244
Cover ratio (%)	111.9	63.5	170.7	16.3	99.4	71.9	24.5	295.9	6.8	113.1	151.3	53.9	400.0	249.2	82.1

Table 5.37

Manufacture of articles of paper and paperboard (NACE Rev. 1 21.2)

Labour related indicators, 1997

	B	DK (1)	D	EL (2)	E	F	IRL	I (2)	L	NL	A	P	FIN	S	UK
Unit personnel costs (thousand ECU per employee)	36.9	37.8	37.1	16.8	22.4	33.7	29.5	31.1	:	:	40.2	11.9	32.2	38.2	29.4
Social charges as a share of personnel costs (%)	37.4	4.9	23.4	31.0	27.2	41.5	16.0	51.0	:	16.6	29.9	34.7	27.2	43.4	13.8
Apparent labour productivity (thousand ECU/pers. empl.)	54.2	45.6	47.4	24.2	40.6	44.2	58.0	57.3	:	:	65.7	20.4	51.7	55.1	46.0
Wage adjusted labour productivity (%)	146.9	148.7	127.6	144.2	181.3	131.4	196.4	184.2	:	:	163.3	171.2	160.5	144.3	156.4
Personnel costs as a share of total operating costs (%)	22.4	30.4	26.5	20.7	18.8	22.9	24.3	17.5	:	20.7	23.5	18.4	24.8	25.8	24.8

(1) Unit personnel costs and wage adjusted labour productivity, 1996; (2) 1996.

Source: Eurostat (SBS, EBT, COMEXT)

_____ Table 5.38

Publishing (NACE Rev. 1 22.1)

Production related indicators in the EU (1)

	1989	1990	1991	1992	1993	1994	1995	1996	1997	1998	1999
Number of persons employed (thousands)	:	:	:	:	:	:	571.4	504.4	:	:	:
Production (million ECU)	:	:	:	:	:	:	80,324	79,475	:	:	:
Domestic producer price index (1995=100)	:	:	:	:	:	:	100.0	104.1	105.6	106.8	108.0
Value added (million ECU)	:	:	:	:	:	:	27,510	29,884	:	:	:

(1) Technically, data before 01/01/1999 are in ECU and after this date in euro. However, as the conversion rate was 1 ECU =1 EUR, for practical purposes the two terms can be used interchangeably.

_____ Table 5.39

Publishing (NACE Rev. 1 22.1)

Trade related indicators in the EU (1)

	1989	1990	1991	1992	1993	1994	1995	1996	1997	1998	1999
Exports (million EUR)	2,590	2,756	2,928	3,120	3,380	3,701	3,953	4,228	4,423	4,487	4,424
Imports (million EUR)	1,317	1,444	1,645	1,727	1,842	1,912	1,968	2,060	2,074	2,193	2,396
Trade balance (million EUR)	1,273	1,312	1,282	1,394	1,538	1,789	1,985	2,168	2,350	2,294	2,029
Cover ratio (%)	196.7	190.9	177.9	180.7	183.5	193.5	200.9	205.2	213.3	204.6	184.7

(1) Technically, data before 01/01/1999 are in ECU and after this date in euro. However, as the conversion rate was 1 ECU =1 EUR, for practical purposes the two terms can be used interchangeably.

_____ Table 5.40

Publishing (NACE Rev. 1 22.1)

Production related indicators, 1997

	B	DK	D	EL (1)	E	F	IRL	I (1)	L	NL	A	P	FIN	S	UK
Number of persons employed (thousands)	10.4	19.2	129.0	6.4	43.5	67.3	3.4	34.7	:	:	:	9.9	16.9	23.7	122.6
Production (million ECU)	2,141	2,032	22,540	437	5,943	13,389	413	7,435	:	4,346	:	1,099	2,095	3,210	18,199
Value added (million ECU)	673	886	9,005	144	2,309	4,322	221	2,252	:	2,030	:	348	878	1,129	7,715
Gross operating surplus (million ECU)	246.4	186.8	2,717.8	26.1	1,040.6	1,016.6	81.0	546.2	:	936.3	:	160.0	305.5	209.2	3,208.1

(1) 1996.

_____ Table 5.41

Publishing (NACE Rev. 1 22.1)

Trade related indicators, 1999

	B	DK	D	EL	E	F	IRL	I	L	NL	A	P	FIN	S	UK
Exports (million EUR)	646	240	2,360	38	843	1,222	168	839	23	826	407	34	175	216	2,909
Imports (million EUR)	865	256	1,416	98	400	1,307	302	497	79	511	614	185	149	326	1,780
Trade balance (million EUR)	-219	-16	944	-59	443	-85	-134	342	-56	315	-207	-152	26	-110	1,129
Cover ratio (%)	74.6	93.8	166.7	39.3	210.7	93.5	55.8	168.9	29.3	161.6	66.3	18.2	117.8	66.3	163.4

_____ Table 5.42

Publishing (NACE Rev. 1 22.1)

Labour related indicators, 1997

	B	DK (1)	D	EL (2)	E	F	IRL	I (2)	L	NL	A	P	FIN	S	UK
Unit personnel costs (thousand ECU per employee)	45.5	38.0	47.6	18.5	29.6	49.1	41.5	49.8	:	:	:	20.2	34.4	38.8	37.3
Social charges as a share of personnel costs (%)	35.4	6.0	23.2	23.6	22.7	41.5	20.8	48.4	:	18.0	:	32.3	28.0	43.8	13.4
Apparent labour productivity (thousand ECU/pers. empl.)	64.6	46.2	69.8	22.5	53.1	64.2	65.0	64.8	:	:	:	35.2	52.1	47.6	62.9
Wage adjusted labour productivity (%)	142.2	125.6	146.5	121.6	179.4	130.8	156.7	130.3	:	:	:	174.6	151.5	122.7	168.8
Personnel costs as a share of total operating costs (%)	22.6	37.7	31.2	26.9	23.6	25.5	41.8	25.1	:	31.9	:	19.9	31.5	30.3	29.8

(1) Unit personnel costs and wage adjusted labour productivity, 1996. (2) 1996.

Source: Eurostat (SBS, EBT, COMEXT)

Table 5.43

Printing and service activities related to printing (NACE Rev. 1 22.2)

Production related indicators in the EU (1)

	1989	1990	1991	1992	1993	1994	1995	1996	1997	1998	1999
Number of persons employed (thousands)	:	:	:	:	612.4	609.2	611.8	614.5	:	:	:
Production (million ECU)	:	:	:	:	50,773	53,409	55,407	58,700	:	:	:
Domestic producer price index (1995=100)	:	:	:	:	:	:	:	:	:	101.2	100.8
Value added (million ECU)	:	:	:	:	22,989	23,805	24,250	25,919	:	:	:

(1) Technically, data before 01/01/1999 are in ECU and after this date in euro. However, as the conversion rate was 1 ECU =1 EUR, for practical purposes the two terms can be used interchangeably.

Table 5.44

Printing and service activities related to printing (NACE Rev. 1 22.2)

Trade related indicators in the EU (1)

	1989	1990	1991	1992	1993	1994	1995	1996	1997	1998	1999
Exports (million EUR)	777	823	859	883	1,087	1,230	1,401	1,263	1,448	1,415	1,422
Imports (million EUR)	450	466	567	545	558	621	690	773	787	825	960
Trade balance (million EUR)	327	357	292	338	529	608	711	490	661	590	463
Cover ratio (%)	172.6	176.6	151.4	162.0	194.9	197.9	203.1	163.4	183.9	171.5	148.2

(1) Technically, data before 01/01/1999 are in ECU and after this date in euro. However, as the conversion rate was 1 ECU =1 EUR, for practical purposes the two terms can be used interchangeably.

Table 5.45

Printing and service activities related to printing (NACE Rev. 1 22.2)

Production related indicators, 1997

	B	DK	D	EL (1)	E	F	IRL	I (1)	L	NL	A	P	FIN	S	UK
Number of persons employed (thousands)	25.7	9.9	133.6	2.4	82.1	76.3	9.1	51.8	1.0	:	12.0	29.8	13.4	:	113.3
Production (million ECU)	3,076	1,052	14,638	145	5,516	8,495	733	5,326	99	3,538	1,294	1,214	1,395	:	11,137
Value added (million ECU)	1,194	480	6,715	59	2,243	3,140	350	2,303	51	1,493	652	566	625	:	5,465
Gross operating surplus (million ECU)	391.5	120.5	1,352.2	14.9	723.9	474.8	122.0	651.5	18.7	471.6	162.8	242.4	230.2	:	1,789.6

(1) 1996.

Table 5.46

Printing and service activities related to printing (NACE Rev. 1 22.2)

Trade related indicators, 1999

	B	DK	D	EL	E	F	IRL	I	L	NL	A	P	FIN	S	UK
Exports (million EUR)	474	131	1,321	15	133	686	68	549	17	373	204	15	114	87	338
Imports (million EUR)	235	194	607	30	109	671	60	196	15	261	199	49	53	134	607
Trade balance (million EUR)	239	-62	714	-15	24	15	7	352	2	112	6	-35	61	-46	-269
Cover ratio (%)	202.0	67.8	217.6	49.3	121.8	102.3	112.2	279.3	111.7	142.7	102.8	29.7	216.5	65.4	55.6

Table 5.47

Printing and service activities related to printing (NACE Rev. 1 22.2)

Labour related indicators, 1997

	B	DK	D	EL (1)	E	F	IRL	I (1)	L	NL	A	P	FIN	S	UK
Unit personnel costs (thousand ECU per employee)	36.9	:	40.1	18.3	20.6	34.9	25.4	33.2	34.7	:	41.0	11.5	31.0	:	34.1
Social charges as a share of personnel costs (%)	38.4	6.1	21.3	32.4	25.1	42.2	16.6	51.2	:	18.5	27.8	30.7	27.4	:	13.8
Apparent labour productivity (thousand ECU/pers. empl.)	46.4	48.6	50.3	24.7	27.3	41.2	38.4	44.4	50.1	:	54.4	19.0	46.6	:	48.2
Wage adjusted labour productivity (%)	125.7	:	125.4	134.8	132.8	117.8	151.1	134.0	144.5	:	132.6	165.4	150.5	:	141.5
Personnel costs as a share of total operating costs (%)	29.8	38.1	40.2	36.4	30.9	32.9	37.1	35.2	40.6	32.6	41.5	33.1	33.7	:	37.2

(1) 1996.

Source: Eurostat (SBS, EBT, COMEXT)

Chemicals, rubber and plastics (NACE Rev. 1 24 and 25)

The manufacture of chemicals, rubber and plastics are divided into two Divisions within the NACE Rev. 1 classification. The first (NACE Rev. 1 24) covers the chemicals industry, whilst rubber and plastics are included within NACE Rev. 1 25. This is a heterogeneous industry, which covers a wide variety of production processes starting with the manufacture of basic chemicals from primary resources coming from the petrochemicals, mining and minerals industries. Vertical integration links these basic chemicals to often complex, technically advanced materials and products further along the production chain.

The EU chemicals, rubber and plastics industries had a combined production value of 572.5 billion EUR in 1999. Together they formed the second most important manufacturing industry in the EU in 1999 in terms of production value (following the grouping of activities used in this publication), with output almost equal to that of transport equipment (572.8 billion EUR). Chemicals, rubber and plastics accounted for 14.3% of the EU's total manufacturing output, a share which rose to 16.0% for value added (193.5 billion EUR generated in 1999). Some 2.89 million persons were employed in 1999, an under-proportional share of the EU manufacturing total (12.4%).

The chemical industry was between two and a half and three times the size of the rubber and plastics industry in 1999, the former accounting for 73.0% of production. In terms of value added the shares were fairly similar with a 70.4% and 29.6% split. However, there were relatively more persons employed in the rubber and plastics industry, 41.9% of the total.

Figure 6.1

Chemicals, rubber and plastics
(NACE Rev. 1 24 and 25)
Share of total manufacturing value added
in the EU, 1999 (%)

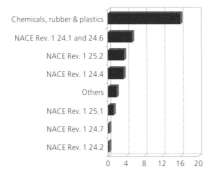

Source: Eurostat (SBS)

The activities covered in this chapter (in terms of NACE Rev. 1) include:

24: manufacture of chemicals and chemical products;
24.1: manufacture of basic chemicals;
24.2: manufacture of pesticides and other agro-chemical products;
24.3: manufacture of paints, varnishes and similar coatings, printing ink and mastics;
24.4: manufacture of pharmaceuticals, medicinal chemicals and botanical products;
24.5: manufacture of soap and detergents, cleaning and polishing preparations, perfumes and toilet preparations;
24.6: manufacture of other chemical products;
24.7: manufacture of man-made fibres;
25: manufacture of rubber and plastic products;
25.1: manufacture of rubber products;
25.2: manufacture of plastic products.

The manufacture of basic industrial chemicals (the first of the sub-chapters covered) was the largest sub-sector, with just over a third (36.7%) of total chemicals, rubber and plastics' output in 1999[1]. Plastics (20.9%), pharmaceuticals (18.8%), rubber (6.0%), man-made fibres (2.1%) and pesticides and agrochemicals (1.5%) followed.

(1) There is no data available for soaps, detergents and toiletries or paints, varnishes and printing inks in 1999, although they accounted for 9.4% and 4.8% respectively of total chemicals, rubber and plastics' output in 1995.

Table 6.1

Chemicals, rubber and plastics (NACE Rev. 1 24 and 25)
Breakdown of turnover and employment by employment size class, 1997 (%)

	Micro (0-9)		Small (10-49)		Medium (50-249)		Large (250+)	
	Turnover (1)	Employment (2)	Turnover (3)	Employment (4)	Turnover (3)	Employment (4)	Turnover (3)	Employment (4)
EU-15	3.7	5.7	9.9	14.1	20.1	20.5	66.3	59.6
B	8.1	4.5	7.8	10.7	18.7	20.5	65.4	64.3
DK	:	:	:	:	:	:	:	:
D	1.0	3.0	5.1	9.7	9.7	12.6	84.2	74.8
EL	:	:	:	:	:	:	:	:
E	4.6	11.1	15.5	23.3	28.6	29.4	51.3	36.3
F	5.9	3.8	9.4	12.2	20.1	22.0	64.6	62.0
IRL	:	:	6.8	17.0	43.6	33.7	48.8	46.9
I	4.8	9.6	19.4	25.8	26.0	24.0	49.9	40.5
L	:	:	:	:	:	:	:	:
NL	:	:	:	:	:	:	:	:
A	1.7	2.9	8.5	11.9	:	:	:	:
P	5.7	9.9	19.4	27.4	39.2	37.8	35.7	24.8
FIN	4.6	5.5	12.4	13.0	23.2	24.9	59.8	56.7
S	3.3	6.2	9.5	14.4	23.9	26.3	63.3	53.1
UK	4.7	8.1	8.1	11.4	17.9	22.0	69.2	58.6

(1) EU-15, E, F, I, P and S, 1996.
(2) EU-15, F, I, P and S, 1996.
(3) EU-15, E, F, IRL, I, P and S, 1996.
(4) EU-15, F, IRL, I, P and S, 1996.

Source: Eurostat (SME)

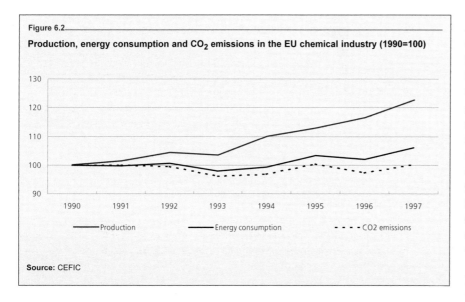

Figure 6.2

Production, energy consumption and CO$_2$ emissions in the EU chemical industry (1990=100)

Production — Energy consumption — - - - CO2 emissions

Source: CEFIC

An important industry within the Benelux countries
Germany was by far the largest EU producer, accounting for over a quarter (26.4%) of the EU's production in 1997, followed by France (17.7%) and the United Kingdom (14.5%)[2]. However, chemicals, rubber and plastics accounted for its highest share of national manufacturing output in Ireland (21.8%) in 1997. The Netherlands (20.7%), Belgium (19.6%) and Luxembourg (19.3%) took the next three places in the ranking of most specialised countries. No other country reported a share of more than 16.0%, whilst these industries had a relatively low importance in Portugal (8.1%) and Finland (8.0%), the only Member States to report shares in total manufacturing output below 10.0%.

(2) I, no data available; although I accounted for a 13.6% share of the EU total in 1996.

—————————————————————Box 6.1

In 1999, CEFIC estimates that 17 of the 30 largest companies in the world were from the EU. German enterprises dominated the sector, with three of the world's top four companies in terms of turnover (Bayer, BASF and Hoechst). The next largest EU enterprises (in 9th and 10th places in the world ranking) were ICI (UK) and Rhône Poulenc (F). Subsequently the creation of Aventis, the merger of Hoechst and Rhône-Poulenc, took place on December 15th 1999.

—————————————————————Table 6.2

Top ten chemical companies in the world, 1999 (million EUR) (1)

	Turnover
BASF	27,842
Bayer	25,808
Du Pont	25,257
Aventis	19,318
Novartis	19,132
Dow	17,761
AstraZeneca	17,307
Roche	16,246
ExxonMobil (2)	14,919
Mitsubishi Chemical (3)	14,854

(1) Reproduced with the kind permission of Reed Business Publishing - Chemical Insight, adjusted by using average rather than year-end exchange rates.
(2) Chemicals only.
(3) Consolidated data; year to March 31st 2000.

Source: Chemical Insight

Chemicals dominated by large enterprises, whilst small and medium-sized enterprises flourish in the rubber and plastics sector

CEFIC[3] estimates that the top 30 global chemical enterprises accounted for 30% of world chemicals' turnover in 1998. The formation of large enterprise groups has been an ever-present characteristic throughout the 1990s. Despite this relatively high degree of concentration, the EU chemical industry was made-up of almost 34 thousand enterprises in 1996, of which 95.9% had less than 250 employees. These small and medium-sized enterprises accounted for 26.4% of turnover and 28.0% of employment in 1996.

In the rubber and plastics industry, small and medium-sized enterprises were much more important, accounting for 98.5% of all enterprises and over half of total turnover (54.0%). They also employed 56.6% of all persons employed in 1996.

————————————————————————

(3) The European Chemical Industry Council.

STRUCTURE AND PERFORMANCE

The production value of the EU chemicals, rubber and plastics industry rose from 322.2 billion ECU in 1985 to 572.5 billion EUR in 1999. In constant price terms production grew at an average rate of 3.3% per annum between 1990 and 1998 (compared to 2.2% for total manufacturing). Between 1991 and 1998 there was only one year when output in these industries fell in real terms (1993, down by 1.4%). Whilst chemicals, rubber and plastics weathered the recession of the early 1990s better than manufacturing in general, annual growth rates of EU production in constant prices between 1995 and 1998 were, with the exception of 1997 (1.9 percentage points higher, at 9.9%), equal to or below manufacturing averages.

Unequal sectoral performances

The structural change in the composition of this industry over the ten-year period 1989 to 1999 shows that the rubber and plastics industry has grown at a more rapid pace than the chemical industry. In 1989, chemicals accounted for more than three-quarters of output (75.6% of the total), a share which had fallen to 73.0% by 1999. However, the shift in production was accounted for entirely by the plastics industry, registering a 3.1 percentage point increase in its share of total EU chemicals, rubber and plastics' output during the period considered (whilst the rubber industry lost 0.5 percentage points). Within the chemicals industry there were even larger disparities, as the manufacture of basic chemicals (NACE Rev. 1 24.1) lost 7.3 percentage points of EU chemicals, rubber and plastics production. The leading growth area was pharmaceuticals, which saw its share of total output rise by 4.7 percentage points over the ten-year period considered.

—————————————————————Figure 6.3

Chemicals, rubber and plastics (NACE Rev. 1 24 and 25)

EU production and value-added in constant prices and employment compared to total manufacturing (1990=100)

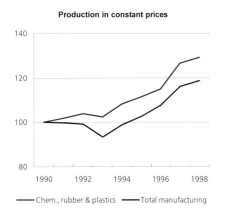

Production in constant prices

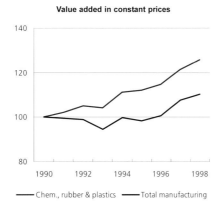

Value added in constant prices

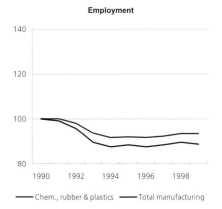

Employment

Source: Eurostat (SBS)

Table 6.3

Chemicals, rubber and plastics (NACE Rev. 1 24 and 25)
Composition of the labour force, 1999 (%)

	Chemicals			Rubber and plastics		
	Women (1)	Part-time (2)	Highly-educated (3)	Women (4)	Part-time (5)	Highly-educated (6)
EU-15	30.7	6.0	27.0	26.9	6.4	12.1
B	25.5	6.3	40.9	19.5	:	19.4
DK	43.4	11.0	49.8	39.5	:	17.2
D	29.8	7.2	28.1	29.7	9.0	14.9
EL	33.5	:	31.0	31.1	:	:
E	29.0	:	37.4	23.7	:	22.3
F	39.2	4.0	31.0	27.9	3.6	13.4
IRL	41.3	:	42.1	26.6	:	:
I	27.1	3.0	17.5	32.9	4.2	4.7
L	:	:	:	:	:	13.6
NL	25.2	22.3	24.9	22.3	17.4	14.0
A	33.1	9.0	11.6	24.9	9.0	:
P	36.9	:	9.6	28.5	:	:
FIN	34.3	:	32.7	34.4	:	28.4
S	42.0	:	:	38.2	:	:
UK	29.9	6.0	34.4	25.4	8.5	9.6

(1) EU-15 and EL, 1998.
(2) EU-15 and B, 1998; DK, 1997.
(3) EL, 1998; EU-15, IRL and UK, 1997.
(4) EU-15 and EL, 1998; S, 1997.
(5) EU-15, 1998.
(6) DK, 1998; EU-15, L, NL and UK, 1997.

Source: Eurostat (LFS)

Cost structure dependent on the price of oil...
Purchases of goods and services by the EU's chemicals,
rubber and plastics industry accounted for almost
70% of turnover in 1999. Whilst no official statistics
exist on the breakdown of these purchases, CEFIC estimates that goods purchased and resold in their original condition accounted for 11% of turnover in 1998,
whilst direct energy costs accounted for 9% on average. This latter figure rose to above 50% for the manufacture of some basic chemicals, an area where EU
manufacturers have progressively lost global market
share. Indeed, the price and efficient use of energy
(and in particular oil) is a major factor in determining
international competitiveness within the chemicals
industry (see sub-chapter 1.2 for more details concerning the price of oil).

... whilst profit rates remain relatively high
In 1999, the remaining 30.7% of turnover (not covered by the purchase of goods and services) was split
12.4% for the gross operating surplus and 18.3% for
personnel costs. This combined share covered by the
gross operating surplus and personnel costs was
somewhat lower than in 1989, when it had reached
32.4% of turnover.

The gross operating rate of the chemicals, rubber and
plastics industry (12.4% in 1999) was consistently
above the manufacturing average between 1989 and
1999, the difference ranging between 1.7 percentage
points (1990) and 3.5 percentage points (1995), with
the latest difference for 1999 some 2.9 points higher.

LABOUR AND PRODUCTIVITY

The number of persons employed in the EU chemicals,
rubber and plastics industry fell from 3.06 million to
2.89 million between 1989 and 1999, equivalent to
an average reduction of 0.6% per annum (whilst the
corresponding reduction for total manufacturing in
the EU was 1.1%). The decline in the number of persons employed ended in 1996, when a low of 2.84
million persons employed was recorded. Between
1996 and 1999 there was a net increase of 52 thousand jobs in the EU.

In 1998, the EU workforce within the chemicals, rubber and plastics industry displayed fairly typical characteristics for industry, this means that the proportions
of women in employment (29.2%) and part-time staff
(6.2%) were similar to the EU manufacturing averages
of 28.2% and 7.3%. The proportion of women in
employment in 1999 ranged from as high as 43.4% in
the chemicals industry in Denmark, to a low of 19.5%
in the rubber and plastics industry in Belgium. The proportion of women employed was higher in the chemicals industry, with only Italy and Finland reporting that
women accounted for a higher share of total employment in the rubber and plastics industry.

High labour productivity and unit personnel costs
The EU's chemical, rubber and plastics industry
recorded high apparent labour productivity in 1999,
when each person employed generated an average of
66.9 thousand EUR of value added (15.1 thousand
EUR more than the EU manufacturing average). The
simple wage adjusted labour productivity ratio (value
added divided by personnel costs) was also well above
the manufacturing average at 167.3% (16.4 percentage points more).

In 1997, unit personnel costs within the chemicals,
rubber and plastics industry were higher than national
manufacturing averages in every Member State of the
EU[4]. The differences ranged between just 0.8 thousand ECU more in Finland and 11.9 thousand ECU per
employee more in Belgium although both these figures were outliers as all other countries lay within the
range of 2.8 to 6.5 thousand ECU.

(4) NL, no data available; DK, EL and I, 1996.

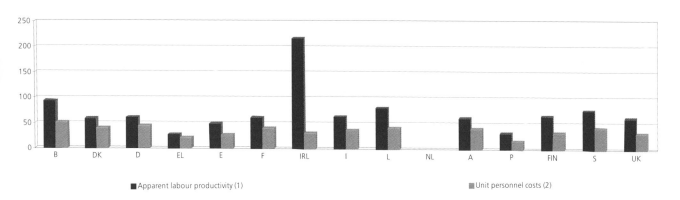

Figure 6.4

Chemicals, rubber and plastics (NACE Rev. 1 24 and 25)

Apparent labour productivity and unit personnel costs, 1997 (thousand ECU)

■ Apparent labour productivity (1)   ▨ Unit personnel costs (2)

(1) EL and I, 1996; NL, not available.
(2) DK, EL and I, 1996; NL, not available.

Source: Eurostat (SBS)

INTERNATIONAL TRENDS AND FOREIGN TRADE

The EU accounted for 40.5% of the Triad's production of chemicals, rubber and plastics in 1997, followed by the USA (37.5%) and Japan (22.0%). These shares were very similar to those observed in 1989 with differences in the relative shares not greater than +/-1.2 percentage points (EU, +0.6 percentage points; Japan, -1.2 points; and the USA +0.6 points).

Quality the key to competitive trade performance
The EU exported 118.8 billion EUR of chemical, rubber and plastic products in 1999. Throughout the 1990s, these industries ran a sizeable trade surplus, which grew to 43.2 billion EUR in 1999 (the highest figure during the ten year period 1989 to 1999). The chemical sectors which exhibited the most successful trade performance were generally those characterised by

competition based on quality (as opposed to price), for example, perfumes, soaps and detergents, pharmaceuticals, speciality chemicals and plastics. The EU also enjoyed successful price competition in the paints and varnishes industry. On the other hand, the EU organic chemicals, fertilisers and man-made fibres industries faced strong competition in price elastic markets, resulting in trade deficits in many product markets.

Figure 6.5

Chemicals, rubber and plastics (NACE Rev. 1 24 and 25)

International comparison of production, value added and employment

Production (million ECU)

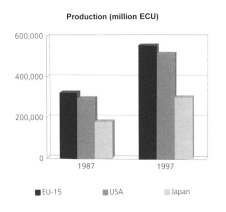

■ EU-15   ▨ USA   ▨ Japan

Value added (million ECU)

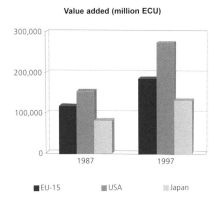

■ EU-15   ▨ USA   ▨ Japan

Employment (units)

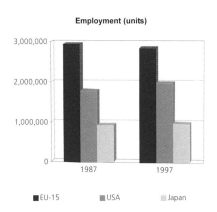

■ EU-15   ▨ USA   ▨ Japan

Source: Eurostat (SBS)

USA accounts for just over a quarter of the EU's exports

The USA was the main destination for EU exports of chemicals, rubber and plastics, accounting for 25.4% of total exports in 1999 (some 29.3 billion EUR in value terms). Whilst the share of the USA rose by 8.2 percentage points between 1989 and 1999, the respective shares of Switzerland and Japan (the next two largest destinations) fell (to 9.5% and 5.9% respectively).

The main origins of EU imports were also the USA, Switzerland and Japan, with almost a third (32.1%) of the EU's imports in 1999 originating from the USA. The combined share of these three countries fell from 64.4% of total EU imports in 1989 to 61.0% by 1999, as imports originating from Asia (notably China, South Korea and Singapore) and Eastern Europe (notably the Czech Republic and Poland) increased.

Figure 6.6

**Chemicals, rubber and plastics
(NACE Rev. 1 24 and 25)
Destination of EU exports, 1999 (%)**

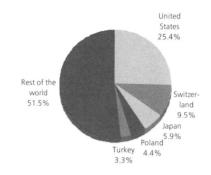

Source: Eurostat (COMEXT)

Figure 6.7

**Chemicals, rubber and plastics
(NACE Rev. 1 24 and 25)
Origin of EU imports, 1999 (%)**

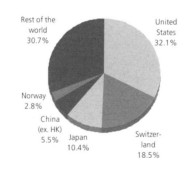

Source: Eurostat (COMEXT)

SUB-CHAPTER 6.1
BASIC INDUSTRIAL CHEMICALS
(INCLUDING PETROCHEMICALS)
AND OTHER CHEMICALS
(NACE Rev. 1 24.1 AND 24.6)

The manufacture of basic chemicals (NACE Rev. 1 24.1) may be broken down into industrial and medical gases (other than for fuels), chemical elements, acids, alkalis, hydrocarbons, dyes and pigments and fertilisers, as well as the manufacture of plastics and synthetic rubber in their primary forms. Other chemicals (NACE Rev. 1 24.6) include the manufacture of explosives, glues, gelatine, natural and aromatic oils, photographic materials and unrecorded media (for music, video or computers).

The EU basic and industrial chemicals industry (NACE Rev. 1 24.1 and 24.6) had combined production value of 210 billion EUR in 1999, accounting for more than a third (36.7%) of the output of the EU's chemicals, rubber and plastics industry (or 5.3% of total manufacturing output). There were 734.2 thousand persons employed in 1999, equivalent to a quarter (25.4%) of the chemicals, rubber and plastics workforce. The considerably higher shares of production and value added are due to the capital-intensive nature of this industry, with new production facilities having a high cost, resulting in large plants being built to achieve efficient scales of production[5].

Downstream markets strongly influenced by cyclical fluctuations in demand
Key markets for basic chemical producers (outside of downstream chemical segments) include the automotive, metals, construction and agricultural sectors that use basic plastics, acids, pigments, industrial gases and fertilisers. These markets are often very cyclical and result in chemical producers often facing supply and demand imbalances.

The breakdown of the data presented in this sub-chapter is heavily weighted in favour of the manufacture of basic chemicals (NACE Rev. 1 24.1) which accounted for 82.0% of total EU basic and industrial chemicals output in 1999.

(5) To give some idea of the physical concentration of the industry, at the end of 1998 there were just 50 steam crackers operating in the whole of Western Europe.

_____ Figure 6.8

Basic industrial chemicals (including petrochemicals) and other chemicals (NACE Rev. 1 24.1 and 24.6)
Production and export specialisation (%)

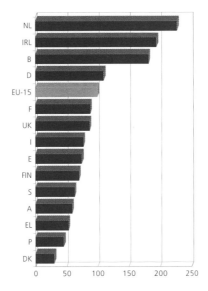

Production specialisation (1997) (1)

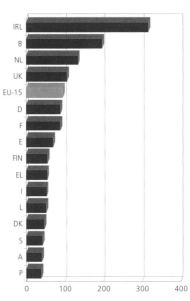

Export specialisation (1999)

(1) IRL, 1994; EL and I, 1995; L, not available.

Source: Eurostat (SBS, COMEXT)

_____ Box 6.3

The production of petrochemicals may be broken down into three main product groups: ethylene, propylene and benzene. APPE (the Association of Petroleum Producers in Europe) estimates that Western European[6] production of ethylene reached 19.0 million tonnes in 1998, with polyethylene the main derivative, accounting for 57% of consumption in 1998.

Western European propylene output reached 12.9 million tonnes in 1998, which was not enough to satisfy demand (with a deficit of 240 thousand tonnes). Polypropylene is the main derivative, accounting for more than half (53%) of consumption in 1998.

Benzene production in Western Europe (6.7 million tonnes) was also less than consumption, resulting in 586 thousand tonnes of imports in 1998 (a 39% increase on 1997). The main derivative in this segment is ethylbenzene (used to produce polystyrene), which accounted for almost half (49.3%) of all benzene consumed in 1998.

(6) EU-15 (excluding DK and IRL), Norway and Switzerland.

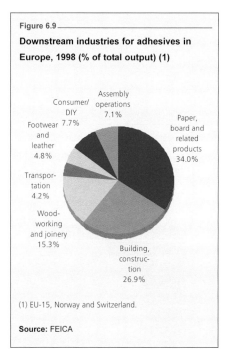

Figure 6.9

Downstream industries for adhesives in Europe, 1998 (% of total output) (1)

- Paper, board and related products 34.0%
- Building, construction 26.9%
- Wood-working and joinery 15.3%
- Consumer/DIY 7.7%
- Assembly operations 7.1%
- Footwear and leather 4.8%
- Transportation 4.2%

(1) EU-15, Norway and Switzerland.

Source: FEICA

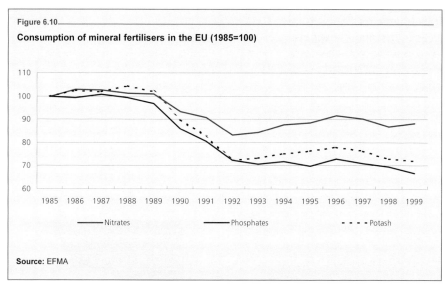

Figure 6.10

Consumption of mineral fertilisers in the EU (1985=100)

Nitrates ——— Phosphates ——— Potash - - - -

Source: EFMA

STRUCTURE AND PERFORMANCE

EU production of basic chemicals (NACE Rev. 1 24.1) rose by 25.9% between 1985 and 1999 in nominal terms (well below the average growth for the whole of chemicals, rubber and plastics, 77.7%). Over this same period the EU focused output on higher value products, resulting in value added growth of 44.2%.

The share of basic chemicals (NACE Rev. 1 24.1) in the total output of the EU's chemicals, rubber and plastics industry fell from 42.4% of the total in 1985 to 30.1% by 1999 although this structural shift in production took place exclusively between 1985 and 1993. Equally, there was little evolution in the share of other chemicals between 1993 and 1999, losing 0.2 percentage points to record a 6.6% share of the chemicals, rubber and plastics total.

Specialisation within the Benelux countries
Germany was the largest producer of basic and other chemicals in the EU, with output equal to 147.2 billion ECU in 1997 (a 26.4% share of the EU total), corresponding to a somewhat higher than average level of specialisation (110.1%)[7]. The most specialised countries were the Netherlands (226.7%) and Belgium (181.9%)[8]. The United Kingdom was relatively specialised in the manufacture of other chemicals (111.6%). No other countries reported specialisation rates in either activity above 100%.

Profitability within the basic and other chemicals industry (12.8% in 1999) is driven largely by the manufacturers ability to match supply and demand through their product mix, whilst maintaining capacity utilisation rates at high levels and achieving economies of scale to make cost savings. In other words there is not a great deal of product differentiation in this industry, with competition largely based on price differentials.

LABOUR AND PRODUCTIVITY

There was a net reduction of more than a quarter (27.9%) in the number of persons employed in the EU basic chemicals industry between 1985 and 1999. Whilst jobs were lost in almost every year of this period, the majority of labour was shed during the period 1991 to 1995, with the share of personnel costs in production falling from 23.1% in 1993 to 18.3% by 1995. This trend continued through to 1997, when a share of 16.8% was recorded (3.2 points less than the chemicals, rubber and plastics average).

Apparent labour productivity in the EU basic and other chemicals industry was equal to 89.2 thousand EUR per person employed in 1999, considerably above the chemicals, rubber and plastics average of 66.9 thousand EUR. When relatively high unit personnel costs (49.3 thousand ECU per employee in 1995) were taken into account, there was still a large difference in the simple wage adjusted productivity ratios of the basic and other chemicals industry (184.6% in 1999) and the chemicals, rubber and plastics average (167.3%).

---

(7) On closer inspection specialisation in D was confined to the manufacture of basic chemicals (113.4%), whilst for other chemical products a specialisation ratio of 94.2% was recorded in 1997.
(8) EL, IRL, I and L, no data available; IRL, production specialisation ratio for 1994 was 194.7%.

INTERNATIONAL TRENDS AND FOREIGN TRADE

The EU and USA had similar levels of output in 1997, with respective production values of basic and other chemicals equal to 209.8 and 204.4 billion ECU (both producing over 40% of the Triad total).

Almost half of the EU's chemical, rubber and plastics imports are concentrated in these activities
Basic and other chemicals accounted for 42.0% of the EU's exports of chemicals, rubber and plastics in 1999 (a share which rose to over 50% in Belgium, Ireland and Finland). The EU ran a trade surplus of 12.8 billion EUR in 1999 despite almost half (49.1%) of the EU's imports of chemicals, rubber and plastics being accounted for by these two activities.

In 1999, the main destination of EU exports was, by far, the USA, with 29.3% of the total (equal to 14.1 billion EUR in value terms), well ahead of Switzerland and Japan (7.4% and 6.3% respectively). The USA was also the main origin of EU imports in 1999 (32.2% or 11.5 billion EUR), followed again by Switzerland and Japan (12.9% and 12.6% respectively). China and Singapore saw their exports to the EU increase at a rapid pace between 1989 and 1999 from 582.0 and 155.8 million ECU to 1.4 billion and 1.1 billion EUR respectively.

Figure 6.11

Basic industrial chemicals (including petrochemicals) and other chemicals (NACE Rev. 1 24.1 and 24.6) Destination of EU exports, 1999 (%)

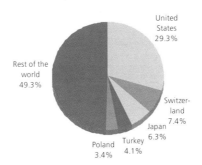

Source: Eurostat (COMEXT)

Figure 6.12

Basic industrial chemicals (including petrochemicals) and other chemicals (NACE Rev. 1 24.1 and 24.6) Origin of EU imports, 1999 (%)

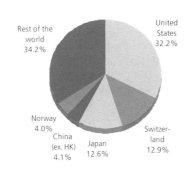

Source: Eurostat (COMEXT)

SUB-CHAPTER 6.2
PESTICIDES AND OTHER AGRO-CHEMICALS (NACE Rev. 1 24.2)

The manufacture of pesticides and agrochemicals includes insecticides, fungicides, herbicides and plant growth regulators. The information presented does not cover the manufacture of fertilisers and nitrogen compounds (which are included in sub-chapter 6.1).

Pesticides are designed to combat attacks of various pests on agricultural and horticultural crops. They fall into three major classes: insecticides (to fight insects), fungicides (to fight diseases) and herbicides (to fight weeds). The term agro-chemicals is broader as it also includes chemicals which enhance the growth and yield of crops[9].

A relatively small industry

EU production of agro-chemicals was equal to 8.6 billion EUR in 1999, just 1.5% of the total output within the chemicals, rubber and plastics industry. The value added rate for the EU's agro-chemicals industry was 26.7%, somewhat lower than the corresponding figure for the whole of chemicals, rubber and plastics (33.8%).

---

(9) The term agro-chemicals will be used to refer to the whole of NACE Rev. 1 24.2 within this sub-chapter.

Figure 6.13 _____

Pesticides and other agro-chemicals (NACE Rev. 1 24.2)
Production and export specialisation (%)

Production specialisation (1997) (1)

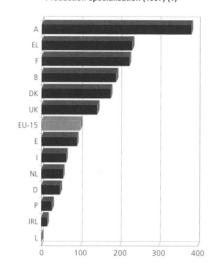

Export specialisation (1999)

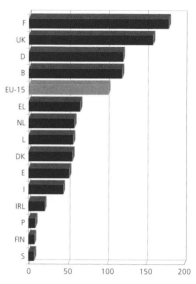

(1) EL, I and A, 1994; FIN and S, not available.

Source: Eurostat (SBS, COMEXT)

Box 6.4 _____

Demand for agro-chemicals is linked to a number of factors including the area of land farmed, the price of agricultural commodities on world markets, the type of land use and the incidence of insects, diseases and weeds in any given year. The total area devoted to growing wheat and barley in the EU decreased in 1998, whilst that of oilseed rape grew. There was higher disease and weed pressure in the northern arable areas than there had been in 1997.

In March 1999, the Council of Agriculture Ministers reached a compromise agreement on the reform of the Common Agricultural Policy, which, amongst other measures, retained the proportion of compulsory set-aside at 10% between 2000 and 2006[10].

---

(10) In 1998, set-aside was equal to 5%.

France had both the highest demand for and production of agro-chemicals in the EU, with output accounting for more than a third (36.7%) of the EU total in 1997 (3.1 billion ECU). The United Kingdom was the second largest producer, with more than a fifth (21.7%) of the EU total. Production was relatively specialised in 1997 in France (224.5%), Belgium (190.8%), Denmark (177.0%) and the United Kingdom (144.2%). No other Member State[11] was relatively specialised in the manufacture of agro-chemicals.

---

(11) EL, I, A, FIN and S, no data available; EL (231.8%) and A (383.7%) were highly specialised in 1994.

STRUCTURE AND PERFORMANCE

Production of agro-chemicals in the EU grew in nominal terms from 5.6 billion ECU in 1993 to 8.6 billion EUR in 1999. This was equivalent to absolute growth of 53.1%, which was above the chemicals, rubber and plastics average of 38.8%. As a result, the share of agro-chemicals in total EU chemicals, rubber and plastics output rose by 0.1 percentage points between 1993 and 1999 (to 1.5%).

_____ **Box 6.5**

The ECPA (European Crop Protection Association) estimates that the crop protection market in Western Europe[12] was valued at 6.1 billion ECU in 1998. This figure represented growth of 3.7%, when compared to that for 1997, whilst in real terms output rose by 1.1%. The leading growth sectors in 1998 included cereal fungicides and herbicides, as well as fruit and vegetable fungicides, insecticides and herbicides.

Some of the largest producers of crop protection products in the EU included BASF, Bayer and Hoechst Schering AgrEvo (all D) and Rhône-Poulenc (F), as well as American companies producing within the EU (such as DuPont de Nemours, Cyanamid Agro, Dow AgroSciences and Monsanto), as well as Novartis Crop Protection (CH).

---
(12) EU-15 and EFTA.

LABOUR AND PRODUCTIVITY

There were 28.3 thousand persons employed in the EU agro-chemicals industry in 1994. More recent data shows that France was the largest employer in the EU in 1997, with more than 7 thousand persons.

Another capital-intensive chemicals
industry with high productivity

Eurostat estimates that the apparent labour productivity of the EU agro-chemicals industry was equal to 82.2 thousand ECU per person employed in 1997, whilst unit personnel costs were equal to 47.9 thousand ECU. The highest unit personnel costs[13] were found in Belgium and France (two of the most specialised producers of agro-chemicals), 61.7 and 55.7 thousand ECU per employee in 1997.

As with basic and other chemicals (in the previous sub-chapter), the EU agro-chemicals industry reported a low share of personnel costs in production value, 16.1% in 1999 (4.1 percentage points below the chemicals, rubber and plastics average).

---
(13) DK, L, NL, A, FIN and S, no data available.

INTERNATIONAL TRENDS AND FOREIGN TRADE

ECPA state that the global agro-chemicals market (excluding genetically modified crops) was essentially static in 1998, with real growth of just 0.1%. Triad production in 1997 was equal to 20.4 billion ECU, with the USA accounting for the largest share (45.8%), ahead of the EU (40.9%) and Japan (13.3%). When compared to the low-point of the EU recession in 1993, the relative share of the EU rose at a rapid pace, gaining 7.4 percentage points, whilst both Japan (4.3 points) and the USA (3.1 points) lost ground.

The share of the EU agro-chemicals industry in total chemicals, rubber and plastics exports fell in relative terms between 1989 and 1999 from 2.7% to 1.9%. This declining trend was particularly evident in the Netherlands and the United Kingdom, where reductions of 2.6 and 2.5 percentage points were recorded over the same period, resulting in the Netherlands falling to 1.6%, below the EU average.. On the other hand, agro-chemicals reported both a higher than average and rising share of chemicals, rubber and plastics exports in both France (4.0%) and Greece (2.7%).

Almost three-quarters of the EU's imports of agro-chemicals originated from either Switzerland (52.8%) or the USA (21.6%) in 1999. The destination of the EU's exports was far more diversified, with the most important export destination in 1999 the USA (12.6% of the total). Indeed, the EU had as many as 28 different export partners that accounted for between 1.0% and 6.4% (Poland, the second most important destination) of its exports.

_____Figure 6.14

Pesticides and other agro-chemicals
(NACE Rev. 1 24.2)
Destination of EU exports, 1999 (%)

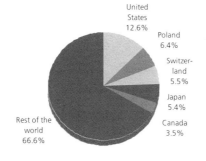

Source: Eurostat (COMEXT)

_____Figure 6.15

Pesticides and other agro-chemicals
(NACE Rev. 1 24.2)
Origin of EU imports, 1999 (%)

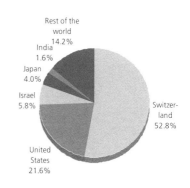

Source: Eurostat (COMEXT)

SUB-CHAPTER 6.3
PAINTS, VARNISHES AND PRINTING INKS
(NACE Rev. 1 24.3)

This sub-chapter includes information relating to the manufacture of paints, varnishes, enamels, lacquers, solvents, thinners, varnish removers, as well as printing inks. The manufacture of dyestuffs and pigments are included within sub-chapter 6.1, as is the manufacture of writing and drawing ink.

EU production of paints, varnishes and printing inks reached 26.8 billion ECU in 1997[14]. There were more recent figures available for the number of persons employed in these industries, 154 thousand in 1999 (or 5.3% of the chemicals, rubber and plastics total).

The home decoration market (do-it-yourself or D.I.Y.), as well as general economic activity (for example, construction activity and the output of motor vehicles) fuel demand within the paint industry, whilst the consumption of printing inks is largely a function of output in the consumer goods sector, which results in increased demand for printed materials, packaging and advertising.

Two distinct enterprise structures
The paint industry has undergone considerable changes in recent years, from an industry characterised by a fragmented national structure of small and medium-sized enterprises to one that at the end of the 1990s has an increasing number of large, multinational players. This changing face may in part be attributed to trends amongst downstream customers (such as vehicle and can-making manufacturers), where large enterprises increasingly expect service from multinational paint suppliers (see box 6.6 for more details). In the same way that downstream industries may influence the structure of the paint industry, the diversified nature of printing and graphics industries may explain the more significant role of small and medium-sized print ink manufacturers, offering value added services to local print-shops.

German output reached 8.0 billion ECU in 1997, which was almost twice the level of the second most important producer, the United Kingdom (4.2 billion ECU). Denmark (138.0%), the Netherlands (129.1%), Belgium (126.1%), Portugal (121.3%) and Spain (115.0%) were all relatively more specialised than either Germany or the United Kingdom in 1995.

(14) EL and I, 1996; L, no data available.

Figure 6.16

Paints, varnishes and printing inks (NACE Rev. 1 24.3)
Production and export specialisation (%)

Production specialisation (1995) (1)

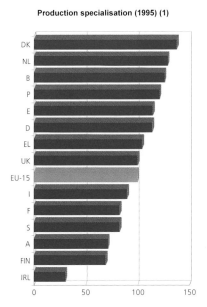

Export specialisation (1999)

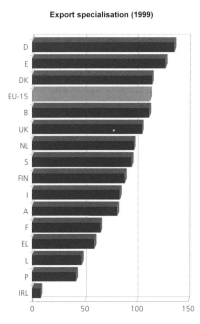

(1) A, 1994; L, not available.

Source: Eurostat (SBS, COMEXT)

Box 6.6

CEPE, the European Council of the Paint, Printing Ink and Artists' Colours Industry, estimates that 43% of the 23 billion litres of paint produced worldwide in 1998 were manufactured by the 10 largest global companies. The remainder came from an estimated 10 thousand small and medium-sized enterprises. During the late 1990s the paints, varnishes and printing inks industry in Europe became more concentrated, DuPont (USA) purchased Herberts (D), Akzo Nobel (NL) took-over Courtaulds (UK) and Kalon merged with Sigma (NL). In the print ink sector, Sun Chemical (JAP) took-over Coates Lorilleux (F).

The effects of the concentration process were particularly noticeable in the decorative paints sector, where European production stood at around 3.2 million tonnes in 1998. In the United Kingdom, CEPE estimates that around 85% of the decorative paints market was in the hands of the three largest producers, whilst in France and Germany the share of the largest multinational producers was only 40%. Concentration was even higher in some specialist sectors, such as industrial coatings, where 2.6 million tonnes of paints were produced in Europe in 1998. CEPE estimates that multinational groups had an estimated 90% share of the marine coatings and can coatings markets and an 88% share of the original equipment (OE) automotive market.

(15) EU-15, Norway and Switzerland.

STRUCTURE AND PERFORMANCE

The paints, varnishes and printing inks industry accounted for between 8.0% of total chemicals, rubber and plastics output in Portugal and just 0.8% in Ireland in 1997. Between 1990 and 1997[16], the relative share of paints, varnishes and printing inks fell in Denmark (2.1 percentage points), Ireland (1.2 points) and France (0.6 points), whilst it rose in all other countries, particularly in the Netherlands (+1.5 points).

The gross operating rate of the EU's paints, varnishes and printing inks industry was estimated at 10.4% in 1997. Amongst the individual Member States, the high rates were recorded in Finland (16.7%) and Portugal (15.9%), and low ones in Belgium (7.9%) and Denmark (7.3%) in 1997. According to CEPE, lower profits predominated in the printing ink industry as a result of price levels not fully reflecting the additional services offered by print ink manufacturers to their customers (research and development).

(16) D, L and A, no data available; EL and I, 1996 instead of 1997.

LABOUR AND PRODUCTIVITY

There was a net reduction of 8.7% in the number of persons employed in the EU paints, varnishes and printing inks industry between 1993 and 1999. The majority of the job losses were recorded in the United Kingdom[17] (where 2.1 thousand jobs were shed between 1990 and 1997), whilst a net increase of more than 3 thousand positions was recorded in Italy[18]. The largest employer in 1997 was Germany, accounting for 46.7 thousand persons (30.7% of the EU total).

Eurostat estimates that apparent labour productivity in the EU paints, varnishes and printing inks industry was equal to 57.7 thousand ECU per person employed in 1997, whilst unit personnel costs were 37.5 thousand ECU. This industry was relatively labour-intensive (in comparison to other sectors of the chemicals industry), with personnel costs estimated to account for 21.9% of the EU's total operating costs in 1997.

(17) No time-series employment data available for D, L, NL and A.
(18) Between 1990 and 1996.

INTERNATIONAL TRENDS AND FOREIGN TRADE

The EU's paints, varnishes and printing inks industry was the largest in the Triad in 1995, accounting for 45.9% of total Triad output, well ahead of the USA with 33.5% and Japan with 20.6%.

Growth in EU exports to Eastern Europe and the Mediterranean

EU exports of paints, varnishes and printing inks were valued at 4.0 billion EUR in 1999, more than four times the level of imports (969 million EUR). Exports of paints, varnishes and printing inks accounted for 3.4% of the chemicals, rubber and plastics total, 0.2 percentage points higher than in 1989.

Imports of paints, varnishes and printing inks into the EU come essentially from just two countries in 1999, Switzerland (39.7%) and the USA (31.5%).

EU exports were more diversified, with Poland (10.2%) the main destination in 1999, followed by the USA and Switzerland. The Polish share of EU exports rose rapidly from just 2.2% in 1989 and was the leading example of a more general trend of growing EU exports to Eastern European (Czech Republic, Hungary, Slovenia and Romania) and Mediterranean markets (Turkey, Egypt and Israel).

————Figure 6.17

Paints, varnishes and printing inks
(NACE Rev. 1 24.3)
Destination of EU exports, 1999 (%)

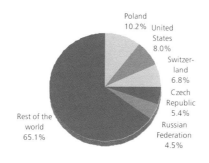

Source: Eurostat (COMEXT)

————Figure 6.18

Paints, varnishes and printing inks
(NACE Rev. 1 24.3)
Origin of EU imports, 1999 (%)

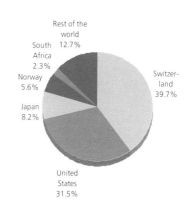

Source: Eurostat (COMEXT)

SUB-CHAPTER 6.4
PHARMACEUTICALS (NACE Rev. 1 24.4)

The manufacture of pharmaceuticals is broken down into two Classes within the European activity classification: the first covering the manufacture of basic pharmaceutical products (NACE Rev. 1 24.41), such as the manufacture of medicinal substances, the processing of blood or the manufacture of pure sugars. The second covers the manufacture of pharmaceutical preparations (NACE Rev. 1 24.42), such as vaccines, homeopathic preparations, contraceptives, dental fillings, as well as bandages, gauzes and dressings.

The manufacture of pharmaceuticals is one of the EU's most high-technology manufacturing sectors, with production value equal to 107.4 billion EUR in 1999, equivalent to almost a fifth (18.8%) of the chemicals, rubber and plastics industry.

Demand expected to rise with an ageing population
The European population is ageing and these changing demographics mean that is likely that there will be increased spending on pharmaceuticals in coming years. Other areas where demand for pharmaceutical products is growing at a rapid pace include self-medication products (in particular herbal remedies, vitamin and mineral supplements). On the other hand, national and private health services are increasingly turning to so-called generic drugs[19] in an attempt to contain or reduce spending on medicines.

France was the leading producer of pharmaceuticals in the EU, accounting for almost a quarter (23.3%) of the EU's output in 1997. Denmark (208.7%), Ireland (147.5%), France (142.5%) and Sweden (133.2%) were the most specialised producers within the EU. There was relatively low geographical concentration within the EU pharmaceuticals industry, as the five largest EU economies produced 75.3% of total output (compared to 79.5% for total manufacturing).

(19) Generic drugs often sell for 50% to 90% less than named brands and may erode 80% of a branded drug's business within a year of a patent expiring.

Figure 6.19

Pharmaceuticals (NACE Rev. 1 24.4)

Production and export specialisation (%)

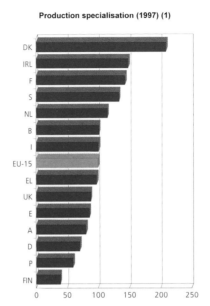

Production specialisation (1997) (1)

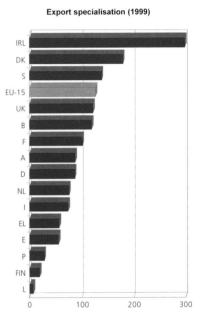

Export specialisation (1999)

(1) EL and I, 1995; L, not available.

Source: Eurostat (SBS, COMEXT)

Box 6.7

According to EFPIA (the European Federation of Pharmaceutical Industries and Associations), the largest European pharmaceutical companies during the financial year of 1998/99 were: Aventis (F/D), GlaxoWellcome (UK), Novartis (CH), AstraZeneca (UK), Roche (CH), Bayer (D), SmithKline Beecham (UK) and Sanofi-Synthélabo (F). All of these companies were in the global top twenty, which featured ten American companies.

An announcement was made on January 17th 2000 for a proposed merger between GlaxoWellcome and SmithKline Beecham, to form the world's leading pharmaceuticals' company with an estimated 7.3% of the global pharmaceuticals market. Other merger and acquisition activity during the first half of 2000 involving European pharmaceuticals' enterprises included Elan Corporation's (IRL) purchase of Liposome (USA); Galen Holdings (UK) take-over of Warner Chilcott (USA); and Qiagen's (NL) bid for Operon Technologies (also USA).

Box 6.8

Upon the discovery of a new drug, pharmaceuticals companies are generally granted a patent for a period of 20 years[20]. Patent protection is seen as necessary to encourage the huge sums of investment that are required to research and develop new medicines. Indeed, production costs of pharmaceuticals are generally considerably lower than their market value, as such the patent period acts as a mechanism to allow manufacturers to recoup their research costs. However, once a patent has expired, generic drugs may be produced by other manufacturers, which usually result in much lower prices.

(20) The period starts when a pharmaceutical compound is registered with the patent office, not when a medicinal product comes to market, which is generally about a decade later (following development work and clinical trials).

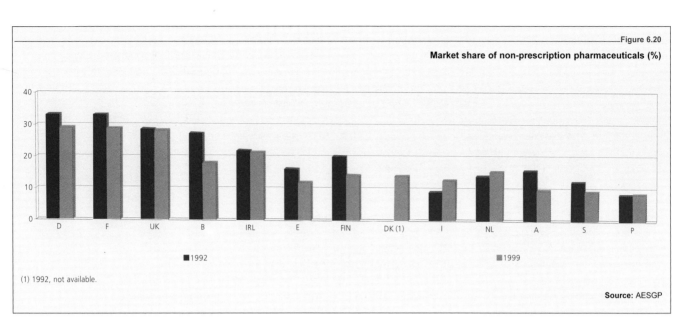

Figure 6.20

Market share of non-prescription pharmaceuticals (%)

■1992 ■1999

(1) 1992, not available.

Source: AESGP

STRUCTURE AND PERFORMANCE

The EU pharmaceuticals industry has recorded rapid growth in the last 15 years. Between 1985 and 1999, production rose by 172.2% in nominal terms (compared to 77.7% for the whole of chemicals, rubber and plastics). As a result the share of pharmaceuticals in the EU's output of chemicals, rubber and plastics increased from 12.2% to 18.8%. The majority of this shift in output took place in the late 1980s, as by 1992 pharmaceuticals already accounted for 17.7% of the total. Despite this relative slowdown, annual average growth for production in constant prices was equal to 5.6% between 1992 and 1997 (0.9 percentage points above the corresponding figure for chemicals, rubber and plastics).

A highly profitable industrial sector

The gross operating rates of pharmaceuticals enterprises (15.1% in 1999) are generally well above manufacturing industry averages (9.4%). The gross operating rate was between 20% and 25% in 1997 in the Nordic Member States, Belgium and the United Kingdom, and rose to as high as 45.1% in Ireland. These high operating profit rates are probably due to many products having very low price elasticity. However, profits are often used to "finance" further research and development and financial deficits. Indeed, EFPIA estimates that some 14.2 billion ECU of research and development spending took place in Europe[21] in 1998 (when the EU's gross operating surplus was 17.5 billion ECU).

(21) EU-15 (excluding L), Norway and Switzerland.

Figure 6.21

Pharmaceuticals (NACE Rev. 1 24.4)

International comparison of production in constant prices and employment (1990=100)

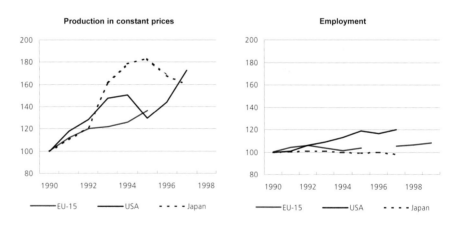

Production in constant prices

Employment

——EU-15 ——USA - - - Japan

Source: Eurostat (SBS)

Box 6.9

One area of the pharmaceuticals industry that has seen rapid growth in recent years is that of self-medication products. According to AESGP (the Association of the European Self-Medication Industry) the largest self-medication markets in Europe[22] are Germany (30.8% of the 13.6 billion EUR[23] market in 1999), the United Kingdom (17.0%) and France (14.2%).

The self-medication market could be broken down into the following constituent parts: treatments for coughs and colds (21.8%), analgesics (18.0%), indigestion (14.9%), vitamins and minerals (11.9%) and skin treatments (10.6%).

(22) EU-15 (excluding EL and L), Czech Republic, Hungary, Norway, Romania, Slovak Republic, Slovenia, and Switzerland.
(23) At public price levels.

LABOUR AND PRODUCTIVITY

There was a net increase of 82.8 thousand persons in employment in the pharmaceuticals industry between 1985 and 1999 (equivalent to average growth of 1.4% per annum). The 475.3 thousand persons employed in 1999 generated on average almost 20 thousand EUR more value added than the chemicals, rubber and plastics average, with apparent labour productivity equal to 86.5 thousand EUR.

Large number of research staff with
higher than average salaries

The share of personnel costs in total operating costs in the EU pharmaceuticals industry was equal to 22.8% in 1999 (which was 1.9 percentage points above the chemicals, rubber and plastics average). This relatively high share may be explained in part by the large number of persons engaged in research and development activities (estimated by EFPIA to be 82.5 thousand in 1998) allied to unit personnel costs that were higher on average than for the whole of the chemicals, rubber and plastics industry. The higher average personnel costs were present in every Member State[24] in 1997, except for Finland (-3.2 thousand ECU per employee difference), with the highest differentials recorded in France, Sweden and the United Kingdom (where unit personnel costs were between 9 and 10 thousand ECU higher in the pharmaceuticals industry).

---

(24) DK, EL, I, L and NL, no data available; although DK, EL and I all reported the same trend in 1996.

INTERNATIONAL TRENDS AND FOREIGN TRADE

The EU was the largest producer of pharmaceuticals in the Triad in 1997, accounting for 45.3% of total output, followed by the USA with just over a third (35.9%) of the Triad's production and Japan (18.8%).

The EU exported 33.3 billion EUR of pharmaceuticals in 1999, which was almost double the level of imports (17.1 billion EUR). This ratio of exports being valued at almost double imports was maintained during the last decade, as the EU's cover ratio progressed from 186.7% in 1989 to 195.0% in 1999.

The overwhelming majority of the EU's imports of pharmaceuticals come from either the USA (42.8% in 1999) or Switzerland (35.1%). EU exports were increasingly destined for the USA (29.8%), Switzerland (13.1%) and Japan (7.6%), with all three of these countries reporting an expansion in their relative shares of total EU exports, with respect to figures for 1989.

Figure 6.22 —————————————

Pharmaceuticals (NACE Rev. 1 24.4)
Destination of EU exports, 1999 (%)

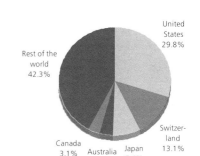

Source: Eurostat (COMEXT)

Figure 6.23 —————————————

Pharmaceuticals (NACE Rev. 1 24.4)
Origin of EU imports, 1999 (%)

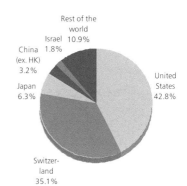

Source: Eurostat (COMEXT)

SUB-CHAPTER 6.5
SOAPS, DETERGENTS AND TOILETRIES
(NACE Rev. 1 24.5)

This sub-chapter includes information on soaps, washing products (for clothes and dishes) and cleaning products (such as waxes, polishes and scouring pastes), which are all classified within NACE Rev. 1 24.51. Perfumes, toilet waters, make-up, bath salts, shaving products, deodorants and sun-creams are all included within NACE Rev. 1 24.52.

EU production of soaps, detergents and toiletries was valued at 47.0 billion ECU in 1995, which represented almost a tenth (9.4%) of the output within the chemicals, rubber and plastics industry.

─────Figure 6.24

Soaps, detergents and toiletries (NACE Rev. 1 24.5)
Production and export specialisation (%)

Production specialisation (1995) (1)

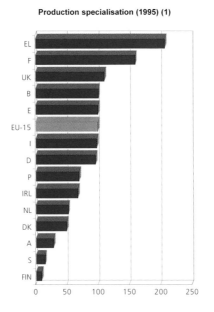

Export specialisation (1999)

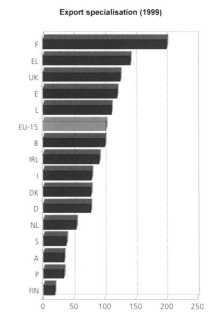

(1) DK, 1994; L, not available.

Source: Eurostat (SBS, COMEXT)

─────────── Box 6.10

The European soaps, detergents and toiletries industry is a world leader, with considerable investment in product innovation and scientific research and development. Marketing and advertising are a key means to develop brand identities within these industries, particularly in areas such as washing powders and perfumes.

Whilst brand names account for a significant share of many product markets, some retailers have recently increased the shelf space they devote to low-price, own label brands. In addition, retailers have increasingly pressed manufacturers to invest in automated warehouses and electronic ordering systems, improving efficiency and reducing stock handling costs.

According to COLIPA (The European Cosmetic, Toiletry and Perfumery Association), average per capita consumption of cosmetics and toiletries within the EU was equal to 117 ECU in 1998. France was the Member States with the highest per capita consumption of cosmetics and toiletries (around 140 ECU per capita), followed by Austria (122 ECU) and the United Kingdom (121 ECU).

In 1998, just over a quarter of the EU personal care market was accounted for by toiletries (26.9%) and another quarter by hair care products (25.5%), whilst the share of skin care products was a fifth (20.7%), followed by perfumes (15.1%) and decorative cosmetics (11.8%).

The predominance of brand names within these industries explains to a large degree the enterprise structure, which is dominated by large multinational players. The main Europeans in the cleaning products industry include Reckitt Benckiser plc (created from the merger of Reckitt & Colman (UK) and Benckiser (D) in 1999), Unilever (UK/NL) and Henkel (D), whilst external competition is largely from the USA (Colgate-Palmolive and Procter & Gamble). Within the perfumes and toiletries industry the largest players include l'Oréal (F) and Schwarzkopf (D), as well as multinationals such as Unilever and Procter & Gamble who have diversified into these areas through the acquisition of several brand names.

─────Figure 6.25

Breakdown of the cosmetics, toiletries and
perfume market in the EU, 1998 (%)

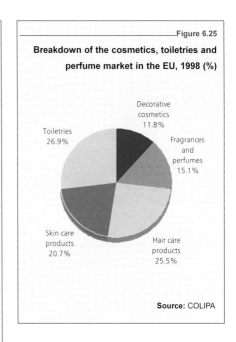

Source: COLIPA

STRUCTURE AND PERFORMANCE

France had the highest level of output within the soaps, detergents and toiletries industry in 1997, some 13.3 billion ECU, followed by Germany (9.9 billion ECU) and the United Kingdom (8.4 billion ECU)[25]. In terms of relative output, France (159.6%) recorded the second highest production specialisation ratio in 1995, behind Greece (206.9%), and was followed by the United Kingdom (110.4%) and Belgium (100.8%)[26].

Between 1987 and 1997, soaps, detergents and toiletries saw their relative share of chemicals, rubber and plastics output rise by 1.1 percentage points in France to 13.5%. This was contrary to the general negative evolution seen in most other Member States (for example, there was a decline of 0.9 percentage points in both Germany and Spain over the same period, whilst the United Kingdom registered no change). Greece again recorded the highest relative gain, with soaps, detergents and toiletries accounting for 22.6% of total chemicals, rubber and plastics output in 1996 (3.6 percentage points more than in 1987).

France specialises in toiletries
and personal care products
The breakdown of activity between soaps, detergents and cleaning products on the one hand and toiletries and personal care products on the other is split almost 50:50 within the EU. Toiletries and personal care products accounted for 51.2% of EU output in 1997[27], largely due to France (where these products accounted for as much as 71.4% of the total). Within eight of the Member States, soaps, detergents and cleaning products accounted for the majority of activity in terms of production value, with the highest relative shares recorded in Denmark (89.3%), Austria (85.2%) and Portugal (83.5%).

LABOUR AND PRODUCTIVITY

There were 224.4 thousand persons employed in the EU soaps, detergents and toiletries industry in 1999. This was equivalent to a net loss of 20.7 thousand jobs between 1989 and 1999, at an average annual rate of -0.9%.

Apparent labour productivity was estimated at 59.2 thousand ECU per person employed in the EU in 1997, whilst personnel costs as a share of total operating costs were estimated to be 18.0% in 1997 (almost 3.0 percentage points below the chemicals, rubber and plastics average).

(25) EL, I and L, no data available; production value of I stood at 7.7 billion ECU in 1996.
(26) DK and L, no data available; no other country was relatively specialised in the manufacture of soaps, detergents and toiletries.
(27) D, EL and L, no data available; I and S, 1996.

Figure 6.26

Soaps, detergents and toiletries (NACE Rev. 1 24.5)

International comparison of production in constant prices and employment (1990=100)

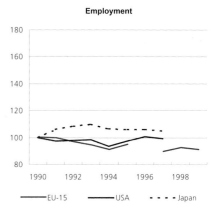

Source: Eurostat (SBS)

INTERNATIONAL TRENDS AND FOREIGN TRADE

The EU accounted for 44.1% of the Triad's output of soaps, detergents and toiletries in 1995, and was followed by the USA (36.0%) and Japan (19.9%), whilst accounting for more than half (55.9%) of the Triad's workforce in 1997.

EU exports of soaps, detergents and toiletries rose to 8.2 billion EUR in 1999, which was 5.9 billion EUR more than the value of imports. The cover ratio of the soaps, detergents and toiletries industry was equal to 352.6% in 1999, somewhat below the 400% to 470% ratios recorded during the remainder of the 1990s.

Imports to the EU dominated
by the USA and Switzerland
The main origin of the EU's imports of soaps, detergents and toiletries was the USA, accounting for 42.6% of the total in 1999, well ahead of Switzerland (with 25.5%), whilst no other country had a share of more than 5.0%. The main destinations for EU exports were the same two countries, USA (14.1%) and Switzerland (9.3%), whilst the relative importance of Poland and the Czech Republic rose between 1989 and 1999.

Figure 6.27

Soaps, detergents and toiletries (NACE Rev. 1 24.5)

Destination of EU exports, 1999 (%)

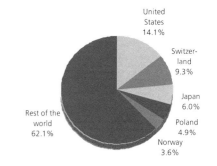

Source: Eurostat (COMEXT)

Figure 6.28

Soaps, detergents and toiletries (NACE Rev. 1 24.5)

Origin of EU imports, 1999 (%)

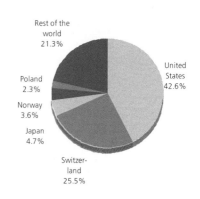

Source: Eurostat (COMEXT)

SUB-CHAPTER 6.6
MAN-MADE FIBRES (NACE Rev. 1 24.7)

The information contained within this sub-chapter refers to the manufacture of artificial and synthetic fibres, yarns and filaments. The data does not cover the spinning of synthetic and artificial fibres or the manufacture of sewing thread (both of which are included within sub-chapter 4.1).

EU production of man-made fibres was equal to 11.8 billion EUR in 1999, which was equivalent to 2.1% of the total for chemicals, rubber and plastics. European manufacturers have increasingly faced foreign competition in this industry during the last three decades. There was a 1.0 percentage point reduction in the share of man-made fibres in total chemicals, rubber and plastics output between 1970 and 1999 (see box 6.11 for more details).

Man-made fibres are normally intermediate products that are further processed into end-use products such as clothing, carpets and household textiles. In addition, there are also a wide range of more specialist, technical end-use products, such as tyres, conveyor belts, fire-, cold- and water-resistant materials, as well as reinforcements within composites (as used in aircraft) that are supplied to other manufacturing sectors.

Germany accounted for over a third (36.8%) of the EU's output of man-made fibres in value terms in 1997, significantly ahead of all other Member States, none of them reported a double-digit share. However, relative to total manufacturing output, Germany (138.4% in 1997) was not the most specialised country within the EU, as both Belgium (197.0%) and the Netherlands (147.6%) had higher production specialisation ratios.

Figure 6.29

Man-made fibres (NACE Rev. 1 24.7)

Production and export specialisation (%)

Production specialisation (1997) (1)

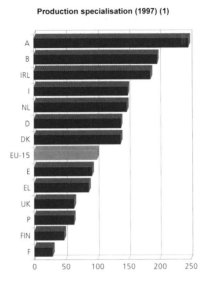

Export specialisation (1999)

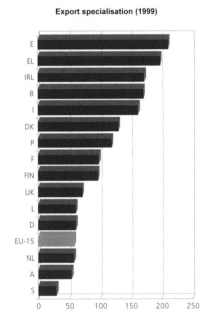

(1) IRL and A, 1994; EL, I and FIN, 1996; L and S, not available.

Source: Eurostat (SBS, COMEXT)

Box 6.11

According to CIRFS (International Rayon and Synthetic Fibres Committee) worldwide production of man-made fibres increased by 4.0% in volume terms in 1999 to reach 29.5 million tonnes of output. The breakdown of fibre output in the world shows the importance of man-made fibres, as they accounted for 59% of total fibre output in 1999, followed by cotton (38%) and wool (3%).

Synthetic fibres are oil or gas based derivatives from the petrochemicals industry, characterised by their durability. Cellulosic fibres (such as viscose) are made from renewable raw material sources such as wood. As such, environmental considerations are very important within the industry, both in terms of clean manufacturing, and in terms of renewing natural resources.

The breakdown of world production between synthetics and cellulosic fibres was largely in favour of the former, which accounted for 91.0% of the total in 1999. Synthetics have taken an increasing share of man-made fibre output, rising from 57.3% of world production in 1970. This trend continued in 1999, when synthetic fibre output increased by 5% to 26.9 million tons, whilst the production of cellulosic fibres decreased by 5% to 2.6 million tons. The most important product category within the synthetics sector is polyester, which accounted for 60% of total man-made fibre output in 1999, followed by polyamides (13%) and acrylics (8%).

Figure 6.30

Breakdown of production of cotton, wool and man-made fibres in the world, 1998 (%)

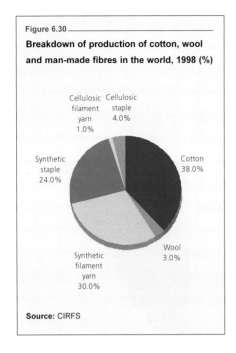

Source: CIRFS

Figure 6.31

Man-made fibres (NACE Rev. 1 24.7)

International comparison of production in constant prices and employment (1990=100)

Production in constant prices

Employment

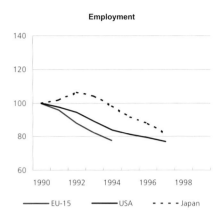

Source: Eurostat (SBS)

STRUCTURE AND PERFORMANCE

Between 1985 and 1999 there was little development in the output of the EU's man-made fibres industry in value terms. Production rose from 10.1 billion ECU in 1985 to 11.8 billion ECU in 1999, equivalent to an absolute gain of 16.4% (whilst chemicals, rubber and plastics rose by 77.7% over the same period). These figures hide the fact that output in real terms was rising at a much faster pace (due to declining producer prices). Average growth in real terms between 1993 and 1998 was equal to 7.6% per annum (2.9 percentage points above the chemicals, rubber and plastics' average).

LABOUR AND PRODUCTIVITY

There were 60.3 thousand persons employed in the EU man-made fibres industry in 1994 (some 30.1 thousand less than in 1985). More recent data for some of the Member States shows that the largest employer within the Union was by far Germany (with 24.5 thousand persons in 1997).

Rapid reduction in relative personnel costs

Simple wage adjusted labour productivity was relatively low within the man-made fibres industry in the early to mid-1990s (falling to 115.8% in 1993). There were marked improvements in the second half of the decade as this productivity measure rose to 142.0% in 1999. Underlying these productivity gains there was a relative reduction in the cost of the labour input, as the share of personnel costs in production value was reduced from 27.3% in 1993 to 21.3% by 1999, despite total personnel costs rising by 9.3% between these two dates.

Box 6.12

According to CIRFS, man-made fibre production was dominated by producers from the Far East and southern Asia in 1999, whilst the USA was estimated to have produced 15% of global output in volume terms, Western Europe[28] 12% (or 3.6 million tonnes) and Japan 6%.

The Triad members have seen their respective shares of world output decline at a rapid pace since 1970, when together they accounted for 76% of world production in volume terms (Western Europe 31%, USA 27% and Japan 18%). There was however positive output growth in all three Triad economies, with the fastest rates between 1970 and 1999 recorded in the USA, where production almost doubled (95.2%) to reach 4.4 million tonnes. In Western Europe output rose by 36.0%, whilst in Japan there was an increase of 17.1%.

(28) EU-15, Norway, Switzerland, Turkey and Yugoslavia.

INTERNATIONAL TRENDS AND FOREIGN TRADE

In value terms the USA was comfortably the largest producer of man-made fibres within the Triad in 1997, accounting for a 47.4% share of total output, ahead of the EU (35.3%) and Japan (17.3%). Since a low-point in 1993 (27.9% of the Triad total), EU output in relative terms rose by 7.4 percentage points through to 1997 (almost entirely at the expense of Japan).

A chemicals sector reporting a trade deficit in the EU
With a declining share of world output, it was no surprise to find that during the course of the 1990s the EU trade deficit for man-made fibres grew from 62.6 million ECU in 1989 to 1.1 billion EUR by 1999 (although this was a 237 million EUR improvement on 1998).

The main origin of EU imports of man-made fibres was the USA, with an 18.7% share of the total in 1999, which was equivalent to an 7.8 percentage point reduction when compared to 1989. Imports originating from Asia and Eastern Europe saw their relative shares rise, in particular those from South Korea, India, Indonesia, Poland and the Slovak Republic.

Figure 6.32

Man-made fibres (NACE Rev. 1 24.7)
Destination of EU exports, 1999 (%)

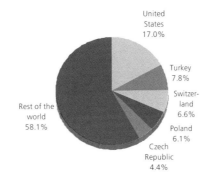

Source: Eurostat (COMEXT)

Figure 6.33

Man-made fibres (NACE Rev. 1 24.7)
Origin of EU imports, 1999 (%)

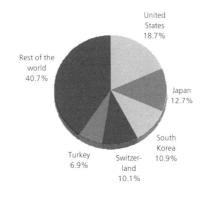

Source: Eurostat (COMEXT)

SUB-CHAPTER 6.7
RUBBER (NACE Rev. 1 25.1)

There are three distinct product divisions within the rubber industry and these are reflected in the activity classification. NACE Rev. 1 25.11 covers the manufacture of rubber tyres and inner tubes, whilst NACE Rev. 1 25.12 covers the retreading and rebuilding of tyres. Other rubber products (such as pipe, floor coverings, textiles, clothes and hygienic articles) are included within NACE Rev. 1 25.13.

The rubber products industry had production valued at 34.6 billion EUR in 1999 in the EU. The industry accounted for 6.7% of total chemicals, rubber and plastics output, whilst it employed 293.8 thousand persons (10.2% of the total).

Retreading a relatively small activity
There is a limited set of information[29] to measure the relative importance of each of the three Classes within the rubber products industry. In 1997, tyres accounted for 49.3% of total output, followed by other rubber products (47.2%), whilst retreading represented just 3.5% of the total. Within the Member States there was greater specialisation in the manufacture of tyres in France (62.7% of the rubber products total) and Spain (59.7%) whilst Italy (60.1%) and the United Kingdom (57.4%) were more orientated towards other rubber products.

High level of dependency on
the motor vehicles industry
Whilst industrial rubber products are used by many industries, the most dominant downstream industry by far is that of motor vehicles, where the largest single application of rubber is in the form of tyres. The world tyre industry is characterised by the dominance of a few large companies: with Goodyear (USA), Michelin (F) and Bridgestone/Firestone (JAP) the three largest global players. The activity of tyre retreading is particularly important in relation to the truck and aircraft sectors.

Non-tyre markets for rubber may be split between the transport sector (where use is also made of rubber in wiper blades, hose, belts, gaskets, weather stripping, doors, windows and seals) and other industrial sectors where the most important products include conveyor belts for mining, floor coverings, footwear and hygienic products.

(29) E, F, P and UK, 1997; DK and I, 1996.

Figure 6.34

Rubber (NACE Rev. 1 25.1)
Production and export specialisation (%)

Production specialisation (1997) (1)

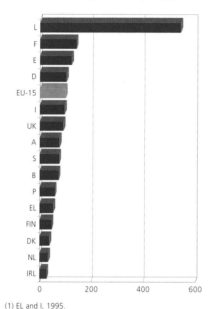

Export specialisation (1999)

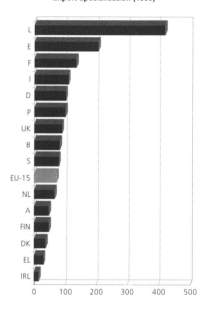

(1) EL and I, 1995.

Source: Eurostat (SBS, COMEXT)

Geographical concentration within
the larger Member States
The manufacture of rubber products is highly concentrated within the five largest EU economies. These countries accounted for 84.7% of total output of rubber products in 1997[30], which was 5.2 percentage points more than their relative share of total manufacturing production. The largest producer was Germany (9.2 billion ECU, or 27.7% of the EU total), followed by France (23.2%) and the United Kingdom (13.9%).

The relative importance of the rubber products industry ranged from as high as 8.4% of chemicals, rubber and plastics output in Spain and 7.9% in France to just 1.4% in the Netherlands and 1.1% in Ireland. One country stood outside this range, as almost a quarter (24.8%) of the chemicals, rubber and plastics produced in Luxembourg were from the rubber industry.

(30) Comparison is based on 1997 data for the majority of Member States; EL and I, 1996.

Figure 6.35

Consumption of rubber in the production
of tyres and related products, 1998
(thousand tonnes)

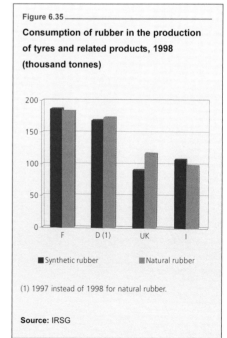

■ Synthetic rubber   ■ Natural rubber

(1) 1997 instead of 1998 for natural rubber.

Source: IRSG

STRUCTURE AND PERFORMANCE

Production of rubber products in the EU rose from 21.7 billion ECU in 1985 to 34.6 billion EUR in 1999. The relative importance of the rubber industry within chemicals, rubber and plastics has declined in almost every Member State during the 1990s. In the EU the relative share fell from 6.7% to 6.0% between 1985 and 1999. Within the majority of Member States the same trend was observed between 1990 and 1997, with only Finland (+1.2 percentage points) and Spain (+1.1 points)[31] reporting a relative increase in the importance of the rubber products industry.

Nevertheless, in real terms the growth of the rubber products industry in the EU in the mid- to late 1990s was at a similar speed to the average for the whole of chemicals, rubber and plastics, with the annual average growth rate of production equal to 4.9% between 1993 and 1998 (compared to 4.8%). As can be deduced from the difference between nominal and real growth rates, the producer price index for the rubber processing industry rose at a relatively slow pace, up by 3.1% between 1993 and 1998 compared to 7.7% for the chemicals industry. The manufacture of synthetic rubber is particularly influenced by the price of crude oil.

LABOUR AND PRODUCTIVITY

There were 293.8 thousand persons employed in the EU rubber processing industry in 1999, which was a net reduction of 73.6 thousand persons compared to 1985.

(31) EL, I, L and A, no data available.

Relatively high labour intensity

The apparent labour productivity of the EU's rubber products industry (48.6 thousand EUR per person employed in 1999) was relatively low in comparison to the chemicals, rubber and plastics' average (66.9 thousand EUR). If this figure is adjusted by taking account of personnel costs, the simple wage adjusted productivity ratio for rubber products (141.5% in 1999) remained well below the average for chemicals, rubber and plastics (167.3%).

The rubber products industry in the EU is relatively labour-intensive, as personnel costs accounted for 28.2% of total operating costs in 1999 (compared to an average of 20.9% for the whole of chemicals, rubber and plastics).

INTERNATIONAL TRENDS AND FOREIGN TRADE

In 1997, the EU was the largest producer of rubber products in the Triad, accounting for 39.9% of total Triad output, ahead of the USA (35.2%) and Japan (24.9%).

The trade position of the EU has deteriorated during the last ten-year period, from a surplus of 1.1 billion ECU in 1989 to a deficit of 483 million EUR by 1999. The relative importance of rubber products as exports has also declined during this period, from 6.2% of the chemicals, rubber and plastics total in 1989 to 4.3% ten years later. The main origin of EU imports was Asia, and in particular Japan, which accounted for 18.0% of the total in 1999. South Korea (8.5%) and Malaysia (6.5%) also featured within the five most important partners.

Figure 6.36

Rubber (NACE Rev. 1 25.1)

International comparison of production in constant prices and employment (1990=100)

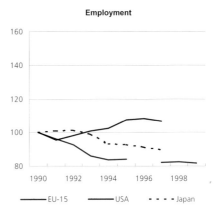

Source: Eurostat (SBS)

Figure 6.37

Rubber (NACE Rev. 1 25.1)

Destination of EU exports, 1999 (%)

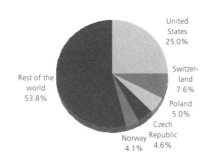

Source: Eurostat (COMEXT)

Figure 6.38

Rubber (NACE Rev. 1 25.1)

Origin of EU imports, 1999 (%)

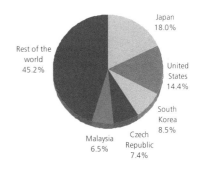

Source: Eurostat (COMEXT)

SUB-CHAPTER 6.8
PLASTICS (NACE Rev. 1 25.2)

This final sub-chapter covers the plastics processing industries. The industry is sub-divided into four Classes within the activity classification, the first of which covers the manufacture of plastic sheets, pipes and tubes (NACE Rev. 1 25.21). The manufacture of plastic packaging goods, such as plastic bags, containers and bottles are included within NACE Rev. 1 25.22, whilst various builders' wares that are made from plastic (such as doors, window frames, baths, showers, floor or wall coverings) are classified under NACE Rev. 1 25.23. Finally, the manufacture of other plastic products, such as insulating and lighting fittings, office supplies, clothing (excluding footwear) and furniture fittings are included within NACE Rev. 1 25.24.

The plastic products industry is one of the fastest growing manufacturing sectors of the EU economy. It is characterised by a high number of small and medium-sized enterprises. Production value in the EU rose to 119.7 billion EUR in 1999, which was approximately one-fifth (20.9%) of the output of the EU chemicals, rubber and plastics industries.

Plastics are widely used in almost every sector of the economy

The unique attributes of plastics (including their light weight and corrosion resistance) means that plastics are increasingly used as substitutes for traditional materials such as paper, glass, wood and metals. The production of plastic products in the EU in 1997[32] may be broken down as follows: plastic plates, sheets, tubes and profiles (22.6%); plastic packing goods (21.7%); plastic builders' ware (13.8%) and other plastic products (41.8% of the total).

(32) D, EL and L, no data available; I, 1996.

Box 6.14

Whilst the plastic products industry consumes large amounts of energy, uses petroleum as an important input in the manufacturing process and faces environmental questions as to the friendliness of products made from PVC, the use of plastics as a substitute for other materials has not had a purely negative effect on sustainable development. Plastics are used to replace metal parts within the motor vehicles industry and have subsequently improved fuel efficiency, whilst reductions in the weight and volume of packaged products also reduces energy consumption with respect to transport costs.

Figure 6.39

Plastics (NACE Rev. 1 25.2)

Production and export specialisation (%)

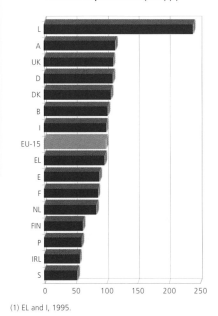
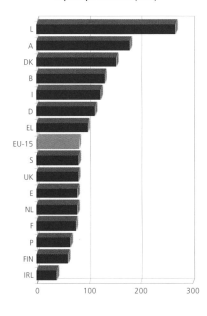

(1) EL and I, 1995.

Source: Eurostat (SBS, COMEXT)

Germany and the United Kingdom lead plastics manufacturing

Germany was by far the largest producer of plastic products in the EU in 1997, accounting for 29.6% of the EU's output (33.5 billion ECU), followed by the United Kingdom with just under 17% (19 billion ECU). After Luxembourg (239.9%), the highest relative production specialisation rates were recorded in Austria (115.3%), the United Kingdom (111.7%) and Germany (111.3%).

STRUCTURE AND PERFORMANCE

In nominal terms, the output of the plastic products industry rose by more than 160% between 1985 and 1999 in the EU (twice the rate of growth recorded for the whole of chemicals, rubber and plastics). As a result, plastic products' share in the chemicals, rubber and plastics' total output rose from 14.2% to 20.3% between these two years. The majority of the EU Member States followed this trend[33], with the two largest producers, the United Kingdom (8.5 percentage points) and Germany (7.2 points), recording the highest relative gains.

High growth and profitability

The gross operating rate of the plastic products industry in the EU was well above the manufacturing average throughout the 1990s, with a difference between 2 and 4 percentage points. In 1999, the EU gross operating rate was 2.8 percentage points higher at 12.2%. The highest spreads were recorded in Germany and the United Kingdom, where profits in the plastic products industry ran 3.6 and 3.0 percentage points above domestic manufacturing averages in 1997.

(33) IRL recorded a loss of 2 percentage points, whilst DK, FIN and S reported a relative decline between 1990 and 1997.

———————————————————————————————— Figure 6.40

Plastics (NACE Rev. 1 25.2)

International comparison of production in constant prices and employment (1990=100)

Production in constant prices

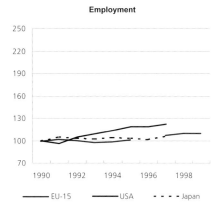

Employment

Source: Eurostat (SBS)

LABOUR AND PRODUCTIVITY

The plastic products industry recorded a net increase of 273.2 thousand jobs between 1985 and 1999, equivalent to an average annual increase of 2.6%. The plastic products industry accounted for 31.7% of those employed in the EU's chemicals, rubber and plastics industry in 1999, with relative shares rising to over 40% in both Luxembourg (42.7%) and Austria (41.7%) in 1997. Apparent labour productivity (47.0 thousand EUR per person employed in 1999) and wage adjusted labour productivity (155.1%) of the EU's plastic products industry were below the EU chemicals, rubber and plastics averages.

INTERNATIONAL TRENDS AND FOREIGN TRADE

Triad output of plastic products was split quite evenly, with Japan (34.1%) the largest producer in 1997, just ahead of the EU (34.1%) and the USA (31.5%).

The growth of EU imports and exports of plastic products followed similar trends during the 1990s, as the cover ratio increased by just 2.7 percentage points between 1990 and 1999 to reach 138.7%. As the EU already ran a surplus of 1.4 billion ECU in 1990, the EU's trade position improved such that by 1999 the surplus was equal to 3.5 billion EUR. In 1998, the EU accounted for just over half (52.8%) of the Triad's exports of plastic products.

China becomes a major trade partner
The USA was the principal origin of EU imports of plastic products in 1999, with a 23.4% share of the total. China followed with almost a fifth (19.6%), which was a 14.8 percentage point increase when compared to 1989. The USA was also the main destination for EU exports, accounting for 14.5% of the total in 1999. A group of applicant countries within close proximity of the EU followed, with exports to Poland (9.5%), the Czech Republic (6.8%), Hungary (4.8%) and Turkey (3.1%) increasing at a rapid pace.

———————————————————————————————— Figure 6.41

Plastics (NACE Rev. 1 25.2)

Destination of EU exports, 1999 (%)

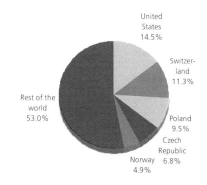

Source: Eurostat (COMEXT)

———————————————————————————————— Figure 6.42

Plastics (NACE Rev. 1 25.2)

Origin of EU imports, 1999 (%)

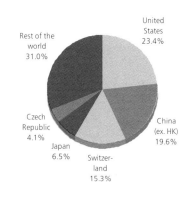

Source: Eurostat (COMEXT)

Table 6.4

Manufacture of basic chemicals (NACE Rev. 1 24.1)

Production related indicators in the EU (1)

	1989	1990	1991	1992	1993	1994	1995	1996	1997	1998	1999
Number of persons employed (thousands)	767.0	752.5	729.6	698.7	651.4	613.1	587.8	:	574.0	564.7	565.4
Production (million EUR)	148,209	140,143	133,721	127,096	120,983	134,516	156,983	:	173,420	170,497	172,158
Domestic producer price index (1995=100)	:	92.1	89.1	84.1	82.0	85.9	100.0	93.6	94.9	89.9	86.6
Value added (million EUR)	49,845	43,702	40,250	39,136	37,699	43,960	53,015	:	53,014	52,365	52,808

(1) Technically, data before 01/01/1999 are in ECU and after this date in euro. However, as the conversion rate was 1 ECU =1 EUR, for practical purposes the two terms can be used interchangeably.

Table 6.5

Manufacture of basic chemicals (NACE Rev. 1 24.1)

Trade related indicators in the EU (1)

	1989	1990	1991	1992	1993	1994	1995	1996	1997	1998	1999
Exports (million EUR)	19,550	18,509	19,373	19,453	23,511	26,926	29,200	30,209	32,386	30,572	35,405
Imports (million EUR)	16,469	16,637	16,960	16,970	16,303	19,688	23,847	22,802	26,892	28,180	27,866
Trade balance (million EUR)	3,081	1,872	2,412	2,483	7,208	7,238	5,353	7,407	5,494	2,392	7,539
Cover ratio (%)	118.7	111.3	114.2	114.6	144.2	136.8	122.4	132.5	120.4	108.5	127.1

(1) Technically, data before 01/01/1999 are in ECU and after this date in euro. However, as the conversion rate was 1 ECU =1 EUR, for practical purposes the two terms can be used interchangeably.

Table 6.6

Manufacture of basic chemicals (NACE Rev. 1 24.1)

Production related indicators, 1997

	B	DK	D	EL (1)	E	F	IRL	I (1)	L	NL	A	P	FIN	S	UK
Number of persons employed (thousands)	25.9	2.9	223.1	4.0	33.3	74.8	6.1	52.4	0.2	:	6.9	6.4	8.0	13.7	76.0
Production (million ECU)	12,276	568	52,326	561	9,532	24,664	7,325	15,555	129	16,321	2,085	1,346	2,543	3,657	21,507
Value added (million ECU)	3,308	193	17,674	165	2,680	6,545	4,564	4,100	41	4,150	548	374	814	1,180	6,437
Gross operating surplus (million ECU)	1,752.7	91.8	4,947.2	43.7	1,474.7	2,747.5	4,278.9	2,077.4	33.9	2,532.0	190.8	217.7	503.2	569.8	3,335.6

(1) 1996.

Table 6.7

Manufacture of basic chemicals (NACE Rev. 1 24.1)

Trade related indicators, 1999

	B	DK	D	EL	E	F	IRL	I	L	NL	A	P	FIN	S	UK
Exports (million EUR)	18,540	1,013	20,622	227	3,853	12,973	10,017	5,981	68	12,419	1,146	505	1,360	1,671	12,436
Imports (million EUR)	13,824	1,716	20,276	958	6,536	14,598	2,021	13,652	327	8,203	2,175	1,291	1,473	3,134	11,391
Trade balance (million EUR)	4,716	-704	345	-731	-2,683	-1,624	7,996	-7,671	-259	4,216	-1,028	-786	-113	-1,464	1,044
Cover ratio (%)	134.1	59.0	101.7	23.7	59.0	88.9	495.7	43.8	20.9	151.4	52.7	39.1	92.3	53.3	109.2

Table 6.8

Manufacture of basic chemicals (NACE Rev. 1 24.1)

Labour related indicators, 1997

	B	DK (1)	D	EL (2)	E	F	IRL	I (2)	L	NL	A	P	FIN	S	UK
Unit personnel costs (thousand ECU per employee)	60.5	39.8	57.1	30.2	33.0	50.8	46.5	38.8	42.7	:	51.8	24.9	40.7	44.7	40.8
Social charges as a share of personnel costs (%)	42.1	4.9	29.5	31.7	25.5	53.1	22.3	47.8	:	21.8	28.5	45.7	27.7	47.6	17.9
Apparent labour productivity (thousand ECU/pers. empl.)	127.5	66.9	79.2	41.0	80.4	87.5	744.7	78.2	238.7	:	79.5	58.8	101.8	86.5	84.7
Wage adjusted labour productivity (%)	210.8	192.5	138.8	136.0	243.3	172.4	1,601.0	201.4	559.5	:	153.5	236.3	250.1	193.3	207.3
Personnel costs as a share of total operating costs (%)	14.8	19.5	22.9	23.7	11.7	15.5	8.7	12.9	8.0	10.2	17.6	11.5	14.6	16.8	14.7

(1) Unit personnel costs and wage adjusted labour productivity, 1996; (2) 1996.

Source: Eurostat (SBS, EBT, COMEXT)

———Table 6.9

Manufacture of pesticides and other agro-chemical products (NACE Rev. 1 24.2)

Production related indicators in the EU (1)

	1989	1990	1991	1992	1993	1994	1995	1996	1997	1998	1999
Number of persons employed (thousands)	:	:	:	:	28.7	28.3	:	:	:	:	:
Production (million EUR)	:	:	:	:	5,609	6,662	:	:	8,362	8,319	8,589
Domestic producer price index (1995=100)	:	97.2	100.3	101.3	101.7	100.1	100.0	101.7	102.5	100.3	99.4
Value added (million EUR)	:	:	:	:	2,029	2,118	:	:	2,205	2,295	2,293

(1) Technically, data before 01/01/1999 are in ECU and after this date in euro. However, as the conversion rate was 1 ECU =1 EUR, for practical purposes the two terms can be used interchangeably.

———Table 6.10

Manufacture of pesticides and other agro-chemical products (NACE Rev. 1 24.2)

Trade related indicators in the EU (1)

	1989	1990	1991	1992	1993	1994	1995	1996	1997	1998	1999
Exports (million EUR)	1,406	1,411	1,502	1,399	1,625	1,929	1,944	2,222	2,463	2,560	2,260
Imports (million EUR)	593	622	644	496	462	499	618	704	667	649	730
Trade balance (million EUR)	813	789	858	904	1,163	1,430	1,326	1,518	1,796	1,911	1,530
Cover ratio (%)	237.0	226.7	233.1	282.4	351.9	386.7	314.6	315.7	369.3	394.3	309.6

(1) Technically, data before 01/01/1999 are in ECU and after this date in euro. However, as the conversion rate was 1 ECU =1 EUR, for practical purposes the two terms can be used interchangeably.

———Table 6.11

Manufacture of pesticides and other agro-chemical products (NACE Rev. 1 24.2)

Production related indicators, 1997

	B	DK	D	EL (1)	E	F	IRL	I (1)	L	NL	A	P	FIN (1)	S	UK
Number of persons employed (thousands)	1.5	1.1	4.6	0.7	2.4	7.0	0.2	2.0	0.0	:	:	0.3	0.0	:	6.1
Production (million ECU)	634	206	1,071	85	557	3,065	19	574	0	184	:	36	0	:	1,816
Value added (million ECU)	125	86	393	23	159	509	5	103	0	60	:	10	0	:	716
Gross operating surplus (million ECU)	32.7	42.3	138.8	5.2	84.1	117.2	1.5	26.4	0.0	30.4	:	4.6	0.0	:	446.1

(1) 1996.

———Table 6.12

Manufacture of pesticides and other agro-chemical products (NACE Rev. 1 24.2)

Trade related indicators, 1999

	B	DK	D	EL	E	F	IRL	I	L	NL	A	P	FIN	S	UK
Exports (million EUR)	565	71	1,727	15	147	1,616	38	291	13	295	:	6	9	16	1,136
Imports (million EUR)	258	127	616	100	310	1,378	74	390	65	269	79	86	46	69	469
Trade balance (million EUR)	307	-57	1,111	-85	-164	238	-36	-99	-51	27	:	-80	-37	-52	666
Cover ratio (%)	218.6	55.4	280.5	15.4	47.2	117.3	51.6	74.7	20.3	109.9	:	7.2	19.7	24.0	242.0

———Table 6.13

Manufacture of pesticides and other agro-chemical products (NACE Rev. 1 24.2)

Labour related indicators, 1997

	B	DK	D	EL (1)	E	F	IRL	I (1)	L	NL	A	P	FIN	S	UK
Unit personnel costs (thousand ECU per employee)	61.7	:	55.0	24.3	28.9	55.7	21.2	39.3	:	:	:	19.0	:	:	44.2
Social charges as a share of personnel costs (%)	47.8	5.1	32.6	29.4	25.0	46.6	25.9	48.2	:	21.5	:	36.1	:	:	21.4
Apparent labour productivity (thousand ECU/pers. empl.)	83.3	78.3	84.8	31.4	67.4	72.4	30.1	52.3	:	:	:	36.3	:	:	116.7
Wage adjusted labour productivity (%)	135.0	:	154.3	129.5	233.4	129.9	141.8	132.8	:	:	:	191.5	:	:	264.1
Personnel costs as a share of total operating costs (%)	16.6	26.6	24.6	15.8	11.8	10.3	11.8	12.6	:	16.2	:	14.2	:	:	16.3

(1) 1996.

Source: Eurostat (SBS, EBT, COMEXT)

Table 6.14

Manufacture of paints, varnishes and similar coatings, printing ink and mastics (NACE Rev. 1 24.3)

Production related indicators in the EU (1)

	1989	1990	1991	1992	1993	1994	1995	1996	1997	1998	1999
Number of persons employed (thousands)	:	:	:	:	169.0	168.8	148.1	:	152.2	154.1	154.3
Production (million ECU)	:	:	:	:	24,058	26,014	24,013	:	:	:	:
Domestic producer price index (1995=100)	:	85.6	90.6	92.1	94.9	96.2	100.0	102.7	103.1	104.3	105.2
Value added (million ECU)	:	:	:	:	8,272	8,711	7,619	:	:	:	:

(1) Technically, data before 01/01/1999 are in ECU and after this date in euro. However, as the conversion rate was 1 ECU =1 EUR, for practical purposes the two terms can be used interchangeably.

Table 6.15

Manufacture of paints, varnishes and similar coatings, printing ink and mastics (NACE Rev. 1 24.3)

Trade related indicators in the EU (1)

	1989	1990	1991	1992	1993	1994	1995	1996	1997	1998	1999
Exports (million EUR)	1,657	1,710	1,748	1,933	2,150	2,478	2,788	3,203	3,708	3,792	3,988
Imports (million EUR)	458	470	508	537	541	601	669	710	839	895	968
Trade balance (million EUR)	1,199	1,240	1,240	1,395	1,609	1,877	2,119	2,493	2,869	2,897	3,020
Cover ratio (%)	361.8	364.0	344.3	359.6	397.6	412.2	416.7	451.3	441.9	423.6	411.8

(1) Technically, data before 01/01/1999 are in ECU and after this date in euro. However, as the conversion rate was 1 ECU =1 EUR, for practical purposes the two terms can be used interchangeably.

Table 6.16

Manufacture of paints, varnishes and similar coatings, printing ink and mastics (NACE Rev. 1 24.3)

Production related indicators, 1997

	B	DK	D	EL (1)	E	F	IRL	I (1)	L	NL	A	P	FIN	S	UK
Number of persons employed (thousands)	4.3	3.0	46.7	1.4	15.3	18.8	0.7	16.4	:	:	3.0	4.5	1.9	3.4	27.2
Production (million ECU)	1,517	477	7,971	143	2,282	3,325	100	3,489	:	1,400	405	397	424	670	4,221
Value added (million ECU)	341	140	2,897	42	736	1,078	35	1,085	:	474	155	137	151	223	1,434
Gross operating surplus (million ECU)	119.3	38.2	823.8	18.9	319.7	300.2	12.9	477.6	:	184.4	42.2	64.9	85.1	88.0	574.8

(1) 1996.

Table 6.17

Manufacture of paints, varnishes and similar coatings, printing ink and mastics (NACE Rev. 1 24.3)

Trade related indicators, 1999

	B	DK	D	EL	E	F	IRL	I	L	NL	A	P	FIN	S	UK
Exports (million EUR)	849	232	3,121	22	577	937	24	879	17	785	239	47	172	352	1,198
Imports (million EUR)	521	213	821	118	407	983	132	625	43	445	347	217	136	256	808
Trade balance (million EUR)	328	19	2,300	-95	169	-45	-108	254	-25	340	-108	-170	36	96	390
Cover ratio (%)	163.0	108.9	380.0	19.0	141.5	95.4	18.3	140.5	40.8	176.3	68.8	21.5	126.6	137.3	148.2

Table 6.18

Manufacture of paints, varnishes and similar coatings, printing ink and mastics (NACE Rev. 1 24.3)

Labour related indicators, 1997

	B	DK (1)	D	EL (2)	E	F	IRL	I (2)	L	NL	A	P	FIN	S	UK
Unit personnel costs (thousand ECU per employee)	52.5	37.5	44.5	16.3	27.6	41.4	33.2	37.7	:	:	37.9	16.2	34.8	39.4	31.8
Social charges as a share of personnel costs (%)	42.9	5.7	23.8	30.0	25.0	43.4	24.4	47.8	:	18.8	29.6	35.8	27.5	42.8	15.0
Apparent labour productivity (thousand ECU/pers. empl.)	79.7	47.1	62.0	29.5	48.2	57.4	52.1	66.1	:	:	51.9	30.4	78.3	65.1	52.8
Wage adjusted labour productivity (%)	152.0	141.0	139.4	180.8	174.9	138.6	156.7	175.4	:	:	137.1	187.8	224.9	165.2	165.9
Personnel costs as a share of total operating costs (%)	15.6	20.7	25.1	19.7	19.0	22.7	22.2	19.2	:	20.6	25.6	20.5	15.5	19.7	21.1

(1) Unit personnel costs and wage adjusted labour productivity, 1996; (2) 1996.

Source: Eurostat (SBS, EBT, COMEXT)

Table 6.19

Manufacture of pharmaceuticals, medicinal chemicals and botanical products (NACE Rev. 1 24.4)

Production related indicators in the EU (1)

	1989	1990	1991	1992	1993	1994	1995	1996	1997	1998	1999
Number of persons employed (thousands)	425.4	440.5	456.5	465.7	455.8	443.1	454.8	:	462.9	468.5	475.3
Production (million EUR)	55,650	60,383	68,329	74,357	75,451	78,813	86,287	:	102,895	104,621	107,405
Domestic producer price index (1995=100)	:	:	:	:	:	:	100.0	102.2	103.4	104.3	105.8
Value added (million EUR)	22,554	24,096	27,107	29,394	30,487	32,207	33,997	:	38,338	40,152	41,114

(1) Technically, data before 01/01/1999 are in ECU and after this date in euro. However, as the conversion rate was 1 ECU =1 EUR, for practical purposes the two terms can be used interchangeably.

Table 6.20

Manufacture of pharmaceuticals, medicinal chemicals and botanical products (NACE Rev. 1 24.4)

Trade related indicators in the EU (1)

	1989	1990	1991	1992	1993	1994	1995	1996	1997	1998	1999
Exports (million EUR)	9,189	9,592	10,961	12,500	15,334	17,348	18,766	20,104	25,338	29,592	33,330
Imports (million EUR)	4,921	5,443	6,219	7,096	7,919	9,004	9,835	11,296	12,886	14,785	17,090
Trade balance (million EUR)	4,268	4,149	4,742	5,404	7,415	8,344	8,932	8,808	12,452	14,807	16,241
Cover ratio (%)	186.7	176.2	176.2	176.2	193.6	192.7	190.8	178.0	196.6	200.1	195.0

(1) Technically, data before 01/01/1999 are in ECU and after this date in euro. However, as the conversion rate was 1 ECU =1 EUR, for practical purposes the two terms can be used interchangeably.

Table 6.21

Manufacture of pharmaceuticals, medicinal chemicals and botanical products (NACE Rev. 1 24.4)

Production related indicators, 1997

	B	DK	D	EL (1)	E	F	IRL	I (1)	L	NL	A	P	FIN	S	UK
Number of persons employed (thousands)	14.1	17.0	111.2	5.4	36.5	88.4	6.9	73.0	:	:	7.7	8.1	6.2	16.0	66.0
Production (million ECU)	4,153	2,983	19,397	511	6,478	23,931	2,217	15,046	:	4,681	1,596	979	745	4,232	13,711
Value added (million ECU)	1,576	1,351	7,527	106	2,405	7,302	1,207	5,505	:	1,178	671	363	355	1,736	6,452
Gross operating surplus (million ECU)	814.7	673.0	1,916.9	-12.3	1,011.0	2,879.2	989.7	2,147.4	:	628.5	320.7	178.3	179.2	907.3	3,714.5

(1) 1996.

Table 6.22

Manufacture of pharmaceuticals, medicinal chemicals and botanical products (NACE Rev. 1 24.4)

Trade related indicators, 1999

	B	DK	D	EL	E	F	IRL	I	L	NL	A	P	FIN	S	UK
Exports (million EUR)	6,721	2,704	14,784	160	1,868	10,842	6,609	5,791	19	4,545	1,913	234	281	3,808	10,304
Imports (million EUR)	5,424	927	8,504	1,076	3,465	8,343	1,461	6,411	161	4,657	2,296	935	718	1,390	7,771
Trade balance (million EUR)	1,298	1,776	6,280	-917	-1,597	2,498	5,148	-620	-142	-112	-383	-701	-437	2,418	2,533
Cover ratio (%)	123.9	291.6	173.8	14.9	53.9	129.9	452.5	90.3	11.8	97.6	83.3	25.0	39.2	273.9	132.6

Table 6.23

Manufacture of pharmaceuticals, medicinal chemicals and botanical products (NACE Rev. 1 24.4)

Labour related indicators, 1997

	B	DK (1)	D	EL (2)	E	F	IRL	I (2)	L	NL	A	P	FIN	S	UK
Unit personnel costs (thousand ECU per employee)	54.2	48.1	50.5	21.8	35.0	50.0	31.5	46.2	:	:	45.3	23.0	29.9	51.8	41.5
Social charges as a share of personnel costs (%)	35.1	7.8	27.2	30.0	23.6	44.9	21.4	46.0	:	22.7	29.2	35.5	25.5	49.2	15.7
Apparent labour productivity (thousand ECU/pers. empl.)	111.7	79.3	67.7	19.6	65.9	82.6	175.1	75.5	:	:	86.8	45.0	57.6	108.5	97.8
Wage adjusted labour productivity (%)	206.3	168.2	134.1	89.6	188.5	165.1	555.4	163.2	:	:	191.6	195.4	192.9	209.6	235.5
Personnel costs as a share of total operating costs (%)	22.9	29.0	28.5	19.0	19.7	19.8	17.2	22.6	:	12.3	22.1	19.8	26.6	24.3	23.9

(1) Unit personnel costs and wage adjusted labour productivity, 1996; (2) 1996.

Source: Eurostat (SBS, EBT, COMEXT)

Table 6.24

Manufacture of soap and detergents, cleaning and polishing preparations, perfumes and toilet preparations (NACE Rev. 1 24.5)

Production related indicators in the EU (1)

	1989	1990	1991	1992	1993	1994	1995	1996	1997	1998	1999
Number of persons employed (thousands)	245.1	247.4	245.3	238.4	232.1	223.9	233.5	:	220.6	227.5	224.4
Production (million ECU)	35,703	37,692	40,408	42,097	42,384	42,904	47,037	:	:	:	:
Domestic producer price index (1995=100)	:	89.6	90.5	94.0	96.9	98.3	100.0	100.8	101.3	102.2	103.3
Value added (million ECU)	10,520	11,196	12,032	12,367	12,761	12,549	13,595	:	:	:	:

(1) Technically, data before 01/01/1999 are in ECU and after this date in euro. However, as the conversion rate was 1 ECU =1 EUR, for practical purposes the two terms can be used interchangeably.

Table 6.25

Manufacture of soap and detergents, cleaning and polishing preparations, perfumes and toilet preparations (NACE Rev. 1 24.5)

Trade related indicators in the EU (1)

	1989	1990	1991	1992	1993	1994	1995	1996	1997	1998	1999
Exports (million EUR)	3,491	3,701	3,906	4,384	4,955	5,747	6,258	7,007	7,811	7,812	8,176
Imports (million EUR)	740	792	949	1,054	1,169	1,358	1,518	1,597	1,744	1,953	2,318
Trade balance (million EUR)	2,751	2,909	2,957	3,330	3,786	4,389	4,740	5,411	6,067	5,859	5,857
Cover ratio (%)	471.8	467.3	411.5	415.9	424.0	423.1	412.2	438.9	448.0	400.0	352.6

(1) Technically, data before 01/01/1999 are in ECU and after this date in euro. However, as the conversion rate was 1 ECU =1 EUR, for practical purposes the two terms can be used interchangeably.

Table 6.26

Manufacture of soap and detergents, cleaning and polishing preparations, perfumes and toilet preparations (NACE Rev. 1 24.5)

Production related indicators, 1997

	B	DK	D	EL (1)	E	F	IRL	I (1)	L	NL	A	P	FIN	S	UK
Number of persons employed (thousands)	5.3	1.7	52.1	4.2	23.4	51.4	3.1	27.4	:	:	1.8	4.1	0.6	1.1	41.0
Production (million ECU)	1,504	315	9,895	604	3,749	13,291	543	7,701	:	1,052	298	477	58	178	8,356
Value added (million ECU)	380	91	3,083	171	1,005	3,353	251	1,866	:	321	92	116	21	61	2,420
Gross operating surplus (million ECU)	156.9	34.0	693.5	72.7	348.2	1,118.2	171.9	781.4	:	127.3	16.0	49.0	6.4	18.8	1,147.8

(1) 1996.

Table 6.27

Manufacture of soap and detergents, cleaning and polishing preparations, perfumes and toilet preparations (NACE Rev. 1 24.5)

Trade related indicators, 1999

	B	DK	D	EL	E	F	IRL	I	L	NL	A	P	FIN	S	UK
Exports (million EUR)	1,717	357	4,013	121	1,224	6,536	611	1,877	93	978	224	83	82	314	3,222
Imports (million EUR)	1,291	535	2,416	344	942	2,154	457	1,474	97	1,111	564	399	236	503	2,272
Trade balance (million EUR)	426	-178	1,598	-223	282	4,382	154	403	-4	-133	-340	-317	-154	-189	950
Cover ratio (%)	133.0	66.7	166.1	35.1	129.9	303.4	133.7	127.4	95.6	88.0	39.8	20.7	34.7	62.5	141.8

Table 6.28

Manufacture of soap and detergents, cleaning and polishing preparations, perfumes and toilet preparations (NACE Rev. 1 24.5)

Labour related indicators, 1997

	B	DK (1)	D	EL (2)	E	F	IRL	I (2)	L	NL	A	P	FIN	S	UK
Unit personnel costs (thousand ECU per employee)	42.6	36.4	46.0	23.3	26.9	43.5	25.8	39.9	:	:	42.1	16.8	27.1	38.2	31.1
Social charges as a share of personnel costs (%)	40.1	6.0	29.4	30.1	24.2	40.7	17.3	46.9	:	15.8	34.4	34.9	25.6	42.4	10.8
Apparent labour productivity (thousand ECU/pers. empl.)	71.3	52.3	59.2	40.4	43.0	65.2	82.0	68.1	:	:	50.8	28.6	37.0	55.1	59.0
Wage adjusted labour productivity (%)	167.5	161.9	128.8	173.4	159.8	150.0	318.1	170.4	:	:	120.7	170.2	136.4	144.3	189.6
Personnel costs as a share of total operating costs (%)	16.6	18.0	23.1	16.6	16.4	17.5	20.2	14.7	:	17.0	20.4	13.9	23.5	23.7	15.7

(1) Unit personnel costs and wage adjusted labour productivity, 1996; (2) 1996.

Source: Eurostat (SBS, EBT, COMEXT)

Table 6.29

Manufacture of other chemical products (NACE Rev. 1 24.6)
Production related indicators in the EU (1)

	1989	1990	1991	1992	1993	1994	1995	1996	1997	1998	1999
Number of persons employed (thousands)	:	:	:	:	176.3	177.9	164.1	174.3	166.0	171.4	168.8
Production (million EUR)	:	:	:	:	28,098	30,361	31,846	35,016	36,425	36,622	37,819
Domestic producer price index (1995=100)	:	95.7	97.6	97.7	97.5	97.6	100.0	100.1	100.4	100.4	100.2
Value added (million EUR)	:	:	:	:	10,262	11,011	10,850	12,170	12,189	12,417	12,694

(1) Technically, data before 01/01/1999 are in ECU and after this date in euro. However, as the conversion rate was 1 ECU =1 EUR, for practical purposes the two terms can be used interchangeably.

Table 6.30

Manufacture of other chemical products (NACE Rev. 1 24.6)
Trade related indicators in the EU (1)

	1989	1990	1991	1992	1993	1994	1995	1996	1997	1998	1999
Exports (million EUR)	6,563	6,718	7,110	7,357	8,943	9,890	10,558	11,729	13,653	13,294	14,540
Imports (million EUR)	5,775	6,191	6,580	6,688	6,309	6,775	6,814	7,245	8,088	8,457	9,267
Trade balance (million EUR)	788	527	530	669	2,633	3,115	3,743	4,484	5,566	4,838	5,273
Cover ratio (%)	113.6	108.5	108.1	110.0	141.7	146.0	154.9	161.9	168.8	157.2	156.9

(1) Technically, data before 01/01/1999 are in ECU and after this date in euro. However, as the conversion rate was 1 ECU =1 EUR, for practical purposes the two terms can be used interchangeably.

Table 6.31

Manufacture of other chemical products (NACE Rev. 1 24.6)
Production related indicators, 1997

	B	DK	D	EL (1)	E	F	IRL	I (1)	L	NL	A	P	FIN	S	UK
Number of persons employed (thousands)	9.7	2.4	47.0	0.7	12.3	28.6	:	19.1	:	:	1.6	2.1	1.2	2.4	31.6
Production (million ECU)	2,879	313	9,127	62	1,905	5,683	:	5,196	:	2,510	285	169	213	440	6,118
Value added (million ECU)	879	135	3,266	3	614	1,769	:	1,564	:	821	107	48	74	159	2,343
Gross operating surplus (million ECU)	295.1	42.8	1,055.1	-11.1	243.0	499.3	:	730.2	:	422.3	34.3	18.8	31.5	53.3	1,234.1

(1) 1996.

Table 6.32

Manufacture of other chemical products (NACE Rev. 1 24.6)
Trade related indicators, 1999

	B	DK	D	EL	E	F	IRL	I	L	NL	A	P	FIN	S	UK
Exports (million EUR)	3,631	382	9,597	74	782	5,851	3,848	2,160	215	3,723	583	122	213	645	5,535
Imports (million EUR)	2,291	618	5,717	417	1,976	5,008	594	3,622	196	2,813	991	450	480	909	4,416
Trade balance (million EUR)	1,339	-236	3,880	-343	-1,194	843	3,254	-1,462	18	909	-408	-328	-267	-265	1,119
Cover ratio (%)	158.5	61.8	167.9	17.8	39.6	116.8	647.7	59.6	109.2	132.3	58.8	27.1	44.3	70.9	125.3

Table 6.33

Manufacture of other chemical products (NACE Rev. 1 24.6)
Labour related indicators, 1997

	B	DK (1)	D	EL (2)	E	F	IRL	I (2)	L	NL	A	P	FIN	S	UK
Unit personnel costs (thousand ECU per employee)	60.1	43.4	47.1	19.4	29.2	44.4	:	44.5	:	:	46.6	14.7	36.2	43.1	35.4
Social charges as a share of personnel costs (%)	41.9	5.9	25.4	28.4	25.0	43.6	:	47.2	:	18.9	31.5	38.6	30.2	47.8	14.9
Apparent labour productivity (thousand ECU/pers. empl.)	90.3	56.5	69.5	4.0	49.9	61.9	:	82.0	:	:	68.6	22.8	60.5	64.9	74.3
Wage adjusted labour productivity (%)	150.2	147.6	147.6	20.7	170.5	139.3	:	184.5	:	:	147.2	154.7	167.3	150.6	209.6
Personnel costs as a share of total operating costs (%)	22.7	31.8	23.9	24.5	17.3	22.7	:	13.9	:	17.8	22.3	18.3	21.2	21.3	19.9

(1) Unit personnel costs and wage adjusted labour productivity, 1996; (2) 1996.

Source: Eurostat (SBS, EBT, COMEXT)

Table 6.34

Manufacture of man-made fibres (NACE Rev. 1 24.7)

Production related indicators in the EU (1)

	1989	1990	1991	1992	1993	1994	1995	1996	1997	1998	1999
Number of persons employed (thousands)	81.9	77.4	74.3	68.4	63.9	60.3	:	:	:	:	:
Production (million EUR)	9,850	9,162	8,730	8,737	8,402	9,325	:	10,743	12,685	12,442	11,754
Domestic producer price index (1995=100)	:	:	:	:	:	:	100.0	96.5	94.1	92.8	88.6
Value added (million EUR)	3,172	3,053	2,917	2,891	2,652	3,011	:	3,157	3,873	3,748	3,551

(1) Technically, data before 01/01/1999 are in ECU and after this date in euro. However, as the conversion rate was 1 ECU =1 EUR, for practical purposes the two terms can be used interchangeably.

Table 6.35

Manufacture of man-made fibres (NACE Rev. 1 24.7)

Trade related indicators in the EU (1)

	1989	1990	1991	1992	1993	1994	1995	1996	1997	1998	1999
Exports (million EUR)	1,217	1,083	1,103	1,027	1,076	1,169	1,090	1,012	821	788	830
Imports (million EUR)	1,280	1,290	1,245	1,252	1,115	1,393	1,601	1,538	1,867	2,127	1,932
Trade balance (million EUR)	-63	-207	-143	-226	-39	-225	-512	-527	-1,046	-1,339	-1,102
Cover ratio (%)	95.1	83.9	88.5	82.0	96.5	83.9	68.1	65.8	44.0	37.1	43.0

(1) Technically, data before 01/01/1999 are in ECU and after this date in euro. However, as the conversion rate was 1 ECU =1 EUR, for practical purposes the two terms can be used interchangeably.

Table 6.36

Manufacture of man-made fibres (NACE Rev. 1 24.7)

Production related indicators, 1997

	B	DK	D	EL (1)	E	F	IRL	I (1)	L	NL	A	P	FIN (1)	S	UK
Number of persons employed (thousands)	2.7	1.4	24.5	0.9	5.8	2.8	:	11.9	:	:	:	0.7	0.6	:	5.3
Production (million ECU)	992	242	4,669	54	849	599	:	2,276	:	741	:	128	90	:	1,218
Value added (million ECU)	189	82	1,532	16	257	128	:	623	:	250	:	29	17	:	438
Gross operating surplus (million ECU)	88.5	29.5	451.7	0.5	81.7	14.6	:	215.0	:	56.5	:	14.6	-2.5	:	241.9

(1) 1996.

Table 6.37

Manufacture of man-made fibres (NACE Rev. 1 24.7)

Trade related indicators, 1999

	B	DK	D	EL	E	F	IRL	I	L	NL	A	P	FIN	S	UK
Exports (million EUR)	522	106	561	30	384	571	206	688	9	187	63	53	76	44	327
Imports (million EUR)	704	113	1,162	82	596	1,053	70	1,484	123	684	225	200	79	95	947
Trade balance (million EUR)	-182	-7	-602	-52	-212	-482	136	-796	-114	-497	-162	-147	-3	-52	-619
Cover ratio (%)	74.2	93.9	48.2	36.7	64.5	54.2	293.8	46.4	7.4	27.4	28.2	26.7	96.0	45.7	34.6

Table 6.38

Manufacture of man-made fibres (NACE Rev. 1 24.7)

Labour related indicators, 1997

	B	DK	D	EL (1)	E	F	IRL	I (1)	L	NL	A	P	FIN (1)	S	UK
Unit personnel costs (thousand ECU per employee)	37.5	:	44.0	17.0	28.8	40.2	:	34.3	:	:	:	21.6	35.0	:	36.8
Social charges as a share of personnel costs (%)	41.1	7.1	26.5	29.9	30.6	72.0	:	48.1	:	22.5	:	41.2	32.2	:	14.1
Apparent labour productivity (thousand ECU/pers. empl.)	69.8	57.6	62.5	17.6	44.4	45.4	:	52.2	:	:	:	43.2	30.0	:	82.0
Wage adjusted labour productivity (%)	186.2	:	141.8	103.3	154.5	112.8	:	152.0	:	:	:	199.7	85.7	:	222.9
Personnel costs as a share of total operating costs (%)	11.1	24.9	22.3	30.6	20.2	16.8	:	19.1	:	28.0	:	12.7	21.0	:	18.6

(1) 1996.

Source: Eurostat (SBS, EBT, COMEXT)

Table 6.39

Manufacture of rubber products (NACE Rev. 1 25.1)

Production related indicators in the EU (1)

	1989	1990	1991	1992	1993	1994	1995	1996	1997	1998	1999
Number of persons employed (thousands)	359.7	358.0	345.2	331.4	309.0	300.1	301.4	:	294.4	296.2	293.8
Production (million EUR)	26,128	26,587	27,021	27,676	25,942	28,191	31,443	:	33,355	34,102	34,634
Domestic producer price index (1995=100)	:	90.3	92.3	95.9	96.7	97.0	100.0	102.0	100.8	99.7	99.2
Value added (million EUR)	11,676	11,633	12,085	12,338	11,700	12,608	13,293	:	13,756	14,246	14,272

(1) Technically, data before 01/01/1999 are in ECU and after this date in euro. However, as the conversion rate was 1 ECU =1 EUR, for practical purposes the two terms can be used interchangeably.

Table 6.40

Manufacture of rubber products (NACE Rev. 1 25.1)

Trade related indicators in the EU (1)

	1989	1990	1991	1992	1993	1994	1995	1996	1997	1998	1999
Exports (million EUR)	3,243	2,981	3,013	3,151	3,461	3,558	3,694	4,154	4,628	5,006	5,149
Imports (million EUR)	2,193	2,238	2,450	2,784	2,809	3,198	3,781	4,114	4,482	5,218	5,632
Trade balance (million EUR)	1,050	743	563	367	652	360	-87	41	145	-212	-483
Cover ratio (%)	147.9	133.2	123.0	113.2	123.2	111.2	97.7	101.0	103.2	95.9	91.4

(1) Technically, data before 01/01/1999 are in ECU and after this date in euro. However, as the conversion rate was 1 ECU =1 EUR, for practical purposes the two terms can be used interchangeably.

Table 6.41

Manufacture of rubber products (NACE Rev. 1 25.1)

Production related indicators, 1997

	B	DK	D	EL (1)	E	F	IRL	I (1)	L	NL	A	P	FIN	S	UK
Number of persons employed (thousands)	4.3	2.2	79.4	0.7	29.9	67.7	1.8	37.1	1.6	:	4.0	5.1	2.4	6.4	48.4
Production (million ECU)	970	178	9,249	80	2,990	7,732	133	4,491	304	438	491	314	292	786	4,638
Value added (million ECU)	233	82	3,997	21	1,286	3,038	51	1,746	129	177	211	120	138	323	2,085
Gross operating surplus (million ECU)	47.9	11.9	796.5	3.3	388.3	756.0	12.0	617.7	42.6	56.1	52.4	59.2	60.0	111.6	689.0

(1) 1996.

Table 6.42

Manufacture of rubber products (NACE Rev. 1 25.1)

Trade related indicators, 1999

	B	DK	D	EL	E	F	IRL	I	L	NL	A	P	FIN	S	UK
Exports (million EUR)	1,253	156	4,638	23	1,856	3,882	91	2,313	310	1,064	282	225	186	590	2,050
Imports (million EUR)	1,621	394	4,356	212	1,519	2,467	213	1,973	93	1,454	786	412	254	781	2,365
Trade balance (million EUR)	-368	-238	282	-189	337	1,415	-123	340	218	-389	-503	-188	-68	-191	-314
Cover ratio (%)	77.3	39.6	106.5	10.9	122.2	157.4	42.5	117.2	335.3	73.2	35.9	54.5	73.1	75.5	86.7

Table 6.43

Manufacture of rubber products (NACE Rev. 1 25.1)

Labour related indicators, 1997

	B	DK (1)	D	EL (2)	E	F	IRL	I (2)	L	NL	A	P	FIN	S	UK
Unit personnel costs (thousand ECU per employee)	43.5	34.9	40.3	26.4	27.2	33.7	22.1	30.8	52.5	:	39.7	12.1	33.4	33.2	29.1
Social charges as a share of personnel costs (%)	37.5	5.1	25.4	27.1	28.3	42.4	15.5	50.4	:	17.5	32.9	32.8	27.8	46.7	15.3
Apparent labour productivity (thousand ECU/pers. empl.)	54.1	36.4	50.3	31.3	43.1	44.9	28.8	47.1	78.4	:	52.9	23.6	57.2	50.7	43.1
Wage adjusted labour productivity (%)	124.5	122.1	125.0	118.4	158.3	133.1	130.0	152.6	149.2	:	133.0	194.3	171.2	152.8	147.9
Personnel costs as a share of total operating costs (%)	20.1	41.1	29.4	17.3	26.0	31.4	32.3	25.2	24.6	27.2	26.5	21.5	30.9	30.2	30.3

(1) Unit personnel costs and wage adjusted labour productivity, 1996; (2) 1996.

Source: Eurostat (SBS, EBT, COMEXT)

Table 6.44

Manufacture of plastic products (NACE Rev. 1 25.2)

Production related indicators in the EU (1)

	1989	1990	1991	1992	1993	1994	1995	1996	1997	1998	1999
Number of persons employed (thousands)	788.7	831.9	849.2	837.4	811.3	820.1	844.1	:	893.6	916.9	917.4
Production (million EUR)	70,607	76,165	80,928	82,876	81,639	88,874	99,585	:	113,088	115,856	119,670
Domestic producer price index (1995=100)	:	93.6	92.8	92.7	92.3	92.9	100.0	99.2	98.8	98.2	97.2
Value added (million EUR)	25,281	28,012	30,356	31,533	31,104	33,345	35,027	:	40,079	41,571	43,093

(1) Technically, data before 01/01/1999 are in ECU and after this date in euro. However, as the conversion rate was 1 ECU =1 EUR, for practical purposes the two terms can be used interchangeably.

Table 6.45

Manufacture of plastic products (NACE Rev. 1 25.2)

Trade related indicators in the EU (1)

	1989	1990	1991	1992	1993	1994	1995	1996	1997	1998	1999
Exports (million EUR)	5,184	5,290	5,563	5,895	6,680	7,768	9,219	9,893	11,708	12,299	12,656
Imports (million EUR)	3,610	3,889	4,409	4,636	4,949	5,622	6,301	6,610	7,790	8,373	9,124
Trade balance (million EUR)	1,574	1,401	1,154	1,259	1,731	2,147	2,918	3,283	3,918	3,926	3,532
Cover ratio (%)	143.6	136.0	126.2	127.2	135.0	138.2	146.3	149.7	150.3	146.9	138.7

(1) Technically, data before 01/01/1999 are in ECU and after this date in euro. However, as the conversion rate was 1 ECU =1 EUR, for practical purposes the two terms can be used interchangeably.

Table 6.46

Manufacture of plastic products (NACE Rev. 1 25.2)

Production related indicators, 1997

	B	DK	D	EL (1)	E	F	IRL	I (1)	L	NL	A	P	FIN	S	UK
Number of persons employed (thousands)	21.4	16.7	268.3	6.9	70.7	126.3	8.2	96.8	2.3	:	20.4	16.0	11.2	13.7	180.0
Production (million ECU)	4,640	1,705	33,492	569	7,424	16,174	941	14,625	453	3,806	2,495	1,098	1,317	1,869	19,016
Value added (million ECU)	1,382	730	12,888	166	2,388	5,064	378	4,930	157	1,328	1,006	326	533	690	7,563
Gross operating surplus (million ECU)	547.2	228.4	3,582.7	55.8	886.2	1,241.9	179.5	2,134.4	71.9	539.3	314.1	150.0	238.0	227.7	3,089.3

(1) 1996.

Table 6.47

Manufacture of plastic products (NACE Rev. 1 25.2)

Trade related indicators, 1999

	B	DK	D	EL	E	F	IRL	I	L	NL	A	P	FIN	S	UK
Exports (million EUR)	4,357	1,360	11,307	163	1,544	4,772	504	5,691	434	2,765	2,322	317	517	1,318	4,004
Imports (million EUR)	3,156	1,034	6,891	367	2,099	5,937	812	2,725	225	2,782	1,702	717	525	1,185	4,961
Trade balance (million EUR)	1,201	327	4,416	-204	-555	-1,165	-308	2,966	209	-17	620	-400	-7	134	-957
Cover ratio (%)	138.0	131.6	164.1	44.4	73.5	80.4	62.1	208.8	193.1	99.4	136.4	44.2	98.6	111.3	80.7

Table 6.48

Manufacture of plastic products (NACE Rev. 1 25.2)

Labour related indicators, 1997

	B	DK (1)	D	EL (2)	E	F	IRL	I (2)	L	NL	A	P	FIN	S	UK
Unit personnel costs (thousand ECU per employee)	40.0	35.1	34.7	16.1	21.3	30.3	24.2	29.7	37.1	:	34.0	11.2	28.7	33.8	25.4
Social charges as a share of personnel costs (%)	38.3	5.1	22.5	29.5	27.8	41.0	17.5	49.5	:	15.7	30.1	29.9	27.8	41.0	12.5
Apparent labour productivity (thousand ECU/pers. empl.)	64.5	43.8	48.0	24.1	33.8	40.1	45.8	50.9	68.6	:	49.4	20.4	47.8	50.4	42.0
Wage adjusted labour productivity (%)	161.4	149.6	138.5	149.8	158.7	132.5	189.4	171.6	184.8	:	145.2	182.7	166.4	149.2	165.8
Personnel costs as a share of total operating costs (%)	20.5	31.7	29.3	19.9	20.6	24.5	25.0	21.3	19.7	22.5	29.2	17.8	26.7	26.3	26.5

(1) Unit personnel costs and wage adjusted labour productivity, 1996; (2) 1996.

Source: Eurostat (SBS, EBT, COMEXT)

Non-metallic mineral products (NACE Rev. 1 26)

This chapter includes information on the manufacture of other non-metallic mineral products covered by Division 26 of the NACE Rev. 1 classification. It includes activities which provide building material, such as clay (NACE Rev. 1 26.4) or cement and concrete (NACE Rev. 1 26.5 and 26.6). In addition, other industries such as glass (NACE Rev. 1 26.1) or ceramic products (NACE Rev. 1 26.2 and 26.3) cover a far broader range of products and end-uses. It should be noted that this Division does not cover optical fibre cables, which are part of chapter 11.

The manufacture of non-metallic mineral products transforms items that have generally been mined or quarried into products for use in downstream activities, such as the construction sector, electrical engineering, chemicals, packaging and steel production, as well as consumer goods (such as glass tableware). In 1999, production value of the non-metallic mineral products industry was equal to 137.6 billion EUR across the EU, contributing 3.4% to total manufacturing. In terms of value added, these activities generated 54.7 billion EUR, or 4.5% of the manufacturing total.

There were over one million persons employed in the non-metallic mineral products industry in 1999, which was equal to 4.5% of the EU manufacturing total.

Figure 7.1

Non-metallic mineral products (NACE Rev. 1 26)
Share of total manufacturing value added in the
EU, 1996 (%)

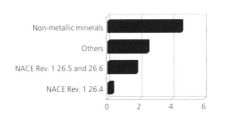

Source: Eurostat (SBS)

Demand closely linked to developments
within the construction sector

The construction sector is a very important downstream market for non-metallic minerals, especially building and civil engineering. In recent years there has been a broad reduction in public spending on civil engineering projects across the Member States, which has resulted in reduced demand for building materials in an already saturated market.

To improve their market position, large EU manufacturers have adopted a strategy to pursue growth through mergers and acquisitions. An alternative strategy for market growth has been to invest in the research and development of new materials. These approaches are all the more necessary as the weight, volume and fragility of many non-metallic mineral products (in relation to their value) often makes it difficult for manufacturers to develop markets outside of their local region (geographical diversification).

The activities covered in this chapter (in terms of NACE Rev. 1) include:

26: manufacture of other non-metallic mineral products;
26.1: manufacture of glass and glass products;
26.2: manufacture of non-refractory ceramic goods other than for construction purposes; manufacture of refractory ceramic products;
26.3: manufacture of ceramic tiles and flags;
26.4: manufacture of bricks, tiles and construction products, in baked clay;
26.5: manufacture of cement, lime and plaster;
26.6: manufacture of articles of concrete, plaster and cement;
26.7: cutting, shaping and finishing of stone;
26.8: manufacture of other non-metallic mineral products.

Table 7.1 _____

Non-metallic mineral products (NACE Rev. 1 26)

Breakdown of turnover and employment by employment size class, 1997 (%)

	Micro (0-9)		Small (10-49)		Medium (50-249)		Large (250+)	
	Turnover (1)	Employment (2)	Turnover (3)	Employment (4)	Turnover (3)	Employment (4)	Turnover (3)	Employment (4)
EU-15	8.8	15.6	20.7	22.6	26.2	23.2	44.2	38.6
B	9.9	17.1	20.8	20.2	19.8	19.0	49.5	43.7
DK	8.5	9.2	22.6	19.7	19.6	19.2	49.2	52.0
D	6.7	12.3	18.4	17.2	23.7	21.1	51.2	49.4
EL	:	:	:	:	:	:	:	:
E	11.9	18.8	27.4	32.4	35.6	28.3	25.1	20.5
F	7.7	12.3	16.1	19.0	20.7	20.4	55.5	48.3
IRL	:	:	18.7	23.7	8.5	31.0	69.2	39.8
I	13.2	23.8	30.3	32.5	28.9	22.3	27.6	21.4
L	:	:	:	:	:	:	:	:
NL	:	:	:	:	:	:	:	:
A	7.0	8.3	16.6	17.1	:	:	:	:
P	8.0	16.3	22.7	30.0	29.5	30.6	39.9	23.1
FIN	8.7	11.6	16.4	17.3	31.4	27.5	43.5	43.6
S	7.2	10.3	14.0	13.6	40.0	32.5	38.7	43.6
UK	9.6	14.2	11.5	11.8	19.5	19.5	59.4	54.4

(1) EU-15, DK, E, F, I, P and S, 1996.
(2) EU-15, DK, F, I, P and S, 1996.
(3) EU-15, DK, E, F, IRL, I, P and S, 1996.
(4) EU-15, DK, F, IRL, I, P and S, 1996.

Source: Eurostat (SME)

No major shifts in the structural composition of the sector

Looking closer at the structure of the non-metallic mineral products industry, data from the lid-1990s suggests that the cement and concrete industry (sub-chapter 7.4) was the principal producer in value terms within the non-metallic mineral products industry, responsible for 40-45% of total output. Clay (sub-chapter 7.3), another building material, was the smallest activity covered in this chapter (with around 5% of output). Stone and other non-metallic mineral products (sub-chapter 7.5) accounted for between 10% and 15%, whilst ceramic products (sub-chapter 7.2) had a sixth of the total and glass (sub-chapter 7.1) in excess of a fifth. Looking at longer time-series (back to the mid-1980s) there were no major changes in the structure of the non-metallic mineral products industry over time.

Supply-side characterised by medium-sized and large enterprises

In 1998 almost one in ten enterprises (9.2%) had no employees, compared to 7.2% in total manufacturing. Whilst the craft nature of some of these industries may explain the higher proportion of enterprises with no employees, large capital investment costs may explain the above average incidence of medium-sized and large enterprises. In 1996, enterprises with 50 or more employees accounted for 4.4% of the enterprises active in the EU non-metallic mineral products industry (compared to 3.9% for total manufacturing).

STRUCTURE AND PERFORMANCE

In the eight years between 1990 and 1998, EU production of non-metallic mineral products rose at a moderate pace (in real terms) from 122.9 billion ECU to 128.0 billion ECU (equivalent to an average increase of 0.5% per annum). This was well below the growth rate for total manufacturing in the EU, which was equal to 2.2% per annum during the same period. Value added declined by 0.1% per annum (again in constant price terms) to 50.4 billion ECU in 1998 (whilst the EU average rose by 1.2% per annum for total manufacturing between the same dates).

Slow growth during the mid-1990s

Looking in more detail at the time-series, the manufacture of non-metallic mineral products recovered slowly from the general economic recession of 1993. Throughout the 1990s, the trend of EU production in constant prices within the non-metallic minerals industry was consistently lower than the corresponding rates of growth for total manufacturing. This may be explained in part by the fact that non-metallic mineral products are a mature industry, relying heavily on the construction sector, which also recorded modest growth in the 1990s. Furthermore, high levels of competition and price elasticity could explain the decline in value added.

Figure 7.2

Non-metallic mineral products (NACE Rev. 1 26)

EU production and value-added in constant prices and employment compared to total manufacturing (1990=100)

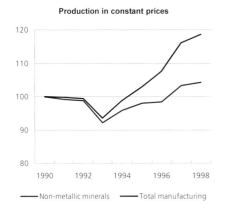

Production in constant prices

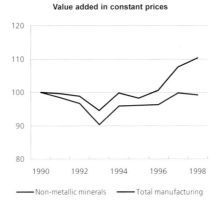

Value added in constant prices

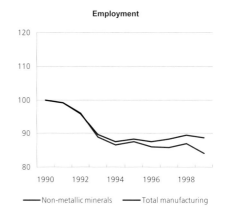

Employment

Source: Eurostat (SBS)

A vital activity in the smaller Member States

Looking at the data by Member State, two distinct trends emerged: whilst the production trend of the non-metallic mineral products industry was subdued in the five largest Member States, high growth rates were recorded in many of the remaining countries during the 1990s. In Portugal production value in constant price terms increased by 4.9% per annum between 1990 and 1997 that was explained to a large extent by an expansion of the manufacture of cement and concrete. In Ireland and Luxembourg, the output of non-metallic mineral products grew by 6.0% and 3.8% per annum between 1990 and 1997 in real terms.

Italy (the second largest producer within the EU) recorded a considerable reduction in output between 1992 and 1995, when production decreased from 22.8 billion ECU to 17.3 billion ECU, whilst Germany reported a decline of 9.8% between 1996 and 1997 to 33.2 billion ECU (following consistent growth in the early and mid-1990s).

LABOUR AND PRODUCTIVITY

Employment in the non-metallic mineral products industry followed the general downward trend displayed within the manufacturing sector as a whole. In the ten years to 1999, the number of persons employed was reduced by 15.5% to 1.05 million persons, a faster rate than the 10.2% reduction for manufacturing as a whole. The reduction in employment was partly the result of restructuring. As a result, between 1990 and 1998 productivity gains and increased automation meant that 16.5% less persons were required in the production process to generate the same output (in constant price terms).

The reductions in employment were not spread evenly over the years: major reductions occurred in the early 1990s (between 1991 and 1993 down by 10.5% in absolute terms) and more recently in 1999 (down by 3.4%, despite growth in production of 5.1%).

An industry dominated by men
in full-time employment...

The proportion of men employed in the EU non-metallic mineral products industry was equal to 77.9% in 1998, which was higher than in manufacturing as a whole (71.8%). The proportion of men employed was particularly high in the Netherlands and Greece (88.8% and 86.4% in 1998). Only Denmark and Portugal reported significantly lower shares (67.3% and 66.8%, both 1999).

Table 7.2

Non-metallic mineral products (NACE Rev. 1 26)

Composition of the labour force, 1999 (%)

	Women (1)	Part-time (2)	Highly-educated (3)
EU-15	22.1	5.5	12.3
B	18.4	:	11.9
DK	32.7	17.0	:
D	26.1	7.8	12.8
EL	13.6	:	:
E	14.3	2.1	16.0
F	22.9	5.2	11.7
IRL	17.7	:	:
I	26.7	3.2	3.1
L	:	:	:
NL	11.2	13.3	:
A	23.1	7.5	:
P	33.2	3.1	:
FIN	25.2	:	26.7
S	:	:	:
UK	24.3	8.4	14.3

(1) EU-15, EL and NL, 1998.
(2) EU-15, DK and P, 1998; NL, 1997.
(3) EU-15 and UK, 1997.

Source: Eurostat (LFS)

Figure 7.3

Non-metallic mineral products (NACE Rev. 1 26)

Apparent labour productivity and unit personnel costs, 1997 (thousand ECU)

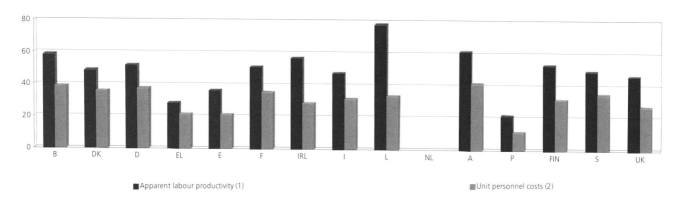

■ Apparent labour productivity (1)   ■ Unit personnel costs (2)

(1) EL and I, 1996; NL, not available.
(2) DK, EL and I, 1996; NL, not available.

Source: Eurostat (SBS)

This industry can also be described as "traditional" in terms of the incidence of part-time employment. In the EU there were only 5.5% of the workforce employed on a part-time basis in 1998 (once more below the manufacturing average of 7.3%). The breakdown by gender showed that 98.1% of men worked with a full-time contract, compared to 81.8% of the women employed.

... with almost half the workforce lowly qualified
The non-metallic mineral products industry employed a relatively high share of persons with a lower level of education. In the EU, 47.5% of those employed had completed a primary or lower secondary education in 1997, underlining the manual nature of the work. This proportion was 8.8 percentage points above the manufacturing average, with the difference being evenly spread between persons employed with an upper secondary education (39.5%) and those employed with a higher education (12.3%), compared to 43.9% and 16.3% for manufacturing as a whole.

A labour-intensive activity with
relatively low unit personnel costs
Apparent labour productivity is an indicator that measures (amongst other things) changes in the production process, including technological innovations. During the 1990s there were improvements reported in apparent labour productivity (gross value added per person employed) within the non-metallic mineral products industry. Between 1989 and 1999 this ratio increased by 16.9 thousand ECU to reach 52.3 thousand EUR per person employed, just above the EU manufacturing average of 51.8 thousand EUR in 1999.

Looking at simple wage adjusted labour productivity, the EU non-metallic mineral products industry was considerably more productive, with a ratio of 163.2% compared to 150.9% for manufacturing in 1999. However, the 1999 figure was largely influenced by a substantial reduction in the number of persons employed and was the highest value reported during the period 1989 to 1999.

The share of personnel costs in production is another way to investigate the structure of costs and allocation of resources within an industry. In the ten years to 1999, this ratio fell by 2.1 percentage points to 24.4%, despite an increase in total personnel costs from 27.6 billion ECU in 1989 to 33.5 billion EUR in 1999. When compared to the same ratio for total manufacturing (20.0% in 1999) the relatively high labour intensity of the non-metallic minerals industry was again apparent.

INTERNATIONAL TRENDS AND FOREIGN TRADE
In 1997 the three Triad economies reported combined output of 282.7 billion ECU. The EU contributed the largest share (45.5%), followed by the USA (29.0%). In the early 1990s, Japan had been the second largest producer in the Triad. However, with slow growth in the ceramic goods, stone and to a less extent cement industries, Japan reported a diminishing share of total Triad production (down by 3.2 percentage points to 25.5% between 1989 and 1997).

EU accounted for more than half of those employed
Employment in the non-metallic mineral products industry fell at an average annual rate of 0.9% in the Triad between 1987 and 1997. The losses reported in the EU were at a faster rate, down by 1.2% per annum on average. In 1997, European manufacturers employed 52.9% of the 2.02 million persons employed in the Triad (compared to 54.5% in 1987). This high share may be partly explained by the relatively low apparent labour productivity in the EU (48.0 thousand ECU in 1997): as manufacturers in Japan reported 90 thousand ECU of value added per person employed and the corresponding ratio in the USA was 80 thousand ECU.

Non-metallic mineral products (NACE Rev. 1 26)
International comparison of production, value added and employment

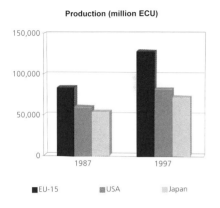

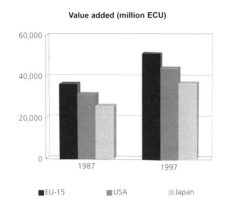

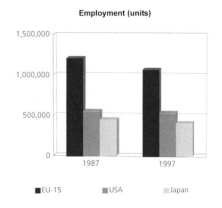

Source: Eurostat (SBS)

EU trade balance increases, although
imports grow at a faster pace

The EU was a net exporter of non-metallic mineral products during the 1990s, with the trade balance increasing from 5.6 billion ECU in 1989 to 7.0 billion EUR by 1999. However, the cover ratio (exports divided by imports) showed that imports into the EU grew at a faster pace than exports to non-Community countries, as the ratio dropped from 298.7% in 1989 to 198.5% by 1999.

The USA was the only Triad member to report a trade deficit, with imports exceeded exports by 5.5 billion ECU in 1998 and a cover ratio of 46.5%. Compared to the other two Triad economies, the EU exported a relatively large amount of non-metallic mineral products, some 2.0% of total manufacturing exports in 1998. The proportion of Japanese non-metallic mineral products in total manufacturing exports was just 1.1%, still higher than in the USA (0.9%).

Intensified trade with Eastern Europe

Over the ten-year period 1989 to 1999, external trade of non-metallic mineral products increased. EU manufacturers faced increasing imports, to a large extent of mass and low-value products. Between 1989 and 1999 imports from China rose by nearly 700% to reach 800.5 million EUR, with China becoming the second largest origin of EU imports. During the same period Eastern European countries also increased their respective shares, for example Polish imports increased five-fold to reach 487.2 million EUR in 1999.

At the same time EU producers also looked to Eastern Europe as a developing export market. EU exports to Poland increased ten-fold between 1989 and 1999 to reach 740.9 million EUR, whilst those to the Czech Republic grew six-fold to reach 369.2 million EUR.

Non-metallic mineral products (NACE Rev. 1 26)
Destination of EU exports, 1999 (%)

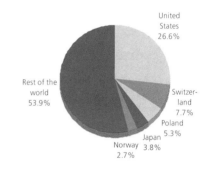

Source: Eurostat (COMEXT)

Non-metallic mineral products (NACE Rev. 1 26)
Origin of EU imports, 1999 (%)

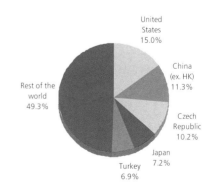

Source: Eurostat (COMEXT)

SUB-CHAPTER 7.1
GLASS (NACE Rev. 1 26.1)

The glass industry covers the manufacture of flat glass, including mirrors (NACE Rev. 1 26.11 and 26.12); hollow glass, such as bottles and glasses (NACE Rev. 1 26.13); glass fibres (NACE Rev. 1 26.14); and specialised glass products for laboratories, clocks and watches, imitation jewellery or rods and tubes (NACE Rev. 1 26.15). The data presented excludes woven fabrics made of glass (chapter 4), as well as optical fibres for data transmission (chapter 11).

The EU glass industry produced goods to the value of 27.7 billion ECU in 1995, which equated to a quarter of the total output of non-metallic mineral products.

Increased competitive pressure

Glass is a mature industry, which faces competition from low-cost producing countries, as well as from substitute materials such as plastics and metals in the container glass sector. As a result, there is permanent pressure on glass manufacturers to reduce costs, develop new markets and innovate new products. The construction sector, the food and beverages industry, transport equipment and electrical engineering are the main downstream industries for glass products.

Figure 7.7

Glass (NACE Rev. 1 26.1)

Production and export specialisation (%)

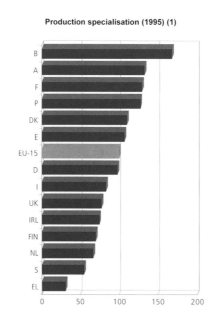

Production specialisation (1995) (1)

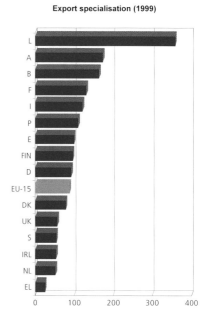

Export specialisation (1999)

(1) L, not available.

Source: Eurostat (SBS, COMEXT)

Box 7.1

Recycled glass has become an increasingly important raw material, which has helped reduce both energy consumption and production times in the glass industry. In 1998, there were 7.6 million tonnes of container glass collected in the EU (excluding Luxembourg), 5.3% more than in 1997.

Contrary to the general upward trend, Austria and Denmark reported falling volumes of collected glass (down by 6.0% and 4.8% in 1998). Despite this decline, Austria still reported the highest recycling rate in the EU (86% in 1998)[1]. At the other extreme Greece and the United Kingdom reported recycling rates as low as 27% and 24% respectively (although the United Kingdom recorded a 7.9% increase in collected glass in 1997 (equal to 441 thousand tonnes).

(1) The second highest rate in Europe behind Switzerland (91%).

Figure 7.8

Recycling rates for glass, 1998 (%)

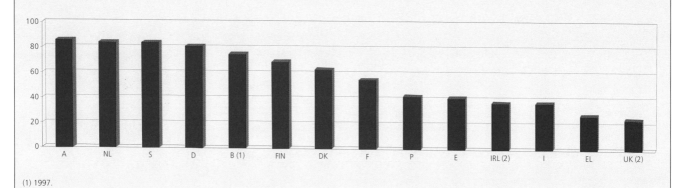

(1) 1997.
(2) Estimate.

Source: FEVE

Within the Member States, the highest production specialisation rate for the glass industry was recorded in Belgium (167.7%), with glass output equal to 2.2 billion ECU in 1997 (or 1.5% of the domestic manufacturing total). In Austria the corresponding share was 1.2%, whilst amongst the larger Member States, France was the most specialised (129.8%), the glass industry representing 1.0% of total French manufacturing output in 1997.

STRUCTURE AND PERFORMANCE

In the five years to 1997 the glass industry in the EU[2] saw its production rise by 3.8% per annum in real terms, a faster pace than the manufacturing average (3.2% per annum) and well ahead of the figure for non-metallic mineral products (0.9% per annum).

---

(2) EL, IRL, I, L and A, no data available.

Figure 7.9

Glass (NACE Rev. 1 26.1)

International comparison of production in constant prices and employment (1990=100)

Production in constant prices

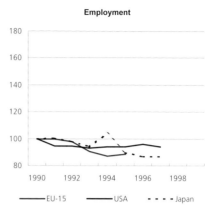

Employment

Source: Eurostat (SBS)

Box 7.2

In 1998 the European glass industry produced 27.9 million tonnes of glass (2.2% more than in 1997). Container glass contributed the largest share with more than 60% of total glass output in 1998 (17.7 million tonnes, up by 2.1%).

Over the period 1990 to 1998 (not taking account of changes in EU membership), glass fibres and technical glassware were the fastest growing sectors, with average growth rates of 3.9% and 8.8% per annum in volume terms. The slowest growing sub-sector was that of glass tableware. EU production rose at an average rate of 0.6% per annum between 1990 and 1998 and even fell by 2.0% in volume terms in 1998 (compared to a year before). The competitive nature of this sector was evident, as apparent consumption of glass tableware rose at an average annual rate of 2.0% between 1990 and 1998 (1.4 percentage points above the corresponding figure for production, the largest difference recorded for any glass sector).

Figure 7.10

Annual average growth rates of apparent consumption and production for selected glass products within the EU, 1990-1998 (%)

Source: CPIV

LABOUR AND PRODUCTIVITY

In 1995 there were 255.2 thousand persons employed in the glass industry. Individual Member State data for 1997 indicated that there was a continuation of the decline in employment levels across the EU. Between 1992 and 1997 the number of persons employed decreased in Germany by 4.1% per annum, whilst Finland was the only Member State to report substantial growth, with employment increasing by 5.2% per annum[3].

The share of personnel costs in total operating costs was estimated to be 31.5% in the EU glass industry in 1997, higher than the non-metallic mineral products average of 27.6% and considerably above the EU manufacturing average of 21.3%.

(3) IRL, employment grew at an annual average rate of 0.3%; EL, I, L and NL, no data available.

INTERNATIONAL TRENDS AND FOREIGN TRADE

In 1995 total glass industry production reached 58.3 billion ECU in the Triad. EU output was nearly twice as high as in either the USA or Japan. In terms of employment the EU's share was even higher, accounting for 56.6% of the 450.7 thousand persons employed in the Triad in 1995.

In the ten years to 1999, EU imports from non-Community countries increased by 150.6% to reach 2.8 billion EUR, whilst EU exports grew by 69.0% to 4.2 billion EUR.

Increased imports from China and Eastern Europe
Changes in the ranking of the EU's main trading partners within the glass industry reflected increased competition from low-cost countries. Between 1989 and 1999 imports from Eastern European countries more than doubled, whilst imports of glass from China increased by more than 700%.

Figure 7.11

Glass (NACE Rev. 1 26.1)
Destination of EU exports, 1999 (%)

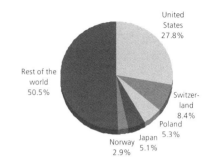

Source: Eurostat (COMEXT)

Figure 7.12

Glass (NACE Rev. 1 26.1)
Origin of EU imports, 1999 (%)

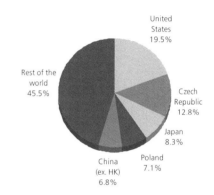

Source: Eurostat (COMEXT)

SUB-CHAPTER 7.2
CERAMIC GOODS
(NACE Rev. 1 26.2 AND 26.3)

The NACE Rev. 1 classification divides the manufacture of ceramic goods between those used for construction purposes, such as tiles and flags for walls, hearths and paving (NACE Rev. 1 26.3) and those used for other purposes (NACE Rev. 1 26.2). In this latter Group are a diverse range of products including tableware, sanitaryware, ornaments, specialised technical products used in laboratories, as well as refractory products (such as bricks and mortars).

In 1999 production of ceramic goods in the EU reached 22.8 billion EUR, which equated 0.6% of total manufacturing output or 16.6% of the total for non-metallic mineral products. The major downstream industries for these goods is the construction sector (tiles, refractory bricks or sanitary fixtures), whilst other products are sold direct to consumers and the hotel and catering trade (ornaments and tableware). Most of these product markets are characterised by fairly static demand and increasing competition from low-cost imports. Higher-end European manufacturers (particularly of tableware) tend to rely on design and brand image to maintain their market share, with relatively low price elasticity.

Product innovation

Through the introduction of new material properties, ceramics have become a leading-edge industry in terms of technological development, resulting in the opening-up of new markets beyond the more traditional, mature markets outlined above. Advanced ceramics are now used in the automotive industry, electrical engineering industry, as well as for medical equipment.

High production specialisation
in Portugal, Spain and Italy

Italy had the largest ceramics industry in the EU in 1996, when production amounted to 5.9 billion ECU (compared to 3.8 billion ECU in Germany (1997)). This figure represented 1.2% of domestic manufacturing output in Italy. Higher rates of specialisation were recorded in Portugal and Spain, where in 1997 ceramic goods contributed 1.4% and 1.3% respectively to the domestic manufacturing total. Together, Italy, Portugal and Spain accounted for almost half of total European output of ceramics in the mid-1990s.

Figure 7.13

Ceramic goods (NACE Rev. 1 26.2 and 26.3)
Production and export specialisation (%)

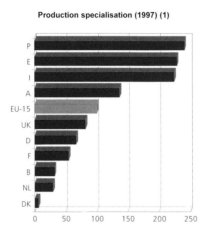

Production specialisation (1997) (1)

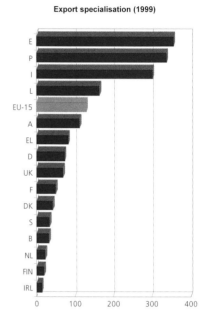

Export specialisation (1999)

(1) DK, 1994; I and NL, 1995; EL, IRL, L, FIN and S, not available.

Source: Eurostat (SBS, COMEXT)

STRUCTURE AND PERFORMANCE

Between 1993 and 1998 EU production of ceramics increased by 2.4% per annum in real terms, a similar rate to the average for all non-metallic mineral products (2.5% per annum), whilst being well below the manufacturing average of 4.9% per annum.

The value added rate (which measures the share of value added in production) is a measure used to study the vertical integration within an industry; a higher share may suggest that there are more integrated steps in the production process. In 1997 the EU ceramic industry had an estimated 41.5% share of value added in production, above the average for non-metallic mineral products (37.5%) and well over the manufacturing average of 27.9%.

LABOUR AND PRODUCTIVITY

The EU ceramic industry employed 222.1 thousand persons in 1995. Looking at individual Member States, Germany stood out with an absolute reduction of 18.6% between 1995 and 1997, resulting in 45.4 thousand persons employed. However, in the three highly-specialised countries, Italy, Spain and Portugal, employment expanded: for example, in Spain employment increased by 8.0% in 1997 (compared to a year before) to reach 42.0 thousand persons.

Improved labour productivity in Spain

One measure to assess changes in labour input is the share of personnel costs in total operating costs. Between 1995 and 1999 this ratio fell by 2.5 percentage points to 32.3% in the EU ceramics industry. During the same period total personnel costs increased by 14.7% to reach 7.0 billion EUR in the EU.

Apparent labour productivity (value added per person employed) is relatively low in the EU ceramics industry and was estimated to be equal to 36.3 thousand ECU per person employed in 1997. Simple wage adjusted labour productivity takes into account the relationship between value added and personnel costs. This ratio remained almost unchanged during the mid-1990s in the EU ceramics industry and was estimated to be 140.1% in 1997.

Within the Member States there were more pronounced changes, with the southern Member States increasing their competitive advantage: for example, in Spain the simple wage adjusted labour productivity ratio increased by 10.5 percentage points in 1997 to 168.9%. In the northern Member States there were generally low levels of productivity (for example, Germany and France reported simple wage adjusted labour productivity equal to 118.9% and 118.2% in 1997) or declining rates (for example, in the United Kingdom the ratio fell by 9.4 percentage points to 141.5%).

INTERNATIONAL TRENDS AND FOREIGN TRADE

Within the Triad the EU was the largest producer of ceramic goods, accounting for 56.1% of total Triad output in 1997. Japan saw its share reduced from 31.7% in 1993 to 26.0% in 1997. The EU was also, by far, the most important exporter within the Triad, accounting for 73.3% of Triad exports in 1998.

Intensified trade with Eastern European countries
The trade balance of the EU continued to grow in the 1990s, even though imports from non-Community countries were increasing twice as fast as exports. China and Eastern Europe became increasingly important origins for EU imports. Indeed, China was the most important partner country with 438.5 million EUR of imports in 1999 (compared to 86.7 million ECU in 1989).

Whilst China was not a major destination for EU ceramic exports, EU manufacturers increased their exports to Eastern European countries at a rapid pace, for example EU exports to Poland rose by 763% between 1989 and 1999.

Figure 7.14

Ceramic goods (NACE Rev. 1 26.2 and 26.3)
Destination of EU exports, 1999 (%)

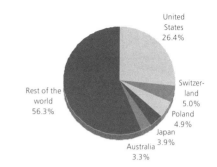

Source: Eurostat (COMEXT)

Figure 7.15

Ceramic goods (NACE Rev. 1 26.2 and 26.3)
Origin of EU imports, 1999 (%)

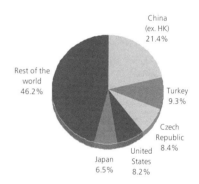

Source: Eurostat (COMEXT)

SUB-CHAPTER 7.3
CLAY PRODUCTS (NACE Rev. 1 26.4)

Clay products are covered by NACE Rev. 1 Group 26.4 and include the manufacture of building materials such as bricks, roofing tiles, chimney pots and pipes, as well as flooring blocks made of baked clay.

With a production value of 6.1 billion ECU in 1996, the EU clay products industry was the smallest of the sub-chapters covered within this section on non-metallic mineral products. It accounted for approximately 5.0% of non-metallic mineral products output in 1996, which was equivalent to 0.2% of the EU's total manufacturing output. In terms of employment the relative shares of this industry were somewhat larger: as clay products accounted for 6.1% of those employed within the non-metallic minerals industry, with some 63.5 thousand persons employed in 1999.

High dependence on the construction sector
Demand for clay products is strongly linked to the fortunes of the construction industry, not only new buildings, but also maintenance and renovation. Subdued demand from the construction sector, coupled with an increased number of mergers and acquisitions, has resulted in a reduced number of clay products' manufacturers within the EU. Wienerberger Baustoffindustrie (A), one of the world's leading brick producers, had over 200 factories worldwide in 2000, following an acquisitions policy that included the purchase of General Shale (USA), Cherokee Sanford (USA) and Later Chrudim (CZ).

In Germany the output of clay products reached 1.7 billion ECU in 1997 (the highest figure in the EU), followed by Italy with 985.3 million ECU of output in 1996 (16.1% of the EU total). However, the highest specialisation was in Portugal (198.5% in 1996), where clay products contributed 0.5% to domestic manufacturing output. At the other extreme, the French and Irish clay products industries contributed less than 0.1% to their domestic manufacturing output[4].

(4) L, no output; FIN and S, no data available.

Figure 7.16

Clay products (NACE Rev. 1 26.4)
Production and export specialisation (%)

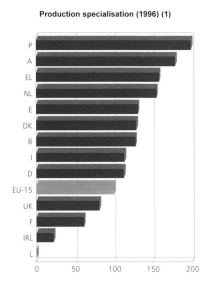

Production specialisation (1996) (1)

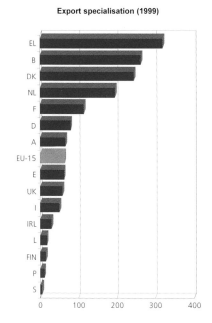

Export specialisation (1999)

(1) A, 1994; FIN and S, not available.

Source: Eurostat (SBS, COMEXT)

The restructuring process in the EU clay products industry also influenced the number of brick works in operation within the EU[5]. There were 1.3 thousand units active in 1998, which was a reduction of more than one-third (36.2%) when compared to 1985.

During the same period, the average sales of bricks per unit increased from 20.7 thousand cubic metres to 38.8 thousand cubic metres. However, in 1998 there was still a great divide in the average size of EU brick producing units. Larger units were the norm in Belgium, Germany, Italy and Austria (an average of around 60 thousand cubic metres of sales per brickwork), whilst in Denmark, Spain, France, the Netherlands and the United Kingdom, sales averaged 20-25 thousand cubic metres per unit.

(5) EL, IRL, L, P, FIN and S are not covered by TBE (European Federation of bricks and tiles producers).

Figure 7.17

Breakdown of sales of bricks in the EU,
1998 (%) (1)

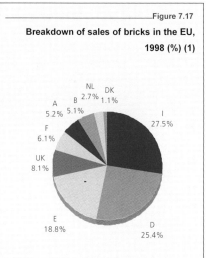

(1) EL, IRL, L, P, FIN and S are not covered by TBE.

Source: TBE

STRUCTURE AND PERFORMANCE

Between 1990 and 1996 the output of clay products in the EU decreased by 1.1% per annum on average in real terms, equivalent to a net reduction of 417 million ECU. Most of the decrease occurred in 1996, when production fell by 9.0%.

Subdued production in Italy whilst constant growth in Spain

More recent data was available for a number of Member States, which showed contrasting fortunes amongst the EU Member States (on the basis of a comparison between data for 1996 and 1997). Whilst production fell in real terms in Germany (-11.0%) and Denmark (-17.4%), output expanded in Belgium (9.2%) and Portugal (41.2%).

Italian production fell in real terms in every year between 1992 and 1996 (except for growth of 3.2% in 1995), the largest loss being recorded in 1996 (-9.8%). In Spain, the opposite trend was seen, with production in constant prices growing throughout the period 1990 to 1997 (other than a 2.0% decrease in 1992), although there was a slowdown in Spanish growth, with the latest figure up by just 0.4% in 1997.

LABOUR AND PRODUCTIVITY

In the ten years to 1999, employment within the EU clay products industry decreased by 3.2% per annum on average (a net loss of 24.8 thousand persons) such that 63.5 thousand persons were employed. This was well in excess of the corresponding rates for either non-metallic mineral products (-1.7% per annum) or total manufacturing (-1.1% per annum). As with the production figures, the largest losses for employment were recorded in 1996, when more than a tenth (10.2%) of the posts were lost. Whilst 1998 was the first year in the 1990s to record an increase in employment levels (up by 1.6%), there was a reduction of 2.7% in 1999.

Between 1989 and 1996 apparent labour productivity in the EU increased by 13 thousand ECU of value added per person employed to 45 thousand ECU. Simple wage adjusted labour productivity remained almost unchanged at 167.4% in 1996.

Figure 7.18

Clay products (NACE Rev. 1 26.4)

International comparison of production in constant prices and employment (1990=100)

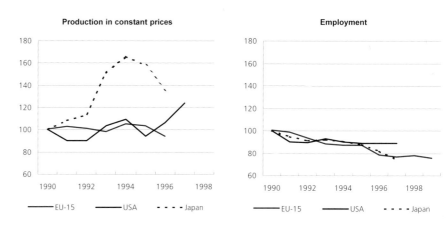

Source: Eurostat (SBS)

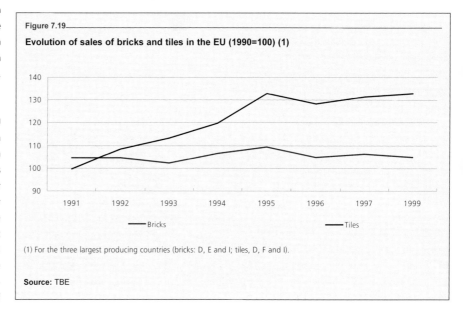

Figure 7.19

Evolution of sales of bricks and tiles in the EU (1990=100) (1)

(1) For the three largest producing countries (bricks: D, E and I; tiles: D, F and I).

Source: TBE

INTERNATIONAL TRENDS AND FOREIGN TRADE

The EU was the leading producer of clay products within the Triad. In 1996, its share of total Triad output (8.7 billion ECU) was 70.8%, whilst Japan and the USA reported similar shares (14.7% and 14.5% respectively in 1996).

Low levels of external trade

External trade of clay products is limited as a result of high transportation costs relative to the value of the product. The increase in trade flows has been largely a result of increasing trade with the emerging markets of Eastern Europe. In 1999, Poland was both the principal origin of EU imports and the main destination for EU exports.

_____Figure 7.20

Clay products (NACE Rev. 1 26.4)
Destination of EU exports, 1999 (%)

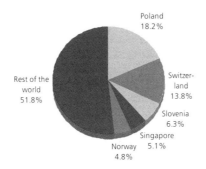

Source: Eurostat (COMEXT)

_____Figure 7.21

Clay products (NACE Rev. 1 26.4)
Origin of EU imports, 1999 (%)

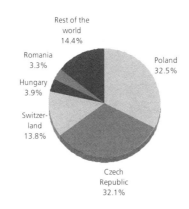

Source: Eurostat (COMEXT)

SUB-CHAPTER 7.4
CEMENT AND CONCRETE
(NACE Rev. 1 26.5 AND 26.6)

This sub-chapter covers the manufacture of cement, quicklime and plaster which are included within (NACE Rev. 1 26.5). These products are then used as inputs to create building materials (classified under NACE Rev. 1 26.6). The latter Group includes the manufacture of precast concrete and cement (for use in making articles such as flagstones, bricks and pipes), the manufacture of structural components for building work, as well as plaster boards and panels. In addition, the data presented also covers the manufacture of ready-mixed concrete, powdered mortars and various items made from concrete, plaster or cement, such as furniture or flowerpots.

The cement and concrete industry is the largest activity covered in this chapter on non-metallic mineral products. EU production was equal to 52.9 billion ECU in 1996, which was equivalent to 43.4% of the non-metallic minerals total (or 1.5% of manufacturing).

Highest production specialisation in Greece
The output of cement and concrete in Germany reached 16.2 billion ECU in 1997, around 30% of the EU total. The highest production specialisation ratios in 1996 were recorded in the smaller (and generally southern) Member States: for example, 282.1% in Greece, 195.4% in Austria and 164.2% in Portugal. Within the larger Member States only Spain reported a similar specialisation ratio (146.5%). These rates were largely influenced by the choice of building materials within a given region, with concrete and cement often being used in the southern Member States.

Geographical diversification in a mature market
Subdued demand from the construction sector and reduced public spending on civil engineering projects during the 1990s has led to European manufacturers seeking to diversify their activities in an attempt to develop new markets.

Figure 7.22

Cement and concrete (NACE Rev. 1 26.5 and 26.6)
Production and export specialisation (%)

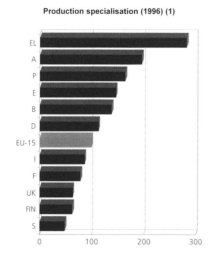

Production specialisation (1996) (1)

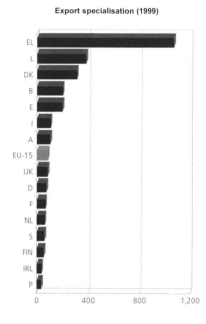

Export specialisation (1999)

(1) A, 1994; DK, IRL, L and NL, not available.

Source: Eurostat (SBS, COMEXT)

Figure 7.23

Cement and concrete (NACE Rev. 1 26.5 and 26.6)
International comparison of production in constant prices and employment (1990=100)

Production in constant prices

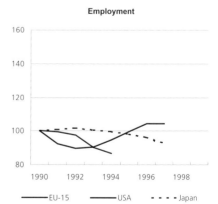

Employment

Source: Eurostat (SBS)

Box 7.4

The ready-mixed concrete industry produced more than 60% of the concrete used on building sites in the EU[6]. Production of ready-mixed concrete increased by 25.8% in absolute terms between 1988 and 1998 to reach 273.2 million cubic metres. Within the Member States Portugal and Spain reported annual average growth rates of 12.1% and 10.5% respectively during this period, whilst production was reduced in Sweden and the United Kingdom (down by 7.0% and 2.2% per annum respectively). Consumption of ready-mixed concrete per capita differed widely across Europe: from 1.3 cubic metres per capita in Austria to just 0.23 cubic metres per capita in Sweden.

(6) EL and L, no data available.

Figure 7.24

Average number of plants per enterprise in the ready-mixed concrete industry (units)

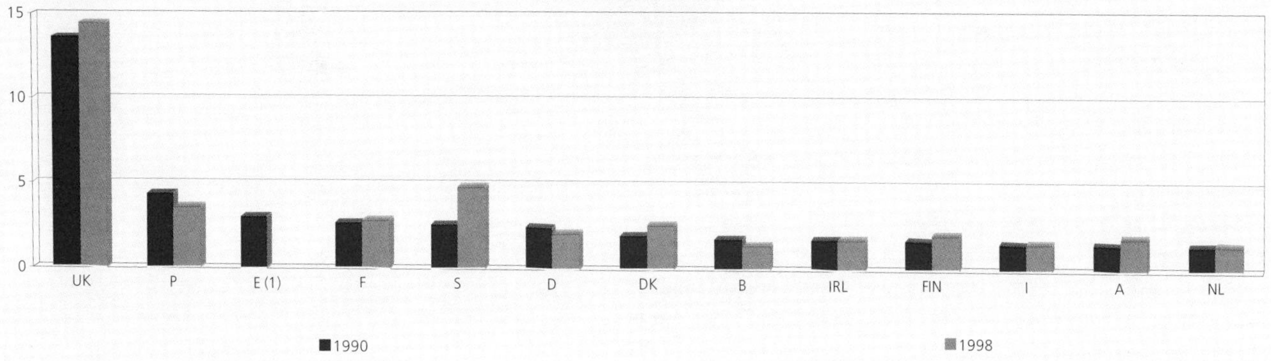

| ■1990 | ■1998 |

(1) 1998, not available.

Source: ERMCO

STRUCTURE AND PERFORMANCE

Production of cement and concrete decreased on average by 0.9% per annum in real terms between 1990 and 1996, equivalent to a loss of 3.0 billion ECU. This rate of decline was faster than the average for the whole of the non-metallic mineral products industry (where real output fell on average by 0.2% per annum between 1990 and 1996). The largest losses for the EU cement and concrete industry occurred in 1993 (down by 7.9% to reach a low of 51.1 billion ECU). In 1997, Germany recorded a continued downward trend in production (losing 3.5% in real terms), whilst in the United Kingdom and Spain there was growth of 25.5% and 5.1% respectively.

Decreasing profitability

During the period 1990 to 1996, the EU's cement and concrete industry has seen its value added decrease at twice the rate of production (down on average by 1.8% per annum in real terms). In 1997, the gross operating rate was estimated to be equal to 13.6% in the EU, similar to the average for the whole of non-metallic mineral products (13.7%), below the 1990 rate of 16.3%.

LABOUR AND PRODUCTIVITY

There were 363.4 thousand persons employed in the EU cement and concrete industry in 1994, almost 45 thousand less than in 1985.

In 1997 simple wage adjusted labour productivity was estimated to be equal to 167.3% in the EU, some 11.2 percentage points below the 1990 figure. The highest simple wage adjusted labour productivity ratios were recorded in Portugal, Spain and the United Kingdom (314.8%, 206.2% and 204.3%, for 1997), countries with comparatively low unit personnel costs of 15.2 thousand ECU per employee, 23.0 thousand ECU and 28.6 thousand ECU in 1997.

INTERNATIONAL TRENDS AND FOREIGN TRADE

The EU is the largest producer of cement and concrete in the Triad, accounting for 43.9% of total Triad output in 1996. The USA's share was equal to a quarter (25.2%) of the total, a rising share as a result of a rapid expansion in output (rising on average by 7.9% per annum in real terms between 1992 and 1997).

The EU recorded a positive trade balance (422.7 million EUR) within the cement and concrete industry, although the cover ratio (exports divided by imports) fell from 265.1% in 1989 to 152.2% by 1999. A breakdown by activity showed that cement, lime and plaster (NACE Rev. 1 26.5) ran a small deficit in 1999 (equal to just 20.2 million EUR).

Competition from Eastern Europe

It is normal for the majority of trade to be carried out with neighbouring countries due to the specificity of cement and concrete Between 1989 and 1999 EU imports of cement and concrete increased by more than 200% to reach 810.2 million EUR. Eastern Europe was the main origin of imports, with the Czech and Slovak Republics together accounting for a 17.5-fold increase on the 1989 figure for Czechoslovakia. Despite the share of EU exports to Eastern Europe increasing, the main destinations for EU cement and concrete products remained the USA, Switzerland and Norway.

Figure 7.25 ────────────────

Cement and concrete
(NACE Rev. 1 26.5 and 26.6)
Destination of EU exports, 1999 (%)

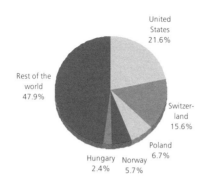

Source: Eurostat (COMEXT)

Figure 7.26 ────────────────

Cement and concrete
(NACE Rev. 1 26.5 and 26.6)
Origin of EU imports, 1999 (%)

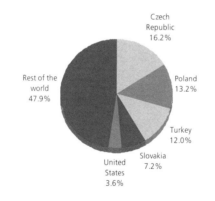

Source: Eurostat (COMEXT)

SUB-CHAPTER 7.5
STONE AND OTHER NON-METALLIC
MINERAL PRODUCTS
(NACE Rev. 1 26.7 AND 26.8)

This sub-chapter covers the cutting, shaping and processing of stone (NACE Rev. 1 26.7), which results in the creation of products such as stone blocks for the construction sector, head-stones for cemeteries, kerb-stones for roads and slate for roofing. Other non-metallic mineral products (NACE Rev. 1 26.8) covers a wide-range of diverse products, including abrasive products (generally used in the sharpening and polishing of stone) and mineral insulating materials (for sound or heat insulation).

Stone industry relatively important
for the Iberian Peninsula

Production of stone and other non-metallic mineral products in the EU was valued at 12.9 billion ECU or 0.4% of total manufacturing output in 1994. Within the EU production was split 60% to 40% in favour of other non-metallic mineral products. This structure was not reflected in the Member States: as in Denmark and the United Kingdom other non-metallic mineral products accounted for 93.5% and 91.3% of aggregated production in 1997, whilst the stone processing industry was considerably more important in Portugal and Spain (82.6% and 71.0% of the total). The relatively high importance of the stone industry in the Iberian Peninsula was shown when studying the production specialisation ratios, which were as high as 480.5% and 399.6% in Portugal and Spain in 1997. The highest specialisation ratios for other non-metallic mineral products were recorded in Denmark and Austria (301.5% and 166.3% respectively in 1996).

—————Figure 7.27

Stone and other non-metallic mineral products (NACE Rev. 1 26.7 and 26.8)
Production and export specialisation (%)

Production specialisation (1994) (1)

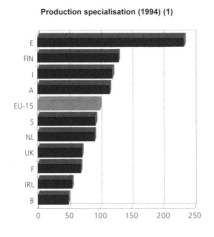

Export specialisation (1999)

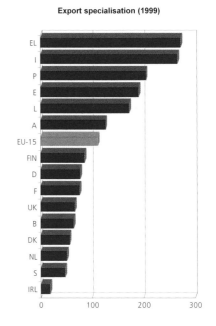

(1) DK, D, EL, L and P, not available.

Source: Eurostat (SBS, COMEXT)

—————Figure 7.28

Stone and other non-metallic mineral products (NACE Rev. 1 26.7 and 26.8)
International comparison of production in constant prices and employment (1990=100)

Production in constant prices

Employment

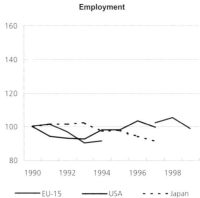

Source: Eurostat (SBS)

STRUCTURE AND PERFORMANCE

Both the EU stone and other non-metallic mineral products industries reported increasing output during the 1990s, the former at a faster pace, whilst both had growth rates of production in constant prices above the average for the whole of non-metallic mineral products. Between 1990 and 1998 output rose by an average of 3.0% per annum in real terms in the stone industry to reach 6.4 billion ECU, although growth in the second half of the 1990s was at a slower pace, with a decrease in production recorded in 1998.

The other non-metallic mineral products industry saw output rise on average by 1.2% per annum between 1990 and 1996 to reach 9.2 billion ECU. Real increases in output were limited to the years after 1993.

Diverging production trends
within the Member States
Production trends in the Member States were varied during the period 1990 to 1997. Looking first at the stone processing industry, Portugal and Spain recorded average increases of 7.6% and 5.8% per annum, whilst Germany (down by 3.4% per annum) was one of a few countries (Sweden and the United Kingdom being the others) to report a decrease in output. However, in the other non-metallic mineral products industry the picture was the contrary, with Germany reporting an average increase of 1.8% per annum, whilst Spanish production was down on average by 1.7% per annum.

LABOUR AND PRODUCTIVITY

In 1999, the stone and other non-metallic mineral products industry employed 147.5 thousand persons in the EU, 2.2 thousand less than in 1990. This figure was the result of diverging trends in the two industries. Whilst employment within the other non-metallic mineral products industry was reduced by 11.6% to 70.3 thousand persons, the stone processing industry increased its employment levels by as much as 10.0% to reach 77.2 thousand persons (even accounting for a loss of 8.5% in 1999 alone).

Decline in labour productivity in France
Between 1990 and 1997 the apparent labour productivity of the stone and other non-metallic mineral products industry in the EU improved by 7.7 thousand ECU per person employed to reach an estimated 38.3 thousand ECU. Apparent labour productivity was lower in the stone processing industry (32.6 thousand EUR, 1999).

Taking account of personnel costs, the simple wage adjusted labour productivity ratios for the stone and other non-metallic mineral products industries were similar (149.9% in 1997 and 144.2% in 1996 respectively).

Within the Member States, there was a reduction of 34.3 percentage points in the simple wage adjusted labour productivity ratio for France to 114.8% (between 1990 and 1997). This was mainly as a result of low productivity in the stone processing industry (102.5% for 1997).

INTERNATIONAL TRENDS AND FOREIGN TRADE

The EU stone processing industry contributed 48.1% to the total production value of the Triad (13.7 billion ECU) in 1997. Since the late-1980s the EU's share has been increasing, whilst the Japanese share has been in decline (down by 8 percentage points to 44% in 1997). The USA recorded a relative small stone processing industry, with just 7.8% of total Triad output in 1997. On the other hand, American output of other non-metallic mineral products was equal to 49.7% of the Triad's 33.8 billion ECU of production in 1996, with the EU and Japan accounting for 27.6% and 22.8% shares respectively.

In 1998, the EU was responsible for 68.1% of total Triad exports and 42.3% of total Triad imports of stone and other non-metallic mineral products. The EU had a trade surplus of 1.8 billion ECU in 1998.

Stone from China and India
Between 1989 and 1999, the USA and Switzerland remained the major trading partners of the EU. There was intensified trade of other non-metallic mineral products with Eastern European countries, especially as a destination for EU exports. On the other hand, imports of processed stone from non-Community countries more than quadrupled between 1989 and 1999, with China (2.4 million ECU to 104.5 million EUR) and India (9.7 million ECU with 91.8 million EUR) the countries that increased their respective shares the most.

Figure 7.29

Stone and other non-metallic mineral products (NACE Rev. 1 26.7 and 26.8)
Destination of EU exports, 1999 (%)

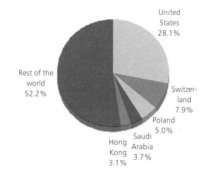

Source: Eurostat (COMEXT)

Figure 7.30

Stone and other non-metallic mineral products (NACE Rev. 1 26.7 and 26.8)
Origin of EU imports, 1999 (%)

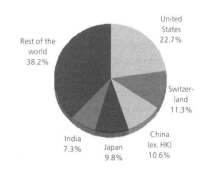

Source: Eurostat (COMEXT)

Table 7.3

Manufacture of glass and glass products (NACE Rev. 1 26.1)

Production related indicators in the EU (1)

	1989	1990	1991	1992	1993	1994	1995	1996	1997	1998	1999
Number of persons employed (thousands)	288.3	288.2	287.3	281.6	260.5	251.9	255.2	:	:	:	:
Production (million ECU)	23,083	23,662	24,397	24,570	23,451	25,023	27,712	:	:	:	:
Domestic producer price index (1995=100)	:	95.6	96.4	96.5	96.0	96.6	100.0	99.9	98.3	98.2	97.7
Value added (million ECU)	10,164	10,156	10,588	10,327	9,890	10,743	11,929	:	:	:	:

(1) Technically, data before 01/01/1999 are in ECU and after this date in euro. However, as the conversion rate was 1 ECU =1 EUR, for practical purposes the two terms can be used interchangeably.

Table 7.4

Manufacture of glass and glass products (NACE Rev. 1 26.1)

Trade related indicators in the EU (1)

	1989	1990	1991	1992	1993	1994	1995	1996	1997	1998	1999
Exports (million EUR)	2,488	2,410	2,439	2,453	2,727	3,138	3,366	3,663	4,239	4,146	4,205
Imports (million EUR)	1,122	1,172	1,395	1,444	1,462	1,622	1,974	1,955	2,252	2,559	2,812
Trade balance (million EUR)	1,366	1,238	1,044	1,009	1,266	1,516	1,392	1,708	1,986	1,587	1,393
Cover ratio (%)	221.7	205.6	174.9	169.9	186.6	193.5	170.5	187.3	188.2	162.0	149.6

(1) Technically, data before 01/01/1999 are in ECU and after this date in euro. However, as the conversion rate was 1 ECU =1 EUR, for practical purposes the two terms can be used interchangeably.

Table 7.5

Manufacture of glass and glass products (NACE Rev. 1 26.1)

Production related indicators, 1997

	B	DK	D	EL (1)	E	F	IRL	I (1)	L	NL	A	P	FIN	S	UK
Number of persons employed (thousands)	12.1	3.7	64.2	0.8	23.9	49.2	3.8	27.0	:	:	7.6	9.1	4.3	4.9	32.1
Production (million ECU)	2,222	435	7,503	51	2,283	6,142	342	3,160	:	793	842	536	469	561	3,217
Value added (million ECU)	694	174	3,169	19	945	2,514	184	1,420	:	331	491	224	203	220	1,510
Gross operating surplus (million ECU)	194.8	67.8	806.3	5.5	376.6	754.9	66.5	562.7	:	130.1	204.7	98.8	69.5	51.7	611.7

(1) 1996.

Table 7.6

Manufacture of glass and glass products (NACE Rev. 1 26.1)

Trade related indicators, 1999

	B	DK	D	EL	E	F	IRL	I	L	NL	A	P	FIN	S	UK
Exports (million EUR)	1,663	214	2,838	13	603	2,531	213	1,712	178	560	685	165	252	268	866
Imports (million EUR)	969	299	2,067	133	751	1,905	154	1,185	47	636	549	183	135	366	1,243
Trade balance (million EUR)	694	-85	771	-120	-148	626	59	527	131	-76	136	-18	117	-98	-377
Cover ratio (%)	171.6	71.6	137.3	9.5	80.3	132.8	138.1	144.5	381.0	88.0	124.7	90.0	186.2	73.2	69.7

Table 7.7

Manufacture of glass and glass products (NACE Rev. 1 26.1)

Labour related indicators, 1997

	B	DK (1)	D	EL (2)	E	F	IRL	I (2)	L	NL	A	P	FIN	S	UK
Unit personnel costs (thousand ECU per employee)	41.4	34.2	36.9	17.8	22.7	35.7	30.7	32.3	:	:	38.0	14.1	31.4	34.3	28.3
Social charges as a share of personnel costs (%)	39.9	4.5	25.3	30.2	28.6	41.0	21.6	53.7	:	17.2	34.3	32.3	28.8	44.0	13.1
Apparent labour productivity (thousand ECU/pers. empl.)	57.1	47.4	49.3	24.7	39.5	51.1	47.9	52.6	:	:	65.0	24.6	47.2	44.8	47.1
Wage adjusted labour productivity (%)	137.9	151.0	133.8	138.8	174.0	142.9	155.7	162.8	:	:	171.1	174.8	150.5	130.7	166.4
Personnel costs as a share of total operating costs (%)	24.7	28.1	33.1	30.0	26.3	31.1	37.7	32.0	:	28.7	41.2	26.1	29.2	30.6	33.0

(1) Unit personnel costs and wage adjusted labour productivity, 1996; (2) 1996.

Source: Eurostat (SBS, EBT, COMEXT)

Table 7.8

Manufacture of non-refractory ceramic goods other than for construction purposes; manufacture of refractory ceramic products (NACE Rev. 1 26.2)
Production related indicators in the EU (1)

	1989	1990	1991	1992	1993	1994	1995	1996	1997	1998	1999
Number of persons employed (thousands)	:	:	:	:	185.2	177.5	150.2	:	:	:	:
Production (million EUR)	:	:	:	:	10,476	10,879	10,600	11,608	12,271	12,238	12,940
Domestic producer price index (1995=100)	:	92.4	91.6	94.0	96.3	97.8	100.0	102.1	103.4	104.6	105.4
Value added (million EUR)	:	:	:	:	4,921	5,252	5,198	5,646	5,810	5,862	6,200

(1) Technically, data before 01/01/1999 are in ECU and after this date in euro. However, as the conversion rate was 1 ECU =1 EUR, for practical purposes the two terms can be used interchangeably.

Table 7.9

Manufacture of non-refractory ceramic goods other than for construction purposes; manufacture of refractory ceramic products (NACE Rev. 1 26.2)
Trade related indicators in the EU (1)

	1989	1990	1991	1992	1993	1994	1995	1996	1997	1998	1999
Exports (million EUR)	1,987	2,019	2,033	2,077	2,224	2,533	2,839	2,795	3,234	3,067	3,086
Imports (million EUR)	738	770	948	1,044	1,051	1,130	1,153	1,263	1,457	1,599	1,785
Trade balance (million EUR)	1,249	1,250	1,085	1,034	1,173	1,403	1,685	1,532	1,777	1,468	1,301
Cover ratio (%)	269.2	262.4	214.6	199.1	211.7	224.3	246.1	221.3	221.9	191.8	172.9

(1) Technically, data before 01/01/1999 are in ECU and after this date in euro. However, as the conversion rate was 1 ECU =1 EUR, for practical purposes the two terms can be used interchangeably.

Table 7.10

Manufacture of non-refractory ceramic goods other than for construction purposes; manufacture of refractory ceramic products (NACE Rev. 1 26.2)
Production related indicators, 1997

	B	DK	D	EL (1)	E	F	IRL	I (1)	L	NL	A	P	FIN	S	UK
Number of persons employed (thousands)	2.1	2.0	36.1	1.7	20.0	17.5	:	19.3	:	:	4.7	24.5	0.9	2.4	38.4
Production (million ECU)	260	126	2,989	66	1,278	1,510	:	1,600	:	107	558	605	88	268	2,472
Value added (million ECU)	110	74	1,404	32	565	659	:	759	:	59	254	307	43	114	1,327
Gross operating surplus (million ECU)	33.8	15.6	244.5	0.6	176.0	110.1	:	227.6	:	16.2	29.7	95.6	21.2	31.7	391.3

(1) 1996.

Table 7.11

Manufacture of non-refractory ceramic goods other than for construction purposes; manufacture of refractory ceramic products (NACE Rev. 1 26.2)
Trade related indicators, 1999

	B	DK	D	EL	E	F	IRL	I	L	NL	A	P	FIN	S	UK
Exports (million EUR)	282	99	1,789	25	356	720	47	777	73	180	390	349	40	145	923
Imports (million EUR)	322	129	966	77	334	649	95	524	20	270	212	93	83	161	536
Trade balance (million EUR)	-40	-30	823	-52	22	70	-48	253	52	-91	178	255	-44	-15	388
Cover ratio (%)	87.6	76.7	185.3	32.1	106.6	110.8	49.7	148.2	360.1	66.4	183.9	373.5	47.5	90.4	172.3

Table 7.12

Manufacture of non-refractory ceramic goods other than for construction purposes; manufacture of refractory ceramic products (NACE Rev. 1 26.2)
Labour related indicators, 1997

	B	DK (1)	D	EL (2)	E	F	IRL	I (2)	L	NL	A	P	FIN	S	UK
Unit personnel costs (thousand ECU per employee)	37.7	30.7	32.1	18.0	20.3	31.4	:	28.1	:	:	48.3	9.0	28.0	34.4	24.4
Social charges as a share of personnel costs (%)	39.4	4.7	25.3	32.8	29.4	41.4	:	52.7	:	23.3	40.4	30.1	25.6	42.6	12.8
Apparent labour productivity (thousand ECU/pers. empl.)	53.1	36.6	38.8	18.3	28.3	37.7	:	39.3	:	:	54.6	12.5	49.0	47.8	34.5
Wage adjusted labour productivity (%)	140.8	116.2	120.9	101.9	139.7	120.0	:	140.2	:	:	113.2	139.7	174.7	138.7	141.5
Personnel costs as a share of total operating costs (%)	34.2	47.4	38.3	46.1	28.6	36.9	:	36.2	:	35.1	35.5	37.7	30.2	31.1	42.1

(1) Unit personnel costs and wage adjusted labour productivity, 1996; (2) 1996.

Source: Eurostat (SBS, EBT, COMEXT)

_____Table 7.13

Manufacture of ceramic tiles and flags (NACE Rev. 1 26.3)
Production related indicators in the EU (1)

	1989	1990	1991	1992	1993	1994	1995	1996	1997	1998	1999
Number of persons employed (thousands)	:	:	:	:	74.0	74.5	71.9	:	:	:	:
Production (million EUR)	:	:	:	:	7,280	7,659	7,913	:	9,054	9,439	9,839
Domestic producer price index (1995=100)	:	:	:	:	:	:	:	:	:	:	:
Value added (million ECU)	:	:	:	:	3,159	3,316	3,342	:	3,689	:	:

(1) Technically, data before 01/01/1999 are in ECU and after this date in euro. However, as the conversion rate was 1 ECU =1 EUR, for practical purposes the two terms can be used interchangeably.

_____Table 7.14

Manufacture of ceramic tiles and flags (NACE Rev. 1 26.3)
Trade related indicators in the EU (1)

	1989	1990	1991	1992	1993	1994	1995	1996	1997	1998	1999
Exports (million EUR)	1,132	1,093	1,065	1,153	1,369	1,654	1,743	1,958	2,273	2,385	2,448
Imports (million EUR)	106	114	134	159	182	191	201	193	220	228	268
Trade balance (million EUR)	1,026	979	931	995	1,187	1,463	1,541	1,765	2,053	2,157	2,179
Cover ratio (%)	1,066.7	956.1	796.5	727.5	754.0	865.5	866.0	1,012.7	1,031.8	1,043.8	912.3

(1) Technically, data before 01/01/1999 are in ECU and after this date in euro. However, as the conversion rate was 1 ECU =1 EUR, for practical purposes the two terms can be used interchangeably.

_____Table 7.15

Manufacture of ceramic tiles and flags (NACE Rev. 1 26.3)
Production related indicators, 1997

	B	DK (1)	D	EL	E	F	IRL	I(1)	L	NL	A	P	FIN	S	UK
Number of persons employed (thousands)	0.1	0.0	9.3	:	22.0	4.5	:	34.6	0.0	:	0.0	4.2	:	:	2.2
Production (million ECU)	9	0	807	:	2,262	394	:	4,347	0	:	0	215	:	:	150
Value added (million ECU)	5	0	389	:	932	147	:	1,759	0	:	0	83	:	:	74
Gross operating surplus (million ECU)	0.6	0.0	40.1	:	419.7	14.3	:	613.1	0.0	:	0.0	37.3	:	:	19.2

(1) 1996.

_____Table 7.16

Manufacture of ceramic tiles and flags (NACE Rev. 1 26.3)
Trade related indicators, 1999

	B	DK	D	EL	E	F	IRL	I	L	NL	A	P	FIN	S	UK
Exports (million EUR)	14	3	223	13	1,567	149	0	3,036	1	37	10	103	6	5	28
Imports (million EUR)	153	44	832	138	36	638	35	79	15	98	159	100	35	46	340
Trade balance (million EUR)	-139	-41	-608	-125	1,531	-489	-35	2,957	-14	-60	-150	2	-30	-41	-312
Cover ratio (%)	8.9	5.9	26.8	9.4	4,375.9	23.4	0.1	3,852.9	5.2	38.1	6.0	102.5	15.6	11.8	8.4

_____Table 7.17

Manufacture of ceramic tiles and flags (NACE Rev. 1 26.3)
Labour related indicators, 1997

	B	DK	D	EL	E	F	IRL	I(1)	L	NL	A	P	FIN	S	UK
Unit personnel costs (thousand ECU per employee)	30.1	:	37.8	:	23.2	29.8	:	33.5	:	:	:	10.9	:	:	24.5
Social charges as a share of personnel costs (%)	37.9	:	28.1	:	27.8	39.2	:	52.0	:	:	:	29.6	:	:	12.1
Apparent labour productivity (thousand ECU/pers. empl.)	33.7	:	42.1	:	42.3	33.0	:	50.9	:	:	:	19.7	:	:	32.9
Wage adjusted labour productivity (%)	111.9	:	111.4	:	182.7	110.8	:	152.0	:	:	:	179.8	:	:	134.5
Personnel costs as a share of total operating costs (%)	47.0	:	35.4	:	25.0	27.8	:	28.1	:	:	:	25.4	:	:	38.7

(1) 1996.

Source: Eurostat (SBS, EBT, COMEXT)

Table 7.18

Manufacture of bricks, tiles and construction products, in baked clay (NACE Rev. 1 26.4)

Production related indicators in the EU (1)

	1989	1990	1991	1992	1993	1994	1995	1996	1997	1998	1999
Number of persons employed (thousands)	88.3	84.3	82.9	78.2	74.1	73.3	73.0	65.5	64.2	65.2	63.5
Production (million ECU)	5,690	5,705	6,185	6,295	6,236	6,784	6,807	6,129	:	:	:
Domestic producer price index (1995=100)	:	86.8	91.8	94.9	96.8	97.8	100.0	98.9	99.4	101.4	105.4
Value added (million ECU)	2,825	2,766	2,958	3,084	3,053	3,324	3,395	2,950	:	:	:

(1) Technically, data before 01/01/1999 are in ECU and after this date in euro. However, as the conversion rate was 1 ECU =1 EUR, for practical purposes the two terms can be used interchangeably.

Table 7.19

Manufacture of bricks, tiles and construction products, in baked clay (NACE Rev. 1 26.4)

Trade related indicators in the EU (1)

	1989	1990	1991	1992	1993	1994	1995	1996	1997	1998	1999
Exports (million EUR)	64	60	66	64	67	81	84	91	95	109	129
Imports (million EUR)	8	10	16	26	36	49	44	35	40	48	41
Trade balance (million EUR)	56	50	49	38	31	32	40	56	55	61	87
Cover ratio (%)	852.5	605.3	402.4	243.6	185.5	164.9	190.6	262.6	239.6	227.8	311.4

(1) Technically, data before 01/01/1999 are in ECU and after this date in euro. However, as the conversion rate was 1 ECU =1 EUR, for practical purposes the two terms can be used interchangeably.

Table 7.20

Manufacture of bricks, tiles and construction products, in baked clay (NACE Rev. 1 26.4)

Production related indicators, 1997

	B	DK	D	EL (1)	E	F	IRL	I (1)	L	NL	A	P	FIN	S	UK
Number of persons employed (thousands)	2.7	0.7	14.4	1.1	9.4	5.1	0.2	9.9	0.0	:	1.4	7.2	0.2	:	9.3
Production (million ECU)	358	97	1,683	56	569	628	21	985	0	367	193	287	18	:	809
Value added (million ECU)	157	53	803	17	238	308	11	396	0	211	97	136	9	:	438
Gross operating surplus (million ECU)	63.7	31.0	272.1	1.0	87.1	145.0	5.2	111.6	0.0	136.9	39.3	65.5	4.5	:	195.2

(1) 1996.

Table 7.21

Manufacture of bricks, tiles and construction products, in baked clay (NACE Rev. 1 26.4)

Trade related indicators, 1999

	B	DK	D	EL	E	F	IRL	I	L	NL	A	P	FIN	S	UK
Exports (million EUR)	113	28	104	7	16	94	5	30	0	90	11	1	2	1	37
Imports (million EUR)	56	9	137	1	12	28	5	13	5	45	37	5	1	3	25
Trade balance (million EUR)	58	19	-33	6	4	66	-1	17	-4	45	-26	-4	1	-2	13
Cover ratio (%)	203.8	308.4	75.7	667.2	135.0	339.7	87.3	222.4	7.5	198.3	29.3	14.4	196.5	33.1	151.3

Table 7.22

Manufacture of bricks, tiles and construction products, in baked clay (NACE Rev. 1 26.4)

Labour related indicators, 1997

	B	DK (1)	D	EL (2)	E	F	IRL	I (2)	L	NL	A	P	FIN	S	UK
Unit personnel costs (thousand ECU per employee)	35.6	36.6	37.3	15.1	16.4	32.0	24.4	29.6	:	:	41.0	9.9	29.7	:	26.7
Social charges as a share of personnel costs (%)	38.5	4.3	24.5	30.3	31.0	43.3	15.4	52.9	:	17.4	27.9	27.1	28.9	:	13.7
Apparent labour productivity (thousand ECU/pers. empl.)	57.9	76.2	55.8	15.8	25.5	60.6	45.3	40.2	:	:	68.8	18.9	51.5	:	47.1
Wage adjusted labour productivity (%)	162.5	208.8	149.9	104.5	155.5	189.3	185.6	135.8	:	:	167.8	190.4	173.2	:	176.7
Personnel costs as a share of total operating costs (%)	31.8	30.2	33.0	32.3	28.7	33.9	35.3	30.4	:	27.5	33.9	31.3	34.3	:	40.2

(1) Unit personnel costs and wage adjusted labour productivity, 1996; (2) 1996.

Source: Eurostat (SBS, EBT, COMEXT)

Table 7.23

Manufacture of cement, lime and plaster (NACE Rev. 1 26.5)

Production related indicators in the EU (1)

	1989	1990	1991	1992	1993	1994	1995	1996	1997	1998	1999
Number of persons employed (thousands)	82.5	82.7	80.3	77.2	73.6	71.3	:	:	:	:	:
Production (million EUR)	13,447	14,165	14,212	13,911	12,799	13,838	:	14,317	14,971	15,358	15,608
Domestic producer price index (1995=100)	:	91.6	87.9	91.1	93.8	97.2	100.0	101.8	104.4	106.3	108.1
Value added (million EUR)	6,325	6,549	6,163	6,230	5,731	6,403	:	6,078	6,456	6,411	6,560

(1) Technically, data before 01/01/1999 are in ECU and after this date in euro. However, as the conversion rate was 1 ECU =1 EUR, for practical purposes the two terms can be used interchangeably.

Table 7.24

Manufacture of cement, lime and plaster (NACE Rev. 1 26.5)

Trade related indicators in the EU (1)

	1989	1990	1991	1992	1993	1994	1995	1996	1997	1998	1999
Exports (million EUR)	348	321	340	341	390	520	505	583	626	578	512
Imports (million EUR)	163	230	311	378	392	437	479	443	488	465	532
Trade balance (million EUR)	185	91	30	-37	-2	83	25	141	139	113	-20
Cover ratio (%)	213.9	139.6	109.5	90.3	99.5	119.0	105.3	131.8	128.4	124.3	96.2

(1) Technically, data before 01/01/1999 are in ECU and after this date in euro. However, as the conversion rate was 1 ECU =1 EUR, for practical purposes the two terms can be used interchangeably.

Table 7.25

Manufacture of cement, lime and plaster (NACE Rev. 1 26.5)

Production related indicators, 1997

	B	DK	D	EL (1)	E	F	IRL	I (1)	L	NL	A	P	FIN (1)	S	UK
Number of persons employed (thousands)	3.3	:	17.1	4.4	9.6	6.8	:	13.1	:	:	1.8	2.1	0.2	0.8	5.3
Production (million ECU)	999	:	3,365	609	2,012	2,167	:	2,180	:	:	339	795	70	182	1,122
Value added (million ECU)	429	:	1,404	226	996	952	:	740	:	:	136	375	34	69	452
Gross operating surplus (million ECU)	255.4	:	600.5	85.9	648.0	612.6	:	282.6	:	:	54.0	312.5	26.3	35.9	246.9

(1) 1996.

Table 7.26

Manufacture of cement, lime and plaster (NACE Rev. 1 26.5)

Trade related indicators, 1999

	B	DK	D	EL	E	F	IRL	I	L	NL	A	P	FIN	S	UK
Exports (million EUR)	240	71	258	153	168	170	17	112	38	59	19	4	5	30	113
Imports (million EUR)	76	21	285	3	177	204	49	95	15	264	73	68	33	28	139
Trade balance (million EUR)	164	50	-27	150	-9	-34	-32	16	23	-205	-55	-64	-28	2	-26
Cover ratio (%)	316.4	330.5	90.5	5,398.9	95.0	83.4	35.2	117.1	254.8	22.4	25.5	5.6	14.3	108.5	81.4

Table 7.27

Manufacture of cement, lime and plaster (NACE Rev. 1 26.5)

Labour related indicators, 1997

	B	DK	D	EL (1)	E	F	IRL	I (1)	L	NL	A	P	FIN (1)	S	UK
Unit personnel costs (thousand ECU per employee)	53.4	:	47.1	32.0	34.3	49.9	:	35.1	:	:	46.4	30.0	36.8	41.7	38.4
Social charges as a share of personnel costs (%)	43.3	:	30.8	32.1	25.4	46.5	:	51.5	:	:	29.6	70.5	31.1	46.5	12.9
Apparent labour productivity (thousand ECU/pers. empl.)	131.8	:	82.2	51.6	104.0	140.2	:	56.3	:	:	76.7	178.8	158.9	86.8	84.7
Wage adjusted labour productivity (%)	246.7	:	174.3	161.4	303.6	280.8	:	160.6	:	:	165.5	596.4	431.9	208.4	220.3
Personnel costs as a share of total operating costs (%)	23.9	:	27.3	30.0	23.3	21.7	:	24.6	:	:	27.5	12.5	15.8	21.6	23.1

(1) 1996.

Source: Eurostat (SBS, EBT, COMEXT)

Table 7.28

Manufacture of articles of concrete, plaster and cement (NACE Rev. 1 26.6)

Production related indicators in the EU (1)

	1989	1990	1991	1992	1993	1994	1995	1996	1997	1998	1999
Number of persons employed (thousands)	325.4	336.5	336.0	330.3	303.6	292.1	287.5	282.4	:	:	:
Production (million ECU)	31,994	34,492	35,927	38,031	36,109	37,454	38,562	38,562	:	:	:
Domestic producer price index (1995=100)	:	:	:	:	:	:	100.0	100.7	101.8	103.1	104.5
Value added (million ECU)	11,517	12,323	12,637	12,954	12,372	13,172	13,573	13,338	:	:	:

(1) Technically, data before 01/01/1999 are in ECU and after this date in euro. However, as the conversion rate was 1 ECU =1 EUR, for practical purposes the two terms can be used interchangeably.

Table 7.29

Manufacture of articles of concrete, plaster and cement (NACE Rev. 1 26.6)

Trade related indicators in the EU (1)

	1989	1990	1991	1992	1993	1994	1995	1996	1997	1998	1999
Exports (million EUR)	358	342	391	358	373	439	533	580	677	711	721
Imports (million EUR)	104	140	146	156	165	188	212	212	238	236	278
Trade balance (million EUR)	254	202	245	202	208	251	321	369	439	475	443
Cover ratio (%)	345.5	244.7	267.9	230.0	225.9	233.0	251.2	274.1	284.6	300.8	259.4

(1) Technically, data before 01/01/1999 are in ECU and after this date in euro. However, as the conversion rate was 1 ECU =1 EUR, for practical purposes the two terms can be used interchangeably.

Table 7.30

Manufacture of articles of concrete, plaster and cement (NACE Rev. 1 26.6)

Production related indicators, 1997

	B	DK	D	EL (1)	E	F	IRL	I (1)	L	NL	A	P	FIN	S	UK
Number of persons employed (thousands)	12.8	8.1	85.1	3.3	39.4	31.3	:	30.5	0.5	:	10.2	11.2	5.2	4.9	30.4
Production (million ECU)	2,186	885	12,844	259	4,043	4,761	:	4,345	78	1,943	1,495	895	829	642	4,656
Value added (million ECU)	648	382	4,723	51	1,212	1,402	:	1,355	26	777	641	239	279	235	1,621
Gross operating surplus (million ECU)	200.9	137.8	1,473.6	-1.9	447.6	345.7	:	455.4	7.7	361.1	223.0	106.2	115.9	67.2	811.6

(1) 1996.

Table 7.31

Manufacture of articles of concrete, plaster and cement (NACE Rev. 1 26.6)

Trade related indicators, 1999

	B	DK	D	EL	E	F	IRL	I	L	NL	A	P	FIN	S	UK
Exports (million EUR)	379	185	428	11	193	211	26	335	20	140	106	11	38	57	278
Imports (million EUR)	149	61	345	13	38	287	74	54	41	169	90	30	14	47	122
Trade balance (million EUR)	230	123	83	-2	155	-76	-47	282	-21	-29	16	-18	24	10	156
Cover ratio (%)	254.2	300.6	123.9	85.9	511.2	73.6	35.8	623.8	48.1	82.6	117.8	37.8	271.5	121.8	228.2

Table 7.32

Manufacture of articles of concrete, plaster and cement (NACE Rev. 1 26.6)

Labour related indicators, 1997

	B	DK (1)	D	EL (2)	E	F	IRL	I (2)	L	NL	A	P	FIN	S	UK
Unit personnel costs (thousand ECU per employee)	36.1	36.1	38.4	16.2	20.2	33.8	:	30.4	35.4	:	41.1	12.3	32.2	34.0	26.9
Social charges as a share of personnel costs (%)	41.6	5.8	25.1	31.9	27.9	45.0	:	53.8	:	17.0	29.5	34.0	29.6	43.7	12.6
Apparent labour productivity (thousand ECU/pers. empl.)	50.6	47.2	55.5	15.5	30.8	44.9	:	44.4	49.7	:	62.9	21.3	53.8	47.6	53.4
Wage adjusted labour productivity (%)	139.9	148.9	144.7	95.7	152.5	132.7	:	146.0	140.3	:	152.8	172.9	167.0	140.0	198.4
Personnel costs as a share of total operating costs (%)	21.8	30.0	26.5	21.6	19.7	21.8	:	22.1	25.9	23.8	28.9	16.6	22.6	28.6	20.4

(1) Unit personnel costs and wage adjusted labour productivity, 1996; (2) 1996.

Source: Eurostat (SBS, EBT, COMEXT)

_____Table 7.33

Cutting, shaping and finishing of stone (NACE Rev. 1 26.7)

Production related indicators in the EU (1)

	1989	1990	1991	1992	1993	1994	1995	1996	1997	1998	1999
Number of persons employed (thousands)	68.5	70.2	76.0	73.2	69.1	70.9	79.0	:	81.3	84.4	77.2
Production (million EUR)	4,216	4,364	4,884	5,005	4,747	4,944	5,750	:	6,620	6,736	6,821
Domestic producer price index (1995=100)	:	:	:	:	:	:	:	:	:	104.9	107.5
Value added (million EUR)	1,518	1,549	1,858	1,897	1,810	1,927	2,227	:	2,408	2,457	2,517

(1) Technically, data before 01/01/1999 are in ECU and after this date in euro. However, as the conversion rate was 1 ECU =1 EUR, for practical purposes the two terms can be used interchangeably.

_____Table 7.34

Cutting, shaping and finishing of stone (NACE Rev. 1 26.7)

Trade related indicators in the EU (1)

	1989	1990	1991	1992	1993	1994	1995	1996	1997	1998	1999
Exports (million EUR)	1,088	1,079	1,047	1,019	983	1,129	1,194	1,358	1,502	1,441	1,388
Imports (million EUR)	65	69	85	108	119	145	168	191	235	275	349
Trade balance (million EUR)	1,023	1,010	962	911	865	984	1,026	1,167	1,268	1,166	1,039
Cover ratio (%)	1,663.1	1,557.3	1,230.0	944.7	829.4	781.0	711.1	712.1	640.3	524.4	398.0

(1) Technically, data before 01/01/1999 are in ECU and after this date in euro. However, as the conversion rate was 1 ECU =1 EUR, for practical purposes the two terms can be used interchangeably.

_____Table 7.35

Cutting, shaping and finishing of stone (NACE Rev. 1 26.7)

Production related indicators, 1997

	B	DK	D	EL (1)	E	F	IRL	I (1)	L	NL	A	P	FIN	S	UK
Number of persons employed (thousands)	3.2	0.2	7.8	1.6	31.6	4.8	0.6	12.3	0.1	:	1.6	13.2	1.3	0.4	2.3
Production (million ECU)	346	16	632	81	1,924	395	44	1,863	5	49	121	508	126	29	143
Value added (million ECU)	100	8	273	28	752	138	19	570	3	18	71	177	58	14	76
Gross operating surplus (million ECU)	37.1	2.4	30.9	6.1	270.2	3.4	6.4	228.7	1.4	5.5	16.1	64.0	25.0	2.0	24.7

(1) 1996.

_____Table 7.36

Cutting, shaping and finishing of stone (NACE Rev. 1 26.7)

Trade related indicators, 1999

	B	DK	D	EL	E	F	IRL	I	L	NL	A	P	FIN	S	UK
Exports (million EUR)	100	17	60	70	493	120	9	1,639	1	19	13	155	33	3	23
Imports (million EUR)	108	31	513	7	53	214	27	52	19	83	78	27	5	11	125
Trade balance (million EUR)	-8	-14	-453	62	440	-94	-19	1,588	-18	-64	-65	128	28	-7	-102
Cover ratio (%)	92.3	55.9	11.7	944.2	927.9	55.9	31.6	3,169.5	5.7	23.3	16.8	581.5	617.8	30.7	18.5

_____Table 7.37

Cutting, shaping and finishing of stone (NACE Rev. 1 26.7)

Labour related indicators, 1997

	B	DK	D	EL (1)	E	F	IRL	I (1)	L	NL	A	P	FIN	S	UK
Unit personnel costs (thousand ECU per employee)	26.0	:	31.6	14.0	17.1	28.0	20.4	29.1	21.5	:	34.1	9.2	27.7	29.7	24.6
Social charges as a share of personnel costs (%)	48.7	3.8	26.2	30.8	30.2	42.6	20.4	63.6	:	20.8	29.4	31.1	29.8	40.9	13.5
Apparent labour productivity (thousand ECU/pers. empl.)	30.8	39.7	35.1	17.8	23.8	28.7	29.9	46.5	41.4	:	44.0	13.4	44.4	34.6	33.0
Wage adjusted labour productivity (%)	118.1	:	110.9	126.8	139.7	102.5	146.6	159.5	192.3	:	128.9	146.0	160.3	116.5	133.9
Personnel costs as a share of total operating costs (%)	19.9	37.2	36.2	31.0	27.8	33.3	32.0	20.2	32.4	25.6	45.9	24.9	29.6	45.9	41.2

(1) 1996.

Source: Eurostat (SBS, EBT, COMEXT)

Table 7.38

Manufacture of other non-metallic mineral products (NACE Rev. 1 26.8)

Production related indicators in the EU (1)

	1989	1990	1991	1992	1993	1994	1995	1996	1997	1998	1999
Number of persons employed (thousands)	92.3	79.5	75.8	71.4	65.7	65.7	:	72.0	71.5	72.7	70.3
Production (million ECU)	8,850	7,834	7,692	7,503	7,252	7,946	:	9,321	:	:	:
Domestic producer price index (1995=100)	:	:	:	:	:	:	100.0	101.6	102.3	101.8	101.4
Value added (million ECU)	3,442	3,030	2,996	2,964	2,915	3,177	:	3,594	:	:	:

(1) Technically, data before 01/01/1999 are in ECU and after this date in euro. However, as the conversion rate was 1 ECU =1 EUR, for practical purposes the two terms can be used interchangeably.

Table 7.39

Manufacture of other non-metallic mineral products (NACE Rev. 1 26.8)

Trade related indicators in the EU (1)

	1989	1990	1991	1992	1993	1994	1995	1996	1997	1998	1999
Exports (million EUR)	879	870	900	895	1,093	1,193	1,304	1,406	1,651	1,685	1,672
Imports (million EUR)	488	536	582	628	671	727	755	815	932	1,030	1,069
Trade balance (million EUR)	390	334	318	267	421	466	549	591	719	655	603
Cover ratio (%)	180.0	162.4	154.7	142.6	162.8	164.0	172.8	172.5	177.2	163.6	156.4

(1) Technically, data before 01/01/1999 are in ECU and after this date in euro. However, as the conversion rate was 1 ECU =1 EUR, for practical purposes the two terms can be used interchangeably.

Table 7.40

Manufacture of other non-metallic mineral products (NACE Rev. 1 26.8)

Production related indicators, 1997

	B	DK	D	EL	E	F	IRL	I (1)	L	NL	A	P	FIN	S	UK
Number of persons employed (thousands)	1.0	2.1	21.8	:	6.1	9.7	0.5	5.6	0.2	:	3.3	1.2	1.6	2.0	12.8
Production (million ECU)	242	235	2,991	:	786	1,385	78	828	19	446	437	107	233	264	1,497
Value added (million ECU)	61	103	1,191	:	268	488	25	261	8	196	184	33	92	100	645
Gross operating surplus (million ECU)	22.6	36.6	316.5	:	105.1	77.4	11.5	98.8	0.6	91.5	50.2	16.6	40.7	32.8	276.5

(1) 1996.

Table 7.41

Manufacture of other non-metallic mineral products (NACE Rev. 1 26.8)

Trade related indicators, 1999

	B	DK	D	EL	E	F	IRL	I	L	NL	A	P	FIN	S	UK
Exports (million EUR)	278	71	1,323	10	172	736	32	530	48	300	275	22	96	132	567
Imports (million EUR)	205	111	919	33	231	526	70	425	30	290	214	60	65	133	467
Trade balance (million EUR)	74	-41	404	-23	-59	210	-38	104	18	10	62	-38	32	-1	100
Cover ratio (%)	136.0	63.5	144.0	30.0	74.6	139.8	46.3	124.5	160.6	103.4	128.8	36.7	148.7	99.1	121.5

Table 7.42

Manufacture of other non-metallic mineral products (NACE Rev. 1 26.8)

Labour related indicators, 1997

	B	DK (1)	D	EL	E	F	IRL	I (2)	L	NL	A	P	FIN	S	UK
Unit personnel costs (thousand ECU per employee)	40.8	37.7	40.1	:	26.1	42.5	28.9	29.7	32.3	:	40.5	13.9	32.4	33.9	29.1
Social charges as a share of personnel costs (%)	40.0	3.9	24.2	:	27.3	44.7	25.5	52.5	:	16.8	32.8	30.9	26.2	51.7	14.0
Apparent labour productivity (thousand ECU/pers. empl.)	59.8	48.5	54.6	:	43.7	50.5	53.7	46.3	34.9	:	55.7	27.7	56.7	50.4	50.2
Wage adjusted labour productivity (%)	146.6	157.3	135.9	:	167.4	118.8	185.9	155.9	108.2	:	137.5	199.1	175.0	148.9	172.6
Personnel costs as a share of total operating costs (%)	17.5	32.1	28.4	:	19.9	24.8	19.7	19.7	40.4	24.2	30.0	14.9	26.4	24.9	27.8

(1) Unit personnel costs and wage adjusted labour productivity, 1996; (2) 1996.

Source: Eurostat (SBS, EBT, COMEXT)

Basic metal processing (NACE Rev. 1 27)

The manufacture of basic metals (NACE Rev. 1 27) is analysed within two sub-chapters in this publication, one dealing with ferrous metals, the other with non-ferrous metals. The former includes the manufacture of basic iron, steel and ferro-alloys, as well as tubes, other first processing and the casting of iron and steel (NACE Rev. 1 Groups 27.1 to 27.3 and NACE Rev. 1 Classes 27.51 and 27.52). The non-ferrous metals industry consists of basic precious and non-ferrous metals and the casting of light and other non-ferrous metals (NACE Rev. 1 Group 27.4 and NACE Rev. 1 Classes 27.53 and 27.54).

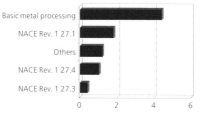

————————————————Figure 8.1

Basic metal processing (NACE Rev. 1 27)
Share of total manufacturing value added
in the EU, 1996 (%)

Source: Eurostat (SBS)

The activities covered in this chapter (in terms of NACE Rev. 1) include:

27:   manufacture of basic metals;
27.1: manufacture of basic iron and steel and of ferro-alloys (ECSC[1]);
27.2: manufacture of tubes;
27.3: other first processing of iron and steel and production of non-ECSC[1] ferro-alloys;
27.4: manufacture of basic precious and non-ferrous metals;
27.5: casting of metals.

---

(1) ECSC: European Coal and Steel Community.

Total EU output of basic metals amounted to 171 billion ECU in 1996, 4.8% of total manufacturing production. As regards the size of the workforce, 917 thousand persons were employed in basic metals in the EU in 1996 (equivalent to 4.0% of the manufacturing workforce in the Union).

Iron and steel accounted for more
than 40% of production
The ferrous metals industry was significantly larger in terms of manufacturing output than the non-ferrous metals sector. The three ferrous metal producing activities for which data was available (NACE Rev. 1 27.1, 27.2 and 27.3) had a combined output of 104 billion ECU[1] in 1996. The largest individual Group was the manufacture of basic iron and steel and ferro-alloys (NACE Rev. 1 27.1), which accounted for 41.8% of production amongst those industries covered in this chapter in 1996. Compared to this, the principal non-ferrous metals Group was the manufacture of basic precious and non-ferrous metals (NACE Rev. 1 27.4) which accounted for 27.8% of the total. The casting of metals (NACE Rev. 1 27.5) accounted for approximately 11.0% of basic metals output[2]. Figures for production in the Member States indicate that ferrous metals casting was generally somewhat more important, as in 1997 it accounted for 59.8% of output in the United Kingdom, 51.9% in France and 69.6% in Spain.

---

(1) IRL and A, no data available for NACE Rev. 1 27.2.

(2) DK, IRL, L and A, no data available.

Majority of employment in ferrous metals production
Ferrous metals was also largest sub-sector in this chapter in terms of the size of the EU workforce in 1996, with NACE Rev. 1 Groups 27.1 to 27.3[3] accounting for approximately 52% of the total number of persons employed in the industry. Basic iron and steel and ferro-alloys (NACE Rev. 1 27.1 was responsible for 34.1% of the employment total. The equivalent figure for the largest non-ferrous metals industry was 21.9% for basic precious and non-ferrous metals (NACE Rev. 1 27.4). The casting of metals (NACE Rev. 1 27.5) is divided between ferrous and non-ferrous metals, and employed almost a quarter of the workforce, despite being responsible for just over 10%[4] of the output in this industry.

Important role for large enterprises in this industry
There were 16.7 thousand enterprises in this industry in 1996, a figure that represented just 0.8% of the manufacturing total (considerably lower than other measures of the size that are recorded for this industry). Generally, large enterprises played an important role, which was borne out when studying the composition of employment broken down between enterprise size classes. Large enterprises (of which there were 737 in the EU in 1996) accounted for 697 thousand persons employed (or 70.3% of the total).

(3) IRL, NL and A, no data available for NACE Rev. 1 Groups 27.1 and 27.2; DK, IRL, NL and A, no data available for NACE Rev. 1 Groups 27.3 and 27.5; DK, IRL, L, NL and A, no data available for NACE Rev. 1 Group 27.5; EU total calculated using all available data.
(4) DK, IRL, L and A, no data available.

Table 8.1 _____

Basic metal processing (NACE Rev. 1 27)

Breakdown of turnover and employment by employment size class, 1997 (%)

	Micro (0-9)		Small (10-49)		Medium (50-249)		Large (250+)	
	Turnover (1)	Employment (2)	Turnover (1)	Employment (3)	Turnover (1)	Employment (4)	Turnover (1)	Employment (3)
EU-15	1.7	3.1	7.6	9.6	15.4	16.9	75.3	70.3
B	0.9	1.5	3.3	5.5	7.9	9.0	87.8	84.1
DK	:	:	:	:	:	:	:	:
D	0.5	1.7	3.3	7.0	7.5	10.0	88.7	81.3
EL	:	:	:	:	:	:	:	:
E	2.7	5.9	10.4	15.6	21.5	20.9	65.4	57.6
F	2.2	1.6	10.0	6.7	13.4	17.8	74.5	73.9
IRL	:	:	:	:	:	:	:	:
I	1.8	4.1	15.8	18.6	28.8	25.3	53.6	52.1
L	:	:	:	:	:	:	:	:
NL	:	:	:	6.1	:	10.2	:	79.3
A	1.1	0.9	3.6	2.4	25.4	15.5	69.9	81.2
P	3.7	10.0	9.5	16.7	35.9	38.9	51.0	34.5
FIN	0.6	1.5	1.8	3.6	7.5	13.8	90.0	81.0
S	1.0	:	3.4	5.0	21.3	:	74.3	73.1
UK	4.1	7.4	7.1	10.1	15.8	20.9	73.1	61.5

(1) EU-15, E, F, I, P and S, 1996.
(2) EU-15, F, I and P, 1996.
(3) EU-15, F, I, NL, P and S, 1996.
(4) EU-15, F, I, NL and P, 1996.

Source: Eurostat (SME)

_____Box 8.1

Competition in the global steel industry is fierce. Firms such as Posco (South Korea) and China Steel (Taiwan) have grown rapidly in recent years, whilst in mature markets new technologies have facilitated the entry of companies like Riva (I) and LNM (NL). As global steel production has failed to evolve during the past decade (770 million tons in 1990, 788 million tons in 1999, source: International Iron and Steel Institute), established enterprises have started to specialise in niche markets, or have consolidated through merger activity in an attempt to benefit from economies of scale. The EU has seen a spate of mergers and acquisitions in the late 1990s. Corus was formed from the amalgamation of British Steel (UK) and Hoogovens (NL), and followed the mergers of Thysen (D) and Krupp (D), Stahlwerke (D) and Sidstahl (B), Usinor (F) and Cockerill-Sambre (B) and Arbed (L) and Aceralia (E).

STRUCTURE AND PERFORMANCE

Nominal production increased by only 20.3% in the EU between 1986 and 1996 (to reach 28.8 billion ECU). This rate of increase was considerably less than the 37.7% increase for total manufacturing. As such, basic metals was responsible for just 2.2% of the expansion of EU manufacturing during this period (well below its 4.8% share of output) The absolute change in value added was lower still, rising by 14.1% over the same period.

In real terms, production was often in decline in the basic metals industry, as demonstrated by the negative annual average rate of change between 1991 and 1996 of 0.7% per annum. This could be compared to the average annual growth rate for manufacturing of 1.5% per annum over the same period.

The output of the basic metals industry fell at a moderate pace to 1993 in constant price terms, when there was a significant reduction of 12.3%. Subsequently, there was a marked recovery, with real growth of 12.0% in 1994 and 8.5% in 1995, followed by a further contraction of 9.0% in the following year. This trend contrasted with that seen for total manufacturing, where the decline in output in 1993 was much less pronounced (-4.3%) and the subsequent recovery continued to be sustained in 1996.

In volume terms the production and consumption of basic metals have increased substantially in the last five years. Nevertheless, the world price of most metals has decreased, probably as a result of high levels of competition and globalisation within the sector.

Below average growth in most Member States over the latest ten-year period

The annual average growth rates over the most recent ten-year period indicate that in most Member States real output increased at a significantly lower rate than manufacturing as a whole. Germany was an exception to this rule, as average growth over the ten years to 1997 was 2.7%, just a tenth of a percentage point lower than the manufacturing average. In the United Kingdom (0.5%, 1997), France (2.2%, 1996) and Italy (0.4%, 1996) output rose by at least 1.5 percentage points less than the domestic manufacturing average. Only Denmark (3.2%, 1997) and Greece (2.0%, 1996) reported growth of basic metals above that of domestic manufacturing norms.

_____Figure 8.2

Basic metal processing (NACE Rev. 1 27)

EU production and value-added in constant prices and employment compared to total manufacturing (1990=100)

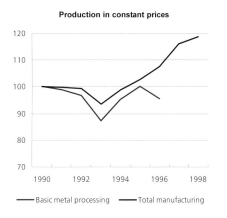

Production in constant prices

— Basic metal processing   — Total manufacturing

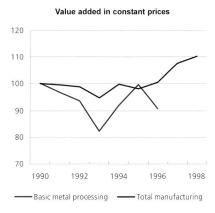

Value added in constant prices

— Basic metal processing   — Total manufacturing

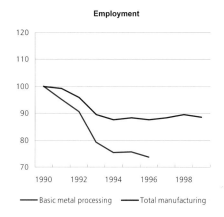

Employment

— Basic metal processing   — Total manufacturing

Source: Eurostat (SBS)

LABOUR AND PRODUCTIVITY

The decline in employment was generally a gradual process, except for the large-scale reductions in 1993, when the number of persons employed fell by 12.5%. The only year between 1986 and 1996 when there was an expansion in employment levels was 1995, with a slight increase of 0.3%. The downward trend continued in 1996, when a 2.4% reduction took place.

Workforce reduced by over one third since the mid-eighties

There were over 511 thousand fewer persons employed in the EU basic metals industry in 1996 than ten years before, with the workforce falling from 1.43 million to 917 thousand persons. EU manufacturing employment fell by 10.0% over this period, and one-fifth of the net reduction was accounted for by job losses within the basic metals industry.

Translated into an annual average rate of change, employment fell by 4.3% per annum between 1986 and 1996; this compared unfavourably with the figure for manufacturing as a whole, -1.0% per annum. The rapid reduction of the workforce in the basic metals industry led to the share of basic metals in total manufacturing employment falling from 5.6% in 1986 to 4.0% by 1996.

High proportion of males and persons employed full time

The labour characteristics of this industry closely follow the stereotypical traditional, mature industry. There was a high degree of reliance on a male labour force, working full-time, within large enterprises where there were relatively low levels of labour flexibility. Furthermore, there is a low level of entrepreneurial activity (probably due to high start-up costs and a relatively large minimum efficient scale of production). Indeed, only 2.4% of the workforce were self-employed in 1999[5].

Employment in this industry was almost exclusively on a full-time basis in 1998, with 96.9% of the persons employed working full-time (compared to 92.7% who worked full-time in the whole manufacturing sector in 1998). This was the third highest figure amongst the 22 NACE Rev. 1 manufacturing Divisions. There was little development in this figure since 1993 when the same ratio was equal to 96.3%.

Accompanying the decline in the number of persons employed, there was an increase in persons employed with a temporary or fixed-duration contract. In the EU[6] in 1999, 90.8% of those employed had a permanent contract, as opposed to 94.5% in 1994, suggesting that employers were turning to more flexible working patterns, in an attempt to efficiently meet fluctuations in demand.

(5) EL, no data available.
(6) EL, no data available.

Table 8.2

Basic metal processing (NACE Rev. 1 27)
Composition of the labour force, 1999 (%)

	Women (1)	Full-time (2)	Highly-educated (3)
EU-15	12.1	96.9	13.5
B	5.7	98.8	10.7
DK	33.4	100.0	25.9
D	15.2	96.7	15.6
EL	:	100.0	:
E	9.1	99.6	26.0
F	12.2	95.6	17.2
IRL	:	94.4	:
I	13.7	97.7	3.5
L	:	98.4	8.6
NL	:	88.0	17.5
A	17.5	96.5	6.6
P	18.8	100.0	:
FIN	20.8	100.0	27.1
S	:	98.8	:
UK	12.9	96.2	15.0

(1) EU-15, 1998; DK, 1997.
(2) 1998.
(3) NL, 1998; EU-15, DK, L and UK, 1997.

Source: Eurostat (LFS)

Productivity rose faster than the manufacturing average

The rationalisation process influenced the figures for apparent labour productivity, which rose from 29.1 thousand ECU in 1986 to 51.7 thousand ECU in 1996. As such, the apparent labour productivity of basic metals was 5.2 thousand ECU higher than the manufacturing average, a considerable improvement on the situation for 1986 when the difference was just 0.5 thousand ECU per person employed.

Figure 8.3

Basic metal processing (NACE Rev. 1 27)
Apparent labour productivity and unit personnel costs, 1997 (thousand ECU)

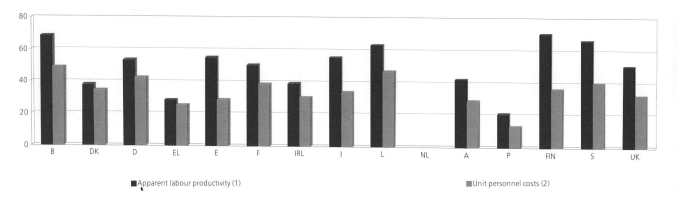

■ Apparent labour productivity (1)   ▨ Unit personnel costs (2)

(1) EL, F and I, 1996; NL, not available.
(2) DK, EL, F and I, 1996; NL, not available.

Source: Eurostat (SBS)

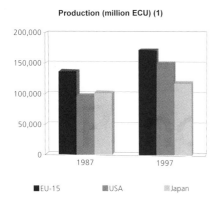

_____ Figure 8.4

Basic metal processing (NACE Rev. 1 27)

International comparison of production, value added and employment

Production (million ECU) (1)

Value added (million ECU) (2)

Employment (units) (2)

■EU-15 ■USA Japan

(1) EU-15, 1996.
(2) EU-15 and JAP, 1996.

Source: Eurostat (SBS)

INTERNATIONAL TRENDS AND FOREIGN TRADE

The EU produced 40.2% of total Triad output (425 billion ECU) in this industry in 1996, a share that was consistent with the data from 1991 (40.1%). The other two members of the Triad had similar levels of output 128 billion ECU (30.2%) in the USA and 126 billion ECU (29.7%) in Japan. However, since 1991, there was a considerable shift in the respective shares of Japan (-5 percentage points) and the USA (+5 percentage points). This trend continued in 1997, when American production rose to 150 billion ECU, whilst Japanese output fell below its 1990 figure (118 billion ECU).

Basic metals is a declining industry
in both the EU and Japan...

Of the Triad members, only the USA basic metals industry maintained its relative importance within domestic manufacturing output between 1992 and 1997, with a 4.3% share. In Japan, over the same period, basic metals lost 0.8 percentage points, to finish with a 5.4% share of total Japanese manufacturing output in 1997. In the EU the share of this industry in the manufacturing total fell from 6.5% in 1986 to 4.8% in 1996.

... whilst maintaining its position in the USA

As with production, the EU was the largest employer in the Triad in 1996, with 48.2% of the 1.9 million persons employed. The average annual reduction of 5.0% per annum between 1991 and 1996, was at a faster pace than in Japan (-3.8% per annum). However, in the USA the number of persons employed

remained relatively stable (average annual rate of change of 0.4% per annum between 1992 and 1997) to result in 617 thousand persons employed. As a result, the relative share of USA employment in the Triad total rose from 28.2% in 1992 to 32.7% in 1996.

EU a net importer...

The EU ran a trade deficit of 11.7 billion EUR in 1999, a figure that has changed little since 1995 (when there was a surge in the level of imports). One of the contributing factors to this trend was the increase in imports from the Russian Federation (the largest origin of imports in 1999). Indeed, Russian imports increased to 4.6 billion EUR in 1999 (compared to 2.3 billion ECU from the USSR in 1989).The USA was the second largest importer in 1999 (4.1 billion EUR), with Switzerland and Norway close behind. South Africa had been the largest importer in 1989, but with 3.6 billion EUR ten years later it slipped to fifth position.

... with a falling share of total manufacturing exports

The declining relative importance of the basic metals industry was also reflected when analysing its export share in total manufacturing exports, which declined from 7.4% in 1989 to 3.9% in 1999. The USA and Switzerland were the two main destination markets for EU exports (in both 1989 and 1999), with values of 5.5 billion EUR and 3.3 billion EUR in 1999. Norway was the third most important destination, with 1.2 billion EUR.

_____ Figure 8.5

Basic metal processing (NACE Rev. 1 27)

Destination of EU exports, 1999 (%)

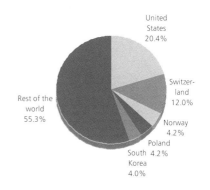

United States 20.4%

Switzerland 12.0%

Rest of the world 55.3%

Norway 4.2%

Poland 4.2%

South Korea 4.0%

Source: Eurostat (COMEXT)

_____ Figure 8.6

Basic metal processing (NACE Rev. 1 27)

Origin of EU imports, 1999 (%)

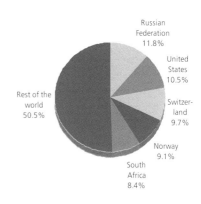

Russian Federation 11.8%

United States 10.5%

Switzerland 9.7%

Rest of the world 50.5%

Norway 9.1%

South Africa 8.4%

Source: Eurostat (COMEXT)

SUB-CHAPTER 8.1
FERROUS METALS
(NACE Rev. 1 27.1, 27.2 AND 27.3)

This ferrous metals sub-chapter covers both first processing and basic processing activities. The data presented generally cover three NACE Rev. 1 Groups
27.1 to 27.3: the manufacture of basic iron and steel
and of ferro-alloys (NACE Rev. 1 27.1), the manufacture of tubes (NACE Rev. 1 27.2) and other first processing of iron and steel and the production of other
ferro-alloys (NACE Rev. 1 27.3).

The EU was the largest steel producer in the world in
1998 with output of crude steel equal to 159.9 million
metric tons in volume terms. NAFTA consumed more
crude steel than the EU, accounting for just over one
fifth of the world's crude steel consumption in 1998.
The increase in supply of steel in recent years can be
largely attributed to expanding production in China,
the Ukraine and Russia. Indeed, the C.I.S. saw its output exceed consumption by 44.8 million metric tons in
1998. It is likely that excess supply was largely responsible for the falling price of crude steel in 1998.

Basic iron and steel (NACE Rev. 1 27.1) was the largest
of the three NACE Rev. 1 Groups covered in this sub-
chapter in 1996, with 71.4 billion ECU of output
(approximately two thirds of ferrous metals production). The manufacture of tubes (NACE Rev. 1 27.2)
followed with 16.8 billion ECU[7], whilst other first processing of iron and steel (NACE Rev. 1 27.3) had a production value of 15.5 billion ECU.

Germany was the largest producer, but
Luxembourg was the most specialised
Germany produced ferrous metal goods to the value
of 29.3 billion ECU in 1997, equivalent to 2.9% of
total domestic manufacturing output. Italy was the
second largest EU producer with 17.5 billion ECU of
production value in 1996 (3.5% of the national manufacturing total). Luxembourg's manufacturing economy relied heavily on the ferrous metals industry, with
23.2% of domestic manufacturing output (1.5 billion
ECU[8] in 1997). Belgium was the next most specialised
country in this industry, as its 6.9 billion ECU of production accounted for 4.6% of domestic manufacturing.

(7) IRL and A, no data available.
(8) NACE Rev. 1 27.2 and 27.3, no data available.

Figure 8.7

Ferrous metals (NACE Rev. 1 27.1, 27.2 and 27.3)
Production and export specialisation (%)

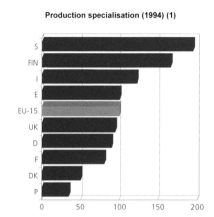

Production specialisation (1994) (1)

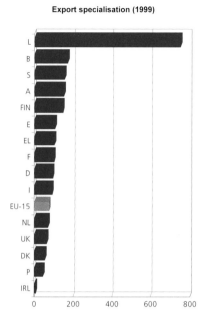

Export specialisation (1999)

(1) B, EL, IRL, L, NL and A, not available.

Source: Eurostat (SBS, COMEXT)

STRUCTURE AND PERFORMANCE
European Union ferrous metal (NACE Rev. 1 27.1 to
27.3) production value increased by 11.2% between
1986 (93.1 billion ECU) and 1996 (104 billion ECU)[9],
a figure much lower than the nominal increase recorded for the whole of manufacturing (60.5%). Value
added rose at an even slower pace, up by 5.2% in
nominal terms compared to a 46.4% increase in manufacturing.

Growth rates adjusted for producer price inflation
indicated that in real terms there was a significant
decline in output between 1990 and 1993 (for example, -10.1% in 1993). Nevertheless, there was growth
of 18.9% in the following year. In the largest activity,
the manufacture of basic iron and steel (NACE Rev. 1
27.1), production in constant prices declined at an
annual average rate of 2.2% in the five years to 1996.
This reduction was also marked by highly fluctuating
rates of change, with real growth of 11.1% in 1994
and 20.5% in 1995 being cancelled out by declines of
11.2% in 1993 and 26.0% in 1996.

(9) IRL and A, no data available for NACE Rev. 1 27.2 in 1996.

Profitability generally below
the manufacturing average
The gross operating rate (defined as value added
minus personnel costs divided by turnover) gives an
indication of the profitability of an activity. During the
recession of the early 1990s, the operating rate for the
EU ferrous metals industry (NACE Rev. 1 27.1, 27.2
and 27.3) was well below the manufacturing average
(3.0% in 1993, which was 5.2 percentage points
lower than the manufacturing average). There was a
recovery in 1994, as the operating rate rose to 8.1%.

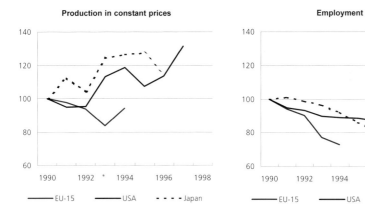

Figure 8.8

Ferrous metals (NACE Rev. 1 27.1, 27.2 and 27.3)

International comparison of production in constant prices and employment (1990=100)

Production in constant prices

Employment

EU-15　　USA　　- - - Japan

EU-15　　USA　　- - - Japan

Source: Eurostat (SBS)

Table 8.3

Cold drawing of steel bars (NACE Rev. 1 27.31)

Main indicators in volume terms, EU-12 (1)

	1988	1989	1990	1991	1992	1993	1994	1995	1996	1997	1998	1999
Production (thousand tonnes)	2,598	2,627	2,609	2,307	2,217	2,066	2,429	2,542	2,253	2,492	2,573	2,509
Number of persons employed	:	:	8,498	8,281	8,243	8,158	8,004	8,014	7,716	7,563	7,240	7,208
Labour productivity (tonnes/person employed)	:	:	307	279	269	253	304	317	292	330	355	348

(1) Excluding A, FIN and S.

Source: EBA

Table 8.4

Cold rolling of steel strip (NACE Rev. 1 27.32)

Main indicators in volume terms, EU-12 (1)

	1988	1989	1990	1991	1992	1993	1994	1995	1996	1997	1998	1999
Production (thousand tonnes)	3,017	3,232	3,147	2,966	2,763	2,556	2,940	3,029	2,777	3,229	3,744	3,979
Number of persons employed	16,400	16,200	15,684	15,311	14,940	14,895	14,735	14,121	13,752	13,425	13,642	13,629
Labour productivity (tonnes/person employed)	184	200	201	194	185	172	200	215	202	241	274	292

(1) Excluding A, FIN and S.

Source: CIELFFA

Table 8.5

Cold forming or folding of steel - long sections only (part of NACE Rev. 1 27.33)

Main indicators in volume terms, EU-12 (1)

	1988	1989	1990	1991	1992	1993	1994	1995	1996	1997	1998	1999
Production (thousand tonnes)	1,223	1,238	1,230	1,387	1,722	1,678	1,809	1,786	1,821	1,991	2,143	2,171
Number of persons employed	:	:	8,151	7,907	8,650	8,215	8,677	8,522	8,481	8,722	8,512	8,577
Labour productivity (tonnes/person employed)	:	:	151	175	199	204	209	210	215	228	252	253

(1) Excluding A, FIN and S.

Source: CIPF

Table 8.6

Cold drawing of steel wire (NACE Rev. 1 27.34)

Main indicators in volume terms, EU-12 (1)

	1988	1989	1990	1991	1992	1993	1994	1995	1996	1997	1998	1999
Production (thousand tonnes)	4,500	4,685	4,943	4,838	4,926	4,692	5,144	5,047	4,675	5,057	5,307	5,392
Number of persons employed	:	:	35,361	34,110	32,385	31,394	31,307	30,411	30,340	29,327	28,151	27,370
Labour productivity (tonnes/person employed)	:	:	140	142	152	150	164	166	154	172	189	197

(1) Excluding A, FIN and S.

Source: CET

Table 8.7

Top twenty steel producing countries in the world

(million metric tons of crude steel production)

Rank		1993	1994	1995	1996	1997	1998	1999 (1)	1998/99 (%)
1	Mainland China	89.5	92.6	95.4	101.2	108.9	114.6	123.3	7.6
2	United States	88.8	91.2	95.2	95.5	98.5	97.7	97.2	-0.5
3	Japan	99.6	98.3	101.6	98.8	104.5	93.5	94.2	0.7
4	Russia	58.3	48.8	51.6	49.3	48.5	43.8	49.8	13.5
5	Germany	37.6	40.8	42.1	39.8	45.0	44.0	42.1	-4.5
6	R.of Korea	33.0	33.7	36.8	38.9	42.6	39.9	41.0	2.9
7	Ukraine	32.6	24.1	22.3	22.3	25.6	24.4	27.0	10.6
8	Brazil	25.2	25.7	25.1	25.2	26.2	25.8	25.0	-3.0
9	Italy	25.7	26.2	27.8	23.9	25.8	25.7	25.0	-2.9
10	India	18.2	19.3	22.0	23.8	24.4	23.5	24.3	3.5
11	France	17.1	18.0	18.1	17.6	19.8	20.1	20.2	0.4
12	United Kingdom	16.6	17.3	17.6	18.0	18.5	17.3	16.3	-5.8
13	Canada	14.4	13.9	14.4	14.7	15.6	15.9	16.3	2.3
14	Taiwan	12.0	11.6	11.6	12.4	16.0	16.9	15.4	-9.1
15	Mexico	9.2	10.3	12.1	13.2	14.2	14.2	15.3	7.7
16	Spain	13.0	13.4	13.8	12.2	13.7	14.8	14.6	-1.4
17	Turkey	11.5	12.6	13.2	13.6	14.5	14.1	14.4	1.5
18	Belgium	10.2	11.3	11.6	10.8	10.7	11.4	11.0	-4.0
19	Poland	9.9	11.1	11.9	10.4	11.6	9.9	8.8	-11.5
20	Australia	7.9	8.4	8.5	8.4	8.8	8.9	8.2	-8.5

(1) Provisional.

Source: IISI (International Iron and Steel Institute)

LABOUR AND PRODUCTIVITY

There were 480 thousand persons employed[10] in the ferrous metals industry (NACE Rev. 1 27.1 to 27.3) in 1996. This represented a reduction of 47.7% on the 918 thousand persons employed in 1986. As such, ferrous metals accounted for nearly one in five of the net reduction in jobs for total manufacturing during the period 1986 to 1996.

The shedding of labour in the early 1990s took place at a slower rate than the reduction in economic activity, as wage adjusted labour productivity fell to 116.7% in 1993, but rebounded to 143.1% in 1996. The increase in the relative importance of personnel costs during the recession was reflected when analysing the share of personnel costs in production, which rose as high as 23.8% in 1992, subsequently falling to 18.6% by 1997 (some 1.2 percentage points above the manufacturing average).

(10) IRL and NL, no data available for NACE Rev. 1 27.1; IRL, NL and A, no data available for NACE Rev. 1 27.2; DK, IRL, L, NL and A, no data available for NACE Rev. 1 27.3.

—————— Box 8.2

POSCO (South Korea) was the largest steel producing company in the world with 26.5 million tons of crude steel output in 1999, just ahead of Nippon Steel (JAP) with 25.2 million tons. The three largest EU based firms all saw their production volumes increase (partly as a result of recent acquisitions), with Arbed (L) and Usinor (F) both producing 22.2 million tons of crude steel, followed by Corus (UK) with 21.3 million tons.

—————— Table 8.8

Top ten largest steel producing companies in the world (million metric tons)

	1998		1999	
	Crude steel production	Ranking	Crude steel production	Ranking
POSCO (South Korea)	25.6	1	26.5	1
Nippon Steel (Japan)	25.1	2	25.2	2
Arbed (L)	20.1	3	22.2	3
Usinor (F) (1)	18.9	4	22.2	4
Corus (UK)	16.3	6	21.3	5
LNM (NL)	17.1	5	20.0	6
Baoshan (China)	9.9	13	16.7	7
Thyssen Krupp (D) (2)	14.8	7	16.1	8
Riva (I)	13.3	8	14.1	9
NKK (Japan)	11.5	9	12.8	10

(1) Includes Cockerill-Sambre.
(2) Includes 50% of HKM.

Source: IISI (International Iron and Steel Institute)

INTERNATIONAL TRENDS AND FOREIGN TRADE

The EU's share of Triad production of ferrous metals fell in the 1990s by 2.7 percentage points to 41.7%[11] in 1996. The USA increased its share, up by four percentage points to 24.0% between 1990 and 1996, and reported a further increase in output equal to 10.0 billion ECU in 1997 (resulting in total output of 69.6 billion ECU). The Japanese share of Triad production remained fairly stable between 1990 and 1996 (34.3%), with the latest production value available for 1997 (78.7 billion ECU).

EU trade balance narrowing

Extra-EU exports remained relatively stable during the 1990s, close to the 15.3 billion EUR recorded in 1999 (other than a high of 19.6 billion ECU in 1997). The share of EU ferrous metal exports in total manufacturing exports fell from 4.8% in 1989 to 2.2% in 1999. Imports on the other hand increased from 7.2 billion ECU in 1989 to 11.1 billion EUR ten years later. As a result the EU trade surplus was equal to 4.2 billion EUR in 1999.

Russian Federation of growing importance
as an origin of imports

The Russian Federation was the main origin of imports into the EU in 1999, with goods to a value of 1.2 billion EUR, more than double the value imported from the former Soviet Union ten years earlier (533 million ECU). Norway was the main origin of imports in 1989, but slipped to second in the ranking in 1999 (with 801 million EUR). The USA was the principal export market for EU ferrous metal goods in 1999, with a value of 3.3 billion EUR. Switzerland was the second largest export market (1.3 billion EUR), followed by Poland (713 million ECU).

(11) IRL and A, no data available for NACE Rev. 1 27.2 in 1996.

—————— Figure 8.9

Ferrous metals
(NACE Rev. 1 27.1, 27.2 and 27.3)
Destination of EU exports, 1999 (%)

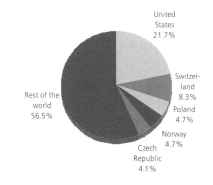

Source: Eurostat (COMEXT)

—————— Figure 8.10

Ferrous metals
(NACE Rev. 1 27.1, 27.2 and 27.3)
Origin of EU imports, 1999 (%)

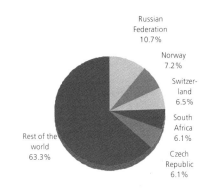

Source: Eurostat (COMEXT)

SUB-CHAPTER 8.2
BASIC PRECIOUS AND
NON-FERROUS METALS
(NACE Rev. 1 27.4)

The data presented in this sub-chapter are comprised of precious metals (NACE Rev. 1 27.41), aluminium (NACE Rev. 1 27.42), lead, zinc and tin (NACE Rev. 1 27.43), copper (NACE Rev. 1 27.44) and other non-ferrous metals (NACE Rev. 1 27.45). Production and semi-manufacturing are the principal processes included in the definition.

In terms of total production value, basic precious and non-ferrous metals (NACE Rev. 1 27.4) was the second largest NACE Rev. 1 Group within the basic metals industry, behind basic iron and steel. Total EU output in 1996 amounted to 47.6 billion ECU or 27.8% of the basic metals total. The share of value added at factor cost was considerably lower, 22.7% of the total. Just over a fifth of employment within the EU basic metals industry was accounted for by non-ferrous metals; 21.5% or 197 thousand persons in 1996.

Germany the largest producer, but smaller Member States were more specialised
Germany produced more basic precious and non-ferrous metals than any other Member State in 1997 (15.8 billion ECU), followed by France (7.0 billion ECU) and the United Kingdom (6.5 billion ECU). However, this industry had its highest share of national manufacturing output in Greece (4.7%), followed by Luxembourg (3.9%).

STRUCTURE AND PERFORMANCE
The value of EU basic precious and non-ferrous metals production increased from 35.6 billion ECU in 1986 to 47.6 billion ECU ten years later (a nominal increase of 33.5%). When adjusted to take account of changes in producer prices, EU production grew at an average annual rate of just 0.9% during the five-year period 1991 to 1996. This average hid the fact that there was a decline in real output in the early 1990s, with a subsequent recovery in 1996, when production in constant prices rose by 6.8% in real terms. Value added at factor cost rose in real terms by 1.4% per annum between 1991 and 1996 (some 1.2 percentage points above the manufacturing average).

Figure 8.11

Basic precious and non-ferrous metals (NACE Rev. 1 27.4)
Production and export specialisation (%)

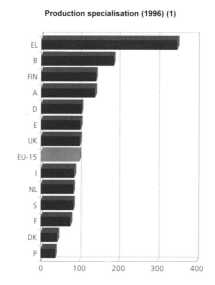

Production specialisation (1996) (1)

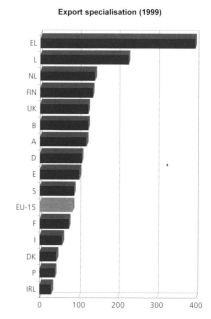

Export specialisation (1999)

(1) IRL and L, not available.

Source: Eurostat (SBS, COMEXT)

Figure 8.12

Production in volume terms of metal casting in the EU, 1998 (%) (1)

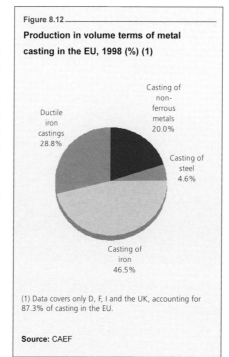

(1) Data covers only D, F, I and the UK, accounting for 87.3% of casting in the EU.

Source: CAEF

Figure 8.13

Production in volume terms of non-ferrous metal casting in the EU, 1998 (%) (1)

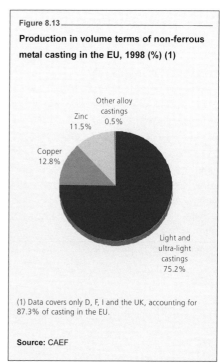

(1) Data covers only D, F, I and the UK, accounting for 87.3% of casting in the EU.

Source: CAEF

EU profitability trails the manufacturing average

Despite value added expanding at a faster rate than the manufacturing average, the gross operating rate remained low. In 1996, the operating rate was equal to 6.5%, 2.1 percentage points below the basic metal processing average. In 1997, Spain (11.4%), Luxembourg (11.2%) and the United Kingdom (10.0%) had the highest operating ratios.

LABOUR AND PRODUCTIVITY

Employment within the basic precious and non-ferrous metals industry fell at a more moderate pace than the basic metals average. However, employment was still reduced by almost a quarter (24.2%) between 1986 and 1996 (a net reduction of 62.9 thousand persons). The number of persons employed fell by over 6% in 1992 and 1993, but the rate of decline moderated subsequently, with an increase of 3.8% reported in 1996. Over the five years to 1996, the average annual rate of decline was 3.9%.

Apparent labour productivity was relatively stable at the start of the 1990s and close to the EU total manufacturing average. However, by 1996 apparent labour productivity was 8.2 thousand ECU per person employed higher for basic precious and non-ferrous metals, at 54.7 thousand ECU. There was a similar development observed in the figures for wage adjusted labour productivity, up from 119.8% in 1993 to 145.1% in 1996 (overtaking the manufacturing average).

INTERNATIONAL TRENDS AND FOREIGN TRADE

The USA become the largest producer in the Triad in 1996, accounting for 39.9% of total Triad non-ferrous metals output (just ahead of the EU with 38.4%). The differential between EU and American shares of total Triad value added widened, with the USA gaining 4.0 percentage points between 1991 and 1996, to attain a 45.8% share. Over the same period the EU lost 3.2 percentage points, to finish with 32.3% of Triad value added in 1996.

USA the largest trading partner of the EU

EU exports almost doubled during the 1990s to reach 12.1 billion EUR in 1999, equivalent to a 1.7% share of total EU manufacturing exports. Nevertheless, the EU's trade deficit grew to 16.1 billion EUR in 1999. Indeed, in 1998 all three Triad members ran trade deficits: 20.3 billion ECU in the EU, 6.9 billion ECU in the USA and 4.5 billion ECU in Japan.

7The main origin of imports into the EU was the USA (3.5 billion EUR in 1999), closely followed by Russia (3.4 billion EUR). These two countries significantly improved their positions, rising from fourth (USA) and fifth (former USSR) most important importers in 1989. South Africa dropped from first place in 1989 to fifth place in 1999 (below Switzerland and Norway).

The USA was also the largest export market for the EU in 1999 (2.2 billion EUR). Switzerland was the second most important export destination (it had been the most important in 1989), with an export value of 2.0 billion EUR. South Korea was the third biggest export destination for EU non-ferrous metals (861 million EUR), reporting a considerable increase on the 118 million ECU of exports in 1989.

_____ Figure 8.14

Basic precious and non-ferrous metals (NACE Rev. 1 27.4)

International comparison of production in constant prices and employment (1990=100)

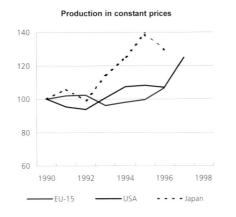

Production in constant prices

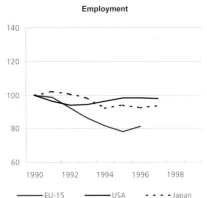

Employment

Source: Eurostat (SBS)

_____ Figure 8.15

Basic precious and non-ferrous metals (NACE Rev. 1 27.4)

Destination of EU exports, 1999 (%)

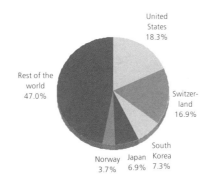

Source: Eurostat (COMEXT)

_____ Figure 8.16

Basic precious and non-ferrous metals (NACE Rev. 1 27.4)

Origin of EU imports, 1999 (%)

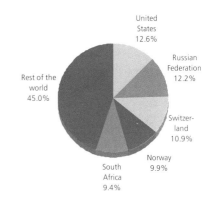

Source: Eurostat (COMEXT)

Table 8.9

Manufacture of basic iron and steel and of ferro-alloys (ECSC) (NACE Rev. 1 27.1)

Production related indicators in the EU (1)

	1989	1990	1991	1992	1993	1994	1995	1996	1997	1998	1999
Number of persons employed (thousands)	528.3	513.9	473.9	451.5	372.7	351.7	330.2	:	:	:	:
Production (million ECU)	89,886	79,832	71,222	65,992	59,144	70,169	82,591	71,410	:	:	:
Domestic producer price index (1995=100)	:	:	:	:	:	:	:	:	:	94.2	85.8
Value added (million ECU)	29,258	24,453	20,641	18,383	15,730	19,573	25,266	18,987	:	:	:

(1) Technically, data before 01/01/1999 are in ECU and after this date in euro. However, as the conversion rate was 1 ECU =1 EUR, for practical purposes the two terms can be used interchangeably.

Table 8.10

Manufacture of basic iron and steel and of ferro-alloys (ECSC) (NACE Rev. 1 27.1)

Trade related indicators in the EU (1)

	1989	1990	1991	1992	1993	1994	1995	1996	1997	1998	1999
Exports (million EUR)	10,040	8,557	8,544	8,096	11,264	10,995	10,980	11,309	11,279	9,560	8,482
Imports (million EUR)	3,935	3,695	3,071	3,330	2,719	4,084	6,608	5,025	5,942	8,453	6,567
Trade balance (million EUR)	6,105	4,862	5,473	4,767	8,545	6,911	4,372	6,284	5,337	1,107	1,915
Cover ratio (%)	255.2	231.6	278.2	243.2	414.2	269.2	166.2	225.1	189.8	113.1	129.2

(1) Technically, data before 01/01/1999 are in ECU and after this date in euro. However, as the conversion rate was 1 ECU =1 EUR, for practical purposes the two terms can be used interchangeably.

Table 8.11

Manufacture of basic iron and steel and of ferro-alloys (ECSC) (NACE Rev. 1 27.1)

Production related indicators, 1997

	B	DK	D	EL (1)	E	F (1)	IRL	I (1)	L	NL	A	P	FIN	S	UK
Number of persons employed (thousands)	21.7	2.0	87.4	2.4	23.0	41.9	:	38.2	5.2	:	15.2	1.8	10.1	13.4	40.2
Production (million ECU)	5,304	293	20,070	508	6,352	9,844	:	9,612	1,473	2,261	1,395	368	2,309	3,500	10,286
Value added (million ECU)	1,510	80	5,077	45	1,537	2,605	:	2,319	324	987	494	60	743	927	2,464
Gross operating surplus (million ECU)	411.0	21.5	1,113.6	-21.1	787.4	705.4	:	962.7	70.8	421.3	151.0	25.3	373.5	363.9	949.1

(1) 1996.

Table 8.12

Manufacture of basic iron and steel and of ferro-alloys (ECSC) (NACE Rev. 1 27.1)

Trade related indicators, 1999

	B	DK	D	EL	E	F	IRL	I	L	NL	A	P	FIN	S	UK
Exports (million EUR)	6,252	351	7,672	175	1,880	5,652	92	2,434	1,446	2,394	1,497	223	1,277	2,025	2,731
Imports (million EUR)	3,423	766	5,969	546	3,208	4,990	311	5,416	806	2,065	798	875	503	1,564	2,423
Trade balance (million EUR)	2,829	-415	1,702	-371	-1,328	661	-219	-2,982	640	329	699	-652	774	460	308
Cover ratio (%)	182.6	45.8	128.5	32.1	58.6	113.3	29.6	44.9	179.3	115.9	187.6	25.5	253.9	129.4	112.7

Table 8.13

Manufacture of basic iron and steel and of ferro-alloys (ECSC) (NACE Rev. 1 27.1)

Labour related indicators, 1997

	B	DK (1)	D	EL (2)	E	F (2)	IRL	I (2)	L	NL	A	P	FIN	S	UK
Unit personnel costs (thousand ECU per employee)	50.7	33.9	45.4	27.2	31.6	45.3	:	35.6	48.7	:	22.6	19.0	37.7	42.0	37.8
Social charges as a share of personnel costs (%)	45.9	3.4	30.4	29.0	29.4	45.1	:	43.3	:	35.6	31.7	41.4	25.8	43.5	13.1
Apparent labour productivity (thousand ECU/pers. empl.)	69.6	39.5	58.1	18.5	66.7	62.1	:	60.6	62.3	:	32.6	32.9	73.2	69.2	61.3
Wage adjusted labour productivity (%)	137.2	125.3	128.1	68.1	211.3	137.1	:	170.3	128.0	:	144.0	172.9	194.1	164.7	162.4
Personnel costs as a share of total operating costs (%)	22.5	21.2	20.4	14.1	12.5	21.0	:	15.7	17.4	30.8	26.4	10.1	18.6	17.9	16.3

(1) Unit personnel costs and wage adjusted labour productivity, 1996; (2) 1996.

Source: Eurostat (SBS, EBT, COMEXT)

_____Table 8.14

Manufacture of tubes (NACE Rev. 1 27.2)
Production related indicators in the EU (1)

	1989	1990	1991	1992	1993	1994	1995	1996	1997	1998	1999
Number of persons employed (thousands)	162.2	148.5	147.1	139.4	128.6	120.0	113.8	:	:	:	:
Production (million ECU)	17,581	15,433	15,915	15,440	13,934	16,572	18,382	:	:	:	:
Domestic producer price index (1995=100)	:	:	:	:	:	:	:	:	:	95.5	91.9
Value added (million ECU)	5,129	4,545	4,652	4,533	3,979	4,983	5,511	:	:	:	:

(1) Technically, data before 01/01/1999 are in ECU and after this date in euro. However, as the conversion rate was 1 ECU =1 EUR, for practical purposes the two terms can be used interchangeably.

_____Table 8.15

Manufacture of tubes (NACE Rev. 1 27.2)
Trade related indicators in the EU (1)

	1989	1990	1991	1992	1993	1994	1995	1996	1997	1998	1999
Exports (million EUR)	4,431	3,435	3,929	3,343	3,378	3,831	3,737	4,386	5,516	5,604	4,057
Imports (million EUR)	888	989	1,073	1,057	891	1,058	1,331	1,371	1,452	1,772	1,560
Trade balance (million EUR)	3,543	2,446	2,856	2,285	2,486	2,773	2,406	3,015	4,063	3,832	2,497
Cover ratio (%)	499.0	347.4	366.1	316.1	379.0	361.9	280.8	320.0	379.8	316.2	260.1

(1) Technically, data before 01/01/1999 are in ECU and after this date in euro. However, as the conversion rate was 1 ECU =1 EUR, for practical purposes the two terms can be used interchangeably.

_____Table 8.16

Manufacture of tubes (NACE Rev. 1 27.2)
Production related indicators, 1997

	B	DK	D	EL (1)	E	F	IRL	I (1)	L (1)	NL	A	P	FIN	S	UK
Number of persons employed (thousands)	1.0	3.8	41.4	0.8	5.0	15.6	:	19.1	0.0	:	4.1	0.7	0.9	2.1	17.2
Production (million ECU)	158	428	5,905	115	916	3,028	:	4,068	0	267	351	95	162	322	2,174
Value added (million ECU)	42	138	2,044	22	278	808	:	1,088	0	70	138	19	46	107	713
Gross operating surplus (million ECU)	6.7	26.2	362.1	6.6	118.6	223.8	:	429.9	0.0	23.0	31.5	11.1	17.8	30.1	182.9

(1) 1996.

_____Table 8.17

Manufacture of tubes (NACE Rev. 1 27.2)
Trade related indicators, 1999

	B	DK	D	EL	E	F	IRL	I	L	NL	A	P	FIN	S	UK
Exports (million EUR)	344	242	2,759	37	447	1,326	11	2,069	44	404	559	31	260	512	756
Imports (million EUR)	462	275	1,516	62	438	986	103	718	19	537	325	130	163	376	737
Trade balance (million EUR)	-118	-33	1,243	-25	9	340	-92	1,352	25	-133	234	-99	96	136	19
Cover ratio (%)	74.4	87.9	181.9	59.2	102.0	134.4	10.7	288.4	228.1	75.2	172.0	23.9	159.1	136.2	102.6

_____Table 8.18

Manufacture of tubes (NACE Rev. 1 27.2)
Labour related indicators, 1997

	B	DK (1)	D	EL (2)	E	F	IRL	I (2)	L	NL	A	P	FIN	S	UK
Unit personnel costs (thousand ECU per employee)	37.0	33.4	40.6	19.9	30.2	37.5	:	34.8	:	:	26.2	10.1	32.9	35.7	31.0
Social charges as a share of personnel costs (%)	34.4	6.0	25.3	31.1	28.3	44.6	:	52.3	:	15.3	30.5	29.3	29.0	45.7	13.2
Apparent labour productivity (thousand ECU/pers. empl.)	43.7	36.7	49.3	28.1	55.2	51.9	:	57.0	:	:	34.0	24.9	52.8	49.8	41.4
Wage adjusted labour productivity (%)	118.2	150.4	121.4	140.8	182.5	138.3	:	163.7	:	:	129.7	246.1	160.7	139.3	133.8
Personnel costs as a share of total operating costs (%)	23.1	27.0	28.5	13.7	18.3	20.1	:	18.2	:	18.4	30.8	8.8	19.6	25.5	25.4

(1) Unit personnel costs and wage adjusted labour productivity, 1996; (2) 1996.

Source: Eurostat (SBS, EBT, COMEXT)

Table 8.19

Other first processing of iron and steel and production on non-ECSC ferro-alloys (NACE Rev. 1 27.3)

Production related indicators in the EU (1)

	1989	1990	1991	1992	1993	1994	1995	1996	1997	1998	1999
Number of persons employed (thousands)	89.5	90.2	87.9	86.5	78.2	74.4	:	:	:	:	:
Production (million EUR)	13,061	12,868	12,367	12,388	11,223	13,465	:	15,505	14,777	15,527	15,183
Domestic producer price index (1995=100)	:	:	:	:	:	:	:	:	:	95.0	91.6
Value added (million EUR)	3,252	3,291	3,251	3,327	3,041	3,506	:	4,221	4,398	4,548	4,265

(1) Technically, data before 01/01/1999 are in ECU and after this date in euro. However, as the conversion rate was 1 ECU =1 EUR, for practical purposes the two terms can be used interchangeably.

Table 8.20

Other first processing of iron and steel and production on non-ECSC ferro-alloys (NACE Rev. 1 27.3)

Trade related indicators in the EU (1)

	1989	1990	1991	1992	1993	1994	1995	1996	1997	1998	1999
Exports (million EUR)	2,042	1,827	1,659	1,579	1,891	2,280	2,425	2,415	2,771	2,958	2,738
Imports (million EUR)	2,397	1,783	1,693	1,701	1,704	2,224	3,121	2,814	3,091	3,320	3,003
Trade balance (million EUR)	-355	44	-34	-122	188	56	-696	-399	-320	-362	-265
Cover ratio (%)	85.2	102.5	98.0	92.8	111.0	102.5	77.7	85.8	89.7	89.1	91.2

(1) Technically, data before 01/01/1999 are in ECU and after this date in euro. However, as the conversion rate was 1 ECU =1 EUR, for practical purposes the two terms can be used interchangeably.

Table 8.21

Other first processing of iron and steel and production on non-ECSC ferro-alloys (NACE Rev. 1 27.3)

Production related indicators, 1997

	B	DK	D	EL (1)	E	F	IRL	I (1)	L	NL	A	P	FIN	S	UK
Number of persons employed (thousands)	7.0	:	17.7	1.6	6.2	10.4	:	14.5	:	:	:	2.5	0.4	6.6	10.4
Production (million ECU)	1,416	:	3,303	194	1,367	2,077	:	3,768	:	106	:	329	121	1,296	1,610
Value added (million ECU)	484	:	942	29	337	559	:	856	:	27	:	67	37	453	414
Gross operating surplus (million ECU)	143.4	:	217.1	-11.8	155.1	164.5	:	404.1	:	11.7	:	31.0	22.2	202.3	106.6

(1) 1996.

Table 8.22

Other first processing of iron and steel and production on non-ECSC ferro-alloys (NACE Rev. 1 27.3)

Trade related indicators, 1999

	B	DK	D	EL	E	F	IRL	I	L	NL	A	P	FIN	S	UK
Exports (million EUR)	891	52	2,153	11	420	1,403	30	1,045	110	446	518	36	117	773	738
Imports (million EUR)	572	146	2,098	50	572	1,353	86	1,120	46	787	387	117	235	359	789
Trade balance (million EUR)	319	-95	55	-38	-152	50	-56	-74	63	-341	132	-82	-118	414	-51
Cover ratio (%)	155.7	35.2	102.6	22.7	73.4	103.7	34.8	93.4	236.9	56.6	134.0	30.3	49.9	215.3	93.6

Table 8.23

Other first processing of iron and steel and production on non-ECSC ferro-alloys (NACE Rev. 1 27.3)

Labour related indicators, 1997

	B	DK	D	EL (1)	E	F	IRL	I (1)	L	NL	A	P	FIN	S	UK
Unit personnel costs (thousand ECU per employee)	49.6	:	41.0	25.0	28.8	37.9	:	31.9	:	:	:	15.0	36.5	38.0	29.5
Social charges as a share of personnel costs (%)	50.7	:	24.0	35.6	28.9	47.9	:	50.7	:	15.5	:	41.6	26.5	46.9	14.3
Apparent labour productivity (thousand ECU/pers. empl.)	69.4	:	53.2	17.8	54.6	53.7	:	59.1	:	:	:	26.6	93.6	68.7	39.6
Wage adjusted labour productivity (%)	140.0	:	129.5	71.2	189.5	141.7	:	185.2	:	:	:	177.7	256.7	180.6	134.3
Personnel costs as a share of total operating costs (%)	33.1	:	22.7	21.5	14.1	19.9	:	13.0	:	15.7	:	11.0	14.4	21.9	19.9

(1) 1996.

Source: Eurostat (SBS, EBT, COMEXT)

Table 8.24

Manufacture of basic precious and non-ferrous metals (NACE Rev. 1 27.4)

Production related indicators in the EU

	1989	1990	1991	1992	1993	1994	1995	1996	1997	1998	1999
Number of persons employed (thousands)	245.1	243.0	239.8	224.6	209.6	198.2	189.7	197.0	:	:	:
Production (million ECU)	52,625	46,842	42,445	40,739	37,303	41,506	48,163	47,575			
Domestic producer price index (1995=100)	:	101.8	86.7	82.9	80.7	87.8	100.0	92.5	98.1	93.9	91.1
Value added (million ECU)	11,819	10,302	9,394	9,155	8,446	9,681	10,760	10,767	:	:	:

(1) Technically, data before 01/01/1999 are in ECU and after this date in euro. However, as the conversion rate was 1 ECU =1 EUR, for practical purposes the two terms can be used interchangeably.

Table 8.25

Manufacture of basic precious and non-ferrous metals (NACE Rev. 1 27.4)

Trade related indicators in the EU (1)

	1989	1990	1991	1992	1993	1994	1995	1996	1997	1998	1999
Exports (million EUR)	8,362	6,554	6,778	6,258	7,219	8,190	9,188	9,981	11,954	11,478	12,096
Imports (million EUR)	23,356	20,584	20,503	20,317	20,383	23,089	26,885	23,946	28,113	31,747	28,168
Trade balance (million EUR)	-14,993	-14,030	-13,725	-14,059	-13,164	-14,899	-17,697	-13,965	-16,159	-20,269	-16,073
Cover ratio (%)	35.8	31.8	33.1	30.8	35.4	35.5	34.2	41.7	42.5	36.2	42.9

(1) Technically, data before 01/01/1999 are in ECU and after this date in euro. However, as the conversion rate was 1 ECU =1 EUR, for practical purposes the two terms can be used interchangeably.

Table 8.26

Manufacture of basic precious and non-ferrous metals (NACE Rev. 1 27.4)

Production related indicators, 1997

	B	DK	D	EL (1)	E	F	IRL	I (1)	L	NL	A (1)	P	FIN	S	UK
Number of persons employed (thousands)	9.4	2.1	65.5	5.0	14.1	23.9	1.1	21.9	0.7	:	5.6	2.6	4.0	5.2	25.9
Production (million ECU)	4,290	333	15,780	970	4,118	7,028	197	5,917	245	1,819	1,450	236	1,444	1,458	6,521
Value added (million ECU)	723	88	3,805	186	921	1,283	52	1,237	59	462	298	55	323	334	1,515
Gross operating surplus (million ECU)	258.5	19.1	926.1	56.2	477.6	273.5	14.8	496.9	27.4	198.1	63.7	23.1	177.7	129.7	717.7

(1) 1996.

Table 8.27

Manufacture of basic precious and non-ferrous metals (NACE Rev. 1 27.4)

Trade related indicators, 1999

	B	DK	D	EL	E	F	IRL	I	L	NL	A	P	FIN	S	UK
Exports (million EUR)	3,785	354	9,941	604	1,854	4,367	360	2,472	338	4,609	1,419	177	1,063	1,324	5,708
Imports (million EUR)	3,728	706	11,120	480	2,112	6,085	375	9,391	243	5,145	1,828	664	547	1,360	9,066
Trade balance (million EUR)	57	-352	-1,179	124	-258	-1,719	-15	-6,919	95	-536	-409	-487	516	-36	-3,358
Cover ratio (%)	101.5	50.1	89.4	125.9	87.8	71.8	96.1	26.3	139.3	89.6	77.6	26.6	194.3	97.4	63.0

Table 8.28

Manufacture of basic precious and non-ferrous metals (NACE Rev. 1 27.4)

Labour related indicators, 1997

	B	DK (1)	D	EL (2)	E	F	IRL	I (2)	L	NL	A (2)	P	FIN	S	UK
Unit personnel costs (thousand ECU per employee)	49.8	37.2	44.0	26.1	30.2	42.3	33.8	34.1	43.4	:	:	12.7	37.0	39.3	30.8
Social charges as a share of personnel costs (%)	46.2	5.6	25.6	30.3	28.9	46.0	15.0	49.9	:	14.9	32.5	31.7	28.6	42.7	13.7
Apparent labour productivity (thousand ECU/pers. empl.)	77.2	41.3	58.1	37.4	65.3	53.7	47.4	56.4	80.9	:	53.0	21.4	81.1	64.2	58.4
Wage adjusted labour productivity (%)	155.0	141.8	132.1	143.0	216.3	127.1	140.4	165.4	186.5	:	:	169.0	219.2	163.4	189.4
Personnel costs as a share of total operating costs (%)	11.4	21.8	18.3	15.8	11.1	12.9	20.1	13.4	14.5	15.7	16.3	14.2	11.9	13.8	12.6

(1) Unit personnel costs and wage adjusted labour productivity, 1996; (2) 1996.

Source: Eurostat (SBS, EBT, COMEXT)

Table 8.29

Casting of metals (NACE Rev. 1 27.5)

Production related indicators in the EU (1)

	1989	1990	1991	1992	1993	1994	1995	1996	1997	1998	1999
Number of persons employed (thousands)	249.6	248.1	234.7	223.8	196.1	192.1	203.2	:	202.3	204.6	196.5
Production (million EUR)	17,394	17,548	16,564	16,244	13,917	16,028	18,752	:	:	:	:
Domestic producer price index (1995=100)	:	:	:	:	:	:	100.0	101.2	102.3	101.5	100.2
Value added (million EUR)	7,156	7,403	7,251	7,132	6,009	6,621	7,517	:	8,714	9,084	8,703

(1) Technically, data before 01/01/1999 are in ECU and after this date in euro. However, as the conversion rate was 1 ECU =1 EUR, for practical purposes the two terms can be used interchangeably.

Table 8.30

Casting of metals (NACE Rev. 1 27.5)

Production related indicators, 1997

	B	DK	D	EL (1)	E	F	IRL	I (1)	L	NL	A	P	FIN	S	UK
Number of persons employed (thousands)	3.5	:	61.0	0.2	20.1	33.0	0.1	32.4	:	:	5.0	6.9	2.5	0.4	34.2
Production (million ECU)	512	:	6,073	11	1,986	3,159	6	4,132	:	492	515	277	234	47	2,901
Value added (million ECU)	168	:	2,787	6	710	1,136	3	1,502	:	186	238	105	112	22	1,367
Gross operating surplus (million ECU)	33.3	:	462.7	2.2	232.4	168.4	1.0	501.4	:	51.4	68.3	28.4	41.1	8.9	420.3

(1) 1996.

Table 8.31

Casting of metals (NACE Rev. 1 27.5)

Labour related indicators, 1997

	B	DK	D	EL (1)	E	F	IRL	I (1)	L	NL	A	P	FIN	S	UK
Unit personnel costs (thousand ECU per employee)	39.1	:	38.2	15.9	23.8	29.3	12.7	31.4	:	:	33.8	11.3	28.9	33.8	27.9
Social charges as a share of personnel costs (%)	35.4	:	23.8	29.6	30.2	41.4	14.3	53.3	:	14.4	31.6	35.3	32.3	39.1	13.0
Apparent labour productivity (thousand ECU/pers. empl.)	47.9	:	45.7	25.8	35.3	34.4	19.8	46.3	:	:	47.3	15.2	45.6	57.2	39.9
Wage adjusted labour productivity (%)	122.5	:	119.6	162.1	148.1	117.4	155.9	147.2	:	:	139.9	133.7	158.1	169.4	143.0
Personnel costs as a share of total operating costs (%)	28.1	:	40.6	41.2	26.0	32.5	30.8	27.1	:	29.9	36.1	30.3	35.6	33.4	36.8

(1) 1996.

Source: Eurostat (SBS, EBT)

Metal products (NACE Rev. 1 28)

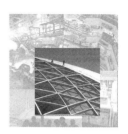

The manufacture of metal products has been divided into three sections for the purposes of this publication. Constructional steelwork deals with the manufacture of structural metal products (NACE Rev. 1 28.1) that are largely used in the building sector. There follows a sub-chapter on boilers, metal containers and packaging (NACE Rev. 1 28.2 and NACE Rev. 1 28.3). The final sub-chapter is entitled "other metal products", it encompasses NACE Rev. 1 28.4 to 28.7, which includes a wide range of production processes (forging, pressing, stamping, roll forming, treatment and coating), as well as the manufacture of metal products (cutlery, tools, general hardware and miscellaneous fabricated metal products).

Figure 9.1

Metal products (NACE Rev. 1 28)

Share of total manufacturing value added in the EU, 1995 (%)

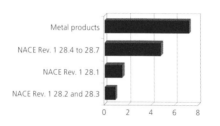

Source: Eurostat (SBS)

The activities covered in this chapter (in terms of NACE Rev. 1) include:

28: manufacture of fabricated metal products, except machinery and equipment;
28.1: manufacture of structural metal products;
28.2: manufacture of tanks, reservoirs and containers of metal; manufacture of central heating radiators and boilers;
28.3: manufacture of steam generators, except central heating hot water boilers;
28.4: forging, pressing, stamping and roll forming of metal; powder metallurgy;
28.5: treatment and coating of metals; general mechanical engineering;
28.6: manufacture of cutlery, tools and general hardware;
28.7: manufacture of other fabricated metal products.

Demand for metal products is strongly linked to the state of the economy as a whole, as the principal downstream markets such as the automotive and construction industries are vulnerable to changing confidence amongst consumers. Some activities may be less affected by such variations, as for instance the manufacture of containers and packaging for food and drink. The threat to the EU metal products industry comes from two different areas: replacement materials and low-value imports from non-Community countries. Alternatives such as plastics, glass and ceramics are increasingly being used in downstream industries, whilst imports of metal products from Eastern Europe and Asia have led to EU manufacturers seeking new production methods to develop more sophisticated products, as low-end markets are increasingly penetrated by foreign competition.

In 1996, 202.4 billion ECU of production value was created by the metal products industry, which amounted to 5.7% of total EU manufacturing output. This industry generated 79.6 billion ECU of value added, or some 7.4% of the Union's manufacturing total. The relative size of this industry was at its largest when considering the number of persons employed, some 2.06 million persons in 1996 (or 8.9% of the manufacturing workforce).

The miscellaneous category of "other metal products" was by far the largest of the metal product activities, accounting for just under two-thirds of production, value added and employment. The remaining two activities were relatively small in terms of production value, with construction steelwork accounting for over 23% of the industry, with the boilers, metal containers and packaging industry half the size.

The role of steel at the heart of the manufacturing economy has been challenged by the introduction of other metals and new materials (for example, vehicle and aircraft industries are using increasing quantities of magnesium, aluminium and titanium, as well as non-metallic alternatives such as plastics and ceramics). To counter these trends, the steel industry has combined to launch programmes that research areas such as light vehicle bodies. The steel industry has also turned towards potentially high growth products, such as quick-assembly solutions and pre-engineered building units.

Small and medium-sized enterprises dominated this industry. They were often best placed to exploit niche markets, as more basic, low-value products were increasingly imported from non-Community countries. The metal products industry consisted of 308 thousand enterprises, or 15.4% of the manufacturing total in 1996. The majority of enterprises were very small (with 0-9 employees), of which there were 249 thousand. Small-sized enterprises (with between 10-19 employees) numbered 50.4 thousand. There were 1.04 million persons employed in small enterprises (which represented 17.1% of the total number of persons employed in all small manufacturing enterprises), whilst 606.7 thousand persons were employed in large enterprises.

STRUCTURE AND PERFORMANCE

Production of metal products grew in nominal terms by 89.1 billion ECU between 1986 and 1996, accounting for 6.7% of the expansion observed in total manufacturing output in the EU during this period. The metal products industry grew at a similar pace to the manufacturing average between 1991 and 1996, with production in constant prices increasing at an average annual rate of 1.5%, just below the manufacturing average. There was a high growth rate in 1994, when output rose by 7.3% in real terms. Positive growth rates continued in 1996, when production in constant prices increased by 3.6%.

Over the same period value added at factor cost rose by 32.6 billion ECU, which amounted to almost a tenth of the increase observed for total manufacturing in the EU. As such, manufacturers were seen to be specialising in higher value products.

Table 9.1

Metal products (NACE Rev. 1 28)

Breakdown of turnover and employment by employment size class, 1997 (%)

	Micro (0-9)		Small (10-49)		Medium (50-249)		Large (250+)	
	Turnover (1)	Employment (2)	Turnover (1)	Employment (2)	Turnover (3)	Employment (4)	Turnover (5)	Employment (6)
EU-15	14.8	24.5	29.5	33.4	25.9	22.6	29.9	19.5
B	18.0	27.6	33.9	34.4	27.8	21.8	20.3	16.2
DK	:	:	:	:	:	:	17.0	17.0
D	9.5	20.1	17.9	24.4	21.8	22.6	50.8	32.8
EL	:	:	:	:	:	:	:	:
E	25.2	37.7	36.9	36.7	26.4	17.8	11.5	7.8
F	12.3	17.2	33.5	37.8	27.1	25.0	27.1	20.0
IRL	:	:	:	:	:	:	:	:
I	21.9	34.1	45.1	44.4	24.7	16.6	8.3	5.0
L	:	:	:	:	:	:	:	:
NL	:	:	:	:	:	35.1	:	18.6
A	8.1	12.9	20.5	25.3	35.6	33.2	36.7	30.2
P	21.3	36.2	30.5	31.7	36.2	24.1	11.9	8.0
FIN	18.0	23.8	29.2	34.0	30.6	29.3	22.1	12.9
S	16.1	24.3	30.1	32.1	25.4	23.9	28.4	19.6
UK	19.6	23.1	28.1	30.1	25.6	26.3	26.7	20.5

(1) EU-15, E, F, I, P and S, 1996.
(2) EU-15, F, I, P and S, 1996.
(3) EU-15, E, F, I, A, P and S, 1996.
(4) EU-15, F, I, NL, A, P and S, 1996.
(5) EU-15, DK, E, F, I, A, P and S, 1996.
(6) EU-15, DK, F, I, NL, A, P and S, 1996.

Source: Eurostat (SME)

Figure 9.2

Metal products (NACE Rev. 1 28)
EU production and value-added in constant prices and employment compared to total manufacturing (1990=100)

Production in constant prices

Value added in constant prices

Employment

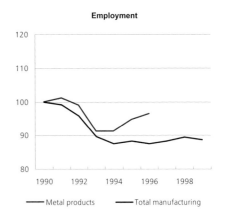

Source: Eurostat (SBS)

Production distributed quite evenly
across the European Union

The German metal products industry had one of the highest shares in its domestic manufacturing total at 6.3% in 1997 (EU, 5.7% in 1996). German output was the highest in the Union, equal to 63.4 billion ECU, despite sluggish real growth of 0.7% per annum during the five-year period to 1997. There was a similar scenario in Spain and Italy, where metal products accounted for more than 6.0% of domestic manufacturing output, whilst recent years saw low production growth rates (up 0.4% and 0.7% per annum in real terms). On the other hand the countries with higher growth rates tended to be those that were relatively unspecialised in the manufacture of metal products, for example, France and the United Kingdom, where production rose by almost 3.0% per annum in real terms in the mid-1990s. The fastest growing industry was found in Finland, where output rose by 13.4% per annum on average in real terms during the five years to 1997. There was also high growth in real terms in Sweden (7.5%) during the same period.

Luxembourg had the highest relative production specialisation rate (198.1% in 1996), with metal products accounting for 12.2% of domestic manufacturing output in 1997 and an average annual growth rate of production in constant prices equal to 5.7% between 1992 and 1997.

LABOUR AND PRODUCTIVITY

European employment rose by 6.3% between 1986 and 1996 in this activity (whilst the EU workforce for total manufacturing fell by 10.0%). The number of persons employed totalled 2.06 million in 1996, or 8.9% of the manufacturing total, a significant increase on the 7.6% share reported in 1986. Employment growth was strongest in the five-year period up until 1991, when the annual average growth rate was 2.2%. Indeed, from a high of 2.16 million persons, employment fell significantly in 1992 (-2.2%) and 1993 (-7.8%), whilst there was no change in 1994. Growth of 3.8% in 1995 and 1.9% in 1996 served to redress some of these losses.

The share of personnel costs in
production fell as productivity rose

Despite an increase in the share of personnel costs in production during the 1992/3 recession, this ratio fell from 31.6% in 1986 to 29.6% in 1996. These shares remained high relative to total manufacturing, at least 7.0 percentage points above the manufacturing average. Apparent labour productivity rose progressively from 24.3 thousand ECU per person employed in 1986 to 33.5 thousand ECU in 1993; in the following years there was more rapid growth, up to 38.7 thousand ECU in 1996. Combining labour productivity and personnel costs, wage-adjusted labour productivity was broadly stable, varying between a high of 137.0% in 1988 and a low of 125.0% in 1993, with the latest figure 132.9% in 1996.

Table 9.2

Metal products (NACE Rev. 1 28)
Composition of the labour force, 1999 (%)

	Women (1)	Part-time (2)	Highly-educated (3)
EU-15	16.5	5.0	11.1
B	20.8	:	12.3
DK	12.7	:	10.1
D	18.6	6.0	15.4
EL	6.6	:	:
E	7.1	2.8	15.8
F	15.2	3.7	10.5
IRL	11.3	:	:
I	19.0	4.9	3.3
L	:	:	:
NL	13.6	12.5	8.6
A	20.4	3.8	2.6
P	16.8	:	3.8
FIN	14.4	:	20.8
S	17.9	12.4	:
UK	16.8	5.1	13.6

(1) EU-15 and IRL, 1998; EL, 1997.
(2) EU-15, 1998.
(3) EU-15, P and UK, 1997.

Source: Eurostat (LFS)

Figure 9.3

Metal products (NACE Rev. 1 28)

Apparent labour productivity and unit personnel costs, 1997 (thousand ECU)

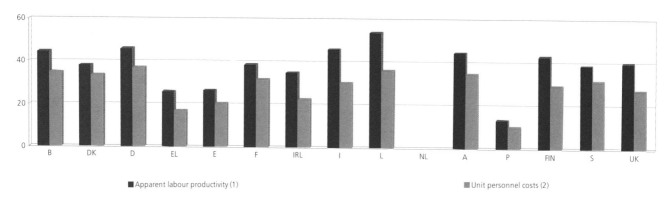

■ Apparent labour productivity (1)　　　　　■ Unit personnel costs (2)

(1) EL, F and I, 1996; NL, not available.
(2) DK, EL, F and I, 1996; NL, not available.

Source: Eurostat (SBS)

Relatively low-skilled workforce

The automated nature of the work carried out by the metal products labour force was reflected in the educational attainment figures for 1997, with only 11.1% of those employed having completed a higher education (compared to the 16.3% for manufacturing as a whole).

The workforce was 83.5% male in 1998, marginally lower than the 85.0% reported in 1994, although this was a much higher share than the figures for total manufacturing, where 71.8% of the labour force were male in 1998. There was a gradual reduction in the number of employees with a permanent contract, with a 2.3 percentage point reduction to 89.7% in 1998, a figure that was equal to the manufacturing average (89.7%).

INTERNATIONAL TRENDS AND FOREIGN TRADE

EU production totalled 202 billion ECU in 1996, 41.4% of the Triad total. In the same year the USA and Japan accounted for 30.9% and 27.7% of output respectively. Latest figures for 1997 showed a diverging trend in the other two members of the Triad, American output increased by 2.1% to 176 billion ECU, whilst Japanese production fell to 130 billion ECU. Employment increased in all three Triad members over the 1986 to 1996 period, with shares of the Triad employment total remaining relatively stable. Employment was divided between the members of the Triad as follows in 1996: EU (48.0%), USA (33.1%) and Japan (19.0%).

The EU trade surplus narrowed
somewhat in the late 1990s

Extra-EU trade was of relatively low importance within this industry, as in 1999 basic metals accounted for only 3.1% of total manufacturing exports (lower than their production share of 5.7%). The EU trade balance increased in absolute terms from 5.3 billion ECU in 1989 to 8.9 billion ECU in 1997 but the cover ratio fell from 193.3% to 173.6%. By 1999, the surplus was 7.2 billion EUR, with the cover ratio down to 148.9%. Exports almost doubled over the ten-year period to 1999 (21.9 billion EUR), whilst imports nearly tripled to 14.7 billion EUR.

The trade deficit of the USA changed very little between 1989 and 1998 (when it stood at -4.8 billion ECU). Over the same period, the Japanese surplus also remained fairly constant, standing at 2.7 billion ECU in 1998. However, as was the case for the EU, the Japanese cover ratio fell from 294.2% in 1989 to 201.4% in 1998, as exports did not keep pace with imports.

Figure 9.4

Metal products (NACE Rev. 1 28)
International comparison of production, value added and employment

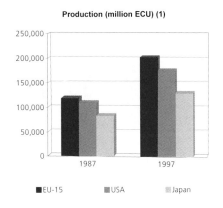

Production (million ECU) (1)

Value added (million ECU) (2)

Employment (units) (2)

■EU-15 ■USA ■Japan

(1) EU-15, 1996.
(2) EU-15 and JAP, 1996.

Source: Eurostat (SBS)

USA remained the EU's largest trading partner

As far as the EU was concerned, the USA was the most important origin of imports (2.4 billion EUR) and the main destination for EU exports (3.4 billion EUR) in 1999. In 1989 Switzerland accounted for slightly more imports than the USA, but ten years later it was the third largest origin of imports (1.9 billion EUR) and the second largest destination for EU exports (1.9 billion EUR). China moved from fifth to second place in terms of imports into the EU over this period, whilst becoming the fifth largest export market for EU metal products (compared to the thirteenth largest in 1989).

Figure 9.5

Metal products (NACE Rev. 1 28)
Destination of EU exports, 1999 (%)

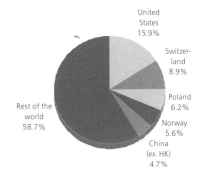

United States 15.9%
Switzerland 8.9%
Poland 6.2%
Norway 5.6%
China (ex. HK) 4.7%
Rest of the world 58.7%

Source: Eurostat (COMEXT)

Figure 9.6

Metal products (NACE Rev. 1 28)
Origin of EU imports, 1999 (%)

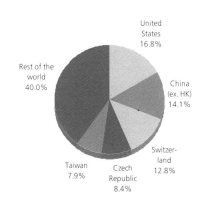

United States 16.8%
China (ex. HK) 14.1%
Switzerland 12.8%
Czech Republic 8.4%
Taiwan 7.9%
Rest of the world 40.0%

Source: Eurostat (COMEXT)

SUB-CHAPTER 9.1
STRUCTURAL METAL PRODUCTS
(NACE Rev. 1 28.1)

Structural metal products (NACE Rev. 1 28.1) encompass constructional steelwork and metal products used in house-building, such as doors, windows, gates etc.

In 1999, the structural metal products activity achieved a production value of 52.4 billion EUR and employed 517.5 thousand persons. Its share of total manufacturing output was 1.3%, whilst it employed as many as 2.2% of the total number of person employed in manufacturing.

Smaller countries the most specialised
Germany was the largest producer of structural metal products in 1997, with 15.1 billion ECU of output, almost three times higher than the second most important producer in the Union, the United Kingdom (5.7 billion ECU), followed by Spain (5.5 billion ECU). Germany and Spain were both relatively specialised in producing structural metal products. However, the most specialised Member States were the Netherlands and Austria, where this industry accounted for 40.6% and 43.2% of total metal products' output in 1997. In several other Member States, this activity contributed close to 35% of output in the metal products industry: Belgium (36.9%), Spain (34.9%), Luxembourg (35.7%) and Ireland (36.4%).

STRUCTURE AND PERFORMANCE
Production increased in real terms during the five-year period to 1998, with the latest growth rate of 4.5% being the second highest recorded (behind the 5.5% increase of 1996). The average annual growth rate between 1993 to 1998 was 4.1%, which was 0.8 percentage points below the average figure for total manufacturing. The recession of 1993 saw real output decline by 9.7%. Value added generated within the structural metal products industry was increasing at a faster rate than the manufacturing average (0.8 percentage points quicker), up by 3.9% per annum on average between 1993 and 1998.

Figure 9.7

Structural metal products (NACE Rev. 1 28.1)

Production and export specialisation (%)

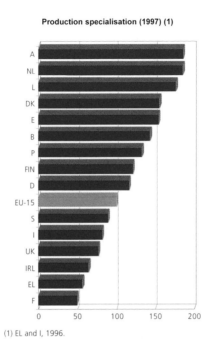
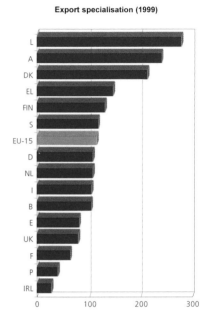

(1) EL and I, 1996.

Source: Eurostat (SBS, COMEXT)

Figure 9.8

Structural metal products (NACE Rev. 1 28.1)

International comparison of production in constant prices and employment (1990=100)

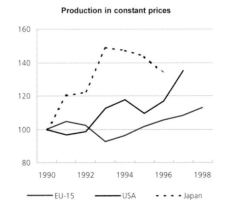

Source: Eurostat (SBS)

Profitability lagged behind the manufacturing average throughout the 1990s

The gross operating rate (value added minus personnel costs divided by turnover) for EU structural metal products was consistently lower than the manufacturing average during recent years. Profitability fell from a high of 9.3% in 1990 to 6.0% in 1993 (some 2.2 percentage points lower than the manufacturing average). As the industry recovered following the recession, this differential narrowed, but remained more than 1.0 percentage point. The highest EU gross operating rate for structural metal products in the latter part of the 1990s was 8.5% in 1998, falling to 7.6% a year later.

LABOUR AND PRODUCTIVITY

In 1999, 518 thousand persons were employed in this industry, 30.1 thousand or 6.2% more than in 1989. Employment grew at an average annual rate of 2.4% during the five years to 1999, whereby the job losses incurred between 1992 and 1994 were fully reversed. The increase in the number of persons employed was considerably above the manufacturing average of 0.2% between 1994 and 1999.

Productivity lower than the metal products average

Apparent labour productivity in the structural metal products industry (35.9 thousand ECU per person employed) was some 15.9 thousand ECU lower than the average for the whole of metal products in 1999.

The share of personnel costs in production remained fairly stable during the 1990s, at around 27.5% (1999). Wage adjusted labour productivity rose gradually between 1993 (120.7%) and 1999 (128.9%), as value added grew at a somewhat faster pace than personnel costs.

INTERNATIONAL TRENDS AND FOREIGN TRADE

Japan maintained its position as the largest producer in the Triad, with 53.8 billion ECU of output in 1997, equivalent to 36.8% of the Triad total. The EU was the smallest producer of structural metal products in 1987 (31.3%), but ten years later had seen its share increase to 33.5% (or 48.9 billion ECU) of Triad output, above the share of the USA (29.8%).

Japan had the highest output in the Triad from the smallest workforce

Conversely, Japan had the lowest number of persons employed within the Triad, some 288 thousand persons (or 25.4% of the Triad total). The EU was the largest employer, with nearly twice as many persons employed (492 thousand persons or 43.4% of the Triad total). Employment fell at a rapid pace in the first half of the 1990s, with a subsequent recovery in the EU and the USA, whilst Japanese employment levels continued to decline.

EU trade balance rose, whilst the cover ratio was reduced

The EU's trade surplus of 1.9 billion EUR in 1999 was higher in absolute terms than in 1989, although imports rose at a much faster pace, resulting in the cover ratio falling from 538.4% in 1989 to 236.2% in 1999. In the USA, a surge in imports during 1998 saw the trade balance turn slightly negative (172 million ECU). Japan also ran a modest trade deficit for structural metal products from 1994 onwards, which increased to 174 million ECU in 1997, moderating to 89.4 million ECU in the following year.

EU's near neighbours were the principal trading partners

This industry would appear to be one area where the opening up of Eastern European markets has had significant effects on European trade. Poland was the largest origin of imports (283 million EUR) in 1999, whilst at the same time being the third largest destination for EU structural metal products (237 million EUR). The Czech Republic was the second largest origin of imports in 1999 (262 million EUR). In both cases, there was a considerable change when compared to 1989, when Poland was the fourth most important origin of imports and Czechoslovakia the tenth most important. Switzerland was the second most important export destination for EU goods in 1999 (371 million EUR), losing its position as the most important origin of imports and destination of exports from 1989.

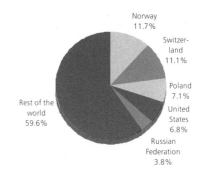

Figure 9.9

Structural metal products (NACE Rev. 1 28.1)
Destination of EU exports, 1999 (%)

Source: Eurostat (COMEXT)

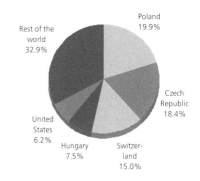

Figure 9.10

Structural metal products (NACE Rev. 1 28.1)
Origin of EU imports, 1999 (%)

Source: Eurostat (COMEXT)

SUB-CHAPTER 9.2
TANKS, BOILERS, RADIATORS AND STEAM
GENERATORS (NACE Rev. 1 28.2 AND 28.3)

This sub-chapter covers the manufacture of tanks, reservoirs and containers of metal; central heating radiators and boilers (NACE Rev. 1 28.2) as well as the manufacture of steam generators (NACE Rev. 1 28.3).

In the countries for which data was available, production value reached 25.7 billion ECU[1] in 1996 (equivalent to 12.7% of total metal products output). The share of value added was similar at 12.1% (or 9.7 billion ECU). There were relatively fewer persons employed, 10.5% of the total for metal products (or 216 thousand persons)[2].

The two NACE Rev. 1 activities covered by this sub-chapter were fairly similar in size, with the manufacture of steam generators being slightly the larger activity, 13.6 billion ECU of output in 1996, whilst production of metal tanks, reservoirs, containers, heating radiators and boilers was equal to 12.1 billion ECU[3]. Similar relative differences were observed for value added and employment (where 119.1 thousand persons were employed in the steam generators industry).

France was the most specialised
and the second largest producer
This activity accounted for 1.2% of total manufacturing output in France in 1996, with production value equal to 7.1 billion ECU. Almost a quarter (22.5%) of total metal products output in France was generated in this industry in 1996. This share was considerably higher than in the other Member States, with Belgium the second placed country (14.5% of metal products output in 1997).

Germany had the highest output (8.4 billion ECU) in 1997, equivalent to 13.3% of metal products output, well ahead of Italy (2.9 billion ECU in 1996) and the United Kingdom (2.3 billion ECU in 1997), where this industry accounted for less than 8.0% of total metal products output.

(1) DK, IRL, L and A, no data available for NACE Rev. 1 28.2.
(2) DK, IRL, L, NL and A, no data available for NACE Rev. 1 28.2.
(3) DK, IRL, L and A, no data available.

Figure 9.11 ─────

Tanks, boilers, radiators and stream generators (NACE Rev. 1 28.2 and 28.3)
Production and export specialisation (%)

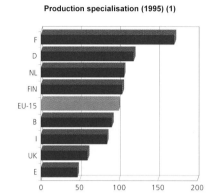

Production specialisation (1995) (1)

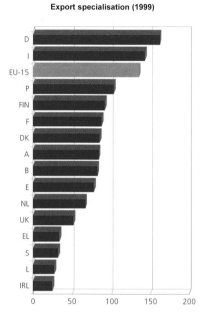

Export specialisation (1999)

(1) DK, EL, IRL, L, A, P and S, not available.

Source: Eurostat (SBS, COMEXT)

STRUCTURE AND PERFORMANCE

Nominal output rose from 17.4 billion ECU in 1986 to 25.7 billion ECU[4] in 1996, an increase of 8.3 billion ECU. As such, this industry accounted for 0.6% of the increase observed in total manufacturing output over the period 1986 to 1996. This was in line with the relative share of the industry in the manufacturing total (representing 0.7% of total manufacturing in 1996).

Annual average growth rates of real production showed that there was moderate growth in this industry, with gains of just 0.8% per annum between 1990 and 1995 (a figure 0.3 percentage points higher than the manufacturing average). This modest figure hid large volatility in the pattern of growth, with significant real increases in 1991 (7.7%) and 1994 (5.1%) being countered by output declining by 1.7% in 1992, 6.0% in 1993 and 0.3% in 1995. The evolution of value added followed a similar trend over the period considered, although declining by a considerably larger margin in 1995 (-5.8%).

Below average profitability
The gross operating rate did not exceed 8.0% between 1986 and 1995, and towards the end of this period fell quite strongly. The highest gross operating rates were reported in 1988 (7.8%) and 1990 (7.5%), although these figures were around 2.0 percentage points lower than the manufacturing average. The recession of the early 1990s had a significant impact, such that by 1995 the gross operating rate was equal to 5.6% (3.6 percentage points lower than the manufacturing EU total).

(4) DK, IRL, L and A, no data available for NACE Rev. 1 28.2.

Figure 9.12

Tanks, boilers, radiators and stream generators (NACE Rev. 1 28.2 and 28.3)
International comparison of production in constant prices and employment (1990=100)

Production in constant prices

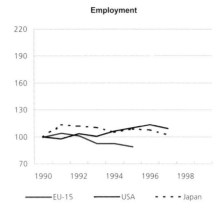

Employment

Source: Eurostat (SBS)

China by far the largest export market
With 669 million EUR, EU exports to China in 1999 were much higher than to any other country. This figure was a considerable increase on the 87 million ECU of exports reported ten years before, when China was the fourth largest export destination for EU products. A similar picture was observed for Poland, with EU exports growing from 8.4 million ECU in 1989 to 247 million EUR in 1999. The USA was the third most important export market for the EU in 1999, worth 200 million EUR.

EU imports originated largely from countries that had a close geographical proximity to the Union. Switzerland was the largest origin of imports in 1999 (134 million EUR), ahead of the Czech Republic (101 million EUR) and Poland (87.6 million EUR), the latter two reported rapidly expanding imports into the EU.

LABOUR AND PRODUCTIVITY

Between 1986 and 1996, employment fell by 57.6 thousand to 216 thousand persons employed[5], equivalent to a reduction of 21.0% (which was more than twice the rate of decline for manufacturing as a whole). Other than 1989 and 1990, employment declined at a regular pace. The average rate of decline between 1990 and 1995 was 2.4% per annum (a similar figure to that for total manufacturing).

Little evolution in wage adjusted labour productivity
Apparent labour productivity increased progressively from 26.4 thousand ECU per person employed in 1986 to 40.8 thousand ECU per person employed in 1995, always at a slightly lower level than the total manufacturing average. Wage adjusted labour productivity was broadly unchanged over the period 1986 to 1995, +/-5 percentage points from 120.0%. As there was no larger change in this ratio, the differential with the manufacturing average widened from -18.8 percentage points in 1986 to -28.0 percentage points in 1995. Unit personnel costs were equal to 36.1 thousand ECU per employee in 1995.

(5) DK, IRL, L, NL and A, no data available for NACE Rev. 1 28.2.

INTERNATIONAL TRENDS AND FOREIGN TRADE

The EU accounted for more than half of the Triad's output throughout the 1985 to 1995 period, 54.4% of the total in 1995. The share of Japanese output increased from 21.9% in 1985 to 29.8% ten years later (or 14.0 billion ECU). Much of the relative increase in Japan came at the expense of the USA, where nominal production levels changed little (7.4 billion ECU of production in 1995). However, by 1997, American output had risen from its 1995 level by more than 2 billion ECU, whilst the Japanese figure fell by a similar margin (-1.7 billion ECU). Employment declined in both the EU and Japan, whilst there was a net increase of 10 thousand persons employed in the USA between 1985 and 1995, reaching 1.01 million persons in 1997.

EU trade surplus of 2.7 billion EUR in 1999
Over the ten-year period to 1999, the EU ran a trade surplus in this industry, which grew from 824 million ECU in 1989 to 3.3 billion ECU in 1998, before falling to 2.7 billion EUR in 1999. Imports grew at a faster pace than exports, as the cover ratio of 471% in 1999 was much lower than it had been in 1994 (715%). The latest data available for the USA and Japan in 1998 revealed that all three Triad members were running surpluses, equal to 683 million ECU in the USA and 652 million ECU in Japan.

Figure 9.13

Tanks, boilers, radiators and stream generators
(NACE Rev. 1 28.2 and 28.3)
Destination of EU exports, 1999 (%)

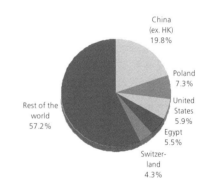

Source: Eurostat (COMEXT)

Figure 9.14

Tanks, boilers, radiators and stream generators
(NACE Rev. 1 28.2 and 28.3)
Origin of EU imports, 1999 (%)

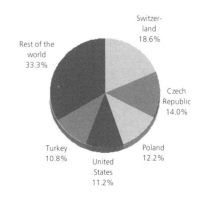

Source: Eurostat (COMEXT)

SUB-CHAPTER 9.3
MISCELLANEOUS METAL PRODUCTS
(NACE Rev. 1 28.4, 28.5, 28.6 AND 28.7)

This sub-chapter covers a number of miscellaneous industrial metal processing techniques (such as forging, pressing, stamping, roll forming and the treatment of metal), as well as the manufacture of a number of specific metal products (such as cutlery, tools, hardware, wire and fasteners).

Miscellaneous metal products had a production value of 128.5 billion ECU[6] in the EU in 1996 which was equivalent to 63.5% of total output in the metal products industry (or 3.6% of total manufacturing output). These activities accounted for 64.5% of employment in metal products, equivalent to 1.33 million persons[7].

Other fabricated metal products (NACE Rev. 1 28.7) accounted for over a third (38.0%) of the production value in this sub-chapter (49.2 billion ECU)[8] in 1996. Its share of total employment was lower at 33.2% or 440.6 thousand persons. Treatment and coating of metals; general mechanical engineering (NACE Rev. 1 28.5) accounted for 23.7% of production (30.5 billion ECU), whilst the remaining two activities were similar in size. Forging, pressing, stamping and roll forming of metal; powder metallurgy (NACE Rev. 1 28.4) produced 22.7 billion ECU compared to 26.1 billion ECU for manufacture of cutlery, tools and general hardware (NACE Rev. 1 28.6).

Germany was the principal EU producer
In these industries, Germany produced almost twice as much as any other Member State, with 39.8 billion ECU of output in 1997. This amounted to 3.9% of the German manufacturing total. France was the next largest producer (22.1 billion ECU) in 1997, with this industry accounting for 3.6% of French manufacturing activity. Italy (21.6 billion ECU, 1996) and Spain (12.1 billion ECU, 1997) were amongst the most specialised countries in the Union, with the industries covered by this sub-chapter accounting for 4.3% and 4.4% of their respective manufacturing totals.

(6) L, no data available for NACE Rev. 1 28.7.
(7) L and NL, no data available for NACE Rev. 1 28.7.
(8) L, no data available.

Figure 9.15

Miscellaneous metal products (NACE Rev. 1 28.4, 28.5, 28.6 and 28.7)
Production and export specialisation (%)

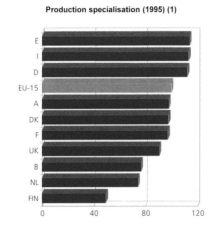

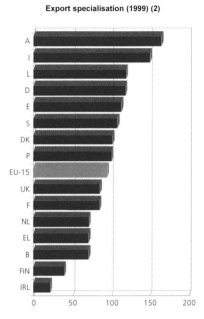

(1) EL, IRL, L, P and S, not available.
(2) Excluding NACE Rev. 1 28.4 and 28.5.

Source: Eurostat (SBS, COMEXT)

STRUCTURE AND PERFORMANCE
Aggregated data for the two largest industries in this sub-chapter (namely other fabricated metal products (NACE Rev. 1 28.8) and the treatment and coating of metals; general mechanical engineering (NACE Rev. 1 28.5)) reported a production value of 53.5 billion EUR in 1999, equivalent to 1.3% of total EU manufacturing output. Annual average growth rates of production during the five-year period 1993 to 1998 reported a real increase in output of 3.1% per annum, which was more than a percentage point lower than the manufacturing average.

There was a rapid increase in the value added generated within the treatment and coating of metals industry (NACE Rev. 1 28.5), almost doubling from 7.7 billion ECU in 1986 to 14.0 billion ECU in 1996. However, this high net increase hid large cyclical fluctuations, as value added fell by more than 10.0% in 1993, followed by double-digit growth between 1994 and 1996 (the highest figure being a 26.3% increase in 1995).

Figure 9.16

Intermediate consumption of steel tinplate, 1998 (1)

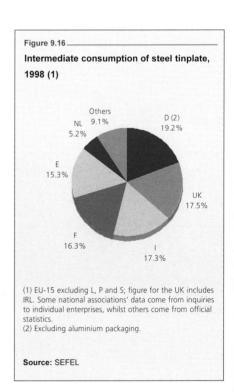

(1) EU-15 excluding L, P and S; figure for the UK includes IRL. Some national associations' data come from inquiries to individual enterprises, whilst others come from official statistics.
(2) Excluding aluminium packaging.

Source: SEFEL

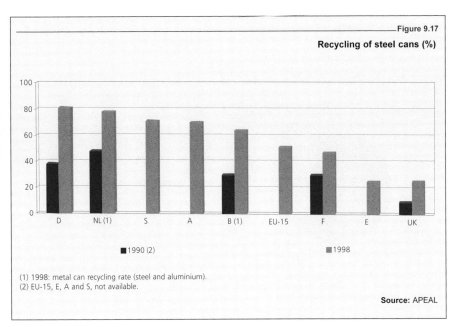

Figure 9.17

Recycling of steel cans (%)

■1990 (2)   ■1998

(1) 1998: metal can recycling rate (steel and aluminium).
(2) EU-15, E, A and S, not available.

Source: APEAL

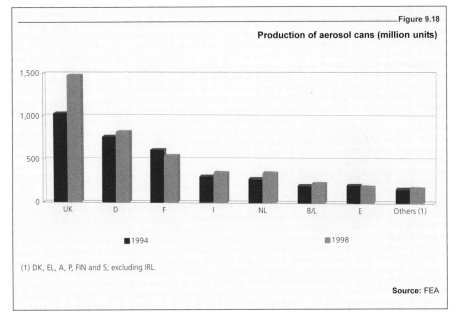

Figure 9.18

Production of aerosol cans (million units)

■1994   ■1998

(1) DK, EL, A, P, FIN and S; excluding IRL.

Source: FEA

Profits remained robust throughout the recession
The industries covered by this sub-chapter generally reported high profit rates (gross operating rate in relation to turnover). Although value added fluctuated considerably in relation to the general economic conditions, the gross operating rate remained above the manufacturing average during the whole of the 1990s. At the lowest point in the economic cycle in 1993, the operating rate of miscellaneous metal products was 8.7% (0.5 percentage points above the manufacturing average). However, by 1995 the operating rate had grown to 11.2% (2.0 percentage points above the manufacturing average).

LABOUR AND PRODUCTIVITY
Employment in these industries grew between 1993 and 1996, when a total of 1.33 million persons were employed[9]. This meant there was a moderate increase on the 1.24 million persons that were employed in 1993. These industries together accounted for between 5% and 6% of the total employed in EU manufacturing.

*Highest wage adjusted labour
productivity within metal products*
At 139.3%, wage adjusted labour productivity for miscellaneous metal products was highest amongst those industries covered in this chapter in 1995, although still 7.0 percentage points below the manufacturing average. Wage adjusted labour productivity increased at a rapid pace following the recession of 1993 (when it stood at 127.5%). Much of the productivity gains seem to have been made through a reduction in the relative cost of labour, as the share of personnel costs in production fell from 33.4% in 1993 to 29.7% in 1995. Nevertheless, labour remained an important input factor in these industries as the share of personnel costs in production were still 8.4 percentage points above the manufacturing average.

(9) L and NL, no data available for NACE Rev. 1 28.7.

INTERNATIONAL TRENDS AND FOREIGN TRADE

EU output of 122 billion ECU in 1995 was 41.4% of the Triad total, higher than the respective figures for the USA (99.3 billion ECU, 33.8%) and Japan (73.0 billion ECU, 24.8%). Subsequently, American production expanded at a rapid rate, rising to 123 billion ECU in 1997, whilst Japanese output was reduced to 63.8 billion ECU.

There was a similar look to the employment data in 1995, with the EU's 1.28 million persons accounting for almost half of the Triad total (47.0%), with 983 thousand persons employed in the USA (36.1%) and 458 thousand in Japan. By 1997, American employment levels had risen to over the one million mark.

EU trade surplus changed little,
whilst the cover ratio fell

Both the EU and Japan reported similar trade positions with trade surpluses of 2.4 billion EUR in 1999 and 2.1 billion ECU in 1998 respectively. Imports rose at a faster pace than exports, with the EU cover ratio falling to 119.3% in 1999 from 149.9% reported in 1990. Likewise in Japan, the cover ratio fell from 269.1% to 198.2%. In the USA exports increased at a faster rate than imports, but despite this the trade deficit widened from -3.2 billion ECU in 1990 to -5.2 billion ECU in 1998.

The USA was the principal origin of EU imports (2.3 billion EUR), as well as being the main destination for EU exports (3.0 billion EUR) in 1999, as was the case ten years before. Switzerland was the second most important export destination, accounting for 1.4 billion EUR of the EU's miscellaneous metal product exports. However, in 1999 the situation had changed as China became the second most important origin of EU imports (2.0 billion EUR), followed by Switzerland (1.5 billion EUR) and Taiwan (1.1 billion EUR).

Figure 9.19 ───────────────

Miscellaneous metal products
(NACE Rev. 1 28.4, 28.5, 28.6 and 28.7)
Destination of EU exports, 1999 (%)

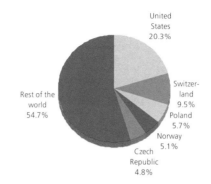

Source: Eurostat (COMEXT)

Figure 9.20 ───────────────

Miscellaneous metal products
(NACE Rev. 1 28.4, 28.5, 28.6 and 28.7)
Origin of EU imports, 1999 (%)

Source: Eurostat (COMEXT)

Table 9.3

Manufacture of structural metal products (NACE Rev. 1 28.1)

Production related indicators in the EU (1)

	1989	1990	1991	1992	1993	1994	1995	1996	1997	1998	1999
Number of persons employed (thousands)	487.4	490.8	510.2	504.4	467.9	459.5	462.4	488.1	492.4	515.8	517.5
Production (million EUR)	37,737	40,408	43,321	43,461	39,441	41,093	45,033	47,446	48,920	52,164	52,411
Domestic producer price index (1995=100)	:	:	:	:	:	:	100.0	101.4	102.1	104.3	105.5
Value added (million EUR)	13,169	14,340	15,618	15,508	14,062	14,476	15,472	16,560	17,295	18,469	18,591

(1) Technically, data before 01/01/1999 are in ECU and after this date in euro. However, as the conversion rate was 1 ECU =1 EUR, for practical purposes the two terms can be used interchangeably.

Table 9.4

Manufacture of structural metal products (NACE Rev. 1 28.1)

Trade related indicators in the EU (1)

	1989	1990	1991	1992	1993	1994	1995	1996	1997	1998	1999
Exports (million EUR)	1,945	2,026	2,190	2,005	2,218	2,252	2,841	2,832	3,253	3,463	3,367
Imports (million EUR)	361	444	560	715	724	779	961	1,052	1,146	1,259	1,425
Trade balance (million EUR)	1,584	1,582	1,631	1,290	1,494	1,473	1,880	1,780	2,107	2,204	1,941
Cover ratio (%)	538.4	456.0	391.4	280.3	306.2	289.1	295.7	269.2	283.9	275.1	236.2

(1) Technically, data before 01/01/1999 are in ECU and after this date in euro. However, as the conversion rate was 1 ECU =1 EUR, for practical purposes the two terms can be used interchangeably.

Table 9.5

Manufacture of structural metal products (NACE Rev. 1 28.1)

Production related indicators, 1997

	B	DK	D	EL (1)	E	F	IRL	I (1)	L	NL	A	P	FIN	S	UK
Number of persons employed (thousands)	22.7	11.4	130.5	1.8	90.7	32.7	4.3	54.3	1.4	:	16.7	26.6	9.9	10.7	53.5
Production (million ECU)	2,782	1,057	15,141	157	5,495	3,982	463	5,529	144	3,596	1,743	1,040	1,107	1,353	5,697
Value added (million ECU)	914	435	5,227	46	1,815	1,324	141	2,074	51	1,156	692	307	413	486	2,235
Gross operating surplus (million ECU)	205.3	103.3	714.8	15.1	425.2	307.7	49.1	596.9	2.2	312.4	136.5	85.7	137.8	128.3	719.2

(1) 1996.

Table 9.6

Manufacture of structural metal products (NACE Rev. 1 28.1)

Trade related indicators, 1999

	B	DK	D	EL	E	F	IRL	I	L	NL	A	P	FIN	S	UK
Exports (million EUR)	654	359	2,036	46	302	761	69	913	86	717	587	37	211	361	748
Imports (million EUR)	423	259	1,584	66	240	678	148	231	66	374	491	113	74	194	512
Trade balance (million EUR)	230	100	452	-20	62	82	-79	682	19	343	95	-76	137	167	236
Cover ratio (%)	154.4	138.5	128.5	69.0	126.1	112.2	46.8	395.7	128.8	191.6	119.4	32.7	283.9	186.1	146.2

Table 9.7

Manufacture of structural metal products (NACE Rev. 1 28.1)

Labour related indicators, 1997

	B	DK (1)	D	EL (2)	E	F	IRL	I (2)	L	NL	A	P	FIN	S	UK
Unit personnel costs (thousand ECU per employee)	33.7	32.2	34.8	16.6	17.5	31.0	21.6	28.3	35.3	:	33.4	9.3	29.4	33.6	29.0
Social charges as a share of personnel costs (%)	39.0	4.4	23.1	30.3	27.6	46.3	15.1	48.6	:	14.6	29.1	28.1	27.1	41.3	12.4
Apparent labour productivity (thousand ECU/pers. empl.)	40.2	38.2	40.1	24.8	20.0	40.4	32.4	38.2	35.4	:	41.4	11.5	41.8	45.6	41.8
Wage adjusted labour productivity (%)	119.4	132.0	115.2	148.9	114.2	130.3	149.9	134.7	100.4	:	124.0	124.5	142.3	135.9	144.2
Personnel costs as a share of total operating costs (%)	27.4	34.4	30.4	21.7	25.8	26.4	21.1	28.5	32.2	24.6	31.6	22.9	27.7	28.7	29.6

(1) Unit personnel costs and wage adjusted labour productivity, 1996; (2) 1996.

Source: Eurostat (SBS, EBT, COMEXT)

Table 9.8

Manufacture of tanks, reservoirs and containers of metal, manufacture of central heating radiators and boilers (NACE Rev. 1 28.2)

Production related indicators in the EU (1)

	1989	1990	1991	1992	1993	1994	1995	1996	1997	1998	1999
Number of persons employed (thousands)	117.4	117.1	120.9	120.5	106.6	105.1	110.0	:	:	:	:
Production (million ECU)	9,219	9,870	11,096	11,544	10,460	10,693	12,197	:	:	:	:
Domestic producer price index (1995=100)	:	:	:	:	:	:	100.0	101.5	102.0	102.8	102.0
Value added (million ECU)	3,489	3,805	4,255	4,458	4,045	4,159	4,558	:	:	:	:

(1) Technically, data before 01/01/1999 are in ECU and after this date in euro. However, as the conversion rate was 1 ECU =1 EUR, for practical purposes the two terms can be used interchangeably.

Table 9.9

Manufacture of tanks, reservoirs and containers of metal, manufacture of central heating radiators and boilers (NACE Rev. 1 28.2)

Trade related indicators in the EU (1)

	1989	1990	1991	1992	1993	1994	1995	1996	1997	1998	1999
Exports (million EUR)	492	529	552	601	710	870	943	1,150	1,259	1,318	1,215
Imports (million EUR)	157	195	261	314	316	352	388	425	473	501	567
Trade balance (million EUR)	336	335	291	287	394	518	554	725	787	816	648
Cover ratio (%)	314.3	271.8	211.2	191.2	225.0	246.9	242.7	270.7	266.5	262.9	214.3

(1) Technically, data before 01/01/1999 are in ECU and after this date in euro. However, as the conversion rate was 1 ECU =1 EUR, for practical purposes the two terms can be used interchangeably.

Table 9.10

Manufacture of tanks, reservoirs and containers of metal, manufacture of central heating radiators and boilers (NACE Rev. 1 28.2)

Production related indicators, 1997

	B	DK	D	EL (1)	E	F (1)	IRL	I (1)	L	NL	A	P	FIN	S	UK
Number of persons employed (thousands)	5.8	2.1	31.7	1.2	11.2	12.4	:	17.2	:	:	4.2	2.8	2.0	1.3	12.9
Production (million ECU)	824	162	3,940	61	746	1,572	:	2,636	:	985	445	152	227	145	1,396
Value added (million ECU)	315	71	1,639	25	293	592	:	919	:	308	196	55	90	54	640
Gross operating surplus (million ECU)	103.9	12.8	390.8	7.0	64.1	157.8	:	390.9	:	87.7	34.9	17.9	30.0	9.3	298.3

(1) 1996.

Table 9.11

Manufacture of tanks, reservoirs and containers of metal, manufacture of central heating radiators and boilers (NACE Rev. 1 28.2)

Trade related indicators, 1999

	B	DK	D	EL	E	F	IRL	I	L	NL	A	P	FIN	S	UK
Exports (million EUR)	379	58	1,113	9	127	535	46	949	5	318	144	81	52	58	251
Imports (million EUR)	231	51	717	159	211	434	61	257	20	258	200	47	14	42	488
Trade balance (million EUR)	148	7	396	-150	-84	101	-14	692	-14	60	-57	33	38	16	-236
Cover ratio (%)	164.2	114.3	155.2	5.5	60.2	123.3	76.6	368.8	27.1	123.4	71.8	171.1	375.5	137.9	51.5

Table 9.12

Manufacture of tanks, reservoirs and containers of metal, manufacture of central heating radiators and boilers (NACE Rev. 1 28.2)

Labour related indicators, 1997

	B	DK	D	EL (1)	E	F (1)	IRL	I (1)	L	NL	A	P	FIN	S	UK
Unit personnel costs (thousand ECU per employee)	37.0	:	39.4	14.7	21.3	35.0	:	31.2	:	:	38.1	13.4	31.4	33.2	26.6
Social charges as a share of personnel costs (%)	40.5	5.6	23.0	31.3	27.2	41.9	:	48.8	:	14.2	29.1	31.2	28.2	43.2	12.6
Apparent labour productivity (thousand ECU/pers. empl.)	54.8	34.7	51.6	20.5	26.2	47.8	:	53.3	:	:	46.3	19.7	44.9	40.2	49.7
Wage adjusted labour productivity (%)	148.1	:	131.0	139.5	123.0	136.3	:	171.0	:	:	121.4	146.5	142.9	121.0	186.7
Personnel costs as a share of total operating costs (%)	29.6	39.0	29.8	30.6	31.6	29.3	:	23.7	:	23.5	35.6	25.6	30.8	32.0	29.2

(1) 1996.

Source: Eurostat (SBS, EBT, COMEXT)

Table 9.13

Manufacture of steam generators, except central heating hot water boilers (NACE Rev. 1 28.3)

Production related indicators in the EU

	1989	1990	1991	1992	1993	1994	1995	1996	1997	1998	1999
Number of persons employed (thousands)	141.4	146.0	152.9	145.0	136.8	137.5	123.6	119.1	:	:	:
Production (million ECU)	11,519	12,433	13,604	13,093	12,832	13,947	13,331	13,581	:	:	:
Domestic producer price index (1995=100)	:	:	:	:	:	:	:	100.8	102.1	103.3	103.1
Value added (million ECU)	4,416	4,945	5,393	5,248	5,184	5,571	4,974	5,079	:	:	:

(1) Technically, data before 01/01/1999 are in ECU and after this date in euro. However, as the conversion rate was 1 ECU =1 EUR, for practical purposes the two terms can be used interchangeably.

Table 9.14

Manufacture of steam generators, except central heating hot water boilers (NACE Rev. 1 28.3)

Trade related indicators in the EU (1)

	1989	1990	1991	1992	1993	1994	1995	1996	1997	1998	1999
Exports (million EUR)	547	701	563	645	1,790	2,268	2,261	2,325	2,420	2,548	2,185
Imports (million EUR)	59	44	95	72	85	86	145	111	105	103	156
Trade balance (million EUR)	489	657	468	573	1,704	2,181	2,115	2,214	2,315	2,445	2,030
Cover ratio (%)	933.3	1,583.7	590.8	898.4	2,097.8	2,628.5	1,553.9	2,093.5	2,294.6	2,463.5	1,404.7

(1) Technically, data before 01/01/1999 are in ECU and after this date in euro. However, as the conversion rate was 1 ECU =1 EUR, for practical purposes the two terms can be used interchangeably.

Table 9.15

Manufacture of steam generators, except central heating hot water boilers (NACE Rev. 1 28.3)

Production related indicators, 1997

	B	DK	D	EL	E	F	IRL	I (1)	L	NL	A	P	FIN	S	UK
Number of persons employed (thousands)	3.2	1.6	35.3	:	2.8	57.5	:	1.9	0.1	:	1.7	0.2	2.1	0.2	7.1
Production (million ECU)	413	186	4,496	:	185	5,600	:	261	0	166	161	6	427	18	864
Value added (million ECU)	140	58	1,743	:	80	2,438	:	95	0	23	58	3	94	8	325
Gross operating surplus (million ECU)	10.0	-1.7	60.0	:	15.6	450.5	:	19.3	-1.0	-7.1	-0.8	0.6	15.2	1.5	19.2

(1) 1996.

Table 9.16

Manufacture of steam generators, except central heating hot water boilers (NACE Rev. 1 28.3)

Trade related indicators, 1999

	B	DK	D	EL	E	F	IRL	I	L	NL	A	P	FIN	S	UK
Exports (million EUR)	63	64	1,520	0	123	358	7	116	2	66	31	1	75	27	168
Imports (million EUR)	66	13	61	6	33	62	6	31	1	18	25	3	5	35	98
Trade balance (million EUR)	-2	51	1,458	-6	90	296	0	85	1	48	6	-2	70	-8	70
Cover ratio (%)	96.4	482.5	2,485.9	4.6	371.6	581.0	103.1	373.4	258.2	373.2	126.0	30.4	1,370.6	77.6	171.3

Table 9.17

Manufacture of steam generators, except central heating hot water boilers (NACE Rev. 1 28.3)

Labour related indicators, 1997

	B	DK	D	EL	E	F	IRL	I (1)	L	NL	A	P	FIN	S	UK
Unit personnel costs (thousand ECU per employee)	41.3	:	47.7	:	23.4	34.5	:	40.0	11.7	:	33.9	11.7	37.6	31.4	43.3
Social charges as a share of personnel costs (%)	36.0	5.1	24.1	:	26.5	41.8	:	43.7	:	19.1	24.9	35.3	27.2	41.3	11.7
Apparent labour productivity (thousand ECU/pers. empl.)	44.0	36.4	49.4	:	28.7	42.4	:	49.5	0.0	:	33.4	14.6	44.7	38.5	46.0
Wage adjusted labour productivity (%)	106.6	:	103.4	:	122.4	122.6	:	123.7	-0.2	:	98.4	124.9	118.8	122.4	106.3
Personnel costs as a share of total operating costs (%)	32.1	31.4	37.9	:	36.9	37.7	:	31.1	:	17.6	33.2	40.4	19.2	38.5	35.5

(1) 1996.

Source: Eurostat (SBS, EBT, COMEXT)

Table 9.18

Forging, pressing, stamping and roll forming of metal; powder metallurgy (NACE Rev. 1 28.4)

Production related indicators in the EU (1)

	1989	1990	1991	1992	1993	1994	1995	1996	1997	1998	1999
Number of persons employed (thousands)	205.8	209.3	206.2	200.9	186.2	188.2	223.6	207.0	217.8	226.4	226.7
Production (million EUR)	17,376	18,010	17,953	18,060	16,313	18,168	22,264	22,704	:	:	:
Domestic producer price index (1995=100)	89.6	91.1	91.2	91.9	91.8	93.2	100.0	102.1	102.0		
Value added (million EUR)	6,342	6,723	6,841	7,120	6,501	7,132	8,391	8,603	:	:	:

(1) Technically, data before 01/01/1999 are in ECU and after this date in euro. However, as the conversion rate was 1 ECU =1 EUR, for practical purposes the two terms can be used interchangeably.

Table 9.19

Forging, pressing, stamping and roll forming of metal; powder metallurgy (NACE Rev. 1 28.4)

Production related indicators, 1997

	B	DK	D	EL	E	F	IRL	I (1)	L	NL	A	P	FIN	S	UK
Number of persons employed (thousands)	2.2	0.0	69.9	:	22.0	42.3	0.3	31.7	:	:	3.1	2.0	0.3	1.4	34.2
Production (million ECU)	251	0	7,721	:	2,054	5,387	22	4,715	:	945	351	59	22	142	2,839
Value added (million ECU)	94	0	3,495	:	733	1,659	11	1,695	:	344	146	21	10	64	1,221
Gross operating surplus (million ECU)	35.3	0.0	841.9	:	261.1	357.3	5.2	691.7	:	126.4	43.3	6.1	4.5	16.5	359.7

(1) 1996.

Table 9.20

Forging, pressing, stamping and roll forming of metal; powder metallurgy (NACE Rev. 1 28.4)

Labour related indicators, 1997

	B	DK	D	EL	E	F	IRL	I (1)	L	NL	A	P	FIN	S	UK
Unit personnel costs (thousand ECU per employee)	33.3	:	38.1	:	22.5	30.8	17.2	32.6	:	:	33.4	9.2	27.6	33.9	25.6
Social charges as a share of personnel costs (%)	36.4	:	23.3	:	28.6	42.1	18.4	51.1	:	14.7	30.3	33.3	29.5	42.6	12.1
Apparent labour productivity (thousand ECU/pers. empl.)	41.8	:	50.0	:	33.4	39.2	32.2	53.5	:	:	47.2	10.9	41.3	45.6	35.7
Wage adjusted labour productivity (%)	125.7	:	131.2	:	148.4	127.4	187.3	163.9	:	:	141.3	118.8	149.9	134.4	139.3
Personnel costs as a share of total operating costs (%)	26.5	:	37.9	:	25.5	25.9	34.1	24.7	:	24.6	32.9	28.1	33.1	37.4	34.2

(1) 1996.

Source: Eurostat (SBS, EBT)

Table 9.21

Treatment and coating of metals; general mechanical engineering (NACE Rev. 1 28.5)
Production related indicators in the EU

	1989	1990	1991	1992	1993	1994	1995	1996	1997	1998	1999
Number of persons employed (thousands)	309.5	324.1	318.3	307.1	275.8	297.7	337.2	392.9	:	:	:
Production (million ECU)	19,014	20,356	20,424	19,972	17,938	20,966	26,588	30,491	:	:	:
Domestic producer price index (1995=100)	:	:	:	:	:	:	:	:	:	:	:
Value added (million ECU)	8,707	9,349	9,566	9,195	8,316	9,477	12,443	13,969	:	:	:

Table 9.22

Treatment and coating of metals; general mechanical engineering (NACE Rev. 1 28.5)
Production related indicators, 1997

	B	DK	D	EL (1)	E	F	IRL	I (1)	L (1)	NL	A	P	FIN	S	UK
Number of persons employed (thousands)	16.7	4.1	63.6	0.4	58.2	83.5	0.9	59.4	0.9	:	5.2	20.8	9.5	15.4	64.5
Production (million ECU)	1,925	292	5,593	19	3,598	6,995	68	5,682	320	843	503	780	778	949	4,197
Value added (million ECU)	767	160	2,734	9	1,575	3,062	30	2,645	49	393	236	274	393	436	2,220
Gross operating surplus (million ECU)	287.1	33.0	705.1	2.1	469.1	490.0	11.4	929.9	21.7	135.6	63.6	104.0	142.6	-1.6	673.7

(1) 1996.

Table 9.23

Treatment and coating of metals; general mechanical engineering (NACE Rev. 1 28.5)
Labour related indicators, 1997

	B	DK (1)	D	EL (2)	E	F	IRL	I (2)	L (2)	NL	A	P	FIN	S	UK
Unit personnel costs (thousand ECU per employee)	32.9	36.0	32.0	17.3	20.8	30.8	20.3	30.3	31.1	:	32.9	10.8	27.7	28.4	25.4
Social charges as a share of personnel costs (%)	38.5	4.2	21.3	28.3	27.2	40.9	15.4	48.7	:	14.1	29.2	33.9	28.0	40.7	12.7
Apparent labour productivity (thousand ECU/pers. empl.)	45.9	38.9	43.0	22.1	27.1	36.7	32.2	44.5	52.4	:	44.9	13.1	41.4	28.3	34.4
Wage adjusted labour productivity (%)	139.7	125.9	134.1	128.3	130.4	119.0	158.9	147.2	168.6	:	136.5	121.8	149.7	99.6	135.6
Personnel costs as a share of total operating costs (%)	29.3	49.1	40.9	41.0	33.6	40.2	33.5	35.0	9.2	35.6	37.0	24.1	38.9	45.0	43.6

(1) Unit personnel costs and wage adjusted labour productivity, 1996; (2) 1996.

Source: Eurostat (SBS)

Table 9.24

Manufacture of other fabricated metal products (NACE Rev. 1 28.7)

Production related indicators in the EU (1)

	1989	1990	1991	1992	1993	1994	1995	1996	1997	1998	1999
Number of persons employed (thousands)	:	:	:	:	490.0	475.6	448.0	:	464.9	481.6	464.4
Production (million EUR)	:	:	:	:	43,502	46,333	47,890	:	51,788	52,797	53,476
Domestic producer price index (1995=100)	:	96.5	96.5	97.3	96.8	96.9	100.0	101.1	101.1	100.7	100.5
Value added (million EUR)	:	:	:	:	17,218	18,078	17,905	:	19,330	19,617	20,101

(1) Technically, data before 01/01/1999 are in ECU and after this date in euro. However, as the conversion rate was 1 ECU =1 EUR, for practical purposes the two terms can be used interchangeably.

Table 9.25

Manufacture of other fabricated metal products (NACE Rev. 1 28.7)

Trade related indicators in the EU (1)

	1989	1990	1991	1992	1993	1994	1995	1996	1997	1998	1999
Exports (million EUR)	4,734	4,702	4,814	4,977	5,332	6,004	6,736	7,590	8,330	8,862	8,811
Imports (million EUR)	2,945	3,064	3,440	3,507	3,752	4,342	5,199	5,461	6,357	7,219	7,712
Trade balance (million EUR)	1,789	1,638	1,375	1,469	1,581	1,662	1,537	2,129	1,973	1,643	1,099
Cover ratio (%)	160.8	153.4	140.0	141.9	142.1	138.3	129.6	139.0	131.0	122.8	114.2

(1) Technically, data before 01/01/1999 are in ECU and after this date in euro. However, as the conversion rate was 1 ECU =1 EUR, for practical purposes the two terms can be used interchangeably.

Table 9.26

Manufacture of other fabricated metal products (NACE Rev. 1 28.7)

Production related indicators, 1997

	B	DK	D	EL (1)	E	F	IRL	I (1)	L	NL	A	P	FIN	S	UK
Number of persons employed (thousands)	8.2	13.4	137.4	3.4	48.3	55.3	3.6	59.9	0.9	:	7.7	18.5	5.8	27.0	58.6
Production (million ECU)	1,360	1,136	15,733	325	4,473	6,973	364	7,954	92	1,757	856	801	594	2,011	6,260
Value added (million ECU)	380	515	6,355	97	1,532	2,434	131	2,914	43	620	332	286	242	744	2,537
Gross operating surplus (million ECU)	94.5	143.1	1,228.6	38.1	538.8	668.7	49.9	1,215.6	5.8	229.3	66.8	105.8	89.0	5.3	1,040.6

(1) 1996.

Table 9.27

Manufacture of other fabricated metal products (NACE Rev. 1 28.7)

Trade related indicators, 1999

	B	DK	D	EL	E	F	IRL	I	L	NL	A	P	FIN	S	UK
Exports (million EUR)	1,740	631	6,197	88	1,523	4,023	191	4,828	111	1,629	1,129	296	218	863	2,459
Imports (million EUR)	1,803	628	4,998	207	1,537	3,657	425	1,585	129	1,914	1,487	445	347	800	2,771
Trade balance (million EUR)	-63	3	1,200	-119	-14	365	-234	3,243	-17	-284	-358	-149	-129	62	-312
Cover ratio (%)	96.5	100.5	124.0	42.6	99.1	110.0	44.9	304.5	86.6	85.1	75.9	66.6	62.9	107.8	88.8

Table 9.28

Manufacture of other fabricated metal products (NACE Rev. 1 28.7)

Labour related indicators, 1997

	B	DK (1)	D	EL (2)	E	F	IRL	I (2)	L	NL	A	P	FIN	S	UK
Unit personnel costs (thousand ECU per employee)	36.9	32.1	37.4	17.4	21.8	31.9	22.8	29.3	43.5	:	34.4	10.5	28.4	27.3	26.7
Social charges as a share of personnel costs (%)	37.3	4.8	23.2	29.9	28.7	41.2	15.9	50.8	:	16.0	27.8	37.3	27.7	41.4	13.4
Apparent labour productivity (thousand ECU/pers. empl.)	46.4	38.5	46.3	28.3	31.7	44.0	36.2	48.6	50.1	:	42.9	15.4	41.4	27.5	43.3
Wage adjusted labour productivity (%)	125.5	133.2	123.6	163.3	145.7	137.9	159.0	165.7	115.1	:	124.7	147.3	145.5	100.7	162.1
Personnel costs as a share of total operating costs (%)	22.6	35.3	32.6	19.6	23.3	26.8	25.1	24.6	43.5	22.5	31.5	24.4	27.2	35.3	26.5

(1) Unit personnel costs and wage adjusted labour productivity, 1996; (2) 1996.

Source: Eurostat (SBS, EBT, COMEXT)

Machinery and equipment (NACE Rev. 1 29)

The manufacture of machinery and equipment not elsewhere classified is covered in Division 29 of NACE Rev. 1. For the purposes of this publication, the structure is broken down into industrial processing machinery (NACE Rev. 1 Groups 29.1, 29.2, 29.4 and 29.5), agricultural machines and tractors (NACE Rev. 1 Group 29.3), and weapons and ammunitions (NACE Rev. 1 Group 29.6). Domestic appliances (NACE Rev. 1 Group 29.7) are covered within chapter 11.

Figure 10.1

Machinery and equipment (NACE Rev. 1 29)
Share of total manufacturing value added
in the EU, 1995 (%)

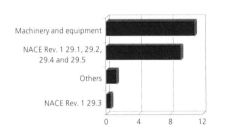

Source: Eurostat (SBS)

The activities covered in this chapter (in terms of NACE Rev. 1) include:

29:    manufacture of machinery and equipment n.e.c.;
29.1: manufacture of machinery for the production and use of mechanical power, except aircraft, vehicle and cycle engines;
29.2: manufacture of other general purpose machinery;
29.3: manufacture of agricultural and forestry machinery;
29.4: manufacture of machine-tools;
29.5: manufacture of other special purpose machinery;
29.6: manufacture of weapons and ammunition.

The manufacture of machinery and equipment[1] is one of the largest activities within the European manufacturing economy. In 1999, machinery and equipment contributed 9.0% or 360.0 billion EUR of production value to the EU's manufacturing total. In terms of value added the relative share was higher at 11.1% (or 134.1 billion EUR), whilst 11.1% (or 2.6 million persons) of the total manufacturing workforce were employed within these activities in 1999.

Custom-made products in a global marketplace
The machinery and equipment industry in the EU provides both simple products, like gears and pumps, though to complete machinery solutions for whole manufacturing plants. Many manufacturers are highly specialised and their output is often made for a narrowly defined downstream industry. As such, even relatively small enterprises can be international players in this industry.

Many enterprises increasingly offer custom-made products starting from design through to the training of the workforce, to provide a complete solution. In the market for standardised products there was intensified competition from low-cost countries, and EU enterprises often shifted their production to countries with lower labour costs.

(1) The analysis in the overview is based on data including domestic appliances (NACE Rev. 1 29.7) for reasons of data availability.

Industrial processing machinery dominates
the machinery and equipment sector

The EU machinery and equipment industry[2] was dominated by industrial processing machinery which was responsible for around 80% of the total in 1999. Breaking this figure down further, 35.0% of output was accounted for by special purpose machinery (NACE Rev. 1 29.4 and 29.5) and around 45% by general purpose machinery (NACE Rev. 1 29.1 and 29.2). Agricultural machines and tractors (NACE Rev. 1 29.3) had a 5.6% share of the EU's machinery and equipment total, whilst the manufacture of weapons and ammunitions formed the smallest activity with 2.3% (in 1994). Between 1988 and 1999 there was little change in the structure of the machinery and equipment industry, with the largest movement in the relative importance of agricultural machinery, which declined by almost 2 percentage points from 7.3% in 1988.

---

(2) Again based on figures including domestic appliances (NACE Rev. 29.7) which accounted for 10% of total production value in the machinery and equipment industry in 1999.

An industry characterised by
medium-sized enterprises

Small (10 to 49 persons employed) and medium-sized enterprises (50 to 249 persons employed) characterised this industry in the EU. They accounted for 20.7% and 5.4% respectively of the total enterprise population in 1996 (compared to shares of 14.9% and 3.1% for total manufacturing). However, there was a lower proportion of very small enterprises (less than 10 persons employed) than the average for the whole of manufacturing (72.4% and 81.2% respectively), whilst there was a high proportion of large enterprises (250 and more persons employed), 1.5% and 0.8%.

Within the Member States, Germany reported the most concentrated industrial structure, with very small enterprises accounting for 53.6% of the total enterprise population and large enterprises accounting for 3.9% of the total in 1997. Finland was at the other end of the ranking, with respective shares of 85.3% and 1.1%.

Box 10.1

The large enterprises in the EU's machinery and equipment industry were generally not exclusively engaged in the production of machinery and equipment. Examples of enterprises operating across several activities include Metallgesellschaft (D) and Linde (D) with product divisions in chemicals; Invensys (UK) in electrical engineering; SKF (S) in steel products; or Weir Group (UK) in maintenance and repair services. CNH (NL) is one of the largest producers of agricultural and construction equipment in the EU, and has diversified into financial services for dealers and end-users. Rheinmetall (D) is involved in the industrial processing machinery industry, as well as the defence industry. On the other hand there were also large enterprises that were specialised within one product category, such Heidelberger Druckmaschinen (D), the world's largest producer of machinery for the printing and publishing industry.

Table 10.1

Machinery and equipment (NACE Rev. 1 29)

Breakdown of turnover and employment by employment size class, 1997 (%)

	Micro (0-9)		Small (10-49)		Medium (50-249)		Large (250+)	
	Turnover (1)	Employment (2)	Turnover (3)	Employment (4)	Turnover (5)	Employment (6)	Turnover (5)	Employment (6)
EU-15	5.7	9.3	15.5	19.8	22.5	23.2	56.3	47.7
B	8.0	11.2	14.9	19.6	22.5	21.9	54.7	47.3
DK	7.3	6.4	16.2	19.0	:	:	:	:
D	1.5	3.7	8.4	13.6	14.9	17.6	75.3	65.0
EL	:	:	:	:	:	:	:	:
E	12.5	19.8	26.8	32.2	29.8	24.0	31.0	24.1
F	7.8	10.7	15.5	20.0	25.1	24.4	51.5	45.0
IRL	:	:	20.0	26.6	52.8	35.8	22.4	31.6
I	8.4	14.5	25.4	28.9	28.7	26.4	37.5	30.2
L	:	:	:	:	:	:	:	:
NL	:	:	:	:	:	:	:	:
A	4.4	5.4	11.9	14.6	33.4	33.2	50.3	46.7
P	20.2	17.3	29.5	36.6	28.5	31.3	21.7	14.9
FIN	6.0	9.2	9.6	13.7	23.9	27.3	60.5	49.8
S	4.3	8.4	10.3	14.0	19.0	20.4	66.4	57.2
UK	8.8	10.7	17.2	17.9	23.5	26.6	50.5	44.9

(1) EU-15, DK, E, F, I, P and S, 1996.
(2) EU-15, DK, F, I, P and S, 1996.
(3) EU-15, DK, E, F, IRL, I, P and S, 1996.
(4) EU-15, DK, F, IRL, I, P and S, 1996.
(5) E, F, IRL, I, P and S, 1996.
(6) EU-15, F, IRL, I, P and S, 1996.

Source: Eurostat (SME)

STRUCTURE AND PERFORMANCE

Between 1990 and 1998 EU production of machinery and equipment grew by 27.2 billion ECU to 340.3 billion ECU in real terms. This was equivalent to an annual average growth rate of 1.0%, well below the 2.2% growth per annum experienced within manufacturing as a whole. During the same period value added grew by 0.8% per annum to reach 127.6 billion ECU in 1998, this was also at a slower pace than the EU total manufacturing average of 1.2% per annum.

Output reflects investment cycles in world regions
A closer look at the evolution of production in constant prices showed that output in the machinery and equipment industry followed closely the evolution of the business cycle, although output fluctuations had a far greater amplitude. Between 1990 and 1993 production in constant prices fell on average by 4.3% per annum, 2.1 percentage points more than the total manufacturing average. This was followed by a fast increase in the three years to 1996, when real output growth was equal to 5.9% per annum, against 4.8% for total manufacturing. Between 1996 and 1998 real production growth of machinery and equipment in the EU slowed to 2.2% per annum, whilst manufacturing output grew at an average annual rate of 5.1%.

Production reduced in Germany in the 1990s
Germany reported a decrease in production in constant prices equal to 0.6% per annum between 1990 and 1997, whilst in Denmark output increased by 4.3% per annum over the same period. During the same period, the production specialisation ratio fell in Germany from 143.0% to 136.5%, whilst in Denmark it increased by 21.1 percentage points to 149.7%. Increases of a similar magnitude were recorded in Finland, Italy and Sweden.

—Figure 10.2

Machinery and equipment (NACE Rev. 1 29)

EU production and value-added in constant prices and employment compared to total manufacturing (1990=100)

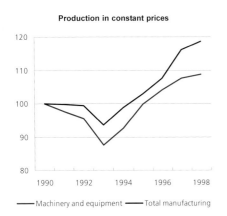

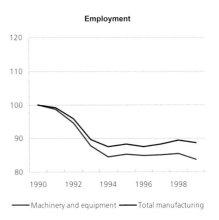

Source: Eurostat (SBS)

LABOUR AND PRODUCTIVITY

In 1999 the EU machinery and equipment industry employed 2.6 million persons, which was 414.7 thousand less than in 1989. This net reduction in the number of persons employed was equivalent to an average annual decrease of 1.5% (compared to a decrease of 1.1% per annum for total manufacturing).

An increased incidence of weekend work

During the six years to 1999, the proportion of the workforce working on a Saturday increased in the Netherlands by 11.9 percentage points to 35.3% and in Italy by 3.7 percentage points to 39.9%. The highest share was recorded in the United Kingdom (63.0% in 1999), whilst in Portugal only 9.0% of the workforce were working on Saturdays.

Part-time contracts were less common in the machinery and equipment industry than in total manufacturing (4.5% compared to 7.3% in 1998). However, several Member States recorded increases in the proportion of staff working on a part-time basis between 1993 and 1999: for example, the Netherlands (up by 2.0 percentage points to 8.1%) and France (up by 1.8 percentage points to 4.3%).

In 1997 the EU machinery and equipment industry employed relatively more persons with an upper secondary or higher education (50.3% and 20.9%) than manufacturing averages (43.9% and 16.3%).

Moderate gains in labour productivity

The EU's machinery and equipment industry reported rising apparent labour productivity between 1989 and 1999 (up from 33.3 thousand ECU to 51.9 thousand EUR of value added per person employed). When looking at the relation between value added and personnel costs, the machinery and equipment industry reported simple wage adjusted labour productivity below total manufacturing averages (134.1% and 150.9% respectively in 1999), with a modest increase of just 3.3 percentage points since 1989.

Table 10.2

Machinery and equipment (NACE Rev. 1 29)
Composition of the labour force, 1999 (%)

	Women (1)	Part-time (2)	Highly-educated (3)
EU-15	17.0	4.5	20.9
B	16.5	:	21.9
DK	25.6	3.6	27.1
D	17.5	5.3	27.2
EL	9.6	:	16.9
E	11.3	1.5	25.2
F	18.7	4.3	16.0
IRL	16.6	:	24.1
I	18.5	3.4	6.0
L	:	:	:
NL	11.0	8.1	17.7
A	17.7	7.9	6.1
P	23.6	:	:
FIN	12.5	:	32.8
S	14.1	:	22.4
UK	16.9	5.9	19.4

(1) EU-15 and EL, 1998.
(2) EU-15 and E, 1998.
(3) EL, 1998; EU-15, IRL and UK, 1997.

Source: Eurostat (LFS)

Figure 10.3

Machinery and equipment (NACE Rev. 1 29)
Apparent labour productivity and unit personnel costs, 1997 (thousand ECU)

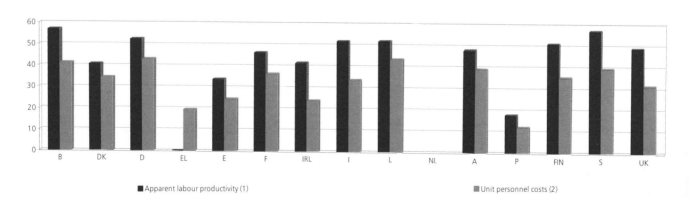

■ Apparent labour productivity (1)   ■ Unit personnel costs (2)

(1) EL and I, 1996; NL, not available.
(2) DK, EL and I, 1996; NL, not available.

Source: Eurostat (SBS)

―――――――――――――――――――――――――――――Figure 10.4

Machinery and equipment (NACE Rev. 1 29)

International comparison of production, value added and employment

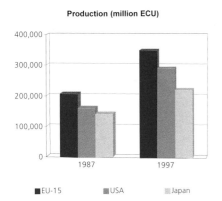

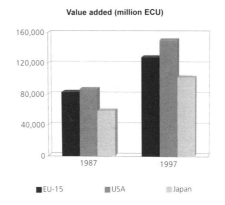

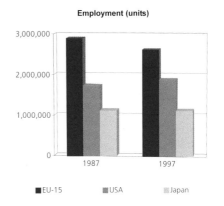

Source: Eurostat (SBS)

INTERNATIONAL TRENDS AND FOREIGN TRADE

The machinery and equipment industry in the Triad had a combined output of 862.6 billion ECU in 1997 (in current prices), of which 40.6% was manufactured in the EU, 33.7% in the USA and 25.7% in Japan. Since 1990, Triad production increased by 3.7% per annum in real terms, with the fastest growth rates in the USA and Japan (up by 7.0% and 4.2% per annum, between 1990 and 1997), whilst expansion in the EU was more subdued (up by 1.0% per annum). The evolution of employment over the same period saw the USA report a 0.9% per annum increase in the number of persons employed, whilst the EU (-2.3% per annum) and Japan (-1.4% per annum) both saw their respective workforces decline.

*Cross-border investment strongest
between the EU and the USA*

In 1997, foreign direct investment (F.D.I.) stocks from non-Community countries within the machinery and equipment industry were valued at 6.1 billion ECU in six EU Member States[3], of which 75.0% originated from the USA. On the other side, the same six Member States had investment positions that accounted for 6.0 billion ECU of stocks in 1997 within the machinery and equipment industries. These stocks of FDI were largely concentrated in the USA and Canada (66.3%), although in 1997 both Germany and the United Kingdom withdrew investments (293 million ECU and 69 million ECU respectively) from the USA.

―――――――――――――――――

(3) D, NL, A, P, FIN and UK.

Important export sector

The machinery and equipment industry was one of the EU's leading export industries. In 1999 machinery and equipment accounted for 15.2% of the EU's manufacturing exports to non-Community countries, with a trade surplus of 54.0 billion EUR. The majority (55.6%) of the Triad's exports of machinery and equipment came from the EU in 1998, with the USA accounting for a quarter (25.5%) of the total.

When looking at the origin of imports the USA, Japan and Switzerland were the largest trading partners in 1999, as they had been in 1989. However, China and the Czech Republic gained in relative importance, with Chinese imports increasing more than 12-fold between 1989 and 1999 to reach 3.1 billion EUR. During the same period EU exports of machinery and equipment to China were doubled (4.5 billion EUR in 1999).

―――――――――――――――――――――Figure 10.5

Machinery and equipment (NACE Rev. 1 29)

Destination of EU exports, 1999 (%)

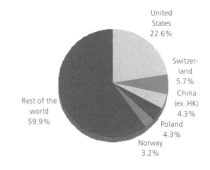

Source: Eurostat (COMEXT)

―――――――――――――――――――――Figure 10.6

Machinery and equipment (NACE Rev. 1 29)

Origin of EU imports, 1999 (%)

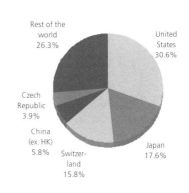

Source: Eurostat (COMEXT)

SUB-CHAPTER 10.1
INDUSTRIAL PROCESSING MACHINERY
(NACE Rev. 1 29.1, 29.2, 29.4 AND 29.5)

Industrial processing machinery can be divided into general purpose machinery (NACE Rev. 1 Groups 29.1 and 29.2) and special purpose machinery (NACE Rev. 1 Groups 29.4 and 29.5). The former is composed of two Groups, machinery for the production and use of mechanical power, except aircraft, vehicles and cycle engines (NACE Rev. 1 29.1) and other general purpose machinery (NACE Rev. 1 29.2) that include furnaces, lifting and handling equipment, cooling and ventilation equipment. Within special purpose machinery the manufacture of machine-tools (NACE Rev. 1 29.4) forms one Group, whilst other special purpose machinery (NACE Rev. 1 29.5) covers, amongst others, the manufacture of machinery for metallurgy, construction or food processing. This sub-chapter does not cover agricultural and forestry machinery (sub-chapter 10.2).

The industrial processing machinery industry in the EU reported a production value of 258.7 billion ECU, whilst employing 2.2 million persons in 1995. It was the largest activity within the machinery and equipment industry (accounting for between 80% and 85% of both production value and employment). Output was split 55% to 45% between general and special purpose machinery.

Germany had by far the largest industrial processing machinery industry, accounting for 42.7% of total EU output in 1995. Looking at the production specialisation ratio the industrial processing machinery industry was relatively important in Denmark, Germany and Sweden (with ratios of 145.0%, 143.4% and 136.5% respectively in 1995).

Figure 10.7

Industrial processing machinery (NACE Rev. 1 29.1, 29.2, 29.4 and 29.5)

Production and export specialisation (%)

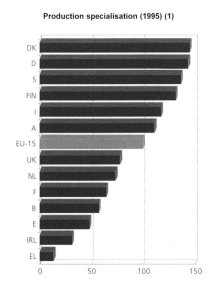

Production specialisation (1995) (1)

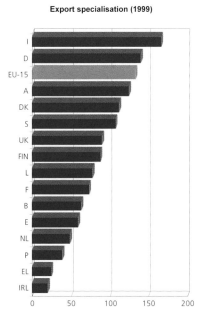

Export specialisation (1999)

(1) L and P, not available.

Source: Eurostat (SBS, COMEXT)

Box 10.2

According to FEM (the European Federation of Handling Equipment), the lifting and handling equipment industry (NACE Rev. 1 29.22) in the EU[4] reported production valued at 21.9 billion ECU in 1997, which represented an increase of 5.3 billion ECU or 3.5% per annum since 1989 (at current prices). Finland and Germany recorded the fastest expansion in output, up by 10.1% and 6.9% per annum between 1989 and 1998, whilst in Italy production decreased by 2.0% per annum.

During the 1990s, the number of companies operating within this industry grew, with growth most pronounced in the United Kingdom (up by 61.3% between 1989 and 1998 to reach 221 companies). In 1998 the largest companies making lifting and handling equipment were found in Finland and Germany, where the average number of employees per company was equal to 233 and 214 respectively. The smallest average size was observed in Spain (34 employees per company).

(4) EU-15, excluding EL and A.

STRUCTURE AND PERFORMANCE

Production value of the EU's industrial processing machinery industry remained almost unchanged in the five years between 1990 and 1995, with output increasing by 1.4 billion ECU or 0.1% per annum in real terms. A breakdown of the activity showed growth for general purpose machinery (up by 1.4% per annum), whilst special purpose machinery saw its output decline by 1.4% per annum (again between 1990 and 1995).

Fastest growth in production in the
Netherlands, Denmark and Spain

Between 1987 and 1997 production in constant prices expanded in the Netherlands (up on average by 5.5% per annum), which was almost matched by an average annual growth of 4.5% in Denmark and Spain. Germany and the United Kingdom recorded slower increases in production (up by 2.0% and 1.5% per annum in real terms).

Low profitability in Germany and France

The gross operating rate for the EU's industrial processing machinery industry was estimated to be equal to 9.0% in 1997, just below the total manufacturing average of 9.2%. Amongst the Member States there were wide fluctuations from 18.4% in Ireland to 5.5% in France. Germany also recorded a gross operating rate well below the EU average (6.7%), whilst in the United Kingdom this rate was equal to 12.4%.

LABOUR AND PRODUCTIVITY

In 1995 there were 1.2 million persons employed in the general purpose machinery industries of the EU, whilst there were 927.4 thousand persons working in the EU's special purpose machinery industry.

The estimated share of personnel costs in total operating costs in the EU's industrial processing machinery industry was equal to 29.8% in 1997, well above the manufacturing average (21.3%). Apparent labour productivity (estimated at 49.5 thousand ECU per person employed in 1997) was broadly in line with the manufacturing average (49.3 thousand ECU).

_____ Figure 10.8

Industrial processing machinery (NACE Rev. 1 29.1, 29.2, 29.4 and 29.5)

International comparison of production in constant prices and employment (1990=100)

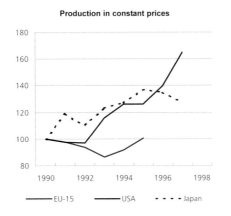

Production in constant prices

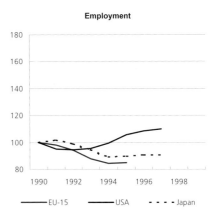

Employment

Source: Eurostat (SBS)

_____ Figure 10.9

Labour intensity in the manufacture of lifting and handling equipment (units) (1)

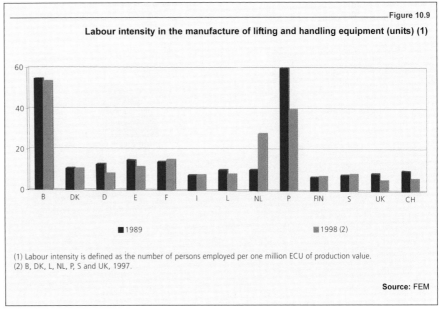

■ 1989   ■ 1998 (2)

(1) Labour intensity is defined as the number of persons employed per one million ECU of production value.
(2) B, DK, L, NL, P, S and UK, 1997.

Source: FEM

_____ Figure 10.10

Production of metalworking machine-tools (1988=100)

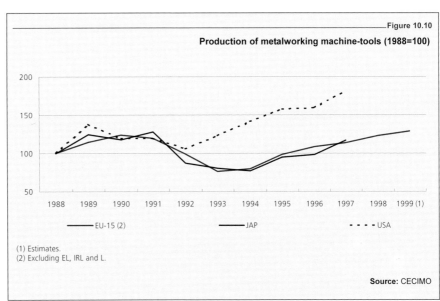

——— EU-15 (2)   ——— JAP   - - - - USA

(1) Estimates.
(2) Excluding EL, IRL and L.

Source: CECIMO

INTERNATIONAL TRENDS AND FOREIGN TRADE

Triad production of industrial processing machinery reached 633.9 billion ECU in 1995, with the EU contributing 40.8% of the total, ahead of either Japan or the USA (29.9% and 29.3% respectively). Since 1995 production in the USA increased by 29.8% to reach 241.1 billion ECU in 1997, supported by strong demand from the automotive sector, whilst in Japan there was a decrease of 12.3% to 166.2 billion ECU (over the same period).

The industrial processing machinery industry was one of the main export sectors of the EU manufacturing economy. Its trade surplus was equal to 50.3 billion EUR in 1999, up by 19.1 billion ECU when compared to 1989, although a high of 64.1 billion ECU was recorded in 1997. Between 1989 and 1999, the USA remained the main trading partner of the EU, whilst there was intensified trade with Eastern European and south-east Asian countries, as well as increased exports to Brazil and Mexico.

Figure 10.11 ────────────────────

Industrial processing machinery
(NACE Rev. 1 29.1, 29.2, 29.4 and 29.5)
Destination of EU exports, 1999 (%)

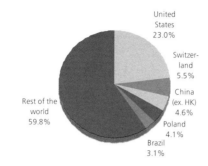

Source: Eurostat (COMEXT)

Figure 10.12 ────────────────────

Industrial processing machinery
(NACE Rev. 1 29.1, 29.2, 29.4 and 29.5)
Origin of EU imports, 1999 (%)

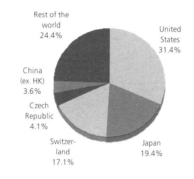

Source: Eurostat (COMEXT)

SUB-CHAPTER 10.2
AGRICULTURAL MACHINES AND
TRACTORS (NACE Rev. 1 29.3)

The NACE Rev. 1 activity classification distinguishes between two types of agricultural and forestry machinery: agricultural tractors (NACE Rev. 1 Class 29.31) and other agricultural and forestry machinery (NACE Rev. 1 Class 29.32), which includes, for example, mowers and milking machines. The information presented in this sub-chapter does not cover road trailers and semi-trailers, works trucks or agricultural hand-tools.

In 1999 the production value of the agricultural machinery and tractors industry in the EU was equal to 20.2 billion EUR. This was equivalent to 5.6% of the total output generated within the whole of the machinery and equipment industry in the EU. There were 117.6 thousand persons employed in 1999, which was equal to 4.6% of the total workforce within the EU's machinery and equipment industry.

The agricultural machinery and tractors industry was relatively important in Denmark, Finland and Austria. The production specialisation ratios of these three countries were between 180% and 200% in 1997, with the next most specialised country Italy (137.9% in 1996).

The agricultural machinery and tractors industry has faced slowly, but steadily decreasing demand. There has been a falling number of farms in the EU[5], down from 5.8 million holdings in 1975 to 4.2 million holdings in 1997, with the agricultural workforce in the EU[6] reduced from 11.5 million persons employed on a full-time equivalents basis in 1980 to 6.8 million by 1998.

---

(5) EU-9, excluding EL, E, A, P, FIN and S.
(6) 1980, excluding former East Germany; 1998, unified Germany.

Figure 10.13

Agricultural machines and tractors (NACE Rev. 1 29.3)
Production and export specialisation (%)

Production specialisation (1997) (1)

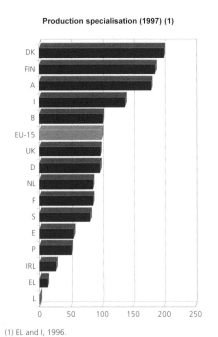

Export specialisation (1999)

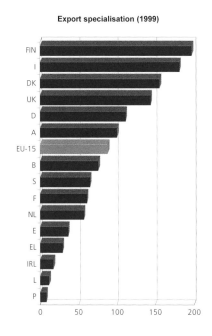

(1) EL and I, 1996.

Source: Eurostat (SBS, COMEXT)

Box 10.3

Two manufacturers dominate the world market for agricultural machinery and tractors: John Deere (USA) and CNH (NL; part of the FIAT group). CNH was formed in 1999 when New Holland (NL) bought Case (USA). The third largest player is AGCO (USA) which bought the largest German manufacturer Fendt in 1996. Within the EU, Deutz Landwirtschaft (D) bought SAME (I), CNH acquired Steyr Landmaschinentechnik (A) and Renault Agriculture (F) has signed co-operation agreements with Massey Ferguson (a subsidiary of AGCO), John Deere, JCB Agri (UK) and Agritalia (I). Claas (D) is a global player in the harvesting and baling equipment sector (accounting for one in three combine harvesters sold in Europe).

STRUCTURE AND PERFORMANCE

The evolution of EU production in the agricultural machinery and tractors industry followed a downward trend in the 1990s. Production value in constant prices was equal to 18.0 billion ECU in 1998, 1.9 billion ECU less than in 1990. This was equivalent to a decline of 1.3% in terms of the annual average rate of change (compared to an annual average increase of 1.0% for the whole of machinery and equipment).

The downward trend in production was not observed throughout the EU, as Sweden, Finland and France all achieved real production growth between 1990 and 1997 (up by 4.7%, 2.5% and 1.3% per annum respectively). However, Germany and Italy, the largest agricultural machinery and tractor manufacturers in the EU both recorded falling output, down by 2.8% per annum and 4.7% per annum respectively (1990 to 1996 for Italy).

LABOUR AND PRODUCTIVITY

The number of persons employed in the EU's agricultural machinery and tractors industry fell by 40.5 thousand persons between 1989 and 1999. This was equivalent to a reduction of 2.9% per annum, a much faster rate than for the whole of machinery and equipment (1.5% per annum). The decrease in employment stopped in the mid- to late 1990s, when there was average growth of 1.1% per annum during the three-year period 1995 to 1998.

High simple wage adjusted labour productivity
Between 1989 and 1999 apparent labour productivity (measured as value added per person employed) within the agricultural machinery and tractors industry of the EU increased by 17.7 thousand ECU per person employed to 52.0 thousand EUR. The EU's agricultural machinery industry reported a high simple wage adjusted labour productivity ratio (value added divided by personnel costs) in 1999, at 160.5%, which was 9.6 percentage points above the EU's manufacturing average and 26.5 percentage points above the average for the whole of machinery and equipment.

INTERNATIONAL TRENDS AND FOREIGN TRADE

Triad output of agricultural machinery and tractors reached 49.1 billion ECU in nominal terms in 1997, a net increase of 18.3 billion ECU compared to 1987. The USA accounted for 45.8% of Triad output in 1997, followed by the EU (39.0%).

Triad exports exceed imports
During the course of the 1990s, the USA cover ratio for agricultural machinery and tractors improved from 99.9% (1989) to 144.4% (1998), resulting in a trade surplus of 1.2 billion ECU. The other two Triad members had even higher cover ratios, 345.8% for Japan and 245.6% for the EU.

EU's main trading partners increasingly in Eastern Europe
The majority of the EU's imports of agricultural machinery and tractors originated from the other two Triad economies and Norway. In the ten-year period to 1999 there was a large increase in EU imports originating from Hungary, Poland and the Czech Republic (imports from all of these countries quadrupled over the period considered). Important export markets for EU agricultural machinery and tractors included North America, Australia, as well as Switzerland and Norway.

Figure 10.14

Agricultural machines and tractors (NACE Rev. 1 29.3)

International comparison of production in constant prices and employment (1990=100)

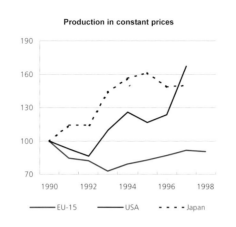

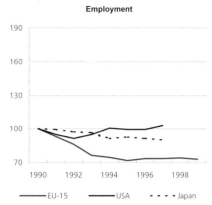

Source: Eurostat (SBS)

Figure 10.15

Agricultural machines and tractors (NACE Rev. 1 29.3)

Destination of EU exports, 1999 (%)

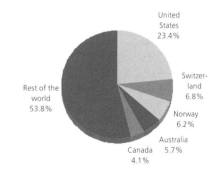

Source: Eurostat (COMEXT)

Figure 10.16

Agricultural machines and tractors (NACE Rev. 1 29.3)

Origin of EU imports, 1999 (%)

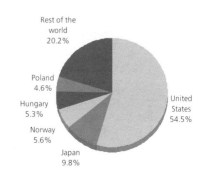

Source: Eurostat (COMEXT)

SUB-CHAPTER 10.3
WEAPONS AND AMMUNITIONS
(NACE Rev. 1 29.6)

Weapons and ammunitions are covered by Group 29.6 of the NACE Rev. 1 classification. The manufacturing activities covered in this sub-chapter include hunting and sporting fire-arms, as well as products for military use, such as tanks, artillery material, small arms, bombs and mines. The information presented does not include armoured vehicles, aeroplanes for defence use or articles made of metal, such as swords.

The production value of the EU's weapons and ammunitions industry was equal to 6.4 billion ECU in 1994, which was equivalent to 2.3% of the machinery and equipment total. Sweden and the United Kingdom were both relatively specialised, with output equal to 645.6 million ECU and 2.7 billion ECU respectively in 1997.

Regulated market with high
dependency on public orders

The market structure of the weapons and ammunitions industry differs from the rest of machinery and equipment industry. The industry is characterised by monopolistic or oligopolistic structure, with governments often the main customer and demand determined by the evolution of defence budgets. Since the early 1990s, European manufacturers of weapons and ammunitions have faced falling defence expenditures, which has resulted in manufacturers diversifying into civilian product lines.

Box 10.4

Within the EU there are two large companies producing weapons and ammunitions, these groups also specialise in the manufacture of aircraft and spacecraft. BAE Systems (UK) was created from a merger of British Aerospace and Marconi Electronic Systems, whilst EADS (European Aeronautic Defence and Space Company) was created from a merger of DaimlerChrysler Aerospace (D), Aerospatiale Matra (F) and Construcciones Aeronauticas (E).

Figure 10.17

Weapons and ammunitions (NACE Rev. 1 29.6)
Production and export specialisation (%)

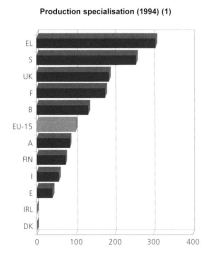

Production specialisation (1994) (1)

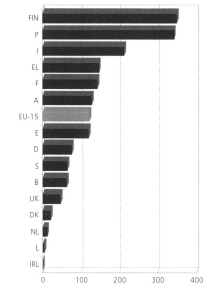

Export specialisation (1999)

(1) D, L, NL and P, not available.

Source: Eurostat (SBS, COMEXT)

STRUCTURE AND PERFORMANCE

Between 1993 and 1997 production in constant prices in the United Kingdom increased by 8.0% per annum to reach 2.6 billion ECU. In Sweden output grew in real terms by 2.7% per annum between 1990 and 1997, whilst French output fell on average by 7.3% per annum over the same period.

LABOUR AND PRODUCTIVITY

In 1994 there were 70.2 thousand persons employed in the EU's weapons and ammunitions industry. Apparent labour productivity was estimated at 54.2 thousand ECU of value added per person employed in 1997, which was nearly double the level of 1994 (28.7 thousand ECU).

INTERNATIONAL TRENDS AND FOREIGN TRADE

In 1994 the output of the USA's weapons and ammunitions industry was similar to that of the EU, with each country accounting for almost two-fifths of total Triad output (38.7% and 39.9% respectively). Japanese output declined between 1997 and 1997 from 3.4 billion ECU to 2.9 billion ECU, whilst in the USA the weapons and ammunitions industry recorded a net gain of 7.3% in production, which rose to 6.6 billion ECU.

In 1998 the USA reported a trade surplus of 2.1 billion ECU in the weapons and ammunitions industry, which was more than eight times higher than the EU surplus of 248.3 million ECU, whilst Japan recorded a deficit of 86.7 million ECU.

Shift in export partners towards south-east Asia
The USA was the main trading partner of the EU, with exports of weapons and ammunition to the USA worth twice the value of imports from the USA (105 million EUR and 237 million EUR in 1999). There was a clear shift in the destination of the EU's exports away from North Africa and the Middle East towards south-east Asia and to a lesser extent other European countries (notably Turkey).

Figure 10.18

Weapons and ammunitions (NACE Rev. 1 29.6)
Destination of EU exports, 1999 (%)

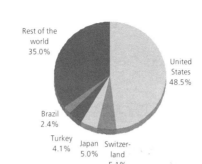

Source: Eurostat (COMEXT)

Figure 10.19

Weapons and ammunitions (NACE Rev. 1 29.6)
Origin of EU imports, 1999 (%)

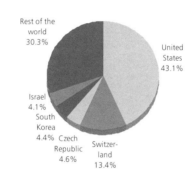

Source: Eurostat (COMEXT)

_____Table 10.3

Manufacture of machinery for the production and use of mechanical power, except aircraft, vehicle and cycle engines (NACE Rev. 1 29.1)

Production related indicators in the EU (1)

	1989	1990	1991	1992	1993	1994	1995	1996	1997	1998	1999
Number of persons employed (thousands)	655.3	668.3	661.2	636.8	591.1	559.8	552.7	:	:	:	:
Production (million ECU)	52,960	56,593	58,005	58,557	56,688	60,239	65,616	:	:	:	:
Domestic producer price index (1995=100)	:	:	:	:	:	:	100.0	102.4	104.0	104.9	105.7
Value added (million ECU)	22,664	23,656	23,969	24,497	23,199	24,476	26,025	:	:	:	:

(1) Technically, data before 01/01/1999 are in ECU and after this date in euro. However, as the conversion rate was 1 ECU =1 EUR, for practical purposes the two terms can be used interchangeably.

_____Table 10.4

Manufacture of machinery for the production and use of mechanical power, except aircraft, vehicle and cycle engines (NACE Rev. 1 29.1)

Trade related indicators in the EU (1)

	1989	1990	1991	1992	1993	1994	1995	1996	1997	1998	1999
Exports (million EUR)	11,535	12,130	13,001	13,154	15,653	16,774	18,270	20,355	22,825	24,023	24,058
Imports (million EUR)	6,015	6,515	6,700	7,113	7,323	8,464	9,407	10,210	11,676	13,499	14,283
Trade balance (million EUR)	5,520	5,615	6,301	6,041	8,330	8,310	8,864	10,145	11,148	10,524	9,775
Cover ratio (%)	191.8	186.2	194.0	184.9	213.7	198.2	194.2	199.4	195.5	178.0	168.4

(1) Technically, data before 01/01/1999 are in ECU and after this date in euro. However, as the conversion rate was 1 ECU =1 EUR, for practical purposes the two terms can be used interchangeably.

_____Table 10.5

Manufacture of machinery for the production and use of mechanical power, except aircraft, vehicle and cycle engines (NACE Rev. 1 29.1)

Production related indicators, 1997

	B	DK	D	EL (1)	E	F	IRL	I (1)	L	NL	A	P	FIN	S	UK
Number of persons employed (thousands)	7.5	25.1	219.6	1.2	18.8	64.5	2.5	83.1	:	:	7.7	4.0	9.0	15.9	84.5
Production (million ECU)	1,764	2,401	26,671	50	1,979	8,724	270	13,049	:	1,938	824	183	1,582	2,232	9,588
Value added (million ECU)	573	1,153	11,445	22	659	3,642	130	4,373	:	597	385	63	471	925	4,427
Gross operating surplus (million ECU)	244.8	349.2	2,006.8	2.0	191.5	1,267.1	59.1	1,636.6	:	174.4	95.3	19.7	171.7	272.5	1,815.4

(1) 1996.

_____Table 10.6

Manufacture of machinery for the production and use of mechanical power, except aircraft, vehicle and cycle engines (NACE Rev. 1 29.1)

Trade related indicators, 1999

	B	DK	D	EL	E	F	IRL	I	L	NL	A	P	FIN	S	UK
Exports (million EUR)	2,592	1,147	17,789	29	1,422	7,076	265	9,013	118	1,766	1,486	232	652	1,997	6,970
Imports (million EUR)	2,596	1,027	9,075	378	2,526	6,335	447	4,840	113	2,101	1,745	447	654	1,850	6,267
Trade balance (million EUR)	-5	120	8,713	-349	-1,104	741	-182	4,173	5	-336	-259	-215	-2	148	703
Cover ratio (%)	99.8	111.7	196.0	7.7	56.3	111.7	59.2	186.2	104.7	84.0	85.2	52.0	99.7	108.0	111.2

_____Table 10.7

Manufacture of machinery for the production and use of mechanical power, except aircraft, vehicle and cycle engines (NACE Rev. 1 29.1)

Labour related indicators, 1997

	B	DK (1)	D	EL (2)	E	F	IRL	I (2)	L	NL	A	P	FIN	S	UK
Unit personnel costs (thousand ECU per employee)	44.1	33.5	43.0	17.2	25.2	36.9	28.2	33.4	:	:	37.9	11.2	36.1	41.0	31.1
Social charges as a share of personnel costs (%)	40.4	3.7	23.8	29.9	28.4	43.2	16.2	49.9	:	17.6	30.1	29.9	26.5	45.2	13.8
Apparent labour productivity (thousand ECU/pers. empl.)	76.3	46.0	52.1	18.9	35.1	56.5	51.3	52.6	:	:	50.3	15.7	52.2	58.1	52.4
Wage adjusted labour productivity (%)	173.1	137.0	121.1	110.0	138.8	153.4	182.2	157.5	:	:	132.7	141.2	144.7	141.8	168.3
Personnel costs as a share of total operating costs (%)	21.1	36.1	35.1	42.1	22.9	27.6	32.1	23.5	:	21.7	34.0	26.0	21.4	27.0	30.6

(1) Unit personnel costs and wage adjusted labour productivity, 1996; (2) 1996.

Source: Eurostat (SBS, EBT, COMEXT)

Table 10.8

Manufacture of other general purpose machinery (NACE Rev. 1 29.2)

Production related indicators in the EU (1)

	1989	1990	1991	1992	1993	1994	1995	1996	1997	1998	1999
Number of persons employed (thousands)	725.8	751.8	745.1	730.1	693.6	681.6	682.0	726.1	724.1	735.3	725.3
Production (million EUR)	61,507	67,080	69,577	69,696	66,005	71,709	80,061	90,424	91,634	94,963	95,691
Domestic producer price index (1995=100)	:	:	:	:	:	:	100.0	102.0	103.2	104.2	105.5
Value added (million EUR)	23,728	25,657	26,788	27,045	25,822	27,945	29,966	34,336	34,032	35,565	35,710

(1) Technically, data before 01/01/1999 are in ECU and after this date in euro. However, as the conversion rate was 1 ECU =1 EUR, for practical purposes the two terms can be used interchangeably.

Table 10.9

Manufacture of other general purpose machinery (NACE Rev. 1 29.2)

Trade related indicators in the EU (1)

	1989	1990	1991	1992	1993	1994	1995	1996	1997	1998	1999
Exports (million EUR)	12,227	13,380	13,631	14,231	15,751	18,151	20,496	23,346	25,898	26,309	24,810
Imports (million EUR)	4,670	4,977	5,587	5,745	5,520	6,001	6,945	7,955	8,742	10,062	11,402
Trade balance (million EUR)	7,556	8,403	8,045	8,486	10,231	12,150	13,550	15,391	17,156	16,246	13,408
Cover ratio (%)	261.8	268.8	244.0	247.7	285.3	302.5	295.1	293.5	296.3	261.5	217.6

(1) Technically, data before 01/01/1999 are in ECU and after this date in euro. However, as the conversion rate was 1 ECU =1 EUR, for practical purposes the two terms can be used interchangeably.

Table 10.10

Manufacture of other general purpose machinery (NACE Rev. 1 29.2)

Production related indicators, 1997

	B	DK	D	EL (1)	E	F	IRL	I (1)	L	NL	A	P	FIN	S	UK
Number of persons employed (thousands)	12.6	19.9	246.7	2.3	49.3	80.2	4.9	109.8	0.4	:	17.5	13.7	15.6	28.8	100.5
Production (million ECU)	1,901	2,054	32,056	124	4,434	10,751	641	16,205	47	3,224	2,074	704	2,125	4,712	11,109
Value added (million ECU)	606	788	12,938	49	1,740	3,210	227	6,014	21	1,139	825	227	739	1,658	4,488
Gross operating surplus (million ECU)	135.3	160.3	2,301.6	9.1	534.1	293.5	109.1	2,262.7	2.4	280.3	141.5	73.2	227.9	507.2	1,420.6

(1) 1996.

Table 10.11

Manufacture of other general purpose machinery (NACE Rev. 1 29.2)

Trade related indicators, 1999

	B	DK	D	EL	E	F	IRL	I	L	NL	A	P	FIN	S	UK
Exports (million EUR)	2,735	1,793	16,988	64	1,818	6,473	639	9,668	195	2,489	2,143	178	1,076	2,838	5,514
Imports (million EUR)	2,978	961	6,601	703	3,024	5,630	773	3,670	208	2,406	1,651	745	734	1,428	5,362
Trade balance (million EUR)	-243	832	10,388	-639	-1,207	843	-134	5,999	-13	83	492	-568	342	1,410	151
Cover ratio (%)	91.8	186.6	257.4	9.1	60.1	115.0	82.7	263.5	93.5	103.5	129.8	23.9	146.6	198.7	102.8

Table 10.12

Manufacture of other general purpose machinery (NACE Rev. 1 29.2)

Labour related indicators, 1997

	B	DK (1)	D	EL (2)	E	F	IRL	I (2)	L	NL	A	P	FIN	S	UK
Unit personnel costs (thousand ECU per employee)	38.7	36.0	43.2	17.5	24.7	36.4	24.1	35.0	41.9	:	39.2	11.9	34.0	39.9	30.9
Social charges as a share of personnel costs (%)	36.4	4.5	23.0	30.9	27.7	43.3	16.7	51.7	:	16.2	29.8	33.4	28.5	43.2	14.0
Apparent labour productivity (thousand ECU/pers. empl.)	48.3	39.5	52.5	21.3	35.3	40.0	46.1	54.8	47.4	:	47.2	16.6	47.4	57.5	44.7
Wage adjusted labour productivity (%)	124.6	114.0	121.3	121.9	142.8	110.1	191.1	156.4	112.9	:	120.4	140.1	139.6	144.1	144.4
Personnel costs as a share of total operating costs (%)	26.5	31.5	34.4	31.4	27.9	27.5	21.8	25.8	40.6	27.7	34.0	23.9	26.2	26.0	28.8

(1) Unit personnel costs and wage adjusted labour productivity, 1996; (2) 1996.

Source: Eurostat (SBS, EBT, COMEXT)

Table 10.13

Manufacture of agricultural and forestry machinery (NACE Rev. 1 29.3)

Production related indicators in the EU (1)

	1989	1990	1991	1992	1993	1994	1995	1996	1997	1998	1999
Number of persons employed (thousands)	158.1	161.0	150.1	139.2	123.0	119.7	115.1	118.1	118.1	119.1	117.6
Production (million EUR)	16,857	17,387	14,805	14,871	13,543	15,152	16,508	17,914	19,140	19,191	20,211
Domestic producer price index (1995=100)	:	:	:	:	:	:	100.0	103.5	105.2	106.7	108.1
Value added (million EUR)	5,421	5,648	4,732	4,947	4,530	4,858	4,828	5,500	5,853	5,982	6,119

(1) Technically, data before 01/01/1999 are in ECU and after this date in euro. However, as the conversion rate was 1 ECU =1 EUR, for practical purposes the two terms can be used interchangeably.

Table 10.14

Manufacture of agricultural and forestry machinery (NACE Rev. 1 29.3)

Trade related indicators in the EU (1)

	1989	1990	1991	1992	1993	1994	1995	1996	1997	1998	1999
Exports (million EUR)	2,623	2,762	2,778	2,520	2,742	3,062	3,147	3,634	4,136	4,161	3,502
Imports (million EUR)	1,100	968	1,053	1,093	1,106	1,179	1,376	1,504	1,648	1,694	1,846
Trade balance (million EUR)	1,523	1,794	1,725	1,427	1,636	1,883	1,772	2,130	2,488	2,466	1,656
Cover ratio (%)	238.4	285.3	263.9	230.6	247.9	259.7	228.8	241.7	251.0	245.6	189.7

(1) Technically, data before 01/01/1999 are in ECU and after this date in euro. However, as the conversion rate was 1 ECU =1 EUR, for practical purposes the two terms can be used interchangeably.

Table 10.15

Manufacture of agricultural and forestry machinery (NACE Rev. 1 29.3)

Production related indicators, 1997

	B	DK	D	EL (1)	E	F	IRL	I (1)	L	NL	A	P	FIN	S	UK
Number of persons employed (thousands)	4.1	6.3	30.9	0.2	9.3	15.8	0.8	18.2	0.0	:	4.7	3.9	3.3	3.0	11.7
Production (million ECU)	774	533	4,936	13	762	2,672	74	3,508	0	649	659	156	667	476	2,817
Value added (million ECU)	205	215	1,631	4	244	742	20	966	0	233	200	57	153	168	817
Gross operating surplus (million ECU)	64.7	47.0	400.8	1.2	87.3	242.6	5.5	372.4	0.1	73.7	34.8	19.1	113.4	52.5	432.7

(1) 1996.

Table 10.16

Manufacture of agricultural and forestry machinery (NACE Rev. 1 29.3)

Trade related indicators, 1999

	B	DK	D	EL	E	F	IRL	I	L	NL	A	P	FIN	S	UK
Exports (million EUR)	643	353	2,858	12	180	986	55	2,133	5	517	331	10	430	271	1,838
Imports (million EUR)	485	384	1,132	137	668	2,155	239	549	32	434	313	216	203	344	930
Trade balance (million EUR)	159	-31	1,726	-125	-488	-1,169	-184	1,583	-28	83	18	-207	226	-74	908
Cover ratio (%)	132.7	92.0	252.5	8.8	27.0	45.8	23.2	388.1	14.2	119.1	105.7	4.4	211.2	78.6	197.6

Table 10.17

Manufacture of agricultural and forestry machinery (NACE Rev. 1 29.3)

Labour related indicators, 1997

	B	DK (1)	D	EL (2)	E	F	IRL	I (2)	L	NL	A	P	FIN	S	UK
Unit personnel costs (thousand ECU per employee)	38.6	31.0	39.9	12.3	19.4	31.6	19.3	33.4	17.7	:	35.6	10.4	33.2	38.7	33.7
Social charges as a share of personnel costs (%)	40.3	4.5	24.6	30.0	29.8	40.9	13.1	51.0	:	16.1	30.8	30.8	28.2	44.3	14.4
Apparent labour productivity (thousand ECU/pers. empl.)	49.7	34.0	52.8	18.0	26.3	47.0	25.8	53.2	9.7	:	43.0	14.4	45.6	56.3	70.0
Wage adjusted labour productivity (%)	128.8	133.3	132.3	146.5	135.3	148.6	133.7	159.2	54.9	:	120.8	139.3	137.3	145.7	208.0
Personnel costs as a share of total operating costs (%)	● 19.4	32.8	24.7	22.2	17.1	16.9	21.3	17.4	0.0	25.1	23.5	25.5	15.6	23.2	13.3

(1) Unit personnel costs and wage adjusted labour productivity, 1996; (2) 1996.

Source: Eurostat (SBS, EBT, COMEXT)

Table 10.18

Manufacture of machine-tools (NACE Rev. 1 29.4)

Production related indicators in the EU (1)

	1989	1990	1991	1992	1993	1994	1995	1996	1997	1998	1999
Number of persons employed (thousands)	339.8	351.1	341.7	311.5	269.3	258.8	234.9	241.5	237.5	235.4	231.7
Production (million EUR)	28,638	31,718	30,451	27,409	23,041	26,223	26,198	29,161	30,540	31,969	31,921
Domestic producer price index (1995=100)	:	:	:	:	:	:	:	:	:	105.2	106.2
Value added (million EUR)	11,442	12,607	12,319	11,079	9,306	10,328	10,237	11,536	11,717	12,559	12,719

(1) Technically, data before 01/01/1999 are in ECU and after this date in euro. However, as the conversion rate was 1 ECU =1 EUR, for practical purposes the two terms can be used interchangeably.

Table 10.19

Manufacture of machine-tools (NACE Rev. 1 29.4)

Trade related indicators in the EU (1)

	1989	1990	1991	1992	1993	1994	1995	1996	1997	1998	1999
Exports (million EUR)	7,338	7,535	7,465	6,860	7,627	8,594	9,645	10,658	10,855	10,784	10,452
Imports (million EUR)	4,460	4,848	4,874	4,243	3,867	4,550	5,610	6,105	6,883	8,016	8,227
Trade balance (million EUR)	2,878	2,686	2,591	2,618	3,760	4,043	4,035	4,553	3,972	2,768	2,225
Cover ratio (%)	164.5	155.4	153.2	161.7	197.2	188.9	171.9	174.6	157.7	134.5	127.0

(1) Technically, data before 01/01/1999 are in ECU and after this date in euro. However, as the conversion rate was 1 ECU =1 EUR, for practical purposes the two terms can be used interchangeably.

Table 10.20

Manufacture of machine-tools (NACE Rev. 1 29.4)

Production related indicators, 1997

	B	DK	D	EL	E	F	IRL	I (1)	L	NL	A	P	FIN	S	UK
Number of persons employed (thousands)	2.2	2.0	116.1	:	12.1	13.8	0.9	43.7	:	:	5.3	2.5	3.6	8.9	22.9
Production (million ECU)	350	192	13,951	:	1,201	1,734	73	6,686	:	331	540	99	518	1,411	2,801
Value added (million ECU)	113	80	5,984	:	431	587	31	2,385	:	108	234	38	183	538	1,211
Gross operating surplus (million ECU)	27.5	20.4	1,030.0	:	132.2	71.3	11.5	913.3	:	29.6	34.1	11.9	74.5	229.4	507.3

(1) 1996.

Table 10.21

Manufacture of machine-tools (NACE Rev. 1 29.4)

Trade related indicators, 1999

	B	DK	D	EL	E	F	IRL	I	L	NL	A	P	FIN	S	UK
Exports (million EUR)	1,147	211	8,428	20	756	1,356	86	4,809	44	743	821	52	257	1,010	2,121
Imports (million EUR)	1,453	415	3,885	181	1,186	2,829	236	2,237	67	909	832	307	332	705	2,332
Trade balance (million EUR)	-306	-204	4,544	-161	-430	-1,473	-150	2,572	-23	-166	-11	-256	-76	305	-211
Cover ratio (%)	78.9	50.8	217.0	11.1	63.8	47.9	36.3	215.0	65.5	81.7	98.7	16.8	77.2	143.3	91.0

Table 10.22

Manufacture of machine-tools (NACE Rev. 1 29.4)

Labour related indicators, 1997

	B	DK (1)	D	EL	E	F	IRL	I (2)	L	NL	A	P	FIN	S	UK
Unit personnel costs (thousand ECU per employee)	39.6	35.2	42.8	:	25.2	37.3	22.2	34.5	:	:	38.0	10.9	31.0	34.7	32.0
Social charges as a share of personnel costs (%)	38.3	4.3	22.4	:	28.5	43.0	16.0	49.4	:	17.8	29.4	27.9	27.8	46.3	13.6
Apparent labour productivity (thousand ECU/pers. empl.)	50.2	40.3	51.6	:	35.7	42.5	34.8	54.6	:	:	44.4	15.3	51.4	60.5	52.8
Wage adjusted labour productivity (%)	127.0	141.5	120.5	:	141.5	113.8	156.8	158.3	:	:	116.8	140.5	165.8	174.3	164.8
Personnel costs as a share of total operating costs (%)	26.3	33.7	36.5	:	26.6	30.2	31.2	24.1	:	22.2	37.3	30.1	24.1	23.8	26.8

(1) Unit personnel costs and wage adjusted labour productivity, 1996; (2) 1996.

Source: Eurostat (SBS, EBT, COMEXT)

_____Table 10.23

Manufacture of other special purpose machinery (NACE Rev. 1 29.5)

Production related indicators in the EU (1)

	1989	1990	1991	1992	1993	1994	1995	1996	1997	1998	1999
Number of persons employed (thousands)	754.3	781.3	756.1	725.4	680.1	650.3	692.5	674.3	675.8	680.7	671.1
Production (million EUR)	68,375	74,229	72,198	70,938	67,241	70,875	86,799	87,923	94,011	94,778	94,080
Domestic producer price index (1995=100)	:	87.2	90.2	92.9	94.9	96.5	100.0	103.0	104.9	106.3	107.0
Value added (million EUR)	26,088	28,348	28,127	27,667	26,622	27,121	31,404	31,694	33,359	34,355	33,803

(1) Technically, data before 01/01/1999 are in ECU and after this date in euro. However, as the conversion rate was 1 ECU =1 EUR, for practical purposes the two terms can be used interchangeably.

_____Table 10.24

Manufacture of other special purpose machinery (NACE Rev. 1 29.5)

Trade related indicators in the EU (1)

	1989	1990	1991	1992	1993	1994	1995	1996	1997	1998	1999
Exports (million EUR)	22,636	24,312	23,825	24,995	29,573	32,330	34,961	38,216	42,676	41,237	38,009
Imports (million EUR)	7,438	7,728	7,803	7,501	7,210	8,106	9,125	9,311	10,848	12,175	13,084
Trade balance (million EUR)	15,198	16,584	16,022	17,494	22,362	24,225	25,835	28,904	31,828	29,062	24,925
Cover ratio (%)	304.3	314.6	305.3	333.2	410.1	398.9	383.1	410.4	393.4	338.7	290.5

(1) Technically, data before 01/01/1999 are in ECU and after this date in euro. However, as the conversion rate was 1 ECU =1 EUR, for practical purposes the two terms can be used interchangeably.

_____Table 10.25

Manufacture of other special purpose machinery (NACE Rev. 1 29.5)

Production related indicators, 1997

	B	DK	D	EL (1)	E	F	IRL	I (1)	L	NL	A	P	FIN	S	UK
Number of persons employed (thousands)	13.0	14.5	283.1	0.4	42.0	56.8	2.4	89.8	1.9	:	22.0	17.9	22.1	22.1	67.7
Production (million ECU)	2,697	1,399	38,127	22	3,365	8,901	222	14,225	263	3,208	2,969	821	3,258	3,741	9,151
Value added (million ECU)	780	584	14,876	8	1,297	2,288	107	4,497	102	1,170	1,103	343	1,203	1,342	3,360
Gross operating surplus (million ECU)	222.7	103.6	2,499.1	2.4	364.0	125.5	47.8	1,415.0	21.8	445.4	183.9	125.2	384.7	478.8	1,176.4

(1) 1996.

_____Table 10.26

Manufacture of other special purpose machinery (NACE Rev. 1 29.5)

Trade related indicators, 1999

	B	DK	D	EL	E	F	IRL	I	L	NL	A	P	FIN	S	UK
Exports (million EUR)	3,387	1,510	23,017	77	1,496	6,781	234	12,550	234	3,090	3,080	422	1,539	2,361	6,460
Imports (million EUR)	2,620	993	6,857	665	3,123	5,741	765	4,496	239	2,378	1,751	1,009	845	1,502	5,246
Trade balance (million EUR)	767	517	16,160	-588	-1,627	1,040	-532	8,054	-5	713	1,328	-587	694	859	1,213
Cover ratio (%)	129.3	152.0	335.7	11.5	47.9	118.1	30.5	279.2	98.0	130.0	175.9	41.8	182.1	157.2	123.1

_____Table 10.27

Manufacture of other special purpose machinery (NACE Rev. 1 29.5)

Labour related indicators, 1997

	B	DK (1)	D	EL (2)	E	F	IRL	I (2)	L	NL	A	P	FIN	S	UK
Unit personnel costs (thousand ECU per employee)	43.6	36.9	43.8	14.7	23.8	38.1	24.7	35.1	43.0	:	41.9	12.6	37.3	39.0	32.5
Social charges as a share of personnel costs (%)	42.4	4.3	22.7	27.9	27.4	43.4	16.2	48.9	:	17.3	28.4	30.7	30.6	44.6	13.2
Apparent labour productivity (thousand ECU/pers. empl.)	60.0	40.4	52.6	20.7	30.9	40.3	44.1	50.0	54.3	:	50.2	19.1	54.5	60.6	49.6
Wage adjusted labour productivity (%)	137.4	121.3	119.9	140.3	130.1	105.8	178.2	142.4	126.3	:	119.9	152.1	146.0	155.5	152.8
Personnel costs as a share of total operating costs (%)	22.7	35.2	33.4	27.9	29.3	24.5	30.9	22.4	27.3	24.8	30.8	30.7	27.9	25.0	25.1

(1) Unit personnel costs and wage adjusted labour productivity, 1996; (2) 1996.

Source: Eurostat (SBS, EBT, COMEXT)

Table 10.28

Manufacture of weapons and ammunitions (NACE Rev. 1 29.6)

Production related indicators in the EU

	1989	1990	1991	1992	1993	1994	1995	1996	1997	1998	1999
Number of persons employed (thousands)	:	:	:	:	75.1	70.2	:	:	:	:	:
Production (million ECU)	:	:	:	:	6,927	6,356	:	:	:	:	:
Domestic producer price index (1995=100)	:	:	:	:	:	:	:	:	:	:	:
Value added (million ECU)	:	:	:	:	2,220	2,018	:	:	:	:	:

Table 10.29

Manufacture of weapons and ammunitions (NACE Rev. 1 29.6)

Trade related indicators in the EU (1)

	1989	1990	1991	1992	1993	1994	1995	1996	1997	1998	1999
Exports (million EUR)	305	353	379	344	445	727	502	1,269	462	515	491
Imports (million EUR)	267	374	334	445	396	466	240	477	360	267	244
Trade balance (million EUR)	39	-22	45	-102	50	262	263	792	102	248	246
Cover ratio (%)	114.5	94.2	113.6	77.2	112.6	156.2	209.6	266.0	128.4	193.1	200.9

(1) Technically, data before 01/01/1999 are in ECU and after this date in euro. However, as the conversion rate was 1 ECU =1 EUR, for practical purposes the two terms can be used interchangeably.

Table 10.30

Manufacture of weapons and ammunitions (NACE Rev. 1 29.6)

Production related indicators, 1997

	B	DK	D	EL	E	F	IRL	I (1)	L	NL	A	P	FIN	S	UK
Number of persons employed (thousands)	1.7	0.0	9.7	:	2.8	5.4	0.0	4.5	:	:	1.2	0.8	1.3	5.8	18.9
Production (million ECU)	265	0	1,066	:	266	1,048	0	464	:	97	183	31	104	646	2,699
Value added (million ECU)	79	0	494	:	81	605	0	184	:	37	73	8	48	290	1,023
Gross operating surplus (million ECU)	7.8	0.0	66.4	:	-25.2	332.8	0.0	25.0	:	13.5	18.9	-4.2	9.3	46.5	280.0

(1) 1996.

Table 10.31

Manufacture of weapons and ammunitions (NACE Rev. 1 29.6)

Trade related indicators, 1999

	B	DK	D	EL	E	F	IRL	I	L	NL	A	P	FIN	S	UK
Exports (million EUR)	53	5	195	6	61	233	0	253	0	11	43	43	77	27	60
Imports (million EUR)	43	21	113	19	53	77	3	69	2	10	46	42	48	25	116
Trade balance (million EUR)	10	-16	82	-13	9	155	-3	185	-2	0	-3	1	29	2	-56
Cover ratio (%)	123.0	22.6	171.8	32.8	116.3	300.6	0.3	368.9	8.0	104.0	93.3	101.6	159.4	106.4	51.8

Table 10.32

Manufacture of weapons and ammunitions (NACE Rev. 1 29.6)

Labour related indicators, 1997

	B	DK	D	EL	E	F	IRL	I (1)	L	NL	A	P	FIN	S	UK
Unit personnel costs (thousand ECU per employee)	43.1	:	44.1	:	35.8	50.2	:	35.5	:	:	44.4	14.7	31.7	41.9	39.3
Social charges as a share of personnel costs (%)	40.6	:	23.6	:	29.3	41.1	:	45.9	:	15.8	25.9	47.0	27.5	46.3	13.8
Apparent labour productivity (thousand ECU/pers. empl.)	47.6	:	51.0	:	28.7	111.6	:	40.7	:	:	59.8	9.3	38.0	49.9	54.1
Wage adjusted labour productivity (%)	110.4	:	115.5	:	80.2	222.1	:	114.6	:	:	134.7	63.2	120.0	119.2	137.6
Personnel costs as a share of total operating costs (%)	28.7	:	41.6	:	31.4	27.1	:	37.8	:	28.2	28.7	35.3	39.0	40.6	30.6

(1) 1996.

Source: Eurostat (SBS, EBT, COMEXT)

Electrical machinery and electronics
(NACE Rev. 1 29.7, 30, 31 and 32)

This chapter covers three Divisions of the NACE Rev. 1 classification, 30 to 32. Division 30 is composed of the manufacture of computers and office equipment. Division 31 contains the manufacture of electric motors, generators and transformers, electricity distribution and control apparatus, as well as insulated wires and cables, accumulators, batteries and lighting equipment. Division 32 is composed of the manufacture of electronic components, television, radio and video equipment, as well as telephones. The manufacture of domestic appliances n.e.c. (NACE Rev. 1 Group 29.7) is also covered in this chapter.

10% of the EU's manufacturing production total
In 1996, the production value of office machinery and computers amounted to 54.3 billion ECU, or 1.5% of the EU's manufacturing total. In 1997, production had risen to 56.0 billion ECU[1]. The production value of the electrical machinery and apparatus industry (NACE Rev. 1 31) was equal to 168.7 billion EUR in 1999, or a 4.2% share of the EU manufacturing total. The production level of the manufacture of radio, television and communications equipment (NACE Rev. 1 32) reached 159.9 billion EUR in 1999, a 4.0% share of the manufacturing total. It can therefore be concluded that the three NACE Rev. 1 Divisions which are covered within this chapter account for around 10% of total EU manufacturing output, whilst generating almost 11% of value added and employing slightly less than 10% of those employed in EU manufacturing. Domestic appliances accounted for 0.7% of EU manufacturing output in 1997 (see sub-chapter 11.2).

(1) EL, I and L, no data available.

Figure 11.1

Electrical machinery and electronics
(NACE Rev. 1 30, 31 and 32)
Share of total manufacturing value added
in the EU, 1994 (%)

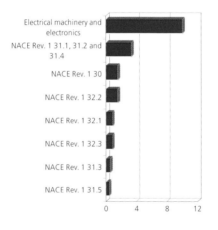

Source: Eurostat (SBS)

The activities covered in this chapter (in terms of NACE Rev. 1) include:

29.7: manufacture of domestic appliances n.e.c.;
30: manufacture of office machinery and computers;
31: manufacture of electrical machinery and apparatus n.e.c.;
31.1: manufacture of electric motors, generators and transformers;
31.2: manufacture of electricity distribution and control apparatus;
31.3: manufacture of insulated wire and cable;
31.4: manufacture of accumulators, primary cells and primary batteries;
31.5: manufacture of lighting equipment and electric lamps;
31.6: manufacture of electrical equipment n.e.c.;
32: manufacture of radio, television and communication equipment and apparatus;
32.1: manufacture of electronic valves and tubes and other electronic components;
32.2: manufacture of television and radio transmitters and apparatus for line telephony and line telegraphy;
32.3: manufacture of television and radio receivers, sound or video recording or reproducing apparatus and associated goods.

Box 11.1 _____

Today's society is increasingly based on information and communications. This so-called "information society" needs an underlying infrastructure of hardware in order to be operative. The manufacture of this hardware forms the focus of this chapter.

The penetration of the PC into the home environment is expected to continue growing at a rapid pace, with more people getting connected to the Internet. The European Commission recently launched the eEurope initiative. One of the key objectives of this initiative is "to bring every citizen, home and school, every business and administration, into the digital age and on-line". E-commerce is becoming increasingly important, especially in the business-to-business sector. These forces, together with technological gains, have resulted in demand for certain products growing exponentially. Telecommunications is one such area, with mobile phones getting smaller and lighter, whilst technological developments such as the introduction of wireless technologies have increased demand.

Electricity distribution and control apparatus the largest activity

Within electrical machinery and electronics, the manufacture of electricity distribution and control apparatus (NACE Rev. 1 31.2) was the largest single activity (at the level of NACE Rev. 1 Groups), accounting for more than one fifth of the production value in the industries covered by this chapter (21.3% in 1997)[2]. It was followed by the manufacture of televisions, radios and telephone equipment (NACE Rev. 1 32.2) with almost a fifth of the total (18.8%) and the manufacture of office machinery and computers (NACE Rev. 1 30) with 18.3%.

_____

(2) EL, I and L, no data available.

Large enterprises dominant

Large enterprises dominate the electrical machinery and electronics sector. According to data from the SME database, they represented 1.8% of the total enterprise population, a full percentage point more than the total manufacturing average. In terms of turnover, large enterprises accounted for almost three-quarters (74.6%) of the turnover generated in electrical machinery and electronics sectors (compared to 59.2% for manufacturing as a whole), whilst they employed 65.7% of the workforce (compared to a manufacturing average of 44.5%).

Table 11.1 _____

Electrical machinery and electronics (NACE Rev. 1 30, 31 and 32)

Breakdown of turnover and employment by employment size class, 1997 (%)

	Micro (0-9)		Small (10-49)		Medium (50-249)		Large (250+)	
	Turnover (1)	Employment (2)	Turnover (3)	Employment (4)	Turnover (5)	Employment (5)	Turnover (6)	Employment (6)
EU-15	4.2	7.4	7.9	11.7	13.4	15.2	74.6	65.7
B	6.6	4.4	6.4	7.8	:	:	:	:
DK	:	:	:	:	:	:	:	:
D	1.9	4.1	6.0	8.9	6.9	8.5	85.2	78.6
EL	:	:	:	:	:	:	:	:
E	6.5	8.8	14.3	17.9	:	21.7	:	51.6
F	2.4	4.8	5.9	10.5	11.9	15.7	79.7	69.0
IRL	:	:	:	:	:	:	:	:
I	6.9	15.2	18.4	23.3	17.4	16.7	57.3	44.7
L	:	:	:	:	:	:	:	:
NL	:	:	:	:	:	:	:	:
A	1.3	2.3	2.6	4.3	:	:	83.1	76.2
P	:	:	:	:	:	:	:	:
FIN	1.7	3.7	:	:	:	:	82.7	72.6
S	3.4	8.2	5.2	9.2	10.7	14.8	80.7	67.7
UK	6.5	9.5	7.8	10.3	:	:	:	:

(1) EU-15, E, F, I, FIN and S, 1996.
(2) EU-15, F, I, FIN and S, 1996.
(3) EU-15, E, F, I, A and S, 1996.
(4) EU-15, F, I, A and S, 1996.
(5) EU-15, F, I and S, 1996.
(6) EU-15, F, I, A, FIN and S, 1996.

Source: Eurostat (SME)

STRUCTURE AND PERFORMANCE

In real terms, the production value of electrical machinery and electronics increased by 51.6% between 1986 and 1996, equal to an annual average growth rate of 4.2%[3], some 1.8 percentage points higher than the EU manufacturing total[4].

Fluctuating growth patterns in the 1990s

Growth within the electrical machinery and electronics sector was seen to fluctuate in response to general economic conditions. The period between 1989 and 1993 saw a reduction in production values in constant price terms, whilst in the period thereafter large increases were reported. During the second half of the

(3) EL, IRL, L, A and P, no data available.
(4) L, A, P and FIN, no data available.

1990s, the use of computers and communications equipment (such as mobile phones) led to a rapid acceleration in output. Output in the whole of the electrical machinery and electronics industry increased by 8.6% in real terms in 1995 and by 6.1% in 1996[5]. During the period 1986 to 1996, the manufacture of office machinery and computers recorded annual average growth rates of 4.0% for production in constant prices[6]. Over the same period, there were growth rates of 2.3% per annum for electrical machinery and apparatus n.e.c.[7] and 7.0% per annum for radio, television and communications equipment[8].

(5) EL, L and A, no data available for both 1995 and 1996.
(6) EL, L, A and P, no data available.
(7) L, A and P, no data available.
(8) IRL, L, A and P, no data available.

Declining profits

The profit rate experienced a downfall in the period between 1986 and 1996. In 1986 gross operating surplus divided by turnover stood at 11.0%[9], 1.9 percentages points higher than in manufacturing. However, ten years later this rate had dropped to 7.6%[10], 1.0 point below the reported rate in manufacturing.

(9) B, EL, E, L, A and P, no data available.
(10) EL, L and A, no data available.

Figure 11.2

Office machinery and computers (NACE Rev. 1 30)

EU production and value-added in constant prices and employment compared to total manufacturing (1990=100)

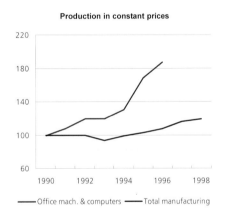
Production in constant prices

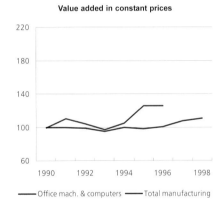
Value added in constant prices

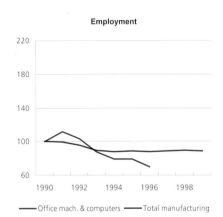
Employment

Source: Eurostat (SBS)

Figure 11.3

Electrical machinery and apparatus n.e.c. (NACE Rev. 1 31)

EU production and value-added in constant prices and employment compared to total manufacturing (1990=100)

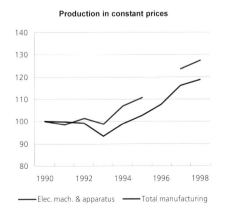
Production in constant prices

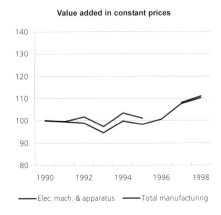
Value added in constant prices

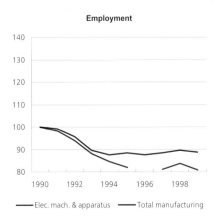
Employment

Source: Eurostat (SBS)

LABOUR AND PRODUCTIVITY

In 1996, almost 2 million persons were employed in the electrical machinery and electronics industry[11]. During the course of the ten year period between 1986 and 1996, a large number of jobs were lost in the industry. A reduction of 15.7% in the number of persons employed was registered, equivalent to an annual average decline of 1.7%[12]. This was 0.7 percentage points more than the decline in total manufacturing in the same period.

Highly skilled labour force

The industry is reliant on a highly skilled workforce, especially in the manufacture of office machinery and computers. In 1997, the Labour Force Survey reports that no less than 42.5% of those employed in the manufacture of office machinery and computers had completed a higher education degree, and another 38.3% possessed an upper secondary level of education. Only in computer and related activities (NACE Rev. 1 Division 72) did more of the workforce possess a higher education degree (54.4%). These figures contrasted with the manufacturing averages, where only 16.3% of the workforce had a higher education degree.

Higher apparent labour productivity...

Apparent labour productivity was slightly higher in electrical machinery and electronics than in manufacturing. In 1996, it stood at 49.3 thousand ECU per person employed in electrical machinery and electronics[13], some 2.8 thousand ECU above the manufacturing average. Ten years before, the gap was somewhat wider at 3.8 thousand ECU per person employed.

...but lower wage adjusted labour productivity

However, when taking account of the unit cost of labour (personnel costs) the relative productivity of these industries fell below the manufacturing norm, with a wage adjusted labour productivity ratio equal to 134.4% in 1996[14], some 10 percentage points below the manufacturing average of 144.3%. Ten years earlier the difference had been much smaller, at just 3.5 percentage points[15], suggesting that increasing personnel costs (linked to a highly skilled workforce) were largely responsible for the deterioration in productivity.

INTERNATIONAL TRENDS AND FOREIGN TRADE

After being the largest producer in the Triad for many years, Japan was overtaken by the USA in 1997, when American production climbed to almost 460 billion ECU, whilst Japanese output fell to 365 billion ECU. The year before, Japanese output (411.5 billion ECU) was 92.2 billion ECU higher than the corresponding American figure (319.3 billion ECU), whilst EU production could be estimated at 308.0 billion ECU in 1996[16].

Almost the same number of people were employed in Japan and the USA in the electrical machinery and electronics industries in 1987, with 1.8 million persons employed in both countries. Ten years later, employment had declined in both Japan (down 134 thousand persons) and the USA (down 60 thousand persons). Whilst no complete figure exists for the EU, it is possible to sum existing data, which shows that there were more than 2 million persons employed) in 1997[17].

(16) EL, no data available for electrical machinery & apparatus n.e.c. (NACE Rev. 1 31); L and A, no data available for radio, television and communications equipment (NACE Rev. 1 32).
(17) EL, L, I and NL, no data available for office machinery and computers (NACE Rev. 1 30).

(13) EL, L, NL and A, no data available.
(14) EL, L and A, no data available.
(15) B, EL, L, A and P, no data available for electrical machinery and electronics.

(11) EL, L, NL and A, no data available.
(12) EL, L, NL, P and A, no data available.

Table 11.2

Electrical machinery and electronics (NACE Rev. 1 30, 31 and 32)

Composition of the labour force, 1999 (%)

	Office machinery and computers			Electrical machinery and apparatus			Radio, TV, communications		
	Women (1)	Part-time (2)	Highly-educated (3)	Women (4)	Part-time (5)	Highly-educated (6)	Women (5)	Part-time (7)	Highly-educated (8)
EU-15	28.1	:	42.5	28.8	6.5	22.8	33.8	6.1	30.8
B	26.6	:	53.8	24.9	:	31.3	21.6	:	44.5
DK	:	:	:	33.6	:	17.5	45.5	:	25.8
D	29.2	7.9	39.8	30.1	7.2	30.8	32.3	8.9	34.3
EL	:	:	:	23.9	:	:	:	:	:
E	22.6	:	68.7	20.7	:	33.6	18.8	:	47.0
F	30.2	9.0	57.1	30.5	5.2	22.5	43.6	10.0	32.2
IRL	43.4	:	48.2	44.0	:	29.4	41.5	:	:
I	22.0	5.8	15.9	29.5	4.1	4.4	33.7	5.4	9.4
L	:	:	:	:	:	:	:	:	:
NL	:	:	:	:	:	:	17.4	13.5	34.6
A	:	:	:	39.9	13.7	:	21.1	9.1	15.1
P	:	:	:	50.3	:	:	54.8	:	:
FIN	:	:	:	33.0	:	37.8	36.2	:	51.5
S	:	:	:	:	:	:	40.0	:	:
UK	28.4	:	43.0	26.3	6.2	22.8	29.2	6.4	31.0

(1) EU-15, 1998; B, 1996.
(2) I, 1996.
(3) B, 1998; EU-15, F, IRL and UK, 1997.
(4) EU-15, 1998; EL, 1996.
(5) EU-15, 1998.
(6) EU-15, IRL and UK, 1997.
(7) EU-15, 1998; UK, 1997.
(8) EU-15 and UK, 1997.

Source: Eurostat (LFS)

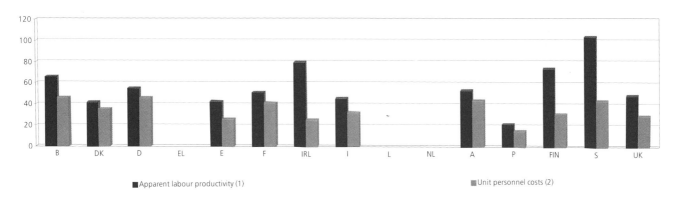

Figure 11.4

Electrical machinery and electronics (NACE Rev. 1 30, 31 and 32)

Apparent labour productivity and unit personnel costs, 1997 (thousand ECU)

■ Apparent labour productivity (1)　　　　　　　■ Unit personnel costs (2)

(1) I, 1996; EL, L and NL, not available.
(2) DK and I, 1996; EL, L and NL, not available.

Source: Eurostat (SBS)

EU exports growing at a faster pace than imports
EU exports to non-Community countries reached 119.5 billion EUR in 1999. Imports from non-Community countries stood at 155.2 billion EUR, and as such the EU ran a trade deficit of 35.7 billion EUR. The cover ratio (which measures the ratio of exports to imports) stood at 77.0% in 1999, compared to 61.3% in 1989.

China gains importance as a trading partner
In 1999, the most important origin of EU imports was the USA (23.6%), followed by Japan (16.5%). A decade earlier, their shares were much higher, at 33.4% for Japan, and 32.7% for the USA. Much of the shift in the composition of EU imports away from fellow Triad members could be explained by rising imports originating from China, whose share in total EU imports rose from 1.5% in 1989 to 8.7% in 1999 (the third most important trading partner of the EU).

The most important export destinations for EU electrical and electronic goods were the USA (18.7%), Switzerland (6.9%) and China (4.6%) in 1999. Again the latter reported an increase in its relative share of the EU total between 1989 and 1999 (from 1.8%).

Box 11.2
Foreign direct investment (FDI) data for NACE Rev. 1 30 and 32 combined (office machinery and computers, and radio, television and communications equipment) shows that at the end of 1997, the EU held 58.2 billion ECU of direct investment assets abroad. This was a sharp increase when compared with 1996 (34.7 billion ECU). There was a 50-50 split between intra-EU holdings and extra-EU holdings. The USA was the largest partner country for EU investors, with 11.9 billion ECU of FDI stocks, which was equal to just over a fifth of the total (20.5%). In contrast, EU investors held FDI stocks in Japan worth only 1.0 billion ECU.

Direct investment liabilities in the EU reached 47.4 billion ECU in 1997, which was 10.6 billion ECU higher than the value at the end of 1996. The USA held 13.4 billion ECU of FDI stocks in the EU, a 28.2% share of the total, Japan had stocks worth 3.0 billion ECU (6.2% of the total).

When analysing the reported FDI flows in 1998, net EU flows abroad for equity capital plus other capital reached 9.5 billion ECU. One third of these flows went to non-Community countries, mainly the USA (2.9 billion ECU). There was an even higher inflow of FDI into the EU in 1998, some 13.9 billion ECU, which originated almost exclusively from the USA (11.9 billion ECU).

Figure 11.5

Electrical machinery and electronics (NACE Rev. 1 30, 31 and 32)

Destination of EU exports, 1999 (%)

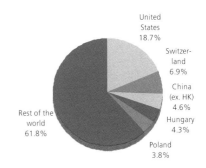

United States 18.7%
Switzerland 6.9%
China (ex. HK) 4.6%
Hungary 4.3%
Poland 3.8%
Rest of the world 61.8%

Source: Eurostat (COMEXT)

Figure 11.6

Electrical machinery and electronics (NACE Rev. 1 30, 31 and 32)

Origin of EU imports, 1999 (%)

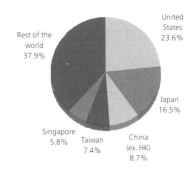

United States 23.6%
Japan 16.5%
China (ex. HK) 8.7%
Taiwan 7.4%
Singapore 5.8%
Rest of the world 37.9%

Source: Eurostat (COMEXT)

SUB-CHAPTER 11.1
MOTORS, GENERATORS, BATTERIES AND ACCUMULATORS AND ELECTRICITY DISTRIBUTION EQUIPMENT
(NACE Rev. 1 31.1, 31.2 AND 31.4)

This sub-chapter covers three Groups of the NACE Rev. 1 classification, the manufacture of electric motors, generators and transformers (NACE Rev. 1 Group 31.1), the manufacture of electricity distribution and control apparatus (such as switches, fuses, junction boxes, relays and sockets (NACE Rev. 1 Group 31.2) and the manufacture of accumulators, primary cells and primary batteries (NACE Rev. 1 Group 31.4).

The production value of motors, generators, batteries and accumulators and electricity distribution equipment reached 90.8 billion ECU in 1996[18], whilst employing 702 thousand persons[19]. The three Groups covered in this sub-chapter accounted for just under a third of the production value generated within electrical machinery and electronics industries (30.2%).

Electricity distribution and control apparatus dominant

The manufacture of electricity distribution and control apparatus was by far the largest of the three Groups, accounting for 72.2% of output in 1996 and 70.1% of employment. Electric motors, generators and transformers accounted for almost a quarter (22.3%) of production in 1996 (and a similar share of employment, 24.8%), whilst accumulators, primary cells and primary batteries accounted for the remaining 5.5% of output and 5.1% of employment.

Germany responsible for more than half of the EU's output

Germany had by far the highest level of production in these industries in 1997, with output reaching 53.1 billion ECU, which was more than half of EU total. France occupied a distant second place (13.0 billion ECU), followed by Italy (8.9 billion ECU, 1996) and the United Kingdom (7.7 billion ECU).

There were almost 364 thousand persons employed in Germany within these industries, whilst no other Member State employed more than 100 thousand persons, as the next largest employers were France (95.4 thousand persons), the United Kingdom (84.3 thousand) and Italy (67.6 thousand, 1996).

(18) DK, EL, L and A, no data available.
(19) DK, EL, L, NL and A, no data available.

Figure 11.7

Motors, generators, batteries and accumulators and electricity distribution equipment (NACE Rev. 1 31.1, 31.2 and 31.4)

Production and export specialisation (%)

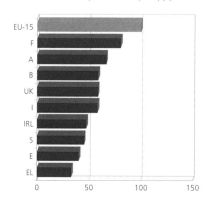

Production specialisation (1994) (1)

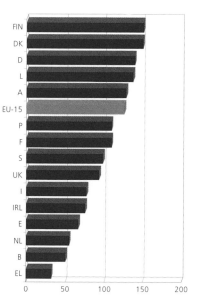

Export specialisation (1999)

(1) DK, D, L, NL, P and FIN, not available.

Source: Eurostat (SBS, COMEXT)

Box 11.3

In 1997, 56.5 million accumulators of more than 5kg and 15Ah were sold in Europe[20]. This was an increase of 3.2% compared with 1996. The two preceding years saw higher demand growth, 4.1% in 1996, and 10.7% in 1995.

To satisfy domestic demand, 30.7% of the batteries used in Europe were imported (excluding imports by battery manufacturers). Of the domestically produced batteries, 30.0% were bought by car manufacturers (including imports by battery manufacturers).

(20) EU-15 (excluding EL, IRL and L), Norway, Switzerland and Turkey.

STRUCTURE AND PERFORMANCE

In Germany (the largest producer within the EU) output rose by 4.6% in real terms between 1995 and 1997, an annual average increase of 2.3%. In France the annual average growth was equal to 6.0% between 1990 and 1997, whilst Italy recorded an increase of 1.0% per annum between 1992 and 1996 (again in real terms). In the United Kingdom the annual average increase of production in constant prices was equal to 5.6% between 1993 and 1997.

Combining the results for a limited set of countries for which data are available for both 1993 and 1996[21], gives an increase of 5.9% on average per annum in real terms.

Turnover in Germany reached 161.8 thousand ECU per person employed in 1997, which was amongst the highest in the EU. Only Belgium reported a higher figure (182.9 thousand ECU per person employed).

Eurostat estimates that turnover per person employed attained 146.6 thousand ECU in the EU in 1997. In the same year, the gross operating rate of the EU is estimated to have been 7.6%, whilst the gross operating surplus per person employed was estimated at 11.1 thousand ECU.

LABOUR AND PRODUCTIVITY

The number of persons employed in six of the Member States[22] rose slightly between 1993 and 1996, up by 2.0% (or a net increase of 5.8 thousand persons). However, in Germany employment went down by 38.7 thousand persons between 1995 and 1997, more than off-setting the gains reported in the aforementioned countries.

Eurostat estimates that apparent labour productivity stood at 51.0 thousand ECU per person employed in 1997, whilst unit personnel costs were equal to 39.7 thousand ECU per employee.

(21) E, F, I, S and UK.
(22) E, F, IRL, I, S and UK.

INTERNATIONAL TRENDS AND FOREIGN TRADE

The EU was the largest Triad producer of motors, generators, batteries and accumulators and electricity distribution equipment in 1996, when it accounted for 47.7% of total Triad output[23], whilst Japan had a share of 27.3% and the USA the remaining quarter (25.0%).

EU was the largest exporter, but
Japan had the highest cover ratio
EU exports to non-Community countries of motors, generators, batteries and accumulators and electricity distribution equipment reached 22.1 billion EUR in 1999, whilst imports stood at 16.6 billion EUR. Consequently, the EU had a surplus of 5.5 billion EUR and a cover ratio of 133.2%. In 1998, Japan ran a trade surplus of 8.8 billion ECU, with exports exceeding imports by a ratio of three to one (300.6%). The USA, on the other hand, recorded a trade deficit of 5.5 billion ECU in 1998 (with a cover ratio of 70.3%).

The USA was the most important
trading partner of the EU
Intra-EU imports accounted for 57.2% of total EU trade in 1999, which was 10.6 percentage points less than in 1989, indicating that trade with non-Community countries became increasingly important in the 1990s. The USA was the most important origin of EU imports, accounting for almost a quarter of the total (23.3%) in 1999, followed by Japan (15.6%), China (10.7%), Switzerland (10.4%) and the Czech Republic (6.0%).

The most important destination for EU exports was also the USA, accounting for 18.1% of total exports to non-Community countries in 1999. The list of main export destinations was similar to that for the origin of imports, as Switzerland was the second most important country (6.4%), followed by China (4.8%), the Czech Republic (4.6%) and Poland (3.8%).

(23) DK, EL, L and A, no data available.

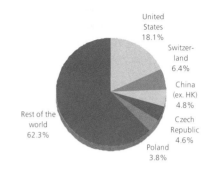

Figure 11.8

Motors, generators, batteries and accumulators and electricity distribution equipment (NACE Rev. 1 31.1, 31.2 and 31.4) Destination of EU exports, 1999 (%)

Source: Eurostat (COMEXT)

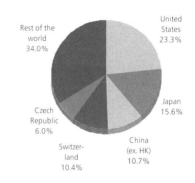

Figure 11.9

Motors, generators, batteries and accumulators and electricity distribution equipment (NACE Rev. 1 31.1, 31.2 and 31.4) Origin of EU imports, 1999 (%)

Source: Eurostat (COMEXT)

SUB-CHAPTER 11.2

DOMESTIC APPLIANCES (NACE Rev. 1 29.7)

This industry covers the manufacture of domestic electrical appliances (such as refrigerators and freezers, dishwashers, washing machines and vacuum cleaners), the manufacture of heating appliances (such as electric water heaters, blankets, ovens, microwaves, cookers, toasters and grills) as well as the manufacture of non-electric domestic cooking and heating equipment (such as space heaters, cooking ranges, stoves, water heaters, cooking appliances and plate warmers). The manufacture of sewing machines and machinery for the preparation of food in commercial kitchens is included within sub-chapter 10.1.

In 1996, domestic appliances reported production value of 32.8 billion ECU[24], which was equal to a 0.9% share of total EU manufacturing output. This industry generated 11.0 billion ECU of value added[25], whilst employing 258 thousand persons[26]. In 1996 the division between electric and non-electric appliances was split 9:1 in favour of electric appliances[27].

Germany and Italy accounted for
more than 60% of production

Germany was the largest producer in the EU, with output equal to 10.3 billion ECU in 1997. Italy followed close behind, with production valued at 9.8 billion ECU in 1996. Hence, these two countries produced in excess of 60% of total EU production. The United Kingdom (3.9 billion ECU) and France (3.7 billion ECU) followed with considerably lower levels of output.

(24) L, no data available.
(25) L, no data available.
(26) L and NL, no data available.
(27) D, EL, IRL, L and A, no data available.

Figure 11.10

Domestic appliances (NACE Rev. 1 29.7)

Production and export specialisation (%)

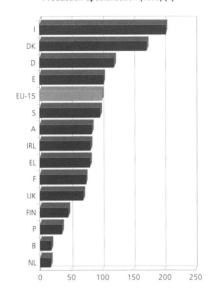

Production specialisation (1995) (1)

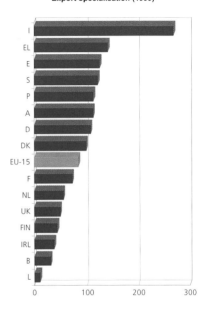

Export specialisation (1999)

(1) S, 1994; L, not available.

Source: Eurostat (SBS, COMEXT)

In terms of value added and employment, Germany had an even larger share of the EU total, generating 4.1 billion ECU of value added in 1997 (a share of 37.3% in 1996[28]) and employing 76.6 thousand persons (31.2% in 1996[29]).

(28) L, no data available.
(29) L and NL, no data available.

STRUCTURE AND PERFORMANCE

The demand for domestic appliances is linked to the general economic situation (which tends to influence if people decide to make or postpone replacement acquisitions), as well as the introduction of new technologies that aim to stimulate demand in a sector that is often characterised by saturated markets.

In 1991, output in domestic appliances increased by 9.0% in real terms when compared with 1990. A substantial decrease was recorded in 1993 (6.1%), which was followed by a fluctuating trend in the mid-1990s. In 1996 there was an 8.1%[30] increase in production. Over the period 1990 to 1996, production in constant prices rose at an average annual rate of 1.4%. Growth in Italy was equal to 5.7% per annum on average during the ten-year period 1986 to 1996 (again in real terms), higher than the corresponding German growth rate between 1987 and 1997 (2.8% per annum).

(30) L and A, no data available.

Box 11.4

Domestic appliances consume about one third of the electricity used in developed countries. Increasing the efficiency of domestic appliances can save large amounts of energy and money, as well as helping to reduce CO_2 emissions caused by power generation.

DG Environment of the European Commission has set up an Eco-label scheme, which is part of a broader strategy, aimed at promoting sustainable production and consumption. The primary function of the Eco-label is to stimulate the supply and demand of products such as washing machines and refrigerators with a reduced environmental impact.

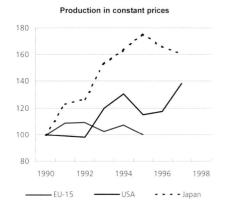
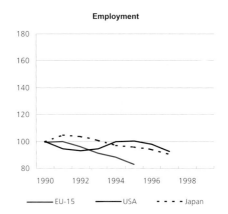

Figure 11.11

Domestic appliances (NACE Rev. 1 29.7)

International comparison of production in constant prices and employment (1990=100)

Production in constant prices

Employment

Source: Eurostat (SBS)

China accounted for a third of the domestic appliance imports in the EU

China was the main origin of EU imports in 1999, accounting for almost one-third (31.1%) of total EU imports. The USA followed with a 10.5% share, ahead of Switzerland (7.2%), Hungary (7.1%) and Slovenia (7.1%). Ten years earlier, in 1989, China accounted only for 6.1% of EU imports. In that year, Japan was the main origin for EU imports, accounting for 15.1% of the total. In 1999, the Japanese share had dropped to 3.2%. One underlying reason could be that Japanese manufacturers have relocated their manufacturing plants from Japan to China during the 1990s.

The USA was the main export destination for EU exports, accounting for 13.1% of exports to non-Community countries in 1999. Switzerland ranked second, with a 9.8% share, followed by Poland (8.2%), Norway (5.8%) and Russia (5.1%).

LABOUR AND PRODUCTIVITY

A large amount of jobs were shed during the 1990s in the domestic appliances industry. Between 1991 and 1996, the number of persons employed was reduced by 14.0%[31], equivalent to an annual average decrease of 3.0%. In the two largest producing countries there was a diverging trend to employment growth patterns. In Germany, the workforce was reduced by a third (33.8%) between 1991 and 1997, whilst in Italy employment rose by 29.9% between 1990 and 1996 (an annual average growth rate of 4.5%).

Eurostat estimates apparent labour productivity in the domestic appliances industry was equal to 44.4 thousand ECU per person employed in 1997. If taking personnel costs and the share of employees in the number of persons employed into account, the wage adjusted labour productivity ratio was equal to 140.9% (again in 1997). These measures were generally below manufacturing averages.

(31) L and NL, no data available.

INTERNATIONAL TRENDS AND FOREIGN TRADE

Japan was the largest producer of domestic appliances in the Triad, with output equal to 42.3 billion ECU in 1997. The American production level reached 20.4 billion ECU in the same year. Expressed as relative shares of the Triad total, Japan accounted for 46.9% in 1996, followed by the EU[32] (34.7%) and the USA (18.4%). However, in terms of employment the EU had the largest share of the Triad total, almost half (49.0%) of the total number of persons employed in 1996[33], whilst Japan accounted for 30.6% and the USA for 20.5%.

EU largest exporter

EU exports to non-Community countries were valued at 6.0 billion EUR in 1999, whilst imports stood at 4.4 billion EUR. The ratio of exports to imports (the cover ratio) was therefore equal to 136.6% in 1999. Whilst this figure was 10.4 percentage points above the cover ratio of 1989, it was considerably lower than the high of 189.3% recorded in 1997.

Nevertheless, in 1998 the EU was the by far largest exporter of domestic appliances in the Triad, accounting for 64.9% of total Triad exports. The USA accounted for 27.4% of the total, whilst Japan exported the remaining 7.7%. The USA was the largest importer, accounting for more than half of the Triad's imports (55.9%), followed by the EU (35.3%) and Japan (8.8%).

(32) L, no data available.
(33) L and NL, no data available.

Figure 11.12

Domestic appliances (NACE Rev. 1 29.7)

Destination of EU exports, 1999 (%)

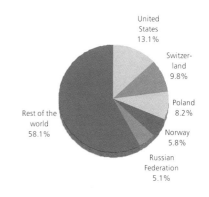

Source: Eurostat (COMEXT)

Figure 11.13

Domestic appliances (NACE Rev. 1 29.7)

Origin of EU imports, 1999 (%)

Source: Eurostat (COMEXT)

SUB-CHAPTER 11.3
ELECTRIC LIGHTING (NACE Rev. 1 31.5)

This subchapter covers the manufacture of lighting equipment and electric lamps, which includes the manufacture of electric filaments, discharge lamps and lighting fittings.

In 1999, the production value of the electric lighting industry stood at 12.7 billion EUR (equal to a 0.3% share of manufacturing production), whilst it generated 5.2 billion EUR of value added and employed 114.6 thousand persons.

In 1996, the production value of the electric lighting industry contributed 3.3% towards the total output of the electrical machinery and electronics industries covered in this chapter[34]. The corresponding shares of value added[35] and employment[36] were 3.9% and 5.0% respectively.

Germany produced one third
of the EU's output in 1997
In 1997, Germany was the largest producer of electric lighting goods in the EU, with a production value of 3.8 billion ECU (or 33.4% of the EU total). The United Kingdom accounted for 16.3% of the EU's production (1.9 billion ECU) and France for 12.0% (1.4 billion ECU). However, in 1996, Italy was the second largest producer in the EU, with an output share of 14.8% (or 1.5 billion ECU). None of the Member States was particularly specialised in the manufacture of electric lighting equipment in 1997, with the highest production specialisation ratio being recorded in Belgium (169.6%).

(34) EL, L and A, no data available.
(35) EL, L and A, no data available.
(36) EL, L, NL and A, no data available.

Box 11.5

The global electric lighting market is dominated by three large enterprises, Philips, Osram and General Electric (the first two are EU companies). Philips is the leading company in the electric lighting market, with Philips Lighting employing around 50 thousand persons in various manufacturing locations both within the EU, as well as in Poland, Brazil, Canada, Mexico, the United States, China, India, Indonesia, South Korea and Thailand. Osram employs around 30 thousand persons and has its headquarters in Munich. In the 1998/99 fiscal year, Osram had sales of 3.7 billion EUR, three-quarters of which were derived from their general lighting and automotive lighting divisions. Osram's sales outside of Germany accounted for 87% of their turnover.

Figure 11.14

Electric lighting (NACE Rev. 1 31.5)
Production and export specialisation (%)

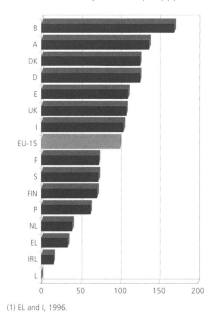

Production specialisation (1997) (1)

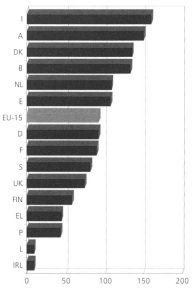

Export specialisation (1999)

(1) EL and I, 1996.

Source: Eurostat (SBS, COMEXT)

STRUCTURE AND PERFORMANCE

After a reduction in output of 3.9% in real terms in 1991, the electric lighting industry experienced four years of moderate growth. There followed a more expansive period of growth, with output rising by 7.1% in real terms in 1996 and by 16.0% in 1997 (although there was a downturn of 7.3% in 1998). Over the whole period 1990 to 1998, a net real increase of 18.9% was observed, equal to an annual average growth rate of 2.2%.

Sustained profit rates during the 1990s
The gross operating rate for the electric lighting industry was equal to 11.7% in 1999, up from 10.4% in 1989. The performance of the lighting industry was somewhat better than that of total manufacturing during the 1990s. The largest difference between the two rates was recorded in 1999 (with electric lighting 2.3 percentage points higher). The lighting industry also out-performed the electrical machinery and electronics average operating rate during the 1990s.

Figure 11.15

Electric lighting (NACE Rev. 1 31.5)
International comparison of production in constant prices and employment (1990=100)

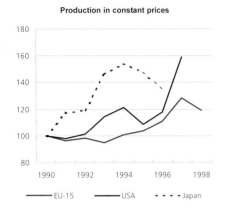

Production in constant prices

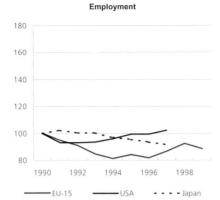

Employment

Source: Eurostat (SBS)

China became the most popular origin of imports
In 1999, China was by far the leading origin of EU imports, accounting for 43.4% of the total. Hungary accounted for 11.3%, followed by the USA (9.1%), Poland (7.7%) and Taiwan (4.9%). Ten years earlier, the USA had been the most important origin for EU imports, with a 17.4% share of the total, well ahead of Japan (16.7%) and Taiwan (16.5%), with China (7.8%) only in fourth place. The data presented seems to suggest that there has been a relocation of manufacturing plants within Asia towards China during the 1990s. The same phenomenon could also explain the increase in the shares of EU imports accounted for by Poland and Hungary, as EU manufacturers switch their production facilities to Eastern Europe.

On the export side, the USA was the principal destination for EU exports in 1999, accounting for 16.1% of the total, followed by Switzerland (10.0%), Norway (6.7%), Poland (6.0%) and Japan (4.8%).

LABOUR AND PRODUCTIVITY

Between 1989 and 1999 employment levels fell by 17.7 thousand persons in the electric lighting industry (an annual average reduction of 1.4%). However, job losses were confined to the first half of this period, as employment fell at an annual average rate of 4.5% between 1989 and 1994, whilst during the period 1994 to 1999 there was average growth of 1.7% per annum.

Low apparent labour productivity
Apparent labour productivity in the lighting industry was equal to 45.0 thousand EUR per person employed in 1999, which was 6.8 thousand EUR per person employed below the manufacturing average. When compared with electrical machinery and electronics[37], apparent labour productivity for electric lighting was also lower (10.1 thousand ECU less in 1996 - the latest comparison available).

(37) EL, L, NL and A, no data available.

INTERNATIONAL TRENDS AND FOREIGN TRADE

In 1997, the USA accounted for 42.2% of Triad output (15.4 billion ECU), ahead of the EU (31.4% or 11.5 billion ECU) and Japan (26.4% or 9.7 billion ECU). In the seven years from the beginning of the 1990s, the USA gained a 9.0 percentage point share, at the expense of both the EU (-5.6 percentage points) and Japan (-3.4 percentage points). The EU had the highest employment share, with 41.6% of the Triad total in 1997, ahead of the USA (38.3%) and Japan (20.2%).

The EU ran its first trade deficit in ten years in 1999
The EU exported 2.6 billion EUR of lighting equipment to non-Community countries in 1999. However, for the first time in the ten-year period 1989 to 1999, the value of imports from non-Community countries was higher (2.9 billion EUR). In 1998, the EU had the highest share of Triad exports, accounting for 57.8% of the total. The USA followed with 29.6% and Japan closed the ranking with 12.7%. The USA was the largest importer within the Triad (58.6% of the total), followed by the EU (35.2%) and Japan (6.1%).

Figure 11.16

Electric lighting (NACE Rev. 1 31.5)
Destination of EU exports, 1999 (%)

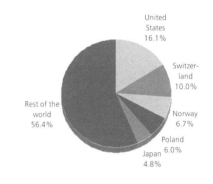

United States 16.1%

Switzerland 10.0%

Norway 6.7%

Poland 6.0%

Japan 4.8%

Rest of the world 56.4%

Source: Eurostat (COMEXT)

Figure 11.17

Electric lighting (NACE Rev. 1 31.5)
Origin of EU imports, 1999 (%)

Rest of the world 23.5%

China (ex. HK) 43.4%

Taiwan 4.9%

Poland 7.7%

United States 9.1%

Hungary 11.3%

Source: Eurostat (COMEXT)

SUB-CHAPTER 11.4
INSULATED WIRE AND CABLE
(NACE Rev. 1 31.3)

The manufacture of insulated wire and cable includes the manufacture of insulated wire, cable, strip and other insulated conductors, whether or not fitted with connectors, and the manufacture of fibre optic cables for coded data transmission, such as telecommunications, video, control and data. The manufacture of metal cable not being used as a conductor of electricity (see sub-chapter 9.3) and the manufacture of optical fibres (see sub-chapter 12.3) are not included.

Production value of wires and cables reached 16.1 billion EUR in 1999, whilst 4.7 billion EUR of value added was generated. In 1996, 94.2 thousand persons were employed in the insulated wire and cable industry[38]. This relatively small activity accounted for 4.6% of the output of electrical machinery and electronics industries in 1997[39] and for 4.9% of employment[40].

Germany largest producer, high specialisation in Portugal and Greece

Germany was the largest producer in the EU in 1997, with output equal to 3.4 billion ECU, followed by France (3.0 billion ECU) and the United Kingdom (2.7 billion ECU). Italy, for which there are no 1997 data available, produced 2.2 billion ECU of wires and cables in 1996. In relative terms however, the industry was of more importance to Portugal, who had the highest production specialisation ratio in 1997 (223.9%). The Greek ratio (which is not available for 1997) was the highest in 1996 at 309.7%[41].

---

(38) NL and A, no data available.
(39) EL, I and L, no data available.
(40) EL, I, L and NL, no data available.
(41) A, no data available.

Figure 11.18

Insulated wire and cable (NACE Rev. 1 31.3)
Production and export specialisation (%)

Production specialisation (1997) (1)

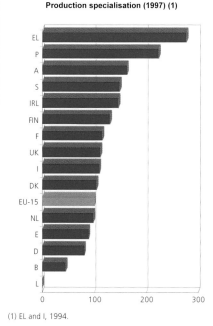

Export specialisation (1999)

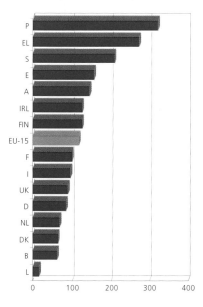

(1) EL and I, 1994.

Source: Eurostat (SBS, COMEXT)

Box 11.6

The globalisation of the wire and cable industry is moving at an increasing pace, with rapid developments in telecommunications, cable TV and Internet applications. Fibre optic cables are being deployed in increasing quantities to fill the need for high speed, wide-band applications. The European cable industry faces an increasing number of challenges, such as the liberalisation of national markets, privatisation of major customers, the emergence of new operators in the telecoms sector, global competition and technological developments.

In 1998, production of cables accounted for just under 90% of total output of insulated wires and cables in Europe (EU-15, Norway and Switzerland), whilst enamelled wires accounted for the remaining 10.4%. Cable production can be further broken down into the production of general wiring cable (accounting for 38.2% of the whole wire and cables total), electricity utility cables (19.2%) and communication cables (32.2%).

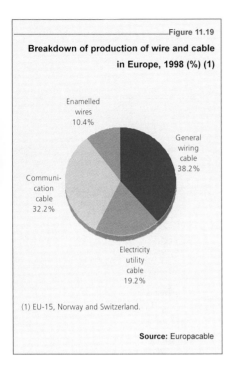

Figure 11.19

Breakdown of production of wire and cable in Europe, 1998 (%) (1)

Enamelled wires 10.4%

General wiring cable 38.2%

Communication cable 32.2%

Electricity utility cable 19.2%

(1) EU-15, Norway and Switzerland.

Source: Europacable

Table 11.3

Production of wire and cable in Europe, 1998 (million ECU)

	Benelux (1)	D	E	F	I	UK	Northern Europe (2)	Southern Europe (3)	Other Europe (4)
General wiring cable	318.8	1,218.8	322.7	672.3	699.7	418.4	413.5	149.8	330.8
Electricity utility cable	169.1	597.2	61.9	434.1	190.4	147.1	411.2	111.3	157.2
Communication cable	152.5	1,194.9	248.3	571.4	306.1	575.7	387.6	78.2	315.9
Enamelled wires	44.4	306.8	110.0	157.8	383.8	87.9	62.1	0.0	84.5
Total	684.8	3,317.7	742.9	1,835.7	1,580.0	1,229.2	1,274.5	339.3	888.4

(1) Enamelled wires, 1996.
(2) DK, FIN, S and Norway.
(3) EL and P.
(4) IRL, A and Switzerland.

Source: Europacable

STRUCTURE AND PERFORMANCE

Between 1993 and 1998 output of the wire and cable industry increased by 4.0% on average per annum in real terms. This was 0.9 percentage points below the manufacturing average. In nominal terms, output grew by 4.1% in 1999, which was 1.1 percentage point higher than the total manufacturing average.

Large fluctuations of output in Member States

For three of the four largest Member States longer time-series are available. France recorded an average annual growth rate of 2.5% in real terms between 1987 and 1997. In Italy, after large fluctuations in the 1990s, the output level in 1996 was almost at the same level as in 1986 (with net real growth of 1.7% reported). Finally, in the United Kingdom, also after considerable fluctuations, a net decrease of 4.3% was registered in real terms during the period 1987 to 1997.

Declining profits in the 1990s

In 1990, the gross operating rate in the wires and cables industry was at a relatively high level of 12.2%[42], 2.6 percentage points above the average rate for the whole of electrical machinery and electronics[43] and 3.0 percentage points higher than the total manufacturing average. By 1999, the gross operating rate for wires and cables had lost 4.1 percentage points, falling to 8.1%, which was 1.3 percentage points below the manufacturing average.

LABOUR AND PRODUCTIVITY

Between 1990 and 1996 there was a large reduction in the workforce of the EU wires and cables industry as the employment level fell by almost a quarter (24.9%). This reduction was equivalent to an annual average decline of 4.7%[44]. It should be noted that if Germany, the second largest employer in the EU, would be included, the reduction would probably have been larger, as between 1995 and 1996 employment fell by 2.7 thousand persons in Germany, a net reduction of 12.7%. In 1997 however, employment grew again by 8.5% in Germany, and by 4.1% in the EU[45] as a whole.

Low apparent labour productivity

Eurostat estimates that apparent labour productivity in the EU wires and cables industry was equal to 44.9 thousand ECU per person employed in 1997. In the same year, apparent labour productivity for the whole of electrical machinery and electronics stood at 54.4 thousand ECU per person employed[46], whilst the total manufacturing average was 49.3 thousand ECU per person employed.

Wage adjusted labour productivity was estimated by Eurostat to be 142.5% in 1997. The equivalent figures for electrical machinery and electronics were 142.0% in 1997[47] and 148.8% for total manufacturing.

(42) B, D, E, L, A and P, no data available.
(43) B, EL, E, L, A and P, no data available.

(44) D, L, NL and A, no data available.
(45) EL, I, NL and A, no data available.
(46) EL, I, L and NL, no data available.
(47) EL, I and L, no data available.

INTERNATIONAL TRENDS AND FOREIGN TRADE

The EU was the largest producer of wires and cables in the Triad in 1997, with production valued at 16.1 billion ECU, or a 40.7% share in Triad production. Japan followed closely behind with output worth 15.3 billion ECU (38.7%), ahead of the USA (8.1 billion ECU or 20.6%). In terms of employment, the EU employed the majority of persons occupied within the wires and cables industry. In 1996, there were 94.2 thousand persons employed in the EU[48] (51.9%), whilst there were 45.7 thousand employed in Japan (25.2%) and 41.5 thousand in the USA (22.9%).

Declining cover ratio in the EU
EU exports to non-Community countries reached 3.5 billion EUR in 1999. Imports from non-Community countries stood at 2.8 billion EUR in the same year. The resulting trade surplus translated into a cover ratio of 127.8% in 1999, which was considerably lower than in 1997 (160.3%). The EU was the largest exporter within the Triad in 1998, accounting for 47.1% of the Triad's exports of wires and cables, ahead of the USA (35.2%) and Japan (17.7%). The USA accounted for the largest share of imports in 1998 (44.3%), just ahead of the EU (41.2%), whilst Japan imported a relatively small share of the total (14.5%).

Rapid increase in EU imports originating from China
The main destination for EU exports in 1999 was the USA, accounting for 8.5% of extra-EU exports. The next three positions were occupied by Eastern European countries, Poland (7.8%), Hungary (6.8%) and Czech Republic (6.1%). Switzerland followed with a 5.1% share.

The USA was also the most important origin for EU imports with a 21.0% share of the total in 1999. China accounted for 14.0%, which was a notable increase on its relative share of 1989, up by 13.4 percentage points (this phenomenon has also been observed within other industries covered by this chapter). The origin of EU imports was otherwise concentrated within neighbouring countries in 1999, such as the Czech Republic (8.3%), Switzerland (8.0%) and Poland (6.5%).

(48) NL and A, no data available.

Figure 11.20 _____

Insulated wire and cable (NACE Rev. 1 31.3)
Destination of EU exports, 1999 (%)

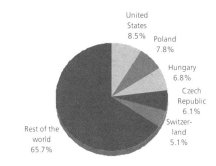

Source: Eurostat (COMEXT)

Figure 11.21 _____

Insulated wire and cable (NACE Rev. 1 31.3)
Origin of EU imports, 1999 (%)

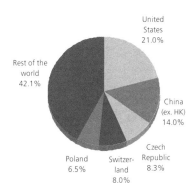

Source: Eurostat (COMEXT)

SUB-CHAPTER 11.5
ELECTRONIC COMPONENTS
(NACE Rev. 1 32.1)

This industry covers the manufacture of electronic valves and tubes and other electronic components, such as diodes, transistors, photosensitive semiconductor devices, mounted piezoelectric crystals, electronic integrated circuits and micro-assemblies, printed circuits, electrical capacitors and resistors. The data presented in this sub-chapter does not include the manufacture of heating resistors (within sub-chapter 11.2), nor the manufacture of transformers or the manufacture of switches (both within sub-chapter 11.1).

Production value of the EU's electronic components industry reached 38.7 billion EUR in 1999. In the same year, value added of 14.6 billion EUR was generated, whilst employment was equal to 241.1 thousand persons. In 1997, production value of electronic components within the EU accounted for 8.6% of the total output of electrical machinery and electronics[49].

United Kingdom largest producer,
Ireland most specialised

The United Kingdom was the largest producer of electronic components in the EU in 1997, accounting for almost a quarter (24.1%, or 7.3 billion ECU), followed by France with 22.3% (6.8 billion ECU) and Germany with 17.1% (5.2 billion ECU). In relative terms however, Ireland stood out as the most specialised country within the EU, with a production specialisation ratio of 541.6%, well ahead of Portugal (170.8%) and the United Kingdom (160.2%).

---

(49) EL, I and L, no data available.

Figure 11.22

Electronic components (NACE Rev. 1 32.1)
Production and export specialisation (%)

Production specialisation (1997) (1)

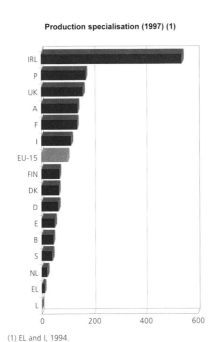

Export specialisation (1999)

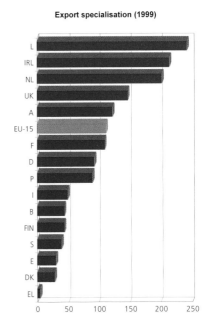

(1) EL and I, 1994.

Source: Eurostat (SBS, COMEXT)

Box 11.7

Electronic components can be divided into three main product categories: active components (such as semiconductors, cathode-ray tubes, flat screens and electro-optical components), passive components (such as capacitors, resistors, inductors and ferrites) and electro-mechanical components (such as printed circuits, connectors, hybrid circuits, MCMs and relays). Active components accounted for the largest share of the components market in the EU[50]. According to estimates from the European Electronic Component Manufacturers Association (EECA), their share of the components market was 62.9% in 1998 (24.2 billion ECU), which was expected to rise to 69.3% (37.3 billion EUR) by 2001. The share of electromechanical components is forecast to fall from 25.8% (9.9 billion ECU) to 21.1% (11.4 billion EUR) during the same period, whilst a reduction from 11.3% (4.3 billion ECU) to 9.5% (5.1 billion EUR) is forecast for passive components.

---

(50) DK, EL, IRL, L, P and FIN, no data available.

Table 11.4

Market developments in the EU electronic components industry (1)

	1998 million ECU	Share (%)	1999 million ECU	Share (%)	2000 million ECU	Share (%)	2001 million ECU	Share (%)
Active components	24,206	62.9	27,540	64.8	32,767	67.4	37,253	69.3
Passive components	4,349	11.3	4,531	10.7	4,939	10.2	5,127	9.5
Electromechanical components	9,939	25.8	10,439	24.6	10,945	22.5	11,355	21.1
Electronic components	38,494	100.0	42,509	100.0	48,651	100.0	53,735	100.0

(1) Excluding DK, EL, IRL, L, P and FIN.

Source: EECA

STRUCTURE AND PERFORMANCE

Output of the electronic components industry grew rapidly in the second half of the 1990s. Between 1993 and 1998, production in constant price terms more than doubled (compared to the period 1988 to 1993), with average annual growth of 17.9%. Growth was at a much faster pace than the average for the whole of the electrical machinery and electronics industry, where annual average growth of 5.3% was recorded between 1993 and 1997[51].

High and increasing profits

The gross operating rate of the EU's electronic components industry followed an upward trend in the second half of the 1990s, rising from 11.5% in 1993 to 15.8% by 1999. The average rate for the whole of the EU's electrical machinery and electronics industry was 5.1 percentage points lower in 1993, and 4.0 points lower in 1997[52].

LABOUR AND PRODUCTIVITY

Employment within the electronic components industry rose by 34.8% between 1994 and 1999, equivalent to an annual average growth rate of 6.2%. This trend appeared to be maintained in the late 1990s, as there was a net increase of 6.6% between 1998 and 1999.

Labour productivity on the rise

In 1993, apparent labour productivity within the EU electronic components industry (38.3 thousand ECU per person employed) was slightly below the average for the whole of electrical machinery and electronics (42.5 thousand ECU per person employed). By 1999 however, this productivity measure was substantially higher for electronic components (60.7 thousand ECU per person employed). The ratio between value added and personnel costs (simple wage adjusted labour productivity), was equally on the rise, up from 141.6% in 1993 to 182.0% by 1999.

(51) EL, IRL, I, L and A, no data available.
(52) EL, I and L, no data available for electrical machinery and electronics.

INTERNATIONAL TRENDS AND FOREIGN TRADE

Whilst the electronic components industry has recorded rapid growth in recent years, the EU recorded a relatively low share of Triad output. In 1997, the USA accounted for 52.8% of Triad production (166.6 billion ECU), Japan accounted for 37.6% (118.7 billion ECU) and the EU for the remaining 9.6% (30.3 billion ECU). The share of value added generated in the USA was even higher at 64.7% (108.5 billion ECU), followed by Japan with 28.4% (47.7 billion ECU) and the EU with 6.9% (11.5 billion ECU).

Increasing cover ratio in the EU

EU exports to non-Community countries attained 18.4 billion EUR in 1999, whilst imports stood at 25.9 billion EUR, resulting in a trade deficit of 7.5 billion EUR. The ratio of exports to imports (the cover ratio) increased during the 1990s, from 49.6% in 1989 to 71.1% in 1999. The USA was the main origin of imports, accounting for a quarter (25.6%) of the EU's imports from non-Community countries in 1999, followed by Asian countries such as Japan (19.7%), Malaysia (8.5%), South Korea (8.3%) and Singapore (8.2%). The USA was also the main destination of EU exports to non-Community countries, 19.7% of the total in 1999, followed by Malaysia (10.7%), Singapore (10.4%), Taiwan (6.6%) and Hungary (5.8%).

Figure 11.23

Electronic components (NACE Rev. 1 32.1)
Destination of EU exports, 1999 (%)

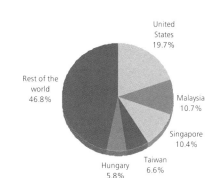

Source: Eurostat (COMEXT)

Figure 11.24

Electronic components (NACE Rev. 1 32.1)
Origin of EU imports, 1999 (%)

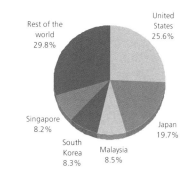

Source: Eurostat (COMEXT)

SUB-CHAPTER 11.6
OFFICE MACHINERY AND COMPUTERS
(NACE Rev. 1 30)

This industry covers the manufacture of office machinery, such as typewriters, addressing machines, calculating machines, cash registers and automatic banknote dispensers, as well as a variety of office machines such as perforating or stapling machines. The data presented also includes information relating to the manufacture of computers and peripheral units, such as printers, terminals and magnetic or optical readers. The data presented does not cover the manufacture of electronic parts found in computers (see sub-chapter 11.5), nor the manufacture of electronic games (sub-chapter 14.3) or the repair and maintenance of computer systems (sub-chapter 21.3).

The EU produced office machinery and computers valued at 54.3 billion ECU in 1996, generating 14.3 billion ECU of value added, whilst employing 208.3 thousand persons. In 1997, the output of the EU's office machinery and computers industry accounted for 18.3% of the total produced within electrical machinery and electronics[53].

As with electronic components, Ireland was again the most specialised

As with electronic components, the United Kingdom was the largest producer of office machinery and computers in the EU in 1997, with production valued at 17.7 billion ECU in 1997, followed by Germany (12.3 billion ECU) and France (11.6 billion ECU). However, in relative terms Ireland surpassed all other Member States, with a production specialisation ratio of 981.3% (1996). The United Kingdom (198.1%) and France (128.5%) were the other two Member States with a specialisation ratio in excess of 100% in 1996.

(53) EL, I and L, no data available.

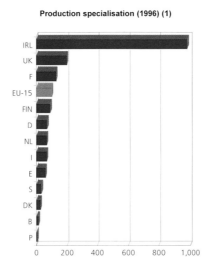

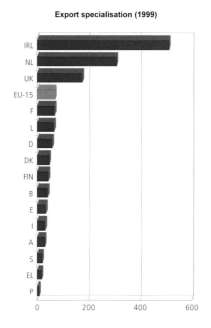

Figure 11.25

Office machinery and computers (NACE Rev. 1 30)
Production and export specialisation (%)

Production specialisation (1996) (1)

Export specialisation (1999)

(1) EL, L and A, not available.

Source: Eurostat (SBS, COMEXT)

Box 11.8

The European Information Technology Observatory (EITO) estimates that the value of the information technology (IT) hardware market in the EU was 92.9 billion EUR in 1999, up 7.6% when compared with 1998. EITO expect further growth of 7.0% in 2000 and 6.5% for 2001. The largest share of the market (78.5%) was accounted for by computer hardware, which could be further broken down into PCs (36.5% of the total), servers (27.5%), add-ons such as printers (12.2%) and workstations (2.4%). Data communications hardware accounted for an 11.6% share of the total, whilst office equipment had a 9.9% share.

STRUCTURE AND PERFORMANCE

Office machinery and computers experienced buoyant growth during the 1990s. Between 1991 and 1996 output rose on average by 11.6% per annum in real terms[54]. The highest single growth rate was in 1995, when production increased by 25.2% in real terms.

Profit rates falling sharply

In 1987, the gross operating rate of the EU's office machinery and computers industry stood at 16.9%, almost 8 percentage points higher than the manufacturing average (9.1%). However, due to increasing competition and falling prices, the gross operating rate declined sharply in the following ten years to 6.8% by 1997[55], below the level recorded for the whole of the electrical machinery and electronics industry (8.7%[56]) as well as below the manufacturing average (9.2%). The largest reduction occurred in 1992, when the operating rate fell from 12.1% to 6.3%.

LABOUR AND PRODUCTIVITY

After an increase of 47.9 thousand persons employed between 1986 and 1991, there was a reduction in employment of 125.6 thousand persons between 1991 and 1996 in the EU's office machinery and computers industry. Over the ten-year period 1986 to 1996 the annual average reduction was equal to 3.1%.

Labour productivity high, but losing ground

Apparent labour productivity in the EU office machinery and computers industry stood at 70.0 thousand ECU per person employed in 1997[57], significantly higher than the average for electrical machinery and electronics (54.4 thousand ECU per person employed[58]). However, ten years before the gap was considerably wider, with apparent labour productivity for the office machinery and computers industry at 61.7 thousand ECU per person employed, compared to only 34.4 thousand ECU for the whole of electrical machinery and electronics[59].

Simple wage adjusted labour productivity for the EU's office machinery and computers industry fell by no less than 26.1 percentage points between 1987 and 1997 (when it was 151.6%[60]).

Figure 11.26

Office machinery and computers (NACE Rev. 1 30)

International comparison of production in constant prices and employment (1990=100)

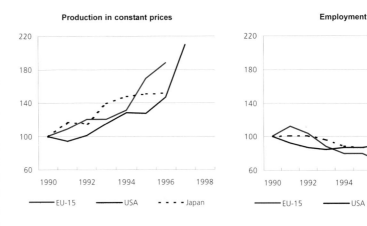

Source: Eurostat (SBS)

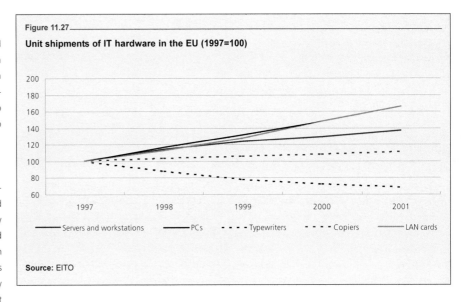

Figure 11.27

Unit shipments of IT hardware in the EU (1997=100)

Source: EITO

---

(54) It is important to note that price indices may not take account of the changes in the quality and specification of products. As the average specification of a computer has risen at a rapid pace during the period considered it is likely that the growth in real terms is even higher than that reported.
(55) EL, I and L, no data available.
(56) EL, I and L, no data available.
(57) EL, I, L and NL, no data available.
(58) EL, I, L and NL, no data available.
(59) B, EL, L, A and P, no data available.
(60) EL, I and L, no data available.

_____Table 11.5

Value of the IT hardware market in the EU (million EUR)

	1997	1998	1999	2000	2001
Total server	21,954	23,740	25,573	27,613	29,495
- Unix servers	4,970	5,515	6,033	6,531	6,976
- NT servers	2,022	2,578	3,064	3,774	4,507
- other servers	7,024	7,138	7,241	7,301	7,321
- server add-ons	7,937	8,509	9,234	10,006	10,691
Workstations	2,469	2,308	2,193	2,129	2,056
PCs	29,350	31,619	33,929	36,502	39,100
- portable	6,761	7,507	8,289	9,079	9,872
- desktop	22,590	24,111	25,640	27,424	29,228
PC/workstation add-ons	9,579	10,131	11,293	11,876	12,469
- PC printers	6,122	6,180	6,196	6,171	6,182
- other add-ons	3,457	3,951	5,097	5,705	6,288
Computer hardware	63,351	67,797	72,987	78,120	83,120
Office equipment	9,018	9,138	9,211	9,350	9,486
- copiers	5,171	5,252	5,315	5,414	5,508
- other office equipment	3,848	3,885	3,896	3,936	3,978
Data communications hardware	8,170	9,470	10,738	11,955	13,259
- LAN hardware	4,855	5,647	6,465	7,092	7,607
- packet switching and routing equipment	1,472	1,800	2,171	2,640	3,191
- other data communication	1,844	2,023	2,102	2,223	2,461
IT hardware	80,540	86,405	92,937	99,425	105,865

Source: EITO

INTERNATIONAL TRENDS AND FOREIGN TRADE

In 1997, the USA overtook Japan as the largest producer of office machinery and computers in the Triad. Japanese output fell from 91.9 billion ECU in 1996 to 79.7 billion ECU in 1997, whilst in the USA production increased from 81.3 billion ECU to 115.9 billion ECU.

EU ran a large trade deficit

In 1999, EU exports to non-Community countries reached 24.2 billion EUR, whilst imports stood at 59.2 billion EUR. As such, the EU ran a trade deficit of 35.0 billion EUR. The EU's cover ratio, exports divided by imports, was equal to 40.9%. Ten years before in 1989, the EU was even more dependent on imports, as the cover ratio had been 33.8%. The USA also ran a large trade deficit of 32.9 billion ECU in 1998, with exports worth 35.9 billion ECU and imports worth almost twice as much (68.9 billion ECU). Japan on the other hand, had a large surplus, exporting 29.6 billion ECU of office machinery and computer products in 1998, whilst importing less than half that level (14.9 billion ECU).

The USA was the most important origin of EU imports, accounting for 23.1% of total imports from non-Community countries in 1999, ahead of Japan (15.5%), Taiwan (12.4%), Singapore (9.2%) and China (8.1%). China's share is noteworthy, as when compared with ten years before it had risen by 7.8 percentage points. The USA was also the main destination for EU exports, accounting for more than a quarter of the total (26.4% in 1999), followed by Switzerland (12.5%), Japan (5.5%), Norway (5.2%) and Hungary (4.9%).

_____Figure 11.28

**Office machinery and computers
(NACE Rev. 1 30)
Destination of EU exports, 1999 (%)**

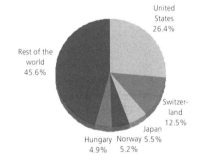

Source: Eurostat (COMEXT)

_____Figure 11.29

**Office machinery and computers
(NACE Rev. 1 30)
Origin of EU imports, 1999 (%)**

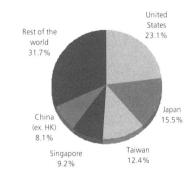

Source: Eurostat (COMEXT)

SUB-CHAPTER 11.7
TELECOMMUNICATIONS EQUIPMENT
(NACE Rev. 1 32.2)

The data presented in this sub-chapter covers the manufacture of apparatus for television transmission, television cameras, transmission apparatus for radio-broadcasting, fixed transmitters and transmitter-receivers, radio-telephony apparatus for transport equipment, radio-telephones, telephone sets, fax machines, automatic and non-automatic switch-boards and exchanges, telex machines and tele-print-er apparatus. The information presented does not cover the manufacture of television or radio sets (which are in the next sub-chapter).

Output of the television, radio and telephone trans-mission equipment industries reached 88.3 billion EUR in 1999, whilst offering employment to 376.9 thou-sand persons. In 1997, this was the second largest sub-activity within the electrical machinery and elec-tronics sector, accounting for 18.8%[61] of total output.

Sweden and Finland most specialised
France was the largest producer of television, radio and telephone transmission equipment in the EU in 1997, accounting for 19.3% of the total, followed by Sweden (18.1%) and Germany (13.5%). Driven by Ericsson (S) and Nokia (FIN), Sweden (584.8%) and Finland (495.0%) were the two countries that were most specialised in within this area of the economy, largely due to a strong presence in the telecommuni-cations market.

---

(61) EL, I and L, no data available.

Figure 11.30

Telecommunications equipment (NACE Rev. 1 32.2)
Production and export specialisation (%)

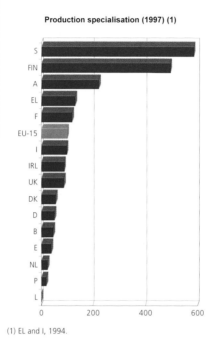

Production specialisation (1997) (1)

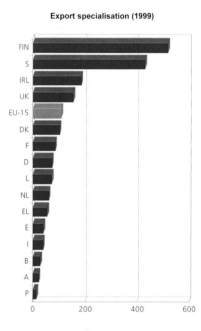

Export specialisation (1999)

(1) EL and I, 1994.

Source: Eurostat (SBS, COMEXT)

Box 11.9

According to data from the European Information Technology Observatory (EITO), the telecommunications hardware market in the EU was worth 55.5 billion EUR in 1999, of which 33.6 billion EUR was end-user equipment and 21.9 billion EUR was network equipment products.

Mobile telephone sets formed three-quarters of the end-user equipment market. The market for mobile phones is rapidly growing, up by 55.0% in 1999. EITO forecasts that growth rates of 33.1% and 22.1% will be recorded in 2000 and 2001 respectively.

The market for network equipment evolves at a slower pace, although there was still growth of 6.9% in 1999, and EITO forecasts further expansion in 2000 and 2001 (8.5% and 7.0% respectively).

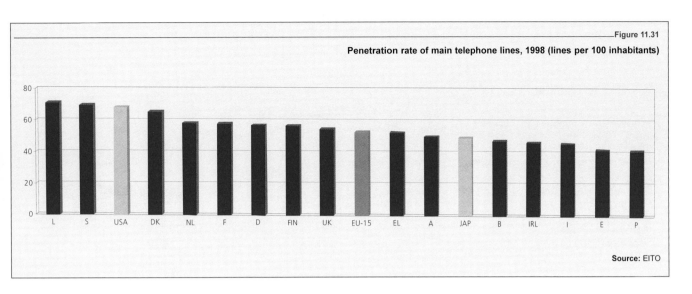

Figure 11.31

Penetration rate of main telephone lines, 1998 (lines per 100 inhabitants)

Source: EITO

STRUCTURE AND PERFORMANCE

The manufacture of television, radio and telephone transmission equipment experienced vigorous growth in the second half of the 1990s. Driven by rapid developments in (mobile) telephone technology, output increased on average by 16.5% per annum in real terms between 1993 and 1998. In 1999, production rose by a further 17.9% (in current prices).

The gross operating rate of the EU's television, radio and telephone transmission equipment industries stood at 14.1% in 1999, up from 8.0% in 1993. As such there was a marked change in relative profit levels, as manufacturing averages rose by just 1.1 percentage points over the same period from 8.3% to 9.4%.

LABOUR AND PRODUCTIVITY

In 1999, there was a net increase of 10.6% in the number of persons employed within the EU's television, radio and telephone transmission equipment industry. During the five-year period from 1993 to 1998, employment grew on average by 2.1% a year.

Employment and labour productivity on the rise
Apparent labour productivity also grew at a rapid pace within the television, radio and telephone transmission equipment industry, up from 47.3 thousand ECU per person employed in 1993 to 80.4 thousand ECU per person employed in 1999 (which was 28.6 thousand ECU higher than the EU manufacturing average). Comparing the apparent labour productivity of the television, radio and telephone transmission equipment industry in the EU with the average for the whole of electrical machinery and electronics sector, there was a difference of 4.8 thousand ECU per person employed in 1993, which widened to 19.5 thousand ECU by 1997[62].

---

(62) EL, I, L and NL, no data available for electrical machinery and electronics.

Table 11.6

Value of telecommunications hardware market in the EU (million EUR)

	1997	1998	1999	2000	2001
Telephone sets	4,855	5,055	5,227	5,384	5,539
Mobile telephone sets	9,795	16,266	25,209	33,551	40,638
Other terminal equipment	2,708	2,945	3,172	3,345	3,531
End-user equipment	17,358	24,266	33,607	42,280	49,708
Transmission	3,470	3,878	3,971	4,175	4,353
Circuit switching equipment	5,929	5,285	5,027	4,733	4,416
PBX & key systems	3,601	3,683	3,781	3,870	3,971
Cellular mobile radio infrastructure	3,679	4,730	5,691	6,863	7,848
Other network equipment	2,459	2,919	3,448	4,133	4,842
Network equipment	19,138	20,494	21,918	23,774	25,429

Source: EITO

INTERNATIONAL TRENDS AND FOREIGN TRADE

In 1997, the EU was the largest producer of television, radio and telephone transmission equipment, with a 40.2% share of total Triad output, just ahead of the USA (39.5%), whilst Japan accounted for 18.5%.

EU reported a trade surplus

EU exports to non-Community countries stood at 21.6 billion EUR in 1999, whilst imports reached 14.6 billion EUR in the same year. The EU's cover ratio was equal to 147.3% in 1999, a considerable increase on the 1989 figure of 94.2%. Nevertheless, this masked the fact that between 1997 and 1999, the EU's cover ratio for television, radio and telephone transmission equipment products declined by 51.3 percentage points.

The USA was the main origin of imports from non-Community countries in 1999, with a 44.0% share of EU imports. China accounted for 7.9% of the total and was followed by South Korea (7.1%), Japan (6.4%) and Israel (5.3%). In 1989 the ranking of import partners had been very different, with Japan accounting for a majority share (63.9%), ahead of the USA (14.4%), with China accounting for just 1.2% of the total. The USA was also the principal destination for extra-EU exports, with over a tenth (11.7%) of the EU's exports in 1999, followed by China (8.9%), Turkey (6.8%), Switzerland (5.8%) and Poland (4.1%).

Figure 11.32

Telecommunications equipment
(NACE Rev. 1 32.2)
Destination of EU exports, 1999 (%)

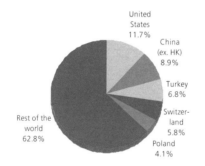

Source: Eurostat (COMEXT)

Figure 11.33

Telecommunications equipment
(NACE Rev. 1 32.2)
Origin of EU imports, 1999 (%)

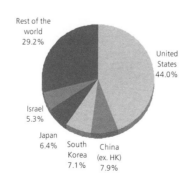

Source: Eurostat (COMEXT)

SUB-CHAPTER 11.8
CONSUMER ELECTRONICS
(NACE Rev. 1 32.3)

The data presented in this sub-chapter covers the manufacture of many well known consumer electronic goods, such as television sets, video recorders, camcorders, radios, tape recorders, telephone answering machines, cassette players, CD players, microphones, loudspeakers, headphones, amplifiers and aerials. Also included are the manufacture of sound apparatus such as intercoms, interpretation apparatus, paging devices and portable sound systems. The publishing and reproduction of pre-recorded audio and video discs and tapes are excluded from the data presented.

The EU's consumer electronics industry produced good to the value of 32.9 billion EUR in 1999, generating 8.5 billion EUR of value added, whilst employing 181.2 thousand persons. In 1997, output from the EU's consumer electronics industry accounted for 9.4% of the total within the electrical machinery and electronics sector[63].

The Netherlands, the largest and
most specialised producer

In 1997, the Netherlands was the largest producer of consumer electronics in the EU, accounting for more than one-fifth (21.6%) of the total, largely as a result of Philips Electronics. Germany also had a share in excess of one-fifth (21.2%) and was followed by the United Kingdom (19.5%). The Netherlands was also the Member State with the highest relative production specialisation ratio in 1997 (545.5%), followed by Austria (194.3%) and Denmark (172.8%).

(63) EL, I and L, no data available.

—————Figure 11.34

Consumer electronics (NACE Rev. 1 32.3)
Production and export specialisation (%)

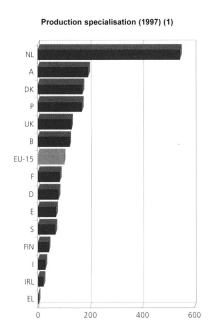

Production specialisation (1997) (1)

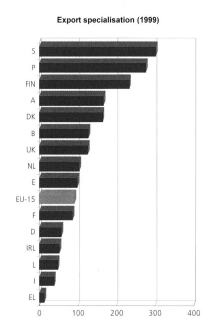

Export specialisation (1999)

(1) EL and I, 1995; L, not available.

Source: Eurostat (SBS, COMEXT)

—————— **Box 11.10**

Sales of video-cassette recorders (VCRs) have been very stable in Europe[64] during the 1990s, fluctuating around 12 million units a year. The latest figures available report sales of VCR's equal to 12.7 million units in 1997, up from 12.5 million a year before. The market for VCRs is quite mature, although there is still room for growth in some EU countries, as markets are not fully saturated. However, it is far more likely that Digital Versatile Disc (DVD) players will increase their share of the market at the expense of VCRs, eventually replacing them (as CDs have replaced vinyl records).

(64) EU-15, Iceland, Norway and Switzerland.

STRUCTURE AND PERFORMANCE

After the recession at the beginning of the 1990s, consumer demand started to increase. As a result, the EU consumer electronics industry grew on average by 7.5% per annum in real terms between 1993 and 1997. In 1998 and 1999, production increased by a further 5.0% and 6.2% in nominal terms.

Low profit rates, high turnover per person employed
The gross operating rate of the EU consumer electronic industry was relatively low at 5.2% in 1999, some 4.2 percentage points below the EU average for the whole of manufacturing.

In 1999, turnover per person employed stood at 234.5 thousand EUR in the consumer electronics industry, almost 50 thousand EUR higher than the EU manufacturing average of 185.3 thousand EUR.

LABOUR AND PRODUCTIVITY

Between 1993 and 1999, the number of persons employed within the EU consumer electronics industry fell by 9.1 thousand, equal to an annual average decline of 0.8%.

Labour productivity below manufacturing averages
Apparent labour productivity within the EU consumer electronics industry reached 46.7 thousand EUR per person employed in 1999, some 5.1 thousand EUR below the manufacturing average of 51.8 thousand EUR.

The simple wage adjusted labour productivity ratio painted a similar picture, 135.8% for consumer electronics in 1999, which was 13.8 percentage points below the manufacturing average of 149.6%.

INTERNATIONAL TRENDS AND FOREIGN TRADE

Japan was the largest producer of consumer electronics within the Triad. In 1997, Japanese output (40.5 billion ECU) accounted for a majority (52.3%) of the consumer electronics produced within the Triad. The EU followed with a 38.1% share, ahead of the USA (9.5%).

Japan dominated production and exports
Japan was also the largest exporter of consumer electronics within the three Triad economies, with total exports valued at 13.3 billion ECU in 1998, some 45.3% of the Triad total. The EU had a 28.3% share and the USA a 26.4% share.

The USA was the largest importer of consumer electronics in 1998, with imports valued at 24.0 billion ECU, whilst the EU imported 14.9 billion ECU of consumer electronics and Japan 4.7 billion ECU.

Japan ran a large trade surplus in 1998, equal to 8.6 billion ECU, with a cover ratio of 283.2%. The USA had the largest trade deficit (16.2 billion ECU in 1998), with a cover ratio of 32.4%. The EU also ran a deficit, equal to 6.6 billion ECU in 1998, which grew to 7.9 billion EUR by 1999. The EU's cover ratio was equal to 52.7% in 1999, an improvement on ten years earlier, when a cover ratio of 28.0% was recorded.

China gaining importance as a trading partner
It was therefore perhaps not surprising to find that Japan was the main origin of EU imports from non-Community countries in 1999, accounting for more than a quarter (27.2%) of the total. China was the second most important import partner of the EU with a 14.3% share, followed by Hungary (9.3%), the USA (9.1%) and Malaysia (7.0%). Ten years before, Japan was much more dominant, with a 47.1% share of the EU's consumer electronics imports. In the same year, China accounted for only 5.7% of the total.

The USA was the main destination for EU exports, accounting for 13.8% of the total exports to non-Community countries in 1999, followed by Hungary (10.1%), China (8.6%, up from 0.4% in 1989), Switzerland (5.3%) and Japan (4.6%).

Table 11.7								
Sales of video-cassette recorders (thousand units)								
	1990	**1991**	**1992**	**1993**	**1994**	**1995**	**1996**	**1997**
B	300	257	258	246	249	268	272	275
DK	235	225	210	195	210	236	315	231
D	3,300	3,325	3,230	3,010	3,090	3,152	3,202	3,330
EL	175	175	189	193	199	201	200	184
E	760	715	670	490	585	495	458	439
F	2,025	1,958	2,025	1,935	1,890	1,845	2,042	1,989
IRL	75	80	85	85	85	72	74	77
I	1,450	1,428	1,350	1,050	1,128	1,196	1,249	1,218
L	9	10	10	10	9	:	:	:
NL	420	575	600	610	630	613	591	604
A	210	275	250	250	260	:	:	:
P	100	125	125	140	140	157	155	162
FIN	185	180	125	102	115	120	127	127
S	270	275	210	275	265	279	287	296
UK	2,150	2,160	2,210	2,400	2,500	2,610	2,835	3,130
EU-15 (1)	**11,984**	**12,100**	**11,918**	**11,355**	**11,752**	**11,934**	**12,507**	**12,738**

(1) Including Iceland, Norway and Switzerland.

Source: IVF

Figure 11.35

Consumer electronics (NACE Rev. 1 32.3)
Destination of EU exports, 1999 (%)

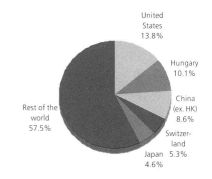

Source: Eurostat (COMEXT)

Figure 11.36

Consumer electronics (NACE Rev. 1 32.3)
Origin of EU imports, 1999 (%)

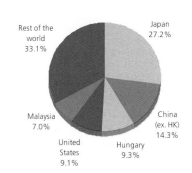

Source: Eurostat (COMEXT)

Table 11.8

Manufacture of domestic appliances n.e.c. (NACE Rev. 1 29.7)

Production related indicators in the EU (1)

	1989	1990	1991	1992	1993	1994	1995	1996	1997	1998	1999
Number of persons employed (thousands)	293.3	302.1	302.9	291.9	276.0	268.5	251.2	:	:	:	:
Production (million ECU)	25,037	26,210	29,467	29,889	28,406	30,235	29,352	:	:	:	:
Domestic producer price index (1995=100)	:	:	:	:	:	:	100.0	101.7	102.9	102.8	102.4
Value added (million ECU)	8,400	9,060	10,406	10,568	10,435	11,015	10,151	:	:	:	:

(1) Technically, data before 01/01/1999 are in ECU and after this date in euro. However, as the conversion rate was 1 ECU =1 EUR, for practical purposes the two terms can be used interchangeably.

Table 11.9

Manufacture of domestic appliances n.e.c. (NACE Rev. 1 29.7)

Trade related indicators in the EU (1)

	1989	1990	1991	1992	1993	1994	1995	1996	1997	1998	1999
Exports (million EUR)	2,482	2,662	2,803	3,205	3,812	4,275	4,993	5,778	6,616	6,343	5,989
Imports (million EUR)	1,966	1,797	2,262	2,365	2,576	2,650	2,703	3,056	3,495	3,806	4,385
Trade balance (million EUR)	516	865	541	840	1,236	1,625	2,290	2,722	3,120	2,537	1,604
Cover ratio (%)	126.2	148.1	123.9	135.5	148.0	161.3	184.7	189.1	189.3	166.7	136.6

(1) Technically, data before 01/01/1999 are in ECU and after this date in euro. However, as the conversion rate was 1 ECU =1 EUR, for practical purposes the two terms can be used interchangeably.

Table 11.10

Manufacture of domestic appliances n.e.c. (NACE Rev. 1 29.7)

Production related indicators, 1997

	B	DK	D	EL (1)	E	F	IRL	I (1)	L	NL	A	P	FIN	S	UK
Number of persons employed (thousands)	1.2	6.4	76.6	1.8	18.6	27.8	3.6	63.4	:	:	5.3	4.3	1.6	7.8	36.0
Production (million ECU)	180	706	10,329	165	2,276	3,685	308	9,828	:	308	539	360	187	1,019	3,871
Value added (million ECU)	56	216	4,088	48	694	1,166	112	2,905	:	95	213	93	70	334	1,322
Gross operating surplus (million ECU)	12.2	32.3	883.8	12.0	254.5	336.8	36.1	1,144.1	:	37.4	48.0	39.8	24.5	33.6	442.8

(1) 1996.

Table 11.11

Manufacture of domestic appliances n.e.c. (NACE Rev. 1 29.7)

Trade related indicators, 1999

	B	DK	D	EL	E	F	IRL	I	L	NL	A	P	FIN	S	UK
Exports (million EUR)	466	404	4,967	107	1,138	2,090	222	5,695	8	896	663	253	171	908	1,120
Imports (million EUR)	1,009	406	3,302	377	1,036	2,700	301	1,108	59	1,347	762	454	327	585	2,562
Trade balance (million EUR)	-544	-2	1,665	-270	102	-611	-79	4,587	-51	-451	-99	-201	-156	322	-1,442
Cover ratio (%)	46.1	99.5	150.4	28.4	109.9	77.4	73.8	514.0	13.6	66.6	87.0	55.7	52.2	155.1	43.7

Table 11.12

Manufacture of domestic appliances n.e.c. (NACE Rev. 1 29.7)

Labour related indicators, 1997

	B	DK (1)	D	EL (2)	E	F	IRL	I (2)	L	NL	A	P	FIN	S	UK
Unit personnel costs (thousand ECU per employee)	36.7	32.7	41.9	19.8	23.3	29.9	21.1	27.9	:	:	31.2	12.3	29.1	38.7	24.6
Social charges as a share of personnel costs (%)	39.4	4.9	25.2	28.4	31.2	39.6	16.3	48.2	:	15.8	30.3	31.4	26.9	46.6	12.6
Apparent labour productivity (thousand ECU/pers. empl.)	46.3	33.7	53.4	26.3	37.3	42.0	31.1	45.8	:	:	40.2	21.4	44.2	43.1	36.8
Wage adjusted labour productivity (%)	126.1	132.7	127.5	133.0	160.3	140.6	147.6	164.0	:	:	128.9	173.9	151.9	111.2	149.6
Personnel costs as a share of total operating costs (%)	26.4	26.5	28.0	18.1	18.1	20.5	28.0	19.4	:	16.2	30.4	15.0	20.6	28.1	23.5

(1) Unit personnel costs and wage adjusted labour productivity, 1996; (2) 1996.

Source: Eurostat (SBS, EBT, COMEXT)

Table 11.13

Manufacture of office machinery and computers (NACE Rev. 1 30)

Production related indicators in the EU (1)

	1989	1990	1991	1992	1993	1994	1995	1996	1997	1998	1999
Number of persons employed (thousands)	304.6	298.6	333.9	307.7	261.6	237.2	235.9	208.3	:	:	:
Production (million ECU)	50,027	51,764	55,433	53,412	47,111	47,681	54,337	54,268	:	:	:
Domestic producer price index (1995=100)	:	191.3	163.4	137.4	124.7	114.4	100.0	90.2	81.6	73.9	67.0
Value added (million ECU)	20,191	20,225	22,111	18,102	14,933	14,934	15,830	14,274	:	:	:

(1) Technically, data before 01/01/1999 are in ECU and after this date in euro. However, as the conversion rate was 1 ECU =1 EUR, for practical purposes the two terms can be used interchangeably.

Table 11.14

Manufacture of office machinery and computers (NACE Rev. 1 30)

Trade related indicators in the EU (1)

	1989	1990	1991	1992	1993	1994	1995	1996	1997	1998	1999
Exports (million EUR)	8,331	8,265	9,059	9,332	11,435	13,412	15,352	16,547	19,587	21,446	24,221
Imports (million EUR)	24,634	24,581	26,998	27,576	28,217	32,323	34,523	37,604	46,028	54,277	59,207
Trade balance (million EUR)	-16,303	-16,315	-17,939	-18,244	-16,782	-18,911	-19,171	-21,057	-26,441	-32,831	-34,986
Cover ratio (%)	33.8	33.6	33.6	33.8	40.5	41.5	44.5	44.0	42.6	39.5	40.9

(1) Technically, data before 01/01/1999 are in ECU and after this date in euro. However, as the conversion rate was 1 ECU =1 EUR, for practical purposes the two terms can be used interchangeably.

Table 11.15

Manufacture of office machinery and computers (NACE Rev. 1 30)

Production related indicators, 1997

	B	DK	D	EL	E	F	IRL	I (1)	L	NL	A	P	FIN	S	UK
Number of persons employed (thousands)	1.3	1.3	58.6	:	7.4	38.2	15.3	18.7	:	:	0.3	0.5	2.5	3.3	57.5
Production (million ECU)	302	122	12,274	:	2,126	11,592	7,810	5,109	:	2,336	32	37	1,185	489	17,653
Value added (million ECU)	84	55	4,082	:	632	2,929	1,310	991	:	438	12	9	147	194	3,577
Gross operating surplus (million ECU)	24.3	10.2	748.4	:	280.4	658.1	923.7	194.3	:	155.1	3.0	3.6	68.0	62.0	1,596.4

(1) 1996.

Table 11.16

Manufacture of office machinery and computers (NACE Rev. 1 30)

Trade related indicators, 1999

	B	DK	D	EL	E	F	IRL	I	L	NL	A	P	FIN	S	UK
Exports (million EUR)	3,058	934	13,070	65	1,483	9,650	15,113	3,194	238	24,912	866	85	843	752	20,129
Imports (million EUR)	4,306	2,409	25,053	658	3,734	14,484	8,231	7,755	457	26,485	2,401	997	1,657	3,165	25,265
Trade balance (million EUR)	-1,247	-1,475	-11,983	-593	-2,251	-4,835	6,882	-4,561	-219	-1,573	-1,535	-912	-814	-2,413	-5,137
Cover ratio (%)	71.0	38.8	52.2	9.8	39.7	66.6	183.6	41.2	52.0	94.1	36.1	8.5	50.9	23.8	79.7

Table 11.17

Manufacture of office machinery and computers (NACE Rev. 1 30)

Labour related indicators, 1997

	B	DK (1)	D	EL	E	F	IRL	I (2)	L	NL	A	P	FIN	S	UK
Unit personnel costs (thousand ECU per employee)	46.3	44.6	56.9	:	41.4	59.4	25.2	43.1	:	:	27.5	11.4	31.3	40.2	34.9
Social charges as a share of personnel costs (%)	32.7	3.5	20.2	:	20.4	43.3	15.9	47.2	:	16.9	29.6	34.2	27.2	45.0	13.1
Apparent labour productivity (thousand ECU/pers. empl.)	64.7	42.8	69.6	:	84.9	76.6	85.4	53.1	:	:	36.6	18.4	59.3	59.1	62.2
Wage adjusted labour productivity (%)	139.9	109.8	122.4	:	205.0	129.0	338.7	123.2	:	:	132.7	161.1	189.3	147.0	178.1
Personnel costs as a share of total operating costs (%)	21.4	38.3	22.6	:	9.6	18.5	5.4	15.6	:	11.4	31.3	15.5	6.7	29.5	9.9

(1) Unit personnel costs and wage adjusted labour productivity, 1996; (2) 1996.

Source: Eurostat (SBS, EBT, COMEXT)

Table 11.18

Manufacture of electric motors, generators and transformers (NACE Rev. 1 31.1)

Production related indicators in the EU (1)

	1989	1990	1991	1992	1993	1994	1995	1996	1997	1998	1999
Number of persons employed (thousands)	:	:	:	:	186.6	183.3	:	:	194.0	201.4	201.8
Production (million ECU)	:	:	:	:	16,844	17,514	:	:	:	:	:
Domestic producer price index (1995=100)	:	:	:	:	:	:	100.0	101.0	101.1	101.2	101.2
Value added (million EUR)	:	:	:	:	6,745	6,714	:	:	9,124	9,817	10,425

(1) Technically, data before 01/01/1999 are in ECU and after this date in euro. However, as the conversion rate was 1 ECU =1 EUR, for practical purposes the two terms can be used interchangeably.

Table 11.19

Manufacture of electric motors, generators and transformers (NACE Rev. 1 31.1)

Trade related indicators in the EU (1)

	1989	1990	1991	1992	1993	1994	1995	1996	1997	1998	1999
Exports (million EUR)	3,351	3,836	3,932	4,194	5,528	6,280	6,783	7,647	8,702	9,501	9,534
Imports (million EUR)	2,326	2,443	2,766	2,854	3,080	3,669	4,330	4,579	6,164	6,997	7,590
Trade balance (million EUR)	1,026	1,393	1,165	1,340	2,448	2,611	2,453	3,068	2,537	2,504	1,944
Cover ratio (%)	144.1	157.1	142.1	147.0	179.5	171.2	156.7	167.0	141.2	135.8	125.6

(1) Technically, data before 01/01/1999 are in ECU and after this date in euro. However, as the conversion rate was 1 ECU =1 EUR, for practical purposes the two terms can be used interchangeably.

Table 11.20

Manufacture of electric motors, generators and transformers (NACE Rev. 1 31.1)

Production related indicators, 1997

	B	DK	D	EL (1)	E	F	IRL	I (1)	L	NL	A	P	FIN	S	UK
Number of persons employed (thousands)	3.8	4.7	59.2	1.2	11.4	23.3	3.6	27.1	:	:	6.5	3.0	6.4	6.9	32.4
Production (million ECU)	619	838	6,499	77	1,603	3,013	526	3,709	:	306	910	198	1,091	926	3,268
Value added (million ECU)	200	198	2,726	30	547	1,060	313	1,166	:	100	295	63	400	370	1,298
Gross operating surplus (million ECU)	42.1	55.5	500.9	6.1	216.9	261.6	215.5	384.3	:	26.9	43.5	15.7	178.3	84.8	412.4

(1) 1996.

Table 11.21

Manufacture of electric motors, generators and transformers (NACE Rev. 1 31.1)

Trade related indicators, 1999

	B	DK	D	EL	E	F	IRL	I	L	NL	A	P	FIN	S	UK
Exports (million EUR)	473	1,219	5,823	18	524	2,669	475	2,069	28	1,002	1,062	229	1,147	798	2,316
Imports (million EUR)	564	552	4,103	156	840	2,374	424	1,461	44	1,190	620	220	317	684	2,494
Trade balance (million EUR)	-91	667	1,719	-138	-316	295	51	608	-15	-188	442	9	831	114	-178
Cover ratio (%)	83.9	220.9	141.9	11.5	62.3	112.4	112.0	141.7	64.6	84.2	171.3	104.3	362.1	116.7	92.9

Table 11.22

Manufacture of electric motors, generators and transformers (NACE Rev. 1 31.1)

Labour related indicators, 1997

	B	DK (1)	D	EL (2)	E	F	IRL	I (2)	L	NL	A	P	FIN	S	UK
Unit personnel costs (thousand ECU per employee)	43.0	33.8	37.6	20.4	28.8	34.3	27.2	29.4	:	:	38.6	17.2	34.3	41.5	27.6
Social charges as a share of personnel costs (%)	38.6	3.9	24.0	30.1	24.8	41.5	17.7	47.9	:	16.1	29.0	27.9	27.4	49.1	13.1
Apparent labour productivity (thousand ECU/pers. empl.)	52.8	41.7	46.1	25.6	48.0	45.5	87.1	43.0	:	:	45.2	21.3	62.4	53.8	40.1
Wage adjusted labour productivity (%)	122.8	109.5	122.5	125.6	166.8	132.8	320.0	146.1	:	:	117.2	124.0	182.2	129.8	145.1
Personnel costs as a share of total operating costs (%)	28.7	17.5	34.8	31.2	22.4	28.8	30.9	23.3	:	21.7	27.9	25.6	23.4	30.4	29.3

(1) Unit personnel costs and wage adjusted labour productivity, 1996; (2) 1996.

Source: Eurostat (SBS, EBT, COMEXT)

Table 11.23

Manufacture of electricity distribution and control apparatus (NACE Rev. 1 31.2)

Production related indicators in the EU (1)

	1989	1990	1991	1992	1993	1994	1995	1996	1997	1998	1999
Number of persons employed (thousands)	:	:	:	:	558.3	529.6	520.7	:	:	:	:
Production (million ECU)	:	:	:	:	54,444	59,076	64,086	:	:	:	:
Domestic producer price index (1995=100)	:	:	:	:	:	:	100.0	101.2	100.9	101.7	102.4
Value added (million ECU)	:	:	:	:	23,474	25,044	26,070	:	:	:	:

(1) Technically, data before 01/01/1999 are in ECU and after this date in euro. However, as the conversion rate was 1 ECU =1 EUR, for practical purposes the two terms can be used interchangeably.

Table 11.24

Manufacture of electricity distribution and control apparatus (NACE Rev. 1 31.2)

Trade related indicators in the EU (1)

	1989	1990	1991	1992	1993	1994	1995	1996	1997	1998	1999
Exports (million EUR)	4,343	4,542	5,088	5,470	6,232	7,319	8,154	9,088	10,466	11,165	11,411
Imports (million EUR)	2,651	2,749	2,840	2,964	3,319	4,022	4,561	4,842	5,764	6,366	6,850
Trade balance (million EUR)	1,692	1,792	2,248	2,505	2,913	3,297	3,593	4,246	4,703	4,799	4,560
Cover ratio (%)	163.8	165.2	179.2	184.5	187.8	182.0	178.8	187.7	181.6	175.4	166.6

(1) Technically, data before 01/01/1999 are in ECU and after this date in euro. However, as the conversion rate was 1 ECU =1 EUR, for practical purposes the two terms can be used interchangeably.

Table 11.25

Manufacture of electricity distribution and control apparatus (NACE Rev. 1 31.2)

Production related indicators, 1997

	B	DK	D	EL (1)	E	F	IRL	I (1)	L	NL	A	P	FIN	S	UK
Number of persons employed (thousands)	9.9	3.2	295.8	1.3	12.8	64.5	3.5	35.9	:	:	7.3	3.0	4.3	5.7	45.3
Production (million ECU)	1,623	320	45,476	71	1,343	8,808	360	4,444	:	936	803	146	523	836	3,675
Value added (million ECU)	596	162	17,295	26	547	3,110	194	1,540	:	360	353	59	205	289	1,644
Gross operating surplus (million ECU)	135.3	65.3	2,808.4	5.2	214.6	620.3	113.0	459.5	:	113.6	84.7	21.0	68.6	49.3	453.4

(1) 1996.

Table 11.26

Manufacture of electricity distribution and control apparatus (NACE Rev. 1 31.2)

Trade related indicators, 1999

	B	DK	D	EL	E	F	IRL	I	L	NL	A	P	FIN	S	UK
Exports (million EUR)	758	241	9,232	32	754	4,418	619	1,660	201	1,047	705	329	269	797	2,440
Imports (million EUR)	1,021	378	4,025	127	1,216	2,388	454	1,966	151	1,149	901	424	417	902	2,506
Trade balance (million EUR)	-263	-138	5,208	-95	-462	2,030	165	-306	50	-101	-195	-95	-147	-105	-66
Cover ratio (%)	74.2	63.6	229.4	25.4	62.0	185.0	136.3	84.4	133.0	91.2	78.3	77.7	64.6	88.3	97.4

Table 11.27

Manufacture of electricity distribution and control apparatus (NACE Rev. 1 31.2)

Labour related indicators, 1997

	B	DK (1)	D	EL (2)	E	F	IRL	I (2)	L	NL	A	P	FIN	S	UK
Unit personnel costs (thousand ECU per employee)	46.9	35.7	49.0	16.1	25.3	38.6	23.0	30.5	:	:	36.9	13.3	31.5	42.0	26.6
Social charges as a share of personnel costs (%)	39.8	3.1	23.5	29.4	28.0	43.7	18.9	42.3	:	18.3	29.3	37.8	24.1	49.5	12.8
Apparent labour productivity (thousand ECU/pers. empl.)	60.4	50.1	58.5	20.1	42.6	48.2	55.1	43.0	:	:	48.4	20.1	47.9	50.7	36.3
Wage adjusted labour productivity (%)	129.0	148.6	119.4	124.9	168.9	124.9	239.4	140.7	:	:	131.4	150.7	152.1	120.6	136.3
Personnel costs as a share of total operating costs (%)	30.9	33.3	30.0	32.9	23.7	30.1	27.7	32.2	:	24.4	33.8	25.2	27.7	28.9	31.5

(1) Unit personnel costs and wage adjusted labour productivity, 1996; (2) 1996.

Source: Eurostat (SBS, EBT, COMEXT)

Table 11.28

Manufacture of insulated wire and cable (NACE Rev. 1 31.3)
Production related indicators in the EU (1)

	1989	1990	1991	1992	1993	1994	1995	1996	1997	1998	1999
Number of persons employed (thousands)	:	:	:	:	108.4	108.2	:	:	:	:	:
Production (million EUR)	:	:	:	:	14,040	15,370	:	:	16,078	15,450	16,079
Domestic producer price index (1995=100)	:	:	:	:	:	:	100.0	97.0	95.0	90.8	86.4
Value added (million EUR)	:	:	:	:	4,525	4,869	:	:	4,708	4,500	4,684

(1) Technically, data before 01/01/1999 are in ECU and after this date in euro. However, as the conversion rate was 1 ECU =1 EUR, for practical purposes the two terms can be used interchangeably.

Table 11.29

Manufacture of insulated wire and cable (NACE Rev. 1 31.3)
Trade related indicators in the EU (1)

	1989	1990	1991	1992	1993	1994	1995	1996	1997	1998	1999
Exports (million EUR)	1,431	1,461	1,489	1,593	1,835	2,053	2,444	2,905	3,413	3,412	3,533
Imports (million EUR)	862	964	1,061	1,065	1,100	1,308	1,688	1,809	2,129	2,377	2,765
Trade balance (million EUR)	570	497	428	529	735	745	756	1,096	1,284	1,036	768
Cover ratio (%)	166.1	151.5	140.4	149.6	166.8	157.0	144.8	160.6	160.3	143.6	127.8

(1) Technically, data before 01/01/1999 are in ECU and after this date in euro. However, as the conversion rate was 1 ECU =1 EUR, for practical purposes the two terms can be used interchangeably.

Table 11.30

Manufacture of insulated wire and cable (NACE Rev. 1 31.3)
Production related indicators, 1997

	B	DK	D	EL (1)	E	F	IRL	I (1)	L	NL	A	P	FIN	S	UK
Number of persons employed (thousands)	1.6	1.7	20.4	1.9	6.5	15.8	3.1	10.5	0.0	:	3.8	6.4	2.2	3.9	23.5
Production (million ECU)	287	233	3,449	272	1,041	3,028	343	2,239	0	626	499	575	390	737	2,704
Value added (million ECU)	84	74	833	39	265	824	113	583	0	217	181	152	112	227	1,000
Gross operating surplus (million ECU)	19.7	21.9	7.8	11.6	102.6	211.5	43.1	274.5	0.0	101.0	16.1	58.1	37.8	70.7	416.0

(1) 1996.

Table 11.31

Manufacture of insulated wire and cable (NACE Rev. 1 31.3)
Trade related indicators, 1999

	B	DK	D	EL	E	F	IRL	I	L	NL	A	P	FIN	S	UK
Exports (million EUR)	394	110	1,642	88	599	1,222	318	859	5	467	361	305	209	660	870
Imports (million EUR)	452	185	1,374	34	364	1,059	216	504	28	477	338	142	183	327	1,019
Trade balance (million EUR)	-58	-75	267	53	235	163	102	355	-23	-11	23	164	26	333	-149
Cover ratio (%)	87.1	59.5	119.4	254.6	164.5	115.4	147.3	170.3	17.4	97.8	106.8	215.4	114.0	201.8	85.4

Table 11.32

Manufacture of insulated wire and cable (NACE Rev. 1 31.3)
Labour related indicators, 1997

	B	DK (1)	D	EL (2)	E	F	IRL	I (2)	L	NL	A	P	FIN	S	UK
Unit personnel costs (thousand ECU per employee)	40.4	37.1	40.4	14.1	24.6	38.8	22.4	29.9	:	:	43.1	14.7	33.7	40.0	25.1
Social charges as a share of personnel costs (%)	38.7	5.7	25.3	27.7	27.5	44.9	15.0	46.0	:	19.2	33.2	38.7	27.9	45.3	11.7
Apparent labour productivity (thousand ECU/pers. empl.)	52.7	44.7	40.8	20.1	40.6	52.2	36.3	55.7	:	:	47.3	23.7	50.8	58.0	42.6
Wage adjusted labour productivity (%)	130.3	172.9	100.9	142.4	165.2	134.5	161.7	186.2	:	:	109.8	161.6	150.7	145.2	169.9
Personnel costs as a share of total operating costs (%)	24.0	24.1	22.6	10.9	16.4	22.7	21.5	15.5	:	18.5	30.3	18.1	19.8	22.2	23.6

(1) Unit personnel costs and wage adjusted labour productivity, 1996; (2) 1996.

Source: Eurostat (SBS, EBT, COMEXT)

Table 11.33

Manufacture of accumulators, primary cells and primary batteries (NACE Rev. 1 31.4)

Production related indicators in the EU (1)

	1989	1990	1991	1992	1993	1994	1995	1996	1997	1998	1999
Number of persons employed (thousands)	:	:	:	:	42.2	41.1	37.0	:	:	:	:
Production (million EUR)	:	:	:	:	4,761	5,053	5,003	5,184	5,441	5,536	5,624
Domestic producer price index (1995=100)	:	:	:	:	:	:	100.0	100.5	99.4	95.2	93.2
Value added (million EUR)	:	:	:	:	1,752	1,784	1,625	1,734	1,921	1,959	1,981

(1) Technically, data before 01/01/1999 are in ECU and after this date in euro. However, as the conversion rate was 1 ECU =1 EUR, for practical purposes the two terms can be used interchangeably.

Table 11.34

Manufacture of accumulators, primary cells and primary batteries (NACE Rev. 1 31.4)

Trade related indicators in the EU (1)

	1989	1990	1991	1992	1993	1994	1995	1996	1997	1998	1999
Exports (million EUR)	425	449	505	523	666	828	1,009	1,035	1,207	1,199	1,187
Imports (million EUR)	597	605	767	786	921	1,238	1,473	1,477	1,922	1,987	2,176
Trade balance (million EUR)	-171	-155	-262	-263	-255	-409	-464	-442	-715	-788	-989
Cover ratio (%)	71.3	74.3	65.8	66.6	72.3	66.9	68.5	70.1	62.8	60.4	54.6

(1) Technically, data before 01/01/1999 are in ECU and after this date in euro. However, as the conversion rate was 1 ECU =1 EUR, for practical purposes the two terms can be used interchangeably.

Table 11.35

Manufacture of accumulators, primary cells and primary batteries (NACE Rev. 1 31.4)

Production related indicators, 1997

	B	DK	D	EL	E	F	IRL	I (1)	L	NL	A	P	FIN	S	UK
Number of persons employed (thousands)	1.9	0.3	8.8	:	2.6	7.6	0.2	4.7	:	:	:	0.9	0.4	1.4	6.6
Production (million ECU)	673	21	1,117	:	385	1,145	14	736	:	32	:	69	71	183	792
Value added (million ECU)	222	5	424	:	127	433	3	202	:	12	:	25	12	77	287
Gross operating surplus (million ECU)	116.7	-3.0	54.3	:	43.0	148.3	0.6	55.2	:	2.5	:	7.9	3.2	25.1	98.1

(1) 1996.

Table 11.36

Manufacture of accumulators, primary cells and primary batteries (NACE Rev. 1 31.4)

Trade related indicators, 1999

	B	DK	D	EL	E	F	IRL	I	L	NL	A	P	FIN	S	UK
Exports (million EUR)	658	49	771	9	213	714	19	303	23	147	106	45	41	218	524
Imports (million EUR)	418	194	981	55	232	752	107	388	10	277	113	57	202	260	691
Trade balance (million EUR)	240	-146	-211	-46	-19	-38	-89	-85	13	-130	-7	-12	-161	-42	-167
Cover ratio (%)	157.4	25.0	78.5	17.1	91.8	95.0	17.6	78.1	232.6	53.1	93.4	79.5	20.4	84.0	75.8

Table 11.37

Manufacture of accumulators, primary cells and primary batteries (NACE Rev. 1 31.4)

Labour related indicators, 1997

	B	DK	D	EL	E	F	IRL	I (1)	L	NL	A	P	FIN	S	UK
Unit personnel costs (thousand ECU per employee)	56.4	:	42.1	:	30.4	37.6	17.2	31.9	:	:	:	19.1	23.6	36.9	28.7
Social charges as a share of personnel costs (%)	38.7	3.8	24.6	:	28.0	42.5	13.0	44.5	:	17.7	:	34.6	17.9	39.8	15.4
Apparent labour productivity (thousand ECU/pers. empl.)	118.9	20.7	48.2	:	48.7	57.1	21.1	43.5	:	:	:	27.9	30.2	54.6	43.6
Wage adjusted labour productivity (%)	210.8	:	114.6	:	159.9	152.0	123.0	136.5	:	:	:	146.3	127.9	147.9	151.8
Personnel costs as a share of total operating costs (%)	18.7	34.9	27.4	:	23.0	27.3	17.8	21.4	:	24.8	:	22.6	14.1	27.1	24.5

(1) 1996.

Source: Eurostat (SBS, EBT, COMEXT)

Table 11.38

Manufacture of lighting equipment and lamps (NACE Rev. 1 31.5)

Production related indicators in the EU (1)

	1989	1990	1991	1992	1993	1994	1995	1996	1997	1998	1999
Number of persons employed (thousands)	132.3	129.7	122.4	117.8	109.2	105.1	108.7	105.4	111.7	119.2	114.6
Production (million EUR)	9,303	9,831	9,867	9,921	9,526	10,039	10,330	10,447	11,479	11,993	12,656
Domestic producer price index (1995=100)	:	:	:	:	:	:	:	:	:	100.6	100.5
Value added (million EUR)	3,823	4,087	4,055	4,026	3,962	4,100	4,165	4,128	4,790	4,786	5,157

(1) Technically, data before 01/01/1999 are in ECU and after this date in euro. However, as the conversion rate was 1 ECU =1 EUR, for practical purposes the two terms can be used interchangeably.

Table 11.39

Manufacture of lighting equipment and lamps (NACE Rev. 1 31.5)

Trade related indicators in the EU (1)

	1989	1990	1991	1992	1993	1994	1995	1996	1997	1998	1999
Exports (million EUR)	1,205	1,191	1,208	1,478	1,729	1,987	2,143	2,349	2,565	2,534	2,583
Imports (million EUR)	783	792	949	1,078	1,314	1,506	1,660	1,777	2,096	2,445	2,880
Trade balance (million EUR)	422	399	259	400	415	482	483	572	469	89	-298
Cover ratio (%)	153.9	150.4	127.3	137.1	131.6	132.0	129.1	132.2	122.4	103.7	89.7

(1) Technically, data before 01/01/1999 are in ECU and after this date in euro. However, as the conversion rate was 1 ECU =1 EUR, for practical purposes the two terms can be used interchangeably.

Table 11.40

Manufacture of lighting equipment and lamps (NACE Rev. 1 31.5)

Production related indicators, 1997

	B	DK	D	EL (1)	E	F	IRL	I (1)	L	NL	A	P	FIN	S	UK
Number of persons employed (thousands)	5.6	1.7	35.7	0.4	11.0	11.3	0.4	10.8	0.0	:	2.7	3.3	1.5	2.5	23.2
Production (million ECU)	773	201	3,840	21	920	1,379	26	1,547	0	178	302	116	153	259	1,865
Value added (million ECU)	284	75	1,820	8	288	481	11	491	0	63	126	42	64	110	795
Gross operating surplus (million ECU)	78.2	23.5	504.5	3.6	85.6	116.8	4.0	191.2	0.0	16.7	24.5	12.4	24.6	28.8	242.8

(1) 1996.

Table 11.41

Manufacture of lighting equipment and lamps (NACE Rev. 1 31.5)

Trade related indicators, 1999

	B	DK	D	EL	E	F	IRL	I	L	NL	A	P	FIN	S	UK
Exports (million EUR)	800	217	1,669	13	383	1,019	22	1,336	3	693	349	38	89	239	669
Imports (million EUR)	544	254	1,615	84	422	1,140	111	570	33	699	407	132	142	354	1,090
Trade balance (million EUR)	255	-37	54	-71	-39	-121	-89	766	-30	-6	-58	-94	-53	-115	-421
Cover ratio (%)	146.9	85.5	103.3	15.7	90.7	89.4	19.4	234.3	8.2	99.2	85.8	28.7	62.9	67.6	61.4

Table 11.42

Manufacture of lighting equipment and lamps (NACE Rev. 1 31.5)

Labour related indicators, 1997

	B	DK (1)	D	EL (2)	E	F	IRL	I (2)	L	NL	A	P	FIN	S	UK
Unit personnel costs (thousand ECU per employee)	37.1	33.7	36.9	13.1	19.4	32.3	16.8	28.6	:	:	38.0	9.3	27.5	32.2	24.2
Social charges as a share of personnel costs (%)	38.5	4.4	23.1	29.7	27.4	42.5	11.7	48.7	:	15.1	31.3	30.7	26.8	44.5	12.5
Apparent labour productivity (thousand ECU/pers. empl.)	50.6	44.1	51.0	22.6	26.2	42.7	26.4	45.5	:	:	47.2	12.6	43.4	43.6	34.4
Wage adjusted labour productivity (%)	136.2	116.7	138.2	172.9	135.1	132.1	156.7	159.3	:	:	123.9	135.6	157.5	135.4	142.3
Personnel costs as a share of total operating costs (%)	29.4	28.0	33.9	26.4	22.1	21.6	29.1	20.1	:	27.5	30.5	27.2	26.3	33.1	29.9

(1) Unit personnel costs and wage adjusted labour productivity, 1996; (2) 1996.

Source: Eurostat (SBS, EBT, COMEXT)

Table 11.43

Manufacture of electronic valves and tubes and other electronic components (NACE Rev. 1 32.1)

Production related indicators in the EU (1)

	1989	1990	1991	1992	1993	1994	1995	1996	1997	1998	1999
Number of persons employed (thousands)	:	:	:	:	173.0	178.8	:	:	226.3	226.2	241.1
Production (million EUR)	:	:	:	:	15,342	18,638	:	:	30,300	31,461	38,747
Domestic producer price index (1995=100)	:	:	:	:	:	:	100.0	95.4	89.1	:	:
Value added (million EUR)	:	:	:	:	6,618	7,781	:	:	11,536	12,337	14,639

(1) Technically, data before 01/01/1999 are in ECU and after this date in euro. However, as the conversion rate was 1 ECU =1 EUR, for practical purposes the two terms can be used interchangeably.

Table 11.44

Manufacture of electronic valves and tubes and other electronic components (NACE Rev. 1 32.1)

Trade related indicators in the EU (1)

	1989	1990	1991	1992	1993	1994	1995	1996	1997	1998	1999
Exports (million EUR)	4,069	4,082	4,813	4,991	6,680	8,486	10,523	11,903	14,702	16,004	18,442
Imports (million EUR)	8,204	7,915	8,878	9,172	11,847	15,702	18,589	19,352	22,259	23,678	25,945
Trade balance (million EUR)	-4,135	-3,834	-4,065	-4,181	-5,166	-7,216	-8,067	-7,450	-7,557	-7,674	-7,502
Cover ratio (%)	49.6	51.6	54.2	54.4	56.4	54.0	56.6	61.5	66.1	67.6	71.1

(1) Technically, data before 01/01/1999 are in ECU and after this date in euro. However, as the conversion rate was 1 ECU =1 EUR, for practical purposes the two terms can be used interchangeably.

Table 11.45

Manufacture of electronic valves and tubes and other electronic components (NACE Rev. 1 32.1)

Production related indicators, 1997

	B	DK	D	EL (1)	E	F	IRL	I (1)	L	NL	A	P	FIN	S	UK
Number of persons employed (thousands)	3.7	3.6	41.2	0.2	11.5	45.0	8.9	27.2	0.0	:	7.6	7.3	4.1	3.7	59.3
Production (million ECU)	538	279	5,187	12	1,119	6,753	2,397	3,874	0	260	810	826	392	387	7,307
Value added (million ECU)	229	107	1,997	4	465	2,224	1,069	1,323	0	92	395	199	165	156	3,217
Gross operating surplus (million ECU)	80.8	-1.7	433.2	1.0	203.4	622.8	819.1	506.5	0.0	19.0	149.1	56.6	53.5	36.5	1,396.3

(1) 1996.

Table 11.46

Manufacture of electronic valves and tubes and other electronic components (NACE Rev. 1 32.1)

Trade related indicators, 1999

	B	DK	D	EL	E	F	IRL	I	L	NL	A	P	FIN	S	UK
Exports (million EUR)	1,534	265	9,934	8	630	7,374	2,954	2,412	417	7,588	1,669	468	394	676	7,804
Imports (million EUR)	1,396	503	11,461	111	1,183	7,115	2,763	3,416	297	5,094	1,397	662	1,478	2,021	9,183
Trade balance (million EUR)	138	-238	-1,527	-103	-554	259	190	-1,004	119	2,494	273	-194	-1,084	-1,345	-1,378
Cover ratio (%)	109.9	52.6	86.7	7.3	53.2	103.6	106.9	70.6	140.2	149.0	119.5	70.7	26.7	33.4	85.0

Table 11.47

Manufacture of electronic valves and tubes and other electronic components (NACE Rev. 1 32.1)

Labour related indicators, 1997

	B	DK (1)	D	EL (2)	E	F	IRL	I (2)	L	NL	A	P	FIN	S	UK
Unit personnel costs (thousand ECU per employee)	40.4	35.5	37.9	14.3	23.5	35.6	28.0	30.4	:	:	32.5	19.6	27.9	32.2	30.9
Social charges as a share of personnel costs (%)	42.3	4.8	21.8	29.2	27.1	41.5	19.8	46.8	:	13.5	32.9	34.8	26.9	41.5	13.3
Apparent labour productivity (thousand ECU/pers. empl.)	62.2	30.1	48.5	18.7	40.4	49.4	119.8	48.7	:	:	52.1	27.1	40.2	42.0	54.3
Wage adjusted labour productivity (%)	154.0	97.0	127.8	131.1	171.7	138.9	428.1	160.4	:	:	160.6	138.7	144.1	130.5	175.9
Personnel costs as a share of total operating costs (%)	32.4	35.5	31.0	27.4	26.6	22.1	15.8	23.3	:	29.4	29.9	17.4	32.6	33.1	23.7

(1) Unit personnel costs and wage adjusted labour productivity, 1996; (2) 1996.

Source: Eurostat (SBS, EBT, COMEXT)

Table 11.48

Manufacture of television and radio transmitters and apparatus for line telephony and line telegraphy (NACE Rev. 1 32.2)

Production related indicators in the EU (1)

	1989	1990	1991	1992	1993	1994	1995	1996	1997	1998	1999
Number of persons employed (thousands)	:	:	:	:	307.0	304.5	:	:	323.8	340.7	376.9
Production (million EUR)	:	:	:	:	37,251	41,379	:	:	67,237	74,897	88,295
Domestic producer price index (1995=100)	:	:	:	:	:	:	100.0	97.9	97.7	95.7	93.0
Value added (million EUR)	:	:	:	:	14,535	15,192	:	:	23,918	26,819	30,308

(1) Technically, data before 01/01/1999 are in ECU and after this date in euro. However, as the conversion rate was 1 ECU =1 EUR, for practical purposes the two terms can be used interchangeably.

Table 11.49

Manufacture of television and radio transmitters and apparatus for line telephony and line telegraphy (NACE Rev. 1 32.2)

Trade related indicators in the EU (1)

	1989	1990	1991	1992	1993	1994	1995	1996	1997	1998	1999
Exports (million EUR)	3,870	4,066	4,779	5,398	6,535	8,719	10,573	13,094	16,547	18,648	21,558
Imports (million EUR)	4,110	4,287	5,425	5,389	5,232	5,897	6,744	8,177	8,334	10,947	14,637
Trade balance (million EUR)	-240	-222	-645	9	1,303	2,822	3,829	4,917	8,214	7,700	6,921
Cover ratio (%)	94.2	94.8	88.1	100.2	124.9	147.9	156.8	160.1	198.6	170.3	147.3

(1) Technically, data before 01/01/1999 are in ECU and after this date in euro. However, as the conversion rate was 1 ECU =1 EUR, for practical purposes the two terms can be used interchangeably.

Table 11.50

Manufacture of television and radio transmitters and apparatus for line telephony and line telegraphy (NACE Rev. 1 32.2)

Production related indicators, 1997

	B	DK	D	EL (1)	E	F	IRL	I (1)	L	NL	A	P	FIN	S	UK
Number of persons employed (thousands)	7.8	3.0	54.2	2.1	11.6	66.2	3.6	61.6	0.0	:	18.0	2.3	21.9	33.1	37.6
Production (million ECU)	1,199	521	9,079	242	1,893	12,983	868	8,720	0	619	2,877	199	6,220	12,143	8,863
Value added (million ECU)	634	147	3,384	70	612	3,400	262	2,928	0	261	1,135	74	2,198	5,119	2,803
Gross operating surplus (million ECU)	154.7	44.7	358.0	25.5	145.5	142.0	149.9	778.2	0.0	105.2	92.7	26.2	1,506.7	3,526.2	1,478.7

(1) 1996.

Table 11.51

Manufacture of television and radio transmitters and apparatus for line telephony and line telegraphy (NACE Rev. 1 32.2)

Trade related indicators, 1999

	B	DK	D	EL	E	F	IRL	I	L	NL	A	P	FIN	S	UK
Exports (million EUR)	1,189	1,151	9,308	115	1,021	6,841	3,053	2,320	148	2,759	360	82	5,611	8,860	9,856
Imports (million EUR)	1,654	1,091	5,445	651	3,076	3,842	1,435	4,180	284	4,003	1,464	649	626	1,685	8,893
Trade balance (million EUR)	-464	59	3,862	-536	-2,056	2,999	1,618	-1,860	-136	-1,244	-1,103	-567	4,985	7,175	962
Cover ratio (%)	71.9	105.4	170.9	17.7	33.2	178.1	212.8	55.5	52.0	68.9	24.6	12.7	895.9	525.9	110.8

Table 11.52

Manufacture of television and radio transmitters and apparatus for line telephony and line telegraphy (NACE Rev. 1 32.2)

Labour related indicators, 1997

	B	DK (1)	D	EL (2)	E	F	IRL	I (2)	L	NL	A	P	FIN	S	UK
Unit personnel costs (thousand ECU per employee)	61.5	41.7	55.9	21.3	33.0	49.2	31.2	35.1	:	:	57.9	21.8	31.6	48.2	35.5
Social charges as a share of personnel costs (%)	44.8	5.1	30.3	27.4	24.4	43.8	17.8	42.7	:	19.0	28.9	29.2	26.8	56.3	13.1
Apparent labour productivity (thousand ECU/pers. empl.)	81.3	49.6	62.5	33.7	52.6	51.4	72.7	47.6	:	:	63.0	33.0	100.5	154.8	74.6
Wage adjusted labour productivity (%)	132.2	115.3	111.8	157.9	159.4	104.4	233.2	135.3	:	:	108.9	151.0	317.6	321.4	210.0
Personnel costs as a share of total operating costs (%)	43.8	20.5	30.0	25.9	22.0	25.8	14.1	26.4	:	25.6	23.5	20.2	14.3	18.5	15.9

(1) Unit personnel costs and wage adjusted labour productivity, 1996; (2) 1996.

Source: Eurostat (SBS, EBT, COMEXT)

Table 11.53

Manufacture of television and radio receivers, sound or video recording or reproducing apparatus and associated goods (NACE Rev. 1 32.3)

Production related indicators in the EU (1)

	1989	1990	1991	1992	1993	1994	1995	1996	1997	1998	1999
Number of persons employed (thousands)	:	:	:	:	190.3	188.3	178.6	:	173.5	173.0	181.2
Production (million EUR)	:	:	:	:	22,823	24,994	27,472	:	29,471	30,954	32,887
Domestic producer price index (1995=100)	:	:	:	:	:	:	100.1	100.8	98.8	97.6	95.7
Value added (million EUR)	:	:	:	:	7,573	7,896	8,089	:	8,197	8,421	8,458

(1) Technically, data before 01/01/1999 are in ECU and after this date in euro. However, as the conversion rate was 1 ECU =1 EUR, for practical purposes the two terms can be used interchangeably.

Table 11.54

Manufacture of television and radio receivers, sound or video recording or reproducing apparatus and associated goods (NACE Rev. 1 32.3)

Trade related indicators in the EU (1)

	1989	1990	1991	1992	1993	1994	1995	1996	1997	1998	1999
Exports (million EUR)	2,885	3,184	3,058	3,174	3,732	4,541	5,356	6,557	8,610	8,308	8,759
Imports (million EUR)	10,318	10,955	11,684	10,471	10,460	10,812	10,272	11,112	13,599	14,916	16,615
Trade balance (million EUR)	-7,433	-7,770	-8,626	-7,298	-6,728	-6,271	-4,917	-4,554	-4,989	-6,608	-7,856
Cover ratio (%)	28.0	29.1	26.2	30.3	35.7	42.0	52.1	59.0	63.3	55.7	52.7

(1) Technically, data before 01/01/1999 are in ECU and after this date in euro. However, as the conversion rate was 1 ECU =1 EUR, for practical purposes the two terms can be used interchangeably.

Table 11.55

Manufacture of television and radio receivers, sound or video recording or reproducing apparatus and associated goods (NACE Rev. 1 32.3)

Production related indicators, 1997

	B	DK	D	EL (1)	E	F	IRL	I (1)	L	NL	A	P	FIN	S	UK
Number of persons employed (thousands)	5.7	6.4	42.1	0.1	6.5	18.7	1.0	6.8	:	:	4.6	7.8	1.4	2.8	34.1
Production (million ECU)	1,428	708	6,245	3	1,482	4,027	90	1,131	:	6,362	1,097	795	231	608	5,754
Value added (million ECU)	455	269	1,989	1	255	651	25	272	:	2,112	246	201	61	165	1,437
Gross operating surplus (million ECU)	224.3	92.2	99.1	0.1	93.2	81.3	6.5	95.2	:	663.4	52.1	73.2	19.1	56.5	573.1

(1) 1996.

Table 11.56

Manufacture of television and radio receivers, sound or video recording or reproducing apparatus and associated goods (NACE Rev. 1 32.3)

Trade related indicators, 1999

	B	DK	D	EL	E	F	IRL	I	L	NL	A	P	FIN	S	UK
Exports (million EUR)	2,649	907	3,516	13	1,208	3,366	416	1,079	48	2,277	1,331	837	1,237	3,048	3,934
Imports (million EUR)	1,879	958	6,743	321	2,158	4,758	362	2,499	100	2,849	1,176	628	826	1,956	5,477
Trade balance (million EUR)	770	-50	-3,227	-309	-950	-1,392	54	-1,420	-52	-572	156	209	411	1,092	-1,543
Cover ratio (%)	141.0	94.7	52.1	4.0	56.0	70.7	114.9	43.2	47.9	79.9	113.2	133.3	149.8	155.8	71.8

Table 11.57

Manufacture of television and radio receivers, sound or video recording or reproducing apparatus and associated goods (NACE Rev. 1 32.3)

Labour related indicators, 1997

	B	DK (1)	D	EL (2)	E	F	IRL	I (2)	L	NL	A	P	FIN	S	UK
Unit personnel costs (thousand ECU per employee)	40.5	31.6	44.9	15.3	24.6	30.5	18.5	26.1	:	:	42.3	16.5	28.9	38.5	25.7
Social charges as a share of personnel costs (%)	39.6	4.2	26.1	25.0	27.7	41.4	14.0	48.5	:	8.4	30.3	45.6	25.7	43.3	10.1
Apparent labour productivity (thousand ECU/pers. empl.)	79.8	42.0	47.2	16.7	39.4	34.8	24.9	39.7	:	:	53.6	25.8	42.7	58.6	42.2
Wage adjusted labour productivity (%)	196.9	160.4	105.2	109.1	160.0	114.3	134.6	152.0	:	:	126.8	156.6	147.8	152.0	164.1
Personnel costs as a share of total operating costs (%)	19.2	27.4	21.1	44.0	9.1	10.6	20.8	16.8	:	15.0	15.8	15.6	17.5	19.4	15.5

(1) Unit personnel costs and wage adjusted labour productivity, 1996; (2) 1996.

Source: Eurostat (SBS, EBT, COMEXT)

Instrument engineering (NACE Rev. 1 33)

The instrument engineering industry is defined within the NACE Rev. 1 classification as the manufacture of medical, precision and optical instruments, as well as the manufacture of watches and clocks.

The EU instrument engineering industry had its output valued at 67.8 billion ECU in 1996, equating to 1.9% of the EU manufacturing total. In the same year, value added and employment accounted for a greater share of the manufacturing total, both 2.7%; equivalent to 29.1 billion ECU and 621.4 thousand persons employed.

The well-being of this sector is strongly linked to the level of demand from downstream industries and consumer confidence. The instrument engineering industry is characterised on the one hand by relatively mature product markets, whilst on the other there are certain niches where new technological improvements or new fashions lead to increased opportunities for growth.

Measuring, precision and process control equipment was the principal sub-activity

The largest sub-chapter within this chapter on instrument engineering was the manufacture of measuring, precision and process control equipment (NACE Rev. 1 33.2 and 33.3). Output within these two Groups totalled nearly 39.6 billion ECU[1], or 58.4% of the instrument engineering total in 1996, with value added representing a slightly lower proportion, at around 55.9%, or 16.3 billion ECU[2]. The measuring, precision and process control equipment workforce was equal to 325.3 thousand persons[3] or around 52.4% of the instrument engineering total.

(1) L, no data available for NACE Rev. 1 33.2.
(2) L, no data available for NACE Rev. 1 33.2.
(3) L and NL, no data available for NACE Rev. 1 33.2; DK, L, NL and A, no data available for NACE Rev. 1 33.3.

Figure 12.1

Instrument engineering (NACE Rev. 1 33)
Share of total manufacturing value added
in the EU, 1995 (%)

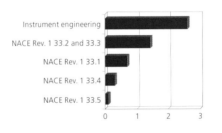

Source: Eurostat (SBS)

... followed by medical and surgical equipment manufacture

The medical/surgical equipment and orthopaedic appliances industry (NACE Rev. 1 33.1) accounted for the majority of the remaining production in 1996, valued at 18.0 billion ECU or a 26.5% share of the instrument engineering total.

Production in the optical and photographic instruments industry (NACE Rev. 1 33.4) amounted to around 8.0 billion ECU[4] or 11.8% of the instrument engineering total, with clocks and watches (NACE Rev. 1 33.5) production valued at 1.4 billion ECU (or 2.1%).

(4) DK, EL, IRL, L, A and S, no data available.

The activities covered in this chapter (in terms of NACE Rev. 1) include:

33:     manufacture of medical, precision and optical instruments, watches and clocks;
33.1: manufacture of medical and surgical equipment and orthopaedic appliances;
33.2: manufacture of instruments and appliances for measuring, checking, testing, navigating and other purposes, except industrial process control equipment;
33.3: manufacture of industrial process control equipment;
33.4: manufacture of optical instruments and photographic equipment;
33.5: manufacture of watches and clocks.

Table 12.1

Instrument engineering (NACE Rev. 1 33)

Breakdown of turnover and employment by employment size class, 1997 (%)

	Micro (0-9)		Small (10-49)		Medium (50-249)		Large (250+)	
	Turnover (1)	Employment (2)	Turnover (1)	Employment (2)	Turnover (3)	Employment (4)	Turnover (5)	Employment (6)
EU-15	11.3	18.7	18.6	20.2	23.3	22.1	46.8	39.1
B	15.2	33.1	19.8	25.0	20.8	18.2	44.2	23.8
DK	:	:	:	:	36.8	31.8	:	:
D	9.5	14.8	20.6	24.2	17.9	15.7	51.9	45.3
EL	:	:	:	:	:	:	:	:
E	20.3	36.9	25.5	24.4	28.6	22.5	25.7	16.2
F	10.7	19.9	15.6	20.1	20.9	22.9	52.8	37.1
IRL	:	:	:	:	:	:	:	:
I	20.7	39.8	27.8	23.4	25.5	17.3	26.0	19.5
L	:	:	:	:	:	:	:	:
NL	:	12.9	:	22.9	:	22.8	:	41.4
A	12.0	21.1	19.2	21.9	37.7	33.0	28.3	22.6
P	13.2	22.4	17.8	19.0	35.8	22.0	33.3	36.6
FIN	10.8	16.1	11.3	12.7	17.7	16.9	60.2	54.3
S	7.3	15.9	14.5	15.1	14.9	16.4	63.3	52.6
UK	12.0	13.2	14.8	14.4	26.3	23.9	46.8	48.5

(1) EU-15, E, F, I, P and S, 1996.
(2) EU-15, F, I, NL, P and S, 1996.
(3) EU-15, DK, E, F, I, A, P and S, 1996.
(4) EU-15, DK, F, I, NL, A, P and S, 1996.
(5) EU-15, E, F, I, A, P and S, 1996.
(6) EU-15, F, I, NL, A, P and S, 1996.

Source: Eurostat (SME)

Above average proportion of very small enterprises
Nearly 85% of the enterprises in the EU instrument engineering industry had less than ten employees (66.8 thousand). However, enterprises with over 250 and more employees accounted for the largest share of the workforce (39.1%), with the other size classes (very small, small and medium) each employing around 20% of the total.

STRUCTURE AND PERFORMANCE

Production in current prices rose from 47.5 billion ECU in 1986 to 67.8 billion ECU ten years later, a 42.7% net increase in nominal terms. The majority of the increase in output came prior to 1991, as production value had reached 60.3 billion ECU by this date. The percentage increase in value added at factor cost in current prices over the same period was lower at 30.5%.

Production declined significantly in real terms during the recession, down 3.0% in 1992 and 6.2% in 1993. Since then, real growth in output was strong, in particular in 1996 when a 7.6% increase was reported (which was 3.7 points higher than the EU manufacturing average for that year). The annual average growth rate of production in constant prices over the five years to 1996 was 0.6%. Value added followed a similar trend to that of production during the 1990s, but a real decline of 2.5% in 1995 contributed to a lower five-year annual average (0.2%).

Profitability and performance measures converge towards manufacturing averages
The gross operating rate (a measure of profitability) of the EU's instrument engineering industry was consistently lower than the manufacturing average during the first half of the 1990s, but by 1996 the profit rate had increased to 10.3% (above the manufacturing average of 8.6%). The ratio of the gross operating surplus divided by value added for the EU instrument engineering industry rose from 19.6% in 1986 to 25.5% ten years later, leading to the difference with the manufacturing average narrowing from 13.3 to 8.2 percentage points.

Figure 12.2

Instrument engineering (NACE Rev. 1 33)

EU production and value-added in constant prices and employment compared to total manufacturing (1990=100)

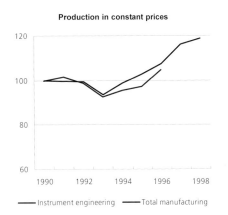

Production in constant prices

— Instrument engineering — Total manufacturing

Value added in constant prices

— Instrument engineering — Total manufacturing

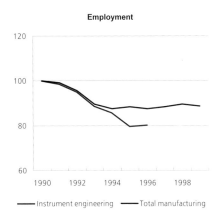

Employment

— Instrument engineering — Total manufacturing

Source: Eurostat (SBS)

LABOUR AND PRODUCTIVITY

The net decline of 22.3% in the EU's instrument engineering workforce over the period 1986 to 1996 was significantly higher than the corresponding rate of decline for the whole of EU manufacturing (10.0%). There were 621.4 thousand persons employed in 1996 within the EU, which was 178 thousand fewer than ten years before. As a result, the relative share of the instrument engineering workforce in the manufacturing total fell from 3.1% to 2.7%.

Most job losses occurred in the
first five years of the 1990s
Employment was hardest hit during the economic downturn that occurred during the first half of the 1990s, although job losses continued even after this date. Net losses of 3.5% and 6.8% were recorded in 1992 and 1993, however, the highest year on year reduction was registered in 1995 (down 7.0%). In the five years to 1995, the workforce fell from 764.2 thousand persons to 617.5 thousand, with an annual average rate of decline equal to 4.4%. This figure was 2.0 percentage points above the EU manufacturing average. In 1996 there was a year of consolidation, as the number of persons employed within the EU's instrument engineering industry rose by 0.6%.

EU workforce was highly educated
In 1997, 27.2% of the instrument engineering workforce in the EU had gained a higher education qualification, the second highest figure of all manufacturing activities behind the manufacture of office machinery and computers (NACE Rev. 1 30). This figure was 10.9 percentage points higher than the EU manufacturing average. Indeed, the proportion with an upper secondary education qualification was also high at 48.8%, 4.9 percentage points above the EU manufacturing average.

The proportion of men working in this industry was 65.9% in 1998, a figure broadly unchanged since 1995, which compared to 71.2% for manufacturing as a whole. For other characteristics of the EU's instrument engineering workforce, there was a similar profile to that of total manufacturing. The proportion of employees was equal to 90.3% in 1997, 1.9 points lower than the manufacturing average, whilst 91.7% worked on a full time basis (just 1.0 point lower than the manufacturing average) and 90.7% had a permanent contract (1.0 point higher than the manufacturing average).

Table 12.2

Instrument engineering (NACE Rev. 1 33)

Composition of the labour force, 1999 (%)

	Women (1)	Part-time (2)	Highly-educated (3)
EU-15	34.1	8.1	27.2
B	42.0	:	44.7
DK	32.2	:	30.7
D	39.8	12.5	30.2
EL	:	:	:
E	23.8	:	46.8
F	31.6	7.2	29.2
IRL	57.1	:	27.3
I	31.4	7.1	10.0
L	:	:	:
NL	30.6	17.6	33.5
A	29.6	7.1	9.3
P	37.1	:	:
FIN	33.0	:	60.8
S	29.8	:	:
UK	30.6	9.2	33.9

(1) EU-15 and B, 1998; P and S, 1996.
(2) EU-15, 1998.
(3) DK, A and FIN, 1998; EU-15 and IRL, 1997.

Source: Eurostat (LFS)

Figure 12.3

Instrument engineering (NACE Rev. 1 33)

Apparent labour productivity and unit personnel costs, 1997 (thousand ECU)

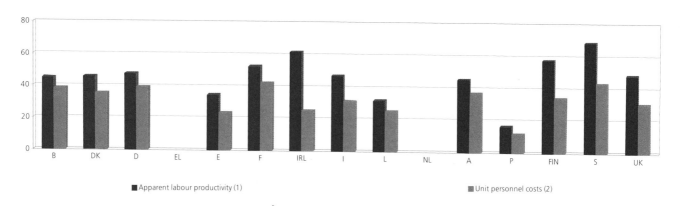

■ Apparent labour productivity (1)   ■ Unit personnel costs (2)

(1) I, 1996; EL and NL, not available.
(2) DK and I, 1996; EL and NL, not available.

Source: Eurostat (SBS)

Productivity grew faster than manufacturing averages in the mid-1990s

Both apparent labour productivity and simple wage adjusted productivity increased at somewhat faster rate within the instrument engineering industry when compared to equivalent rates for the whole of manufacturing between 1995 and 1996. Over a longer timeframe (1986 to 1996) apparent labour productivity in the EU's instrument engineering industry rose steadily each year, from 27.9 thousand ECU per person employed in 1986 to 37.6 thousand ECU by 1993, remaining around 2.0 to 3.0 thousand ECU below the EU manufacturing average. Then this ratio rose quickly to 44.0 thousand ECU per person employed in 1995 and a year later in 1997 apparent labour productivity in the instrument engineering industry was 0.3 thousand ECU per person employed above the EU manufacturing average, at 46.8 thousand ECU. Likewise, simple wage adjusted labour productivity remained around 20 points below the manufacturing average between 1986 and 1994, with the figure for the latter date being 126.0%. Over the following two years, the ratio rose to 134.3%, and the difference to the manufacturing average narrowed to 9.9 percentage points.

INTERNATIONAL TRENDS AND FOREIGN TRADE

Output in current prices increased by 42.7% in the EU between 1986 and 1996, leading to a gradual increase in the share of Triad output from 29.0% in 1987 to 31.8% over this period. A similar nominal rate of increase was recorded in the USA between 1987 and 1997 resulting in total production of 117.8 billion ECU. The 24.6% increase in current prices in Japan over the ten years to 1997 gave production of 38.3 billion ECU and a declining share of Triad output (18.9% in 1996).

Large scale job losses in the Triad

Triad employment in the instrument engineering industry fell by 19.5% between 1986 and 1996, with the EU (-22.3%) and Japan (-23.8%) reporting larger than average decreases whilst the USA (-15.6%) fared slightly better. Average annual rates of change in employment during the five years between 1990 and 1995 showed the EU and Japan losing jobs at a similar rate (4.4% and 4.3% per annum respectively), whilst the figure for the USA was somewhat lower at -3.2% per annum.

Mixed picture for the EU trade balance

The EU ran a trade deficit for the first five years of the 1989 to 1999 period, but subsequently there was a surplus, up until 1999. The trade deficit was at its largest (2.1 billion ECU) in 1991, but then exports began to grow substantially each year, up from 14.8 billion ECU in 1991 to 30.5 billion EUR in 1999. As import growth was more subdued, the first surplus was reported in 1995 (446.8 million ECU) and this rose to 1.9 billion ECU by 1997. However, imports began to rise again from this date and by 1999 a deficit of 430.7 million EUR emerged.

... whilst the other Triad economies increased or maintained their surpluses

The trade surplus in the USA remained around 3 billion ECU between 1989 and 1995, but it then rose strongly to between 4.3 billion ECU and 6.3 billion ECU in the subsequent three years. The Japanese surplus over the same period varied between 6.8 billion ECU (in 1990 and 1998) and 8.8 billion ECU (in 1995).

─────────Figure 12.4

Instrument engineering (NACE Rev. 1 33)
International comparison of production, value added and employment

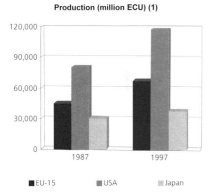

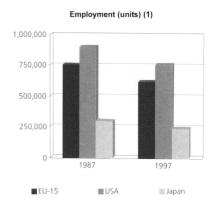

(1) EU-15, 1996.

Source: Eurostat (SBS)

USA dominated trade with the EU

The USA's trade with the EU in this industry more than doubled in nominal terms between 1989 and 1999, sustaining its position as the EU's most important trading partner. Imports into the EU from the USA totalled 13.3 billion EUR in 1999 (43.2% of total EU imports), whilst EU exports to the USA amounted to 9.7 billion EUR (32.1% of total EU exports). These figures were significantly higher than those for the next largest trading nations, where the respective totals for imports to and exports from the EU in 1999 were 4.7 billion EUR and 2.2 billion EUR for Switzerland and 4.2 billion EUR and 2.3 billion EUR for Japan.

─────────Figure 12.5

Instrument engineering (NACE Rev. 1 33)
Destination of EU exports, 1999 (%)

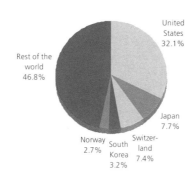

Source: Eurostat (COMEXT)

─────────Figure 12.6

Instrument engineering (NACE Rev. 1 33)
Origin of EU imports, 1999 (%)

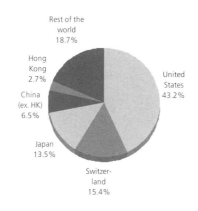

Source: Eurostat (COMEXT)

SUB-CHAPTER 12.1
MEDICAL AND SURGICAL EQUIPMENT
AND ORTHOPAEDIC APPLIANCES
(NACE Rev. 1 33.1)

This sub-chapter groups together activities that manufacture a variety of medical, surgical, dental and veterinary instruments and appliances, covering highly technical items such as electro-diagnostic apparatus, electro-cardiographs and dental drills, but also more basic items such as syringes and specialist mirrors. Also included is medical furniture such as hospital beds and dentists' chairs, as well as orthopaedic appliances like crutches and hearing aids.

Medical and surgical equipment and orthopaedic appliances were the second largest activity within the instrument engineering sector, accounting for over a quarter (26.5%) of production in 1996. More recent data exists for 1999, when EU production of medical and surgical equipment and orthopaedic appliances amounted to 20.7 billion EUR (just 0.5% of the EU's manufacturing total). The medical and surgical equipment and orthopaedic appliances industry generated 9.3 billion EUR of value added in 1999 and employed 181.9 thousand persons.

Europe's ageing population is
expected to drive demand
An ageing population in Europe and advances in medical technology are two of the most important motors for driving production in these industries. However, advances in medical science and the accompanying equipment which supports such discoveries often come at a price to health care systems.

Figure 12.7

Medical and surgical equipment and orthopaedic appliances (NACE Rev. 1 33.1)
Production and export specialisation (%)

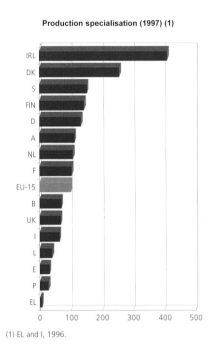

Production specialisation (1997) (1)

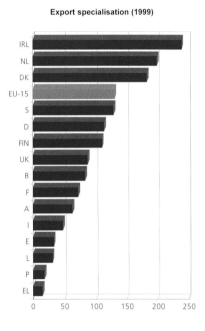

Export specialisation (1999)

(1) EL and I, 1996.

Source: Eurostat (SBS, COMEXT)

German output more than double
that of any other Member State
In terms of the value of production, the manufacture of medical and surgical equipment and orthopaedic appliances was dominated by the larger Member States in 1997. Germany was the largest producer in the EU with 6.8 billion ECU of output, followed by France with under half this figure (3.2 billion ECU), the United Kingdom (2.0 billion ECU) and Italy (1.6 billion ECU in 1996).

However, relative to the size of the national manufacturing economy, Ireland was by far the most specialised Member State in this industry, with 1.2 billion ECU of output in 1997, which represented 2.1% of total manufacturing output. By way of comparison, the figure for Germany equated to 0.7% of total manufacturing output, and in France and the United Kingdom the relative importance of the medical and surgical equipment and orthopaedic appliances industries was even lower (0.5% and 0.3% respectively).

Figure 12.8

Medical and surgical equipment and orthopaedic appliances (NACE Rev. 1 33.1)
International comparison of production in constant prices and employment (1990=100)

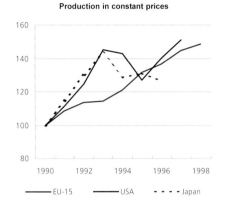

Production in constant prices

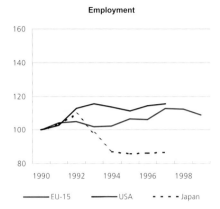

Employment

Source: Eurostat (SBS)

Figure 12.9

Medical and surgical equipment and orthopaedic appliances (NACE Rev. 1 33.1)
Destination of EU exports, 1999 (%)

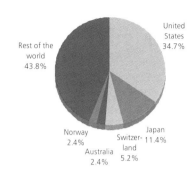

Source: Eurostat (COMEXT)

STRUCTURE AND PERFORMANCE

EU production of medical and surgical equipment and orthopaedic appliances increased in real terms throughout the 1990s, with annual rates of growth frequently exceeding 5.0%, and growth only slowing in 1993 (0.6%). The average annual growth rate of production in constant prices over the five-year period 1993 to 1998 was equal to 5.4%, which was 0.5 percentage points above the manufacturing average.

Rising profitability

In 1989, the gross operating rate for the EU's medical and surgical equipment and orthopaedic appliances industry was equal to 11.2%, which was 1.1 percentage points above the EU manufacturing average. Profit rates were maintained during the mid-1990s and then rose in the latter 1990s, reaching 14.5% in 1999 (5.1 points higher than the manufacturing average).

LABOUR AND PRODUCTIVITY

A net total of 20.7 thousand jobs were created between 1989 and 1999 in the EU's medical and surgical equipment and orthopaedic appliances industry, equal to a 12.8% increase. Nevertheless, the most recent data available showed that there was a 3.0% decline in the number of persons employed between 1998 and 1999 (the second largest reduction of the 1990s).

Labour productivity rises above manufacturing averages

Apparent labour productivity of the EU's medical and surgical equipment and orthopaedic appliances industry was higher than the manufacturing average throughout the 1990s. It rose in almost every year during the period considered from 30.8 thousand ECU per person employed in 1989 to 51.0 thousand EUR by 1999 (4.5 thousand EUR higher than the EU manufacturing average).

Simple wage adjusted labour productivity in the EU's medical and surgical equipment and orthopaedic appliances industry was lower than the manufacturing average (by around 10 percentage points) at the start of the 1990s. This situation was reversed in 1994 and by 1999 simple wage adjusted labour productivity was equal to 157.1% (some 12.8 percentage points higher than EU manufacturing average).

INTERNATIONAL TRENDS AND FOREIGN TRADE

The USA was the principal producer of medical and surgical equipment and orthopaedic appliances in the Triad, accounting for around 60% of the Triad total in 1997. The EU's share increased from 26.0% to 29.4% between 1987 and 1997, at the experience of Japan where the relative share fell to 9.9%.

Figure 12.10

Medical and surgical equipment and orthopaedic appliances (NACE Rev. 1 33.1)
Origin of EU imports, 1999 (%)

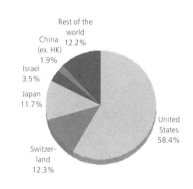

Source: Eurostat (COMEXT)

The main origin of EU imports was the USA, with rapid growth between 1989 and 1999, as imports rose from 1.8 billion ECU to 5.4 billion EUR (or 58.4% of total EU imports). Imports of medical and surgical equipment and orthopaedic appliances from Switzerland and Japan rose by around 100% over the same period, resulting in imports from both countries being valued at 1.1billion EUR in 1999.

Exports from the EU destined for the USA almost tripled over the period 1989 to 1999, reaching 3.4 billion EUR (or 34.7% of total EU exports). Exports from the EU to Japan more than tripled to reach 1.1 billion EUR and those to Switzerland almost doubled to reach 511 million EUR.

SUB-CHAPTER 12.2
MEASURING, PRECISION AND
PROCESS CONTROL EQUIPMENT
(NACE Rev. 1 33.2 AND 33.3)

The manufacture of instruments and appliances for measuring, checking, testing, navigating and other purposes (NACE Rev. 1 33.2) and the manufacture of industrial process control equipment (NACE Rev. 1 33.3) are analysed together in this sub-chapter. The former encompasses a wide variety of activities including the manufacture of balances, drawing instruments, gauges, microscopes, navigational equipment and utility supply meters (such as water, gas or electricity), whilst the latter relates to the design and assembly of automated production plants consisting of various machines.

Production of measuring, precision and process control equipment within the EU had a production value of 39.6 billion ECU[5] in 1996, which was around 58.4% of the EU's instrument engineering output. The measuring, precision and process control equipment industry generated 16.3 billion ECU[6] of value added and employed 325.3 thousand persons[7] in 1996.

The health of this industry is strongly related to the investment decisions of downstream manufacturing industries. Therefore, demand will rise as manufacturers modernise or open-up new production facilities. Also, niche markets have emerged, such as increased demand for pollution measuring devices.

Germany, France and the United Kingdom all relatively specialised
Total German output of measuring, precision and process control equipment amounted to 12.1 billion ECU in 1997, which represented 1.2% of national manufacturing output. Only three Member States reported higher relative shares, France and the United Kingdom with 1.7% and 1.5%, as well as Sweden, which was the most specialised country in the EU with a 1.9% share of the national manufacturing total (2.2 billion ECU).

(5) L, no data available for NACE Rev. 1 33.2.
(6) L, no data available for NACE Rev. 1 33.2.
(7) L and NL, no data available for NACE Rev. 1 33.2; DK, L, NL and A, no data available for NACE Rev. 1 33.3.

Figure 12.11

Measuring, precision and process control equipment (NACE Rev. 1 33.2 and 33.3)
Production and export specialisation (%)

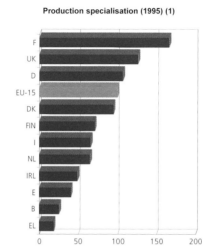

Production specialisation (1995) (1)

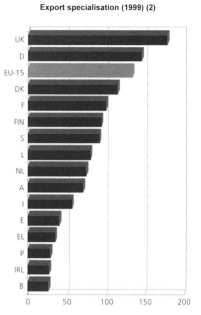

Export specialisation (1999) (2)

(1) DK and NL, 1994; L, A, P and S, not available.
(2) Excluding NACE Rev. 1 33.3.

Source: Eurostat (SBS, COMEXT)

STRUCTURE AND PERFORMANCE
Production in current prices increased between 1993 (34.9 billion ECU) and 1995 (36.0 billion ECU), with a more significant rise in nominal terms reported in 1996 when output was equal to 39.6 billion ECU[8].

Low profit rates
Despite rising from 6.3% in 1994 to 7.6% a year later, the gross operating rate for the EU's measuring, precision and process control equipment industry remained below the figure of 9.2% for total manufacturing. The gross operating surplus divided by value added equalled 18.8% in 1995, which was 12.7 percentage points lower than that for total manufacturing.

(8) L, no data available for NACE Rev. 1 33.2.

LABOUR AND PRODUCTIVITY
The number of persons employed in the EU's measuring, precision and process control equipment declined at a rapid pace between 1993 and 1996, as the workforce fell by around a fifth from 405.1 thousand persons employed to 325.3 thousand[9]. The largest net reduction of employment was recorded in 1995, down by 11.9%.

Productivity rose quickly
As the size of the workforce fell, the figures for apparent labour productivity rose rapidly, up by 7.5 thousand ECU per person employed between 1993 and 1995, to reach 44.8 thousand ECU, which was 6.0 thousand ECU higher than the EU manufacturing average. Simple wage adjusted labour productivity also rose quickly, from 110.5% to 123.3%, with the difference to the figure for total manufacturing reduced from -33.3 percentage points to -13.0 points in just two years.

(9) L and NL, no data available for NACE Rev. 1 33.2; DK, L, NL and A, no data available for NACE Rev. 1 33.3.

INTERNATIONAL TRENDS AND FOREIGN TRADE

The USA was responsible for 46.1% of total Triad production of measuring, precision and process control equipment in 1995 (107.4 billion ECU), with the EU producing a third (33.5%) of the total and Japan a fifth (20.5%).

All three Triad members reported a positive trade position in the measuring, precision and process control equipment industries in the 1990s. From 170.7 million ECU in 1989, the EU trade balance grew to 2.9 billion ECU by 1997 but declined to 2.0 billion EUR two years later. This compares to the USA where the surplus rose from 5.0 billion ECU in 1989 to 11.2 billion ECU nine years later. In Japan, the surplus recorded by the measuring, precision and process control equipment industries more than doubled between 1989 and 1997, reaching 6.3 billion ECU, before falling away to 4.9 billion ECU in 1998.

EU's trade deficit with the USA stable

The EU increased its exports to the USA from 1.9 billion ECU in 1989 to 4.2 billion EUR in 1999, although imports from the USA rose at a similar rate, to reach 6.4 billion EUR in 1999, thus continuing a trade deficit of around 2.2 billion EUR. The USA dominated trade with the EU in 1999, as imports of measuring, precision and process control equipment products from the USA represented more than half (52.6%) of total EU imports in 1999. The EU's trade position in relation to other developed world economies such as Switzerland and Japan deteriorated, with trade surpluses in 1989 becoming deficits ten years later.

Figure 12.12

**Measuring and precision equipment
(NACE Rev. 1 33.2)
Destination of EU exports, 1999 (%)**

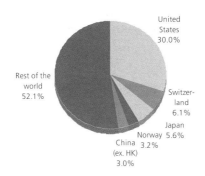

Source: Eurostat (COMEXT)

Figure 12.13

**Measuring and precision equipment
(NACE Rev. 1 33.2)
Origin of EU imports, 1999 (%)**

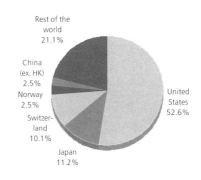

Source: Eurostat (COMEXT)

SUB-CHAPTER 12.3
OPTICAL AND PHOTOGRAPHIC
INSTRUMENTS (NACE Rev. 1 33.4)

Optical instruments include microscopes, binoculars and lasers, but also so-called optical elements such as lenses, filters, as well as spectacle frames. Cameras are the principal products within the photographic equipment industry, although image projectors, flashlights and other similar products are also included in the definition.

The EU's optical and photographic industries had a combined production value of 10.6 billion EUR in 1999, whilst they generated close to 3.5 billion ECU[10] of value added and employed around 80.2 thousand persons[11] in 1996.

The majority of the products from these industries are consumer-orientated, especially in areas such as spectacles, where fashion considerations rather than clinical needs are increasingly driving the market. Whilst the majority of markets are mature industries there is a great deal of innovation, which results in the development of new product lines, such as increasingly smaller or digital cameras, in an attempt to stimulate demand.

Homogenous specialisation figures
The only countries to report relatively high production specialisation figures in these industries were Italy (1.8 billion ECU of production value in 1996) and Denmark (222.5 million ECU in 1997), where optical and photographic industries had 0.4% shares of national manufacturing output, 0.1 percentage points above the EU average. Germany was the largest producer within the EU, with production valued at 2.8 billion ECU in 1997, followed by Italy, the United Kingdom (1.4 billion ECU) and France (1.3 billion ECU).

(10) DK, EL, IRL, L, A and S, no data available.
(11) DK, EL, IRL, L, NL, A and S, no data available.

Figure 12.14

Optical and photographic instruments (NACE Rev. 1 33.4)

Production and export specialisation (%)

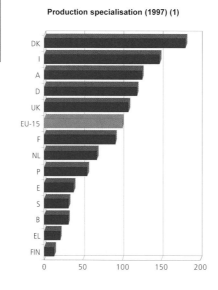

Production specialisation (1997) (1)

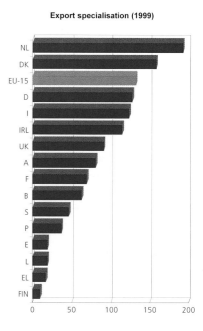

Export specialisation (1999)

(1) A, 1994; EL, I and S, 1995; IRL and L, not available.

Source: Eurostat (SBS, COMEXT)

Figure 12.15

Optical and photographic instruments (NACE Rev. 1 33.4)

International comparison of production in constant prices and employment (1990=100)

Production in constant prices

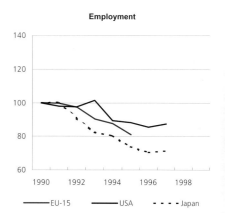

Employment

Source: Eurostat (SBS)

STRUCTURE AND PERFORMANCE

The EU's optical and photographic industries recorded a nominal increase of 77.8% for production between 1989 and 1999 (substantially higher than the 43.4% rise reported over the same period for total manufacturing).

There was only one year when a reduction in production in constant prices was recorded between 1989 and 1999 (-7.4% in 1993). Real growth in the mid-1990s was particularly high, 6.3% in 1994 and 4.7% in 1995. In real terms, production within the EU's optical and photographic industries rose by an average of 1.3% during the five-year period 1990 to 1995, whilst the equivalent figure for total manufacturing was 0.6%.

The gross operating rate of the EU's optical and photographic industries was equal to 6.3% in 1989. However, profitability subsequently began to increase, reaching 11.3% by 1995, well above the average for total manufacturing (9.2%).

LABOUR AND PRODUCTIVITY

Employment within the EU's optical and photographic industries fell at a faster pace than the rates observed for total manufacturing. The number of persons employed in the EU's optical and photographic industries was equal to 98.1 thousand persons in 1986, which fell to 80.2 thousand[12] by 1996, equivalent to an 18% reduction. The most notable reductions were recorded in 1993 (7.4%) and 1995 (7.6%).

Rapid productivity growth in the mid-1990s

Apparent labour productivity of the EU's optical and photographic industries rose consistently but relatively slowly from 21.7 thousand ECU per person employed in 1985 to 27.7 thousand ECU in 1990. However, from this point onwards, apparent labour productivity increased at a more rapid pace, by 4.3 thousand ECU in 1991, 3.0 thousand ECU in 1994 and 5.5 thousand ECU in 1995. These increases resulted in apparent labour productivity for the EU's optical and photographic industries rising to 43.2 thousand ECU per person employed in 1995, which was 2.1 thousand ECU below the manufacturing average.

(12) DK, EL, L, NL, A and S, no data available.

INTERNATIONAL TRENDS AND FOREIGN TRADE

Over the ten years to 1997, EU production of optical and photographic instruments rose by 78.0% in nominal terms, significantly higher than the 43.4% increase recorded in the USA, whilst in Japan there was a decline of 12.7%. As a result, the EU became the second largest producer within the Triad, with 27.9% of total Triad output in 1997, just ahead of Japan (24.3%), but well behind the USA (47.8%).

EU reports a stable trade deficit

Imports into the EU exceeded exports by between 500 million ECU and 1 billion ECU during the 1990s. In 1999 this situation did not change, with the EU's trade deficit equal to 671 million EUR. Japan and the USA both reported increasing trade surpluses during the period 1989 to 1998, up by 2.2 billion ECU in Japan to 5.1 billion ECU and up by 1.4 billion ECU in the USA to 2.3 billion ECU.

Emergence of the Far East as a major trading partner

Japan (1.6 billion EUR, or 28.1% of total EU imports) and the USA (1.5 billion EUR, or 27.1% of total EU imports) were the principal sources of imports into the EU in 1999. China emerged as an important trading partner, with imports totalling 784.9 million EUR in 1999 (or 14.2% of the total).

As regards exports from the EU, the USA was the main destination in 1999, with EU exports valued at 1.9 billion EUR (or 38.4% of the total). South Korea became the second largest export market for EU optical and photographic instruments, valued at 401 million EUR in 1999 (or 8.2% of the total), ahead of Japan (355.0 million EUR) in third place.

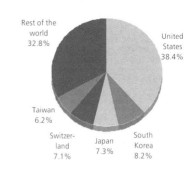

—————————————————————Figure 12.16

**Optical and photographic instruments
(NACE Rev. 1 33.4)
Destination of EU exports, 1999 (%)**

Source: Eurostat (COMEXT)

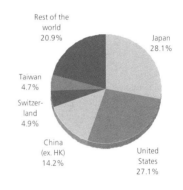

—————————————————————Figure 12.17

**Optical and photographic instruments
(NACE Rev. 1 33.4)
Origin of EU imports, 1999 (%)**

Source: Eurostat (COMEXT)

SUB-CHAPTER 12.4
CLOCKS AND WATCHES (NACE Rev. 1 33.5)

The information in this sub-chapter includes data on the manufacture of clocks and watches of all kinds, whether they are of the stand-alone variety, or incorporated in other devices such as time switches.

This sub-chapter had by far the lowest level of output amongst those presented within this chapter on instrument engineering. Total output of the EU's watches and clocks industry totalled 1.6 billion EUR in 1999, whilst value added was equal to 617 million EUR. In 1996, there were 13.7 thousand persons employed[13] in the EU's watches and clocks industry.

The bulk of the EU's production of clocks and watches (approximately 85%) came from the four largest Member States. Germany was responsible for the highest value of output, 520.1 million ECU in 1997, ahead of France (440.9 million ECU).

(13) IRL, NL, A and S, no data available.

Box 12.1
According to the Federation of the Swiss Watch Industry, world production of watches, movements, basic components and other watch products was estimated to be equal to 1.2 billion pieces in 1999, with a combined value of over 10 billion EUR. The majority of these pieces came from Hong Kong, China, Japan and India, whilst in value terms Switzerland accounted for over half of total output.

World production of finished watches totalled around 500 million pieces in 1999, with China and Hong Kong accounting for 80% of the total, compared to 33 million pieces in Switzerland, 19.5 million in Japan and 7.4 million in France.

Figure 12.18

Clocks and watches (NACE Rev. 1 33.5)

Production and export specialisation (%)

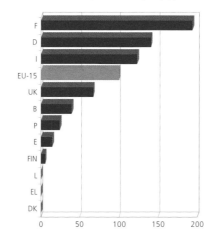

Production specialisation (1997) (1)

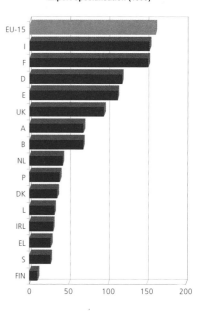

Export specialisation (1999)

(1) EL and I, 1996; IRL, NL, A and S, not available.

Source: Eurostat (SBS, COMEXT)

Figure 12.19

Clocks and watches (NACE Rev. 1 33.5)

International comparison of production in constant prices and employment (1990=100)

Production in constant prices

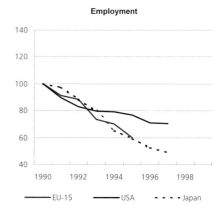

Employment

Source: Eurostat (SBS)

STRUCTURE AND PERFORMANCE

There was little evolution to the output of the EU's clocks and watches industry between 1989 and 1999 in nominal terms. In real terms, the average annual decline of production in constant prices was equal to 1.6% between 1988 and 1998. There was a fluctuating evolution of output, with 11.3% real growth in 1990 followed by a period of five years when real output declined on average by 5.7% per annum. There was a slight upturn towards the end of the decade, with, for example, a 1.2% real increase in 1998.

The gross operating rate of the EU's watches and clocks industry rose from 8.7% in 1998 to 10.6% in 1999, the first time during the 1990s that a figure in excess of the manufacturing average was recorded.

LABOUR AND PRODUCTIVITY

Employment in the EU's watches and clocks industry fell by more than 50% during the period 1986 to 1996, falling from 29.9 thousand persons to around 13.7 thousand persons[14]. In every year of this ten-year period there was a reduction in the workforce, with the sharpest declines in the first half of the 1990s, when the average annual rate of decline was 9.8%. The largest contractions in employment came in 1991 (down 9.0%), 1993 (down 17.2%), 1995 (down 14.5%) and 1996 (down by approximately 10%[15]).

There was a steady increase in apparent labour productivity levels in the EU's watches and clocks industry between 1985 and 1995, from 19.0 thousand ECU per person employed to 35.2 thousand ECU. As such, the watches and clocks industry continued to report apparent labour productivity some 10 thousand ECU per person employed below the EU manufacturing average. Simple wage adjusted labour productivity was some 25 percentage points lower than the EU manufacturing average in both 1985 and 1995, rising from 115.8% to 121.7%.

(14) IRL, NL, A and S, no data available.
(15) IRL, NL, A and S, no data available.

INTERNATIONAL TRENDS AND FOREIGN TRADE

Triad production of watches and clocks reached 7.5 billion ECU in 1997. Japan accounted for the majority of production (67.5%) and was the only Triad economy to report growth in current prices between 1987 and 1997, a net gain of 7.5%. In real terms, the average annual growth rate of production during the ten-year period 1987 to 1997 was negative for all three Triad economies (EU -1.7%, USA -4.1% and Japan -0.5% to 1996).

Switzerland and Far East account for the majority of the EU's imports

The EU's trade gap increased from 1.5 billion ECU to 2.6 billion EUR over the period 1989 to 1999. Switzerland was the main origin of EU imports in 1999, accounting for over half of the total (2.1 billion EUR or 53.1%). Imports from China increased at a rapid pace from 146.3 million ECU in 1989 to 728.5 million EUR in 1999, equivalent to 18.4% of the total. This increase relegated Hong Kong to third place with 603.9 million EUR.

Figure 12.20

Clocks and watches (NACE Rev. 1 33.5)
Destination of EU exports, 1999 (%)

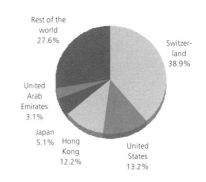

Source: Eurostat (COMEXT)

Figure 12.21

Clocks and watches (NACE Rev. 1 33.5)
Origin of EU imports, 1999 (%)

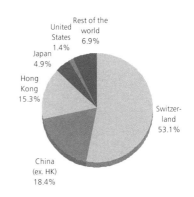

Source: Eurostat (COMEXT)

Table 12.3

Manufacture of medical and surgical equipment and orthopaedic appliances (NACE Rev. 1 33.1)

Production related indicators in the EU (1)

	1989	1990	1991	1992	1993	1994	1995	1996	1997	1998	1999
Number of persons employed (thousands)	161.2	166.7	174.0	175.4	169.9	171.0	177.5	176.9	188.1	187.6	181.9
Production (million EUR)	10,423	11,550	12,984	13,951	14,390	15,371	16,912	17,989	19,163	19,859	20,730
Domestic producer price index (1995=100)	:	:	:	:	:	:	100.0	102.4	103.0	103.7	105.0
Value added (million EUR)	4,963	5,514	6,166	6,606	6,913	7,473	7,790	8,407	8,768	9,021	9,283

(1) Technically, data before 01/01/1999 are in ECU and after this date in euro. However, as the conversion rate was 1 ECU =1 EUR, for practical purposes the two terms can be used interchangeably.

Table 12.4

Manufacture of medical and surgical equipment and orthopaedic appliances (NACE Rev. 1 33.1)

Trade related indicators in the EU (1)

	1989	1990	1991	1992	1993	1994	1995	1996	1997	1998	1999
Exports (million EUR)	3,847	4,124	4,604	4,858	5,742	6,187	6,714	7,344	8,305	9,049	10,162
Imports (million EUR)	3,196	3,315	4,035	4,309	4,605	4,969	5,286	6,024	7,027	7,576	9,271
Trade balance (million EUR)	652	809	569	549	1,137	1,218	1,428	1,319	1,278	1,472	892
Cover ratio (%)	120.4	124.4	114.1	112.7	124.7	124.5	127.0	121.9	118.2	119.4	109.6

(1) Technically, data before 01/01/1999 are in ECU and after this date in euro. However, as the conversion rate was 1 ECU =1 EUR, for practical purposes the two terms can be used interchangeably.

Table 12.5

Manufacture of medical and surgical equipment and orthopaedic appliances (NACE Rev. 1 33.1)

Production related indicators, 1997

	B	DK	D	EL (1)	E	F	IRL	I (1)	L	NL	A	P	FIN	S	UK
Number of persons employed (thousands)	4.4	7.2	78.1	0.2	8.7	22.9	9.5	14.4	0.3	:	4.4	2.2	4.6	5.7	21.1
Production (million ECU)	530	681	6,767	7	431	3,222	1,145	1,611	13	811	410	85	516	901	1,954
Value added (million ECU)	161	305	3,421	3	199	1,116	589	690	8	293	196	32	270	381	950
Gross operating surplus (million ECU)	53.2	92.5	749.2	0.3	64.5	219.1	357.6	242.7	1.8	105.2	33.5	12.4	129.1	152.8	400.3

(1) 1996.

Table 12.6

Manufacture of medical and surgical equipment and orthopaedic appliances (NACE Rev. 1 33.1)

Trade related indicators, 1999

	B	DK	D	EL	E	F	IRL	I	L	NL	A	P	FIN	S	UK
Exports (million EUR)	1,389	815	5,716	13	325	2,280	1,562	1,099	25	3,532	407	44	472	1,052	2,194
Imports (million EUR)	1,656	396	3,990	299	1,176	2,728	717	2,056	50	2,262	634	286	259	682	2,005
Trade balance (million EUR)	-267	419	1,726	-287	-851	-448	845	-957	-25	1,270	-227	-242	213	370	189
Cover ratio (%)	83.9	205.9	143.3	4.2	27.6	83.6	217.8	53.4	49.4	156.1	64.1	15.3	182.5	154.3	109.4

Table 12.7

Manufacture of medical and surgical equipment and orthopaedic appliances (NACE Rev. 1 33.1)

Labour related indicators, 1997

	B	DK (1)	D	EL (2)	E	F	IRL	I (2)	L	NL	A	P	FIN	S	UK
Unit personnel costs (thousand ECU per employee)	34.0	34.3	34.3	15.4	17.6	39.2	24.4	31.7	24.3	:	37.5	10.4	31.8	40.0	27.4
Social charges as a share of personnel costs (%)	34.8	3.7	22.0	31.6	26.9	42.2	18.6	47.7	:	16.7	28.6	28.1	26.7	46.7	14.0
Apparent labour productivity (thousand ECU/pers. empl.)	36.4	42.7	43.8	17.1	22.9	48.8	61.9	47.9	27.5	:	45.0	14.6	59.0	66.7	45.0
Wage adjusted labour productivity (%)	107.2	142.6	127.7	110.6	130.4	124.4	254.1	151.1	113.6	:	120.2	141.1	185.4	166.9	164.3
Personnel costs as a share of total operating costs (%)	22.6	36.1	39.7	41.0	31.4	26.1	22.4	28.3	54.8	18.3	37.1	26.6	29.7	26.2	29.6

(1) Unit personnel costs and wage adjusted labour productivity, 1996; (2) 1996.

Source: Eurostat (SBS, EBT, COMEXT)

Table 12.8

Manufacture of instruments and appliances for measuring, checking, testing, navigating and other purposes, except industrial process control equipment (NACE Rev. 1 33.2): Production related indicators in the EU (1)

	1989	1990	1991	1992	1993	1994	1995	1996	1997	1998	1999
Number of persons employed (thousands)	:	:	:	:	321.6	300.2	297.0	:	:	:	:
Production (million ECU)	:	:	:	:	27,575	27,918	31,204	:	:	:	:
Domestic producer price index (1995=100)	:	:	:	:	:	:	:	:	:	102.9	104.0
Value added (million ECU)	:	:	:	:	11,969	12,561	13,270	:	:	:	:

(1) Technically, data before 01/01/1999 are in ECU and after this date in euro. However, as the conversion rate was 1 ECU =1 EUR, for practical purposes the two terms can be used interchangeably.

Table 12.9

Manufacture of instruments and appliances for measuring, checking, testing, navigating and other purposes, except industrial process control equipment (NACE Rev. 1 33.2): Trade related indicators in the EU (1)

	1989	1990	1991	1992	1993	1994	1995	1996	1997	1998	1999
Exports (million EUR)	6,999	7,261	7,233	7,422	8,202	8,877	9,630	10,902	13,212	13,862	14,103
Imports (million EUR)	6,828	6,892	7,447	7,280	7,262	7,812	8,213	9,113	10,295	11,529	12,145
Trade balance (million EUR)	171	370	-214	142	940	1,065	1,417	1,789	2,918	2,332	1,958
Cover ratio (%)	102.5	105.4	97.1	101.9	112.9	113.6	117.3	119.6	128.3	120.2	116.1

(1) Technically, data before 01/01/1999 are in ECU and after this date in euro. However, as the conversion rate was 1 ECU =1 EUR, for practical purposes the two terms can be used interchangeably.

Table 12.10

Manufacture of instruments and appliances for measuring, checking, testing, navigating and other purposes, except industrial process control equipment (NACE Rev. 1 33.2): Production related indicators, 1997

	B	DK	D	EL (1)	E	F	IRL	I (1)	L	NL	A	P	FIN	S	UK
Number of persons employed (thousands)	1.9	4.8	98.0	0.6	9.5	56.5	2.0	21.2	:	:	3.1	0.9	3.1	9.7	72.4
Production (million ECU)	282	472	11,047	48	1,004	9,189	289	2,421	:	1,051	301	32	409	1,524	7,659
Value added (million ECU)	106	215	4,932	14	412	3,453	112	1,091	:	430	151	16	186	723	3,596
Gross operating surplus (million ECU)	30.4	53.7	775.5	3.6	141.3	752.4	58.0	342.2	:	121.8	39.5	5.7	80.8	292.7	1,323.6

(1) 1996.

Table 12.11

Manufacture of instruments and appliances for measuring, checking, testing, navigating and other purposes, except industrial process control equipment (NACE Rev. 1 33.2): Trade related indicators, 1999

	B	DK	D	EL	E	F	IRL	I	L	NL	A	P	FIN	S	UK
Exports (million EUR)	604	692	9,928	40	545	4,292	243	1,769	88	1,792	619	96	545	1,008	6,074
Imports (million EUR)	1,138	453	5,046	201	1,501	4,273	330	2,506	46	1,850	910	323	390	1,022	4,655
Trade balance (million EUR)	-534	238	4,883	-161	-956	19	-87	-736	42	-57	-291	-227	155	-14	1,419
Cover ratio (%)	53.0	152.5	196.8	19.7	36.3	100.4	73.7	70.6	190.2	96.9	68.0	29.8	139.7	98.6	130.5

Table 12.12

Manufacture of instruments and appliances for measuring, checking, testing, navigating and other purposes, except industrial process control equipment (NACE Rev. 1 33.2): Labour related indicators, 1997

	B	DK (1)	D	EL (2)	E	F	IRL	I (2)	L	NL	A	P	FIN	S	UK
Unit personnel costs (thousand ECU per employee)	40.6	37.5	42.4	16.0	27.8	47.8	26.9	35.9	:	:	35.8	11.1	34.3	44.3	31.7
Social charges as a share of personnel costs (%)	37.8	3.0	22.4	33.3	26.4	43.2	21.5	47.8	:	15.0	30.3	33.8	25.7	43.0	14.2
Apparent labour productivity (thousand ECU/pers. empl.)	55.8	44.8	50.4	21.6	43.2	61.1	55.7	51.4	:	:	48.4	16.5	59.9	74.5	49.7
Wage adjusted labour productivity (%)	137.2	135.1	118.7	135.0	155.8	127.9	207.4	143.3	:	:	135.3	147.8	175.0	168.0	156.6
Personnel costs as a share of total operating costs (%)	30.6	37.9	38.0	23.1	27.9	30.6	21.8	32.9	:	30.5	40.1	38.1	31.1	34.3	33.6

(1) Unit personnel costs and wage adjusted labour productivity, 1996; (2) 1996.

Source: Eurostat (SBS, EBT, COMEXT)

Table 12.13

Manufacture of industrial process control equipment (NACE Rev. 1 33.3)

Production related indicators in the EU

	1989	1990	1991	1992	1993	1994	1995	1996	1997	1998	1999
Number of persons employed (thousands)	:	:	:	:	83.5	82.4	39.9	:	:	:	:
Production (million ECU)	:	:	:	:	7,369	7,965	4,741	5,481	:	:	:
Domestic producer price index (1995=100)	:	:	:	:	:	:	:	:	:	:	:
Value added (million ECU)	:	:	:	:	3,147	3,311	1,819	2,144	:	:	:

Table 12.14

Manufacture of industrial process control equipment (NACE Rev. 1 33.3)

Production related indicators, 1997

	B	DK	D	EL (1)	E	F	IRL	I (1)	L	NL	A	P	FIN	S	UK
Number of persons employed (thousands)	1.1	0.1	7.9	0.0	2.6	12.7	0.3	9.1	:	:	0.8	1.4	1.7	3.8	8.4
Production (million ECU)	154	9	1,055	0	292	1,407	34	1,177	:	:	79	93	256	680	1,101
Value added (million ECU)	64	5	425	0	105	506	15	440	:	:	38	26	93	236	420
Gross operating surplus (million ECU)	11.1	0.9	36.6	0.0	32.6	12.7	4.9	123.0	:	:	4.5	6.2	22.4	57.7	122.3

(1) 1996.

Table 12.15

Manufacture of industrial process control equipment (NACE Rev. 1 33.3)

Labour related indicators, 1997

	B	DK	D	EL	E	F	IRL	I (1)	L	NL	A	P	FIN	S	UK
Unit personnel costs (thousand ECU per employee)	50.4	:	48.9	:	27.9	38.8	31.0	35.7	:	:	42.8	14.7	40.8	47.4	35.8
Social charges as a share of personnel costs (%)	40.9	5.0	22.3	:	26.1	42.2	14.8	47.4	:	:	27.4	28.3	25.5	45.8	15.1
Apparent labour productivity (thousand ECU/pers. empl.)	58.3	36.7	53.5	:	41.2	39.8	45.2	48.4	:	:	48.5	18.9	54.3	62.7	49.9
Wage adjusted labour productivity (%)	115.6	:	109.3	:	147.5	102.6	145.7	135.6	:	:	113.4	128.1	133.0	132.3	139.5
Personnel costs as a share of total operating costs (%)	36.5	48.8	36.2	:	25.9	35.9	31.7	29.6	:	:	37.9	21.9	28.4	28.7	27.5

(1) 1996.

Source: Eurostat (SBS)

Table 12.16

Manufacture of optical instruments and photographic equipment (NACE Rev. 1 33.4)

Production related indicators in the EU (1)

	1989	1990	1991	1992	1993	1994	1995	1996	1997	1998	1999
Number of persons employed (thousands)	103.1	104.1	103.3	101.2	93.7	91.2	84.2	:	:	:	:
Production (million EUR)	5,935	6,278	6,826	7,131	6,821	7,389	7,891	:	8,864	9,297	10,553
Domestic producer price index (1995=100)	:	85.1	89.8	93.1	96.1	97.9	100.0	101.7	102.7	104.1	104.8
Value added (million ECU)	2,708	2,887	3,309	3,341	3,254	3,439	3,639	:	:	:	:

(1) Technically, data before 01/01/1999 are in ECU and after this date in euro. However, as the conversion rate was 1 ECU =1 EUR, for practical purposes the two terms can be used interchangeably.

Table 12.17

Manufacture of optical instruments and photographic equipment (NACE Rev. 1 33.4)

Trade related indicators in the EU (1)

	1989	1990	1991	1992	1993	1994	1995	1996	1997	1998	1999
Exports (million EUR)	1,972	1,921	1,997	2,179	2,490	2,727	3,088	3,580	4,327	4,513	4,908
Imports (million EUR)	2,916	2,829	3,141	3,112	3,191	3,523	3,690	4,079	4,449	4,930	5,579
Trade balance (million EUR)	-944	-908	-1,144	-933	-700	-797	-601	-499	-122	-418	-671
Cover ratio (%)	67.6	67.9	63.6	70.0	78.1	77.4	83.7	87.8	97.3	91.5	88.0

(1) Technically, data before 01/01/1999 are in ECU and after this date in euro. However, as the conversion rate was 1 ECU =1 EUR, for practical purposes the two terms can be used interchangeably.

Table 12.18

Manufacture of optical instruments and photographic equipment (NACE Rev. 1 33.4)

Production related indicators, 1997

	B	DK	D	EL	E	F	IRL	I (1)	L	NL	A	P	FIN	S	UK
Number of persons employed (thousands)	0.7	1.5	26.9	:	2.9	12.7	:	17.9	:	:	:	1.8	0.2	:	14.5
Production (million ECU)	109	223	2,801	:	245	1,316	:	1,836	:	239	:	79	21	:	1,435
Value added (million ECU)	37	100	1,317	:	107	531	:	695	:	133	:	33	9	:	708
Gross operating surplus (million ECU)	11.9	49.5	239.6	:	32.4	103.5	:	284.5	:	79.5	:	13.0	3.5	:	329.5

(1) 1996.

Table 12.19

Manufacture of optical instruments and photographic equipment (NACE Rev. 1 33.4)

Trade related indicators, 1999

	B	DK	D	EL	E	F	IRL	I	L	NL	A	P	FIN	S	UK
Exports (million EUR)	498	336	3,067	7	90	1,042	356	1,363	7	1,635	248	43	20	180	1,084
Imports (million EUR)	560	205	2,374	84	563	1,403	176	1,039	30	1,217	313	158	153	288	1,787
Trade balance (million EUR)	-63	131	693	-77	-473	-362	180	323	-22	418	-65	-116	-133	-108	-703
Cover ratio (%)	88.8	164.1	129.2	8.0	16.0	74.2	202.6	131.1	24.9	134.4	79.2	27.0	13.1	62.5	60.7

Table 12.20

Manufacture of optical instruments and photographic equipment (NACE Rev. 1 33.4)

Labour related indicators, 1997

	B	DK	D	EL	E	F	IRL	I (1)	L	NL	A	P	FIN	S	UK
Unit personnel costs (thousand ECU per employee)	35.7	:	40.1	:	23.6	33.7	:	23.4	:	:	:	11.2	27.2	:	26.4
Social charges as a share of personnel costs (%)	36.1	3.9	25.7	:	27.6	43.9	:	47.2	:	16.2	:	26.3	26.7	:	12.4
Apparent labour productivity (thousand ECU/pers. empl.)	51.0	66.5	48.9	:	37.2	41.9	:	38.9	:	:	:	18.5	39.0	:	48.7
Wage adjusted labour productivity (%)	142.7	:	122.1	:	157.7	124.2	:	166.4	:	:	:	164.7	143.6	:	184.5
Personnel costs as a share of total operating costs (%)	25.3	28.4	36.8	:	24.6	34.5	:	26.2	:	27.0	:	26.1	30.7	:	31.3

(1) 1996.

Source: Eurostat (SBS, EBT, COMEXT)

Table 12.21

Manufacture of watches and clocks (NACE Rev. 1 33.5)

Production related indicators in the EU (1)

	1989	1990	1991	1992	1993	1994	1995	1996	1997	1998	1999
Number of persons employed (thousands)	26.3	25.8	23.5	22.8	18.9	18.0	15.4	:	:	:	:
Production (million EUR)	1,549	1,753	1,606	1,638	1,455	1,511	1,425	1,435	1,392	1,461	1,593
Domestic producer price index (1995=100)	:	:	:	:	:	:	:	:	:	102.5	103.4
Value added (million EUR)	634	685	623	650	619	623	544	540	560	572	617

(1) Technically, data before 01/01/1999 are in ECU and after this date in euro. However, as the conversion rate was 1 ECU =1 EUR, for practical purposes the two terms can be used interchangeably.

Table 12.22

Manufacture of watches and clocks (NACE Rev. 1 33.5)

Trade related indicators in the EU (1)

	1989	1990	1991	1992	1993	1994	1995	1996	1997	1998	1999
Exports (million EUR)	965	1,017	991	1,029	1,113	1,259	1,360	1,299	1,441	1,327	1,349
Imports (million EUR)	2,467	2,627	2,825	2,882	2,971	3,155	3,209	3,219	3,647	3,936	3,966
Trade balance (million EUR)	-1,502	-1,611	-1,834	-1,853	-1,857	-1,896	-1,849	-1,920	-2,206	-2,609	-2,617
Cover ratio (%)	39.1	38.7	35.1	35.7	37.5	39.9	42.4	40.4	39.5	33.7	34.0

(1) Technically, data before 01/01/1999 are in ECU and after this date in euro. However, as the conversion rate was 1 ECU =1 EUR, for practical purposes the two terms can be used interchangeably.

Table 12.23

Manufacture of watches and clocks (NACE Rev. 1 33.5)

Production related indicators, 1997

	B	DK	D	EL (1)	E	F	IRL	I (1)	L	NL	A	P	FIN	S	UK
Number of persons employed (thousands)	0.2	0.0	5.0	0.0	0.2	5.1	:	0.7	0.0	:	:	0.2	0.0	:	1.7
Production (million ECU)	22	0	520	0	14	441	:	251	0	:	:	5	1	:	142
Value added (million ECU)	9	0	198	0	5	179	:	65	0	:	:	2	0	:	49
Gross operating surplus (million ECU)	1.5	0.0	20.0	0.0	0.7	27.0	:	45.0	0.0	:	:	-0.4	0.1	:	13.0

(1) 1996.

Table 12.24

Manufacture of watches and clocks (NACE Rev. 1 33.5)

Trade related indicators, 1999

	B	DK	D	EL	E	F	IRL	I	L	NL	A	P	FIN	S	UK
Exports (million EUR)	123	17	638	2	119	516	21	381	3	81	48	10	5	24	255
Imports (million EUR)	174	51	998	73	516	716	31	853	14	204	160	88	33	84	727
Trade balance (million EUR)	-51	-34	-360	-70	-396	-200	-10	-472	-11	-123	-112	-78	-29	-60	-472
Cover ratio (%)	70.6	32.9	63.9	3.4	23.2	72.1	68.8	44.7	20.5	39.6	29.9	11.5	14.1	28.2	35.1

Table 12.25

Manufacture of watches and clocks (NACE Rev. 1 33.5)

Labour related indicators, 1997

	B	DK	D	EL	E	F	IRL	I (1)	L	NL	A	P	FIN	S	UK
Unit personnel costs (thousand ECU per employee)	35.4	:	35.3	:	20.1	29.8	:	28.2	:	:	:	11.3	24.7	:	22.8
Social charges as a share of personnel costs (%)	37.0	:	21.3	:	25.8	39.2	:	52.7	:	:	:	73.3	50.0	:	12.5
Apparent labour productivity (thousand ECU/pers. empl.)	41.3	:	39.3	:	22.8	35.1	:	88.2	:	:	:	8.9	30.1	:	29.7
Wage adjusted labour productivity (%)	116.5	:	111.3	:	113.5	117.8	:	313.3	:	:	:	79.0	121.9	:	129.9
Personnel costs as a share of total operating costs (%)	37.0	:	30.1	:	28.3	33.7	:	9.6	:	:	:	45.6	23.1	:	23.8

(1) 1996.

Source: Eurostat (SBS, EBT, COMEXT)

Transport equipment (NACE Rev. 1 34 and 35)

The NACE Rev. 1 classification of economic activities distinguishes the manufacture of motor vehicles, including their parts, components and equipment (NACE Rev. 1 34) from the manufacture of other transport equipment (NACE Rev. 1 35), which includes the manufacture of ships, railway equipment, aircraft and spacecraft, as well as motorcycles and bicycles.

This activity is one of the cornerstones of economic activity, as developed economies increasingly require an efficient transport system to act as a lubricant for modern economic flows. The production of transport equipment is also of major importance to upstream economic activities, most notably metal processing, rubber, plastics, electronics and engineering.

Transport equipment was the largest manufacturing industry in the EU in 1999

Transport equipment accounted for 14.3% of EU manufacturing activity in terms of production value in 1999 and for 12.4% in terms of value added, making it the largest manufacturing industry (in terms of NACE Rev. 1 Subsection headings). Total EU output reached 573 billion EUR, and this industry employed 2.54 million persons in 1999, which was more than a tenth of all the persons employed in EU manufacturing (10.9%).

Figure 13.1

Transport equipment (NACE Rev. 1 34 and 35)
Share of total manufacturing value added
in the EU, 1995 (%)

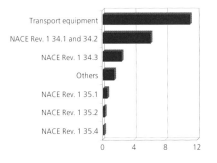

Source: Eurostat (SBS)

The activities covered in this chapter (in terms of NACE Rev. 1) include:

34: manufacture of motor vehicles, trailers and semi-trailers;
34.1: manufacture of motor vehicles;
34.2: manufacture of bodies (coachwork) for motor vehicles; manufacture of trailers and semi-trailers;
34.3: manufacture of parts and accessories for motor vehicles and their engines;
35: manufacture of other transport equipment;
35.1: building and repairing of ships and boats;
35.2: manufacture of railway and tramway locomotives and rolling stock;
35.3: manufacture of aircraft and spacecraft;
35.4: manufacture of motorcycles and bicycles;
35.5: manufacture of other transport equipment n.e.c.

Having pioneered mass production processes in the first half of the century, the motor vehicles industry (in particular) has become a leader in the use of new production and management techniques. Of these, perhaps the best known are "just-in-time" and "lean" production, "total quality management" and "continuous re-engineering".

The process of globalisation has greatly affected the transport equipment industry and resulted in the world's leading manufacturers setting-up transplants and negotiating alliances throughout the world. This has often led to the development of transport specific geographical "clusters" - for example, motor vehicles in Baden-Württemberg and Bavaria (both Germany), Piemonte (Italy) and the Midlands (United Kingdom), or aerospace around Toulouse (France).

Transport equipment is dominated by the manufacture of motor vehicles, trailers and semi-trailers (NACE Rev. 1 34) that accounted for over four-fifths of EU production within the industries covered by this chapter. By far the most important sub-activity was the manufacture of motor vehicles (NACE Rev. 1 34.1), which alone accounted for almost 60% of the EU transport equipment industry in 1995. The second most important industry was the manufacture of parts and accessories for motor vehicles (NACE Rev. 1 34.3) which accounted for 17.0% of the transport equipment total (1995), followed by the manufacture of aircraft and spacecraft (NACE Rev. 1 35.3) with a 13.0% share (1999).

Germany had the highest absolute production and relative specialisation

Some 17.1% of domestic manufacturing output in Germany was generated within the transport equipment industry in 1997, equivalent to 172 billion ECU (the vast majority derived from the motor vehicles industry). The next most important relative shares were found in France and Sweden (where 16.6% and 16.1% of domestic manufacturing output was generated in 1997). Transport equipment accounted for less than 4.0% of total domestic manufacturing output in Greece (1996), Ireland, Luxembourg and Finland in 1997 (the lowest shares within the EU).

Production within the French transport equipment industry was spread across a range of industries including motor vehicles (production specialisation ratio of 126.6%) and aerospace (179.0%), whilst the United Kingdom was relatively specialised in aerospace (238.5%) and Italy in the manufacture of motorcycles and bicycles (322.5%).

An industry dominated by large enterprises

More than four-fifths (82.1%) of the total number of persons employed in the EU transport equipment industry were working in a large enterprise (with 250 or more employees) in 1996. This was well above the average for total industry (46.1%), with only the manufacture of coke, refined petroleum products and nuclear fuel reporting a higher figure (89.5%). In terms of turnover, the share of large enterprises was higher still, as they accounted for 89.1% of the turnover generated by the transport equipment industry. These figures suggest that economies of scale play an important role in this highly capital-intensive industry.

Table 13.1

Transport equipment (NACE Rev. 1 34 and 35)

Breakdown of turnover and employment by employment size class, 1997 (%)

	Micro (0-9)		Small (10-49)		Medium (50-249)		Large (250+)	
	Turnover (1)	Employment (2)	Turnover (3)	Employment (4)	Turnover (5)	Employment (6)	Turnover (7)	Employment (8)
EU-15	1.3	3.1	3.5	5.7	6.1	9.0	89.1	82.1
B	1.6	2.4	2.9	6.0	3.9	6.3	91.6	85.3
DK	:	:	11.6	12.9	:	:	:	:
D	0.4	1.2	1.1	3.1	1.6	2.7	96.9	92.9
EL	:	:	:	:	:	:	:	:
E	1.8	5.0	3.1	10.3	8.7	14.8	86.4	69.8
F	1.0	2.2	3.0	4.3	4.5	7.4	91.6	86.2
IRL	:	:	:	:	:	:	:	:
I	1.7	3.7	7.0	9.9	12.2	14.3	79.1	72.2
L	:	:	:	:	:	:	:	:
NL	:	:	:	:	:	19.6	:	57.0
A	0.6	2.1	2.6	6.1	8.0	15.7	86.6	76.1
P	2.4	4.7	4.5	13.5	12.7	21.5	80.3	60.2
FIN	4.7	7.0	8.6	13.3	23.5	17.4	63.3	62.2
S	1.5	:	2.7	4.8	7.0	11.8	88.8	:
UK	2.7	6.1	3.2	5.2	:	:	84.5	:

(1) EU-15, E, F, I, P and S, 1996.
(2) EU-15, F, I and P, 1996.
(3) EU-15, DK, E, F, I, A, P and S, 1996.
(4) EU-15, DK, F, I, A, P and S, 1996.
(5) EU-15, E, F, I, A, P and S, 1996.
(6) EU-15, F, I, NL, A, P and S, 1996.
(7) EU-15, E, F, I, A, P, S and UK, 1996.
(8) EU-15, F, I, NL, A and P, 1996.

Source: Eurostat (SME)

Figure 13.2

Transport equipment (NACE Rev. 1 34 and 35)

EU production and value-added in constant prices and employment compared to total manufacturing (1990=100)

Production in constant prices

Value added in constant prices

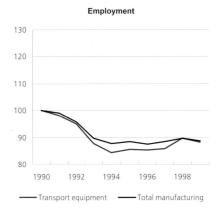

Employment

Source: Eurostat (SBS)

STRUCTURE AND PERFORMANCE

EU production rose on average by 3.1% each year in real terms between 1990 and 1998, above the figure for the whole of EU manufacturing (2.2%). There were nevertheless large fluctuations reported during the 1990s, as production in constant prices fell by as much as 14.2% in 1993. This was one of just two years during the 1990s (1991 was the other) when production fell in real terms. In both these cases output decreased at a faster pace than the manufacturing average. The recovery was equally pronounced, as transport equipment registered production growth in excess of the manufacturing average in each year between 1994 and 1998, rising by as much as 15.0% in real terms in 1997 (some 7.0 percentage points over the manufacturing average).

Motor vehicle parts and accessories
accounted for an increasing share of
the transport equipment industry…
Structural change in the composition of the transport equipment industry can be analysed over the period 1985 to 1995, when the shares of the different transport activities shifted in favour of motor vehicle production away from other transport sectors (reinforcing the dominant position of the motor vehicles industry,

with a swing of +/-5.7 percentage points). This change was largely a result of rapidly increasing output in the motor vehicles parts and accessories industry (+4.1 percentage points). This could well be due to the fact that an increasing share of motor vehicle production is being carried out by manufacturers of parts and accessories (see sub-chapter 13.2 for more details), as a result of a tiered outsourcing system. On the downside, the relative share of shipbuilding declined by 2.8 percentage points, whilst the aerospace industry lost approximately 2.6 percentage points.

… whilst its production transferred
to the Iberian peninsula
In 1985, 81.0% of the manufacture of transport equipment was concentrated within the four largest EU economies. By 1997[1], this share had fallen by 3.1 percentage points (although the German share rose by 0.2 percentage points). The transfer of production away from Italy (-0.2 percentage points), France (-0.5 percentage points) and the United Kingdom (-1.4 percentage points) shifted in the main towards Spain (+2.1 percentage points). Based upon the available data for the other 14 Member States it is likely that the relative share of Portugal also improved considerably over this period.

LABOUR AND PRODUCTIVITY

Transport equipment industries accounted for 10.4% of the manufacturing workforce in the EU in 1999. There were 2.54 million persons employed, with 274 thousand posts lost between 1989 and 1999. This decline was equivalent to an average annual reduction of 1.0%, similar to the rate of change recorded for the whole of EU manufacturing (-1.1%). In both relative and absolute terms, employment declined the most in the United Kingdom and France (losing 146 thousand and 140 thousand net jobs between 1985 and 1997). These losses were more than three times as large as those recorded in either Germany or Italy[2]. With the exception of Ireland (with a net increase of 4.1 thousand posts) all countries reported a declining workforce between 1985 and 1997[3]. In terms of relative shares of the EU total, the German, Spanish and the Portuguese labour markets grew in the 1990s.

An industry dominated by male employment…
A large proportion of men were employed within the transport equipment industry in the EU in 1998. Men held 85.1% of all posts in this industry, the third highest share in the economy (in terms of all economic activities, at the level of NACE Rev. 1 Sections and Subsections), behind construction and mining and quarrying.

---

(1) EL and I, 1996 instead of 1997; FIN, 1986 instead of 1985; P, no data available.

(2) I, calculated on the basis of the change between 1985 and 1996.
(3) EL and I, 1996 instead of 1997; FIN, 1986 instead of 1985; P, no data available.

In 1999, the proportion of men employed in transport equipment was between 11.8 and 14.1 percentage points higher than the manufacturing industry average in at least half of the Member States[4]. In Finland (19.5 percentage points difference from the manufacturing average) and Denmark (17.7 percentage points) there was an even higher proportion of men employed, whilst in neighbouring Sweden, the lowest difference was recorded (7.8 percentage points). Portugal had the lowest share of men employed in transport equipment in 1999[5] (69.0% of the total), whilst two countries reported men accounting for more than 90% of their transport equipment workforce, Spain (90.5%) and the Netherlands (91.3%).

... and the lowest proportion of part-time work
Part-time work was of low importance, as it accounted for just 3.1% of the total number of persons in employment in EU transport equipment industries (compared to an EU manufacturing average of 7.3%) in 1998. This was the lowest share of part-time work for any industrial or service activity (in terms of all economic activities, at the level of NACE Rev. 1 Sections and Subsections).

Apparent labour productivity of the transport equipment industry was equal to 59.2 thousand EUR per person employed in 1999, above the EU manufacturing average of 51.8 thousand EUR. The differential between the manufacturing average and transport equipment was less than 3 thousand ECU per person employed in favour of transport equipment during the

(4) EL and L, no data available.
(5) EL and L, no data available.

period 1989 to 1996. However, since 1997 transport equipment industries have seen their apparent labour productivity grow at a more rapid pace.

Unit personnel costs in the EU were some 4.7 thousand ECU per employee higher in the transport equipment industry than the manufacturing average in 1995, at 38.3 thousand ECU per employee. By combining the two indicators on apparent labour productivity and unit personnel costs it is possible to derive a wage adjusted labour productivity ratio (124.2% for transport equipment in 1995), which showed that the industry was less productive than the manufacturing average (134.7%) when the cost of labour was taken into account. Closer inspection of the data showed that this was largely due to other transport activities, where the wage adjusted labour productivity ratio was equal to 104.7% in 1995.

INTERNATIONAL TRENDS AND FOREIGN TRADE
The EU accounted for 38.7% of total Triad output in 1997, a 4.2 percentage point gain compared to 1987. As such, the EU was the largest manufacturer of transport equipment (overtaking the USA in 1995). American output reached 478 billion ECU in 1997 (or 37.0% of the total), whilst Japan produced 314 billion ECU of transport equipment goods (or 24.3% of the total).

The decline in employment levels in the EU during the early 1990s was mirrored in both the USA and Japan. In 1997, the EU accounted for nearly half (48.9%) of the Triad workforce, whilst a third (33.4%) worked in the USA and the remaining 17.7% were employed in Japan.

Table 13.2

Transport equipment (NACE Rev. 1 34 and 35)
Composition of the labour force, 1999 (%)

	Women (1)	Part-time (2)	Highly-educated (3)
EU-15	14.9	3.1	19.1
B	10.2	:	17.6
DK	19.5	:	17.8
D	16.6	4.1	22.7
EL	:	:	:
E	9.5	1.1	27.0
F	16.4	4.1	19.1
IRL	:	:	:
I	14.8	1.5	6.4
L	:	:	:
NL	8.7	:	18.7
A	11.8	:	7.0
P	31.0	:	6.9
FIN	11.3	:	21.4
S	17.8	:	26.7
UK	13.8	2.3	20.0

(1) EU-15 and DK, 1998; FIN, 1996.
(2) EU-15, 1998.
(3) DK, 1998; EU-15, P and UK, 1997.

Source: Eurostat (LFS)

Figure 13.3

Transport equipment (NACE Rev. 1 34 and 35)
Apparent labour productivity and unit personnel costs, 1997 (thousand ECU)

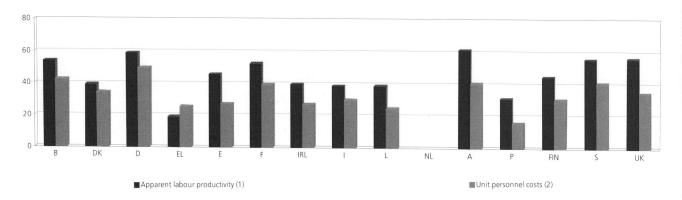

(1) EL and I, 1996; NL, not available.
(2) DK, EL and I, 1996; NL, not available.

Source: Eurostat (SBS)

Figure 13.4

Transport equipment (NACE Rev. 1 34 and 35)

International comparison of production, value added and employment

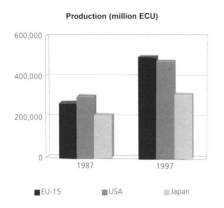

Production (million ECU)

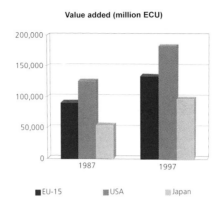

Value added (million ECU)

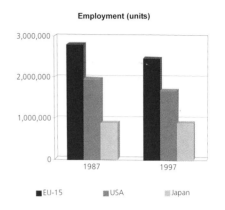

Employment (units)

Source: Eurostat (SBS)

There was a high degree of investment by south-east Asian motor vehicle producers in Europe in the early 1990s, often justified as being in anticipation of the creation of the Single Market. Foreign direct investment inflows were more subdued in the second half of the 1990s, and transport equipment accounted for just 3.2% of total manufacturing FDI coming into the EU in 1998 (991 million ECU).

On the other hand, investments (equity and other capital) made by EU manufacturers abroad rose to a record level of 38.5 billion ECU in 1998 (almost 70% of the manufacturing total). Germany was by far the most important contributor, carrying out almost three-quarters of the EU's investment abroad.

The late 1990s saw the leading firms growing through mergers and acquisitions rather than by internal growth. This trend has led to consolidation in the transport equipment industry, with some large mergers or take-overs, such as DaimlerChrysler or Aerospatiale Matra and DaimlerChrysler Aerospace.

Almost 18% of the EU's manufacturing exports were transport equipment goods

Transport equipment accounted for a rising share of the EU's manufacturing exports to non-Community countries during the course of the 1990s (up from 15.2% in 1989 to 17.7% in 1999). The EU was by far the most important exporter of transport equipment goods within the Triad, its share of Triad exports rising from 30.6% in 1989 to 38.0% in 1998. In 1999, EU exports were valued at 125 billion EUR, almost 28 billion EUR above the corresponding level of imports. Nevertheless, during the late 1990s imports grew at a faster pace, with the cover ratio falling in successive years from a high of 191.5% in 1995 to 128.4% by 1999.

The main destination of EU exports remained fairly similar when comparing data for 1989 and 1999. The USA was the most important export market, accounting for almost a third (32.5%) of the EU's exports in 1989, rising to 37.0% in 1999. Switzerland and Japan occupied second and third places respectively, with their shares in 1999 somewhat reduced (8.0% and 4.7% compared to 9.0% and 7.0%).

The majority of EU imports in 1999 originated from just two countries, namely the USA (38.7%) and Japan (19.3%). There was however a decline in their respective shares, as in 1989 they accounted for more than three-quarters of the EU's imports from non-Community countries (USA 41.7% and Japan 35.4%). The main beneficiaries in 1999, recording rising shares of total EU imports, were South Korea (4.2%), the Czech Republic (3.4%) and Poland (2.4%).

Figure 13.5

Transport equipment (NACE Rev. 1 34 and 35)

Destination of EU exports, 1999 (%)

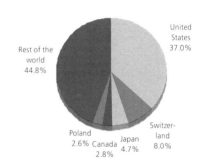

Source: Eurostat (COMEXT)

Figure 13.6

Transport equipment (NACE Rev. 1 34 and 35)

Origin of EU imports, 1999 (%)

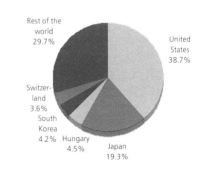

Source: Eurostat (COMEXT)

SUB-CHAPTER 13.1
MOTOR VEHICLES
(NACE Rev. 1 34.1 AND 34.2)

This sub-chapter covers the manufacture of motor vehicles (NACE Rev. 1 34.1), as well as the manufacture of motor vehicle bodies (NACE Rev. 1 34.2). The data included in this sub-chapter does not include the manufacture of tractors (sub-chapter 8.3), parts and accessories for motor vehicles (sub-chapter 13.2), nor the retail sale or repair of motor vehicles (sub-chapter 16.1).

EU output of motor vehicles and bodies reached 259.6 billion ECU in 1995, with 1.2 million persons employed. More recent figures for the individual Member States showed that output increased in the second half of the 1990s, as production reached 301.3 billion ECU in 1997[6].

The manufacture of motor vehicles and bodies is approximately twice the size of the parts and accessories industry

The information covered in this sub-chapter accounted for just over two-thirds (67.4%) of the whole motor vehicles industry in 1995, with parts and accessories (covered in the next sub-chapter) accounting for the remaining third. The manufacture of motor vehicles (NACE Rev. 1 34.1) was significantly more important than the manufacture of motor vehicle bodies (NACE Rev. 1 34.2), as it represented 94.0% of total output and 89.0% of the total number of persons employed within the data presented in this sub-chapter.

Germany was the largest producer of motor vehicles and bodies in 1997, with output equal to 118.2 billion ECU (approximately 40% of the EU total). This high share was also reflected in the relative production specialisation figures, with Germany (134.1%) the second most specialised country in 1995, behind Sweden (139.8%).

(6) On the basis of 1997 information summed across Member States: EL and I, 1996; NL, 1994; L, no data available.

Figure 13.7

Motor vehicles (NACE Rev. 1 34.1 and 34.2)

Production and export specialisation (%)

Production specialisation (1995) (1)

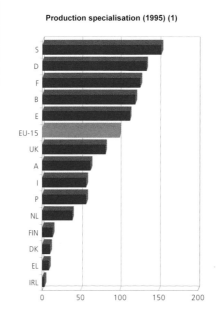

Export specialisation (1999)

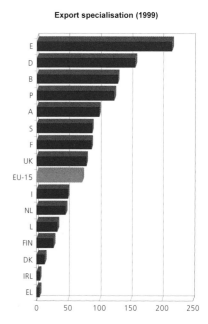

(1) A, 1994; L, not available.

Source: Eurostat (SBS, COMEXT)

Table 13.3

Automobile production in the EU, 1999 (units)

Automobile Group	Passenger cars	Light commercial vehicles	Trucks	Buses	Total
Volkswagen	2,985,715	177,890	0	0	3,163,605
PSA Peugeot Citroën	1,969,102	415,367	0	0	2,384,469
Ford (1)	2,079,412	198,495	0	0	2,277,907
GM	1,916,279	58,249	0	0	1,974,528
Renault	1,645,670	263,285	42,182	2,355	1,953,492
Fiat	1,402,698	217,474	66,108	4,197	1,690,477
DaimlerChrysler	1,127,085	178,259	94,848	6,423	1,406,615
BMW Rover	1,048,046	24,155	0	0	1,072,201
Volvo	0	0	50,505	5,698	56,203
Man	0	0	50,025	3,943	53,968
Paccar-Daf-Leyland Trucks-Foden	0	0	32,466	1,795	34,261
Scania	0	0	41,580	2,633	44,213
Porsche	46,167	0	0	0	46,167
Other European manufacturers	0	1,532	12,913	6,744	21,189
Japanese manufacturers	713,296	82,225	3,584	0	799,105
TOTAL	14,933,470	1,616,931	394,211	33,788	16,978,400

(1) Volvo cars production is included in Ford.

Source: ACEA

According to the European Automobile Manufacturers Association (ACEA), the EU produced an estimated 17.0 million passenger cars, trucks and buses in 1999. This was 2.3% more than in 1998. Passenger cars (14.9 million units) were by far the most important group, followed by light commercial trucks (1.6 million units), trucks (394 thousand units) and buses (34 thousand units).

Volkswagen (20.0%), Ford[7] (13.9%), PSA Peugeot Citroen (13.2%), General Motors (12.8%) and Renault (11.0%) produced the majority of the passenger cars made in the EU in 1999. Fiat, DaimlerChrysler and BMW Rover also produced in excess of one million units each in 1999 (representing at least 7.0% of the total), whilst Japanese manufacturers were responsible for 4.8% of the EU's output of passenger cars. The main producer of light commercial vehicles was PSA Peugeot Citroen, with more than a quarter (25.7%) of the EU's output, followed by Renault (16.3%) and Fiat (13.4%). In the heavy trucks sector, DaimlerChrysler (24.1%), Fiat (16.8%), Volvo (12.8%) and MAN (12.7%) were the leading manufacturers. Scania and Renault also produced more than 10% of the EU's output of heavy trucks.

(7) Includes Volvo's car making business.

──────────────── Figure 13.8

Number of passenger cars in use per thousand inhabitants, as of 31st December 1998 (units)

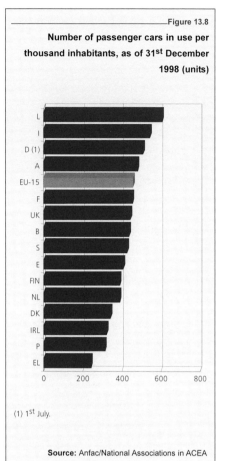

(1) 1st July.

Source: Anfac/National Associations in ACEA

STRUCTURE AND PERFORMANCE

The motor vehicles and bodies industry recorded declining output between 1990 and 1995, with production in constant prices falling at an average rate of 1.2% per annum. This negative rate of change was in stark contrast to the evolution of the parts and accessories industry (+7.2% per annum) and was also below the transport equipment average (-0.3% per annum). During the second half of 1990s, there was however a rapid expansion in production as consumer demand recovered. Production grew in real terms by as much as 27.0% in Ireland and 19.3% in the United Kingdom between 1996 and 1997. All Member States[8] reported growth in excess of 4.0% between these two years except for Belgium (-7.4%).

EU gross value added as a share of production fell from 30.3% in 1985 to 24.8% by 1995. This rate of change was considerably more pronounced than the reduction recorded for the whole of manufacturing (-0.4 percentage points) and may point to an increase in out-sourcing which is a common feature of many transport equipment industries.

(8) EL, I, L and A, no data available.

──────────────── Figure 13.9

Motor vehicles (NACE Rev. 1 34.1 and 34.2)
International comparison of production and employment (1990=100)

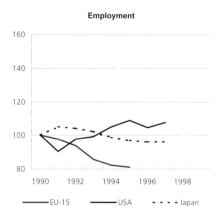

Source: Eurostat (SBS)

Leading vehicle manufacturers have devoted large amounts of money to research. The increase in oil prices during the course of 1999 further fuelled research efforts to develop cheaper, alternative means of powering cars (such as natural gas, LPG or electric vehicles driven by batteries). The European motor vehicles industry agreed to cut vehicle emissions of carbon dioxide by a quarter between 1995 and 2008.

Another area where research is concentrated is safety issues (with a more widespread introduction of air bags and ABS breaking systems). These initiatives (together with legislation on the use of seat belts) have resulted in a significant decrease in the number of persons killed in car accidents in the EU (from 64.2 thousand in 1980 to 42.7 thousand in 1998).

Demand fluctuated by a large margin
between the Member States

There were 14.6 million new passenger car registrations in the EU in 1999. Demand for new passenger cars grew at an average rate of 1.2% per annum between 1990 and 1999 masking a slump in demand during the mid-1990s; the low was reached in 1993 when there were just 10.9 million new car registrations. The fastest expanding markets for new passenger cars during the 1990s were Greece (9.5% per annum), Ireland (8.6%), Denmark (6.6%) and Spain (4.0%). On the other hand, the four largest EU markets reported little change in demand, the United Kingdom (+1.0% per annum), Italy (+0.2%), France (-0.8%) and Germany (-1.1%)[9].

LABOUR AND PRODUCTIVITY

The total number of persons employed in the motor vehicles and bodies industry in the EU fell by 273 thousand between 1985 and 1995, down by 18.4%, a somewhat larger decline than that observed for the whole of transport equipment (-15.0%).

Eurostat estimate that apparent labour productivity in the EU was equal to 56.6 thousand ECU per person employed in 1997, whilst unit personnel costs were estimated to be as high as 42.8 thousand ECU per employee. Portugal (246.7%) and to a lesser degree Spain (195.1%) and the United Kingdom (177.4%) reported the highest wage adjusted labour productivity ratios in 1997, whilst Germany (118.9%) closed the ranking.

---

(9) Annual average growth rate between 1991 and 1999. Reunification in D may have affected consumer spending in 1991 and 1992, resulting in a negative rate of change as figures stabilised in the following years.

INTERNATIONAL TRENDS AND FOREIGN TRADE

The EU was the leading producer of motor vehicles and bodies in the Triad, accounting for 42.0% of output in 1995 (more than 6.0 percentage points above the EU's share of the Triad transport equipment industry). The USA accounted for one third (33.0%) of total Triad production, leaving Japan with the remaining quarter (25.0%).

The EU exported 52.3 billion EUR of motor vehicles and bodies in 1999. Its trade surplus stood at 19.9 billion EUR, which was down compared to the high of 28.2 billion EUR reached in 1997 (but still above the levels recorded during the late 1980s and early to mid-1990s). Japan also ran a large trade surplus, which grew during the 1990s to reach 50.6 billion ECU in 1998 (when the value of Japanese exports was more than ten times that of Japanese imports).

Decreasing importance for Japanese imports?

Japan was the origin of 71.3% of the EU's imports of motor vehicles and bodies in 1989, a share which had fallen to 39.1% by 1999[10]. Specific import arrangements on Japanese imports entering the EU were ended at the start of 2000 (following the expiry of the "Elements of Consensus"). The importance of Eastern Europe as an origin for EU imports grew rapidly during the 1990s. Hungary, the Czech Republic, Slovakia, Poland and Slovenia were all present within the top eight importing countries, and together they accounted for 28.2% of total EU imports in 1999. There was also a significant increase in the share of South Korean imports from 0.8% in 1989 to 10.2% in 1999.

---

(10) It is important to note that data relating to Japanese-owned transplants within Europe are attributed to the country where production took place. The share of Japanese brands in the EU motor vehicles market is therefore higher than these import figures suggest.

In 1999, the main destination of EU exports was the USA (38.6% of the total), followed by Japan (8.7%) and Switzerland (8.3%). There was little change in the respective shares of these three countries between 1989 and 1999. Poland, Turkey, Hungary and the Czech Republic all became increasingly important as a destination for EU exports during the 1990s.

Figure 13.10

Motor vehicles (NACE Rev. 1 34.1 and 34.2)
Destination of EU exports, 1999 (%)

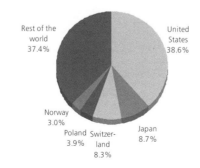

Source: Eurostat (COMEXT)

Figure 13.11

Motor vehicles (NACE Rev. 1 34.1 and 34.2)
Origin of EU imports, 1999 (%)

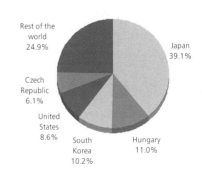

Source: Eurostat (COMEXT)

SUB-CHAPTER 13.2
MOTOR VEHICLES PARTS AND
ACCESSORIES (NACE Rev. 1 34.3)

The information contained within this sub-chapter covers the manufacture of diverse parts and accessories for motor vehicles, such as brakes, gear boxes, axles, road wheels, radiators, exhaust pipes, clutches, steering wheels, safety belts, doors and bumpers. The data presented does not cover the majority of the electrical and electronic components or batteries used in motor vehicles (chapter 11), the manufacture of tyres (sub-chapter 6.7) or the repair of motor vehicles (sub-chapter 16.2).

The industry is traditionally broken down into two main segments. Firstly, the market for original equipment (OE), which comprises parts and accessories that car manufacturers buy from specialised producers for the assembly of new vehicles. Secondly, the replacement or after-market (AM), which comprises of parts and accessories destined for maintenance and repairs.

An industry employing more than
half a million persons in the EU...
The latest figures available for the output of the EU motor vehicles parts and accessories industry show that production value was equal to 69.7 billion ECU in 1995. As such the industry represented 17.0% of output within the transport equipment industry (making it the second largest activity behind the manufacture of motor vehicles). In terms of employment, motor vehicle parts and accessories accounted for an even higher share of the total number of persons employed, 22.9% in 1995 (or 565 thousand persons).

_____ **Box 13.6**
Demand for OE automotive components is linked to the level of motor vehicle production, which fluctuates with the general economic cycle. Some components benefit from much faster growth rates, as previously optional parts become standard fittings (for example, anti-lock brakes, air bags and anti-theft devices). Demand for AM parts is largely dependent on the market for used cars, the average age of motor vehicles, the average annual mileage per vehicle, the existence of specific legislation with regard to the obligatory inspection of vehicles, as well as extreme weather conditions.

_____ Figure 13.12

Motor vehicle parts and accessories (NACE Rev. 1 34.3)
Production and export specialisation (%)

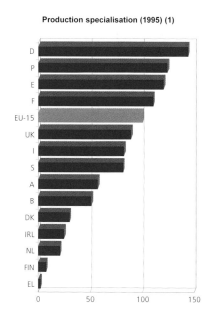

Production specialisation (1995) (1)

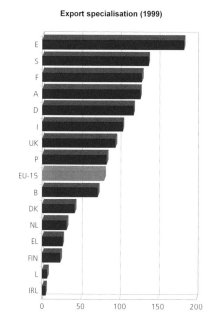

Export specialisation (1999)

(1) A, 1994; L, not available.

Source: Eurostat (SBS, COMEXT)

Germany was by far the leading EU manufacturer of motor vehicle parts and accessories (33.8 billion ECU in 1997), with output almost three times that of France - the second most important producer. The German share of EU output was in excess of 40.0% in 1995. As such, Germany was more specialised than any other Member State (143.7%), followed by Portugal (123.8%) and Spain (120.3%). In all three countries, motor vehicles parts and accessories accounted for approximately one-fifth of total transport equipment output.

STRUCTURE AND PERFORMANCE

In the first half of the 1990s, the motor vehicles parts and accessories industry displayed far more rapid expansion than the transport equipment average. Between 1990 and 1995, the average annual rate of growth for production in constant prices was equal to 7.6%, whilst the general economic recession of the early 1990s resulted in a negative rate (-0.3% per annum) for the whole of transport equipment over the same period. Growth rates in the second half of the 1990s were generally at an even faster pace, especially in those countries that were relatively specialised in this industry. Output rose in real terms by 19.2% in Spain and 15.1% in Germany in 1997.

There was a shift in the geographical location of EU production between 1985 and 1995. The United Kingdom (-3.6 percentage points), France (-2.6 points) and Belgium (-2.5 points) recorded the largest losses in terms of their shares of EU output. The main beneficiary was Germany, which recorded a 6.6 percentage point gain in its share of EU output, whilst Italy (+1.2 points) and Portugal (+1.1 points, between 1990 and 1995) also benefited.

LABOUR AND PRODUCTIVITY

More than 65 thousand net jobs were created in the motor vehicles parts and accessories industry in the EU between 1985 and 1995 (whilst transport equipment as a whole lost 436 thousand posts). These figures hide a cyclical evolution, whereby the number of persons employed increased at a steady pace between 1985 and 1990, declined to a low of 487 thousand persons in 1993, only to rise in dramatic fashion between 1994 and 1995 (+15.0%).

In 1997, unit personnel costs in the EU were estimated at 35.0 thousand ECU per employee. Of the 9 countries for which data were available, all (except Spain, where no difference was observed) reported that unit personnel costs were lower for the manufacture of motor vehicle parts and accessories than for transport equipment as a whole. Apparent labour productivity was estimated to be 48.3 thousand ECU per person employed in 1997.

Figure 13.13

Motor vehicle parts and accessories (NACE Rev. 1 34.3)

International comparison of production in constant prices and employment (1990=100)

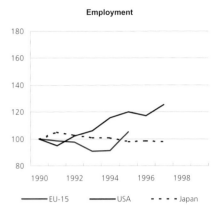

Source: Eurostat (SBS)

INTERNATIONAL TRENDS AND FOREIGN TRADE

Japan accounted for just less than half of the output of the motor vehicle parts and accessories industry in the Triad in 1995 (49.8%), whilst the remainder was split almost equally between the USA (25.4%) and the EU (24.8%). In terms of employment the shares were considerably different, as the EU employed more persons (37.3% of the total) than Japan (35.2%), whilst the share of the USA was quite consistent with that recorded for production (27.4%).

Increasing importance of Eastern Europe as an origin of imports and a destination for exports
Almost 15% of the EU's transport equipment exports were accounted for by the motor vehicles parts and accessories industry in 1999. EU exports were valued at 18.6 billion EUR, some 7.1 billion EUR more than imports. The main destination for EU exports was the USA, accounting for more than a quarter of the total in both 1989 and 1999 (25.4%). There were several countries that became relatively more important over this ten-year period: Poland, Hungary, Brazil, Mexico and the Czech Republic all accounted for between 5% and 6% of the EU's exports by 1999.

In 1989, two-thirds of the EU's imports originated in Japan (41.5%) and the USA (25.7%). Whilst there was almost no evolution in the relative share of the USA (26.3%) in 1999, there was a marked reduction for Japan (22.1%). The main beneficiaries were from Eastern Europe, with the Czech Republic (9.5%), Hungary (6.1%) and Poland (4.9%) next in the ranking.

Figure 13.14

Motor vehicle parts and accessories (NACE Rev. 1 34.3)

Destination of EU exports, 1999 (%)

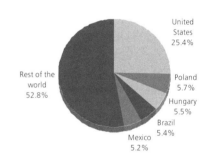

Source: Eurostat (COMEXT)

Figure 13.15

Motor vehicle parts and accessories (NACE Rev. 1 34.3)

Origin of EU imports, 1999 (%)

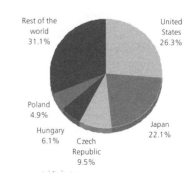

Source: Eurostat (COMEXT)

SUB-CHAPTER 13.3
MOPEDS, MOTORCYCLES AND BICYCLES
(NACE Rev. 1 35.4)

This sub-chapter concludes the coverage of the manufacture of road transport vehicles, focusing on motorcycles, mopeds and bicycles. The data presented includes the manufacture of parts and accessories for these modes of transport, as well as the manufacture of invalid carriages. This sub-chapter does not cover the manufacture of children's cycles other than bicycles, which are covered under the section on toys (sub-chapter 14.3).

Bicycles and motorised two-wheelers (mopeds, scooters and motorcycles) are used mainly for commuting or for leisure purposes. Their cost is relatively low, both in terms of purchasing price and operational costs (with a simple moped costing about an eighth of a small car to purchase and a fifth of a small car to run).

An industry dominated in the
EU by Italian manufacturers

In 1999, EU production value of the motorcycle and bicycle industry reached 7.6 billion EUR (1.3% of the transport equipment total), whilst there were 47.7 thousand persons employed (1.9% of the transport equipment total).

Italy had a dominant position with respect to other Member States, with output equal to 2.9 billion ECU in 1996 (approximately 45% of the EU total). Italian production of motorcycles and bicycles accounted for 0.6% of domestic manufacturing output, whilst in all other Member States the equivalent figure was less than 0.2%. The only other country to be relatively specialised in the manufacture of motorcycles and bicycles was the Netherlands with a production specialisation ratio of 121.8% in 1997 (compared to 332.3% in Italy in 1995).

Figure 13.16

Mopeds, motorcycles and bicycles (NACE Rev. 1 35.4)
Production and export specialisation (%)

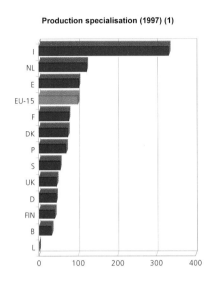

Production specialisation (1997) (1)

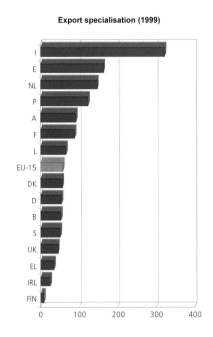

Export specialisation (1999)

(1) B, 1994; I and S, 1995; EL, IRL and A, not available.

Source: Eurostat (SBS, COMEXT)

Figure 13.17

Number of motorcycles and mopeds in use per thousand inhabitants, 1996 (units)

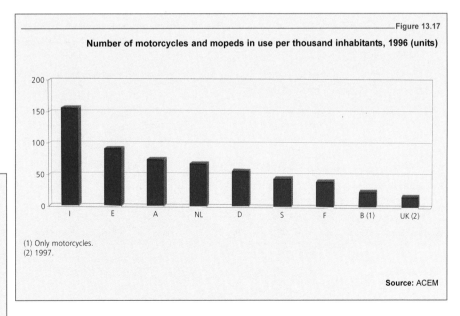

(1) Only motorcycles.
(2) 1997.

Source: ACEM

Figure 13.18

Production and consumption of bicycles, 1998 (thousand units)

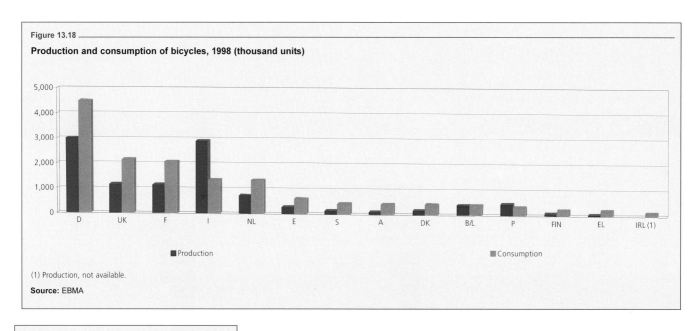

(1) Production, not available.

Source: EBMA

Box 13.9

According to ACEM (Association des Constructeurs Européens de Motocycle) there were almost 2 million mopeds and motorcycles produced in the EU in 1998, of these more than a million were produced in Italy (1.03 million).

More than half of the powered two-wheelers in use in Europe were found in the southern Member States (E, EL, I and P), reflecting both income levels and climatic conditions. In 1995, the highest number of powered two-wheelers was recorded in Italy, 7.8 million units, twice as many as in Germany (3.9 million), the next highest. Italy was also the country with the highest rate of ownership, with 137 powered two-wheelers per thousand inhabitants. Between 1980 and 1995 there was significant growth in vehicle ownership in the southern Member States, rising from 92‰ (92 vehicles per thousand inhabitants) to 137‰ in Italy, 48‰ to 86‰ in Spain, 26‰ to 52‰ in Greece and 72‰ to 92‰ in Portugal. Of the remaining Member States only Luxembourg (+16‰ to 49‰) and Finland (+10‰ to 38‰) reported a double-digit increase in their number of powered two-wheelers owned per thousand inhabitants. The lowest penetration of motorcycles and mopeds was recorded in the United Kingdom, where there were just 15 per thousand inhabitants.

However, it is interesting to note the breakdown of activity between the manufacture of powered two-wheelers and bicycles within the Member States[11]. Whilst powered two-wheelers accounted for by far the largest share of production in Spain (90.4% of the total) and Italy (71.9% of the total), the manufacture of bicycles was far more important in Belgium (98.4%) and the Netherlands (91.8%).

(11) Data exists for B, E, I, L, NL, P, FIN and UK for 1996 or 1997.

STRUCTURE AND PERFORMANCE

EU production of motorcycles and bicycles rose from 5.3 billion ECU in 1990 to 7.6 billion EUR by 1999. Production grew in real terms at an average rate of 2.4% per annum between 1990 and 1998 (whilst the equivalent figure for transport equipment was 3.1% per annum). There was rapid growth in the motorcycles and bicycles industry in the mid-1990s, when output rose in real terms by 7.5% (1994) and 9.0% (1995).

Figure 13.19

Mopeds, motorcycles and bicycles (NACE Rev. 1 35.4)

International comparison of production in constant prices and employment (1990=100)

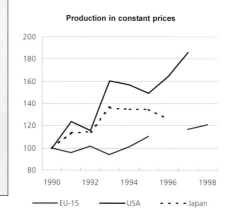

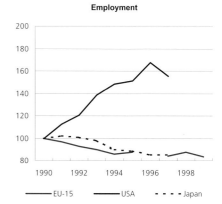

Source: Eurostat (SBS)

	1991	1992	1993	1994	1995	1996	1997	1998
EU-15 (1)	643,693	657,397	587,966	546,731	561,194	674,571	818,091	986,217
B	11,183	13,231	14,827	14,000	14,603	15,717	17,534	20,534
DK	1,651	1,181	1,652	2,022	2,288	3,020	3,254	3,394
D	144,063	175,911	204,936	216,183	218,245	271,770	313,669	289,879
EL	21,771	24,092	23,033	23,099	18,132	19,098	34,055	45,307
E	113,683	96,805	48,338	33,262	32,877	30,132	41,451	55,346
F	115,391	115,590	99,691	84,870	85,028	116,006	148,369	172,346
IRL	3,197	2,884	1,914	1,837	1,685	2,171	2,717	2,980
I	129,606	123,437	90,482	73,879	80,405	91,500	114,905	228,346
L	:	:	:	712	985	963	1,040	1,086
NL	19,981	22,608	23,056	18,401	17,799	17,010	16,466	15,085
A	11,214	12,661	15,055	16,789	18,704	21,144	20,861	24,978
P	10,543	17,310	18,171	12,903	17,628	19,646	12,180	14,300
FIN	3,215	2,025	1,230	852	1,006	1,304	2,325	3,793
S	6,389	5,677	4,611	3,903	4,380	5,762	8,672	10,988
UK	51,806	43,985	40,970	44,731	47,429	59,328	80,593	97,855
NO	610	829	1,664	2,331	2,824	3,540	6,119	7,214
CH	31,488	30,947	30,053	28,457	29,524	33,176	25,679	25,200

_____ Table 13.4

Number of motorcycle registrations (units)

(1) Excluding L, 1991 to 1993.

Source: ACEM

LABOUR AND PRODUCTIVITY

There was a net reduction of 8.6 thousand persons employed in the EU motorcycle and bicycle industries between 1989 and 1999 (equivalent to an average rate of 1.6% per annum). The jobs lost within this activity accounted for just 3.1% of the total lost within transport equipment during the period 1989 to 1999 (275 thousand posts).

In 1999, the share of the motorcycle and bicycle industries personnel costs in total operating costs was equal to 17.4%, slightly below the ratio observed for the whole of transport equipment (18.0%)[12]. Apparent labour productivity and unit personnel costs in the motorcycle and bicycle industry were relatively low when compared to most other transport equipment activities. Eurostat estimates that apparent labour productivity was equal to 35.5 thousand ECU per person employed in 1997, whilst unit personnel costs were estimated to be 26.7 thousand ECU per employee in the same year. Dividing these two ratios, the simple wage adjusted labour productivity ratio (value added / personnel costs) was equal to 133.0%.

(12) Although it should be noted that this ratio is dominated by the motor vehicles industry, whilst other transport equipment industries reported considerably higher shares.

INTERNATIONAL TRENDS AND FOREIGN TRADE

Japan was by far the leading producer of motorcycles and bicycles in the Triad, accounting for almost three-quarters (74.5%) of Triad production in 1998 (EU, 17.1%; the USA, 8.4%). After rapid growth in the early 1990s, growth tailed-off in Japan in the second half of the decade, whilst EU output started to expand. Despite such a dominant share of Triad production, Japan employed an almost identical number of persons (48.5 thousand) in 1997 as in the EU (48.0 thousand) in this industry. Whilst Japan was the leading Triad producer, south-east Asia as a whole was the centre of motorcycle and bicycle manufacture in the world, with China, India, Japan, Malaysia, Taiwan, Thailand and Vietnam all producing significant numbers of two-wheeled vehicles.

More than half of the EU's imports originate in Japan
It is therefore no surprise to see Japan account for an absolute majority (56.8%) of the EU's imports of motorcycles and bicycles in 1999, followed by Taiwan (18.3%), the USA (9.1%) and China (3.2%). In the same year, EU exports were largely destined for developed world economies, with the USA accounting for almost a third of them (32.9%), followed by Switzerland (13.1%) and Japan (8.5%).

_____ Figure 13.20

**Mopeds, motorcycles and bicycles
(NACE Rev. 1 35.4)
Destination of EU exports, 1999 (%)**

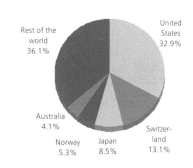

Source: Eurostat (COMEXT)

_____ Figure 13.21

**Mopeds, motorcycles and bicycles
(NACE Rev. 1 35.4)
Origin of EU imports, 1999 (%)**

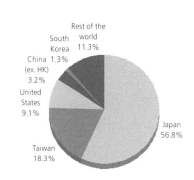

Source: Eurostat (COMEXT)

SUB-CHAPTER 13.4
AEROSPACE EQUIPMENT
(NACE Rev. 1 35.3)

This sub-chapter covers the manufacture of aeroplanes for the transport of goods or passengers, for use by defence forces, as well as for sporting activities. It also includes the space industry (launch vehicles, satellites, orbital stations and shuttles), the manufacture of helicopters, gliders, hang-gliders and balloons (but not parachutes). Parts and accessories for aircraft (such as fuselage, wings and landing gear) are also included, with the exception of instruments for navigational purposes (sub-chapter 12.2) and ignition systems for combustion engines (sub-chapter 10.1).

The EU aerospace industry had a production value of 74.4 billion EUR in 1999, whilst 22.7 billion EUR of value added was generated in the same year. Aerospace equipment can be broken down into two main product categories: civilian and military. During the last two decades there has been a significant switch towards civilian aerospace equipment, which has resulted from increased sales of civil aircraft due to the rapid growth in the number of air passengers. At the same time there has been a reduction in government spending on defence contracts (following the end of the Cold War). According to AECMA (the European Association of Aerospace Industries), between 1980 and 1998 the share of EU aerospace turnover accounted for by government spending fell from 52.4% of total turnover to 25.6%.

Figure 13.22

Aerospace equipment (NACE Rev. 1 35.3)
Production and export specialisation (%)

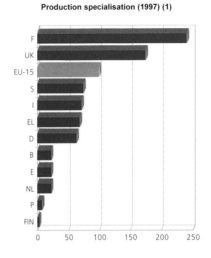

Production specialisation (1997) (1)

Export specialisation (1999)

(1) EL and I, 1994; DK, IRL, L and A, not available.

Source: Eurostat (SBS, COMEXT)

Box 13.10

There has been consolidation in the EU aerospace industry in recent years. By far the largest merger to date took place in 1999, when DaimlerChrysler Aerospace merged with Aerospatiale Matra to form the European Aeronautical, Defence & Space Company (EADS). The deal created the world's third largest aerospace and defence concern, behind Boeing and Lockheed (both USA). EADS holds an 80% share in Airbus Industrie (which took 55% of world orders for big airliners in 1999). The remaining 20% of Airbus Industrie is held by BAE Systems (formerly British Aerospace), which is the second largest aerospace manufacturer in the EU. BAE Systems has also been involved in take-over activity in the late 1990s, purchasing the electronics defence unit of Marconi, as well as the USA-based Tracor.

France (26.2 billion ECU of production value) and the United Kingdom (17.6 billion ECU of production value) were the leading aerospace manufacturers in the EU in 1997, some way ahead of Germany (11.2 billion ECU). Indeed, in terms of relative production specialisation, only France (241.1%) and the United Kingdom (175.2%) reported that the manufacture of aerospace equipment contributed more than the European average to their national manufacturing totals. Of the remaining Member States, only Italy (4.9 billion ECU, 1996), Sweden (1.5 billion ECU, 1997) and Spain (1.1 billion ECU, 1997) reported output in excess of 600 million ECU.

Figure 13.23

Breakdown of aerospace industry turnover by product segment in the EU, 1998 (%) (1)

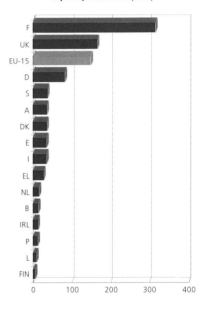

(1) Based on consolidated turnover.
(2) Data comprises EU and non-EU supplied aerostructures, engines and equipment.
(3) Excluding maintenance.

Source: AECMA

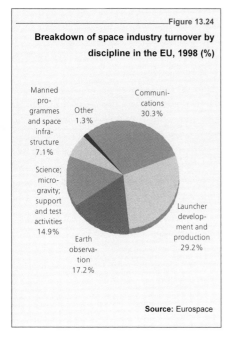

Figure 13.24

Breakdown of space industry turnover by discipline in the EU, 1998 (%)

Manned programmes and space infrastructure 7.1%

Other 1.3%

Communications 30.3%

Science; microgravity; support and test activities 14.9%

Earth observation 17.2%

Launcher development and production 29.2%

Source: Eurospace

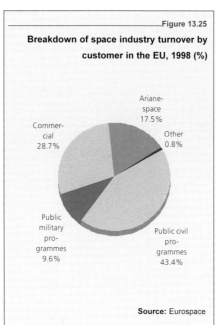

Figure 13.25

Breakdown of space industry turnover by customer in the EU, 1998 (%)

Commercial 28.7%

Ariane-space 17.5%

Other 0.8%

Public military programmes 9.6%

Public civil programmes 43.4%

Source: Eurospace

Box 13.11

AECMA estimates that in 1998 the largest aerospace product segment was final aircraft products, which accounted for 41.5% of turnover in the EU. This category can be further broken down into large civil aircraft (45.6%), military aircraft (33.9%), helicopters (11.3%), regional aircraft (4.9%) and business jets (4.3%). The second largest product segment (in terms of turnover) was aircraft maintenance (22.5%), which has become one of the most competitive areas of the industry in recent years, as rival manufacturers and servicing companies have started to compete for contracts linked to the maintenance of (each other's) planes.

STRUCTURE AND PERFORMANCE

Between 1989 and 1999 EU production rose by 33.6 billion ECU in current price terms. Production increased at an average rate of 3.3% per annum between 1990 and 1998 in real terms (slightly above the transport equipment average of 3.1%) although there was a substantial decline in production in 1993 (compared to 1992), equal to 11.3% in real terms.

The share of EU aerospace production in the transport equipment total rose from 12.5% to 13.0% between 1985 and 1999. Aerospace accounted for just over a quarter (25.5%) of French transport equipment output in 1997, a 3.5 percentage point increase on the share recorded in 1985. This was the largest gain[13] recorded by any of the Member States, consolidating the French position as Europe's leading aerospace manufacturer. During the same period the largest relative decline was recorded in the Netherlands where the share of aerospace manufacture in the transport equipment total fell from 16.7% to 7.5%.

Whilst there was an increasing move towards consolidation of the main aerospace manufacturers, this industry (in common with other transport equipment industries) has at the same time turned to sub-contracting and out-sourcing. AECMA estimates that there were around 700 companies in the EU operating as prime contractors and/or suppliers to the main aerospace manufacturers and around 80 thousand suppliers of hardware, software and services at the next level (serving prime contractors). This move towards sub-contracting and outsourcing was evident in the data for the value added rate (the share of value added in production value) which fell from 40.5% to 30.5% between 1985 to 1999 (whilst the total manufacturing average fell from 31.5% to 30.2% over the same period).

An industry that devotes a high share of turnover to R&D

Aerospace is one of the EU's leading high-technology industries. R&D expenditure was estimated by AECMA to be equal to more than 16% of turnover in 1999. Profitability (measured by the gross operating rate) in the aerospace industry were higher than the transport equipment average during the period 1985 to 1999 (other than during the recessionary period 1992 to 1994). In 1999, the gross operating rate of the EU aerospace industry was equal to 8.4% (1.7 percentage points above the transport equipment average).

(13) In EL, aerospace output was more than halved between 1985 and 1996, whilst its relative share of the domestic transport equipment total tripled.

Figure 13.26

Aerospace equipment (NACE Rev. 1 35.3)
International comparison of production in constant prices and employment (1990=100)

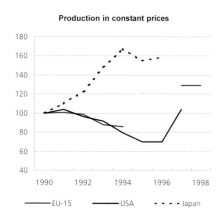

Production in constant prices

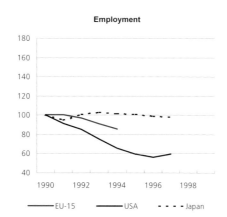

Employment

Source: Eurostat (SBS)

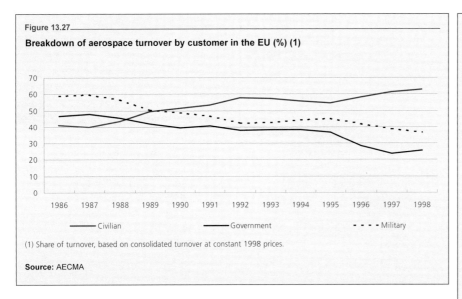

Figure 13.27

Breakdown of aerospace turnover by customer in the EU (%) (1)

(1) Share of turnover, based on consolidated turnover at constant 1998 prices.

Source: AECMA

Box 13.12

Eurospace estimates that consolidated turnover in the EU space industry was equal to 5.2 billion ECU in 1998, whilst there were 34.3 thousand persons employed. The European space industry leads the world in the area of the commercial launch market with Arianespace. The two major areas of European space activity (which were also the two most commercially developed) were telecommunications and launcher production and development. They accounted for 1.5 billion EUR and 1.6 billion EUR of turnover respectively in 1998. Next in importance was earth observation, which is not a commercially mature market, followed by scientific domains such as microgravity and human spaceflight-related developments (activities which are largely funded by public budgets).

LABOUR AND PRODUCTIVITY

The EU aerospace industry employed 321 thousand persons in 1997[14], which could be compared with 407 thousand in 1985. However, the tiered hierarchy that has resulted from the out-sourcing of production means that many more jobs are likely to depend on the aerospace industry. Indeed, AECMA estimates that the supply chain accounts for an additional 800 thousand jobs in the EU.

French employees well-paid compared to their transport equipment counterparts

In 1997[15], unit personnel costs of the aerospace industry were higher than the transport equipment average in every Member State except Finland (0.7 thousand ECU per employee difference). The largest difference was recorded in France, where aerospace employees earned an average of 12.5 thousand ECU more than their transport equipment counterparts.

Simple wage adjusted labour productivity (the ratio of value added to personnel costs) in the EU fell as low as 112.3% in 1993 at the low point of the recession, by 1999, labour productivity (using this measure) rose to 141.2%, the first time during the period 1985 to 1999 that it was higher than the transport equipment average (139.9%).

(14) DK, EL and I, 1996; IRL, L, NL and A, no data available.
(15) DK, EL and I, 1996; IRL, L, NL and A, no data available.

INTERNATIONAL TRENDS AND FOREIGN TRADE

The USA was the leading aerospace manufacturer in the Triad in 1997, with output equal to 119.5 billion ECU (or 62.3% of the Triad total). Boeing dominates American production of civilian aircraft, and is also the principal contractor for NASA's space shuttle and the International Space Station programmes. Boeing purchased McDonnell Douglas (the leading producer of military aircraft in the world) and Rockwell (one of the largest defence manufacturers) during the late 1990s. Three companies lead the USA aerospace industry: Boeing, Lockheed Martin, and Raytheon (largely a defence manufacturer).

Small by global standards, 5.7 billion ECU (or 3.0% of the Triad total), Japanese aerospace industry production is increasing. Targeted by the Japanese government, aerospace research and development efforts have focused on aircraft fuselage and systems components, electronics, high-speed propulsion systems, and space launch vehicles.

Export markets become increasingly important for EU manufacturers

Exports have become increasingly important to the EU aerospace industry as there has been a shift from domestic military sales (which have been significantly reduced during the 1990s) to export sales. In 1999, 6.1% of the EU's manufacturing exports were accounted for by the aerospace industry (some 2.0 percentage points more than in 1989).

The EU ran a small trade deficit in 1999 (855 million ECU), the first time a negative figure was recorded for the trade balance since 1991 (the surplus had risen as high as 8.0 billion ECU in 1995). Almost half (44.8%) of the EU's exports were destined for the USA in 1999, followed by Switzerland (11.3%), Canada (5.6%), China (2.9%) and Brazil (2.4%). The USA was also by far the most important origin of EU imports, accounting for 70.9% of the total.

Figure 13.28

Aerospace equipment (NACE Rev. 1 35.3)
Destination of EU exports, 1999 (%)

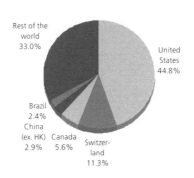

Source: Eurostat (COMEXT)

Figure 13.29

Aerospace equipment (NACE Rev. 1 35.3)
Origin of EU imports, 1999 (%)

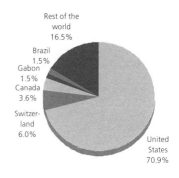

Source: Eurostat (COMEXT)

SUB-CHAPTER 13.5
RAILWAY ROLLING STOCK
(NACE Rev. 1 35.2)

This sub-chapter includes information on the manufacture of both electric and diesel locomotives, railway rolling stock (such as goods' wagons and coaches) and parts and accessories (such as bogies, axles, wheels, brakes and buffers). The information presented does not include the manufacture of rails (sub-chapter 8.1), engines (sub-chapter 10.1) or electric motors (sub-chapter 11.1). The railway equipment sector also includes companies which design and manufacture rolling stock used for metropolitan underground systems and tramways.

In 1999, the manufacture of railway rolling stock accounted for 2.3% of the total production value of the transport equipment sector in the EU, equivalent to 13.2 billion EUR. The corresponding share of the total number of persons employed was considerably higher at 3.6%[16], or some 88 thousand persons.

Germany accounted for just over a third (33.6%) of the EU's production of railway rolling stock in 1997, with output equal to 3.9 billion ECU. This was almost twice the level of output recorded in France (the second largest producer in the EU in 1997), 2.0 billion ECU or 17.3% of the EU total. Whilst Germany (production specialisation ratio of 126.2%) and France (106.1%) were both relatively specialised in the manufacture of railway rolling stock, they fell short of the ratios recorded in Austria (317.1%) and Sweden (173.9%).

STRUCTURE AND PERFORMANCE
The production value of the railway rolling stock industry grew at an average rate of 4.1% per annum in real terms between 1990 and 1998. This was above the average for the whole of transport equipment (3.1% per annum over the same period). Production grew at a rapid pace in 1993, with output up by 11.4% in real terms (compared to the transport equipment average of -13.5%). There was also double-digit growth during the preceding year (1992), when real output rose by 10.5%. However, since 1993 output growth was less spectacular, rising by just 414 million ECU in real terms between 1993 and 1998 (equivalent to an average rate of 0.8% per annum). During the period 1987 to 1997, Germany (8.3% per annum) and France (8.2%) recorded the highest average growth rates in real terms.

(16) Although this figure was only available for 1995 (when the share of railway rolling stock production was again equal to 2.3%).

Figure 13.30

Railway rolling stock (NACE Rev. 1 35.2)

Production and export specialisation (%)

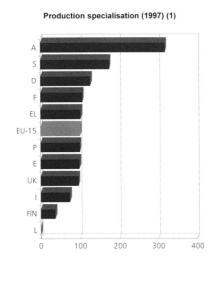

Production specialisation (1997) (1)

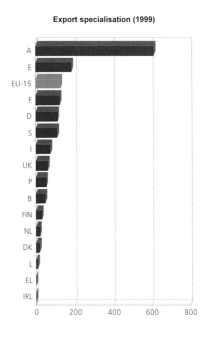

Export specialisation (1999)

(1) EL and I, 1995; B, DK, IRL and NL, not available.

Source: Eurostat (SBS, COMEXT)

Figure 13.31

Railway rolling stock (NACE Rev. 1 35.2)

International comparison of production and employment (1990=100)

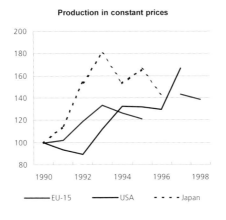

Production in constant prices

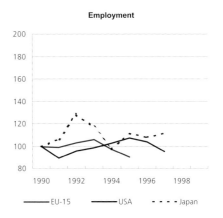

Employment

Source: Eurostat (SBS)

Box 13.13

In the passenger rail market, railways face stiff competition from both cars and cheap air travel. However, demand for railway equipment is expected to increase as rail becomes more competitive for intercity journeys of between one and five hours (in terms of safety, reliability, speed, as well as with respect to the environment). For more details on transport services please refer to chapter 18.

In the freight market, rail faces its stiffest competition from long distance road haulage. Demand is expected to increase with the development of Trans-European Networks (TENs) that will start to link the network of national railway systems (each currently with its own standards and regulations).

Another area where investment in transport infrastructure is likely to benefit this sector is the expansion/development of urban rail networks and tramways, which are increasingly being used to combat the problems of road congestion.

LABOUR AND PRODUCTIVITY

There were 88 thousand persons employed in EU railway rolling stock industries in 1995. Looking at data on the number of persons employed for the 7 Member States[17] where data is available for both 1995 and 1997, there was a net loss of 1.4 thousand jobs.

Low productivity levels and ratios

Apparent labour productivity (gross value added per person employed) was equal to 38.2 thousand ECU in 1995 (which was 9.4 thousand ECU below the transport equipment average in the same year).

Dividing personnel costs by value added it is possible to create a simple wage adjusted labour productivity ratio. During the period 1985 to 1999, this ratio fell within the range 101.0% (1998) to 117.1% (1993) for railway rolling stock, which can be compared with 119.6% (1993) to 142.0% (1989) for transport equipment as a whole. The latest figure available, for 1999, showed that both industries were approaching their respective maxima over the period considered (116.0% for railway rolling stock and 139.9% for transport equipment).

As with most other transport equipment activities, the share of personnel costs in total operating costs fell at a rapid pace in the railway rolling stock industry from 31.8% in 1995 to 26.3% by 1999, although this remained well above the transport equipment average of 18.0%.

(17) D, EL, E, F, P, FIN and UK.

INTERNATIONAL TRENDS AND FOREIGN TRADE

The EU accounted for more than half (53.5%) of the Triad's production of railway rolling stock in 1997, whilst the USA produced a third of the total (33.2%) and Japan the remaining 13.3%. The EU's share of Triad exports was very similar to its share of Triad production, equal to 54.2% in 1998. EU exports of railway rolling stock were valued at 1.6 billion EUR in 1999, with exports exceeding imports by 661 million EUR (the lowest EU surplus recorded since 1990).

The most important export destination in 1999 was the USA (11.6% of the total), followed by South Korea (9.8%), Switzerland (7.6%) and Brazil (7.2%). The remaining export destinations were either located close geographically to the EU (Norway, Czech Republic or Poland, with between 5.9% and 4.3% of total EU exports) or in Asia (China, Thailand, Taiwan and Japan, all with between 6.7% and 3.4% of total EU exports).

Imports of railway rolling stock totalled 922.9 million EUR in 1999, with the most important origin being Canada (25.9% of the total), followed by Switzerland and the Czech Republic. Of the top five countries of origin in 1999, Switzerland was the only one that was also present in 1989.

Box 13.14

Major international locomotive builders include GEC Alsthom (F and UK), Brush Electric (UK), Krupp (D), Asea Brown Boveri (S), General Motors and General Electric (both USA) and Hitachi (JAP).

The majority of urban equipment manufacturers are diversified, multinational enterprises, such as Siemens, MAN and AEG Westinghouse (all D), GEC Alsthom, Ansaldo (I), Asea Brown Boveri, Kawasaki (JAP), Hitachi and Hyundai (Republic of Korea).

Figure 13.32

Railway rolling stock (NACE Rev. 1 35.2)
Destination of EU exports, 1999 (%)

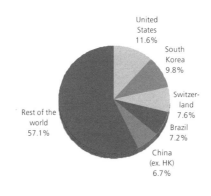

Source: Eurostat (COMEXT)

Figure 13.33

Railway rolling stock (NACE Rev. 1 35.2)
Origin of EU imports, 1999 (%)

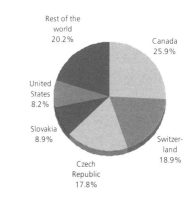

Source: Eurostat (COMEXT)

SUB-CHAPTER 13.6
SHIPBUILDING (NACE Rev. 1 35.1)

This sub-chapter includes data concerning the building and repairing of ships, whether they be commercial vessels, fishing boats, warships, sail, pleasure or sports boats, hovercraft, inflatables, canoes or kayaks. The data also covers floating structures (such as drilling platforms, landing stages and buoys). The information does not however cover the manufacture of propellers (sub-chapter 9.3), engines (sub-chapter 10.1) or navigational instruments (sub-chapter 12.2).

EU shipbuilding had a production value of 23.3 billion EUR in 1999, which represented 4.1% of the transport equipment total (or just less than 0.6% of total manufacturing output in the EU). There were almost 174 thousand persons employed in this industry in 1999, which was a substantially higher share of the transport equipment total (6.8%) than the corresponding production share.

High production specialisation
rates in Denmark and Finland
In 1997, almost one fifth of the EU's shipbuilding production was recorded in Germany (18.9%), ahead of the United Kingdom (16.8%). Spain accounted for 10.6% of EU production and was the only other country to report a double-digit share of the EU total in 1997[18]. In two of the Nordic Member States, shipbuilding accounted for over half of the national transport equipment production total in 1997: Finland (55.5%) and Denmark (51.6%). High shares were also recorded in Greece (38.9%, 1996) and the Netherlands (23.6%). As a result, in 1997 the highest relative production specialisation ratios in shipbuilding were in Denmark (387.6%), Finland (348.1%), the Netherlands (228.3%) and Greece (189.9%, 1996).

An activity dominated by the manufacture of ships
It is possible to look in more detail at shipbuilding activity in the EU, with the production and repair of ships (NACE Rev. 1 35.11) larger in terms of output when compared to the manufacture and repair of pleasure and sporting boats (NACE Rev. 1 35.12). Data is available for 11 of the Member States in 1997[19], with the share of the manufacture and repair of ships accounting for as much as 96.4% of total shipbuilding and repair activity in Spain and 95.8% in Portugal. The lowest shares were recorded in Ireland (65.3% of the total) and Sweden (64.8%).

(18) Output in I accounted for a 15.1% share of the total in 1996.
(19) I, 1996; B, D, EL and A, no data available.

—————— Figure 13.34

Shipbuilding (NACE Rev. 1 35.1)
Production and export specialisation (%)

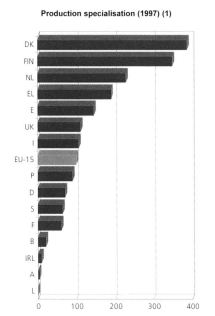

Production specialisation (1997) (1)

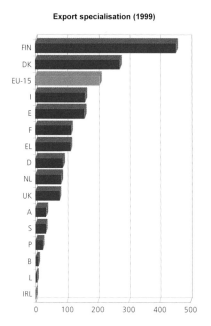

Export specialisation (1999)

(1) EL and I, 1996.

Source: Eurostat (SBS, COMEXT)

—————— Figure 13.35

Completions by region and type of ship, 1997 (%) (1)

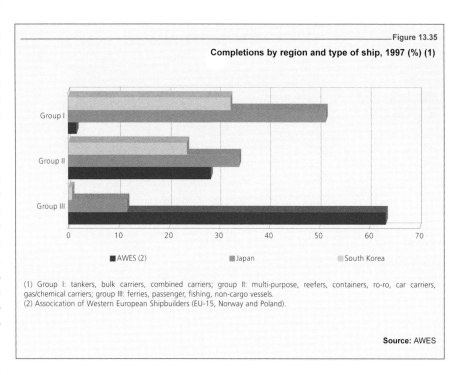

■ AWES (2)   ▨ Japan   ▧ South Korea

(1) Group I: tankers, bulk carriers, combined carriers; group II: multi-purpose, reefers, containers, ro-ro, car carriers, gas/chemical carriers; group III: ferries, passenger, fishing, non-cargo vessels.
(2) Association of Western European Shipbuilders (EU-15, Norway and Poland).

Source: AWES

Figure 13.36 _____

New orders by region and type of ship, 1997 (%) (1)

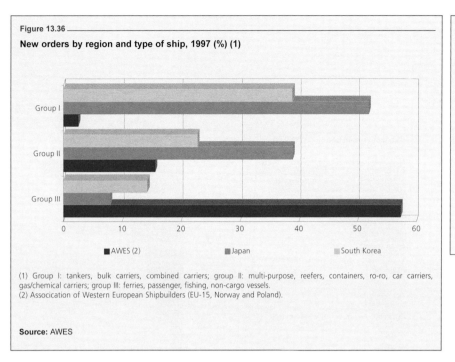

(1) Group I: tankers, bulk carriers, combined carriers; group II: multi-purpose, reefers, containers, ro-ro, car carriers, gas/chemical carriers; group III: ferries, passenger, fishing, non-cargo vessels.
(2) Association of Western European Shipbuilders (EU-15, Norway and Poland).

Source: AWES

Box 13.15 _____

Demand for ships is mainly linked to the movement of cargo between countries (especially over long distances). The European Community Shipowners' Association (ECSA) estimates that over 90% of external trade and 35% of intra-EU trade is carried by sea. ECSA also estimate that the world's fleet of ships was equal to 44.7 thousand vessels or 773.2 million DWT[20] in 1999, whilst the global order book was equal to 69.6 million DWT. Demand for oil tankers and bulk carriers was down on 1998 figures, whilst that for container vessels rose.

_____

(20) Dead weight tonnes.

STRUCTURE AND PERFORMANCE

Nominal output within the EU shipbuilding industry grew at a very moderate pace during the 1980s and 1990s, rising from 17.5 billion ECU in 1985 to 23.3 billion EUR in 1999 (a net increase of 33.3%, compared to 70.9% for transport equipment as a whole).

Output sinking during the 1990s

In real terms there was a reduction in output, which fell by 0.7% per annum between 1990 and 1998. The largest decline was recorded in 1993, when production fell by 14.5% (marking the end of a period of three years of declining output). The largest gain was recorded in 1996 when production rose by 9.0% (0.4 percentage points above the transport equipment average). During the period 1991 to 1998 the only other year when shipbuilding production grew at a faster pace than the transport equipment average was 1991 (when the difference was 0.5 percentage points).

Whilst changes in production fluctuated during the 1990s, value added in constant price terms fell each year between 1990 and 1997 and remained stable in 1998, with an average rate of decline equal to 4.4% per annum between 1990 and 1998.

Figure 13.37 _____

Shipbuilding (NACE Rev. 1 35.1)

International comparison of production in constant prices and employment (1990=100)

Production in constant prices

Employment

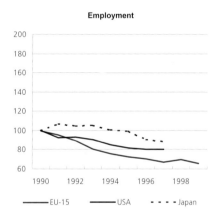

Source: Eurostat (SBS)

LABOUR AND PRODUCTIVITY

More than a third (34.9%) of the net job losses in the transport equipment sector between 1989 and 1999 were accounted for by the shipbuilding industry. Employment fell from 269.7 thousand persons to 173.8 thousand between these two dates, a net loss of almost 96 thousand posts (at an average annual rate of -4.3%). During the 1990s there was just one year when the number of persons employed in EU shipbuilding activities increased, namely 1998 when the number of persons employed rose by 3.5%.

Extremely slow growth in value added results in low levels of apparent labour productivity

Apparent labour productivity in shipbuilding rose at a moderate pace from 28.4 thousand ECU per person employed in 1989 to 37.5 thousand EUR per person employed by 1999. This net increase of 32.0% was 21 percentage points below the average increase for transport equipment (where apparent labour productivity reached 59.2 thousand ECU per person employed by 1999). Simple wage adjusted labour productivity (value added divided by personnel costs) was at a much lower level (111.3% in 1999) than the transport equipment average in the second half of the 1990s (139.9% in 1999). The difference between the two ratios widened during this period from 11.0 percentage points in 1996 to 28.6 percentage points in 1999.

In 1997 there were just 2 out of 10 Member States[21] that reported higher unit personnel costs in the shipbuilding industry than their respective national transport equipment averages, Belgium (3.7 thousand ECU per employee more) and Finland (0.5 thousand ECU).

INTERNATIONAL TRENDS AND FOREIGN TRADE

The production value of shipbuilding in the Triad was equal to 50.7 billion ECU in 1997. The EU accounted for the largest share of this figure (44.0%), followed by Japan (29.6%) and the USA (26.4%).

The EU (46.6%) and Japan (47.9%) together accounted for almost all of the Triad's exports. Whilst the EU's cover ratio (206% in 1999) showed exports to be worth double the value of imports, in Japan exports were worth more than 50 times the value of imports (with a cover ratio of 5,687% in 1998).

(21) DK, EL, I, L and NL, no data available; however, there was data available for the first three of these countries in 1996, when DK (1.5 thousand ECU higher), EL (1.1 thousand ECU) and I (0.9 thousand ECU) all had higher unit personnel costs in shipbuilding.

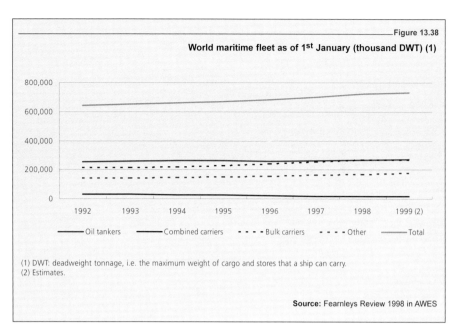

Figure 13.38

World maritime fleet as of 1st January (thousand DWT) (1)

Oil tankers — Combined carriers — ▪ ▪ Bulk carriers — ▪ ▪ Other — Total

(1) DWT: deadweight tonnage, i.e. the maximum weight of cargo and stores that a ship can carry.
(2) Estimates.

Source: Fearnleys Review 1998 in AWES

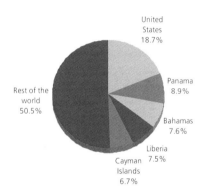

Figure 13.39

Shipbuilding (NACE Rev. 1 35.1)
Destination of EU exports, 1999 (%)

United States 18.7%
Panama 8.9%
Bahamas 7.6%
Liberia 7.5%
Cayman Islands 6.7%
Rest of the world 50.5%

Source: Eurostat (COMEXT)

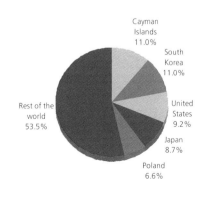

Figure 13.40

Shipbuilding (NACE Rev. 1 35.1)
Origin of EU imports, 1999 (%)

Cayman Islands 11.0%
South Korea 11.0%
United States 9.2%
Japan 8.7%
Poland 6.6%
Rest of the world 53.5%

Source: Eurostat (COMEXT)

The increasing importance of South Korea was seen when looking at the origin of EU imports, where South Korea increased its share of total EU imports from 6.1% to 11.0% between 1989 and 1999. Poland's share of EU imports also rose over this period to attain 6.6% in 1999.

The main destination for EU exports in 1999 was the USA (18.7% of the total), followed by countries with flags of convenience, such as Panama (8.9%), the Bahamas (7.6%) and Liberia (7.5%).

Box 13.16

In 1998 AWES[22] estimates there were 1,653 ships delivered within the world with a volume of 18.0 million CGT[23]. AWES members delivered 482 of these (or 4.5 million CGT, which was equivalent to 24.8% of the global market in volume terms). AWES members specialised in the production of passenger vessels, which were generally high value ships (indeed, the market for cruise ships has developed rapidly in recent years as disposable incomes have risen). Japanese and South Korean manufacturers tended to specialise in container ships and oil tankers.

Japan had a much higher share of this market in volume terms (38.0%), whilst South Korea accounted for just over a fifth of world production (20.3%) in 1998, increasing its share of world production from 11.0% in 1985 to 20.3% by 1998, almost single-handedly accounting for the expansion in world output during this period.

(22) Association of European Shipbuilders and Shiprepairers: DK, D, EL, E, F, I, NL, P, FIN, UK, Norway and Poland.
(23) Compensated gross tons.

Table 13.5

Manufacture of motor vehicles (NACE Rev. 1 34.1)

Production related indicators in the EU (1)

	1989	1990	1991	1992	1993	1994	1995	1996	1997	1998	1999
Number of persons employed (thousands)	1,286.4	1,327.7	1,300.5	1,254.1	1,151.4	1,095.6	1,078.4	:	:	:	:
Production (million ECU)	207,136	217,264	221,584	232,400	201,102	230,331	243,858	:	:	:	:
Domestic producer price index (1995=100)	:	:	:	:	:	:	:	:	:	103.0	103.6
Value added (million ECU)	59,591	59,648	60,573	61,908	52,745	59,447	59,644	:	:	:	:

(1) Technically, data before 01/01/1999 are in ECU and after this date in euro. However, as the conversion rate was 1 ECU =1 EUR, for practical purposes the two terms can be used interchangeably.

Table 13.6

Manufacture of motor vehicles (NACE Rev. 1 34.1)

Trade related indicators in the EU (1)

	1989	1990	1991	1992	1993	1994	1995	1996	1997	1998	1999
Exports (million EUR)	24,925	26,249	23,984	24,068	29,152	36,288	39,546	43,138	48,749	50,161	50,658
Imports (million EUR)	13,855	13,779	15,549	16,404	14,097	14,030	14,809	16,329	21,692	27,538	31,668
Trade balance (million EUR)	11,071	12,470	8,435	7,664	15,055	22,259	24,737	26,809	27,058	22,623	18,990
Cover ratio (%)	179.9	190.5	154.2	146.7	206.8	258.7	267.0	264.2	224.7	182.2	160.0

(1) Technically, data before 01/01/1999 are in ECU and after this date in euro. However, as the conversion rate was 1 ECU =1 EUR, for practical purposes the two terms can be used interchangeably.

Table 13.7

Manufacture of motor vehicles (NACE Rev. 1 34.1)

Production related indicators, 1997

	B	DK	D	EL (1)	E	F	IRL	I (1)	L	NL	A	P	FIN	S	UK
Number of persons employed (thousands)	39.5	0.0	485.4	1.1	78.3	171.9	0.3	103.8	:	:	:	10.1	2.6	48.3	118.5
Production (million ECU)	11,508	0	111,634	104	23,827	57,047	40	20,179	:	3,939	:	3,116	305	13,551	33,478
Value added (million ECU)	2,114	0	31,410	27	4,688	9,218	9	3,598	:	863	:	577	118	3,350	8,369
Gross operating surplus (million ECU)	385.5	0.0	4,983.1	2.3	2,154.7	2,574.1	2.0	582.7	:	432.9	:	359.3	37.0	1,272.7	3,810.8

(1) 1996.

Table 13.8

Manufacture of motor vehicles (NACE Rev. 1 34.1)

Trade related indicators, 1999

	B	DK	D	EL	E	F	IRL	I	L	NL	A	P	FIN	S	UK
Exports (million EUR)	19,209	372	71,046	33	19,594	24,873	292	10,006	234	7,336	5,651	2,789	970	6,165	17,928
Imports (million EUR)	13,435	2,343	32,341	2,264	16,072	21,260	2,335	21,577	850	10,047	5,534	4,615	1,795	3,977	26,967
Trade balance (million EUR)	5,775	-1,972	38,705	-2,231	3,522	3,613	-2,042	-11,571	-615	-2,711	116	-1,826	-825	2,188	-9,039
Cover ratio (%)	143.0	15.9	219.7	1.5	121.9	117.0	12.5	46.4	27.6	73.0	102.1	60.4	54.0	155.0	66.5

Table 13.9

Manufacture of motor vehicles (NACE Rev. 1 34.1)

Labour related indicators, 1997

	B	DK	D	EL (1)	E	F	IRL	I (1)	L	NL	A	P	FIN	S	UK
Unit personnel costs (thousand ECU per employee)	43.8	:	54.5	21.6	29.8	38.7	21.0	29.0	:	:	:	21.7	32.9	43.0	38.5
Social charges as a share of personnel costs (%)	42.1	:	28.3	32.8	30.5	43.2	14.3	48.8	:	15.5	:	38.9	28.6	48.7	12.5
Apparent labour productivity (thousand ECU/pers. empl.)	53.6	:	64.7	23.6	59.9	53.6	26.8	34.6	:	:	:	57.3	45.5	69.4	70.6
Wage adjusted labour productivity (%)	122.3	:	118.9	109.1	201.0	138.7	127.2	119.3	:	:	:	264.5	138.1	161.3	183.3
Personnel costs as a share of total operating costs (%)	15.5	:	21.3	28.6	8.7	11.1	16.1	13.4	:	11.0	:	6.0	28.4	12.3	12.6

(1) 1996.

Source: Eurostat (SBS, EBT, COMEXT)

Table 13.10

Manufacture of bodies (coachwork) for motor vehicles; manufacture of trailers and semi-trailers (NACE Rev. 1 34.2)

Production related indicators in the EU (1)

	1989	1990	1991	1992	1993	1994	1995	1996	1997	1998	1999
Number of persons employed (thousands)	164.6	168.6	164.2	150.9	133.3	133.6	133.7	:	141.5	149.3	143.3
Production (million ECU)	13,209	14,112	15,026	13,932	11,939	13,376	15,689	:	:	:	.
Domestic producer price index (1995=100)	:	85.8	90.5	94.0	96.0	97.1	100.0	102.9	104.0	105.1	106.1
Value added (million ECU)	4,337	4,548	4,695	4,594	3,992	4,460	4,738	:	:	:	:

(1) Technically, data before 01/01/1999 are in ECU and after this date in euro. However, as the conversion rate was 1 ECU =1 EUR, for practical purposes the two terms can be used interchangeably.

Table 13.11

Manufacture of bodies (coachwork) for motor vehicles; manufacture of trailers and semi-trailers (NACE Rev. 1 34.2)

Trade related indicators in the EU (1)

	1989	1990	1991	1992	1993	1994	1995	1996	1997	1998	1999
Exports (million EUR)	763	758	812	867	866	976	1,123	1,189	1,657	1,895	1,686
Imports (million EUR)	209	233	288	299	304	316	419	439	496	650	727
Trade balance (million EUR)	554	525	524	568	562	660	704	750	1,162	1,245	960
Cover ratio (%)	365.2	324.8	282.2	289.7	284.8	308.8	268.2	270.6	334.2	291.7	232.0

(1) Technically, data before 01/01/1999 are in ECU and after this date in euro. However, as the conversion rate was 1 ECU =1 EUR, for practical purposes the two terms can be used interchangeably.

Table 13.12

Manufacture of bodies (coachwork) for motor vehicles; manufacture of trailers and semi-trailers (NACE Rev. 1 34.2)

Production related indicators, 1997

	B	DK	D	EL (1)	E	F	IRL	I (1)	L	NL	A	P	FIN	S	UK
Number of persons employed (thousands)	6.6	4.6	41.6	0.2	11.1	20.8	0.7	12.9	:	:	3.1	3.3	3.5	2.0	25.3
Production (million ECU)	1,202	553	6,558	15	1,107	2,466	78	1,918	:	807	330	145	393	261	3,309
Value added (million ECU)	285	179	1,776	4	285	664	22	568	:	229	119	40	137	94	1,018
Gross operating surplus (million ECU)	59.2	50.6	311.7	0.8	89.6	60.3	8.9	184.5	:	47.5	24.7	8.9	40.6	27.6	296.9

(1) 1996.

Table 13.13

Manufacture of bodies (coachwork) for motor vehicles; manufacture of trailers and semi-trailers (NACE Rev. 1 34.2)

Trade related indicators, 1999

	B	DK	D	EL	E	F	IRL	I	L	NL	A	P	FIN	S	UK
Exports (million EUR)	681	149	2,080	2	143	768	28	631	15	304	306	8	106	505	518
Imports (million EUR)	523	261	868	26	232	752	63	236	19	715	339	73	61	177	461
Trade balance (million EUR)	158	-112	1,213	-24	-89	15	-36	395	-4	-411	-32	-64	46	328	57
Cover ratio (%)	130.3	57.1	239.8	6.1	61.6	102.1	43.7	267.7	80.0	42.5	90.4	11.5	175.6	285.8	112.4

Table 13.14

Manufacture of bodies (coachwork) for motor vehicles; manufacture of trailers and semi-trailers (NACE Rev. 1 34.2)

Labour related indicators, 1997

	B	DK (1)	D	EL (2)	E	F	IRL	I (2)	L	NL	A	P	FIN	S	UK
Unit personnel costs (thousand ECU per employee)	34.4	31.8	35.3	16.0	18.8	29.0	18.4	30.3	:	:	31.0	9.7	27.5	33.7	28.7
Social charges as a share of personnel costs (%)	38.6	4.1	23.8	33.3	29.6	41.6	14.3	61.2	:	14.1	30.3	29.2	27.8	41.1	12.6
Apparent labour productivity (thousand ECU/pers. empl.)	43.2	39.3	42.7	19.3	25.6	31.9	30.6	43.9	:	:	38.7	12.3	38.7	47.7	40.3
Wage adjusted labour productivity (%)	125.4	127.9	120.9	120.6	136.5	110.0	166.3	144.8	:	:	124.8	126.7	140.8	141.5	140.5
Personnel costs as a share of total operating costs (%)	19.6	24.9	22.2	21.8	16.8	23.8	17.0	21.5	:	22.0	28.4	21.7	26.1	22.6	22.9

(1) Unit personnel costs and wage adjusted labour productivity, 1996; (2) 1996.

Source: Eurostat (SBS, EBT, COMEXT)

Table 13.15

Manufacture of parts and accessories for motor vehicles and their engines (NACE Rev. 1 34.3)

Production related indicators in the EU (1)

	1989	1990	1991	1992	1993	1994	1995	1996	1997	1998	1999
Number of persons employed (thousands)	528.8	538.2	529.0	525.4	487.9	491.0	564.8	:	:	:	:
Production (million ECU)	44,070	46,070	47,001	51,496	47,482	53,905	69,686	:	:	:	:
Domestic producer price index (1995=100)	:	:	:	:	:	:	:	:	:	100.1	100.0
Value added (million ECU)	16,684	17,248	17,491	19,310	17,915	20,496	25,654	:	:	:	:

(1) Technically, data before 01/01/1999 are in ECU and after this date in euro. However, as the conversion rate was 1 ECU =1 EUR, for practical purposes the two terms can be used interchangeably.

Table 13.16

Manufacture of parts and accessories for motor vehicles and their engines (NACE Rev. 1 34.3)

Trade related indicators in the EU (1)

	1989	1990	1991	1992	1993	1994	1995	1996	1997	1998	1999
Exports (million EUR)	8,084	7,847	8,325	8,228	9,398	10,653	12,219	13,937	17,034	18,013	18,644
Imports (million EUR)	3,811	3,695	3,971	4,478	5,265	6,167	7,061	7,414	8,595	9,777	11,520
Trade balance (million EUR)	4,274	4,152	4,354	3,751	4,133	4,486	5,158	6,523	8,439	8,237	7,124
Cover ratio (%)	212.2	212.4	209.6	183.8	178.5	172.7	173.0	188.0	198.2	184.2	161.8

(1) Technically, data before 01/01/1999 are in ECU and after this date in euro. However, as the conversion rate was 1 ECU =1 EUR, for practical purposes the two terms can be used interchangeably.

Table 13.17

Manufacture of parts and accessories for motor vehicles and their engines (NACE Rev. 1 34.3)

Production related indicators, 1997

	B	DK	D	EL (1)	E	F	IRL	I (1)	L	NL	A	P	FIN	S	UK
Number of persons employed (thousands)	7.8	3.6	243.2	0.2	60.7	75.9	2.3	69.0	:	:	:	10.9	1.0	16.9	95.4
Production (million ECU)	1,722	304	33,817	9	8,041	11,730	277	9,103	:	768	:	941	97	2,283	10,490
Value added (million ECU)	502	131	13,112	4	2,623	3,735	76	3,029	:	214	:	260	43	820	4,109
Gross operating surplus (million ECU)	202.2	30.4	2,531.2	1.1	1,021.0	1,230.7	28.6	1,067.3	:	61.9	:	127.3	13.6	240.2	1,395.7

(1) 1996.

Table 13.18

Manufacture of parts and accessories for motor vehicles and their engines (NACE Rev. 1 34.3)

Trade related indicators, 1999

	B	DK	D	EL	E	F	IRL	I	L	NL	A	P	FIN	S	UK
Exports (million EUR)	3,579	557	17,745	64	5,428	12,170	85	7,179	15	1,675	2,445	608	298	3,346	7,094
Imports (million EUR)	6,526	607	11,289	457	8,737	7,587	229	3,810	83	3,024	3,140	1,332	705	2,761	10,824
Trade balance (million EUR)	-2,946	-50	6,456	-392	-3,309	4,583	-144	3,369	-68	-1,350	-695	-724	-407	586	-3,730
Cover ratio (%)	54.9	91.8	157.2	14.1	62.1	160.4	37.0	188.4	18.1	55.4	77.9	45.7	42.2	121.2	65.5

Table 13.19

Manufacture of parts and accessories for motor vehicles and their engines (NACE Rev. 1 34.3)

Labour related indicators, 1997

	B	DK (1)	D	EL (2)	E	F	IRL	I (2)	L	NL	A	P	FIN	S	UK
Unit personnel costs (thousand ECU per employee)	38.8	32.2	43.5	13.5	25.4	33.0	21.0	28.7	:	:	:	12.3	29.3	34.2	28.6
Social charges as a share of personnel costs (%)	37.9	4.1	25.1	33.3	29.3	42.4	14.0	48.3	:	16.9	:	33.8	26.5	42.9	12.6
Apparent labour productivity (thousand ECU/pers. empl.)	64.6	36.6	53.9	18.8	43.2	49.2	33.5	43.9	:	:	:	24.0	42.8	48.4	43.1
Wage adjusted labour productivity (%)	166.3	129.9	123.9	139.3	170.2	149.1	159.7	152.8	:	:	:	194.0	146.2	141.5	150.5
Personnel costs as a share of total operating costs (%)	19.8	35.1	29.7	37.3	21.3	22.1	19.3	23.6	:	19.7	:	16.0	33.3	27.9	28.7

(1) Unit personnel costs and wage adjusted labour productivity, 1996; (2) 1996.

Source: Eurostat (SBS, EBT, COMEXT)

_____Table 13.20

Building and repairing of ships and boats (NACE Rev. 1 35.1)

Production related indicators in the EU (1)

	1989	1990	1991	1992	1993	1994	1995	1996	1997	1998	1999
Number of persons employed (thousands)	269.7	262.1	251.2	235.3	212.4	200.0	191.1	184.9	177.0	183.2	173.8
Production (million EUR)	18,823	20,770	21,130	20,773	17,977	18,845	19,104	21,211	22,331	23,164	23,334
Domestic producer price index (1995=100)	:	:	:	:	:	:	:	:	:	:	:
Value added (million EUR)	7,664	8,113	8,101	8,125	6,783	6,673	6,623	6,590	6,475	6,648	6,516

(1) Technically, data before 01/01/1999 are in ECU and after this date in euro. However, as the conversion rate was 1 ECU =1 EUR, for practical purposes the two terms can be used interchangeably.

_____Table 13.21

Building and repairing of ships and boats (NACE Rev. 1 35.1)

Trade related indicators in the EU (1)

	1989	1990	1991	1992	1993	1994	1995	1996	1997	1998	1999
Exports (million EUR)	3,458	4,186	4,077	5,031	6,248	5,658	6,367	7,063	7,853	8,173	8,347
Imports (million EUR)	2,170	2,150	2,630	2,318	3,108	2,535	2,032	2,949	2,990	3,664	4,051
Trade balance (million EUR)	1,288	2,036	1,447	2,712	3,139	3,123	4,334	4,114	4,863	4,509	4,295
Cover ratio (%)	159.3	194.7	155.0	217.0	201.0	223.2	313.3	239.5	262.7	223.1	206.0

(1) Technically, data before 01/01/1999 are in ECU and after this date in euro. However, as the conversion rate was 1 ECU =1 EUR, for practical purposes the two terms can be used interchangeably.

_____Table 13.22

Building and repairing of ships and boats (NACE Rev. 1 35.1)

Production related indicators, 1997

	B	DK	D	EL (1)	E	F	IRL	I (1)	L	NL	A	P	FIN	S	UK
Number of persons employed (thousands)	1.7	9.5	27.4	6.6	31.2	14.5	0.5	21.6	0.0	:	0.2	6.0	9.5	3.1	37.0
Production (million ECU)	186	1,202	4,215	234	2,366	2,219	31	3,212	0	2,018	16	322	1,453	446	3,743
Value added (million ECU)	76	402	1,355	85	684	104	12	967	0	434	8	138	449	127	1,434
Gross operating surplus (million ECU)	1.8	105.9	275.4	-91.1	-104.0	-359.4	2.5	306.0	0.0	31.9	0.9	48.0	158.6	16.0	225.5

(1) 1996.

_____Table 13.23

Building and repairing of ships and boats (NACE Rev. 1 35.1)

Trade related indicators, 1999

	B	DK	D	EL	E	F	IRL	I	L	NL	A	P	FIN	S	UK
Exports (million EUR)	70	625	2,297	49	814	1,892	2	1,926	2	750	114	28	1,004	137	994
Imports (million EUR)	93	206	984	459	545	1,632	46	423	5	305	112	42	74	63	334
Trade balance (million EUR)	-23	419	1,313	-410	268	260	-44	1,503	-3	445	2	-14	930	74	660
Cover ratio (%)	75.2	303.8	233.5	10.6	149.2	115.9	5.0	454.8	36.7	246.0	102.2	67.5	1,351.0	218.0	297.4

_____Table 13.24

Building and repairing of ships and boats (NACE Rev. 1 35.1)

Labour related indicators, 1997

	B	DK (1)	D	EL (2)	E	F	IRL	I (2)	L	NL	A	P	FIN	S	UK
Unit personnel costs (thousand ECU per employee)	46.2	36.0	39.5	26.7	24.9	32.0	21.1	31.0	:	:	33.9	15.4	31.0	35.3	33.0
Social charges as a share of personnel costs (%)	30.4	3.7	25.1	23.9	29.5	43.5	12.8	53.7	:	16.5	25.9	37.0	26.4	41.1	11.6
Apparent labour productivity (thousand ECU/pers. empl.)	45.0	42.1	49.5	12.9	21.9	7.2	26.1	44.8	:	:	38.2	22.9	47.3	40.4	38.8
Wage adjusted labour productivity (%)	97.3	74.5	125.4	48.2	88.1	22.5	123.7	144.5	:	:	112.8	148.6	152.7	114.4	117.6
Personnel costs as a share of total operating costs (%)	41.2	26.9	26.1	70.5	29.7	22.1	33.2	22.5	:	19.5	42.2	29.0	22.3	25.7	34.3

(1) Unit personnel costs and wage adjusted labour productivity, 1996; (2) 1996.

Source: Eurostat (SBS, EBT, COMEXT)

Table 13.25

Manufacture of railway and tramway locomotives and rolling stock (NACE Rev. 1 35.2)

Production related indicators in the EU (1)

	1989	1990	1991	1992	1993	1994	1995	1996	1997	1998	1999
Number of persons employed (thousands)	92.6	97.0	96.1	99.9	103.1	94.4	88.0	:	:	:	:
Production (million EUR)	5,849	7,027	7,404	8,723	9,890	9,544	9,539	:	11,551	11,475	13,222
Domestic producer price index (1995=100)	:	:	:	:	:	:	:	:	:	:	:
Value added (million EUR)	2,393	2,773	2,950	3,293	3,714	3,468	3,362	:	3,383	3,404	3,782

(1) Technically, data before 01/01/1999 are in ECU and after this date in euro. However, as the conversion rate was 1 ECU =1 EUR, for practical purposes the two terms can be used interchangeably.

Table 13.26

Manufacture of railway and tramway locomotives and rolling stock (NACE Rev. 1 35.2)

Trade related indicators in the EU (1)

	1989	1990	1991	1992	1993	1994	1995	1996	1997	1998	1999
Exports (million EUR)	683	711	1,482	1,761	1,393	1,342	1,331	1,488	1,541	1,757	1,584
Imports (million EUR)	132	176	337	359	337	558	489	365	434	625	923
Trade balance (million EUR)	551	536	1,145	1,402	1,056	784	842	1,123	1,107	1,133	661
Cover ratio (%)	518.0	405.0	440.1	490.2	412.9	240.4	272.2	408.2	354.8	281.4	171.6

(1) Technically, data before 01/01/1999 are in ECU and after this date in euro. However, as the conversion rate was 1 ECU =1 EUR, for practical purposes the two terms can be used interchangeably.

Table 13.27

Manufacture of railway and tramway locomotives and rolling stock (NACE Rev. 1 35.2)

Production related indicators, 1997

	B	DK	D	EL (1)	E	F	IRL	I	L	NL	A	P	FIN	S	UK
Number of persons employed (thousands)	:	:	26.2	2.2	8.0	15.4	:	:	0.0	:	3.8	3.1	0.1	3.4	11.3
Production (million ECU)	:	:	3,878	72	827	2,002	:	:	0	:	701	184	79	620	1,667
Value added (million ECU)	:	:	1,087	54	358	473	:	:	0	:	212	81	6	150	532
Gross operating surplus (million ECU)	:	:	-67.4	6.7	97.9	-122.3	:	:	0.0	:	27.5	20.6	1.1	12.5	153.3

(1) 1996.

Table 13.28

Manufacture of railway and tramway locomotives and rolling stock (NACE Rev. 1 35.2)

Trade related indicators, 1999

	B	DK	D	EL	E	F	IRL	I	L	NL	A	P	FIN	S	UK
Exports (million EUR)	126	13	891	0	293	622	0	275	1	56	633	21	21	142	244
Imports (million EUR)	170	57	530	58	67	269	12	128	21	32	190	51	33	124	548
Trade balance (million EUR)	-44	-44	361	-58	225	352	-12	147	-20	24	443	-31	-13	18	-303
Cover ratio (%)	74.2	22.9	168.0	0.2	435.8	230.8	2.4	215.0	5.1	176.5	333.7	40.3	62.6	114.1	44.6

Table 13.29

Manufacture of railway and tramway locomotives and rolling stock (NACE Rev. 1 35.2)

Labour related indicators, 1997

	B	DK	D	EL (1)	E	F	IRL	I	L	NL	A	P	FIN	S	UK
Unit personnel costs (thousand ECU per employee)	:	:	44.1	21.3	30.2	38.7	:	:	:	:	48.4	19.2	37.2	39.9	33.6
Social charges as a share of personnel costs (%)	:	:	22.4	28.1	29.3	43.9	:	:	:	:	27.9	37.7	24.4	43.2	11.0
Apparent labour productivity (thousand ECU/pers. empl.)	:	:	41.5	24.3	44.7	30.8	:	:	:	:	55.7	25.8	45.1	43.6	46.9
Wage adjusted labour productivity (%)	:	:	94.1	114.1	147.8	79.5	:	:	:	:	114.9	134.4	121.1	109.1	139.6
Personnel costs as a share of total operating costs (%)	:	:	29.3	73.3	33.9	32.3	:	:	:	:	26.2	36.0	6.8	22.1	24.8

(1) 1996.

Source: Eurostat (SBS, COMEXT)

_____Table 13.30

Manufacture of aircraft and spacecraft (NACE Rev. 1 35.3)

Production related indicators in the EU (1)

	1989	1990	1991	1992	1993	1994	1995	1996	1997	1998	1999
Number of persons employed (thousands)	407.1	422.8	423.0	409.4	382.9	360.1	:	:	:	:	:
Production (million EUR)	40,798	44,982	46,655	46,246	41,531	41,308	:	:	66,622	68,477	74,408
Domestic producer price index (1995=100)	:	:	:	:	:	:	:	:	:	:	:
Value added (million EUR)	16,374	17,670	18,107	16,199	15,579	15,675	:	:	20,170	20,675	22,663

(1) Technically, data before 01/01/1999 are in ECU and after this date in euro. However, as the conversion rate was 1 ECU =1 EUR, for practical purposes the two terms can be used interchangeably.

_____Table 13.31

Manufacture of aircraft and spacecraft (NACE Rev. 1 35.3)

Trade related indicators in the EU (1)

	1989	1990	1991	1992	1993	1994	1995	1996	1997	1998	1999
Exports (million EUR)	14,115	14,685	17,722	19,885	22,654	23,190	25,392	27,137	36,030	40,548	43,334
Imports (million EUR)	16,087	16,344	18,796	16,187	17,882	18,046	17,417	20,246	29,765	36,486	43,989
Trade balance (million EUR)	-1,972	-1,659	-1,074	3,698	4,773	5,144	7,975	6,892	6,265	4,063	-655
Cover ratio (%)	87.7	89.9	94.3	122.8	126.7	128.5	145.8	134.0	121.0	111.1	98.5

(1) Technically, data before 01/01/1999 are in ECU and after this date in euro. However, as the conversion rate was 1 ECU =1 EUR, for practical purposes the two terms can be used interchangeably.

_____Table 13.32

Manufacture of aircraft and spacecraft (NACE Rev. 1 35.3)

Production related indicators, 1997

	B	DK (1)	D	EL (1)	E	F	IRL	I (1)	L	NL	A	P	FIN	S	UK
Number of persons employed (thousands)	4.4	0.6	63.3	4.4	10.8	80.7	:	41.2	:	:	:	1.8	0.7	11.4	102.0
Production (million ECU)	596	53	11,280	160	1,092	26,220	:	4,850	:	590	:	82	39	1,535	17,577
Value added (million ECU)	295	18	3,811	112	568	5,905	:	1,593	:	248	:	37	29	196	6,470
Gross operating surplus (million ECU)	86.8	-4.2	263.0	-13.2	205.3	1,707.0	:	102.0	:	92.1	:	7.1	6.8	-301.8	2,624.6

(1) 1996.

_____Table 13.33

Manufacture of aircraft and spacecraft (NACE Rev. 1 35.3)

Trade related indicators, 1999

	B	DK	D	EL	E	F	IRL	I	L	NL	A	P	FIN	S	UK
Exports (million EUR)	884	597	15,445	86	1,308	37,386	321	3,020	27	1,068	875	115	93	1,140	15,543
Imports (million EUR)	802	754	13,127	156	2,608	30,657	1,504	3,285	796	1,481	1,213	488	861	1,198	12,806
Trade balance (million EUR)	82	-157	2,318	-70	-1,300	6,728	-1,183	-265	-768	-413	-338	-373	-767	-58	2,737
Cover ratio (%)	110.3	79.1	117.7	55.1	50.2	121.9	21.3	91.9	3.4	72.1	72.1	23.7	10.8	95.2	121.4

_____Table 13.34

Manufacture of aircraft and spacecraft (NACE Rev. 1 35.3)

Labour related indicators, 1997

	B	DK (1)	D	EL (1)	E	F	IRL	I (1)	L	NL	A	P	FIN	S	UK
Unit personnel costs (thousand ECU per employee)	47.6	37.2	56.1	28.6	33.0	52.0	:	36.3	:	:	:	16.7	29.8	43.5	37.9
Social charges as a share of personnel costs (%)	53.4	4.7	25.0	34.2	27.5	45.7	:	46.4	:	16.6	:	26.0	24.6	49.1	15.0
Apparent labour productivity (thousand ECU/pers. empl.)	67.4	30.3	60.2	25.6	52.8	73.2	:	38.7	:	:	:	20.2	38.9	17.1	63.4
Wage adjusted labour productivity (%)	141.5	81.3	107.4	89.5	160.1	140.7	:	106.7	:	:	:	121.3	130.5	39.3	167.5
Personnel costs as a share of total operating costs (%)	40.8	40.9	32.2	80.6	38.4	16.8	:	31.5	:	27.8	:	38.6	67.7	27.0	24.8

(1) 1996.

Source: Eurostat (SBS, COMEXT)

Table 13.35

Manufacture of motorcycles and bicycles (NACE Rev. 1 35.4)

Production related indicators in the EU (1)

	1989	1990	1991	1992	1993	1994	1995	1996	1997	1998	1999
Number of persons employed (thousands)	56.3	57.0	55.2	53.0	51.3	48.9	49.8	:	48.0	49.9	47.7
Production (million EUR)	4,724	5,268	5,203	5,566	5,218	5,707	6,473	:	7,062	7,499	7,582
Domestic producer price index (1995=100)	:	:	:	:	:	:	:	:	:	:	:
Value added (million ECU)	1,530	1,802	1,771	1,765	1,594	1,677	1,910	:	:	:	:

(1) Technically, data before 01/01/1999 are in ECU and after this date in euro. However, as the conversion rate was 1 ECU =1 EUR, for practical purposes the two terms can be used interchangeably.

Table 13.36

Manufacture of motorcycles and bicycles (NACE Rev. 1 35.4)

Trade related indicators in the EU (1)

	1989	1990	1991	1992	1993	1994	1995	1996	1997	1998	1999
Exports (million EUR)	483	525	531	517	590	719	803	859	893	964	1,044
Imports (million EUR)	1,851	2,345	3,009	3,203	3,344	3,142	3,075	3,304	3,759	4,279	4,710
Trade balance (million EUR)	-1,368	-1,820	-2,478	-2,687	-2,753	-2,422	-2,272	-2,445	-2,866	-3,315	-3,666
Cover ratio (%)	26.1	22.4	17.6	16.1	17.7	22.9	26.1	26.0	23.8	22.5	22.2

(1) Technically, data before 01/01/1999 are in ECU and after this date in euro. However, as the conversion rate was 1 ECU =1 EUR, for practical purposes the two terms can be used interchangeably.

Table 13.37

Manufacture of motorcycles and bicycles (NACE Rev. 1 35.4)

Production related indicators, 1997

	B (1)	DK	D	EL	E	F	IRL	I (1)	L	NL	A	P	FIN	S (1)	UK
Number of persons employed (thousands)	0.5	0.7	7.0	:	3.5	7.2	:	20.3	0.0	:	:	2.0	0.4	0.9	4.4
Production (million ECU)	89	73	832	:	528	884	:	2,905	0	340	:	79	53	140	475
Value added (million ECU)	21	17	254	:	126	261	:	750	0	98	:	25	18	45	153
Gross operating surplus (million ECU)	4.3	-3.4	19.9	:	38.0	49.3	:	228.5	0.0	38.5	:	6.7	5.5	13.7	53.2

(1) 1996.

Table 13.38

Manufacture of motorcycles and bicycles (NACE Rev. 1 35.4)

Trade related indicators, 1999

	B	DK	D	EL	E	F	IRL	I	L	NL	A	P	FIN	S	UK
Exports (million EUR)	204	59	639	7	384	660	37	1,767	13	619	140	72	8	97	266
Imports (million EUR)	444	152	1,756	157	564	1,349	49	1,219	22	930	278	136	77	173	1,035
Trade balance (million EUR)	-240	-93	-1,117	-151	-180	-689	-12	548	-9	-311	-138	-64	-69	-76	-769
Cover ratio (%)	45.9	38.9	36.4	4.2	68.1	48.9	75.1	144.9	57.7	66.6	50.3	52.9	9.8	55.9	25.7

Table 13.39

Manufacture of motorcycles and bicycles (NACE Rev. 1 35.4)

Labour related indicators, 1997

	B (1)	DK (2)	D	EL	E	F	IRL	I (1)	L	NL	A	P	FIN	S (1)	UK
Unit personnel costs (thousand ECU per employee)	33.1	32.6	33.6	:	24.3	29.4	:	26.1	:	:	:	9.2	31.2	34.6	23.1
Social charges as a share of personnel costs (%)	40.2	4.1	22.8	:	29.2	39.3	:	51.2	:	14.8	:	30.0	22.8	:	12.4
Apparent labour productivity (thousand ECU/pers. empl.)	39.1	24.3	36.4	:	35.6	36.3	:	37.0	:	:	:	12.6	45.0	49.8	34.9
Wage adjusted labour productivity (%)	118.1	109.7	108.2	:	146.7	123.3	:	141.8	:	:	:	136.3	144.0	143.8	150.9
Personnel costs as a share of total operating costs (%)	20.5	25.5	25.6	:	13.1	23.6	:	18.6	:	18.3	:	23.0	25.4	22.9	22.8

(1) 1996; (2) Unit personnel costs and wage adjusted labour productivity, 1996.

Source: Eurostat (SBS, COMEXT)

Other manufacturing industries (NACE Rev. 1 36)

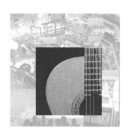

This chapter covers the manufacture of furniture classified within NACE Group 36.1, the manufacture of jewellery and related articles (NACE Rev. 1 Group 36.2) and other manufacturing not elsewhere classified (NACE Rev. 1 Groups 36.3 to 36.6). Together this makes up NACE Rev. 1 Division 36. Note that this chapter does not cover recycling (NACE Rev. 1 Division 37), nor the manufacture of sports clothes (which are included in Chapter 4).

_____ **Figure 14.1**

**Other manufacturing industries
(NACE Rev. 1 36)
Share of total manufacturing value added
in the EU, 1999 (%)**

Source: Eurostat (SBS)

The activities covered in this chapter (in terms of NACE Rev. 1) include:

36: manufacture of furniture; manufacturing n.e.c.;
36.1: manufacture of furniture;
36.2: manufacture of jewellery and related articles;
36.3: manufacture of musical instruments;
36.4: manufacture of sports goods;
36.5: manufacture of games and toys;
36.6: miscellaneous manufacturing n.e.c.

This is the last of twelve manufacturing chapters. Its activity coverage is rather heterogeneous and is defined as furniture plus other manufacturing or, as it is more correctly known, manufacturing not elsewhere classified.

Strong competition from developing countries
Looking deeper within this mixed heading it is possible to identify some distinct industries, some of them producing consumer durables such as jewellery and musical instruments and others producing consumer non-durables such as sports goods and games and toys. As such the demand for the products of most of the activities grouped under this heading is strongly influenced by consumer confidence. Although there are some large enterprises in most of these industries, a high proportion of the enterprises are small, often reflecting craft production methods. All these industries have faced strong competition from developing countries for many years, particularly for mass-produced products, although the origin of this competition is quite different: Eastern Europe and Indonesia for furniture, India for jewellery and China and other south-east Asian countries for musical instruments, sports goods and toys.

A small industry, but one that
employs a million people in the EU
The manufacture of furniture and other manufacturing not elsewhere classified generated an estimated 37 billion EUR of value added in 1999 across the EU. This equates to 3.0% of value added in manufacturing as a whole. The share of production value in manufacturing was lower at 2.6% indicating relatively high value added activities compared to manufacturing as a whole. These shares rank this industry as one of the smallest manufacturing industries. Nevertheless more than a million persons were employed in 1999. This corresponded to 4.6% of total manufacturing employment, indicating that although value added was high compared to production value, the workforce had a below average apparent labour productivity. As will be seen in the following sub-chapters, these aggregate figures for furniture manufacture and other manufacturing as a whole mask a great diversity in the performance of the individual industries that make up this aggregate.

Table 14.1

Other manufacturing industries (NACE Rev. 1 36)
Breakdown of turnover and employment by employment size class, 1997 (%)

	Micro (0-9)		Small (10-49)		Medium (50-249)		Large (250+)	
	Turnover (1)	Employment (2)	Turnover (1)	Employment (3)	Turnover (4)	Employment (5)	Turnover (4)	Employment (5)
EU-15	16.2	22.7	26.2	23.6	26.4	20.8	31.2	32.8
B	28.5	37.2	38.4	28.8	19.2	22.2	13.9	11.9
DK	10.1	14.3	24.7	29.1	:	:	:	:
D	7.2	9.0	14.5	15.6	18.1	28.0	60.2	47.5
EL	:	:	:	:	:	:	:	:
E	28.8	40.2	37.3	38.1	23.2	15.4	10.7	6.3
F	17.9	31.8	20.6	22.0	27.4	22.1	34.1	24.0
IRL	:	:	:	:	:	:	:	:
I	18.3	38.5	41.7	38.4	27.6	16.8	12.4	6.3
L	:	:	:	:	:	:	:	:
NL	:	:	:	16.5	:	18.1	:	45.7
A	14.2	26.0	24.8	31.2	36.4	24.2	24.5	18.7
P	22.2	34.5	37.1	39.7	32.5	21.0	8.2	4.8
FIN	20.2	23.8	26.7	27.8	25.7	22.8	27.4	25.6
S	13.3	19.6	19.1	22.3	41.1	37.5	26.5	20.6
UK	25.7	31.3	19.9	18.8	25.7	25.0	28.7	25.0

(1) EU-15, DK, E, F, I, P and S, 1996.
(2) EU-15, DK, F, I, P and S, 1996.
(3) EU-15, DK, F, I, NL, P and S, 1996.
(4) EU-15, E, F, I, P and S, 1996.
(5) EU-15, F, I, NL, P and S, 1996.

Source: Eurostat (SME)

A stable structure, dominated by furniture manufacture

The manufacture of furniture (sub-chapter 14.1) dominates the data presented within this chapter, accounting for 70-75% of production, value added and the number of persons employed in the EU. Jewellery (sub-chapter 14.2) accounted for 6-8% of the EU totals for the same indicators. Amongst the heterogeneous activities treated in sub-chapter 14.3, the manufacture of musical instruments (NACE Rev. 1 Group 36.3) accounted for only 1% of output and employment in this chapter, sports goods (NACE Rev. 1 Group 36.4) for about 3 to 4%, games and toys (NACE Group 36.5) for 5-6% and miscellaneous manufacturing (NACE Group 36.6) for 11-12%. All of the above figures are for 1995 except for the manufacture of furniture (1999). Comparing the growth rates of the incomplete data set for individual Member States between 1995 and 1997 it seems unlikely that the EU shares of these activities have changed greatly. Furthermore, a longer time comparison, back to 1989, shows that the relative importance of the different activities within furniture manufacture and other manufacturing has been relatively stable for a longer period.

A manufacturing industry dominated by very small and small enterprises

1997 data on enterprises classified by employment size employment shows that all of these activities, from furniture to miscellaneous manufacturing were dominated by small enterprises. Although totals for the EU are not available, an analysis of the data for a large number of Member States shows a greater concentration in the number of very small enterprises (less than 10 persons employed) than in manufacturing as a whole, except for the manufacture of furniture. This analysis is supported by the relatively low share of employees in these activities and the correspondingly large numbers of self-employed and family workers.

STRUCTURE AND PERFORMANCE

Between 1989 and 1999 the EU production value for furniture manufacture and other manufacturing increased in value terms (current prices) by 35.1 billion ECU to 104.2 billion EUR, an absolute increase of 50.8%, which lies above the manufacturing average increase of 43.4%. This was equivalent to a growth rate of 4.2% per annum over the ten-year period. Value added increased over the same period (3.4% per annum), although by a smaller percentage than output, whilst still faster than in manufacturing as a whole (2.8% per annum).

Slower growth experienced in the mid- to late-1990s than in total manufacturing

The fastest annual growth rates were experienced between 1989 and 1991 and between 1995 and 1998; only in 1993 did output and value added actually fall in value terms. The fact that the ten-year growth rate in these industries was higher than in manufacturing can be mainly attributed to the period 1989 to 1993 which saw initially high growth followed by a comparatively small contraction. Since then these industries have continued to grow, but at a slower pace than manufacturing as a whole. This can be seen clearly in an analysis in volume or real terms over a five-year period. Output rose in these industries by an average of 3.3% per annum in real terms during the five years to 1998 and value added by 1.9% over the same period. This is considerably below the 4.9% annual growth in output and 3.1% annual growth in value added recorded in real terms for manufacturing as a whole during the same period.

Figure 14.2

Other manufacturing industries (NACE Rev. 1 36)

EU production and value-added in constant prices and employment compared to total manufacturing (1990=100)

Production in constant prices

Value added in constant prices

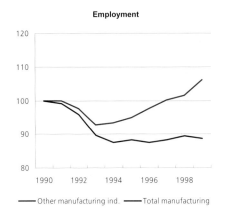

Employment

Source: Eurostat (SBS)

An important industry in some of the EU's smaller Member States

The Member States where furniture manufacture and other manufacturing industries accounted for a considerably greater share of manufacturing value added than in the EU as a whole were Denmark, Austria and Portugal. This can be seen from the production specialisation ratio relative to the EU, which was 207.5% in Denmark, 151.6% in Portugal and 148.7% in Austria. Not only do these industries represent a relatively large proportion of manufacturing in Denmark, but they have also seen considerable growth in both absolute and real terms. For example value added in constant prices increased at an average compound rate of 3.8% per annum during the ten years to 1997.

LABOUR AND PRODUCTIVITY

Unlike manufacturing as a whole, furniture manufacture and other manufacturing saw an increase in employment over the 10 years to 1999. A net gain of 96 thousand jobs was recorded taking the total in the EU over the one million threshold. Although difficult to confirm because of incomplete time series in other industries, it is likely that this 9.8% increase was one of the three largest in manufacturing during the 1990s.

A manufacturing industry with growing employment and less severe contractions

Growth was not steady; total employment in the EU had already passed one million in 1990 only to fall in each of the next three years to 938 thousand persons by 1993. Throughout the 1990s employment growth was stronger than in manufacturing as a whole and the contractions observed were less severe. The employment figures confirm the findings from the analysis of value added that these industries are particularly important in Denmark, Portugal, Spain and Austria.

Low apparent labour productivity and low average personnel costs

The apparent labour productivity of the EU labour force in furniture manufacture and other manufacturing has grown in absolute terms from 26.7 thousand ECU of value added in current prices per head in 1989 to 34.1 thousand EUR per head in 1999, slightly down on the 1998 high of 34.6 thousand ECU. Throughout this period, apparent labour productivity in these industries has been consistently lower than the manufacturing average. Simple wage adjusted labour productivity, which shows the relation between value added and personnel costs, has fallen from 1989 to a low in 1995 since when it has steadily increased through to 1999. However, at 139.2% it still remained below its 1989 level and also 11.8 percentage points below the manufacturing average.

Table 14.2

Other manufacturing industries (NACE Rev. 1 36)

Composition of the labour force, 1999 (%)

	Women (1)	Part-time (2)	Highly-educated (3)
EU-15	25.4	8.3	10.3
B	28.6	:	15.2
DK	37.4	7.7	10.8
D	27.8	10.1	19.8
EL	18.3	:	7.1
E	14.3	4.3	10.8
F	30.9	8.5	12.3
IRL	23.7	:	:
I	27.2	5.5	1.9
L	:	:	:
NL	19.5	21.4	5.1
A	21.3	9.6	:
P	20.5	:	:
FIN	28.5	:	20.1
S	33.5	:	:
UK	26.1	11.0	12.3

(1) EU-15 and EL, 1998.
(2) EU-15, 1998.
(3) B and EL, 1998; EU-15 and UK, 1997.

Source: Eurostat (LFS)

Figure 14.3

Other manufacturing industries (NACE Rev. 1 36)

Apparent labour productivity and unit personnel costs, 1997 (thousand ECU)

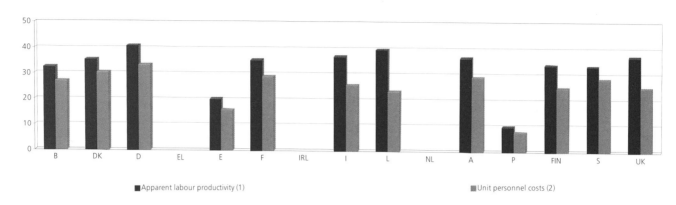

■ Apparent labour productivity (1)　　　　　　■ Unit personnel costs (2)

(1) I, 1996; EL, IRL and NL, not available.
(2) DK and I, 1996; EL, IRL and NL, not available.

Source: Eurostat (SBS)

Personnel costs in furniture manufacture and other manufacturing were 26.2 thousand ECU per employee in 1995, lower than the 33.6 thousand ECU average for manufacturing as a whole. Despite these relatively low personnel costs, the proportion of total operating costs spent on personnel (26% in 1999) in these industries was 5 percentage points higher than in manufacturing.

An industry with a small but
growing female workforce

Like most manufacturing industries the proportion of men in employment in this NACE Rev. 1 Division was much higher than the average for the economy. In 1998, across the EU, approximately 75% of the persons employed in these industries were men compared to 58% for the whole economy; this was only about 3 percentage points higher than the manufacturing average. The similarity in the proportion of men in employment in these industries and in manufacturing as a whole holds true for most countries with the exception of Portugal where nearly 78% of employment in these industries was male, compared to 56% in manufacturing as a whole.

Low qualification levels

The furniture manufacture and other manufacturing industries rely heavily on labour with relatively low qualification levels: 46.0% of persons in employment had completed primary or lower secondary education which was one of the highest proportions of any NACE Rev. 1 Division and was considerably above the manufacturing average of 38.8% for 1997. Unsurprisingly the proportion of those employed in furniture manufacture and other manufacturing having completed higher education was 6 percentage points less than the manufacturing average of 16.0%.

Highest proportion of self-employment
in manufacturing

The craft nature of several of the industries within furniture manufacture and other manufacturing, notably jewellery, musical instruments and furniture manufacture, leads to a very high proportion of self-employed persons within these activities. In 1998 this proportion reached 17.9%. Whilst this is considerably below some service activities such as HORECA (26.6%), retail trade (27.7%) and also some way below construction (24.4%), it is the highest proportion for any manufacturing NACE Rev. 1 Division except for the manufacture of wood and of wood products and more than double the manufacturing average (7.8%).

The proportion of full-time work in 1998 in furniture manufacture and other manufacturing (91.7%) was lower than the average for manufacturing (92.6%). Turning to the number of hours worked per week, the range in 1998 was from 36.0 in the Netherlands to 45.2 in Greece.

INTERNATIONAL TRENDS AND FOREIGN TRADE

In 1997, Triad production in current prices in furniture manufacture and other manufacturing reached 244.1 billion ECU. The EU's share of this was 39.7%, just below the USA's 40.7% share. 1997 was the first year since 1987 that the USA's share had been greater than the EU's. Over the same period the Japanese share of Triad production fell from 23.6% to 19.7%. This relatively low Japanese share of Triad production was reflected in the contribution of furniture manufacture and other manufacturing to total manufacturing which in Japan was 2.2%, compared to 2.5% in the EU and 2.8% in the USA (all figures for 1997).

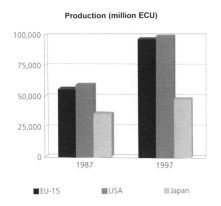
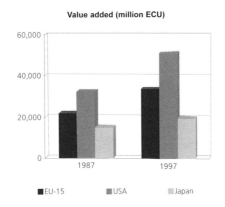
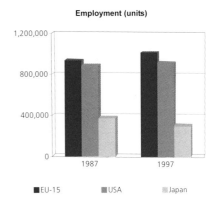

Figure 14.4

Other manufacturing industries (NACE Rev. 1 36)
International comparison of production, value added and employment

Production (million ECU)

Value added (million ECU)

Employment (units)

■ EU-15   ■ USA   ▨ Japan

■ EU-15   ■ USA   ▨ Japan

■ EU-15   ■ USA   ▨ Japan

Source: Eurostat (SBS)

Low apparent labour productivity, falling further behind Japan and the USA

Triad value added in 1997 was equal to 104.3 billion ECU, representing 42.8% of production value, a rate higher than the manufacturing average of 38.0% (1996). This value added was generated by 2.2 million persons, at a rate of 46.8 thousand ECU per person. Large differences in this measure of apparent labour productivity can be seen between the Triad members; for 1997, each person employed in Japan generated 64.6 thousand ECU of value added on average, in the USA the figure was 55.9 thousand ECU, whilst in the EU it was just above half the Japanese level at 33.1 thousand ECU. This divergence in apparent labour productivity between the EU and Japan grew substantially over the 5 years to 1997 as, measured in current prices, the EU's apparent labour productivity grew by 9.8% compared to 19.6% in Japan. Over the same period the USA appeared to have been closing the gap with Japan, as value added in the USA grew considerably faster than employment and apparent labour productivity in current prices rose by 37.6%.

EU moves from being a net exporter to a net importer

During the ten-year period from 1989 to 1999 the EU moved from being a net exporter in furniture manufacture and other manufacturing to a net importer. Exports grew from 14.5 billion ECU to 24.0 billion EUR, whilst imports more than doubled from 12.4 billion ECU to 28.3 billion EUR. The cover ratio (exports divided by imports) fell below 100% in 1991, moved back above 100% from 1994 to 1996, before falling to 84.9% in 1999.

Both the USA and Japan were net importers in furniture manufacture and other manufacturing throughout the same period. In 1998 these countries had cover ratios significantly lower than the EU: 71.5% in Japan and 20.0% in the USA, the latter reflecting a trade deficit in these industries of 37.1 billion ECU.

Eastern European chairs and tables and Asian toys and games

As noted at the beginning of this chapter, the origin of imports into the EU varies significantly between NACE Rev. 1 Groups within furniture manufacture and other manufacturing. However, China was clearly a major exporter to the EU in nearly all activities covered in this chapter. Since 1989 Chinese imports into the EU rose from 1.4 billion ECU to 7.0 billion EUR in 1999. Other countries from which EU imports have grown in value or percentage terms over the period considered included Indonesia and Poland and, to a lesser extent, Turkey.

The main export markets for EU producers in 1999 were the same as in 1989, namely the other members of the Triad (Japan and USA) and the two largest EFTA countries (Norway and Switzerland), as well as Hong Kong. However, an analysis of some of the smaller EU export markets shows the growing importance of Eastern European countries such as Poland, the Russian Federation, the Czech Republic and Hungary.

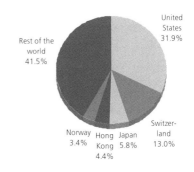

Figure 14.5

Other manufacturing industries
(NACE Rev. 1 36)
Destination of EU exports, 1999 (%)

Rest of the world 41.5%

United States 31.9%

Switzerland 13.0%

Norway 3.4%   Hong Kong 4.4%   Japan 5.8%

Source: Eurostat (COMEXT)

Figure 14.6

Other manufacturing industries
(NACE Rev. 1 36)
Origin of EU imports, 1999 (%)

China (ex. HK) 24.8%

Rest of the world 45.4%

United States 10.5%

Japan 7.6%

Switzerland 5.9%

Poland 5.8%

Source: Eurostat (COMEXT)

SUB-CHAPTER 14.1
FURNITURE (NACE Rev. 1 36.1)

The structure of the NACE Rev. 1 classification within the manufacture of furniture is built up by reference to products such as chairs and seats (NACE Rev. 1 36.11) and mattresses (NACE Rev. 1 36.15) and also by reference to the different use of furniture products such as office and shop furniture (NACE Rev. 1 36.12), as well as kitchen furniture (NACE Rev. 1 36.13). A residual Class (NACE Rev. 1 36.14) covers other furniture which is generally household furniture for gardens or rooms other than kitchens and also includes finishing activities such as spraying, painting and polishing.

Overlap of the office and home furniture market segments

One of the main factors that influences the market for furniture is consumer confidence. This is mainly driven by the level of disposable income for households and general economic performance for businesses. Interest rates play an important role with a dual influence on the demand for furniture: as low, stable interest rates influence directly the demand for furniture and also stimulate the housing market, indirectly encouraging expenditure on furniture, particularly for fitted furniture such as kitchens and bedrooms. Global trends show an increase in demand for SOHO[1] furniture derived from the greater propensity for people to work at least some time at home and from an increased penetration of computers into the home. Not only does this have a direct impact on the demand for furniture globally but also reflects a fusion between two previously separate market segments, office and household furniture.

_____
(1) Small office/home office.

Figure 14.7 _____

Furniture (NACE Rev. 1 36.1)

Production and export specialisation (%)

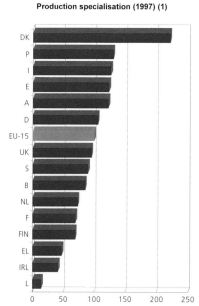

Production specialisation (1997) (1)

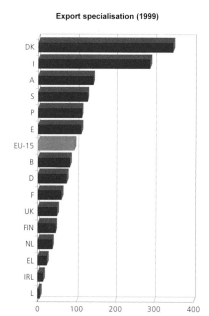

Export specialisation (1999)

(1) EL and I, 1995.

Source: Eurostat (SBS, COMEXT)

STRUCTURE AND PERFORMANCE

By 1999 the output of the EU furniture industry reached nearly 74 billion EUR in current prices, 1.9% of manufacturing output. In the ten years since 1989 it had increased from just under 50 billion EUR at an annual average growth rate of 4.3%, marginally above the total manufacturing average. In real terms, output grew by 3.0% in the five years to 1998. These growth rates hide the sharp fall in output and value added that occurred in 1993 and more moderate reductions during a number of subsequent years, as well as the high rates of annual growth (in current prices) recorded in 1989 (10.4%) and 1990 (9.1%).

High specialisation in furniture production in Denmark, Austria and Portugal

The five largest Member States had the highest output with production in current prices in 1997 ranging from 19.3 billion ECU in Germany to 6.2 billion ECU in Spain. However some smaller Member States recorded the highest production specialisation in this industry, notably Denmark, where production in 1997 accounted for 4.1% of manufacturing output, far ahead of Austria and Portugal (both 2.9%). The least specialised in this industry were Ireland (0.7% of manufacturing output) and Luxembourg (0.4%). This strong Danish position in furniture has been strengthening over the ten years to 1997. In current prices Danish production increased on average each year by 7.3%, 1.5 percentage points ahead of the EU average. Despite the very small absolute size of the industry in Ireland, considerable growth was recorded over the same period, from 129.9 million ECU of output in 1987 to 412.9 million ECU in 1997, an annual average growth rate of 12.3%, which was above the Irish average annual growth rate for total manufacturing.

Figure 14.8

Furniture (NACE Rev. 1 36.1)

International comparison of production in constant prices and employment (1990=100)

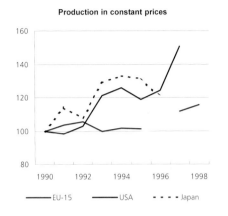

Production in constant prices

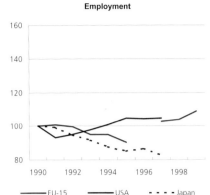

Employment

Source: Eurostat (SBS)

EUR and from Mexico to 56.6 million EUR. Looking at countries that have dropped down the rankings, Japan stood out as the country from which EU imports fell the most in absolute terms between 1989 and 1999.

The main destination of EU exports within the furniture industry remained unchanged between 1989 and 1999 (the USA, Switzerland and Norway). Looking below these top destinations the importance of Eastern European countries grew significantly, particularly the Russian Federation, Poland, the Czech Republic and Hungary, replacing countries such as Australia and Canada.

LABOUR AND PRODUCTIVITY

Employment in the EU furniture industry increased substantially between 1989 and 1999, from 696 thousand to 788 thousand persons, an overall increase of 13.2%. Hence, the furniture industry was almost entirely responsible for the 96.1 thousand person increase in employment observed for furniture manufacture and other manufacturing as a whole. Most Member States have seen employment grow over the ten-year period to 1997, although Finland registered an annual average reduction of 1.9% during this period. More recently, over the five years to 1997, the level of employment in the furniture industry fell in Spain, France, Austria and Germany.

The expansion of output in this industry over the ten years to 1999 has come partly from the increase in employment noted above and partly from an increase of apparent labour productivity which rose from 25.6 thousand ECU per head in 1989 to 32.8 thousand EUR per head in 1999, having peaked in 1998 at 33.3 thousand ECU per head. However, looking at simple wage adjusted labour productivity which shows the value added generated in relation to the personnel cost, productivity in 1999 (134.8%) was at a similar level to 1989 (135.9%) having fallen to 128.7% in 1995. This improvement since 1995 in wage adjusted labour productivity was also reflected in the share of personnel costs in total operating costs which fell from 28.2% in 1995 to 26.8% in 1999, although this remained significantly above the manufacturing average of 21.0% (1999).

INTERNATIONAL TRENDS AND FOREIGN TRADE

Over the ten years from 1987 to 1997 the EU share of Triad production rose from 43.3% to 46.5%, mainly at the expense of Japan where the share of Triad production fell from 17.1% to 13.4%. Over the same ten-year period, employment fell at an annual average rate of 1.6% in Japan but grew in the EU and USA. As a result Japan's share of Triad employment fell from 12.2% to 9.9%.

From 1989 to 1999 exports of furniture from the EU doubled to 8.4 billion EUR while imports increased more dramatically from 1.9 billion ECU to 8.3 billion EUR. Throughout the period considered the EU maintained a positive trade balance although it shrunk to close to zero in 1999. Behind this overall figure, Germany's extra-EU trade balance turned from a surplus in 1989 of 99.0 million ECU to a deficit in 1999 of 1.8 billion EUR. France also saw its extra-EU trade surplus turn into a deficit over the same period, whilst the extra-EU trade deficits of the United Kingdom and the Netherlands increased by a large proportion. In the other direction Italy recorded a significant improvement in its extra-EU trade surplus, which more than doubled between 1989 and 1999 to 2.9 billion EUR.

Increased imports from Indonesia, China and Malaysia and more trade with Eastern Europe
Analysing the growth of imports into the EU in percentage and absolute terms between 1989 and 1999, Indonesia, China, Malaysia and Brazil ranked high for both measures. Vietnam and Mexico also recorded considerable growth in their export performance: in 1989 the EU imported less than 1 million ECU of furniture from each of them but by 1999 EU imports of furniture from Vietnam had increased to 129.0 million

Figure 14.9

Furniture (NACE Rev. 1 36.1)

Destination of EU exports, 1999 (%)

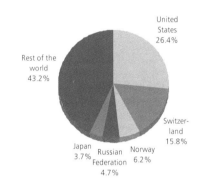

Source: Eurostat (COMEXT)

Figure 14.10

Furniture (NACE Rev. 1 36.1)

Origin of EU imports, 1999 (%)

Source: Eurostat (COMEXT)

SUB-CHAPTER 14.2
JEWELLERY (NACE Rev. 1 36.2)

In terms of the NACE Rev. 1 classification the Group 36.2 is split between the striking of coins and medals on the one hand and the manufacture of jewellery and related articles on the other. The first of these activities includes all coins and medals, regardless of whether they are made from precious metals or not. The second, concerning jewellery, includes all working of precious and semi-precious stones and metals, including pearls, but excludes the preparation of parts for watches which is included in chapter 12.

STRUCTURE AND PERFORMANCE

The last year for which the EU production value for the jewellery industry is available is 1995, when output reached 7.4 billion ECU, just 0.2% of manufacturing production.

Jewellery production concentrated
in Italy and Belgium

In 1996 production value in current prices was 3.0 billion ECU in Italy, which was about 40% of total EU production, making it easily the largest producer in the EU. The next largest EU producer in absolute terms was Belgium with just under 1 billion ECU of production value in 1997. Whilst the jewellery industry was a relatively important manufacturing industry in Belgium in production terms, accounting for 0.6% (1997) of the manufacturing total compared to the EU's average of 0.2% (1995), its value added represented only 0.2% of the total Belgian manufacturing value added. As such, value added in the Belgium jewellery industry was equivalent to only 10.9% of production. Similarly low shares of value added in production were recorded in Italy (19.2%), Portugal (16.4%) and Austria (10.2%), where the jewellery industry's share of manufacturing production also significantly exceeded the EU average.

Figure 14.11

Jewellery (NACE Rev. 1 36.2)

Production and export specialisation (%)

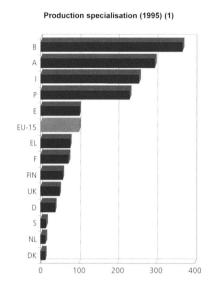

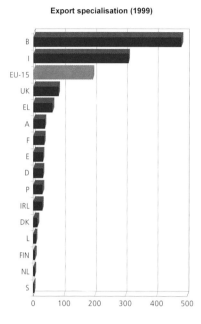

(1) IRL and L, not available.

Source: Eurostat (SBS, COMEXT)

Figure 14.12

Jewellery (NACE Rev. 1 36.2)

International comparison of production in constant prices and employment (1990=100)

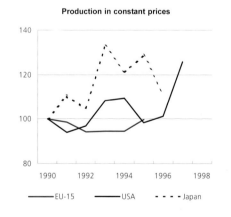

Source: Eurostat (SBS)

*Growth in Spain and contraction
in Germany and Denmark*

Time series for this industry are quite fragmented and so it is difficult to draw conclusions on the dynamics of the EU industry, however it is possible to contrast the trends of the jewellery industry between a selection of Member States that indicate varying fortunes. Spain recorded high growth rates for production and value added over the ten-year period from 1987 to 1997, mainly due to exceptional growth early in the period considered. The annual average growth over the ten-year period was between 10% and 13% in constant and current prices for production and value added, despite some contraction in the Spanish jewellery industry between 1993 and 1995. The German and Danish jewellery industries on the other hand saw production and value added decline in real terms over the same ten-year period. In constant prices German value added fell by an average of 1.9% per year and Danish value added by an average of 2.2% per year. In 1997 production in Germany in current prices was 737.8 million ECU, a fall of just over 60 million ECU since 1987. Most of this contraction in the German jewellery industry took place after 1991 as jewellery output grew steadily between 1987 and 1990. Production in the Danish jewellery industry oscillated throughout the nineties but both production and value added recorded large rises in 1997, value added in current prices for example rising from 4.4 million ECU to 6.2 million ECU.

LABOUR AND PRODUCTIVITY

The latest estimate of EU employment in the jewellery industry was 58.5 thousand persons for the 1995 reference year. Data for 1997 for several Member States indicated a fall in employment since then, for example 1.3 thousand less persons employed in the United Kingdom and 1.7 thousand less in Germany. A significant expansion in employment took place in the Portuguese jewellery industry as employment grew from 4.2 thousand in 1992 to 6.4 thousand persons in 1997 overtaking the employment level in the United Kingdom in 1996. Apparent labour productivity in the EU fell in current prices from 41.5 thousand ECU of value added per head in 1989 to an estimated 32.5 thousand ECU per head in 1997, most of the reduction took place between 1989 and 1991. Simple wage adjusted labour productivity also fell sharply between the same years from 212.4% (1989) to 159.0% (1991) due to a 17.5% increase in personnel costs allied to a fall (-12.0%) in value added. Since 1991 the value of this indicator has remained relatively stable as both value added and personnel costs have generally fallen.

INTERNATIONAL TRENDS AND FOREIGN TRADE

Whilst the jewellery industry in the EU was very small in terms of production, its contribution to exports was more significant although it fell from 2.0% of total manufacturing exports in 1989 to 1.4% in 1999.

*Expanding exports and a growing
extra-EU trade surplus*

The EU jewellery industry was the only industry within this chapter that started the ten-year period from 1989 to 1999 with a trade surplus and finished with an even larger one. Exports grew in most of the ten years from 6.8 billion ECU to 9.7 billion EUR whilst imports initially fell from 4.3 billion ECU in 1989 to 4.0 billion ECU in 1992 before rising to 6.8 billion EUR in 1999, leading to an increase in the trade surplus over the ten-year period of 11.5%.

The top countries of origin for EU imports in 1999 were India, the United States, Switzerland, Israel and Thailand, all of which figured in the top six in 1989. EU imports from these countries as well as Hong Kong and China all recorded growth in excess of 200 million ECU between 1989 and 1999. Amongst the large importers into the EU, China, Turkey, South Korea and the United Arab Emirates saw the greatest growth in percentage terms.

Exports of the EU jewellery industry to the USA, Switzerland, Hong Kong, Japan and Israel each exceeded half a billion euro in 1999. The export markets that expanded the most in absolute terms between 1989 and 1999 were the USA, the United Arab Emirates and Israel. Amongst the major EU export markets Japan, Brunei, Saudi Arabia and Oman reduced their imports from the EU over the same period.

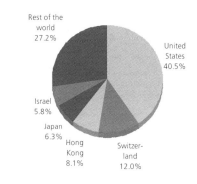

Figure 14.13

**Jewellery (NACE Rev. 1 36.2)
Destination of EU exports, 1999 (%)**

Source: Eurostat (COMEXT)

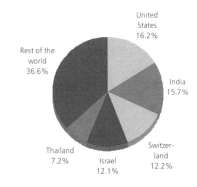

Figure 14.14

**Jewellery (NACE Rev. 1 36.2)
Origin of EU imports, 1999 (%)**

Source: Eurostat (COMEXT)

SUB-CHAPTER 14.3
MUSICAL INSTRUMENTS, SPORTS
GOODS, TOYS AND GAMES
(NACE Rev. 1 36.3, 36.4 AND 36.5)

This mixed collection of manufacturing industries covers an extremely wide range of activities. Clothing, footwear and specialist horse-riding equipment are excluded, as well as most sports vehicles (and boats and boat sails) and weapons.

MUSICAL INSTRUMENTS:
STRUCTURE AND PERFORMANCE

EU production of musical instruments in 1999 was 736 million EUR, unchanged compared to ten years earlier. Value added increased by 26 million EUR over the same period to 376 million EUR and as a result its share of production exceeded 50%, the only manufacturing industry in which this was the case. Germany had by far the largest musical instrument industry in the EU, with production and value added accounting for around 45% of the EU total in 1997. As a share of manufacturing, this is one of the smallest industries in the EU accounting for only 0.02% of total manufacturing output. From the Member States for which data is available, France, Spain and the Netherlands recorded growth over the ten years to 1997. Both the German and Finnish industries contracted over five and ten-year periods to 1997, Finland experiencing a particularly large reduction with production falling in most years from 22.6 million ECU in 1986 (earliest available data) to 3.3 million ECU in 1997.

LABOUR AND PRODUCTIVITY

The manufacture of musical instruments employed only 11.9 thousand persons in 1995, 4.4 thousand persons less than five years earlier. Approximately half of all EU employment in the manufacture of musical instruments was in Germany which recorded a steady fall in employment from 8.1 thousand in 1990 through 5.9 thousand persons in 1995 down to 5.2 thousand in 1997, equivalent to a decline of 35.9% over this seven-year period.

Figure 14.15

Musical instruments (NACE Rev. 1 36.3)
Production and export specialisation (%)

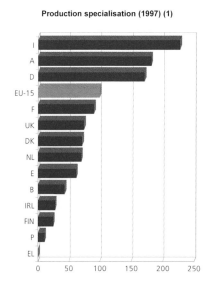

Production specialisation (1997) (1)

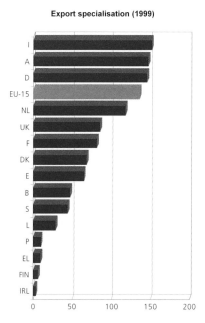

Export specialisation (1999)

(1) EL and I, 1995; L and S, not available.

Source: Eurostat (SBS, COMEXT)

Figure 14.16

Musical instruments (NACE Rev. 1 36.3)
International comparison of production in constant prices and employment (1990=100)

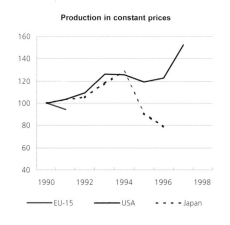

Production in constant prices

Employment

Source: Eurostat (SBS)

INTERNATIONAL TRENDS AND FOREIGN TRADE

Japan accounted for 55.6% of Triad production and 49.9% of Triad value added. Over the ten years from 1987 the EU's share of both of these measures stayed well below the manufacturing average at around 15-20%, whilst the USA's share increased at the expense of Japan.

Falling but enduring trade deficit

Exports of musical instruments from the EU rose during the ten years to 1999, imports stayed at the same level and hence the cover ratio (the ratio of exports to imports) strengthened, but the EU still had a trade deficit of 303.7 million EUR in this industry in 1999. In 1989 all Member States had an extra-EU trade deficit in musical instruments, but by 1999 both Italy and Austria had established an extra-EU trade surplus. Considerable growth (in absolute terms) over the ten years to 1999 was recorded in EU imports from China, the USA and Taiwan. EU imports from Indonesia and Malaysia also increased from less than 1 million ECU each in 1989 to 36.2 million EUR and 11.6 million EUR respectively in 1999. Between 1989 and 1999 there were no major changes in EU export markets for musical instruments. However, the largest market, the USA, expanded significantly, importing nearly 90 million EUR more of musical instruments in 1999 (161.5 million ECU) than ten years earlier (72.4 million ECU in 1989).

―――――――――――――――――――――Figure 14.17

Musical instruments (NACE Rev. 1 36.3)
Destination of EU exports, 1999 (%)

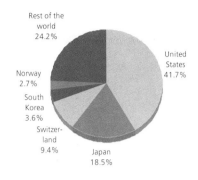

Source: Eurostat (COMEXT)

―――――――――――――――――――――Figure 14.18

Musical instruments (NACE Rev. 1 36.3)
Origin of EU imports, 1999 (%)

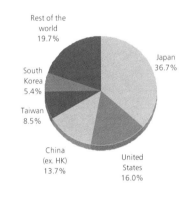

Source: Eurostat (COMEXT)

SPORTS GOODS:

STRUCTURE AND PERFORMANCE

Output in the sports goods industry reached 2.9 billion ECU in 1995, the last year for which an EU total is available, with value added equivalent to 36.6% of that figure. Data for many Member States is available through to 1997 from which it is clear that EU production passed the 3 billion ECU mark.

Austria's winter sports goods boost EU production
Amongst the Member States the Austrian sports goods industry stands out as the 1997 production value (398.3 million ECU) was of the same order of magnitude as in Italy (404.4 million ECU for 1996). The production of winter sports goods (skis, bindings and ski poles) was largely responsible for this. In most Member States the sports goods industry accounted for somewhere between 0.01% and 0.15% of total manufacturing production with Austrian sports goods output considerably more significant at 0.55%.

LABOUR AND PRODUCTIVITY

It is estimated that the EU sports goods industry employed 27.5 thousand persons in 1995, a figure which is likely to have increased since, judging from the results reported for 1997 for most Member States. The one large sports goods producing Member state that saw employment fall throughout most of the nineties was Austria where 1.7 thousand jobs were lost between 1991 and 1997, equivalent to 31.1% of the 1991 employment level.

INTERNATIONAL TRENDS AND FOREIGN TRADE

Production in the USA in 1997 was 9.6 billion ECU and dwarfed the production in Japan (3.0 billion ECU in 1997) and the EU (2.9 billion ECU in 1995). This was also apparent in employment terms as 57.4% of Triad employment in 1995 was in the USA.

Increasing trade deficit mainly due to imports from China and the USA
The EU's trade deficit in sports goods worsened from 245.0 million ECU to 809.9 million EUR between 1989 and 1999. The cover ratio also fell from 75.3% to 58.9% reflecting a proportionately more rapid rise in imports than in exports, the former having topped 2 billion ECU in 1997 before declining slightly in 1998 and 1999. In 1999 China, the USA, Taiwan, Pakistan and South Korea were the countries from which the EU imported the most sports goods. China recorded the highest growth in exports to the EU of any country, increasing from 35.6 million ECU in 1989 to 535.4 million EUR in 1999. The top three export markets for EU sports goods in 1999 were the same as they had been ten years earlier, namely the USA, Japan and Switzerland. There was nevertheless considerable growth in exports to some of the Eastern European

countries such as the Czech Republic, Poland, Hungary and the Russian Federation, all of which passed Australia in the value of sports goods they imported from the EU.

Figure 14.19

Sports goods (NACE Rev. 1 36.4)

Production and export specialisation (%)

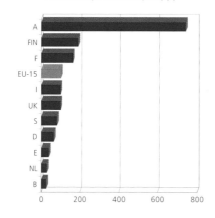

Production specialisation (1995) (1)

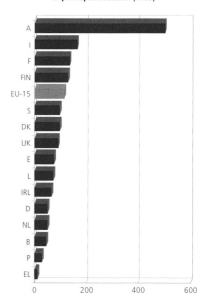

Export specialisation (1999)

(1) S, 1994; DK, EL, IRL, L and P, not available.

Source: Eurostat (SBS, COMEXT)

Figure 14.20

Sports goods (NACE Rev. 1 36.4)

Destination of EU exports, 1999 (%)

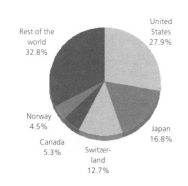

Source: Eurostat (COMEXT)

Figure 14.21

Sports goods (NACE Rev. 1 36.4)

Origin of EU imports, 1999 (%)

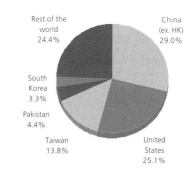

Source: Eurostat (COMEXT)

GAMES AND TOYS:

STRUCTURE AND PERFORMANCE

The manufacture of games and toys in the EU was worth 5.6 billion EUR in production terms in 1999, an increase of 804 million ECU in current prices compared to five years earlier. At 3.2% per year on average, growth was below the EU manufacturing average and below the average for furniture manufacture and other manufacturing.

The Danes, specialists in games and toys

Most Member States' activity in this industry in 1997 accounted for somewhere between 0.02% (the Netherlands) and 0.24% (Austria) of total manufacturing value added. The share in Denmark (1.01%) was considerably above this range as it was to a lesser extent in Spain (0.33%). Austria, France and Denmark reported overall growth between 1992 and 1997, interspersed with years of contraction. Spain appeared to have the strongest growing games and toys industry within the EU as production and value added expanded in real terms in each of the three years to 1997 (production grew by a total of 23.4% and value added by a total of 28.4% between 1994 and 1997).

LABOUR AND PRODUCTIVITY

Estimates of employment in the EU games and toys industry exceeded 50 thousand for the third successive year in 1999, approximately 0.22% of EU total manufacturing employment. Apparent labour productivity was 39.3 thousand EUR per head, 5.2 thousand EUR higher than the average for furniture manufacture and other manufacturing, but still considerably below the total manufacturing average.

INTERNATIONAL TRENDS AND FOREIGN TRADE

The share of Triad production of games and toys was evenly split between all three members in 1997. In spite of the similar production levels, the USA generated slightly more than half of Triad value added and Japan less than one-fifth. The EU's 45% share of Triad employment in this industry in 1997 combined with its share of value added contributed to a lower apparent labour productivity than the USA and Japan.

Expansion of exports to Eastern Europe and Brazil

By 1997 the EU's cover ratio for sports goods had fallen to nearly 20%, indicating that imports were close to five times as large as exports in this industry, one of the lowest of all manufacturing cover ratios. The EU's trade deficit of 4.7 billion EUR for sports goods in 1999 was one of the largest in manufacturing. All Member States contributed to this extra-EU trade deficit in 1999 with the United Kingdom (-1.3 billion EUR) and Germany (-1.1 billion EUR) recording the largest extra-EU trade deficits, despite also being the

largest extra-EU exporters. The main source of EU imports of games and toys in 1999 was China as it had been in 1989. The value of these imports had however increased from 840.4 million ECU to 3.3 billion EUR over these ten years - Japan and China together accounted for 76% of all games and toys imports into the EU. Amongst the other sources of EU imports, Indonesia, the USA and Vietnam also recorded increases. The USA was by far the largest export market for

the EU's games and toys industry and also recorded the largest growth in absolute terms between 1989 and 1999. Hungary, the Czech Republic, Hong Kong and Brazil increased in importance as an export destination for EU goods.

Figure 14.22

Games and toys (NACE Rev. 1 36.5)
Production and export specialisation (%)

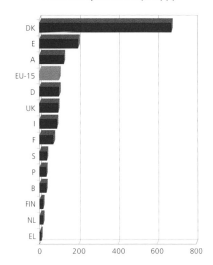

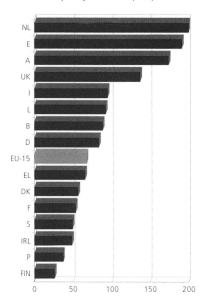

(1) EL and I, 1994; IRL and L, not available.

Source: Eurostat (SBS, COMEXT)

Figure 14.23

Games and toys (NACE Rev. 1 36.5)
Destination of EU exports, 1999 (%)

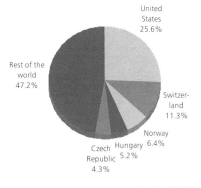

Source: Eurostat (COMEXT)

Figure 14.24

Games and toys (NACE Rev. 1 36.5)
Origin of EU imports, 1999 (%)

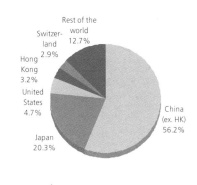

Source: Eurostat (COMEXT)

Table 14.3

Manufacture of furniture (NACE Rev. 1 36.1)

Production related indicators in the EU (1)

	1989	1990	1991	1992	1993	1994	1995	1996	1997	1998	1999
Number of persons employed (thousands)	695.6	722.4	729.2	720.2	686.5	686.6	652.0	:	742.0	752.3	787.6
Production (million EUR)	48,491	52,912	56,554	58,175	55,696	57,896	59,879	:	68,593	72,001	73,913
Domestic producer price index (1995=100)	:	:	:	:	:	:	100.0	102.4	103.6	105.2	106.7
Value added (million EUR)	17,797	19,225	20,676	21,220	20,616	20,671	20,846	:	23,702	25,031	25,814

(1) Technically, data before 01/01/1999 are in ECU and after this date in euro. However, as the conversion rate was 1 ECU =1 EUR, for practical purposes the two terms can be used interchangeably.

Table 14.4

Manufacture of furniture (NACE Rev. 1 36.1)

Trade related indicators in the EU (1)

	1989	1990	1991	1992	1993	1994	1995	1996	1997	1998	1999
Exports (million EUR)	4,216	4,232	4,099	4,134	4,557	5,434	6,157	6,820	7,834	8,103	8,445
Imports (million EUR)	1,927	2,061	2,540	2,877	3,275	3,706	4,309	4,877	5,862	6,831	8,321
Trade balance (million EUR)	2,288	2,171	1,558	1,257	1,283	1,729	1,848	1,943	1,972	1,272	124
Cover ratio (%)	218.7	205.3	161.3	143.7	139.2	146.7	142.9	139.8	133.6	118.6	101.5

(1) Technically, data before 01/01/1999 are in ECU and after this date in euro. However, as the conversion rate was 1 ECU =1 EUR, for practical purposes the two terms can be used interchangeably.

Table 14.5

Manufacture of furniture (NACE Rev. 1 36.1)

Production related indicators, 1997

	B	DK	D	EL (1)	E	F	IRL	I (1)	L	NL	A	P	FIN	S	UK
Number of persons employed (thousands)	21.4	22.3	168.0	3.4	116.9	72.9	5.6	92.1	0.3	:	21.6	53.3	11.6	19.6	107.7
Production (million ECU)	2,323	2,108	19,309	171	6,160	7,836	413	11,642	16	1,989	1,611	1,425	887	1,902	9,864
Value added (million ECU)	702	775	6,913	71	2,187	2,461	148	3,220	8	689	752	475	380	658	4,034
Gross operating surplus (million ECU)	193.4	197.5	1,160.1	28.1	545.3	404.9	52.8	955.6	2.3	199.4	140.2	139.1	114.7	112.2	1,389.1

(1) 1996.

Table 14.6

Manufacture of furniture (NACE Rev. 1 36.1)

Trade related indicators, 1999

	B	DK	D	EL	E	F	IRL	I	L	NL	A	P	FIN	S	UK
Exports (million EUR)	1,580	1,784	4,332	23	1,279	2,256	104	7,710	6	778	1,056	318	227	1,198	1,451
Imports (million EUR)	1,814	696	5,974	186	701	3,251	249	825	148	1,772	1,371	304	271	846	2,895
Trade balance (million EUR)	-234	1,088	-1,642	-163	577	-995	-145	6,885	-142	-994	-315	14	-44	352	-1,445
Cover ratio (%)	87.1	256.4	72.5	12.4	182.3	69.4	41.7	934.3	4.0	43.9	77.0	104.8	83.9	141.6	50.1

Table 14.7

Manufacture of furniture (NACE Rev. 1 36.1)

Labour related indicators, 1997

	B	DK (1)	D	EL (2)	E	F	IRL	I (2)	L	NL	A	P	FIN	S	UK
Unit personnel costs (thousand ECU per employee)	27.7	30.4	34.4	13.1	15.4	28.2	17.4	25.5	23.9	:	28.6	7.0	24.5	27.9	25.3
Social charges as a share of personnel costs (%)	47.5	4.9	22.7	29.6	28.3	39.9	13.7	48.7	:	14.8	30.0	29.8	25.7	41.1	11.6
Apparent labour productivity (thousand ECU/pers. empl.)	32.8	34.7	41.1	21.2	18.7	33.8	26.4	35.0	28.1	:	34.8	8.9	32.7	33.6	37.4
Wage adjusted labour productivity (%)	118.3	136.2	119.7	161.7	121.5	119.7	151.9	137.2	117.8	:	121.9	126.8	133.4	120.6	148.1
Personnel costs as a share of total operating costs (%)	24.0	29.5	30.0	30.1	27.9	27.0	25.7	19.7	33.5	25.6	36.8	25.5	28.4	29.9	29.8

(1) Unit personnel costs and wage adjusted labour productivity, 1996; (2) 1996.

Source: Eurostat (SBS, EBT, COMEXT)

_____Table 14.8

Manufacture of jewellery and related articles (NACE Rev. 1 36.2)

Production related indicators in the EU (1)

	1989	1990	1991	1992	1993	1994	1995	1996	1997	1998	1999
Number of persons employed (thousands)	58.8	62.3	62.0	61.4	57.7	56.7	58.5	:	:	:	:
Production (million ECU)	6,727	6,627	6,752	6,508	6,602	6,736	7,393	:	:	:	:
Domestic producer price index (1995=100)	:	:	:	:	:	:	100.0	101.1	100.3	100.3	101.2
Value added (million ECU)	2,440	2,351	2,147	2,092	2,012	1,993	1,961	:	:	:	:

(1) Technically, data before 01/01/1999 are in ECU and after this date in euro. However, as the conversion rate was 1 ECU =1 EUR, for practical purposes the two terms can be used interchangeably.

_____Table 14.9

Manufacture of jewellery and related articles (NACE Rev. 1 36.2)

Trade related indicators in the EU (1)

	1989	1990	1991	1992	1993	1994	1995	1996	1997	1998	1999
Exports (million EUR)	6,846	6,344	6,447	6,479	7,648	8,189	7,905	8,427	9,495	9,038	9,692
Imports (million EUR)	4,262	4,175	4,134	3,964	5,217	5,593	5,229	5,886	6,716	6,554	6,810
Trade balance (million EUR)	2,584	2,169	2,313	2,515	2,431	2,596	2,676	2,541	2,779	2,484	2,882
Cover ratio (%)	160.6	151.9	155.9	163.4	146.6	146.4	151.2	143.2	141.4	137.9	142.3

(1) Technically, data before 01/01/1999 are in ECU and after this date in euro. However, as the conversion rate was 1 ECU =1 EUR, for practical purposes the two terms can be used interchangeably.

_____Table 14.10

Manufacture of jewellery and related articles (NACE Rev. 1 36.2)

Production related indicators, 1997

	B	DK	D	EL (1)	E	F	IRL	I (1)	L	NL	A	P	FIN	S	UK
Number of persons employed (thousands)	3.6	0.1	7.3	0.6	10.0	7.7	:	14.2	0.0	:	0.6	6.4	0.8	:	5.5
Production (million ECU)	955	15	738	33	632	937	:	3,015	2	51	381	565	76	:	544
Value added (million ECU)	104	6	289	11	206	306	:	578	1	20	39	93	30	:	204
Gross operating surplus (million ECU)	49.4	1.6	71.5	2.7	60.5	52.8	:	217.0	0.0	6.0	19.3	42.8	11.7	:	67.9

(1) 1996.

_____Table 14.11

Manufacture of jewellery and related articles (NACE Rev. 1 36.2)

Trade related indicators, 1999

	B	DK	D	EL	E	F	IRL	I	L	NL	A	P	FIN	S	UK
Exports (million EUR)	5,145	38	987	33	195	710	121	4,599	5	49	152	47	14	12	1,312
Imports (million EUR)	4,141	46	1,124	64	279	895	74	751	16	149	174	122	34	64	1,980
Trade balance (million EUR)	1,004	-7	-137	-31	-84	-185	46	3,847	-12	-100	-22	-75	-20	-52	-668
Cover ratio (%)	124.2	83.7	87.8	51.5	69.9	79.3	162.4	612.2	27.8	33.1	87.4	38.9	41.2	19.4	66.3

_____Table 14.12

Manufacture of jewellery and related articles (NACE Rev. 1 36.2)

Labour related indicators, 1997

	B	DK (1)	D	EL (2)	E	F	IRL	I (2)	L	NL	A	P	FIN	S	UK
Unit personnel costs (thousand ECU per employee)	19.5	39.2	29.7	15.4	16.4	32.9	:	26.8	23.9	:	34.7	9.3	26.8	:	26.5
Social charges as a share of personnel costs (%)	32.0	4.5	22.0	30.8	26.6	40.7	:	47.3	:	14.8	24.7	26.2	25.7	:	12.3
Apparent labour productivity (thousand ECU/pers. empl.)	29.1	46.3	39.8	20.0	20.6	39.8	:	40.8	18.6	:	68.1	14.6	36.8	:	37.3
Wage adjusted labour productivity (%)	148.8	128.9	133.8	129.9	126.1	120.8	:	152.2	77.8	:	196.4	156.6	137.2	:	141.1
Personnel costs as a share of total operating costs (%)	5.9	33.1	29.5	29.5	23.4	28.0	:	12.6	24.0	30.6	5.4	9.1	27.4	:	25.9

(1) Unit personnel costs and wage adjusted labour productivity, 1996; (2) 1996.

Source: Eurostat (SBS, EBT, COMEXT)

Table 14.13

Manufacture of musical instruments (NACE Rev. 1 36.3)

Production related indicators in the EU (1)

	1989	1990	1991	1992	1993	1994	1995	1996	1997	1998	1999
Number of persons employed (thousands)	16.0	16.3	15.7	:	:	:	11.9	:	:	:	:
Production (million EUR)	733	841	822	:	:	:	834	:	713	755	736
Domestic producer price index (1995=100)	:	:	:	:	:	:	:	:	:	108.6	110.6
Value added (million EUR)	350	384	393	:	:	:	388	:	376	377	376

(1) Technically, data before 01/01/1999 are in ECU and after this date in euro. However, as the conversion rate was 1 ECU =1 EUR, for practical purposes the two terms can be used interchangeably.

Table 14.14

Manufacture of musical instruments (NACE Rev. 1 36.3)

Trade related indicators in the EU (1)

	1989	1990	1991	1992	1993	1994	1995	1996	1997	1998	1999
Exports (million EUR)	249	259	267	270	286	326	346	359	394	383	395
Imports (million EUR)	695	692	705	679	651	679	643	660	698	715	699
Trade balance (million EUR)	-445	-432	-439	-409	-365	-353	-297	-302	-304	-332	-304
Cover ratio (%)	35.9	37.5	37.8	39.8	44.0	48.0	53.8	54.4	56.5	53.6	56.5

(1) Technically, data before 01/01/1999 are in ECU and after this date in euro. However, as the conversion rate was 1 ECU =1 EUR, for practical purposes the two terms can be used interchangeably.

Table 14.15

Manufacture of musical instruments (NACE Rev. 1 36.3)

Production related indicators, 1997

	B	DK	D	EL (1)	E	F	IRL	I (1)	L	NL	A	P	FIN	S	UK
Number of persons employed (thousands)	0.2	0.2	5.2	0.0	0.8	1.6	0.0	1.3	:	:	0.4	0.1	0.1	:	1.2
Production (million ECU)	12	7	325	0	32	106	3	184	:	20	25	1	3	:	81
Value added (million ECU)	5	5	177	0	17	54	2	67	:	9	15	1	2	:	40
Gross operating surplus (million ECU)	2.6	0.2	7.9	0.0	5.2	3.2	1.0	35.0	:	2.5	3.1	0.1	0.7	:	9.6

(1) 1996.

Table 14.16

Manufacture of musical instruments (NACE Rev. 1 36.3)

Trade related indicators, 1999

	B	DK	D	EL	E	F	IRL	I	L	NL	A	P	FIN	S	UK
Exports (million EUR)	30	11	273	0	24	96	1	130	1	78	35	1	1	14	80
Imports (million EUR)	37	26	253	13	62	141	8	95	5	90	38	14	14	27	201
Trade balance (million EUR)	-8	-15	20	-13	-38	-45	-7	36	-4	-11	-3	-13	-13	-14	-121
Cover ratio (%)	79.5	43.7	107.9	2.2	38.7	68.1	10.0	137.8	19.5	87.2	92.9	6.3	7.3	49.5	39.8

Table 14.17

Manufacture of musical instruments (NACE Rev. 1 36.3)

Labour related indicators, 1997

	B	DK (1)	D	EL	E	F	IRL	I (2)	L	NL	A	P	FIN	S	UK
Unit personnel costs (thousand ECU per employee)	24.4	31.0	32.2	:	16.6	31.4	16.9	24.9	:	:	29.3	7.1	21.1	:	24.3
Social charges as a share of personnel costs (%)	47.1	4.2	23.2	:	29.0	39.6	16.7	76.5	:	12.5	33.3	33.3	30.0	:	13.3
Apparent labour productivity (thousand ECU/pers. empl.)	21.6	29.7	33.9	:	22.5	33.4	42.8	50.2	:	:	36.5	6.1	20.2	:	31.9
Wage adjusted labour productivity (%)	88.2	116.1	105.3	:	135.9	106.3	253.2	201.5	:	:	124.6	86.3	95.6	:	131.5
Personnel costs as a share of total operating costs (%)	26.0	68.5	48.4	:	37.5	48.4	31.6	20.3	:	36.2	55.7	36.4	37.1	:	37.5

(1) Unit personnel costs and wage adjusted labour productivity, 1996; (2) 1996.

Source: Eurostat (SBS, EBT, COMEXT)

Table 14.18

Manufacture of sports goods (NACE Rev. 1 36.4)
Production related indicators in the EU

	1989	1990	1991	1992	1993	1994	1995	1996	1997	1998	1999
Number of persons employed (thousands)	:	:	:	:	28.3	28.4	27.5	:	:	:	:
Production (million ECU)	:	:	:	:	2,823	2,803	2,940	:	:	:	:
Domestic producer price index (1995=100)	:	:	:	:	:	:	:	:	:	:	:
Value added (million ECU)	:	:	:	:	1,026	1,043	1,076	:	:	:	:

Table 14.19

Manufacture of sports goods (NACE Rev. 1 36.4)
Trade related indicators in the EU (1)

	1989	1990	1991	1992	1993	1994	1995	1996	1997	1998	1999
Exports (million EUR)	746	751	719	770	936	1,069	1,204	1,126	1,124	1,063	1,160
Imports (million EUR)	991	956	1,091	1,152	1,231	1,360	1,400	1,799	2,001	1,980	1,970
Trade balance (million EUR)	-245	-205	-371	-382	-294	-291	-196	-674	-877	-917	-810
Cover ratio (%)	75.3	78.6	66.0	66.8	76.1	78.6	86.0	62.6	56.2	53.7	58.9

(1) Technically, data before 01/01/1999 are in ECU and after this date in euro. However, as the conversion rate was 1 ECU =1 EUR, for practical purposes the two terms can be used interchangeably.

Table 14.20

Manufacture of sports goods (NACE Rev. 1 36.4)
Production related indicators, 1997

	B	DK	D	EL	E	F	IRL (1)	I (1)	L	NL	A	P	FIN	S	UK
Number of persons employed (thousands)	0.2	0.3	5.3	:	1.2	6.5	0.7	2.6	:	:	3.8	0.5	1.2	0.7	5.7
Production (million ECU)	20	38	542	:	95	837	57	404	:	44	398	47	106	72	492
Value added (million ECU)	8	12	220	:	32	259	28	123	:	17	155	7	48	35	214
Gross operating surplus (million ECU)	2.8	1.8	54.3	:	10.2	45.0	16.0	53.3	:	4.8	25.5	3.2	17.7	11.3	72.8

(1) 1996.

Table 14.21

Manufacture of sports goods (NACE Rev. 1 36.4)
Trade related indicators, 1999

	B	DK	D	EL	E	F	IRL	I	L	NL	A	P	FIN	S	UK
Exports (million EUR)	98	56	336	1	97	556	56	495	8	118	424	9	72	104	299
Imports (million EUR)	180	85	602	25	174	542	49	297	9	217	231	38	71	140	615
Trade balance (million EUR)	-82	-29	-265	-23	-77	13	7	198	-1	-99	193	-29	1	-37	-316
Cover ratio (%)	54.4	65.8	55.9	5.1	55.9	102.4	114.3	166.9	87.4	54.5	183.6	24.0	101.5	73.8	48.6

Table 14.22

Manufacture of sports goods (NACE Rev. 1 36.4)
Labour related indicators, 1997

	B	DK (1)	D	EL	E	F	IRL (2)	I (2)	L	NL	A	P	FIN	S	UK
Unit personnel costs (thousand ECU per employee)	35.8	33.6	31.5	:	18.5	32.9	16.8	27.4	:	:	34.5	9.7	25.9	33.0	26.0
Social charges as a share of personnel costs (%)	40.0	6.0	22.9	:	28.2	42.3	14.9	48.5	:	13.3	29.8	50.0	31.6	41.2	12.1
Apparent labour productivity (thousand ECU/pers. empl.)	35.9	36.8	41.6	:	26.0	39.8	39.2	47.4	:	:	41.2	15.7	38.2	49.0	37.3
Wage adjusted labour productivity (%)	100.3	135.9	131.9	:	140.4	121.0	233.8	172.8	:	:	119.5	161.7	147.4	148.5	143.7
Personnel costs as a share of total operating costs (%)	29.7	23.9	31.0	:	23.1	24.0	26.8	18.3	:	28.3	28.8	9.4	30.2	28.2	23.6

(1) Unit personnel costs and wage adjusted labour productivity, 1996; (2) 1996.

Source: Eurostat (SBS, COMEXT)

Table 14.23

Manufacture of games and toys (NACE Rev. 1 36.5)

Production related indicators in the EU (1)

	1989	1990	1991	1992	1993	1994	1995	1996	1997	1998	1999
Number of persons employed (thousands)	:	:	:	:	45.6	47.7	:	:	51.1	52.1	51.5
Production (million EUR)	:	:	:	:	4,327	4,755	:	:	5,386	5,733	5,559
Domestic producer price index (1995=100)	:	:	:	:	:	:	100.0	101.9	102.9	104.2	104.6
Value added (million EUR)	:	:	:	:	1,756	1,812	:	:	1,937	1,935	2,021

(1) Technically, data before 01/01/1999 are in ECU and after this date in euro. However, as the conversion rate was 1 ECU =1 EUR, for practical purposes the two terms can be used interchangeably.

Table 14.24

Manufacture of games and toys (NACE Rev. 1 36.5)

Trade related indicators in the EU (1)

	1989	1990	1991	1992	1993	1994	1995	1996	1997	1998	1999
Exports (million EUR)	609	680	756	806	904	1,031	1,057	1,035	1,174	1,165	1,205
Imports (million EUR)	2,374	2,588	3,872	4,832	4,655	4,106	3,968	4,126	5,496	5,639	5,920
Trade balance (million EUR)	-1,765	-1,908	-3,117	-4,026	-3,751	-3,075	-2,911	-3,091	-4,322	-4,475	-4,715
Cover ratio (%)	25.7	26.3	19.5	16.7	19.4	25.1	26.6	25.1	21.4	20.7	20.4

(1) Technically, data before 01/01/1999 are in ECU and after this date in euro. However, as the conversion rate was 1 ECU =1 EUR, for practical purposes the two terms can be used interchangeably.

Table 14.25

Manufacture of games and toys (NACE Rev. 1 36.5)

Production related indicators, 1997

	B	DK	D	EL (1)	E	F	IRL (1)	I (1)	L	NL	A	P	FIN	S	UK
Number of persons employed (thousands)	0.6	4.8	14.8	0.1	7.0	5.1	1.0	3.2	:	:	1.7	1.0	0.2	0.7	9.0
Production (million ECU)	70	504	1,421	2	772	619	97	609	:	36	127	29	17	61	769
Value added (million ECU)	29	189	601	1	262	201	31	154	:	10	63	10	7	22	306
Gross operating surplus (million ECU)	7.5	53.1	163.2	0.4	122.2	56.7	14.0	65.7	:	3.6	17.8	3.3	3.0	-1.6	113.6

(1) 1996.

Table 14.26

Manufacture of games and toys (NACE Rev. 1 36.5)

Trade related indicators, 1999

	B	DK	D	EL	E	F	IRL	I	L	NL	A	P	FIN	S	UK
Exports (million EUR)	337	58	965	12	435	387	72	503	17	814	258	21	25	93	788
Imports (million EUR)	615	179	1,793	131	740	1,314	130	696	31	1,194	277	160	65	222	1,903
Trade balance (million EUR)	-278	-121	-827	-119	-305	-927	-57	-193	-14	-380	-18	-139	-40	-129	-1,114
Cover ratio (%)	54.8	32.4	53.8	9.5	58.7	29.5	55.8	72.2	55.7	68.1	93.4	12.9	38.7	41.7	41.4

Table 14.27

Manufacture of games and toys (NACE Rev. 1 36.5)

Labour related indicators, 1997

	B	DK (1)	D	EL (2)	E	F	IRL (2)	I (2)	L	NL	A	P	FIN	S	UK
Unit personnel costs (thousand ECU per employee)	35.8	29.7	29.4	9.2	20.5	28.2	18.2	28.1	:	:	26.2	7.3	23.2	34.6	22.3
Social charges as a share of personnel costs (%)	36.9	7.5	23.0	20.0	26.5	38.7	16.2	50.0	:	14.5	29.5	29.4	25.0	44.7	12.4
Apparent labour productivity (thousand ECU/pers. empl.)	47.6	39.3	40.6	15.5	37.4	39.2	32.6	47.7	:	:	36.3	10.2	35.1	32.3	33.8
Wage adjusted labour productivity (%)	133.1	208.9	138.1	167.8	182.9	139.2	179.2	169.6	:	:	138.9	140.9	151.5	93.3	151.8
Personnel costs as a share of total operating costs (%)	35.0	22.4	31.2	42.9	19.5	24.8	20.3	16.3	:	15.9	36.3	22.7	25.3	25.5	26.5

(1) Unit personnel costs and wage adjusted labour productivity, 1996; (2) 1996.

Source: Eurostat (SBS, EBT, COMEXT)

_____Table 14.28

Miscellaneous manufacturing (NACE Rev. 1 36.6)

Production related indicators in the EU (1)

	1989	1990	1991	1992	1993	1994	1995	1996	1997	1998	1999
Number of persons employed (thousands)	122.1	126.5	122.7	117.3	109.2	112.7	112.1	:	:	:	:
Production (million ECU)	7,197	7,870	7,881	8,258	7,886	8,497	9,151	:	:	:	:
Domestic producer price index (1995=100)	:	:	:	:	:	:	100.0	102.0	102.9	103.8	104.3
Value added (million ECU)	3,187	3,478	3,478	3,633	3,450	3,599	3,752	:	:	:	:

(1) Technically, data before 01/01/1999 are in ECU and after this date in euro. However, as the conversion rate was 1 ECU =1 EUR, for practical purposes the two terms can be used interchangeably.

_____Table 14.29

Miscellaneous manufacturing (NACE Rev. 1 36.6)

Trade related indicators in the EU (1)

	1989	1990	1991	1992	1993	1994	1995	1996	1997	1998	1999
Exports (million EUR)	1,869	1,884	2,102	2,150	2,433	2,643	2,765	2,923	3,313	3,088	3,085
Imports (million EUR)	2,191	2,237	2,811	2,962	2,988	3,098	3,131	3,168	3,652	3,902	4,470
Trade balance (million EUR)	-322	-352	-709	-813	-556	-455	-366	-245	-339	-813	-1,386
Cover ratio (%)	85.3	84.2	74.8	72.6	81.4	85.3	88.3	92.3	90.7	79.2	69.0

(1) Technically, data before 01/01/1999 are in ECU and after this date in euro. However, as the conversion rate was 1 ECU =1 EUR, for practical purposes the two terms can be used interchangeably.

_____Table 14.30

Miscellaneous manufacturing (NACE Rev. 1 36.6)

Production related indicators, 1997

	B	DK	D	EL (1)	E	F	IRL	I (1)	L	NL	A	P	FIN	S	UK
Number of persons employed (thousands)	2.0	1.5	29.2	0.5	13.4	17.1	:	16.6	:	:	2.8	7.2	1.7	2.6	22.2
Production (million ECU)	223	120	2,615	19	848	1,659	:	1,870	:	384	215	277	128	166	1,712
Value added (million ECU)	66	55	1,205	8	313	646	:	660	:	165	103	87	61	64	810
Gross operating surplus (million ECU)	19.2	14.7	314.5	2.1	106.1	156.5	:	246.0	:	83.4	35.3	28.9	22.1	-5.5	321.6

(1) 1996.

_____Table 14.31

Miscellaneous manufacturing (NACE Rev. 1 36.6)

Trade related indicators, 1999

	B	DK	D	EL	E	F	IRL	I	L	NL	A	P	FIN	S	UK
Exports (million EUR)	403	157	1,936	20	318	1,123	180	1,165	11	619	366	71	63	227	892
Imports (million EUR)	458	256	1,659	129	524	1,332	128	786	34	681	383	181	103	261	1,521
Trade balance (million EUR)	-55	-99	277	-109	-206	-210	53	379	-23	-62	-18	-110	-40	-34	-629
Cover ratio (%)	88.0	61.3	116.7	15.6	60.7	84.3	141.5	148.2	31.8	90.9	95.4	39.3	61.2	86.8	58.6

_____Table 14.32

Miscellaneous manufacturing (NACE Rev. 1 36.6)

Labour related indicators, 1997

	B	DK (1)	D	EL (2)	E	F	IRL	I (2)	L	NL	A	P	FIN	S	UK
Unit personnel costs (thousand ECU per employee)	28.7	30.5	30.1	11.8	16.9	28.6	:	25.7	:	:	24.7	9.0	25.5	27.0	23.4
Social charges as a share of personnel costs (%)	35.5	5.2	22.9	27.3	26.8	39.5	:	51.3	:	17.5	29.7	32.1	27.2	40.9	12.9
Apparent labour productivity (thousand ECU/pers. empl.)	32.5	37.0	41.3	15.8	23.3	37.7	:	39.7	:	:	37.3	12.1	36.8	24.8	36.5
Wage adjusted labour productivity (%)	113.3	132.7	137.2	134.4	137.6	131.9	:	154.8	:	:	151.2	133.9	144.2	92.0	156.1
Personnel costs as a share of total operating costs (%)	22.9	32.8	33.7	32.2	24.5	29.4	:	24.0	:	22.4	30.1	20.7	28.3	37.5	30.3

(1) Unit personnel costs and wage adjusted labour productivity, 1996; (2) 1996.

Source: Eurostat (SBS, EBT, COMEXT)

Construction and real estate (NACE Rev. 1 45 and 70)

The EU statistical classification of economic activities covers construction activities and real estate services within NACE Rev. 1 Section F and NACE Rev. 1 Division 70 (part of Section K: business services). Other activities that also contribute to the construction sector, such as architects or construction economists are not covered here, but rather in chapter 20 on business services. Please note that structural data presented in this chapter relates to the whole enterprise population, and is not limited to enterprises that generally employed 20 or more persons (as is the case for the other industrial chapters within this publication).

STRUCTURE AND PERFORMANCE

According to 1997 National Accounts, the branch of building and construction contributes about 5.1% to the total value added of the EU, although this share was in decline from 1990 onwards, the year when building and construction accounted for 6.2% of total wealth created. Austria and Spain displayed the highest degree of specialisation: in these two countries, the contribution of construction to national value added was 50% above the EU average, at 7.8% and 7.7% (1997). Three other Member States displayed above average proportions: Greece (7.4%), Finland (6.2%) and Portugal (6.0%). This contrasts with Germany and France where the contribution of construction to total value added was below 4.5%.

16% of all European enterprises

In 1996, 2.5 million construction enterprises were active in the EU, in addition to 828 thousand real estate enterprises, which represented 16.0% of the number of manufacturing, construction and services (NACE Rev. 1 Sections D to K) enterprises in the EU. Construction activities are characterised by a very high presence of small enterprises, with a majority of enterprises having no employees at all (i.e. self-employed persons), accounting for 54.8% of construction enterprises and as many as 73.6% of real estate enterprises (both 1996). The comparable ratio for manufacturing activities was 34.1% (NACE Rev. 1 Section D, 1996), whilst it was 51.9% in services (NACE Rev. 1 Sections G to K, 1996). Very small enterprises with fewer than 10 employees made up 92.6% of all construction enterprises (against 81.2% for total manufacturing), whilst accounting for 49.5% of employment in this activity (15.2% for total manufacturing) and 33.9% of turnover (7.0% for total manufacturing). Similarly, 98.2% of real estate services enterprises had less than 10 employees (95.0% for all services), and they accounted for 69.4% of employment and 53.6% of turnover (39.2% and 20.8% respectively for all services).

The activities covered in this chapter (in terms of NACE Rev. 1) include:

45:   construction;
45.1: site preparation;
45.2: building of complete constructions or parts thereof; civil engineering;
45.3: building installation;
45.4: building completion;
45.5: renting of construction or demolition equipment with operator;
70   real estate activities;
70.1: real estate activities with own property;
70.2: letting of own property;
70.3: real estate activities on a fee or contract basis.

Table 15.1

Construction (NACE Rev. 1 45)

Breakdown of turnover and employment by employment size class, 1997 (%)

	Micro (0-9)		Small (10-49)		Medium (50-249)		Large (250+)	
	Turnover	Employment	Turnover	Employment	Turnover	Employment	Turnover	Employment
EU-15	33.9	49.5	28.9	27.0	18.4	12.3	18.8	11.2
B	44.9	55.0	27.5	25.3	16.9	12.3	10.7	7.3
DK	36.2	40.4	28.3	33.1	14.6	13.3	20.8	13.3
D	20.2	32.1	36.9	41.4	25.8	16.1	17.1	10.4
EL	19.8	46.1	32.1	25.0	25.5	15.7	22.5	13.1
E	42.1	51.0	31.2	27.7	14.5	12.1	12.2	9.2
F	34.7	50.3	27.6	26.3	15.5	10.9	22.3	12.5
IRL	41.3	47.4	27.9	27.5	21.6	19.1	9.2	6.1
I	54.9	65.8	26.8	23.9	10.5	6.0	7.8	4.4
L	16.9	16.2	38.0	40.1	31.6	34.3	13.4	9.4
NL	21.1	47.9	33.9	15.7	26.9	23.0	18.2	13.4
A	15.5	19.6	33.6	35.7	26.4	26.1	24.5	18.5
P	30.5	43.8	23.8	24.8	19.5	16.4	26.3	15.0
FIN	35.0	45.1	24.4	25.2	14.8	10.6	25.8	19.1
S	24.2	40.3	23.2	22.0	10.8	9.6	41.8	28.1
UK	46.2	65.0	16.8	13.2	12.1	7.9	24.9	13.9

Source: Eurostat (SME)

Table 15.2

Real estate services (NACE Rev. 1 70)

Breakdown of turnover and employment by employment size class, 1997 (%)

	Micro (0-9)		Small (10-49)		Medium (50-249)		Large (250+)	
	Turnover (1)	Employment (2)	Turnover (1)	Employment (1)	Turnover (3)	Employment (3)	Turnover (4)	Employment (5)
EU-15	53.6	69.4	20.3	12.9	20.2	10.8	6.0	7.0
B	83.7	88.4	12.4	7.7	:	:	:	:
DK	83.2	69.3	14.8	11.8	:	:	:	:
D	44.4	69.5	24.4	13.4	26.4	10.9	4.7	6.3
EL	:	:	:	:	:	:	:	:
E	:	78.1	:	15.2	:	:	:	:
F	55.8	70.7	14.1	11.0	19.0	11.3	11.2	7.0
IRL	:	:	:	:	:	:	0.0	0.0
I	91.4	94.9	5.6	3.6	:	:	:	:
L	:	:	:	:	:	:	:	:
NL	:	:	:	:	:	:	:	:
A	35.6	36.6	25.4	22.0	:	:	:	:
P	77.9	72.3	17.5	19.5	4.6	8.1	0.0	0.0
FIN	35.6	51.4	38.5	24.8	7.7	13.3	18.2	10.5
S	50.7	:	10.5	12.1	17.1	19.8	21.6	:
UK	60.5	57.0	19.8	15.4	14.4	10.9	7.1	14.7

(1) EU-15, DK, F, I, P and S, 1996.
(2) EU-15, DK, F, I and P, 1996.
(3) EU-15, F, P, S and UK, 1996.
(4) EU-15, F, IRL, P, S and UK, 1996.
(5) EU-15, F, IRL, P and UK, 1996.

Source: Eurostat (SME)

*Enterprises in Austria and Luxembourg
are larger than the European average*
The small average size of construction and real estate enterprises is also confirmed by the average number of persons employed per enterprise. This ratio was equal to 4 persons per enterprise in the EU (1997), as compared to 15 persons in manufacturing and 5 persons in services (NACE Rev. 1 Sections G to K).

Average employment for construction activities was comprised between 4 and 6 persons per enterprise in most Member States, except in Austria (14 persons) and Luxembourg (16 persons) where it was markedly higher, and in the United Kingdom (2 persons) where it was lower. Real estate enterprises were smaller with 2 persons employed on average in the EU (1996), and between 2 and 3 persons employed on average in most countries, except in Denmark (5 persons) and Austria (6 persons).

Average turnover of construction enterprises in the EU was equal to 376 thousand ECU (1997), ranging from 173 thousand ECU in Portugal and 207 thousand ECU in Italy up to 1.0 million ECU in Luxembourg and 1.3 million ECU in Austria. The average turnover of real estate enterprises reached 310 thousand ECU in the EU (1996), with minima[1] recorded in Italy (139 thousand ECU) and Sweden (173 thousand ECU) and maxima in Austria (1.5 million ECU) and Ireland (1.6 million ECU).

---

(1) E, L and NL, no data available.

Box 15.1

Construction activities can be broken down into four main categories: private house-building; non-residential construction; renovation and maintenance; and civil engineering. Non-residential construction accounted for 29% of the total EU production value in 1997. It was the largest activity, preceding house-building (individual dwellings, apartment blocks and social housing schemes) with 27%. Civil engineering (roads, railways, bridges, tunnels and hydraulic structures) was the smallest construction activity generating 19% of production value. Finally, one quarter of total construction activity was accounted for by rehabilitation and maintenance activities.

According to the European Construction Industry Federation (FIEC), construction output rose by 2.3% in 1999, the second-highest growth rate in the decade after the record year in 1994 (3.2%), and following two years of modest results in 1997 (0.5%) and 1998 (0.6%). Growth can be mainly attributed to non-residential construction, where an increase of 3.3% was reported. Rehabilitation and maintenance of existing constructions progressed by 2.4%, more than new house-building (0.8%). Civil engineering picked up by 2.2% after 5 years of decline or stagnation.

Table 15.3

Annual growth rate of production value in real terms in construction (%)

	1991	1992	1993	1994	1995	1996	1997	1998	1999 (1)
EU-15 (2)	-1.0	0.8	-2.9	3.2	-0.7	-0.4	0.5	0.6	2.3
B	:	2.1	-5.0	2.0	3.2	-3.1	6.2	3.6	1.8
DK	-9.3	0.4	-1.3	2.2	5.4	6.1	6.1	1.5	-3.1
D	:	10.7	1.8	11.1	-5.5	-2.9	-1.4	-3.9	0.1
EL	:	:	:	:	:	:	:	:	:
E	:	-6.1	-6.4	1.6	5.7	0.1	2.2	5.7	9.0
F	1.3	-2.8	-5.1	-0.4	-1.4	-3.7	-1.1	0.8	4.2
IRL	3.4	1.1	-6.1	11.0	13.6	18.3	14.9	8.1	14.2
I	2.2	-1.3	-6.6	-6.3	0.9	1.7	-1.8	0.1	2.0
L	:	:	:	:	:	:	:	:	:
NL	0.6	-0.1	-2.3	1.5	7.8	2.5	2.7	2.1	3.3
A	:	5.4	-1.6	5.0	-3.2	2.4	1.3	3.0	1.5
P	:	2.9	-0.2	13.6	4.9	3.9	12.3	6.0	3.2
FIN	-16.4	-17.2	-13.2	-2.5	2.8	6.5	11.7	11.0	6.0
S	-3.8	-8.1	-11.4	-4.6	-0.9	1.1	-6.6	2.9	3.4
UK	-6.8	-4.0	-1.9	3.3	-0.2	2.3	3.1	1.9	0.8

(1) Estimates.
(2) EL and L, not available.

Source: FIEC

Figure 15.1

Annual average growth rate of production value in real terms in construction (%) (1)

■ 1990-94   ■ 1994-99

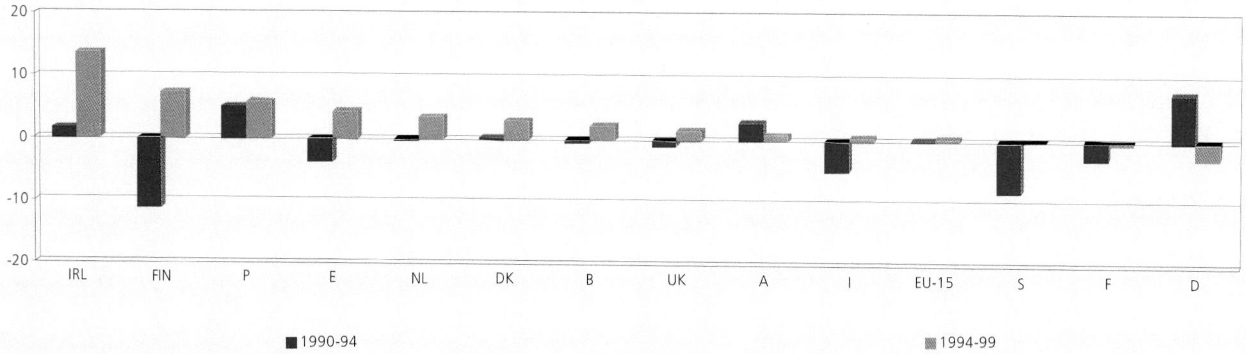

(1) EL and L, not available.

Source: FIEC

LABOUR AND PRODUCTIVITY

Employment in enterprises active in construction exceeded 10.1 million persons in 1997, to which must be added another 1.8 million working in real estate services (1996). As measured by National Accounts, employment in the construction branch accounted for 6.6% of the total number of occupied persons in the EU. Although the construction industry's share of total employment experienced decline from 1990 (when it accounted for 7.2% of the total), in absolute terms employment in construction grew over the period 1987 to 1997 (at an average rate of 0.2% per annum in the EU). This modest growth rate hides very contrasting situations across the EU, as employment declined by as much as 2.9% per year in Finland and 2.7% in Sweden, whilst it increased by 2.0% in Ireland, 2.3% in Spain and even 4.6% in Luxembourg (again 1987 to 1997).

A high share of self-employed persons
Self-employment was relatively important in construction activities as it represented 24.4% of total employment in 1998, as compared to 11.8% in industry as a whole (NACE Rev. 1 Sections C to F). As regards real estate services, the rate of self-employment was also significant, at an average of 17.5% in 1998 with rates as high as 35.9% in Belgium or 41.0 % in Portugal and up to 51.3% in Italy. The rate of self-employment in France (10.4%) and Austria (6.9%) lay well below the EU average.

Construction a predominantly male activity, with a low share of permanent duration contracts
In construction activities male employment and temporary work contracts show above average shares in total employment. At 91.5%, the share of male employment was the second highest found in any economic activity in 1998 (NACE Rev. 1 Divisions A to Q), the industrial average for the EU being 77.4%. In addition, 19.4% of the persons employed in construction activities had a temporary job or a work contract of limited duration, the highest rate of all industrial activities, whilst the industry average was 12.3%.

Real estate services displayed a totally different picture as regards these two characteristics. Women occupied exactly half of all jobs, although they were less represented Denmark (39.2%), Belgium (39.1%) or Sweden (29.8%), compared to 69.7% in Austria.

Some 10.4% of all persons employed in real estate services worked on the base of temporary work contract, less than the 12.0% average recorded for services (NACE Rev. 1 Sections G to K). Two countries, Spain and Portugal, displayed a particularly high share of temporary work contracts equal to 44.9% and 46.1% respectively.

Low average education level... except in real estate
Education of the construction workforce is highly spread, between engineers having completed a third level education and low-skilled workers that have reached only lower secondary education. Overall, the education level was lower than average, as only 11.6% of the persons employed had a third level education compared to 15.4% in industry as a whole, whilst as many as 41.4% of those employed had a lower secondary education against 38.9% in industry (1997). Women employed in construction had generally a higher education level than men: 16.9% possessed a higher education degree and only 24.3% a lower secondary education.

Table 15.4

Construction and real estate (NACE Rev. 1 45 and 70)

Composition of the labour force, 1999 (%)

	Construction			Real estate		
	Women (1)	Part-time (2)	Highly-educated (3)	Women (4)	Part-time (5)	Highly-educated (6)
EU-15	8.5	5.3	11.6	50.0	23.0	23.8
B	9.4	3.5	10.3	39.1	21.9	44.5
DK	11.3	5.1	12.0	39.2	25.6	20.3
D	12.8	6.5	20.4	48.7	25.1	26.2
EL	1.4	4.1	4.0	:	:	:
E	3.9	1.4	11.0	48.0	12.1	45.2
F	9.5	5.4	6.0	57.6	21.6	20.2
IRL	4.3	6.1	14.8	47.0	:	:
I	6.3	4.4	3.7	47.9	9.9	10.3
L	7.0	4.1	3.8	:	:	:
NL	7.2	10.7	6.0	43.3	30.3	26.1
A	8.1	5.3	1.4	69.7	33.6	:
P	3.5	3.5	2.7	45.8	:	37.5
FIN	6.9	5.2	20.7	45.6	18.9	28.1
S	9.7	6.8	10.1	29.8	18.2	:
UK	9.0	6.5	13.6	52.6	25.1	32.5

(1) EU-15, 1998; EL, 1997.
(2) EU-15, B and EL, 1998.
(3) EL, 1998; EU-15, IRL, P and UK, 1997.
(4) EU-15, 1998.
(5) EU-15 and B, 1998; S, 1997.
(6) EU-15 and UK, 1997; P, 1996.

Source: Eurostat (LFS)

In real estate services, the average education level was noticeably higher with 23.8% of the persons employed having completed a higher education, a share that reached 29.5% for men. This compares with an average for services (NACE Rev. 1 Sections G to K) equal to 19.3% (all 1997).

Unit personnel costs lower than the manufacturing average

The low average education level of persons employed in construction is mirrored in unit personnel costs that were generally below those faced in manufacturing. Unit personnel costs were spread between 29.0 thousand ECU (Ireland, 1997) and 33.0 thousand ECU (Germany and the United Kingdom, 1997) in most Member States, although much lower figures were recorded in Portugal (10.4 thousand ECU, 1997) and somewhat higher ones in Denmark and Austria (37.0 thousand ECU and 37.5 thousand ECU respectively, 1996 and 1997). The value added generated by each person employed (apparent labour productivity) generally ranged between 30.9 thousand ECU (Belgium, 1997) and 44.7 thousand ECU (United Kingdom, 1997). Portugal (15.3 thousand ECU) and Ireland (53.6 thousand ECU, 1997) recorded outlying values.

Unit personnel costs in real estate services were ranging between 27.9 thousand ECU (in Finland, 1996) and 33.3 thousand ECU (in Austria, 1997). Portugal again recorded the lowest value, 12.1 thousand ECU (1997). Apparent labour productivity was estimated at 53.7 thousand ECU in 1997, ranging from 37.2 thousand ECU in Portugal up to 106.2 thousand ECU in Austria.

Box 15.2

Construction is mainly a local activity, with few large firms and little export activity. However, EU firms are successful in world markets. Intra- and extra-EU activity is increasing on large projects and there is extensive use of non-national labour.

The geographical distribution of construction activity is very diversified and varies according to cultural, geographical and historical criteria. Spanish construction firms have a strong presence in Latin America; British construction firms are present in North America and Asia; German construction firms are present in Eastern Europe and Asia; Finnish construction firms are present in the Commonwealth of Independent States.

Table 15.5

Value of new international construction contracts by region, 1998 (million ECU)

	B	DK	D	EL	E	F (1)	NL	P	FIN	S	UK
EU	2,111	132	3,196	51	703	6,400	4,792	1	48	4,307	491
Africa	167	65	538	28	216	2,300	217	6,132	2	0	2,290
North America	0	13	3,422	0	167	1,900	545	60	0	4,889	3,158
South America	30	1	253	:	1,472	600	403	12	0	0	187
Asia	338	2	155	:	3	2,300	502	1	11	0	1,494
Australia/Pacific	36	0	1,967	0	0	:	2	0	0	0	430
Middle East	188	154	1,007	:	:	1,100	121	:	354	:	265
Other	131	26	192	0	149	800	195	0	3	0	753

(1) Turnover.

Source: FIEC

SUB-CHAPTER 15.1
SITE PREPARATION AND CONSTRUCTION
(NACE Rev. 1 45.1 AND 45.2)

The NACE Rev. 1 activity classification divides construction activities according to the stages of the construction process. Site preparation and general construction, the first of these stages, are covered by Groups 45.1 and 45.2 and will be addressed in this sub-chapter. It is estimated that around 60% of all construction work falls into this category.

Site preparation includes relatively diverse activities, ranging from test drilling and boring to determine ground conditions, through demolition of existing buildings and structures, site clearance, ground stabilisation, excavation, earth moving, and trench digging, to landscaping. General construction activities cover the building of complete constructions (or parts thereof) and civil engineering.

Average employment between
4 and 8 persons per enterprise
From the countries for which data is available, Italy numbered the highest number of site preparation and building enterprises[2], almost 219 thousand (1996). This was more than double the figure reported by France (114 thousand in 1997) or the United Kingdom (93.9 thousand in 1997). In Portugal there was also a relatively high number of enterprises recorded, 49.9 thousand in 1997.

Average employment per enterprise was spread in most Member States between four persons (Italy, 1996) and eight persons (Denmark, 1997). Austrian enterprises stood out with an average of some 24 persons employed per enterprise (1997). They also recorded the largest average turnover per enterprise (2.6 million ECU in 1997), whilst the corresponding ratios were well below one million ECU in most of the other Member States, with a minimum of 328 thousand ECU in Italy.

(2) B, D, EL, E and IRL, no data available.

Box 15.3

FIEC states there was growth in construction activity across all Member States in 1999, except in Denmark (-3.1%). The highest growth rate for 1999 was recorded in Ireland with an expansion of 14.2%, ahead of Spain (9.0%) and Finland (6.0%). FIEC forecasts a continuation of growth in 2000, although at a lower rate, with the exception of Belgium (-0.4%). Ireland was the country where construction experienced the most rapid expansion over the 1990s, with only one year of contraction in 1993 and six years of double-digit growth. Portugal also fared well, boasting six years of continuous growth from 1994. Germany had a mixed record: the first half of the decade enjoyed rapid expansion following reunification, but construction activity has decreased since 1995, and experienced a first year of modest, positive growth (0.1%) in 1999. Despite this, the level of construction activity was still 9.0% higher in 1999 than it had been in 1991. France, Italy and Sweden all reported low levels of construction activity during the 1990s.

Growth during the decade has been mainly in the area of house-building. In 1999, EU house-building activity was 12.9% above its level of 1991, with not a single year of decline. On the contrary, non-residential construction and civil engineering in the EU experienced a downturn from 1993, from which they have yet to recover. Their production value in 1999 was still more than 4% below the levels of 1991. According to FIEC, the main reason for this poor performance could be attributed to the contraction of publicly financed projects.

Figure 15.2

Investment in construction in the EU (1991=100) (1)

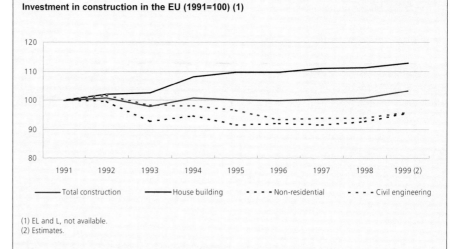

(1) EL and L, not available.
(2) Estimates.

Source: FIEC

———Figure 15.3

Site preparation and construction (NACE Rev. 1 45.1 and 45.2)

Number of persons employed, 1997 (thousands) (1)

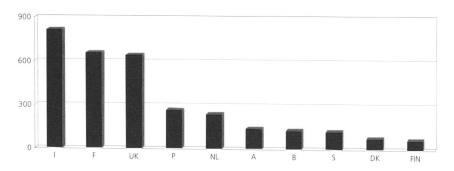

(1) I, 1996; D, EL, E, IRL and L, not available.

Source: Eurostat (SBS)

———Figure 15.4

Site preparation and construction (NACE Rev. 1 45.1 and 45.2)

Apparent labour productivity, 1997 (thousand ECU per person employed) (1)

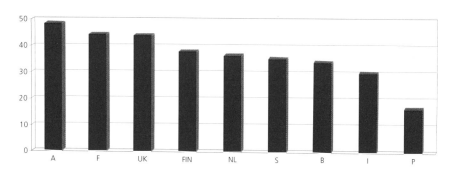

(1) I, 1996; DK, D, EL, E, IRL and L, not available.

Source: Eurostat (SBS)

———Figure 15.5

Site preparation and construction (NACE Rev. 1 45.1 and 45.2)

Unit personnel costs, 1997 (thousand ECU per employee) (1)

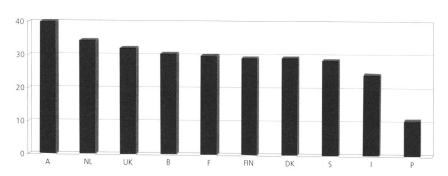

(1) DK and I, 1996; D, EL, E, IRL and L, not available.

Source: Eurostat (SBS)

Apparent labour productivity and profitability lower than in manufacturing

Value added accounted for around 30.0% of turnover, and when compared to the number of persons employed, apparent labour productivity was between 33.7 thousand ECU (Belgium, 1997) and 44.1 thousand ECU (France, 1997) in the majority of Member States. Extreme values were recorded in Austria (48.3 thousand ECU, 1997) and Portugal (16.2 thousand ECU, 1997).

Profitability of site preparation and building enterprises, as measured by the gross operating surplus generated on each ECU of turnover (the gross operating rate), was lower than for manufacturing enterprises in a majority of countries. The Netherlands reported the lowest rate, with an average gross operating rate equal to 5.1% (1997). The ratio ranged in most of the other countries between 8.0% (Belgium, 1997) and 10.8% (United Kingdom, 1997), with Italian (15.4%, 1996) and French enterprises (16.7%, 1997) performing well above the average.

Low unit personnel costs

These low productivity levels were matched by unit personnel costs somewhat lower than the average manufacturing enterprise, although usually higher than in construction as a whole. Whilst Portugal reported the minimum level (10.5 thousand ECU, 1997), unit personnel costs varied between 28.6 thousand ECU (Sweden, 1997) and 34.2 thousand ECU (the Netherlands, 1997) in a majority of Member States. Austria recorded the highest level, 39.8 thousand ECU (1997).

SUB-CHAPTER 15.2
INSTALLATION AND COMPLETION
(NACE Rev. 1 45.3, 45.4 AND 45.5)

Installation and completion work for buildings, both residential and non-residential, and for civil engineering works is divided into nine categories at the Class level of NACE Rev. 1 (4-digit codes): installation of electrical wiring and fittings (NACE Rev. 1 45.31); insulation (NACE Rev. 1 45.32); plumbing (NACE Rev. 1 45.33); plastering (NACE Rev. 1 45.41); joinery installation (NACE Rev. 1 45.42); floor and wall covering (NACE Rev. 1 45.43); painting and glazing (NACE Rev. 1 45.44); and other building installation and completion activities (NACE Rev. 1 45.34 and 45.45). This sub-chapter also covers the activities of renting construction or demolition equipment with an operator (NACE Rev. 1 Group 45.5).

Several of the installation categories described here contain important sub-divisions. The principal divisions of electrical work for buildings include, general electrical wiring and fitting, the installation of equipment for communications and for security of buildings, and the installation of lifts and escalators. Plumbing work is defined as including all heating and ventilation work, as well as the installation of water services, drains and gas services.

Smallest enterprises within the construction sector
Italy numbered more than 242.4 thousand enterprises in the activities covered by this sub-chapter in 1996, the largest figure amongst the countries for which data is available[3]. There were 192.3 thousand enterprises in France (1997) and 84.8 thousand in the United Kingdom (1997). Amongst the smaller Member States, the Netherlands and Sweden both had under 26 thousand enterprises, Denmark 18.0 thousand and Portugal 14.4 thousand (all 1997).

Enterprises active in these sectors were generally smaller than in other construction activities. In most countries, average employment per enterprise was comprised between two persons (Italy, 1996) and four persons per enterprise (Portugal and the United Kingdom, 1997), approximately half the values recorded in site preparation and construction activities. Larger average enterprise size was reported in the Netherlands (almost eight persons per enterprise, 1997) and Austria (almost ten persons, 1997).

(3) B, D, EL, E and IRL, no data available.

Figure 15.6

Installation and completion (NACE Rev. 1 45.3, 45.4 and 45.5)

Number of persons employed, 1997 (thousands) (1)

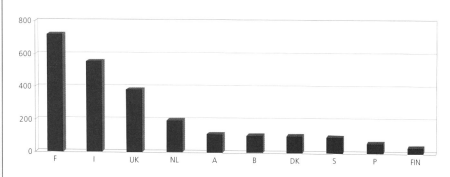

(1) I, 1996; D, EL, E, IRL and L, not available.

Source: Eurostat (SBS)

Figure 15.7

Installation and completion (NACE Rev. 1 45.3, 45.4 and 45.5)

Apparent labour productivity, 1997 (thousand ECU per person employed) (1)

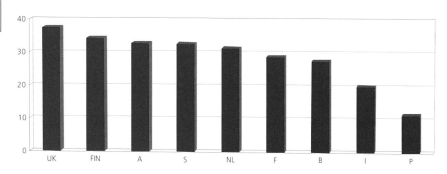

(1) I, 1996; DK, D, EL, E, IRL and L, not available.

Source: Eurostat (SBS)

Figure 15.8

Installation and completion (NACE Rev. 1 45.3, 45.4 and 45.5)

Unit personnel costs, 1997 (1) (thousand ECU per employee)

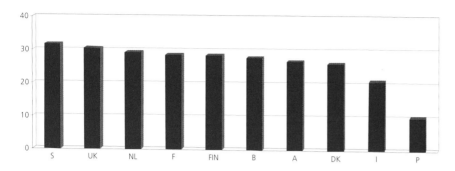

(1) DK and I, 1996; D, EL, E, IRL and L, not available.

Source: Eurostat (SBS)

Average turnover per enterprise was equal to 400 thousand ECU or less in most of the Member States, with minima of 146.6 thousand ECU in Portugal (1997) and 112.5 thousand ECU in Italy (1996). Dutch and Austrian enterprises reported on average much higher turnover at 595.1 thousand ECU and 667.9 thousand ECU respectively (both 1997). Installation enterprises displayed generally higher average turnover than those of other activities, and even exceeded one million ECU in Luxembourg (1.1 million, 1997) and the Netherlands (1.0 million, 1997).

Higher profitability rates despite
labour productivity lag

Apparent labour productivity, as measured by the gross value added generated by each person employed, was in all countries lower than the average for construction activities. The ratio ranged between 27.5 thousand ECU (Belgium, 1997) and 34.2 thousand ECU (Finland,1997). Italy (19.6 thousand ECU, 1996) and Portugal (11.3 thousand ECU, 1997) reported figures well below these limits, whilst the apparent labour productivity in the United Kingdom was somewhat higher (37.6 thousand ECU, 1997).

Despite this productivity lag, the sector boasted higher profitability rates than the average for construction activities in the majority of countries. Indeed the gross operating rate, was for a majority of countries, comprised between 9.1% (Portugal, 1997) and 12.0% (Belgium, 1997). British (14.7%, 1997) and Italian enterprises (21.3%, 1996) displayed higher rates, in contrast to their French (7.2%, 1997) and Swedish (7.0%, 1997) counterparts. In general, the gross operating rate for this sector was two to three percentage point higher than that for construction as a whole, with exception of France, Portugal and Sweden.

Unit personnel costs lower than
the construction average

As for many other industrial activities, Portugal reported the lowest level of unit personnel costs, at 9.9 thousand ECU per year, or about 0.5 thousand ECU less than the national average for construction activities. The same could be observed in most Member States, where unit personnel costs ranged between 26.0 thousand ECU (Denmark, 1997) and 30.4 thousand ECU (United Kingdom, 1997). Only Sweden recorded unit personnel costs above the construction average, with 31.7 thousand ECU in 1997. A more detailed analysis across the sector reveals that building completion enterprises faced generally lower personnel costs than those active in building installation. Unit personnel costs in building completion ranged between 25.9 thousand ECU (Belgium, 1997) and 28.7 thousand ECU (Sweden, 1997), with extreme values in Portugal (8.7 thousand ECU, 1997) and the Netherlands (32.4 thousand ECU, 1997).

Box 15.4

As regards repair, maintenance and improvement of residential buildings, FIEC estimates that growth rates in this sector in recent years have exceeded those for total construction and for new house-building. In 1999 this activity expanded by 2.4% in the EU, six times the rate of new house-building (0.4%). FIEC forecasts further growth of 2.4% for 2000. The average growth rate between 1991 and 1999 was equal to 2.1% per annum, compared to 1.4% for new house-building.

Figure 15.9

Evolution of construction renovation and maintenance production value in real terms in the EU (1991=100) (1)

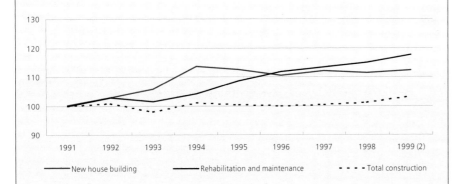

(1) EL and L, not available.
(2) Estimates.

Source: FIEC

Portugal stands out as the country that enjoyed the fastest expansion in this activity, with production value in 1999 almost twice as high as in 1991 (corresponding to an annual average growth rate of 8.3%). Portugal was also the only country with Spain that displayed a positive growth rate in every year during the period covered. All countries but two ended the decade with a positive balance as compared with 1991. The two exceptions were Sweden (-3.2% per annum on average) and Belgium (-0.9% per annum), despite a steady recovery in the latter country from 1994 onwards.

Table 15.6

Annual growth of construction renovation and maintenance production value in real terms (%)

	1991	1992	1993	1994	1995	1996	1997	1998	1999 (1)
EU-15 (2)	-2.1	2.9	-1.5	2.7	4.4	2.9	1.3	1.3	2.4
B	:	-1.9	-18.9	3.1	2.6	3.6	1.2	2.8	2.3
DK	1.6	7.0	23.5	6.5	-0.4	-3.0	-9.1	-1.4	-1.5
D	:	8.1	-8.0	-2.7	6.5	6.1	0.2	-1.1	1.1
EL	:	:	:	:	:	:	:	:	:
E	:	3.1	4.3	6.2	9.8	7.2	5.2	3.7	5.1
F	1.5	0.0	3.0	1.2	0.2	-1.8	1.0	1.7	2.0
IRL	5.8	7.9	-12.2	23.8	12.1	31.0	-2.1	-11.8	-5.5
I	-1.1	2.5	4.7	10.7	4.3	1.3	1.8	4.9	5.9
L	:	:	:	:	:	:	:	:	:
NL	-0.3	7.8	-2.9	-2.8	21.2	1.6	2.5	1.5	2.6
A	:	20.6	-5.0	12.5	-7.8	6.0	3.5	15.5	7.1
P	:	13.1	6.4	13.2	8.0	3.3	10.3	7.5	5.1
FIN	-19.4	0.0	4.8	9.2	12.6	5.6	11.5	5.6	5.3
S	-3.1	-3.2	-7.7	-5.9	-8.7	4.6	-7.7	-0.4	4.3
UK	-12.0	-6.7	-1.2	5.1	1.7	0.4	2.2	-1.5	0.4

(1) Estimates.
(2) EL and L, not available.

Source: FIEC

SUB-CHAPTER 15.3
REAL ESTATE SERVICES (NACE Rev. 1 70)

In the NACE Rev. 1 classification, real estate activities are found in Division 70, part of Section K (together with renting, computer services, research and development and business services). The Division is composed of three distinct areas. Groups 70.1 and 70.2 cover activities relating to property, the former the development, buying and selling of real estate, the latter the letting of property. Group 70.3 in contrast covers real estate activities on a fee or contract basis, including the activities of real estate agencies and of real estate management companies.

Almost three-quarters of
enterprises with no employees

The number of enterprises active in real estate services was estimated to be over 828 thousand in 1996. No less than 73.6% of these were enterprises without any employee, such as, for example, self-employed real-estate agents, and another 24.6% were very small enterprises with between one and nine employees. When compared to the corresponding averages for services (51.9% with no employees and 43.0% with one to nine employees, NACE Rev. 1 Sections G to K), these figures highlight, the higher presence of very small enterprises and the greater proportion of those that were one-man businesses.

On average just two to three
persons employed per enterprise

Enterprises in real estate services have a smaller average size compared to other activities. Average employment was comprised in most Member States between two and three persons per enterprise, except in Austria where it was markedly higher at six persons per enterprise. Similarly, average turnover of real estate enterprises reported by most countries ranged between 139.4 thousand ECU in Italy (1996) and 1.7 million ECU in Austria (1997).

Box 15.5

The property sector has experienced growth in the second half of the 1990s, after a difficult start at the beginning of the decade due to the recession and high real interest rates. Most Member States experienced growth in their number of housing transactions since 1993, with the notable exception of Germany where they plunged from 754 thousand in 1993 to 570 thousand in 1997, before picking up to 595 thousand in 1998. One should also note that the market in the United Kingdom saw almost double the number of housing transactions, when compared to France or Germany.

Table 15.7

Number of housing transactions (units)

	1990	1991	1992	1993	1994	1995	1996	1997	1998
B	99,773	99,654	104,875	104,118	104,101	96,262	102,444	105,601	109,250
DK	56,750	52,441	60,052	63,232	71,350	74,050	76,900	78,068	80,635
D	554,000	543,000	612,500	754,300	662,200	619,500	600,000	570,000	595,000
EL	93,070	43,883	59,887	61,421	65,984	67,159	68,675	100,228	:
E	:	:	:	:	:	:	:	:	:
F (1)	754,000	712,500	611,100	623,700	684,300	639,100	773,100	:	:
IRL	34,812	37,058	44,433	45,390	50,204	49,288	61,006	64,652	68,925
I	517,085	555,888	465,373	501,891	495,178	502,468	483,782	523,646	:
L	2,893	3,082	3,667	3,030	:	:	:	:	:
NL (2)	202,100	211,100	245,300	198,000	215,000	224,000	259,000	281,000	291,000
A	:	:	:	:	:	:	:	:	:
P	103,403	150,182	166,030	178,073	186,920	185,980	:	:	:
FIN	56,315	62,128	67,994	75,175	71,088	68,225	83,305	81,400	:
S	54,300	57,200	33,300	35,700	42,700	41,900	46,600	54,700	52,200
UK	1,398,000	1,305,000	1,138,000	1,195,000	1,275,000	1,134,000	1,241,000	1,440,000	1,348,000

(1) Break in series as of 1992.
(2) Break in series as of 1993.

Source: European Mortgage Federation

Between 1990 and 1997 the price of dwellings in nominal terms increased in most Member States, with the exception of Finland. In the United Kingdom prices remained (on a national average) below their level of 1990 until 1996. The highest rates of increase for the price of dwellings were recorded in Ireland and the Netherlands, where dwelling prices rose by an average of 12% and 8% per year.

Table 15.8

Trend in the price of dwellings (1990=100)

	1990	1991	1992	1993	1994	1995	1996	1997	1998
B	100	106	115	123	132	138	144	146	150
DK	100	101	95	101	108	108	118	128	134
D	100	109	115	123	136	133	133	133	137
EL	:	:	:	:	:	:	:	:	:
E	100	114	113	112	113	117	120	121	127
F	:	:	:	:	:	:	:	:	:
IRL	100	102	105	106	111	120	132	154	190
I	100	112	119	120	116	118	118	:	:
L	:	:	:	:	:	:	:	:	:
NL	100	103	112	122	131	137	151	163	181
A	100	105	110	118	123	127	130	132	134
P	:	:	:	:	:	:	:	:	:
FIN	100	86	90	65	69	67	70	82	91
S	100	107	97	86	90	91	91	98	107
UK	100	99	95	93	95	95	99	108	120

Source: European Mortgage Federation

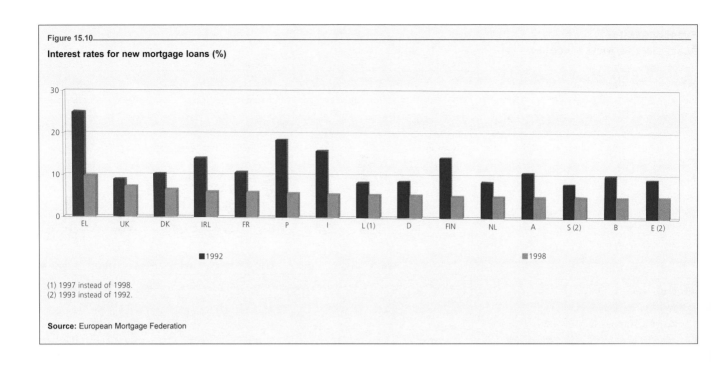

Figure 15.10

Interest rates for new mortgage loans (%)

■1992   ■1998

(1) 1997 instead of 1998.
(2) 1993 instead of 1992.

Source: European Mortgage Federation

Figure 15.11

Real estate services (NACE Rev. 1 70)
Number of persons employed, 1997 (thousands) (1)

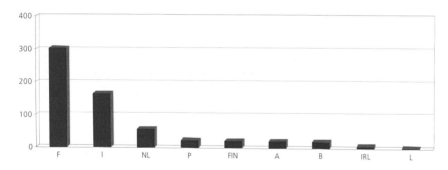

(1) I, 1996; DK, D, EL, E, S and UK, not available.

Source: Eurostat (SBS)

High productivity and profitability

Apparent labour productivity in real estate services was generally at the upper-end of the scale when compared to other service activities. It is estimated that 53.7 thousand ECU of gross value added was generated by each person employed in this sector in 1997. This average figure for the EU masks great divergences across the Member States, with values ranging from 35.3 thousand ECU in Portugal up to 106.2 thousand ECU in Austria.

Profitability rates were also relatively high, as the gross operating surplus of the sector represented between 14.5% (Portugal, 1997) and 43.5% of turnover (Italy, 1996).

Unit personnel costs faced by real estate enterprises were generally comprised between 27.9 thousand ECU per employee (Finland, 1996) and 33.3 thousand ECU (Austria, 1997), although lower levels were reported in the United Kingdom (21.0 thousand ECU, 1997), Italy (20.0 thousand ECU, 1996) and Portugal (12.1 thousand ECU, 1997).

Figure 15.12

Real estate services (NACE Rev. 1 70)
Apparent labour productivity, 1997 (thousand ECU per person employed) (1)

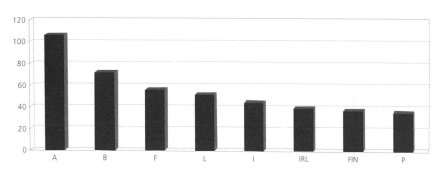

(1) I, 1996; DK, D, EL, E, NL, S and UK, not available.

Source: Eurostat (SBS)

Figure 15.13

Real estate services (NACE Rev. 1 70)
Unit personnel costs, 1997 (thousand ECU per employee) (1)

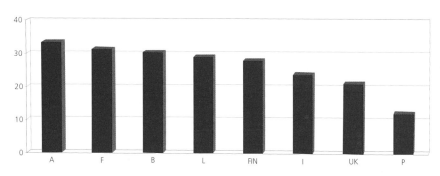

(1) DK and I, 1996; D, EL, E, IRL and L, not available.

Source: Eurostat (SBS)

Table 15.9

Site preparation (NACE Rev. 1 45.1)

Employment related indicators, 1997

	B	DK (1)	D	EL	E	F	IRL	I(2)	L	NL	A	P	FIN	S	UK
Number of persons employed (thousands)	5.8	2.0	:	:	:	77.3	:	29.6	:	10.3	5.3	4.6	8.9	16.2	10.9
Employees/number of persons employed (%)	69.5	84.6	:	:	:	91.1	:	51.7	:	85.7	82.5	94.3	78.2	78.5	90.5
Average no. of persons employed/enterprise (units)	:	4.0	:	:	:	6.0	:	2.5	:	6.0	5.0	8.0	2.0	3.0	7.0

(1) Employees as a share of the number of persons employed, 1996; (2) 1996.

Table 15.10

Site preparation (NACE Rev. 1 45.1)

Turnover related indicators, 1997

	B	DK	D	EL	E	F	IRL	I(1)	L	NL	A	P	FIN	S	UK
Turnover (million ECU)	654	204	:	:	:	7,535	:	2,132	:	1,005	437	250	968	1,450	1,411
Turnover per enterprise (million ECU)	:	0.4	:	:	:	0.6	:	0.2	:	0.6	0.4	0.4	0.2	0.2	0.9
Turnover per person employed (thousand ECU)	111.8	100.0	:	:	:	97.5	:	72.1	:	97.3	81.8	54.2	108.3	89.7	130.0

(1) 1996.

Table 15.11

Site preparation (NACE Rev. 1 45.1)

Performance related indicators, 1997

	B	DK (1)	D	EL	E	F	IRL	I(2)	L	NL	A	P	FIN	S	UK
Value added (million ECU)	257	:	:	:	:	2,267	:	932	:	378	234	87	394	546	583
Value added as a share of turnover (%)	39.3	:	:	:	:	30.1	:	43.7	:	37.6	53.6	34.7	40.7	37.7	41.3
Apparent labour productivity (thousand ECU/person employed)	43.9	:	:	:	:	29.3	:	31.5	:	36.6	43.8	18.8	44.1	33.8	53.7
Unit personnel costs (thousand ECU)	29.0	27.4	:	:	:	29.8	:	25.4	:	28.6	32.0	10.7	26.8	26.2	31.1
Simple wage adjusted labour productivity (%)	217.7	:	:	:	:	108.1	:	239.9	:	149.3	166.1	186.2	210.8	164.2	190.7
Gross operating surplus (million ECU)	139	20	:	:	:	170	:	544	:	125	93	40	207	214	277

(1) Unit personnel costs, 1996; (2) 1996.

Table 15.12

Building of complete constructions or parts thereof; civil engineering (NACE Rev. 1 45.2)

Employment related indicators, 1997

	B	DK (1)	D	EL	E	F	IRL	I(2)	L	NL	A	P	FIN	S	UK
Number of persons employed (thousands)	118.6	68.9	:	:	:	575.6	:	783.0	13.6	225.6	131.5	258.6	50.8	101.9	626.0
Employees/number of persons employed (%)	82.9	92.1	:	:	:	91.5	:	67.2	96.1	86.8	98.0	86.2	90.8	90.5	87.5
Average no. of persons employed/enterprise (units)	:	8.0	:	:	:	6.0	:	3.8	23.0	9.0	28.0	5.0	5.0	6.0	7.0

(1) Employees as a share of the number of persons employed, 1996; (2) 1996.

Table 15.13

Building of complete constructions or parts thereof; civil engineering (NACE Rev. 1 45.2)

Turnover related indicators, 1997

	B	DK	D	EL	E	F	IRL	I(1)	L	NL	A	P	FIN	S	UK
Turnover (million ECU)	13,056	7,823	:	:	:	58,513	:	69,749	969	29,285	14,314	19,444	6,329	11,915	90,837
Turnover per enterprise (million ECU)	:	0.9	:	:	:	0.6	:	0.3	1.7	1.2	3.1	0.4	0.6	0.7	1.0
Turnover per person employed (thousand ECU)	110.1	113.6	:	:	:	101.7	:	89.1	71.5	129.8	108.9	75.2	124.5	116.9	145.1

(1) 1996.

Table 15.14

Building of complete constructions or parts thereof; civil engineering (NACE Rev. 1 45.2)

Performance related indicators, 1997

	B	DK (1)	D	EL	E	F	IRL	I(2)	L	NL	A	P	FIN	S	UK
Value added (million ECU)	3,943	:	:	:	:	26,520	:	23,230	438	8,171	6,367	4,177	1,860	3,600	27,252
Value added as a share of turnover (%)	30.2	:	:	:	:	45.3	:	33.3	45.2	27.9	44.5	21.5	29.4	30.2	30.0
Apparent labour productivity (thousand ECU/person employed)	33.3	:	:	:	:	46.1	:	29.7	32.3	36.2	48.4	16.2	36.6	35.3	43.5
Unit personnel costs (thousand ECU)	30.3	29.2	:	:	:	29.7	:	24.2	25.6	34.5	40.1	10.5	29.6	28.9	32.0
Simple wage adjusted labour productivity (%)	132.1	:	:	:	:	169.4	:	182.6	131.2	120.9	123.3	179.3	136.4	135.2	155.5
Gross operating surplus (million ECU)	959	498	:	:	:	10,867	:	10,510	104	1,411	1,205	1,847	496	937	9,727

(1) Unit personnel costs, 1996; (2) 1996.

Source: Eurostat (SBS)

_____Table 15.15

Building installation (NACE Rev. 1 45.3)

Employment related indicators, 1997

	B	DK (1)	D	EL	E	F	IRL	I (2)	L	NL	A	P	FIN	S	UK
Number of persons employed (thousands)	47.8	49.8	:	:	:	347.9	:	358.1	6.0	116.1	67.2	39.4	24.2	62.6	226.8
Employees/number of persons employed (%)	68.5	91.6	:	:	:	86.2	:	56.8	92.8	90.1	93.7	90.0	87.6	88.9	82.3
Average no. of persons employed/enterprise (units)	:	8.0	:	:	:	5.0	:	3.1	15.0	12.0	12.0	7.0	4.0	5.0	5.0

(1) Employees as a share of the number of persons employed, 1996; (2) 1996.

_____Table 15.16

Building installation (NACE Rev. 1 45.3)

Turnover related indicators, 1997

	B	DK	D	EL	E	F	IRL	I (1)	L	NL	A	P	FIN	S	UK
Turnover (million ECU)	4,114	3,777	:	:	:	26,863	:	20,462	447	10,122	4,931	1,511	2,292	5,856	20,210
Turnover per enterprise (million ECU)	:	0.6	:	:	:	0.4	:	0.2	1.1	1.0	0.9	0.3	0.4	0.4	0.5
Turnover per person employed (thousand ECU)	86.0	75.9	:	:	:	77.2	:	57.1	75.0	87.2	73.4	38.3	94.6	93.5	89.1

(1) 1996.

_____Table 15.17

Building installation (NACE Rev. 1 45.3)

Performance related indicators, 1997

	B	DK (1)	D	EL	E	F	IRL	I (2)	L	NL	A	P	FIN	S	UK
Value added (million ECU)	1,395	:	:	:	:	10,910	:	8,015	185	3,572	2,195	482	835	2,163	8,307
Value added as a share of turnover (%)	33.9	:	:	:	:	40.6	:	39.2	41.4	35.3	44.5	31.9	36.4	36.9	41.1
Apparent labour productivity (thousand ECU/person employed)	29.2	:	:	:	:	31.4	:	22.4	31.1	30.8	32.7	12.2	34.5	34.5	36.6
Unit personnel costs (thousand ECU)	29.6	27.1	:	:	:	30.2	:	21.0	27.3	27.6	26.8	10.3	29.0	33.0	31.5
Simple wage adjusted labour productivity (%)	144.2	:	:	:	:	120.7	:	187.3	122.4	123.6	130.3	132.1	135.7	117.6	141.2
Gross operating surplus (million ECU)	427	338	:	:	:	1,874	:	3,736	34	682	511	117	220	323	2,424

(1) Unit personnel costs, 1996; (2) 1996.

_____Table 15.18

Building completion (NACE Rev. 1 45.4)

Employment related indicators, 1997

	B	DK (1)	D	EL	E	F	IRL	I (2)	L	NL	A	P	FIN	S	UK
Number of persons employed (thousands)	55.2	51.1	:	:	:	367.0	:	195.9	4.6	73.0	44.1	20.4	9.8	30.8	133.7
Employees/number of persons employed (%)	62.1	81.4	:	:	:	80.0	:	24.3	88.4	68.3	87.9	65.8	80.1	76.9	76.6
Average no. of persons employed/enterprise (units)	:	4.0	:	:	:	3.0	:	1.6	9.0	5.0	7.0	2.0	3.0	3.0	4.0

(1) Employees as a share of the number of persons employed, 1996; (2) 1996.

_____Table 15.19

Building completion (NACE Rev. 1 45.4)

Turnover related indicators, 1997

	B	DK	D	EL	E	F	IRL	I (1)	L	NL	A	P	FIN	S	UK
Turnover (million ECU)	3,942	3,619	:	:	:	22,837	:	6,753	272	4,483	2,807	567	663	2,001	12,524
Turnover per enterprise (million ECU)	:	0.3	:	:	:	0.2	:	0.1	0.5	0.3	0.5	0.1	0.2	0.2	0.4
Turnover per person employed (thousand ECU)	71.5	70.8	:	:	:	62.2	:	34.5	58.7	61.4	63.7	27.8	67.8	65.0	93.7

(1) 1996.

_____Table 15.20

Building completion (NACE Rev. 1 45.4)

Performance related indicators, 1997

	B	DK (1)	D	EL	E	F	IRL	I (2)	L	NL	A	P	FIN	S	UK
Value added (million ECU)	1,410	:	:	:	:	9,581	:	2,974	128	2,215	1,443	185	309	877	5,019
Value added as a share of turnover (%)	35.8	:	:	:	:	42.0	:	44.0	46.9	49.4	51.4	32.6	46.6	43.8	40.1
Apparent labour productivity (thousand ECU/person employed)	25.6	:	:	:	:	26.1	:	15.2	27.6	30.4	32.7	9.1	31.6	28.5	37.6
Unit personnel costs (thousand ECU)	25.9	24.8	:	:	:	26.8	:	19.3	25.7	32.4	26.7	8.7	26.9	28.7	28.4
Simple wage adjusted labour productivity (%)	158.9	:	:	:	:	121.6	:	324.4	121.3	136.9	139.4	157.7	146.5	128.8	172.7
Gross operating surplus (million ECU)	523	440	:	:	:	1,701	:	2,057	22	603	408	68	98	196	2,114

(1) Unit personnel costs, 1996; (2) 1996.

Source: Eurostat (SBS)

Table 15.21

Renting of construction or demolition equipment with operator (NACE Rev. 1 45.5)

Employment related indicators, 1997

	B	DK (1)	D	EL	E	F	IRL	I (2)	L	NL	A	P	FIN	S	UK
Number of persons employed (thousands)	0.6	0.8	:	:	:	3.1	:	1.0	:	6.1	0.1	0.6	1.3	2.3	21.7
Employees/number of persons employed (%)	94.3	93.5	:	:	:	97.7	:	51.1	:	92.2	85.7	90.1	90.4	58.0	76.6
Average no. of persons employed/enterprise (units)	:	6.0	:	:	:	10.0	:	2.5	:	8.0	4.0	6.0	4.0	2.0	5.0

(1) Employees as a share of the number of persons employed, 1996; (2) 1996.

Table 15.22

Renting of construction or demolition equipment with operator (NACE Rev. 1 45.5)

Turnover related indicators, 1997

	B	DK	D	EL	E	F	IRL	I (1)	L	NL	A	P	FIN	S	UK
Turnover (million ECU)	85	72	:	:	:	318	:	69	:	674	24	29	108	197	1,688
Turnover per enterprise (million ECU)	:	0.6	:	:	:	1.0	:	0.2	:	0.8	0.7	0.3	0.4	0.2	0.4
Turnover per person employed (thousand ECU)	149.6	93.3	:	:	:	104.2	:	68.9	:	109.8	188.6	51.1	80.5	86.2	77.7

(1) 1996.

Table 15.23

Renting of construction or demolition equipment with operator (NACE Rev. 1 45.5)

Performance related indicators, 1997

	B	DK (1)	D	EL	E	F	IRL	I (2)	L	NL	A	P	FIN	S	UK
Value added (million ECU)	41	:	:	:	:	141	:	28	:	323	11	14	65	82	1,031
Value added as a share of turnover (%)	48.4	:	:	:	:	44.5	:	40.0	:	48.0	47.5	46.9	60.6	41.8	61.1
Apparent labour productivity (thousand ECU/person employed)	72.3	:	:	:	:	46.3	:	27.6	:	52.7	89.5	24.0	48.8	36.1	47.5
Unit personnel costs (thousand ECU)	31.7	22.0	:	:	:	31.4	:	28.3	:	33.3	36.2	11.2	29.1	29.9	30.9
Simple wage adjusted labour productivity (%)	242.0	:	:	:	:	151.1	:	191.0	:	171.5	289.7	238.6	185.8	208.1	200.3
Gross operating surplus (million ECU)	24	9	:	:	:	48	:	13	:	135	7	8	30	43	516

(1) Unit personnel costs, 1996; (2) 1996.

Table 15.24

Real estate activities (NACE Rev. 1 70)

Employment related indicators, 1997

	B	DK	D	EL	E	F	IRL	I (1)	L	NL (2)	A	P	FIN (2)	S	UK
Number of persons employed (thousands)	19.9	:	:	:	:	302.5	6.9	165.2	1.6	57.7	20.8	23.6	22.3	:	:
Employees/number of persons employed (%)	56.8	:	:	:	:	70.0	54.1	24.3	64.1	85.3	86.7	75.2	82.4	:	:
Average no. of persons employed/enterprise (units)	:	:	:	:	:	4.0	3.0	1.6	2.0	3.0	6.0	3.0	2.0	:	:

(1) 1996; (2) Employees as a share of the number of persons employed, 1996.

Table 15.25

Real estate activities (NACE Rev. 1 70)

Turnover related indicators, 1997

	B	DK	D	EL	E	F	IRL	I (1)	L	NL	A	P	FIN	S	UK
Turnover (million ECU)	3,481	:	107,369	:	:	53,886	501	14,630	278	:	5,604	4,264	2,290	:	33,269
Turnover per enterprise (million ECU)	:	:	0.5	:	:	0.8	0.2	0.1	0.4	:	1.7	0.5	0.2	:	0.6
Turnover per person employed (thousand ECU)	175.2	:	:	:	:	178.1	72.6	88.6	179.1	:	269.3	181.0	102.6	:	:

(1) 1996.

Table 15.26

Real estate activities (NACE Rev. 1 70)

Performance related indicators, 1997

	B	DK	D	EL	E	F	IRL	I (1)	L	NL	A	P	FIN (2)	S	UK
Value added (million ECU)	1,427	:	:	:	:	16,872	270	7,315	80	:	2,211	831	831	:	:
Value added as a share of turnover (%)	41.0	:	:	:	:	31.3	53.8	50.0	28.8	:	39.4	19.5	36.3	:	:
Apparent labour productivity (thousand ECU/person employed)	71.8	:	:	:	:	55.8	39.1	44.3	51.5	:	106.2	35.3	37.2	:	:
Unit personnel costs (thousand ECU)	30.3	:	:	:	:	31.2	:	23.8	29.0	:	33.3	12.1	27.9	:	21.0
Simple wage adjusted labour productivity (%)	417.3	:	:	:	:	255.2	:	766.2	277.2	:	368.6	387.7	210.3	:	:
Gross operating surplus (million ECU)	1,085	:	:	:	:	10,262	:	6,360	51	:	1,611	617	436	:	:

(1) 1996; (2) Unit personnel costs, 1996.

Source: Eurostat (SBS)

Distributive trades (NACE Rev. 1 50, 51 and 52)

Distributive trades primarily provide a link between producers and consumers. The NACE Rev. 1 classification splits distribution into three main forms: motor trades, wholesale and retail trade. Repair is included under motor trades for motor vehicles and motorcycles and under retail trade for personal and household goods. Commission trade is included with wholesale trade.

By all major measures of size, distribution ranks amongst the largest industries in the EU economy. Eurostat estimates place the number of enterprises active in distribution in 1996 at around 4.5 to 5 million, which is more than one in four of all non-agricultural businesses. Between 22 million and 23 million persons were employed in distribution in the late 1990s generating around 13% of EU value added.

Distribution is the most basic link between producers and consumers. A traditional and still common model involves one or several wholesalers and retailers intervening between a product leaving the factory gate and reaching the final consumer. A small proportion of economic activity that receives a great deal of media exposure bypasses these conventional distribution channels as producers sell directly to consumers, for example via the Internet or factory stores. In may cases these sales still rely on traditional distribution and transport enterprises to process orders and/or physically distribute and deliver merchandise. However, there is no doubt that the ability of consumers and retailers to order directly from manufacturers has increased pressure on retailers and wholesalers to be more competitive and to provide other value added services and to increase productivity.

The growing market share accounted for by a small number of large retailers in many EU Member States has lead not only to economies of scale but also to a shift in bargaining power from manufacturers to retailers. There is however concern about the social impact of the relocation of retail outlets from town centres to out-of-town shopping areas, as this may reduce the potential for competition at a local level giving further advantage to established networks.

The activities covered in this chapter (in terms of NACE Rev. 1) include:

50: sale, maintenance and repair of motor vehicles and motorcycles; retail sale of automotive fuel;
50.1: sale of motor vehicles;
50.2: maintenance and repair of motor vehicles;
50.3: sale of motor vehicle parts and accessories;
50.4: sale, maintenance and repair of motorcycles and related parts and accessories;
50.5: retail sale of automotive fuel;
51: wholesale trade and commission trade, except of motor vehicles and motorcycles;
51.1: wholesale on a fee or contract basis;
51.2: wholesale of agricultural raw materials and live animals;
51.3: wholesale of food, beverages and tobacco;
51.4: wholesale of household goods;
51.5: wholesale of non-agricultural intermediate products, waste and scrap;
51.6: wholesale of machinery, equipment and supplies;
51.7: other wholesale;
52: Retail trade, except of motor vehicles and motorcycles; repair of personal and household goods;
52.1: retail sale in non-specialised stores;
52.2: retail sale of food, beverages and tobacco in specialised stores;
52.3: retail sale of pharmaceuticals and medical goods, cosmetic and toilet articles;
52.4: other retail sale of new goods in specialised stores;
52.5: retail sale of second-hand goods in stores;
52.6: retail sale not in stores;
52.7: repair of personal and household goods.

Box 16.1
Cross border trade within the EU was boosted by the development of the Single Market and it is expected to receive further support from the introduction of the euro. Stability in exchange rates between the 11 countries that adopted the euro on 1st January 1999 has already facilitated price comparisons between these countries and this will become easier still as the proportion of goods and services whose prices are quoted in euro increase. The principal issues facing the distribution sector, particularly retail trade (as well as other sectors such as HORECA, passenger transport and personal services) are: the need to help and educate customers and staff; the cost of managing the circulation of two currencies; and investment in IT to make systems euro-compatible.

Table 16.1

Fixed exchange rates for the euro (1 euro=...)

B (BEF)	40.3399
D (DEM)	1.95583
E (ESP)	166.386
F (FRF)	6.55957
IRL (IEP)	0.787564
I (ITL)	1,936.27
L (LUF)	40.3399
NL (NLG)	2.20371
A (ATS)	13.7603
P (PTE)	200.482
FIN (FIM)	5.94573

Source: Eurostat (MNY)

Multi-national chains and corner shops

The traditional characterisation of distribution as a sector dominated by very small and small enterprises holds true particularly for motor trades where the share of EU turnover generated by very small enterprises with less than 10 employees in 1996 was 33.5%. Small and medium-sized enterprises accounted for the largest proportion of turnover in wholesale trade reflecting the larger average size of these enterprises (2.1 million ECU turnover per enterprise in 1996), compared to motor trades (1.1 million ECU) and retail trade (0.5 million ECU).

Retail trade showed a more complex structure with very small enterprises and large enterprises both generating more than a third of EU turnover in 1996 whilst small and medium-sized enterprises together accounted for only 23.5%. This reflects the image of the retail trade sector being composed essentially of a few very large groups or chains exploiting economies of scale mixed with many small shops serving a local market. The figures also reflect the differences in the structure of this sector between Member States as a clear distinction can be drawn between Italy, Portugal, Spain and Belgium where the importance of very small enterprises is considerably above the EU average and the United Kingdom and the Netherlands where large enterprises account for a much greater share of turnover and employment.

Large enterprises: a larger share of turnover and employment

The increasingly important role of large enterprises in EU retail trade can be seen from their share in total turnover, which grew steadily from 37.8% in 1993 to 41.4% in 1996 at the expense of the share of very small enterprises. A similar but smaller shift can be seen in employment terms as large enterprises employed 30.9% of retail workers in 1996 (up 3.3 percentage points from 1993) whilst the share of retail employment provided by very small enterprises fell. This trend in employment is most pronounced in the Netherlands and the United Kingdom but can be seen in the employment figures of the majority of Member States.

Figure 16.1

Recovery and repair services, wholesale and retail trade services (NACE-CLIO 56)

Share of total market services value added and employment, 1997 (%)

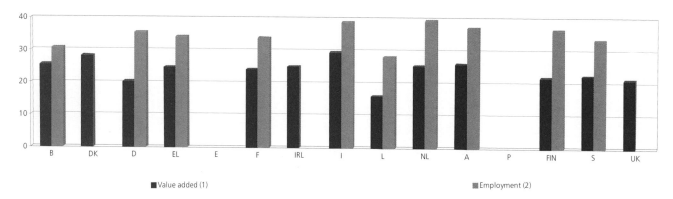

(1) D, EL, F, L and A, value added at market prices; DK, D, IRL, S and UK, 1996; E and P, not available.
(2) B, D, A and S, 1996; DK, E, IRL, P and UK, not available.

Source: Eurostat (SEC2)

Table 16.2

Distributive trades (NACE Rev. 1 50, 51 and 52)

Breakdown of turnover and employment by employment size class, 1997 (%)

	Micro (0-9)		Small (10-49)		Medium (50-249)		Large (250+)	
	Turnover (1)	Employment (2)	Turnover (1)	Employment (3)	Turnover (1)	Employment (3)	Turnover (1)	Employment (2)
EU-15	29.1	46.6	24.7	19.4	19.7	9.5	26.5	24.5
B	40.0	64.7	28.4	15.5	13.0	6.4	18.6	13.5
DK	:	:	:	:	:	:	:	:
D	17.7	34.8	23.9	22.6	30.0	8.9	28.3	33.6
EL	:	:	:	:	:	:	:	:
E	35.5	63.5	18.2	17.7	17.1	7.4	29.2	11.4
F	26.7	43.8	28.2	23.9	19.4	12.9	25.7	19.4
IRL	:	:	:	:	:	:	:	:
I	47.4	72.9	25.8	14.8	11.6	4.9	15.2	7.3
L	:	:	:	:	:	:	:	:
NL	:	:	:	23.2	:	12.6	:	:
A	24.6	29.7	25.2	23.8	:	:	:	:
P	37.5	61.2	29.7	22.9	21.6	10.2	11.2	5.8
FIN	24.5	36.4	23.1	22.2	16.6	13.8	35.8	27.5
S	:	40.7	:	24.2	:	14.3	:	20.9
UK	21.7	29.2	20.5	14.7	14.0	9.4	43.7	46.7

(1) EU-15, E, F, I and P, 1996.
(2) EU-15, F, I, P and S, 1996.
(3) EU-15, F, I, NL, P and S, 1996.

Source: Eurostat (SME)

Box 16.2

The European Information Technology Observatory (EITO) estimates the worldwide value of goods and services traded electronically in 1998 at 262 billion ECU and forecasts that this will rise to 717 billion EUR by 2002. E-commerce is still relatively small but has grown rapidly in a number of product markets and could potentially have major social and economic implications, such as changing fundamentally the relationship between enterprises and consumers and also the skills of the workforce.

For distribution and several other industries[1], e-commerce can be seen as an opportunity to develop a new trading form with lower transaction costs. This form could involve:

- increased independence from opening hours;
- more frequent updates of prices/special offers;
- fewer, smaller or simpler shops and showrooms;
- better stock control;
- more efficient use of personnel;
- reduced errors in order taking and processing;
- on-line automatic support and after-sales service.

Alternatively it can be seen as a threat to bypass one or several layers of distribution intermediaries, increasing costs for the delivery of physical goods and leading customers to incur higher search costs, whilst reducing the "emotional" value added of more traditional forms of distribution. In practice it is likely that distribution enterprises will see a change in the balance of their roles between transmitting goods along the distribution chain from producer to customer and transmitting information on customer requirements back towards producers.

(1) Examples are travel agents, banking, direct marketing, software houses, advertising and entertainment/news and information services.

STRUCTURE AND PERFORMANCE

National Accounts estimates suggest that valued added at market prices in current prices in distribution has grown each year between 1985 and 1997 from just under 450 billion ECU to over 800 billion ECU, an annual average growth rate exceeding 5% but slower than in market services as a whole. Most of the growth in value added in distribution (and market services) occurred between 1985 and 1991. Amongst the Member States, Ireland stands out as its value added in current prices in distribution more than tripled during the period 1985 to 1997. Portugal, Luxembourg, Spain, Greece, Belgium and Germany also saw increases in value added in current prices close to or in excess of 100% over this twelve-year period.

LABOUR AND PRODUCTIVITY

National Accounts data shows that employment in distribution grew from an estimated 20.7 million in 1985 to 22.1 million in 1990 since when it has remained between 22.0 and 22.5 million through to 1996, the latest year available.

Labour Force Survey data gives similar levels of employment and indicates that employment did not change greatly between 1996 and 1998, but is likely to have reached or even passed 23 million in 1999. Ireland and Spain both saw double-digit growth in employment over the five-year period from 1994 to 1999. Growth in excess of 10% over shorter periods was also recorded in Greece (1994 to 1998) and Finland (1995 to 1999). In the five years to 1999 employment fell in Italy (-4.5%) and Luxembourg (-3.6%) as well as in Germany (-0.3%) between 1995 and 1999.

More employees and less self-employment

From a social perspective one of the changes that has accompanied the relative decline in importance of smaller enterprises and growth in larger ones has been the increase in the share of paid employees in the persons in employment total, with a corresponding fall in the share of self-employed and unpaid family workers. For the EU the share of paid employees rose from 70.4% in 1995 to 72.6% in 1998 and nearly all of the Member States for which 1999 data is available have recorded a further rise. In most countries this has been largely due to stability or a fall in the number of self-employed persons and a contraction in the number of unpaid family workers between 1995 and 1999. There were approximately 260 thousand less self-employed persons in distribution in the EU in 1998 than in 1995 and 47 thousand less family workers. Although motor and wholesale trades both saw a fall in the share of the self-employed, the most rapid reduction was recorded in retail trade, from 30.1% of persons in employment in 1995 to 27.7% in 1998.

In 1998 men accounted for 54.4% of persons in employment in distribution, a lower share than any industrial Section (defined here as Sections C to F of NACE Rev. 1) but higher than in HORECA (Section H) and financial intermediation (Section J) amongst the services. The share of men in employment in motor trades was 83.0% in 1998, above the manufacturing average for comparison. In wholesale trade the share was much lower at 68.4% and in retail trade it was 41.9%, the second lowest of all Divisions in the industrial and service Sections C to K of NACE Rev. 1.

Table 16.3

Distributive trades (NACE Rev. 1 50, 51 and 52)

Composition of the labour force, 1999 (%)

	Motor trade			Wholesale trade			Retail trade		
	Women (1)	Part-time (2)	Highly-educated (3)	Women (1)	Part-time (2)	Highly-educated (4)	Women (1)	Part-time (2)	Highly-educated (4)
EU-15	17.0	9.1	9.9	31.6	10.8	17.1	58.1	29.5	11.0
B	21.6	8.4	10.6	36.6	7.9	31.3	57.0	23.6	21.5
DK	20.9	23.7	11.9	27.4	8.6	18.9	57.0	34.9	14.6
D	21.0	9.6	20.4	37.1	15.6	16.9	66.8	36.0	12.1
EL	10.0	2.9	7.3	27.3	3.2	24.9	48.5	4.9	12.6
E	10.7	3.2	12.9	30.0	4.9	22.2	56.1	10.5	16.2
F	17.9	9.2	8.5	31.2	8.1	24.5	58.4	25.6	15.1
IRL	17.7	13.5	12.5	28.8	9.9	26.8	60.2	34.3	16.8
I	14.5	4.3	1.3	30.6	6.4	7.5	45.6	10.2	4.3
L	24.7	:	:	23.8	:	17.6	63.4	14.0	7.1
NL	18.8	24.8	5.1	26.8	17.7	19.0	60.3	59.3	5.4
A	21.5	10.0	:	39.3	13.7	5.7	68.0	32.0	5.0
P	10.9	2.5	3.4	23.7	5.3	5.6	54.1	9.0	2.8
FIN	19.8	6.5	17.2	32.8	6.5	41.6	65.4	31.9	28.7
S	13.4	12.2	:	33.1	10.8	28.3	61.7	40.0	13.7
UK	20.2	15.5	7.2	30.9	12.9	16.8	60.6	48.9	11.5

(1) EU-15 and EL, 1998.
(2) EU-15, B and EL, 1998.
(3) EL, 1998; EU-15, P and UK, 1997; DK and IRL, 1996.
(4) EL, 1998; EU-15, IRL and UK, 1997.

Source: Eurostat (SME)

*High and growing part-time
employment in retail trade*

The proportion of part-time employment increased between 1995 and 1998 in distribution from 20.1% to 21.9%. This proportion is one of the highest in the economy with only hotels and restaurants (NACE Rev. 1 Section H) recording a higher proportion amongst the industrial and service Sections C to K. Within distribution large variations can be seen, as the incidence of part-time employment in retail trade (29.5%) was substantially higher than wholesale trade (10.8%) and motor trades (9.1%) in 1998. There is a great difference in the incidence of part-time employment between men and women although the trends are similar. The proportion of women working part-time in distribution has increased from 36.4% to 38.9% in the three years to 1998 while the share of men working part-time has grown from 6.6% to 7.7%.

This high incidence of part-time employment is reflected in the figures on hours worked. In 1998 the proportion of persons in employment working less than 30 hours a week ranged from 34.6% in the United Kingdom and 33.0% in the Netherlands to 3.7% in Greece, with Portugal, Spain and Italy also recording percentages below 10%. In 1999, in nearly all Member States the proportion of persons working less than 30 hours a week was between two and four times higher in retail trade than in either wholesale or motor trades, the only significant exception to this was Denmark.

The increase in greater flexibility in the forms of employment can be seen clearly, as most countries recorded falls in the proportion of their respective workforces that never worked on Saturdays, Sundays, evenings or nights as these atypical work practices became more widespread. Amongst the three types of distribution the proportion of persons never working Saturdays, Sundays or evenings was lowest in retail trade and highest in wholesale trade.

INTERNATIONAL TRENDS

Distribution in Japan in 1996 employed 11.4 million persons, a 17.6% share of the total labour force, higher than the EU's share of just over 15% in 1997. In the USA the share of the labour force was higher still, at 18.5% in 1997 which represented more than 23 million persons.

*Growth in the US distribution sector
and signs of a slowing decline in Japan*

The Japanese Ministry of International Trade and Industry in its preliminary report (May 2000) on the current survey of commerce records sales in retail trade in the 1999 financial year at 1,109 billion EUR, down 2.0% compared to 1998 (in current Japanese Yen) and in wholesale trade at 3,461 billion EUR, down 4.3% (in current Japanese Yen) compared to 1998. Whilst continuing the trend experienced in 1997 and 1998 the rate of decline was lower in 1999 than in 1998.

The US Bureau of Labor Statistics reports employment in retail trade (including motor retail trade) having increased by 1.8 million persons in the ten years to 1998 to a total of 14.5 million, an annual average growth rate of 1.3%. Output in constant price US dollars was recorded as having grown by 3.5% per annum. The same source indicates a similar rate of growth in employment in wholesale trade, growing by 802 thousand persons in the ten years to 1998, to a total of 6.8 million persons (annual average growth rate of 1.3%). Output in constant price US dollars in wholesale trade grew faster than retail trade, reaching an annual average of 5.1%.

SUB-CHAPTER 16.1
SALE OF MOTOR VEHICLES
(NACE Rev. 1 50.1, 50.3 AND 50.4)

These activities cover the wholesale, retail and commission sale of new and used motor vehicles (Group 50.1) and motorcycles (Group 50.4), as well as parts and accessories (Group 50.3), including specialist vehicles, lorries, trailers and caravans. In addition, it includes the maintenance and repair of motorcycles but not of motor vehicles. It does not include the renting of motor vehicles.

Car retailing has traditionally been a mix of mass-production of standardised models and customer driven orders for cars with particular specifications. Whilst customers have had this choice of different models and options for a long time, these have often come with a high price tag and lengthy delays, rarely accepted on lower price range makes and models. Many manufacturers are now trying to provide customer driven orders for high-volume car sales with the aim of reducing their stock of finished products that need to be pushed through distribution channels. Apart from the technological revolution in manufacturing techniques, one of the ways of reducing the time to delivery is to squeeze the time between order, production and delivery. As elsewhere in distribution the Internet is regarded as one of the main means by which this will be done, firstly by allowing consumers to access up-to-date specification and price information for standard and customised models and secondly, to a lesser extent, by directly accepting orders. In some ways this may be a threat to existing intermediaries as customers can order directly from the manufacturer or through specialised Internet dealers, however dealers' showrooms are unlikely to disappear altogether.

STRUCTURE AND PERFORMANCE

Turnover for the sale of motor vehicles (including motorcycles and parts) in 1996 was in excess of 486 billion ECU[2]. More recent data available for most Member States suggest that this figure increased in 1997. An analysis of the structure of the sale of motor vehicles (including motorcycles and parts) industry is possible on the base of 1997 data for 8 Member States[3]. This data indicates that motorcycle trade (Group 50.4) is the smallest of the three activities, accounting for less than 5% of total turnover, followed by the sale of motor vehicle parts and accessories (Group 50.3) which accounts for between 10% and 20%. Group 50.1 (the sale of motor vehicles, excluding motorcycles and parts) dominates this

industry with between 79% and 88% of sales. 1996 data shows Italy significantly outside of these limits in motorcycle trade where sales exceeded 6% of the total. Value added shows a similar ranking of the three Groups but with a greater share for parts and accessories.

The United Kingdom in the fast lane

The United Kingdom and Germany had the largest motor vehicle sales industries (including motorcycles and parts) in 1997, with turnover valued at 139.7 billion ECU and 115.2 billion ECU respectively. In the United Kingdom the industry grew by 47.7% in nominal terms between 1995 and 1997 compared to 4.9% in Germany, such that by 1997 the United Kingdom had become the largest Member State in turnover terms. Part of this increase can be attributed to changes in the exchange rates (notably the increase in the Pound Sterling) against the ECU during this period and partly to a real increase in activity[4]. Italy, Sweden and Belgium also saw turnover increase by more than 10% between 1995 and 1996 (again partly due to exchange rate movements in the case of Italy and Sweden), as did Finland between 1996 and 1997. Of the countries reporting data for at least two years between 1995 and 1997, only France reported a fall in turnover (between 1996 and 1997) and this was by less than 1%.

---

(4) For example new vehicle registrations increased by 10.9% in the UK during the same period.

In terms of average turnover the largest enterprises[5] were in Austria (4.9 million ECU, 1997), whilst the smallest were in Portugal (1.4 million ECU, 1997). The breakdown within the different activities showed that enterprises distributing parts and accessories tended to have an average turnover of between 1.5 and 2.0 million ECU, whilst motorcycle trade enterprises reported average turnover of less than 1.5 million ECU. Enterprises classified as selling motor vehicles (Group 50.1) were considerably larger, with turnover ranging between 2.4 million ECU (France) and 6.2 million ECU (Austria)[6].

*High investment in Portuguese
motor vehicle distribution*

From the limited available data on investment it is clear that investment in Portugal has been very high; the investment rate (investment as a share of value added) was 43.6% in 1997. In comparison, the highest rate for this indicator amongst the five other Member States for which data is available was 21.2% in Finland. The sale of motor vehicles (Group 50.1) is largely responsible for this high Portuguese figure, as investment in this activity exceeded half (56.4%) of value added in 1997.

---

(5) 1996 and 1997 data considered together.
(6) For these average turnover size comparisons, data was unavailable for 1996 and 1997 for B, DK, EL and E; IRL was only available for Group 50.1.

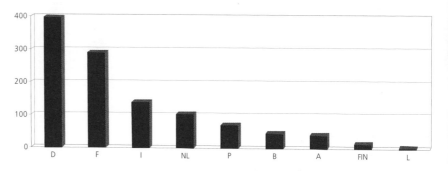

Figure 16.2

Sale of motor vehicles (NACE Rev. 1 50.1, 50.3 and 50.4)

Number of persons employed, 1997 (thousands) (1)

(1) I and L, 1996; DK, EL, E, IRL, S and UK, not available.

Source: Eurostat (SBS)

---

(2) A, 1997; DK, 1995; EL, E and IRL, no data available.
(3) B, D, F, NL, A, P, FIN and UK.

─────Figure 16.3

Sale of motor vehicles (NACE Rev. 1 50.1, 50.3 and 50.4)

Apparent labour productivity, 1997 (thousand ECU per person employed) (1)

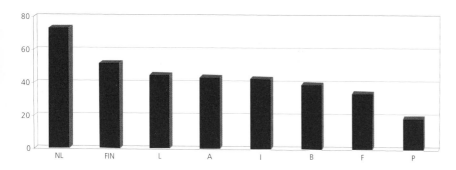

(1) I and L, 1996; DK, D, EL, E, IRL, S and UK, not available.

Source: Eurostat (SBS)

─────Figure 16.4

Sale of motor vehicles (NACE Rev. 1 50.1, 50.3 and 50.4)

Unit personnel costs, 1997 (thousand ECU per employee) (1)

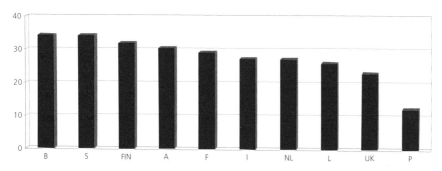

(1) I, L and S, 1996; DK, D, EL, E and IRL, not available.

Source: Eurostat (SBS)

LABOUR AND PRODUCTIVITY

A combination of data available for the sale of motor vehicles industry (including motorcycles and parts) shows that the number of persons employed in 1996 in the EU was in excess of 1.5 million persons[7]. The labour force in the sale of motor vehicles industry (including motorcycles and parts) appears to have been relatively stable between 1995 and 1997. Germany, the largest employer with the United Kingdom, saw a fall of 1.4% in the number of persons employed between these two years, but most other Member States providing data indicated stability or a small rise.

High personnel costs for a distribution activity

The following analysis of personnel costs and apparent labour productivity is limited to data for Belgium, France, the Netherlands, Austria, Portugal and Finland (who all provided data for 1997). Value added per person employed, a simple measure of apparent labour productivity, ranged from 18.8 thousand ECU in Portugal to 73.0 thousand ECU in the Netherlands. Unit personnel costs (personnel costs per employee) were generally higher in the sale of motor vehicles industry (including motorcycles and parts) than in distribution as a whole. The lowest value was recorded in Portugal (12.1 thousand ECU), whilst most Member States were in the range 27.0 thousand ECU to 34.1 thousand ECU. Belgium and France recorded the lowest wage adjusted labour productivity ratios[8], with value added 114.3% and 116.1% of personnel costs respectively, the Netherlands still recorded the highest figure (270.4%), whilst Portugal joined the remaining Member States within the range of 140% to 165%.

(7) DK, 1995; A, 1997; S, number of employees; UK, number of employees for 1997; EL, E and IRL, no data available.
(8) Value added divided by personnel costs multiplied by the share of employees in the number of persons employed.

Mixed fortunes in the USA and Japan

The North American dealers association reported a 5% increase in sales from the franchised new-car dealerships part of the industry in 1998, following a slightly smaller rise in 1997. In all, sales reached 475.9 billion ECU with an average dealership size of 21.2 million ECU of sales. Breaking down these sales through franchised new-car dealerships, 59.4% of income came from the sale of new vehicles, 28.6% from the sale of used vehicles and 12.0% from servicing and parts. Compared to ten years earlier this represented an increase of 5.8 percentage points for used vehicle sales with a reduction of 2 to 3 percentage points for the share of the other categories. The US Bureau of Census reports that resale margins as a share of sales for automotive dealers fell from 19.0% in 1988 to 17.0% in 1998, the lowest level during this ten-year period.

According to the Japan Automobile Dealers Association the motor trade industry of Japan suffered its second successive year of falling new motor vehicle registrations in 1998, with all of the three main categories (cars, trucks and buses) failing to reach their 1997 levels. New car registrations fell by just under 400 thousand units, the second largest reduction (after 1992) in absolute terms since 1974. Compared to 1997, new truck registrations fell by 20.1% (or 445 thousand units) to under 1.8 million units in 1998, the lowest level since 1977.

SUB-CHAPTER 16.2
REPAIR OF MOTOR VEHICLES
(NACE Rev. 1 50.2)

Maintenance and repair of motor vehicles includes all types of repairs (mechanical, bodywork and electrical), spraying and painting, ordinary servicing, washing and polishing, as well as the installation of parts and accessories. Equally it covers tyre repair and fitting, towing and roadside assistance.

This activity is essentially made up of enterprises specialising in fitting replacement parts, repairs and servicing or motor related services such as towing or washing.

Internationalisation of replacement parts groups
There are a number of national and international chains replacing parts that normally wear out once or more during the lifetime of a vehicle, such as tyres, filters, wiper blades, batteries and spark plugs. European chains have developed such as the Euromaster group and there have been recent acquisitions such as Kwik-Fit's purchase of Speedy and Pit Stop in 1999. As well as expanding their geographical coverage some of these motor vehicle replacement parts enterprises have expanded the range of services that provide, notably into regular vehicle servicing. There has also been a recent trend of motor vehicle manufacturers moving into this part of the industry, notably Ford (acquiring Kwik-Fit in 1999) and General Motors. In addition, there are a number of very specialised firms competing for parts of the same market, for example Belron, which trades within the EU as Carglass and Autoglass and is the largest automotive glass replacement and repair business.

Small independent repair workshops
Another part of the industry contains a large number of generally small, independent repair shops that carry out mechanical, body and electrical repairs as well as services. Both the replacement part fitters and these repair workshops compete with motor sales dealers (classified in NACE Rev. 1 Groups 50.1) and generally take a progressively larger share of the market as cars age, whether it be for repair work, servicing or replacement parts. The independent part of this industry is faced by the challenge posed by the growing complexity of motor vehicles and the need to invest in increasingly sophisticated equipment.

A large number of generally small enterprises provide specialised services such as car-washes and vehicle recovery. There are a few large networks in these areas, such as l'Eléphant bleu for self-washing and IMO for automated (tunnel) car washes.

STRUCTURE AND PERFORMANCE
EU turnover in the repair of motor vehicles industry in 1996 totalled 47.4 billion ECU before taking into account Germany (which was possibly the largest national market in the EU), Greece or Spain. The French industry saw turnover grow between 1996 and 1997 by 1.2% and the Italian industry grew by 13.1% between 1995 and 1996. The remaining large market, the United Kingdom, grew by 8.4% between 1995 and 1997 to reach 11.5 billion ECU. The Belgian industry on the other hand recorded a fall in turnover in current prices compared to the preceding year for both 1996 and 1997, falling by a total of 39.1% in these two years.

Figure 16.5 _____

Repair of motor vehicles (NACE Rev. 1 50.2)
Number of persons employed, 1997 (thousands) (1)

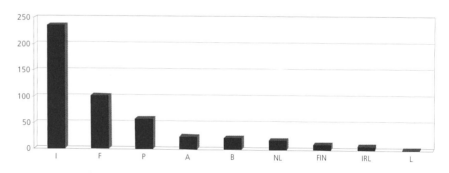

(1) IRL, I and L, 1996; DK, D, EL, E, S and UK, not available.

Source: Eurostat (SBS)

Figure 16.6 _____

Repair of motor vehicles (NACE Rev. 1 50.2)
Apparent labour productivity, 1997 (thousand ECU per person employed) (1)

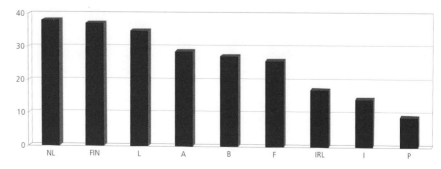

(1) IRL, I and L, 1996; DK, D, EL, E, S and UK, not available.

Source: Eurostat (SBS)

Low share of motor trades turnover,
but important in value added terms

As a share of turnover in motor trades, the repair of motor vehicles industry accounted in 1997 for as little as 2.7% in the Netherlands and as much as 18.7% in Finland[9]. Its share in motor trades value added was generally much higher, ranging from 7.9% in Luxembourg (1997) to 32.0% in Italy (1996). This increased share of value added is reflected in the gross operating rate which is between 40% and 175% higher for the repair of motor vehicles than the motor trades average in all of the Member States for 1996 or 1997[10].

LABOUR AND PRODUCTIVITY

The number of persons employed in the EU in the repair of motor vehicles industry in 1996 exceeded two-thirds of a million[11]. The Netherlands (20.5%) and Portugal (10.4%) recorded strong growth in the number of persons employed between 1996 and 1997 and growth in Ireland also exceeded 10% between 1995 and 1996. Belgium recorded a fall in the number of persons employed of 9.7% between 1995 and 1996 and a further reduction of 10.8% the following year. Italian data for the number of employees recorded an even larger decrease between 1995 and 1996 (16.3%).

Low labour productivity compared
to motor trades as a whole

A number of labour ratios are available for 1997 for Belgium, France, the Netherlands, Austria, Portugal and Finland, as well as for 1996 for Ireland, Italy and Luxembourg. Apparent labour productivity was generally lower in the repair of motor vehicles industry than in motor trades as a whole (subject to data availability). It was lowest in Portugal (9.0 thousand ECU per head) and highest in the Netherlands (38.1 thousand ECU). It should be noted that the strong increase in employment in the Netherlands contributed to the reduction in productivity from 45.1 thousand ECU the year before. At the same time, the increase in employment in Portugal was accompanied by near stability in productivity.

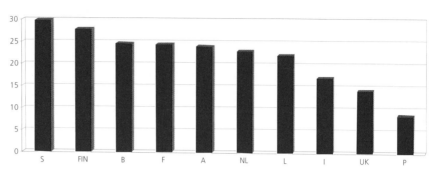

Figure 16.7

Repair of motor vehicles (NACE Rev. 1 50.2)

Unit personnel costs, 1997 (thousand ECU per employee) (1)

(1) I, L and S, 1996; DK, D, EL, E and IRL, not available.

Source: Eurostat (SBS)

Adjusted for personnel costs and for the share of employees in persons employed, the ratio of value added to personnel costs rose in Italy from 79.0% in 1995, but was still below the 100% threshold at 86.0% in 1996. The other Member States recorded wage adjusted labour productivity above the 100% threshold, between 106.8% in France and 166.3% in the Netherlands. As with the more simple measure of apparent labour productivity, wage adjusted labour productivity was consistently lower in the repair of motor vehicles than in motor trades in general.

---

(9) D, EL or E, no data available.
(10) DK, D, EL, E or IRL, no data available.
(11) DK, 1995; A, 1997; S, number of employees; UK, number of employees for 1997; D, EL and E, no data available.

SUB-CHAPTER 16.3
RETAIL SALE OF AUTOMOTIVE FUEL
(NACE Rev. 1 50.5)

This specialist activity covers the retail sale of automotive fuel, lubricating and cooling products for motor vehicles and motorcycles. It does not include the wholesale trade of automotive fuel which is classified as wholesale trade rather than motor trades and is included with the wholesale of all fuel products regardless of their physical state or purpose.

The role of service stations in the retailing network has changed during the last twenty years. Firstly there has been a change in the product mix provided by service stations with non-fuel sales being derived from forecourt shops, related motor trade services such as car washes and non-motor trade services such as catering. Secondly, there has been increased competition, notably with other retailers such as supermarkets and hypermarkets entering the sector.

STRUCTURE AND PERFORMANCE

In 1998 there were 113 thousand retail outlets in the EU with combined retail motor fuels sales of 238 million m³, according to EUROPIA. This was a slight increase on the 1997 sales figures of 233 million m³.

Germany is the largest market
but Italy has a larger network
According to this same source the two largest markets in terms of their share of EU sales volume were Germany (21.6%) and France (17.4%). The largest retail outlets in terms of average sales volume were found in Luxembourg (6.4 thousand m³ on average). Greece (0.9 thousand m³) and Ireland (0.8 thousand m³) had the smallest outlets.. The average size of retail outlets for the remaining Member States ranged between 1.3 thousand m³ (Belgium) and 3.4 thousand m³ (Spain), with the EU-15 average at 2.1 thousand m³.

The largest number of retail motor fuel outlets was found in Italy (25.4 thousand, 22.5% of the EU total) and France (17.1 thousand, 15.2%). The number of outlets per ten-thousand population in 1998 ranged from 1.8 in the United Kingdom to 7.2 in Ireland, with Greece (7.0) and Luxembourg (6.0) the only other Member States to exceed 5 outlets per ten-thousand population (the EU average was 3.0).

Operators and owners: dealers and oil companies
Service station outlets are placed into a number of categories by EUROPIA. The largest is the dealer owned and operated category selling petroleum products of one of the major brands. These account for approximately 39% of the EU network and many of them have an exclusive purchasing agreement with an oil company. The second largest category covers the major brand oil company owned and operated outlets of which there were some 30 thousand in 1997, accounting for about 26% of the EU network. A hybrid of these two categories is the oil company owned and dealer operated outlet where the supply of major brand petroleum products may take a number of formats. Approximately 10 thousand outlets are in this category and account for just under 9% of all outlets.

In 1997 there were approximately 6 thousand outlets owned by supermarkets and hypermarkets and 24 thousand other outlets. As such, the major brands accounted for a total of 85 thousand outlets, approximately 74% of all outlets and had a slightly higher (78%) share of sales volume.

Table 16.4

Retail sales of motor fuel and number of motor fuel outlets, 1998

| | Sales | | Outlets | | Average sales per outlet |
	Volume (thousand m³)	Share of EU total (%)	Number (units)	Share of EU total (%)	(thousand m³)
EU-15	238,200	100.0	112,675	100.0	2.1
B	6,600	2.8	5,060	4.5	1.3
DK	3,850	1.6	2,500	2.2	1.5
D	51,350	21.6	16,625	14.8	3.1
EL	6,700	2.8	7,350	6.5	0.9
E	24,000	10.1	7,025	6.2	3.4
F	41,550	17.4	17,125	15.2	2.4
IRL	2,150	0.9	2,650	2.4	0.8
I	35,500	14.9	25,400	22.5	1.4
L	1,525	0.6	240	0.2	6.4
NL	8,750	3.7	4,000	3.6	2.2
A	4,900	2.1	3,140	2.8	1.6
P	5,750	2.4	2,500	2.2	2.3
FIN	3,125	1.3	1,760	1.6	1.8
S	5,650	2.4	3,550	3.2	1.6
UK	36,800	15.4	13,750	12.2	2.7

Source: EUROPIA

Figure 16.8

Retail sale of automotive fuel (NACE Rev. 1 50.5)

Number of persons employed, 1997 (1) (thousands)

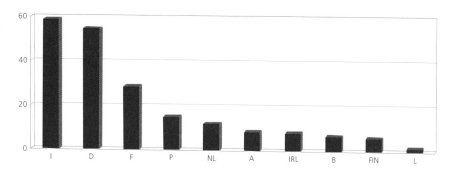

(1) I and L, 1996; DK, EL, E, S and UK, not available.

Source: Eurostat (SBS)

Figure 16.9

Retail sale of automotive fuel (NACE Rev. 1 50.5)

Apparent labour productivity, 1997 (thousand ECU per person employed) (1)

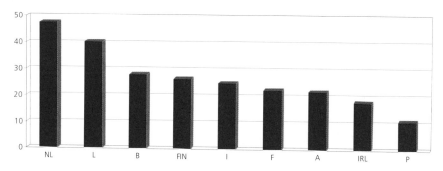

(1) I and L, 1996; DK, D, EL, E, S and UK, not available.

Source: Eurostat (SBS)

Figure 16.10

Retail sale of automotive fuel (NACE Rev. 1 50.5)

Unit personnel costs, 1997 (thousand ECU per employee) (1)

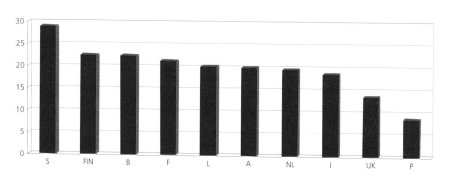

(1) I, L and S, 1996; DK, D, EL, E and IRL, not available.

Source: Eurostat (SBS)

LABOUR AND PRODUCTIVITY

The number of persons employed in the EU in the retail sale of automotive fuels was in excess of 270 thousand persons in 1997[12]. The German, Italian and British industries were the largest employers with the number of persons employed exceeding 50 thousand in each country. Belgium (35.9%) and Finland (14.2%) recorded growth in the number of persons employed in excess of 10% in 1997 compared to 1996, as did the Netherlands (31.1%) and Ireland (15.7%) in 1996 compared to 1995. Germany recorded a fall of 9.8% in 1996 (compared to 1995) and a further reduction of 23.4% in 1997.

High specialisation of labour in the retail sale of automotive fuels in Ireland and Luxembourg

In most Member States there were less persons employed in this industry than in the sale of motor vehicles or the repair of motor vehicles. Exceptions to this rule in 1997 were Luxembourg and Ireland, where the retail sale of automotive fuels industry employed more persons than the repair of motor vehicles. Employment within the retail sale of automotive fuels accounted for 32.2% of total motor trade employment in Ireland and 23.5% in Luxembourg in 1996. The next highest share was 17.6% in Italy.

High Dutch productivity

Labour ratios are available for Belgium, France, the Netherlands, Austria, Portugal and Finland for 1997 and for Ireland, Italy and Luxembourg for 1996. A ranking by apparent labour productivity left the Netherlands (47.5 thousand ECU) and Portugal (10.7 thousand ECU) determining the range for EU Member States as they had for the repair of motor vehicles. Both of these Member States recorded increases compared to 1996, as had Ireland and Belgium.

Wage adjusted labour productivity for the retail sale of automotive fuels ranged from 104.6% in France to 128.6% in Portugal, with only the Netherlands outside of this range (244.4%). Wage adjusted labour productivity in this industry was higher than the motor trades average in Luxembourg, Italy and Belgium.

(12) DK, 1995; I, L, 1996; S, 1996, number of employees; UK, number of employees; EL and E, no data available.

SUB-CHAPTER 16.4
WHOLESALE ON A FEE OR CONTRACT
BASIS (NACE Rev. 1 51.1)

This wholesale activity covers agents trading on behalf and on account of others, those involved in bringing sellers and buyers together and those undertaking commercial transactions on behalf of a principal. It does not include financial intermediaries such as insurance or real estate agents, nor any retail sale by agents.

Wholesale agents and brokers are distinguished from merchant wholesalers essentially by the fact that they buy and sell merchandise on behalf of a principal for a commission or fee and hence do not purchase merchandise on their own account. These enterprise generally make up a small part of wholesaling in terms of employment and financial measures such as turnover or value added.

STRUCTURE AND PERFORMANCE

In 1997[13] turnover by agents in the EU exceeded 87 billion ECU. Looking in more detail at the Classes within Group 51.1 of NACE Rev. 1 in 1997[14] the share of turnover accounted for by specialist agents was 40.4% for consumer goods (Classes 51.15, 51.16 and 51.17), 9.6% for intermediate goods (Classes 51.11, 51.12 and 51.13) and 5.8% for capital goods (Class 51.14). Of the remainder, 16.3% came from agents specialised in other products not specified (Class 51.18) and over a quarter (27.9%) came from agents involved in unspecialised trading, in other words agents involved in the wholesale of a variety of goods (Class 51.19).

A common and growing type of wholesale trade in France; minor industry in Ireland

Agents represented between 0.5% (Ireland) and 11.7% (France) of wholesale trade turnover in 1997. Growth rates between 1995 and 1996 and between 1996 and 1997 can be calculated for five countries in each case. They show a growth in turnover (in current prices) between 1995 and 1997 in Austria and Finland totalling 16.9% and 13.7% respectively. France recorded growth of 6.9% in current price terms between 1996 and 1997, whilst Ireland and Portugal both saw reductions in excess of 10% between the same years.

(13) DK, 1995; I, L, S and UK, 1996; D, EL, E and NL, no data available.
(14) DK, 1995; I, L and S, 1996; D, EL, E, NL and UK, no data available.

Figure 16.11

Wholesale on a fee or contractual basis (NACE Rev. 1 51.1)

Number of persons employed, 1997 (thousands) (1)

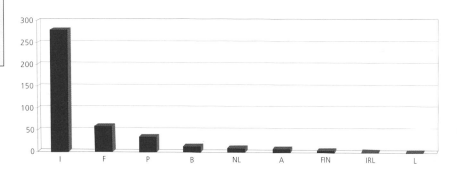

(1) I and L, 1996; DK, D, EL, E, S and UK, not available.

Source: Eurostat (SBS)

Figure 16.12

Wholesale on a fee or contractual basis (NACE Rev. 1 51.1)

Apparent labour productivity, 1997 (thousand ECU per person employed) (1)

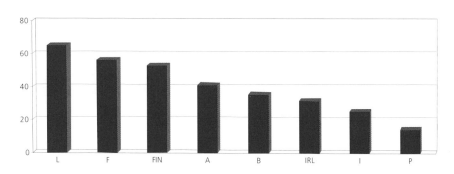

(1) I and L, 1996; DK, D, EL, E, NL, S and UK, not available.

Source: Eurostat (SBS)

LABOUR AND PRODUCTIVITY

Agents employed in excess of 470 thousand persons in 1997[15]. Between 1996 and 1997 employment grew in Finland (2.3%) and Ireland (4.9%), whilst it fell in the Netherlands (-14.3%), Belgium (-14.1%) and Portugal (-6.0%). The proportion of employees in the total number of persons employed was particularly low in Italy (10.4%, 1996) and Belgium (29.3%, 1997) and consistently lower than in wholesale trade activities in general in all Member States, even in France which had the highest share (94.3%, 1997 compared with 98.4%).

(15) DK, 1995; I, L and S 1996; S and UK, number of employees; D, EL and E, no data available.

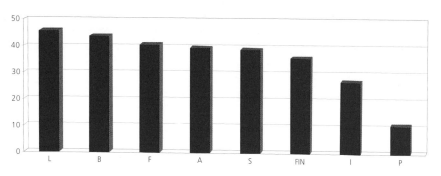

Figure 16.13

Wholesale on a fee or contractual basis (NACE Rev. 1 51.1)

Unit personnel costs, 1997 (thousand ECU per employee) (1)

(1) I, L and S, 1996; DK, D, EL, E, IRL, NL and UK, not available.

Source: Eurostat (SBS)

SUB-CHAPTER 16.5
OTHER WHOLESALE TRADE
(NACE Rev. 1 51.2 TO 51.7)

This grouping of activities covers all wholesale trade except that undertaken by agents and that concerning motor trades products. It covers resale (sale without transformation) of new and used goods to retailers, industrial, commercial, institutional or professional users or to other wholesalers. It also includes services common to wholesaling such as assembling, sorting and grading of goods, break of bulk, repackaging, bottling, redistribution, storage, refrigeration, delivery and installation.

Wholesaling other than through agents can be referred to as merchant wholesaling, in other words the activity of buying and reselling merchandise. Merchant wholesalers have traditionally relied on their strength of small order handling allied with other services such as credit terms, stock management, packaging, labelling, coding, transportation logistics, product selection and product advice for clients. The structural changes occurring in distribution channels place pressure on merchant wholesalers to improve their productivity and to emphasise the strengths of their related value added services. This is particularly true as technological developments reduce the lead-time between preparation and execution of an order and the implementation of just-in-time production methods reduce the importance of small-order handling.

High density of wholesalers in
Luxembourg and Belgium

The number of merchant wholesalers in the EU exceeded 615 thousand in 1997[16]. Italy and France had the largest network of merchant wholesalers with over 120 thousand each. Calculated as the number of wholesale enterprises per ten-thousand population, Luxembourg (54.0) and Belgium (49.8) had the highest density of merchant wholesalers and Germany the lowest (9.1)[17].

(16) DK, 1995; I, L, S and UK, 1996; B, EL and E, no data available.
(17) B, EL and E, no data available.

Figure 16.14 _____

Other wholesale trade (NACE Rev. 1 51.2 to 51.7)

Number of persons employed, 1997 (thousands) (1)

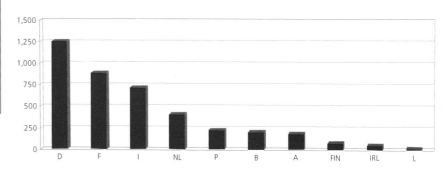

(1) I and L, 1996; DK, EL, E, S and UK, not available.

Source: Eurostat (SBS)

Figure 16.15 _____

Other wholesale trade (NACE Rev. 1 51.2 to 51.7)

Apparent labour productivity, 1997 (thousand ECU per person employed) (1)

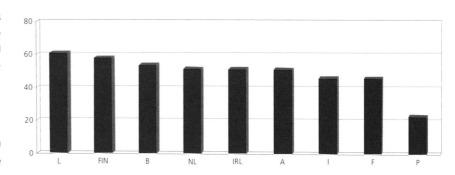

(1) I and L, 1996; DK, D, EL, E, S and UK, not available.

Source: Eurostat (SBS)

STRUCTURE AND PERFORMANCE

EU turnover by merchant wholesalers exceeded 2.2 billion ECU in 1997[18]. These merchant wholesalers accounted for 88.3% of wholesaling turnover in France (the smallest share) and 99.5% in Ireland (the largest share). Like agents, merchant wholesalers are generally distinguished by the type of product they trade and the relative importance of these product categories can be seen in their share of EU wholesale trade turnover in 1997: agricultural raw materials and live animals 6.7%; consumer durables and non-durables 40.7%; intermediate goods 31.5%; and capital goods 15.6%. Non-specialised wholesaling and other specialised trading not covered elsewhere accounted for the remaining 5.5% of turnover in 1997[19]. Wholesalers specialising in capital goods accounted for a larger proportion of value added (26.6%) than they did of turnover while wholesalers of agricultural raw materials and live animals (3.9%) and intermediate goods (23.8%) accounted for a smaller proportion by this measure.

Merchant wholesaling is the largest type of distribution measured in turnover

The Member States with the largest merchant wholesale industries (in turnover terms) were Germany and the United Kingdom. Specialisation in merchant wholesaling, measured here by the industry's share in total distribution turnover, was highest in the Netherlands, Denmark and Belgium, accounting for between 58% and 62% of total distribution turnover[20]. The least specialised countries in merchant wholesaling (using this measure) were Portugal, Ireland, France and Italy, although even in these Member States merchant wholesaling accounted for more than 45% of total distribution turnover.

The importance of Germany and the United Kingdom in turnover terms and of Italy and France in terms of the number of enterprises is confirmed by their average enterprise size. German merchant wholesalers generated on average 7.4 million ECU of turnover in 1997 compared to the British average of 4.2 million ECU (1996). In Italy the average size was 1.9 million ECU (1996) and in France 3.0 million ECU (1997). Amongst the remaining Member States Portugal (1.4 million ECU) had the smallest average size (using this measure) and Austria the largest (5.0 million ECU).

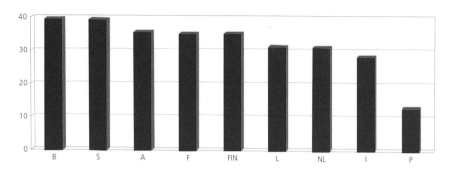

—————————————————————————————————————Figure 16.16

Other wholesale trade (NACE Rev. 1 51.2 to 51.7)

Unit personnel costs, 1997 (thousand ECU per employee) (1)

(1) I, L and S, 1996; DK, D, EL, E, IRL and UK, not available.

Source: Eurostat (SBS)

LABOUR AND PRODUCTIVITY

The number of persons employed in the EU in merchant wholesale exceeded 5.3 million in 1997[21]. Compared to the turnover breakdown, wholesalers of consumer goods accounted for a larger share of employment (44.4%), as did wholesalers of capital goods (22.0%). Wholesalers of intermediate products accounted for almost a quarter of merchant wholesale employment (23.6%), 7.9 percentage points less than their share of turnover.

The largest employers were Germany and the United Kingdom, both registering more than one million persons employed in this industry. Of the seven Member States providing data for 1996 and 1997, Ireland was the only one to record employment growth in excess of 10% between these years, although no Member State saw employment fall by more than 1%.

The share of employees in persons employed in merchant wholesaling is generally higher than in distribution as a whole, indicating a smaller role for the self-employed and family workers. As with wholesale agents, the lowest share of employees in persons employed for merchant wholesalers was in Italy (71.4%, 1996) and the highest in France (98.4%, 1997).

Higher productivity than distribution in general

Based on data for eight Member States for 1996 and 1997, turnover per person employed in merchant wholesale was between one and a half and two times higher than the average for the whole of distribution, ranging from 211.4 thousand ECU in Portugal to 593.2 thousand ECU in Belgium[22]. Wage adjusted labour productivity ratios ranged from 128.8% in France (1997) to 192.5% in Luxembourg (1996)[23] and, for every Member State for which data was available, was higher in merchant wholesaling than distribution in general.

—————————————————————————
(22) EL, E, S and UK, no data available.
(23) Based on data available for B, F, I, L, NL, A, P and FIN in 1996 and/or 1997.

—————————————————————————
(21) DK, 1995; I, L and S, 1996; S and UK, number of employees; EL and E, no data available.

—————————————————————————
(18) DK, 1995; I, L, S and UK, 1996; D, EL, E and NL, no data available.
(19) DK, 1995; I, L, S and UK, 1996; EL and E, no data available.
(20) D and NL, total distribution turnover is estimated; EL and E, no data available; the calculation is based on a mixture of data from 1995 to 1997 (subject to availability).

SUB-CHAPTER 16.6
RETAIL TRADE OF FOOD ITEMS
(NACE Rev. 1 52.11 AND 52.2)

These activities cover retail sale of food, beverages and tobacco, either in specialised stores (Group 52.2) or in non-specialised stores which have a predominance of these products (Class 52.11).

European food retailing continues to grow as does the size of its largest players. In 1998 the biggest European retailers of food in terms of turnover were Carrefour-Promodès, Intermarché, Metro, Rewe, Tesco, Aldi, Edeka, Auchan and Sainsbury, each of whom had food turnover in excess of 15 billion ECU (according to M+M EUROdATA, Frankfurt). Most of these food retailers figure amongst the 50 largest business groups in Europe.

The trend towards increased size has been powered by a desire to take advantage of economies of scale (for example in marketing and logistics) and to increase bargaining power with suppliers. International expansion has grown partly from a perceived saturation of home markets and from a belief that new markets, notably in Eastern Europe, will provide opportunities for profits.

Box 16.3

The Single Market has had two distinct impacts on distribution, directly in the way that retail and wholesale markets have opened up cross-border competition between enterprises in these industries and also indirectly as transport costs have fallen. Visibly for the consumer this has contributed to the greater internationalisation of retail networks and to a wider range of goods and services being available. An example can be given for food retailing where the 50 largest retail groups in Europe accounted for 75.3% of European food retail turnover in 1998 (according to M+M EUROdATA, Frankfurt). This figure can be contrasted with the situation in 1992, on the eve of the Single Market, when the 50 largest retailers accounted for 62.2% of European food retail turnover. The same source shows that during the period 1992 to 1998 the number of these groups operating in (current) EU applicant countries grew from 9 to 19.

1998 saw the entry of Wal-Mart, the world's largest retailer, into the EU market
Retail groups within the EU have also been the target for non-EU retailers with Wal-Mart (USA) entering the German (Supercenters) and the UK (ASDA[24]) markets in 1998 and 1999 respectively.

Household expenditure on food, beverages and tobacco, down to 17.4% in 1997
National Accounts show that EU household consumption on food, beverages and tobacco in 1997 exceeded 765 billion ECU. In the 10 years since 1987 household expenditure on these items has increased in (1990) constant prices by only 11.9% whilst total household expenditure has risen by 26.4%. The proportion of household expenditure on these items fell in current price terms from 21.0% in 1987 to 17.4% in 1997. The reduction was steady and uniform as the share fell in each and every year during the ten-year period considered. Over the same period the share of expenditure taken up by gross rent, fuel and power increased by 2.6 percentage points and in 1993 expenditure on these items in the EU overtook that on food, beverages and tobacco.

(24) In addition to its acquisition of Asda, in July 2000 Wal-Mart opened its first Wal-Mart Supercentre in the UK.

STRUCTURE AND PERFORMANCE

In 1997 the density of retail food enterprises in the EU ranged from 7.7 per ten-thousand population in Germany to 35.0 per ten-thousand in Portugal and 35.2 per ten-thousand in Italy[25]. Hence, there were in excess of 525 thousand retail food enterprises in the EU. Average turnover per enterprise ranged from 288.8 thousand ECU in Portugal to 1.9 million ECU in Germany, with Ireland and Italy the only other Member States recording average enterprise turnover below 1 million ECU.

In 1997[26] total turnover in the retail food sector of the EU exceeded 541 billion ECU. Of this (incomplete) total, France accounted for just over one-quarter and Germany and the United Kingdom around one-fifth each.

Food retailing growing in real terms by more than 2.5% per year
Annualised data from short-term statistics provides a sales volume index[27] for the EU from 1995 to 1999. This indicates that food retailing turnover has grown steadily since 1995 by a total of 7.6%, with growth exceeding 2.5% per year in both 1998 and 1999. Sales volumes grew by more than 10% between 1995 and 1999 in Ireland (26.0%), France (23.6%), Finland (21.9%), the United Kingdom (17.8%) and Belgium (11.2%). Germany was the only Member State not to have recorded growth in sales volumes over this period[28].

(25) I, L, S and UK, 1996; B, EL and E, no data available.
(26) L, 1995; I, S and UK, 1996; EL and E, no data available.
(27) Working-day adjusted.
(28) P, no data available.

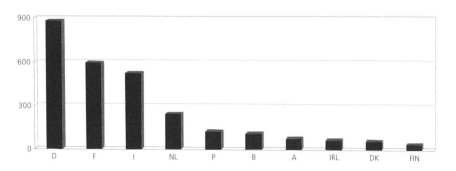

Figure 16.17

Retail trade of food items (NACE Rev. 1 52.11 and 52.2)
Number of persons employed, 1997 (thousands) (1)

(1) I, 1996; EL, E, L, S and UK, not available.

Source: Eurostat (SBS)

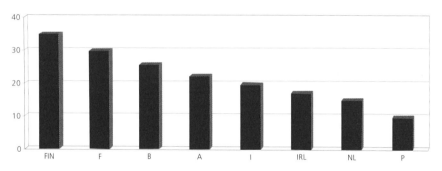

Figure 16.18

Retail trade of food items (NACE Rev. 1 52.11 and 52.2)
Apparent labour productivity, 1997 (thousand ECU per person employed) (1)

(1) I, 1996; DK, D, EL, E, L, S and UK, not available.

Source: Eurostat (SBS)

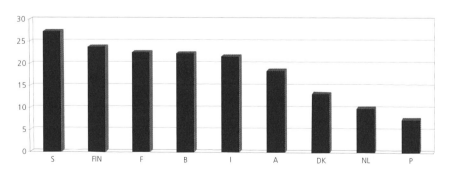

Figure 16.19

Retail trade of food items (NACE Rev. 1 52.11 and 52.2)
Unit personnel costs, 1997 (thousand ECU per employee) (1)

(1) DK, I and S, 1996; D, EL, E, IRL, L and UK, not available.

Source: Eurostat (SBS)

LABOUR AND PRODUCTIVITY

The average enterprise size in employment terms showed similarities to the average turnover figures in that Italy (2.6) and Portugal (3.5) had the smallest enterprises and Germany (14.0) was amongst the largest. The main difference was the average size of Dutch food retailers, 14.3 persons employed per enterprise, which made these the largest enterprises by this measure. The average number of persons employed per enterprise in the food retail sector in 1997 in most other Member States was between 6 and 9 persons.

Germany employed over 8.8 million persons in this sector in 1997, France 5.9 million and Italy 5.2 million. As a share of total distribution employment, the food retail sector accounted for as little as 14.3% of the total in Austria and as much as 30.6% in Ireland.

Very low unit personnel costs and
low apparent labour productivity

Unit personnel costs were lower in food retailing than on average in distribution (except in Italy), ranging from 7.5 thousand ECU in Portugal to 27.3 thousand ECU in Sweden[29]. These were often amongst the lowest in the economy, comparable with the average for hotels and restaurants.

Apparent labour productivity in food retailing was also lower in all Member States than on average in distribution[30]. After adjusting this productivity measure for the generally low personnel costs per employee, wage adjusted labour productivity in food retailing generally came closer to the average for distribution, but only surpassed it in France.

(29) D, EL, E, IRL and UK, no data available.
(30) DK, D, EL, E, S and UK, no data available.

SUB-CHAPTER 16.7
RETAIL TRADE OF NON-FOOD ITEMS
(NACE Rev. 1 52.12 AND 52.3 TO 52.6)

These activities cover retail sale other than food, beverages and tobacco. Retail sales may be the sale of new goods from specialised stores (Group 52.3 and 52.4), the sale of new goods from non-specialised stores (Class 52.12), the sale of used or second-hand goods in stores (Group 52.5) or sales not in stores (Group 52.6). Note that the retail sale of second-hand motor vehicles is excluded, as is all renting and hiring of personal and household goods to the general public.

Non-food retail trading through stores is a collection of mature industries with relatively slow growth. This can be compared with the small activity of remote-selling through the Internet that receives a great deal of media attention for its actual and potential growth.

Non-food retailing is more seasonally sensitive than food retailing

Non-food retailing is heavily dependent on consumer confidence with the retail sale of consumer durables in particular suffering when confidence falls. Furthermore non-food retail industries are seasonal. Figure 16.20 compares a simple working-day adjusted (w.d.a.) index of sales with a seasonally adjusted (s.a.) index for 1999; the difference between these two indices is the seasonal effect and hence the months where the w.d.a. index is above the s.a. index are the ones where sales are concentrated. From this recent example for 1999 it is clear that this is particularly the case around the Christmas period of November and December, whilst a relatively low proportion of sales are made in January, February and August. Whilst total turnover in food retailing is also seasonal, the seasonal component of sales in non-food retailing is more significant.

Slow growth in household expenditure and a falling share

National Accounts show that EU household expenditure on furniture, furnishings, household equipment, clothing and footwear in 1997 exceeded 607 billion ECU. In the 10 years to 1997 household expenditure on these items has increased in (1990) constant prices by 20.7%, 5.7 percentage points slower than total household expenditure and hence the proportion of household expenditure (in current prices) on these

items has fallen from 15.9% in 1987 to 13.8% in 1997. The reduction in the proportion of household expenditure given over to clothing and footwear has been particularly marked, although even here expenditure in constant prices increased at an annual average growth rate of 1.4% between 1987 and 1997.

Figure 16.20

Non-food retail sales volumes in the EU, 1999 (1995=100)

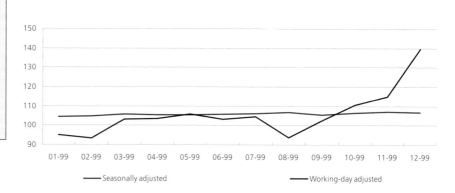

Source: Eurostat (EBT)

Figure 16.21

Retail trade of non-food items (NACE Rev. 1 52.12 and 52.3 to 52.6)
Number of persons employed, 1997 (thousands) (1)

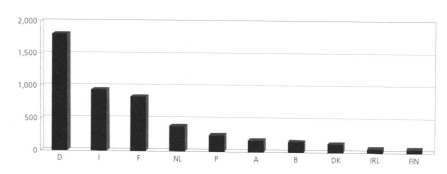

(1) I, 1996; EL, E, L, S and UK, not available.

Source: Eurostat (SBS)

STRUCTURE AND PERFORMANCE

Non-food retailing accounted for an estimated 56% of retailing (excluding repair) turnover in the EU in 1997[31]. This ranged from 45.9% in France[32] to 65.1% in Denmark. Apart from France, the only countries where this proportion was less than 50% were Ireland and Sweden.

The non-specialised sector (for example, department stores) accounted for approximately one-third of non-food retail turnover in Denmark and Finland in 1997 while in the other Member States it accounted for between 1.7% (Portugal) and 16.6% (United Kingdom, 1996). Amongst the specialised industries, the main activities in the non-food retail industry concern the retail sale of new goods in stores (for example, clothes, footwear and electrical goods, as well as pharmaceutical, medical and cosmetic goods). These activities accounted for more than half of non-food retail turnover in every Member State, a proportion that rose as high as 95.6% in Portugal. The turnover of second-hand goods stores was the smallest in all Member States, never accounting for more than 1.4% of non-food retail turnover in any Member State. Retail sale not in stores (for example, mail-order) accounted for between 8.7% and 16.9% of non-food retail turnover in the four largest Member States and between 1.8% and 5.7% of turnover in the remaining EU Member States[33].

Strong sales growth in 1998 but weaker in 1999
Annualised data from short-term statistics provides a sales volume index[34] for the EU from 1995 to 1999. This indicates that non-food retail turnover remained stable between 1995 and 1996, growing by 1.0%, 3.0% and 1.7% in subsequent years. Sales volumes grew by more than 10% between 1995 and 1999 in Finland (26.0%), Sweden (23.6%), Luxembourg (21.9%), Spain (17.8%) and Austria (11.2%). Italy and Germany recorded stable sales volume figures over this period[35].

---

(31) EL, E and NL, no data available; mixed years 1995 to 1997.
(32) It should be noted that in 1999, 19.7% of all non-food retail sales in France were accounted for by supermarkets and hypermarkets classified as food-retail (source: Comptes de commerce, INSEE).
(33) EL, E and NL, no data available.
(34) Working-day adjusted.
(35) B, DK, EL, F, IRL, NL, P, UK, no data available.

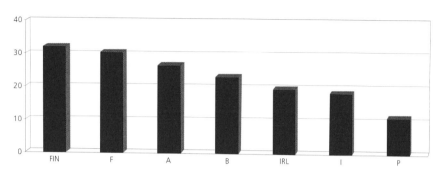

_____Figure 16.22

Retail trade of non-food items (NACE Rev. 1 52.12 and 52.3 to 52.6)
Apparent labour productivity, 1997 (thousand ECU per person employed) (1)

(1) I, 1996; DK, D, EL, E, L, NL, S and UK, not available.

Source: Eurostat (SBS)

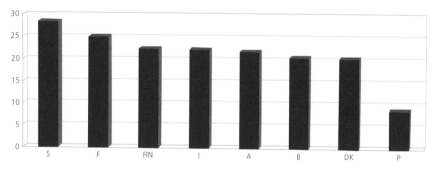

_____Figure 16.23

Retail trade of non-food items (NACE Rev. 1 52.12 and 52.3 to 52.6)
Unit personnel costs, 1997 (thousand ECU per employee) (1)

(1) DK, I and S, 1996; D, EL, E, IRL, L, NL and UK, not available.

Source: Eurostat (SBS)

LABOUR AND PRODUCTIVITY

Germany had by far the largest[36] number of persons employed in non-food retailing, with over 1.8 million, nearly double the number in Italy (949 thousand, 1996) and more than double the number in France (841 thousand). Eurostat estimates that non-food retailing accounted for approximately 64% of retailing (excluding repair) employment in the EU in 1997, ranging from 50.2% in Ireland to as much as 70.6% in Austria[37]. The share of employees in the number of persons employed was generally lower in non-food retailing than in food retailing (except in Portugal) and was always lower than the average for distribution as a whole, with only Italy (33.7%, 1996) outside of the range from 79.0% (Luxembourg, 1995) to 87.2% (Finland, 1997)[38].

Unit personnel costs and labour productivity very similar to food retailing
Unit personnel costs in non-food retail trade rarely differ greatly from those recorded in the retail trade of food and were generally lower than for distribution as a whole, with Italy the only known exception. Apparent labour productivity in non-food retailing was also generally close to that of food retailing and as such was systematically lower than the average for distribution. Even after adjustment for low unit personnel costs the wage adjusted labour productivity ratio for non-food retailing remained consistently below the distribution average.

---

(36) I and S, 1996; L, 1995; S, number of employees; EL, E and UK, no data available.
(37) EL, E, S and UK, no data available.
(38) D, EL, E, S and UK, no data available; mixed years 1995 to 1997.

Table 16.5

Sale of motor vehicles (NACE Rev. 1 50.1)

Employment related indicators, 1997

	B	DK	D	EL	E	F	IRL	I (1)	L (1)	NL	A	P	FIN	S	UK
Number of persons employed (thousands)	33.4	:	309.4	:	:	219.4	10.8	80.2	3.3	85.1	31.2	45.8	8.5	:	:
Employees/number of persons employed (%)	71.6	:	:	:	:	95.4	91.5	78.9	92.0	81.5	95.3	95.4	94.6	:	:
Average no. of persons employed/enterprise (units)	:	:	14.0	:	:	7.0	11.0	6.5	9.0	6.0	17.0	10.0	6.0	:	:

(1) 1996.

Table 16.6

Sale of motor vehicles (NACE Rev. 1 50.1)

Turnover related indicators, 1997

	B	DK	D	EL	E	F	IRL	I (1)	L (1)	NL	A	P	FIN	S (1)	UK
Turnover (million ECU)	25,236	:	95,492	:	:	70,511	5,623	46,127	1,156	33,999	11,299	12,838	5,811	12,303	122,761
Turnover per enterprise (million ECU)	:	:	4.2	:	:	2.4	5.7	3.7	3.2	2.5	6.2	2.8	4.3	3.3	3.6
Turnover per person employed (thousand ECU)	754.9	:	308.6	:	:	321.3	522.4	575.5	348.9	399.4	362.7	280.5	685.9	:	:

(1) 1996.

Table 16.7

Sale of motor vehicles (NACE Rev. 1 50.1)

Performance related indicators, 1997

	B	DK	D	EL	E	F	IRL	I (1)	L (1)	NL	A	P	FIN	S (1)	UK
Value added (million ECU)	1,293	:	:	:	:	7,292	484	4,165	152	6,451	1,311	946	496	1,164	15,672
Value added as a share of turnover (%)	5.1	:	:	:	:	10.3	8.6	9.0	13.1	19.0	11.6	7.4	8.5	9.5	12.8
Apparent labour productivity (thousand ECU/person employed)	38.7	:	:	:	:	33.2	45.0	52.0	45.8	75.8	42.1	20.7	58.5	:	:
Unit personnel costs (thousand ECU)	34.8	:	:	:	:	29.0	:	27.8	25.4	27.0	30.7	12.8	34.0	33.9	25.8
Simple wage adjusted labour productivity (%)	155.2	:	:	:	:	120.1	:	236.6	196.1	344.2	143.9	169.2	182.0	148.6	282.3
Gross operating surplus (million ECU)	460	:	:	:	:	1,220	:	2,405	74	4,576	400	387	224	381	10,120

(1) 1996.

Table 16.8

Maintenance and repair of motor vehicles (NACE Rev. 1 50.2)

Employment related indicators, 1997

	B	DK	D	EL	E	F	IRL (1)	I (1)	L (1)	NL	A	P	FIN	S	UK
Number of persons employed (thousands)	22.7	:	:	:	:	101.5	7.1	235.2	0.5	18.3	24.6	58.3	10.4	:	:
Employees/number of persons employed (%)	67.4	:	:	:	:	81.8	67.8	39.3	78.6	76.2	88.4	76.7	79.5	:	:
Average no. of persons employed/enterprise (units)	:	:	:	:	:	3.0	3.0	2.2	4.0	6.0	8.0	3.0	2.0	:	:

(1) 1996.

Table 16.9

Maintenance and repair of motor vehicles (NACE Rev. 1 50.2)

Turnover related indicators, 1997

	B	DK	D	EL	E	F	IRL (1)	I (1)	L (1)	NL	A	P	FIN	S (1)	UK
Turnover (million ECU)	3,039	:	:	:	:	9,656	578	10,772	66	1,240	2,791	2,597	1,963	3,072	11,501
Turnover per enterprise (million ECU)	:	:	:	:	:	0.3	0.3	0.1	0.6	0.4	0.9	0.1	0.4	0.3	0.5
Turnover per person employed (thousand ECU)	134.1	:	:	:	:	95.1	82.0	45.8	131.6	67.7	113.5	44.6	189.2	:	:

(1) 1996.

Table 16.10

Maintenance and repair of motor vehicles (NACE Rev. 1 50.2)

Performance related indicators, 1997

	B	DK	D	EL	E	F	IRL (1)	I (1)	L (1)	NL	A	P	FIN	S (1)	UK
Value added (million ECU)	619	:	:	:	:	2,634	121	3,414	18	698	705	523	386	707	4,192
Value added as a share of turnover (%)	20.4	:	:	:	:	27.3	21.0	31.7	26.5	56.3	25.3	20.1	19.7	23.0	36.4
Apparent labour productivity (thousand ECU/person employed)	27.3	:	:	:	:	26.0	17.2	14.5	34.9	38.1	28.7	9.0	37.3	:	:
Unit personnel costs (thousand ECU)	24.5	:	:	:	:	24.3	:	16.9	21.9	22.9	23.9	8.4	27.7	29.7	14.0
Simple wage adjusted labour productivity (%)	165.3	:	:	:	:	130.7	:	219.0	202.3	218.3	135.4	139.6	169.5	148.2	187.2
Gross operating surplus (million ECU)	244	:	:	:	:	619	:	1,855	9	378	184	148	158	230	1,953

(1) 1996.

Source: Eurostat (SBS)

Table 16.11

Sale of motor vehicle parts and accessories (NACE Rev. 1 50.3)

Employment related indicators, 1997

	B	DK	D	EL	E	F	IRL	I (1)	L (1)	NL	A	P	FIN	S	UK
Number of persons employed (thousands)	11.0	:	80.0	:	:	58.1	:	41.8	0.6	15.8	9.4	18.9	6.3	:	:
Employees/number of persons employed (%)	81.6	:	:	:	:	97.9	:	61.8	85.8	88.2	92.5	93.5	90.6	:	:
Average no. of persons employed/enterprise (units)	:	:	11.0	:	:	9.0	:	3.9	5.0	7.0	12.0	6.0	5.0	:	:

(1) 1996.

Table 16.12

Sale of motor vehicle parts and accessories (NACE Rev. 1 50.3)

Turnover related indicators, 1997

	B	DK	D	EL	E	F	IRL	I (1)	L (1)	NL	A	P	FIN	S (1)	UK
Turnover (million ECU)	3,743	:	17,102	:	:	10,575	:	8,671	137	4,305	2,156	2,020	1,404	2,142	15,106
Turnover per enterprise (million ECU)	:	:	2.4	:	:	1.7	:	0.8	1.3	2.0	2.9	0.6	1.0	1.3	2.3
Turnover per person employed (thousand ECU)	340.7	:	213.9	:	:	182.1	:	207.5	232.0	273.1	230.1	107.1	224.5	:	:

(1) 1996.

Table 16.13

Sale of motor vehicle parts and accessories (NACE Rev. 1 50.3)

Performance related indicators, 1997

	B	DK	D	EL	E	F	IRL	I (1)	L (1)	NL	A	P	FIN	S (1)	UK
Value added (million ECU)	474	:	:	:	:	2,120	:	1,367	22	923	442	327	269	317	3,292
Value added as a share of turnover (%)	12.7	:	:	:	:	20.0	:	15.8	16.2	21.4	20.5	16.2	19.1	14.8	21.8
Apparent labour productivity (thousand ECU/person employed)	43.1	:	:	:	:	36.5	:	32.7	37.7	58.6	47.1	17.3	43.0	:	:
Unit personnel costs (thousand ECU)	33.0	:	:	:	:	29.7	:	27.1	29.0	26.6	29.2	10.9	28.8	35.0	17.8
Simple wage adjusted labour productivity (%)	160.3	:	:	:	:	125.5	:	195.4	151.7	249.1	174.3	170.2	164.9	152.1	186.2
Gross operating surplus (million ECU)	178	:	:	:	:	431	:	667	8	553	188	135	106	108	1,524

(1) 1996.

Table 16.14

Sale, maintenance and repair of motorcycles and related parts and accessories (NACE Rev. 1 50.4)

Employment related indicators, 1997

	B	DK	D	EL	E	F	IRL	I (1)	L (1)	NL	A	P	FIN	S	UK
Number of persons employed (thousands)	1.7	:	8.6	:	:	12.7	:	18.9	0.1	2.3	0.9	7.2	0.3	:	:
Employees/number of persons employed (%)	37.9	:	:	:	:	82.0	:	35.6	80.0	77.4	80.1	62.8	72.9	:	:
Average no. of persons employed/enterprise (units)	:	:	5.0	:	:	3.0	:	2.0	5.0	3.0	4.0	2.0	2.0	:	:

(1) 1996.

Table 16.15

Sale, maintenance and repair of motorcycles and related parts and accessories (NACE Rev. 1 50.4)

Turnover related indicators, 1997

	B	DK	D	EL	E	F	IRL	I (1)	L (1)	NL	A	P	FIN	S (1)	UK
Turnover (million ECU)	447	:	2,561	:	:	2,873	:	3,852	17	759	280	718	88	273	1,852
Turnover per enterprise (million ECU)	:	:	1.5	:	:	0.6	:	0.4	1.5	1.1	1.3	0.2	0.5	0.5	1.2
Turnover per person employed (thousand ECU)	258.3	:	298.0	:	:	227.0	:	203.7	341.0	329.6	295.2	99.7	280.8	:	:

(1) 1996.

Table 16.16

Sale, maintenance and repair of motorcycles and related parts and accessories (NACE Rev. 1 50.4)

Performance related indicators, 1997

	B	DK	D	EL	E	F	IRL	I (1)	L (1)	NL	A	P	FIN	S (1)	UK
Value added (million ECU)	31	:	:	:	:	370	:	425	2	153	38	78	11	39	300
Value added as a share of turnover (%)	6.9	:	:	:	:	12.9	:	11.0	11.2	20.2	13.5	10.9	12.1	14.4	16.2
Apparent labour productivity (thousand ECU/person employed)	17.8	:	:	:	:	29.3	:	22.5	37.0	66.6	39.9	10.8	34.1	:	:
Unit personnel costs (thousand ECU)	23.6	:	:	:	:	25.9	:	20.5	24.0	28.0	27.0	9.5	25.9	28.8	11.0
Simple wage adjusted labour productivity (%)	198.7	:	:	:	:	137.7	:	308.0	190.0	307.4	184.4	182.5	181.4	167.5	223.7
Gross operating surplus (million ECU)	15	:	:	:	:	101	:	287	1	104	17	35	5	16	166

(1) 1996.

Source: Eurostat (SBS)

Table 16.17

Retail sale of automotive fuel (NACE Rev. 1 50.5)

Employment related indicators, 1997

	B	DK	D	EL	E	F	IRL	I (1)	L (1)	NL	A	P	FIN	S	UK
Number of persons employed (thousands)	6.5	:	54.5	:	:	28.5	7.9	58.6	1.4	11.9	8.4	14.8	5.8	:	:
Employees/number of persons employed (%)	46.3	:	:	:	:	92.0	80.8	32.4	81.3	85.2	78.3	96.4	80.6	:	:
Average no. of persons employed/enterprise (units)	:	:	8.0	:	:	4.0	6.0	2.4	6.0	7.0	4.0	8.0	5.0	:	:

(1) 1996.

Table 16.18

Retail sale of automotive fuel (NACE Rev. 1 50.5)

Turnover related indicators, 1997

	B	DK	D	EL	E	F	IRL	I (1)	L (1)	NL	A	P	FIN	S (1)	UK
Turnover (million ECU)	3,072	:	6,189	:	:	4,826	1,311	25,663	808	5,462	1,313	3,799	1,230	4,355	21,108
Turnover per enterprise (million ECU)	:	:	0.9	:	:	0.7	1.0	1.1	3.3	3.2	0.7	2.0	1.0	1.9	2.8
Turnover per person employed (thousand ECU)	469.6	:	113.6	:	:	169.4	166.0	437.8	590.5	459.3	157.0	257.5	211.3	:	:

(1) 1996.

Table 16.19

Retail sale of automotive fuel (NACE Rev. 1 50.5)

Performance related indicators, 1997

	B	DK	D	EL	E	F	IRL	I (1)	L (1)	NL	A	P	FIN	S (1)	UK
Value added (million ECU)	183	:	:	:	:	633	140	1,457	55	565	182	158	153	425	1,823
Value added as a share of turnover (%)	5.9	:	:	:	:	13.1	10.6	5.7	6.8	10.3	13.8	4.2	12.5	9.8	8.6
Apparent labour productivity (thousand ECU/person employed)	27.9	:	:	:	:	22.2	17.7	24.9	40.1	47.5	21.7	10.7	26.3	:	:
Unit personnel costs (thousand ECU)	22.3	:	:	:	:	21.2	:	18.4	20.0	19.4	19.8	8.4	22.4	28.8	13.4
Simple wage adjusted labour productivity (%)	270.5	:	:	:	:	113.7	:	416.6	247.3	286.7	140.2	133.3	145.6	145.5	268.5
Gross operating surplus (million ECU)	115	:	:	:	:	76	:	1,108	33	368	52	40	48	133	1,144

(1) 1996.

Source: Eurostat (SBS)

Table 16.20

Wholesale on a fee or contract basis (NACE Rev. 1 51.1)

Employment related indicators, 1997

	B	DK	D	EL	E	F	IRL	I (1)	L (1)	NL	A	P	FIN	S	UK
Number of persons employed (thousands)	13.9	:	:	:	:	59.4	1.9	279.8	0.6	9.9	8.2	35.0	5.1	:	:
Employees/number of persons employed (%)	29.3	:	:	:	:	94.3	69.4	10.4	57.8	78.4	51.8	68.3	73.0	:	:
Average no. of persons employed/enterprise (units)	:	:	:	:	:	2.0	4.0	1.3	2.0	3.0	2.0	2.0	1.0	:	:

(1) 1996.

Table 16.21

Wholesale on a fee or contract basis (NACE Rev. 1 51.1)

Turnover related indicators, 1997

	B	DK	D	EL	E	F	IRL	I (1)	L (1)	NL	A	P	FIN	S (1)	UK (1)
Turnover (million ECU)	3,247	:	:	:	:	48,980	102	15,797	368	:	704	3,448	635	3,234	9,233
Turnover per enterprise (million ECU)	:	:	:	:	:	1.3	0.2	0.1	0.9	:	0.2	0.2	0.2	1.1	0.7
Turnover per person employed (thousand ECU)	233.9	:	:	:	:	824.8	52.6	56.4	572.8	:	85.9	98.4	124.5	:	:

(1) 1996.

Table 16.22

Wholesale on a fee or contract basis (NACE Rev. 1 51.1)

Performance related indicators, 1997

	B	DK	D	EL	E	F	IRL	I (1)	L (1)	NL	A	P	FIN	S (1)	UK (1)
Value added (million ECU)	494	:	:	:	:	3,339	61	7,100	42	:	337	506	270	441	2,050
Value added as a share of turnover (%)	15.2	:	:	:	:	6.8	60.1	44.9	11.4	:	47.9	14.7	42.6	13.6	22.2
Apparent labour productivity (thousand ECU/person employed)	35.6	:	:	:	:	56.2	31.6	25.4	65.2	:	41.2	14.4	53.0	:	:
Unit personnel costs (thousand ECU)	43.8	:	:	:	:	40.7	:	27.0	45.8	:	39.5	10.6	35.8	38.9	:
Simple wage adjusted labour productivity (%)	277.3	:	:	:	:	146.5	:	902.8	245.9	:	201.5	199.4	202.7	149.0	228.5
Gross operating surplus (million ECU)	316	:	:	:	:	1,060	:	6,313	25	:	170	252	137	145	1,153

(1) 1996.

Table 16.23

Wholesale of agricultural raw materials and live animals (NACE Rev. 1 51.2)

Employment related indicators, 1997

	B	DK	D	EL	E	F	IRL	I (1)	L (1)	NL	A	P	FIN	S	UK
Number of persons employed (thousands)	7.6	:	52.0	:	:	54.4	1.6	25.4	0.4	32.3	16.4	10.0	1.6	:	:
Employees/number of persons employed (%)	45.4	:	:	:	:	94.9	87.8	50.8	75.8	84.2	93.5	81.4	91.4	:	:
Average no. of persons employed/enterprise (units)	:	:	8.0	:	:	7.0	8.0	2.9	4.0	7.0	15.0	4.0	5.0	:	:

(1) 1996.

Table 16.24

Wholesale of agricultural raw materials and live animals (NACE Rev. 1 51.2)

Turnover related indicators, 1997

	B	DK	D	EL	E	F	IRL	I (1)	L (1)	NL	A	P	FIN	S (1)	UK (1)
Turnover (million ECU)	6,360	:	34,119	:	:	47,468	850	13,249	193	21,102	5,730	3,449	783	2,930	8,882
Turnover per enterprise (million ECU)	:	:	5.1	:	:	5.8	4.3	1.5	1.8	4.4	5.2	1.3	2.5	3.4	4.8
Turnover per person employed (thousand ECU)	841.8	:	656.3	:	:	873.2	525.8	521.9	486.9	654.1	349.2	345.6	504.1	:	:

(1) 1996.

Table 16.25

Wholesale of agricultural raw materials and live animals (NACE Rev. 1 51.2)

Performance related indicators, 1997

	B	DK	D	EL	E	F	IRL	I (1)	L (1)	NL	A	P	FIN	S (1)	UK (1)
Value added (million ECU)	282	:	:	:	:	2,462	105	971	19	1,381	566	151	74	247	606
Value added as a share of turnover (%)	4.4	:	:	:	:	5.2	12.4	7.3	9.6	6.5	9.9	4.4	9.4	8.4	6.8
Apparent labour productivity (thousand ECU/person employed)	37.3	:	:	:	:	45.3	65.2	38.2	46.9	42.8	34.5	15.1	47.3	:	:
Unit personnel costs (thousand ECU)	29.2	:	:	:	:	33.0	:	25.8	29.2	28.5	27.0	9.6	30.9	34.0	:
Simple wage adjusted labour productivity (%)	281.4	:	:	:	:	144.5	:	291.3	213.8	178.7	136.7	193.3	167.4	122.0	234.8
Gross operating surplus (million ECU)	182	:	:	:	:	759	:	637	10	608	152	73	30	45	348

(1) 1996.

Source: Eurostat (SBS)

Table 16.26

Wholesale of food, beverages and tobacco (NACE Rev. 1 51.3)

Employment related indicators, 1997

	B	DK	D	EL	E	F	IRL	I (1)	L (1)	NL	A	P	FIN	S	UK
Number of persons employed (thousands)	33.8	:	225.7	:	:	173.9	11.0	166.7	2.8	64.1	37.0	55.4	6.8	:	:
Employees/number of persons employed (%)	80.2	:	:	:	:	98.3	92.9	66.3	92.8	91.7	96.2	93.5	94.9	:	:
Average no. of persons employed/enterprise (units)	:	:	19.0	:	:	8.0	11.0	4.6	9.0	10.0	25.0	7.0	6.0	:	:

(1) 1996.

Table 16.27

Wholesale of food, beverages and tobacco (NACE Rev. 1 51.3)

Turnover related indicators, 1997

	B	DK	D	EL	E	F	IRL	I (1)	L (1)	NL	A	P	FIN	S (1)	UK (1)
Turnover (million ECU)	20,746	:	119,404	:	:	88,749	5,468	63,511	1,821	37,418	12,512	12,657	4,750	14,900	73,818
Turnover per enterprise (million ECU)	:	:	9.9	:	:	4.2	5.4	1.7	5.8	6.1	8.4	1.7	4.2	4.2	4.9
Turnover per person employed (thousand ECU)	613.6	:	529.1	:	:	510.4	495.1	381.1	646.8	584.2	338.3	228.4	694.6	:	:

(1) 1996.

Table 16.28

Wholesale of food, beverages and tobacco (NACE Rev. 1 51.3)

Performance related indicators, 1997

	B	DK	D	EL	E	F	IRL	I (1)	L (1)	NL	A	P	FIN	S (1)	UK (1)
Value added (million ECU)	1,347	:	:	:	:	7,118	485	5,624	150	2,799	1,409	979	351	989	6,616
Value added as a share of turnover (%)	6.5	:	:	:	:	8.0	8.9	8.9	8.2	7.5	11.3	7.7	7.4	6.6	9.0
Apparent labour productivity (thousand ECU/person employed)	39.9	:	:	:	:	40.9	43.9	33.7	53.3	43.7	38.1	17.7	51.3	:	:
Unit personnel costs (thousand ECU)	29.6	:	:	:	:	31.0	:	25.0	26.7	26.1	29.2	10.1	30.4	36.4	:
Simple wage adjusted labour productivity (%)	168.0	:	:	:	:	134.6	:	203.7	215.2	182.7	135.5	187.0	177.9	132.9	210.5
Gross operating surplus (million ECU)	545	:	:	:	:	1,829	:	2,863	80	1,267	369	455	154	245	3,473

(1) 1996.

Table 16.29

Wholesale of household goods (NACE Rev. 1 51.4)

Employment related indicators, 1997

	B	DK	D	EL	E	F	IRL	I (1)	L (1)	NL	A	P	FIN	S	UK
Number of persons employed (thousands)	57.7	:	336.4	:	:	185.9	9.6	241.8	1.9	89.3	45.0	64.5	14.9	:	:
Employees/number of persons employed (%)	80.8	:	:	:	:	98.3	94.3	75.1	82.5	89.6	92.9	95.6	91.6	:	:
Average no. of persons employed/enterprise (units)	:	:	15.0	:	:	5.0	11.0	5.4	4.0	6.0	11.0	7.0	4.0	:	:

(1) 1996.

Table 16.30

Wholesale of household goods (NACE Rev. 1 51.4)

Turnover related indicators, 1997

	B	DK	D	EL	E	F	IRL	I (1)	L (1)	NL	A	P	FIN	S (1)	UK (1)
Turnover (million ECU)	24,105	:	114,605	:	:	70,161	3,067	71,714	706	34,964	14,760	11,553	5,189	16,043	62,320
Turnover per enterprise (million ECU)	:	:	5.1	:	:	1.9	3.6	1.6	1.4	2.5	3.6	1.2	1.4	1.4	2.5
Turnover per person employed (thousand ECU)	418.1	:	340.7	:	:	377.4	318.6	296.6	373.1	391.7	328.0	179.2	349.2	:	:

(1) 1996.

Table 16.31

Wholesale of household goods (NACE Rev. 1 51.4)

Performance related indicators, 1997

	B	DK	D	EL	E	F	IRL	I (1)	L (1)	NL	A	P	FIN	S (1)	UK (1)
Value added (million ECU)	2,953	:	:	:	:	8,598	508	10,580	110	4,703	2,347	1,514	813	2,230	9,650
Value added as a share of turnover (%)	12.2	:	:	:	:	12.3	16.6	14.8	15.5	13.5	15.9	13.1	15.7	13.9	15.5
Apparent labour productivity (thousand ECU/person employed)	51.2	:	:	:	:	46.3	52.8	43.8	57.9	52.7	52.2	23.5	54.7	:	:
Unit personnel costs (thousand ECU)	41.0	:	:	:	:	35.9	:	25.0	30.9	31.0	38.0	14.5	33.7	38.7	:
Simple wage adjusted labour productivity (%)	154.7	:	:	:	:	131.3	:	232.5	227.2	189.5	147.7	170.1	177.4	151.3	220.0
Gross operating surplus (million ECU)	1,044	:	:	:	:	2,050	:	6,030	61	2,221	758	624	355	756	5,263

(1) 1996.

Source: Eurostat (SBS)

Table 16.32

Wholesale of non-agricultural intermediate products, waste and scrap (NACE Rev. 1 51.5)

Employment related indicators, 1997

	B	DK	D	EL	E	F	IRL	I (1)	L (1)	NL	A	P	FIN	S	UK
Number of persons employed (thousands)	46.6	:	354.0	:	:	192.4	10.0	154.0	2.8	79.5	42.9	41.6	16.4	:	:
Employees/number of persons employed (%)	85.0	:	:	:	:	99.1	94.8	72.5	90.0	90.4	94.8	94.0	94.3	:	:
Average no. of persons employed/enterprise (units)	:	:	19.0	:	:	11.0	13.0	5.4	6.0	10.0	15.0	7.0	6.0	:	:

(1) 1996.

Table 16.33

Wholesale of non-agricultural intermediate products, waste and scrap (NACE Rev. 1 51.5)

Turnover related indicators, 1997

	B	DK	D	EL	E	F	IRL	I (1)	L (1)	NL	A	P	FIN	S (1)	UK (1)
Turnover (million ECU)	48,051	:	186,949	:	:	83,854	5,280	87,158	2,657	36,912	22,531	10,579	10,349	24,877	167,146
Turnover per enterprise (million ECU)	:	:	10.3	:	:	4.8	6.9	3.1	5.6	4.8	7.8	1.7	3.9	2.4	10.9
Turnover per person employed (thousand ECU)	1,031.3	:	528.0	:	:	435.7	527.1	565.8	950.5	464.4	525.0	254.1	630.2	:	:

(1) 1996.

Table 16.34

Wholesale of non-agricultural intermediate products, waste and scrap (NACE Rev. 1 51.5)

Performance related indicators, 1997

	B	DK	D	EL	E	F	IRL	I (1)	L (1)	NL	A	P	FIN	S (1)	UK (1)
Value added (million ECU)	2,970	:	:	:	:	8,812	593	8,612	225	4,249	2,470	1,101	1,042	2,885	9,024
Value added as a share of turnover (%)	6.2	:	:	:	:	10.5	11.2	9.9	8.5	11.5	11.0	10.4	10.1	11.6	5.4
Apparent labour productivity (thousand ECU/person employed)	63.8	:	:	:	:	45.8	59.2	55.9	80.4	53.5	57.6	26.5	63.5	:	:
Unit personnel costs (thousand ECU)	39.6	:	:	:	:	34.6	:	30.9	31.7	32.9	36.4	13.2	34.4	38.8	:
Simple wage adjusted labour productivity (%)	189.4	:	:	:	:	133.5	:	249.8	281.1	179.5	166.8	213.0	195.6	167.1	184.2
Gross operating surplus (million ECU)	1,402	:	:	:	:	2,209	:	5,165	145	1,882	989	584	510	1,159	4,124

(1) 1996.

Table 16.35

Wholesale of machinery, equipment and supplies (NACE Rev. 1 51.6)

Employment related indicators, 1997

	B	DK	D	EL	E	F	IRL	I (1)	L (1)	NL	A	P	FIN	S	UK
Number of persons employed (thousands)	49.9	:	198.8	:	:	269.3	11.0	83.8	3.2	118.5	40.9	35.4	27.1	:	:
Employees/number of persons employed (%)	86.8	:	:	:	:	98.8	94.1	75.8	90.0	94.2	92.5	96.0	95.7	:	:
Average no. of persons employed/enterprise (units)	:	:	14.0	:	:	8.0	14.0	5.8	5.0	11.0	10.0	8.0	7.0	:	:

(1) 1996.

Table 16.36

Wholesale of machinery, equipment and supplies (NACE Rev. 1 51.6)

Turnover related indicators, 1997

	B	DK	D	EL	E	F	IRL	I (1)	L (1)	NL	A	P	FIN	S (1)	UK (1)
Turnover (million ECU)	17,899	:	60,453	:	:	77,902	2,943	21,708	1,094	47,328	12,664	5,681	9,638	17,662	61,213
Turnover per enterprise (million ECU)	:	:	4.3	:	:	2.3	3.6	1.5	1.8	4.3	3.1	1.3	2.4	1.8	5.2
Turnover per person employed (thousand ECU)	358.5	:	304.2	:	:	289.3	266.8	259.0	345.3	399.4	309.7	160.5	355.1	:	:

(1) 1996.

Table 16.37

Wholesale of machinery, equipment and supplies (NACE Rev. 1 51.6)

Performance related indicators, 1997

	B	DK	D	EL	E	F	IRL	I (1)	L (1)	NL	A	P	FIN	S (1)	UK (1)
Value added (million ECU)	2,919	:	:	:	:	12,870	565	4,524	171	6,571	2,443	875	1,603	3,022	11,397
Value added as a share of turnover (%)	16.3	:	:	:	:	16.5	19.2	20.8	15.6	13.9	19.3	15.4	16.6	17.1	18.6
Apparent labour productivity (thousand ECU/person employed)	58.5	:	:	:	:	47.8	51.2	54.0	53.8	55.5	59.7	24.7	59.1	:	:
Unit personnel costs (thousand ECU)	46.4	:	:	:	:	38.7	:	37.7	35.6	34.4	42.4	15.8	39.0	42.8	:
Simple wage adjusted labour productivity (%)	145.3	:	:	:	:	125.0	:	188.8	168.1	171.0	152.3	162.8	158.4	144.2	190.4
Gross operating surplus (million ECU)	911	:	:	:	:	2,578	:	2,128	69	2,728	839	338	591	927	5,412

(1) 1996.

Source: Eurostat (SBS)

Table 16.38

Other wholesale (NACE Rev. 1 51.7)

Employment related indicators, 1997

	B	DK	D	EL	E	F	IRL	I (1)	L (1)	NL	A	P	FIN	S	UK
Number of persons employed (thousands)	7.1	:	83.2	:	:	6.2	4.9	41.0	0.4	22.1	2.7	16.0	7.7	:	:
Employees/number of persons employed (%)	84.9	:	:	:	:	93.0	88.6	69.9	65.4	91.2	84.1	88.2	98.4	:	:
Average no. of persons employed/enterprise (units)	:	:	50.0	:	:	1.0	6.0	4.4	2.0	5.0	5.0	4.0	16.0	:	:

(1) 1996.

Table 16.39

Other wholesale (NACE Rev. 1 51.7)

Turnover related indicators, 1997

	B	DK	D	EL	E	F	IRL	I (1)	L (1)	NL	A	P	FIN	S (1)	UK (1)
Turnover (million ECU)	3,043	:	41,102	:	:	2,698	1,023	13,241	179	6,667	2,575	3,205	7,175	274	39,909
Turnover per enterprise (million ECU)	:	:	24.8	:	:	0.5	1.3	1.4	0.8	1.5	5.1	0.9	14.5	0.6	1.4
Turnover per person employed (thousand ECU)	429.3	:	493.8	:	:	434.7	209.2	323.3	446.3	301.4	963.2	200.0	932.4	:	:

(1) 1996.

Table 16.40

Other wholesale (NACE Rev. 1 51.7)

Performance related indicators, 1997

	B	DK	D	EL	E	F	IRL	I (1)	L (1)	NL	A	P	FIN	S (1)	UK (1)
Value added (million ECU)	323	:	:	:	:	230	200	2,143	20	998	127	349	407	52	4,010
Value added as a share of turnover (%)	10.6	:	:	:	:	8.5	19.5	16.2	10.9	15.0	4.9	10.9	5.7	18.8	10.0
Apparent labour productivity (thousand ECU/person employed)	45.6	:	:	:	:	37.0	40.9	52.3	48.8	45.1	47.4	21.8	52.9	:	:
Unit personnel costs (thousand ECU)	33.1	:	:	:	:	30.3	:	34.2	34.8	26.2	35.4	12.2	32.4	30.6	:
Simple wage adjusted labour productivity (%)	162.1	:	:	:	:	131.4	:	218.8	215.4	188.9	159.3	202.0	165.8	142.3	182.0
Gross operating surplus (million ECU)	124	:	:	:	:	55	:	1,163	11	470	47	176	162	15	1,806

(1) 1996.

Source: Eurostat (SBS)

—————Table 16.41

Retail sale in non-specialized stores (NACE Rev. 1 52.1)

Employment related indicators, 1997

	B	DK (1)	D	EL	E	F	IRL	I (2)	L (2)	NL	A	P	FIN	S	UK
Number of persons employed (thousands)	80.5	73.3	893.8	:	:	521.3	63.4	367.8	4.4	227.1	66.1	78.8	49.6	:	:
Employees/number of persons employed (%)	89.0	95.6	:	:	:	96.5	86.4	64.3	93.8	97.8	92.9	86.7	94.8	:	:
Average no. of persons employed/enterprise (units)	:	20.0	28.0	:	:	15.0	11.0	4.3	15.0	53.0	15.0	6.0	11.0	:	:

(1) Employees as a share of the number of persons employed, 1996; (2) 1996.

—————Table 16.42

Retail sale in non-specialized stores (NACE Rev. 1 52.1)

Turnover related indicators, 1997

	B	DK	D	EL	E	F	IRL	I (1)	L (1)	NL	A	P	FIN	S (1)	UK (1)
Turnover (million ECU)	16,300	12,685	127,356	:	:	131,456	6,864	59,678	907	:	9,709	7,358	10,994	15,506	110,169
Turnover per enterprise (million ECU)	:	3.4	4.1	:	:	3.8	1.2	0.7	3.1	:	2.3	0.5	2.4	2.2	2.9
Turnover per person employed (thousand ECU)	202.6	173.1	142.5	:	:	252.2	108.2	162.3	208.2	:	146.8	93.4	221.8	:	:

(1) 1996.

—————Table 16.43

Retail sale in non-specialized stores (NACE Rev. 1 52.1)

Performance related indicators, 1997

	B	DK (1)	D	EL	E	F	IRL	I (2)	L (2)	NL	A	P	FIN	S (2)	UK (2)
Value added (million ECU)	2,357	:	:	:	:	16,013	1,118	8,197	117	:	1,385	904	1,679	2,189	8,849
Value added as a share of turnover (%)	14.5	:	:	:	:	12.2	16.3	13.7	12.9	:	14.3	12.3	15.3	14.1	8.0
Apparent labour productivity (thousand ECU/person employed)	29.3	:	:	:	:	30.7	17.6	22.3	27.0	:	20.9	11.5	33.9	:	:
Unit personnel costs (thousand ECU)	23.9	16.5	:	:	:	22.8	:	23.0	19.1	:	18.7	7.8	22.9	27.4	:
Simple wage adjusted labour productivity (%)	137.7	:	:	:	:	139.8	:	150.6	150.7	:	120.8	170.3	156.5	125.0	85.6
Gross operating surplus (million ECU)	645	289	:	:	:	4,560	:	2,754	40	:	238	373	606	438	-1,487

(1) Unit personnel costs, 1996; (2) 1996.

—————Table 16.44

Retail sale of food, beverages and tobacco in specialized stores (NACE Rev. 1 52.2)

Employment related indicators, 1997

	B	DK (1)	D	EL	E	F	IRL	I (2)	L (2)	NL	A	P	FIN	S	UK
Number of persons employed (thousands)	33.6	16.1	170.0	:	:	100.8	9.7	194.7	2.1	55.7	15.9	47.5	3.3	:	:
Employees/number of persons employed (%)	48.0	74.4	:	:	:	68.3	69.2	15.4	83.7	73.3	68.7	60.4	78.7	:	:
Average no. of persons employed/enterprise (units)	:	3.0	5.0	:	:	2.0	3.0	1.7	6.0	4.0	3.0	2.0	2.0	:	:

(1) Employees as a share of the number of persons employed, 1996; (2) 1996.

—————Table 16.45

Retail sale of food, beverages and tobacco in specialized stores (NACE Rev. 1 52.2)

Turnover related indicators, 1997

	B	DK	D	EL	E	F	IRL	I (1)	L (1)	NL	A	P	FIN	S (1)	UK (1)
Turnover (million ECU)	3,195	1,436	14,148	:	:	10,837	842	16,313	228	4,903	2,484	3,000	552	3,460	17,896
Turnover per enterprise (million ECU)	:	0.3	0.4	:	:	0.2	0.3	0.1	0.6	0.4	0.5	0.1	0.4	0.5	0.3
Turnover per person employed (thousand ECU)	95.2	89.0	83.2	:	:	107.5	86.9	83.8	108.8	88.0	156.4	63.2	165.4	:	:

(1) 1996.

—————Table 16.46

Retail sale of food, beverages and tobacco in specialized stores (NACE Rev. 1 52.2)

Performance related indicators, 1997

	B	DK (1)	D	EL	E	F	IRL	I (2)	L (2)	NL	A	P	FIN	S (2)	UK (2)
Value added (million ECU)	569	:	:	:	:	2,545	167	3,014	61	971	427	310	137	445	1,312
Value added as a share of turnover (%)	17.8	:	:	:	:	23.5	19.8	18.5	26.7	19.8	17.2	10.3	24.8	12.9	7.3
Apparent labour productivity (thousand ECU/person employed)	16.9	:	:	:	:	25.2	17.2	15.5	29.0	17.4	26.9	6.5	41.0	:	:
Unit personnel costs (thousand ECU)	15.5	14.7	:	:	:	23.1	:	17.7	18.5	11.6	19.4	6.7	31.6	27.7	:
Simple wage adjusted labour productivity (%)	227.7	:	:	:	:	159.7	:	570.3	187.9	204.4	201.7	160.5	165.0	144.9	81.7
Gross operating surplus (million ECU)	319	116	:	:	:	951	:	2,485	28	496	216	117	54	138	-294

(1) Unit personnel costs, 1996; (2) 1996.

Source: Eurostat (SBS)

Table 16.47

Retail sale of pharmaceutical and medical goods, cosmetic and toilet articles (NACE Rev. 1 52.3)

Employment related indicators, 1997

	B	DK (1)	D	EL	E	F	IRL	I (2)	L (2)	NL	A	P	FIN	S	UK
Number of persons employed (thousands)	19.0	9.2	253.4	:	:	141.0	7.1	88.1	0.9	36.5	21.7	19.4	7.4	:	:
Employees/number of persons employed (%)	68.8	92.4	:	:	:	86.5	88.4	46.3	82.9	89.3	90.4	89.9	89.9	:	:
Average no. of persons employed/enterprise (units)	:	12.0	10.0	:	:	5.0	6.0	2.7	6.0	10.0	11.0	4.0	6.0	:	:

(1) Employees as a share of the number of persons employed, 1996; (2) 1996.

Table 16.48

Retail sale of pharmaceutical and medical goods, cosmetic and toilet articles (NACE Rev. 1 52.3)

Turnover related indicators, 1997

	B	DK	D	EL	E	F	IRL	I (1)	L (1)	NL (1)	A	P	FIN	S (1)	UK (1)
Turnover (million ECU)	3,215	1,237	29,200	:	:	23,005	755	13,318	167	4,575	2,821	2,372	1,212	2,891	9,061
Turnover per enterprise (million ECU)	:	1.6	1.2	:	:	0.8	0.7	0.4	1.2	1.4	1.5	0.5	1.0	3.1	1.2
Turnover per person employed (thousand ECU)	169.2	134.2	115.2	:	:	163.2	106.6	151.1	192.2	134.3	130.0	122.0	163.4	:	:

(1) 1996.

Table 16.49

Retail sale of pharmaceutical and medical goods, cosmetic and toilet articles (NACE Rev. 1 52.3)

Performance related indicators, 1997

	B	DK (1)	D	EL	E	F	IRL	I (2)	L (2)	NL (2)	A	P	FIN	S (2)	UK (2)
Value added (million ECU)	648	:	:	:	:	5,785	173	2,695	37	1,491	710	446	309	490	678
Value added as a share of turnover (%)	20.2	:	:	:	:	25.1	22.9	20.2	21.8	32.6	25.2	18.8	25.5	16.9	7.5
Apparent labour productivity (thousand ECU/person employed)	34.1	:	:	:	:	41.0	24.4	30.6	41.9	43.8	32.7	22.9	41.6	:	:
Unit personnel costs (thousand ECU)	21.9	24.0	:	:	:	26.6	:	21.3	23.7	18.0	21.2	12.4	25.0	36.8	:
Simple wage adjusted labour productivity (%)	226.4	:	:	:	:	178.1	:	309.9	213.5	272.6	170.4	205.2	185.0	125.9	72.9
Gross operating surplus (million ECU)	362	42	:	:	:	2,536	:	1,826	19	944	293	229	142	101	-252

(1) Unit personnel costs, 1996; (2) 1996.

Table 16.50

Other retail sale of new goods in specialized stores (NACE Rev. 1 52.4)

Employment related indicators, 1997

	B	DK (1)	D	EL	E	F	IRL	I (2)	L (2)	NL	A	P	FIN	S	UK
Number of persons employed (thousands)	124.9	87.4	1,170.2	:	:	573.7	48.4	680.8	9.2	286.1	142.3	219.2	36.0	:	:
Employees/number of persons employed (%)	58.3	83.0	:	:	:	85.6	79.3	33.8	79.9	80.4	85.4	81.6	81.6	:	:
Average no. of persons employed/enterprise (units)	:	5.0	7.0	:	:	3.0	5.0	2.0	4.0	7.0	7.0	4.0	3.0	:	:

(1) Employees as a share of the number of persons employed, 1996; (2) 1996.

Table 16.51

Other retail sale of new goods in specialized stores (NACE Rev. 1 52.4)

Turnover related indicators, 1997

	B	DK	D	EL	E	F	IRL	I (1)	L (1)	NL	A	P	FIN	S (1)	UK (1)
Turnover (million ECU)	17,737	8,964	113,194	:	:	76,460	4,644	64,994	1,208	27,659	15,830	15,237	5,269	13,320	86,616
Turnover per enterprise (million ECU)	:	0.5	0.7	:	:	0.4	0.5	0.2	0.6	0.6	0.8	0.2	0.4	0.4	1.0
Turnover per person employed (thousand ECU)	142.0	102.6	96.7	:	:	133.3	95.9	95.5	131.0	96.7	111.3	69.5	146.5	:	:

(1) 1996.

Table 16.52

Other retail sale of new goods in specialized stores (NACE Rev. 1 52.4)

Performance related indicators, 1997

	B	DK (1)	D	EL	E	F	IRL	I (2)	L (2)	NL	A	P	FIN	S (2)	UK (2)
Value added (million ECU)	2,733	:	:	:	:	16,578	894	12,324	256	6,156	3,639	2,266	1,071	2,780	10,482
Value added as a share of turnover (%)	15.4	:	:	:	:	21.7	19.3	19.0	21.2	22.3	23.0	14.9	20.3	20.9	12.1
Apparent labour productivity (thousand ECU/person employed)	21.9	:	:	:	:	28.9	18.5	18.1	27.8	21.5	25.6	10.3	29.8	:	:
Unit personnel costs (thousand ECU)	20.1	18.9	:	:	:	24.4	:	21.5	20.6	15.1	21.7	8.3	21.9	27.1	:
Simple wage adjusted labour productivity (%)	186.9	:	:	:	:	138.3	:	248.5	168.6	176.9	137.9	151.9	166.8	141.4	107.1
Gross operating surplus (million ECU)	1,271	616	:	:	:	4,591	:	7,365	104	2,675	1,001	774	429	815	691

(1) Unit personnel costs, 1996; (2) 1996.

Source: Eurostat (SBS)

_____Table 16.53

Retail sale of second-hand goods in stores (NACE Rev. 1 52.5)
Employment related indicators, 1997

	B	DK (1)	D	EL	E	F	IRL	I (2)	L (2)	NL	A	P	FIN	S	UK
Number of persons employed (thousands)	2.8	1.4	6.8	:	:	12.8	1.0	4.0	0.1	4.8	1.9	1.3	0.6	:	:
Employees/number of persons employed (%)	14.4	29.9	:	:	:	52.5	38.6	21.6	35.1	48.5	45.6	66.7	39.1	:	:
Average no. of persons employed/enterprise (units)	:	1.0	2.0	:	:	1.0	2.0	1.6	1.0	2.0	2.0	2.0	1.0	:	:

(1) Employees as a share of the number of persons employed, 1996; (2) 1996.

_____Table 16.54

Retail sale of second-hand goods in stores (NACE Rev. 1 52.5)
Turnover related indicators, 1997

	B	DK	D	EL	E	F	IRL	I (1)	L (1)	NL	A	P	FIN	S (1)	UK (1)
Turnover (million ECU)	189	70	415	:	:	1,353	47	207	5	:	110	63	42	147	1,857
Turnover per enterprise (million ECU)	:	0.1	0.1	:	:	0.1	0.1	0.1	0.1	:	0.1	0.1	0.1	0.1	0.4
Turnover per person employed (thousand ECU)	67.6	49.4	61.0	:	:	105.9	48.3	51.5	81.7	:	59.1	47.4	67.5	:	:

(1) 1996.

_____Table 16.55

Retail sale of second-hand goods in stores (NACE Rev. 1 52.5)
Performance related indicators, 1997

	B	DK (1)	D	EL	E	F	IRL	I (2)	L (2)	NL	A	P	FIN	S (2)	UK (2)
Value added (million ECU)	54	:	:	:	:	282	13	58	1	:	34	10	10	28	107
Value added as a share of turnover (%)	28.8	:	:	:	:	20.8	28.6	27.9	25.5	:	31.3	15.9	22.9	19.0	5.8
Apparent labour productivity (thousand ECU/person employed)	19.5	:	:	:	:	22.1	13.9	14.4	20.9	:	18.5	7.6	15.4	:	:
Unit personnel costs (thousand ECU)	13.8	16.1	:	:	:	25.8	:	23.1	20.8	:	19.9	8.8	18.0	20.9	:
Simple wage adjusted labour productivity (%)	971.4	:	:	:	:	162.7	:	288.1	300.0	:	204.8	129.9	220.5	224.2	77.0
Gross operating surplus (million ECU)	49	12	:	:	:	109	:	38	1	:	18	2	5	15	-32

(1) Unit personnel costs, 1996; (2) 1996.

_____Table 16.56

Retail sale not in stores (NACE Rev. 1 52.6)
Employment related indicators, 1997

	B	DK (1)	D	EL	E	F	IRL	I (2)	L (2)	NL	A	P	FIN	S	UK
Number of persons employed (thousands)	9.1	2.9	198.5	:	:	85.4	0.9	134.5	0.5	26.9	7.4	9.3	1.5	:	:
Employees/number of persons employed (%)	29.8	60.0	:	:	:	69.0	80.6	6.5	53.5	50.1	77.1	19.8	84.1	:	:
Average no. of persons employed/enterprise (units)	:	2.0	5.0	:	:	1.0	6.0	1.3	2.0	2.0	5.0	1.0	2.0	:	:

(1) Employees as a share of the number of persons employed, 1996; (2) 1996.

_____Table 16.57

Retail sale not in stores (NACE Rev. 1 52.6)
Turnover related indicators, 1997

	B	DK	D	EL	E	F	IRL	I (1)	L (1)	NL	A	P	FIN	S (1)	UK (1)
Turnover (million ECU)	1,076	284	32,994	:	:	11,366	133	8,435	54	3,032	1,176	436	342	966	11,310
Turnover per enterprise (million ECU)	:	0.2	0.8	:	:	0.2	0.9	0.1	0.3	0.2	0.7	0.1	0.4	0.5	1.8
Turnover per person employed (thousand ECU)	118.3	98.0	166.2	:	:	133.1	149.1	62.7	118.9	112.8	159.3	47.1	225.1	:	:

(1) 1996.

_____Table 16.58

Retail sale not in stores (NACE Rev. 1 52.6)
Performance related indicators, 1997

	B	DK (1)	D	EL	E	F	IRL	I (2)	L (2)	NL	A	P	FIN	S (2)	UK (2)
Value added (million ECU)	152	:	:	:	:	2,031	29	1,431	10	649	257	64	56	178	1,451
Value added as a share of turnover (%)	14.1	:	:	:	:	17.9	21.9	17.0	17.9	21.4	21.8	14.7	16.5	18.4	12.8
Apparent labour productivity (thousand ECU/person employed)	16.7	:	:	:	:	23.8	32.6	10.6	21.4	24.1	34.8	6.9	37.2	:	:
Unit personnel costs (thousand ECU)	22.8	19.0	:	:	:	26.2	:	23.6	19.2	14.3	27.0	11.7	23.6	32.3	:
Simple wage adjusted labour productivity (%)	246.4	:	:	:	:	131.7	:	695.5	206.4	336.3	167.4	299.1	188.0	128.0	128.4
Gross operating surplus (million ECU)	90	13	:	:	:	488	:	1,226	5	456	103	43	26	39	321

(1) Unit personnel costs, 1996; (2) 1996.

Source: Eurostat (SBS)

Table 16.59

Repair of personal and household goods (NACE Rev. 1 52.7)

Employment related indicators, 1997

	B	DK (1)	D	EL	E	F	IRL	I (2)	L (2)	NL	A	P	FIN	S	UK
Number of persons employed (thousands)	3.0	4.3	:	:	:	30.3	1.5	40.7	0.2	7.3	2.8	11.3	2.0	:	:
Employees/number of persons employed (%)	30.5	59.3	:	:	:	61.3	46.2	16.7	63.4	30.1	65.1	43.7	56.3	:	:
Average no. of persons employed/enterprise (units)	:	2.0	:	:	:	2.0	2.0	1.4	3.0	2.0	3.0	2.0	1.0	:	:

(1) Employees as a share of the number of persons employed, 1996; (2) 1996.

Table 16.60

Repair of personal and household goods (NACE Rev. 1 52.7)

Turnover related indicators, 1997

	B	DK	D	EL	E	F	IRL	I (1)	L (1)	NL	A	P	FIN	S (1)	UK (1)
Turnover (million ECU)	164	241	:	:	:	1,520	54	1,327	9	:	117	250	121	419	538
Turnover per enterprise (million ECU)	:	0.1	:	:	:	0.1	0.1	0.0	0.1	:	0.1	0.0	0.1	0.1	0.3
Turnover per person employed (thousand ECU)	55.2	56.3	:	:	:	50.2	35.8	32.6	43.5	:	42.0	22.1	60.2	:	:

(1) 1996.

Table 16.61

Repair of personal and household goods (NACE Rev. 1 52.7)

Performance related indicators, 1997

	B	DK (1)	D	EL	E	F	IRL	I (2)	L (2)	NL	A	P	FIN	S (2)	UK (2)
Value added (million ECU)	61	:	:	:	:	681	25	467	5	:	60	62	49	154	75
Value added as a share of turnover (%)	37.1	:	:	:	:	44.8	45.2	35.2	52.8	:	51.4	24.7	40.2	36.8	13.9
Apparent labour productivity (thousand ECU/person employed)	20.4	:	:	:	:	22.5	16.2	11.5	22.9	:	21.6	5.5	24.2	:	:
Unit personnel costs (thousand ECU)	27.5	23.3	:	:	:	26.5	:	17.2	18.8	:	22.4	8.5	21.3	30.6	:
Simple wage adjusted labour productivity (%)	243.8	:	:	:	:	138.8	:	398.7	195.8	:	148.3	147.4	201.7	145.4	39.9
Gross operating surplus (million ECU)	36	40	:	:	:	190	:	350	2	:	20	20	25	48	-113

(1) Unit personnel costs, 1996; (2) 1996.

Source: Eurostat (SBS)

Tourism (NACE Rev. 1 55, 63.3, 92.33 and 92.53)

Tourism can be defined as a sector serving persons travelling to and staying in places outside their usual environment for not more than one consecutive year for leisure or business purposes. It is a concept involving a wide range of activities that is best viewed as a market rather than a sector. This chapter covers activities which make up a significant part of the tourism market: hotels and restaurants (NACE Rev. 1 55), recreation, zoological and amusement parks (NACE Rev. 1 92.33 and 92.53) and travel agencies (NACE Rev. 1 63.3).

	Table 17.1
Top 10 tourism destinations, 1999	

	International tourist arrivals (millions)
F	71.4
E	52.0
USA	47.0
I	35.8
China	27.0
UK	25.7
Mexico	20.2
Canada	19.6
Poland	17.9
A	17.6

Source: World Tourism Organisation

The activities covered in this chapter (in terms of NACE Rev. 1) include:

55:	hotels and restaurants;
55.1:	hotels;
55.2:	camping sites and other provision of short-stay accommodation;
55.3:	restaurants;
55.4:	bars;
55.5:	canteens and catering;
63.3:	activities of travel agencies and tour operators; tourist assistance activities n.e.c.;
92.33:	fair and amusement park activities;
92.53:	botanical and zoological gardens and nature reserves activities.

Tourism is strongly linked to personal mobility that has rapidly developed in the second half of the 20th century. It has been supported by a dramatic improvement in communications and a growing internationalisation of the world economy. In this context, tourism also assumes a role of redistribution of resources and may become a factor of economic development both at a regional level in Europe and worldwide.

France, Spain and Italy, the most popular destinations, Germany the top spender
Tourism has rapidly developed in the EU over the last fifteen years. The number of international arrivals[1] into the Member States grew by an estimated 4.1% per annum since 1985, despite stagnation in the first half of the 1990s. Countries like Ireland (6.5 million visitors) and the Netherlands (9.8 million) recorded a growth of more than 9% on average per annum between 1993 and 1999, whilst Austria was the only country witnessing a decline in arrivals, from 19.0 million in 1990 to 17.6 million in 1999.

France, with a relatively modest 3.5% average annual growth rate of arrivals in the 1990s, remained the country welcoming the largest number of tourists. In 1999 some 71.4 million international arrivals were recorded in France, or 10.7% of the world total. Within the EU, France was followed by Spain, ranking second in the world with 52.0 million arrivals, and Italy, the fourth most visited destination in the world with 35.8 million arrivals.

(1) Number of visitors who stay at least one night in a collective or private accommodation in the country visited. Please note that when a person visits the same country several times a year, an equivalent number of arrivals is recorded.

Figure 17.1

Lodging and catering services (NACE-CLIO 59)

Share of total market services value added and employment, 1997 (%)

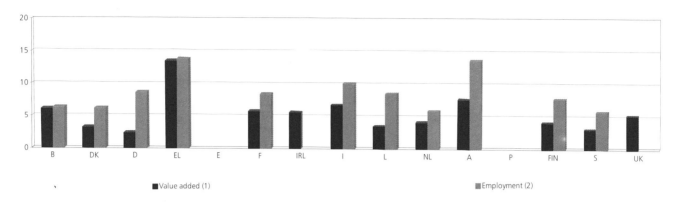

■ Value added (1)   ■ Employment (2)

(1) D, EL, F, L and A, value added at market prices; DK, D, IRL, S and UK, 1996; E and P, not available.
(2) B, DK, D, A and S, 1996; E, IRL, P and UK, not available.

Source: Eurostat (SEC2)

Table 17.2

Top 10 tourism earners, 1998

	International tourism receipts (billion ECU)
USA	63.6
F	26.7
I	26.6
E	26.5
UK	18.7
D	14.7
China	11.2
A	10.0
Canada	8.4
Poland	7.1

Source: World Tourism Organisation

Table 17.3

Top 10 tourism spenders, 1998

	International tourism expenditure (billion ECU)
USA	50.0
D	41.8
UK	28.8
JAP	25.7
F	15.9
I	15.7
NL	10.0
Canada	9.6
A	8.5
China	8.2

Source: World Tourism Organisation

These three countries were also the world's top tourism earners in 1998 behind the USA. Their international tourism receipts[2] were close to each other: 26.7 billion ECU for France, 26.6 billion ECU for Italy and 26.5 billion ECU for Spain, representing altogether a fifth of the world total.

Germany was the world's second largest tourism spender after the USA in 1998. International tourism expenditure of German tourists reached 41.8 billion ECU, compared to 50.0 billion ECU for Americans. British tourists followed with international tourism expenditure reaching 28.8 billion ECU.

(2) International tourism receipts are generally gathered in the framework of the Balance of Payments. Data covers all receipts made by tourists (including same-day visitors) on goods and services in the country visited. This includes lodging, food and beverages, entertainment, gifts and souvenirs exported and transport within the country. It excludes however international transport.

STRUCTURE AND PERFORMANCE

Due to its composite nature and the variety of activities involved either directly or indirectly, the relative importance of tourism in the European economy is not straightforward to assess. According to estimates of the European Commission[3], enterprises directly involved in tourism activities numbered more than 2 million in the European Union in 1998, employing no less than 9 million persons, and accounting for at least 5.5% of GDP and 30% of total external trade in services. Besides these direct jobs, it is also necessary to consider indirect or spin-off jobs created in other sectors of the economy influenced by tourism.

Most are HORECA businesses

Lodging and catering activities constitute the largest share of tourism. Available Eurostat data suggest that hotels and restaurants represented approximately 1.3 million enterprises within the Union. In addition, National Accounts statistics reveal that the branch of hotels and restaurants employed more than 6 million persons in 1997, about 4.3% of the total number of persons employed in the EU. It also accounted for about 2.8% of total EU value added, representing around 182 billion ECU. In Greece (7.1%) and Spain (6.7%) the relative importance of these activities was more than double that of the EU average, whilst it was less than half in the Nordic countries.

(3) Source: "Enhancing Tourism's Potential for Employment", Communication from the Commission to the European Parliament and to the Council, COM(205) final of 28 April 1999.

Table 17.4

Hotels and restaurants (NACE Rev.1 55)

Breakdown of turnover and employment by employment size class, 1997 (%)

	Micro (0-9)		Small (10-49)		Medium (50-249)		Large (250+)	
	Turnover (1)	Employment (2)	Turnover (1)	Employment (2)	Turnover (1)	Employment (2)	Turnover (1)	Employment (2)
EU-15	49.7	53.2	20.2	21.0	10.7	8.6	19.4	17.2
B	58.8	70.9	20.4	17.6	8.0	4.4	12.9	7.2
DK	56.4	60.2	24.9	24.2	10.7	8.2	8.0	7.5
D	52.0	53.2	26.5	27.3	11.4	9.6	10.0	9.9
EL	:	:	:	:	:	:	:	:
E	46.7	63.1	15.2	18.1	21.0	10.0	17.1	8.8
F	54.9	62.4	20.8	18.8	7.1	5.5	17.3	13.3
IRL	:	:	:	:	:	:	:	:
I	60.5	66.9	21.1	18.9	6.9	5.5	11.6	8.6
L	:	:	:	:	:	:	:	:
NL	:	59.0	:	20.1	:	11.4	:	9.6
A	48.3	53.4	32.9	31.5	12.5	10.8	6.2	4.3
P	53.1	61.0	21.3	20.2	14.2	10.1	11.3	8.6
FIN	42.2	40.1	22.1	21.2	11.1	11.3	24.6	27.5
S	33.2	39.2	33.2	29.3	17.3	14.9	16.4	16.6
UK	28.8	26.7	16.3	16.3	8.5	7.6	46.4	49.4

(1) EU-15, DK, E, F, I, P and S, 1996.
(2) EU-15, DK, F, I, NL, P and S, 1996.

Source: Eurostat (SME)

LABOUR AND PRODUCTIVITY

Different work patterns may be found within the tourism sector than those generally found in other more traditional industries. There are more flexible working patterns, often characterised by a high seasonal component, whilst there is a high degree of precariousness for many job holders. Only 72.6% of the total number of persons employed in hotels and restaurants in the EU in 1998 worked full-time, amongst the lowest shares of all economic activities, compared to 82.7% for the whole EU economy. Differences amongst Member States were wide-ranging: the Netherlands (39.8%), the United Kingdom (49.5%) and Denmark (53.0%) recorded the lowest proportion of full-time employment, whilst more than 90.0% of the persons employed in Luxembourg, Portugal and Greece were working full-time.

Hotels and restaurants also displayed a higher than average proportion of temporary jobs or limited-duration contracts. Only 78.2% of the persons employed in hotels and restaurants in 1998 in the EU had a permanent contract, down from 80.3% in 1992. Again variability across the EU was considerable: the shares ranged from as low as 54.8% in Spain and 65.4% in Sweden, to as high as 90.6% in Belgium and 98.3% in Luxembourg.

Finally, it is in this sector that the highest proportion of "atypical" working patterns can be found: only a small proportion of persons employed never worked on Saturdays (12.2% in 1999), Sundays (21.0%), evenings (22.6%) or nights (42.8%).

High proportion of female employment

This flexibility in work patterns may explain the attraction that the sector has for women and young people, with many jobs often constituting the first step on the employment ladder or a return to the employment market after a period of not working. The Labour Force Survey reveals that women accounted for 52.9% of the labour force in hotels and restaurants in 1998, a much higher share than in the whole economy (41.9%). The share of females in the total varied from 41.5% in Greece and 45.8% Spain to 66.5% in Denmark and 68.0% in Finland. In contrast, the share of persons employed in hotels and restaurants with a higher education level was one of the lowest of all service activities, at just 8.3%[4]. In Italy, Austria and Portugal the share of highly educated persons was below 3.0%. Only two countries displayed a share clearly above the average: Finland (16.7%) and Ireland (18.7%).

Low labour costs and apparent productivity

The combination of flexible working patterns and a high presence of unskilled manpower may explain the low level of labour costs. EU unit personnel costs

Table 17.5

Hotels and restaurants (NACE Rev.1 55)

Composition of the labour force, 1999 (%)

	Women (1)	Part-time (2)	Highly-educated (3)
EU-15	52.9	27.2	7.6
B	53.0	25.9	11.1
DK	66.5	47.0	12.4
D	58.1	29.0	9.5
EL	41.5	6.0	7.7
E	46.2	14.0	10.1
F	46.9	24.0	10.2
IRL	59.2	37.7	18.7
I	45.8	11.7	2.5
L	47.9	9.8	:
NL	51.9	60.2	5.0
A	63.7	20.2	1.8
P	58.4	7.6	2.4
FIN	68.0	27.4	16.7
S	57.4	32.7	12.0
UK	60.6	50.5	9.7

(1) EU-15 and EL, 1998.
(2) EU-15, B and EL, 1998.
(3) EL, 1998; EU-15, IRL and UK, 1997.

Source: Eurostat (LFS)

in the activities covered in this chapter could be estimated at around 20.0 thousand ECU in 1997, with travel agencies recording the highest average (29.8 thousand ECU), followed by hotels (20.3 thousand ECU) and restaurants and bars (under 17.0 thousand ECU).

(4) 1999, excluding EL.

Apparent labour productivity in the activities covered by this chapter was estimated at 21.3 thousand ECU of value added per person employed in 1997. In terms of profitability, however, the gross operating rate (operating surplus as a share of turnover) could be estimated at a respectable level of 14.1% in 1997.

INTERNATIONAL COMPARISON

Europe the world's tourism market leader

Between 1985 and 1999, according to the World Tourism Organisation, the number of international tourist arrivals grew at an average annual rate of 5.1% worldwide, rising from 327 million to 657 million. Europe (using its geographical definition which includes eastern European countries) maintained its position as the market leader, despite a declining market share. Almost 59% of international tourists chose Europe as their destination in 1999, compared to 64.8% in 1985. The EU makes up the largest part of this market, accounting for around 40%.

It should be noted that these figures exclude domestic tourism, as well as same-day visitors, but that intra-European tourism is considered as international. It is estimated that about two-thirds of the total number of holidays taken by European residents can be classified as domestic, whilst more than one fifth concern international tourism between Member States. The statistics also neglect the growing importance of day trips to neighbouring countries that can constitute up to 50% of all trips abroad.

America constitutes the second most popular tourism destination in the world. Its market share in 1999 was 19.3%, only slightly lower than its level of 1985 thanks to an increase in visitors to South America (from 2.1% to 2.9%) that compensated slower growth in North America, whose market share fell from 14.8% to 13.2%.

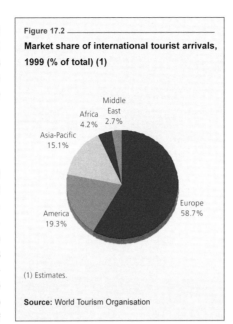

Figure 17.2

Market share of international tourist arrivals, 1999 (% of total) (1)

Middle East 2.7%
Africa 4.2%
Asia-Pacific 15.1%
America 19.3%
Europe 58.7%

(1) Estimates.

Source: World Tourism Organisation

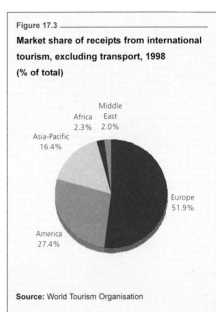

Figure 17.3

Market share of receipts from international tourism, excluding transport, 1998 (% of total)

Middle East 2.0%
Africa 2.3%
Asia-Pacific 16.4%
America 27.4%
Europe 51.9%

Source: World Tourism Organisation

Table 17.6

International tourist arrivals by region of departure, 1998 (%)

from:	World	Africa	America	East Asia/ Pacific	Europe	Middle East	South Asia	Other
to:								
Africa	3.7	66.0	0.7	0.6	2.6	10.4	1.9	6.1
America	19.2	2.3	71.6	10.5	6.0	3.2	6.5	6.9
East Asia/Pacific	14.2	2.7	5.5	72.6	3.1	3.2	25.2	1.2
Europe	59.7	70.3	21.2	14.5	86.5	21.1	25.6	80.0
Middle East	2.4	7.8	0.6	1.1	1.2	59.5	16.9	5.8
South Asia	0.8	0.9	0.4	0.7	0.7	2.6	23.9	0.0

Source: World Tourism Organisation

The fastest growing tourist destination in the world was East Asia and the Pacific (including countries such as Japan, China, Thailand or Australia) where international tourist arrivals increased by an annual average rate of 8.2% between 1985 and 1999, despite two years of decline in 1997 and 1998, to reach 93.7 million visitors in 1999.

As a general rule, tourists from a given world region stay inside that region. This is the case for 59.5% of Middle East tourists up to 86.5% of European tourists. But less than one quarter of southern Asian tourists (from India, Iran, Nepal or Pakistan) stayed in their region. Europe was the destination of more than a fifth of African, American and Middle-Eastern tourists and more than a quarter of South Asians.

More generally, the concentration of tourist destinations has strongly decreased over the last thirty years. Whilst the five most popular destinations attracted 43% of the world's tourists in 1970, and 65% for the top 10, these shares fell to 35% and 50% respectively in 1999.

Box 17.1

According to a Eurobarometer survey carried out on behalf of the European Commission in 1998, every second European goes away from home on holiday (53%), a proportion higher in the northern countries and amongst the 25-39 age group (59%). The typical European holiday maker leaves in August (41%) for 2 weeks or more (35.6%), and uses his own car (58%) to drive to Spain or France with his partner (61%) and/or children (25%). He arranged his holidays himself (75%) rather than relying on a travel agency (15%), and chose his destination for the scenery (49%) and the climate (45%), preferably on the seaside (63%) and in a hotel or holiday club (42%). In total he spent about 2,000 ECU for his holidays (67%), mainly in cash (44%).

SUB-CHAPTER 17.1
HOTELS AND CAMPING SITES
(NACE Rev. 1 55.1 AND 55.2)

Hotels and other provision of short-stay accommodation are covered by two NACE Rev. 1 Groups: Group 55.1 includes the provision of short-stay lodging in hotels, motels and inns, excluding the rental of long-stay accommodation and timeshare operations; Group 55.2 covers camping sites and other provision of short-stay accommodation, including youth hostels, holiday chalets or cottages.

185 thousand hotels with 48 rooms on average
According to EU official statistics (Tour database) there were more than 185 thousand hotels and similar establishments in the EU in 1998, down from 188 thousand in 1994. The EU had a total of 9 million bedplaces, up from 8.7 million in 1994. The United Kingdom alone numbered more than one quarter of all the establishments (47.5 thousand) and Germany

more than one fifth (38.9 thousand), but they were generally smaller than in the other Member States. The average European establishment had 48 rooms, compared to only 5.5 in Ireland, 11.6 in the United Kingdom (where bed & breakfast was a common form of tourist accommodation) and 21.4 in Germany. In contrast, establishments in Spain were the largest with 67.4 rooms per establishment respectively.

—————Table 17.7

Main indicators for hotels and similar establishments, 1998 (thousands)

	B	DK (1)	D	EL	E	F	IRL	I	L	NL	A	P	FIN	S	UK
Number of establishments (2)	2.0	0.5	38.9	7.9	7.5	19.6	5.2	33.5	0.3	2.8	15.8	1.8	1.0	1.9	47.5
Number of bedrooms (3)	51.1	30.5	833.4	304.8	508.5	653.3	28.5	949.8	7.7	:	310.6	94.8	53.6	94.3	553.0
Number of bedplaces (2)	116	60	1,547	585	979	1,451	107	1,782	15	169	585	216	110	185	1,096
Arrivals of residents (4)	1,740	1,550	62,982	5,375	25,583	55,345	:	35,552	16	:	5,299	4,021	5,202	9,299	31,169
Arrivals of non-residents (5)	4,859	1,305	14,457	6,785	20,199	32,339	:	25,927	525	:	12,803	4,974	1,655	2,143	17,188
Nights spent, residents (2)	3,498	4,339	147,274	13,984	66,552	96,696	5,583	126,178	81	12,622	16,483	9,164	9,494	15,643	81,093
Nights spent, non-residents (2)	9,483	4,462	29,735	42,565	111,803	66,330	13,220	87,192	1,089	14,262	53,503	23,241	3,226	4,409	69,309

(1) Number of establishments, bedrooms and bedplaces refer to hotels with at least 40 bedplaces only.
(2) 1997, IRL.
(3) 1997, EL and A; 1995, IRL.
(4) 1997, EL and S.
(5) 1997, EL.

Source: Eurostat (TOUR)

—————Table 17.8

Main hotel chains in the world by number of rooms, 1999

		Country	Brands	Number of rooms (thousands)	Number of sites (units)	Average number of rooms per site (units)
1	Cendant Corp	USA	Days Inn, Ramada, Super 8, H. Johnson, Travelodge, Knights Inn	519	5,813	89
2	Bass Hotels & Resorts	UK	Holiday Inn, Crowne Plaza, Inter-Continental	471	2,757	171
3	Choice Hotels Intl.	USA	Comfort Inn, Econo Lodge, Quality Inn, Clarion	421	5,147	82
4	Marriott	USA	Marriott, Renaissance, Courtyard, Residence Inn, Fairfield Inn	329	1,664	198
5	Best Western	USA	Best Western	312	4,012	78
6	Accor	F	Sofitel, Novotel, Mercure, Ibis, Etap Hôtel, Formule 1, Motel 6	294	2,663	110
7	Starwood	USA	Sheraton, Four Points, Westin, W Hotels	241	675	357
8	Promus Hotel Corp. (1)	USA	Hampton Inn, Embassy Suites, Homewood Suites, Doubletree	192	1,325	145
9	Hilton Hotels Corp. (1)	USA	Hilton, Conrad	140	418	336
10	Carlson Hospitality	USA	Regent, Radisson, Country Inn	108	560	193
11	Hyatt	USA	Hyatt	85	186	454
12	Grupo Sol Meliá	E	Meliá Hotels, Sol Hotels	65	244	267
13	La Société du Louvre	F	Concorde, Campanile, Première Classe, Bleu Marine, Clarine	52	668	78
14	Golden Tulip Intl.	UK	Golden Tulip, Tulip Inn	49	373	130
15	Granada Plc	UK	Le Meridien, Forte Posthouse, Forte Heritage	44	249	176

(1) Hilton Hotels Corporation acquired Promus Hotel Corporation in 1999.

Source: Trade press, company data

These figures illustrate a general trend in the EU towards reduction in the number of establishments and a gradual increase in accommodation capacity in absolute terms as well as in terms of average size. This can in part be explained by a trend witnessed within the hotel industry towards greater concentration, the development of partnership agreements between hotel chains and the emergence of regional, national or global hotel networks. Hotel chains may for example achieve economies of scale through centralised reservation systems or grouped marketing initiatives. There is also a strong trend in the hotel industry towards the development of franchising and contract management of hotels, as distinct from direct ownership. One of the factors explaining the success of the franchising formula is that it associates a hotel with a well-known national or international brand.

Low apparent productivity but
good profitability ratios

Apparent labour productivity in hotels and similar establishments was relatively low compared to other service activities. It was estimated at 27.6 thousand ECU of value added per person employed in the EU in 1997. Available data for individual Member States revealed that it ranged between 14.2 thousand ECU in Portugal and 51.1 thousand ECU in the Netherlands. For most other countries (apparent labour productivity) was close to 30.0 thousand ECU.

Profitability (as measured by the ratio of gross operating surplus to turnover) was estimated at 20.4% in 1997. Sweden (8.0%), France (12.1%) and Finland (12.5%) were clearly below the average, as opposed to Luxembourg (22.8%), Italy (23.1%) and the Netherlands (53.0%).

A recent worldwide hotel industry study by Horwath Consulting revealed that only about half of the revenue of European hotels was accounted for by room rental (51.3%), whilst the worldwide average was 56.3%, and in North American hotels it was equivalent to 64.8% of total revenue. Conversely, food and beverages accounted for as much as 41.3% of hotel revenue in Europe, compared to only 27.9% in North America.

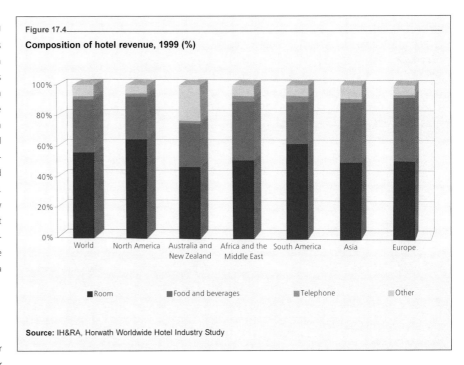

Figure 17.4

Composition of hotel revenue, 1999 (%)

■ Room   ■ Food and beverages   ■ Telephone   ▨ Other

Source: IH&RA, Horwath Worldwide Hotel Industry Study

High fluctuation of demand

One of the major problems facing the hotel industry is the fluctuation of demand: calculated on a weekly basis, the share of rooms sold on Wednesdays is almost 50% higher than the share sold on Sundays within the European hotel industry. Similarly, August records 11.5% of the yearly room sales, twice as much as in December or January. The long-term trend towards multiple holidays and the growth of the "short breaks" market, which hotels and travel operators have actively courted through special packages and discounts helps to smooth the seasonality of demand for tourist accommodation to some degree.

Box 17.2

Technological change pervades across many areas of the hotel trade, although it is difficult to assess its impact on EU hotel operators, notably on small- and medium-sized establishments. Significant process and product innovations have occurred in areas such as operations management (for example, specific software applications used for purchasing, sales and catering management systems), client interfaces (in-room services, room check-out, etc.), business services and entertainment (video-conferencing, interactive TV communication systems) and reservation systems. On this latter point it is interesting to note that advance reservation through Internet sites or via e-mail, represented only 1.8% of the total reservations made in 1999 (1.2% in Europe and 3.1% in North America). Whilst print advertising remains by far the most common marketing medium (used by more than 92.2% of hotels worldwide), 65.8% of those companies taking part in the Horwath survey used their own web page for advertising in 1999 (64.6% in Europe and 72.7% in North America) and 36.1% a third-party Internet site. Bookings through the Internet are expected to become much more significant in the future as hotels further increase their presence on the Internet and on-line reservation sites become more accessible to travellers.

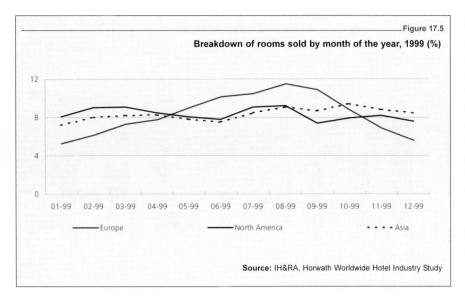

Figure 17.5

Breakdown of rooms sold by month of the year, 1999 (%)

Source: IH&RA, Horwath Worldwide Hotel Industry Study

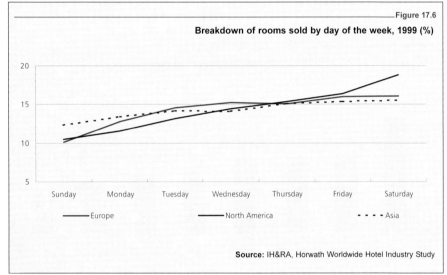

Figure 17.6

Breakdown of rooms sold by day of the week, 1999 (%)

Source: IH&RA, Horwath Worldwide Hotel Industry Study

The rate of utilisation of hotels' bedplaces can be estimated with the net occupancy rate, a ratio between the number of registered overnight stays and the number of bedplaces, adjusted by the number of days when the bedplaces are actually available for use (i.e. excluding seasonal closures or other temporary closures). Spain was the country where hotels recorded the highest net occupancy rate in 1998, at 61.2%. Amongst the other Member States, only Greece and France recorded rates above 50%. Belgium (31.6%) and Luxembourg (23.5%) closed the ranking.

Residents are more frequent clients but stay shorter
The primary clients of European hotels are, as a general rule, persons living in the country itself. Non-residents represented on average only 34.4% of the persons checking in to hotels and similar establishments in the EU in 1998, although they accounted for a much larger share in smaller countries like Austria (70.7%), Belgium (73.6%) and Luxembourg (97.0%). These countries were also the only ones[5] with Greece and Portugal where arrivals of non-residents outnumbered those of residents. In contrast, only 18.7% of the persons arriving in hotels in Germany and Sweden were people visiting from a foreign country.

(5) IRL and NL, no data available.

Figure 17.7

Net use of bed-places in hotels and similar establishements (%)

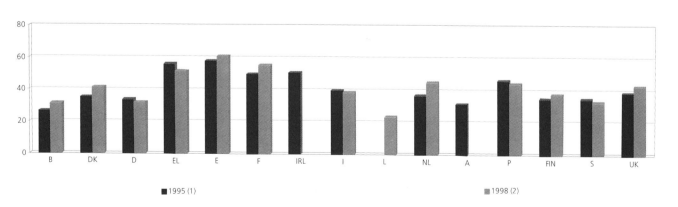

■ 1995 (1)　　　■ 1998 (2)

(1) L, not available.
(2) IRL and A, not available.

Source: Eurostat (TOUR)

Non-residents, however, tended to stay somewhat longer than residents: 3.7 nights against 2.5. They represented 46.7% of all nights spent in EU hotels. In some countries, the length of stay varies noticeably according to the residence criteria. This was for example the case in those Mediterranean countries that are very popular international destinations for - generally longer - summer holidays, such as Greece, Spain and Portugal. The average length of stay of non-residents in those countries was more than twice as long as for residents, and was the highest amongst the Member States: 6.3 nights in Greece, 5.5 in Spain and 4.7 in Portugal. The opposite situation was witnessed only in Luxembourg, where residents stayed on average 5.0 nights against 2.1 for non-residents.

Other accommodation establishments

Besides hotels and similar establishments, the EU tourism infrastructure can also count on nearly 90 thousand other types of tourists collective accommodation establishments, with a total capacity of nearly 12 million bedplaces in 1998. This category chiefly includes camping sites, holiday dwellings, youth hostels and collective dormitories for tourists. Whilst Italy was the country with the highest number of these establishments, representing 40% of the EU total, it was France that boasted the largest capacity with over 2.9 million bedplaces, or one quarter of the EU total.

Table 17.9

Main indicators for collective accomodation establishments other than hotels, 1998 (thousands)

	Number of establishments (1)	Number of bed-places (2)
B	1.7	1,068.2
DK	0.6	317.8
D	16.5	1,460.6
EL (3)	0.3	97.3
E (3)	1.1	667.0
F	9.2	2,979.2
IRL	2.4	55.0
I	36.6	1,772.3
L	0.3	52.6
NL	2.2	713.2
A	5.2	323.6
P	0.2	267.2
FIN	0.5	99.8
S	1.6	365.2
UK	11.2	1,759.7

(1) 1997, IRL, NL and P.
(2) 1997, I, NL and P.
(3) Only tourist campsites.

Source: Eurostat (TOUR)

Figure 17.8

Hotels and other lodging (NACE Rev. 1 55.1 and 55.2)
Number of persons employed, 1997 (thousands) (1)

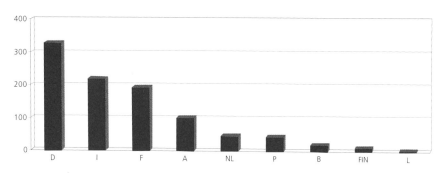

(1) I, 1996; DK, EL, E, IRL, S and UK, not available.

Source: Eurostat (SBS)

Figure 17.9

Hotels and other lodging (NACE Rev. 1 55.1 and 55.2)
Apparent labour productivity, 1997 (thousand ECU per person employed) (1)

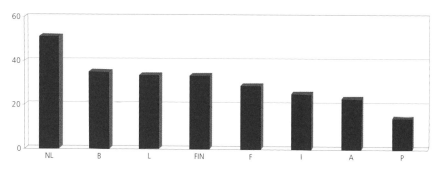

(1) I, 1996; DK, D, EL, E, IRL, S and UK, not available.

Source: Eurostat (SBS)

Figure 17.10

Hotels and other lodging (NACE Rev. 1 55.1 and 55.2)
Unit personnel costs, 1997 (thousand ECU per employee) (1)

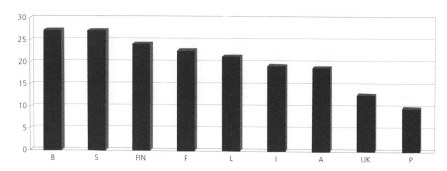

(1) I and S, 1996; DK, D, EL, E, IRL and NL, not available.

Source: Eurostat (SBS)

SUB-CHAPTER 17.2
RESTAURANTS, BARS AND CATERING
(NACE Rev. 1 55.3, 55.4 AND 55.5)

Restaurants and bars are present in virtually every local community. In addition to their economic worth, restaurants and bars also play a significant social role in villages and cities throughout the EU. For statistical purposes, the activities of the sale of meals and drinks for consumption are classified under NACE Rev. 1 Groups 55.3 (restaurants), 55.4 (bars) and 55.5 (canteens and catering). These activities represent together a substantial share of the hotels and restaurants sector of the economy, accounting for more than two-thirds of it in terms of turnover and employment.

This sector is a very diverse one from a number of perspectives. Businesses can be very different in size and shape, from small, family-run outlets to multinational franchises, or from popular bars, snack outlets and fast-food chains to high-class establishments dealing in haute cuisine. All of these are covered by the statistics presented here, in so far that the provision of drinks and meals is their principal activity. These statistics do not include the numerous enterprises active in different areas that also offer this service as a complement to their core business. Most notable amongst these exclusions are hotels, cinemas, recreation parks, railways, ferries or night-clubs. In some cases, the sale of food and drinks may represent an important part of their revenue, as was for example highlighted in the section on hotels above.

One million enterprises, often very small

The number of restaurants, bars and catering enterprises can be estimated at around 1 million in the EU in 1997[6], most of which were relatively small in size. They employed on average between 3 (France, Italy, Portugal) and 4 persons (Luxembourg, Austria, Finland) each and generated turnover usually under 300 thousand ECU per year, ranging in 1997 from a minimum of 80 thousand ECU in Portugal to a maximum of 548 thousand ECU in the United Kingdom. Portuguese enterprises also recorded the lowest average profitability level, with a gross operating surplus that represented just 5.4% of turnover, against an estimated 16% for the EU.

(6) B and EL, no data available.

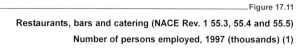

Figure 17.11

Restaurants, bars and catering (NACE Rev. 1 55.3, 55.4 and 55.5)
Number of persons employed, 1997 (thousands) (1)

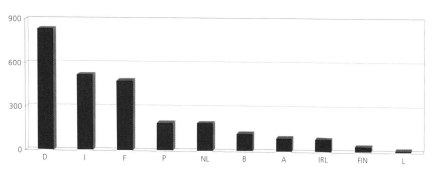

(1) I, 1996; DK, EL, E, S and UK, not available.

Source: Eurostat (SBS)

Figure 17.12

Restaurants, bars and catering (NACE Rev. 1 55.3, 55.4 and 55.5)
Apparent labour productivity, 1997 (thousand ECU per person employed) (1)

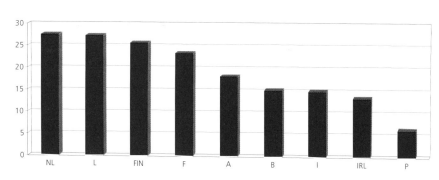

(1) I, 1996; DK, D, EL, E, S and UK, not available.

Source: Eurostat (SBS)

The low qualification level of most of the workforce and the importance of part-time work may explain the relatively low personnel costs faced by enterprises in this sector. They were generally under 20 thousand ECU per employee, ranging from a minimum of 6 thousand ECU in Portugal to a maximum of 23.5 thousand ECU in Sweden. Mirroring personnel costs, apparent labour productivity, as measured by the value added generated by each person employed in the sector, was also relatively low compared to other service activities. In 1997, there was a low of 6 thousand ECU in Portugal and a maximum of 27 thousand ECU in Luxembourg and the Netherlands. It should be noted that these two indicators are not directly comparable one to the other, considering the large proportion of the workforce that is not paid (for example self-employed persons or family workers that do not receive a wage or salary). In 1996/97, employees accounted for as little as 45% of employment in restaurants and bars in Italy, 63% in Belgium and about 75% in Austria and Portugal.

Larger enterprises in contract catering

Tourism flows have a great importance in the evolution of this sector, both through business and leisure travellers. However, in addition to restaurants and bars, this activity also comprises catering services that display a markedly different structure. Enterprises are generally much larger: average employment was for example 30 persons per enterprise in Italy with a turnover of over 1.5 million ECU per enterprise in 1996, close to ten times the average figure for the sector.

Figure 17.13

Restaurants, bars and catering (NACE Rev. 1 55.3, 55.4 and 55.5)

Unit personnel costs, 1997 (thousand ECU per employee) (1)

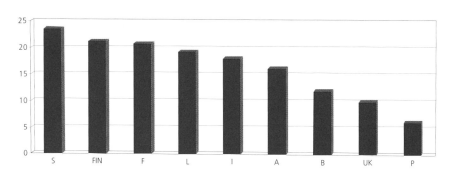

(1) I and S, 1996; DK, D, EL, E, IRL and NL, not available.

Source: Eurostat (SBS)

Box 17.3

This activity has in recent years greatly benefited from the trend of industries outsourcing activities that are not part of their core business (see chapter on business services). Enterprises, schools and public administrations that used to run their own restaurant facilities for their personnel, students or pupils have increasingly subcontracted this activity to specialised independent enterprises. These enterprises are hence perhaps better viewed as business services' enterprises, as are cleaning services and security services. The European market for catering services is led by the French group Sodexho Alliance. They generated turnover of almost 3.2 billion ECU in 1997, ahead of the Compass Group (UK) with a turnover of 2.5 billion ECU. It is estimated that the segments related to clients in education and health each account for a third of the catering service market, the remainder being largely shared between enterprises and public-sector canteens.

SUB-CHAPTER 17.3
RECREATION PARKS
(NACE Rev. 1 92.33 AND 92.53)

The recreation parks sector includes a wide variety of establishments in terms of size, style and service offered. They vary from theme parks, other amusement parks and water parks, through holiday camps, to zoological gardens and safari parks. NACE Rev. 1 92.33 covers fairs and amusement parks, whilst NACE Rev. 1 92.53 covers botanical and zoological gardens and nature reserve activities.

	EU (1)	USA (2)
Average number of operating days (units)	170.4	162.8
Average length of visitors stay (hours)	4.8	5.2
Annual attendance (thousands)	511.0	865.8
Average number of persons employed during peak month (units)	262.3	723.1
Share of admissions in revenue (%)	50.9	45.5

_____Table 17.10

Main indicators of amusement and theme parks, 1997 (average of surveyed parks)

(1) Including Norway.
(2) Including Canada.

Source: IAAPA

Although a significant segment of the tourism industry, this sector lacks comprehensive statistical coverage, and very few official statistics exist at the present time. Analysis of this area is therefore based on estimates from professional trade associations and consultants. Figures should therefore be considered with precaution and readers are advised not to compare directly these data with those found for other activities of the economy.

100 million visitors each year in Europe
According to the European Association of Zoos and Aquaria (EAZA), almost 81 million persons visited their 238 member zoos that were open to the public in 1997. The total attendance, including free tickets and multiple visits by annual ticket holders was estimated at approximately 100 million visitors. It must be noted that EAZA members originate from EU Member States, as well as most central European countries, plus Russia, Turkey and Israel.

Based on the most recent estimates, more than 110 million visitors went to amusement and theme parks in Europe. The largest single recreation park in the EU is Disneyland Paris, with more than 12.5 million visitors in 1999 (a figure comparable to the year before) and turnover of around 920 million EUR.

EU parks smaller than in the USA
North America is the standard reference for international comparisons of amusement and theme parks. Theme parks in the USA are a very important element of the tourism industry, both for domestic and international visitors. In Europe, parks are as a general rule smaller than in the USA. The average European park welcomed 511 thousand visitors in 1997, 350 thousand fewer than its American counterpart. Average employment during peak months was equal to 262 persons in the EU, just over a third of the level in the USA.

The structure of revenue was also different, with admission revenues in major European amusement parks accounting for over half of all revenues (excluding accommodation), a level somewhat higher than in the USA. There was also a lower level of expenditure on ancillary products in European theme parks.

Highly seasonal employment and attendance
Recreation parks are important employers of both skilled and unskilled workers. It is estimated that 40 to 50 thousand persons worked in recreation parks in the EU in 1997. Permanent core staff are generally well-qualified, including administrative and marketing staff as well as skilled workers, such as carpenters, painters, electricians, mechanics and specialised designers. For zoos and aquaria, the requisite qualifications are usually even higher. However, seasonal staff outnumber permanent staff in this activity by a ratio of around 4 to 1, with many temporary and seasonal staff with often no related qualifications.

At present, most parks are idle throughout the winter. The average amusement and theme park in the EU was open 24 weeks a year in 1997, one week more than in the USA. However, the increasing popularity of indoor and water-based attractions has increased the scope for extending the season. This development is both demand and supply driven. One recent feature of the tourism sector is increased demand for short breaks during the off-season. This trend coincides with the wishes of park operators to increase the utilisation level. Also, many recreation parks are increasingly turning to the corporate sector to boost demand during off-peak periods.

Another important trend has emerged in recent years whereby consumers are encouraged to consider recreation parks as tourist destinations per se. Traditionally amusement parks were either a day trip attraction or one of the entertainment activities and attractions offered to tourists at holiday resort destinations. However, Europe's major theme parks (following the example of Disneyland Paris), are now increasingly positioning themselves as overnight destinations or fully-fledged resorts.

In total, the number of recreation parks in Europe has increased over the last decade. However, expansion has not been uniform and amusement parks have enjoyed far greater growth than zoos, aquaria and safari parks. Greenfield investment in amusement parks is a relatively high-risk activity, with capital costs of investment high and demand difficult to predict.

SUB-CHAPTER 17.4
TRAVEL AGENCIES (NACE Rev. 1 63.3)

Travel services encompass all firms engaged in arranging transport, accommodation and catering on behalf of travellers. The activity covered by the NACE Rev. 1 63.3 includes furnishing travel information, advice and planning, arranging made-to-measure tours, accommodation and transportation for travellers and tourists, furnishing tickets, the sale of packaged tours and the activities of tour operators and of tourist guides.

Small enterprises with high
turnover but low profitability

Travel agencies are generally small enterprises employing between 5 and 10 persons, with Italy and Luxembourg at the lower end of the ranking and France and Ireland at the upper end. Their average turnover may appear relatively high when compared to their size, ranging from 1 million ECU in Italy up to 3.5 million ECU in Ireland. But in their role of intermediaries between travel services providers and end consumers, travel agencies face constant pressure on their margins (see below). This is reflected in the relatively low level of profitability they display compared to other service activities. The gross operating surplus was estimated in 1997 at just 3.1% of turnover. The lowest level was recorded in France with only 0.8%, whilst Spain (5.7%) and Italy (5.2%) displayed the highest rates.

Unit personnel costs tend to be somewhat lower in travel agencies when comparing to other service activities, but higher than in the other tourism related activities covered in this chapter. In most countries for which data is available annual unit personnel costs were below 30 thousand ECU per employee, with an EU average of 29.8 thousand ECU in 1997. Figures were somewhat lower in Portugal (at 14 thousand ECU per employee), whilst they reached a high of 32 thousand ECU per employee in France and Sweden.

Figure 17.14

Travel agencies (NACE Rev. 1 63.3)

Number of persons employed, 1997 (thousands) (1)

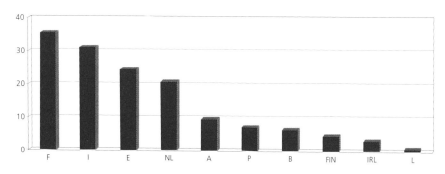

(1) I and L, 1996; DK, D, EL, S and UK, not available.

Source: Eurostat (SBS)

Figure 17.15

Travel agencies (NACE Rev. 1 63.3)

Apparent labour productivity, 1997 (thousand ECU per person employed) (1)

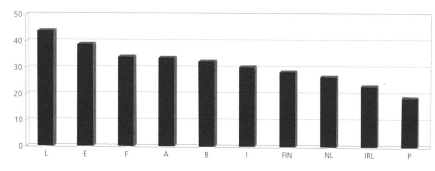

(1) I and L, 1996; DK, D, EL, S and UK, not available.

Source: Eurostat (SBS)

Productivity was also in the lower range of service activities. Apparent labour productivity, as measured by the valued added generated by each person employed, was estimated at 30 thousand ECU in the EU in 1997. It was markedly below the average in Portugal (18.4 thousand ECU), as opposed to Luxembourg where it reached a high of 43.7 thousand ECU. When adjusted to take into account wage level differences across the Member States, productivity was still the highest in Luxembourg, with gross value added per capita exceeding unit personnel costs by 55%, compared to barely 6% in France.

Demand stimulated by air travel

One of the key variables affecting demand for leisure and business travel and related travel services is that of airfare prices. They are particularly significant given the sector's reliance on travel bookings to medium and long-haul destinations, whereas domestic holidays and the bulk of rail and road transport bookings tend to by-pass travel agencies. The increasing liberalisation of air transport in Europe has been reflected in a sharp increase in passenger growth since the mid-80s (see chapter on transport services). The gradual liberalisation of domestic and intra-regional air transport markets is expected to put further downward pressure on airfares, and hence further stimulate demand for services from travel agents.

Significant impact of new technologies

Information technologies (IT) may be expected to drastically change the face of the sector in years to come. IT is now almost universally present in the daily operations of a travel agent, for both desk and back-office operations (from data exchange to ticketing and payments). There is heavy reliance on computer reservation systems, which can be easily linked to the Internet to allow people to make their travel purchases directly from their home PC. The Travel Industry Association of America estimates that 85 million persons used the Internet for travel-related purposes in 1999 in the USA, up from 29 million in 1996. The number of travellers that used the Internet for travel planning (getting information on destinations, checking prices or schedules) reached 52 million persons, of which 16.5 million used the Internet to make actual reservations.

In Europe, according to 1999 research by Datamonitor, the travel industry was expected to be one of the fastest growing sectors for on-line sales over the next few years. The sale of on-line travel products in Europe is expected to be worth 1.7 billion EUR by the year 2002, whilst it was valued at just 6.8 million ECU in 1997. The key drivers of growth are expected to be on-line flight reservation systems as well as purchases for business travellers, travelling regularly and at short notice.

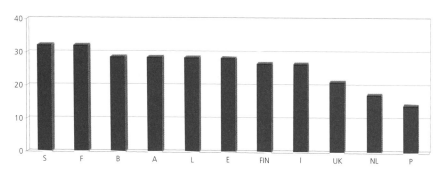

Figure 17.16

Travel agencies (NACE Rev. 1 63.3)

Unit personnel costs, 1997 (thousand ECU per employee) (1)

(1) I, L, NL, FIN and S, 1996; DK, D, EL and IRL, not available.

Source: Eurostat (SBS)

Development of direct sales and e-ticketing

Travel agencies (including on-line ones) may have to face increasing competition from airlines and tour operators, attracted by the opportunity to make direct sales and thus eliminating agents' commissions. Already several airlines companies, led by discount operators, offer the opportunity to book a flight from their Internet site. This is sometimes further facilitated by the absence of tickets as such (e-ticketing), as only the reservation confirmation number is required to check-in for the flight. Tour operators are embarking along a similar path by complementing their paper catalogues with web sites offering tourists the opportunity to gather information, visit and eventually book their stay on-line.

Business travel specialists have pre-empted the threat of direct distribution by increasing the range of services they provide to corporate clients. Leading operators have re-positioned themselves as travel "management" companies, able to advise clients on their business travel policy by interpreting travel patterns and monitoring travel costs.

Table 17.11

Hotels, camping sites and other short stay accommodation (NACE Rev. 1 55.1 and 55.2)

Employment related indicators, 1997

	B	DK	D	EL	E	F	IRL	I (1)	L	NL (2)	A	P	FIN	S	UK
Number of persons employed (thousands)	20.3	:	329.0	:	:	194.1	:	220.1	3.1	47.0	102.5	45.3	11.8	:	:
Employees/number of persons employed (%)	87.1	:	:	:	:	90.3	:	74.4	90.6	88.3	79.6	95.3	94.9	:	:
Average no. of persons employed/enterprise (units)	:	:	8.0	:	:	4.0	:	6.0	8.0	10.0	6.0	13.0	9.0	:	:

(1) 1996; (2) Employees as a share of the number of persons employed, 1996.

Table 17.12

Hotels, camping sites and other short stay accommodation (NACE Rev. 1 55.1 and 55.2)

Turnover related indicators, 1997

	B	DK	D	EL	E	F	IRL	I (1)	L	NL	A	P	FIN	S (1)	UK
Turnover (million ECU)	1,446	:	13,864	:	:	13,405	:	10,328	190	2,952	4,688	1,299	982	1,873	17,026
Turnover per enterprise (million ECU)	:	:	0.3	:	:	0.3	:	0.3	0.5	0.7	0.3	0.4	0.8	0.7	1.2
Turnover per person employed (thousand ECU)	71.3	:	42.1	:	:	69.1	:	46.9	61.9	62.8	45.7	28.7	83.4	:	:

(1) 1996.

Table 17.13

Hotels, camping sites and other short stay accommodation (NACE Rev. 1 55.1 and 55.2)

Performance related indicators, 1997

	B	DK	D	EL	E	F	IRL	I (1)	L	NL	A	P	FIN	S (1)	UK
Value added (million ECU)	710	:	:	:	:	5,600	:	5,542	103	2,405	2,363	643	393	755	8,129
Value added as a share of turnover (%)	49.1	:	:	:	:	41.8	:	53.7	54.1	81.5	50.4	49.5	40.0	40.3	47.7
Apparent labour productivity (thousand ECU/person employed)	35.0	:	:	:	:	28.9	:	25.2	33.5	51.1	23.0	14.2	33.4	:	:
Unit personnel costs (thousand ECU)	27.2	:	:	:	:	22.7	:	19.3	21.4	:	18.9	9.7	24.2	27.2	12.7
Simple wage adjusted labour productivity (%)	147.6	:	:	:	:	140.6	:	175.4	172.8	286.2	153.5	153.8	145.5	124.6	212.9
Gross operating surplus (million ECU)	229	:	:	:	:	1,617	:	2,382	43	1,564	823	225	123	149	4,312

(1) 1996.

Table 17.14

Restaurants, bars and catering (NACE Rev. 1 55.3, 55.4 and 55.5)

Employment related indicators, 1997

	B	DK	D	EL	E	F	IRL	I (1)	L	NL (2)	A	P	FIN	S	UK
Number of persons employed (thousands)	116.8	:	831.6	:	:	475.8	81.1	516.6	7.7	188.4	89.0	189.2	33.4	:	:
Employees/number of persons employed (%)	63.3	:	:	:	:	83.2	81.1	44.9	90.9	80.3	73.1	75.9	86.8	:	:
Average no. of persons employed/enterprise (units)	:	:	5.0	:	:	3.0	7.0	3.0	4.0	6.0	4.0	3.0	4.0	:	:

(1) 1996; (2) Employees as a share of the number of persons employed, 1996.

Table 17.15

Restaurants, bars and catering (NACE Rev. 1 55.3, 55.4 and 55.5)

Turnover related indicators, 1997

	B	DK	D	EL	E	F	IRL	I (1)	L	NL	A	P	FIN	S (1)	UK
Turnover (million ECU)	4,772	:	27,567	:	:	25,781	3,410	22,836	517	8,010	3,608	4,609	2,461	3,986	51,859
Turnover per enterprise (million ECU)	:	:	0.2	:	:	0.2	0.3	0.1	0.3	0.2	0.2	0.1	0.3	0.3	0.5
Turnover per person employed (thousand ECU)	40.9	:	33.2	:	:	54.2	42.1	44.2	67.2	42.5	40.5	24.4	73.7	:	:

(1) 1996.

Table 17.16

Restaurants, bars and catering (NACE Rev. 1 55.3, 55.4 and 55.5)

Performance related indicators, 1997

	B	DK	D	EL	E	F	IRL	I (1)	L	NL	A	P	FIN	S (1)	UK
Value added (million ECU)	1,735	:	:	:	:	11,035	1,067	7,601	209	5,165	1,597	1,127	850	1,373	18,908
Value added as a share of turnover (%)	36.4	:	:	:	:	42.8	31.3	33.3	40.4	64.5	44.3	24.4	34.5	34.4	36.5
Apparent labour productivity (thousand ECU/person employed)	14.9	:	:	:	:	23.2	13.2	14.7	27.2	27.4	18.0	6.0	25.5	:	:
Unit personnel costs (thousand ECU)	11.9	:	:	:	:	20.7	:	18.0	19.2	:	16.1	6.1	21.2	23.5	9.9
Simple wage adjusted labour productivity (%)	196.6	:	:	:	:	134.6	:	182.1	155.7	272.8	152.3	128.1	138.3	126.9	195.7
Gross operating surplus (million ECU)	852	:	:	:	:	2,835	:	3,426	75	3,272	549	247	235	291	9,247

(1) 1996.

Source: Eurostat (SBS)

Table 17.17

Activities of travel agencies and tour operators; tourist assistance activities n.e.c. (NACE Rev. 1 63.3)

Employment related indicators, 1997

	B	DK	D	EL	E	F	IRL	I (1)	L (1)	NL (2)	A	P	FIN (2)	S	UK
Number of persons employed (thousands)	6.3	:	:	:	24.3	35.3	2.9	30.9	0.5	20.6	9.3	7.0	4.5	:	:
Employees/number of persons employed (%)	83.8	:	:	:	76.8	99.5	90.7	71.4	94.3	90.7	90.3	96.4	96.0	:	:
Average no. of persons employed/enterprise (units)	:	:	:	:	5.1	9.0	10.0	4.5	5.0	11.0	9.0	8.0	9.0	:	:

(1) 1996; (2) Employees as a share of the number of persons employed, 1996.

Table 17.18

Activities of travel agencies and tour operators; tourist assistance activities n.e.c. (NACE Rev. 1 63.3)

Turnover related indicators, 1997

	B	DK	D	EL	E	F	IRL	I (1)	L (1)	NL	A	P	FIN	S (1)	UK
Turnover (million ECU)	2,983	:	:	:	7,270	8,643	1,016	6,651	341	2,988	2,875	1,605	1,174	4,393	18,723
Turnover per enterprise (million ECU)	:	:	:	:	1.5	2.2	3.5	1.0	3.1	1.5	2.7	1.8	2.4	2.7	3.1
Turnover per person employed (thousand ECU)	472.3	:	:	:	299.0	244.8	344.6	215.2	665.1	144.7	307.7	229.2	263.5	:	:

(1) 1996.

Table 17.19

Activities of travel agencies and tour operators; tourist assistance activities n.e.c. (NACE Rev. 1 63.3)

Performance related indicators, 1997

	B	DK	D	EL	E	F	IRL	I (1)	L (1)	NL (2)	A	P	FIN (2)	S (1)	UK
Value added (million ECU)	203	:	:	:	938	1,192	67	926	22	544	313	129	126	373	2,779
Value added as a share of turnover (%)	6.8	:	:	:	12.9	13.8	6.6	13.9	6.6	18.2	10.9	8.0	10.7	8.5	14.8
Apparent labour productivity (thousand ECU/person employed)	32.2	:	:	:	38.6	33.8	22.8	30.0	43.7	26.3	33.5	18.4	28.2	:	:
Unit personnel costs (thousand ECU)	28.5	:	:	:	28.0	31.9	:	26.3	28.2	17.2	28.3	14.0	26.4	32.0	21.0
Simple wage adjusted labour productivity (%)	135.1	:	:	:	179.3	106.5	:	159.4	163.5	138.2	131.0	136.4	115.2	129.6	138.0
Gross operating surplus (million ECU)	53	:	:	:	415	73	:	345	9	150	74	34	17	85	766

(1) 1996; (2) Unit personnel costs, 1996.

Source: Eurostat (SBS)

Transport services (NACE Rev. 1 60, 61, 62 and 63)

The transport services industry covers enterprises primarily engaged in the conveyance of goods and passengers. This includes both direct involvement in transport activities, i.e. the actual conveyance of goods and passengers by various modes of transport, and indirect involvement, such as handling, traffic guidance, travel arrangements, freight brokerage and storage. In the nomenclature of economic activities, transport services are broken down into: land transport, which includes railways, urban transport, road and road freight transport, as well as transport by pipelines (NACE Rev. 1 60), water transport (NACE Rev. 1 61), air transport, which includes space transport (NACE Rev. 1 62), and supporting and auxiliary transport activities, which cover cargo handling and storage, the operation of railway stations, ports and airports, travel agencies and tourist assistance activities (NACE Rev. 1 63). All these activities are covered in this chapter, except for travel agencies (NACE Rev. 1 63.3) that have been included in the chapter on tourism.

Transport services are at the centre of economic activities and flows. As a consequence, the overall competitiveness of an economy is greatly affected by the quality and efficiency of its transport system. In addition, in recent years enterprises have increasingly adopted more flexible production management systems, whereby transport services have become an integral and essential part of the production process, for example just-in-time (J.I.T.) production systems, where materials deliveries are made in close co-ordination with production schedules.

The importance of transport services in the European economy may be measured using National Accounts data, which indicate that transport services generated between 3.0% (in Greece) and more than 6.0% (in Belgium or Denmark) of the wealth created within the EU[1].

Inland transport[2] makes up the largest share of transport services in the majority of Member States; for example in Austria it accounted for as much as two-thirds of total transport services' value added in 1997[3].

In the majority of countries land transport accounted for between 2.0% and 2.5% of total GDP, with a share of more than 3.0% in Finland and Denmark, and less than 2.0% in Germany and Ireland.

Growing demand for transport services...
Enterprises have increasingly tried to reduce their costs by keeping inventories as low as possible, leading to more frequent deliveries of smaller quantities of materials. In addition, movement of goods and passengers has also been affected by the relocation of business away from city centres, towards major transport arteries. From an international perspective, the completion of the Internal Market and the process of globalisation have also contributed to increase demand for international freight transport. As for passenger transport, urban spread has boosted the demand for commuter services, whereas leisure transport has benefited from a continuous increase in personal mobility and reductions in the cost of certain forms of transport, notably airborne.

The activities covered in this chapter (in terms of NACE Rev. 1) include:

60:    land transport; transport via pipelines;
60.1: transport via railways;
60.2: other land transport;
60.3: transport via pipelines;
61:    water transport;
61.1: sea and coastal water transport;
61.2: inland water transport;
62:    air transport;
62.1: scheduled air transport;
62.2: non-scheduled air transport;
62.3: space transport;
63:    supporting and auxiliary transport activities; activities of travel agencies;
63.1: cargo handling and storage;
63.2: other supporting transport activities;
63.4: activities of other transport agencies

---

(1) Latest years available: B and EL, 1997; DK, 1994.
(2) In the National Accounts sense, which classifies transport services as either inland, maritime or air.
(3) Not surprising, as A (together with L) is one of only two land-locked Member States.

Figure 18.1 _____

Transport services (NACE-CLIO 61, 63 and 65)

Share of total market services value added and employment, 1997 (%)

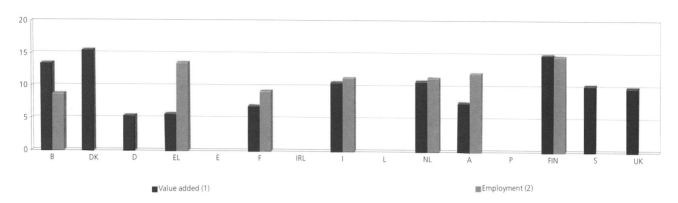

■ Value added (1)   ■ Employment (2)

(1) D, EL, F and A, value added at market prices; DK, D, S and UK, 1996; E, IRL, L and P, not available.
(2) B and A, 1996; DK, D, E, IRL, L, P, S and UK, not available.

Source: Eurostat (SEC2)

Table 18.1 _____

Transport services (NACE Rev. 1 60, 61 and 62)

Breakdown of turnover and employment by employment size class, 1997 (%)

	Micro (0-9)		Small (10-49)		Medium (50-249)		Large (250+)	
	Turnover (1)	Employment (2)	Turnover (1)	Employment (3)	Turnover (1)	Employment (1)	Turnover (4)	Employment (5)
EU-15	23.5	33.5	18.9	17.9	14.9	10.5	42.8	38.0
B	19.5	23.9	33.6	21.0	:	:	:	:
DK	:	:	:	:	:	:	31.9	17.5
D	14.2	29.7	21.1	28.1	14.9	12.3	49.8	29.9
EL	:	:	:	:	:	:	:	:
E	:	63.8	:	12.9	:	:	:	:
F	17.2	22.5	19.9	18.9	17.4	13.7	45.5	44.8
IRL	:	:	:	:	:	:	:	:
I	34.5	35.5	18.9	13.0	13.9	7.9	32.7	43.7
L	:	:	:	:	:	:	:	:
NL	:	17.5	:	26.5	:	:	:	:
A	:	:	:	:	:	:	:	:
P	:	:	:	16.0	:	:	:	:
FIN	:	39.6	:	14.2	:	:	:	:
S	24.8	:	25.5	20.1	17.3	13.2	32.4	:
UK	21.0	31.5	12.4	11.9	:	:	:	:

(1) EU-15, F, I and S, 1996.
(2) EU-15, F, I, NL and UK, 1996.
(3) EU-15, F, I, NL, P and S, 1996.
(4) EU-15, DK, F, I and S, 1996.
(5) EU-15, DK, F and I, 1996.

Source: Eurostat (SME)

As a result, the transportation of goods and passengers has witnessed strong and consistent growth during the period 1990 to 1997. Combining road, rail, inland waterways, pipelines and sea transport, there were more than 2,700 billion tonne-kilometres[4] of goods moved in 1997 within the EU. Looking back over the last thirty years, this corresponds to an average increase of 2.7% per annum. Passenger transport by car, bus, rail and air totalled 4,800 billion passenger-kilometres[5] within the EU in 1997, rising at an average rate of 3.0% per annum since 1970.

... particularly for road haulage...

The main area of growth with respect to the transport of goods has been road freight transport, which increased on average by 4.0% per annum between 1970 and 1997, rising from 412 billion tonne-kilometres to 1,200 billion tonne-kilometres by 1997. In 1990, road became the most popular mode of transport for goods in the EU, overtaking intra-EU sea transport. Sea transport has however also experienced strong growth, rising on average by 3.3% per annum during the last three decades, resulting in a total volume of 1,124 billion tonne-kilometres transported in 1997. Rail transport remained the third largest mode of goods transport, although this sector lost ground in relative and absolute terms, with transported volumes falling from 283 billion tonne-kilometres in 1970 to 240 billion tonne-kilometres by 1998.

(4) Number of tonnes multiplied by the number of kilometres.
(5) Number of passengers multiplied by the number of kilometres.

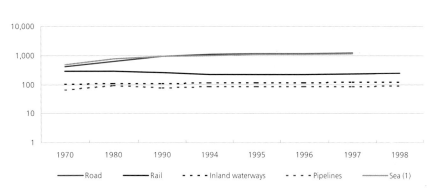

_____**Figure 18.2**

Evolution of goods transported in the EU (billion tonne-kilometres, log scale)

(1) Intra-EU traffic only.

Source: Eurostat, ECMT, UIC

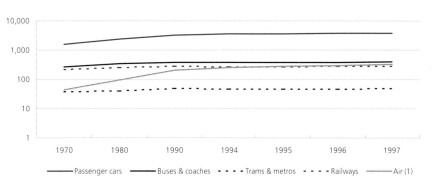

_____**Figure 18.3**

Evolution of passenger transport in the EU (billion passenger-kilometres, log scale)

(1) Intra-EU traffic only.

Source: Eurostat, ECMT, UIC, AEA, IACA

... and passenger air transport

The evolution of passenger transport over the last thirty years shows that air transport experienced by far the highest rates of growth, rising by 7.7% per annum on average between 1970 and 1997. As such, the volume of air passenger traffic rose from 43 billion passenger-kilometres in 1970 to 322 billion passenger-kilometres by 1997. In 1995, European air transport overtook railways in terms of the volume of passengers carried. If current rates of growth continue, air will quickly surpass buses and coaches (393 billion passenger-kilometres in 1997) and become the second most important mode of passenger transport after cars. Nevertheless, the car remains by far the principal mode of passenger transport, with 3,787 billion passenger-kilometres in 1997.

STRUCTURE AND PERFORMANCE

National Accounts allow a rough estimate of transport services value added to be made for the second half of the 1990s at 261 billion ECU[6], up from 209 billion ECU in 1990[7]. This corresponded to an annual average growth rate of 3.2% or a net gain of 25% between 1990 and 1997, which was superior to the growth in the volume of traffic over the same period, when the number of tonne-kilometres of goods transported increased by 21% and the number of passenger-kilometres travelled was up by 15%.

However, the evolution of value added for transport services lagged that of other market services during the 1990s. Market services' value added progressed by more than 45% in nominal terms between 1990 and 1997, reaching 3,500 billion ECU by 1997, equivalent to an average growth rate of 5.5% per annum. Closer examination of the data for the various transport services' activities shows that the value added generated by land transport services grew at a relatively slow pace, with annual average growth of 2.7% between 1990 and 1997, compared to 3.3% for maritime, air and auxiliary transport services.

Neighbouring Denmark and Germany the extremes in terms of the weight of transport services in their respective economies

Transport services contributed more than 6.4% of Denmark's total gross value added[8]. This was the highest share in the EU ahead of Belgium (6.3%), the only other country reporting a share greater than 6.0%. Most of the other Member States displayed shares close to 4.0%, whilst Germany recorded the lowest figure, just 2.8%.

---

(6) Inland, maritime, air and auxiliary transport services; IRL and L, no data available; B, DK, EL, F, I, NL, A and FIN, 1997; D, S and UK, 1996; E and P, 1995.
(7) EL, 1991; IRL, 1992 for inland transport only.
(8) Figures quoted in this paragraph refer to 1997, the latest National Accounts data available, except for D, S and UK (1996) and E and P (1995).

Inland transport services created the largest share of value added amongst the transport services, with more than half of the wealth created in practically all Member States, and more than 60% of the total in Denmark, Greece, Spain, Italy, Austria and Finland. Only Belgium reported a considerably lower share, with auxiliary transport services' accounted for no less than 63% of total transport services' value added. Other countries with a comparatively large auxiliary transport services branch included the United Kingdom (36%), Portugal and France (both 35%). Air and maritime transport services generated their highest share of transport services' value added in the Netherlands (24%), Greece and Sweden (both 23%).

A sector dominated by SMEs

A very large number of the 934 thousand transport services' enterprises active within the EU in 1996 were small in size, with 93.1% of them classified as micro enterprises (with less than 10 employees). The average size of the typical transport services' enterprise varied considerably according to the type of transport considered. Air transport enterprises tend to be larger, with an average number of persons employed of more than 100 in 1996. In contrast, land transport enterprises employed just 5 persons on average, with the figures for water transport and auxiliary transport services twice as high at 10.2 and 11.6 persons respectively.

The small size of enterprises is reflected in the relatively low average turnover per enterprise, 640 thousand ECU in 1996. By activity, the figures ranged from 320 thousand ECU per enterprise in land transport to as much as 21.2 million ECU in air transport. On average each person employed in transport services generated an average of just under 100 thousand ECU of turnover per year in 1996. Land transport enterprises with no employees recorded the lowest turnover levels amongst all transport services enterprises at 46 thousand ECU per enterprise and 35 thousand ECU per person employed. Air transport enterprises, on the other hand, boasted the highest figures with average turnover of 197 thousand ECU per person employed.

LABOUR AND PRODUCTIVITY

Transport services provided work in the 1990s to more than 5.0% of those employed in Denmark, Greece, Italy, the Netherlands, Austria and Finland, and accounted for more than 4.0% of the workforce in Belgium, Spain and the United Kingdom.

According to the Labour Force Survey there were 6.4 million persons employed in the EU in 1998 in transport services, of which 3.9 million (around 60%) were employed within land transport, 360 thousand in air transport and 260 thousand in water transport. Auxiliary transport services employed the remaining 1.9 million persons.

Only 10% of the workforce were highly-educated

Only a tenth of those employed in transport services within the EU in 1997 had completed a higher education degree, compared to the market services average (NACE Rev. 1 Sections G to K) of 19.3%. Closer examination reveals that the proportions ranged from as high as 28.3% for air transport and 24.0% for water transport (two activities where relatively small numbers of persons were employed), to as low as 7.0% for land transport (the largest transport services' employer). Indeed, within the land transport activities almost half (48.4% in 1997) of the workforce had completed a lower education level (primary or lower secondary), one of the highest proportions amongst service activities.

Table 18.2

Transport services (NACE Rev. 1 60, 61 and 62) Composition of the labour force, 1999 (%)

	Women (1)	Part-time (2)	Highly-educated (3)
EU-15	14.7	7.6	10.1
B	14.4	6.0	15.4
DK	19.0	9.7	13.3
D	19.9	8.9	14.7
EL	3.9	:	11.8
E	10.6	4.0	13.5
F	15.9	6.4	11.4
IRL	19.2	8.2	13.2
I	10.9	3.7	2.6
L	22.4	:	9.2
NL	19.4	23.0	8.0
A	15.0	7.9	2.8
P	11.6	2.8	4.3
FIN	17.6	7.2	14.2
S	15.4	12.5	10.7
UK	15.4	10.9	10.4

(1) EU-15 and EL, 1998.
(2) EU-15 and B, 1998; P, 1997.
(3) EL, 1998; EU-15, IRL and UK 1997.

Source: Eurostat (LFS)

Transport services, a mainstay of male employment within the service sector

Women occupied just 12.6% of the posts in the EU's land transport activities in 1998, a proportion that rose to 31.4% for auxiliary transport services and 35.4% for air transport services. These figures were noticeably below the market services (NACE Rev. 1 Section G to K) average, where women accounted for 42.8% of the total number of persons employed.

Germany (19.9%) and Luxembourg (22.4%) boasted the highest female participation rates in land, maritime and air transport services (NACE Rev. 1 Divisions 60, 61 and 62), whilst Greece (3.9%) was the only Member State to report that women represented less than a tenth of its workforce.

The incidence of part-time working within the EU transport services sector was below the market services (NACE Rev. 1 Sections G to K) average of 19.4% in the EU in 1998. Only 7.6% of those employed in land, water and air transport services worked on a part-time basis, although this proportion rose to 25.4% for women, whilst just 7.6% of the workforce in auxiliary transport services (22.3% for women) worked part-time.

Labour productivity for inland transport drags down the transport services average

The average value added generated by each person employed in EU transport services in 1997 ranged from 24 thousand ECU in Portugal to 55 thousand ECU in the Netherlands, if the extreme values recorded in Greece (12 thousand ECU) and Belgium (90 thousand ECU) are excluded. Apparent labour productivity was below the average for the whole of market services in most Member States. However, the differences could be largely attributed to inland transport services, as maritime, air and auxiliary transport services usually reported considerably higher ratios.

INTERNATIONAL TRENDS

Transport services contributed 5.3% of Japanese GDP in 1997, a proportion that was in line with the most transport service intensive countries of the EU. In contrast, transport services accounted for only 3.5% of American GDP in 1997, a low level by European standards. Much of the difference could be explained by the relatively low weight of maritime and auxiliary transport services in the USA.

Europe relies heavily on road transport

By comparing the share of each mode of transport in the total traffic for a given country with the same ratio at a world level it is possible to derive a specialisation rate for transport services. For both passenger transport and freight transport there is evidence that Europe relies heavily on road transport (especially use of personal car), whilst the Japanese tend to favour public transport by rail. Buses and coaches had low levels of penetration across the whole of the Triad.

As regards freight transport, Europe and Japan transport a considerably higher share of goods by road than the USA, where pipelines, inland navigation and rail contribute more significantly (to the detriment of sea transport).

Figure 18.4

Specialisation ratios for passenger transport, 1997 (%) (1)

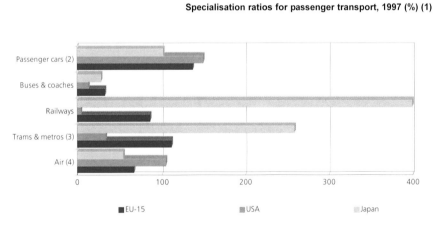

(1) Share of the transport mode in the region considered / share of the transport mode in the world total.
(2) Including light trucks in the USA and Japan.
(3) For Japan: results for trams & metros have been subtracted from official railway figures.
(4) Domestic air travel only.

Source: Eurostat, UN, UIC, IRF

SUB-CHAPTER 18.1
ROAD TRANSPORT (NACE Rev. 1 60.2)

Other land transport activities (NACE Rev. 1 60.2) covers road freight transport, as well as passenger transport (other than railways), scheduled or not, such as urban, suburban or inter-city public transport, taxi operations or charters, excursions and other occasional coach services. This definition includes a diverse number of agents, ranging from independent lorry or taxi drivers to large national or metropolitan public transport companies.

The main modes of transport by road are the passenger car, bus, lorries and vans. Increased mobility and flexibility have dramatically affected the demand for road transport, both for passenger travel and freight transport. One example of the switch to road transport is the development of services such as door-to-door deliveries (for both business and consumers). Over longer distances, road transport for freight also allows for door-to-door delivery without transhipment.

Demand for road freight transport continues to grow
Road transport represented 43.4% of total freight transport inside the EU in 1997. In comparison, only one third of the freight transported in the EU at the beginning of the 1980s was made by road. Nominal growth of 29% between 1990 and 1997 has seen road freight significantly outperform other means of freight transport, resulting in more than 1.2 thousand billion tonne-kilometres of freight being transported by road in 1997.

There were wide disparities in the use of road freight transport across the Member States, from just 39.3% of total inland transport in Austria to 98.1% of the total in Greece. This ratio is affected by criteria such as the quality of the transport infrastructure, climatic and geographical conditions or the density of the population, as well as by cost[9].

(9) It should be noted that these figures refer only to inland transport. The exclusion of sea transport from the calculation has a significant effect on the results presented for countries such as EL.

Box 18.2

The number of registered road vehicles has increased at a rapid rate in the recent decades. This growth has been largely confined to passenger cars and goods vehicles, whilst buses and coaches have seen little evolution in their numbers since the 1980s. There were no fewer than 170 million cars and 19 million goods' vehicles on the EU's roads in 1997, whilst there were just half a million buses and coaches.

There is great diversity across Europe when comparing the number of passenger cars in circulation to the size of the road network. Ireland displayed the lowest ratio with just 11 cars per kilometre of road. At the opposite end of the spectrum, Italy had 107 cars for each kilometre of road (more than twice the EU average).

The motorisation rate allows a comparison of the number of cars in relation to the population of a given country. The EU averaged 457 cars per thousand inhabitants at the end of 1998. The highest rates were recorded in Luxembourg (608 cars per thousand inhabitants) and Italy (545), whilst the lowest rates were recorded in Portugal (316) and Greece (244).

Figure 18.5

Share of road transport in total goods transported, 1997 (%) (1)

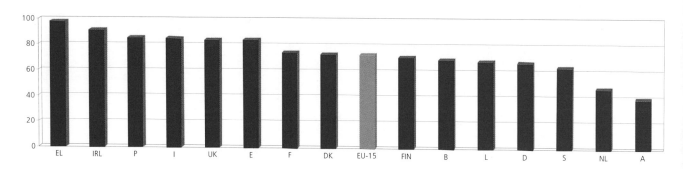

(1) Excluding sea transport.

Source: Eurostat, ECMT, UIC

The EU's road transport infrastructure had 3.5 million kilometres of road network in 1996, of which 63.8% were municipal roads and 28.5% state roads. Motorways totalled 47.6 thousand kilometres in 1997, a 54% increase on 1980. As a consequence of their high population density and their geographical situation at the centre of the EU, Belgium and the Netherlands had the highest density of roads, 4.7 kilometres per kilometre² (of which 55 metres were motorways) and 3.1 kilometres per kilometre² (including 58 metres of motorways). In comparison, lowly populated Nordic countries, such as Sweden and Finland, had just 307 metres and 230 metres of road per kilometre² of land, of which 3 meters or less were motorways.

─────────────────── Table 18.3

Breakdown of land passenger transport, 1997 (% of passenger-kilometres)

	Passenger cars	Powered two-wheelers	Buses & coaches	Trams & metros	Railways
EU-15	81.8	2.6	8.5	1.0	6.1
B	81.7	1.3	10.3	0.7	6.1
DK	79.0	1.0	13.7	:	6.3
D	82.1	1.6	7.5	1.6	7.1
EL	66.0	10.1	21.2	0.8	1.9
E	81.4	3.2	10.2	1.1	4.0
F	84.5	1.5	5.2	1.2	7.6
IRL	86.3	0.5	10.5	:	2.7
I	76.1	6.4	10.6	0.6	6.3
L	86.7	0.7	7.2	:	5.3
NL	82.0	1.6	7.9	0.8	7.8
A	73.7	1.7	13.7	1.7	9.1
P	83.1	3.0	10.0	0.4	3.5
FIN	80.2	1.4	12.5	0.6	5.3
S	83.5	1.2	8.4	1.2	5.7
UK	87.7	0.6	6.0	0.9	4.8

Source: Eurostat, ECMT, UIC

─────────────────── Figure 18.6

Road density, 1996 (kilometres per kilometre²) (1)

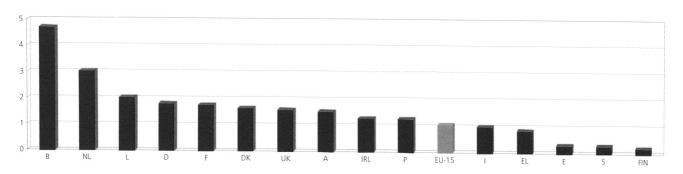

(1) Motorways, national roads, state roads and municipal roads.

Source: Eurostat, UN, ECMT, IRF

─────────────────── Figure 18.7

Evolution of land passenger transport in the EU (1970=100) (1)

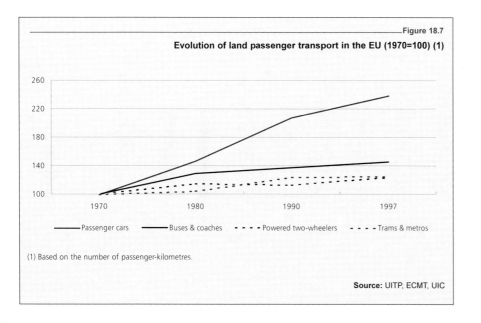

(1) Based on the number of passenger-kilometres.

Source: UITP, ECMT, UIC

Car the favourite mode of passenger transport

The dominant mode of inland passenger transport in 1997 was the passenger car (82%), followed by buses and coaches (8%) and railways (6%). Road was also the means of transport that experienced the highest growth rates between 1980 and 1997. Passenger car traffic in the EU reached 3.8 thousand billion passenger-kilometres in 1997, up by 15% in nominal terms since 1990 and 62% since 1980. In comparison, buses and coaches transported 380 billion passenger-kilometres in 1997, powered two-wheelers 114 billion passenger-kilometres and trams and metros just 42 billion passenger-kilometres. In all three of these cases the volume of passenger traffic was broadly similar to figures from 1980.

STRUCTURE AND PERFORMANCE

Road transport enterprises account for a majority of the EU's transport services' enterprises. There were an estimated 934 thousand enterprises active in the whole of transport services in the EU in 1996, of which 83.3% (or 778 thousand) were land transport enterprises.

Total turnover reached an estimated 37 billion ECU for road passenger transport enterprises and 132 billion ECU for road freight transport enterprises in 1997. Average turnover per enterprise was higher for road haulage enterprises at 300 thousand ECU than it was for road passenger transport enterprises (200 thousand ECU).

The enterprises in this sector are generally small in size, with the largest road transport enterprises found in the Netherlands and Luxembourg. In these two countries average turnover per road transport enterprise was equal to approximately 1 million ECU. At the other end of the spectrum, Spanish enterprises generated just 73 thousand ECU of turnover each on average.

Table 18.4

Land transport; transport via pipelines (NACE Rev. 1 60)

Composition of the labour force, 1999 (%)

	Women (1)	Part-time (2)	Highly-educated (3)
EU-15	12.6	7.4	4.1
B	8.7	4.7	12.1
DK	18.8	9.8	7.4
D	17.4	8.0	12.0
EL	:	:	4.0
E	7.6	3.3	10.9
F	13.9	6.1	7.8
IRL	11.5	9.1	:
I	9.5	3.5	2.0
L	17.1	:	:
NL	15.8	20.7	2.7
A	13.2	7.8	2.4
P	8.7	3.7	:
FIN	11.8	7.7	8.4
S	11.7	13.1	:
UK	13.0	11.4	7.7

(1) EU-15, 1998.
(2) EU-15 and B, 1998; P, 1996.
(3) EU-15 and EL, 1998.

Source: Eurostat (LFS)

Table 18.5

Land transport; transport via pipelines (NACE Rev. 1 60)

Breakdown of turnover and employment by employment size class, 1997 (%)

	Micro (0-9)		Small (10-49)		Medium (50-249)		Large (250+)	
	Turnover (1)	Employment (2)	Turnover (3)	Employment (4)	Turnover (5)	Employment (6)	Turnover (5)	Employment (6)
EU-15	30.2	36.8	23.4	19.4	15.1	10.4	31.3	33.4
B	23.1	25.9	36.1	22.3	12.6	7.3	28.2	44.5
DK	:	:	38.3	36.8	13.4	13.2	4.2	3.8
D	16.2	33.2	23.7	30.6	15.4	12.6	44.6	23.7
EL	:	:	:	:	:	:	:	:
E	:	68.2	:	13.3	:	5.1	:	13.4
F	21.1	24.3	26.7	20.6	21.7	14.6	30.5	40.4
IRL	:	:	13.8	18.5	:	:	:	:
I	43.2	37.9	22.6	13.5	12.0	7.0	22.1	41.7
L	:	:	:	:	:	:	:	:
NL	:	17.2	:	30.9	:	14.9	:	37.0
A	19.0	17.3	28.7	19.3	:	:	:	:
P	:	31.6	:	17.3	:	14.6	:	36.5
FIN	50.3	49.5	19.6	16.9	8.6	8.8	21.5	24.9
S	37.3	40.1	32.8	24.0	14.3	12.0	15.7	23.9
UK	29.2	35.2	16.3	13.3	9.9	9.1	47.4	42.5

(1) EU-15, F, I and S, 1996.
(2) EU-15, F, I, NL, P and S, 1996.
(3) EU-15, DK, F, IRL, I and S, 1996.
(4) EU-15, DK, F, IRL, I, NL, P and S, 1996.
(5) EU-15, DK, F, I, S and UK, 1996.
(6) EU-15, DK, F, I, NL, P, S and UK, 1996.

Source: Eurostat (SME)

In terms of profitability, Finland ranked amongst the countries recording the highest gross operating rates (operating surplus as a share of turnover) for road haulage enterprises, with this ratio reaching 28% in 1997. Rates close to 20% were also recorded in Austria, Italy and the Netherlands, whilst France completed the ranking with a gross operating rate of just 6%.

LABOUR AND PRODUCTIVITY

Employment in road transport activities exceeded 2.6 million persons. Road freight transport alone accounted for 1.7 million persons, with the average road haulage enterprise employing approximately 4 persons (one less than the passenger transport average).

Sole proprietors common in Spain for road haulage
Spain was the European country with the lowest average number of persons employed in road transport, with less than 2 persons employed on average by each road haulage enterprise. This figure could be compared with averages of more than 10 persons in both Luxembourg and the Netherlands. These differences could be explained, in part, by the high number of sole-proprietors in Spain. Independent lorry drivers represented 53% of total employment within the road freight sector in Spain, as opposed to less than 10% in Luxembourg.

Using the wage adjusted labour productivity ratio, Portugal ranked in 1997 as the most productive country in the road haulage sector (147%), largely as a result of low unit personnel costs. At the other end of the range was France, where the relatively low value added resulted in a productivity ratio of 104%.

Unit personnel costs in road transport enterprises were within a narrow range for most Member States, between 27 thousand ECU per employee in France and Finland and 33 thousand ECU per employee in Belgium and the Netherlands (1997). Only Portugal (13 thousand ECU per employee) recorded significantly lower unit personnel costs. This figure was equivalent to less than 20% of total operating costs, whilst the corresponding proportions for the majority of the other Member States were close to a third, rising to as high as 45% in the Netherlands.

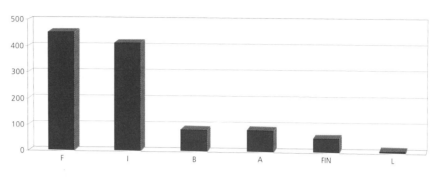

Figure 18.8

Road transport (NACE Rev. 1 60.2)
Number of persons employed, 1997 (thousands) (1)

(1) F, I and L, 1996; DK, D, EL, E, IRL, NL, P, S and UK, not available.

Source: Eurostat (SBS)

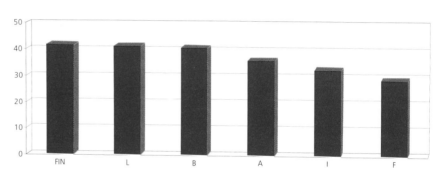

Figure 18.9

Road transport (NACE Rev. 1 60.2)
Apparent labour productivity, 1997 (thousand ECU per person employed) (1)

(1) F, I and L, 1996; DK, D, EL, E, IRL, NL, P, S and UK, not available.

Source: Eurostat (SBS)

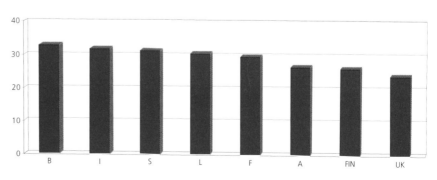

Figure 18.10

Road transport (NACE Rev. 1 60.2)
Unit personnel costs, 1997 (thousand ECU per employee) (1)

(1) F, I, L, FIN and S, 1996; DK, D, EL, E, IRL, NL and P, not available.

Source: Eurostat (SBS)

SUB-CHAPTER 18.2
AIR TRANSPORT
(NACE Rev. 1 62 AND 63.23)

The air transport industry comprises enterprises which are exclusively or primarily engaged in the transport of passengers and goods by air on scheduled services (NACE Rev. 1 62.1) as well as unscheduled services, helicopter and air taxi services and the employment of aircraft for private use (NACE Rev. 1 62.2). Space transport activities (NACE Rev. 1 62.3), essentially the launching of satellites and space vehicles, completes the coverage of Division 62. This sub-chapter also encompasses supporting air transport activities which are covered by NACE Rev. 1 63.23, which includes the operation of terminal facilities and airports, as well as air-traffic-control activities.

Air transport has witnessed strong growth in recent decades, intra-European passenger traffic grew at an average annual rate of 7.8% in the 1980's and by 6.7% per annum between 1990 and 1997, jumping from 96 billion passenger-kilometres in 1980 to 322 billion passenger-kilometres in 1997. Air transport accounted for 6.7% of total passenger transport within the EU, up from 4.9% in 1990 and 3.0% in 1980. Worldwide traffic of EU carriers was over 600 billion passenger kilometres in 1997.

More than 2,500 enterprises,
generally larger than average

The European air transport sector (NACE Rev. 1 Division 62) numbered more than 2.5 thousand enterprises in 1997[10] and generated turnover in excess of 75.9 billion ECU[11].

Air transport enterprises tend to be larger than in other transport activities. As many as 5.6% of all enterprises were large companies employing more than 250 persons, or an average of more than 3 thousand persons each (1996). Average employment for all size classes exceeded 100 persons per enterprise, more than ten times the levels of the other transport sectors. Average turnover per enterprise was equal to 21.2 million ECU.

(10) B and EL, no data available; I, L, NL and S, 1996.
(11) EL, no data available; I, FIN and S, 1996; L, 1995; NL, 1994.

Airbus share in the fleet on the rise

Data on prominent airline companies in Europe is available from the Association of European Airlines[12] (AEA). In 1999, its 27 members boasted a fleet of 2,099 aircraft, 136 more than the preceding year. One-quarter of the jet fleet was composed of aircraft made by the European consortium Airbus and 59% by Boeing and McDonnell Douglas. However, a look at the order book revealed that these figures were expected to change in the near future. No less than 59% of the 604 aircraft on order in 1999 were Airbuses, against only 21% for Boeing and McDonnell Douglas. In 1999, AEA airlines placed 66 new jet aircraft orders (of which 52 were Airbuses and 13 Boeings), down from a record 334 units in 1998.

Capacity grew faster than traffic in 1999

Total scheduled passenger traffic on EU airlines expanded by 5.9% in 1999, reaching 501.3 billion revenue passenger-kilometres[13] or 1,337 kilometres per inhabitant. Approximately one-fifth of the traffic was accounted for by European routes. The carrying capacity of airlines grew faster than traffic, by 7.0% to 703 billion seat-kilometres. As a consequence the passenger load factor, in other words, the average rate of seating capacity which was actually sold and utilised, decreased to 71.3% although it was still within a percentage point of the all-time high recorded in 1997 (72.0%). Passenger load factors were higher on international routes (71.9%) than on European routes (62.4%). The highest passenger load factor was achieved by KLM (77.3%), followed by Air France (76.2%) and Lufthansa (74.1%), whilst the lowest was recorded by Luxair (49.7%).

(12) Adria Airways Slovenia, Aer Lingus Ireland, Air France, Air Malta, Alitalia, Austrian Airlines, Balkan Bulgarian Airlines, British Airways, British Midland airways, Cargolux Airlines, Croatia Airlines, CSA Czech Airlines, Cyprus Airways, Finnair, Iberia (E), Icelandair, JAT Yugoslav Airlines, KLM (NL), Lufthansa (D), Luxair, Malev Hungarian Airlines, Olympic (EL), Sabena (B), SAS (DK, S, NO), Swissair, TAP-Air Portugal, Turkish Airlines.
(13) Revenue passenger kilometres: one fare-paying passenger transported one kilometre, counted on a point-to-point basis, carried at 25% or more of the normal applicable fare for the journey. RPKs are computed by multiplying the number of revenue passengers by the kilometres they are flown.

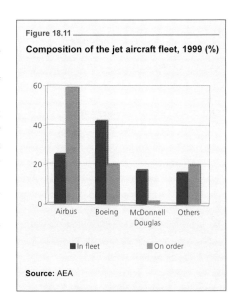

Figure 18.11

Composition of the jet aircraft fleet, 1999 (%)

■ In fleet   ■ On order

Source: AEA

Table 18.6

Air transport (NACE Rev. 1 62)

Breakdown of turnover and employment by employment size class, 1997 (%)

	Micro (0-9)		Small (10-49)		Medium (50-249)		Large (250+)	
	Turnover (1)	Employment (2)	Turnover (3)	Employment (4)	Turnover (5)	Employment (5)	Turnover (6)	Employment (7)
EU-15	2.3	1.8	3.6	3.0	8.0	5.5	86.0	89.7
B	4.9	2.2	16.5	5.7	9.4	6.6	70.8	85.5
DK	:	:	:	:	:	:	0.0	0.0
D	0.3	2.4	1.2	4.2	1.8	4.7	96.8	88.8
EL	:	:	:	:	:	:	:	:
E	:	0.7	:	3.0	:	9.5	:	86.7
F	2.2	1.0	1.5	1.7	2.9	2.7	93.4	94.6
IRL	:	:	:	:	:	:	:	:
I	0.9	1.2	3.9	3.0	6.9	7.0	88.3	88.8
L	:	:	:	:	:	:	:	:
NL	:	0.8	:	0.7	:	:	:	:
A	:	:	:	:	:	:	:	:
P	:	:	5.7	3.2	:	:	:	93.1
FIN	1.9	1.6	1.7	1.8	:	:	:	:
S	1.8	:	4.4	3.8	6.3	5.5	87.4	:
UK	3.8	3.4	4.5	2.3	:	:	:	:

(1) EU-15, F, I and S, 1996.
(2) EU-15, F, I and NL, 1996.
(3) EU-15, F, I, P and S, 1996.
(4) EU-15, F, I, NL, P and S, 1996.
(5) EU-15, B, F, I and S, 1996.
(6) EU-15, B, DK, F, I and S, 1996.
(7) EU-15, B, DK, F, I and P, 1996.

Source: Eurostat (SME)

Table 18.7

AEA airlines scheduled passenger traffic, 1999

	Country	Passenger traffic (million passenger-kilometres)	Share of traffic on European routes (%)	Annual growth of traffic (%)	Passenger load (%)	Passenger load on European routes (%)
Sabena	B	17,693	36.8	15.4	65.7	61.4
SAS	DK, S, NO	21,160	41.3	1.6	63.7	58.2
Lufthansa	D	86,154	19.4	14.2	74.1	62.7
Olympic	EL	8,306	39.1	-3.0	62.0	55.9
Iberia	E	34,607	21.4	6.4	68.9	66.2
Air France	F	83,823	11.2	12.5	76.2	66.5
Aer Lingus	IRL	7,602	36.2	17.6	73.9	73.7
Alitalia	I	36,690	19.9	3.2	67.4	59.7
Luxair	L	738	74.8	62.6	49.7	49.4
KLM	NL	58,113	12.8	1.5	77.3	68.5
Austrian	A	7,891	29.8	8.3	66.1	58.2
TAP	P	9,380	37.3	0.3	67.8	62.5
Finnair	FIN	7,803	43.9	-27.2	61.9	55.6
British Airways	UK	118,016	14.2	1.7	70.1	62.7
British Midland	UK	3,401	60.4	10.8	62.5	62.4
EU-15	EU-15	501,373	19.6	5.9	71.3	62.4
Icelandair	IS	3,658	49.6	-1.5	71.4	71.3
Swissair	CH	31,767	22.2	13.3	72.4	60.2
Adria Airways	SI	515	100.0	25.1	55.1	55.1
Air Malta	MT	1,978	87.3	3.1	67.5	69.8
Balkan	BG	1,486	47.6	-26.6	57.9	54.1
Croatia Airlines	HR	560	82.9	2.8	49.7	48.0
CSA Czech Airlines	CZ	2,871	47.9	8.8	64.7	57.7
Cyprus Airways	CY	2,687	95.7	-0.9	69.1	70.7
JAT	YU	269	25.0	-63.2	49.6	44.0
Malev	HU	2,861	60.9	14.0	63.4	58.8
Turkish Airlines	TR	13,350	42.5	2.4	60.0	60.4

Source: AEA

American airlines largest due to domestic traffic

North American airlines accounted for the largest share of world passenger traffic. No fewer than six of the world's top ten airlines were American, including the four largest. United Airlines topped the ranking with 201.8 billion passenger-kilometres carried in 1999, ahead of American Airlines (177.3 billion) and Delta Airlines (168.5 billion). The first European company was British Airways, in fifth place with 118.0 billion passenger-kilometres. European companies fared better when taking into account only international traffic. British Airways was the leading carrier in the world for international routes with more than 114.5 billion passenger-kilometres carried in 1999, of which 97.7 billion were on routes outside Europe. British Airways preceded Lufthansa (80.5 billion passenger-kilometres on international routes), Air France (74.6 billion) and United Airlines (73.9 billion).

Box 18.4

Airline strategies will continue to be influenced by the progressive liberalisation and privatisation of the EU air transport sector, which has been accompanied by the formation of very large alliances between airlines. In September 2000 the "Star Alliance" network (19.1% of world traffic[14]) regrouped Air Canada, Air New Zealand, All Nippon, Ansett Australia, Austrian, British Midland, Lauda Air (A), Lufthansa, Mexicana, SAS, Singapore, Thai, United and VARIG (BR). The "One World" alliance (13.0% of world traffic) included Aer Lingus, American Airlines, British Airways, Cathay Pacific (HK), Iberia, LanChile, Finnair and Qantas (AU). The "Qualiflyer Group" (3.1% of world traffic) is an alliance of eleven European airlines including Swissair, Sabena (B), TAP (P), Turkish, Crossair (CH), LOT (PL), Portugalia, AOM (F), Air Littoral (F), Air Europe (I) and Volare (I).

---

(14) According to 1998 figures for passenger traffic.

Table 18.8

Top twenty airlines in the world by passengers flown, 1999

		Country	Total scheduled passenger traffic (million passenger-kilometres)	Share of international destinations (%)	World ranking by international traffic
1	United Airlines	USA	201,785	36.6	4
2	American Airlines	USA	177,299	34.3	7
3	Delta Air Lines	USA	168,512	23.8	12
4	Northwest Airlines	USA	119,411	44.3	9
5	British Airways	UK	118,016	97.0	1
6	Continental Airlines	USA	89,997	32.8	17
7	Lufthansa	D	86,154	93.3	2
8	Air France	F	83,823	89.0	3
9	Japan Airlines	JAP	82,904	79.1	5
10	US Airways	USA	66,751	12.9	39
11	Singapore Airlines	SG	64,529	100.0	6
12	Qantas	AU	59,249	75.0	10
13	KLM	NL	58,113	100.0	8
14	All Nippon Airways	JAP	56,725	39.1	22
15	TWA	USA	41,858	17.5	48
16	Cathay Pacific	HK	41,435	100.0	11
17	Air Canada	CA	38,993	64.9	20
18	Thai Airways	TH	38,345	91.4	13
19	Alitalia	I	36,690	80.6	16
20	Korean Air Lines	KR	36,401	88.6	14

Source: IATA, AEA

Table 18.9

Top twenty EU airports by number of passengers, 1999

		Country	Number of passengers (thousands)	World ranking
1	London Heathrow	UK	62,264	4
2	Frankfurt/Main	D	45,858	7
3	Paris Ch. de Gaulle	F	43,597	8
4	Amsterdam Schiphol	NL	36,781	11
5	London Gatwick	UK	30,559	21
6	Madrid Barajas	E	27,532	27
7	Paris Orly	F	25,349	32
8	Roma Fiumicino	I	24,024	33
9	München F.J. Strauss	D	21,283	40
10	Bruxelles National	B	20,025	44
11	Palma de Mallorca	E	19,227	47
12	Manchester Ringway Intl	UK	17,760	50
13	København Kastrup	DK	17,404	52
14	Barcelona Transoceanico	E	17,368	53
15	Stockholm Arlanda	S	17,364	54
16	Milano Malpensa	I	16,914	55
17	Düsseldorf Rhein-Ruhr	D	15,926	58
18	Dublin Collinstown	IRL	12,802	72
19	Wien Schwechat	A	11,204	78
20	Berlin Tegel	D	9,606	85

Source: ACI

London Heathrow largest airport in
the EU with 62 million passengers

North America accounted for fourteen airports in the world's top twenty in 1999, including the top three, whilst only four of the top twenty were airports located in the EU. The largest airport in the world was Atlanta Hartsfield International Airport with more than 77.9 million passengers per annum. With a notable rise in traffic of 6.1% it overtook the long-time leader Chicago O'Hare (72.6 million passengers) and preceded Los Angeles (63.9 million passengers). The first EU airport in the ranking was London Heathrow in fourth place with 62.3 million passengers. At a European level, Heathrow preceded Frankfurt, Paris Charles de Gaulle and Amsterdam (all with in excess of 30 million passengers per annum).

25.8 billion tonnes-kilometres
of freight transported by air

Freight transported by EU airlines grew by 2.6% in 1999 to reach 25.8 billion tonne-kilometres, of which only 2.6% concerned European routes. The total revenue load factor (the percentage of total capacity available for freight and mail which is actually sold and utilised) was equal to 67.7% on all routes (and just 54.2% on European routes).

Box 18.5

The largest freight airline in the world in 1999 was Federal Express (USA) with traffic that exceeded 10.0 billion tonne-kilometres, of which only 39.9% were on international routes. It was followed by Lufthansa (D) with more than 6.6 billion tonne-kilometres, almost exclusively on international routes, which made Lufthansa the largest international freight carrier in the world. In general, EU air companies were better placed in the world ranking of freight transport compared to passenger transport. Air France, the sixth freight carrier in the world with 4.7 billion tonnes-kilometres, ranked fourth for international traffic ahead of British Airways (4.2 billion tonnes-kilometres).

Table 18.10

AEA airlines scheduled freight traffic, 1999

	Country	Freight traffic (million tonne-kilometres)	Share of traffic on European routes (%)	Annual growth of traffic (%)	Total revenue load factor (%)	Total revenue load factor on European routes (%)
Sabena (1)	B	:	:	:	65.7	61.4
SAS	DK, S, NO	693	5.1	-8.2	64.3	51.8
Lufthansa	D	6,603	3.1	6.1	72.5	57.2
Olympic	EL	103	31.1	-8.3	50.2	47.5
Iberia	E	774	6.0	2.5	56.5	52.5
Air France	F	4,732	0.4	3.0	71.4	59.0
Aer Lingus	IRL	138	5.1	6.4	68.7	66.0
Alitalia	I	1,611	1.5	8.4	67.5	58.1
Cargolux	L	2,405	0.2	7.1	86.9	:
Luxair	L	6	5.6	:	44.9	46.4
KLM	NL	3,806	2.0	2.6	76.5	61.6
Austrian	A	221	10.1	37.8	66.8	54.6
TAP	P	204	15.3	-11.5	57.2	53.7
Finnair	FIN	252	12.4	-11.2	53.0	45.3
British Airways	UK	4,249	3.3	5.0	61.9	48.0
British Midland	UK	7	66.1	26.8	49.0	49.0
EU-15	EU-15	25,805	2.6	4.3	67.7	54.2
Icelandair	IS	74	40.9	26.8	65.1	62.4
Swissair	CH	1,776	3.2	-6.3	71.8	53.3
Adria Airways	SI	4	100.0	8.1	43.7	46.5
Air Malta	MT	13	73.1	12.3	61.3	67.1
Balkan	BG	12	47.7	-59.2	55.7	41.5
Croatia Airlines	HR	2	84.9	0.5	43.0	41.5
CSA Czech Airlines	CZ	26	23.9	5.9	47.3	49.9
Cyprus Airways	CY	41	95.8	6.9	65.1	62.3
JAT	YU	1	34.5	-78.0	46.5	37.7
Malev	HU	43	18.4	16.5	50.3	44.6
Turkish Airlines	TR	313	28.9	28.7	39.2	48.4

(1) At the beginning of 1997, the responsibility for selling air freight capacity on Sabena services was transferred to Swisscargo.

Source: AEA

Table 18.11

Top twenty airlines in the world by freight flown, 1999

		Country	Total scheduled freight traffic (million tonne-kilometres)	Share of international destinations (%)	World ranking by international traffic
1	Federal Express	USA	10,069	39.9	7
2	Lufthansa	D	6,603	99.7	1
3	United Parcel Service	USA	5,975	29.2	16
4	Korean Air Lines	KR	5,858	98.4	2
5	Singapore Airlines	SG	5,482	100.0	3
6	Air France	F	4,732	99.7	4
7	Japan Airlines	JAP	4,423	93.6	6
8	British Airways	UK	4,249	99.8	5
9	KLM	NL	3,806	100.0	8
10	Cathay Pacific	HK	3,771	100.0	9
11	United Airlines	USA	3,582	73.3	10
12	Northwest Airlines	USA	3,017	74.6	12
13	American Airlines	USA	2,489	76.9	14
14	Cargolux	L	2,405	100.0	11
15	Delta Air Lines	USA	1,985	72.1	20
16	Nippon Cargo	JAP	1,976	100.0	13
17	Swissair	CH	1,776	99.9	15
18	Thai Airways	TH	1,671	98.0	17
19	Alitalia	I	1,611	99.4	18
20	Qantas	AU	1,589	91.5	19

Source: IATA, AEA

Table 18.12

Top twenty EU airports by freight traffic, 1999

		Country	Freight traffic (thousand tonnes) (1)	World ranking
1	Frankfurt/Main	D	1,539	9
2	London Heathrow	UK	1,355	13
3	Paris Ch. de Gaulle	F	1,226	14
4	Amsterdam Schiphol	NL	1,225	15
5	Bruxelles National	B	656	27
6	Luxembourg Findel	L	448	38
7	Köln/Bonn	D	410	43
8	København Kastrup	DK	389	46
9	Madrid Barajas	E	318	55
10	London Gatwick	UK	314	56
11	Milano Malpensa	I	251	69
12	Liège Bierset	B	208	76
13	London Stansted	UK	194	78
14	Roma Fiumicino	I	185	82
15	Stockholm Arlanda	S	144	93
16	East Midlands	UK	142	94
17	München F.J. Strauss	D	138	95
18	Paris Orly	F	135	96
19	Wien Schwechat	A	126	105
20	Manchester Ringway Intl	UK	112	111

(1) Loaded & unloaded freight and mail in metric tonnes.

Source: ACI

The busiest airport in the world for freight traffic in 1999 was Memphis, a major express courier hub that ranked only 82nd in terms of passenger traffic (2.4 million tonnes of freight loaded and unloaded). The first EU airport was ranked in ninth place, Frankfurt (with 1.5 million tonnes), followed by London Heathrow, Amsterdam and Paris Charles de Gaulle, the only EU airports that exceeded 1 million tonnes of annual freight traffic.

Rising trends in employment

Total employment in the air transport sector (NACE Rev. 1 62) exceeded 309 thousand persons in 1997[15]. Virtually all persons employed were employees, self-employed persons representing less than 1.0% of the workforce in most Member States. Figures from AEA airlines indicate that employment in this sector has been on a rising trend in the second half of the 1990s, up from 265 thousand employees in 1995 to 310 thousand in 1999 (EU airlines only).

Women represented 35.4% of the workforce in 1998, a share higher than in the rest of the transport sector, but lower than the average for EU service activities. As regards the education level of the workforce, a relatively high share (20.2%, 1998) of the persons employed in EU air transport activities had completed a higher education university degree or equivalent.

(15) EL and S, no data available; I and FIN, 1996; L, 1995; NL and UK, 1994.

Table 18.13

Air transport (NACE Rev.1 62)

Composition of the labour force, 1999 (%)

	Women (1)	Part-time (2)	Highly-educated (3)
EU-15	35.4	:	20.2
B	36.9	15.1	29.8
DK	44.9	:	28.4
D	41.6	17.3	27.8
EL	38.1	:	:
E	46.4	10.5	41.9
F	37.0	9.1	43.4
IRL	52.3	:	:
I	37.6	:	11.1
L	33.5	:	:
NL	38.7	34.8	32.5
A	46.4	:	:
P	41.9	:	18.4
FIN	41.7	:	28.7
S	:	:	:
UK	36.8	:	28.7

(1) EU-15, 1998; DK and EL, 1997.
(2) B, 1998.
(3) EU-15, 1998; I, 1997; DK and P, 1996.

Source: Eurostat (LFS)

Frequent atypical work patterns

Air transport activities also recorded a higher than average proportion of atypical work patterns. In 1997, just 29.1% of the persons employed never worked on Saturdays and 35.7% never worked on Sundays (compared to service sector (NACE Rev. 1 Sections G to K) averages of 40.8% and 69.6%).

Modest profitability

Value added represented approximately one-quarter of the turnover generated by the EU's air transport sector (25.7%, 1997). Apparent labour productivity levels were relatively high, ranging between 47.1 thousand ECU per person employed in Portugal (1997) and 93.8 thousand ECU in Luxembourg (again 1997).

It was estimated that as much as 85.0% of the value added generated by the sector in 1997 was accounted for by personnel costs, one of the highest proportions in all services activities. The EU gross operating rate was low at an estimated 3.9% in 1997, with even lower rates recorded in France (2.3%, 1997) and Belgium (2.6%, 1997), well below the figures of Spain (12.4%, 1997) and Luxembourg (17.4%, 1995).

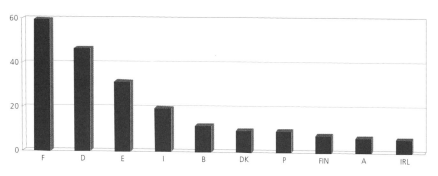

Figure 18.12

Air transport (NACE Rev. 1 62)

Number of persons employed, 1997 (thousands) (1)

(1) I and FIN, 1996; EL, L, NL, S and UK, not available.

Source: Eurostat (SBS)

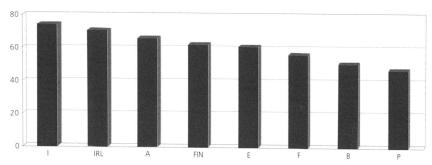

Figure 18.13

Air transport (NACE Rev. 1 62)

Apparent labour productivity, 1997 (thousand ECU per person employed) (1)

(1) I and FIN, 1996; DK, D, EL, L, NL, S and UK, not available.

Source: Eurostat (SBS)

Figure 18.14

Air transport (NACE Rev. 1 62)

Unit personnel costs, 1997 (thousand ECU per employee) (1)

(1) F, I, L, FIN and S, 1996; DK, D, EL, E, IRL, NL and P, not available.

Source: Eurostat (SBS)

SUB-CHAPTER 18.3
RAILWAY TRANSPORT (NACE Rev. 1 60.1)

This sub-chapter includes activities that are exclusively or primarily engaged in the transport of passengers and goods by rail. It also includes the equipment and facilities required to provide this transport, including private railway lines. Not included in this sector are: metropolitan rail networks (NACE Rev. 1 60.21), repair and maintenance of rolling stock (NACE Rev. 1 35.20), sleeping car services (NACE Rev. 1 55.23) and dining car services (NACE Rev. 1 55.30).

Rail accounts for a declining
share of transport services

The European rail network encompassed 155 thousand kilometres (44.4% electrified) in 1998. Rail remains an important mode of transport, accounting for 5.8% of passenger transport and 14.5% of goods inland transport[16] in 1997. It has however lost significant ground relative to other transport modes. Indeed, railways accounted for 10.1% of passenger transport in 1970 before dropping to 8.2% in 1980 and 6.5% in 1990. As regards goods transport, the negative trends was similar and as strong, with a modal share for rail that declined from 32.7% in 1970 to 25.9% in 1980 and 18.7% in 1990.

---

(16) Road, rail, pipelines and inland waterways; 8.6% including intra-EU sea transport.

Modest increase of passenger traffic...

Rail passenger traffic progressed only moderately over the last couple of decades, reaching 282 billion passenger-kilometres in the EU in 1997, 3% above its level of 1990 (274 billion passenger-kilometres) and 12% above that of 1980 (253 billion passenger-kilometres). Related to population, each EU citizen travelled on average 760 km by train in 1998. The French (1,093 km), Danish (1,056 km) and Austrian (1,015 km) were the most active train users as opposed to the Irish (378 km) and the Greek (171 km). Urban rail transport (such as tram or metro transport) accounted for an additional 48 billion passenger-kilometres in 1997.

... but declining freight traffic

For rail freight, there has been a downward trend in the volume of goods transported, falling to 237 billion tonne-kilometres in 1997 (from 255 billion tonne-kilometres in 1990 and 283 billion tonne-kilometres in 1980). Rail freight transport declined by 1.2% on average during the 1980's, a trend that continued during the period 1990-1997, despite growth of 7.8% in 1997. The main beneficiary of this decline has been road transport that boasted average annual growth rates close to 4.0% through the 1970's, 1980's and 1990's.

Table 18.14

Passengers transported by rail
(billion passenger-kilometres) (1)

	1970	1980	1990	1998
EU-15	216.4	252.7	273.8	278.9
B	7.6	7.0	6.5	7.1
DK	3.6	4.5	5.1	5.4
D	56.9	63.0	62.1	59.2
EL	1.5	1.5	2.0	1.8
E	15.0	14.8	16.7	18.3
F	41.0	54.7	63.8	64.3
IRL	0.8	1.0	1.2	1.4
I	34.9	42.9	48.3	47.3
L (2)	0.2	0.2	0.2	0.3
NL	8.0	8.9	11.1	14.8
A	6.4	7.6	8.7	8.0
P	3.5	6.1	5.7	4.6
FIN	2.2	3.2	3.3	3.4
S	4.6	7.0	6.0	7.0
UK	30.4	30.3	33.2	36.1

(1) Including non-UIC railways.
(2) 1997.

Source: ECMT, UIC

Figure 18.15

Share of rail in total goods transported, 1997 (%) (1)

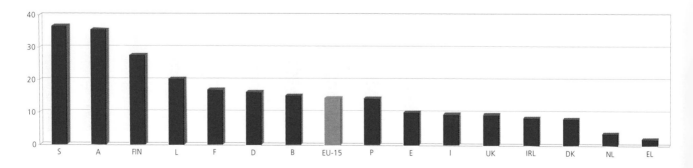

(1) Excluding sea transport.

Source: Eurostat, ECMT, UIC

Table 18.15 — Goods transported by rail (billion tonne-kilometres) (1)				
	1970	1980	1990	1998
EU-15	282.8	287.3	256.2	235.5
B	7.9	8.0	8.4	7.6
DK	1.9	1.6	1.7	1.7
D	113.0	121.3	101.7	73.3
EL	0.7	0.8	0.6	0.3
E	9.7	11.3	11.6	11.6
F	67.6	66.4	50.7	54.0
IRL	0.5	0.6	0.6	0.5
I	18.1	18.4	19.5	22.4
L	0.8	0.7	0.6	0.6
NL	3.7	3.4	3.1	3.8
A	10.0	11.2	12.8	15.4
P	0.8	1.0	1.5	2.0
FIN	6.3	8.3	8.4	9.9
S	17.3	16.6	19.1	14.3
UK	24.5	17.6	16.0	18.2

(1) Including non-UIC railways.

Source: ECMT, UIC

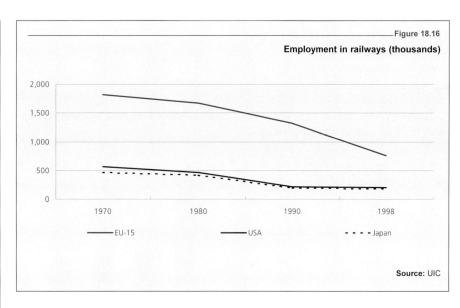

Figure 18.16

Employment in railways (thousands)

Source: UIC

Continued reduction of employment

There were under 760 thousand people working in railway transport services in the EU in 1998, down from 1.3 million in 1990. Employment in European railways has declined continuously since the beginning of the 1980s and the number of persons employed has been more than halved between 1980 and 1998.

USA favour freight transport by rail more than the EU or Japan

Comparison of EU railways to those of the USA and Japan reveals significant differences in orientation. The US railway system is heavily dominated by freight traffic that is moved over a large geographical area with longer distances between population centres. In contrast, passenger usage of the US railway network was comparatively low compared to the EU. Japan, by contrast, was dominated by passenger traffic, due to population concentrations in many parts of the country and extreme road traffic congestion.

About 50 meters of rail track per square kilometre in the EU and Japan

The length of railway lines in the EU (155.4 thousand kilometres, 1998) was much greater than in Japan (20.1 thousand kilometres, 1998) and far less than in the USA (232.2 thousand kilometres, 1998). On average however, the density of railway tracks was comparable in the EU and Japan, with around 50 metres of track per square kilometre, about double the density found in the USA. The EU and Japan had higher proportions of electric track, with 44% and 60% of track electrified respectively, against practically none in the USA.

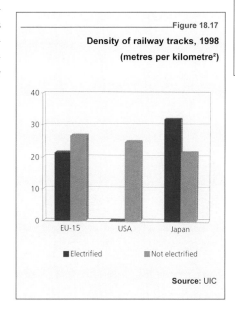

Figure 18.17

Density of railway tracks, 1998 (metres per kilometre²)

■ Electrified   ■ Not electrified

Source: UIC

Box 18.6

One of the priorities on the agenda of the EU is to create Trans-European Networks (TENs). This program also constitutes the cornerstone of European policy in terms of transport infrastructure. In terms of passenger transport, the focus is on extending the high-speed network, to increase the market share of rail in the passenger transport market. The network to be developed also seeks to optimise the co-ordination of rail services with other means of transport. The intention is to integrate the rail network with other transport systems: metros, trams, airports, as well as private means of transport. For freight, co-ordination is also being pursued, to create flexibility and ease of transfer of rail freight to and from other means of transport. Development of new lines, for example, the Channel Tunnel, gives distinct advantages to rail freight.

SUB-CHAPTER 18.4:
WATER TRANSPORT
(NACE Rev. 1 61 AND 63.22)

This sub-chapter covers all water transport activities included in NACE Rev. 1 Division 61, both sea and coastal transport (NACE Rev. 1 61.1) and inland water transport (NACE Rev. 1 61.2), as well as other supporting water transport activities (NACE Rev.1 63.22) such as for example the operation of harbours and piers.

Almost 30 thousand kilometres of inland waterways
There were 29.8 thousand kilometres of inland waterways[17] in the EU in 1997, a level that has remained stable during recent decades. The highest density was found in the Netherlands with no less than 120 metres per square kilometre, followed by Belgium with 50 metres per square kilometre, whilst the EU average lay at 9 metres per square kilometre. Four major axis could be identified when looking at the European inland waterways' network. The Basle-Rotterdam axis with the Rhine as its backbone is the most important in the EU. The Main-Danube axis, extending from Bamberg on the Main to Kelheim on the Danube, and connected to the first by the Rhine-Main-Danube canal is the second most important. The third major axis (East-West) is formed by the rivers Elbe, Weser and Ems. The fourth (North-South) serves the regions of Belgium, the Netherlands and France not connected to the Rhine. The main rivers of this axis are the Meuse, Scheldt, Lys and Sambre.

---

(17) Navigable canals, rivers and lakes regularly used for transport.

Figure 18.18

Share of goods transported by inland waterways, 1997 (%) (1)

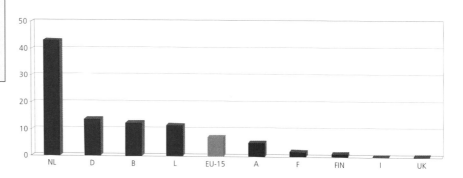

(1) Excluding sea transport.

Source: Eurostat, ECMT, UIC

Building materials and fuel products are the main goods transported by inland waterways
Inland shipping specialises in the transport of large quantities of bulk products, such as sand, ores, coal, chemicals, and oil. The largest volumes of goods transported are cement and building materials (34% of total tonnes-kilometres transported in 1996), petroleum (19%) and coal and other solid mineral fuels (19%). Total goods transported were equal to 118 billion tonne-kilometres in 1997 (120.9 billion tonnes-kilometres in 1998), half the level of rail and a tenth of road transport, equivalent to a market share of 7.2% of all goods transported. The country displaying the highest specialisation in inland water transport was the Netherlands, where over two-fifths of goods were transported by inland waterways, some 41 billion tonne-kilometres in 1997 (40.7 billion tonnes-kilometres in 1998). Germany (13.8%), Belgium (12.4%) and Luxembourg (11.5%) were the only other countries where more than 10% of goods were moved using this transport mode.

Slow growth of traffic
Over the years, growth in inland waterways shipping has been fairly limited compared to other means of transportation, equal to 0.1% per annum during the 1980's, accelerating to 1.3% per annum between 1990 and 1997. The busiest inland EU port in 1998 was Duisburg (D) with almost 50 million tonnes of freight loaded and unloaded, followed by Liège (B) and Paris (F) with over 18 million tonnes each.

Table 18.16

Water transport (NACE Rev. 1 61)

Breakdown of turnover and employment by employment size class, 1997 (%)

	Micro (0-9)		Small (10-49)		Medium (50-249)		Large (250+)	
	Turnover (1)	Employment (2)	Turnover (1)	Employment (3)	Turnover (1)	Employment (4)	Turnover (5)	Employment (6)
EU-15	14.7	17.0	14.8	12.7	25.5	23.4	45.0	46.9
B	27.2	24.0	54.2	25.6	:	:	:	:
DK	13.7	11.2	13.8	9.5	15.8	11.6	56.8	67.7
D	16.6	13.7	28.9	28.5	35.2	26.5	19.3	31.3
EL	:	:	:	:	:	:	:	:
E	:	7.3	:	21.3	:	:	:	:
F	22.1	23.8	7.4	8.8	17.5	18.4	52.9	49.1
IRL	:	:	:	:	:	:	:	:
I	2.1	6.3	6.8	9.5	39.1	30.9	51.9	53.3
L	:	:	:	:	:	:	:	:
NL	:	49.6	:	12.5	:	17.5	:	20.3
A	:	:	:	:	:	:	0.0	0.0
P	:	11.3	:	24.1	:	:	:	:
FIN	6.0	3.8	13.1	6.5	:	:	51.0	66.6
S	12.4	:	23.4	7.2	31.8	27.4	32.4	:
UK	21.9	18.9	11.6	9.1	:	:	:	:

(1) EU-15, DK, F, I and S, 1996.
(2) EU-15, DK, F, I, NL and P, 1996.
(3) EU-15, DK, F, I, NL, P and S, 1996.
(4) EU-15, DK, F, I, NL and S, 1996.
(5) EU-15, DK, F, I, FIN and S, 1996.
(6) EU-15, DK, F, I, NL and FIN, 1996.

Source: Eurostat (SME)

Table 18.17

Top twenty inland ports in the EU ranked by traffic (million tonnes) (1)

		Country	1996	1997	1998
1	Duisburg	D	44.4	49.3	49.7
2	Liège	B	15.8	17.5	18.3
3	Paris	F	18.5	17.0	18.1
4	Strasbourg	F	9.3	9.3	9.4
5	NV Zeekanaal, Brabant	B	8.6	8.7	8.7
6	Köln	D	7.6	7.9	8.6
7	Mannheim	D	7.9	7.8	8.6
8	Ludwigshafen	D	7.7	8.0	7.5
9	Karlsruhe	D	10.3	8.4	6.2
10	Neuss	D	4.7	4.3	5.6
11	Dortmund	D	4.8	5.4	5.5
12	Heilbronn	D	5.2	4.9	5.4
13	Ports Rhénans Alsace	F	4.5	4.8	5.0
14	Frankfurt am Main	D	3.8	3.7	3.9
15	Saarlouis/Dillingen	D	3.6	3.3	3.5
16	Düsseldorf	D	3.0	3.2	3.5
17	Bruxelles/Brussel	B	4.8	4.9	3.4
18	Kehl	D	2.9	2.9	3.1
19	Regensburg	D	1.9	2.0	3.1
20	Vänerhamn	S	2.3	2.4	3.0

(1) Fluvial and fluvio-maritime traffic.

Source: EFIP

12% of the world sea merchant fleet under EU flag

Turning to sea transport, the EU merchant fleet numbered 5,343 vessels in 1999. This was equivalent to 61.9 million gross tonnes (GT), or about 12.1% of total world tonnage. The European Economic Area (EEA) registered a fleet of 6,817 ships or 83.9 million GT, representing 16.4% of world tonnage. That share has been in constant decline between 1985 when it still accounted for 27.7% of the total and the all-time low recorded in 1998 (16.0%). It should be noted that these figures refer only to ships registered in EEA countries. According to Lloyd's figures, some 60% of the total fleet controlled by owners from EEA countries fly a third country flag. It is estimated that the real tonnage of EEA-controlled ships reached 196 million GT in 1999, well over a third of the world fleet. EEA-flagged ships can be broken down by type: with 18.3% dry bulk, 41.6% liquid bulk and 38.1% other dry cargo (of which 15.7% were container vessels alone). Passenger and cruise vessels accounted for only 2.0% of the gross tonnage.

Table 18.18

World fleet, as of 31st December 1998

	Number of ships (units)	Gross tonnage (thousand GT)
B	183	127
DK (1)	1,056	5,790
D	1,158	8,083
EL	1,545	25,225
E (1)	1,570	1,838
F (1)	808	4,848
IRL	150	184
I	1,329	6,819
L	45	932
NL (1)	1,358	5,233
A	22	68
P (1)	444	1,132
FIN	284	1,629
S	562	2,552
UK (1)	1,686	8,335
EU-15	12,200	72,795
China	3,214	16,503
Japan	8,922	17,780
South Korea	2,381	5,694
USA	5,626	11,852
World	85,828	531,893

(1) Including International Register and other affiliated flags.

Source: Lloyd's Register of Shipping

Table 18.19

Water transport (NACE Rev. 1 61)

Composition of the labour force, 1999 (%)

	Women (1)	Part-time	Highly-educated (2)
EU-15	:	:	24.0
B	35.7	:	:
DK	18.3	:	60.9
D	23.8	:	34.0
EL	:	:	36.3
E	:	:	27.5
F	36.0	:	47.8
IRL	:	:	:
I	12.7	:	:
L	:	:	:
NL	:	:	:
A	:	:	:
P	:	:	:
FIN	36.0	:	46.0
S	:	:	:
UK	26.0	:	30.1

(1) D and F, 1998; DK, 1997; I, 1996.
(2) EL, 1998; EU-15, 1997.

Source: Eurostat (LFS)

A male dominated workforce with frequent atypical working patterns

EU employment in water transport activities was estimated at some 157 thousand persons (1996). It is a transport mode that is largely male dominated, as women represented only 17.4% of the workforce (1998), a share much lower than the average service activity. One other characteristic of the workforce is its relatively high education level as 24.0% (1997) of the persons employed possessed a third level education degree, a proportion above the average (19.3%).

Box 18.7

The European Community Shipowners' Association (ECSA) estimate that about 155 thousand seafarers were working on-board EU flagged vessels in 1998, a figure similar to 1995, down from 169 thousand in 1992. Whilst the majority of seafarers were EU nationals, there has recently been a trend towards a greater proportion of non-EU nationals, whose share reached 22% in 1998 (up from 15% in 1992 and 10% in 1983).

Water transport activities also display more frequent atypical work patterns than the average. Only 20.8% of the persons employed never worked on Saturdays (1997) and 27.7% never on Sundays (40.8% and 69.6% respectively for services, NACE Rev. 1 Sections G to K). Night work concerned 54.1% of the workforce, against only 15.0% in the average service activity.

Intra-EU sea shipping the second largest transport mode for goods

As far as shipping is concerned, a distinction can be made between deep-sea transport, that refers to shipping on long sea routes, and short-sea shipping, that covers transport services of passengers and goods between national or European ports. Short-sea shipping was in 1997 the second most important freight transport mode in the EU. Intra-EU traffic reached 1,124 billion tonne-kilometres, a level only slightly below that of road transport. Growth recorded in the 1980's for short-sea transport reached 1.7% per annum, rising to 2.9% per annum between 1990 and 1997.

World sea borne trade declined in 1998

Looking at world trade, sea borne freight transport experienced a moderate decline of 1.1% in 1998 to 21.4 thousand billion tonne-miles. Transport of crude oil alone accounted for over a third of the total (36.5%) and was the only product category witnessing a traffic increase (1.9%) in 1998. Other important goods categories included iron ore (11.3%), coal (10.3%), oil products (9.2%) and grain (4.9%), all of which lost ground in 1998. This was especially the case for grain (-10.2%) and coal (-5.0%).

Rotterdam the largest sea port in the EU

The busiest sea-port in the EU in 1997 was Rotterdam (NL) with traffic of more than 300 million tonnes, practically three times more than the next largest port, Antwerp (B). Rotterdam was also the largest port in terms of container transport, with 6.0 million TEUs[18] in 1998, ahead of Hamburg (3.5 million) and Antwerp (3.3 million). One of the main trends in the port industry is to switch to containers, away from conventional general cargo transportation. This is clearly reflected in the growth rates recorded in the largest ports. General cargo traffic in the top five sea-ports grew at an average rate of 1.4% per annum between 1990 and 1997, whilst container traffic grew by more than 6% per annum.

(18) TEU: Twenty Foot Equivalent Unit: a measurement of carrying capacity on a containership, referring to a common container size of 20ft in length.

_____ Table 18.20

Top twenty sea ports in the EU ranked by traffic (million tonnes)

		Country	1970	1980	1990	1997
1	Rotterdam	NL	226	276	288	303
2	Antwerpen	B	78	82	102	112
3	Marseille	F	74	103	90	94
4	Hamburg	D	47	63	61	77
5	Le Havre	F	58	77	54	60
6	Amsterdam	NL	21	34	47	57
7	London	UK	64	48	58	56
8	Teese & Hartlepool	UK	23	38	40	51
9	Trieste	I	27	38	34	46
10	Genova	I	53	51	44	43
11	Forth ports	UK	:	29	25	43
12	Algeciras	E	8	22	25	40
13	Dunkerque	F	25	41	37	37
14	Wilhelmshaven	D	22	32	16	36
15	Milford Haven	UK	41	39	32	35
16	Bremen/Bremerhaven	D	23	25	28	34
17	Southampton	UK	28	25	29	33
18	Zeebrugge	B	8	12	30	32
19	Tarragona	E	4	20	24	31
20	Liverpool	UK	31	13	23	31

Source: ISL

_____ Table 18.21

Top twenty ports in the EU ranked by container traffic (thousand TEU)

		Country	1990	1995	1997	1998
1	Rotterdam	NL	3,667	4,787	5,495	6,011
2	Hamburg	D	1,969	2,890	3,337	3,547
3	Antwerpen	B	1,549	2,329	2,969	3,266
4	Felixstowe	UK	1,436	1,924	2,237	2,500
5	Gioia Tauro	I	:	16	1,449	2,126
6	Bremen/B'haven	D	1,198	1,524	1,538	1,826
7	Algeciras	E	553	1,155	1,703	1,812
8	Le Havre	F	858	970	1,185	1,319
9	Genoa	I	310	615	1,180	1,266
10	Barcelona	E	448	689	972	1,095
11	Valencia	E	387	672	832	1,005
12	Zeebrugge	B	342	528	648	776
13	La Spezia	I	450	965	616	:
14	Southampton	UK	345	681	:	:
15	Piraeus	EL	426	600	:	:
16	Marseille	F	482	498	:	:
17	Gothenburg	S	352	458	:	:
18	Liverpool	UK	239	406	:	:
19	Livorno	I	416	424	:	:
20	Tilbury	UK	363	338	:	:

Source: Containerisation International Yearbook, Port of Rotterdam

Figure 18.19

Water transport (NACE Rev. 1 61)

Number of persons employed, 1997 (thousands) (1)

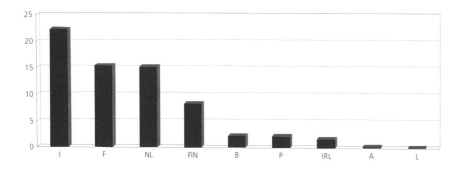

(1) I, L and FIN, 1996; DK, D, EL, E, S and UK, not available.

Source: Eurostat (SBS)

Figure 18.20

Water transport (NACE Rev. 1 61)

Apparent labour productivity, 1997 (thousand ECU per person employed) (1)

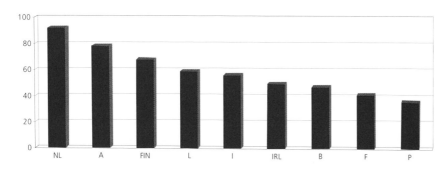

(1) I, L and FIN, 1996; DK, D, EL, E, S and UK, not available.

Source: Eurostat (SBS)

Figure 18.21

Water transport (NACE Rev. 1 61)

Unit personnel costs, 1997 (thousand ECU per employee) (1)

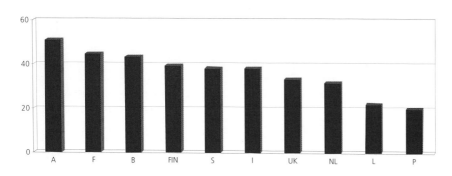

(1) I, L, NL, FIN and S, 1996; DK, D, EL, E and IRL, not available.

Source: Eurostat (SBS)

_____Table 18.22

Land transport; transport via pipelines (NACE Rev. 1 60)

Employment related indicators, 1997

	B	DK	D	EL	E	F	IRL	I (1)	L (1)	NL (1)	A	P	FIN (2)	S	UK
Number of persons employed (thousands)	122.2	:	:	:	:	637.7	21.5	559.8	9.0	179.3	139.1	94.2	63.0	:	:
Employees/number of persons employed (%)	91.6	:	:	:	:	92.2	87.1	70.7	94.1	91.5	93.3	89.3	80.6	:	:
Average no. of persons employed/enterprise (units)	:	:	:	:	:	8.0	8.0	4.0	15.0	16.0	15.0	6.0	3.0	:	:

(1) 1996. (2) Employees as a share of the number of persons employed, 1996.

_____Table 18.23

Land transport; transport via pipelines (NACE Rev. 1 60)

Turnover related indicators, 1997

	B	DK	D	EL	E	F	IRL	I (1)	L (1)	NL	A	P	FIN	S (1)	UK
Turnover (million ECU)	8,582	:	:	:	:	44,460	1,253	34,257	736	:	7,022	4,187	4,319	9,466	40,786
Turnover per enterprise (million ECU)	:	:	:	:	:	0.6	0.5	0.2	1.3	:	0.8	0.2	0.2	0.4	0.9
Turnover per person employed (thousand ECU)	70.3	:	:	:	:	69.7	58.2	61.2	82.2	:	50.5	44.5	68.6	:	:

(1) 1996.

_____Table 18.24

Land transport; transport via pipelines (NACE Rev. 1 60)

Performance related indicators, 1997

	B	DK	D	EL	E	F	IRL	I (1)	L (1)	NL	A	P	FIN (2)	S (1)	UK
Value added (million ECU)	5,800	:	:	:	:	18,890	517	18,779	425	:	5,383	1,447	2,636	3,159	18,444
Value added as a share of turnover (%)	67.6	:	:	:	:	42.5	41.2	54.8	57.8	:	76.7	34.6	61.0	33.4	45.2
Apparent labour productivity (thousand ECU/person employed)	47.5	:	:	:	:	29.6	24.0	33.5	47.5	:	38.7	15.4	41.9	:	:
Unit personnel costs (thousand ECU)	39.9	:	:	:	:	32.0	:	35.9	37.2	:	29.8	14.2	31.2	31.1	25.7
Simple wage adjusted labour productivity (%)	130.0	:	:	:	:	100.4	:	132.0	135.6	:	139.1	121.1	183.4	122.0	157.7
Gross operating surplus (million ECU)	1,337	:	:	:	:	82	:	4,548	112	:	1,514	252	1,199	570	6,750

(1) 1996; (2) Unit personnel costs, 1996.

_____Table 18.25

Water transport (NACE Rev. 1 61)

Employment related indicators, 1997

	B	DK	D	EL	E	F	IRL	I (1)	L (1)	NL (2)	A	P	FIN (1)	S	UK
Number of persons employed (thousands)	2.2	:	:	:	:	15.4	1.7	22.3	0.1	15.2	0.3	2.1	8.3	:	:
Employees/number of persons employed (%)	78.2	:	:	:	:	90.9	98.7	92.8	60.3	90.7	71.3	96.7	98.6	:	:
Average no. of persons employed/enterprise (units)	:	:	:	:	:	8.0	37.0	24.5	3.0	3.0	3.0	22.0	29.0	:	:

(1) 1996; (2) Employees as a share of the number of persons employed, 1996.

_____Table 18.26

Water transport (NACE Rev. 1 61)

Turnover related indicators, 1997

	B	DK	D	EL	E	F	IRL	I (1)	L (1)	NL	A	P	FIN (1)	S (1)	UK
Turnover (million ECU)	1,900	:	:	:	:	4,611	305	3,949	6	4,075	74	418	1,739	3,252	5,607
Turnover per enterprise (million ECU)	:	:	:	:	:	2.4	6.8	4.3	0.3	0.9	1.0	4.3	6.1	4.9	4.7
Turnover per person employed (thousand ECU)	845.1	:	:	:	:	299.3	183.3	177.2	91.2	268.1	288.1	195.7	210.2	:	:

(1) 1996.

_____Table 18.27

Water transport (NACE Rev. 1 61)

Performance related indicators, 1997

	B	DK	D	EL	E	F	IRL	I (1)	L (1)	NL (2)	A	P	FIN (1)	S (1)	UK
Value added (million ECU)	106	:	:	:	:	629	82	1,248	4	1,393	20	76	560	762	2,433
Value added as a share of turnover (%)	5.6	:	:	:	:	13.6	26.9	31.6	64.5	34.2	27.1	18.1	32.2	23.4	43.4
Apparent labour productivity (thousand ECU/person employed)	47.0	:	:	:	:	40.8	49.4	56.0	58.8	91.7	78.0	35.5	67.7	:	:
Unit personnel costs (thousand ECU)	43.4	:	:	:	:	44.6	:	38.0	22.0	31.6	51.0	19.9	39.2	38.1	33.2
Simple wage adjusted labour productivity (%)	138.5	:	:	:	:	100.7	:	158.9	444.4	302.3	213.8	184.2	175.1	148.9	364.5
Gross operating surplus (million ECU)	29	:	:	:	:	4	:	463	3	932	11	35	240	250	1,765

(1) 1996; (2) Unit personnel costs, 1996.

Source: Eurostat (SBS)

Table 18.28

Air transport (NACE Rev. 1 62)

Employment related indicators, 1997

	B	DK	D	EL	E	F	IRL	I (1)	L	NL	A	P	FIN (1)	S	UK
Number of persons employed (thousands)	12.0	9.9	46.6	:	31.7	59.7	6.2	19.7	:	:	6.8	9.7	7.8	:	:
Employees/number of persons employed (%)	99.4	99.7	99.1	:	100.0	100.0	99.6	99.5	:	:	99.3	99.9	99.6	:	:
Average no. of persons employed/enterprise (units)	:	55.0	154.0	:	1,320.1	111.0	183.0	223.8	:	:	84.0	389.0	113.0	:	:

(1) 1996.

Table 18.29

Air transport (NACE Rev. 1 62)

Turnover related indicators, 1997

	B	DK	D	EL	E	F	IRL	I (1)	L	NL	A	P	FIN (1)	S (1)	UK
Turnover (million ECU)	2,747	2,073	15,140	:	4,782	12,160	1,372	5,157	:	:	1,704	1,106	1,209	2,264	20,999
Turnover per enterprise (million ECU)	:	11.6	50.0	:	199.3	22.6	40.3	58.6	:	:	21.0	44.2	17.5	12.8	24.1
Turnover per person employed (thousand ECU)	228.1	210.4	324.9	:	150.9	203.7	220.7	261.9	:	:	250.4	113.7	155.4	:	:

(1) 1996.

Table 18.30

Air transport (NACE Rev. 1 62)

Performance related indicators, 1997

	B	DK	D	EL	E	F	IRL	I (1)	L	NL	A	P	FIN (1)	S (1)	UK
Value added (million ECU)	612	:	:	:	1,934	3,352	440	1,461	:	:	449	458	484	701	4,816
Value added as a share of turnover (%)	22.3	:	:	:	40.4	27.6	32.1	28.3	:	:	26.3	41.4	40.0	31.0	22.9
Apparent labour productivity (thousand ECU/person employed)	50.8	:	:	:	61.0	56.2	70.7	74.2	:	:	65.9	47.1	62.2	:	:
Unit personnel costs (thousand ECU)	45.1	47.8	:	:	42.3	51.5	:	57.9	:	:	50.1	33.9	44.2	49.9	48.5
Simple wage adjusted labour productivity (%)	113.4	:	:	:	144.3	109.1	:	128.7	:	:	132.4	139.0	141.2	134.1	135.1
Gross operating surplus (million ECU)	72	:	:	:	594	279	:	326	:	:	110	128	141	178	1,252

(1) 1996.

Source: Eurostat (SBS)

Financial services (NACE Rev. 1 65, 66 and 67)

The financial services sector encompasses financial intermediation as offered by credit institutions, investment firms, leasing enterprises (NACE Rev. 1 65), insurance and pension funding services (NACE Rev. 1 66), as well as activities providing auxiliary services, such as the administration of financial markets, security brokering or fund management (NACE Rev. 1 67).

Efficient financial services are a prerequisite to aid economic flows. They are the indispensable medium between lenders and borrowers, savers and investors, whilst offering tools to manage risk. Their main functions can be identified as offering payment and saving products; fiduciary services; corporate and private lending services; underwriting and issuance of equity and debt; as well as insurance and risk management products.

STRUCTURE AND PERFORMANCE

Services of credit and insurance enterprises accounted for between 4% and 6% of GDP in the majority of Member States in 1997 (according to National Accounts), although some countries diverged from this trend. Luxembourg was the EU economy where financial services had the highest weight in the domestic economy, with a share of than 18.7% of GDP in 1997. Next came Austria, with a share of 7.6%, followed by Ireland (6.0%, 1996). At the other end of the scale were the Nordic Member States (Denmark, Sweden and Finland) that displayed relatively low shares, below 3.5%.

More than 300 thousand enterprises

It is estimated that the EU numbered some 308 thousand financial services enterprises in 1996 (as classified within Section J of NACE Rev. 1), a relatively small share (2.7%) of the services (NACE Rev. 1 Sections G to K) total. Of these, more than half (56.3%) had no employees at all (mainly self-employed persons) and over a third (37.8%) had between 1 and 9 employees. Altogether, however, these very small enterprises (most of which were financial auxiliaries), whilst numerous, did not account for a significant share of activity, as they accounted for just 12.2% of employment and 3.9% of turnover[1].

Larger enterprises dominate the sector

Indeed, financial services were the service activity (at NACE Rev. 1 Section level) where the proportional weight of large enterprises was at its greatest. The few large companies employing more than 250 employees (0.2% of all enterprises in 1996) attracted almost three-quarters (73.2%) of the sector's employment, with an average of 1,670 employees each, whilst they generated over two-thirds (66.8%) of its turnover. Average turnover of these large enterprises was high at 1.3 billion ECU, against 202.1 million ECU for enterprises with between 50 and 249 employees and 25.6 million ECU for enterprises with between 10 and 49 employees.

(1) Turnover is defined as interests and commissions received for banking activities and gross premiums written/gross contributions for insurance and pension funds.

The activities covered in this chapter (in terms of NACE Rev. 1) include:

65: financial intermediation, except insurance and pension funding;
65.1: monetary intermediation;
65.2: other financial intermediation;
66: insurance and pension funding, except compulsory social security;
67: activities auxiliary to financial intermediation;
67.1: activities auxiliary to financial intermediation, except insurance and pension funding;
67.2: activities auxiliary to insurance and pension funding.

Figure 19.1

Services of credit and insurance institutions (NACE-CLIO 69)

Share of total market services value added and employment, 1997 (%)

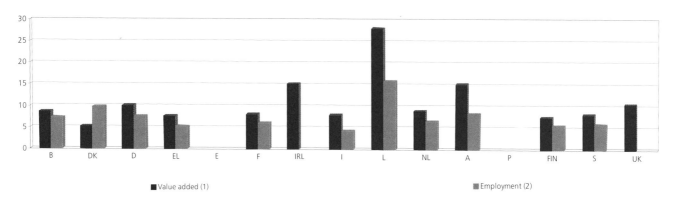

(1) D, EL, F, L and A, value added at market prices; DK, D, IRL, S and UK, 1996; E and P, not available.
(2) B, DK, D, A and S, 1996; E, IRL, P and UK, not available.

Source: Eurostat (SEC2)

LABOUR AND PRODUCTIVITY

According to National Accounts more than four million persons were working in the EU financial services' sector in 1997[2], about 3.0% of total employment. Differences amongst Member States were not large, except for Luxembourg where the share reached a level twice as high as any other Member State (8.8% in 1997). Only two countries displayed a share lower than 2%, Italy and Portugal (lowest with 1.8%).

Part-time work less frequent than average
Women were well represented within financial services, with a 47.0% share of the labour force in 1998. Part-time work accounted for 12.9% of the jobs within financial services in 1998, a relatively low share compared to other service activities (19.4% for NACE Rev. 1 Sections G to K), and beneath the average for the whole EU economy (17.2%). The importance of part-time work was highly variable across the Member States. The Netherlands recorded by far the highest figure, with around one quarter of the labour force (24.7%) employed part-time in financial services. This strongly contrasted with Spain, Portugal and Greece, where the share of part-time workers was under 5.0%.

(2) Earlier years had to be used for some countries.

A well educated workforce
The educational level of people working in financial services ranked amongst the highest of all economic activities. At 26.7%, the proportion of persons with a higher education degree was above the average for services activities (19.3%, NACE Rev. 1 Sections G to K) in 1997. Belgium and Ireland boasted the highest ratios, with 51.5% and 42.4% of all persons employed in the financial services sector holding a higher education degree. The lowest ratios were found in Italy (16%) and Austria (9%).

—————Table 19.1

Financial services (NACE Rev.1 65, 66 and 67)
Composition of the labour force, 1999 (%)

	Financial intermediation			Insurance and pension fuding			Auxilliary financial intermediation		
	Women (1)	Part-time (2)	Highly-educated (3)	Women (4)	Part-time (5)	Highly-educated (3)	Women (6)	Part-time (7)	Highly-educated (8)
EU-15	47.5	12.5	26.9	47.4	12.5	25.8	44.5	15.1	27.3
B	40.4	13.5	54.9	43.8	12.9	48.6	28.3	:	44.4
DK	46.7	13.3	19.3	39.3	12.1	31.2	:	:	:
D	55.5	17.2	23.2	45.6	13.8	25.5	37.2	17.9	:
EL	47.2	:	38.7	47.9	:	:	:	:	:
E	30.3	2.1	44.1	41.7	8.9	43.8	42.4	:	38.0
F	49.8	13.4	38.8	62.3	13.3	35.5	58.1	15.5	35.5
IRL	60.2	12.0	:	56.0	:	:	46.1	:	:
I	31.4	5.0	16.8	44.5	9.2	18.0	35.9	:	15.6
L	38.4	6.0	28.6	50.9	:	:	42.4	:	55.6
NL	49.9	26.0	31.5	36.5	22.1	32.7	36.8	25.6	26.1
A	54.4	18.5	10.6	41.4	12.1	7.5	:	:	:
P	30.2	2.8	27.4	33.9	11.6	27.1	:	:	:
FIN	73.1	8.3	57.1	64.6	:	:	:	:	:
S	61.6	18.7	:	51.3	:	:	:	:	:
UK	55.9	17.3	24.2	51.5	11.9	28.1	46.0	13.9	25.3

(1) EU-15 and EL, 1998.
(2) EU-15 and B, 1998; P, 1997.
(3) EL, 1998; EU-15 and UK, 1997.
(4) EU-15, EL and L, 1998.
(5) EU-15 and B, 1998; DK, 1997; P, 1996.
(6) EU-15 and B, 1998.
(7) EU-15, 1998.
(8) B, 1998; EU-15 and UK, 1997.

Source: Eurostat (LFS)

INTERNATIONAL TRENDS

Financial services are becoming increasingly globalised. Products are becoming more homogeneous across borders, whilst competitive pressure is increasing as markets are opened and liberalised. The resulting integration has broadened the choice of market participants: issuers have increased access to foreign markets to raise capital, whilst investors have tended to internationalise their portfolios.

—————Table 19.2

Top 20 EU banks, as of 31/12/1997

Name	Country	Assets (million ECU)	Profits (million ECU)	Number of employees (units)	World ranking
Deutsche Bank	D	530,465	519	76,100	2
HSBC	UK	413,564	5,361	133,000	7
Crédit Agricole	F	379,972	1,588	84,700	10
ABN-AMRO	NL	378,020	1,864	74,900	11
Société Générale	F	371,897	955	55,500	12
Dresdner Bank	D	344,272	858	46,200	15
Barclays Bank	UK	338,857	1,696	84,300	16
BNP	F	307,448	940	52,400	18
WestLB	D	307,099	369	29,800	19
NatWest	UK	267,733	132	77,000	21
Commerzbank	D	262,920	681	28,700	22
Lloyds TSB	UK	228,313	3,392	82,600	27
Crédit Lyonnais	F	226,437	252	51,000	28
BayernLB	D	215,160	305	7,300	29
Abbey National (1)	UK	218,775	1,384	24,100	31
Bay. Vereinsbank (2)	D	215,160	414	22,000	33
Caisses d'épargne et de prévoyance	F	194,386	311	39,400	34
Rabobank	NL	191,165	897	38,900	36
DG Bank	D	190,001	163	12,000	37
Halifax	UK	189,315	1,576	27,300	38

(1) Estimates.
(2) Before the merger with Bayerische Hypotheken- und Wechselbank, effective 9/1998.

Source: Trade Press

Japanese banks dominate the top of the world rankings. At the end of 1997, six of the 10 largest banks in the world ranked by assets were Japanese, three were from the EU and one was Swiss. But a broader view of the ranking shows that EU banks have significant weight on the international financial scene. The total assets of the top 40 global banks exceeded 12 thousand billion ECU as of 31/12/1997. Looking at the breakdown between the Triad members, half of the total assets were accounted for by 22 EU banks, 30% by 10 Japanese banks and 12% by 6 North American banks. Germany was the main European player with aggregate assets of 2.3 thousand billion ECU, followed by France and the United Kingdom with 1.7 thousand billion ECU each.

As regards the insurance market, 23 EU companies accounted for 60% of the value of premiums written in 1997 by the 40 largest companies in the world[3]. This was double the share of the 13 top USA companies. The United Kingdom was the largest contributor within the EU, with 7 companies accounting for 90 billion ECU of premiums written, followed by Germany (5 companies and 84 billion ECU) and France (4 companies and 82 billion ECU).

___

(3) JAP, no data available, although existing information suggests that the largest insurance companies in the world are based in this country.

Table 19.3

Top 20 EU insurance companies, as of 31/12/1997

Name	Country	Premiums (million ECU)	Profits (million ECU)	Number of employees (units)	World ranking (9)
AXA (1)	F	46,467	1,992	80,600	1
Allianz	D	43,537	1,371	73,300	2
Generali	I	21,000	711	41,400	4
Standard Life (2)	UK	17,636	4,074	9,500	7
CNP Assurances (3)	F	16,744	280	2,500	8
Münchener Rückvers. (4)	D	16,368	355	18,000	10
Prudential	UK	15,324	1,209	22,120	12
ING Group	NL	14,287	1,855	64,200	14
Aegon (3)	NL	14,149	997	23,400	15
Legal and General Group	UK	13,629	705	7,200	16
Royal Sun Alliance (5)	UK	13,321	879	43,500	17
Commercial Union (6)	UK	12,331	504	26,200	19
AGF (7)	F	10,814	387	30,700	24
Allianz Lebensvers. (8)	D	10,670	108	4,800	25
General Accident (6)	UK	9,102	994	25,600	30
Fortis	B	8,969	1,113	35,200	31
RAS (8)	I	8,377	265	12,900	32
Norwich Union	UK	8,264	389	16,300	33
Skandia Group	S	8,225	415	9,700	34
AMB	D	7,731	205	18,300	35

(1) After the merger with UAP.
(2) Estimates, as of 30/11/1997.
(3) Turnover (no premiums).
(4) As of 30/06/1997.
(5) Net premiums.
(6) Commercial Union and General Accident merged in 1998.
(7) Take-over by Allianz in 1998.
(8) Estimates.
(9) Excluding JAP.

Source: Trade Press

SUB-CHAPTER 19.1
FINANCIAL INTERMEDIATION
(NACE Rev. 1 65)

The activities covered by this sub-chapter include all financial intermediation activities, whether they are monetary (NACE Rev. 1 65.1) or not (NACE Rev. 1 65.2), with the exception of insurance and pension funds and financial auxiliaries.

Financial intermediation fulfils various functions: accepting deposits and converting them into loans and credits for enterprises, public authorities and consumers; managing payment systems and clearing mechanisms; providing services with capital transactions; performing various other services like the provision of guarantees or commission based services such as bank custody services. It must be noted however that some of these activities are not performed only by credit institutions. Consumer and industrial credit can be provided by finance companies (many of which have links with banks) and mortgage loans by life insurance companies or pension funds.

As regards credit institutions, they can be classified in two broad categories:

- universal banks: multi-purpose banks that offer the whole range of financial services. Most of them are commercial banks, but in certain countries savings banks, co-operative and public banks are also universal banks;
- specialised banks: which include merchant banks, investment banks and mortgage banks.

A declining number of enterprises

Due to on-going market liberalisation, the market structure of credit institutions has changed noticeably. The number of enterprises has declined in most countries in recent years, which can be explained by a wave of mergers within the banking industry resulting in fewer, large credit institutions (see the ranking of the top 20 provided). According to structural business statistics, there were 8,618 credit institutions in the EU in 1998[4], down from 9,938 in 1994, a net reduction of 12.9%.

---

(4) IRL, no data available.

Table 19.4

Financial intermediation, except insurance and pension funding (NACE Rev. 1 65)
Breakdown of turnover and employment by employment size class, 1997 (%)

	Micro (0-9)		Small (10-49)		Medium (50-249)		Large (250+)	
	Turnover (1)	Employment (1)	Turnover (1)	Employment (1)	Turnover (1)	Employment (2)	Turnover (1)	Employment (2)
EU-15	4.1	2.7	7.3	5.4	23.6	8.3	65.0	83.7
B	19.2	1.7	26.1	7.3	22.2	7.5	32.5	83.4
DK	1.7	1.4	3.6	4.3	9.4	9.4	85.3	84.9
D	:	0.6	:	7.4	:	10.5		81.5
EL	:	:	:	:	:	:	:	:
E	:	1.1	:	2.0	:	4.8	:	92.1
F	4.3	3.6	2.7	3.5	3.4	5.7	89.6	87.2
IRL	:	:	:	:	:	:	:	:
I	:	:	:	:	:	:	:	:
L	:	:	:	:	:	:	:	:
NL	:	:	:	:	:	3.9	:	92.5
A	:	:	9.5	18.6	5.9	18.1	81.2	60.4
P	6.4	1.5	4.5	5.5	8.9	5.3	80.3	87.8
FIN	4.9	5.0	13.5	13.8	15.0	15.5	66.6	65.6
S	:	:	:	:	:	:	:	:
UK	4.8	5.8	9.2	2.6	23.7	5.3	62.2	86.2

(1) EU-15, DK, F and P, 1996.
(2) EU-15, DK, F, NL and P, 1996.

Source: Eurostat (SME)

The consolidation of the banking industry has not only affected small, local and regional enterprises, but also involved cross-border mergers between major players within the European Union. Of the 90 mergers and acquisitions recorded in 1999 concerning European banks, 60 concerned transnational operations, worth a total of 50.8 billion EUR[5]. Intra-European operations accounted for 7.0 billion EUR of the total, down from 19.0 billion ECU the year before. More than half of the value of international deals involved American banks, including the take-overs of the Republic National Bank of New York by HSBC (UK) for 9.6 billion EUR and Bankers Trust by Deutsche Bank (D) for 8.4 billion EUR. The most important intra-European deals in 1999 concerned ING (NL) increasing its stake in BHF (D) and the acquisition by BSCH (E) of part of the Champalimaud group (P).

(5) Source: "Éclairages", monthly bulletin of the Crédit Agricole (F), 1/2000. Covers operations of more than approximately 75 million ECU involving banks of the EEA and Switzerland.

Figure 19.2 ——————

Mergers and acquisitions involving European banks

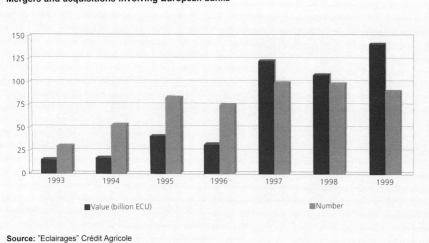

Source: "Eclairages" Crédit Agricole

On the other hand, the number of local units[6] has not been severely affected by the trend towards larger credit institutions. Indeed, the number of local units in the EU has risen from 189.7 thousand in 1994 to 203.2 thousand in 1998[7]. Neither the development of banking technology (for example the development of phone or on-line banking), nor the increasing number of mergers and acquisitions in the industry have yet replaced traditional local units as distribution outlets. It must be noted however that statistical methodology may also have affected these figures with the inclusion of newly privatised institutions in the statistics (for example Deutsche Postbank). Indeed, if one takes the identical cohort of enterprises, the number of local units has fallen in most Member States.

Banks proximity the highest in Luxembourg

The average number of business units (sum of enterprises and local units) per 10 thousand inhabitants gives some idea of the density and geographical distribution of banking outlets. This measure can be regarded as a rough measure of the proximity of credit institutions to their clients. Apart from Luxembourg where there were 19 business units per 10 thousand inhabitants, the highest presence of business units was observed in those countries where small regional or co-operative banks still play an important role, for example, Spain (10.0), Germany (8.1) and Austria (8.0), whilst the EU average was equal to 5.7 business units per 10 thousand inhabitants.

Each EU credit institution numbered on average 24 local units. There were great differences according to the country studied, with larger networks present in Spain (97 local units per enterprise), Belgium (62 per enterprise) and Greece (56 per enterprise). Banks established in Austria, Finland and Luxembourg had on average less than ten local units each (6, 5 and 3 respectively).

(6) Local units are normally defined as part of a credit institution, located separately and employing at least one person; they include branch offices and other comparable outlets, but exclude automated teller machines (ATMs).
(7) IRL, no data available.

Table 19.5 ——————

Co-operative banks: main indicators as of 31/12/1998

	Regional/local banks (units)	Outlets (units)	Staff (units)	Total assets (million ECU)
EU-15	4,827	51,724	505,468	1,919,689
B	1	1	172	3,229
DK	40	87	437	898
D	2,248	18,681	170,000	522,300
IRL	:	584	2,348	7,127
E	95	3,668	13,271	31,010
F	140	13,685	144,376	671,319
EL	27	41	263	351
I	653	8,054	79,300	291,000
L	35	87	331	2,194
NL	445	2,426	49,465	249,700
A	737	3,009	29,805	100,906
P	150	515	3,400	5,647
FIN	247	728	8,366	23,300
S	10	10	95	2,981
UK	:	149	4,011	7,727

Source: GEBC (European Association of Co-operative Banks)

_____Table 19.6

Commercial banks: main indicators as of 31/12/1998

	Banks	Outlets (1)	Staff (2)	Total assets (million ECU)
EU-15	2,639	97,407	1,791,816	11,986,100
B	120	7,129	76,274	727,500
DK	191	2,185	40,288	194,600
D	323	6,999	217,200	1,295,600
EL	40	2,025	49,710	102,400
E	149	17,593	133,899	564,400
F	382	10,138	224,000	1,403,000
IRL	75	922	29,400	135,600
I	359	23,488	314,034	1,431,000
L	209	395	19,814	544,800
NL	166	6,121	123,400	1,213,700
A	70	733	15,274	134,400
P	54	4,354	56,467	218,000
FIN	15	528	16,227	88,300
S	32	1,797	38,629	245,100
UK	454	13,000	437,200	3,687,700

(1) Figures exclude foreign bank branches, except for B, F, I and P.
(2) Full-time employees or equivalent, except for B, F and I (number of employees).

Source: FBE (Banking Federation of the European Union)

_____Table 19.7

Savings banks: main indicators as of 01/01/1999

	Banks (units)	Outlets (units)	Staff (units)	Total assets (million EUR)
EU-15	881	54,956	648,272	2,420,317
B	3	2,333	9,763	91,977
DK	11	113	939	2,234
D	594	17,882	287,646	910,994
EL	1	130	1,290	9,216
E	51	17,598	94,846	313,522
F	34	4,200	38,568	201,981
IRL	1	80	1,170	2,248
I	67	6,206	78,782	294,956
L	1	96	1,772	26,990
NL	1	290	3,116	18,700
A	70	1,428	25,010	173,024
P	5	957	14,612	49,572
FIN	40	248	1,828	5,203
S	1	695	11,734	76,700
UK	1	2,700	77,196	243,000

Source: ESBG (European Savings Bank Group)

Growth of 4.4% per year in the mid-1990s

Interests and commissions[8] grew by an average of 4.4% per annum in the EU between 1994 and 1997 to reach 998 billion ECU. Most countries experienced an increase in business volume, with the exception of Spain, Austria and Finland. Particularly positive results were recorded in France (partly explained by the fact that derivatives used for hedging purposes were included in the figures) and the United Kingdom.

Stable employment levels

More than 2.7 million persons were employed in credit institutions in the EU in 1998, a modest decline of 0.7% compared to the level of 1994[9]. According to the Labour Force Survey, an estimated 47.5% of the persons employed in the whole of financial intermediation (Division 65) were women.

Divergent employment characteristics by sex

Behind this apparent gender balance, there were large differences in the employment characteristics for men and women working within the financial intermediation sector. Whilst 26.7% of those employed possessed a third-level education degree in 1997, this was the case for only 18.9% of the women, compared to 33.4% of the men employed.

(8) Interests and commissions received can be regarded as a proxy for the volume of business carried out by credit institutions. Interests received normally include income from interest-bearing assets such as loans, debt securities, treasury bills, etc. Commissions received include charges for services rendered in loan administration, securities transactions, brokerage services, etc.
(9) IRL, no data available.

Box 19.3

Property and mortgage markets have experienced strong growth in recent years, fuelled by the sharp decline of interest rates until 1999. According to the European Mortgage Federation, total loans on residential property exceeded 2.7 thousand billion ECU in the EU in 1998 (excluding Austria), a level approximately 7.1% higher than the year before. Total mortgage loans recorded double-digit growth in 1998 in six of the Member States, both on commercial and residential property. In Portugal (36.9%), Spain (21.7%) and Italy (21.5%) growth even exceeded 20%. Sweden was the only country that witnessed a rather sharp decline in mortgage loans, down to 115 billion ECU (although the Swedish figures only cover specialised mortgage institutions).

Table 19.8

Outstanding loans against mortgage, 1998

	Residential and commercial property (million ECU) (1)	Growth 1997/1998 (%)	Residential property (million ECU) (2)	Growth 1997/1998 (%)
B	53,748	:	55,528	11.9
DK (3)	138,076	8.4	104,823	9.5
D	1,212,056	7.4	1,012,998	7.4
EL (3)	8,593	12.3	7,037	14.2
E	179,624	21.7	122,637	18.2
F	:	:	262,121	4.4
IRL	24,298	18.9	20,888	19.0
I (4)	138,245	21.5	81,449	8.9
L	:	:	3,615	:
NL	299,949	13.6	220,537	15.3
A (3)	9,531	1.9	:	:
P	38,382	36.9	31,941	36.5
FIN	:	:	33,765	8.2
S (5)	107,009	-7.2	98,998	-8.0
UK	:	:	647,284	0.0

(1) B, 1997.
(2) L, 1997.
(3) For residential and commercial property: only members of the association.
(4) End of third quarter.
(5) For residential and commercial property: specialised mortgage credit institutions only.

Source: EMF (European Mortgage Federation)

Table 19.9

Finance houses: main indicators, 1998

	Number of enterprises	Number of branches (1)	Number of persons employed	New credit granted (million ECU)		
				Industrial credit	Consumer credit	Car finance
B	93	6,000	3,200	:	5,410	1,534
D	64	1,058	19,285	2,314	6,542	19,259
E	51	:	:	156	3,159	4,003
F	89	:	15,900	871	20,704	6,928
IRL	22	850	1,160	1,180	85	1,559
I	38	360	4,812	:	5,290	8,969
NL	50	:	:	:	8,766	:
P	23	:	:	:	608	1,052
FIN	6	20	864	597	962	662
S	39	500	2,106	443	640	2,866
UK	665	6,750	30,000	1,694	47,533	31,028

(1) 1997.

Source: Eurofinas

The proportion of those employed working on a part-time basis in 1998 was estimated at 12.5% within financial intermediation, less than the services average (19.4%, NACE Rev. 1 Sections G to K). However, a breakdown by sex reveals that only 2.3% of the men employed in financial intermediation worked on a part-time basis, whilst the corresponding proportion for women was almost a quarter (23.9%).

Atypical working patterns concerned principally evening work (affecting 28.7% of the workforce in 1997) and Saturday work (24.4% of the workforce). The share of persons working shifts (3.7%), nights (4.6%), Sundays (8.4%) or from home (10.8%) was below the corresponding figures recorded for services as a whole (NACE Rev. 1 Sections G to K).

Figure 19.3

Credit institutions (NACE Rev. 1 65.12)

Unit personnel costs, 1997 (thousand ECU per employee) (1)

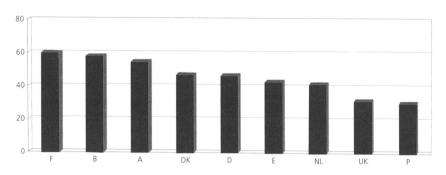

(1) EL, IRL, I, L, FIN and S, not available.

Source: Eurostat (SBS)

SUB-CHAPTER 19.2
INSURANCE AND PENSION FUNDING
(NACE Rev. 1 66)

The activities analysed in this sub-chapter include insurance and pension fund services covered by Division 66 of NACE Rev. 1. A distinction is made in the activity classification between life insurance (NACE Rev. 1 66.01), pension funding (NACE Rev. 1 66.02) and non-life insurance (NACE Rev. 1 66.03). The classification does not yet consider reinsurance as a separate activity as most of the general insurance companies also underwrite reinsurance. As such this activity is assigned to one of the three NACE Rev. 1 Groups above, according to the type of risk being reinsured.

The insurance activity can be described as embracing all enterprises exclusively or primarily engaged in converting individual risks into collective risks. Compulsory social security services are excluded. Insurance is thus defined in terms of the economic function of converting and mutualising risks. Life insurance embraces conventional life insurance contracts, as well as life reinsurance, with or without a substantial savings element. Pension funding includes the provision of retirement incomes. In non-life insurance, the risks covered are those not included in the previous categories, such as accident, motor or health insurance.

Fewer insurance enterprises

There were 4,212 insurance enterprises operating in the EU in 1997, down from 5,422 in 1990. Whilst this decreasing trends was experienced in most Member States, the number of insurance enterprises grew between 1990 and 1997 in Luxembourg (from 196 to 330) and Ireland (from 81 to 101). This can be explained by the attractiveness of these countries as financial centres, due to taxation or other advantages.

The largest number of insurance enterprises active in the EU in 1997 were dealing with non-life insurance (2,626, or 62.3% of the total), ranging from 49.1% of the national total in Portugal[10] to 88.2% in Finland. Life insurance (948 enterprises in 1997) accounted for 22.5% of the total number of insurance enterprises in the EU, ranging from 8.3% of the national total in Finland to 36.4% in Denmark.

---

(10) Excluding L, where 255 specialist reinsurance enterprises accounted for 77.3% of the national total.

Life insurance the largest insurance business in terms of gross premiums

The gross premiums written by EU insurance enterprises amounted to 609.6 billion ECU in 1997, broken down as 262.0 billion ECU (43.0%) for life insurance enterprises, 193.4 billion ECU (31.7%) for non-life insurance enterprises, 112.6 billion ECU (18.5%) for composite insurance enterprises[11] and 41.6 billion ECU (6.8%) for specialist reinsurance enterprises.

Total gross premiums written grew by 7.5% in the EU compared to 1996, ranging from 39.4% growth in Ireland, 24.4% in Luxembourg and 20.3% in Italy to decreases of 0.3% in Austria (estimate) and 2.0% in Finland. As a general rule, premiums on life insurance showed more progress than those of non-life insurance, as 22.8% more life insurance premiums were written in the EU in 1997 compared to 1995, whilst non-life insurance premiums experienced a 7.9% decline.

---

(11) Enterprises allowed to carry out both life and non-life business. These exist only in a limited number of Member States.

Box 19.4

As with the banking sector, insurance companies have responded to the completion of the Single Market for financial services with a wave of mergers and acquisitions. Although most merger activities remain on the domestic scene, some large-scale international moves are worth noting, such as Allianz's (D) acquisition of AGF (F), AXA's (F) take-over of Guardian Royal Exchange (UK) or Aegon's (NL) purchase of Transamerica (USA).

Underlying the acquisition strategy of many insurers are both the objectives of strengthening their position on their home market and gaining European or even global market share. Many companies now operate in several EU countries other than their domestic base. As cross-border moves through mergers continue, completion of the Single European Insurance market, as a result of the third generation Directives[12] not only offered EU companies better possibilities to operate internationally within the EU, but they also made it easier for non-EU insurance companies to operate within the EU through a single licence. This opening up of the Single Market has also paved the way for a series of take-overs and mergers between banks and insurance companies. Through the emergence of "bancassurance" a clear distinction between insurance companies, banks and "bancassurance" companies cannot be made anymore, with banks increasingly offering insurance products and insurers providing asset management services.

---

(12) The third generation insurance Directives came into force in July 1994. The most significant feature of these Directives is the attempt to move the regulatory focus from host-country control to home-country control.

———Table 19.10

Insurance and pension funding, except compulsory social security (NACE Rev. 1 66)

Breakdown of turnover and employment by employment size class, 1997 (%)

	Micro (0-9)		Small (10-49)		Medium (50-249)		Large (250+)	
	Turnover (1)	Employment (2)	Turnover (1)	Employment (2)	Turnover (3)	Employment (4)	Turnover (3)	Employment (4)
EU-15	6.6	2.4	6.1	3.0	15.2	8.7	72.2	85.9
B	4.1	0.1	2.3	0.8	6.2	4.2	87.4	94.8
DK	1.3	1.0	3.3	3.8	18.3	18.4	77.1	76.8
D	:	0.6	:	1.4	:	2.0	:	96.0
EL	:	:	:	:	:	:	:	:
E	:	3.3	:	5.3	:	22.9	:	68.5
F	12.3	0.8	12.6	2.0	26.6	10.8	48.5	86.4
IRL	:	:	:	:	:	:	:	:
I	:	:	:	:	:	:	:	:
L	:	:	:	:	:	:	:	:
NL	:	2.1	:	5.4	:	13.5	:	79.0
A	:	:	1.8	1.8	4.4	4.4	93.4	93.4
P	:	:	:	:	:	:	:	:
FIN	4.1	4.5	8.5	6.3	13.6	13.0	74.8	76.3
S	:	:	:	:	:	:	:	:
UK	10.4	4.1	7.4	2.4	17.8	:	67.2	:

(1) EU-15, DK and F, 1996.
(2) EU-15, DK, F and NL, 1996.
(3) EU-15, DK, F, FIN and UK, 1996.
(4) EU-15, DK, F, NL and FIN, 1996.

Source: Eurostat (SME)

Average expenditure of 1,629 ECU per person

Large differences exist in insurance services expenditure across the EU Member States. The average EU citizen spent around 700 ECU on life insurance premiums in 1997 and 517 ECU of non-life insurance premiums. An additional 301 ECU were accounted for by composite insurance enterprises.

The highest level of gross premiums written per capita were found in Luxembourg, with as much as 16,264 ECU, of which more than half (8,872 ECU) was for life insurance and over a third (5,831 ECU) was for reinsurance.

Amongst the other Member States, life insurance expenditure per capita was particularly high in the United Kingdom (1,549 ECU per inhabitant), the Netherlands (1,106 ECU) and Denmark (1,103 ECU). It was the lowest in Portugal (127 ECU), Austria (114 ECU) and Greece (75 ECU). Non-life insurance expenditure ranged from 886 ECU in Germany and 871 ECU in the Netherlands down to 127 ECU in Portugal and 81 ECU per capita in Greece.

———Table 19.11

Gross premiums written of insurance enterprises, 1997 (million ECU)

	Total enterprises	Life insurance enterprises	Non-life insurance enterprises	Composite insurance enterprises	Specialist reinsurance enterprises
EU-15	609,607	261,972	193,431	112,614	41,588
B	14,544	1,690	3,469	9,385	:
DK	10,232	5,827	3,786	:	619
D	154,578	50,298	72,707	:	31,572
EL (1)	1,640	791	849	:	:
E	25,037	7,173	5,313	12,022	529
F	127,957	56,515	41,504	26,457	3,482
IRL	6,287	3,659	2,629	:	:
I	47,035	12,362	9,632	23,306	1,735
L	6,847	3,735	656	:	2,455
NL	30,869	17,267	13,602	:	:
A (2)	12,124	924	1,296	8,737	1,167
P	4,499	1,265	1,262	1,965	7
FIN	4,109	1,937	2,168	:	4
S	12,561	7,088	5,454	:	18
UK	151,288	91,441	29,104	30,742	:

(1) 1996.
(2) 1996 data for life insurance; estimate for composite insurance and total.

Source: Eurostat

One third of non-life insurance premiums written for motor vehicles

Motor vehicle insurance was the largest category of non-life insurance in the EU, accounting for about a third of the non-life gross premiums written (77.4 billion ECU in 1997, or 33.4%). Accident and health insurance (58.3 billion ECU, or 25.2%) and fire and other damage to property (47.6 billion ECU, or 20.6%) were the other major products.

Almost one million persons employed

Employment in insurance services was estimated at just under one million persons (967 thousand) in 1996. The Labour Force Survey estimates that 47.4% of the persons employed in 1998 were women. However, as with banking the employment characteristics between men and women diverged considerably. Whilst 25.7% of the persons employed in insurance possessed a third-level education degree in 1997, this was the case for less than a fifth (19.3%) of the women employed but almost a third (31.2%) of the men. Similarly, only 4.3% of the men employed in insurance activities worked on a part-time basis in 1998, whilst as many as 21.8% of women did so. Atypical working patterns concerned principally evening work, affecting as much as 34.6% of the workforce in 1997 and Saturday work (29.8%).

Figure 19.4 ────────────

Gross premiums written of non-life insurance products, 1997 (million ECU) (1)

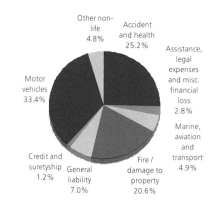

(1) Preliminary data for EL; premium income for UK.

Source: Eurostat

SUB-CHAPTER 19.3
FINANCIAL INTERMEDIARIES
(NACE Rev. 1 67)

The activities covered in this sub-chapter are classified under Division 67 of NACE Rev. 1, covering the "provision of services involved in or closely related to financial intermediation, but not themselves involving financial intermediation". The definition includes the administration of financial markets, securities brokering and fund management (part of NACE Rev. 1 67.1), as well as activities of insurance brokers and agents (part of NACE Rev. 1 67.2).

Financial intermediaries have experienced dramatic changes in their business environment in recent years. Standing at the centre of economic flows, financial markets have to adapt to the evolution of world business. On the one hand, companies increasingly operate on an international or even global basis, which leads them to issue bonds and equity outside of their domestic market. On the other hand, investors are also operating worldwide, helped by the emergence of electronic markets and Internet.

The reorganisation of stock markets has also played an important role in stimulating the supply of financial services and the competition between financial intermediaries. Key elements include:

- the end to brokers' monopoly and the liberalisation of commissions;
- the creation of secondary listings, allowing medium-sized businesses unable to meet the conditions for a full listing to improve their access to capital;
- and the computerisation of stock markets and market operations in all European exchanges, that greatly improved market liquidity by making information more rapidly available.

Activities auxiliary to financial intermediation have a supporting function in capital markets, performing functions that are complementary to banking and insurance activities, as well as providing some financial services that compete with banks and insurance companies. The liberalisation of capital markets has led to the emergence of a sizeable number of financial auxiliaries, present for example in corporate finance, stock markets or broking.

Table 19.12

Activities auxiliary to insurance and pension funding (NACE Rev. 1 67)

Breakdown of turnover and employment by employment size class, 1997 (%)

	Micro (0-9)		Small (10-49)		Medium (50-249)		Large (250+)	
	Turnover (1)	Employment (1)	Turnover (1)	Employment (1)	Turnover (2)	Employment (3)	Turnover (2)	Employment (3)
EU-15	8.1	61.0	13.2	11.4	9.2	9.9	69.4	17.7
B	33.7	62.2	18.2	8.8	5.2	8.4	42.9	20.7
DK	31.2	20.4	33.2	21.8	27.5	44.4	8.1	13.5
D	:	87.5	:	5.0	:	4.0	:	3.6
EL	:	:	:	:	:	:	:	:
E	:	81.5	:	9.5	:	6.0	:	3.0
F	34.2	48.1	26.1	16.9	22.7	18.4	17.0	16.6
IRL	:	:	:	:	:	:	:	:
I	89.3	94.0	10.7	6.0	0.0	0.0	0.0	0.0
L	:	:	:	:	:	:	:	:
NL	:	:	:	:	:	20.8	:	24.8
A	23.7	69.5	52.9	19.1	23.5	11.5	0.0	0.0
P	:	:	:	:	:	:	:	:
FIN	15.0	32.4	12.0	25.4	:	:	:	:
S	:	:	:	:	:	:	:	:
UK	2.1	30.7	23.9	14.4	7.1	:	76.8	:

(1) EU-15, DK, F and I, 1996.
(2) EU-15, DK, F, I and UK, 1996.
(3) EU-15, DK, F, I and NL, 1996.

Source: Eurostat (SME)

Box 19.5

The London Stock Exchange was the largest in Europe in 1999, with an aggregate total of 2,274 listed shares (excluding investment funds). This was above the level of Paris with 1,114. The German stock exchanges followed with 851 listed shares. The number of companies listed has increased in the majority of European countries, and this was noticeably the case in Spain, where Madrid saw 50% growth in the number of listed companies between 1998 and 1999.

Table 19.13

Stock markets, main indicators 1999

	Country	Total number of companies listed, excluding investment funds	Of which: national	foreign	Share trading, including investment funds (million EUR)	Trading view (1)	Market capitalisation of domestic companies (million EUR)
Brussels	B	268	146	122	207,703	REV	172,771
Copenhagen	DK	242	233	9	62,494	REV	98,794
Germany	D	851	617	234	1,455,711	TSV	1,343,774
Athens	EL	262	262	0	177,598	TSV	184,698
Madrid	E	727	718	9	693,132	REV	:
Barcelona	E	500	496	4	184,411	REV	:
Bilbao	E	275	273	2	201,478	REV	:
Paris	F	1,144	968	176	2,713,788	REV	1,410,190
Ireland	IRL	103	84	19	44,673	REV	64,528
Italy	I	270	264	6	506,154	TSV	683,293
Luxembourg	L	277	51	226	1,319	TSV	33,721
Amsterdam	NL	387	233	154	442,142	REV	652,288
Vienna	A	114	97	17	11,948	TSV	30,985
Lisbon	P	125	125	0	37,981	TSV	63,941
Helsinki	FIN	150	147	3	103,118	TSV	327,829
Stockholm	S	300	277	23	294,318	REV	350,239
London	UK	2,274	1,826	448	3,189,571	REV	2,679,119
NYSE	USA	3,025	2,619	406	8,393,107	TSV	10,731,668
NASDAQ	USA	4,829	4,400	428	9,821,323	REV	4,883,391
Toronto	CA	1,456	1,409	47	335,381	TSV	740,471
Hong Kong	HK	708	695	13	215,835	TSV	571,497
Tokyo	JAP	1,935	1,892	43	1,572,220	TSV	4,180,364
Singapore	SG	399	354	45	100,777	TSV	185,816
Taiwan	TW	462	462	0	857,222	TSV	353,270

(1) TSV (Trading System View) count only those transactions which pass through the trading system or which take place on the exchange's trading floor.
REV (Regulated Environment View) includes all transactions subject to supervision by the market authority.

Source: FIBV

The 1990s have been characterised by an enormous growth in equity turnover in Europe and North America. During the period 1990 to 1994, the value of share trading almost doubled in the EU and the New York Stock Exchange, whilst during the period 1994 to 1997 the value was doubled again, and again between 1997 and 1999. The NASDAQ market witnessed impressive growth, with a share trading value that grew ten-fold between 1990 and 1997 and was further multiplied by 2.5 between 1997 and 1999. In Europe, similar increases were witnessed on the smaller markets of Bilbao, Helsinki, Luxembourg and Stockholm. This could be contrasted with the Tokyo market, where share turnover in 1998 was still below the level of 1990.

Figure 19.5

The world's largest stock markets by market capitalisation, 1999 (billion EUR)

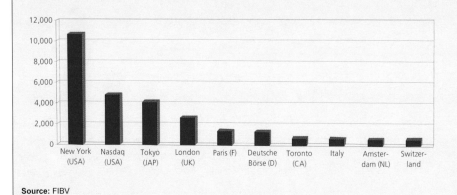

Source: FIBV

Box 19.5 (continued)

All European stock markets witnessed a sharp rise in capitalisation[13] during the course of the 1990s, a trend that accelerated in the second half of the decade. As with the two years that proceeded it, 1999 will be remembered as a buoyant year for European equity markets. Market capitalisation of EU markets rose by 34.8% in 1999 to reach 8.5 thousand billion EUR, a level almost five times higher than in 1990. Athens and Helsinki were the two markets that recorded the highest growth between 1990 and 1999, with capitalisation being multiplied by 15-fold and 18-fold respectively.

In 1999, European shares represented 29% of the world's total, up from 25% in 1994, but down from 32% in 1998. North American equities accounted for 50% of the world's total capitalisation, up from 37% in 1994.

(13) Data on market capitalisation excludes foreign companies, investment funds, rights, warrants and convertibles.

Figure 19.6

Value of share trading including investment funds (1990=100)

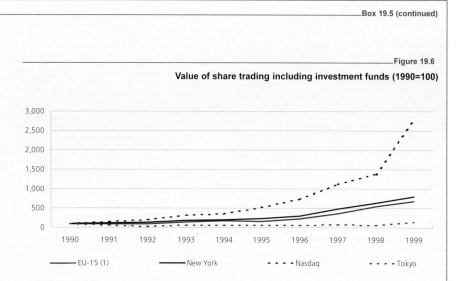

(1) Amsterdam, Athens, Barcelona, Bilbao, Brussels, Copenhagen, Helsinki, London, Madrid, Paris, Stockholm, Vienna and stock exchanges from Italy and Germany.

Source: FIBV

Figure 19.7

Market capitalisation (billion ECU)

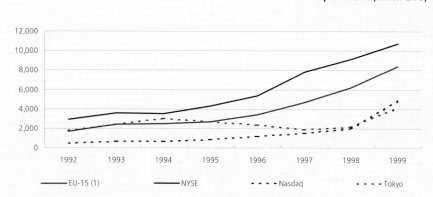

(1) Amsterdam, Athens, Brussels, Copenhagen, Helsinki, Lisbon, London, Luxembourg, Paris, Stockholm, Vienna and stock exchanges from Germany, Italy and Spain.

Source: FIBV

Figure 19.8

Market capitalisation of domestic companies' shares (%)

Source: FIBV

A sector dominated by small enterprises...

Amongst the estimated 247 thousand enterprises active in this sector in 1996, the vast majority (59.2%) did not have a single employee. Another large proportion (38.6%) of the enterprise population was accounted for by very small enterprises with less than 10 employees.

The average size of financial auxiliary enterprises was generally small, with each enterprise employing on average just three persons, two less than the services (NACE Rev. 1 Sections G to K) average. Even enterprises of the largest size class (250 employees and more) employed only 850 persons on average, as compared to a services' average of 1,303 persons for the same size-class.

Financial intermediaries generally had high average turnover, with the average for all size-classes equal to 1.7 million ECU, compared to 1.0 million ECU for services as a whole. Within the different size classes average turnover ranged between 249 thousand ECU for enterprises with between 1 and 9 employees up to 1.8 billion ECU for the enterprises with 250 or more employees (where the services average was 316 million ECU).

One-fifth of the persons employed worked in enterprises with no employees

Employment in financial auxiliary activities was estimated at some 769 thousand persons in 1996. Over one-fifth of those employed (21.8%) were working in enterprises with no employees and 39.2% worked in small enterprises with between 1 and 9 employees. Large enterprises of more than 250 employees accounted for just 17.7% of the workforce.

In 1998 approximately 44.5% of the workforce were women, a proportion slightly above the average for service activities (42.8%, NACE Rev. 1 Sections G to K). Their education level, although higher than the average for services activities, was still well below that of men. Only 19.6% of women had a third-level education degree in 1997, as opposed to 33.8% of men.

One characteristic of this sector as compared to the other financial services is the high presence of persons with only a lower education level. They represented 24.6% of the persons employed in 1997, 26.7% amongst women and 22.7% amongst men. In comparison, the proportion was equal to 19.7% in insurance services and 21.0% in banking.

Part-time work and atypical working patterns less frequent

Part-time work concerned 15.1% of the financial intermediaries workforce in 1998, more than in insurance or banking (12.5% in both), but far less than in services as a whole (35.2%, NACE Rev. 1 Section G to K). As in most other sectors, women were more prone to work part-time (23.9%) than men (2.3%).

Atypical working patterns concerned mainly home work, that affected 31.9% of the workforce in 1997, compared to a services average of just 13.3%. In contrast, only 47.5% of those employed worked on Saturdays (regularly or not), whilst the average for services was as high as 59.2%.

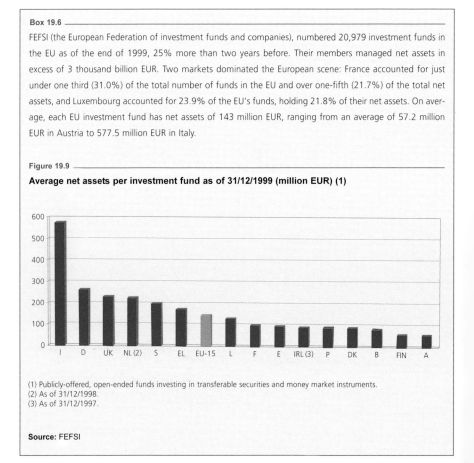

Box 19.6

FEFSI (the European Federation of investment funds and companies), numbered 20,979 investment funds in the EU as of the end of 1999, 25% more than two years before. Their members managed net assets in excess of 3 thousand billion EUR. Two markets dominated the European scene: France accounted for just under one third (31.0%) of the total number of funds in the EU and over one-fifth (21.7%) of the total net assets, and Luxembourg accounted for 23.9% of the EU's funds, holding 21.8% of their net assets. On average, each EU investment fund has net assets of 143 million EUR, ranging from an average of 57.2 million EUR in Austria to 577.5 million EUR in Italy.

Figure 19.9

Average net assets per investment fund as of 31/12/1999 (million EUR) (1)

(1) Publicly-offered, open-ended funds investing in transferable securities and money market instruments.
(2) As of 31/12/1998.
(3) As of 31/12/1997.

Source: FEFSI

Business services (NACE Rev. 1 71, 73 and 74)

Business services include the technical, professional and operational services generally supplied to firms or administrations, rather than to households, for the support of their production process or their organisation. The most important business services generally include activities such as legal, tax and management consultancy, engineering services, computer services, personnel recruitment and selection, cleaning and maintenance services, security services, advertising and market research activities and call centres. All of these are covered by Section K of the NACE Rev. 1 classification (Divisions 70 to 74) and will be addressed in this chapter, with the exception of real estate services (NACE Rev. 1 70) and computer services (NACE Rev. 1 72) studied in chapters 15 and 21 respectively.

The significant development of business services activities over the past thirty years can be mainly attributed to two main factors. Firstly, there has been a clear shift in the structure of the European economy towards service activities, stemming from manufacturing enterprises out-sourcing activities to independent service providers. In other words, a series of activities that used to be executed "in-house", such as accounting, cleaning or security services have been sub-contracted to specialised firms, with the hope that this would achieve flexibility, as well as lower costs and a better quality of service. Secondly, the sector has benefited from strong internal growth, thanks to an ever-increasing demand for this category of service, in response to the growing complexity of business processes, increasing pressure from competitors worldwide and the emergence of new technologies. These factors have spurred demand for example for consultancy, training or R&D services.

The activities covered in this chapter (in terms of NACE Rev. 1) include:

71: renting of machinery and equipment without operator and of personal and household goods;
71.1: renting of automobiles;
71.2: renting of other transport equipment;
71.3: renting of other machinery and equipment;
71.4: renting of personal and household goods n.e.c.;
73: research and development;
73.1: research and experimental development on natural sciences and engineering;
73.2: research and experimental development on social sciences and humanities;
74: other business activities;
74.1: legal, accounting, book-keeping and auditing activities; tax consultancy; market research and public opinion polling; business and management consultancy; holdings;
74.2: architectural and engineering activities and related technical consultancy;
74.3: technical testing and analysis;
74.4: advertising;
74.5: labour recruitment and provision of personnel;
74.6: investigation and security activities;
74.7: industrial cleaning;
74.8: miscellaneous business activities n.e.c.

Figure 20.1 _____

Other market services (NACE-CLIO 74)

Share of total market services value added and employment, 1997 (%)

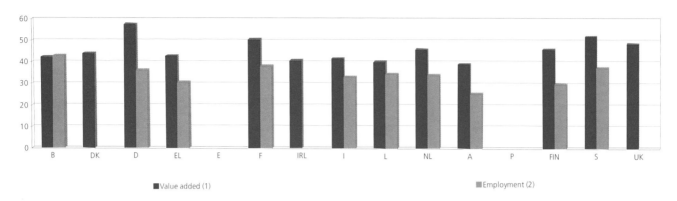

■ Value added (1)   ■ Employment (2)

(1) D, EL, F, L and A, value added at market prices; DK, D, IRL, S and UK, 1996; E and P, not available.
(2) B, D, A and S, 1996; DK, E, IRL, P and UK, not available.

Source: Eurostat (SEC2)

STRUCTURE AND PERFOMANCE

All these elements have driven business services to become the largest branch of the European economy. According to National Accounts, the value added they generate each year is equal to more than one-fifth of total GDP, ranging from a maximum of 27.1% in Germany and 26.6% in Luxembourg to a minimum of 16.1% in Ireland and 14.7% in Portugal[1]. In terms of employment, the share of business services is slightly lower (although still considerable) at over 15% in most European countries, ranging from a tenth of total employment in Finland to over a fifth in Belgium[2].

Business services are a key element
for competitiveness and growth
Besides their importance in economic terms, business services are widely recognised as being a key element concerning the competitiveness of enterprises and an important factor driving long-term growth. This central role has been highlighted by the Commission in a communication to the Council that sets the framework for a common policy aimed at strengthening the competitiveness of European industry[3]. The communication underlines the dynamic relationship between business services and industry, not only as a result of out-sourcing, but also because of their growing inte-

gration into industrial production. This is for example the case when industrial firms call upon business services enterprises to seek improved flexibility in their production chain, to improve the quality of the human and technological production factors, to cope with rapid technological developments or to face more complex and international markets.

According to the Commission's communication, these intangible contributions to the value added chain of industry are becoming more important than traditional tangible investments. In other words, a growing proportion of the production costs faced by industrial firms are generated not within manufacturing but in the business services sector. In turn, business services can provide industry with key competitive advantages such as cost reductions, improved quality or better access to knowledge, skills, expertise and new technologies.

Smaller average enterprise size
than in other service activities
The EU numbered more than 2.4 million enterprises in the business service activities covered by Division 74 of NACE Rev. 1 in 1997[4] and 115 thousand additional enterprises in Division 71 (renting activities, 1996 data). Of these, 94.7% were very small enterprises (38.2% with between 1 and 10 employees and 56.5% with no employees at all (mainly self-employed persons).

Altogether very small enterprises dominated this sector of the European business economy, accounting for 34.9% of total employment and 33.3% of turnover in Divisions 71, 73 and 74. In comparison, large firms employing more than 250 persons represented only 0.2% of the number of enterprises, 34.8% of the persons employed and 29.4% of turnover.

(4) Comprised of legal, accounting and consultancy services, architectural and engineering services, technical testing and analysis, advertising, labour recruitment and personnel services, investigation and security services and industrial cleaning.

(1) These figures relate to 1995 to 1997, depending upon the country studied.
(2) It must be noted, however, that these figures are based on the National Accounts classification that is slightly different from that used for business statistics (the NACE Rev. 1 classification), which is the basis of the information presented in the majority of this chapter. Nevertheless, a large number of activities are common to both classifications and hence the data presented is probably the best available approximation.
(3) "The Contribution of Business Services to Industrial Performance", Communication from the Commission to the Council, COM(1998)534, 1998.

Table 20.1

Business services (NACE Rev.1 71, 73 and 74)
Breakdown of turnover and employment by employment size class, 1997 (%)

	Micro (0-9)		Small (10-49)		Medium (50-249)		Large (250+)	
	Turnover (1)	Employment (2)	Turnover (3)	Employment (4)	Turnover (5)	Employment (6)	Turnover (5)	Employment (7)
EU-15	33.3	34.9	20.5	17.1	16.8	13.2	29.4	34.8
B	35.1	37.0	:	8.8	21.1	8.7	:	:
DK	:	:	:	:	:	:	:	:
D	18.3	20.7	18.5	16.6	13.5	8.4	49.7	54.3
EL	:	:	:	:	:	:	:	:
E	:	43.9	:	13.9	:	:	:	:
F	33.0	29.4	22.5	19.6	16.4	16.4	28.1	34.6
IRL	:	:	:	:	:	:	:	:
I	54.4	65.5	21.9	13.4	:	:	:	:
L	:	:	:	:	:	:	:	:
NL	:	:	:	:	:	:	:	:
A	41.9	38.7	28.9	22.8	:	:	:	:
P	:	:	:	:	:	:	:	:
FIN	:	40.2	:	19.4	:	:	:	:
S	40.0	:	28.9	:	17.4	14.5	13.7	:
UK	34.1	38.2	17.7	16.7	:	:	:	:

(1) EU-15, F, I and S, 1996.
(2) EU-15, F and I, 1996.
(3) EU-15, F, I, A and S, 1996.
(4) EU-15, F, I, A and FIN, 1996.
(5) EU-15, F and S, 1996.
(6) EU-15, B, F and S, 1996.
(7) EU-15 and F, 1996.

Source: Eurostat (SME)

LABOUR AND PRODUCTIVITY

Business services have been responsible for a great deal of job creation in recent years. National Accounts show that employment in this branch has been rising by 2.0% to 4.0% per annum on average in most Member States since 1985. As a consequence, the number of persons employed was in 1997 well over a third higher than ten years before in the majority of Member States. It is estimated that 12 million persons were employed in NACE Rev. 1 Division 74 in 1997 and 445 thousand in renting activities the preceding year.

Part-time work frequent, mainly amongst women
In business services (NACE Rev. 1 Section K), part-time work is of particular importance. It accounted for over a fifth (20.2%) of the persons employed in 1999, 0.7 percentage points above the services average (NACE Rev. 1 Sections G to K)[5]. The highest penetration of part-time work was found in the Netherlands (32.0%) and Austria (26.0%), whilst only Greece (1998) reported less than a tenth of those employed working part-time (5.1%). Women were much more inclined to work on a part-time basis than men, 35.1% of those employed (compared to only 8.8% for men).

On the other hand, this high share of part-time work was not accompanied, as is often the case, by an above average level of job insecurity. In 1999, 13.1% of those employed had a temporary job or a work contract of limited duration, a share similar to the average for the whole European economy. Spain (30.8%) and Portugal (26.7%) displayed the highest shares of such contracts, whilst the figures in Austria (5.4%) and Luxembourg (3.1%) showed there was little reliance on this form of work arrangement.

Gender balance reached in numbers...
but not in education level
Gender balance was relatively even within business services in 1999, as women represented 44.5% of the total number of persons employed, compared to 42.4% in the whole economy (NACE Rev. 1 Sections A to Q) and 43.4% in services (NACE Rev. 1 Sections G to K). There was a rapid development in the share of women employed within this field of the economy over the past decade, as women made up only 38.6% of the workforce in 1992. In 1999, they out-numbered men in Austria (53.6%) and Portugal (50.8%), as opposed to Sweden where they accounted for only 38.1% of total employment.

Table 20.2

Business services (NACE Rev.1 Section K)
Composition of the labour force, 1999 (%)

	Women (1)	Part-time (2)	Highly-educated (3)
EU-15	44.4	20.5	39.7
B	44.1	15.5	57.0
DK	42.1	21.0	42.7
D	48.3	25.5	38.0
EL	43.7	5.1	61.8
E	46.3	14.0	46.9
F	46.1	18.2	41.2
IRL	45.9	15.0	58.1
I	42.0	12.9	32.0
L	42.2	12.8	42.0
NL	39.7	32.0	41.1
A	53.6	26.0	21.2
P	50.8	11.1	26.1
FIN	44.9	15.4	49.7
S	38.1	17.4	45.1
UK	41.6	20.1	43.6

(1) EU-15 and EL, 1998.
(2) EU-15, B and EL, 1998.
(3) EL, 1998; EU-15 and IRL, 1997.

Source: Eurostat (LFS)

(5) Latest data for 1999 within this section on employment characteristics excludes EL.

Business services competitiveness essentially relies on high quality human capital, which directly depends on the level of education possessed by the workforce. In business services, the general level of education was higher than in other sectors of the economy. Indeed, about 39.7% of the persons employed in 1997 possessed a higher-education degree, one of the highest ratios in service activities and almost 20.0 percentage points above the services average. This high qualification level, however, applied principally to men. Women employed in the sector had a markedly lower education level, as only 29.4% possessed a third-level degree, compared to 48.6% of the men employed. These figures suggest there may be a high presence of women in lower-qualified posts: such as support roles, back-office staff or secretarial jobs, as well as business services with per se low qualification requirements, for example cleaning services. The highest presence of highly-educated persons was found in Greece (61.8% in 1998), Ireland (58.1%, 1997 data) and Belgium (57.0%), the only countries where highly-educated persons outnumbered persons with a lower education level. Portugal (26.1%) and Austria (21.2%) recorded the lowest levels of persons employed with a third-level education degree.

Higher than average apparent labour productivity

Measuring labour productivity of business services usually relies on estimating the value added generated by each person they employ. National Accounts suggest that business services labour productivity is generally higher than in the other service activities, a trend confirmed by the structural business statistics that are available. Eurostat estimate that apparent labour productivity was equal to 111.1 thousand ECU per person employed in 1997 within renting activities[6] (NACE Rev. 1 Division 71) and at 31.8 thousand ECU for other business services (NACE Rev. 1 Division 74), amongst which legal, accounting and management consultancy activities (NACE Rev. 1 Group 74.1) had the highest ratio, with 47.4 thousand ECU per person employed.

---

(6) This figure should be interpreted with care due to the nature of renting activities, which may have high financial costs and depreciation charges (especially for renting or leasing of machinery or vehicles) that are included in gross value added, which may therefore be over-estimated compared to other activities.

INTERNATIONAL TRENDS

Whilst business services represent a significant share of the European economy, it was lower than in the other Triad countries. National Accounts statistics show that business services accounted for 27.6% of American GDP in 1996, well above the average of most EU Member States, placing the USA at the same level as the Member States where business services recorded their highest shares. Japan, similarly, reported business services accounting for a share of total value added that was higher than in the majority of Member States, some 25.8% in 1997.

The same conclusions could be drawn looking at the structure of employment. Business services accounted for no less than 21.9% of the American workforce in 1997 and 17.1% in Japan. In both cases, this would place them amongst the top European countries, such as Belgium (21.6%) or Luxembourg (19.2%).

SUB-CHAPTER 20.1
LEGAL, ACCOUNTANCY AND
MANAGEMENT CONSULTANCY
(NACE Rev. 1 74.1)

The activities analysed in this sub-chapter cover a variety of professional activities that include: legal services, accounting, book-keeping and auditing services, tax consultancy, market research and public opinion polling, business and management consultancy services, as well as management activities of holding companies.

Small enterprises with high profitability levels

Italy displayed the largest number of enterprises with 193.8 thousand (1996 data), followed by Germany (127.8 thousand, 1997), Spain (127.3 thousand) and France (124.8 thousand). Amongst the smaller Member States, Sweden and the Netherlands stood out (relative to their size) with a large number of enterprises, in excess of 30 thousand. In comparison, Austria, Portugal and Finland all numbered approximately 9 thousand enterprises.

According to structural business statistics, the average European enterprise in this sector of the economy was small in size, employing between 3 and 5 persons. Average turnover per person employed was relatively high at an estimated 99.5 thousand ECU. Value added accounted for a 47.3% share of turnover, and when divided by the number of persons employed, resulted in an estimated apparent labour productivity of 47.4 thousand ECU per person employed. The highest figure was recorded in Luxembourg with 67.2 thousand ECU of value added per person employed in 1997. Finland (59.1 thousand ECU) and France (57.2 thousand ECU) also stood markedly above the average, as opposed to Italy (38.5 thousand ECU) and Portugal (20.9 thousand ECU).

Profitability (as measured by the gross operating surplus generated on each ECU of turnover, the gross operating rate) was amongst the highest in service activities, at an estimated 19.7% in 1997. This average, however, hides significant differences across the EU. The gross operating rate was as high as 49.1% in Italy (1996 data) and 34.1% in Finland, falling to as low as 8.8% in Sweden (1996 data) or 6.1% in France.

Figure 20.2

Legal, accountancy and management consultancy (NACE Rev. 1 74.1)

Number of persons employed, 1997 (thousands) (1)

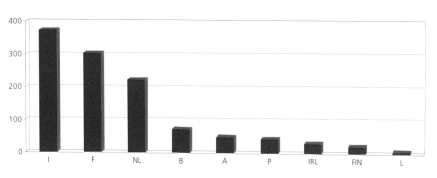

(1) I, 1996; DK, D, EL, E, S and UK, not available.

Source: Eurostat (SBS)

Figure 20.3

Legal, accountancy and management consultancy (NACE Rev. 1 74.1)

Apparent labour productivity, 1997 (thousand ECU per person employed) (1)

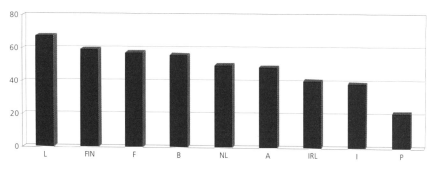

(1) I, 1996; DK, D, EL, E, S and UK, not available.

Source: Eurostat (SBS)

Legal services

Legal services are defined as activities of advocates, barristers and solicitors, notaries, registered lawyers and legal consultants, but they exclude the activities of law courts. The few available official statistics on legal services (NACE Rev. 1 Class 74.11) allow an estimate to be made that they represent roughly one third of the activities covered in this sub-chapter in terms of enterprises, turnover and employment. There were for example 24.8 thousand legal services enterprises in France (1994 data), representing 31.4% of the total for this sub-chapter, employing 132.9 thousand persons (32.9%) and generating 9.6 billion ECU of turnover (26.8%). Data for Italy reported that there were 77.4 thousand enterprises in 1996 (39.9% of the sub-chapter total), employing 131.4 thousand persons (35.2%) with a total turnover of 7.8 billion ECU (36.7%). As a comparison, in the United Kingdom 22.3 thousand enterprises generated turnover of 12.7 billion ECU in 1996.

A large share of the persons employed in legal services activities were not employees, such as for example self-employed lawyers or notaries. The share of employees in the total number of persons employed was equal to 64.2% in France (1994 data), but it was as low as 35.2% in Spain (1996) and 33.0% in Italy (1996).

Accountancy services

Another third of the activities covered in this sub-chapter are classified within accountancy services. These services consist mainly of account keeping and auditing, but often extend to tax consultancy, financial advisory, mergers & acquisitions or management consultancy. Italy numbered the highest number of accountancy enterprises within the Member States for which data was available. There were 70.7 thousand in 1996 (36.5% of the sub-chapter total), employing 144.7 thousand persons (38.8%) and generating 6.7 billion ECU of turnover (31.2%). In France, the weight of this sector was somewhat lower with 14.5 thousand enterprises (19%, 1994 data), employing 117.7 thousand persons (29%) with turnover of 7.2 billion ECU (20.0%). As a comparison, the United Kingdom numbered 21.4 thousand enterprises (1996) generating 9.3 billion ECU of turnover.

Figure 20.4

Legal, accountancy and management consultancy (NACE Rev. 1 74.1)

Unit personnel costs, 1997 (thousand ECU per employee) (1)

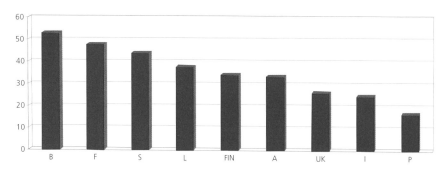

(1) I, FIN and S, 1996; DK, D, EL, E, IRL and NL, not available.

Source: Eurostat (SBS)

The profession is dominated by a few large international firms (known as the "big five": PricewaterhouseCoopers (PwC), Ernst & Young, KPMG, Deloitte & Touche and Arthur Andersen) that usually work for large national and international companies (although they have increasingly started to work for medium-sized enterprises too). However, the bulk of the profession consists of small enterprises, and a large share of persons employed are not employees, but self-employed accountants. Only 47.6% of the persons employed in Italy were employees (1996) and 72.3% in Denmark (1993), whilst the share was somewhat higher in France at 89.9% (1994).

A typical characteristic of accountancy services is the multitude of rules and regulations to which they are subject, including accession to the profession itself. This leads to a high fragmentation of this activity as regulations on accountancy, taxation, company law or social legislation still differ to a large degree across the EU.

Box 20.1

According to the Council of the Bars and Law Societies of the European Community (CCBE) there were in 1996/97 more than 436 thousand registered lawyers in the EU. In addition, the association of notaries (the Council for European affairs of the UINL, Union Internationale du Notariat Latin) estimate that Germany was the EU country with the largest number of notaries' offices, more than 10 thousand, ahead of Italy (4,543) in 1996.

Box 20.2

According to ESOMAR, the European Society for Opinion and Marketing Research, market research activities generated 4.84 billion ECU of turnover in the EU in 1998, an increase of 12.1% when compared to 1997. The main clients of market research services were manufacturing industries, accounting for over half of the turnover generated (51.9%), whilst media enterprises were the second largest group (10.2%). On average, some 72.0% of turnover was generated in the area of consumer research. The largest company in the EU was AC Nielsen with turnover equal to 460 million ECU, about a third of its global turnover. Three companies followed close behind: IMS Health (387 million ECU), TN Sofres (379 million ECU) and Kantar Group (376 million ECU).

Market research and public opinion polling

Market research deals with analysing markets for products and services. It is generally used by businesses to identify and evaluate market conditions and emerging trends, and to define and assess marketing strategies. This service also covers the surveying of public attitudes to political, economic and social issues.

Italy was the country with the largest number of enterprises active in this area (3.8 thousand in 1995), followed by France (3.6 thousand in 1997) and Spain (3.1 thousand in 1997). It is interesting to note the importance of the activity in the Netherlands, where as many as 2.3 thousand enterprises were reported in 1997, with employment reaching 12.4 thousand persons, ahead of Spain (11.3 thousand, 1993 data) and Italy (10.0 thousand, 1995).

EU turnover for market research and opinion polling activities is estimated at around 10 billion ECU in 1997[7]. Two countries were responsible for practically half of this amount: the United Kingdom (2.6 billion ECU) and Germany (2.4 billion ECU). The highest levels of profitability were recorded in Luxembourg and the Netherlands, where enterprises generated approximately 40% of their gross operating surplus from each ECU of turnover.

(7) This figure is the sum of the latest available figures for each Member State; EL, no data available; S, 1996; I, 1995; DK and E, 1993.

Management consultancy

Management consultancy services cover the provision of advice on management matters to businesses or the public sector, sometimes extending to the implementation of solutions. This service also has a highly fragmented supply, as beyond the large multinational enterprises (such as McKinsey, BCG, ATK, Bain, Arthur D Little or Booz-Allen) the majority of enterprises are very small in size, with many consisting of just self-employed persons. In Italy, for example, only 45.6% of the persons employed in 1996 were employees, whilst the equivalent figure in the Netherlands (1993) was 68.2%, a share that was somewhat higher in Spain (81.9%, 1993).

Amongst the countries for which data is available, Italy had the highest number of management consultancy enterprises with more than 40.7 thousand in 1996, employing 83.5 thousand persons and generating turnover of 5.2 billion ECU. Italian enterprises were generally smaller than those of other Member States with average turnover of just 127.5 thousand ECU, compared with 267.9 thousand ECU for the 23.4 thousand enterprises in France (1994), 311.0 thousand ECU for the 33.4 thousand enterprises in the United Kingdom (1996) and 560.3 thousand ECU for the 1.3 thousand enterprises in Spain (1993).

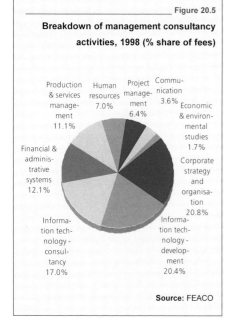

————————————————— Figure 20.5

Breakdown of management consultancy activities, 1998 (% share of fees)

Source: FEACO

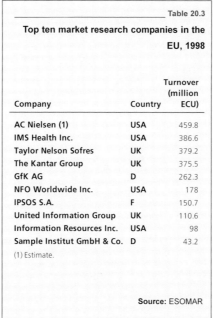

————————————————— Table 20.3

Top ten market research companies in the EU, 1998

Company	Country	Turnover (million ECU)
AC Nielsen (1)	USA	459.8
IMS Health Inc.	USA	386.6
Taylor Nelson Sofres	UK	379.2
The Kantar Group	UK	375.5
GfK AG	D	262.3
NFO Worldwide Inc.	USA	178
IPSOS S.A.	F	150.7
United Information Group	UK	110.6
Information Resources Inc.	USA	98
Sample Institut GmbH & Co.	D	43.2

(1) Estimate.

Source: ESOMAR

————————————————— Table 20.4

Breakdown of market research clients in Europe (1), 1998

	Share of research turnover (%)
Manufacturing	51.9
Media	10.2
Research institutes	7.2
Public sector	6.2
Others	5.0
Financial services	4.8
Distributive trades	4.4
Post & telecom	4.0
Other services	2.7
Advertising agencies	2.6
Utilities	1.0

(1) Average for EEE, Switzerland, Central and Eastern European countries, Cyprus and Turkey.

Source: ESOMAR

SUB-CHAPTER 20.2
ARCHITECTS AND ENGINEERING
ACTIVITIES
(NACE Rev. 1 74.2)

This sub-chapter covers a number of services that are related to the construction industry. They include areas such as architectural consulting activities (building design and drafting, supervision of construction, town and city planning and landscape architecture), machinery and industrial plan design, engineering, project management and technical activities, elaboration of projects using air-conditioning, refrigerating, sanitary and pollution control engineering, acoustical engineering, geological and prospecting activities, weather forecasting activities, and geodetic surveying activities.

The activities of architects, engineering and related technical consultancy are characterised by the presence of a very large number of small companies. The few available official statistics on the sector for the mid-1990s indicated that there were over 43.7 thousand enterprises in France (1994 data), 48.9 thousand in the United Kingdom (1996), 61.0 thousand in Spain (1994) and no fewer than 181.4 thousand in Italy (1996). Average employment per enterprise was equal to just 1.4 persons per enterprise in Italy, 2.2 in Spain and 4.6 in France. The 11.8 thousand enterprises active in the Netherlands in 1995 had a higher than average number of persons employed (6.5).

Unit personnel costs were as a general rule at the upper-end of the scale when compared to other service activities, ranging from 26.2 thousand ECU per employee in Spain (1992 data) to more than 41.0 thousand ECU in France and Denmark (1994 and 1995).

Box 20.4

The Architects' Council of Europe (ACE) estimate that there were some 320 thousand architects active in the EU between 1997 and 1999. One characteristic of this activity is that professional registration is compulsory in most Member States. In addition, certain activities may be restricted to architects only, usually those related to the drawing up of plans, the delivery of the building permits or the supervision of the way the work is carried out. In Spain, even urban and rural development planning is reserved as a domain of architects. In contrast, housing construction in France can sometimes largely avoid the involvement of an architect. Regulatory barriers may partly explain why only a marginal number of architects work abroad. According to ACE, non-nationals make up less than 1.0% of registered architects in most Member States, except in Luxembourg where about half are foreigners.

Table 20.5

Number of architects in the EU (units)

	1997	1998	1999
B	9,869	:	:
DK	6,165	6,205	6,295
D	103,852	:	103,737
EL	13,888	:	:
E	26,945	28,101	30,098
F	26,970	27,080	:
IRL	2,000	:	:
I	79,000	:	:
L	447	:	:
NL	:	:	:
A	2,824	:	:
P	6,654	8,176	8,839
FIN	3,755	:	:
S	4,750	:	:
UK	:	:	:

Source: ACE

Box 20.5

Construction economists are professionals who assist building owners or promoters in contractual, financial, managerial and economic matters, with the objective of optimising the value of a construction project over its lifetime. They are usually engineers, architects or quantity/building surveyors. According to the European Committee of Construction Economists (CEEC), there were about 90 thousand construction economists registered in the national professional associations of the EU in the second half of the 1990s. This must be considered as a rough estimation, though, as data availability and definitions may vary from one country to another.

Services focus on cost-modelling for investors, design management and operational electronic information services. In most Member States the majority of construction economists are employed in private consulting companies. However, in some countries, notably the Netherlands and Spain, a substantial share work as employees within contracting organisations. The average number of qualified staff per enterprise was less than 10, except in the United Kingdom (20).

Another activity contributing to the optimisation of investment projects is that of engineering consultancy. Its objective is to advise, design, implement and/or manage engineering solutions providing the lowest cost and highest investment productivity, for part or the entirety of a construction project.

The European Federation of Engineering Consultancy Associations (EFCA) estimate that there were more than 8 thousand engineering consultancy firms in the EU in 1997 (excluding Finland), employing over 185 thousand persons and generating annual turnover in excess of 16 billion ECU.

The activity of engineering consultancy is greatly affected by international developments. Exports represented up to 42% of turnover in the United Kingdom in 1997, and more than 20% of turnover in five other Member States. International aid programmes and foreign direct investment were often essential components of demand. Whilst they traditionally concentrated on developing countries or emerging economies, demand in the 1990s strongly increased from Central and Eastern European countries, the Commonwealth of Independent Sates and the Eastern Länder of Germany. Domestically, demand has only slightly increased during the last decade in the EU, as a result of a slowdown in public investment, whilst it was stimulated by major projects for transport infrastructure, such as the Channel tunnel. Environmental concerns are expected to further benefit the sector, for example through the construction of waste management facilities.

————————————————————————————————————— Table 20.6

Top ten engineering consulting groups by turnover in the EU, 1998

	Group	Country	Employees (units)	Turnover (million ECU)
1	WS Atkins	UK	8,522	600
2	Arcadis Group	NL	6,635	579
3	Jaakko Pöyrö Group	FIN	5,554	379
4	Fugro	NL	5,136	578
5	Mott MacDonald Group	UK	4,536	269
6	Ove Arup Partnership	UK	4,440	306
7	Maunsell Group	UK	3,419	225
8	Hyder Consulting Group	UK	3,255	196
9	Halcrow Group	UK	3,140	211
10	DHV Group	NL	3,074	230

Source: EFCA

The International Federation of Surveyors defines a geodetic surveyor as a professional whose responsibilities are to assemble and assess land and geographic related information, and to use that information for the purpose of planning and implementing the efficient administration of the land, the sea and structures thereon.

The Council of European Geodetic Surveyors (CLGE) numbers almost 18 thousand members in the EU. The average number of square kilometres for each geodetic surveyor ranges from about 60 in Denmark and Belgium up to 480 in Finland, a large country with low population density. The public sector plays a central role in this activity as CLGE estimates that it accounts for over half of the employment total in most Member States.

Land and geographic information systems (LIS and GIS) represent about three-quarters of the services provided by geodetic surveyors in the EU. New technologies have had a strong influence on the provision of these services. Land measurement can now be carried out with satellite systems. GIS and LIS accounted for about 15% of the market for geodetic services, a share that is expected to grow rapidly in the future.

Landscaping includes the installation, renovation and maintenance of private and public gardens, sports grounds, parks and leisure centres. Specific activities such as tree maintenance and transplantation, landscaping of public works and installations for noise prevention also fall within this sector. Renovation of pre-existing sites and on-going maintenance is a significant field of work for landscape contractors.

The European Landscape Contractors Association (ELCA) estimate that there are approximately 38 thousand landscaping companies in the EU (excluding Greece, Luxembourg, Portugal and Finland), employing more than 205 thousand persons, of which 8.0% were apprentices. Reduced public spending in Europe in recent years has led to a reduction in public contracts, and the ELCA does not expect a reversal of this trend in the near future. The importance of public contracts varies between the individual Member States, ranging from 5.0% in Denmark up to 60.0% in France and Italy.

SUB-CHAPTER 20.3
ADVERTISING AND DIRECT MARKETING
(NACE Rev. 1 74.4)

Advertising and direct marketing enterprises engage in communication services aimed at promoting ideas, goods and services to the general public, to specific target groups, to individuals and to other businesses. They are covered by Group 74.4 of the NACE Rev. 1 classification, which includes the activities of creating and placing of outdoor advertising, the sale of advertisement time and space or the distribution or delivery of advertising material. These activities also cover direct marketing, sponsorship and sales promotion services.

Advertising and marketing services play an essential role in an economy. They allow companies to create awareness of their products and services and to market these as efficiently as possible using product differentiation and positioning. On the other hand, they help consumers obtain information on the marketplace and compare the various offers of each supplier. One of the main trends witnessed in the 1990s has been the increasing fragmentation of the mass media as a consequence of the liberalisation of broadcasting, its progressive conversion to digital technologies and the plummeting costs of publishing systems with the emergence of mainstream "desktop publishing". Mass media has created multiple choices for advertising with fragmented audiences, which has in turn fragmented advertising expenditures. The number of specialised publications and television channels is rapidly expanding, and each one is targeted at a specific group of persons.

Average employment of 3 to 4 persons per enterprise
There were approximately 122 thousand advertising enterprises[8] in the EU in 1997, of which 92.3 thousand were located in the five largest Member States (34.7 thousand in Germany, 20.2 thousand in France, 15.5 thousand in Spain, 11.1 thousand in the United Kingdom and 10.9 thousand in Italy). Each enterprise employed an average of 3 to 4 persons, except in France (5 persons), Portugal (6 persons) and Ireland (where the average was much higher at 12 persons).

(8) B and EL, no data available; DK, 1995; I and S, 1996.

Box 20.9

Global advertising expenditure continued to follow a rising trend and was estimated by the European Group of Television Advertising (EGTA) to have increased by almost 10% in Europe during 1998 to more than 64 billion ECU. Amongst EU countries, the United Kingdom displayed the highest advertising expenditure per capita at 250 ECU per inhabitant in 1998, ahead of France with 192 ECU per capita. This contrasted with Spain, where expenditure did not reach half that amount (97 ECU per inhabitant).

The share of television was however highly variable from one country to another. It ranged from under one-quarter of advertising expenditure in Austria and Finland to about 60% in Italy and Portugal in 1998. Over the long-term, there has been a clear shift in advertising budgets towards television at the expense of printed press. The deregulation of television, a loosening grip on advertising monopolies by government-run television channels and the proliferation of new broadcasting services have largely fuelled these trends.

Figure 20.6

Evolution of advertisement expenditure in Europe by medium (billion ECU) (1)

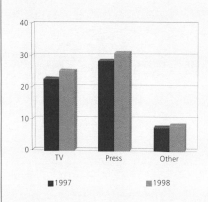

■ 1997   ■ 1998

(1) EU-15 (excluding DK, EL, L and S), Bulgaria, Croatia, Czech Republic, Estonia, Hungary, Norway, Poland, Romania, Slovenia and Switzerland.

Source: EGTA

Figure 20.7

Share of TV in total advertising expenditure, 1998 (%)

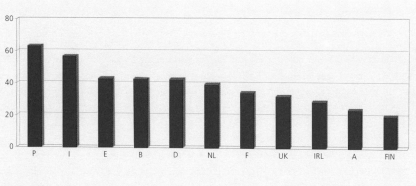

Source: EGTA

High productivity levels but profitability remains low
Unit personnel costs were in all countries for which data was available above 30 thousand ECU per employee, and as a general rule close to 35 thousand ECU, a relatively high figure compared to other economic activities. The extreme values were recorded in Portugal (12.0 thousand ECU) and Denmark (41.9 thousand ECU). High unit personnel costs were often accompanied by high apparent labour productivity. The value added generated by each person employed in advertising activities was estimated at 45.4 thousand ECU in the EU in 1997, with a minimum of 16.5 thousand ECU in Portugal and a maximum of 52.0 thousand ECU in Austria.

Advertising activities did not boast notable profitability rates. It was estimated that the gross operating surplus as a share of turnover (the gross operating rate) was equal to 10.4% in the EU in 1997. Enterprises in Portugal (4.6%) and France (5.6%) recorded the lowest rates, well behind their Italian (20.3%, 1996 data) and Dutch (22.0%) counterparts.

─────────────────────────────────────── **Box 20.10**

FEDMA, the Federation of European Direct Marketing, defines direct marketing as "a part of the commercial communication services sector (...) used by most organisations and companies to sell products at a distance, provide customer care, raise funds, inform customers of offers, etc. It is supported by a variety of service industries (direct marketing agencies, call centres, tele-shopping broadcasters, printers and letter shops)". Although direct marketing is traditionally considered in terms of direct mail and un-addressed mail, other techniques are growing rapidly, such as direct response to printed press, tele-shopping, tele-marketing, Internet and other on-line services.

FEDMA estimate that the largest share of the 31 billion ECU expenditure within direct marketing in the EU in 1997 was dedicated to direct mail, as opposed to tele-marketing or Internet/on-line expenditure. This pattern is expected to change, as direct marketing is increasingly likely to rely on telecommunications rather than post. Already a large share of orders or contacts for direct marketing are made by phone or fax, and FEDMA expects this to grow.

─────────────────────────────────────── **Figure 20.8**

Volume of direct marketing addressed mail per capita, 1997 (items/inhabitant)

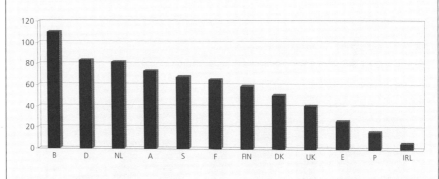

Source: FEDMA

In terms of volume, Belgium was the country with the largest number of items sent per capita in 1997, with no fewer than 110 addressed mails for each inhabitant. Inhabitants received more than 80 mails during a year in only two other countries: Germany (83) and the Netherlands (82). In contrast, the Portuguese received a mere 16 addressed marketing mails, and the Irish only 5. When combined with un-addressed mailings, Dutch citizens received as many as 575 items per year, the highest figure in the EU ahead of Austrians (487).

The main users of direct marketing have always been mail-order traders, publishers, specialised clubs (books, records, etc.) and business-to-business relations. However, as database systems become more sophisticated, they are increasingly being used for activities such as fund-raising or membership campaigns for charities and political parties, as well as customer care (including inquiries, information and after-sales services).

Figure 20.9

Advertising and direct marketing (NACE Rev. 1 74.4)

Number of persons employed, 1997 (thousands) (1)

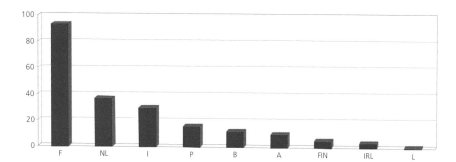

(1) I, 1996; DK, D, EL, E, S and UK, not available.

Source: Eurostat (SBS)

Figure 20.10

Advertising and direct marketing (NACE Rev. 1 74.4)

Apparent labour productivity, 1997 (thousand ECU per person employed) (1)

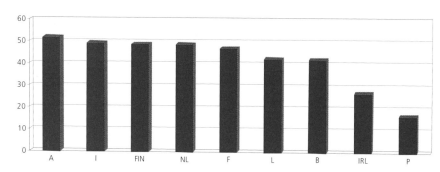

(1) I, 1996; DK, D, EL, E, S and UK, not available.

Source: Eurostat (SBS)

Figure 20.11

Advertising and direct marketing (NACE Rev. 1 74.4)

Unit personnel costs, 1997 (thousand ECU per employee) (1)

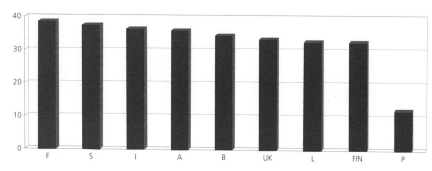

(1) I, FIN and S, 1996; DK, D, EL, E, IRL and NL, not available.

Source: Eurostat (SBS)

SUB-CHAPTER 20.4
LABOUR RECRUITMENT AND
PROVISION OF PERSONNEL
(NACE Rev. 1 74.5)

Activities covered in this section include personnel search, selection referral and placement in connection with employment supplied to the potential employer or to the prospective employee, head-hunters and labour-contracting activities (for example, temporary work agencies). The following activities are excluded: farm labour contractors, personal theatrical or artistic agents and cinema, television and other theatrical casting activities.

Business services related to human resources have developed rapidly over the last twenty years. A series of factors underlie this growth, such as deregulation of labour markets, out-sourcing of selection and recruitment activities, and increasing labour market flexibility (stemming from the needs of both enterprises and individuals, see box 20.11).

Strong growth in the number of enterprises
More than 21 thousand enterprises were active in labour recruitment and the provision of personnel services in the EU[9] in 1997. The United Kingdom accounted for nearly half of the total with 9.3 thousand enterprises, up 14.4% when compared to 1996, followed by Germany (2.6 thousand enterprises, up 13.4%) and France (2.3 thousand, up 0.3%). The Netherlands clearly stood out from the other smaller Member States with a much higher number of enterprises (2.2 thousand, up 25.0%), exceeding Spain (2.1 thousand, up 3.8%).

Average employment per enterprise for these activities was considerably higher than in the majority of other business services. In France for example, there were on average 177 persons employed per enterprise in 1997, and there were 154 in the Netherlands. It is however important to note the particularity of employment figures for these specific activities, as a consequence of their nature. Indeed, employees such as agency or temporary workers are normally considered as persons employed by the employment agency and not by the client enterprise.

(9) B and EL, no data available; DK and I, 1995; S, 1996.

Box 20.11

Temporary work businesses supply workers to their clients for a wide range of short term, specialised requirements. For workers, temporary work businesses may satisfy particular individual needs and preferences. For enterprises, they allow for greater flexibility in organisation and operation, for example to face unexpected variations in demand, to meet a contract demanding unusual skills or to fill the temporary absence of permanent staff.

In addition, temporary work may contribute to a more flexible labour market, as a growing number of jobless workers resort to temporary work businesses to find a temporary occupation with the expectation of finding a permanent position at a later stage. Conversely, companies may treat temporary work contracts as trial contracts before offering a permanent position to workers. CIETT, the International Confederation of Temporary Work Business estimate that on average well over one-third of temporary workers find permanent jobs as a result of temporary contracts.

CIETT estimate that about 1.8 million persons carry out temporary work on any given day and that temporary work accounts for about 1.5% of total employment in the EU. France, Belgium, and more precisely the Netherlands and the United Kingdom were the countries with the highest propensity to use temporary workers. In these latter two countries temporary work accounted for more than 3.5% of total employment in 1996, an average of 220 thousand and 880 thousand persons a day respectively.

In the USA, where labour laws are generally less strict than in European countries, there is also evidence of a high recourse to temporary work businesses, that accounted for 2.0% of total employment. This corresponded to about 2.3 million persons working daily, and contrasts with Japan where only 320 thousand persons, less than 1.0% of the total number employed, were employed through a temporary work enterprise.

Table 20.7

Main indicators of temporary work, 1996

	Number of enterprises	Daily temporary work employment	Share of total employment (%)
B	91	44,000	1.1
DK	100	2,000	0.1
D	2,601	177,000	0.5
E (1)	125	60,000	0.5
F	850	350,000	1.7
IRL	260	3,300	0.2
L	31	2,200	1.1
NL	575	225,000	3.6
A	593	15,000	0.4
P	210	:	:
S (1)	18	7,000	0.2
UK	5,000	880,000	3.4
JAP (1)	264	320,000	0.5
USA	6,000	2,310,000	1.9

(1) For the number of enterprises: members of national associations only.

Source: CIETT

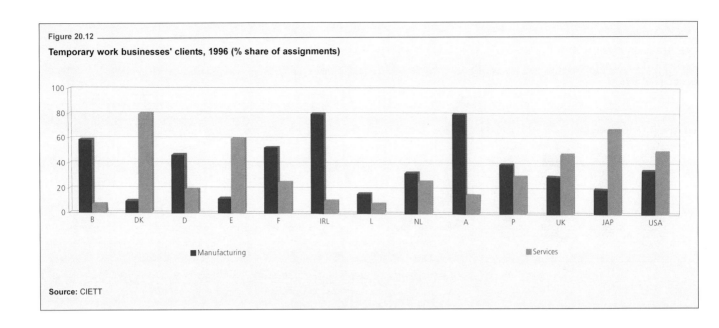

Figure 20.12

Temporary work businesses' clients, 1996 (% share of assignments)

■Manufacturing   ■Services

Source: CIETT

Low productivity and profitability levels

Apparent labour productivity was relatively low in this activity when compared to other services. It was estimated at only 18.9 thousand ECU of value added per person employed in 1997, ranging from a minimum of 9.3 thousand ECU in Portugal to a maximum of 30.6 thousand ECU in Austria.

Similarly, the average profitability level of personnel services enterprises was also relatively low compared to the other service activities. The share of gross operating surplus in turnover (the gross operating rate) was estimated at 10.7% in 1997. France displayed the lowest average rate (3.4%), together with Belgium, Austria and Portugal (all between 4.0% and 5.0%), whilst Italy (27.8%, 1995 data) and Sweden (28.8%, 1996 data) boasted the highest rates.

Figure 20.13

Labour recruitment and provision of personnel (NACE Rev. 1 74.5)

Number of persons employed, 1997 (thousands) (1)

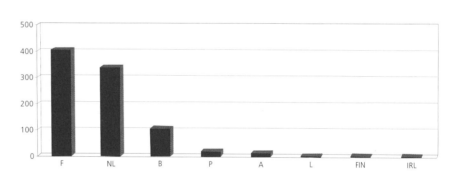

(1) DK, D, EL, E, I, S and UK, not available.

Source: Eurostat (SBS)

Figure 20.14

Labour recruitment and provision of personnel (NACE Rev. 1 74.5)

Apparent labour productivity, 1997 (thousand ECU per person employed) (1)

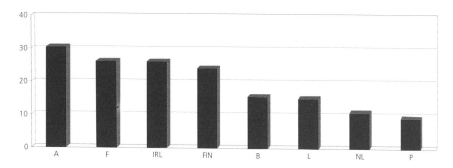

(1) DK, D, EL, E, I, S and UK, not available.

Source: Eurostat (SBS)

Figure 20.15

Labour recruitment and provision of personnel (NACE Rev. 1 74.5)

Unit personnel costs, 1997 (thousand ECU per employee) (1)

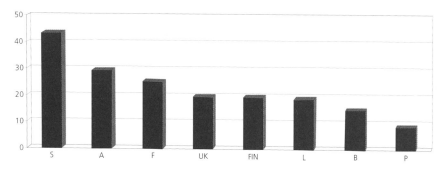

(1) FIN and S, 1996; DK, D, EL, E, IRL, I and NL, not available.

Source: Eurostat (SBS)

SUB-CHAPTER 20.5
SECURITY SERVICES (NACE Rev. 1 74.6)

The services covered by this sub-chapter include investigation activities, surveillance and protective activities, transport of valuables, bodyguard activities, guard and watchman activities for apartment buildings, offices and factories, as well as consultancy in the field of security and training of dogs for security reasons. It however excludes the installation of alarm systems.

Security service activities emerged after the Second World War due to a number of factors, such as the fast growth in living standards of the population and increased demand from businesses. As with the other business services covered in this chapter, this sector has greatly benefited from the trends in out-sourcing, whereby enterprises increasingly rely on specialised companies for their security needs, for example to guard their premises or to transport their valuables.

476 thousand employees working in
more than 17 thousand enterprises
More than 17.0 thousand enterprises were active in security services in 1997 in the EU[10], of which a large share were established in France (4.9 thousand enterprises, or 28.8% of the EU total). Amongst the larger Member States, Germany and the United Kingdom numbered more than 3 thousand enterprises, almost twice as many as in Italy or Spain (1.8 thousand[11] and 1.7 thousand respectively). In Austria there were very few enterprises active (84 in 1997). As such, Austrian enterprises were significantly larger than in the other countries, with an average of 70 persons employed per and turnover exceeding 2.1 million ECU. As a comparison, average employment per enterprise in most of the other Member States was comprised between 20 and 30 persons and average turnover between 450 thousand ECU and 850 thousand ECU.

(10) B and EL, no data available; DK and I, 1995; S, 1996.
(11) 1995.

Turning to employment, there were an estimated 476 thousand employees working in security services enterprises in 1996/97 in the EU[12], representing 97% to 99% of the total number of persons employed in most countries. Only Italy (94.1%), the Netherlands (93.7%) and Denmark (47.7%) recorded much lower shares of employees in their respective total number of persons employed. The United Kingdom alone accounted for more than one-fifth of the workforce with 107.7 thousand employees in 1997, ahead of France (95.1 thousand) and Germany (94.6 thousand).

Productivity and profitability
amongst the lowest in services
Apparent labour productivity of security services was at the lower-end of the scale when compared to other service activities, with an estimated 20.0 thousand ECU of value added generated by each person employed in 1997. Amongst the Member States, the range was from 10.7 thousand ECU in Portugal to 33.0 thousand ECU in Belgium. Profitability rates were also low, as the gross operating surplus of the sector represented an estimated 7.1% of total turnover in 1997. Higher gross operating rates were recorded in the United Kingdom (15.7%) and Italy (14.7%, 1995 data), but this ratio fell as low as 5.4% in Austria and 2.2% in France.

(12) EL, no data available; DK, I and L, 1995.

Box 20.12

According to European Security Transport Association (ESTA), there were 422 European enterprises active in this sector in 1998. This very small number is an indication of the relatively high concentration within the market. More than three-quarters of these companies were located in Italy (220) and Germany (130).

Cash transport activities (including coin processing, cash and notes processing, cheque encoding or automatic teller machine (ATM) servicing) employed almost 32 thousand employees in 1998, with an 11 thousand-strong fleet of armoured vehicles. Average enterprise size was highest in the United Kingdom, where enterprises numbered approximately 400 vehicles and one thousand employees each. The average fleet of vehicles per enterprise exceeded 100 units in only three other countries: Spain (240), the Netherlands (130) and Portugal (100). This contrasted with Italy, Luxembourg and Germany where the typical cash transport enterprise numbered fewer than 20 vehicles and 40 employees.

The total market for cash transport services was estimated at 3.8 billion ECU in 1998. Of this amount, about 2 billion ECU was out-sourced to independent transport companies, which corresponded to a market penetration rate of about 52%. In all countries except for the United Kingdom, independent companies made up more than half the total market, ranging from 50% in Germany to 92% in Spain.

Table 20.8

Main indicators of security transport services in Europe, 1998

	Number of enterprises	Number of vehicles	Number of cash processing centres	Number of employees in cash transportation	Number of employees in cash processing centres	Turnover (million ECU)	Turnover from cash processing (million ECU)
EU-15	422	11,166	568	31,563	10,500	1,985.2	511.5
B	4	285	5	1,200	200	70.6	8.6
DK	2	56	7	200	:	47.0	23.5
D	130	2,000	150	5,000	300	306.8	92.0
EL	5	150	10	320	50	6.6	0.6
E	5	1,200	60	2,200	1,800	132.2	52.9
F	19	1,200	150	5,300	2,200	365.9	117.4
IRL	3	140	4	400	:	25.4	:
I	220	1,600	85	4,500	820	284.0	123.9
L	3	45	2	100	20	4.2	0.5
NL	2	260	3	1,150	140	61.4	7.7
A	5	200	8	800	:	19.3	4.7
P	2	200	11	493	320	27.8	6.0
FIN	3	80	20	400	350	30.3	13.5
S	10	210	10	500	:	41.2	4.2
UK	9	3,540	43	9,000	1,600	562.5	56.5
Czech Republic	12	210	1	3,500	50	15.0	2.0
Estonia	2	33	2	168	17	2.0	0.6
Hungary	20	300	5	1,500	300	23.9	7.9
Norway	8	30	5	80	50	19.8	2.9
Poland	50	600	5	7,000	:	12.4	0.6
Slovakia	25	61	:	150	:	5.4	:
Switzerland	8	100	10	250	100	13.6	3.6

Source: ESTA

Figure 20.16

Market penetration by independent cash transport companies, 1998 (% share of total market value)

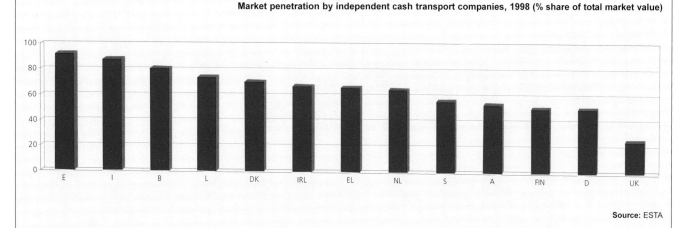

Source: ESTA

Figure 20.17

Security services (NACE Rev. 1 74.6)

Number of persons employed, 1997 (thousands) (1)

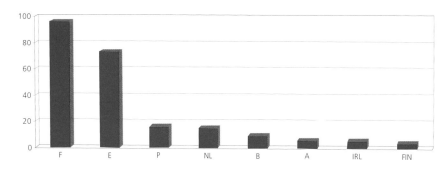

(1) E, 1996; DK, D, EL, I, L, S and UK, not available.

Source: Eurostat (SBS)

Figure 20.18

Security services (NACE Rev. 1 74.6)

Apparent labour productivity, 1997 (thousand ECU per person employed) (1)

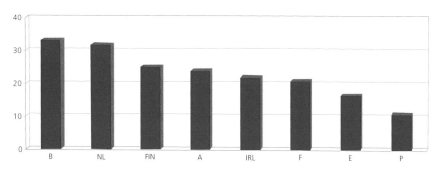

(1) E, 1996; DK, D, EL, I, L, S and UK, not available.

Source: Eurostat (SBS)

Figure 20.19

Security services (NACE Rev. 1 74.6)

Unit personnel costs, 1997 (thousand ECU per employee) (1)

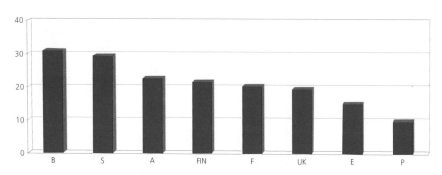

(1) E, FIN and S, 1996; DK, D, EL, IRL, I, L and NL, not available.

Source: Eurostat (SBS)

SUB-CHAPTER 20.6
INDUSTRIAL CLEANING SERVICES
(NACE Rev. 1 74.7)

Industrial cleaning services include the interior clean-ing of buildings of all types, including offices, hospi-tals, factories or multi-unit residential buildings, the cleaning of public means of transport, window clean-ing, chimney cleaning, but also disinfecting and exter-minating activities for buildings, ships and trains. However, it excludes agricultural pest control, or steam-cleaning, sand blasting and similar activities for building exteriors.

Industrial cleaning services constitute a sizeable activi-ty within business services, especially in terms of employment, accounting for between 13.1% of NACE Rev. 1 Division 74 in Belgium (1997) and 26.2% in Denmark (1995). Cleaning services are one of the main beneficiaries of the out-sourcing trends men-tioned in the introduction to this chapter. In-house cleaning staff have hence increasingly been replaced by employees from industrial cleaning enterprises, whilst demand has also been stimulated by higher liv-ing standards.

1.6 million employees in over
100 thousand enterprises
Some 103.9 thousand industrial cleaning enterprises were active in the EU in 1997[13]. Almost one half of them were found in Italy (25.0 thousand) and Germany (21.9 thousand). As a comparison, France had just 13.6 thousand cleaning enterprises and the United Kingdom a mere 7.9 thousand, only slightly ahead of Denmark (6.3 thousand).

Industrial cleaning enterprises employed on average more persons than most other business service activi-ties. Denmark recorded the lowest rate of average employment with 6 persons employed per enterprise in 1997, whilst the range went as high as 40 persons in Luxembourg (1996 data) and 59 in Ireland. Average turnover, however, was relatively modest, ranging from 135.1 thousand ECU per enterprise in Denmark (1995 data) and 186.8 thousand ECU per enterprise in Italy (1996 data) to 640.7 thousand ECU in the United Kingdom and 938.5 thousand ECU in Luxembourg (1996 data).

(13) B and EL, no data available; DK, 1995; I and S, 1996.

There were approximately 1.6 million employees working for industrial cleaning enterprises in 1996/97[14] in the EU. This represented 96% to 99% of the total number of persons employed in the activity for the majority of countries (excluding Italy and Denmark where the share of employees was much lower at respectively 84.7% and 42.7% of the total number of persons employed). The largest employer in the EU was the United Kingdom, with 393.2 thousand employees. Germany (292.6 thousand) and Spain (222.3 thousand, 1995 data) followed. The Netherlands stood out amongst the smallest countries with 131.1 thousand employees (1996 data), three to four times as many as in countries such as Belgium, Austria or Portugal.

Average personnel costs per employee (unit personnel costs) within industrial cleaning activities were particu-larly low when compared to other service activities. They reached a maximum of 31.1 thousand ECU per employee in Denmark (1995 data), down to 5.0 thou-sand ECU in Portugal (1997 data), with an average in the EU of approximately 15.0 thousand ECU. These figures may be interpreted with respect to the low average level of qualifications within the workforce. In addition, these figures are brought down by the high number of part time employees working in this sector (as employment data is often not adjusted to full-time equivalents). Furthermore, labour market policies have been introduced in several EU countries that allow employers to hire on the basis of contracts with tax and social security advantages (usually at low wages or for a limited number of hours in the working week).

(14) EL, no data available; DK and E, 1995.

Amongst the lowest apparent
labour productivity in services
Productivity of the industrial cleaning workforce was amongst the lowest in services. Apparent labour pro-ductivity was estimated at just 15.6 thousand ECU of value added per person employed in 1997. The lowest levels were recorded in Portugal and Ireland with just 5.6 thousand ECU and 7.7 thousand ECU. In Belgium and Italy, the countries where apparent labour pro-ductivity was highest, levels rose to 19.1 thousand ECU and 20.0 thousand ECU (1996 data).

Similarly, profitability rates were also modest. Industrial cleaning enterprises made on average an estimated 13.1 ECU of gross operating surplus on each 100 ECU of turnover in 1997, a rate that ranged between 5.0% in Portugal and 6.0% in France up to maxima of 19.7% in the United Kingdom and 26.2% in the Netherlands.

Box 20.13

Industrial cleaning enterprises are represented at European level by the European Federation of Cleaning Industries (EFCI/FENI). They include enterprises active in areas corresponding to NACE Rev. 1 Group 74.7, but also other activities carried out by cleaning companies such as waste management services, chimney sweeping, façade cleaning or green space maintenance. This is due to the growing number of auxiliary services being incorporated into the services offered by cleaning enterprises and may result from clients demanding a full "facility management" solution aimed at reducing the number of sub-contractors.

As regards cleaning services, office cleaning was by far the largest market segment in 1997, as it accounted for more than half of total turnover. Industry (including factories, nuclear power stations and agro-food industries) was the second largest segment (10.6%), ahead of hospitals (7.6%).

Figure 20.20

Main market segments of industrial cleaning, 1997 (% share of turnover)

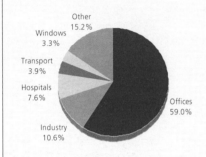

Other 15.2%
Windows 3.3%
Transport 3.9%
Hospitals 7.6%
Industry 10.6%
Offices 59.0%

Source: FENI

Table 20.9

Main characteristics of employment in industrial cleaning, 1997

	Share of part-time employees (%)	Total labour costs per hour (ECU)	Average daily working time (hours)
B	69	15.4	4.4
DK	60	14.2	4.5
D	80	14.6	4.0
E	70	8.7	4.0
F	70	16.7	5.0
I	80	8.0	4.0
L	90	13.1	5.0
NL	82	9.8	4.0
P	78	3.0	6.0
FIN	60	8.4	4.6
S	60	11.3	:
UK	74	5.7	2.7

Source: FENI

Employment characteristics of cleaning services enterprises include a high feminine presence. Indeed, women represented no fewer than 74% of the workforce in 1998. A large number of employees, about a fifth, were migrant workers[15], ranging from just 1% in the United Kingdom to 48% in Belgium. Another striking characteristic was the prevalence of part-time work, which was carried out by more than three-quarters of all employees, with an average working time of just 4.4 hours a day in 1997. Only 15% of these hours were performed during normal working hours, with some 62% carried out during the evening or at night.

Labour costs were relatively low, although they varied considerably across the EU. The total hourly cost of an employee ranged from 3.0 ECU in Portugal to more than five times that amount in Belgium (15.4 ECU) and France (16.6 ECU) in 1997.

(15) Either from other Member States or from non-Community countries.

─────────Figure 20.21

Industrial cleaning services (NACE Rev. 1 74.7)

Number of persons employed, 1997 (thousands) (1)

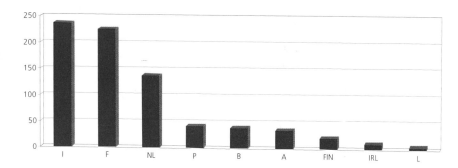

(1) I and L, 1996; DK, D, EL, E, S and UK, not available.

Source: Eurostat (SBS)

─────────Figure 20.22

Industrial cleaning services (NACE Rev. 1 74.7)

Apparent labour productivity, 1997 (thousand ECU per person employed) (1)

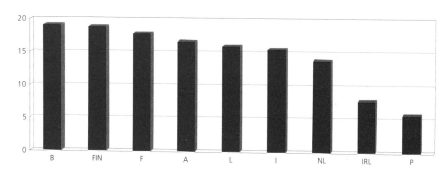

(1) I and L, 1996; DK, D, EL, E, S and UK, not available.

Source: Eurostat (SBS)

─────────Figure 20.23

Industrial cleaning services (NACE Rev. 1 74.7)

Unit personnel costs, 1997 (thousand ECU per employee) (1)

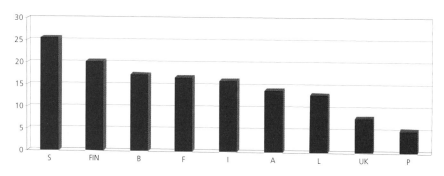

(1) I, L, FIN and S, 1996; DK, D, EL, E, IRL and NL, not available.

Source: Eurostat (SBS)

SUB-CHAPTER 20.7
RENTING (NACE Rev. 1 71)

The data presented in this chapter covers the activities of renting of machinery and equipment without operators and the renting of personal and household goods. This service activity includes amongst other things the renting of transport equipment (automobiles, boats, aeroplanes, etc...), the renting of agricultural, construction or office equipment. It should be noted that operational leasing, which is normally long-term rental, is included within this sub-chapter, whilst financial leasing is not (as it is considered a special form of credit granting).

Almost 100 thousand enterprises

The EU numbered approximately 99.5 thousand renting enterprises in 1997[16]. Almost half of them were located in just two of the Member States: Germany (25.0 thousand) and France (20.0 thousand). Amongst the other larger Member States, Italy had the lowest number of renting enterprises (7.9 thousand in 1996), less than half the figure in Spain (16.8 thousand). Average employment was generally very low, ranging in a majority of countries between 1 and 3 persons per enterprise. Dutch enterprises, however, were significantly larger with 6 persons employed on average. Renting enterprises are generally smaller than the average service enterprise. Enterprises without any employees (normally self-employed) represented 58.3% of the total number of enterprises in 1996, compared to 51.9% for the same size-class in the whole of service activities (NACE Rev. 1 Sections G to K). These enterprises accounted for 16.6% of the number of persons employed in renting activities and generated 10.9% of the turnover. Corresponding shares for the whole of services were lower, at 12.2% and 4.2% respectively. Similarly, the immediately superior size-class (enterprises with 1 to 9 employees) represented 36.7% of the total number of enterprises (43.0% for services), 27.7% of employment (27.0%) and 20.1% of turnover (16.6%).

(16) B and EL, no data available; DK, 1995; E, I and S, 1996.

Average turnover per enterprise was very similar to the average for service activities. It varied between a minima of 204 thousand ECU in Italy (1996 data) and 213 thousand ECU in Denmark (1995) and a maxima of 1.3 million ECU in Luxembourg and 1.6 million ECU in the United Kingdom (1997 in both cases).

High productivity and profitability indicators

The interpretation of financial ratios within renting activities should be carried out with great caution, bearing in mind the specific nature of this activity. Renting enterprises may indeed face much higher financial income and costs or depreciation compared to enterprises active in other service areas.

As a consequence, ratios relying on indicators such as gross value added may appear over-estimated. Apparent labour productivity, for example, was the highest of all service activities (NACE Rev. 1 Sections G to K) at an estimated 111.1 thousand ECU of gross value added per person employed in 1997. The lowest value was recorded in Ireland (34.1 thousand ECU, 1997 data), far below the maxima of 211.8 thousand ECU of Austria (1997) and 297.4 thousand ECU in Luxembourg (1997).

The gross operating rate was also one of the highest amongst service activities, with an estimated 43.9 ECU of gross operating surplus being generated from each 100 ECU of turnover in 1997. Within the Member States the shares ranged from 25.2% in Italy (1996) up to as much as 58.5% in Austria (1997).

Box 20.14

According to the latest estimates from the European Car and Truck Rental Association (ECATRA) for 1994, the largest car rental markets were found in Germany, France and the United Kingdom. Together these countries had a total fleet of 420 thousand cars for short-term rentals. The United Kingdom had the largest fleet with 155 thousand rental vehicles, followed by France (145 thousand) and Germany (120 thousand). For comparison, the total number of rental vehicles in service in the USA was estimated at 1.6 million in 1998. Within the market for long-term car rental, Germany was by far the largest market with a total number of vehicles equal to 2.2 million cars and an estimated 250 thousand light vans. The United Kingdom ranked second with nearly 1.2 million passenger cars and 85 thousand light vans.

Car rental companies are important clients of car manufacturers, with strong links growing between the two sectors. For example, Hertz is a majority-owned subsidiary of Ford since 1987 and Europcar numbers Volkswagen amongst its largest shareholders. There have however been significant changes in the ownership of car rental companies in the second half of the 1990s. General Motors sold its 25% stake in Avis in 1996, Ford sold approximately 20% of its equity in Hertz in 1997 and Chrysler sold Dollar and Thrifty. Car rental companies continue however to be a party to supply and repurchase agreements with car manufacturers. Under such programmes, a car rental company agrees to purchase a specified minimum number of new vehicles at a given price, whilst the manufacturer agrees to repurchase the vehicles from the car rental company at a future date (typically, six to nine months after the purchase). These programmes limit a car rental company's residual risk with respect to its fleet and enable them to determine a substantial percentage of their depreciation expenses in advance.

SUB-CHAPTER 20.8
LEASING (PART OF NACE Rev. 1 71)

The definition of leasing is not exactly the same in the different Member States. Comparisons across Member States, therefore, have to be interpreted cautiously. Broadly speaking, leasing refers to the transfer of a good from the lessor (the owner) to the lessee, who can make use of the good based upon regular payments for it. While leasing concerns an operation over the medium or long-term, renting refers primarily to the transfer of a good in the short-term (hours, days, etc.) between two natural or legal persons on payment of a fee. According to the NACE Rev. 1 classification, leasing falls under Division 71 which covers renting services of machinery and equipment without operator, and services of personal goods and household goods. The leasing of real estate is excluded and figures only refer to the leasing of movables, or so-called equipment leasing.

Financial lease vs. operational lease

Two major categories of leasing contracts are distinguished: the financial lease and the operational lease. A financial lease refers to a contract with a full payout (full amortisation). It is in principle irrevocable and does not provide for maintenance and service (the legal ownership stays with the lessor, but the economic ownership shifts to the lessee). Furthermore, in several Member States such as the United Kingdom, the Netherlands, Belgium, Germany, France and Spain, the financial lease includes a purchase option for the lessee at the expiration date.

An operational lease refers to a contract with non-full payout (partial amortisation): the lessee only uses the capital equipment for a portion of its normal service life, and there are normally one or more additional users. The leasing rates and payments are calculated at a fraction of the purchase value. Furthermore, an operational lease can normally be cancelled. This form of leasing usually calls for the lessor to maintain and service the leased equipment, whilst the costs of maintenance are either built into the lease payments or contracted for separately. Legal and economic ownership stays with the lessor.

The main actors

Originally, leasing companies were mainly manufacturers trying to stimulate their sales by offering additional services to customers. A second family of leasing companies was formed by financial institutions, which in several Member States overtook the manufacturers

because of their financial expertise. The European market continues to be dominated by bank-owned lessors. However, there is some evidence that this may change, as manufacturer-owned lessors are once again increasing their market share.

Box 20.15

According to Leaseurope figures, total industry turnover reached 108.7 billion ECU in 1998[17], up 14% from the year before. European leasing activities are mainly concentrated in Germany and the United Kingdom, with each of these countries recording turnover close to 30.0 billion ECU. Together they accounted for 54.7% of total EU turnover in 1998, whilst France and Italy accounted for 14.5% and 10.9% respectively.

The European leasing market has gradually undergone significant changes in terms of suppliers, customers and products. Leasing operations used to concentrate on office equipment, but have extended during the 1990s to all kinds of goods, ranging from machines and industrial equipment to road transport vehicles, ships and aircraft.

The decreasing role of office equipment is reflected in a lower share of total turnover of leasing machinery. In 1998, only 13.2% of total turnover could be attributed to office equipment, compared to 15.0% in 1992. Motor vehicles were the largest market segment constituting about 32.5% of total turnover. The shares of the other segments remained fairly stable between 1992 and 1998, with machinery accounting for 26.0% of the leasing market.

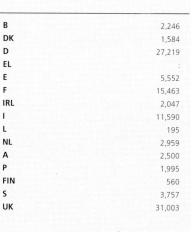

Table 20.10

Turnover from equipment leasing, 1998 (million ECU)

B	2,246
DK	1,584
D	27,219
EL	:
E	5,552
F	15,463
IRL	2,047
I	11,590
L	195
NL	2,959
A	2,500
P	1,995
FIN	560
S	3,757
UK	31,003

Source: Leaseurope

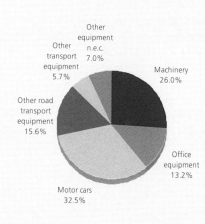

Figure 20.24

Equipment leased by type of asset in the EU, 1998 (share of turnover)

Other equipment n.e.c. 7.0%
Other transport equipment 5.7%
Machinery 26.0%
Other road transport equipment 15.6%
Office equipment 13.2%
Motor cars 32.5%

Source: Leaseurope

More than two-thirds (69.7%) of leasing contracts were concluded for a period of 2 to 5 years. About 13.7% had a duration of up to 2 years, whilst 6.5% of contracts were for a period longer than 10 years (concentrated in just a few Member States, notably the United Kingdom, where they accounted for no less than 13.9% of the total, and Germany (8.0%)).

---

(17) EL, no data available.

SUB-CHAPTER 20.9
FRANCHISING
(NO NACE DEFINITION APPLICABLE)

Franchising is a strategy of business development that has had remarkable success around the world. It is a means of adapting to local market conditions without losing the benefits of global concerns, ideas and scales. The last 25 years have seen a considerable evolution in the channels of distribution. Stronger competition has resulted in increased specialisation and the emergence of new ideas, with franchising being one concept that has developed.

This type of distribution has rapidly evolved, and covers many different types of businesses. In Europe, franchising was first adopted in retail sectors, where, with some exceptions, traditional forms of co-operation were little used. It then rapidly extended to a variety of businesses, ranging from hotels and restaurants to personal services' enterprises. Although North American franchisors found their way to Europe, many national franchise networks were also developed. Despite growing internationalisation, most national markets are still held by national networks.

Box 20.16

The European Franchise Federation accounted for approximately 3.6 thousand franchisors in the EU in 1996, controlling a network comprising of almost 145 thousand franchisees. Altogether, franchising employed almost 1.2 million persons and achieved a turnover of 90.7 billion ECU (all these figures exclude Greece, Ireland, Luxembourg and Finland). France was the leading country with 530 franchisors and 29.7 thousand franchisees (1998 data). There were a similar number of franchisors in Germany (530), along with 22.0 thousand franchisees. German franchising realised a turnover of 14.6 billion ECU in 1996. Germany has become one of the most important franchising countries in Europe; however, because of its co-operatively structured retail trade industry with strong "buying groups", franchising had difficulty in taking-off until the beginning of the 1990s. German franchising mostly developed in the areas of food distribution (with large groups like Spar or Eismann) and household equipment, followed by personal equipment and services. Next came the United Kingdom with 474 franchisors and 25.7 thousand franchisees. One characteristic of the United Kingdom is the great influence of American franchises. Most American franchisors started their European strategies with a British operation. Consequently, almost 30% of the franchise networks in the United Kingdom were American in 1997.

Table 20.11

Main indicators of franchising in the EU, 1996 (units)

	Number of franchisees	Number of franchisors	Number of persons employed	Turnover (million ECU)
B	3,500	170	28,000	3,600
DK	2,500	98	40,000	1,000
D	22,000	530	230,000	14,600
EL	:	:	:	:
E	13,161	288	69,000	6,800
F (1)	29,673	530	350,000	29,880
IRL	:	:	:	:
I	21,390	436	49,660	12,000
L	:	:	:	:
NL	11,825	350	85,300	9,200
A	3,000	210	40,000	1,600
P	2,000	220	35,000	1,000
FIN	:	:	:	:
S	9,150	230	71,000	5,720
UK (2)	26,800	541	264,100	9,700

(1) As of 31/12/1998.
(2) As of 31/12/1997.

Source: EFF

_____Table 20.12

Renting of machinery and equipment without operator and of personal and household goods (NACE Rev. 1 71)

Employment related indicators, 1997

	B	DK	D	EL	E	F	IRL	I (1)	L	NL (2)	A	P	FIN (2)	S	UK
Number of persons employed (thousands)	8.8	:	:	:	:	65.3	5.7	15.1	0.5	22.8	5.9	9.0	2.6	:	:
Employees/number of persons employed (%)	71.2	:	:	:	:	88.4	79.5	40.1	91.4	84.0	79.4	78.0	83.3	:	:
Average no. of persons employed/enterprise (units)	:	:	:	:	:	3.0	5.0	1.9	3.0	6.0	4.0	4.0	3.0	:	:

(1) 1996; (2) Employees as a share of the number of persons employed, 1996.

_____Table 20.13

Renting of machinery and equipment without operator and of personal and household goods (NACE Rev. 1 71)

Turnover related indicators, 1997

	B	DK	D	EL	E	F	IRL	I (1)	L	NL	A	P	FIN	S (1)	UK
Turnover (million ECU)	2,984	:	32,418	:	:	13,540	468	1,616	260	4,554	1,887	965	384	1,902	17,143
Turnover per enterprise (million ECU)	:	:	1.3	:	:	0.7	0.4	0.2	1.3	1.1	1.4	0.4	0.4	0.4	1.6
Turnover per person employed (thousand ECU)	339.0	:	:	:	:	207.5	82.1	107.1	521.8	199.5	320.9	107.2	149.6	:	:

(1) 1996.

_____Table 20.14

Renting of machinery and equipment without operator and of personal and household goods (NACE Rev. 1 71)

Performance related indicators, 1997

	B	DK	D	EL	E	F	IRL	I (1)	L	NL	A	P	FIN (2)	S (1)	UK
Value added (million ECU)	1,239	:	:	:	:	7,692	195	593	148	2,750	1,245	616	188	816	10,045
Value added as a share of turnover (%)	41.5	:	:	:	:	56.8	41.6	36.7	57.0	60.4	66.0	63.8	49.0	42.9	58.6
Apparent labour productivity (thousand ECU/person employed)	140.7	:	:	:	:	117.9	34.1	39.3	297.4	120.5	211.8	68.4	73.3	:	:
Unit personnel costs (thousand ECU)	33.4	:	:	:	:	28.1	:	30.6	38.2	:	30.2	12.1	28.7	32.5	23.0
Simple wage adjusted labour productivity (%)	591.4	:	:	:	:	475.2	:	320.0	852.9	583.9	882.4	724.2	328.7	325.4	325.0
Gross operating surplus (million ECU)	1,029	:	:	:	:	6,073	:	408	131	2,279	1,104	531	131	565	6,954

(1) 1996; (2) Unit personnel costs, 1996.

_____Table 20.15

Legal, accounting, book-keeping and auditing activities; tax consultancy; market research and public opinion polling; business and management consultancy; holdings (NACE Rev. 1 74.1): Employment related indicators, 1997

	B	DK	D	EL	E	F	IRL	I (1)	L	NL (2)	A	P	FIN (2)	S	UK
Number of persons employed (thousands)	71.3	:	:	:	:	302.2	29.6	373.0	5.7	222.4	48.6	43.5	21.0	:	:
Employees/number of persons employed (%)	62.9	:	:	:	:	96.7	77.2	42.5	84.1	75.6	80.7	88.5	82.8	:	:
Average no. of persons employed/enterprise (units)	:	:	:	:	:	2.0	6.0	1.9	3.0	7.0	6.0	5.0	2.0	:	:

(1) 1996; (2) Employees as a share of the number of persons employed, 1996.

_____Table 20.16

Legal, accounting, book-keeping and auditing activities; tax consultancy; market research and public opinion polling; business and management consultancy; holdings (NACE Rev. 1 74.1): Turnover related indicators, 1997

	B	DK	D	EL	E	F	IRL	I (1)	L	NL	A	P	FIN	S (1)	UK
Turnover (million ECU)	9,384	:	87,934	:	:	53,882	1,736	21,340	635	15,050	3,882	2,275	1,825	6,588	44,616
Turnover per enterprise (million ECU)	:	:	0.7	:	:	0.4	0.3	0.1	0.4	0.5	0.4	0.3	0.2	0.2	0.5
Turnover per person employed (thousand ECU)	131.6	:	:	:	:	178.3	58.7	57.2	110.7	67.7	80.0	52.3	87.0	:	:

(1) 1996.

_____Table 16.17

Legal, accounting, book-keeping and auditing activities; tax consultancy; market research and public opinion polling; business and management consultancy; holdings (NACE Rev. 1 74.1): Performance related indicators, 1997

	B	DK	D	EL	E	F	IRL	I (1)	L	NL	A	P	FIN (2)	S (1)	UK
Value added (million ECU)	3,980	:	:	:	:	17,284	1,194	14,371	385	11,075	2,354	908	1,239	2,741	29,244
Value added as a share of turnover (%)	42.4	:	:	:	:	32.1	68.8	67.3	60.7	73.6	60.6	39.9	67.9	41.6	65.5
Apparent labour productivity (thousand ECU/person employed)	55.8	:	:	:	:	57.2	40.3	38.5	67.2	49.8	48.5	20.9	59.1	:	:
Unit personnel costs (thousand ECU)	52.9	:	:	:	:	47.9	:	24.6	37.7	:	33.5	16.6	34.2	43.9	26.1
Simple wage adjusted labour productivity (%)	167.7	:	:	:	:	123.6	:	369.2	211.6	168.7	179.5	142.4	201.0	126.6	207.6
Gross operating surplus (million ECU)	1,607	:	:	:	:	3,302	:	10,479	203	4,510	1,043	270	623	577	15,155

(1) 1996; (2) Unit personnel costs, 1996.

Source: Eurostat (SBS)

Table 20.18

Advertising (NACE Rev. 1 74.4)

Employment related indicators, 1997

	B	DK	D	EL	E	F	IRL	I (1)	L	NL (2)	A	P	FIN (2)	S	UK
Number of persons employed (thousands)	12.3	:	:	:	:	93.9	4.0	30.1	0.6	37.1	10.3	16.0	5.5	:	:
Employees/number of persons employed (%)	63.7	:	:	:	:	96.9	94.9	57.6	87.4	54.3	71.9	91.1	82.9	:	:
Average no. of persons employed/enterprise (units)	:	:	:	:	:	5.0	16.0	2.8	3.0	4.0	4.0	6.0	3.0	:	:

(1) 1996; (2) Employees as a share of the number of persons employed, 1996.

Table 20.19

Advertising (NACE Rev. 1 74.4)

Turnover related indicators, 1997

	B	DK	D	EL	E	F	IRL	I (1)	L	NL	A	P	FIN	S (1)	UK
Turnover (million ECU)	3,517	:	21,439	:	:	16,481	494	4,228	101	5,169	1,974	1,925	999	3,392	22,444
Turnover per enterprise (million ECU)	:	:	0.6	:	:	0.8	2.0	0.4	0.5	0.6	0.7	0.7	0.5	0.4	2.0
Turnover per person employed (thousand ECU)	286.0	:	:	:	:	175.5	123.1	140.6	167.4	139.4	192.4	120.1	182.9	:	:

(1) 1996.

Table 20.20

Advertising (NACE Rev. 1 74.4)

Performance related indicators, 1997

	B	DK	D	EL	E	F	IRL	I (1)	L	NL	A	P	FIN (2)	S (1)	UK
Value added (million ECU)	517	:	:	:	:	4,433	108	1,488	26	1,815	533	264	268	875	4,848
Value added as a share of turnover (%)	14.7	:	:	:	:	26.9	21.9	35.2	25.3	35.1	27.0	13.7	26.8	25.8	21.6
Apparent labour productivity (thousand ECU/person employed)	42.1	:	:	:	:	47.2	26.9	49.5	42.4	48.9	52.0	16.5	49.0	:	:
Unit personnel costs (thousand ECU)	34.5	:	:	:	:	38.7	:	36.5	32.7	:	36.0	12.0	32.6	37.6	33.5
Simple wage adjusted labour productivity (%)	191.7	:	:	:	:	126.0	:	235.6	148.0	268.8	200.5	150.5	159.6	142.8	172.7
Gross operating surplus (million ECU)	247	:	:	:	:	915	:	857	8	1,140	267	89	100	262	2,041

(1) 1996; (2) Unit personnel costs, 1996.

Table 20.21

Labour recruitment and provision of personnel (NACE Rev. 1 74.5)

Employment related indicators, 1997

	B	DK	D	EL	E	F	IRL	I	L	NL (1)	A	P	FIN (1)	S	UK
Number of persons employed (thousands)	106.9	:	:	:	:	406.9	3.9	:	4.8	340.7	15.5	21.0	4.5	:	:
Employees/number of persons employed (%)	99.7	:	:	:	:	100.0	96.1	:	99.9	99.7	98.5	99.8	96.6	:	:
Average no. of persons employed/enterprise (units)	:	:	:	:	:	177.0	21.0	:	94.0	154.0	57.0	104.0	16.0	:	:

(1) Employees as a share of the number of persons employed, 1996.

Table 20.22

Labour recruitment and provision of personnel (NACE Rev. 1 74.5)

Turnover related indicators, 1997

	B	DK	D	EL	E	F	IRL	I	L	NL	A	P	FIN	S (1)	UK
Turnover (million ECU)	1,838	:	4,485	:	:	12,105	207	:	83	7,606	598	284	131	44	16,418
Turnover per enterprise (million ECU)	:	:	1.7	:	:	5.3	1.1	:	1.6	3.4	2.2	1.4	0.5	0.3	1.8
Turnover per person employed (thousand ECU)	17.2	:	:	:	:	29.8	53.5	:	17.3	22.3	38.6	13.5	29.0	:	:

(1) 1996.

Table 20.23

Labour recruitment and provision of personnel (NACE Rev. 1 74.5)

Performance related indicators, 1997

	B	DK	D	EL	E	F	IRL	I	L	NL	A	P	FIN (1)	S (2)	UK
Value added (million ECU)	1,681	:	:	:	:	10,745	102	:	73	3,729	474	196	109	27	11,791
Value added as a share of turnover (%)	91.5	:	:	:	:	88.8	49.1	:	87.7	49.0	79.3	68.9	83.3	61.0	71.8
Apparent labour productivity (thousand ECU/person employed)	15.7	:	:	:	:	26.4	26.3	:	15.2	11.0	30.6	9.3	24.2	:	:
Unit personnel costs (thousand ECU)	14.9	:	:	:	:	25.4	:	:	19.0	:	29.5	8.7	19.6	43.6	19.7
Simple wage adjusted labour productivity (%)	105.6	:	:	:	:	104.0	:	:	80.3	148.7	105.5	107.4	111.6	189.4	117.8
Gross operating surplus (million ECU)	89	:	:	:	:	415	:	:	-18	1,221	25	13	11	13	1,785

(1) Unit personnel costs, 1996; (2) 1996.

Source: Eurostat (SBS)

———Table 20.24

Investigation and security activities (NACE Rev. 1 74.6)

Employment related indicators, 1997

	B	DK	D	EL	E (1)	F	IRL	I	L	NL (2)	A	P	FIN (2)	S	UK
Number of persons employed (thousands)	9.3	:	:	:	73.2	96.2	5.6	:	:	15.1	5.9	16.2	3.9	:	:
Employees/number of persons employed (%)	96.8	:	:	:	98.5	98.9	98.0	:	:	93.7	98.7	97.2	96.0	:	:
Average no. of persons employed/enterprise (units)	:	:	:	:	44.9	20.0	27.0	:	:	31.0	70.0	31.0	13.0	:	:

(1) 1996; (2) Employees as a share of the number of persons employed, 1996.

———Table 20.25

Investigation and security activities (NACE Rev. 1 74.6)

Turnover related indicators, 1997

	B	DK	D	EL	E (1)	F	IRL	I	L	NL	A	P	FIN	S (1)	UK
Turnover (million ECU)	383	:	2,713	:	1,424	2,892	152	:	:	561	178	232	128	480	3,315
Turnover per enterprise (million ECU)	:	:	0.8	:	0.9	0.6	0.7	:	:	1.1	2.1	0.4	0.4	1.1	1.1
Turnover per person employed (thousand ECU)	41.2	:	:	:	19.4	30.1	27.2	:	:	37.2	30.3	14.4	33.1	:	:

(1) 1996.

———Table 20.26

Investigation and security activities (NACE Rev. 1 74.6)

Performance related indicators, 1997

	B	DK	D	EL	E (1)	F	IRL	I	L	NL	A	P	FIN (2)	S (1)	UK
Value added (million ECU)	307	:	:	:	1,201	1,999	122	:	:	478	141	173	97	342	2,604
Value added as a share of turnover (%)	80.0	:	:	:	84.4	69.1	80.4	:	:	85.1	78.9	74.4	75.4	71.2	78.6
Apparent labour productivity (thousand ECU/person employed)	33.0	:	:	:	16.4	20.8	21.9	:	:	31.6	23.9	10.7	25.0	:	:
Unit personnel costs (thousand ECU)	30.9	:	:	:	15.0	20.3	:	:	:	:	22.6	9.8	21.5	29.4	19.4
Simple wage adjusted labour productivity (%)	110.1	:	:	:	110.7	103.4	:	:	:	107.6	107.2	112.1	114.6	117.3	125.0
Gross operating surplus (million ECU)	28	:	:	:	116	65	:	:	:	34	10	19	12	51	521

(1) 1996; (2) Unit personnel costs, 1996.

———Table 20.27

Industrial cleaning (NACE Rev. 1 74.7)

Employment related indicators, 1997

	B	DK	D	EL	E	F	IRL	I (1)	L (1)	NL (2)	A	P	FIN (2)	S	UK
Number of persons employed (thousands)	38.3	:	:	:	:	225.5	9.3	236.3	3.8	137.0	34.4	41.4	20.0	:	:
Employees/number of persons employed (%)	94.4	:	:	:	:	97.2	98.5	84.7	98.9	94.8	96.7	97.6	90.1	:	:
Average no. of persons employed/enterprise (units)	:	:	:	:	:	17.0	59.0	9.4	40.0	24.0	28.0	29.0	9.0	:	:

(1) 1996; (2) Employees as a share of the number of persons employed, 1996.

———Table 16.28

Industrial cleaning (NACE Rev. 1 74.7)

Turnover related indicators, 1997

	B	DK	D	EL	E	F	IRL	I (1)	L (1)	NL	A	P	FIN	S (1)	UK
Turnover (million ECU)	1,119	:	9,935	:	:	5,689	98	4,686	90	2,276	725	591	518	1,182	5,083
Turnover per enterprise (million ECU)	:	:	0.5	:	:	0.4	0.6	0.2	0.9	0.4	0.6	0.4	0.2	0.2	0.6
Turnover per person employed (thousand ECU)	29.3	:	:	:	:	25.2	10.5	19.8	23.5	16.6	21.1	14.3	25.9	:	:

(1) 1996.

———Table 16.29

Industrial cleaning (NACE Rev. 1 74.7)

Performance related indicators, 1997

	B	DK	D	EL	E	F	IRL	I (1)	L (1)	NL	A	P	FIN (2)	S (1)	UK
Value added (million ECU)	729	:	:	:	:	4,012	72	3,662	61	1,888	569	231	376	799	4,084
Value added as a share of turnover (%)	65.1	:	:	:	:	70.5	73.1	78.1	67.7	82.9	78.5	39.0	72.5	67.6	80.3
Apparent labour productivity (thousand ECU/person employed)	19.1	:	:	:	:	17.8	7.7	15.5	15.9	13.8	16.6	5.6	18.8	:	:
Unit personnel costs (thousand ECU)	17.3	:	:	:	:	16.7	:	16.0	12.9	:	13.9	5.0	20.2	25.5	7.8
Simple wage adjusted labour productivity (%)	116.5	:	:	:	:	109.3	:	114.4	125.3	146.2	122.8	114.8	127.2	122.2	132.4
Gross operating surplus (million ECU)	103	:	:	:	:	342	:	460	12	597	106	30	80	145	1,000

(1) 1996; (2) Unit personnel costs, 1996.

Source: Eurostat (SBS)

Information and audio-visual services

(NACE Rev. 1 22.14, 22.31, 64, 72, 92.1 and 92.2)

The activities covered in this chapter share the exchange of information as one of their main goods. They are: post and courier activities and telecommunications (NACE Rev. 1 Division 64), software and computer services (Division 72) for managing and processing information, as well as content industries such as film (Group 92.1), television (Group 92.2) and music recording (Class 22.14).

This chapter encompasses several of the economy's most dynamic activities and constitutes the "software" face of the technology, media and telecommunications sector (the "hardware" side may be found in chapter 11). These activities are often associated with the emergence of the so-called "information society", a society whose wealth and growth is based on its ability to process, store, retrieve and communicate information in whatever form - oral, written or visual. Some commentators see this movement towards an "information society" as significant and far-reaching as last century's industrial revolution, with the Internet as the backbone of this society.

STRUCTURE AND PERFORMANCE

Communications services (that include units engaged in the transmission of packages, documents, images and sounds) contributed around 2.3% to GDP in the Member States in the second half of the 1990's. Luxembourg and Greece clearly stood out from the other countries with shares of 4.0% and 2.9% respectively in 1997, whilst Italy and Denmark were the only countries reporting shares lower than 2.0% (1.9% and 1.8% respectively in 1997).

In most countries, the relative contribution of communications services to GDP has significantly risen over a ten-year period (1987 to 1997), sometimes sharply, as in Greece (up 0.8 percentage points from 2.1% in 1987) or in Luxembourg (doubling from 2.0% in 1987). In other countries there was less spectacular growth, for example the Netherlands (from 2.0% to 2.3%) or Finland (from 2.0% to 2.2%). Some other countries reported no change in the relative share of the communications services branch, such as France and Ireland (2.3% in 1987 and 1996) or Austria (2.4% in 1987 and 1997).

The activities covered in this chapter (in terms of NACE Rev. 1) include:

22.14: publishing of sound recordings;
22.31: reproduction of sound recording;
64:    post and telecommunications;
64.1: post and courier activities;
64.2: telecommunications;
72:    computer and related activities;
72.1: hardware consultancy;
72.2: software consultancy and supply;
72.3: data processing;
72.4: database activities;
72.5: maintenance and repair of office, accounting and computing machinery;
72.6: other computer related activities;
92.1: activities of business, employers' and professional organizations;
92.2: activities of trade unions.

Figure 21.1 _____

Communication services (NACE-CLIO 67)

Share of total market services value added and employment, 1997 (%)

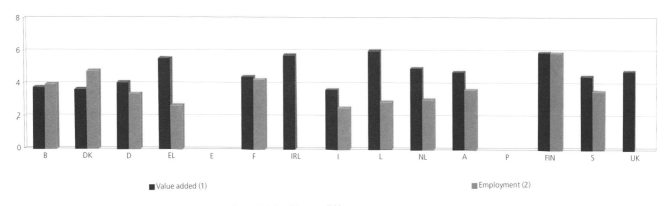

■ Value added (1)   ■ Employment (2)

(1) D, EL, F, L and A, value added at market prices; DK, D, IRL, S and UK, 1996; E and P, not available.
(2) B, DK, D, A and S, 1996; E, IRL, P and UK, not available.

Source: Eurostat (SEC2)

Box 21.1 _____

According to estimates of the European Information Technology Observatory (EITO), the total turnover of information and communications' technologies (ICT) in the EU was worth 445.5 billion EUR in 1999, of which 182.9 billion EUR was accounted for by telecom services alone. As for the audio-visual sector, the European Audiovisual Observatory estimates that the 16 largest European enterprises of the sector each had turnover in excess of 1 billion ECU in 1997 and their aggregated turnover exceeded 43.6 billion ECU.

Table 21.1 _____

ICT turnover in the EU (million EUR)

.	1998	1999	2000	2001
Computer hardware	67,797	72,987	78,120	83,120
Office equipment	9,138	9,211	9,350	9,486
Data communication hardware	9,470	10,738	11,955	13,259
Software	36,283	41,150	46,928	53,666
IT services	64,152	72,988	82,386	91,851
Telecom equipment	44,763	55,526	66,053	75,138
Telecom services	165,872	182,924	198,422	210,995
Total	397,475	445,525	493,215	537,514

Source: EITO

Post and telecommunications enterprises dominated by large enterprises

A total of 42.6 thousand post and telecommunications enterprises were recorded in the EU in 1996 (SME database) and 244.9 thousand enterprises in computer services, representing approximately 2.5% of the total number of services enterprises in the EU (NACE Rev. 1 Sections G to K).

Post and telecommunication services are dominated by a few large enterprises, whilst computer services has an enterprise size distribution that is more closely matched to the services average (i.e. a dominance of small and medium-sized enterprises). In post and telecommunications, 70.2% of the enterprises had no employees at all and 24.4% were small enterprises with between one and nine employees (1996). However, whilst large enterprises with 250 employees or more represented only 0.4% of the total enterprise population, they accounted for as much as 93.7% of employment in the sector and 90.0% of its turnover. Average turnover for a telecommunications enterprise was estimated at 4.6 million ECU per enterprise, ranging from 63 thousand ECU for enterprises without an employee to 335 thousand ECU for enterprises with one to nine employees and up to 1.1 billion ECU for enterprises with more than 250 employees.

Large enterprises account for a quarter of the workforce in computer services

Computer services displayed a different enterprise size class structure. Large enterprises of more than 250 employees represented only 0.2% of the total enterprise population and accounted for 24.4% of employment and 31.3% of turnover. In addition, whilst 39.4% of enterprises had no employees at all, 53.7% had between one and nine employees, this latter size-class accounted for as much as 25.6% of employment and 20.2% of turnover. Whilst the average computer services enterprise employed 5 persons (similar to the services average), large computer services enterprises (with 250 or more employees) employed an average of 637 persons (whilst the services average was 1.3 thousand employees). Similarly, average turnover of these large computer services enterprises was equal to 72.0 million ECU, four times less than the average for the same size-class in services.

LABOUR AND PRODUCTIVITY

According to National Accounts, communications services accounted for between 1.4% (Netherlands, 1997) and 2.0% (Belgium, 1996) of the total number of persons employed in the majority of Member States. The outliers to this range were recorded in Portugal (0.8%, 1995) and Finland (2.2%, 1997).

In 1996 there were around 2.3 million persons employed in post and telecommunications and 1.3 million in computer services.

A male-dominated workforce

Women were under-represented in the workforce as they accounted for only slightly more than one-third of total employment in post and telecommunications services (35.7%, 1998), and just above a quarter of the total in computer services (25.7%, 1998). This compares with average female employment of 41.9% in the whole economy, and 42.8% in service sectors (NACE Rev. 1 Sections G to K).

Computer services ranked amongst the sectors with the lowest share of persons employed working on a part-time basis (9.2% in 1998), compared to 17.2% in the economy as a whole. Austria (20.3%) had the highest proportion of persons working part-time in computer services, whilst less than 5% of the total number of persons employed in Italy and Spain worked part-time.

Particularly high education level in computer services

Turning to the level of education of the workforce, computer services employed one of the highest proportions of highly educated persons in the whole European economy. Indeed, computer services had the highest level of all services activities (NACE Rev. 1 Sections G to K) with more than half of the workforce (54.4%) possessing a higher education degree in 1997. This compares to an average in the whole economy of 23.4% and contrasts with communication services where only 15.3% of those persons employed held a higher education degree. There are however differences between the education level of men (58.3% with a higher education level in computer services, 17.0% in post and telecommunications) and women (42.2% and 12.0% respectively).

Table 21.2

Communications and software and computing services (NACE Rev.1 64 and 72)

Breakdown of turnover and employment by employment size class, 1997 (%)

	Micro (0-9)		Small (10-49)		Medium (50-249)		Large (250+)	
	Turnover (1)	Employment (1)	Turnover (2)	Employment (2)	Turnover (3)	Employment (3)	Turnover (3)	Employment (3)
EU-15	11.4	14.3	9.1	9.1	11.5	8.3	68.1	68.3
B	15.4	21.1	12.0	13.2	11.3	13.2	61.2	52.5
DK	10.5	11.4	:	:	:	:	:	:
D	5.8	7.8	7.5	10.1	15.6	9.8	71.2	72.4
EL	:	:	:	:	:	:	:	:
E	:	20.7	:	13.0	:	12.1	:	54.2
F	7.1	7.7	8.9	8.3	10.9	8.0	73.0	76.0
IRL	:	:	12.4	13.8	:	:	:	:
I	13.8	20.2	8.9	9.6	6.5	5.4	70.8	64.8
L	:	:	:	:	:	:	:	:
NL	:	:	:	:	:	:	:	:
A	8.4	10.2	:	:	:	:	:	:
P	:	:	:	:	:	:	:	:
FIN	8.0	8.5	14.5	8.7	16.5	11.8	61.0	71.0
S	9.9	9.1	7.9	7.1	10.5	7.4	71.7	76.5
UK	21.2	28.1	9.1	6.5	8.6	6.3	61.1	59.1

(1) EU-15, DK, F, I and S, 1996.
(2) EU-15, F, IRL, I and S, 1996.
(3) EU-15, F, I and S, 1996.

Source: Eurostat (SME)

Communications services boast high profitability rates
Post and telecommunications boasted one of the highest profitability rates of any service activity. Eurostat estimates that in 1997 for each 100 ECU of turnover realised in these activities some 26.9 ECU of gross operating surplus was generated. This high gross operating rate was a result of value added accounting for 63.3% of turnover. Luxembourg (45.8%, 1995) and Portugal (41.3%, 1997) reported particularly high gross operating rates, ahead of the Netherlands (34.0%, 1997) and Italy (33.7%, 1996). France (22.0%, 1997) and Sweden (16.0%, 1996) were below the EU average.

As regards computer services, the gross operating rate was estimated at 14.5% in 1997 with value added accounting for a 49.6% share of turnover, whilst the share of personnel costs in value added was considerably higher at 70.8%. Profitability was lowest in France (5.4%, 1997) and Luxembourg (7.1%, 1996), whilst the highest values were recorded in the United Kingdom (23.6%, 1997) and the Netherlands (29.4%, 1997).

Table 21.3

Post and communications, computer and related activities (NACE Rev.1 64 and 72)

Composition of the labour force, 1999 (%)

	Post and communications			Computer and related activities		
	Women (1)	Part-time (2)	Highly-educated (3)	Women (4)	Part-time (5)	Highly-educated (6)
EU-15	35.7	15.2	15.3	25.7	9.2	54.4
B	31.8	7.7	23.9	23.2	:	76.0
DK	37.2	19.0	15.7	17.3	10.4	45.0
D	39.2	20.0	19.3	23.5	11.6	53.7
EL	18.7	:	26.3	48.0	:	:
E	33.6	5.5	36.0	20.9	4.1	63.2
F	44.3	14.4	17.0	29.7	6.0	70.8
IRL	26.2	:	:	33.9	:	75.4
I	32.9	3.3	9.4	29.2	4.8	29.4
L	31.6	12.1	14.6	:	:	:
NL	39.3	36.3	15.7	21.9	14.3	58.5
A	26.8	10.9	:	23.0	20.3	27.5
P	36.1	:	21.2	28.4	:	42.2
FIN	41.7	15.9	24.6	27.5	:	49.8
S	40.1	20.6	13.6	28.8	:	73.5
UK	27.4	15.6	16.5	25.1	9.3	56.7

(1) EU-15 and EL, 1998.
(2) EU-15 and B, 1998.
(1) EL, 1998; EU-15 and UK, 1997; S, 1996.
(4) EU-15, EL and P, 1998.
(5) EU-15, 1998.
(6) FIN, 1998; EU-15, IRL, S and UK, 1997.

Source: Eurostat (LFS)

Box 21.2

EITO estimates that Europe accounted for 30.9% of the world's ICT turnover in 1999, against 35.4% for the USA and 10.8% for Japan. The USA has a strong position in each of the ICT segments: 28.9% of world turnover in telecommunications services, 46.5% of the turnover for software and IT services, and 41.1% of the IT hardware market. Europe nevertheless occupies some strategic markets, especially in areas with high value added. The main European success story is telecommunications, where Europe generated 33.4% of the world's turnover for services in 1999 and 43.3% for hardware. This reflects to a large extent the domination of European GSM technology in digital mobile telephony.

Figure 21.2

Share of ICT turnover by world region, 1999 (%)

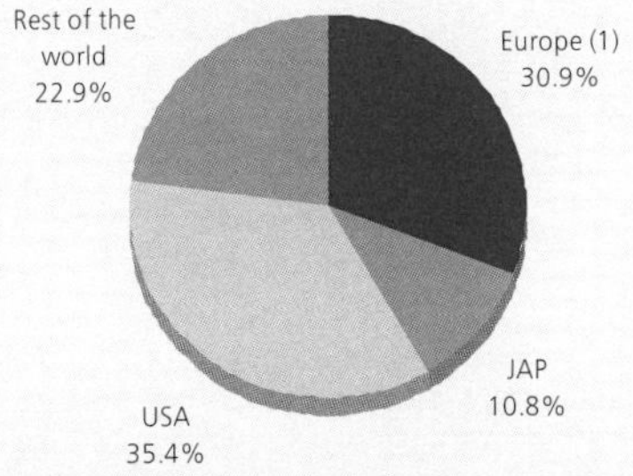

(1) EEA, Czech Republic, Estonia, Hungary, Poland, Russia, Slovakia, Slovenia and Switzerland.

Source: EITO

Table 21.4

ICT turnover by product and region, 1999 (million EUR)

	Western Europe	Eastern Europe	JAP	USA	Rest of the world	World
IT hardware	98,652	4,189	44,313	141,163	55,310	343,627
Software	43,517	813	13,172	68,216	23,265	148,982
IT services	77,646	1,621	37,082	141,389	43,635	301,372
Telecom equipment	58,091	3,190	12,073	23,808	44,374	141,535
Carrier services	192,135	13,255	64,646	189,650	197,575	657,261
Total	470,040	23,067	171,285	564,225	364,159	1,592,777

Source: EITO

SUB-CHAPTER 21.1
POSTAL AND COURIER SERVICES
(NACE Rev. 1 64.1)

Postal and courier services ensure that letters and parcels are moved between businesses, administrations and private customers. This activity is covered by Group 64.1 of the NACE Rev. 1 classification. National post activities (NACE Rev. 1 64.11) include the pick-up, transport and delivery (domestic or international) of mail and parcels, and other services such as mailbox rental, "poste restante" etc. Courier activities other than national post activities are covered by NACE Rev. 1 Group 64.12 and are dominated by express courier deliveries activities, where enterprises have widened their initial focus on business documents towards the transfer of packages and freight, carried by fleets of aircraft, trucks, trains and delivery vans.

Within the EU, national public postal operators dominate the market for letter services. However, the competitive environment in this area of the economy is changing fast and there has been a gradual step by step move towards market liberalisation. Public postal operators provide general letter services and in most cases they still operate as a monopoly with exclusive rights, balanced by the fact that they are bound by a universal service obligation. Private operators dominate the express services market, providing letter and parcel services, specifically to the business-to-business, direct mail and business-to-private segments of the market.

Fewer permanent post offices but not letterboxes
In 1997, the 15 national postal services of the EU operated approximately 85 thousand permanent post offices open to the public, about 15 thousand fewer than ten years before. Despite this, figures indicate that the number of letterboxes did not experience a significant change over the same period. Differences across Member States remained considerable though: the extremes were recorded on the one hand in Sweden, where a letterbox served on average only 241 inhabitants, and on the other hand in Spain where there were as many as 1,220 inhabitants per letterbox. Most of the other countries reported between 360 (Luxembourg) and 585 (Germany) inhabitants per letterbox.

Figure 21.3

Inhabitants per post box, 1997 (units) (1)

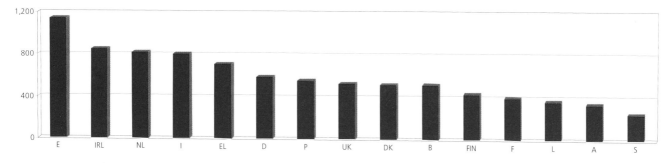

(1) F, NL, A, S and UK, 1996.

Source: Eurostat (COINS)

Figure 21.4

Employment in national post activities (units)

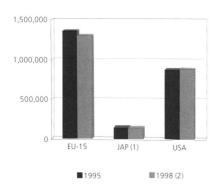

(1) Full-time staff only.
(2) 1997 data for EU-15 (except F, NL, A, S and UK, 1996).

Source: Eurostat (COINS), UPU

Figure 21.5

Average number of letter-post items per inhabitant, 1997 (units)

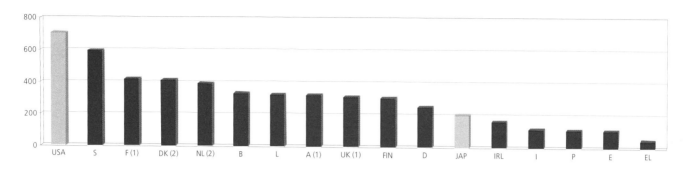

(1) 1996.
(2) 1995.

Source: Eurostat (COINS), UPU

Part-time employment on the rise

Employment in national postal administrations recorded a decline over the period 1987 to 1997, losing over 100 thousand persons, with 1.3 million persons employed in the EU in 1997. One trend of important significance has been the evolution of part-time work, accounting for an 18% share in employment in 1997, twice the level seen in 1987. Particularly high proportions of part-time employment were reported in the Netherlands (50%, 1996), Germany (30%, 1997), Finland (29%, 1997) and Luxembourg (27%, 1997). At the other extreme, part-time work was marginal (1% or less) in Denmark, Greece, Italy and Portugal.

Almost 100 billion items handled per year

National postal services handled a total of approximately 100 billion postal items (letter-post items) in the EU in 1997, including domestic service (national) and international receipt and dispatch. Domestic services accounted for the vast majority of the traffic, with between 92.8% (United Kingdom, 1996) and 96.6% (France, 1996) of the total volume of letter-post items handled in the five largest Member States. A high proportion of domestic traffic was also reported in Finland and Sweden (96.0% in both countries, 1997).

In comparison, geographically smaller countries such as Denmark, Austria or Belgium reported 90% shares. The smallest Member State, Luxembourg, recorded the lowest weight of domestic traffic, 63.9% (1997). Letter-post traffic has witnessed a rising trend over the last decade, much of which can be attributed to domestic traffic, which has risen by 2.7% per year between 1986 and 1996.

Box 21.3

The UPU (Universal Postal Union) expects the rising trends in letter-post traffic volumes to continue. In a study entitled "Post 2005", the UPU forecasts growth of domestic letter traffic in high income countries to be equal to 2.3% per annum on average between 1995 and 2005. Forecasts for international mail are even more optimistic, ranging from 3.4% to 5.2% depending on the region considered.

Businesses (including administrations) remain the most important customers (senders) with a market share of about 90% of postal volumes, broken down as 60% from business-to-private and 30% business-to-business. On the receivers side, the most important segment is the sector of private individuals, whose importance is increasing. Only 10% of traffic concerns private-to-private mail. Businesses also dominate in the parcel services market, accounting for approximately 85% of parcels sent.

Direct marketing mail already accounts for a large proportion of the handled items and its importance is still growing. Mail order is also a promising segment which has developed as a competitor to in-store retailing. New technological developments such as the development of e-commerce and Internet shopping are expected to further fuel demand for parcel traffic.

Conversely, this same technological evolution has a negative influence on postal traffic, with the widespread adoption of fax and e-mail as rapid communications' media. UPU anticipate a 5 percentage point reduction in the share of the communications' market of physical mail between 1995 and 2005, down from 20% to less than 15% of the communications' market. The greatest substitution effect is expected to be seen in the business-to-business segment in high-income countries, where more than 50% of businesses are expected to use electronic mail by the year 2005.

Courier enterprises generally
small with low profitability

Courier activities are activities carried out in enterprises that are generally small in size, employing an average of four (Italy, 1995) to six persons (Austria, 1997) each and generating average turnover of between 200 thousand ECU (Denmark, 1997) and 300 thousand ECU (Netherlands, 1997). Apparent labour productivity was at relatively low levels, ranging between 23.1 thousand ECU per person employed (Finland, 1997) and 25.3 thousand ECU (Austria, 1997). Profitability was also generally inferior to most other service activities, with a gross operating rate (the gross operating surplus divided by turnover) equal to between 4.0% (Austria, 1997) and 9.5% (Italy, 1995).

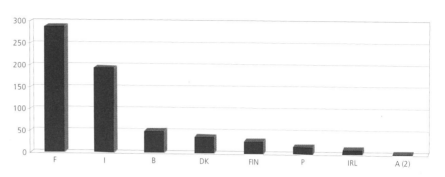

——————————————————Figure 21.6

Postal and courier services (NACE Rev. 1 64.1)
Number of persons employed, 1997 (thousands) (1)

(1) F and I, 1996; D, EL, E, L, NL, S and UK, not available.
(2) Excluding national postal service activities, classified within NACE Rev. 1 64.2.

Source: Eurostat (SBS)

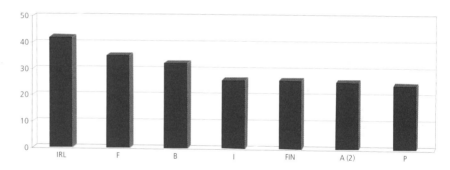

——————————————————Figure 21.7

Postal and courier services (NACE Rev. 1 64.1)
Apparent labour productivity, 1997 (thousand ECU per person employed) (1)

(1) F and I, 1996; DK, D, EL, E, L, NL, S and UK, not available.
(2) Excluding national postal service activities, classified within NACE Rev. 1 64.2.

Source: Eurostat (SBS)

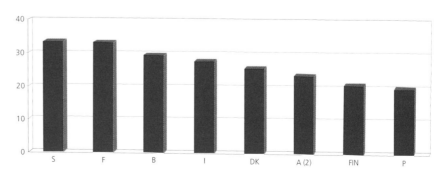

——————————————————Figure 21.8

Postal and courier services (NACE Rev. 1 64.1)
Unit personnel costs, 1997 (thousand ECU per employee) (1)

(1) F, I, FIN and S, 1996; D, EL, E, IRL, L, NL and UK, not available.
(2) Excluding national postal service activities, classified within NACE Rev. 1 64.2.

Source: Eurostat (SBS)

SUB-CHAPTER 21.2
TELECOMMUNICATIONS' SERVICES
(NACE Rev. 1 64.2)

Telecommunications' services as are classified within Group 64.2 of NACE Rev. 1. They embrace the distribution of sound, images, data and other information via cables, broadcasting, relay or satellite. These services include both the management and maintenance of networks and the provision of services using this network, excluding the provision of radio and television programmes (see sub-chapter 21.5).

Until the 1980s, the telecommunications sector was a heavily regulated market based around state-controlled enterprises with a legal and economic monopoly. Over the past two decades, however, market conditions have changed considerably. Liberalisation moves began in the first half of the 1980s and initially concerned value added services or business users, leaving control of basic services in the hands of the national monopolies. The liberalisation of the sector has progressed at faster pace in the 1990s and since January 1998 telecommunication services have been fully liberalised in the majority of EU countries.

Sweden the most equipped country in fixed line telephony, and second to Finland in mobile telephony
The EU telecommunications infrastructure consisted of 193 million telephone lines in 1997, equivalent to 52 lines per 100 inhabitants (ten more than in 1990). Luxembourg and Sweden reported the highest penetration rates, at 66 and 68 lines respectively, whilst Spain (40 lines) and Portugal (38 lines) closed the ranking. The vast majority of telephone lines were used by households, with between 70% and 80% depending on the Member State studied.

A very important trend in telecommunications in recent years has been the adoption of cellular wireless technology, which is expected to replace fixed wire technology in many applications. There were 52.7 million subscriber lines to cellular mobile telephone systems in the EU in 1997, or 14% of the population, up from 33.5 million in 1996 and 21.2 million in 1995. Finland boasted the highest penetration rate of mobile phones, with 42 lines per 100 inhabitants, ahead of Sweden (36%) and Denmark (27%). On the other end, Greece reported just 9 mobile phone lines per 100 inhabitants. EITO estimates that the number of mobile phone subscribers in Europe[1] will more than double between 1999 and 2005, to reach 318.4 million.

(1) EEA, Czech Republic, Estonia, Hungary, Poland, Russia, Slovakia, Slovenia and Switzerland.

Figure 21.9

Telecommunications' services (NACE Rev. 1 64.2)

Number of persons employed, 1997 (thousands) (1)

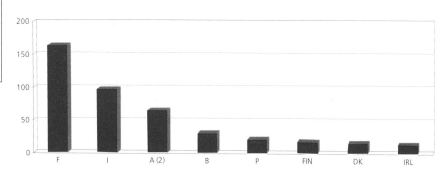

(1) F and I, 1996; D, EL, E, L, NL, S and UK, not available.
(2) Includes national postal service activities.

Source: Eurostat (SBS)

Figure 21.10

Telecommunications' services (NACE Rev. 1 64.2)

Apparent labour productivity, 1997 (thousand ECU per person employed) (1)

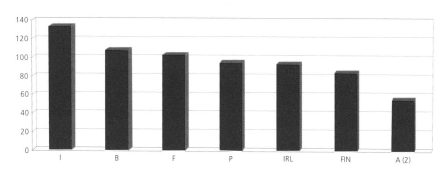

(1) F and I, 1996; DK, D, EL, E, L, NL, S and UK, not available.
(2) Includes national postal service activities.

Source: Eurostat (SBS)

Annually 131 international calls per line

As regards telephone traffic an average of 131 outgoing international calls were made on each telephone line in the EU[2] in 1997, almost 50% more than in 1990 (89 calls). Small countries naturally reported the highest levels, with the maximum in Luxembourg (over one thousand calls per line). Belgium (249 calls), which hosts several international institutions, and Ireland (463 calls), where numerous European call-centres are established, also recorded a significantly higher than average number of international calls per line. Amongst the larger Member States, low numbers of international calls were recorded in Spain (77 calls, 1996) and Italy (90 calls), when compared to the United Kingdom (172 calls).

Almost 900 thousand employees
or 4.7 per thousand lines

Telecommunication enterprises had 899 thousand employees in 1997, down from over one million in 1990. This represented an average of 4.7 employees per thousand telephone lines, down from 6.5 in 1990. Luxembourg (3.0 employees per thousand lines) and the Netherlands (3.4) reported the lowest ratio, whilst the highest ratios were recorded in Finland (6.3) and Ireland (7.3).

High unit personnel costs
matched by high profitability

Unit personnel costs were estimated at 42.7 thousand ECU per employee in 1997, a relatively high figure when compared to other service activities. The highest average unit personnel costs were found in Denmark (69.3 thousand ECU, 1997) and Luxembourg (60.4 thousand ECU, 1995), more than twice the levels seen in Austria (29.9 thousand ECU, 1997) and Portugal (28.0 thousand ECU, 1997). The relatively high cost of labour was matched by high profitability rates, as each 100 ECU of turnover generated 36.8 ECU of operating surplus.

---

(2) E and A, no data available.

Figure 21.11

Telecommunications' services (NACE Rev. 1 64.2)
Unit personnel costs, 1997 (thousand ECU per employee) (1)

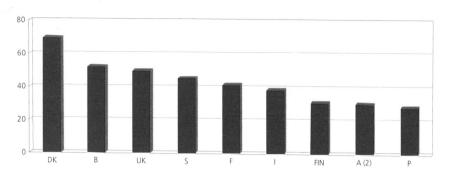

(1) F, I, FIN and S, 1996; D, EL, E, IRL, L and NL, not available.
(2) Includes national postal service activities.

Source: Eurostat (SBS)

Box 21.4

EITO (the European Information Technology Observatory) estimates that the turnover of telecommunication activities in the EU (both equipment and services) was equal to 238 billion EUR in 1999, of which 183 billion EUR was for carrier services alone.

The European[3] telecom market was the largest in the world in 1999, with the turnover of carrier services accounting for 31.2% of the estimated world total of 657 billion EUR. This share was ahead of the USA (190 billion EUR or 28.9%) and Japan (65 billion EUR or 9.8%).

(3) EEA, Czech Republic, Estonia, Hungary, Poland, Russia, Slovakia, Slovenia and Switzerland.

Table 21.5

Telecom turnover in the EU (million EUR)

	1998	1999	2000	2001
Total telecom	**210,634**	**238,449**	**264,475**	**286,132**
Total equipment	**44,760**	**55,525**	**66,054**	**75,137**
End-user equipment	24,266	33,607	42,280	49,708
Telephone sets	5,055	5,227	5,384	5,539
Mobile telephone sets	16,266	25,209	33,551	40,638
Other terminal equipment	2,945	3,172	3,345	3,531
Network equipment	20,494	21,918	23,774	25,429
Transmission	3,878	3,971	4,175	4,353
Circuit switching equipment	5,285	5,027	4,733	4,416
PBX & key systems	3,683	3,781	3,870	3,971
Cellular mobile radio infrastructure	4,730	5,691	6,863	7,848
Other network equipment	2,919	3,448	4,133	4,842
Carrier services	**165,874**	**182,924**	**198,421**	**210,995**
Telephone services (1)	100,188	103,586	107,036	110,140
Mobile phone services	36,492	47,995	57,876	64,969
Switched data and leased lines services	23,316	24,717	25,886	27,193
CaTV services	5,878	6,626	7,623	8,694

(1) Includes Internet and online services.

Source: EITO

Figure 21.12

Share of telecom services turnover by world region, 1999 (%)

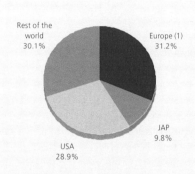

(1) EEA, Czech Republic, Estonia, Hungary, Poland, Russia, Slovakia, Slovenia and Switzerland.

Source: EITO

The turnover of EU telecom services grew by 10.3% in 1999 but growth was expected to slow down to 8.4% in 2000 and 6.3% in the year 2001. Fixed telephone services represented the largest share of telecom services with turnover equal to 104 billion EUR, whilst witnessing the lowest rates of growth (3.4% in 1999) and the lowest growth forecasts (3.3% in 2000 and 2.9% in 2001). This may be explained by the fact that the price of local and long-distance calls should continue to decline as competition intensifies. Mobile telephone services boasted growth of 31.5% in 1999, with turnover estimated at 48 billion EUR, thanks to the growing number of mobile phone subscribers and increasing average call duration.

Table 21.6

Main indicators of telecommunications infrastructure, 1999 (thousands)

	Main telephone lines	of which, digital (%)	ISDN lines	Analogue mobile telephone subscribers	Digital mobile telephone subscribers
Europe (1)	311,438	82.3	28,730	8,676	137,229
JAP	63,676	100.0	10,016	700	48,600
USA	192,258	94.5	9,158	48,000	34,000
Rest of the world	336,877	94.3	3,140	32,935	102,531
World	904,250	90.6	51,044	90,311	322,360

(1) EEA, Czech Republic, Estonia, Hungary, Poland, Russia, Slovakia, Slovenia and Switzerland.

Source: EITO

Figure 21.13

Total mobile phone subscribers (thousands)

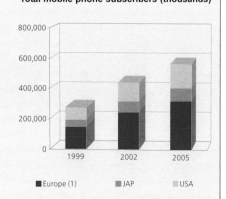

(1) EEA, Czech Republic, Estonia, Hungary, Poland, Russia, Slovakia, Slovenia and Switzerland.

Source: EITO

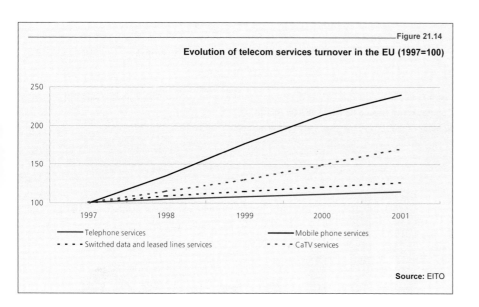

Figure 21.14

Evolution of telecom services turnover in the EU (1997=100)

Telephone services
Mobile phone services
Switched data and leased lines services
CaTV services

Source: EITO

SUB-CHAPTER 21.3
COMPUTER AND RELATED ACTIVITIES
(NACE Rev. 1 72)

Software and computing services are covered by Division 72 of NACE Rev. 1. They include hardware consultancy services (Group 72.1), analysis, design and programming of ready to use software (Group 72.2), data processing and database activities (Groups 72.3 and 72.4 respectively), as well as the maintenance and repair of office machinery (Group 72.5). Excluded are the reproduction of computer media (NACE Rev. 1 22.33), the manufacture of computers (NACE Rev. 1 30.02) and the retail trade of computers and software (NACE Rev. 1 52.48).

Enterprises smaller than average...

There were an estimated 245 thousand enterprises engaged in computer services in the EU in 1996. They employed over 1.3 million persons and generated 116.5 billion ECU of turnover. Each enterprise employed an average of 5 persons, although 39.4% of enterprises had no employees at all and 53.7% had between 1 and 9 employees. This contrasts with other service activities (NACE Rev. 1 Sections G to K) where enterprises with no employees usually constituted the largest share of the enterprise population. In other words, there are more small enterprises with few employees than one-man businesses in computer services activities. In addition, the average number of persons employed in larger enterprises (with 250 or more employees) was equal to 637 persons, compared to 1.3 thousand for services in general (NACE Rev. 1 Sections G to K), and average turnover per enterprise was equal to 72.0 million ECU, compared to 315.9 million ECU. As such, large enterprises in computer services were, on average, smaller than large enterprises active in other services activities.

Figure 21.15

Computer and related activities (NACE Rev. 1 72)

Number of persons employed, 1997 (thousands) (1)

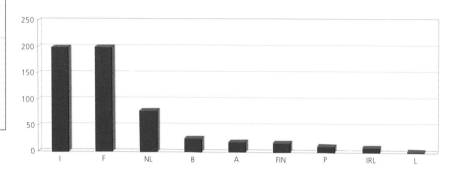

(1) I and L, 1996; DK, D, EL, E, S and UK, not available.

Source: Eurostat (SBS)

Figure 21.16

Computer and related activities (NACE Rev. 1 72)

Apparent labour productivity, 1997 (thousand ECU per person employed) (1)

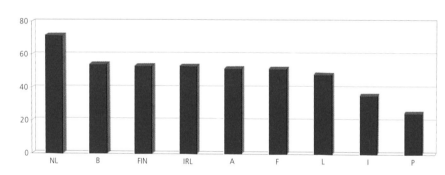

(1) I and L, 1996; DK, D, EL, E, S and UK, not available.

Source: Eurostat (SBS)

...with turnover generally under one million ECU

Within the EU, the United Kingdom had the largest number of computer services enterprises, some 64.3 thousand in 1996. In comparison, Italy numbered 47.3 thousand enterprises (1996), Germany 37.5 thousand (1997) and France 27.4 thousand (1997). Average employment ranged between 4 persons per enterprise in Italy (1996) and Austria (1997) and 9 persons in Ireland and the Netherlands (both 1997). Average turnover per enterprise was below a million ECU in all Member States (giving further supportive evidence of the small average size of enterprises in this sector). Dutch and French enterprises reported the highest levels of average turnover, 864 thousand ECU and 802 thousand ECU each in 1997, practically two and a half times the level recorded in the United Kingdom (339 thousand ECU, 1996) or Spain (304 thousand ECU, 1995).

Unit personnel costs and apparent labour productivity higher than average

The computer services workforce has a generally higher than average level of education, with as many as 54.4% of those employed having completed a university degree (or equivalent). This feeds through into the figures for unit personnel costs, which were above 40.0 thousand ECU per employee in a majority of the Member States, with highs of 49.7 thousand ECU in Belgium (1997) and 49.1 thousand ECU in Sweden (1997). Apparent labour productivity was also higher than average, with value added estimated to account for 49.6% of turnover in 1997. Eurostat estimates that each person employed in computer services in the EU in 1997 generated some 48.3 thousand ECU of value added. The Netherlands recorded the highest level, with an average of 71.8 thousand ECU per person employed, whilst Portugal closed the ranking with 24.8 thousand ECU.

EU gross operating rate equal to 14.5%

Average profitability of computer services activities can be measured by the gross operating surplus generated on each ECU of turnover. Eurostat estimates that this ratio was equal to 14.5% in the EU in 1997, a rate similar to that for other business activities (NACE Rev. 1 Division 74). The Netherlands reported an operating rate almost twice that level (29.4%, 1997), whilst only Portugal (9.7%, 1997), Luxembourg (7.1%, 1996) and France (5.4%, 1997) displayed rates below 10%.

—————————————————————————————————Figure 21.17

Computer and related activities (NACE Rev. 1 72)

Unit personnel costs, 1997 (thousand ECU per employee) (1)

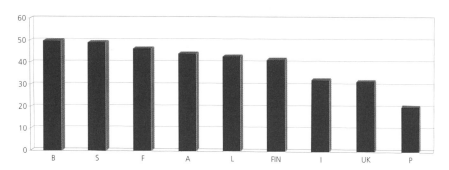

(1) I, L, FIN and S, 1996; DK, D, EL, E, IRL and NL, not available.

Source: Eurostat (SBS)

Box 21.5

EITO (the European Information Technology Observatory) estimated that EU information technology (IT) turnover, including computer hardware, was equal to 207 billion EUR in 1999. Software and IT services alone accounted for 114 billion EUR of turnover or 55% of the total.

World turnover for software and IT services reached 450 billion EUR in 1999 and was expected to increase to 560 billion EUR by 2001. The USA held the largest market share in 1999 (46.5%), compared to 27.4% for Europe[4] and 11.2% for Japan.

(4) EEA, Czech Republic, Estonia, Hungary, Poland, Russia, Slovakia, Slovenia and Switzerland.

Table 21.7

IT turnover in the EU (million EUR)

	1998	1999	2000	2001
IT hardware	86,405	92,937	99,425	105,865
Software	36,283	41,150	46,928	53,666
Application software	18,529	20,974	23,989	27,313
System software	17,754	20,176	22,939	26,353
Services	64,152	72,988	82,386	91,851
Consulting	6,549	7,660	8,946	10,401
Implementation	21,198	25,045	28,940	33,118
Operations management	21,689	24,642	27,894	30,872
Support services	14,716	15,642	16,606	17,460
Total	186,840	207,075	228,739	251,382

Source: EITO

Figure 21.18

Share of software and IT services turnover by world region, 1999 (%)

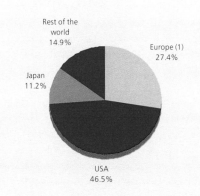

(1) EEA, Switzerland, Czech Republic, Estonia, Hungary, Poland, Russia, Slovakia and Slovenia.

Source: EITO

The EU software and IT services market grew by 13.6% in 1999 and was expected to continue to boast double-digit growth rates in both 2000 and 2001. The software products' sub-sector recorded growth of 13.4% in 1999, with market value (turnover) estimated at 41 billion EUR. Within the software products market, systems software and applications software each shared about half of the total market value (20.2 billion EUR and 21.0 billion EUR respectively). Growth expectations were for double-digit expansions to continue, with somewhat higher growth expected for applications software.

Computing services represented an even larger and faster expanding area, with a market that was worth an estimated 73.0 billion EUR in 1999 (with annual growth of 13.8%). Almost half of the market was accounted for by consulting and implementation services, one-third by operations management services (for example, systems and network management, help-desks, back-up and archiving services) and the rest by support services (for example, maintenance contracts and telephone support, be it bundled or not with software packages). The fastest growing activities in computing services were consulting and implementation services.

Figure 21.19

Evolution of software and IT services turnover in the EU (1997=100)

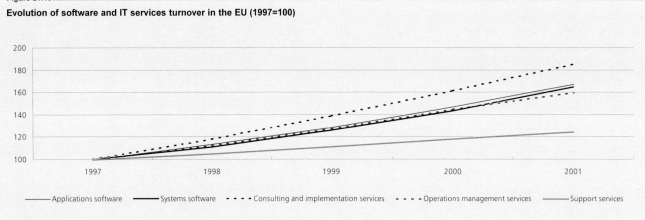

Source: EITO

—Table 21.8

World's top software and IT services companies, 1999

Company	Worldwide revenue (million EUR)
By software licence:	
Microsoft Corp.	20,258
IBM Corp.	11,916
Computer Associates Inc.	4,656
Oracle Corp.	3,634
Hewlett-Packard Co.	2,385
SAP AG	1,826
Sun Microsystems Inc.	1,222
Unisys Corp.	1,133
Compaq Computer Corp.	1,085
Novell Inc.	1,024
By service revenue:	
IBM Corp.	30,213
PricewaterhouseCoopers	16,232
Andersen Consulting LLP	8,389
Compaq Computer Corp.	6,214
Hewlett-Packard Co.	5,810
Oracle Corp.	5,119
SAP AG	2,932
Bull Worldwide Inf. Syst.	2,618
Ernst & Young LLP	1,877
Sun Microsystems Inc.	1,816

Source: Software Magazine's Annual Software 500, June 2000, Wiesner Publishing, Framingham, Mass

SUB-CHAPTER 21.4
FILM AND VIDEO (NACE Rev. 1 92.1)

The film and video industry is covered by Group 92.1 within the NACE Rev. 1 activity classification. It includes services of cinematographic and audiovisual production, including cinematographic films, advertising, television fiction and documentaries and production services such as special effects and dubbing. Distribution services and the management of audiovisual rights are also covered within this sub-chapter. Activities such as the duplication and reproduction of films and videotapes from master copies (Group 22.3) and the retail trade and renting of video tapes to the general public (Groups 52.1 and 71.4) are not included.

More than 10 thousand cinema sites with an average of 2.2 screens and 234 seats per screen
The EU cinema infrastructure was composed in 1998 of 10.2 thousand sites[5] and 22.7 thousand screens, equivalent to 2.2 screens per site. Irish cinema sites were generally larger than in the rest of Europe, with 3.9 screens on average in 1998, ahead of Belgium (3.4 screens), Germany (2.9) and the Netherlands (2.8). Greece and Portugal reported a low presence of multi-screen cinemas, which resulted in an average of just over one screen per site.

In 1998, the average cinema auditorium had 234 seats in the EU[6], with a high of approximately 340 seats per screen in the United Kingdom and Spain. All other countries[7] fell within the range 154 (Denmark) to 261 (Portugal) seats per screen. From 1990, the average size of cinema auditoriums decreased in every country (with the exception of Luxembourg). Indeed, in 1970 the highest average number of seats per screen was 447 in Spain, more than 100 above the corresponding figure for 1997.

(5) P, 1996.
(6) EL and I, no data available; P and UK, 1997.
(7) EL and I, no data available.

Figure 21.20

Average size and occupancy rate of cinemas, 1998 (units)

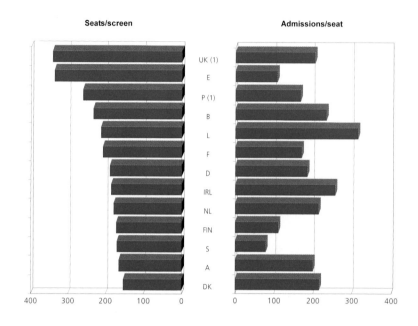

(1) 1997.

Source: Eurostat (AUVIS)

Figure 21.21

Multiplex density in relation to market share of US films, 1998

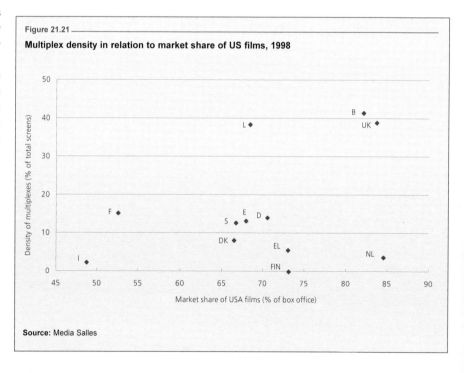

Source: Media Salles

Led by France, the EU amongst the top long-length feature films producers in the world

In 1998, 413 national long-length feature films were produced in the EU in addition to some 220 international co-productions[8]. The EU was therefore one of the largest film producers in the world, with the leader being India (697 films in 1997), whilst 661 long-length feature films were produced in the USA (in 1998) and 249 in Japan.

The largest contributor to the EU film industry was France with 180 long-length movies in 1998 (102 national productions and 78 international co-productions), followed by Italy (92), the United Kingdom (87), Spain (65) and Germany (50).

An average of two admissions per year

Box office revenues are on a rising trend in the EU, supported by an increasing number of admissions. Total receipts reached 4.3 billion ECU in 1998 (+12.4% on the year before), with 796 million admissions (+6.2%). American cinemas had 1.5 billion admissions in the same year (+6.7%), with total box office takings worth 6.2 billion ECU (+10.4%).

The average European went to the movies twice in 1998 and faced total admission costs of 11 ECU. France was the leader in terms of both admissions and box office takings, with 170 million admissions and 907 million ECU in gross takings in 1998, accounting for more than a fifth of the EU total. However, it was in Luxembourg that the highest value of ticket sales per capita was recorded (20.0 ECU per inhabitant), ahead of Austria (17.5 ECU), Ireland (15.8) and France (15.4). In comparison, Americans spent on average 22.9 ECU for cinema tickets in 1998 and the Japanese less than half that amount (10.5 ECU).

The country within the EU where people liked to visit[9] the cinema most was Luxembourg, with 3.6 cinema tickets sold per inhabitant in 1998, followed by Ireland (3.3) and France (2.9). These figures are a long way short of those recorded in the USA (5.5 tickets per inhabitant). The average cinema attendance in Japan was only slightly more than once a year per inhabitant (1.2), the same level as the Greek and Finnish figures (the lowest within the EU).

		Number of multiplex sites by number of screens, as of 1st January 1999 (units)					
	8	9	10	11-15	15-20	20+	Total
EU-15	108	75	63	121	17	5	389
B	3	0	2	8	1	2	16
DK	0	1	0	0	1	0	2
D	23	20	13	13	3	0	72
EL	1	1	1	0	0	0	3
E	20	14	11	11	2	2	60
F	22	7	3	35	5	1	73
IRL	0	2	2	3	0	0	7
I	1	4	2	:	1	0	8
L	0	0	1	0	0	0	1
NL	3	1	0	0	0	0	4
A	4	1	0	3	0	0	8
P	1	1	2	1	1	0	6
FIN	0	0	1	0	0	0	1
S	6	3	3	2	1	0	15
UK	24	20	22	45	2	0	113

Table 21.9

Source: Media Salles

Half of the new releases are American films

American studios dominate the European film marketplace. Figures indicate that more than half of the new films released each year in the EU are of American origin (51.3%, 1997), a share that rises to two-thirds or more in Portugal (66.5%, 1997), Greece (68.5%, 1998) and Ireland (69.3%, 1998). France, on the other hand, displayed the lowest penetration of American films (just 37%), with only three other Member States reporting a penetration ratio by American films below 50%: Belgium (45.2%, 1998), Italy (47.4%, 1997) and Austria (48.6%, 1997).

National productions represented less than one-fifth of the releases in most Member States, including the United Kingdom. However, there was one notable exception, France, where French movies accounted for 37.4% of all releases in 1998. In the USA, 85.5% of all releases were of national origin (1997), whilst in Japan the proportion was 44.9% (1998).

Box 21.6

The emergence of private television channels and the development of pay-TV since the mid-1980s have significantly affected the film industry. Several broadcasters actively finance the film industry, either through co-production or rights acquisitions, with the objective of increasing and securing the programming rights for their ever-expanding number of channels. Several Member States and the European Commission (the Media programme) support their national cinematographic industries, either by requiring television channels to invest in film production (for example, France and Italy), or through direct financing. It is estimated that public and Community-financed investment accounted for less than a quarter of total production costs in Europe.

(8) IRL: 1997 for national productions, excluding international co-productions. UK: 1997 for international co-productions. Figures cannot be added because of double-counting in co-productions at the EU-level.
(9) Cinema visitors may not be resident in the country where they watch a film.

Figure 21.22

Average price indicators for the video market, 1998 (ECU)

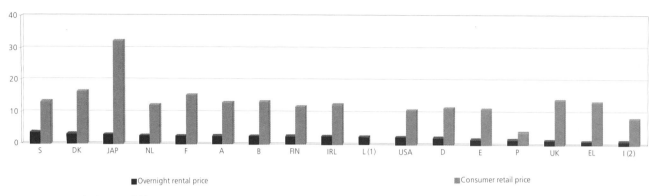

■ Overnight rental price   ■ Consumer retail price

(1) 1997; consumer retail price, not available.
(2) 1997.

Source: Eurostat (AUVIS)

Two-thirds of video cassettes or discs are sold rather than rented

The EU video market has rapidly developed in the 1990s with receipts from sales and rentals reaching 5.5 billion ECU in 1998. An important evolution within this market has been a clear shift from rentals to sales. In 1990, two-thirds of video revenues originated from rentals, whilst by 1998 two-thirds originated from the sale of more than 279 million videos (cassettes or discs). After experiencing a sharp decline between 1990 and 1994, video rental recovered somewhat in the second half of the 1990s. The number of rental transactions rose by 9% in 1998 to reach 699 million units[10], up from 619 million units in 1994 (excluding Luxembourg). Total revenues from video rentals rose by 11% in 1998 to 1.9 billion ECU, up from 1.5 billion ECU in 1994, but still below the 2.3 billion ECU recorded in 1990.

(10) I, 1997.

Figure 21.23

Receipts from pre-recorded video cassettes or discs in the EU (million ECU)

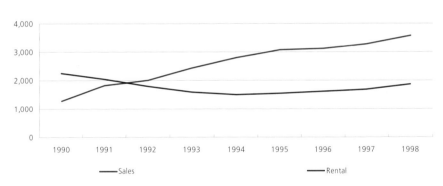

———— Sales   ———— Rental

Source: Eurostat (AUVIS)

SUB-CHAPTER 21.5
RADIO AND TELEVISION
(NACE Rev. 1 92.2)

The radio and television industry consists of three major activities: the production of programmes, the compilation of schedules for those programmes and their transmission to the final consumer. Following the NACE Rev. 1 activity classification, the first two activities are included in Group 92.2, whilst the physical transmission of signals via Hertzian relays, satellite or cable networks is covered by the Group 64.2 (telecommunication services).

_____ Box 21.7

The supply of TV channels is expected to continue rising as broadcasting turns to digital technology. Digitalisation allows a greater number of channels to be transmitted on the same bandwidth, hence reducing transmission costs (notably for the transmission of channel packages). It also provides better images and enhanced transmission capabilities, such as extended pay-per-view services, multiplexing, video on demand, software downloading, etc. According to the European Audiovisual Observatory, the number of pay-per-view operators in Europe expanded from one in 1994 to 28 by 1998, and the number of channels from one to over 260 during the same period.

In this context of rapidly increasing supply there are two key elements to success, access to transmission capabilities (either terrestrial, by cable or through satellite slots) and control over the supply of content (broadcasting rights for films, series, sports events). This has led several broadcasters to pursue a vertical integration strategy. There have been attempts to take control of football clubs (BSkyB with Manchester Utd., Canal+ with Paris St. Germain), the acquisition of cable networks (Canal+ with one of Vivendi's networks) or possible co-operation deals with media groups (Kirch with Viacom/Paramount, the merger of CLT-Ufa and Pearson's television activities). These trends rely somewhat on the willingness of public authorities to maintain competitive conditions within the market. One of the remaining questions concerning the development of digital pay-TV is whether the consumer will accept to pay high fees to watch prime events, considering the abundant offer of free channels.

Radio and television have become part of everyday life within European households in the second half of the 20th Century, with virtually every household equipped with a radio and/or TV set. During the last twenty years, most Member States have opened their audio-visual markets to private operators, pan-European channels have emerged and transmission techniques such as satellite or cable have been introduced.

TV households: 43% multi-set, 27% connected to cable, 14% with satellite dishes

There were 96.6% of EU households equipped with a television set in 1997, up from 95.0% at the beginning of the decade. Within the Member States the range was from 93.6% in France (1998) to 99.7% in Portugal (1998). Approximately 43% of TV households in the EU were equipped with a second television set in 1997, a share much lower than in the USA or Japan, where 74% and 99% of TV households had at least a second television set in 1998.

_____ Table 21.10

Equipment rate of households, 1998

	Number of TV households (thousand) (1)	TV households with 2 TV sets or more (%) (2)	Penetration rate of VCRs (%) (3)
EU-15	144,037	43.0	66.9
B	3,984	19.2	75.1
DK	2,357	42.0	76.0
D	37,007	27.7	65.4
EL	3,663	48.0	37.8
E	11,951	57.9	72.1
F	21,996	37.3	77.6
IRL	1,175	42.6	71.8
I	21,149	45.3	63.8
L	162	47.5	72.2
NL	6,558	40.8	74.5
A	3,032	44.0	77.2
P	3,037	64.5	65.0
FIN	2,233	45.8	74.0
S	3,994	54.0	85.6
UK	23,600	58.0	83.0
JAP	43,900	99.0	85.2
USA	98,500	74.0	84.6

(1) EU-15, B and JAP, 1997.
(2) EU-15, DK, EL, E and UK, 1997.
(3) Share of TV households owning at least one VCR; EU-15, B, NL, E, UK and JAP, 1997.

Source: Eurostat (AUVIS), European Audiovisual Observatory (EAO)

Besides terrestrial (Hertzian) transmission of the TV signals, cable and satellite have emerged as important alternatives. They provide a better quality of reception and a wider choice of programmes, with sometimes additional services such as for example telephony services or high-speed Internet access. In the EU, 27.1% of TV households were subscribing to cable networks in 1997, whilst 14% were connected to satellite dishes. The Benelux countries were the most cabled countries in the world with around 90% of TV households connected to a network. As for satellite dishes, German (32.8%), Austrian (39.2%) and Danish (39.9%) TV households had the highest penetration rates in the EU, despite reporting relatively high cable penetration rates as well (48.1%, 38.6% and 65.6% respectively). With marginal cable and satellite penetration rates, countries such as Greece, Italy and Spain relied most on Hertzian transmission.

Approximately 190 minutes of daily viewing time
Final consumption of television can be measured by the average amount of time that people spend watching each day. Eurostat estimates this length of time to be approximately 190 minutes per person per day within the EU in 1998, varying from 136 minutes in Luxembourg (1997) up to 253 minutes in Greece. Viewing times in the EU have increased in recent years, although generally staying below the levels recorded in the USA (238 minutes) and Japan (222 minutes). Viewing time is Inter alia influenced by economic, social and technological factors, such as employment conditions (the unemployment rate, share of part-time work or the average number of working hours), the occurrence of important events (such as major sports events or international crises) or the number and variety of channels available.

Figure 21.24

Cable and satellite penetration rate in private TV households, 1998 (%)

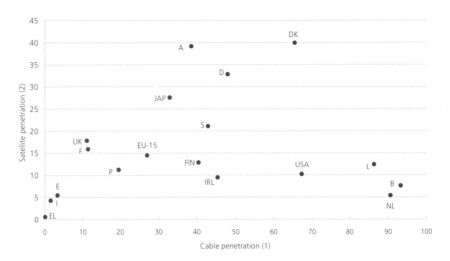

(1) Share of TV households connected to operated cable networks; E, I and L, 1995; EU-15, B, DK, EL and JAP, 1997.
(2) Share of TV households connected to satellite dishes; EU-15, B, EL, E, I, UK and JAP, 1997.

Source: Eurostat (AUVIS), European Audiovisual Observatory (EAO)

Figure 21.25

Average daily viewing or listening time, 1998 (minutes/day)

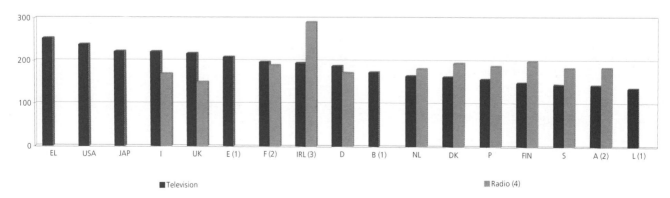

(1) 1997.
(2) TV: average daily viewing time of adults.
(3) Radio, 1996.
(4) B, EL, E, L, JAP and USA, not available.

Source: Eurostat (AUVIS)

*Sharp increase of TV-licence fees receipts -
fragmentation of advertising revenue*

Broadcasters can count on three types of revenues, depending on their legal status and their commercial strategy: TV-licence fees paid each year by every television set owner and/or State subsidies (for public operators); revenues from advertising and sponsorship (for public and commercial operators) and direct receipts from viewers (in the case of pay-TV operators). Revenues from TV-licence fees grew at a rapid pace during the 1990s reaching 11 billion ECU in the EU in 1997, up from 7.8 billion ECU in 1990 (in excess of 30%). At the same time, increasing competition between a rising number of channels has led to a fragmentation of audiences and of advertising revenue.

*Six thousand radio stations, listened to for
more than 180 minutes on average a day*

As regards radio broadcasting, Eurostat estimates there were approximately 6 thousand radio stations active in the EU in 1998, two-thirds of which were established in Spain and Italy alone. In comparison, there were 4.6 thousand radio stations in the USA in 1995 and only 222 in Japan in 1998. The vast majority of radio stations have only regional or local coverage. Only in the Netherlands did national radio stations outnumber local ones (17 compared to 13 in 1998). At the other end of the scale, more than 97% of Greek, Portuguese or Italian radio stations were local.

In the majority of Member States the average radio listening time per day was greater than 180 minutes per day[11]. Average listening time was greater than TV viewing time in several of the smaller Member States, including all Nordic countries. Irish inhabitants listened most to the radio, with an average of 290 minutes per day in 1996, which was almost twice the duration of those living in the United Kingdom (150 minutes in 1998).

_____

(11) B, EL and L, no data available.

_____Figure 21.26

Daily cumulated audience share of the most watched TV channel (%)

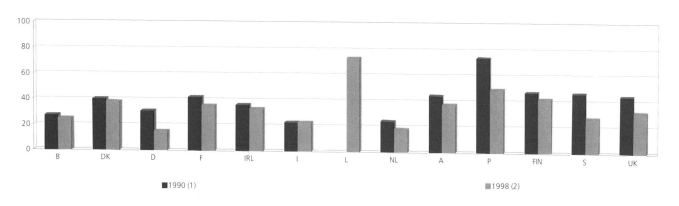

(1) A, 1991; DK and P, 1992; IRL and FIN, 1993; NL, 1995; L, not available.
(2) A, 1997.

Source: Eurostat (AUVIS)

_____Figure 21.27

Breakdown of the number of radio stations according to their coverage (%)

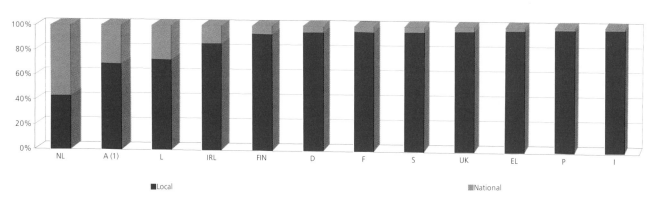

(1) 1996.

Source: Eurostat (AUVIS)

SUB-CHAPTER 21.6
MUSIC RECORDING
(NACE Rev. 1 22.14 AND 22.31)

The music recording industry includes activities that range from the selection, management and production of artists to the manufacturing, marketing and distribution of recorded media such as compact discs, vinyl discs and cassettes. Two Classes of the NACE Rev. 1 classification cover this industry, 22.14 for the publishing side and 22.31 for the reproduction side.

Strong growth of turnover in the EU in the 1990s
Turnover from the sale of music recordings in the EU exceeded 9.5 billion ECU in 1998, a 2.9% rise over the previous year and 47.3% above the level recorded in 1990 (in nominal terms). EU sales increased at an average annual rate of 13.5% (again in nominal terms) between 1985 and 1991. In 1992, sales stagnated, but the market quickly recovered, gaining on average 4.7% per annum in value to 1998.

The largest market for music recording was the USA, where total pre-recorded music sales reached 11.8 billion ECU in 1998, or 43.4% of the sales in the Triad. In Japan turnover was equal to 5.8 billion ECU in the same year (21.5% of the Triad total).

Box 21.8
According to IFPI (the International Federation of the Phonographic Industry), world pre-recorded music turnover was equal to 41 billion EUR in 1999, which was up by 1% compared to 1998. In volume terms there were 3.8 billion units sold. CDs unit sales increased by 2%, representing close to 65% of total unit sales.

The EU represented around a third of world sales, recording a 3% decline in volume terms (with no evolution in value terms). Sales volumes in the United Kingdom dropped by 5% (whilst values grew by 4%), which reflected the declining sale of singles (short-play formats) in favour of (more expensive) CDs (long-play formats). Italy reported growth of 1% in volume terms and 4% in value terms. Sales in France and Spain fell, whilst there was no change in volume terms in Germany.

Figure 21.28

Evolution of turnover of pre-recorded music sales in the Triad (million ECU)

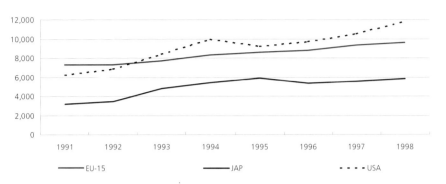

Source: Eurostat (AUVIS)

Figure 21.29

Evolution of the number of music recordings sold in the EU (1991=100) (1)

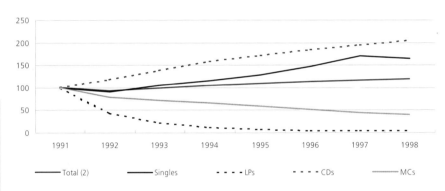

(1) L, no data available.
(2) Three singles are counted as one recording unit (IFPI standards).

Source: Eurostat (AUVIS)

Sales driven by CDs and singles
An analysis of sales in unit terms reveals that turnover growth has been principally fuelled by sales of CDs and singles. The EU recorded sales of more than 890 million units[12] of pre-recorded music in 1998, 79% of which were CDs. Vinyl LPs sales in the EU plummeted from over 140 million units in 1990 to a mere 3.5 million by 1998. Music cassettes peaked at 274 million units in 1991, declining to 108 million units in 1998. In contrast, the number of long format CDs sold more than doubled between 1991 and 1997, reaching 712 million units in 1998, up from 350 million units in 1991.

(12) Total unit sales of CDs, LPs, MCs and singles (45rpm vinyl and 2-title MCs/CDs). Following the definition of IFPI (International Federation of the Phonographic Industry), three singles are counted as one album.

Figure 21.30

Number of sound recordings sold per inhabitant, 1998 (units) (1)

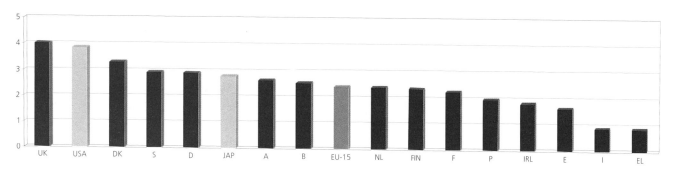

(1) Three singles are counted as one recording unit (IFPI standards).

Source: Eurostat (AUVIS)

Box 21.9

Whilst CD sales continue their steady growth worldwide, other formats such as Sony's MiniDisc have failed to capture a substantial share of the market, whilst other formats (for example Philips' DCC) have been discontinued. New formats such as MPEG-1 layer 3[13], have gained momentum in recent years, with the introduction of cheap portable MP3 players in 1998. This development also raised concerns about wide-scale piracy using the Internet as a reproduction and exchange medium.

A major challenge for the music industry comes from the development of on-line music distribution. Although this distribution channel remains marginal at present, it is commonly agreed that digital diffusion (through Internet or other means) will become an important part of the global market in the future. Major music companies have become increasingly involved in channels through which music is either distributed or played (such as radio, television or computer networks). As a result, global entertainment companies are emerging in the fields of computers, telecommunications, media, broadcasting and entertainment. The two leading examples of this trend are the mergers between TimeWarner/AOL and Seagram/Vivendi. Whilst the majority of music companies have diversified operations into related markets that include film production, book publishing, broadcasting and retailing, others (like Sony) have also expanded into the manufacture of the audio equipment.

(13) Also known after ifs DOS file extension, MP3. MPEG is an ISO/IEC sound compression algorithm standard developed by the Moving Picture Experts Group (MPEG). It is widespread over the Internet and allows music files to be compressed at about a tenth of their original size, whilst keeping near-perfect reproduction quality.

Publishing enterprises usually very small...

Music publishing companies range from small independent labels to large multinational corporations. In general their average size is relatively small, with between one (Finland, 1997) and three persons employed per enterprise (Italy, 1996 and France, the Netherlands and Portugal, 1997). Values outside this range were reported only by Austria (5 persons, 1997) and Spain (8 persons, 1997). Average turnover per enterprise was lowest in Finland and Luxembourg with 101 thousand ECU and 157 thousand ECU per enterprise respectively in 1997, whilst remaining well below one million ECU per enterprise in the majority of the other Member States, except Spain (1.9 million ECU, 1997).

... with high productivity and profitability

Apparent labour productivity in music publishing was high, with a maximum recorded in the United Kingdom where each person employed generated some 160 thousand ECU of valued added in 1997. Apparent labour productivity was also well in excess of manufacturing averages in France (89.9 thousand ECU, 1997) and the Netherlands (81.7 thousand ECU, 1997), whilst most other countries displayed values between 30.0 and 40.0 thousand ECU per person employed. Belgium (21.4 thousand ECU, 1996) and Portugal (16.2 thousand ECU) were well below these levels.

Profitability rates were also generally high, with the gross operating surplus of the sector representing between 5.0% (Portugal) and 50.4% (United Kingdom) of its turnover in 1997.

In a majority of countries, unit personnel costs were higher than in other manufacturing activities in 1997. They generally fluctuated around 25 to 32 thousand ECU per employee, although they were notably lower in Portugal (12.8 thousand ECU) and significantly higher in the Netherlands (43.0 thousand ECU) and France (48.4 thousand ECU).

Reproduction enterprises larger
than publishing ones...

Enterprises active in the reproduction of music recordings were often larger than publishing ones, reflecting their industrial nature. For example, average employment in the seven enterprises active in this sector in Austria in 1997 was equal to 165 persons and average turnover per enterprise was equal to 46.4 million ECU. Amongst the other Member States, Spain (16 persons, 2 million ECU) and the Netherlands (30 persons, 6.3 million ECU) also reported an enterprise structure dominated by larger enterprises. In contrast Italian, Portuguese, Swedish and Finnish enterprises employed less than 4 persons on average and generated annual turnover below 300 thousand ECU each.

... also with high apparent labour productivity and profitability

In the majority of the Member States, each person employed in music reproduction enterprises generated more than 40.0 thousand ECU of value added, with maxima of 89.0 thousand ECU per person employed in the United Kingdom and 173.2 thousand ECU per person employed in Austria. On the other hand, unit personnel costs were in most of the Member States generally lower for music reproduction activities than for music publishing activities. In six Member States[14] for each ECU of turnover generated the gross operating surplus was over 20%, with a maximum of 48.9% in Austria. Four other countries[15] recorded operating rates of between 15% and 17%, whilst France lagged behind (12.7%).

(14) B, E, I, A, P and UK.
(15) DK, NL, FIN and S.

Figure 21.31

Music recording (NACE Rev. 1 22.14 and 22.31)
Number of persons employed, 1997 (thousands) (1)

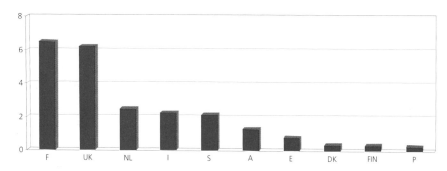

(1) I, 1996; B, D, EL, IRL and L, not available.

Source: Eurostat (SBS)

Figure 21.32

Music recording (NACE Rev. 1 22.14 and 22.31)
Apparent labour productivity, 1997 (thousand ECU per person employed) (1)

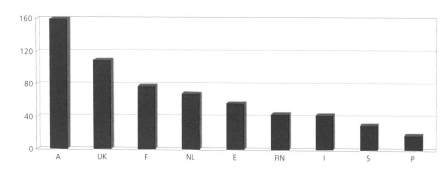

(1) I, 1996; B, DK, D, EL, IRL and L, not available.

Source: Eurostat (SBS)

Figure 21.33

Music recording (NACE Rev. 1 22.14 and 22.31)
Unit personnel costs, 1997 (thousand ECU per employee) (1)

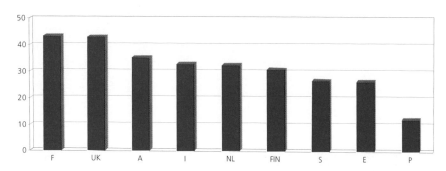

(1) I, 1996; B, DK, D, EL, IRL and L, not available.

Source: Eurostat (SBS)

_____Table 21.11

Post and courier activities (NACE Rev. 1 64.1)

Employment related indicators, 1997

	B	DK	D	EL	E	F (1)	IRL	I (1)	L	NL	A (2)	P	FIN (3)	S	UK
Number of persons employed (thousands)	49.9	36.9	:	:	:	288.3	10.9	193.3	:	:	1.2	16.3	27.7	:	:
Employees/number of persons employed (%)	97.0	98.1	:	:	:	99.8	95.8	99.1	:	:	83.6	100.0	99.7	:	:
Average no. of persons employed/enterprise (units)	:	27.0	:	:	:	225.0	23.0	146.6	:	:	6.0	775.0	121.0	:	:

(1) 1996; (2) Excluding national postal service activities, classified within NACE Rev. 1 64.2; (3) Employees as a share of the number of persons employed, 1996.

_____Table 21.12

Post and courier activities (NACE Rev. 1 64.1)

Turnover related indicators, 1997

	B	DK	D	EL	E	F (1)	IRL	I (1)	L	NL	A (2)	P	FIN	S (1)	UK
Turnover (million ECU)	2,301	1,507	2,130	:	:	13,357	685	6,444	:	:	164	487	1,116	2,639	:
Turnover per enterprise (million ECU)	:	1.1	0.5	:	:	10.4	1.5	4.9	:	:	0.8	23.2	4.9	15.2	:
Turnover per person employed (thousand ECU)	46.1	40.8	:	:	:	46.3	62.9	33.3	:	:	140.6	30.0	40.3	:	:

(1) 1996; (2) Excluding national postal service activities, classified within NACE Rev. 1 64.2.

_____Table 21.13

Post and courier activities (NACE Rev. 1 64.1)

Performance related indicators, 1997

	B	DK	D	EL	E	F (1)	IRL	I (1)	L	NL	A (2)	P	FIN (3)	S (1)	UK
Value added (million ECU)	1,605	:	:	:	:	10,099	456	5,007	:	:	30	392	716	1,486	:
Value added as a share of turnover (%)	69.7	:	:	:	:	75.6	66.5	77.7	:	:	18.0	80.4	64.1	56.3	:
Apparent labour productivity (thousand ECU/person employed)	32.2	:	:	:	:	35.0	41.8	25.9	:	:	25.3	24.1	25.9	:	:
Unit personnel costs (thousand ECU)	29.3	25.5	:	:	:	33.1	:	27.6	:	:	23.4	19.7	20.6	33.3	:
Simple wage adjusted labour productivity (%)	113.2	:	:	:	:	106.2	:	94.9	:	:	129.4	121.9	118.4	98.5	:
Gross operating surplus (million ECU)	187	:	:	:	:	587	:	-271	:	:	7	70	111	-22	:

(1) 1996; (2) Excluding national postal service activities, classified within NACE Rev. 1 64.2; (3) Unit personnel costs, 1996.

_____Table 21.14

Main indicators of postal services, 1997

	EU-15	B	DK	D	EL	E	F	IRL	I	L	NL	A	P	FIN	S	UK
Post offices open to the public (1)	:	1,662	4,227	22,250	1,249	60,587	16,636	1,917	14,097	106	2,309	2,613	5,660	1,619	16,691	19,958
Sorting offices (2)	:	7	8	116	21	141	171	88	135	1	11	31	10	15	55	714
Letter boxes (thousand) (3)	668	20	10	140	15	35	149	4	72	1	19	24	18	12	37	112
Total staff (thousand) (3)	1,326	43	26	267	12	65	287	8	184	2	54	58	16	24	47	209
Share of full-time staff (%) (3)	82	89	100	70	100	91	81	92	100	73	50	94	99	71	84	82
Postal services expenditure (million ECU) (4)	52,189	1,606	1,278	14,532	353	1,185	13,403	475	6,846	89	2,553	2,279	443	847	2,503	5,944
Postal services investment (million ECU) (5)	2,934	77	87	982	7	67	423	29	394	7	913	95	44	52	200	511
Postal services receipts (million ECU) (6)	56,750	1,680	1,300	14,808	268	1,022	12,911	493	5,975	86	3,136	3,027	485	916	2,609	7,827
Post items, domestic service (million) (7)	90,557	3,139	1,678	20,000	394	4,014	23,914	523	6,346	102	5,970	2,438	1,020	1,519	5,160	17,296
Share of letters in domestic service (%) (8)	:	35	56	43	77	72	42	:	43	100	41	23	75	50	65	:
Post items, international dispatch (million) (9)	:	214	130	403	73	156	395	65	140	33	27	136	54	28	89	863
Post items, international receipt (million) (10)	:	204	78	702	41	160	453	124	181	25	12	143	42	36	127	480

(1) A and P, 1996; F and NL, 1995; D and UK, 1992; (2) F, NL, A and UK, 1996; S, 1991; (3) EU-15, F, NL, A, S and UK, 1996; (4) F and A, 1996; NL, 1995; EU-15 and UK, 1992;
(5) NL, S and UK, 1996; F and A, 1995; EU-15 and I, 1993; (6) EU-15, F, NL, A and UK, 1996; (7) F, A and UK, 1996; EU-15 and NL, 1995; (8) A, 1996; F and NL, 1995;
(9) F, A and UK, 1996; EU-15, DK and NL, 1995; (10) EL, F, A and UK, 1996; DK and NL, 1995.

_____Table 21.15

Evolution of main indicators of postal services, EU-15

	1988	1989	1990	1991	1992	1993	1994	1995	1996	1997
Permanent post offices (1)	111,789	116,695	153,886	152,153	144,828	:	:	:	:	:
Letter boxes (thousand) (2)	:	669	614	667	708	705	707	700	650	:
Total staff (thousand)	1,433	1,454	1,462	1,410	1,439	1,433	1,374	1,356	1,326	:
Share of full-time staff (%)	91	91	91	93	85	86	85	85	82	:
Postal services expenditure (million ECU) (3)	42,000	45,228	44,629	49,986	51,238	:	:	:	:	:
Postal services investment (million ECU) (4)	2,568	2,669	2,896	2,902	:	2,931	:	:	:	:
Postal services receipts (million ECU) (3)	39,100	43,293	39,603	47,875	48,992	51,422	55,337	55,074	55,667	:
Post items, domestic service (million) (1)	71,243	71,269	74,976	75,663	79,967	81,998	81,461	81,805	86,147	:
Post items, international dispatch (million) (5)	:	2,361	2,416	2,536	2,376	2,567	2,442	2,503	2,614	:

(1) Excluding NL; (2) Excluding IRL and FIN; (3) Excluding DK; (4) Excluding L; (5) Excluding DK, IRL, NL and S.

Source: Eurostat (SBS, COINS)

Table 21.16

Telecommunications (NACE Rev. 1 64.2)

Employment related indicators, 1997

	B	DK	D	EL	E	F (1)	IRL	I (1)	L	NL	A (2)	P	FIN (3)	S	UK
Number of persons employed (thousands)	29.7	15.3	:	:	:	163.5	13.2	96.3	:	:	64.5	20.5	16.9	:	:
Employees/number of persons employed (%)	99.6	99.9	:	:	:	100.0	99.6	99.7	:	:	99.9	99.8	99.7	:	:
Average no. of persons employed/enterprise (units)	:	92.0	:	:	:	198.0	250.0	404.6	:	:	485.0	178.0	97.0	:	:

(1) 1996; (2) Includes national postal service activities; (3) Employees as a share of the number of persons employed, 1996.

Table 21.17

Telecommunications (NACE Rev. 1 64.2)

Turnover related indicators, 1997

	B	DK	D	EL	E	F (1)	IRL	I (1)	L	NL	A (2)	P	FIN	S (1)	UK
Turnover (million ECU)	4,954	4,355	33,871	:	:	25,238	1,989	19,730	:	:	5,686	2,966	2,597	5,620	38,229
Turnover per enterprise (million ECU)	:	26.4	121.4	:	:	30.5	37.5	82.9	:	:	42.7	25.8	14.8	23.6	:
Turnover per person employed (thousand ECU)	166.6	285.3	:	:	:	154.3	150.4	204.9	:	:	88.1	144.5	153.8	:	:

(1) 1996; (2) Includes national postal service activities.

Table 21.18

Telecommunications (NACE Rev. 1 64.2)

Performance related indicators, 1997

	B	DK	D	EL	E	F (1)	IRL	I (1)	L	NL	A (2)	P	FIN (3)	S (1)	UK
Value added (million ECU)	3,180	:	:	:	:	16,696	1,222	12,769	:	:	3,502	1,928	1,408	2,907	21,804
Value added as a share of turnover (%)	64.2	:	:	:	:	66.2	61.5	64.7	:	:	61.6	65.0	54.2	51.7	57.0
Apparent labour productivity (thousand ECU/person employed)	107.0	:	:	:	:	102.1	92.4	132.6	:	:	54.3	93.9	83.3	:	:
Unit personnel costs (thousand ECU)	51.8	69.3	:	:	:	41.2	:	38.2	:	:	29.9	28.0	30.6	45.1	49.4
Simple wage adjusted labour productivity (%)	207.3	:	:	:	:	247.7	:	348.1	:	:	181.7	336.0	255.0	186.0	243.7
Gross operating surplus (million ECU)	1,646	:	:	:	:	9,955	:	9,101	:	:	1,574	1,354	856	1,344	12,856

(1) 1996; (2) Includes national postal service activities; (3) Unit personnel costs, 1996.

Table 21.19

Main indicators of telecommunications services, 1997

	EU-15	B	DK	D	EL	E	F	IRL	I	L	NL	A	P	FIN	S	UK
Main telephone lines (thousand)	193,340	4,939	3,341	45,200	5,431	15,854	33,700	1,500	25,698	280	8,860	3,969	3,819	2,861	6,010	31,878
Share of residential main lines (%) (1)	:	78	80	76	70	75	75	68	78	65	77	:	79	71	76	74
Mobile phone subscribers (thousand)	52,663	975	1,444	8,170	938	4,338	5,817	533	11,734	67	1,717	1,160	1,507	2,162	3,169	8,933
ISDN lines (thousand) (2)	2,714	99	58	2,887	1	229	1,270	0	335	10	310	86	48	58	20	260
Telex subscriber lines (3)	345,923	3,224	2,153	16,940	15,073	3,568	39,000	2,500	10,430	1,016	6,300	3,569	1,938	1,042	4,650	20,299
Subscriber's telefax stations (thousand) (4)	6,695	190	250	1,800	40	700	125	80	1,800	17	500	207	50	198	450	1,800
Total staff (thousand)	900	21	17	219	23	73	165	11	103	1	30	17	19	18	34	149
Telecom services expenditure (million ECU) (5)	106,816	2,710	2,845	33,499	1,984	8,415	19,461	921	14,307	194	5,738	2,943	3,193	2,463	4,192	13,671
Telecom services receipts (million ECU)	156,798	3,983	3,074	40,725	2,898	9,676	23,702	1,651	21,079	275	7,272	3,296	3,641	2,708	4,276	28,544
Share of receipts from telephone services (%) (6)	76	68	47	71	82	100	83	94	71	70	61	93	76	32	45	59
Gross investment (million ECU) (7)	35,404	1,284	785	7,891	731	2,068	5,052	397	5,908	70	1,680	843	677	770	669	6,577
Outgoing international calls (million) (8)	23,200	1,229	608	4,813	597	1,189	3,407	695	2,315	283	1,535	948	393	371	1,065	5,495

(1) D, EL, E, F, S and UK, 1996; I, 1995; NL, 1994; B, DK and IRL, 1993; (2) EL and IRL, 1996; EU-15, F, S and UK, 1995; (3) D, EL, F, A and UK, 1996; NL and S, 1995; EU-15 and IRL, 1993;
(4) B, D, EL, E, A and S, 1996; DK, F, I, NL, P and UK, 1995; EU-15 and IRL, 1994; (5) D, EL and E, 1996; F, I, NL, A and S, 1995; B, 1994; EU-15, IRL and UK, 1993;
(6) B, D, EL, E, NL and UK, 1996; EU-15, F, IRL, A and S, 1995; (7) Including land and buildings; (8) EU-15, E and A, 1996.

Table 21.20

Evolution of main indicators of telecommunications services, EU-15

	1988	1989	1990	1991	1992	1993	1994	1995	1996	1997
Main telephone lines (thousand)	138,928	145,396	153,439	159,329	165,328	170,881	176,896	182,568	188,197	193,340
Mobile phone subscribers (thousand)	:	:	3,114	4,239	5,629	8,451	13,536	21,160	33,476	52,663
ISDN lines (thousand)	:	:	25	97	:	:	1,618	2,714	:	:
Telex subscriber lines (1)	715,848	658,780	584,113	493,468	411,787	343,423	:	173,441	:	:
Subscriber's telefax stations (thousand) (1)	1,161	1,995	3,114	4,134	4,162	4,663	6,615	7,704	:	:
Total staff (thousand)	1,021	1,026	1,003	997	952	923	926	892	875	900
Telecom services receipts (million ECU)	77,213	86,403	91,311	101,778	110,471	115,063	122,487	128,195	136,507	156,798
Share of receipts from telephone services (%)	:	:	:	81	81	75	:	75	:	:
Gross investment (million ECU) (2)	29,201	34,503	54,060	64,272	64,312	63,013	31,989	31,301	35,494	35,404
Outgoing international calls (million)	10,600	11,900	13,600	15,100	16,800	18,500	19,900	21,700	23,200	:

(1) Excluding IRL; (2) Including land and buildings.

Source: Eurostat (SBS, COINS)

Table 21.21

Computer and related activities (NACE Rev. 1 72)

Employment related indicators, 1997

	B	DK	D	EL	E	F	IRL	I (1)	L (1)	NL (2)	A	P	FIN (2)	S	UK
Number of persons employed (thousands)	26.5	:	:	:	:	200.0	9.7	200.1	2.3	79.0	19.8	11.8	18.1	:	:
Employees/number of persons employed (%)	82.3	:	:	:	:	98.9	92.3	70.3	94.8	86.6	76.1	89.7	92.7	:	:
Average no. of persons employed/enterprise (units)	:	:	:	:	:	7.0	9.0	4.2	6.0	9.0	4.0	5.0	6.0	:	:

(1) 1996; (2) Employees as a share of the number of persons employed, 1996.

Table 21.22

Computer and related activities (NACE Rev. 1 72)

Turnover related indicators, 1997

	B	DK	D	EL	E	F	IRL	I (1)	L (1)	NL	A	P	FIN	S (1)	UK (2)
Turnover (million ECU)	3,311	:	24,932	:	:	21,958	894	16,236	250	7,749	2,315	840	1,869	6,072	33,104
Turnover per enterprise (million ECU)	:	:	0.7	:	:	0.8	0.8	0.3	0.7	0.9	0.5	0.4	0.6	0.5	0.3
Turnover per person employed (thousand ECU)	124.9	:	:	:	:	109.8	92.2	81.2	108.3	98.1	116.7	71.0	103.0	:	:

(1) 1996; (2) Turnover per enterprise, 1996.

Table 21.23

Computer and related activities (NACE Rev. 1 72)

Performance related indicators, 1997

	B	DK	D	EL	E	F	IRL	I (1)	L (1)	NL	A	P	FIN (2)	S (1)	UK
Value added (million ECU)	1,439	:	:	:	:	10,323	516	7,133	111	5,672	1,025	293	968	2,670	18,896
Value added as a share of turnover (%)	43.5	:	:	:	:	47.0	57.7	43.9	44.4	73.2	44.3	34.9	51.8	44.0	57.1
Apparent labour productivity (thousand ECU/person employed)	54.3	:	:	:	:	51.6	53.2	35.7	48.1	71.8	51.7	24.8	53.3	:	:
Unit personnel costs (thousand ECU)	49.7	:	:	:	:	46.3	:	32.1	42.7	:	44.0	20.0	41.3	49.1	31.5
Simple wage adjusted labour productivity (%)	132.7	:	:	:	:	112.9	:	157.9	119.0	167.2	154.3	138.2	139.9	128.9	170.6
Gross operating surplus (million ECU)	355	:	:	:	:	1,176	:	2,614	18	2,279	361	81	276	599	7,819

(1) 1996; (2) Unit personnel costs, 1996.

Source: Eurostat (SBS)

Table 21.24

Main indicators of the cinema industry, 1998

	EU-15	B	DK	D	EL	E	F	IRL	I	L	NL	A	P	FIN	S	UK	JAP	USA
Annual cinema admissions (million) (1)	796.3	25.4	11.0	148.9	12.4	108.4	170.1	12.4	118.5	1.4	20.1	15.2	14.8	6.4	15.8	115.5	153.1	1,480.7
Gross box office receipts (million ECU) (2)	4,323	132	72	813	61	386	908	58	587	8	118	141	47	41	118	835	1,322	6,198
Average price per cinema ticket (ECU)	5.4	5.2	6.5	5.5	4.9	3.6	5.3	4.7	5.0	5.6	5.9	9.3	3.1	6.4	7.4	7.2	8.6	4.2
Cinema sites (3)	10,461	137	166	1,445	319	1,329	2,152	66	2,159	8	186	222	217	234	839	722	:	:
Cinema sites with 8 or more screens (4)	217	16	2	39	3	33	73	7	8	1	4	4	2	0	16	122	:	:
Number of cinema screens (5)	22,665	463	328	4,244	360	2,968	4,764	259	4,603	21	519	454	330	331	1,167	1,854	1,993	34,186
Number of cinema seats (thousand) (6)	4,051	108	51	801	:	1,000	989	48	:	4	93	76	82	57	199	603	:	:
New films released for the first time (7)	276	480	176	287	143	481	465	156	382	218	227	249	200	148	186	276	555	490
of which from the USA (7)	142	217	101	146	98	212	172	114	181	120	130	121	133	82	106	178	152	:

(1) Provisional data for E; (2) Estimated data for EL; provisional data for E and F; (3) EU-15 and P, 1996; (4) DK, E and P, 1997; EU-15 and A, 1996; (5) Provisional data for E and USA;
(6) EU-15 excluding EL and I; provisional data for E; EU-15, P and UK, 1997; (7) Provisional data for A; EU-15, EL, E, I, NL, A, P and UK, 1997.

Table 21.25

Evolution of main indicators of the cinema industry, EU-15

	1990	1991	1992	1993	1994	1995	1996	1997	1998
Annual cinema admissions (million)	577	594	574	653	658	642	702	750	796
Gross box office receipts (million ECU)	2,400	2,608	2,591	2,936	3,043	3,008	3,366	3,846	4,323
Average price per cinema ticket (ECU)	4.2	4.4	4.5	4.5	4.6	4.7	4.8	5.1	5.4
Cinema sites (1)	:	:	:	10,140	10,209	10,311	10,139	9,650	9,665
Cinema sites with 8 or more screens (1)	:	:	:	129	150	168	217	268	327
Number of cinema screens (2)	18,771	18,937	18,775	18,702	19,081	19,669	20,691	21,413	22,665
Number of cinema seats (thousand) (3)	:	:	3,805	3,659	3,685	3,799	3,889	4,051	4,111
New films released for the first time (4)	260	264	250	239	245	258	274	276	265
of which from the USA (5)	146	151	134	132	133	132	141	142	132

(1) Excluding EL; including 1992 data for NL and P in 1993 and 1996 data for B in 1997; excluding P in 1997 and 1998; (2) Excluding EL; including 1996 data for B in 1997 and 1997 data for DK, E and P in 1998; (3) Excluding EL, I, and in 1993-94, IRL; including 1997 data for P and UK in 1998; (4) EU-15 total is an average, excluding UK in 1990-92 and EL, E, I, NL, A, P and UK in 1998; (5) EU-15 total is an average, excluding IRL in 1990-94, UK in 1990-92 and 1994 and EL, E, I, NL, A, P and UK in 1998.

Table 21.26

Main indicators of cinema production, 1998 (units)

	EU-15	B	DK	D	EL	E	F	IRL	I	L	NL	A	P	FIN	S	UK	JAP	USA
Long length films produced (1)	:	7	23	50	22	65	180	17	92	10	18	12	19	9	20	87	249	661
National films (2) (3)	413	1	15	39	16	47	102	:	79	0	13	7	12	4	13	65	241	652
International co-productions (2) (4)	:	6	8	11	6	18	78	:	13	10	5	5	7	5	7	:	3	13

(1) Definition of production may vary. EU-15 total not applicable because of intl co-productions double counting; UK: data exclude domestic production of foreign films; US: data include films never released on cinema screens; (2) The assessment for nationality of films may vary: nationality of main producers, nationality of film director /crew and original language of the film etc;
(3) Production of long length films considered as of 100% national origin; excluding IRL;
(4) International co-production of long length films with national origin producers (majority/equally shared/minority co-productions).

Table 21.27

Cinema: evolution of the number of national film productions (units) (1)

	1990	1991	1992	1993	1994	1995	1996	1997	1998
EU-15 (2)	379	380	376	349	327	325	410	408	413
JAP (3)	239	230	240	237	249	286	275	275	241
USA (4)	:	:	:	:	:	660	672	662	652

(1) Cinematographic long length films produced with 100% national origin producers; (2) Excluding B in 1992 and IRL in 1998; (3) New films released;
(4) Including films never released on cinema screens.

Table 21.28

Cinema: evolution of the number of international film co-productions (units) (1)

	1990	1991	1992	1993	1994	1995	1996	1997	1998
EU-15 (2)	143	187	155	213	178	225	226	218	219
JAP	:	:	:	1	2	3	3	3	8
USA	:	:	:	:	:	37	43	13	9

(1) International co-productions of cinematographic long length films with national origin producers;
(2) For information, as double counting between countries may lead to inaccurate figures; excluding IRL for 1994-98; including 1997 data for UK in 1998; estimated data for EL.

Source: Eurostat (AUVIS)

Table 21.29

Main indicators of the video market, 1998

	EU-15	B	DK	D	EL	E	F	IRL	I	L	NL	A	P	FIN	S	UK	JAP	USA
Number of outlets renting videos (1) (2)	26,203	700	2,025	5,550	525	4,600	900	1,100	2,500	16	1,250	350	787	1,000	600	4,300	10,000	27,944
Video sales/rentals (million ECU) (2) (3)	5,464	170	176	859	19	310	1,006	114	195	5	216	87	45	69	162	2,036	3,984	16,125
Share of rentals in receipts (%) (3)	34.1	37.6	41.8	42.6	64.9	42.5	20.0	67.6	26.0	31.1	45.8	35.1	26.8	34.9	48.4	31.7	65.9	53.3
Number of rental transactions (million) (3)	698	24	22	159	10	73	73	29	39	1	35	11	7	9	21	186	849	3,441
Average price per video rental (4)	2.0	2.7	3.3	2.3	1.2	1.8	2.7	2.7	1.2	2.5	2.8	2.7	1.7	2.7	3.8	1.5	3.1	2.5
Pre-recorded video cassettes sold (million) (3)	279	8	6	43	1	16	52	3	18	:	10	4	9	4	6	100	42	701
Average price per pre-recorded video sold (5)	13.5	13.4	16.5	11.5	13.3	11.1	15.5	12.5	8.2	16.6	12.3	13.0	3.9	11.9	13.4	13.9	32.4	10.7
Number of VCR households (thousand) (6)	102,448	2,990	1,791	24,208	1,385	6,450	17,061	844	13,489	117	4,846	2,340	1,973	1,651	3,418	19,885	37,422	84,100

(1) B, EL, F, FIN and S, 1997; JAP, 1996; USA, 1995; EU-15, sum of available data; (2) Pre-recorded cassettes or discs; total video market (retail level) including VAT; (3) L, 1997; EU-15, excluding L;
(4) EU-15, I and L, 1997; (5) L, 1993; EU-15, average of available data; (6) B, NL, UK and JAP, 1997; E, 1996; EU-15, sum of available data.

Table 21.30

Evolution of the main indicators of the video market, EU-15

	1990	1991	1992	1993	1994	1995	1996	1997	1998
Number of outlets renting videos (1)	40,247	34,688	33,181	27,022	24,618	24,521	24,084	25,500	26,203
Receipts from video sales and rentals (million ECU) (2)	3,555	3,875	3,821	4,045	4,317	4,636	4,766	4,972	5,464
Share of rentals in receipts (%) (3)	63	53	47	39	35	33	34	34	34
Number of rental transactions (million) (4)	921	817	743	668	616	619	654	639	699
Pre-recorded video cassettes sold (million) (5)	96	131	143	182	209	236	248	259	279

(1) Excluding DK in 1991; including 1996 data for P in 1997 and 1997 data for B, EL, F, FIN and S in 1998; (2) Pre-recorded cassettes or discs; total video market (retail level) including VAT;
(3) Excluding L in 1998; (4) Excluding EL in 1990-92, P in 1990-91 and L in 1994-95; including 1997 data for I in 1998; (5) Excluding EL in 1990-92 and L in 1994-98.

Source: Eurostat (AUVIS)

Table 21.31

Cable network operations, 1998 (units)

	EU-15	B	DK	D	EL	E	F	IRL	I	L	NL	A	P	FIN	S	UK	JAP	USA
Number of cable operators (1)	798	31	65	120	:	28	121	5	1	7	120	49	15	100	4	132	720	11,119
Households connected to a network (thousand) (2)	40,500	3,721	751	17,810	2	483	2,538	535	321	132	5,956	1,171	596	906	1,717	3,861	15,817	67,000
Average number of channels per network (3)	:	31	15	25	:	30	:	15	14	32	31	32	30	:	11	:	:	57

(1) EU-15 sum of available data. F, UK, JAP: 1997; L, USA: 1996; A:1995; (2) EU-15 sum of available data. B: 1997; DK, EL: 1996; I, L: 1995; (3) B, IRL: 1997; L, P: 1996.

Table 21.32

Evolution of the number of households connected to operated cable networks (thousands)

	1990	1991	1992	1993	1994	1995	1996	1997	1998
EU-15 (1)	21,364	24,486	27,595	30,043	32,118	34,424	35,556	:	:
B	3,370	3,451	3,510	3,549	3,594	3,629	3,684	3,721	:
DK	861	1,075	1,131	1,186	1,240	1,320	751	:	:
D	8,100	9,900	11,800	13,500	14,600	15,800	16,700	17,610	17,810
EL	:	:	:	:	2	2	2	:	:
E	110	122	122	130	300	400	440	:	483
F	515	762	1,048	1,305	1,626	1,885	2,108	2,280	2,538
IRL	386	390	400	405	415	460	470	:	535
I	:	:	:	:	:	321	:	:	:
L	104	107	110	112	131	132	:	:	:
NL	4,980	5,379	5,594	5,657	5,865	5,769	5,641	5,808	5,956
A	632	759	865	978	1,003	1,080	1,077	1,110	1,171
P	0	:	2	7	11	58	171	383	596
FIN	669	722	753	760	798	817	845	875	906
S	1,482	1,548	1,800	1,825	1,565	1,535	1,652	1,573	1,717
UK	155	271	460	629	968	1,216	2,015	3,098	3,861
JAP	6,768	7,431	8,344	9,228	10,254	11,005	12,629	14,482	15,817
USA	54,929	55,777	57,228	58,188	59,723	62,678	63,965	65,954	67,000

(1) Sum of available data.

Table 21.33

Evolution of the number of households equipped with satellite dishes (thousands)

	1990	1991	1992	1993	1994	1995	1996	1997	1998
EU-15 (1)	:	:	9,690	12,441	15,400	18,489	19,771	21,555	25,099
B	:	:	:	:	:	255	:	300	:
DK	387	465	539	570	700	700	700	:	940
D	850	2,465	5,285	6,800	7,300	10,000	10,700	11,370	12,140
EL	:	:	:	:	20	20	20	:	:
E	:	:	100	145	300	654	738	770	1,270
F	476	548	620	806	902	1,000	1,338	1,862	3,500
IRL	20	24	35	48	62	84	100	110	110
I	:	:	:	:	:	:	:	:	:
L	:	:	:	:	20	20	20	20	20
NL	:	45	186	251	285	292	:	260	350
A	:	196	421	662	805	940	1,078	1,121	1,188
P	:	:	26	38	240	260	290	316	340
FIN	45	60	96	126	164	197	231	261	285
S	111	335	489	608	642	787	766	865	839
UK	1,278	1,734	1,893	2,387	3,960	3,280	3,790	4,300	4,117
JAP	2,340	:	4,970	5,870	6,520	9,129	10,965	12,065	13,371
USA	:	:	:	:	:	4,565	6,563	8,400	10,044

(1) Sum of available data.

Source: Eurostat (AUVIS)

_____Table 21.34

Music recording (NACE Rev. 1 22.14 and 22.31)

Employment related indicators, 1997

	B	DK	D	EL	E	F	IRL	I (1)	L	NL	A	P	FIN	S	UK
Number of persons employed (thousands)	:	0.3	:	:	0.8	6.5	:	2.2	:	2.5	1.3	0.2	0.3	2.1	6.2
Employees/number of persons employed (%)	:	:	:	:	98.6	96.9	:	60.2	:	90.7	96.7	83.5	79.7	64.5	81.1
Average no. of persons employed/enterprise (units)	:	2.3	:	:	11.9	3.2	:	3.1	:	8.1	40.0	3.5	1.1	2.0	4.6

(1) 1996.

_____Table 21.35

Music recording (NACE Rev. 1 22.14 and 22.31)

Turnover related indicators, 1997

	B	DK	D	EL	E	F	IRL	I (1)	L	NL	A	P	FIN	S	UK
Turnover (million ECU)	:	54	:	:	125	1,885	:	379	:	565	335	26	35	237	1,227
Turnover per enterprise (million ECU)	:	0.4	:	:	1.9	0.9	:	0.5	:	1.9	10.5	0.4	0.1	0.2	0.9
Turnover per person employed (thousand ECU)	:	156.1	:	:	163.9	291.0	:	168.7	:	228.1	261.9	107.8	111.7	111.1	197.7

(1) 1996.

_____Table 21.36

Music recording (NACE Rev. 1 22.14 and 22.31)

Performance related indicators, 1997

	B	DK	D	EL	E	F	IRL	I (1)	L	NL	A	P	FIN	S	UK
Value added (million ECU)	:	:	:	:	43	504	:	94	:	169	204	4	14	63	677
Value added as a share of turnover (%)	:	:	:	:	34.5	26.7	:	24.9	:	29.9	60.9	16.4	38.6	26.7	55.2
Apparent labour productivity (thousand ECU/person employed)	:	:	:	:	56.5	77.7	:	42.0	:	68.2	159.6	17.7	43.2	29.7	109.1
Unit personnel costs (thousand ECU)	:	:	:	:	26.1	43.1	:	32.7	:	32.4	35.1	11.8	30.7	26.4	42.9
Simple wage adjusted labour productivity (%)	:	:	:	:	219.4	185.9	:	213.1	:	232.5	470.3	179.2	176.6	174.1	313.6
Gross operating surplus (million ECU)	:	4	:	:	23	233	:	50	:	96	161	2	6	27	461

(1) 1996.

_____Table 21.37

Sales of music recordings, 1998 (thousand units)

	EU-15	B	DK	D	EL	E	F	IRL	I	L	NL	A	P	FIN	S	UK	JAP	USA
Total sound recordings (1)	890,713	25,650	17,468	236,167	8,830	63,630	131,060	6,614	49,466	:	37,100	21,153	19,300	11,967	25,687	236,623	350,400	1,038,167
Singles (2)	67,736	2,900	367	17,267	:	500	13,341	583	1,155	:	2,200	1,033	200	167	1,567	26,458	48,000	29,267
LPs (3)	3,464	50	1	500	30	30	308	14	83	:	200	20	0	0	20	2,208	8,400	3,400
CDs (3)	711,624	22,400	16,900	193,300	8,300	50,200	103,604	4,736	34,169	:	34,100	19,200	15,300	10,500	23,200	175,715	286,100	847,000
MCs (3)	107,889	300	200	25,100	500	12,900	13,807	1,281	14,059	:	600	900	3,800	1,300	900	32,242	7,900	158,500
Turnover (million ECU) (4)	9,543	329	234	2,532	103	608	1,137	61	541	:	501	310	164	125	351	2,549	5,831	11,777

(1) In the total, three singles are counted as one recording unit (IFPI standards); EU-15 excluding L;
(2) Singles include vinyl, MC and CD singles; EU-15 excluding EL and L; (3) EU-15 excluding L; (4) Total retail level value; EU-15 excluding L.

_____Table 21.38

Evolution of main indicators of postal services, EU-15

	1990	1991	1992	1993	1994	1995	1996	1997	1998
Total sound recordings (1)	726,852	752,899	696,591	737,224	786,183	816,388	846,980	869,680	890,713
Singles (2)	46,865	41,048	37,483	43,330	47,375	52,841	60,515	70,055	67,736
LPs (3)	140,298	88,461	37,897	18,539	10,765	6,349	4,069	3,525	3,464
CDs (3)	270,049	349,227	406,682	481,265	551,243	597,404	642,982	676,869	711,624
MCs (3)	269,640	274,163	214,529	194,091	176,800	159,794	139,414	119,231	107,889
Turnover (million ECU) (3) (4)	6,479	7,282	7,240	7,685	8,288	8,513	8,753	9,278	9,543

(1) In the total three singles are counted as one recording unit (IFPI standards); Excluding IRL (1990) and L; 1990 excluding former Eastern Germany;
(2) Singles include vinyl, MC and CD singles; Excluding EL, IRL (1990) and L; 1990 excluding former Eastern Germany; (3) Excluding IRL (1990) and L; 1990 excluding former Eastern Germany;
(4) Total retail level value.

Source: Eurostat (SBS, AUVIS)

European Commission

Panorama of European Business, 2000

Luxembourg: Office for Official Publications of the European Communities

2000 – 563 pp. – 21 x 29.7 cm

Theme 4: Industry, trade and services
Collection: Panorama of the European Union

ISBN 92-894-0180-X

Price (excluding VAT) in Luxembourg: EUR 50

.... Eurostat Data Shops

BELGIQUE/BELGIË

Eurostat Data Shop
Bruxelles/Brussel
Planistat Belgique
Rue du Commerce 124
Handelsstraat 124
B-1000 Bruxelles/Brussel
Tél. (32-2) 234 67 50
Fax (32-2) 234 67 51
E-mail: datashop@planistat.be

DANMARK

DANMARKS STATISTIK
Bibliotek og Information
Eurostat Data Shop
Sejrøgade 11
DK-2100 København Ø
Tlf. (45) 39 17 30 30
Fax (45) 39 17 30 03
E-mail: bib@dst.dk

DEUTSCHLAND

Statistisches Bundesamt
Eurostat Data Shop Berlin
Otto-Braun-Straße 70-72
(Eingang: Karl-Marx-Allee)
D-10178 Berlin
Tel. (49) 1888-644 94 27/28
Fax (49) 1888-644 94 30
E-Mail:
datashop@statistik-bund.de

ESPAÑA

INE
Eurostat Data Shop
Paseo de la Castellana, 183
Oficina 009
Entrada por Estébanez
Calderón
E-28046 Madrid
Tel. (34) 91 583 91 67
Fax (34) 91 579 71 20
E-mail:
datashop.eurostat@ine.es
Member of the MIDAS Net

FRANCE

INSEE Info service
Eurostat Data Shop
195, rue de Bercy
Tour Gamma A
F-75582 Paris Cedex 12
Tél. (33) 1 53 17 88 44
Fax (33) 1 53 17 88 22
E-mail: datashop@insee.fr
Member of the MIDAS Net

ITALIA - ROMA

ISTAT
Centro di informazione
statistica — Sede di Roma
Eurostat Data Shop
Via Cesare Balbo, 11a
I-00184 Roma
Tel. (39) 06 46 73 31 02/06
Fax (39) 06 46 73 31 01/07
E-mail: dipdiff@istat.it
Member of the MIDAS Net

ITALIA - MILANO

ISTAT
Ufficio regionale per la
Lombardia
Eurostat Data Shop
Via Fieno, 3
I-20123 Milano
Tel. (39) 02 80 61 32 460
Fax (39) 02 80 61 32 304
E-mail: mileuro@tin.it
Member of the MIDAS Net

LUXEMBOURG

Eurostat Data Shop Luxembourg
BP 453
L-2014 Luxembourg
4, rue Alphonse Weicker
L-2721 Luxembourg
Tél. (352) 43 35-2251
Fax (352) 43 35-22221
E-mail:
dslux@eurostat.datashop.lu
Member of the MIDAS Net

NEDERLAND

STATISTICS NETHERLANDS
Eurostat Data Shop — Voorburg
Postbus 4000
2270 JM Voorburg
Nederland
Tel. (31-70) 337 49 00
Fax (31-70) 337 59 84
E-mail: datashop@cbs.nl

PORTUGAL

Eurostat Data Shop Lisboa
INE/Serviço de Difusão
Av. António José de Almeida, 2
P-1000-043 Lisboa
Tel. (351) 21 842 61 00
Fax (351) 21 842 63 64
E-mail: data.shop@ine.pt

SUOMI/FINLAND

STATISTICS FINLAND
Eurostat DataShop Helsinki
Tilastokirjasto
PL 2B
FIN-00022 Tilastokeskus
Työpajakatu 13 B, 2. Kerros,
Helsinki
P. (358-9) 17 34 22 21
F. (358-9) 17 34 22 79
Sähköposti:
datashop.tilastokeskus@
tilastokeskus.fi
URL:
http://www.tilastokeskus.fi/tk/k
k/datashop.html

SVERIGE

STATISTICS SWEDEN
Information service
Eurostat Data Shop
Karlavägen 100
Box 24 300
S-104 51 Stockholm
Tfn (46-8) 50 69 48 01
Fax (46-8) 50 69 48 99
E-post: infoservice@scb.se
Internet:
http://www.scb.se/info/
datashop/eudatashop.asp

UNITED KINGDOM

Eurostat Data Shop
Enquiries & advice and
publications
Office for National Statistics
Customers & Electronic
Services Unit B1/05
1 Drummond Gate
London SW1V 2QQ
United Kingdom
Tel. (44-20) 75 33 56 76
Fax (44-1633) 81 27 62
E-mail:
eurostat.datashop@ons.gov.uk
Member of the MIDAS Net

Eurostat Data Shop
Electronic Data Extractions,
enquiries & advice r.cade
1L Mountjoy Research Centre
University of Durham
Durham DH1 3SW
United Kingdom
Tel. (44-191) 374 73 50
Fax (44-191) 384 49 71
E-mail: r-cade@dur.ac.uk
Internet:
http://www-rcade.dur.ac.uk

NORWAY

Statistics Norway
Library and Information Centre
Eurostat Data Shop
Kongens gate 6
Boks 8131 Dep.
N-0033 Oslo
Tel. (47) 21 09 46 42/43
Fax (47) 21 09 45 04
E-mail: Datashop@ssb.no

SCHWEIZ/SUISSE/SVIZZERA

Statistisches Amt des Kantons
Zürich
Eurostat Data Shop
Bleicherweg 5
CH-8090 Zürich
Tel. (41-1) 225 12 12
Fax (41-1) 225 12 99
E-mail: datashop@statistik.zh.ch
Internet:
http://www.zh.ch/statistik

USA

HAVER ANALYTICS
Eurostat Data Shop
60 East 42nd Street
Suite 3310
New York, NY 10165
Tel. (1-212) 986 93 00
Fax (1-212) 986 69 81
E-mail: eurodata@haver.com

EUROSTAT HOME PAGE
www.europa.eu.int/comm/eurostat/

MEDIA SUPPORT
EUROSTAT
(only for professional journalists)
Postal address:
Jean Monnet building
L-2920 Luxembourg
Office: BECH A3/48 —
5, rue Alphonse Weicker
L-2721 Luxembourg
Tel. (352) 43 01-33408
Fax (352) 43 01-32649
E-mail:
Eurostat-mediasupport@cec.eu.in